# Financial Institutions Management

## A Risk Management Approach

# The McGraw-Hill/Irwin Series in Finance, Insurance, and Real Estate

Stephen A. Ross
*Franco Modigliani Professor of Finance and Economics Sloan School of Management Massachusetts Institute of Technology Consulting Editor*

## FINANCIAL MANAGEMENT

Block, Hirt, and Danielsen
**Foundations of Financial Management**
*Fifteenth Edition*

Brealey, Myers, and Allen
**Principles of Corporate Finance**
*Eleventh Edition*

Brealey, Myers, and Allen
**Principles of Corporate Finance, Concise**
*Second Edition*

Brealey, Myers, and Marcus
**Fundamentals of Corporate Finance**
*Seventh Edition*

Brooks
**FinGame Online 5.0**

Bruner
**Case Studies in Finance: Managing for Corporate Value Creation**
*Seventh Edition*

Cornett, Adair, and Nofsinger
**Finance: Applications and Theory**
*Second Edition*

DeMello
**Cases in Finance**
*Second Edition*

Grinblatt (editor)
**Stephen A. Ross, Mentor: Influence Through Generations**

Grinblatt and Titman
**Financial Markets and Corporate Strategy**
*Second Edition*

Higgins
**Analysis for Financial Management**
*Tenth Edition*

Kellison
**Theory of Interest**
*Third Edition*

Ross, Westerfield, and Jaffe
**Corporate Finance**
*Tenth Edition*

Ross, Westerfield, Jaffe, and Jordan
**Corporate Finance: Core Principles and Applications**
*Fourth Edition*

Ross, Westerfield, and Jordan
**Essentials of Corporate Finance**
*Eighth Edition*

Ross, Westerfield, and Jordan
**Fundamentals of Corporate Finance**
*Tenth Edition*

Shefrin
**Behavioral Corporate Finance: Decisions That Create Value**
*First Edition*

White
**Financial Analysis with an Electronic Calculator**
*Sixth Edition*

## INVESTMENTS

Bodie, Kane, and Marcus
**Essentials of Investments**
*Ninth Edition*

Bodie, Kane, and Marcus
**Investments**
*Tenth Edition*

Hirt and Block
**Fundamentals of Investment Management**
*Tenth Edition*

Jordan and Miller
**Fundamentals of Investments: Valuation and Management**
*Sixth Edition*

Stewart, Piros, and Heisler
**Running Money: Professional Portfolio Management**
*First Edition*

Sundaram and Das
**Derivatives: Principles and Practice**
*First Edition*

## FINANCIAL INSTITUTIONS AND MARKETS

Rose and Hudgins
**Bank Management and Financial Services**
*Ninth Edition*

Rose and Marquis
**Financial Institutions and Markets**
*Eleventh Edition*

Saunders and Cornett
**Financial Institutions Management: A Risk Management Approach**
*Eighth Edition*

Saunders and Cornett
**Financial Markets and Institutions**
*Fifth Edition*

## INTERNATIONAL FINANCE

Eun and Resnick
**International Financial Management**
*Sixth Edition*

## REAL ESTATE

Brueggeman and Fisher
**Real Estate Finance and Investments**
*Fourteenth Edition*

Ling and Archer
**Real Estate Principles: A Value Approach**
*Fourth Edition*

## FINANCIAL PLANNING AND INSURANCE

Allen, Melone, Rosenbloom, and Mahoney
**Retirement Plans: 401(k)s, IRAs, and Other Deferred Compensation Approaches**
*Eleventh Edition*

Altfest
**Personal Financial Planning**
*First Edition*

Harrington and Niehaus
**Risk Management and Insurance**
*Second Edition*

Kapoor, Dlabay, and Hughes
**Focus on Personal Finance: An Active Approach to Help You Develop Successful Financial Skills**
*Fourth Edition*

Kapoor, Dlabay, and Hughes
**Personal Finance**
*Tenth Edition*

Walker and Walker
**Personal Finance: Building Your Future**
*First Edition*

# Financial Institutions Management

**A Risk Management Approach**

Eighth Edition

**Anthony Saunders**
*John M. Schiff Professor of Finance*
*Salomon Center*
*Stern School of Business*
*New York University*

**Marcia Millon Cornett**
*Professor of Finance*
*Bentley University*

Mc
Graw
Hill
Education

To all my co-authors over the years.
Anthony Saunders

To my parents, Tom and Sue.
Marcia Millon Cornett

# About the Authors

## Anthony Saunders

Anthony Saunders is the John M. Schiff Professor of Finance and the former Chair of the Department of Finance at the Stern School of Business at New York University. Professor Saunders received his PhD from the London School of Economics and has taught both undergraduate- and graduate-level courses at NYU since 1978. Throughout his academic career, his teaching and research have specialized in financial institutions and international banking. He has served as a visiting professor all over the world, including INSEAD, the Stockholm School of Economics, and the University of Melbourne.

Professor Saunders has held positions on the Board of Academic Consultants of the Federal Reserve Board of Governors as well as the Council of Research Advisors for the Federal National Mortgage Association. In addition, Dr. Saunders has acted as a visiting scholar at the Comptroller of the Currency and at the Federal Reserve Banks of Philadelphia and New York. Currently, he is an academic consultant for the FDIC. He also held a visiting position in the research department of the International Monetary Fund. He is editor of *Financial Markets, Instruments and Institutions.* His research has been published in all the major money and banking and finance journals and in several books. In addition, he has authored or coauthored several professional books, the most recent of which is *Credit Risk Measurement: New Approaches to Value at Risk and Other Paradigms,* 3rd edition, John Wiley and Sons, New York, 2010. In 2008, he was ranked as the most published author in the last 50 years in the top seven journals in finance.

## Marcia Millon Cornett

Marcia Millon Cornett is a Professor of Finance at Bentley University. She received her BS degree in Economics from Knox College in Galesburg, Illinois, and her MBA and PhD degrees in Finance from Indiana University in Bloomington, Indiana. Dr. Cornett has written and published several articles in the areas of bank performance, bank regulation, and corporate finance. Articles authored by Dr. Cornett have appeared in such academic journals as the *Journal of Finance,* the *Journal of Money, Credit and Banking,* the *Journal of Financial Economics, Financial Management,* and the *Journal of Banking and Finance.* In 2008, she was ranked as the 124th most published author in the last 50 years in the top seven journals in finance. Dr. Cornett served as an Associate Editor of *Financial Management* and is currently an Associate Editor for the *Journal of Banking and Finance, Journal of Financial Services Research, FMA Online,* the *Multinational Finance Journal,* and the *Review of Financial Economics.* She has served as a member of the Board of Directors, the Executive Committee, and the Finance Committee of the SIU Credit Union. Dr. Cornett has also taught at the University of Colorado, Boston College, Southern Methodist University, and Southern Illinois University at Carbondale. She is a member of the Financial Management Association, the American Finance Association, and the Western Finance Association.

# Preface

The last 25 years have been dramatic for the financial services industry. In the 1990s and 2000s boundaries between the traditional industry sectors, such as commercial banking and investment banking, broke down, and competition became increasingly global in nature. Many forces contributed to this breakdown in interindustry and intercountry barriers, including financial innovation, technology, taxation, and regulation. Then in 2008–09, the financial services industry experienced the worst financial crisis since the Great Depression. Even into the mid-2010s, the U.S. and world economies have not recovered from this crisis. It is in this context that this book is written. Although the traditional nature of each sector's product activity is analyzed, a greater emphasis is placed on *new* areas of activities such as asset securitization, off-balance-sheet banking, international banking, and on changes occurring as a result of the financial crisis.

When the first edition of this text was released in 1994, it was the first to analyze modern financial institutions management from a risk perspective. Thus, the title, *Financial Institutions Management: A Modern Perspective*. At that time, traditional texts presented an overview of the industry sector by sector, concentrating on balance sheet presentations and overlooking management decision making and risk management. Over the last 20 years other texts have followed this change, such that a risk management approach to analyzing modern financial institutions is now well accepted. Thus, the title: *Financial Institutions Management: A Risk Management Approach*.

The eighth edition of this text takes the same innovative approach taken in the first seven editions and focuses on managing return and risk in modern financial institutions (FIs). *Financial Institutions Management*'s central theme is that the risks faced by FI managers and the methods and markets through which these risks are managed are similar whether an institution is chartered as a commercial bank, a savings bank, an investment bank, or an insurance company.

As in any stockholder-owned corporation, the goal of FI managers should always be to maximize the value of the financial institution. However, pursuit of value maximization does not mean that risk management can be ignored.

Indeed, modern FIs are in the risk management business. As we discuss in this book, in a world of perfect and frictionless capital markets, FIs would not exist and individuals would manage their own financial assets and portfolios. But since real-world financial markets are not perfect, FIs provide the positive function of bearing and managing risk on behalf of their customers through the pooling of risks and the sale of their services as risk specialists.

## INTENDED AUDIENCE

*Financial Institutions Management: A Risk Management Approach* is aimed at upper-level undergraduate and MBA audiences. Occasionally there are more technical sections. *These sections may be included or dropped from the chapter reading, depending on the rigor of the course, without harming the continuity of the chapters.*

# MAIN FEATURES

Throughout the text, special features have been integrated to encourage student interaction with the text and to aid in absorbing the material. Some of these features include:

- **In-chapter Internet Exercises and references,** which detail instructions for accessing important recent financial data online.
- **International material highlights,** which call out material relating to global issues.
- **In-chapter Examples,** which provide numerical demonstrations of the analytics described in various chapters.
- **Bold key terms and marginal glossary,** which highlight and define the main terms and concepts throughout the chapter.
- **In-chapter Concept Questions,** which allow students to test themselves on the main concepts within each major chapter section.
- **Notable Events from the Financial Crisis, Industry Perspectives, and After the Crisis boxes,** which demonstrate the application of chapter material to real current events.

# ORGANIZATION

Since our focus is on return and risk and the sources of that return and risk, this book relates ways in which the managers of modern FIs can expand return with a managed level of risk to achieve the best, or most favorable, return-risk outcome for FI owners.

Chapter 1 introduces the special functions of FIs and takes an analytical look at how financial intermediation benefits today's economy. Chapters 2 through 6 provide an overview describing the key balance sheet and regulatory features of the major sectors of the U.S. financial services industry. We discuss depository institutions in Chapter 2, finance companies in Chapter 3, securities firms and investment banks in Chapter 4, mutual funds and hedge funds in Chapter 5, and insurance institutions in Chapter 6. In Chapter 7 we preview the risk measurement and management sections with an overview of the risks facing a modern FI. We divide the chapters on risk measurement and management into two sections: measuring risk and managing risk.

In Chapters 8 and 9, we start the risk measurement section by investigating the net interest margin as a source of profitability and risk, with a focus on the effects of interest rate volatility and the mismatching of asset and liability durations on FI risk exposure. In Chapter 10, we look at the measurement of credit risk on individual loans and bonds and how this risk adversely affects an FI's profits through losses and provisions against the loan and debt security portfolio. In Chapter 11, we look at the risk of loan (asset) portfolios and the effects of loan concentrations on risk exposure. In addition, as a by-product of the provision of their interest rate and credit intermediation services, FIs face liquidity risk. We analyze the special nature of this risk in Chapter 12.

Modern FIs do more than domestic maturity mismatching and credit extensions. They also are increasingly engaging in foreign exchange activities and overseas financial investments (Chapter 13) and engaging in sovereign lending and securities activities (Chapter 14). In Chapter 15, we analyze market risk, a risk incurred by FIs in trading assets and liabilities due to changes in interest rates, exchange rates, and other asset prices.

In addition, modern FIs do more than generate returns and bear risk through traditional maturity mismatching and credit extensions. They also are increasingly engaging in off-balance-sheet activities to generate fee income (Chapter 16) and making technological investments to reduce costs (Chapter 17). Each of these has implications for the size and variability of an FI's profits and/or revenues.

In Chapter 18 we begin the risk management section by looking at ways in which FIs can insulate themselves from liquidity risk. In Chapter 19 we look at the key role deposit insurance and other guaranty schemes play in reducing liquidity risk. At the core of FI risk insulation is the size and adequacy of the owners' capital or equity investment in the FI, which is the focus of Chapter 20. Chapter 21 analyzes how and why product and geographic diversification—both domestic and international—can improve an FI's return-risk performance and the impact of regulation on the diversification opportunity set. Chapters 22 through 26 review various new markets and instruments that have been innovated or engineered to allow FIs to better manage three important types of risk: interest rate risk, credit risk, and foreign exchange risk. These markets and instruments and their strategic use by FIs include futures and forwards (Chapter 22); options, caps, floors, and collars (Chapter 23); swaps (Chapter 24); loan sales (Chapter 25); and securitization (Chapter 26).

## CHANGES IN THIS EDITION

Each chapter in this edition has been revised thoroughly to reflect the most up-to-date information available. End-of-chapter questions and problem material have also been expanded and updated to provide a complete selection of testing material.

The following are some of the new features of this revision:

- Tables and figures in all chapters have been revised to include the most recently available data.
- New boxes highlighting significant events occurring "After the Crisis" have been added to chapters throughout the book.
- Integrated Minicases have been added to Chapters 9, 13, 16, and 24.
- Updates on the major changes proposed for the regulation of financial institutions are included where appropriate throughout the book.
- Discussion of how financial institutions continue to recover from the financial crisis has been added throughout the book. Virtually every chapter includes new material detailing how the financial crisis has affected risk management in financial institutions.
- Chapters 2, 7, and 14 include discussions of the European debt crisis as it affects the risk and return of financial institutions.
- Chapter 2 includes a discussion of Bank Transfer Day, as well as a summary of the new stress tests imposed on large depository institutions.
- A section on venture capital services has been added to Chapter 5. Also, the chapter includes a discussion of the LIBOR scandal that broke in late 2012.
- Chapter 5 includes a new section on index funds and expanded discussion of ETFs. Further, the chapter includes an update on the regulation of hedge funds.

- An actual interest rate sensitivity report for a depository institution has been added to Chapter 8, and actual duration gap numbers for several banks have been added to Chapter 9.
- Detailed discussion and examples of the new international liquidity standards enacted as a result of the financial crisis have been added to Chapter 12.
- Chapter 13 includes a discussion of the pegging of the Swiss franc to the euro in September 2011.
- Chapter 14 now includes a discussion of the Euromoney Credit Risk measure. This credit risk measure is then used in Chapter 20 as it applies to the new capital standards being phased in at depository institutions.
- Chapter 15 includes a discussion and examples of the newest market risk measures enacted as a result of the financial crisis. The chapter also discusses the changes made to market risk measures as a result of Basel 2.5 and Basel III.
- Chapter 16 includes a discussion of the losses incurred by J.P. Morgan Chase from derivative trading by the "London Whale."
- Chapter 17 includes a new section on advanced technologies in banking and additional discussion of several recent technology related losses incurred by FIs.
- Chapter 18 includes extensive discussion and examples of the new insurance premium system used by depository institutions.
- Chapter 20 includes a discussion of Basel III capital adequacy rules. The major changes are described in detail. Many in-chapter and EOC problems have been added to the chapter to illustrate the many and complex changes to capital adequacy calculations.
- Chapter 21 includes a new section on shadow banks. The chapter also provides an update on implementation of the Wall Street Reform and Consumer Protection Act enacted as a result of the financial crisis.
- Chapter 26 includes a new section on synthetic CDOs.

We have retained and updated these features:

- The **risk approach** of *Financial Institutions Management* has been retained, keeping the first section of the text as an introduction and the last two sections as a risk measurement and risk management summary, respectively.
- We again present a detailed look at **what is new** in each of the different sectors of the financial institutions industry in the first six chapters of the text. We have highlighted the continued **international coverage** with a global issues icon throughout the text.
- Chapter 17 includes material on electronic technology and the Internet's impact on financial services. Technological changes occurring over the last two decades have changed the way financial institutions offer services to customers, both domestically and overseas. The **effect of technology** is also referenced in other chapters where relevant.
- **Coverage of credit risk models** (including newer models, such as Moody's Analytics, CreditMetrics, and CreditRisk+) remains in the text.
- Coverage in the **"Product and Geographic Expansion"** chapter explores the increased inroads of banks into the insurance field, the move toward nationwide banking (in the United States), and the rapid growth of foreign banks and other intermediaries in the United States.

- Numerous highlighted **in-chapter Examples** remain in the chapters.
- **Internet references** remain throughout each chapter and Internet questions are found after the end-of-chapter questions.
- An **extensive problem set,** including web exercises, can be found at the end of each chapter that allows students to practice a variety of skills using the same data or set of circumstances.

# ANCILLARIES

All supplemental materials for both students and instructors can be found on the McGraw-Hill website for the eighth edition of *Financial Institutions Management* at **www.mhhe.com/saunders8e.** Instructor materials are password-protected for your security.

Print versions are available by request only—if interested, please contact your McGraw-Hill/Irwin representative. The following supplements are available for the eighth edition.

## For Students

- *Multiple-Choice Quizzes* for each chapter consist of 10 multiple-choice questions that reflect key concepts from the text. These quizzes have instant grading.
- *Appendices* consist of material that has been removed from previous editions of the print textbook to allow room for new topics.

## For Instructors

- The *Test Bank,* created by Thomas Secrest of Coastal Carolina University, offers multiple-choice and true/false questions that are designed to apply specifically to this text and this edition's revisions. The *Test Bank* is available in Word document format and EZ Test online.
- The *Instructor's Manual,* created by author Marcia Millon Cornett, contains answers to the text's Questions and Problems at the end of each chapter and chapter outlines.
- The *PowerPoint Presentations* summarize the main points of each chapter in a step-by-step fashion. These slideshows can be edited by instructors to customize presentations.
- The *Digital Image Library* contains electronic versions of all figures and tables from the seventh edition of the text.

CourseSmart is a new way for faculty to find and review eTextbooks. It's also a great option for students who are interested in accessing their course materials digitally. CourseSmart offers thousands of the most commonly adopted textbooks across hundreds of courses from a wide variety of higher education publishers. It is the only place for faculty to review and compare the full text of a textbook online. At CourseSmart, students can save up to 50 percent off the cost of a print book, reduce their impact on the environment, and gain access to powerful web tools for learning including full text search, notes and highlighting, and email tools for sharing notes between classmates. Your eBook also includes tech support in case you ever need help.

Finding your eBook is easy. Visit **www.CourseSmart.com** and search by title, author, or ISBN.

# Acknowledgments

Finally, we would like to thank the numerous colleagues who assisted with the previous editions of this book. Of great help were the book reviewers whose painstaking comments and advice guided the text through its seven revisions.

**Jack Aber**
*Boston University*

**Brian J. Adams**
*University of Portland*

**Michael H. Anderson**
*Suffolk University*

**Mounther Barakat**
*University of Houston–Clear Lake*

**Sreedhar Bharath**
*University of Michigan*

**Rita Biswas**
*SUNY–Albany*

**M. E. Bond**
*University of Memphis*

**Qiang Bu**
*Pennsylvania State–Harrisburg*

**Yea-Mow Chen**
*San Francisco State University*

**Jeffrey A. Clark**
*Florida State University*

**Robert A. Clark**
*Butler University*

**S. Steven Cole**
*University of North Texas*

**Douglas Cook**
*University of Mississippi*

**Kenneth Daniels**
*Virginia Commonwealth University*

**Paul Ellinger**
*University of Illinois*

**David Ely**
*San Diego State University*

**Joseph Finnerty**
*University of Illinios*

**Jack Clark Francis**
*Baruch College–CUNY*

**James H. Gilkeson**
*University of Central Florida*

**Anurag Gupta**
*Case Western Reserve University*

**John H. Hand**
*Auburn University*

**Yan He**
*San Francisco State University*

**Alan C. Hess**
*University of Washington–Seattle*

**Ray Jackson**
*University of Massachusetts–Dartmouth*

**Kevin Jacques**
*Georgetown University and Office of the Comptroller of the Currency*

**Julapa Jagtiani**
*Federal Reserve Bank of Chicago*

**Craig G. Johnson**
*California State University–Hayward*

**Nelson J. Lacey**
*University of Massachusetts at Amherst*

**Robert Lamy**
*Wake Forest University*

**Rick LeCompte**
*Wichita State University*

**Barry Marchman**
*Georgia Institute of Technology*

**Patricia C. Matthews**
*Mount Union College*

**Robert McLeod**
*University of Alabama*

**Jamie McNutt**
*Rutgers–Camden*

**Ardavan Mobasheri**
*Bernard M. Baruch College–CUNY*

**Richard Patterson**
*Indiana University*

**Roberto Perli**
*University of Maryland*

**Rose M. Prasad**
*Central Michigan University*

**Andreas Rauterkus**
*University of Alabama–Birmingham*

**Kenneth Rhoda**
*LaSalle University*

**Tara Rice**
*Boston College*

**Don Sabbarese**
*Kennesaw State University*

**Daniel Singer**
*Towson University*

**Richard Stolz**
*California State University–Fullerton*

**Michael Toyne**
*Northeastern State University*

**Haluk Unal**
*University of Maryland*

**James A. Verbrugge**
*University of Georgia*

**Hsinrong Wei**
*Baruch College–CUNY*

**Sonya Williams-Stanton**
*University of Michigan–Ann Arbor*

**Robert Wolf**
*University of Wisconsin–La Crosse*

In addition, we gratefully acknowledge the contributions of the reviewers of the seventh edition:

**Ethan Cohen-Cole**
*University of Maryland–College Park*

**James Conover**
*University of North Texas*

**Elyas Elyasiani**
*Temple University–Philadelphia*

**Margaret Forster**
*University of Notre Dame*

**Deniz Kebabci Tudor**
*San Francisco State University*

**Elinda Kiss**
*University of Maryland–College Park*

**Richard Patterson**
*Indiana University–Bloomington*

**Joe Peek**
*University of Kentucky–Lexington*

**Marcelo Pinheiro**
*George Mason University*

**Alexander Wilson**
*University of Arizona*

**Shaorong Zhang**
*Marshall University*

**Lina Zhou**
*Augustana College*

We very much appreciate the contributions of the book team at McGraw-Hill Education: Chuck Synovec, Executive Brand Manager; Noelle Bathurst, Development Editor; Melissa Caughlin, Senior Marketing Manager; and Judi David, Content Project Manager. We are also grateful to our secretaries and assistants, Robyn Vanterpool, Ingrid Persaud, Anand Srinivasan, Brenda Webb, and Sharon Moore.

*Anthony Saunders*

*Marcia Millon Cornett*

# Brief Contents

# Contents

# Introduction

See Appendices Online at www.mhhe.com/saunders8e
- Appendix 1A: The Financial Crisis: The Failure of Financial Institution Specialness
- Appendix 1B: Monetary Policy Tools

# Why Are Financial Institutions Special?

## INTRODUCTION

Over the last 90 years, the financial services industry has come full cycle. Originally, the banking industry operated as a full-service industry, performing directly or indirectly all financial services (commercial banking, investment banking, stock investing services, insurance providers, etc.). In the early 1930s, the economic and industrial collapse resulted in the separation of some of these activities. In the 1970s and 1980s, new, relatively unregulated financial services industries sprang up (mutual funds, brokerage funds, etc.) that separated financial services functions even further. As we entered the 21st century, regulatory barriers, technology, and financial innovation changes were such that a full set of financial services could again be offered by a single financial services firm under the umbrella of a financial services holding company. For example, J.P. Morgan Chase operates a commercial bank, J.P. Morgan Chase Bank, an investment bank, J.P. Morgan Securities (which also sells mutual funds), and an insurance company, J.P. Morgan Insurance Agency. During the financial crisis, this financial services holding company purchased a savings institution, Washington Mutual, and several investment banks, including Bear Stearns. Not only did the boundaries between traditional industry sectors change, but competition became global in nature as well. For example, J.P. Morgan Chase is the world's eighth largest financial services holding company, operating in 60 countries. Then came the late 2000s when the United States and indeed the world experienced a collapse of financial markets second only to that experienced during the Great Depression. The financial crisis produced a major reshaping of all financial institution (FI) sectors and the end of many major FIs, e.g., Bear Stearns and Lehman Brothers. The result was a call by the Obama administration to again separate activities performed by individual FIs.

As the competitive environment changes, attention to profit and, more than ever, risk becomes increasingly important. The major themes of this book are the measurement and management of the risks of financial institutions. Financial institutions (e.g., banks, credit unions, insurance companies, and mutual funds) perform the essential function of channeling funds from those with surplus funds (suppliers of funds) to those with shortages of funds (users of funds). In 2012, U.S. FIs held assets totaling more than $28.68 trillion. In contrast, the U.S. motor vehicle and parts industry (e.g., General Motors and Ford Motor Corp.) held total assets of $0.48 trillion.

Although we might categorize or group FIs and the services they perform as life insurance companies, banks, investment banks, and so on, they face many common risks. Specifically, all FIs described in this chapter and Chapters 2 through 6 (1) hold some assets that are potentially subject to default or credit risk and (2) tend to mismatch the maturities of their balance sheet assets and liabilities to a greater or lesser extent and are thus exposed to interest rate risk. Moreover, all FIs are exposed to some degree of liability withdrawal or liquidity risk, depending on the type of claims they have sold to liability holders. In addition, most FIs are exposed to some type of underwriting risk, whether through the sale of securities or the issue of various types of credit guarantees on or off the balance sheet. Finally, all FIs are exposed to operating risks because the production of financial services requires the use of real resources and back-office support systems (labor and technology combined to provide services).

Because of these risks and the special role that FIs play in the financial system, FIs are singled out for special regulatory attention. In this chapter, we first examine questions related to this specialness. In particular, what are the special functions that FIs—both depository institutions (banks, savings institutions, and credit unions) and nondepository institutions (insurance companies, securities firms, investment banks, finance companies, and mutual funds)—provide? These functions are summarized in Table 1–1. How do these functions benefit the economy? Second, we investigate what makes some FIs more special than others. Third, we look at how unique and long-lived the special functions of FIs really are. As part of this discussion, we briefly examine how changes in the way FIs deliver services

**TABLE 1–1**   **Areas of Financial Intermediaries' Specialness in the Provision of Services**

**Information costs** The aggregation of funds in an FI provides greater incentive to collect information about customers (such as corporations) and to monitor their actions. The relatively large size of the FI allows this collection of information to be accomplished at a lower average cost (so-called economies of scale) than would be the case for individuals.

**Liquidity and price risk** FIs provide financial claims to household savers with superior liquidity attributes and with lower price risk.

**Transaction cost services** Similar to economies of scale in information production costs, an FI's size can result in economies of scale in transaction costs.

**Maturity intermediation** FIs can better bear the risk of mismatching the maturities of their assets and liabilities.

**Transmission of monetary supply** Depository institutions are the conduit through which monetary policy actions by the country's central bank (the Federal Reserve) impact the rest of the financial system and the economy.

**Credit allocation** FIs are often viewed as the major, and sometimes only, source of financing for particular sectors of the economy, such as farming, small business, and residential real estate.

**Intergenerational wealth transfers** FIs, especially life insurance companies and pension funds, provide savers with the ability to transfer wealth from one generation to the next.

**Payment services** The efficiency with which depository institutions provide payment services such as check clearing directly benefits the economy.

**Denomination intermediation** FIs, such as mutual funds, allow small investors to overcome constraints to buying assets imposed by large minimum denomination size.

played a major part in the events leading up to the severe financial crisis of the late 2000s. A more detailed discussion of the causes of, major events during, and regulatory and industry changes resulting from the financial crisis is provided in Appendix 1A to the chapter (located at the book's website, **www.mhhe.com/ saunders8e**).

# FINANCIAL INSTITUTIONS' SPECIALNESS

To understand the important economic function of FIs, imagine a simple world in which FIs do not exist. In such a world, households generating excess savings by consuming less than they earn would have the basic choice: They could hold cash as an asset or invest in the securities issued by corporations. In general, corporations issue securities to finance their investments in real assets and cover the gap between their investment plans and their internally generated savings such as retained earnings.

As shown in Figure 1–1, in such a world, savings would flow from households to corporations. In return, financial claims (equity and debt securities) would flow from corporations to household savers. In an economy without FIs, the level of fund flows between household savers and the corporate sector is likely to be quite low. There are several reasons for this. Once they have lent money to a firm by buying its financial claims, households need to monitor, or check, the actions of that firm. They must be sure that the firm's management neither absconds with nor wastes the funds on any projects with low or negative net present values. Such monitoring actions are extremely costly for any given household because they require considerable time and expense to collect sufficiently high-quality information relative to the size of the average household saver's investments. Given this, it is likely that each household would prefer to leave the monitoring to others. In the end, little or no monitoring would be done. The resulting lack of monitoring would reduce the attractiveness and increase the risk of investing in corporate debt and equity.

**liquidity**
The ease of converting an asset into cash.

The relatively long-term nature of corporate equity and debt, and the lack of a secondary market in which households can sell these securities, creates a second disincentive for household investors to hold the direct financial claims issued by corporations. Specifically, given the choice between holding cash and holding long-term securities, households may well choose to hold cash for **liquidity** reasons, especially if they plan to use savings to finance consumption expenditures in the near future.

**price risk**
The risk that the sale price of an asset will be lower than the purchase price of that asset.

Finally, even if financial markets existed (without FIs to operate them) to provide liquidity services by allowing households to trade corporate debt and equity securities among themselves, investors also face a **price risk** on sale of securities, and the secondary market trading of securities involves various transaction costs. That is, the price at which household investors can sell securities on secondary markets such as the New York Stock Exchange (NYSE) may well differ from the price they initially paid for the securities.

**FIGURE 1–1**
**Flow of Funds in a World without FIs**

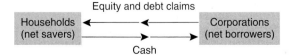

Because of (1) monitoring costs, (2) liquidity costs, and (3) price risk, the average household saver may view direct investment in corporate securities as an unattractive proposition and prefer either not to save or to save in the form of cash. However, the economy has developed an alternative and indirect way to channel household savings to the corporate sector. This is to channel savings via FIs. Because of costs of monitoring, liquidity, and price risk, as well as for some other reasons, explained later, savers often prefer to hold the financial claims issued by FIs rather than those issued by corporations. Consider Figure 1–2, which is a closer representation than Figure 1–1 of the world in which we live and the way funds flow in our economy. Notice how financial institutions or intermediaries are standing, or intermediating, between the household and corporate sectors. These intermediaries fulfill two functions; any given FI might specialize in one or the other or might do both simultaneously.

## FIs Function as Brokers

The first function is the brokerage function. When acting as a pure broker, an FI acts as an agent for the saver by providing information and transaction services. For example, full-service securities firms (e.g., Bank of America Merrill Lynch) carry out investment research and make investment recommendations for their retail (or household) clients as well as conduct the purchase or sale of securities for commission or fees. Discount brokers (e.g., Charles Schwab) carry out the purchase or sale of securities at better prices and with greater efficiency than household savers could achieve by trading on their own. This efficiency results in reduced costs of trading, or **economies of scale** (see Chapter 21 for a detailed discussion). Similarly, independent insurance brokers identify the best types of insurance policies household savers can buy to fit their savings and retirement plans. In fulfilling a brokerage function, the FI plays an extremely important role by reducing transaction and information costs or imperfections between households and corporations. Thus, the FI encourages a higher rate of savings than would otherwise exist.

**economies of scale**
The concept that the cost reduction in trading and other transaction services results in increased efficiency when FIs perform these services.

**asset transformer**
An FI issues financial claims that are more attractive to household savers than the claims directly issued by corporations.

**primary securities**
Securities issued by corporations and backed by the real assets of those corporations.

## FIs Function as Asset Transformers

The second function is the asset-transformation function. In acting as an **asset transformer,** the FI issues financial claims that are far more attractive to household savers than the claims directly issued by corporations. That is, for many households, the financial claims issued by FIs dominate those issued directly by corporations as a result of lower monitoring costs, lower liquidity costs, and lower price risk. In acting as asset transformers, FIs purchase the financial claims issued by corporations—equities, bonds, and other debt claims called **primary securities**—and finance these purchases by selling financial claims to household

**FIGURE 1–2**
**Flow of Funds in a World with FIs**

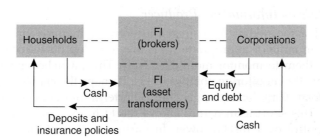

**secondary securities**
Securities issued by FIs and backed by primary securities.

investors and other sectors in the form of deposits, insurance policies, and so on. The financial claims of FIs may be considered **secondary securities** because these assets are backed by the primary securities issued by commercial corporations that in turn invest in real assets. Specifically, FIs are independent market parties that create financial products whose value added to their clients is the transformation of financial risk.

How can FIs purchase the direct or primary securities issued by corporations and profitably transform them into secondary securities more attractive to household savers? This question strikes at the very heart of what makes FIs special and important to the economy. The answer lies in the ability of FIs to better resolve the three costs facing a saver who chooses to invest directly in corporate securities.

## Information Costs

One problem faced by an average saver directly investing in a commercial firm's financial claims is the high cost of information collection. Household savers must monitor the actions of firms in a timely and complete fashion after purchasing securities. Failure to monitor exposes investors to **agency costs,** that is, the risk that the firm's owners or managers will take actions with the saver's money contrary to the promises contained in the covenants of its securities contracts. Monitoring costs are part of overall agency costs. That is, agency costs arise whenever economic agents enter into contracts in a world of incomplete information and thus costly information collection. The more difficult and costly it is to collect information, the more likely it is that contracts will be broken. In this case the saver (the so-called principal) could be harmed by the actions taken by the borrowing firm (the so-called agent).

**agency costs**
Costs relating to the risk that the owners and managers of firms that receive savers' funds will take actions with those funds contrary to the best interests of the savers.

### *FI's Role as Delegated Monitor*

One solution to this problem is for a large number of small savers to place their funds with a single FI. This FI groups these funds together and invests in the direct or primary financial claims issued by firms. This agglomeration of funds resolves a number of problems. First, the large FI now has a much greater incentive to collect information and monitor actions of the firm because it has far more at stake than does any small individual household. In a sense, small savers have appointed the FI as a **delegated monitor** to act on their behalf. Not only does the FI have a greater incentive to collect information, the average cost of collecting information is lower. For example, the cost to a small investor of buying a $100 broker's report may seem inordinately high for a $10,000 investment. For an FI with $10 million under management, however, the cost seems trivial. Such economies of scale of information production and collection tend to enhance the advantages to savers of using FIs rather than directly investing themselves.

**delegated monitor**
An economic agent appointed to act on behalf of smaller agents in collecting information and/or investing funds on their behalf.

### *FI's Role as Information Producer*

Second, associated with the greater incentive to monitor and the costs involved in failing to monitor appropriately, FIs may develop new secondary securities that enable them to monitor more effectively. Thus, a richer menu of contracts may improve the monitoring abilities of FIs. Perhaps the classic example of this is the bank loan. Bank loans are generally shorter-term debt contracts than bond contracts. This short-term nature allows the FI to exercise more monitoring power and control over the borrower. In particular, the information the FI generates regarding the firm is frequently updated as its loan renewal decisions are made. When bank loan contracts are sufficiently short term, the banker becomes almost like an insider to the firm regarding informational familiarity with its operations and financial conditions. Indeed, this more frequent monitoring often replaces the need for the relatively inflexible and hard-to-enforce covenants found in bond contracts. Thus, by acting as a delegated monitor and producing better and more timely information, FIs reduce the degree of information imperfection and asymmetry between the ultimate suppliers and users of funds in the economy.

## Liquidity and Price Risk

In addition to improving the flow and quality of information, FIs provide financial or secondary claims to household and other savers. Often, these claims have superior liquidity attributes compared with those of primary securities such as corporate equity and bonds. For example, depository institutions issue transaction account deposit contracts with a fixed principal value (and often a guaranteed interest rate) that can be withdrawn immediately on demand by household savers. Money market mutual funds issue shares to household savers that allow those savers to enjoy almost fixed principal (depositlike) contracts while often earning interest rates higher than those on bank deposits. Even life insurance companies allow policyholders to borrow against their policies held with the company at very short notice. The real puzzle is how FIs such as depository institutions can offer highly liquid and low price risk contracts to savers on the liability side of their balance sheets while investing in relatively illiquid and higher price risk securities issued by corporations on the asset side. Furthermore, how can FIs be confident enough to guarantee that they can provide liquidity services to investors and savers when they themselves invest in risky asset portfolios? And why should savers and investors believe FIs' promises regarding the liquidity of their investments?

**diversify**
Reducing risk by holding a number of different securities in a portfolio.

The answers to these questions lie in the ability of FIs to **diversify** away some but not all of their portfolio risks. The concept of diversification is familiar to all students of finance. Basically, as long as the returns on different investments are not perfectly *positively* correlated, by exploiting the benefits of size, FIs diversify away significant amounts of portfolio risk—especially the risk specific to the individual firm issuing any given security. Indeed, research has shown that equal investments in as few as 15 securities can bring significant diversification benefits to FIs and portfolio managers. Further, as the number of securities in an FI's asset portfolio increases beyond 15 securities, portfolio risk falls, albeit at a diminishing rate. What is really going on here is that FIs exploit the law of large numbers in their investments, achieving a significant amount of diversification, whereas because of their small size, many household savers are constrained to holding relatively undiversified portfolios. This risk diversification allows an FI to predict more accurately its expected return on its asset portfolio. A domestically and globally diversified FI may be able to generate an almost risk-free return on its assets. As a result, it can credibly fulfill its promise to households to supply highly liquid claims with little price or capital value risk. A good example of this is the ability of a bank to offer highly liquid demand deposits—with a fixed principal value—as liabilities, while at the same time investing in risky loans as assets. As long as an FI is sufficiently large to gain from diversification and monitoring, its financial claims are likely to be viewed as liquid and attractive to small savers compared with direct investments in the capital market.

### Other Special Services

The preceding discussion has concentrated on three general or special services provided by FIs: reducing household savers' monitoring costs, increasing their liquidity, and reducing their price risk exposure. Next, we discuss two other special services provided by FIs: reduced transaction costs and maturity intermediation.

#### Reduced Transaction Costs

Just as FIs provide potential economies of scale in information collection, they also provide potential economies of scale in transaction costs. For example, since May 1, 1975, fixed commissions for equity trades on the NYSE have been abolished. As a result, small retail buyers face higher commission charges or transaction costs than do large wholesale buyers. By grouping their assets in FIs that purchase assets in bulk—such as in mutual funds and pension funds—household savers can reduce the transaction costs of their asset purchases. In addition, bid–ask (buy–sell) spreads are normally lower for assets bought and sold in large quantities.

#### Maturity Intermediation

An additional dimension of FIs' ability to reduce risk by diversification is that they can better bear the risk of mismatching the maturities of their assets and liabilities than can small household savers. Thus, FIs offer maturity intermediation services to the rest of the economy. Specifically, through maturity mismatching, FIs can produce long-term contracts, such as long-term, fixed-rate mortgage loans to households, while still raising funds with short-term liability contracts. Further, while such mismatches can subject an FI to interest rate risk (see Chapters 8 and 9), a large FI is better able to manage this risk through its superior access to markets and instruments for hedging such as loan sales and securitization (Chapters 25 and 26); futures (Chapter 22); swaps (Chapter 24); and options, caps, floors, and collars (Chapter 23).

---

| **Concept Questions** | 1. What are the three major risks to household savers from direct security purchases? |
|---|---|
| | 2. What are two major differences between brokers (such as security brokers) and depository institutions (such as commercial banks)? |
| | 3. What are primary securities and secondary securities? |
| | 4. What is the link between asset diversification and the liquidity of deposit contracts? |

---

## OTHER ASPECTS OF SPECIALNESS

The theory of the flow of funds points to three principal reasons for believing that FIs are special, along with two other associated reasons. In reality, academics, policymakers, and regulators identify other areas of specialness relating to certain specific functions of FIs or groups of FIs. We discuss these next.

### The Transmission of Monetary Policy

The highly liquid nature of depository institution deposits has resulted in their acceptance by the public as the most widely used medium of exchange in the economy. Indeed, at the core of the two most commonly used definitions of the money supply—M1 and M2[1]—lie depository institutions' deposit contracts. Because the liabilities of depository institutions are a significant component of the money supply that impacts the rate of inflation, they play a key role in the *transmission of monetary policy* from the central bank to the rest of the economy. That is, depository institutions are the conduit through which monetary policy actions impact the rest of the financial sector and the economy in general. Indeed, a major reason the United States and world governments bailed out many depository institutions and increased the deposit insurance limit from $100,000 to $250,000 per person per bank during the financial crisis was so that central banks could implement aggressive monetary policy actions to combat collapsing financial markets. Monetary policy actions include open market operations (the purchase and sale of securities in the U.S. Treasury securities market), setting the discount rate (the rate charged on "lender of last resort" borrowing from the Federal Reserve), and setting reserve requirements (the minimum amount of reserve assets depository institutions must hold to back deposits held as liabilities on their balance sheets). Appendix 1B to the chapter (located at the book's website, **www.mhhe.com/saunders8e**) reviews the tools used by the Federal Reserve to implement monetary policy.

www.federalreserve.gov

## Credit Allocation

A further reason FIs are often viewed as special is that they are the major and sometimes the only source of financing for a particular sector of the economy pre-identified as being in special need of financing. Policymakers in the United States and a number of other countries, such as the United Kingdom, have identified *residential real estate* as needing special subsidies. This has enhanced the specialness of FIs that most commonly service the needs of that sector. In the United States, savings associations and savings banks have traditionally served the credit needs of the residential real estate sector. In a similar fashion, farming is an especially important area of the economy in terms of the overall social welfare of the population. The U.S. government has even directly encouraged financial institutions to specialize in financing this area of activity through the creation of Federal Farm Credit Banks.

## Intergenerational Wealth Transfers or Time Intermediation

The ability of savers to transfer wealth across generations is also of great importance to the social well-being of a country. Because of this, life insurance and pension funds (see Chapter 6) are often especially encouraged, via special taxation relief and other subsidy mechanisms, to service and accommodate those needs.

## Payment Services

Depository institutions (see Chapter 2) are special in that the efficiency with which they provide payment services directly benefits the economy. Two important payment services are check-clearing and wire transfer services. For example, on any given day, trillions of dollars worth of payments are effected through Fedwire and

---

[1] M1: ($2,418.6 billion outstanding in October 2012) consists of (1) currency outside the U.S. Treasury, Federal Reserve Banks, and the vaults of depository institutions; (2) traveler's checks of nonbank issuers; (3) demand deposits at all commercial banks other than those owed to depository institutions, the U.S. government, and foreign banks and official institutions, less cash items in the process of collection and Federal Reserve float; and (4) other checkable deposits (OCDs). M2: ($10,221.0 billion outstanding in October 2012) consists of M1 plus (1) savings and small time deposits (time deposits in amounts of less than $100,000) and (2) other nondeposit obligations of depository institutions.

CHIPS, the two large wholesale payment wire networks in the United States (see Chapter 17). Any breakdowns in these systems probably would produce gridlock in the payment system with resulting harmful effects to the economy.

### Denomination Intermediation

Both money market and debt–equity mutual funds are special because they provide services relating to denomination intermediation (see Chapter 5). Because they are sold in very large denominations, many assets are either out of reach of individual savers or would result in savers' holding highly undiversified asset portfolios. For example, the minimum size of a negotiable certificate of deposit (CD) is $100,000 and commercial paper (short-term corporate debt) is often sold in minimum packages of $250,000 or more. Individually, a saver may be unable to purchase such instruments. However, by buying shares in a money market mutual fund along with other small investors, household savers overcome the constraints to buying assets imposed by large minimum denomination sizes. Such indirect access to these markets may allow small savers to generate higher returns on their portfolios as well.

# SPECIALNESS AND REGULATION

**negative externalities**
Action by an economic agent imposing costs on other economic agents.

In the preceding section, FIs were shown to be special because of the various services they provide to sectors of the economy. Failure to provide these services or a breakdown in their efficient provision can be costly to both the ultimate sources (households) and users (firms) of savings. The financial crisis of the late 2000s is a prime example of how such a breakdown in the provision of financial services can cripple financial markets worldwide and bring the world economy into a recession. The **negative externalities**[2] affecting firms and households when something goes wrong in the FI sector of the economy make a case for regulation. That is, FIs are regulated to protect against a disruption in the provision of the services discussed earlier and the costs this would impose on the economy and society at large. For example, bank failures may destroy household savings and at the same time restrict a firm's access to credit. Insurance company failures may leave households totally exposed in old age to catastrophic illnesses and sudden drops in income on retirement. Further, individual FI failures may create doubts in savers' minds regarding the stability and solvency of FIs in general and cause panics and even runs on sound institutions. Indeed, this possibility provided the reasoning in 2009 for an increase in the deposit insurance cap to $250,000 per person per bank. At this time, the FDIC was more concerned about the possibility of contagious runs as a few major depository institutions (DIs) (e.g., IndyMac, Washington Mutual) failed or nearly failed. At this point, the FDIC wanted to instill confidence in the banking system and made the change to avoid massive depositor runs from many of the troubled (and even safer) DIs, more DI failures, and an even larger collapse of the financial system.

---

[2] A good example of a negative externality is the costs faced by small businesses in a one-bank town if the local bank fails. These businesses could find it difficult to get financing elsewhere, and their customers could be similarly disadvantaged. As a result, the failure of the bank may have a negative or contagious effect on the economic prospects of the whole community, resulting in lower sales, production, and employment.

Although regulation may be socially beneficial, it also imposes private costs, or a regulatory burden, on individual FI owners and managers. For example, regulations prohibit commercial banks from making loans to individual borrowers that exceed more than 10 percent of their equity capital even though the loans may have a positive net present value to the bank. Consequently, regulation is an attempt to enhance the social welfare benefits and mitigate the social costs of the provision of FI services. The private costs of regulation relative to the private benefits, for the producers of financial services, is called the **net regulatory burden.**

**net regulatory burden**
The difference between the private costs of regulations and the private benefits for the producers of financial services.

Six types of regulation seek to enhance the net social welfare benefits of financial intermediaries' services: (1) safety and soundness regulation, (2) monetary policy regulation, (3) credit allocation regulation, (4) consumer protection regulation, (5) investor protection regulation, and (6) entry and chartering regulation. Regulations are imposed differentially on the various types of FIs. For example, depository institutions are the most heavily regulated of the FIs. Finance companies, on the other hand, are subject to many fewer regulations. Regulation can also be imposed at the federal or the state level and occasionally at the international level, as in the case of bank capital requirements (see Chapter 20). Finally, because of the historically segmented nature of the U.S. FI system, many regulations in that system are institution-specific, for example, consumer protection legislation imposed on bank credit allocation to local communities. However, these institution-specific regulations are increasingly being liberalized (see Chapter 21).

## Safety and Soundness Regulation

To protect depositors and borrowers against the risk of FI failure due, for example, to a lack of diversification in asset portfolios, regulators have developed layers of protective mechanisms. These mechanisms are intended to ensure the safety and soundness of the FI and thus to maintain the credibility of the FI in the eyes of its borrowers and lenders. Indeed, even during the worst of the financial crisis deposit runs at banks, savings institutions, and credit unions did not occur. This is because the safety and soundness regulations in place protected virtually all depositors from losing their money. Thus, while depository institution failures increased significantly during the crisis, depositors felt little need to run.

In the first layer of protection are requirements encouraging FIs to diversify their assets. Thus, banks are required not to make loans exceeding more than 10 percent of their own equity capital funds to any one company or borrower (see Chapter 10). A bank that has 10 percent of its assets funded by its own capital funds (and therefore 90 percent by deposits) can lend no more than 1 percent of its assets to any one party.

The second layer of protection concerns the minimum level of capital or equity funds that the owners of an FI need to contribute to the funding of its operations (see Chapter 20). For example, bank and insurance regulators are concerned with the minimum ratio of capital to (risk) assets. The higher the proportion of capital contributed by owners, the greater the protection against insolvency risk to outside liability claim holders such as depositors and insurance policyholders. This is because losses on the asset portfolio due, for example, to the lack of diversification are legally borne by the equity holders first, and only after equity is totally wiped out by outside liability holders. For example, in 2008 the near failure and subsequent purchase by J.P. Morgan Chase of Washington Mutual left Washington Mutual shareholders with very little. Consequently, by varying the required degree of equity capital, FI regulators can directly affect the degree of risk exposure faced by nonequity claim holders in FIs. Indeed, part of the TARP program of 2008–2009 (approved by the U.S. Congress in October 2008 as a first response to the financial crisis) was the Capital Purchase Program (CPP). The goal of the CPP was to encourage U.S. financial institutions to build capital to increase the flow of financing to U.S. businesses and consumers and to support the U.S. economy. Further, regulators acted quickly to ensure the largest DIs had sufficient capital to withstand large losses during the financial crisis. In late February 2009, the Obama administration announced that it would conduct a "stress test" of the 19 largest U.S. DIs, which would measure the ability of these DIs to withstand a protracted economic slump: unemployment rate above 10 percent and home prices dropping another 25 percent. Results of the stress test showed that 10 of the 19 DIs needed to raise a total of $74.6 billion in capital. Within a month of the May 7, 2009, release of the results the DIs had raised $149.45 billion of capital. (See Chapter 20 for more discussion on the role of capital in FIs.)

www.fdic.gov
www.sipc.org

The third layer of protection is the provision of guaranty funds such as the Deposit Insurance Fund (DIF) for depository institutions, the Security Investors Protection Corporation (SIPC) for securities firms, and the state guaranty funds established (with regulator encouragement) to meet insolvency losses to small claim holders in the life and property–casualty insurance industries (see Chapter 19). By protecting FI claim holders, when an FI fails and owners' equity or net worth is wiped out, these funds create a demand for regulation of the insured institutions to protect the funds' resources (see Chapter 19 for more discussion). For example, the FDIC monitors and regulates participants in the DIF.

The fourth layer of regulation is monitoring and surveillance itself. Regulators subject all FIs, whether banks, securities firms, or insurance companies, to varying degrees of monitoring and surveillance. This involves on-site examination as well as an FI's production of accounting statements and reports on a timely basis for off-site evaluation. Just as savers appoint FIs as delegated monitors to evaluate the behavior and actions of ultimate borrowers, society appoints regulators to monitor the behavior and performance of FIs. Many of the regulatory changes proposed in reaction to the financial crisis included significant increases in the monitoring and surveillance of any financial institution whose failure could have serious systemic effects.

Finally, note that regulation is not without costs for those regulated. For example, society's regulators may require FIs to have more equity capital than private owners believe is in their own best interests. Similarly, producing the information requested by regulators is costly for FIs because it involves the time of managers, lawyers, and accountants. Again, the socially optimal amount of information may differ from an FI's privately optimal amount.[3] As noted earlier, the differences between the private benefits to an FI from being regulated—such as insurance fund guarantees—and the private costs it faces from adhering to regulation—such as examinations—is called the *net regulatory burden*. The higher the net regulatory burden on FIs, the more inefficiently they produce any given set of financial services from a private (FI) owner's perspective.

---

[3] Also, a social cost rather than social benefit from regulation is the potential risk-increasing behavior (often called *moral hazard*) that results if deposit insurance and other guaranty funds provide coverage to FIs and their liability holders at less than the actuarially fair price (see Chapter 19 for further discussion).

## Monetary Policy Regulation

www.federalreserve.gov

**outside money**
The part of the money supply directly produced by the government or central bank, such as notes and coin.

**inside money**
The part of the money supply produced by the private banking system.

Another motivation for regulation concerns the special role banks play in the transmission of monetary policy from the Federal Reserve (the central bank) to the rest of the economy. The problem is that the central bank directly controls only the quantity of notes and coin in the economy—called **outside money**—whereas the bulk of the money supply consists of deposits—called **inside money.** In theory, a central bank can vary the quantity of cash or outside money and directly affect a bank's reserve position as well as the amount of loans and deposits it can create without formally regulating the bank's portfolio. In practice, regulators have chosen to impose formal controls (these are described in Appendix 1B, located at the book's website, **www.mhhe.com/saunders8e**). In most countries, regulators commonly impose a minimum level of required cash reserves to be held against deposits (see Chapter 18). Some argue that imposing such reserve requirements makes the control of the money supply and its transmission more predictable. Such reserves also add to an FI's net regulatory burden if they are more than the institution believes are necessary for its own liquidity purposes. In general, whether banks or insurance companies, all FIs would choose to hold some cash reserves—even non-interest-bearing—to meet the liquidity and transaction needs of their customers directly. For well-managed FIs, however, this optimal level is normally low, especially if the central bank (or other regulatory body) does not pay interest or pays very little interest on required reserves. As a result, FIs often view required reserves as similar to a tax and as a positive cost of undertaking intermediation.

## Credit Allocation Regulation

Credit allocation regulation supports the FI's lending to socially important sectors such as housing and farming. These regulations may require an FI to hold a minimum amount of assets in one particular sector of the economy or to set maximum interest rates, prices, or fees to subsidize certain sectors. Examples of asset restrictions include the qualified thrift lender (QTL) test, which requires thrifts (i.e., savings institutions) to hold 65 percent of their assets in residential mortgage-related assets to retain a thrift charter, and insurance regulations, such as those in New York State that set maximums on the amount of foreign or international assets in which insurance companies can invest. Examples of interest rate restrictions are the usury laws set in many states on the maximum rates that can be charged on mortgages and/or consumer loans and regulations (now abolished) such as the Federal Reserve's Regulation Q maximums on time and savings deposit interest rates.

Such price and quantity restrictions may have justification on social welfare grounds—especially if society has a preference for strong (and subsidized) housing and farming sectors. However, they can also be harmful to FIs that have to bear the private costs of meeting many of these regulations. To the extent that the net private costs of such restrictions are positive, they add to the costs and reduce the efficiency with which FIs undertake intermediation.

## Consumer Protection Regulation

Congress passed the Community Reinvestment Act (CRA) and the Home Mortgage Disclosure Act (HMDA) to prevent discrimination in lending. For example, since 1975, the HMDA has assisted the public in determining whether banks and other mortgage-lending institutions are meeting the needs of their local communities. HMDA is especially concerned about discrimination on the basis of age, race,

www.ffiec.gov

www.federalreserve.gov
www.fdic.gov
www.occ.treas.gov

sex, or income. Since 1990, depository institutions have reported to their chief federal regulator on a standardized form the reasons credit was granted or denied. To get some idea of the information production cost of regulatory compliance in this area, consider that the Federal Financial Institutions Examination Council (FFIEC) processed information on more than 14.7 million mortgage transactions from more than 7,632 institutions in 2012. (The council is a federal supervisory body comprising the members of the Federal Reserve, the Federal Deposit Insurance Corporation (FDIC), and the Office of the Comptroller of the Currency.)[4]

Many analysts believe that community and consumer protection laws are imposing a considerable net regulatory burden on FIs without providing offsetting social benefits that enhance equal access to mortgage and lending markets. However, as deregulation proceeds and the trend toward consolidation and universal banking (see Chapter 2) continues, it is likely that such laws will be extended beyond banks to other financial service providers, such as insurance companies, that are not currently subject to CRA community lending requirements. Indeed, a new Consumer Financial Protection Bureau to protect consumers across the financial sector from unfair, deceptive, and abusive practices was a part of the Wall Street Reform and Consumer Protection Act passed by the U.S. Congress in 2010. Further, a new credit card reform bill, effective in 2010, put unprecedented restrictions on the actions that may be taken by all credit card issuers against credit card holders. Included in the bill were limits on allowable interest rate increases during the first year, limits on fees and penalties credit card companies may charge, protection against arbitrary interest rate increases, provisions giving credit card holders sufficient time to pay their bills, and the abolition of universal default (a practice in which credit card issuers would raise interest rates on customers' accounts resulting from actions on other accounts, e.g., missing a payment on a utility bill would result in an increase in a credit card rate).

## Investor Protection Regulation

A considerable number of laws protect investors who use investment banks directly to purchase securities and/or indirectly to access securities markets through investing in mutual or pension funds. Various laws protect investors against abuses such as insider trading, lack of disclosure, outright malfeasance, and breach of fiduciary responsibilities (see Chapter 4). Important legislation affecting investment banks and mutual funds includes the Securities Acts of 1933 and 1934, the Investment Company Act of 1940, and the Wall Street Reform and Consumer Protection Act of 2010. As with consumer protection legislation, compliance with these acts can impose a net regulatory burden on FIs.

## Entry Regulation

The entry and activities of FIs are also regulated (e.g., new bank chartering regulations). Increasing or decreasing the cost of entry into a financial sector affects the profitability of firms already competing in that industry. Thus, industries heavily protected against new entrants by high direct costs (e.g., through required equity or capital contributions) and high indirect costs (e.g., by restricting individuals

---

[4] The FFIEC also publishes aggregate statistics and analysis of CRA and HMDA data. The Federal Reserve and other regulators also rate bank compliance. For example, in 2012 the FDIC judged 2.6 percent of the banks examined to be outstanding in CRA compliance, 96.1 percent as satisfactory, and 1.3 percent as needing to improve or as being in noncompliance.

who can establish FIs) of entry produce bigger profits for existing firms than those in which entry is relatively easy (see Chapter 21). In addition, regulations (such as the Financial Services Modernization Act of 1999) define the scope of permitted activities under a given charter (see Chapter 21). The broader the set of financial service activities permitted under a given charter, the more valuable that charter is likely to be. Thus, barriers to entry and regulations pertaining to the scope of permitted activities affect the *charter value* of an FI and the size of its net regulatory burden.

---

| **Concept Questions** | 1. Why should more regulation be imposed on FIs than on other types of private corporations? |
| :--- | :--- |
| | 2. Define the concept of net regulatory burden. |
| | 3. What six major types of regulation do FIs face? |

---

# THE CHANGING DYNAMICS OF SPECIALNESS

At any moment in time, each FI supplies a set of financial services (brokerage related, asset transformation related, or both) and is subject to a given net regulatory burden. As the demands for the special features of financial services change as a result of changing preferences, macroeconomic conditions, and technology, one or more areas of the financial services industry become more or less profitable. Similarly, changing regulations can increase or decrease the net regulatory burden faced in supplying financial services in any given area. These demand, cost, and regulatory pressures are reflected in changing market shares in different financial service areas as some contract and others expand. Clearly, an FI seeking to survive and prosper must be flexible enough to move to growing financial service areas and away from those that are contracting. If regulatory activity restrictions inhibit or reduce the flexibility with which FIs can alter their product mix, this will reduce their competitive ability and the efficiency with which financial services are delivered. That is, activity barriers within the financial services industry may reduce the ability to diversify and potentially add to the net regulatory burden faced by FIs.

## Trends in the United States

In Table 1–2 we show the changing shares of total assets in the U.S. financial services industry from 1860 to 2012. A number of important trends are evident: most apparent is the decline in the total share of depository institutions since the Second World War. Specifically, the share of commercial banks declined from 54.5 to 32.9 percent between 1948 and 2012, while the share of thrifts (savings banks, savings associations, and credit unions) fell from 12.0 to 6.9 percent over the same period. Thus, services provided by depository institutions (payment services, transaction costs services, information cost) have become relatively less significant as a portion of all services provided by FIs. Similarly, insurance companies also witnessed a secular decline in their share, from 26.0 to 14.6 percent.

The most dramatically increasing trend is the rising share of investment companies (mutual funds and money market mutual funds), increasing their share from 0.3 to 19.8 percent between 1948 and 2012. Investment companies differ from

**TABLE 1–2** Percentage Shares of Assets of Financial Institutions in the United States, 1860–2012

Sources: Randall Kroszner, "The Evolution of Universal Banking and Its Regulation in Twentieth Century America," chap. 3 in Anthony Saunders and Ingo Walter, eds., *Universal Banking Financial System Design Reconsidered* (Burr Ridge, IL: Irwin, 1996); and Federal Reserve Board, "Flow of Fund Accounts," various issues. *www.federalreserve.gov*

| | 1860 | 1900 | 1922 | 1929 | 1948 | 1960 | 1970 | 1980 | 2000 | 2005 | 2012 |
|---|---|---|---|---|---|---|---|---|---|---|---|
| Commercial banks | 71.4% | 62.9% | 63.3% | 53.7% | 54.5% | 40.8% | 42.6% | 40.7% | 30.5% | 29.3% | 32.9% |
| Thrift institutions | 17.8 | 18.2 | 13.9 | 14.0 | 12.0 | 21.0 | 23.0 | 25.0 | 10.1 | 10.2 | 6.9 |
| Insurance companies | 10.7 | 13.8 | 16.7 | 18.6 | 26.0 | 24.2 | 19.0 | 16.2 | 15.6 | 15.0 | 14.6 |
| Investment companies | — | — | 0.0 | 2.4 | 0.3 | 0.7 | 0.7 | 2.0 | 15.8 | 13.7 | 19.8 |
| Pension funds | — | 0.0 | 0.0 | 0.7 | 3.8 | 7.7 | 8.0 | 9.5 | 8.8 | 6.2 | 7.6 |
| Finance companies | — | 0.0 | 0.0 | 2.0 | 2.7 | 5.2 | 5.7 | 6.2 | 6.9 | 7.3 | 4.8 |
| Securities brokers and dealers | 0.0 | 3.8 | 5.3 | 8.1 | 0.7 | 0.4 | 0.7 | 0.3 | 12.1 | 17.3 | 12.1 |
| Real estate investment trusts | — | — | — | — | — | 0.0 | 0.3 | 0.1 | 0.2 | 1.0 | 1.3 |
| Total (%) | 100.0% | 100.0% | 100.0% | 100.0% | 100.0% | 100.0% | 100.0% | 100.0% | 100.0% | 100.0% | 100.0% |
| Total ($ trillions) | 0.001 | 0.016 | 0.075 | 0.123 | 0.218 | 0.500 | 1.079 | 3.140 | 15.93 | 23.80 | 28.68 |

banks and insurance companies in that they give savers cheaper access to the direct securities markets. They do so by exploiting the comparative advantages of size and diversification, with the transformation of financial claims, such as maturity transformation, a lesser concern. Thus, open-ended mutual funds buy stocks and bonds directly in financial markets and issue savers shares whose value is linked in a direct pro rata fashion to the value of the mutual fund's asset portfolio. Similarly, money market mutual funds invest in short-term financial assets such as commercial paper, CDs, and Treasury bills and issue shares linked directly to the value of the underlying portfolio. To the extent that these funds efficiently diversify, they also offer price risk protection and liquidity services.

### The Rise of Financial Services Holding Companies

To the extent that the financial services market is efficient and these trends reflect the forces of demand and supply, they indicate a trend: savers increasingly prefer the denomination intermediation and information services provided by mutual funds. These FIs provide investments that closely mimic diversified investments in the *direct* securities markets over the transformed financial claims offered by traditional FIs. This trend may also indicate that the net regulatory burden on traditional FIs—such as banks and insurance companies—is higher than that on investment companies. Indeed, traditional FIs are unable to produce their services as cost efficiently as they could previously.

Recognizing this changing trend, the U.S. Congress passed the Financial Services Modernization (FSM) Act, which repealed the 1933 Glass-Steagall barriers between commercial banking, insurance, and investment banking. The act, promoted as the biggest change in the regulation of financial institutions in 70 years, allowed for the creation of "financial services holding companies" that could engage in banking activities, insurance activities, and securities activities. Thus, after 70 years of partial or complete separation between insurance, investment banking, and commercial banking, the Financial Services Modernization Act of 1999 opened the door for the creation of full-service financial institutions in the United States similar to those that existed before 1933 and that exist in many other countries. As a result, while Table 1–2 lists assets of financial institutions by functional area, the financial services holding company (which combines these activities in a single financial institution) has become the dominant form of financial institution in terms of total assets.

### The Shift Away from Risk Measurement and Management and the Financial Crisis

Certainly, a major event that changed and reshaped the financial services industry was the financial crisis of the late 2000s. As FIs adjusted to regulatory changes brought about by the likes of the FSM Act, one result was a dramatic increase in systemic risk of the financial system, caused in large part by a shift in the banking model from that of "originate and hold" to "originate to distribute." In the traditional model, banks take short term deposits and other sources of funds and use them to fund longer term loans to businesses and consumers. Banks typically hold these loans to maturity, and thus have an incentive to screen and monitor borrower activities even after a loan is made. However, the traditional banking model exposes the institution to potential liquidity, interest rate, and credit risk. In attempts to avoid these risk exposures and generate improved return–risk trade-offs, banks have shifted to an underwriting model in which they originate or warehouse loans, and then quickly sell them. Figure 1–3 shows the growth in bank loan secondary market trading from 1991 through the third quarter of 2012. Note the huge growth in bank loan trading even during the financial crisis of 2008–2009. When loans trade, the secondary market produces information that can substitute for the information and monitoring of banks.[5] Further, banks may have lower incentives to collect information and monitor borrowers if they sell loans rather than keep them as part of the bank's portfolio of assets. Indeed, most large banks are organized as financial service holding companies to facilitate these new activities.

More recently, activities of shadow banks—nonfinancial service firms that perform banking services—have facilitated the change from the originate and hold model of commercial banking to the originate and distribute banking model. Participants in the shadow banking system include structured investment vehicles (SIVs), special-purpose vehicles (SPVs), asset-backed paper vehicles, credit hedge funds, asset-backed commercial paper (ABCP) conduits, limited-purpose finance companies, money market mutual funds (MMMFs), and credit hedge funds (see Chapter 21 for a detailed discussion of these FIs). In the shadow banking system, savers place their funds with money market mutual[6] and similar funds, which invest these funds in the liabilities of other shadow banks. Borrowers get loans and leases from shadow banks such as finance companies rather than from banks. Like the traditional banking system, the shadow banking system intermediates the flow of funds between net savers and net borrowers. However, instead of the bank serving as the middleman, it is the nonbank financial service firm, or shadow bank, that intermediates. Further, unlike the traditional banking system,

**FIGURE 1–3**
**Bank Loan Secondary Market Trading, 1991–2012Q3**

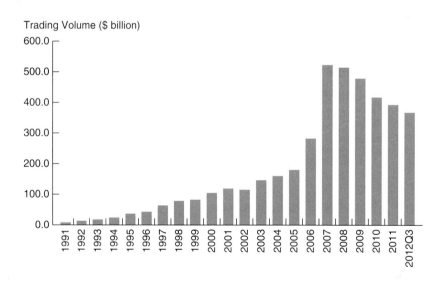

Trading Volume ($ billion)

[5] A. Gande and A. Saunders, "Are Banks Still Special When There Is a Secondary Market for Loans?" *Journal of Finance,* 2012, pp. 1649–1684, find that equity of borrowers whose bank loans trade on secondary markets for the first time receive positive announcement period returns. Further, announcements by banks of new loans to a borrower after the borrower's loans begin trading in the secondary markets show positive announcement period returns.

[6] Recent regulatory proposals recognize that MMMFs are operating as "banks." These proposals include requirements that MMMFs maintain capital levels similar to banks and/or that fund shares be backed by a private deposit insurance scheme.

where the complete credit intermediation is performed by a single bank, in the shadow banking system it is performed through a series of steps involving many nonbank financial service firms.

These innovations remove risk from the balance sheet of financial institutions and shift risk off the balance sheet to other parts of the financial system. Since the FIs, acting as underwriters, are not exposed to the credit, liquidity, and interest rate risks of traditional banking, they have little incentive to screen and monitor activities of borrowers to whom they originate loans. Thus, FIs' role as specialists in risk measurement and management has been reduced.

Adding to FIs' move away from risk measurement and management was the boom ("bubble") in the housing markets, which began building in 2001, particularly after the terrorist attacks of 9/11. The immediate response by regulators to the terrorist attacks was to create stability in the financial markets by providing liquidity to FIs. For example, the Federal Reserve lowered the short-term interest rate that banks and other financial institutions pay in the federal funds market and even made lender of last resort funds available to nonbank FIs such as investment banks. Perhaps not surprisingly, low interest rates and the increased liquidity provided by the central banks resulted in a rapid expansion in consumer, mortgage, and corporate debt financing. Demand for residential mortgages and credit card debt rose dramatically. As the demand for mortgage debt grew, especially among those who had previously been excluded from participating in the market because of their poor credit ratings, FIs began lowering their credit quality cut-off points. Moreover, to boost their earnings, in the market now popularly known as the "subprime market," banks and other mortgage-supplying institutions often offered relatively low "teaser" rates on adjustable rate mortgages (ARMs), i.e., exceptionally low initial interest rates, but, if market rates rose in the future, substantial increases in rates could occur after the initial rate period expired two or three years later. Under the traditional, originate and hold, banking model, banks might have been reluctant to so aggressively pursue low credit quality borrowers for fear that the loans would default. However, under the originate to distribute model of banking, asset securitization and loan syndication allowed banks to retain little or no part of the loans, and hence the default risk on loans that they originated. Thus, as long as the borrower did not default within the first months after a loan's issuance and the loans were sold or securitized without recourse back to the bank, the issuing bank could ignore longer term credit risk concerns. The result was a deterioration in credit quality, at the same time as there was a dramatic increase in consumer and corporate leverage.

Eventually, in 2006, housing prices started to fall. At the same time, the Federal Reserve started to raise interest rates as it began to fear inflation. Since many subprime mortgages originated in the 2001–2005 period had adjustable rates, the cost of meeting mortgage commitments rose to unsustainable levels for many low income households. The confluence of falling house prices, rising interest rates, and rising mortgage costs led to a wave of mortgage defaults in the subprime market and foreclosures that only reinforced the downward trend in house prices. The number of subprime mortgages that were more than 60 days behind on their payments was 17.1 percent in June 2007 and more than 20 percent in August 2007. As this happened, the poor quality of the collateral and credit quality underlying subprime mortgage pools became apparent, with default rates far exceeding those apparently anticipated by the rating agencies in setting their initial subprime mortgage securitizations ratings. In 2007, the percentage of subprime mortgage-backed securities delinquent by 90 days or more was 10.09 percent, substantially higher than the 5.37 percent rate in May 2005. The financial crisis began. Appendix 1A to the chapter (located at the book's website, **www.mhhe.com/saunders8e**) provides a detailed discussion of the causes of, major events during, and regulatory and industry changes resulting from the financial crisis

The economy relies on financial institutions to act as specialists in risk measurement and management. The importance of this was demonstrated in the aftermath of the FIs' failure to perform this critical function during the global financial crisis. The result was a worldwide breakdown in credit markets, as well as an enhanced level of equity market volatility. When FIs failed to perform their critical risk measurement and management functions, the result was a crisis of confidence that disrupted financial markets.

## Global Trends

In addition to these domestic trends, U.S. FIs must now compete not only with other domestic FIs but increasingly with foreign FIs that provide services (such as payment services and denomination intermediation) comparable to those of U.S. FIs. For example, Table 1–3 lists the 10 largest banks in the world, measured by total assets as of October 2012. Notice that only 1 of the top 10 banks is a U.S. bank. Table 1–4 lists foreign versus domestic bank offices' assets held in the United States from 1992 through 2012. Total foreign bank assets over this period increased

**TABLE 1–3**
The 10 Largest
Banks in the World
(in millions of
dollars)

Source: *The Banker,* February
2012. *www.thebanker.com*

| | Total Assets |
|---|---|
| Deutsche Bank (Germany) | $2,809.9 |
| Mitsubishi UFJ Financial Group (Japan) | 2,803.4 |
| Industrial & Commerce Bank of China (China) | 2,763.6 |
| HSBC Holdings (United Kingdom) | 2,721.1 |
| Barclays Bank (United Kingdom) | 2,584.3 |
| BNP Paribas (France) | 2,563.0 |
| Japan Post Bank (Japan) | 2,513.2 |
| J.P. Morgan Chase (United States) | 2,321.3 |
| Crédit Agricole Groupe (France) | 2,317.1 |
| Royal Bank of Scotland (United Kingdom) | 2,295.8 |

**TABLE 1–4**  Domestic versus Foreign Bank Offices' Assets Held in the United States (in billions of dollars)

Source: Federal Reserve Board, "Flow of Fund Accounts," Statistical Releases, various dates. *www.federalreserve.gov*

| | 1992 | 1997 | 1999 | 2002 | 2004 | 2008 | 2012 |
|---|---|---|---|---|---|---|---|
| **Foreign Bank Financial Assets** | $ 510.9 | $ 819.1 | $ 763.5 | $ 823.0 | $ 664.1 | $ 1,624.5 | $ 1,976.7 |
| **Domestic Bank Financial Assets** | 3,824.4 | 4,858.5 | 5,664.4 | 6,979.1 | 8,371.8 | 11,639.0 | 11,747.6 |

from $510.9 billion in 1992 to $1,976.7 billion in 2012. This consistently represents over 10 percent (and has been as high as 21.9 percent) of total assets held in the United States.

| **Concept Questions** | 1. Is the share of bank and thrift assets growing as a proportion of total FI assets in the United States? |
|---|---|
| | 2. What are the fastest growing FIs in the United States? |
| | 3. What were the causes of the financial crisis? |
| | 4. Describe the global challenges facing U.S. FIs in the early 2000s. |

*Internet Exercise* Go to the website of the Board of Governors of the Federal Reserve, and find the latest information available for foreign bank offices' assets and liabilities held in the United States using the following steps. At **www.federalreserve.gov**, click on "Economic Research and Data." Click on "Flow of Funds Accounts of the United States." Click on the most recent date. Click on "Level Tables." This will download a file to your computer that will contain the most recent information in Tables L.110 and L.111.

## Summary

This chapter described various factors and forces impacting financial institutions and the specialness of the services they provide. These forces have resulted in FIs, which have historically relied on making profits by performing traditional special functions (such as asset transformation and the provision of liquidity services), expanding into selling financial services that interface with direct security market transactions, such as asset management, insurance, and underwriting services. This is not to say that specialized or niche FIs cannot survive but rather that only the most efficient FIs will prosper as the competitive value of a specialized FI charter declines.

The major theme of this book is the measurement and management of FI risks. In particular, although we might categorize or group FIs and label them life insurance companies, banks, finance companies, and so on, in fact, they face risks that are more common than different. Specifically, all the FIs described in this and the next five chapters (1) hold some assets that are potentially subject to default or credit risk and (2) tend to mismatch the maturities of their balance sheets to a greater or lesser extent and are thus exposed to interest rate risk. Moreover, all are exposed to some degree of saver withdrawal or liquidity risk depending on the type of claims sold to liability holders. And most are exposed to some type of underwriting risk, whether through the sale of securities or by issuing various types of credit guarantees on or off the balance sheet. Finally, all are exposed to operating cost risks because the production of financial services requires the use of real resources and back-office support systems.

In Chapters 7 through 26 of this textbook, we investigate the ways managers of FIs are measuring and managing this inventory of risks to produce the best return-risk trade-off for shareholders in an increasingly competitive and contestable market environment.

## Questions and Problems

1. What are five risks common to all financial institutions?

2. Explain how economic transactions between household savers of funds and corporate users of funds would occur in a world without financial institutions.

3. Identify and explain three economic disincentives that would dampen the flow of funds between household savers of funds and corporate users of funds in an economic world without financial institutions.

4. Identify and explain the two functions FIs perform that would enable the smooth flow of funds from household savers to corporate users.

5. In what sense are the financial claims of FIs considered *secondary securities,* while the financial claims of commercial corporations are considered *primary securities?* How does the transformation process, or intermediation, reduce the risk, or economic disincentives, to savers?

6. Explain how financial institutions act as delegated monitors. What secondary benefits often accrue to the entire financial system because of this monitoring process?

7. What are five general areas of FI specialness that are caused by providing various services to sectors of the economy?

8. What are agency costs? How do FIs solve the information and related agency costs experienced when household savers invest directly in securities issued by corporations?

9. How do large FIs solve the problem of high information collection costs for lenders, borrowers, and financial markets?

10. How do FIs alleviate the problem of liquidity risk faced by investors who wish to buy securities issued by corporations?

11. How do financial institutions help individual savers diversify their portfolio risks? Which type of financial institution is best able to achieve this goal?

12. How can financial institutions invest in high-risk assets with funding provided by low-risk liabilities from savers?

13. How can individual savers use financial institutions to reduce the transaction costs of investing in financial assets?

14. What is maturity intermediation? What are some of the ways the risks of maturity intermediation are managed by financial institutions?

15. What are five areas of institution-specific FI specialness and which types of institutions are most likely to be the service providers?

16. How do depository institutions such as commercial banks assist in the implementation and transmission of monetary policy?

17. What is meant by credit allocation regulation? What social benefit is this type of regulation intended to provide?

18. Which intermediaries best fulfill the intergenerational wealth transfer function? What is this wealth transfer process?

19. What are two of the most important payment services provided by financial institutions? To what extent do these services efficiently provide benefits to the economy?

20. What is denomination intermediation? How do FIs assist in this process?

21. What is negative externality? In what ways do the existence of negative externalities justify the extra regulatory attention received by financial institutions?

22. If financial markets operated perfectly and costlessly, would there be a need for financial institutions?

23. Why are FIs among the most regulated sectors in the world? When is the net regulatory burden positive?

24. What forms of protection and regulation do the regulators of FIs impose to ensure their safety and soundness?
25. In the transmission of monetary policy, what is the difference between *inside money* and *outside money?* How does the Federal Reserve try to control the amount of inside money? How can this regulatory position create a cost for depository institutions?
26. What are some examples of credit allocation regulation? How can this attempt to create social benefits create costs to a private institution?
27. What is the purpose of the Home Mortgage Disclosure Act? What are the social benefits desired from the legislation? How does the implementation of this legislation create a net regulatory burden on financial institutions?
28. What legislation has been passed specifically to protect investors who use investment banks directly or indirectly to purchase securities? Give some examples of the types of abuses for which protection is provided.
29. How do regulations regarding barriers to entry and the scope of permitted activities affect the *charter value* of financial institutions?
30. What reasons have been given for the growth of investment companies at the expense of "traditional" banks and insurance companies?
31. What events resulted in banks' shift from the traditional banking model of "originate and hold" to a model of "originate and distribute"?
32. How did the boom in the housing market in the early and mid-2000s exacerbate FIs' transition away from their role as specialists in risk measurement and management?

The following questions and problems are based on material in Appendix 1B to the chapter.

33. What are the tools used by the Federal Reserve to implement monetary policy?
34. Suppose the Federal Reserve instructs the Trading Desk to purchase $1 billion of securities. Show the result of this transaction on the balance sheets of the Federal Reserve System and commercial banks.
35. Explain how a decrease in the discount rate affects credit availability and the money supply.
36. What changes did the Fed implement to its discount window lending policy in the early 2000s?
37. Bank Three currently has $600 million in transaction deposits on its balance sheet. The Federal Reserve has currently set the reserve requirement at 10 percent of transaction deposits.
    a. Suppose the Federal Reserve decreases the reserve requirement to 8 percent. Show the balance sheet of Bank Three and the Federal Reserve System just before and after the full effect of the reserve requirement change. Assume that Bank Three withdraws all excess reserves and gives out loans and that borrowers eventually return all of these funds to Bank Three in the form of transaction deposits.
    b. Redo part (a) using a 12 percent reserve requirement.
38. Which of the monetary tools available to the Federal Reserve is most often used? Why?
39. Describe how expansionary activities conducted by the Federal Reserve impact credit availability, the money supply, interest rates, and security prices. Do the same for contractionary activities.

## Web Questions

40. Go to the Federal Reserve Board's website at **www.federalreserve.gov**. Find the latest figures for M1 and M2 using the following steps. Click on "Economic Research and Data." Click on "View All." Click on "Money Stock Measures." This downloads a file onto your computer that contains the relevant data. By what percentage have these measures of the money supply grown over the past year?

41. Go to the Federal Reserve Board's website at **www.federalreserve.gov**. Find the latest figures for financial assets outstanding at various types of financial institutions using the following steps. Click on "Economic Research and Data." Click on "Flow of Funds Accounts of the United States." Click on the most recent date. Click on "Level tables." This downloads a file onto your computer that contains the relevant data. How has the percent of financial assets held by commercial banks changed since that listed in Table 1–2 for 2012?

## Appendix 1A: The Financial Crisis: The Failure of Financial Services Institution Specialness

View Appendix 1A at the website for this textbook **(www.mhhe.com/saunders8e).**

## Appendix 1B: Monetary Policy Tools

View Appendix 1B at the website for this textbook **(www.mhhe.com/saunders8e).**

# Chapter Two

See Appendices Online at www.mhhe.com/saunders8e
- Appendix 2A: Financial Statement Analysis Using a Return on Equity (ROE) Framework
- Appendix 2B: Commercial Banks' Financial Statements and Analysis
- Appendix 2C: Depository Institutions and Their Regulators
- Appendix 2D: Technology in Commercial Banking

# Financial Services: Depository Institutions

## INTRODUCTION

A theme of this book is that the products sold and the risks faced by modern financial institutions are becoming increasingly similar, as are the techniques used to measure and manage those risks. To illustrate this, Tables 2–1A and 2–1B contrast the products sold by the financial services industry in 1950 with those sold in 2013. In 1999, the U.S. Congress passed the Financial Services Modernization Act (FSMA), which repealed regulations that set barriers between commercial banking, insurance, and investment banking. The bill, promoted as the biggest change in the regulation of financial institutions in nearly 70 years, allowed for the creation of "financial services holding companies" that could engage in banking activities,

**TABLE 2–1A** Products Sold by the U.S. Financial Services Industry, 1950

| | Function | | | | | | | |
|---|---|---|---|---|---|---|---|---|
| | | | | Lending | | Underwriting Issuance of | | Insurance and Risk Management |
| Institution | Payment Services | Savings Products | Fiduciary Services | Business | Consumer | Equity | Debt | Products |
| Depository institutions | X | X | X | X | X | | | |
| Insurance companies | | X | | * | | | | X |
| Finance companies | | | | * | X | | | |
| Securities firms | | X | X | | | X | X | |
| Pension funds | | X | | | | | | |
| Mutual funds | | X | | | | | | |

* Minor involvement.

**TABLE 2–1B**    **Products Sold by the U.S. Financial Services Industry, 2013**

| | | | | Lending | | Underwriting Issuance of | | Insurance and Risk Management Products |
|---|---|---|---|---|---|---|---|---|
| Institution | Payment Services | Savings Products | Fiduciary Services | Business | Consumer | Equity | Debt | |
| Depository institutions | X | X | X | X | X | X | X | X |
| Insurance companies | X | X | X | X | X | X | X | X |
| Finance companies | X | X | X | X | X | † | † | X |
| Securities firms | X | X | X | X | X | X | X | X |
| Pension funds | | X | X | X | | | | X |
| Mutual funds | X | X | X | | | | | |

† Selective involvement via affiliates.

insurance activities, *and* securities activities. The bill also allowed large banks to place certian activities, including some securities underwriting, in direct bank subsidiaries. Thus, after nearly 70 years of partial or complete separation between the various functions performed by financial institutions, the FSMA opened the door for the creation of full-service financial institutions in the United States. Legislation enacted as a result of the financial crisis, however, represents a partial reversal of this trend. For example, the "Volcker rule" provision of the Wall Street Reform and Consumer Protection Act prohibits bank holding companies from engaging in proprietary trading and limits their investments in hedge funds, private equity, and related vehicles. Despite these most recent changes, many FIs operate in more than one of the industries discussed in the next five chapters.

Furthermore, during the financial crisis, several nondepository financial institutions (e.g., investment banks Goldman Sachs and Morgan Stanley and finance company GMAC) requested and were allowed to convert to bank holding companies. The change was recognition that their models of finance and investing had become too risky and the FIs needed the cushion of bank deposits that kept some of the bigger commercial banks like J.P. Morgan Chase relatively safe during the crisis. By becoming bank holding companies, the firms agreed to significantly tighter regulations and much closer supervision by bank examiners from government agencies rather than only the Securities and Exchange Commission. The new charters required the FIs to be subject to more disclosure, hold higher capital reserves, and take less risk. However, the new banks would also have access to the full array of the Federal Reserve lending facilities, something the failed investment bank Lehman Brothers did not have.

In this chapter we begin by describing three major FI groups—commercial banks, savings institutions, and credit unions—which are also called *depository institutions* (DIs) because a significant proportion of their funding comes from customer deposits. Historically, commercial banks have operated as more diversified institutions, having a large concentration of residential mortgage assets but holding commercial loans and consumer loans as well. Savings institutions have concentrated primarily on residential mortgages. Finally, credit unions have historically focused on consumer loans funded with member deposits. In Chapters 3 through 6 other (nondepository) FIs will be described. We focus on four major characteristics of each group: (1) size, structure, and composition of the industry group, (2) balance sheets and recent trends, (3) regulation, and (4) industry performance.

**FIGURE 2–1**
A Simple
Depository
Institution Balance
Sheet

Depository Institutions

| Assets | Liabilities and Equity |
|--------|------------------------|
| Loans | Deposits |
| Other assets | Other liabilities and equity |

**TABLE 2–2**
Largest Depository
Institutions, 2012
(Banks and Savings
Institutions Ranked
by Total Assets
on September 30,
2012, in billions of
dollars)

Source: Quarterly reports,
2012.

| Company | Banking Assets | Holding Company Assets |
|---------|----------------|------------------------|
| 1. J.P. Morgan Chase | $1,812.8 | $2,321.3 |
| 2. Bank of America | 1,445.1 | 2,168.0 |
| 3. Citigroup | 1,347.8 | 1,931.3 |
| 4. Wells Fargo | 1,180.2 | 1,374.7 |
| 5. U.S. Bancorp | 342.8 | 352.3 |
| 6. PNC Financial Services Corp. | 291.8 | 301.1 |
| 7. Bank of New York Mellon | 259.1 | 340.1 |
| 8. State Street Corp. | 197.0 | 204.1 |
| 9. TD Bank | 195.9 | 212.5 |
| 10. HSBC North America | 194.0 | 320.8 |

Figure 2–1 presents a very simplified product-based balance sheet for depository institutions. Notice that DIs offer products to their customers on both sides of their balance sheets (loans on the asset side and deposits on the liability side). This joint-product nature of the DI business creates special challenges for management as they deal with the many risks facing these institutions. These risks will be discussed later, in Chapters 7 through 26.

Table 2–2 lists the largest U.S. depository institutions in 2012. The ranking is by size of assets devoted to banking services. The table also lists the assets at the holding company level. Many of these large depository institutions (e.g., J.P. Morgan Chase, Bank of America) operate in other financial service areas (e.g., investment banking and security brokerage) as well. Thus, assets held at the holding company level can be much larger than just those devoted to banking services. Several depository institutions manage assets of over $1 trillion which reflects the dramatic trend toward consolidation and mergers among financial service firms in the 1990s and 2000s. The largest bank is J.P. Morgan Chase, created from the merger of J.P. Morgan, Chase Manhattan, Bank One, and Washington Mutual; the second largest is Bank of America, created by the merger of NationsBank BankAmerica, and FleetBoston; and the third largest is Citigroup, created from the merger of Citicorp and Travelers Insurance.

# COMMERCIAL BANKS

**commercial bank**
A bank that accepts
deposits and makes
consumer, commercial,
and real estate loans.

**Commercial banks** make up the largest group of depository institutions measured by asset size. They perform functions similar to those of savings institutions and credit unions. That is, they accept deposits (liabilities) and make loans (assets). However, they differ in their composition of assets and liabilities, which are much more varied. Commercial bank liabilities usually include several types of nondeposit sources of funds, while their loans are broader in range, including consumer, commercial, and real estate loans. Commercial banking activity is also

**FIGURE 2–2**
**Breakdown of Loan Portfolios**

Source: Federal Deposit Insurance Corporation, September 2012. *www.fdic.gov*

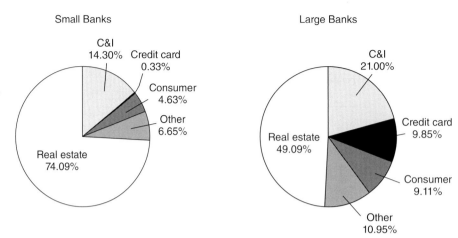

Small Banks

C&I 14.30%   Credit card 0.33%
Consumer 4.63%
Other 6.65%
Real estate 74.09%

Large Banks

C&I 21.00%
Credit card 9.85%
Real estate 49.09%
Consumer 9.11%
Other 10.95%

Note: Small banks are defined as banks with assets less than $1 billion. Large banks are defined as banks with assets of $1 billion or more.

regulated separately from the activities of savings institutions and credit unions. Within the banking industry the structure and composition of assets and liabilities also vary significantly across banks of different asset sizes. For example, as shown in Figure 2–2, small banks make proportionately fewer commercial and industrial (C&I) loans and more real estate loans than do big banks.

## Size, Structure, and Composition of the Industry

In late 2012 the United States had 6,168 commercial banks. Even though this may seem a large number, in fact, the number of banks has been shrinking. For example, in 1985 there were 14,416 banks, and in 1989 there were 12,744. Figure 2–3 illustrates the number of bank mergers, bank failures, and new charters for the period 1980 through 2012. Notice that much of the change in the size, structure, and composition of this industry is the result of mergers and acquisitions. It was

**FIGURE 2–3   Structural Changes in the Number of Commercial Banks, 1980–2012**

Source: Federal Deposit Insurance Corporation, *Quarterly Banking Profile,* various issues. *www.fdic.gov*

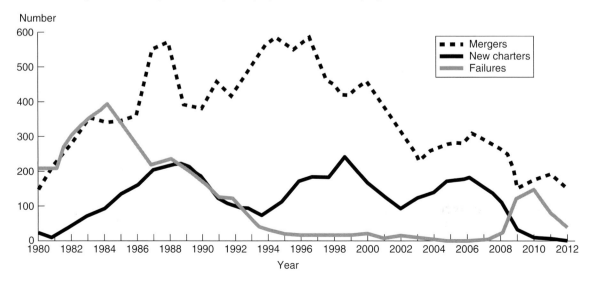

**TABLE 2–3**
Number of
Subsidiaries of
Selected Financial
Services Holding
Companies

Source: D. Avraham,
P. Selvaggi, and J.I. Vickery,
"A Structural View of U.S.
Bank Holding Companies,"
*FRBNY Economic Policy
Review,* July 2012.

| Holding Company Rank | Name | Domestic | | Foreign |
|---|---|---|---|---|
| | | Commercial Bank | Other | |
| 1 | J.P. Morgan Chase | 4 | 2,936 | 451 |
| 2 | Bank of America | 5 | 1,541 | 473 |
| 3 | Citigroup | 2 | 935 | 708 |
| 4 | Wells Fargo | 5 | 1,270 | 91 |
| 5 | Goldman Sachs | 1 | 1,444 | 1,670 |
| 7 | Morgan Stanley | 1 | 1,593 | 1,289 |
| 10 | Bank of New York Mellon | 3 | 211 | 146 |
| 20 | Regions Financial | 1 | 35 | 4 |
| 30 | Comerica | 2 | 72 | 2 |
| 40 | First Horizon National | 1 | 35 | 1 |
| 50 | Webster Financial | 1 | 21 | 0 |

not until the 1980s and 1990s that regulators (such as the Federal Reserve or state banking authorities) allowed banks to merge with other banks across state lines (interstate mergers), and it has only been since 1994 that Congress has passed legislation (the Riegle-Neal Act) easing branching by banks across state lines. Indeed, the number of branches at U.S. banks has increased from 43,293 in 1985 to 83,209 in 2012. Table 2–3 reports the number of subsidiaries for some of the largest financial services holding companies. Many of the nonbank subsidiaries reported in the table manage trusts and investment funds beyond the traditional banking business.

Further, the industry has seen some of the largest mergers and acquisitions ever, such as J.P. Morgan's acquisition of Chase Manhattan (for $33.6 billion) in September 2000, Bank of America's acquisition of FleetBoston Financial (for $49.3 billion) in October 2003, J.P. Morgan Chase's acquisition of Bank One (for $60.0 billion) in January 2004, and Bank of New York's accuisition of Mellon Financial (for $18.3 billion) in 2007. Thus, while back-office operations are being consolidated, bank customers have an increase in the number of branch locations available to them. Finally, it has only been since 1987 that banks have possessed (limited) powers to underwrite corporate securities. Full authority to enter the investment banking (and insurance) business was received only with the passage of the Financial Services Modernization Act in 1999. Thus, commercial banks may now merge with investment banks (and insurance companies). In subsequent chapters, we discuss the impact that changing regulations as well as technological advances have had on the drop in the number of commercial banks (e.g., technology changes [Chapter 17], regulatory changes [Chapter 21], and competition [Chapter 21]).

A comparison of asset concentration by bank size (see Table 2–4) indicates that the consolidations in banking appear to have reduced the asset share of the smallest banks (under $1 billion) from 36.6 percent in 1984 to 9.0 percent in 2012. These smaller or **community banks**—under $1 billion in asset size—tend to specialize in retail or consumer banking, such as providing residential mortgages and consumer loans and accessing the local deposit base. Clearly, this group of banks is decreasing in both number and importance.

**community banks**
Banks that specialize
in retail or consumer
banking.

**TABLE 2–4** U.S. Bank Asset Concentration, 1984 versus 2012

Source: *FDIC Quarterly Banking Profile,* fourth quarter 1984 and third quarter 2012. *www.fdic.gov*

| | 2012 | | | | 1984 | | | |
|---|---|---|---|---|---|---|---|---|
| | Number | Percent of Total | Assets* | Percent of Total | Number | Percent of Total | Assets* | Percent of Total |
| **All FDIC-insured commercial banks** | 6,168 | | 13,069.9 | | 14,483 | | $2,508.9 | |
| 1. Under $100 million | 2,034 | 33.0% | 118.0 | 0.9% | 12,044 | 83.2% | 404.2 | 16.1% |
| 2. $100 million–$1 billion | 3,608 | 58.5 | 1,059.2 | 8.1 | 2,161 | 14.9 | 513.9 | 20.5 |
| 3. $1 billion–$10 billion | 437 | 7.1 | 1,133.6 | 8.7 | 254 | 1.7 | 725.9 | 28.9 |
| 4. $10 billion or more | 89 | 1.4 | 10,759.1 | 82.3 | 24 | 0.2 | 864.8 | 34.5 |

* In billions of dollars.

**regional or superregional banks**
Banks that engage in a complete array of wholesale commercial banking activities.

**federal funds market**
An interbank market for short-term borrowing and lending of bank reserves.

**money center banks**
Banks that have a heavy reliance on nondeposit or borrowed sources of funds.

The relative asset share of the largest banks (more than $1 billion in assets), on the other hand, increased from 63.4 percent in 1984 to 91.0 percent in 2012. The majority of banks in the two largest size classes are often either **regional or superregional banks.** They engage in a more complete array of wholesale commercial banking activities, encompassing consumer and residential lending as well as commercial and industrial lending (C&I loans), both regionally and nationally. In addition, the big banks access markets for purchased funds—such as the interbank or **federal funds market**—to finance their lending and investment activities. However, some of the very biggest banks often have the separate title **money center banks.** Currently, five banking organizations constitute the money center bank group: Bank of New York Mellon, Deutsche Bank (through its U.S. acquisition of Bankers Trust), Citigroup, J.P. Morgan Chase, and HSBC Bank USA (formerly Republic NY Corporation).[1,2] This number has been declining because of the megamergers, discussed earlier.

It is important to note that asset or lending size does not necessarily make a bank a money center bank. Thus, Bank of America Corporation, with $1,445 billion in assets in 2012 (the second-largest U.S. bank organization), is not a money center bank, while Bank of New York Mellon (with only $259 billion in assets) is. What makes a bank a money center bank is partly location[3] and partly its heavy reliance on nondeposit or borrowed sources of funds. In fact, because of its extensive retail branch network,[4] Bank of America tends to be a net supplier of funds on the interbank market (federal funds market). By contrast, money center banks have few retail branches and rely almost entirely on wholesale and borrowed funds as sources of assets or liabilities. Money center banks are also major participants in foreign currency markets and are therefore subject to foreign exchange risk (see Chapter 13).

[1] Bankers Trust was purchased by Deutsche Bank (a German bank) in 1998. The Bankers Trust name, however, has been retained for U.S. operations. Republic NY Corporation was purchased by HSBC (a British bank) in 1999. Republic NY Bank has been retained for U.S. operations under the name HSBC Bank USA.

[2] These banking organizations are mostly holding companies that own and control the shares of a bank or banks.

[3] A money center bank normally is headquartered in New York or Chicago. These are the traditional national and regional centers for correspondent banking services offered to smaller community banks.

[4] In 2012 Bank of America had more than 5,700 branches nationwide.

**TABLE 2–5**
ROA and ROE
of Banks by Size,
1990–2012

Source: Federal Deposit
Insurance Corporation,
Various dates. *www.fdic.gov*

| Percentage Return on Assets (insured commercial banks by consolidated assets) | | | | | |
|---|---|---|---|---|---|
| Year | All Banks | $0–$100 Million | $100 Million– $1 Billion | $1 Billion– $10 Billion | $10 Billion+ |
| 1990 | 0.49% | 0.79% | 0.78% | 0.76% | 0.38% |
| 1995 | 1.17 | 1.18 | 1.25 | 1.28 | 1.10 |
| 2000 | 1.19 | 1.01 | 1.28 | 1.29 | 1.16 |
| 2001 | 1.16 | 0.91 | 1.20 | 1.31 | 1.13 |
| 2003 | 1.40 | 0.94 | 1.27 | 1.46 | 1.42 |
| 2006 | 1.33 | 0.95 | 1.24 | 1.35 | 1.35 |
| 2007 | 0.95 | 0.82 | 1.06 | 1.08 | 0.92 |
| 2008 | 0.16 | 0.36 | 0.38 | −0.10 | 0.16 |
| 2009 | 0.09 | 0.06 | −0.01 | −0.35 | 0.15 |
| 2010 | 0.66 | 0.36 | 0.34 | 0.19 | 0.75 |
| 2012 | 1.02 | 0.78 | 0.89 | 1.25 | 1.01 |

| Percentage Return on Equity (insured commercial banks by consolidated assets) | | | | | |
|---|---|---|---|---|---|
| Year | All Banks | $0–$100 Million | $100 Million– $1 Billion | $1 Billion– $10 Billion | $10 Billion+ |
| 1990 | 7.64% | 9.02% | 9.95% | 10.25% | 6.68% |
| 1995 | 14.68 | 11.37 | 13.48 | 15.04 | 15.60 |
| 2000 | 14.07 | 9.09 | 13.56 | 14.57 | 14.42 |
| 2001 | 13.10 | 8.07 | 12.24 | 13.77 | 13.43 |
| 2003 | 15.31 | 8.19 | 12.80 | 14.00 | 16.37 |
| 2006 | 13.06 | 7.38 | 12.20 | 12.65 | 13.40 |
| 2007 | 9.29 | 6.00 | 10.34 | 9.47 | 9.22 |
| 2008 | 1.62 | 2.76 | 3.68 | −0.90 | 1.70 |
| 2009 | 0.85 | 0.46 | −0.15 | −3.16 | 1.44 |
| 2010 | 5.99 | 3.06 | 3.35 | 1.67 | 6.78 |
| 2012 | 9.06 | 6.69 | 8.36 | 10.66 | 8.97 |

**spread**
The difference
between lending and
deposit rates.

The bigger banks tend to fund themselves in national markets and lend to larger corporations. This means that their **spreads** (i.e., the difference between lending and deposit rates) in the past (the 1990s) often were narrower than those of smaller regional banks, which were more sheltered from competition in highly localized markets. As a result, the largest banks' return on assets (ROA) was below that of smaller banks (see Table 2–5). However, as the barriers to interstate competition and expansion in banking have fallen in recent years and as large banks have focused more on off-balance-sheet activities to generate income (see below), the largest banks' ROAs as well as returns on equity (ROEs) have often outperformed those of the smallest banks, especially those with assets under $100 million (see Table 2–5). Appendix 2A (located at the book's website, **www.mhhe.com/saunders8e**) shows how a bank's ROE can be decomposed to examine the different underlying sources of profitability. This decomposition of ROE is often referred to as *DuPont analysis*. Appendix 2B (also located at the book's website) contains an overview of the evaluation of bank performance and risk exposure.

The U.S. banking system is unique in that it consists of not only very big banks but also a large number of relatively small community banks. This unique banking structure is largely the result of a legal framework that until recently restricted banks' abilities to diversify geographically. Over time, with regulatory change (see below) and financial innovation, large banks have become complex organizations engaged in a wide range of activities worldwide. These large banks provide a variety of services to their customers, but often rely on factual financial information, computer models, and centralized decision making as the basis for conducting business. Small banks focus more on relationship banking, often basing decisions on personal knowledge of customers' creditworthiness and an understanding of business conditions in the communities they serve. As discussed above, with increased merger activity over the last 30 years, the number of community banks (while still large) has declined. Although community banks hold only a small share of the nation's banking assets, they provide important financial services (such as small-business lending) for which there are few, if any, substitutes. Thus, community banks will likely continue to play an important role in the banking industry even as technology and market conditions change.

## Balance Sheet and Recent Trends

### Assets

Figure 2–4 shows the broad trends over the 1951–2012 period in the four principal earning asset areas of commercial banks: business loans (or C&I loans), securities, mortgages, and consumer loans. Although business loans were the major asset on bank balance sheets between 1965 and 1987, there has been a drop in their importance (as a proportion of the balance sheet) since 1987. This drop has been mirrored by an offsetting rise in holdings of securities and mortgages. These trends reflect a number of long-term and temporary influences. One important long-term influence has been the growth of the commercial paper market, which has become an alternative funding source for major corporations. Another has been the securitization of mortgages—the pooling and packaging of mortgage loans for sale in the form of bonds (see Chapter 26). A more temporary influence was the so-called

**FIGURE 2–4**    **Portfolio Shift: U.S. Commercial Banks' Financial Assets**

Source: Federal Deposit Insurance Corporation, Statistics on Depository Institutions. *www.fdic.gov*

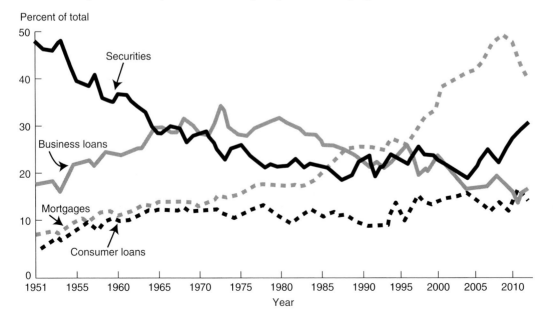

**TABLE 2–6**
**Balance Sheet (All U.S. Commercial Banks) as of September 30, 2012 (in billions of dollars)**

Source: Federal Deposit Insurance Corporation, September 30, 2012. *www.fdic.gov*

| Assets | | | | |
|---|---|---|---|---|
| Loans and securities | | | | $10,653.2 |
| Investment securities | | | $3,909.3 | |
| U.S. government securities | | $1,705.6 | | |
| Other | | 2,203.7 | | |
| Total loans | | | 6,743.9 | |
| Interbank loans | | 104.6 | | |
| Loans excluding interbank | | 6,639.3 | | |
| Commercial and industrial | $1,401.2 | | | |
| Real estate | 3,569.9 | | | |
| Individual | 1,206.9 | | | |
| All other | 619.8 | | | |
| Less: Reserve for loan losses | 158.5 | | | |
| Total cash assets | | | | 1,228.4 |
| Other assets | | | | 1,188.3 |
| Total assets | | | | 13,069.9 |
| **Liabilities** | | | | |
| Total deposits | | | | $ 9,622.4 |
| Deposits held in foreign offices | | | $1,443.9 | |
| Deposits held in domestic offices | | | 8,178.5 | |
| Transaction accounts | | $1,303.0 | | |
| Nontransaction accounts | | 6,875.5 | | |
| Borrowings | | | | 1,568.6 |
| Other liabilities | | | | 378.2 |
| Total liabilities | | | | 11,569.2 |
| Total equity capital | | | | 1,500.7 |

credit crunch and decline in the demand for business loans as a result of the economic downturn and recession in 1989–92 and 2001–02. Further, the financial crisis and the recession of 2007–09 resulted in a reduction in all areas of lending and an increase in the banks' holdings of less risky securities investments (e.g., Treasury securities, federal funds, and U.S. government agency securities).

Look at the detailed balance sheet for all U.S. commercial banks as of September 2012 (Table 2–6). Total loans amount to $6,743.9 billion, or 51.6 percent of total assets, and fall into four broad classes: business or C&I ($1,401.2 billion); commercial and residential real estate ($3,569.9 billion); individual, such as consumer loans for auto purchases and credit card debt ($1,206.9 billion); and all other loans, such as less developed country (LDC) loans ($619.8 billion). In the investment security portfolio of $3,909.3 billion, or 29.9 percent of total assets, U.S. government securities, such as Treasury bonds, constitute $1,705.6 billion, with other securities (in particular, municipal securities and investment-grade corporate bonds) making up the rest.[5]

A major inference we can draw from this asset structure is that credit or default risk exposure is a major risk faced by modern commercial bank managers (see Chapters 10 and 11). Because commercial banks are highly leveraged and therefore

---

[5] The footnotes to commercial bank balance sheets also distinguish between securities held by banks for trading purposes, normally for less than one year, and those held for longer-term investment purposes. The large money center banks are often active in the secondary market trading of government securities, reflecting their important role as primary dealers in government securities at the time of Treasury security auctions.

hold little equity (see below) compared with total assets, even a relatively small number of loan defaults can wipe out the equity of a bank, leaving it insolvent.[6]

### Liabilities

Commercial banks have two major sources of funds other than the equity provided by owners: deposits and borrowed or other liability funds. A major difference between banks and other firms is banks' high leverage. For example, banks had an average ratio of equity to assets of 11.48 percent in 2012. This implies that 88.52 percent of their assets were funded by debt, either deposits or borrowed funds.

Note in Table 2–6, the aggregate balance sheet of U.S. banks, that deposits amounted to $9,622.4 billion, or 73.6 percent of total liabilities and equity, and borrowings and other liabilities were $1,568.6 billion and $378.2 billion, respectively. Of the total stock of deposits, transaction accounts constituted 13.5 percent, or $1,303.0 billion. **Transaction accounts** are checkable deposits that bear no interest (demand deposits) or are interest bearing (most commonly called **NOW accounts,** or negotiable order of withdrawal accounts). Since their introduction in 1980, interest-bearing checking accounts—especially NOW accounts—have dominated the transaction accounts of banks. However, since limitations are imposed on the ability of corporations to hold such accounts and since there are minimum balance requirements for NOW accounts, non-interest-bearing demand deposits are still held. The second major segment of deposits is retail or household savings and time deposits (also called certificates of deposits or CDs), normally individual account holdings of less than $100,000. Important components of bank retail savings accounts are small nontransaction accounts, which include passbook savings accounts and retail time deposits. Small nontransaction accounts constitute 63.6 percent of total deposits, or $6,123.0 billion. However, this disguises an important trend in the supply of these deposits to banks. Specifically, retail savings and time deposits have been falling in recent years, largely as a result of competition from **money market mutual funds.** These funds pay a competitive rate of interest based on wholesale money market rates by pooling and investing funds (see Chapter 5) while requiring relatively small-denomination investments by mutual fund investors.

The third major source of deposit funds consists of large time deposits (over $100,000), which amounted to $752.5 billion, or approximately 7.8 percent of the stock of deposits, in September 2012. These are primarily **negotiable CDs** (deposit claims with promised interest rates and fixed maturities of at least 14 days) that can be resold to outside investors in an organized secondary market. As such, they are usually distinguished from retail time deposits by their negotiability and secondary market liquidity.

Nondeposit liabilities comprise borrowings and other liabilities that together total 16.8 percent of all bank liabilities, or $1,946.8 billion. These categories include a broad array of instruments, such as purchases of federal funds (bank reserves) on the interbank market and repurchase agreements (temporary swaps of securities for federal funds) at the short end of the maturity spectrum to the issuance of notes and bonds at the longer end.[7]

**transaction accounts**
The sum of non-interest-bearing demand deposits and interest-bearing checking accounts.

**NOW accounts**
Interest-bearing checking accounts.

**money market mutual funds**
Specialized mutual funds that offer depositlike interest bearing claims to savers.

**negotiable CDs**
Fixed-maturity interest-bearing deposits with face values over $100,000 that can be resold in the secondary market.

---

[6] Losses such as those due to defaults are charged off against the equity (stockholders' stake) in a bank. Additions to the reserve for loan and lease losses account (and, in turn, the expense account "provisions for losses on loans and leases") to meet *expected* defaults reduce retained earnings and, thus, reduce equity of the bank. *Unexpected* defaults (e.g., due to a sudden major recession) are meant to be written off against the remainder of the bank's equity (e.g., its retained earnings and funds raised from share offerings).

[7] These instruments are explained in greater detail in later chapters, especially Chapter 18.

Overall, the liability structure of bank balance sheets tends to reflect a shorter maturity structure than does the asset portfolio with relatively more liquid instruments, such as deposits and interbank borrowings, used to fund less liquid assets such as loans. Thus, maturity mismatch or interest rate risk and liquidity risk are key exposure concerns for bank managers (see Chapters 8, 9, 12, and 18).

### Equity

Commercial bank equity capital (11.48 percent of total liabilities and equity in 2012) consists mainly of common and preferred stock (listed at par value), surplus or additional paid-in capital, and retained earnings. Regulators require banks to hold a minimum level of equity capital to act as a buffer against losses from their on- and off-balance-sheet activities (see Chapter 20). Because of the relatively low cost of deposit funding, banks tend to hold equity close to the minimum levels set by regulators. As we discuss in subsequent chapters, this impacts banks' exposures to risk and their ability to grow—both on and off the balance sheet—over time.

Part of the TARP program of 2008–2009 was the Capital Purchase Program intended to encourage U.S. financial institutions to build capital to increase the flow of financing to U.S. businesses and consumers and to support the U.S. economy. Under the program, the Treasury purchased more than $200 billion of senior preferred equity. The senior preferred shares rank senior to common stock should the bank be closed. In addition to capital injections received as part of the Capital Purchase Program, TARP provided additional emergency funding to Citigroup ($25 billion) and Bank of America ($20 billion). Through 2012, $245 billion of TARP capital injections had been allocated to DIs, of which $233.7 billion has been paid back plus a return of $33.9 billion in dividends and assessments to the government.

As part of the 2010 Wall Street Reform and Consumer Protection Act, the largest banks are subject to annual stress tests, designed to ensure that the banks are properly capitalized. Scenarios used as part of the stress tests range from mild to calamitous, with the most extreme including a 5 percent decline in gross domestic product, an unemployment rate of 12 percent, and a volatile stock market that loses half its value. The original stress test was announced in late February 2009 when the Obama administration announced that it would conduct a "stress test" of the 19 largest U.S. DIs, which would measure the ability of these DIs to withstand a protracted economic slump: unemployment rate above 10 percent and home prices dropping another 25 percent. Results of this first stress test showed that 10 of the 19 DIs needed to raise a total of $74.6 billion in capital. Within a month of the May 7, 2009, release of the results, the DIs had raised $149.45 billion of capital. As part of the 2013 stress tests, the worst-case scenario includes international events, i.e., the eurozone plunges into recession and a sharp slowdown in China spills into neighboring countries.

---

*Internet Exercise*   Go to the Federal Deposit Insurance Corporation website (**www.fdic.gov**) and find the latest balance sheet information available for commercial banks using the following steps. Click on "Analysts." Click on "Statistics on Banking." Click on "Run Report." This will download a file onto your computer that will contain the most recent balance sheet information for commercial banks.

### *Off-Balance-Sheet Activities*

The balance sheet itself does not reflect the total scope of bank activities. Banks conduct many fee-related activities off the balance sheet. Off-balance-sheet (OBS) activities are important, in terms of their dollar value and the income they generate for banks—especially as the ability of banks to attract high-quality loan applicants and deposits becomes ever more difficult. OBS activities include issuing various types of guarantees (such as letters of credit), which often have a strong insurance underwriting element, and making future commitments to lend. Both services generate additional fee income for banks. Off-balance-sheet activities also involve engaging in derivative transactions—futures, forwards, options, and swaps.

**off-balance-sheet asset**
An item that moves onto the asset side of the balance sheet when a contingent event occurs.

**off-balance-sheet liability**
An item that moves onto the liability side of the balance sheet when a contingent event occurs.

Under current accounting standards, such activities are not shown on the current balance sheet. Rather, an item or activity is an **off-balance-sheet asset** if, when a contingent event occurs, the item or activity moves onto the asset side of the balance sheet or an income item is realized on the income statement. Conversely, an item or activity is an **off-balance-sheet liability** if, when a contingent event occurs, the item or activity moves onto the liability side of the balance sheet or an expense item is realized on the income statement.

By moving activities off the balance sheet, banks hope to earn additional fee income to complement declining margins or spreads on their traditional lending business. At the same time, they can avoid regulatory costs or "taxes" since reserve requirements and deposit insurance premiums are not levied on off-balance-sheet activities (see Chapter 16). Thus, banks have both earnings and regulatory "tax-avoidance" incentives to undertake activities off their balance sheets.

Off-balance-sheet activities, however, can involve risks that add to the overall insolvency exposure of an FI. Indeed, at the very heart of the financial crisis were losses associated with off-balance-sheet mortgage-backed securities created and held by FIs. Losses resulted in the failure, acquisition, or bailout of some of the largest FIs and a near meltdown of the world's financial and economic systems. However, off-balance-sheet activities and instruments have both risk-reducing as well as risk-increasing attributes, and, when used appropriately, they can reduce or hedge an FI's interest rate, credit, and foreign exchange risks.

We show the notional, or face, value of bank OBS activities, and their distribution and growth, for 1992 to 2012 in Table 2–7. Notice the relative growth in the notional dollar value of OBS activities in Table 2–7. By September 2012, the notional value of OBS bank activities was $236,945.3 billion compared with the $13,069.9 billion value of on-balance-sheet activities. It should be noted that the notional, or face, value of OBS activities does not accurately reflect the risk to the bank undertaking such activities. The potential for the bank to gain or lose is based on the possible change in the market value over the life of the contract rather than the notional, or face, value of the contract, normally less than 3 percent of the notional value of an OBS contract.[8]

The use of derivative contracts (futures and forwards, swaps, and options) accelerated during the 1992–2012 period and accounted for much of the growth in OBS activity. Along with the growth in the notional value of OBS activities, banks have seen significant growth in the percentage of their total operating income

---

[8] For example, the market value of a swap (today) is the difference between the present value of the cash flows (expected) to be received minus the present value of cash flows expected to be paid (see Chapter 24).

**TABLE 2–7**   Aggregate Volume of Off-Balance-Sheet Commitments and Contingencies by U.S. Commercial Banks, (in billions of dollars)

Sources: FDIC, *Statistics on Banking,* various issues. *www.fdic.gov*

| | 1992 | 2003 | 2007 | 2009 | 2012* | Distribution 2012 |
|---|---|---|---|---|---|---|
| Commitments to lend | $ 1,272.0 | $ 5,398.9 | $ 7,263.9 | $ 5,406.3 | $ 5,234.6 | 2.2% |
| Future and forward contracts (exclude FX) | | | | | | |
| On commodities and equities | 26.3 | 104.9 | 251.2 | 186.2 | 345.2 | 0.2 |
| On interest rates | 1,738.1 | 7,209.8 | 9,116.9 | 20,995.8 | 30,634.9 | 12.9 |
| Notional amount of credit derivatives | 9.6 | 1,001.2 | 15,862.8 | 14,112.3 | 13,997.6 | 5.9 |
| Standby contracts and other option contracts | | | | | | |
| Option contracts on interest rates | 1,012.7 | 12,539.5 | 20,984.4 | 27,166.2 | 26,332.8 | 11.1 |
| Option contracts on foreign exchange | 494.8 | 1,298.3 | 4,024.7 | 2,714.0 | 4,480.8 | 1.9 |
| Option contracts on commodities | 60.3 | 767.5 | 2,715.9 | 2,001.5 | 2,539.5 | 1.1 |
| Commitments to buy FX (includes $US), spot, and forward | 3,015.5 | 4,351.1 | 10,057.9 | 9,212.5 | 15,321.4 | 6.5 |
| Standby LCs and foreign office guarantees | 162.5 | 348.9 | 1,139.6 | 1,098.5 | 1,257.5 | 0.5 |
| (amount of these items sold to others via participations) | (14.9) | (60.3) | (220.5) | (192.1) | (302.0) | |
| Commercial LCs | 28.1 | 24.2 | 29.7 | 22.5 | 24.2 | 0.0 |
| Participations in acceptances | 1.0 | 0.5 | 0.1 | 0.0 | 0.0 | 0.0 |
| Securities borrowed or lent | 107.2 | 852.0 | 2,052.2 | 1,027.3 | 996.7 | 0.4 |
| Other significant commitments and contingencies | 8.7 | 53.3 | 173.1 | 151.7 | 224.3 | 0.1 |
| Notional value of all outstanding swaps | 2,122.0 | 44,082.7 | 103,091.1 | 139,126.6 | 135,555.8 | 57.2 |
| Total | $10,075.8 | $78,032.8 | $176,763.5 | $223,221.4 | $236,945.3 | 100.0% |
| Total assets (on-balance-sheet items) | $ 3,476.4 | $ 7,602.5 | $ 11,176.1 | $ 11,822.7 | $ 13,069.9 | |

*FX* = foreign exchange; LC = letter of credit.
* As of September.

(interest income plus noninterest income) coming from these non-balance-sheet activities. Indeed, the percentage of noninterest income to total operating income has increased from 22.66 percent in 1979 to 33.73 percent in 2012. As we discuss in detail in Chapters 22 through 24, the significant growth in derivative securities activities by commercial banks has been a direct response to the increased interest rate risk, credit risk, and foreign exchange risk exposures they have faced, both domestically and internationally. In particular, these contracts offer banks a way to hedge these risks without having to make extensive changes on the balance sheet. However, these assets and liabilities also introduce unique risks that must be managed. The failure or near failure of some of the largest U.S. financial institutions during the financial crisis can be attributed to risks associated with OBS activities (e.g., Citigroup). As mortgage borrowers defaulted on their mortgages, financial institutions that held these "toxic" mortgages and "toxic" credit derivatives (in the form of mortgage backed securities) started announcing huge losses on them. Losses from the falling value of OBS securities reached over $1 trillion worldwide through 2009.

The TARP gave the U.S. Treasury funds to buy "toxic" mortgages and other securities from financial institutions. However, the TARP plan was slow to be instituted and not all FIs chose to participate in the program. Better capitalized FIs wanted to hold on to their troubled OBS securities rather than sell them and record losses. Then early 2009 saw a plunge in the market values of financial institutions. Banks such as Citigroup, Bank of America, and J.P. Morgan Chase traded at less than their book value as investors had little confidence in the value of their assets. As a result, a new plan, announced on February 10, 2009, involved a number of initiatives, including offering federal insurance to banks against losses on bad assets and expanding the Fed's Term Asset-Backed Securities Loan Facility (TALF). Further, the Treasury, working with the Federal Reserve, FDIC, and private investors, created the Public–Private Investment Fund (PPIF) to acquire real-estate related OBS assets. By selling to PPIF, financial institutions could reduce balance sheet risk, support new lending, and help improve overall market functioning. The PPIF facility was initially funded at $500 billion with plans to expand the program to up to $1.25 trillion over time. After several months of discussion, in July 2009, the government had selected nine financial firms to manage a scaled-down program; investing $30 billion to start the fund. The selected firms had 12 weeks to raise $500 million of capital each from private investors willing to invest in FI's toxic assets. The total investment would be matched by the federal government. The purchases of $1.25 trillion in OBS mortgage-backed securities were completed in March 2010.

Although the simple notional dollar value of OBS items overestimates their risk exposure amounts, the increase in these activities is still nothing short of phenomenal. Indeed, this phenomenal increase pushed regulators into imposing capital requirements on such activities and explicitly recognizing an FI's solvency risk exposure from pursuing such activities. We describe these capital requirements in Chapter 20. Further, as a result of the role derivatives played in the financial crisis, in spring 2009, regulators proposed a revamping of the U.S. financial regulatory system that included extending regulatory oversight to unregulated OTC derivative securities (see below). The regulation requires that all over-the-counter derivative contracts be subject to regulation, all derivatives dealers subject to supervision, and regulators be empowered to enforce rules against manipulation and abuse.

## Other Fee-Generating Activities

Commercial banks engage in other fee-generating activities that cannot easily be identified from analyzing their on- and off-balance-sheet accounts. Two of these are trust services and correspondent banking.

### Trust Services

The trust department of a commercial bank holds and manages assets for individuals or corporations. Only the largest banks have sufficient staff to offer trust services. Individual trusts represent about one-half of all trust assets managed by commercial banks. These trusts include estate assets and assets delegated to bank trust departments by less financially sophisticated investors. Pension fund assets are the second largest group of assets managed by the trust departments of commercial banks. The banks manage the pension funds, act as trustees for any bonds held by the pension funds, and act as transfer and disbursement agents for the pension funds.

### Correspondent Banking

Correspondent banking is the provision of banking services to other banks that do not have the staff resources to perform the service themselves. These services include check clearing and collection, foreign exchange trading, hedging services, and participation in large loan and security issuances. Correspondent banking services are generally sold as a package of services. Payment for the services is generally in the form of non-interest-bearing deposits held at the bank offering the correspondent services (see Chapter 16).

## Regulation

### The Regulators

Unlike banks in countries that have one or sometimes two regulators, U.S. banks may be subject to the supervision and regulations of up to four separate regulators. The key regulators are the Federal Deposit Insurance Corporation (FDIC), the Office of the Comptroller of the Currency (OCC), the Federal Reserve System (FRS), and state bank regulators. Next, we look at the principal roles played by each regulator. Appendix 2C (located at the book's website, **www.mhhe.com/ saunders8e**) lists in greater detail the regulators that oversee the various activities of depository institutions.

www.fdic.gov    ***The FDIC***   Because of the serious social welfare effects that a contagious run on depository institutions could have, the Federal Deposit Insurance Corporation (FDIC) has established guarantee programs offering deposit holders varying degrees of insurance protection to deter depositor "runs." While a run on an unhealthy DI is not necessarily a bad thing, there is a risk that runs on bad DIs can become contagious and spread to good or well-run DIs. In a contagious run or panic conditions, liability holders do not bother to distinguish between good and bad DIs but, instead, seek to turn their liabilities into cash or safe securities as quickly as possible. Contagious runs can have a major contractionary effect on the supply of credit as well as the money supply regionally, nationally, or even internationally. Moreover, a contagious run on DIs can have serious social welfare effects. For example, a major run on banks can have an adverse effect on the level of savings in all types of FIs and therefore can inhibit the ability of individuals to transfer wealth through time to protect themselves against major risks such as future ill health and falling income in old age. However, if a deposit holder believes a claim is totally secure, even if the DI is in trouble, the holder has no incentive to run. Thus, FDIC deposit insurance deters runs as well as contagious runs and panics.

To see how deposit insurance protects commercial banks from depositor runs, consider the case of Bear Stearns, an investment bank. In the summer of 2007, two Bear Stearns hedge funds suffered heavy losses on investments in the subprime mortgage market. The two funds filed for bankruptcy in the fall of 2007. Bear Stearns' market value was hurt badly from these losses. The losses became so great that by March 2008 Bear Stearns was struggling to finance its day-to-day operations. Lacking of any kind of federal insurance of its liabilities, rumors of Bear Stearns' liquidity crisis became a reality as investors began quickly selling their stock and draining what little liquid assets the firm had left; the first major run on a U.S. FI since the Great Depression. In contrast, during the financial crisis investors, looking for a "safer haven" for their money, deposited funds in FDIC-insured depository institutions.

In exchange for insuring the deposits of member banks, the Federal Deposit Insurance Corporation levies insurance premiums on member banks, manages the deposit insurance fund, and carries out bank examinations. Further, when an insured bank is closed, the FDIC acts as the receiver and liquidator—although the closure decision itself is technically in the hands of the bank chartering or licensing agency, such as the OCC. Because of the problems in the thrift industry and the insolvency of the savings association insurance fund (FSLIC) in 1989, the FDIC managed both the commercial bank insurance fund and the savings association insurance fund. In 2007, the two funds were combined into one, the Deposit Insurance Fund (DIF). The number of FDIC-insured banks and the division between nationally chartered and state chartered banks is shown in Figure 2–5.

www.occ.treas.gov

*Office of the Comptroller of the Currency (OCC)*   The OCC is the oldest bank regulatory agency. Established in 1863, it is a subagency of the U.S. Treasury. Its primary function is to charter so-called national banks as well as to close them. In addition, the OCC examines national banks and has the power to approve or disapprove their merger applications. However, instead of seeking a national charter, banks can be chartered by any of 50 individual state bank regulatory agencies. The choice of being a nationally chartered or state chartered bank lies at the foundation of the **dual banking system** in the United States. While most large banks, such as Bank of America, choose national charters, this is not always the case. For example, Morgan Guaranty, the money center bank subsidiary of J.P. Morgan Chase, is chartered as a state bank under New York state law. In September 2012, 1,273 banks were *nationally* chartered and 4,895 were *state* chartered, with approximately 69 percent and 31 percent of total commercial bank assets, respectively.

**dual banking system**
The coexistence of both nationally chartered and state chartered banks in the United States.

www.federalreserve.gov

*Federal Reserve System*   Apart from being concerned with the conduct of monetary policy, as this country's central bank, the Federal Reserve also has regulatory power over some banks and, when relevant, their holding company parents. All of the 1,273 nationally chartered banks in Figure 2–5 are automatically members of

**FIGURE 2–5**
**Bank Regulators**

Source: FDIC (internal figures), September 2012. *www.fdic.gov*

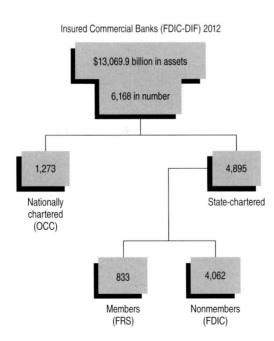

Insured Commercial Banks (FDIC-DIF) 2012

$13,069.9 billion in assets

6,168 in number

1,273 — Nationally chartered (OCC)

4,895 — State-chartered

833 — Members (FRS)

4,062 — Nonmembers (FDIC)

the Federal Reserve system; 833 state-chartered banks also have chosen to become members. Since 1980, all banks have had to meet the same non-interest-bearing reserve requirements whether they are members of the Federal Reserve System (FRS) or not. The primary advantages of FRS membership are direct access to the federal funds wire transfer network for nationwide interbank borrowing and lending of reserves and to the discount window for lender of last resort borrowing of funds. Finally, many banks are often owned and controlled by parent **holding companies.** For example, Citigroup is the parent holding company of Citibank (a bank). Because the holding company's management can influence decisions taken by a bank subsidiary and thus influence its risk exposure, the Federal Reserve System regulates and examines bank holding companies as well as banks.

**holding companies**
Parent companies that own a controlling interest in subsidiary banks or other FIs.

## *Regulations*

Because of the inherent special nature of banking and banking contracts (see Chapter 1), commercial banks are among the most regulated firms in the U.S. economy. Regulators have imposed numerous restrictions on their product and geographic activities. Table 2–8 lists the major laws from the McFadden Act of 1927 to the Wall Street Reform and Consumer Protection Act of 2010 and briefly describes the key features of each act.

**TABLE 2–8**
**Major Bank Laws,**
**Major Features**

### 1927 The McFadden Act
1. Made branching of nationally chartered banks subject to the same branching regulations as state-chartered banks.
2. Liberalized national banks' securities underwriting activities, which previously had to be conducted through state-chartered affiliates.

### 1933 The Banking Acts of 1933
1. The Glass-Steagall Act generally prohibited commercial banks from underwriting securities with four exceptions:
   *a.* Municipal general obligation bonds.
   *b.* U.S. government bonds.
   *c.* Private placements.
   *d.* Real estate loans.
2. In addition, the acts established the FDIC to insure bank deposits.
3. The Glass-Steagall Act prohibited banks from paying interest on demand deposits.

### 1956 The Bank Holding Company Act
1. Restricted the banking and nonbanking acquisition activities of multibank holding companies.
2. Empowered the Federal Reserve to regulate multibank holding companies by:
   *a.* Determining permissible activities.
   *b.* Exercising supervisory authority.
   *c.* Exercising chartering authority.
   *d.* Conducting bank examinations.

### 1970 Amendments to the Bank Holding Company Act of 1956
1. Extended the BHC Act of 1956 to one-bank holding companies.
2. Restricted permissible BHC activities to those "closely related to banking."

### 1978 International Banking Act
1. Regulated foreign bank branches and agencies in the United States.
2. Subjected foreign banks to the McFadden and Glass-Steagall Acts.
3. Gave foreign banks access to Fedwire, the discount window, and deposit insurance.

*(continued)*

**TABLE 2–8**
*(continued)*

**1980 Depository Institutions Deregulation and Monetary Control Act (DIDMCA)**

1. Set a six-year phaseout for Regulation Q interest rate ceilings on small time and savings deposits.
2. Authorized NOW accounts nationwide.
3. Introduced uniform reserve requirements for state-chartered and nationally chartered banks.
4. Increased the ceiling on deposit insurance coverage from $40,000 to $100,000.
5. Allowed federally chartered thrifts to make consumer and commercial loans (subject to size restrictions).

**1982 Garn–St. Germain Depository Institutions Act (DIA)**

1. Introduced money market deposit accounts (MMDAs) and super NOW accounts as interest rate–bearing savings accounts with limited check-writing features.
2. Allowed federally chartered thrifts more extensive lending powers and demand deposit–taking powers.
3. Allowed sound commercial banks to acquire failed savings institutions.
4. Reaffirmed limitations on bank powers to underwrite and distribute insurance.

**1987 Competitive Equality in Banking Act (CEBA)**

1. Redefined the definition of a *bank* to limit the growth of nonbank banks.
2. Sought to recapitalize the Federal Savings and Loan Insurance Corporation (FSLIC).

**1989 Financial Institutions Reform Recovery and Enforcement Act (FIRREA)**

1. Limited savings banks' investments in nonresidential real estate, required divestiture of junk bond holdings (by 1994), and imposed a restrictive asset test for qualifications as a savings institution (the qualified thrift lender [QTL] test).
2. Equalized the capital requirements of thrifts and banks.
3. Replaced the FSLIC with the FDIC-SAIF.
4. Replaced the Federal Home Loan Bank Board as the charterer of federal savings and loans with the Office of Thrift Supervision (OTS), an agency of the Treasury.
5. Created the Resolution Trust Corporation (RTC) to resolve failed and failing savings institutions.

**1991 Federal Deposit Insurance Corporation Improvement Act (FDICIA)**

1. Introduced prompt corrective action (PCA), requiring mandatory interventions by regulators whenever a bank's capital falls.
2. Introduced risk-based deposit insurance premiums beginning in 1993.
3. Limited the use of too-big-to-fail bailouts by federal regulators for large banks.
4. Extended federal regulation over foreign bank branches and agencies in the Foreign Bank Supervision and Enhancement Act (FBSEA).

**1994 Riegle-Neal Interstate Banking and Branching Efficiency Act**

1. Permitted bank holding companies to acquire banks in other states, starting September 1995.
2. Invalidated the laws of states that allowed interstate banking only on a regional or reciprocal basis.
3. Beginning in June 1997, bank holding companies were permitted to convert out-of-state subsidiary banks into branches of a single interstate bank.
4. Newly chartered branches also permitted interstate if allowed by state law.

**1999 Financial Services Modernization Act**

1. Eliminated restrictions on banks, insurance companies, and securities firms entering into each others' areas of business. Allowed for the creation of a financial services holding company.
2. Provided for state regulation of insurance.
3. Streamlined bank holding company supervision, with the Federal Reserve as the umbrella holding company supervisor.
4. Prohibited FDIC assistance to affiliates and subsidiaries of banks and savings institutions.
5. Provided for national treatment of foreign banks engaging in activities authorized under the act.

*(continued)*

**TABLE 2–8**
*(continued)*

| 2010 Wall Street Reform and Consumer Protection Act |
|---|
| 1. Created the Financial Services Oversight Council that would look out for systemic risks at large FIs. |
| 2. Gave the government power to break up FIs that provide a systemic risk to the financial system. |
| 3. Created the Consumer Financial Protection Bureau to regulate products such as credit cards and mortgages. |
| 4. Allowed Congress to order the Government Accountability Office to audit Federal Reserve activities. |
| 5. Gave shareholders the right to a nonbinding proxy vote on corporate pay packages. |
| 6. Required some over-the-counter derivatives be traded through clearinghouses to provide transparency of the value of trades. |

Even though we will go into greater detail about these regulations in later chapters (e.g., product and geographic diversification, Chapter 21), we now note the major objectives of each of these laws. The 1927 McFadden Act sought to restrict interstate bank branching, while the 1933 Glass-Steagall Act sought to separate commercial banking from investment banking by limiting the powers of commercial banks to engage in securities activities. Restrictions on the nonbank activities of commercial banks were strengthened by the Bank Holding Company Act of 1956 and its 1970 amendments, which limited the ability of a bank's parent holding company to engage in commercial, insurance, and other nonbank financial service activities. The 1978 International Banking Act extended federal regulation, such as the McFadden and Glass-Steagall Acts, to foreign branches and agencies in the United States for the first time, thereby seeking to level the competitive playing field between domestic and foreign banks. The 1980 DIDMCA and the 1982 DIA are mainly deregulation acts in that they eliminated interest ceilings on deposits and gave banks (and thrifts) new liability and asset powers. As we discuss in the next section on thrifts, this deregulation is blamed in part for the thrift crisis that resulted in widespread failures and the insolvency of the FSLIC in 1989.

**nonbank banks**
Firms that undertake many of the activities of a commercial bank without meeting the legal definition of a bank.

The Competitive Equality in Banking Act (CEBA) of 1987 sought to impose controls over a growing number of **nonbank banks** that were established to get around interstate banking restrictions and restrictions on nonbank ownership of banks imposed under the 1927 McFadden and the 1956 Bank Holding Company Acts. In 1989 Congress responded to the problems of thrifts and the collapse of the FSLIC with the passage of the FIRREA. In 1991 Congress enacted the FDICIA to deal with a large number of bank failures and the threatened insolvency of the FDIC, the insurance fund for commercial banks. Both the FIRREA and FDICIA sought to pull back from some of the deregulatory elements of the 1980 DIDMCA and the 1982 DIA. In 1994 the Riegle-Neal Act rolled back many of the restrictions on interstate banking imposed by the 1927 McFadden and the 1956 Bank Holding Company Acts. In particular, since June 1997 bank holding companies have been permitted to convert their bank subsidiaries in various states into branches, thus making nationwide branching possible for the first time in 70 years. In 1999 the Financial Services Modernization Act repealed Glass-Steagall barriers between commercial banks and investment banks. The act allowed for the creation of a **financial services holding company** that could engage in banking activities *and* securities underwriting. In 2012, more than 750 banks qualified as financial services holding companies. This act also allows

**financial services holding company**
A financial institution that engages in banking activities and securities underwriting or any other financial activity.

FI customers to opt out of any private information sharing an FI may want to pursue. Thus, FI customers have some control over who will see and have access to their private information.

Finally, in 2010, the U.S. Congress passed the 2010 Wall Street Reform and Consumer Protection Act which sought to prevent a repeat of the market meltdown of 2008. Touted as the most extensive proposal for the overhaul of financial rules since the Great Depression, this bill proposed a sweeping overhaul of the nation's financial system and the rules that govern it. The bill set forth reforms to meet five key objectives:

1. *Promote robust supervision and regulation of financial firms* by establishing (a) a new Financial Services Oversight Council of financial regulators (chaired by Treasury and including the heads of the principal federal financial regulators as members) to identify emerging systemic risks and improve interagency cooperation, (b) a new authority for the Federal Reserve to supervise all firms that could pose a threat to financial stability, even those that do not own banks, (c) stronger capital and other prudential standards for all financial firms, and even higher standards for large, interconnected firms, (d) a new National Bank Supervisor to supervise all federally chartered banks, (e) the elimination of the federal thrift charter for thrifts not dedicated to mortgage lending and other loopholes that allowed some depository institutions to avoid bank holding company regulation by the Federal Reserve, and (f) the registration of advisers of hedge funds and other private pools of capital with the SEC.

2. *Establish comprehensive supervision of financial markets* by establishing (a) the regulation of securitization markets, including new requirements for market transparency, stronger regulation of credit rating agencies, and a requirement that issuers and originators retain a financial interest in securitized loans, (b) comprehensive regulation of all over-the-counter derivatives, and (c) new authority for the Federal Reserve to oversee payment, clearing, and settlement systems.

3. *Protect consumers and investors from financial abuse* by establishing (a) a new Consumer Financial Protection Bureau to protect consumers across the financial sector from unfair, deceptive, and abusive practices, (b) stronger regulations to improve the transparency, fairness, and appropriateness of consumer and investor products and services, and (c) a level playing field and higher standards for providers of consumer financial products and services, whether or not they are part of a bank.

4. *Provide the government with the tools it needs to manage financial crises* by establishing (a) a new regime to resolve nonbank financial institutions whose failure could have serious systemic effects and (b) revisions to the Federal Reserve's emergency lending authority to improve accountability.

5. *Raise international regulatory standards and improve international cooperation* by establishing international reforms to support efforts in the U.S., including strengthening the capital framework; improving oversight of global financial markets; coordinating supervision of internationally active firms; and enhancing crisis management tools.

## Industry Performance

Table 2–9 presents selected performance ratios for the commercial banking industry for various years from 1989 through 2012. With the economic expansion in the U.S. economy and falling interest rates throughout most of the 1990s, U.S. commercial banks flourished for most of that period. In 1999 commercial bank earnings were

**TABLE 2–9**   **Selected Indicators for U.S. Commercial Banks, 1989 through 2012**

Sources: FDIC, *Quarterly Banking Profile*, various issues; and *Historical Statistics*, 1989. *www.fdic.gov*

|  | 2012* | 2010 | 2009 | 2008 | 2007 | 2006 | 2003 | 2001 | 2000 | 1999 | 1989 |
|---|---|---|---|---|---|---|---|---|---|---|---|
| Number of institutions | 6,168 | 6,530 | 6,840 | 7,086 | 7,283 | 7,450 | 7,769 | 8,079 | 8,315 | 8,580 | 12,709 |
| Return on assets (%) | 1.02 | 0.65 | −0.10 | 0.13 | 0.93 | 1.33 | 1.40 | 1.15 | 1.19 | 1.31 | 0.49 |
| Return on equity (%) | 9.06 | 5.86 | −0.93 | 1.33 | 9.12 | 13.02 | 15.34 | 13.09 | 14.07 | 15.31 | 7.71 |
| Provision for loan losses to total assets (%) | 0.30 | 1.21 | 1.94 | 1.30 | 0.54 | 0.26 | 0.47 | 0.67 | 0.47 | 0.38 | 0.94 |
| Net charge-offs to loans (%) | 1.17 | 2.67 | 2.60 | 1.32 | 0.62 | 0.41 | 0.89 | 0.95 | 0.64 | 0.61 | 1.16 |
| Asset growth rate (%) | 4.03 | 2.05 | −3.95 | 10.15 | 10.75 | 11.63 | 7.42 | 4.91 | 8.79 | 5.37 | 5.38 |
| Net operating income growth (%) | 11.94 | 1,088.1 | −137.98 | −80.48 | −21.21 | 11.19 | 14.92 | −1.89 | 2.02 | 20.42 | −38.70 |
| Number of failed/ assisted institutions | 34 | 139 | 120 | 25 | 2 | 0 | 3 | 3 | 6 | 7 | 206 |

* Through September.

a record $71.6 billion. More than two-thirds of all U.S. banks reported a return on assets (ROA) of 1 percent or higher, and the average ROA for all banks was 1.31 percent, up from 1.19 percent for the year 1998.[9] This, despite continued financial problems (or sovereign risk, see Chapter 14) in Southeast Asia, Russia, and South America. With the economic downturn in the early 2000s, however, bank performance deteriorated slightly. For example, commercial banks' string of eight consecutive years of record earnings ended in 2000 as their net income fell to $71.2 billion. Banks' provision for loan losses (or credit risk) rose to $9.5 billion in the fourth quarter of 2000, an increase of $3.4 billion (54.7 percent) from the level of a year earlier. This was the largest quarterly loss provision since the fourth quarter of 1991. Finally, the average ROA was 1.19 in 2000, down from 1.31 percent in 1999.

This downturn was short-lived, however. In 2001, net income of $74.3 billion easily surpassed the old record of $71.6 billion, and net income rose further, to $106.3 billion, in 2003. Moreover, in 2003, both ROA and ROE (return on equity) reached all-time highs of 1.40 percent and 15.34 percent, respectively. The two main sources of earnings strength in 2003 were higher noninterest income (up $18.9 billion, 10.3 percent) and lower loan loss provisions (down $14.2 billion, or 27.6 percent). The greatest improvement in profitability occurred at large institutions, whose earnings had been depressed in the early 2000s by losses on loans to corporate borrowers and by weakness in market-sensitive noninterest revenue. Only 5.7 percent of all institutions were unprofitable in 2003, the lowest proportion since 1997.

Several explanations have been offered for the strong performance of commercial banks during the early 2000s. First, the Federal Reserve cut interest rates 13 times during this period. Lower interest rates made debt cheaper to service and kept many households and small firms borrowing. Second, lower interest rates made home purchasing more affordable. Thus, the housing market boomed throughout the period. Third, the development of new financial instruments, such as credit derivatives and mortgage-backed securities, helped banks shift credit risk from their balance sheets to financial markets and other FIs such as insurance companies. Finally, improved information technology helped banks manage their risk better.

[9] ROA is calculated as net income divided by the book value of total assets. It reflects the earnings per dollar of assets for the bank. ROE is calculated as net income divided by common equity of the bank and measures the return to the bank's common stockholders.

As interest rates rose in the mid-2000s, performance did not deteriorate significantly. Third quarter 2006 earnings represented the second-highest quarterly total ever reported by the industry, and more than half of all banks reported higher earnings in the third quarter of 2006 than in the second quarter. However, increased loan loss provisions, reduced servicing income, and lower trading revenue kept net income reported by commercial banks from setting a new record for the full year. Rising funding costs outstripped increases in asset yields for a majority of banks. Further, mortgage delinquencies, particularly on subprime mortgages, surged in the last quarter of 2006 as homeowners who had stretched themselves financially to buy a home or refinance a mortgage in the early 2000s fell behind on their loan payments. Loan losses at banks in Louisiana, Mississippi, and Texas soared as businesses and consumers hit by Hurricanes Katrina and Rita defaulted on loans. Despite these weaknesses, the industry's core capital ratio increased to 10.36 percent, the highest level since new, risk-based capital ratios were implemented in 1993. Finally, no FDIC-insured banks failed during 2005 or 2006. Both the number and assets of "problem" banks were at historical lows.

**provision for loan losses**
Bank management's recognition of expected bad loans for the period.

The performance of the late 1990s and early and mid-2000s was quite an improvement from the recessionary and high interest rate conditions in which the industry operated in the late 1980s. As reported in Table 2–9, the average ROA and ROE for commercial banks in 2006 were 1.33 percent and 13.02 percent, respectively, compared with 1989 when the ROA and ROE averaged 0.49 percent and 7.71 percent, respectively. **Provision for loan losses** (bank management's expectations of losses on the current loan portfolio) to assets ratio and **net charge-offs** (actual losses on loans and leases) to loans ratio averaged 0.26 percent and 0.41 percent, respectively, in 2006, versus 0.94 percent and 1.16 percent, respectively, in 1989. **Net operating income** (income before taxes and extraordinary items) grew at an annualized rate of 11.19 percent in 2006 versus a *drop* of 38.70 percent in 1989. Finally, note that in 2006 no U.S. commercial banks failed, versus 206 failures in 1989.

**net charge-offs**
Actual losses on loans and leases.

**net operating income**
Income before taxes and extraordinary items.

In the late 2000s, the U.S. economy experienced its strongest recession since the Great Depression. Commercial banks' performance deteriorated along with the economy. For all of 2007, net income was $105.5 billion, a decline of $39.8 billion (27.4 percent) from 2006. Less than half of all institutions (49.2 percent) reported increased earnings in 2007, the first time in 23 years that a majority of institutions had not posted full year earnings increases. The average ROA for the year was 0.93 percent, the lowest yearly average since 1991, and the first time in 15 years that the industry's annual ROA had been below 1 percent. Sharply higher loss provisions and a very rare decline in noninterest income were primarily responsible for the lower industry profits. Things got even worse in 2008. Net income for all of 2008 was $10.2 billion, a decline of $89.8 billion (89.8 percent) from 2007. This was the lowest annual earnings total since 1989, when the industry earned $10.0 billion. The ROA for the year was 0.13 percent, the lowest since 1987. Almost one in four institutions (23.6 percent) was unprofitable in 2008, and almost two out of every three institutions (62.8 percent) reported lower full-year earnings than in 2007. Total noninterest income declined by $25.6 billion (11 percent) as a result of the industry's first ever full-year trading loss ($1.8 billion), a $5.8 billion (27.4 percent) decline in securitization income, and a $6.6 billion drop in proceeds from sales of loans, foreclosed properties, and other assets. Net loan and lease charge-offs totaled $38.0 billion in the fourth quarter, an increase of $21.7 billion (132.7 percent) from the fourth quarter of 2007, the highest charge-off rate in the 25 years that institutions have reported quarterly net charge-offs. Twenty commercial banks failed or were assisted during the year, the largest number of failed and assisted institutions in a year since 1993. At year-end, 252 institutions were on the FDIC's "Problem List," up from 76 institutions at the end of 2007.

As the economy improved in the second half of 2009, so did commercial bank performance. While rising loan-loss provisions continued to dominate industry profitability, growth in operating revenues, combined with appreciation in securities values, helped the industry post an aggregate net profit. Commercial banks earned $2.8 billion in net income in the third quarter of 2009, more than three times the $879 million from 2008. Growth in net interest income, lower realized losses on securities and other assets, higher noninterest income, and lower noninterest expenses, all contributed to the year-over-year increase in net income. The average **net interest margin** (NIM, i.e., interest income minus interest expense divided by earning assets) in the third quarter was 3.51 percent, the highest quarterly average since the third quarter of 2005. Almost two-thirds of all institutions (62.1 percent) reported higher NIMs than in the second quarter. Realized losses on securities and other assets totaled $4.1 billion, which was $3.8 billion less than the $7.9 billion in losses the industry experienced a year earlier. Noninterest income was $4.0 billion (6.8 percent) higher than 2008 due to net gains on loan sales (up $2.7 billion) and servicing fees (up $1.9 billion). However, the industry was still feeling the effects of the long recession. Provisions for loan and lease losses totaled $62.5 billion, the fourth consecutive quarter that industry provisions had exceeded $60 billion. Net charge-offs continued to rise for an 11th consecutive quarter. Commercial banks charged off $50.8 billion in the quarter, an increase of $22.6 billion (80.5 percent) over the third quarter of 2008. Net charge-offs were higher than 2008 at 60 percent of all institutions. As a result, the full year 2009 ROA and ROE fell to −0.10 and −0.93, respectively. Further, 120 commercial banks failed in 2009. This is the largest number of failures since 1992. The number of commercial banks on the FDIC's "Problem List" rose from 416 to 552 during the third quarter of 2009, and total assets of "problem" institutions increased from $299.8 billion to $345.9 billion. Both the number and assets of "problem" institutions were at the highest level since the end of 1993.

As the economy continued to slowly recover in 2010 through 2012, so did bank performance. The 2010 industry ROA and ROE increased to 0.65 percent and 5.86 percent, respectively, the highest in three years. By 2012, industry ROA and ROE increased to 1.02 percent and 9.06 percent, respectively. In 2012, more than half (57.5 percent) of all institutions reported higher year-over-year net income, and only 10 percent reported negative net income (the lowest level in five years). Provisions for loan losses declined for a third consecutive year, and the amount of loans and leases that were noncurrent (90 days or more past due or in nonaccrual status) declined for 11 consecutive quarters. The number of institutions on the FDIC's "Problem List" fell from 732 to 694, while assets of "problem" banks declined from $282.4 billion to $262.2 billion. This is the smallest number of "problem" institutions since third-quarter 2009.

In addition to a changing economy, also certain to affect the future performance of commercial banks (as well as savings institutions and credit unions) is the extent to which banks adopt the newest technology (see Chapter 17), including the extent to which industry participants embrace the Internet and mobile banking. Appendix 2D (located at the book's website, **www.mhhe.com/saunders8e**) provides a short summary of technology-based wholesale and retail services

**net interest margin (NIM)**
Interest income minus interest expense divided by earning assets.

provided by banks and other FIs. The performance of banks that have invested in Internet banking as a complement to their existing services has been similar to the performance of those without Internet banking, despite relatively high initial technology-related expenses. In particular, banks that offer Internet banking services generally have higher noninterest income (which offsets any increased technology expenses). Further, the risk of banks offering Internet-related banking products appears to be similar to the risk of those banks without Internet banking.

| Concept Questions | |
|---|---|
| | 1. What are the major assets held by commercial banks? |
| | 2. What are the major sources of funding for commercial banks? |
| | 3. Describe the responsibilities of the three federal regulatory agencies in the United States. |
| | 4. What are the major regulations that have affected the operations of U.S. commercial banks? |
| | 5. What has the trend in ROA and ROE been in the commercial banking industry over the last decade? |

# SAVINGS INSTITUTIONS

Savings institutions were first created in the early 1800s in response to commercial banks' concentration on serving the needs of business (commercial) enterprises rather than the needs of individuals requiring borrowed funds to purchase homes. Thus, the first savings institutions pooled individual savings and invested them mainly in mortgages and other securities. Today's savings institutions, however, generally perform services similar to those of commercial banks.

**savings institutions**
Depository institutions that specialize in residential mortgages mostly backed by short-term deposits and other funds.

**Savings institutions** comprise two different groups of FIs: savings associations (SAs) and savings banks (SBs). They usually are grouped together because they not only provide important mortgage and/or lending services to households but also are important recipients of household savings. Historically, savings associations have concentrated more on residential mortgages, while savings banks have operated as relatively diversified savings institutions that have a large concentration of residential mortgage assets but hold some commercial loans, corporate bonds, and corporate stock as well. In this section, we review these two groups.

## Size, Structure, and Composition of the Industry

Savings associations were historically referred to as savings and loans (S&Ls) associations. However, in the 1980s, federally chartered savings banks appeared in the United States. The term *savings association* has replaced "S&L association" to capture the resulting change in the structure of the industry.[10] These institutions have the same regulators as traditional savings and loans.

The savings association industry prospered throughout most of the 20th century. These specialized institutions made long-term residential mortgages backed

[10] In 1978, the Federal Home Loan Bank Board (FHLBB), at the time the main regulator of savings associations, began chartering federal savings banks insured by the Federal Savings and Loan Insurance Corporation (FSLIC). In 1982, the FHLBB allowed S&Ls to convert to federal savings banks with bank (rather than S&L) names. As more and more S&Ls converted to savings banks, the title associated with this sector of the thrift industry was revised to reflect this change.

by short-term savings deposits. At the end of the 1970s, slightly fewer than 4,000 savings associations had assets of approximately $0.6 trillion. Over the period October 1979 to October 1982, however, the Federal Reserve's restrictive monetary policy action led to a sudden and dramatic surge in interest rates, with rates on T-bills rising as high as 16 percent. This increase in short-term rates and the cost of funds had two effects. First, savings associations faced negative interest spreads or net interest margins in funding much of their fixed-rate long-term residential mortgage portfolios over this period. Second, they had to pay more competitive interest rates on savings deposits to prevent **disintermediation** and the reinvestment of those funds in money market mutual fund accounts. Their ability to do this was constrained by the Federal Reserve's **Regulation Q ceilings,** which limited the rates savings associations could pay on traditional passbook savings account and retail time deposits.

**disintermediation**
Withdrawal of deposits from savings associations and other depository institutions and their reinvestment elsewhere.

**Regulation Q ceiling**
An interest ceiling imposed on small savings and time deposits at banks and thrifts until 1986.

In part to overcome the effects of rising rates and disintermediation on the savings association industry, Congress passed two acts, the DIDMCA and the DIA (see Table 2–8). These acts expanded the deposit-taking and asset-investment powers of savings associations. For many savings associations, the new powers created safer and more diversified institutions. For a small but significant group whose earnings and shareholders' capital were being eroded in traditional lines of business, this created an opportunity to take more risks in an attempt to return to profitability. However, in the mid-1980s, real estate and land prices in Texas and the Southwest collapsed. This was followed by economic downturns in the Northeast and in western states of the United States. Many borrowers with mortgage loans issued by savings associations in these areas defaulted. In other words, the credit or lending risks incurred by savings associations in these areas often failed to pay off. This risk-taking, or moral hazard, behavior was accentuated by the policies of the savings association insurer, the FSLIC. Due to a lack of funds, the FSLIC could not close many of the capital-depleted, economically insolvent savings associations (a policy of **regulator forbearance**) and maintained deposit insurance premium assessments independent of the risk of the savings institution (see Chapter 19). As a result, there was an increasing number of failures in the 1982–89 period aligned with rapid asset growth of the industry. Thus, savings associations decreased in number from 4,000 in 1980 to 2,600 in 1989, or by 35 percent (however, their assets actually doubled from $600 billion to $1.2 trillion over that period).

**regulator forbearance**
A policy of not closing economically insolvent FIs, but allowing them to continue in operation.

**mutual organizations**
Savings banks in which the depositors are also the legal owners of the bank.

Traditionally, savings banks were established as **mutual organizations** (in which the depositors are also legally the owners of the bank) in states that permitted such organizations. These states were largely confined to the East Coast—for example, New York, New Jersey, and the New England states. As a result, savings banks (unlike savings associations) were not as affected by the oil-based economic shocks that impacted Texas and the Southwest in the 1980s. Nevertheless, the crash in New England real estate values in 1990–91 presented equally troubling problems for this group. Indeed, many of the failures of savings institutions in the early 1990s were savings banks rather than savings associations. As a result, savings banks have decreased in both size and number.

Figure 2–6 shows the number of failures, mergers, and new charters of savings institutions from 1984 through 2012. Notice the large number of failures from 1987 through 1992 and the decline in the number of new charters. These failures, especially in 1988 and 1989, depleted the resources of the FSLIC to such an extent that by 1989 it was massively insolvent (see Chapter 19). Resulting legislation—the FIRREA of 1989—abolished the FSLIC and created a new insurance fund (SAIF)

**FIGURE 2–6**   **Structural Changes in the Number of Savings Institutions, 1984–2012**

Source: Federal Deposit Insurance Corporation, *Quarterly Banking Profile,* various years. *www.fdic.gov*

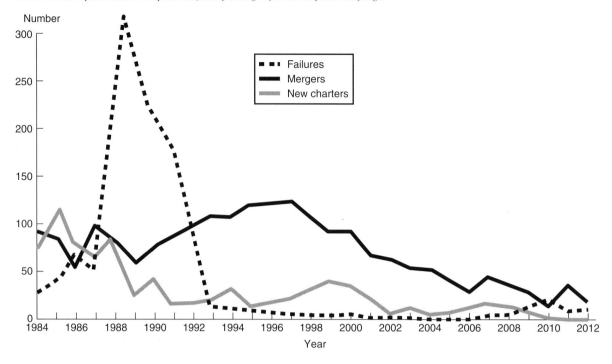

**QTL test**
Qualified thrift lender test that sets a floor on the mortgage related assets held by thrifts (currently 65 percent).

under the management of the FDIC. In addition, the act created the Resolution Trust Corporation (RTC) to close the most insolvent savings associations.[11]

Further, the FIRREA strengthened the capital requirements of savings institutions and constrained their non-mortgage-related asset-holding powers under a newly imposed qualified thrift lender, or **QTL, test.** In 1991, Congress enacted the FDICIA. FDICIA introduced risk-based deposit insurance premiums (starting in 1993) in an attempt to limit excess risk taking by savings institutions. It also introduced a prompt corrective action (PCA) policy, such that regulators could close thrifts (and banks) faster (see Chapter 20). In particular, if a savings institution's ratio of its equity capital to its assets falls below 2 percent, it has to be closed down or recapitalized within three months.

As a result of the closing of weak savings institutions and the strengthening of capital requirements, the industry shrank significantly, both in numbers and in asset size, in the 1990s. Savings institutions decreased in number from 3,677 in 1989 to 2,262 in 1993 (by 38 percent), and assets shrank from $1.427 trillion to $1.001 trillion (by 30 percent) over that same period.

## Balance Sheet and Recent Trends

Even in its new streamlined state, concerns have been raised about the future viability of the savings institution industry in traditional mortgage lending areas. This is partly due to intense competition for mortgages from other financial

---

[11] At the time of its dissolution in 1995, the RTC had resolved or closed more than 700 savings institutions, at an estimated cost of $200 billion to the U.S. taxpayers.

institutions, such as commercial banks and specialized mortgage bankers. It is also due to the securitization of mortgages into mortgage-backed security pools by government-sponsored enterprises, which we discuss further in Chapter 26.[12] In addition, long-term mortgage lending exposes an FI to significant credit, interest rate, and liquidity risks.

Table 2–10 shows the balance sheet of savings institutions in 2012. On this balance sheet, mortgages and mortgage-backed securities (securitized pools of mortgages) account for 65.63 percent of total assets. This compares with 27.31 percent in commercial banks. As noted earlier, the FDICIA uses the qualified thrift lender (QTL) test to establish a minimum holding of 65 percent in mortgage-related assets for savings institutions. Reflecting the enhanced lending powers established under the 1980 DIDMCA and the 1982 DIA, commercial loans and consumer loans amounted to 4.66 and 7.65 percent of assets, respectively, in 2012. Finally, savings institutions are required to hold cash and investment securities for liquidity risk purposes and to meet regulator-imposed reserve requirements. In September 2012, cash and U.S. Treasury securities holdings amounted to 10.14 percent of total assets, compared with 22.45 percent at commercial banks.

On the liability side of the balance sheet, small time and savings deposits are still the predominant source of funds, with total deposits accounting for 76.48 percent of total liabilities and net worth. The second most important source of funds consists of borrowings from the Federal Home Loan Banks (FHLBs), of which there are 12. These banks in turn are owned by the savings institutions themselves. Because of their size and government-sponsored status, FHLBs have access to wholesale money markets and the capital market for notes and bonds

**TABLE 2–10**
Assets and Liabilities of Savings Institutions, September 30, 2012

Source: FDIC, December 2012. *www.fdic.gov*

| | Millions of Dollars | Percent |
|---|---|---|
| Cash and due from | $  110,454 | 9.58% |
| U.S. Treasury securities | 6,398 | 0.56 |
| Mortgage loans | 517,525 | 44.88 |
| MBS (includes CMOs, POs, IOs) | 239,214 | 20.75 |
| Bonds, notes, debentures, and other securities | 59,130 | 5.12 |
| Commercial loans | 53,730 | 4.66 |
| Consumer loans | 88,192 | 7.65 |
| Other loans and financing leases | 17,609 | 1.53 |
| Less: Allowance for loan losses and unearned income | (10,353) | (0.90) |
| Other assets | 71,181 | 6.17 |
| Total assets | $1,153,080 | 100.00% |
| Total deposits | $881,859 | 76.48% |
| Other borrowings | 83,377 | 7.23 |
| Federal funds and repurchase agreements | 30,920 | 2.68 |
| Other liabilities | 19,861 | 1.72 |
| Total liabilities | 1,016,017 | 88.11 |
| Net worth | 137,063 | 11.89 |
| Total liabilities and net worth | $1,153,080 | 100.00% |
| Number of institutions | 1,013 | |

[12] The major enterprises are GNMA, FNMA, and FHLMC.

and can relend the funds borrowed on these markets to savings institutions at a small markup over wholesale cost. Other borrowed funds include repurchase agreements and direct federal fund borrowings. Finally, net worth, the book value of the equity holders' capital contribution, amounted to 11.89 percent of total assets in 2012. This compares with 11.48 percent at commercial banks.

## Regulation

The main regulators of savings institutions are the Office of the Comptroller of the Currency (OCC) and the FDIC.

www.occ.gov

### *The Office the Comptroller of the Currency*

In 1989 FIRREA established the Office of Thrift Supervision. This office chartered and examined all federal savings institutions. Further, when savings institutions were held by parent holding companies, the OTS supervised the holding companies as well. During the financial crisis the U.S. Congress determined that savings bank regulators performed relatively weakly compared with commercial bank regulators. Further, a Government Accountability Office report noted that some of the savings institutions regulated by the OTS were primarily operating in areas other than those traditionally engaged by thrifts, i.e., insurance, securities, and commercial activities. To address these concerns, the Wall Street Reform and Consumer Protection Act mandated the consolidation of the Office of Thrift Supervision with the Office of the Comptroller of the Currency. As a result, the OTS became part of the OCC on July 21, 2011, and on October 19, 2011, the OTS ceased to exist. Thus, the OCC now regulates both national banks and federal savings institutions. Additionally, the bill did not eliminate the charter for savings institutions dedicated to mortgage lending, but did subject savings institution holding companies to supervision by the Federal Reserve.

www.fdic.gov

### *The FDIC-DIF Fund*

Also established in 1989 under the FIRREA and in the wake of the FSLIC insolvency, the FDIC oversaw and managed the Savings Association Insurance Fund (SAIF). In 1996, as part of a plan to recapitalize the SAIF, commercial banks were required to pay for part of the burden. In return, Congress promised to eventually merge bank and thrift charters (and hence insurance funds) into one. In January 2007, the FDIC merged the SAIF and the Bank Insurance Fund (BIF) to form the Deposit Insurance Fund (DIF). Thus, thrifts now operate under the same regulatory structure that applies to commercial banks.

### *Other Regulators*

State-chartered savings institutions (the vast majority) are regulated by state agencies. Savings institutions that adopt federal charters are subject to the regulations of the OTS.

## Industry Performance

Like commercial banks, savings institutions experienced record profits in the mid- to late-1990s as interest rates (and thus the cost of funds to savings institutions) remained low and the U.S. economy expanded. The result was an increase in the spread between interest income and interest expense for savings institutions and consequently an increase in their net income. In 1999, savings institutions reported $10.7 billion in net income and an annualized ROA of 1.00 percent (this compares with an ROA of 1.31 percent over the same period for commercial banks). Only the $10.8 billion of net income reported in 1998 exceeded these results. Asset quality improvements were widespread during 1999, providing the most favorable net operating income that the industry had ever reported. However, as in the commercial banking industry, the downturn in the U.S. economy also resulted in a decline in savings institutions' profitability in 2000. Specifically, their ROA and ROE ratios fell slightly in 2000 to 0.92 percent and 11.14 percent, respectively, from their 1999 levels. Again, as with commercial banks, despite an economic recession, this downturn was short-lived. Both ROA and ROE increased to record levels each year from 2001 through 2003. The industry's net interest margins rose: the cost of funding earning assets declined by 2.70 percent while the yield on earning assets declined by only 2.35 percent. However, net charge-offs in 2003 were almost twice those in 2000. A flat yield curve and increased funding costs contributed to decreased margins in the mid-2000s. The average ROA declined to 1.15 percent in 2005 and 0.99 percent in 2006, while ROE decreased to 10.40 percent in 2005 and 8.68 percent in 2006. Table 2–11 presents several performance ratios for the industry for various years from 1989 through 2012.

In the late 2000s, as the U.S. economy experienced its strongest recession since the Great Depression, savings institutions' performance deteriorated. For all of 2007, net income was $6.0 billion, down $11.1 billion from 2006. The average ROA for the year was 0.13 percent, the lowest yearly average since 1989. In 2008, net income was −$8.6 billion. This was the first negative earnings year since 1991. The ROA for the year was −0.72 percent. However, only six savings institutions failed or were assisted during the year. In this group was Washington Mutual the largest savings institution, with over $300 billion in assets. At year-end, 18 savings institutions were on the FDIC's "Problem List," up from six institutions at the end of 2007. Like commercial banks, as the economy improved in the second half of 2009 through 2012, so did savings institution performance. Savings institutions earned $1.4 billion in net income in the third quarter of 2009, up from −$18.3 million in the second quarter. This trend continued into 2010 as savings institutions earned $8.3 billion for the year, ROA for the industry was 0.65 percent, and ROE was 5.76 percent—up from 0.14 percent and 1.31 percent,

**TABLE 2–11**  Selected Indicators for U.S. Savings Institutions, 1989 through 2012

Source: FDIC, *Quarterly Banking Profile*, various issues, and *Historical Statistics*, 1989. *www.fdic.gov*

| | 2012* | 2010 | 2009 | 2008 | 2007 | 2006 | 2005 | 2003 | 2001 | 2000 | 1999 | 1989 |
|---|---|---|---|---|---|---|---|---|---|---|---|---|
| Number of institutions | 1,013 | 1,128 | 1,172 | 1,219 | 1,251 | 1,279 | 1,307 | 1,413 | 1,535 | 1,590 | 1,642 | 3,677 |
| Return on assets (%) | 1.01 | 0.65 | 0.14 | −0.72 | 0.13 | 0.99 | 1.15 | 1.28 | 1.07 | 0.92 | 1.00 | −0.39 |
| Return on equity (%) | 8.61 | 5.76 | 1.31 | −7.75 | 1.08 | 8.68 | 10.40 | 13.66 | 12.33 | 11.14 | 11.73 | −8.06 |
| Noncurrent assets plus other real estate owned to assets (%) | 2.30 | 3.04 | 3.00 | 2.40 | 1.46 | 0.63 | 0.57 | 0.62 | 0.65 | 0.56 | 0.58 | 2.78 |
| Asset growth rate (%) | −7.60 | −0.84 | −17.50 | −17.53 | 4.97 | −3.70 | 8.64 | 8.49 | 8.17 | 6.41 | 5.60 | −11.14 |
| Net operating income growth (%) | 35.69 | 273.16 | 120.37 | −456.80 | −81.68 | −9.84 | 8.03 | 23.07 | 6.64 | 3.55 | 16.70 | −58.95 |
| Number of failed/ assisted institutions | 9 | 18 | 20 | 6 | 1 | 0 | 0 | 0 | 1 | 1 | 1 | 331 |

* Through September.

**TABLE 2–12** U.S. Savings Institution Asset Concentration, 1992 versus 2012

Source: *FDIC Quarterly Banking Profile,* various issues. *www.fdic.gov*

| | 2012 | | | | 1992 | | | |
|---|---|---|---|---|---|---|---|---|
| | Number | Percent of Total | Assets* | Percent of Total | Number | Percent of Total | Assets* | Percent of Total |
| **All FDIC-insured savings institutions** | 1,013 | | $1,153.1 | | 2,391 | | $1,035.2 | |
| 1. Under $100 million | 253 | 25.0% | 14.3 | 1.2% | 1,109 | 46.4% | 55.9 | 5.4% |
| 2. $100 million–$1 billion | 627 | 61.9 | 219.1 | 19.0 | 1,093 | 45.7 | 315.3 | 30.5 |
| 3. $1 billion–$10 billion | 105 | 10.4 | 218.5 | 19.0 | 181 | 7.6 | 479.5 | 46.3 |
| 4. $10 billion or more | 28 | 2.7 | 701.1 | 60.8 | 8 | 0.3 | 184.5 | 17.8 |

* In billions of dollars.

respectively, in 2009. By 2012, the industry ROA was 1.01 percent and ROE was 8.61 percent. Further, 9 savings institutions failed in 2012, down from 20 in 2009 and 18 in 2010.

Also like commercial banks, savings institutions experienced substantial consolidation in the 1990s. For example, the 1998 acquisition of H. F. Ahmanson & Co. by Washington Mutual Inc. for almost $10 billion was the fourth-largest bank–thrift merger completed in 1998.[13] Washington Mutual was the third-largest savings institutions in the United States early in 1997, while Ahmanson was the largest savings institution. In 1997, Washington Mutual bought Great Western, to become the largest thrift in the country. Then, in March 1998, Washington Mutual bought Ahmanson to combine the two largest U.S. thrifts. However, as mentioned above, Washington Mutual became a victim of the mortgage market meltdown and was seized by regulators in September 2008. The bulk of the institution's operations were sold to J.P. Morgan Chase. Table 2–12 shows the industry consolidation in number and asset size over the period 1992–2012. Notice that over this period, the biggest savings institutions (over $10 billion in assets) grew in number from 8 to 28 and their control of industry assets grew from 17.8 percent to 60.8 percent.

| **Concept Questions** | 1. Are savings institutions likely to be more or less exposed to interest rate risk than are banks? Explain your answer. |
|---|---|
| | 2. How do adjustable-rate mortgages help savings institutions? |
| | 3. Why should savings institutions with little or no equity capital seek to take more risk than well-capitalized savings institutions? |
| | 4. Why could it be argued that the QTL test makes savings institutions more rather than less risky? |
| | 5. Describe the recent performance of savings institutions. |
| | 6. Describe the ways that profit trends for savings institutions have been similar to those of commercial banks in the 1990s through the 2010s. |

[13] Behind Travelers Group–Citigroup ($74 billion), NationsBank–BankAmerica ($67 billion), and BankOne–First Chicago NBD ($30 billion).

# CREDIT UNIONS

**credit unions**
Nonprofit depository institutions, owned by members with a common bond, specializing in small consumer loans.

**Credit unions** (CUs) are nonprofit depository institutions mutually organized and owned by their members (depositors). Credit unions (CUs) were first established in the United States in the early 1900s as self-help organizations intended to alleviate widespread poverty. The first credit unions were organized in the Northeast, initially in Massachusetts. Members paid an entrance fee and invested funds to purchase at least one deposit share in the CU. Members were expected to deposit their savings in the CU, and these funds were lent only to other members.

This limit in the customer base of CUs continues today as, unlike commercial banks and savings institutions, CUs are prohibited from serving the general public. Rather, in organizing a credit union, members are required to have a common bond of occupation (e.g., police CUs) or association (e.g., university-affiliated CUs), or to cover a well-defined neighborhood, community, or rural district. CUs may, however, have multiple groups with more than one type of membership.

The primary objective of credit unions is to satisfy the depository and lending needs of their members. CU member deposits (shares) are used to provide loans to other members in need of funds. Any earnings from these loans are used to pay higher rates on member deposits, charge lower rates on member loans, or attract new members to the CU. Because credit unions do not issue common stock, the members are legally the owners of a CU. Also, because credit unions are nonprofit organizations, their net income is not taxed and they are not subject to the local investment requirements established under the 1977 Community Reinvestment Act. This tax-exempt status allows CUs to offer higher rates on deposits, and charge lower rates on some types of loans, than do banks and savings institutions. This is shown in Figure 2–7 for the period 1991–2012.

## Size, Structure, and Composition of the Industry

Credit unions are the most numerous of the institutions that make up the depository institutions segment of the FI industry, totaling 7,219 in 2012. Moreover, they were less affected by the crises that impacted commercial banks and savings institutions in the 1980s and late 2000s[14] because traditionally, more than 40 percent of their assets have been in the form of small consumer loans, often for amounts less than $10,000. In addition, CUs tend to hold large amounts of government securities (19.9 percent of their assets in 2012) and relatively small amounts of residential mortgages. Their lending activities are funded by savings deposits contributed by more than 95 million members who share some common thread or bond of association, usually geographic or occupational in nature. As a result, in 2008 at the height of the financial crisis, while commercial banks' and savings institutions' average ROAs were 0.13 and −0.72 percent, respectively, credit unions saw an average ROA of 0.31 percent.

To attract and keep customers, CUs have had to expand their services to compete with those of commercial banks and savings institutions. For example, CUs now offer products and services ranging from mortgages and auto loans (their traditional services) to credit lines and mobile banking. Some credit unions now offer business

---

[14] Credit unions have been covered by federal deposit insurance guarantees since 1971 (under the National Credit Union Share Insurance Fund). The depositor coverage cap of $250,000 is the same as that which currently exists for both commercial banks and savings institutions.

**FIGURE 2–7**   Credit Union versus Bank Interest Rates

Source: National Credit Union Administration, December 2012. *www.ncua.gov*

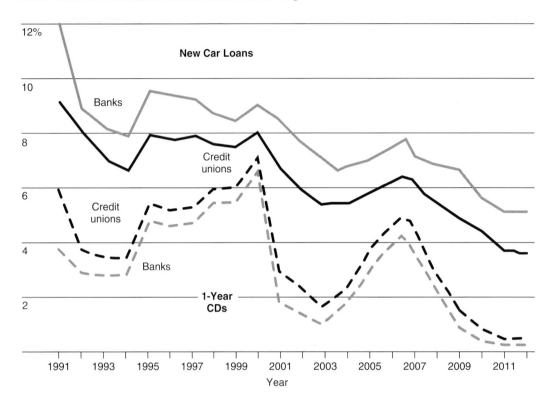

and commercial loans to their employer groups. For example, in 2012, business loans represented 5.1 percent of the industry's lending. Because of their tax-exempt status, CUs can charge lower rates on these loans, providing CUs with a cost advantage over banks and savings institutions that is very attractive to customers.

As CUs have expanded in number, size, and services, bankers have claimed that CUs are unfairly competing with small banks that have historically been the major lenders in small towns. For example, the American Bankers Association has stated that the tax exemption for CUs gives them the equivalent of a $1 billion per year subsidy. The Credit Union National Association's (CUNA) response is that any cost to taxpayers from CUs' tax-exempt status is more than made up in benefits to members and therefore the social good they create. CUNA estimates that the benefits of CU membership can range from $200 to $500 a year per member or, with more than 95 million members, a total benefit of $19 billion to $47.5 billion per year.

In 1997 the banking industry filed two lawsuits in its push to narrow the widening membership rules governing credit unions that followed a 1982 legal interpretation of the original 1934 Federal Credit Union Act's definition of what constitutes a "group having a common bond of occupation or association." The first lawsuit (filed by four North Carolina banks and the American Bankers Association) challenged the ability of an occupation-based credit union (the AT&T Family Credit Union based in North Carolina) to accept members from companies unrelated to the firm that originally sponsored the CU. In the second lawsuit, the American Bankers Association asked the courts to bar the federal government from letting

www.aba.com

occupation-based credit unions convert to community-based charters. Bankers argued in both lawsuits that such actions, broadening the membership of credit unions under other than occupation-based guidelines, would further exploit an unfair advantage allowed by the credit unions' tax-exempt status. In February 1998 the Supreme Court sided with banks, stating that credit unions could no longer accept members who did not share the common bond of membership. In April 1998, however, the U.S. House of Representatives overwhelmingly passed a bill that allowed all existing members to keep their credit union accounts. The bill was passed by the Senate in July 1998 and signed into law by the president in August 1998. This legislation allowed CUs not only to keep their existing members but also to accept new groups of members—including small businesses and low income communities—that were not considered part of the "common bond" of membership by the Supreme Court ruling.

In another hit to commercial banks, credit unions saw record increases in membership in late 2011 and early 2012, with most of the increase coming from commercial bank customers. For the year ending June 30, 2012, credit union membership increased by nearly 2.2 million new members: almost twice the 1.2 million average annual growth experienced in similar 12-month periods over the previous 10 years and four times greater than the 550,000 new members over that same period the prior year. Much of the growth in membership occurred as a part of nationwide campaigns—such as Bank Transfer Day on November 5, 2011—that encouraged consumers to leave their "big" banks for credit unions and community banks, which tend to incur fewer fees. Among the catalysts for these campaigns was Bank of America's plan to impose a monthly fee for debit card use. The plan was scrapped after seeing the strong negative reactions from consumers.

## Balance Sheet and Recent Trends

Table 2–13 shows the assets and liabilities for credit unions in June 2012. In that year 7,219 credit unions had assets of $1,012.8 billion. This compares with $155 billion in assets in 1987. Individually, credit unions tend to be very small, with an average size of $140.3 million in 2012 compared with $2,112.8 million for banks. The total assets of all credit unions are less than half the size of those of the largest U.S. banking organization, J.P. Morgan Chase.

Given their emphasis on retail or consumer lending, discussed above, 23.8 percent of CU assets are in the form of small consumer loans and another 28.1 percent are in the form of home mortgages. Together, these member loans constitute 51.9 percent of total assets. Because of the common bond requirement on credit union customers, relatively few business or commercial loans are issued by CUs.

Credit unions also invest heavily in investment securities (28.3 percent of total assets in 2012). Further, 70.2 percent of the investment portfolios of CUs are in U.S. government Treasury securities or federal agency securities. Their investment portfolio composition, along with their cash holdings (9.5 percent of total assets), allow credit unions ample liquidity to meet their daily cash needs—such as share (deposit) withdrawals. Some CUs have also increased their off-balance-sheet activities. Specifically, unused loan commitments, including credit card limits and home equity lines of credit, totaled more than $152 billion in 2012.

Credit union funding comes mainly from member deposits (85.9 percent of total funding in 2012). Figure 2–8 presents the distribution of these deposits in 2012. Regular share draft transaction accounts (similar to NOW accounts at other depository institutions) accounted for 32.3 percent of all CU deposits, followed

**TABLE 2–13**
Assets and
Liabilities of Credit
Unions, September
2012

Source: *National Credit Union Administration,* December 2012. *www.ncua.gov*

| | Billions of Dollars | Percentage |
|---|---|---|
| **Assets** | | |
| Cash and equivalents | $   95.7 | 9.5% |
| Investment securities: | | |
| U.S. government securities | | |
| Treasury | 11.6 | 1.1 |
| Agency | 190.0 | 18.8 |
| Mortgage-backed securities | 49.7 | 4.9 |
| Other investment securities | 35.9 | 3.5 |
| Total investment securities | 287.2 | 28.3 |
| Loans: | | |
| Home mortgages | 285.0 | 28.1 |
| Consumer loans | 241.4 | 23.8 |
| Business loans | 40.8 | 4.0 |
| Other | 23.9 | 2.4 |
| (Allowance for loan losses) | (8.3) | (0.8) |
| Total loans | 582.8 | 57.5 |
| Other assets | 47.1 | 4.7 |
| Total assets | $1,012.8 | 100.0% |
| **Liabilities and Equity** | | |
| Share drafts | $   109.7 | 10.8% |
| Small time and savings | 687.0 | 67.9 |
| Large time | 73.0 | 7.2 |
| Shares/deposits | $   869.7 | 85.9% |
| Other loans and advances | 26.3 | 2.6 |
| Miscellaneous liabilities | 12.0 | 1.2 |
| Total liabilities | $   908.0 | 89.7% |
| Total ownership shares | $   104.8 | 10.3% |

**FIGURE 2–8**
Composition of
Credit Union
Deposits, 2012

Source: Credit Union National Association, Credit Union Report Mid-Year 2012. *www.cuna.org*

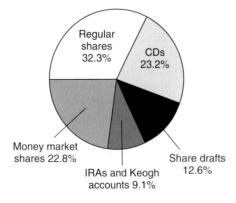

by certificates of deposits (23.2 percent of deposits), money market accounts (22.8 percent of deposits) and share drafts (similar to passbook savings accounts at other depository institutions, but so named to designate the deposit holders' ownership status) (12.6 percent of deposits). Credit unions hold lower levels of equity than other depository institutions. Since CUs are not stockholder owned, this equity is basically the accumulation of past profits from CU activities that are "owned" collectively by member depositors. As we will discuss in Chapters 7 and 20, this equity protects a CU against losses on its loan portfolio as well as against other financial and operating risks. However, these risks are generally lower for credit unions than commercial banks and savings institutions. In June 2012, CUs' capital-to-assets ratio was 10.35 percent compared with 11.89 percent for savings institutions and 11.48 percent for commercial banks.

## Regulation

Like commercial banks and savings institutions, credit unions can be federally or state chartered. As of 2012, 60.5 percent of the 7,219 CUs were federally chartered and subject to National Credit Union Administration (NCUA) regulation, accounting for 54.0 percent of the total credit union membership and 53.5 percent of total assets. In addition, through its insurance fund (the National Credit Union Share Insurance Fund, or NCUSIF), the NCUA provides deposit insurance guarantees of up to $250,000 for insured credit unions. Currently, the NCUSIF covers 98 percent of all credit union deposits.

www.ncua.gov
www.cuna.org

## Industry Performance

Like other depository institutions, the credit union industry grew in asset size in the 1990s and 2000s. Asset growth from 1999 to 2012 was more than 7.5 percent annually. In addition, CU membership increased from 77.5 million to over 95.3 million over the 1999–2012 period. Asset growth was especially pronounced among the largest CUs (with assets of more than $500 million) as their assets increased by 20 percent annually from 1999 through 2012. Figure 2–9 shows

**FIGURE 2–9** **Return on Assets for Credit Unions, 1993 through 2012**

Source: National Credit Union Association, *Year-End Statistics*, 2013. *www.ncua.gov*

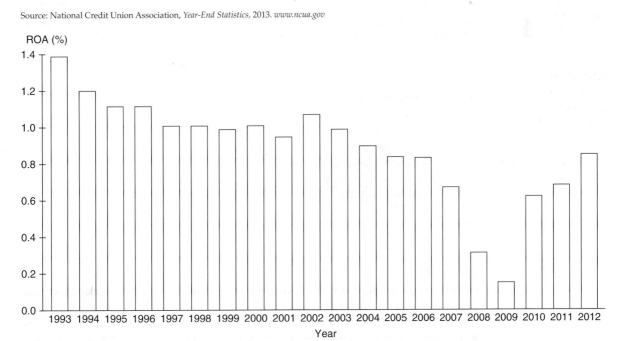

the trend in ROA for CUs from 1993 through 2012. The decrease in ROA over the period is mostly attributed to earnings decreases at the smaller CUs. For example, the largest credit unions experienced an ROA of 0.95 percent in the first six months of 2012, while for the smallest CUs (with assets of less than $5 million) the ROA was −0.11 percent. ROA for the whole industry was 0.84 percent. Smaller CUs generally have a smaller customer base with which to issue quality loans and have higher overhead expenses per dollar of assets. Thus, their ROAs have been hurt.

Given the mutual-ownership status of this industry, however, growth in ROA (or profits) is not necessarily the primary goal of CUs. Rather, as long as capital or equity levels are sufficient to protect a CU against unexpected losses on its credit portfolio as well as other financial and operational risks, this not-for-profit industry has a primary goal of serving the deposit and lending needs of its members. This contrasts with the emphasis placed on profitability by stockholder-owned commercial banks and savings institutions.

| **Concept Questions** | 1. How do credit unions differ from commercial banks and savings institutions? |
|---|---|
| | 2. Why did credit unions prosper in the 1980s and late 2000s compared with commercial banks and savings institutions? |
| | 3. What is the major asset held by credit unions? |
| | 4. Why do commercial banks and savings institutions claim that credit unions have an unfair advantage in providing bank services? |

## GLOBAL ISSUES: THE FINANCIAL CRISIS

Soon after it hit the United States, the financial crisis spread worldwide. As the crisis quickly spread, banks worldwide saw losses driven by their portfolios of structured finance products and securitized exposures to the subprime mortgage market. Losses were magnified by illiquidity in the markets for those instruments. As with U.S. banks, this led to substantial losses in their marked-to-market valuations. In Europe, the general picture of bank performance in 2008 was similar to that in the United States. That is, net income fell sharply at all banks. The largest banks in the Netherlands, Switzerland, and the United Kingdom had net losses for the year. Banks in Ireland, Spain, and the United Kingdom were especially hard hit as they had large investments in mortgages and mortgage-backed securities, both U.S. and domestic. Because they focused on domestic retail banking, French and Italian banks were less affected by losses on mortgage-backed securities. Continental European banks, in contrast to U.K. banks, partially cushioned losses through an increase in their net interest margins.

A number of European banks averted outright bankruptcy thanks to direct support from their central banks and national governments. During the last week of September and first week of October 2008, the German government guaranteed all consumer bank deposits and arranged a bailout of Hypo Real Estate, the country's second largest commercial property lender. The United Kingdom nationalized mortgage lender Bradford & Bingley (the country's eighth largest mortgage lender) and raised deposit guarantees from $62,220 to $88,890 per account. Ireland guaranteed deposits and debt of its six major financial institutions. Iceland rescued its third largest bank with an $860 million purchase of 75 percent of the bank's stock and a few days later seized the country's entire banking system. The Netherlands, Belgium, and Luxembourg central governments together agreed to inject $16.37 billion into Fortis NV (Europe's first ever cross-border financial services company) to keep it afloat. However, five days later this deal fell apart, and the bank was split up. The Dutch bought all assets located in the Netherlands for approximately $23 billion. The central bank in India stepped in to stop a run on the country's second largest bank, ICICI Bank, by promising to pump in cash. Central banks in Asia injected cash into their banking systems as banks' reluctance to lend to each other led the Hong Kong Monetary Authority to inject liquidity into its banking system after rumors led to a run on Bank of East Asia Ltd. South Korean authorities offered loans and debt guarantees to help small and midsize businesses with short-term funding. The United Kingdom, Belgium, Canada, Italy, and Ireland were just a few of the countries to pass an economic stimulus plan and/or bank bailout plan. The Bank of England lowered its target interest rate to a record low of 1 percent, hoping to help the British economy out of a recession. The Bank of Canada, Bank of Japan, and Swiss National Bank also lowered their main interest rate to 1 percent or below. All of these actions were a result of the spread of the U.S. financial market crisis to world financial markets.

However, the worldwide economic slowdown experienced in the later stages of the crisis meant that bank losses have become more closely connected to macroeconomic performance. Countries across the world saw companies scrambling for credit and cutting their growth plans. Additionally, consumers worldwide reduced their spending. Even China's booming economy slowed more than had been predicted, from 10.1 percent in the second quarter of 2008 to 9 percent in the third quarter. This was the first time since 2002 that China's growth was below 10 percent and dimmed hopes that Chinese demand could help keep world economies growing. In late October, the global crisis hit the Persian Gulf as Kuwait's central bank intervened to rescue Gulf Bank, the first bank rescue in the oil rich Gulf. Until this time, the area had been relatively immune to the world financial crisis. However, plummeting oil prices (which had dropped over 50 percent between July and October 2008) left the area's economies vulnerable. In this period, the majority of bank losses were more directly linked to a surge in borrower defaults and to anticipated defaults as evidenced by the increase in the amount and relative importance of loan loss provision expenses.

International banks' balance sheets continued to shrink during the first half of 2009 (although at a much slower pace than in the preceding six months) and, as in the United States, began to recover in the latter half of the year. In the fall of 2009, a steady stream of mostly positive macroeconomic news reassured investors that the global economy had turned around, but investor confidence remained fragile. For example, in late November 2009, security prices worldwide dropped sharply as investors reacted to news that government-owned Dubai World had asked for a delay in some payments on its debt. Further, throughout the spring of 2010, Greece struggled with a severe debt crisis. Early on, some of the healthier European countries tried to step in and assist the debt-ridden country. Specifically, in March 2010, a plan led by Germany and France to bail out Greece with as much as $41 billion in aid began to take shape. However, in late April 2010, Greek bond prices dropped dramatically as traders began betting a debt default was inevitable, even if the country received a massive bailout. The sell-off was the result of still more bad news for Greece, which showed that the 2009 budget deficit was worse than had been previously reported, and as a result, politicians in Germany began to voice opposition to a Greek bailout. Further, Moody's Investors Service downgraded Greece's debt rating and warned that additional cuts could be on the way. Greece's debt created heavy losses across the Greek banking sector. A run on Greek banks ensued. Initially, between €100 and €500 million per day was being withdrawn from Greek banks. At its peak, the run on Greek banks produced deposit withdrawals of as high as €750 million a day, nearly 0.5 percent of the entire €170 billion deposit base in the Greek banking system.

Problems in the Greek banking system then spread to other European nations with fiscal problems, such as Portugal, Spain, and Italy. The risk of a full-blown banking crisis arose in Spain, where the debt rating of 16 banks and four regions were downgraded by Moody's Investors Service. Throughout Europe, some of the biggest banks announced billions of euros lost from write-downs on Greek loans. In 2011, Crédit Agricole reported a record quarterly net loss of €3.07 billion ($4.06 billion U.S.) after a €220 million charge on its Greek debt. Great Britain's Royal Bank of Scotland revalued its Greek bonds at a 79 percent loss—or £1.1 billion ($1.7 billion U.S.)—for 2011. Germany's Commerzbank's fourth-quarter 2011 earnings decreased by €700 million due to losses on Greek sovereign debt. The bank needed to find €5.3 billion to meet the stricter new capital requirements set by Europe's banking regulator. Bailed-out Franco-Belgian bank Dexia warned it risked going out of business due to losses of €11.6 billion from its break-up and exposure to Greek debt and other toxic assets such as U.S. mortgage-backed securities. Even U.S. banks were affected by the European crisis. In late 2010, U.S. banks had sovereign risk exposure to Greece totaling $43.1 billion. In addition, exposures to Ireland totaled $113.9 billion, to Portugal totaled $47.1 billion, and to Spain totaled $187.5 billion. Worldwide, bank exposure to these four countries totaled $2,512.3 billion. Default by a small country like Greece cascaded into something that threatened the world's financial system.

Worried about the effect a Greek debt crisis might have on the European Union, other European countries tried to step in and assist Greece. On May 9, 2010, in return for huge budget cuts, Europe's finance ministers and the International Monetary Fund approved a rescue package worth $147 billion and a "safety net" of $1 trillion aimed at ensuring financial stability across Europe. Through the rest of 2010 and into 2012, eurozone leaders agreed on more measures designed to prevent the collapse of Greece and other member economies. In return, Greece continued to offer additional austerity reforms and agreed to reduce its budget deficits. At times, the extent of these reforms and budget cuts led to worker strikes and protests (some of which turned violent), as well as changes in Greek political leadership. In December 2011, the leaders of France and Germany agreed on a new fiscal pact that they said would help prevent another debt crisis. French President Nicolas Sarkozy outlined the basic elements of the plan to increase budget discipline after meeting with German Chancellor Angela Merkel in Paris. The pact, which involved amending or rewriting the treaties that govern the European Union, was presented in detail at a meeting of European leaders and approved. Efforts by the EU and reforms enacted by the Greek and other European country governments appear to have worked. As of December 18, 2012, Standard & Poor's raised its rating on Greek debt by six notches to B minus from selective default. S&P cited a strong and clear commitment from members of the eurozone to keep Greece in the common currency bloc as the main reason for the upgrade.

## Summary

This chapter provided an overview of the major activities of commercial banks, savings institutions, and credit unions. It also described the agencies that regulate these depository institutions. The Federal Reserve System, the FDIC, the OTS, and the Office of the Comptroller of the Currency, in conjunction with state regulators, are the agencies that oversee the activities of these institutions. Each of these institutions relies heavily on deposits to fund its activities, although borrowed funds are becoming increasingly important for the largest institutions. Historically, commercial banks have concentrated on commercial or business lending and on investing in securities, while savings institutions have concentrated on mortgage lending and credit unions have concentrated on consumer lending. These differences are being eroded as a result of competitive forces, regulation, and changing financial and business technology.

## Questions and Problems

1. What are the differences between community banks, regional banks, and money center banks? Contrast the business activities, location, and markets of each of these bank groups.
2. Use the data in Table 2–5 for banks in the two asset size groups (a) $100 million–$1 billion and (b) more than $10 billion to answer the following questions.
   a. Why have the ratios for ROA and ROE tended to increase for both groups over the 1990–2006 period, decrease in 2007–2009, and increase in 2010–2012? Identify and discuss the primary variables that affect ROA and ROE as they relate to these two size groups.
   b. Why is ROA for the smaller banks generally larger than ROA for the large banks?
   c. Why is the ratio for ROE consistently larger for the large bank group?
   d. Using the information on ROE decomposition in Appendix 2A, calculate the ratio of equity to total assets for each of the two bank groups for the period 1990–2012. Why has there been such dramatic change in the values over this time period, and why is there a difference in the size of the ratio for the two groups?
3. What factors caused the decrease in loan volume relative to other assets on the balance sheets of commercial banks? How has each of these factors been related to the change and development of the financial services industry during the 1990s and 2000s? What strategic changes have banks implemented to deal with changes in the financial services environment?
4. What are the major uses of funds for commercial banks in the United States? What are the primary risks to a bank caused by each of these? Which of the risks is most critical to the continuing operation of a bank?
5. What are the major sources of funds for commercial banks in the United States? How is the landscape for these funds changing and why?
6. What are the three major segments of deposit funding? How are these segments changing over time? Why? What strategic impact do these changes have on the profitable operation of a bank?
7. How does the liability maturity structure of a bank's balance sheet compare with the maturity structure of the asset portfolio? What risks are created or intensified by these differences?

8. The following balance sheet accounts (in millions of dollars) have been taken from the annual report for a U.S. bank. Arrange the accounts in balance sheet order and determine the value of total assets. Based on the balance sheet structure, would you classify this bank as a community bank, regional bank, or money center bank?

| | | | |
|---|---|---|---|
| Premises | $ 1,078 | Net loans | $29,981 |
| Savings deposits | 3,292 | Short-term borrowing | 2,080 |
| Cash | 2,660 | Other liabilities | 778 |
| NOW accounts | 12,816 | Equity | 3,272 |
| Long-term debt | 1,191 | Investment securities | 5,334 |
| Other assets | 1,633 | Demand deposits | 5,939 |
| Intangible assets | 758 | Certificates of deposit (under $100,000) | 9,853 |
| Other time deposits | 2,333 | Federal funds sold | 110 |

9. What types of activities are normally classified as off-balance-sheet (OBS) activities?
   a. How does an OBS activity move onto the balance sheet as an asset or liability?
   b. What are the benefits of OBS activities to a bank?
   c. What are the risks of OBS activities to a bank?
10. Use the data in Table 2–7 to answer the following questions.
    a. What was the average annual growth rate in OBS total commitments over the period 1992–2012?
    b. What categories of contingencies have had the highest annual growth rates?
    c. What factors are credited for the significant growth in derivative securities activities by banks?
11. For each of the following banking organizations, identify which regulatory agencies (OCC, FRB, FDIC, or state banking commission) may have some regulatory supervision responsibility:
    a. State-chartered, nonmember non–holding company bank.
    b. State-chartered, nonmember holding company bank.
    c. State-chartered member bank.
    d. Nationally chartered non–holding company bank.
    e. Nationally chartered holding company bank.
12. What are the main features of the Riegle-Neal Interstate Banking and Branching Efficiency Act of 1994? What major impact on commercial banking activity occured from this legislation?
13. What factors normally are given credit for the revitalization of the banking industry during the 1990s? How is Internet banking expected to provide benefits in the future?
14. What factors are given credit for the strong performance of commercial banks in the early and mid-2000s?
15. What factors are given credit for the weak performance of commercial banks in the late 2000s?
16. How do the asset and liability structures of a savings institution compare with the asset and liability structures of a commercial bank? How do these structural differences affect the risks and operating performance of a savings institution? What is the QTL test?

17. How do savings banks differ from savings associations? Differentiate in terms of risk, operating performance, balance sheet structure, and regulatory responsibility.
18. What happened in 1979 to cause the failure of many savings institutions during the early 1980s? What was the effect of this change on the operating statements of savings institutions?
19. How did two pieces of regulatory legislation—the DIDMCA in 1980 and the DIA in 1982—change the operating profitability of savings institutions in the early 1980s? What impact did these pieces of legislation ultimately have on the risk posture of the savings institutions industry? How did the FSLIC react to this change in operating performance and risk?
20. How did the Financial Institutions Reform, Recovery, and Enforcement Act (FIRREA) of 1989 and the Federal Deposit Insurance Corporation Improvement Act of 1991 reverse some of the key features of earlier legislation?
21. What is the "common bond" membership qualification under which credit unions have been formed and operated? How does this qualification affect the operational objective of a credit union?
22. What are the operating advantages of credit unions that have caused concern among commercial bankers? What has been the response of the Credit Union National Association to the banks' criticism?
23. How does the asset structure of credit unions compare with the asset structure of commercial banks and savings institutions? Refer to Tables 2–6, 2–10, and 2–13 to formulate your answer.
24. Compare and contrast the performance of worldwide depository institutions during and after the financial crisis.

The questions and problems that follow refer to Appendix 2B.

25. The financial statements for First National Bank (FNB) are shown below:

---

### Balance Sheet - First National Bank

| Assets | | Liabilities and Equity | |
|---|---|---|---|
| Cash | $ 450 | Demand deposits | $ 5,510 |
| Demand deposits from other FIs | 1,350 | Small time deposits | 10,800 |
| Investments | 4,050 | Jumbo CDs | 3,200 |
| Federal funds sold | 2,025 | Federal funds purchased | 2,250 |
| Loans | 15,525 | Equity | 2,200 |
| Reserve for loan losses | (1,125) | | |
| Premises | 1,685 | | |
| Total assets | $23,960 | Total liabilities/equity | $23,960 |

---

### Income Statement - First National Bank

| | |
|---|---|
| Interest Income | $2,600 |
| Interest expense | 1,650 |
| Provision for loan losses | 180 |
| Noninterest income | 140 |
| Noninterest expense | 420 |
| Taxes | 90 |

a. Calculate the dollar value of FNB's earning assets.
b. Calculate FNB's ROA.
c. Calculate FNB's asset utilization ratio.
d. Calculate FNB's spread.

26. Megalopolis Bank has the following balance sheet and income statement.

**Balance Sheet (in millions)**

| Assets | | Liabilities and Equity | |
|---|---|---|---|
| Cash and due from banks | $  9,000 | Demand deposits | $  19,000 |
| Investment securities | 23,000 | NOW accounts | 89,000 |
| Repurchase agreements | 42,000 | Retail CDs | 28,000 |
| Loans | 90,000 | Debentures | 19,000 |
| Fixed Assets | 15,000 | Total liabilities | $155,000 |
| Other assets | 4,000 | Common stock | 12,000 |
| Total assets | $183,000 | Paid in capital | 4,000 |
| | | Retained earnings | 12,000 |
| | | Total liabilities and equity | $183,000 |

**Income Statement**

| | |
|---|---|
| Interest on fees and loans | $ 9,000 |
| Interest on investment securities | 4,000 |
| Interest on repurchase agreements | 6,000 |
| Interest on deposits in banks | 1,000 |
| Total interest income | $20,000 |
| Interest on deposits | 9,000 |
| Interest on debentures | 2,000 |
| Total interest expense | $11,000 |
| Operating income | $ 9,000 |
| Provision for loan losses | 2,000 |
| Other income | 2,000 |
| Other expenses | 1,000 |
| Income before taxes | $ 8,000 |
| Taxes | 3,000 |
| Net income | $ 5,000 |

For Megalopolis, calculate:

a. Return on equity
b. Return on assets
c. Asset utilization
d. Equity multiplier
e. Profit margin
f. Interest expense ratio
g. Provision for loan loss ratio
h. Noninterest expense ratio
i. Tax ratio

## Web Questions

27. Go to the FDIC website at **www.fdic.gov** and find the most recent break-down of U.S. bank asset concentrations using the following steps. Click on "Analysts." From there click On "FDIC Quarterly Banking Profile" and then click on "Quarterly Banking Profile." Click on "Commercial Bank Section." Then click on "TABLE III-A. Full Year (or First XXX Quarters) 20XX, FDIC-Insured Commercial Banks." This will bring the files up on your computer that contain the relevant data. How have the number and dollar value of assets held by commercial banks changed since 2012?

28. Go to the Federal Deposit Insurance Corporation website at **www.fdic.gov** and find the latest balance sheet information available for savings institutions using the following steps. Click on "Analysts." Click on "Statistics on Banking." Select "Savings Institutions," then click on "Run Report." This will download a file on to your computer that will contain the most recent balance sheet information for savings institutions. Using information in this file, update Table 2–10. How have the assets and liabilities of credit unions changed since 2012?

29. Go to the National Credit Union Administration website at **www.ncua.gov** to collect the most recent information on number of credit unions, assets of credit unions, and membership in credit unions using the following steps. Click on "Regulations, Publications and Reports." Under "Reports, Plans, & Presentations," click on "Industry At a Glance (IAG)." Click on the most recent date. This will download a file onto your computer that will contain the necessary data. How have these data changed since 2012?

## Appendix 2A: Financial Statement Analysis Using a Return on Equity (ROE) Framework

View Appendix 2A at the website for this textbook **(www.mhhe.com/saunders8e)**.

## Appendix 2B: Commercial Banks' Financial Statements and Analysis

View Appendix 2B at the website for this textbook **(www.mhhe.com/saunders8e)**.

## Appendix 2C: Depository Institutions and Their Regulators

View Appendix 2C at the website for this textbook **(www.mhhe.com/saunders8e)**.

## Appendix 2D: Technology in Commercial Banking

View Appendix 2D at the website for this textbook **(www.mhhe.com/saunders8e)**.

www.mhhe.com/saunders8e

# Chapter **Three**

# Financial Services: Finance Companies

## INTRODUCTION

Like commercial banks, savings institutions, and credit unions, the main financial service provided by finance companies is lending. That is, the primary function of finance companies is to make loans to both individuals and corporations. The services provided by finance companies include consumer lending, business lending, and mortgage financing. Some of their loans are similar to depository institutions loans, such as consumer and auto loans, but others are more specialized. Finance companies differ from depository institutions in that they do not accept deposits but instead rely on short- and long-term debt as a source of funds. Additionally, finance companies often lend to customers depository institutions find too risky. This difference can lead to losses and even failure if the high risk does not pay off.

In this chapter we look at the services provided by finance companies and the competitive and financial situation facing these firms. We discuss the size, structure, and composition of the industry; the services the industry provides; its competitive and financial position; and its regulation. We conclude the chapter with a look at some global issues. From this chapter, the reader should obtain a basic understanding of services provided by finance companies, their performance, and the degree to which they are regulated.

## SIZE, STRUCTURE, AND COMPOSITION OF THE INDUSTRY

www.gecapital.com

The first major finance company was originated during the Depression, when General Electric Corp. created General Electric Capital Corp. (GECC) as a means of financing appliance sales to cash-constrained customers who were unable to get installment credit from banks. Installment credit is a loan that is paid back to the lender with periodic payments (installments) consisting of varying amounts of interest and principal (e.g., auto loans, home mortgages, and student loans). By the late 1950s banks were more willing to make installment loans, and so finance companies began looking outside their parent companies for business. GE Capital's consumer finance and banking businesses today provides millions of customers with loans, including credit card, personal, auto financing, and real estate loans. GE Capital Real Estate's assets total $73 billion, while GE Energy Financial

Services' assets total $21 billion. GECC also now performs commercial lending and leasing in a number of industries, from aviation, health care, and energy financing, to fleet, franchise, and middle market corporate finance. In the United States, Canada, and Mexico, GE Capital is a leading provider of business lending and leasing for companies of all sizes in a wide array of industries. In Europe, GE Capital has more than 350,000 customers, while in Asia, GE Capital provides services for more than 15 million businesses and consumers. Services include acquisition finance, inventory and working capital financing, leveraged and sponsor finance, equity capital, equipment leasing, and fleet management. GE Aviation is a world-leading provider of commercial and military jet engines and components. GE Aviation owns and manages more than 1,800 aircraft, for more than 245 customers in 75 countries.[1]

GE Capital's exposure to the financial crisis resulted in General Electric Corp.'s market value falling by more than half during 2008 (GE Capital accounted for about half of GE's sales and profit). The parent company's stock price fell to $14.58 in November 2008, its lowest level since January 1997. In order to reassure investors and help GE Capital unit compete with banks that already had government protection behind their debt, on November 12, 2008, the FDIC approved GE Capital's application for designation as an eligible entity under the FDIC's Temporary Liquidity Guarantee Program (TLGP). Under the TLGP, as much as $139 billion in debt (or 125 percent of total senior unsecured debt outstanding as of September 30, 2008) issued by GE Capital was guaranteed and backed by the full faith and credit of the United States. Granting this finance company access to the FDIC program was possible because GE Capital also owns a federal savings bank and an industrial loan company, both of which qualified for FDIC assistance. The terms of these agreements included, among other things, a requirement that GE and GE Capital reimburse the FDIC for any amounts that the FDIC paid to holders of debt that was guaranteed by the FDIC. In July 2009, GE Capital received approval to exit the TLGP program.

www.ally.com   Ally Financial (formerly GMAC) is another major finance company, founded in 1919 as the General Motors Acceptance Corporation (GMAC), a provider of financing to automotive customers. Since then, the business has expanded to include insurance, direct banking, mortgage operations, and commercial finance. In November 2006, General Motors sold a 51 percent interest in GMAC to a consortium of investors led by hedge fund Cerberus Capital Management and subsidiaries of Citigroup, Aozora Bank, and PNC Financial. GMAC's existing management team remained in place, but the finance company assumed a separate and independent credit profile and independent governance by a new board of directors. Under terms of the transaction, General Motors and GMAC entered into a 10-year agreement under which GMAC remained the exclusive provider of GM-sponsored auto finance programs.

December 24, 2008, was a key turning point in GMAC's history when it was approved as a bank holding company by the Federal Reserve Board under the Bank Holding Company Act. GMAC had been hit with huge losses in both its mortgage and auto loan businesses. Its mortgage unit, Residential Capital, had suffered significant losses on home loans it made during the housing boom of the early and mid-2000s. The company lost $8 billion in 2007–2008. In light of the impact GMAC's losses were having on financial markets, to help ensure the survival of the company, federal regulators permitted the financing arm of General Motors to become a bank holding company. The move allowed GMAC access to as much as $6 billion

---

[1] See GECC's website, *www.gecapital.com.*

**TABLE 3–1**
Assets and
Liabilities of U.S.
Finance Companies,
2012

Source: Federal Reserve
Board, December 2012.
*www.federalreserve.gov*

| | Billions of Dollars | | Percent of Total Assets | |
|---|---|---|---|---|
| **Assets** | | | | |
| Accounts receivable gross | $1,300.8 | | 74.8% | |
|   Consumer | 578.3 | | 33.3 | |
|   Business | 429.2 | | 24.7 | |
|   Real estate | 293.3 | | 16.8 | |
| Less reserves for unearned income | (24.3) | | (1.4) | |
| Less reserves for losses | (26.5) | | (1.5) | |
| Accounts receivable net | | $1,250.0 | | 71.9% |
| All other | | 488.0 | | 28.1 |
| Total assets | | $1,738.0 | | 100.0% |
| **Liabilities and Capital** | | | | |
| Bank loans | | $76.5 | | 4.4% |
| Commercial paper | | 61.8 | | 3.6 |
| Debt due to parent | | 256.6 | | 14.8 |
| Debt not elsewhere classified | | 771.5 | | 44.4 |
| All other liabilities | | 322.4 | | 18.5 |
| Capital, surplus, and undivided profits | | 249.2 | | 14.3 |
| Total liabilities and capital | | $1,738.0 | | 100.0% |

in government bailout money. As part of the deal, Cerberus Capital Management was forced to cut its stake in the new bank holding company to less than 15 percent and become a passive investor. Cerberus also stopped providing consulting services to GMAC and the two entities would no longer share executives. Also as a condition of the Federal Reserve's approval, General Motors had to reduce its ownership stake in GMAC to less than 10 percent, from 49 percent. As of November 2012, the U.S. Treasury owned 73.8 percent of GMAC, followed by General Motors (9.9 percent), Cerberus (8.7 percent), and other third-party investors (7.6 percent).

The Federal Reserve's decision to approve GMAC's application was particularly controversial. Critics had raised questions about GMAC's financial strength, its ownership by a private equity firm, and whether it was involved in too many commercial activities to become a bank. GMAC had to make several changes to its structure to alleviate concerns. The Fed, which had been considering the proposal since early November, determined that "emergency conditions" made it imperative that it act quickly. Regulators also wanted to approve GMAC's application to become a bank so that it could apply for federal funds before a year-end deadline set by the Treasury Department. The company would also be subject to more stringent federal oversight and had to diversify its business beyond loans to car buyers and dealerships. Despite these changes, GMAC still operates and provides financial services mainly as a finance company.

Because of the attractive rates they offer on some loans (such as new car loans, see below), their willingness to lend to riskier borrowers than depository institutions, their often direct affiliation with manufacturing firms, and the relatively limited amount of regulation imposed on these firms, finance companies have been among the fastest growing FI groups in recent years. In 2012 their assets stood at $1,738.0 billion (see Table 3–1). Comparing this to assets at the end of 1977 (reported in Table 3–2) of $104.3 billion, this industry has experienced growth of almost 1,566 percent in the last 35 years.

**TABLE 3–2**
Assets and
Liabilities of U.S.
Finance Companies
on December 31,
1977

Source: *Federal Reserve Bulletin*, June 1978, p. A39.
*www.federalreserve.gov*

| | Billions of Dollars | Percent of Total Assets |
|---|---|---|
| **Assets** | | |
| Accounts receivable gross | $ 99.2 | 95.1% |
|    Consumer | 44.0 | 42.2 |
|    Business | 55.2 | 52.9 |
| Less reserves for unearned income and losses | (12.7) | (12.2) |
| Accounts receivable net | $ 86.5 | 82.9% |
| Cash and bank deposit | 2.6 | 2.5 |
| Securities | 0.9 | 0.9 |
| All other | 14.3 | 13.7 |
| Total assets | $104.3 | 100.0% |
| **Liabilities and Capital** | | |
| Bank loans | $ 5.9 | 5.7% |
| Commercial paper | 29.6 | 28.4 |
| Debt | | |
|    Short-term | 6.2 | 5.9 |
|    Long-term | 36.0 | 34.5 |
|    Other | 11.5 | 11.0 |
| Capital, surplus, and undivided profits | 15.1 | 14.5 |
| Total liabilities and capital | $104.3 | 100.0% |

www.fordcredit.com
www.hfc.com
www.aigag.com
www.cit.com

**sales finance institutions**
Institutions that specialize in making loans to the customers of a particular retailer or manufacturer.

**personal credit institutions**
Institutions that specialize in making installment and other loans to consumers.

**business credit institutions**
Institutions that specialize in making business loans.

**factoring**
The process of purchasing accounts receivable from corporations (often at a discount), usually with no recourse to the seller if the receivables go bad.

The three major types of finance companies are (1) sales finance institutions, (2) personal credit institutions, and (3) business credit institutions. **Sales finance institutions** (e.g., Ford Motor Credit and Sears Roebuck Acceptance Corp.) specialize in making loans to the customers of a particular retailer or manufacturer. Because sales finance institutions can frequently process loans faster and more conveniently (generally at the location of purchase) than depository institutions, this sector of the industry competes directly with depository institutions for consumer loans. **Personal credit institutions** (e.g., HSBC Finance and AIG American General) specialize in making installment and other loans to consumers. Personal credit institutions will make loans to customers that depository institutions find too risky to lend to (due to low income or a bad credit history). These institutions compensate for the additional risk by charging higher interest rates than depository institutions and/or accepting collateral (e.g., used cars) that depository institutions do not find acceptable. **Business credit institutions** (e.g., CIT Group and U.S. Bancorp Equipment Finance) are companies that provide financing to corporations, especially through equipment leasing and **factoring,** in which the finance company purchases accounts receivable from corporate customers. These accounts are purchased at a discount from their face value, and the finance company specializes in and assumes the responsibility for collecting the accounts receivable. As a result, the corporate customer no longer has the worry of whether the accounts receivable may or may not be delayed and thus receives cash for sales faster than the time it takes customers to pay their bills. Many finance companies perform more than one of these three services (e.g., GMAC).

The industry is quite concentrated, with the largest 20 firms accounting for more than 65 percent of its assets. In addition, many of the largest finance companies, such as Ford Motor Credit Corp., tend to be wholly owned or captive

**TABLE 3–3**   The Largest Finance Companies

Sources: Insurance Information Institute and authors' research.

| Company Name | Total Receivables ($ millions) | Type of Finance Company | Ownership |
|---|---|---|---|
| General Electric Capital Corporation | $285,395 | Sales finance and business credit | Captive of GE |
| Capital One Financial | 203,132 | Personal credit | NYSE-listed independent that also owns Capital One Bank |
| SLM Corp. | 167,166 | Personal credit | NYSE-listed independent |
| J.P. Morgan Chase (credit card business) | 124,537 | Personal credit | Part of J.P. Morgan Chase |
| Ally Financial | 121,259 | Sales finance | Owned by consortium of investors including the U.S. Treasury, Cerberus Capital Management, and GM |
| American Express | 117,380 | Personal credit | NYSE-listed independent that also owns American Express Bank |
| Citigroup (credit card business) | 108,819 | Personal credit | Part of Citigroup |
| Bank of America (credit card business) | 108,659 | Personal credit | Part of Bank of America |
| HSBC Finance Corp. | 86,680 | Personal credit | Subsidiary of HSBC Holdings |
| Ford Motor Credit Company | 71,517 | Sales finance | Captive of Ford |

**captive finance company**
A finance company that is wholly owned by a parent corporation.

subsidiaries of major manufacturing companies. A major role of a **captive finance company** is to provide financing for the purchase of products manufactured by the parent, as Ford Motor Credit Corp. does for cars. In turn, the parent company is often a major source of debt finance for the captive finance company. A benefit of the captive finance subsidiary to the parent company is diversification in revenue streams. For example, as the auto industry suffered from a lack of sales in the mid-2000s, Ford Motor Credit Corp. was producing record profits, as much as 80 percent of the overall profits of Ford Motor Corporation.

Table 3–3 lists some of the top finance companies (in terms of total receivables) as of 2012. GECC is the largest with receivables totaling $285.4 billion. Note that 6 of the 10 finance companies are subsidiaries of financial services holding companies such as Citigroup. Thus, while Citibank cannot make high-risk, high-interest rate loans due to bank regulations that restrict credit risk, Citigroup can indirectly make these loans through its finance company subsidiary.

**Concept Questions**

1. What are the three major types of finance companies? What types of customers does each serve?
2. What is a captive finance company?

# BALANCE SHEET AND RECENT TRENDS

## Assets

As mentioned earlier, finance companies provide three basic lending services: customer lending, consumer lending, and business lending. In Table 3–1 we show the balance sheet of finance companies in 2012. As you can see, business and consumer loans (called *accounts receivable*) are major assets held by finance companies, accounting for 58.0 percent of total assets, while real estate loans are 16.8 percent of total assets. Comparing the figures in Table 3–1 to those in Table 3–2 for 1977, we see that 95.1 percent of total assets were consumer and business loans in 1977, yet no real estate loans were listed. Over the last 35 years, finance companies have replaced consumer and business loans with increasing amounts of real estate loans and other assets, although these loans have not become dominant, as is the case with depository institutions. However, like depository institutions, these activities create credit risk, interest rate risk, and liquidity risk that finance company managers must evaluate and manage. The financial crisis was a period that saw the downside of these risks, producing losses in all lending areas for the industry.

Table 3–4 shows the breakdown of the industry's loans in 1995 and 2012 for consumer, real estate, and business lending. In recent years, the fastest-growing areas of asset business have been in the nonconsumer finance areas, especially leasing and business lending. In 2012, consumer loans constituted 58.5 percent of all finance company loans, mortgages represented 12.8 percent, and business loans comprised 28.7 percent.

### Consumer Loans

Consumer loans consist of motor vehicle loans and leases, other consumer loans, and securitized loans from each category. Motor vehicle loans and leases are traditionally the major type of consumer loan (53.1 percent of the consumer loan portfolio in 2012). As can be seen from Table 3–5, finance companies historically charged higher rates for automobile loans than did commercial banks. In 1995 and 1996, auto finance companies charged interest rates 1.62 and 0.79 percent, respectively, higher than those of commercial banks. Nevertheless, sometimes these rates get lowered dramatically. For example, because new car sales by U.S. firms in the late 1990s were lower than normal, auto finance companies owned by the major auto manufacturers slashed interest rates on new car loans (some to as low as 0.9 percent). Moreover, after the terrorist attacks in September 2001, the major auto manufacturers lowered rates on many new car loans to 0 percent in an attempt to boost sales. Some of these 0 percent rates continued to be offered into 2005 as the U.S. economy struggled to recover and the general level of interest rates remained low. The financial crisis saw the resurrection of 0 percent car loan rates as auto manufacturers tried to boost slumping car sales. Notice that the difference between new car loans at commercial banks and finance companies continued to widen throughout the early 2000s. By 2002 finance companies were charging more than 3.3 percent less on new car loans than commercial banks, mainly due to the zero interest rates offered by the major auto manufacturers' captive finance company loans to new car buyers. However, other than for new car loans, these types of low rates are fairly rare.

**subprime lender**
A finance company that lends to high-risk customers.

The higher rates finance companies charge for consumer loans are mostly due to the fact that finance companies attract riskier customers than commercial banks. Customers who seek individual (or business) loans from finance companies are often those judged too risky to obtain loans from commercial banks or thrifts.[2] It is, in fact, possible for individuals to get a loan from a **subprime lender** finance company (a finance company that lends to high-risk customers) even with

---

[2] We look at the analysis of borrower (credit) risk in Chapter 10.

**TABLE 3–4**
Finance Company
Loans Outstanding,
1995–2012 (in
billions of dollars)

Source: Federal Reserve
Board, "Flow of Fund
Accounts," various issues.
*www.federalreserve.gov*

| | 1995 | Percent of Total, 1995 | 2012 | Percent of Total, 2012 |
|---|---|---|---|---|
| Consumer | $285.8 | $ 41.5% | $ 839.4 | 58.5% |
|   Motor vehicle loans | 81.1 | 11.8 | 294.6 | 20.5 |
|   Motor vehicle leases | 80.8 | 11.7 | 139.9 | 9.7 |
|   Revolving[1] | 28.5 | 4.1 | 74.2 | 5.2 |
|   Other[2] | 42.6 | 6.2 | 312.2 | 21.8 |
|   Securitized assets | | | | |
|     Motor vehicle loans | 34.8 | 5.1 | 11.0 | 0.8 |
|     Motor vehicle leases | 3.5 | 0.5 | 0.0 | 0.0 |
|     Revolving | n.a. | n.a. | 0.0 | 0.0 |
|     Other | 14.7 | 2.1 | 7.4 | 0.5 |
| Real estate | $ 72.4 | 10.5% | $ 183.5 | 12.8% |
|   One- to four-family | n.a. | n.a. | 134.0 | 9.3 |
|   Other | n.a. | n.a. | 49.9 | 3.5 |
|   Securitized real estate assets[3] | | | | |
|     One- to four-family | n.a. | n.a. | 0.0 | 0.0 |
|     Other | n.a. | n.a. | 0.1 | 0.0 |
| Business | $331.2 | 48.0% | $ 411.8 | 28.7% |
|   Motor vehicles | 66.5 | 9.6 | 127.5 | 8.9 |
|     Retail loans | 21.8 | 3.1 | 23.7 | 1.7 |
|     Wholesale loans[4] | 36.6 | 5.3 | 73.0 | 5.1 |
|     Leases | 8.0 | 1.2 | 30.8 | 2.1 |
|   Equipment | 188.0 | 27.3 | 202.6 | 14.1 |
|     Loans | 58.6 | 8.5 | 120.6 | 8.4 |
|     Leases | 129.4 | 18.8 | 82.0 | 5.7 |
|   Other business receivables[5] | 47.2 | 6.8 | 81.7 | 5.7 |
|   Securitized assets[3] | | | | |
|     Motor vehicles | 20.6 | 3.0 | 0.0 | 0.0 |
|       Retail loans | 1.8 | 0.3 | 0.0 | 0.0 |
|       Wholesale loans | 18.8 | 2.7 | 0.0 | 0.0 |
|     Equipment | 8.1 | 1.2 | 0.0 | 0.0 |
|       Loans | 5.3 | 0.8 | 0.0 | 0.0 |
|       Leases | 2.8 | 0.4 | 0.0 | 0.0 |
|     Other business receivables[5] | 0.8 | 0.1 | 0.0 | 0.0 |
| Total | $689.5 | $100.0% | $1,434.7 | 100.0% |

[1] Excludes revolving credit reported as held by depository institutions that are subsidiaries of finance companies.
[2] Includes personal cash loans, mobile home loans, and loans to purchase other types of consumer goods, such as appliances, apparel, boats, and recreation vehicles.
[3] Outstanding balances of pools on which securities have been issued; these balances are no longer carried on the balance sheets of the loan originator.
[4] Credit arising from transactions between manufacturers and dealers, that is, floor plan financing.
[5] Includes loans on commercial accounts receivable, factored commercial accounts, and receivable dealer capital; small loans used primarily for business or farm purposes; and wholesale and lease paper for mobile homes, campers, and travel trailers.

**TABLE 3–5**   Consumer Credit Interest Rates, 1995–2012

Source: Federal Reserve Board, "Flow of Fund Accounts," various dates. *www.federalreserve.gov*

| Type | 1995 | 1996 | 1997 | 2002 | 2007 | 2008 | 2012 |
|---|---|---|---|---|---|---|---|
| Commercial bank new car | 9.57% | 9.05% | 9.02% | 7.62% | 7.77% | 7.02% | 5.73% |
| Auto finance company new car | 11.19 | 9.84 | 7.12 | 4.29 | 4.87 | 5.52 | 4.73 |
| Difference in commercial bank versus finance company rate | 1.62 | 0.79 | −1.90 | −3.33 | −2.90 | −1.50 | −1.00 |

a bankruptcy on their records. For example, Jayhawk Acceptance Corp., one of a group of finance companies that lent money to used-car buyers with poor or no credit, began marketing loans for tummy tucks, hair transplants, and other procedures that are not usually covered by health insurance. Jayhawk entered into contracts with doctors to lend money to their patients who were seeking cosmetic surgery or some types of dental procedures. Borrowers who paid the loans within a year paid an annual rate of 9.9 percent, while those who repaid within the maximum of two years paid 13.9 percent per year. Left unanswered, however, was what Jayhawk could repossess if a borrower defaulted on a loan. Jayhawk eventually declared bankruptcy. Banks would rarely make these types of risky loans. Most finance companies that offer these types of loans charge rates com-

**loan sharks**
Subprime lenders that charge unfairly exorbitant rates to desperate subprime borrowers.

mensurate with the higher risk, and there are a few **loan shark** companies that prey on desperate consumers, charging exorbitant rates as high as 30 percent per year or more.

Another case of a subprime lender is the payday lender. Payday lenders provide short-term cash advances that are often due when borrowers receive their next paycheck. The payday lending industry originated from check cashing outlets in the early 1990s and has exploded in recent years as demand for short-term loans has risen. A typical borrower takes out a two-week loan and pays $15 for every $100 borrowed, or the equivalent of a 390 percent annual interest rate. The typical customer earns between $25,000 and $50,000 per year. Payday lenders generate approximately $44 billion in loans annually and earned about $10 billion in revenue in 2012. The number of storefronts more than doubled between 2000 and 2012, to roughly 24,000 nationwide and hundreds of websites. As of September 2012, payday lender Cash America International had $256.8 million in payday loans on its balance sheet and charged $558.7 million in interest and fees. Critics claim that rates are exorbitant and often trap financially strapped borrowers in a cycle of paying additional fees to renew the same amount of principal. Lenders argue that the high rates are necessary to cover costs, offset higher default rates, and still earn a profit.

The payday loan industry is regulated at the state level. As of 2012, 18 states had effectively banned payday lending. When not explicitly banned, laws that prohibit payday lending are usually in the form of usury limits. Payday lenders have succeeded in getting around usury laws in some states by forming relationships with nationally chartered banks based in a different state with no usury ceiling (such as South Dakota or Delaware). As federal banking regulators became aware of this practice, they began prohibiting these partnerships between commercial banks and payday lenders. The FDIC still allows its member banks to participate in payday lending, but it did issue guidelines in March 2005 that are meant to discourage long-term debt cycles by transitioning to a longer-term loan after six payday loan renewals.

Revolving and other consumer loans include personal cash loans, mobile home loans, and private-label credit card loans (e.g., Discover card) to purchase other types of consumer goods, such as appliances, apparel, general merchandise, and recreational vehicles. In 2012, these loans made up 46.9 percent of the consumer loan portfolio of finance companies.

### Mortgages

Residential and commercial mortgages have become a major component in finance company portfolios, although, referring again to Table 3–2, they did not generally deal in mortgages in 1977. However, since finance companies are not subject to as extensive regulations as are banks, they are often willing to issue mortgages to riskier borrowers than commercial banks. They compensate for this additional risk by charging higher interest rates and fees. Mortgages include all loans secured by liens on any type of real estate. Mortgages can be made either directly or as **securitized mortgage assets.** Securitization of mortgages involves the pooling of a group of mortgages with similar characteristics, the removal of these mortgages from the balance sheet, and the subsequent sale of interests in the pool to secondary market investors. Securitization of mortgages results in the creation of mortgage-backed securities (e.g., government agency securities, collateralized mortgage obligations), which can be traded in secondary mortgage markets.[3] While removed from its balance sheet, the finance company that originates the mortgage may still service the mortgage portfolio for a fee.[4]

The mortgages in the loan portfolio can be first mortgages or second mortgages in the form of home equity loans. **Home equity loans** allow customers to borrow on a line of credit secured with a second mortgage on their home. Home equity loans have become very profitable for finance companies since the Tax Reform Act of 1986 was passed, disallowing the tax deductibility of consumers' interest payments other than those on home mortgages. Specifically, interest on (first and second) mortgages secured by residential real estate is tax deductible. Interest on other types of individual loans—such as consumer (e.g., credit card) loans—is not eligible for a tax deduction. Also, the bad debt expense and administrative costs on home equity loans are lower than those on other finance company loans. As discussed below, in 2007–2008 a sharp rise in late payments and defaults by subprime and even relatively strong credit mortgage and home equity loan borrowers caused large losses for mortgage lenders and mortgage-backed securities investors, and ultimately was the root cause of the financial crisis of 2008–2009.

### Business Loans

Business loans represent 28.7 percent of the loan portfolio of finance companies. Finance companies have several advantages over commercial banks in offering services to small business customers. First, as mentioned earlier, they are not subject to regulations that restrict the types of products and services they can offer. Second,

**securitized mortgage assets**
Mortgages packaged and used as assets backing secondary market securities.

**home equity loans**
Loans that let customers borrow on a line of credit secured with a second mortgage on their home.

---

[3] We discuss the securitization of mortgages in more detail in Chapter 26.

[4] Mortgage servicing is a fee-related business whereby, after mortgages are securitized, the flow of mortgage repayments (interest and principal) has to be collected and passed on (by the mortgage servicer) to investors in either whole mortgage loan packages or securitization vehicles such as pass-through securities (see Chapter 26). In undertaking this intermediation activity, the servicer charges a fee.

because finance companies do not accept deposits, they have no bank-type regulators looking directly over their shoulders.[5] Third, being in many cases subsidiaries of corporate-sector holding companies, finance companies often have substantial industry and product expertise. Fourth, as mentioned in regard to consumer loans, finance companies are more willing to accept risky customers than are commercial banks. Fifth, finance companies generally have lower overheads than banks have; for example, they do not need tellers or branches for taking deposits.

The major subcategories of business loans are retail and wholesale motor vehicle loans and leases (31.0 percent of all business loans in 2012), equipment loans (49.2 percent), other business loans (19.8 percent), and securitized business assets (0.0 percent). Motor vehicle loans consist of retail loans that assist in transactions between the retail seller of the product and the ultimate consumer (i.e., passenger car fleets and commercial land vehicles for which licenses are required). Wholesale loans are loan agreements between parties other than the companies' consumers. For example, Ford Motor Credit Corp. (FMCC) provides wholesale financing to Ford dealers for inventory floor plans in which FMCC pays for Ford dealers' auto inventory received from Ford. FMCC puts a lien on each car on the showroom floor. While the dealer pays periodic interest on the floor plan loan, it is not until the car is sold that the dealer pays for the car. These activities extend to retail and wholesale leasing of motor vehicles as well.

Business-lending activities of finance companies also include equipment loans, with the finance company either owning or leasing the equipment directly to its industrial customer or providing the financial backing for a leveraged lease, a working capital loan, or a loan to purchase or remodel the customer's facility. Finance companies often prefer to lease equipment rather than sell and finance the purchase of equipment. One reason for this is that repossession of the equipment in the event of default is less complicated when the finance company retains its title (by leasing). Further, a lease agreement generally requires no down payment, making a lease more attractive to the business customer. Finally, when the finance company retains ownership of the equipment (by leasing), it receives a tax deduction in the form of depreciation expense on the equipment. Other business loans include loans to businesses to finance accounts receivable, factored commercial accounts, small farm loans, and wholesale and lease paper for mobile homes, campers, and trailers.

## Liabilities and Equity

To finance asset growth, finance companies have relied primarily on short-term commercial paper and other debt (longer-term notes and bonds). Thus, management of liquidity risk is quite different from that in commercial banks that mostly rely on deposits (see Chapter 2). As reported in Table 3–1, in 2012 commercial paper amounted to $61.8 billion (3.6 percent of total assets), while other debt (debt due to parents and debt not elsewhere classified) totaled $1,028.1 billion (59.2 percent) and bank loans totaled $76.5 billion (4.4 percent). Debt due to parent includes all short- and long-term debt owed to the parent company of the finance company, for example, debt Ford Motor Credit Corp. owes to Ford Motor Corp. Debt not elsewhere classified includes all short- and long-term debt (loans, notes, certificates, negotiable paper, or other) owed to external lenders not listed above. If the

---

[5] Finance companies do, of course, have market participants looking over their shoulders and monitoring their activities.

finance company subsidiary has a bad year and cannot make promised payments on its debt, the parent company would be less likely than external fund providers to initiate legal proceedings against the finance company. However, given their large percentage of funding, the parent to a finance company is susceptible to large losses of its own if the finance company subsidiary has a bad year.

Comparing these figures with those for 1977 (in Table 3–2), commercial paper was used more in 1977 (28.4 percent of total liabilities and capital), while other debt (short- and long-term) was less significant as a source of financing (40.4 percent). Finance companies also now rely less heavily on bank loans for financing. In 1977, bank loans accounted for 5.7 percent of total financing. Much of the change in funding sources is due to the strong economy and low interest rates in the U.S. long-term debt markets in the early and mid-2000s and the continued low interest rates during the financial crisis of 2008–2009. Finally, in 2012 finance companies' capital-to-assets ratio was 14.3 percent, only slightly lower than the 14.5 percent in 1977.

As discussed earlier, unlike banks and thrifts, finance companies cannot issue deposits. Rather, to finance assets, finance companies rely heavily on short-term commercial paper, with many having direct sale programs in which commercial paper is sold directly to mutual funds and other institutional investors on a continuous day-by-day basis. Indeed, finance companies are now the largest issuers in the short-term commercial paper market. Most commercial paper issues have maturities of 30 days or less, although they can be issued with maturities of up to 270 days.[6]

## INDUSTRY PERFORMANCE

In the early 2000s, the outlook for the industry as a whole was bright. Interest rates were at historical lows. Mortgage refinancing grew, and loan demand among lower- and middle-income consumers was strong. Because many of their potential borrowers had very low savings, no major slowdown in the demand for finance company services was expected. The largest finance companies—those that lend to less risky individual and business customers and with few subprime borrowers (e.g., HSBC Finance)—experienced strong profits and loan growth. (The industry's assets as a whole grew at a rate of almost 8 percent in the early 2000s.) As such, the most successful finance companies became takeover targets for other financial service as well as industrial firms. For example, Citigroup acquired Associates First Capital to create the largest full-service financial institution in the country. In May 2001 American General (the then 13th-largest finance company) was acquired by American International Group (AIG), one of the country's largest life insurance companies. Finally, in 2003 Household International was acquired by British commercial bank HSBC Holdings for $14.9 billion. This acquisition was one of the largest M&As of any kind in 2003. These are just other examples of integration and consolidation among firms in the financial services sector.

www.hfc.com

Nevertheless, in the mid- and late 2000s problems for industry participants who specialized in loans to relatively lower-quality customers created large losses in the industry and a very big problem for the U.S. economy as a whole. As home prices began to fall in 2005 and 2006 and borrowers faced rising interest rates,

---

[6] Commercial paper issued with a maturity longer than 270 days has to be registered with the SEC (i.e., it is treated the same as publicly placed bonds).

more people defaulted on their mortgages. At the end of 2006, the percentage of subprime mortgage loans on which payments were at least 60 days late was 14 percent, up from 6 percent in early 2005. With delinquencies and defaults by borrowers rising, finance companies started a sharp pullback in subprime lending. Originations of subprime mortgages declined 30 to 35 percent in 2007 from 2006, when they totaled approximately $600 billion, or about one-fifth of the entire mortgage market. The results were sharply lower values for finance companies. For example, shares of New Century Financial, the number-two subprime lender, plunged nearly 79 percent in early March 2007 after the company said it was facing a criminal probe of its practices by the Justice Department and its outside auditor said it believed there was substantial doubt about New Century's ability to continue as a going concern. On March 13, 2007, the NYSE suspended trading on the company's stock and began steps to delist the company. Similarly, Fremont General Corp. lost one-third of its value after it announced it would exit the subprime sector due to demands of regulators and market conditions. Countrywide Financial, the country's leading mortgage lender, lost over half its market value in the summer and fall of 2007 as it announced continued losses in its subprime mortgage portfolio. Only a $2 billion equity investment by Bank of America in 2007 and then an acquisition offer in 2008 kept this finance company alive. However, in March 2008, the FBI announced a probe of Countrywide for possible securities fraud. The inquiry focused on whether company officials made misrepresentations about the company's financial position and the quality of its mortgage loans in securities filings. Other leaders in the subprime mortgage lending market were units of some of the nation's biggest financial services holding companies, including HSBC (the number-one subprime mortgage lender, which took a $10.6 million charge for bad loans in 2006), General Electric, Wells Fargo, and Washington Mutual.

This crash in the subprime mortgage market led to serious problems in the U.S. and worldwide economies. The housing boom of the early 2000s held defaults to very low levels because borrowers who fell behind on payments could easily sell their homes or refinance into a loan with easier terms. Further, roughly two-thirds of mortgages were packaged into securities and sold to investors worldwide. That and other innovations made credit cheaper and more available, helping more people to afford a home. But as home prices flattened and then dropped in most parts of the country, more borrowers fell behind on their mortgage payments. By the end of 2009 mortgage loan delinquencies increased for the 12th straight quarter, hitting an all-time national average high of 6.89 percent. This rate indicated that more than 7.2 million mortgage loans were behind on payments. As the financial crisis developed and spread, other areas of lending saw increased losses. Small business loan failure rates hit the double digits, at 11.9 percent, in 2009; in 2004, the failure rate was 2.4 percent. In 2009, the national default rate for commercial real estate mortgages rose to 2.25 percent from 1.62 percent in the fourth quarter of 2008. This was the largest quarterly increase since at least 1992. Finance company performance suffered along with these decreases in loan performance.

As noted earlier, the crisis resulted in the failure of Countrywide Financial and the forced conversion of GMAC Financial Services to a bank holding company in order to prevent its failure. Another notable failure is that of CIT Group, which filed for Chapter 11 bankruptcy in November 2009. In 2008, CIT was a lender to nearly a million mostly small and midsize businesses and companies. As the financial crisis hit, many of its borrowers became delinquent or defaulted on their loans. While CIT's failure would not affect financial markets to the same extent as the failure of a large commercial bank such as Citigroup, it could hurt the flow of credit to many businesses to which banks traditionally did not lend. As a result, in December 2008, the Federal Reserve approved CIT Group's application to convert to a bank holding company, clearing a key hurdle for the firm to bolster its resources with loans and support from the government's financial rescue fund. However, as the financial crisis wore on, losses mounted, and CIT was forced to file for bankruptcy protection. At the time of bankruptcy, CIT had assets of $71 billion and liabilities of $65 billion. The bankruptcy eliminated $10 billion of this debt, including $2.3 billion extended to CIT in 2008 as part of the taxpayer bailout of the finance company. The bankruptcy of CIT Group was one of the largest filings ever of a U.S. company—trailing only the likes of Lehman Brothers, Washington Mutual, and General Motors.

As was true with depository institutions, as the U.S. economy improved in the late 2000s and early 2010s, the finance company industry improved as well. Employment in the industry increased from 561,700 in 2010 to 562,400 in 2011 (still below the 2007 level of 715,900). Further, in 2011, the median ROE for business credit institutions increased to 9.33 percent from 7.81 percent in 2010. However, the median ROE for personal credit institutions decreased to 13.73 percent in 2011 from 14.12 percent in 2010. Financial crisis issues remained even into 2012. Industry assets totaled $1.74 trillion in 2012 down from $1.75 trillion in 2010 and $2.21 trillion in 2008. Receivables also lagged behind pre-crisis levels. Total receivables dropped from $1.77 trillion in mid-2008 to $1.40 trillion in 2009 and $1.30 trillion in 2012.

| **Concept Questions** | 1. How have the major assets held by finance companies changed in the last 30 years? |
|---|---|
| | 2. How do subprime lender finance company consumer loan customers differ from consumer loan customers at banks? |
| | 3. What advantages do finance companies offer over commercial banks to small business customers? |

# REGULATION

The Federal Reserve defines a finance company as a firm (other than a depository institution) whose primary assets are loans to individuals and businesses.[7] Finance companies, like depository institutions, are financial intermediaries that borrow funds for relending, making a profit on the difference between the interest rate on borrowed funds and the rate charged on the loans. Also like depository institutions, finance companies are subject to any state-imposed usury ceilings on the maximum loan rate assigned to any individual customer and are regulated as to the extent to which they can collect on delinquent loans (e.g., legal mechanisms to be followed). However, because finance companies do not accept deposits, they are not subject to extensive oversight by any specific federal or state regulators as are banks or thrifts—even though they offer services that compete directly with those of depository institutions (e.g., consumer installment loans and mortgages).[8] The lack of regulatory oversight for these companies enables them to offer a wide scope of "bank-like" services and yet avoid the expense of regulatory compliance, such

---

[7] Whereas a bank is defined as an institution that *both* accepts deposits and makes loans.

[8] Like any corporation, they are subject to SEC disclosure rules.

as that imposed on banks and thrifts by the Community Reinvestment Act of 1977, which requires these institutions to keep and file extensive reports showing that they are not discriminating in their lending practices in their local communities.

However, because of the impact that nonbank FIs, including finance companies, had on the U.S. economy during the financial crisis and as a result of the need for the Federal Reserve to rescue several nonbank FIs, regulators proposed that non-bank FIs receive more oversight. Indeed, as discussed earlier, at the height of the financial crisis the Fed stepped in to rescue numerous finance companies, including GMAC, GE Capital, and CIT Group. Credit card lenders American Express and Discover Financial (as well as investment banks Goldman Sachs and Morgan Stanley) also became bank holding companies in 2008. As a result, as part of the 2010 Wall Street Reform and Consumer Protection Act, the federal government was provided with the tools it needs to manage financial crises by establishing (a) a new regime to resolve nonbank financial institutions whose failure could have serious systemic effects and (b) revisions to the Federal Reserve's emergency lending authority to improve accountability. The bill also proposed robust supervision and regulation of all financial firms by establishing (a) a new Financial Services Oversight Council of financial regulators (chaired by Treasury and including the heads of the principal federal financial regulators as members) to identify emerging systemic risks and improve interagency cooperation; (b) a new authority for the Federal Reserve to supervise all firms that could pose a threat to financial stability, even those that do not own banks; and (c) stronger capital and other prudential standards for all financial firms, and even higher standards for large, interconnected firms.

Further, since finance companies are heavy borrowers in the capital markets and do not enjoy the same regulatory "safety net" as banks, they need to signal their solvency and safety to investors.[9] Signals of solvency and safety are usually sent by holding higher equity or capital-to-asset ratios—and therefore lower leverage ratios—than banks hold. For example, in 2012 the aggregate balance sheet (Table 3–1) shows a capital-to-assets ratio of 14.3 percent for finance companies. This can be compared to the capital-to-asset ratio for commercial banks of 11.5 percent reported in Table 2–6. Larger, captive finance companies also use default protection guarantees from their parent companies and/or guarantees such as letters of credit or lines of credit purchased for a fee from high-quality commercial or investment banks as additional protection against insolvency risk and as a device to increase their ability to raise additional funds in the capital and money markets. Thus, this group will tend to operate with lower capital-to-asset ratios than smaller finance companies. Given that there is little regulatory oversight of this industry, having sufficient capital and access to financial guarantees are critical to their continued ability to raise funds. Thus, finance companies operate more like nonfinancial, nonregulated companies than other types of financial institutions examined in this text.

| **Concept Questions** | 1. Since finance companies seem to compete in the same lending markets as banks, why are they not subject to the same regulations as banks? |
| --- | --- |
| | 2. How do finance companies signal solvency and safety to investors? |

[9] That is, they have no access to the deposit insurance fund or to the Federal Reserve discount window (see Chapter 19). On the other hand, they do not have to pay deposit insurance premiums or meet regulatory imposed minimum capital standards.

# GLOBAL ISSUES

While commercial banks are the most important source of credit supply in many foreign countries, particularly emerging market economies, nonbank financial institutions (finance companies, credit unions, and building societies) account for a substantial part of the outstanding credit by all financial institutions and their relative importance has been increasing over the past decade. Specialized consumer finance agencies operate throughout western Europe, Canada, Australia, Japan, and some Latin American countries. For example, from the mid-1990s to the late-2000s, the percentage of aggregate credit issued by nonbank financial institutions increased from 22 to 32 percent in Latin America and from 4 to 17 percent in central Europe. In Thailand, nonbank financial institutions, particularly those specializing in credit card lending, gained market share. This trend also occurred in Mexico, where specialized mortgage institutions dominated low-income mortgage lending. Large sales finance companies specialize in financing purchases of particular commodities and remain closely associated with specific manufacturers. Some also extend credit for wholesale purchases by retail dealers. While the financial crisis affected the operations of finance companies, they still remained a major part of the financial sector in countries worldwide. For example, in New Zealand the financial crisis led to the consolidation, collapse, and restructuring of many of the country's finance companies. Further, in Russia significant finance company staff reductions occurred during the financial crisis. Because regulations in most foreign countries are not as restrictive as those in the United States, finance companies in foreign countries are generally subsidiaries of commercial banks or industrial firms. For those finance companies owned by commercial banks, as the bank goes, so does the finance company. Some of the major multinational business financing companies include Alliance Leicester Commercial Bank (part of Santander Group, United Kingdom), Commercial Lifeline (United Kingdom), Finance Eai (Australia), Five Arrows Commercial Finance (Australia), Lloyds TSB (United Kingdom), Lombard (United Kingdom), and SME Commercial Finance (Australia).

## Summary

This chapter provided an overview of the finance company industry. This industry competes directly with depository institutions for high-quality (prime) loan customers by specializing in consumer loans, real estate loans, and business loans. The industry also services subprime (high-risk) borrowers deemed too risky for most depository institutions. However, because firms in this industry do not accept deposits, they are not regulated to the same extent as are depository institutions. Because they do not have access to deposits for their funding, finance companies rely heavily on short- and long-term debt, especially commercial paper. Currently, the industry is generally growing and profitable, although the subprime lending sector of the industry is experiencing some financial problems as consumer default rates on loans and credit cards rise.

## Questions and Problems

1. What is the primary function of finance companies? How do finance companies differ from depository institution?

2. What are the three major types of finance companies? To which market segments do each of these types of companies provide service?

3. What have been the major changes in the accounts receivable balances of finance companies over the 35-year period 1977–2012?

4. What are the major types of consumer loans? Why are the rates charged by consumer finance companies typically higher than those charged by commercial banks?

5. Why have home equity loans become popular? What are securitized mortgage assets?

6. What advantages do finance companies have over commercial banks in offering services to small business customers? What are the major subcategories of business loans? Which category is the largest?

7. What have been the primary sources of financing for finance companies?

8. How do finance companies make money? What risks does this process entail? How do these risks differ for a finance company versus a commercial bank?

9. Compare Tables 3–1 and 2–6. Which firms have higher ratios of capital to total assets: finance companies or commercial banks? What does this comparison indicate about the relative strengths of these two types of firms?

10. Why do finance companies face less regulation than do commercial banks? How does this advantage translate into performance advantages? What is the major performance disadvantage?

## Web Question

11. Go to the Federal Reserve's website at **www.federalreserve.gov** and get the latest information on finance company consumer, real estate, and business lending using the following steps. Click on "All Statistical Releases." Under "Business Finance," click on "Finance Companies." This downloads a file onto your computer that contains the relevant data. How have these numbers changed since 2012, reported in Table 3–4?

www.mhhe.com/saunders8e

# Chapter **Four**

# Financial Services: Securities Brokerage and Investment Banking

## INTRODUCTION

Securities firms and investment banks primarily help net suppliers of funds (e.g., households) transfer funds to net users of funds (e.g., businesses) at a low cost and with a maximum degree of efficiency. Unlike other types of FIs, securities firms and investment banks do not transform the securities issued by the net users of funds into claims that may be "more" attractive to the net suppliers of funds (e.g., banks and their creation of bank deposits and loans). Rather, they serve as brokers intermediating between fund suppliers and users.

Investment banking involves the raising of debt and equity securities for corporations or governments. This includes the origination, underwriting, and placement of securities in money and capital markets for corporate or government issuers. Securities services involve assistance in the trading of securities in the secondary markets (brokerage services and/or market making). Together these services are performed by securities firms and investment banks. The largest companies in this industry perform both sets of services (i.e., underwriting and brokerage services). These full-line firms (e.g., Bank of America Merrill Lynch) are generally called *investment banks.* Many other firms concentrate their services in one area only (either securities trading or securities underwriting). That is, some firms in the industry specialize in the purchase, sale, and brokerage of existing securities (the retail side of the business) and are called *securities firms,* while other firms specialize in originating, underwriting, and distributing issues of new securities (the commercial side of the business) and are called *investment banks.*

Investment banking also includes corporate finance activities such as advising on mergers and acquisitions (M&As), as well as advising on the restructuring of existing corporations. Figure 4–1 reports merger activity for the period 1990–2012. Total dollar volume (measured by transaction value) of domestic M&As increased from less than $200 billion in 1990 to $1.83 trillion in 2000 (reflecting 10,864 deals).

**FIGURE 4–1**
**Attracting Partners**

Source: Thompson Reuters Deals Intelligence, 2013. *www.thompsonreuters.com*

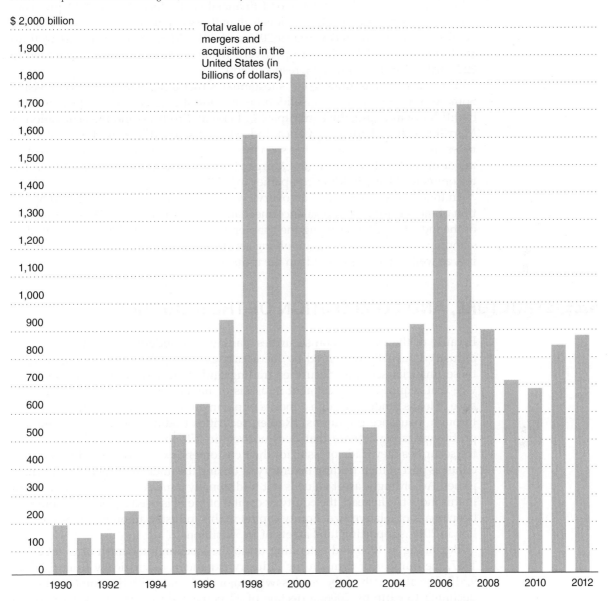

This merger wave was not restricted to the United States. For example, in 2000 there were more than 36,700 merger and acquisition deals globally, valued at more than $3.49 trillion. However, reflecting the downturn in the U.S. economy, M&A transactions fell 53 percent in 2001 to $819 billion on only 7,525 deals (the first time since 1995 there were fewer than 10,000 deals). Similarly, worldwide M&As fell to $1.74 trillion in 2001. Domestic M&A activity bottomed out at $458 billion in 2002 (while worldwide activity fell to $1.2 trillion) before recovering (along with the economy), topping $1.7 trillion in the United States (and $4.5 trillion worldwide)

in 2007. During the financial crisis, domestic M&A activity fell to $903 billion, $713 billion, and $687 billion in 2008, 2009, and 2010, respectively, while worldwide M&As fell to $2.9 trillion, $1.7 trillion, and $1.8 trillion, respectively. Note that while this period included the worst financial crisis since the Great Depression, M&A activity remained at higher levels than those experienced in the early 2000s. As the U.S. economy recovered in 2011 and 2012, M&A activity rose as well (to $861 billion and $882 billion, respectively, while worldwide activity increased to $2.33 trillion and $2.04 trillion, respectively).

The industry has undergone substantial structural changes in recent years. Some of the most recent consolidations include the acquisition of Bear Stearns by J.P. Morgan Chase, the bankruptcy of Lehman Brothers, and the acquisition of Merrill Lynch by Bank of America. Indeed, as discussed later in the chapter, the investment banking industry has seen the failure or acquisition of all but two of its major firms (Goldman Sachs and Morgan Stanley), and these two firms converted to commercial bank holding companies in 2008.

In this chapter we present an overview of (1) the size, structure, and composition of the industry, (2) the balance sheet and recent trends, and (3) the regulation of the industry. After studying the chapter, the reader should have a basic understanding of financial services involving securities brokerage and investment banking, as well as the major trends in the industry.

## SIZE, STRUCTURE, AND COMPOSITION OF THE INDUSTRY

Because of the emphasis on securities trading and underwriting, the size of the industry is usually measured by the equity capital of the firms participating in these financial services. Securities trading and underwriting is a financial service that requires no investment in assets or liability funding (such as the issuance of loans funded through deposits or payments on insurance contracts funded through insurance premiums). Rather, securities trading and underwriting is a profit-generating activity that does not require FIs to actually hold or invest in the securities they trade or issue for their customers, except for very short periods either as part of their trading inventory or during the underwriting period for new issues. Accordingly, asset value is not traditionally a measure of the size of a firm in this industry. Instead, the equity or capital of the FI is used as the most common benchmark of relative size. Equity capital in this industry amounted to $205.9 billion in 2012, supporting total assets of $4.55 trillion.

Beginning in 1980 and extending up to the stock market crash of October 19, 1987, the number of firms in the industry expanded dramatically from 5,248 to 9,515. The aftermath of the crash saw a major shakeout, with the number of firms declining to 6,016 by 2006, a decline of 37 percent since 1987. Concentration of business among the largest firms over this period increased dramatically. Some of the significant growth in size came through M&As among the top ranked firms. Table 4–1 lists major U.S. securities industry M&A transactions, many of which involve repeated ownership changes of the same company. Notice from this table that many recent mergers and acquisitions have been interindustry mergers (i.e., insurance companies and investment banks). Recent regulatory changes such as the Financial Services Modernization Act of 1999 (discussed in Chapter 2 and described in more detail in Chapter 21) are a primary cause for such mergers. In fact, note in Table 4–1 that a majority of the securities' industry mergers

**TABLE 4–1**
Major U.S. Securities Industry Merger and Acquisition Transactions

Sources: Thomson Financial Securities Data; *The Wall Street Journal;* and authors' figures.

| Rank | Deal | Price ($ billions) | Year |
|------|------|-------------------|------|
| 1 | Citicorp merges with Travelers (which owns Smith Barney and Salomon) | $83.0 | 1998 |
| 2 | J.P. Morgan acquires Bank One* | 60.0 | 2004 |
| 3 | Bank of America acquires Merrill Lynch | 50.0 | 2008 |
| 4 | Bank of America acquires FleetBoston* | 49.3 | 2003 |
| 5 | Bank of America acquires Merrill Lynch | 47.1 | 2008 |
| 6 | Chase acquires J.P. Morgan* | 35.0 | 2000 |
| 7 | Bank of America acquires MBNA* | 35.0 | 2005 |
| 8 | Wachovia acquires Golden West Financial* | 25.5 | 2006 |
| 9 | Wachovia acquires Southtrust* | 14.3 | 2004 |
| 10 | BlackRock Inc. acquires Barclays Global | 13.5 | 2009 |
| 11 | UBS acquires Paine Webber Group | 12.0 | 2000 |
| 12 | Credit Suisse First Boston acquires Donaldson Lufkin Jenrette | 11.5 | 2000 |
| 13 | Dean Witter merges with Morgan Stanley[†] | 10.2 | 1997 |
| 14 | Deutsche Bank acquires Bankers Trust* | 10.1 | 1998 |
| 15 | Region's Financial acquires AmSouth* | 10.0 | 2006 |
| 16 | CME Group acquires NYMEX Holdings | 9.5 | 2008 |
| 17 | Travelers acquires Salomon Inc. | 9.0 | 1997 |
| 18 | Intercontinental Exchange acquires NYSE | 8.2 | 2012 |
| 19 | Goldman Sachs acquires Spear, Leeds & Kellogg | 6.5 | 2000 |
| 20 | J.P. Morgan acquires Bear Stearns | 0.2 | 2008 |

\* These organizations own Section 20 securities subsidiaries and/or are established financial service holding companies under the 1999 Financial Services Modernization Act.
† Value of Dean Witter, Discover shares to be exchanged for Morgan Stanley stock, based on closing price of $40.625 on February 5, 1997.

and acquisitions occurring in the 2000s include securities firms that are a part of a financial services holding company.

The financial crisis resulted in a second major change in the structure of the industry. The five largest investment banks in existence at the beginning of 2008 (Lehman Brothers, Bear Stearns, Merrill Lynch, Goldman Sachs, and Morgan Stanley) were all gone as investment banks by the end of the year. Lehman Brothers failed at the start of the financial crisis, Bear Stearns and Merrill Lynch were acquired by financial services holding companies (J.P. Morgan Chase and Bank of America, respectively), and Goldman Sachs and Morgan Stanley requested and were granted commercial bank charters. As of 2011, commercial bank holding companies' fee income from securities brokerage topped $40.28 billion, up from $16.47 billion in 2007, and more than 65 percent of the industry total. Table 4–2 lists the top bank holding companies in terms of securities brokerage fee income. Further, the number of securities firms continued to fall to 4,481 by 2012. The investment banking industry was irrevocably changed.

**broker–dealers**
Assist in the trading of existing securities.

**underwriting**
Assisting in the issue of new securities.

In its changed state, firms in the industry can be divided along a number of dimensions. The largest firms, the so-called national full-line firms, service both retail customers (especially in acting as **broker–dealers**, thus assisting in the trading of existing securities) and corporate customers (such as **underwriting**, thus assisting in the issue of new securities). With the changes in the past few years, national full-line firms now fall into three subgroups. First are the commercial bank

**TABLE 4–2**
Top Bank Holding Companies in Securities Brokerage Fee Income, 2011 (in billions of dollars)

| Bank Holding Company | Securities Brokerage Fee Income |
|---|---|
| Bank of America | $ 9.93 |
| Morgan Stanley | 7.47 |
| Wells Fargo | 4.75 |
| Goldman Sachs | 3.01 |
| J.P. Morgan Chase | 2.75 |
| All bank holding companies | $36.81 |

holding companies that are the largest of the full service investment banks. They have extensive domestic and international operations and offer advice, underwriting, brokerage, trading, and asset management services. The largest of these firms include Bank of America (through their acquisition of Merrill Lynch), Morgan Stanley, and J.P. Morgan Chase (through its many acquisitions, including that of Bear Stearns, for $240 million in 2008). Second are the national full-line firms that specialize more in corporate business with customers and are highly active in trading securities. Examples are Goldman Sachs and Salomon Brothers/Smith Barney, the investment banking arm of Citigroup (created from the merger of Travelers and Citicorp in 1998). Third are the large investment banks. These firms maintain more limited branch networks concentrated in major cities operating with predominantly institutional client bases. These firms include Lazard Ltd. and Greenhill & Co.

The rest of the industry is comprised of firms that perform a mix of primary and secondary market services for a particular segment of the financial markets:

1. Regional securities firms that are often subdivided into large, medium, and small categories and concentrate on servicing customers in a particular region, e.g., New York or California (such as Raymond James Financial).

**discount brokers**
Stockbrokers that conduct trades for customers but do not offer investment advice.

2. Specialized **discount brokers** that effect trades for customers on- or offline without offering investment advice or tips (such as Charles Schwab).

3. Specialized electronic trading securities firms (such as E*trade) that provide a platform for customers to trade without the use of a broker. Rather, trades are enacted on a computer via the Internet.[1]

4. Venture capital firms that pool money from individual investors and other FIs (e.g., hedge funds, pension funds, and insurance companies) to fund relatively small and new businesses (e.g., in biotechnology).[2]

5. Other firms in this industry include research boutiques, floor specialists, companies with large clearing operations, and other firms that do not fit into one of the preceding categories. This would include firms such as Knight Capital Group (a leading firm in off-exchange trading of U.S. equities) and floor specialist LaBranche & Co.

Securities firms and investment banks engage in as many as seven key activity areas investment banking, venture capital, market making, trading, investing,

---

[1] Discount brokers and electronic trading securities firms usually charge lower commissions than do full-service brokers such as Merrill Lynch.

[2] Venture capital firms generally play an active management role in the firms in which they invest, often including a seat on the board of directors, and hold significant equity stakes. This differentiates them from traditional banking and securities firms.

**TABLE 4–3**
Top Underwriters
of Global Debt and
Equity

Source: Thompson Reuters
Deals Intelligence, 2013.
*www.thompsonreuters.com*

| | Full Year 2012 | | Full Year 2011 | | |
|---|---|---|---|---|---|
| **Manager** | **Amount (billions)** | **Market Share** | **Amount (billions)** | **Rank** | **Market Share** |
| J.P. Morgan | $ 488.6 | 7.9% | $ 384.8 | 1 | 6.9% |
| Deutsche Bank | 409.7 | 6.6 | 371.3 | 2 | 6.7 |
| Barclays Capital | 384.6 | 6.2 | 365.9 | 3 | 6.6 |
| Citigroup | 373.6 | 6.0 | 305.6 | 5 | 5.5 |
| Bank of America Merrill Lynch | 339.1 | 5.5 | 325.6 | 4 | 5.9 |
| Top ten | $3,323.2 | 53.6% | $2,958.4 | | 53.2% |
| Industry total | $6,191.7 | 100.0% | $5,569.7 | | 100.0% |

cash management, mergers and acquisitions, and other service functions. As we describe each of these, note that while each activity is available to a firm's customers independently, many of these activities can be and are conducted simultaneously (such as mergers and acquisitions financed by new issues of debt and equity underwritten by the M&A advising firm) for a firm's customers.

### 1. Investment Banking

**IPO**
An initial, or first time, public offering of debt or equity by a corporation.

Investment banking refers to activities related to underwriting and distributing new issues of debt and equity. New issues can be either primary, the first-time issues of companies (sometimes called **IPOs** [initial public offerings]), or secondary issues (the new issues of seasoned firms whose debt or equity is already trading). In 2012, a total of $6.19 trillion of debt and equity was underwritten. This was up from $4.95 trillion underwritten in 2008 during the financial crisis, but well below the pre-crisis amounts of $7.51 and $7.84 trillion in 2007 and 2006, respectively. Table 4–3 lists the top 5 underwriters of global debt and equity for 2011 and 2012. The top 5 underwriters represented 32.2 percent and the top 10 firms represented more than 50 percent of the industry total, suggesting that the industry is dominated by a handful of top-tier underwriting firms. Top-tier rating and the implied reputation this brings has a huge effect in this business. At times, investment banks have refused to participate in an issue because their name would not be placed where they desired it on the "tombstone" advertisement announcing the issue and its major underwriters.

**private placement**
A securities issue placed with one or a few large institutional investors.

Securities underwritings can be undertaken through either public offerings or private offerings. In a private offering, the investment banker acts as a **private placement** agent for a fee, placing the securities with one or a few large institutional investors such as life insurance companies. In a public offering, the securities may be underwritten on a best-efforts or a firm commitment basis, and the securities may be offered to the public at large. With best-efforts underwriting, investment bankers act as *agents* on a fee basis related to their success in placing the issue. In a firm commitment underwriting, the investment banker acts as a *principal,* purchasing the securities from the issuer at one price and seeking to place them with public investors at a slightly higher price. Finally, in addition to investment banking operations in the corporate securities markets, investment banks may participate as an underwriter (primary dealer) in government, municipal, and asset-backed securities. Table 4–4 shows the top-ranked underwriters for 2012 and 2011 in the different areas of securities underwriting.

**TABLE 4–4** Who Is the Lead Underwriter in Each Market?

Source: Thompson Reuters Deals Intelligence, 2013. *www.thompsonreuters.com*

| Type | Full Year 2012 | | Full Year 2011 | |
|---|---|---|---|---|
| | Amount (billions) | Top-Ranked Manager | Amount (billions) | Top-Ranked Manager |
| Total debt | $5,557.2 | J.P. Morgan | $4,952.2 | Barclays Capital |
| Convertible debt | 64.2 | Deutsche Bank | 65.4 | Goldman Sachs |
| Investment-grade debt | 2,655.3 | J.P. Morgan | 2,258.7 | J.P. Morgan |
| Mortgage-backed securities | 462.0 | Deutsche Bank | 521.5 | Bank of America Merrill Lynch |
| Asset-backed securities | 321.0 | J.P. Morgan | 243.0 | Bank of America Merrill Lynch |
| Common stock | 566.2 | Goldman Sachs | 551.9 | Goldman Sachs |
| IPOs | 117.4 | Morgan Stanley | 163.8 | Goldman Sachs |
| Syndicated loans | 3,226.8 | J.P. Morgan | 3,934.0 | J.P. Morgan |

**EXAMPLE 4–1**

*Best Efforts versus Firm Commitment Securities Offering*

An investment bank agrees to underwrite an issue of 20 million shares of stock for Murray Construction Corp. on a firm commitment basis. The investment bank pays $15.50 per share to Murray Construction Corp. for the 20 million shares of stock. It then sells those shares to the public for $16.35 per share. How much money does Murray Construction Corp. receive? What is the profit to the investment bank? If the investment bank can sell the shares for only $14.75, how much money does Murray Construction Corp. receive? What is the profit to the investment bank?

If the investment bank sells the stock for $16.35 per share, Murray Construction Corp. receives $15.50 × 20,000,000 shares = $310,000,000. The profit to the investment bank is ($16.35 − $15.50) × 20,000,000 shares = $17,000,000. The stock price of Murray Construction Corp. is $16.35 since that is what the public agrees to pay. From the perspective of Murray Construction Corp., the $17 million represents the commission that it must pay to issue the stock.

If the investment bank sells the stock for $14.75 per share, Murray Construction Corp. still receives $15.50 × 20,000,000 shares = $310,000,000. The profit to the investment bank is ($14.75 − $15.50) × 20,000,000 shares = −$15,000,000. The stock price of Murray Construction Corp. is $14.75 since that is what the public agrees to pay. From the perspective of the investment bank, the −$15 million represents a loss for the firm commitment it made to Murray Construction Corp. to issue the stock.

Suppose, instead, that the investment bank agrees to underwrite the 20 million shares on a best-efforts basis. The investment bank is able to sell 18.4 million shares for $15.50 per share, and it charges Murray Construction Corp. $0.375 per share sold. How much money does Murray Construction Corp. receive? What is the profit to the investment bank? If the investment bank can sell the shares for only $14.75, how much money does Murray Construction Corp. receive? What is the profit to the investment bank?

If the investment bank sells the stock for $15.50 per share, Murray Construction Corp. receives ($15.50 − $0.375) × 18,400,000 shares = $278,300,000, the investment bank's profit is $0.375 × 18,400,000 shares = $6,900,000, and the stock price is $15.50 per share since that is what the public pays.

If the investment bank sells the stock for $14.75 per share, Murray Construction Corp. receives ($14.75 − $0.375) × 18,400,000 shares = $264,500,000, the investment bank's profit is still $0.375 × 18,400,000 shares = $6,900,000, and the stock price is $14.75 per share since that is what the public pays.

## 2. Venture Capital

**venture capital**
A professionally managed pool of money used to finance new and often high-risk firms.

A difficulty for new and small firms in obtaining debt financing from commercial banks (or CBs) is that CBs are generally not willing or able to make loans to new companies with no assets and business history. In this case, new and small firms often turn to investment banks (and other firms) that make venture capital investments to get capital financing as well as advice. **Venture capital** is a professionally managed pool of money used to finance new and often high-risk firms. Venture capital is generally provided to back an untried company and its managers in return for an equity investment in the firm. Venture capital firms do not make outright loans. Rather, they purchase an equity interest in the firm that gives them the same rights and privileges associated with an equity investment made by the firm's other owners. The terms *venture capital* and *private equity* are often used interchangeably. However, there are distinct differences in the two types of investment institutions. For example, venture capital firms generally, using the pooled investment resources of institutions and wealthy individuals, concern themselves more with startup business concerns. Private equity firms acquire the investment funds they use from sources such as equity securities and non–publicly traded stocks as well as the institutional and individual investment pooling used by venture capital firms. Further, venture capital firms tend to utilize teams of either scientific or business professionals to help identify new and emerging technologies in which to place their money. Private equity firms deal more with existing companies that have already proven themselves in the business field. As a result of the financial crisis, the differences between venture capital firms and private equity firms have become less distinct. With fewer new ventures being brought forth, there has been greater competition between the two types of investment institutions, with both searching for and funding the same types of new and small firms.

**institutional venture capital firms**
Business entities whose sole purpose is to find and fund the most promising new firms.

There are many types of venture capital firms. **Institutional venture capital firms** are business entities whose sole purpose is to find and fund the most promising new firms. Private sector institutional venture capital firms include venture capital limited partnerships (that are established by professional venture capital firms, acting as general partners in the firm: organizing and managing the firm and eventually liquidating their equity investment), financial venture capital firms (subsidiaries of investment or commercial banks), and corporate venture capital firms (subsidiaries of nonfinancial corporations that generally specialize in making startup investments in high-tech firms). Limited partner venture capital firms dominate the industry. In addition to these private sector institutional venture capital firms, the federal government, through the Small Business Administration (SBA), operates small business investment companies (SBICs). SBICs are privately organized venture capital firms licensed by the SBA that make equity investments (as well as loans) to entrepreneurs for startup activities and expansions. As federally sponsored entities, SBICs have relied on their unique opportunity to obtain investment funds from the U.S. Treasury at very low rates relative to private sector institutional venture capital firms. In contrast to institutional venture capital firms, **angel venture capitalists (or angels)** are wealthy individuals who make equity investments. Angel venture capitalists have invested much more in new and small firms than institutional venture capital firms.

**angel venture capitalists (or angels)**
Wealthy individuals who make equity investments.

Venture capital firms receive many unsolicited proposals of funding from new and small firms. A majority of these requests are rejected. Venture capital firms look for two things in making their decisions to invest in a firm. The first is a high return. Venture capital firms are willing to invest in high-risk new and small firms. However, they require high levels of returns (sometimes as high as 700 percent within five to seven years) to take on these risks. The second is an easy exit. Venture capital firms realize a profit on their investments by eventually selling their interests in the firm. They want a quick and easy exit opportunity when it comes time to sell. Basically, venture capital firms provide equity funds to new, unproven, and young firms. This separates venture capital firms from commercial banks, which prefer to invest in existing, financially secure businesses.

### 3. Market Making

Market making involves creating a secondary market in an asset by a securities firm or investment bank. Thus, in addition to being primary dealers in government securities and underwriters of corporate bonds and equities, investment banks make a secondary market in these instruments. Market making can involve either agency or principal transactions. *Agency* transactions are two-way transactions on behalf of *customers,* for example, acting as a *stockbroker* or dealer for a fee or commission. On the NYSE, a market maker in a stock such as IBM may, upon the placement of orders by its customers, buy the stock at $190 from one customer and immediately resell it at $191 to another customer. The $1 difference between the buy and sell price is usually called the bid–ask spread and represents a large portion of the market maker's profit.

In *principal* transactions, the market maker seeks to profit on the price movements of securities and takes either long or short inventory positions for its own account. (Or an inventory position may be taken to stabilize the market in the securities.) In the example above, the market maker would buy the IBM stock at $190 and hold it in its own portfolio in expectation of a price increase later on. Normally, market making can be a fairly profitable business. However, in periods of market stress or high volatility, these profits can rapidly disappear. For example, on the NYSE, market makers, in return for having monopoly power in market making for individual stocks (e.g., IBM), have an affirmative obligation to buy stocks from sellers even when the market is crashing. This caused a number of actual and near bankruptcies for NYSE market makers at the time of the October 1987 market crash. On NASDAQ, which has a system of competing market makers, liquidity was significantly impaired at the time of the crash and a number of firms had to withdraw from market making. Finally, the recent moves toward decimalization of equities markets in the United States (i.e., expressing quotes in integers of 1 cent [e.g., $50.32] rather than rounding to eighths [e.g., $50\frac{3}{8}$]) has cut into traders' profits, as has competition from Internet-based or electronic-based exchanges such as Instinet Group.

### 4. Trading

Trading is closely related to the market-making activities just described, where a trader takes an active net position in an underlying instrument or asset. There are at least six types of trading activities:

1. *Position trading* involves purchasing large blocks of securities on the expectation of a favorable price move. Position traders maintain long or short positions for intervals of up to several weeks or even months. Rather than attempting to profit from very short-term movements in prices, as day traders do, position traders take relatively longer views of market trends. Such positions also facilitate the smooth functioning of the secondary markets in such securities.

2. *Pure arbitrage* entails buying an asset in one market at one price and selling it immediately in another market at a higher price. Pure arbitrage "locks in" profits that are available in the market. This profit position usually occurs with no equity investment, the use of only very short-term borrowed funds, and reduced transaction costs for securities firms. Pure arbitrageurs often attempt to profit from price discrepancies that may exist between the spot, or cash, price of a security and its corresponding futures price. Some important theoretical pricing relationships in futures markets should exist with spot markets and prices. When these relationships get out of line, pure arbitrageurs enter the market to exploit them.

3. *Risk arbitrage* involves buying securities in anticipation of some information release, such as a merger or takeover announcement or a Federal Reserve interest rate announcement. It is termed *risk arbitrage* because if the event does not actually occur—for example, if a merger does not take place or the Federal Reserve does not change interest rates—the trader stands to lose money.

4. *Program trading* is defined by the NYSE as the simultaneous buying and selling of a portfolio of at least 15 different stocks valued at more than $1 million, using computer programs to initiate such trades. Program trading is often associated with seeking a risk arbitrage between a cash market price (e.g., the Standard & Poor's 500 Stock Market Index) and the *futures* market price of that instrument.[3] Because computers are used to continuously monitor stock and futures prices—and can even initiate buy or sell orders—these trades are classified separately as *program trading*.

5. *Stock brokerage* involves the trading of securities on behalf of individuals who want to transact in the money or capital markets. To conduct such transactions, individuals contact their broker (such as Merrill Lynch), which then sends the orders to its representative at the exchange to conduct the trades. Large brokerage firms often have several licenses on the floor of a stock exchange (e.g., NYSE), through which their commission brokers trade orders from the firm's clients or for the firms own account.

6. *Electronic brokerage,* offered by major brokers, involves direct access, via the Internet, to the trading floor, therefore bypassing traditional brokers. Many securities firms and investment banks offer online trading services to their customers as well as direct access to a client representative (stockbroker). Thus, customers may now conduct trading activities from their homes and offices through their accounts at securities firms. Because services provided by a typical brokerage firm are bypassed, the cost per share is generally lower and the price may be advantageous compared with trading directly on the exchanges. Users of the system can often use the network to discover existing sizes and quotes of offers to buy or sell. Interested parties can then negotiate with each other using the system's computers.

As with many activities of securities firms, such trading can be conducted on behalf of a customer as an agent (or broker), or on behalf of the firm as a principal. When trading at the retail level occurs on behalf of customers, it is often called *brokerage* (or stock brokering).

---

[3] An example would be buying the cash S&P index and selling futures contracts on the S&P index. Since stocks and futures contracts trade in different markets, their prices are not always equal. Moreover, program trading can occur between futures and cash markets in other assets, e.g., commodities.

### 5. Investing

Investing involves managing not only pools of assets such as closed- and open end mutual funds but also pension funds in competition with life insurance companies. Securities firms can manage such funds either as agents for other investors or as principals for themselves. The objective in funds management is to choose asset allocations to beat some return–risk performance benchmark such as the S&P 500 index. Since this business generates fees that are based on the size of the pool of assets managed, it tends to produce a more stable flow of income than does either investment banking or trading.

### 6. Cash Management

**cash management accounts**
Money market mutual funds sold by investment banks; most CMAs offer check-writing privileges.

Investment banks offer bank deposit-like **cash management accounts** (CMAs) to individual investors and since the 1999 Financial Services Modernization Act, deposit accounts themselves (Merrill Lynch was the first investment bank to offer a direct deposit account in June 2000, via the two banks it owned). Most of these CMAs allow customers to write checks against some type of mutual fund account (e.g., money market mutual fund). These accounts, when issued in association with commercial banks and thrifts, can even be covered by federal deposit insurance from the FDIC. CMAs were adopted by other security firms under various names (e.g., house account) and spread rapidly. Many of these accounts offer ATM services and debit cards. As a result of CMAs, the distinction between commercial banks and investment banks became blurred. However, the advantage of brokerage firm CMAs over commercial bank deposit accounts is that they make it easier to buy and sell securities. The broker can take funds out of the CMA account when an investor buys a security and deposit funds back into the CMA when the investor sells securities. CMAs were instrumental in the securities industry's efforts to provide commercial banking services prior to the 1999 Financial Services Modernization Act. Since the passage of this regulation, securities firms are allowed to make loans, offer credit and debit cards, provide ATM services, and, most importantly, sell securities.

### 7. Mergers and Acquisitions

Investment banks are frequently involved in providing advice or assisting in mergers and acquisitions. For example, they will assist in finding merger partners, underwriting new securities to be issued by the merged firms, assessing the value of target firms, recommending terms of the merger agreement, and even helping target firms prevent a merger (e.g., seeing that poison-pill provisions are written into a potential target firm's securities contracts). As noted in the introduction to this chapter, U.S. merger and acquisition activity stood at $882 billion in 2012. Panel A of Table 4–5 lists the top 10 investment bank merger advisors ranked by dollar volume of domestic mergers in which they were involved. Panel B of Table 4–5 lists the top 10 investment banks ranked by dollar volume of worldwide M&A activity. Notice that many of the top U.S.-ranked investment banks reported in panel A of Table 4–5 are also top-ranked for worldwide activity in panel B.

### 8. Back-Office and Other Service Functions

These functions include custody and escrow services, clearance and settlement services, and research and other advisory services—for example, giving advice on divestitures and asset sales. In addition, investment banks are making increasing inroads into traditional bank service areas such as small business lending and the

**TABLE 4–5**
Ten Largest Merger and Acquisition Firms Ranked by Value of Mergers, 2012

Source: Thompson Reuters Deals Intelligence, 2013. *www.thompsonreuters.com*

| Panel A: Mergers Completed in U.S. | | | |
|---|---|---|---|
| **Rank** | **Investment Bank** | **Value ($ billions)** | **Number of Deals** |
| 1 | Goldman Sachs | $299.8 | 140 |
| 2 | J.P. Morgan | 241.5 | 114 |
| 3 | Barclays Capital | 229.9 | 120 |
| 4 | Credit Suisse | 216.7 | 86 |
| 5 | Morgan Stanley | 175.2 | 95 |
| 6 | Evercore Partners | 140.9 | 65 |
| 7 | Citigroup | 134.1 | 72 |
| 8 | Bank of America Merrill Lynch | 131.5 | 91 |
| 9 | Lazard | 124.8 | 91 |
| 10 | Deutsche Bank | 101.3 | 66 |
| | Industry total | $882.1 | 6,951 |

| Panel B: Worldwide Mergers | | | |
|---|---|---|---|
| **Rank** | **Investment Bank** | **Credit Lent ($ billions)** | **Number of Deals** |
| 1 | Goldman Sachs | $  570.2 | 352 |
| 2 | J.P. Morgan | 406.4 | 247 |
| 3 | Morgan Stanley | 379.4 | 320 |
| 4 | Credit Suisse | 354.5 | 231 |
| 5 | Barclays Capital | 321.6 | 235 |
| 6 | Bank of America Merrill Lynch | 274.2 | 192 |
| 7 | Deutsche Bank | 265.0 | 216 |
| 8 | Citigroup | 238.1 | 184 |
| 9 | Lazard | 220.0 | 223 |
| 10 | Rothschild | 164.6 | 234 |
| | Industry total | $2,040.6 | 28,454 |

trading of loans (see Chapter 21). In performing these functions, an investment bank normally acts as an agent for a fee. As mentioned above, fees charged are often based on the total bundle of services performed for the client by the firm. The portion of the fee or commission allocated to research and advisory services is called *soft dollars*. When one area in the firm, such as an investment advisor, uses client commissions to buy research from another area in the firm, it receives a benefit because it is relieved from the need to produce and pay for the research itself. Thus, the advisor using soft dollars faces a conflict of interest between the need to obtain research and the client's interest in paying the lowest commission rate available. Because of the conflict of interest that exists, the SEC (the primary regulator of investment banks and securities firms) requires these firms to disclose soft dollar arrangements to their clients.

Nevertheless, in the early and mid-2000s tremendous publicity was generated concerning conflicts of interest in a number of investment banks between analysts' research recommendations on stocks to buy or not buy and whether the firm played a role in underwriting the securities of the firm the analysts were recommending. After an investigation by the New York State Attorney General, Merrill

Lynch agreed to pay a fine of $100 million and to follow procedures more clearly separating analysts' recommendations (and their compensation) from the underwriting activities of the firm. A number of other major Wall Street firms were also placed under investigation (discussed later). The investigation was triggered by the dramatic collapse of many new technology stocks while analysts were still making recommendations to buy or hold them.

| **Concept Questions** | 1. Describe the difference between brokerage services and underwriting services.<br>2. What are the key areas of activities for securities firms and investment banks?<br>3. Describe the difference between a best-efforts offering and a firm commitment offering.<br>4. What are the trading activities performed by securities firms and investment banks? |
| --- | --- |

## BALANCE SHEET AND RECENT TRENDS

### Recent Trends

In this section, we look at the balance sheet and trends in the securities firm and investment banking industry. Trends in this industry depend heavily on the state of the stock market. For example, a major effect of the 1987 stock market crash was a sharp decline in stock market trading volume and thus in brokerage commissions earned by securities firms over the 1987–91 period. The overall decline in brokerage commissions actually began more than 35 years ago, in 1977. The decline is reflective of a long-term fall in the importance of commission income, as a percentage of revenues, for securities firms as a result of the abolition of fixed commissions on securities trades imposed by the Securities and Exchange Commission (SEC) in May 1975 and the fierce competition for wholesale commissions and trades that followed (see Figure 4–2). Commission income began to stabilize and recover only after 1992, with record equity trading volumes being achieved in 1995–2000 when the Dow Jones and S&P indexes hit new highs. Improvements in the U.S. economy in the mid-2000s resulted in even greater increases in stock market values and trading and thus commission income. However, rising oil prices and the subprime mortgage market collapse and the eventual full market crash in 2008–09 pushed stock market values down. As a result, commission income in the securities industry declined as well. As the economy and the stock market recovered in the early 2010s, commission income again rose to almost 20 percent of total revenues.

Also affecting the profitability of the securities industry was the decline in new equity issues over the 1987–90 period as well as a decline in bond and equity underwriting in general (see Table 4–6). This was due partly to the stock market crash, partly to a decline in mergers and acquisitions, partly to a general economic recession, and partly to investor concerns about the high-risk junk-bond market, which crashed during this period. Between 1991 and 2001, however, the securities industry showed a resurgence in profitability. For example, domestic underwriting activity over the 1990–2001 period grew from $192.7 billion in 1990 to $1,623.9 billion in 2001 (see Table 4–6). The principal reasons for this were enhanced trading profits and increased growth in new issue underwritings. In particular, corporate debt issues became highly attractive to corporate treasurers because of relatively low long-term interest rates. Moreover, growth in the asset-backed

**FIGURE 4–2** Commission Income as a Percentage of Total Revenues

Sources: Securities and Exchange Commission, Standard & Poor's *Industry Surveys,* and Securities Industry and Financial Markets Association.

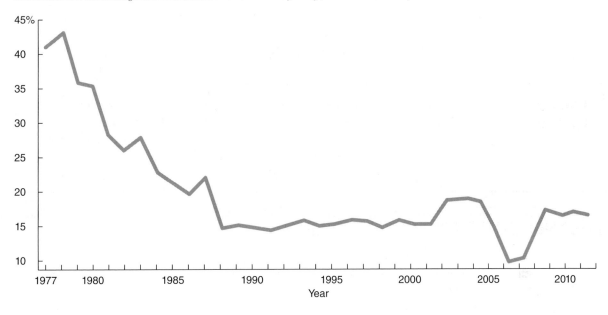

**TABLE 4–6** U.S. Corporate Underwriting Activity (in billions of dollars)

Source: Securities Industry and Financial Markets Association. *www.sifma.com*

| | Straight Corporate Debt | Con-vertible Debt | Asset-Backed Debt | Non agency MBS | Total Debt | Common Stock | Preferred Stock | Total Equity | All IPOs | Total Under-writing |
|---|---|---|---|---|---|---|---|---|---|---|
| 1986 | 134.9 | 9.8 | 10.0 | 62.2 | 216.9 | 43.2 | 13.9 | 57.1 | 22.3 | 274.0 |
| 1987 | 108.5 | 10.3 | 8.9 | 83.3 | 211.0 | 41.5 | 11.4 | 52.9 | 24.0 | 263.9 |
| 1990 | 76.5 | 5.5 | 43.6 | 43.2 | 168.8 | 19.2 | 4.7 | 23.9 | 10.1 | 192.7 |
| 1995 | 279.8 | 12.0 | 113.1 | 36.5 | 441.4 | 82.0 | 15.1 | 97.1 | 30.2 | 538.5 |
| 2000 | 587.5 | 49.6 | 337.0 | 102.1 | 1,076.2 | 189.1 | 15.4 | 204.5 | 76.1 | 1,280.7 |
| 2001 | 776.1 | 78.3 | 383.3 | 216.5 | 1,454.2 | 128.4 | 41.3 | 169.7 | 40.8 | 1,623.9 |
| 2002 | 635.4 | 30.5 | 496.2 | 263.9 | 1,399.0 | 116.4 | 37.6 | 154.0 | 41.2 | 1,553.0 |
| 2005 | 752.8 | 30.1 | 753.5 | 901.2 | 2,437.6 | 160.5 | 29.9 | 190.4 | 62.6 | 2,628.0 |
| 2006 | 1,058.9 | 62.8 | 753.9 | 917.4 | 2,793.0 | 157.2 | 33.4 | 190.5 | 57.9 | 2,983.5 |
| 2007 | 1,128.3 | 76.4 | 509.7 | 773.9 | 2,488.2 | 187.5 | 60.0 | 247.5 | 91.1 | 2,735.7 |
| 2008 | 707.2 | 42.0 | 163.3 | 45.0 | 957.4 | 164.9 | 77.3 | 242.3 | 11.0 | 1,199.7 |
| 2009 | 901.9 | 33.0 | 150.9 | 32.4 | 1,118.2 | 254.6 | 9.6 | 264.2 | 26.9 | 1,382.4 |
| 2010 | 1,062.8 | 29.1 | 107.5 | 19.0 | 1,218.4 | 239.5 | 22.2 | 261.7 | 52.0 | 1,480.0 |
| 2011 | 1,012.1 | 20.7 | 124.8 | 22.9 | 1,180.5 | 185.1 | 13.3 | 198.4 | 47.8 | 1,378.9 |
| 2012 | 1,354.5 | 19.7 | 199.4 | 39.3 | 1,612.9 | 245.1 | 32.5 | 277.6 | 55.4 | 1,890.5 |
| % Change (YTD 2011 to YTD 2012) | 33.8% | −5.1% | 59.8% | 71.1% | 36.6% | 32.4% | 144.4% | 39.9% | 15.7% | 37.1% |

Note: High-yield bonds represent a subset of straight corporate debt. IPOs are a subset of common stock; true and closed-end fund IPOs are subsets of all IPOs.

**FIGURE 4–3** Securities Industry Pretax Profits, 1990–2012

Source: Securities Industry and Financial Markets Association, various years. *www.sifma.com*

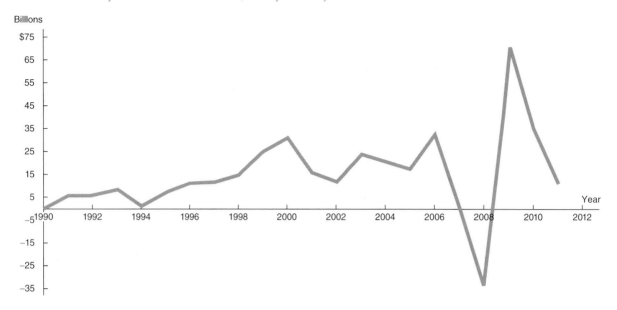

securities market as a result of increased securitization of mortgages (and growth of mortgage debt) added to the value of underwriting.[4]

As a result of enhanced trading profits and growth in new issue underwriting, pretax net income for the industry topped $9 billion each year over the 1996–2000 period (see Figure 4–3). This is despite the collapse of the Russian ruble and bond markets, economic turmoil in Asia, and political uncertainty in Washington during this period. Possibly more surprising is that despite a downturn in the U.S. economy toward the end of 2000, pretax profits soared to an all-time high of $31.6 billion in 2000. The continued slowdown of the U.S. economy in 2001 and the terrorist attacks on the World Trade Center (which housed offices of many securities firms and investment banks) in September 2001, however, brought an end to these record profits. Industry pretax profits for the year 2001 fell 24 percent, to $16 billion. The Bank of New York alone estimated costs associated with the terrorist attacks were $125 million. Citigroup estimated it lost $100–$200 million in business from branches that were closed and because of the four days the stock market did not trade. Morgan Stanley, the largest commercial tenant in the World Trade Center, said the cost of property damage and relocation of its employees was $150 million. Also impacting profit, the securities industry was rocked by several allegations of securities law violations as well as a loss of investor confidence in Wall Street and corporate America as a result of a number of corporate governance failures and accounting scandals involving Enron, Merck, WorldCom, and other major U.S. corporations.

With the recovery of the U.S. economy in the mid-2000s, the U.S. securities industry again earned record profits as revenue growth strengthened and became

---

[4] Another sign of the resurgence in this industry during the 1990s appears in employment figures. Annual U.S. securities industry employment increased by 72 percent (from 486,000 jobs in 1992 to 837,000 in 2000 [peaking at 840,900 in March 2001]).

more broadly based. Domestic underwriting surged to $2,983.5 billion in 2006, from $1,553.0 billion in 2002 (see Table 4–6). Further, the industry increased its profitability through deep cuts in expenses. Total expenses fell 10.4 percent from 2002 levels, largely due to lower interest expenses. Interest expense fell an estimated 22.5 percent from $48.4 billion in 2002 to $37.5 billion in 2003. The results for 2003 were a surge in pretax profits to $24.1 billion (see Figure 4–3). Interest rate increases in 2005 caused interest expense incurred by the securities industry to increase. The result was that, while gross revenues remained high, the increased interest expense caused pretax profits to fall to $17.6 billion in 2005. A surge in revenues from trading gains and corporate advisory services caused pretax profits to bounce back to a record level of $33.1 billion for 2006.

Signs of the impending financial crisis arose in 2007. The industry began 2007 on a strong note but, hit by the subprime mortgage market meltdown that began in the summer of 2007, ended the year with pretax profits of just $0.78 billion. Many revenue lines showed solid growth in 2007, and total revenues reached a record high of $474.2 billion. However, trading and investment account losses were large, totaling a loss of $6 billion in 2007 compared with a gain of $43 billion in 2006. Further, expenses grew faster than revenues, to a record $473.4 billion in 2007. The worst of the financial crisis hit in 2008 as the industry reported a record loss for the year of $34.1 billion. Revenues were $290.5 billion, down 38.7 percent from 2007. Nearly all revenue lines decreased from 2007 levels, with trading and investment account losses being the largest (−$65.0 billion in 2008).

As quickly as industry profits plunged during the financial crisis, they recovered in 2009. Pretax profits were a record $61.4 billion. Revenues totaled $288.1 billion for the year. Commission and fee income was $49.0 billion of the total, reflecting improved trading volume. Trading revenues, which had been negative for six consecutive quarters, grew to $45.3 billion. Industry expenses for 2009 were $212.4 billion, 33.7 percent below 2008 levels. Of this, interest expense fell to just $21.9 billion, 82.2 percent below 2008 levels. While still in a fragile state, the industry seemed to be recovering along with the economy.

The U.S. and world economies grew very slowly after the financial crisis. While interest rates remained at historic lows, concerns about the health of eurozone economies and the U.S. fiscal cliff kept economic growth at a standstill. Memories of the financial crisis were still fresh in the minds of investors. Events such as the May 2010 "flash crash," the October 2011 collapse of MF Global Holdings, and the August 2012 trading glitch at Knight Capital caused individual and institutional investors to limit capital market activity. Industry pretax profits fell to $34.8 billion, $10.6 billion, and $12.4 billion in 2010, 2011, and 2012, respectively.

## Balance Sheet

The consolidated balance sheet for the industry is shown in Table 4–7. Note the current importance of securities trading and underwriting in the consolidated balance sheet of all securities firms. Looking at the asset portfolio, we can see that reverse repurchase agreements—securities purchased under agreements to resell (i.e., the broker gives a short-term loan to the repurchase agreement seller)— accounted for 34.7 percent, receivables from other broker–dealers accounted for 27.9 percent, and long positions in securities and commodities accounted for 23.6 percent of assets. Because of the extent to which this industry's balance sheet consists of financial market securities, the industry is subjected to particularly high levels of market risk (see Chapter 15) and interest rate risk (see Chapters 8 and 9).

**TABLE 4–7**
Assets and
Liabilities of
Broker–Dealers as
of 2012 (in billions
of dollars)

Source: *Focus Report,*
Office of Economic Analysis,
U.S. Securities and
Exchange Commission, 2013.
*www.sec.gov*

| Assets | | Percent of Total Assets |
|---|---|---|
| Cash | $ 117.2 | 2.6% |
| Receivables from other broker–dealers | 1,267.6 | 27.9 |
| Receivables from customers | 192.5 | 4.2 |
| Receivables from noncustomers | 47.0 | 1.0 |
| Long positions in securities and commodities | 1,074.6 | 23.6 |
| Securities and investments not readily marketable | 19.7 | 0.4 |
| Securities purchased under agreements to resell | 1,577.4 | 34.7 |
| Exchange membership | 0.2 | 0.0 |
| Other assets | 254.1 | 5.6 |
| Total assets | $4,550.3 | |
| **Liabilities** | | |
| Bank loans payable | $ 45.0 | 1.0% |
| Payables to other broker–dealers | 621.1 | 13.6 |
| Payables to noncustomers | 71.0 | 1.6 |
| Payables to customers | 681.3 | 15.0 |
| Short positions in securities and commodities | 381.6 | 8.4 |
| Securities sold under repurchase agreements | 2,065.6 | 45.4 |
| Other nonsubordinated liabilities | 356.9 | 2.7 |
| Subordinated liabilities | 121.9 | 2.7 |
| Total liabilities | $4,344.4 | 95.5% |
| **Capital** | | |
| Equity capital | $ 205.9 | 4.5% |
| Total capital (equity capital and subordinate liabilities) | 327.8 | 7.2% |
| Number of firms | 4,481 | |

Further, to the extent that many of these securities are foreign issued securities, FI managers must also be concerned with foreign exchange risk (see Chapter 13) and sovereign risk (see Chapter 14).

With respect to liabilities, repurchase agreements were the major source of funds; these are securities temporarily lent in exchange for cash received. Repurchase agreements—securities sold under agreements to repurchase—amounted to 45.4 percent of total liabilities and equity. The other major sources of funds were payables to customers, payables to other broker–dealers, and securities and commodities sold short for future delivery. Equity capital amounted to only 4.5 percent of total assets, while total capital (equity capital plus subordinated liabilities) accounted for 7.2 percent of total assets. These levels are well below those we saw for depository institutions in Chapter 2 (11.48 percent for commercial banks, 11.89 percent for savings institutions, and 10.35 percent for credit unions). One reason for lower capital levels is that securities firms' balance sheets contain mostly tradable (liquid) securities compared with the relatively illiquid loans that constitute a significant proportion of depository institutions' asset portfolios. Securities firms are required to maintain a net worth (capital) to assets ratio in excess of 2 percent (see Chapter 20).

| **Concept Questions** | 1. Describe the trend in profitability in the securities industry over the past 10 years. |
|---|---|
| | 2. What are the major assets held by broker–dealers? |
| | 3. Why do broker–dealers tend to hold less equity capital than do commercial banks and thrifts? |

# REGULATION

www.sec.gov

The primary regulator of the securities industry is the Securities and Exchange Commission (SEC), established in 1934 largely in response to abuses by securities firms that many at the time felt were partly responsible for the economic problems in the United States. The primary role of the SEC includes administration of securities laws, review and evaluation of registrations of new securities offerings (ensuring that all relevant information is revealed to potential investors), review and evaluation of annual and semiannual reports summarizing the financial status of all publicly held corporations, and the prohibition of any form of security market manipulation. The National Securities Markets Improvement Act (NSMIA) of 1996 reaffirmed the significance of the SEC as the primary regulator of securities firms. According to the NSMIA, states are no longer allowed to require federally registered securities firms to be registered in a state as well. States are also now prohibited from requiring registration of securities firms' transactions and from imposing substantive requirements on private placements. Prior to the NSMIA, most securities firms were subject to regulation from the SEC and from each state in which they operated. While the NSMIA provides that states may still require securities firms to pay fees and file documents to be submitted to the SEC, most of the regulatory burden imposed by states has been removed. Thus, the NSMIA effectively gives the SEC the exclusive regulatory jurisdiction over securities firms.

The early 2000s saw a reversal of this trend toward the dominance of the SEC, with states—especially their attorneys general—increasingly intervening through securities-related investigations. Several highly publicized securities violations resulted in criminal cases brought against securities law violators by mainly state and some federal prosecutors. For example, the New York State attorney general forced Merrill Lynch to pay a $100 million penalty because of allegations that Merrill Lynch brokers gave investors overly optimistic reports about the stock of its investment banking clients.

In the spring of 2003 the issue culminated in an agreement between regulators and 10 of the nation's largest securities firms to pay a record $1.4 billion in penalties to settle charges involving investor abuse. The long-awaited settlement centered on charges that securities firms routinely issued overly optimistic stock research to investors in order to gain favor with corporate clients and win their investment banking business. The agreement also settled charges that at least two big firms, Citigroup and Credit Suisse First Boston, improperly allocated initial public offering (IPO) shares to corporate executives to win banking business from their firms. The SEC and other regulators, including the Financial Industry Regulatory Authority (FINRA) and state regulators, unveiled multiple examples of how Wall Street stock analysts tailored their research reports and ratings to win investment banking business. The agreement forced brokerage companies to make structural

www.finra.org

changes in the way they handle research—preventing analysts, for example, from attending certain investment banking meetings with bankers. The agreement also required securities firms to have separate reporting and supervisory structures for their research and banking operations. Additionally, it required that analysts' pay be tied to the quality and accuracy of their research, rather than the amount of investment banking business they generate. Table 4–8 lists the 10 firms involved in the settlement and the penalties assessed.

Subsequent to these investigations, the SEC instituted rules requiring Wall Street analysts to vouch that their stock picks are not influenced by investment banking colleagues and that analysts disclose details of their compensation that would flag investors to any possible conflicts. If evidence surfaces that analysts have falsely attested to the independence of their work, it could be used to bring enforcement actions. Violators could face a wide array of sanctions, including fines and other penalties, such as a suspension or a bar from the securities industry. In addition, the SEC now requires that top officials from all public companies sign off on financial statements.

Despite all of these changes, in December 2012, Morgan Stanley agreed to pay $5 million to settle allegations that one of its senior investment bankers tried to improperly influence research analysts in the days before Facebook went public in May 2012. Allegations involved in the charge that the senior investment banker arranged phone calls from Facebook to analysts in a way that favored large investors over small investors and that violated restrictions on investment bankers' role in the IPO process.

While the SEC sets the overall regulatory standards for the industry, the Financial Industry Regulatory Authority (FINRA) is involved in the day-to-day regulation of trading practices. The FINRA monitors trading abuses (such as insider trading) trading rule violations, and securities firms' capital (solvency) positions. For example, in January 2013, FINRA announced that it is expanding its oversight of dark pool trading. Dark pools are trades created by institutional orders away from central exchanges. The details of the trades are unavailable to the public. As of 2013, nearly 15 percent of all stock trades in the United States occurred through dark pools, up from 3 percent in 2007. As more financial trading has occurred in dark pools, regulators and investors are concerned that firms are placing orders on exchanges and in dark pools at the same time to move stock prices to their advantage. FINRA's expanded oversight is intended to monitor and determine

**TABLE 4–8**
Securities Firm
Penalties Assessed
for Trading Abuses

Source: Authors' research,
2004.

| Firm | Penalty ($ millions) |
| --- | --- |
| Citigroup | $400 |
| Credit Suisse First Boston | 200 |
| Merrill Lynch | 200 |
| Morgan Stanley | 125 |
| Goldman Sachs | 110 |
| Bear Stearns | 80 |
| J.P. Morgan Chase | 80 |
| Lehman Brothers | 80 |
| UBS Warburg | 80 |
| Piper Jaffray | 32 |

whether orders placed in dark pools are indeed attempts at moving stock prices. FINRA also announced that it is increasing its surveillance of high-speed trading and rapid-fire trading across exchanges.

Also overseeing this industry at the federal level is the U.S. Congress. For example, along with changes instituted by the SEC, the U.S. Congress passed the Sarbanes-Oxley Act in July 2002. This act created an independent auditing oversight board under the SEC, increased penalties for corporate wrongdoers, forced faster and more extensive financial disclosure, and created avenues of recourse for aggrieved shareholders. The goal of the legislation was to prevent deceptive accounting and management practices and to bring stability to jittery stock markets battered in the summer of 2002 by corporate governance scandals of Enron, Global Crossings, Tyco, WorldCom, and others.

More recently, the U.S. Senate Permanent Subcommittee on Investigations was created with the broad mandate to determine whether any changes are required in U.S. law to better protect the public. In the spring of 2010, a subcommittee hearing focused on the role of investment banks in contributing to the financial crisis. Investment banks such as Goldman Sachs bundled toxic mortgages into complex financial instruments, many of which were rated AAA by credit rating agencies, and sold them to investors. Goldman Sachs, in an attempt to manage its own risk on these securities, shorted the mortgage market, setting itself up for gains that would offset losses on the mortgage securities. The subcommittee brought up evidence and internal Goldman documents that showed Goldman knew the housing market was on the brink of collapse but continued to sell mortgage-backed securities to investors. All the while, Goldman allegedly bet against the securities it built and sold with the knowledge that the housing market's collapse would bring the firm a sizable payday.

The 2010 Wall Street Reform and Consumer Protection Act, passed in response to the financial crisis, set forth many changes in the way securities firms and investment banks are regulated. The bill's Financial Services Oversight Council of financial regulators was given oversight of the industry in its charge to identify emerging systemic risks. Also under the act, effective July 21, 2011, the dollar threshold for determining whether an investment advisor must register under federal or state law increased. Specifically, all advisors with assets under management of less than $100 million must register with state regulators and those with more than $100 million under management must register with the SEC. Prior to that date, only advisors with assets under management of less than $25 million registered with a state regulator. The bill also gave new authority for the Federal Reserve to supervise all firms that could pose a threat to financial stability and called for stronger capital and other prudential standards for all financial firms, and even higher standards for large, interconnected firms. Investment banks also saw stricter oversight as the bill called for the regulation of securitization markets, stronger regulation of credit rating agencies, a requirement that issuers and originators retain a financial interest in securitized loans, comprehensive regulation of all over-the-counter derivatives, and new authority for the Federal Reserve to oversee payment, clearing, and settlement systems. Finally, the bill gave authority to the government to resolve nonbank financial institutions whose failure could have serious systemic effects and revised the Federal Reserve's emergency lending authority to improve accountability.

One of the most publicized "missteps" by securities firms and investment banks over the course of the financial crisis was related to executive compensation. Top executives received millions of dollars in bonuses for taking risks that in some cases paid off and in others cases left taxpayers to bailout the firms. As a result, the Obama administration proposed compensation rule changes for all financial institutions. Specifically, the administration called for stronger assurances that compensation committees are independent from senior management. It also proposed regulations that gave shareholders at all publicly traded companies a nonbinding vote on executive compensation packages. Finally, at FIs receiving government support, the administration's "pay czar," Kenneth Feinberg, was given a say over compensation packages given to top executives. While meant to curb what was seen by many as excessive pay, others argued that these restrictions would make it difficult to attract and retain talent sufficient to keep domestic FIs on a competitive footing with their global peers.

Securities firms and investment banks have historically been strongly supportive of efforts to combat money laundering, and the industry has been subject to federal laws that impose extensive reporting and record-keeping requirements. However, the USA Patriot Act, passed in response to the September 11 terrorist attacks, included additional provisions that financial services firms must implement. The new rules, which took effect on October 1, 2003, imposed three requirements on firms in the industry. First, firms must verify the identity of any person seeking to open an account. Second, firms must maintain records of the information used to verify the person's identity. Third, firms must determine whether a person opening an account appears on any list of known or suspected terrorists or terrorist organizations. The rules are intended to deter money laundering without imposing undue burdens that would constrain the ability of firms to serve their customers.

www.sipc.org   Finally, the Securities Investor Protection Corporation (SIPC) protects investors against losses of up to $500,000 caused by securities firm failures. This guaranty fund was created after the passage of the Securities Investor Protection Act in 1970 and is funded with premium contributions from member firms. The fund protects investor accounts against the possibility of a member broker–dealer not being able to meet its financial obligations to customers. The fund does not, however, protect against losses on a customer's account due to poor investment choices that reduce the value of a portfolio.

---

**Concept Questions**

1. What is the major result of the NSMIA?
2. What regulatory changes resulted from the financial crisis?

---

## GLOBAL ISSUES

Much more so than other sectors of the financial institutions industry, securities firms and investment banks operate globally. Both U.S. and European investment banks compete for business worldwide. This can be seen in Table 4–3, as three of the top 5 (and 5 of the top 10) underwriters of global debt and equity are U.S. investment banks (e.g., J.P. Morgan Chase, Bank of America Merrill Lynch) and the rest European banks (e.g., Barclays Capital, Credit Suisse). In 2012, in M&A deals involving U.S. targets, 7 of the top 10 advisors were U.S. investment banks (e.g., Morgan Stanley, Goldman Sachs) and 3 were European banks (e.g., Barclays Capital, Deutsche Bank). Further, U.S. investment banks held 6 of the top 10 spots on M&A deals in Europe and held five of the top spots on deals in Asia.

As domestic securities trading and underwriting have grown in the 1990s and 2000s, so have foreign securities trading and underwriting. Tables 4–9 and 4–10 show foreign transactions in U.S. securities and U.S. transactions in foreign securities from 1991–2012. For example, foreign investors' transactions involving U.S. stocks increased from $211.2 billion in 1991 to $12,037.9 billion in 2008 (an increase of 5,600 percent) before falling to $6,654.0 in 2009, during the financial crisis. As of 2012, stock transactions had increased to only $7,048.6 billion. Similarly, U.S. investors' transactions involving stocks listed on foreign exchanges grew from $152.6 billion in 1991 to $5,423.0 billion in 2008 (an increase of 3,454 percent), before falling to $3,228.9 in 2009 and recovering only slightly to $3,455.2 billion in 2012. Table 4–11 reports the total dollar value of international security offerings from 1995–2012. Over this period, total offerings increased from $570.5 billion to $6,547.2 billion in 2009, then decreased to $5,503.5 billion in 2011. Of the amounts in 2011, U.S. security issuers offered $2,558.2 billion in international markets, up from $184.7 billion in 1995.

One result of the financial crisis in the late 2000s was that large investment banks around the world became more concerned than ever with capital, liquidity, and leverage. However, they did not want to lose ground in the global competition for clients. The result was that global investment banks looked for strategic alliances that would allow them to compete in foreign markets or they exited foreign markets altogether. For example, in 2008, Morgan Stanley, in need of capital to bolster its balance sheet, sold a 21 percent stake in the firm to Japanese financial

**TABLE 4–9**
Foreign Transactions in U.S. Securities Markets (in billions of dollars)

Source: *Treasury Bulletin,* U.S. Treasury, various dates. *www.ustreas.gov*

| Year | Corporate Stock Transactions | Corporate Bond Transactions |
|---|---|---|
| 1991 | $    211.2 | $    85.9 |
| 1995 | 451.7 | 168.1 |
| 2000 | 3,605.2 | 479.5 |
| 2006 | 6,868.6 | 1,678.5 |
| 2007 | 10,639.3 | 1,913.3 |
| 2008 | 12,037.9 | 1,467.0 |
| 2009 | 6,654.0 | 1,189.4 |
| 2010 | 6,747.2 | 971.2 |
| 2011 | 7,720.3 | 996.1 |
| 2012 | 7,048.6 | 937.6 |

**TABLE 4–10**
U.S. Transactions in Foreign Securities Markets (in billions of dollars)

Source: *Treasury Bulletin,* U.S. Treasury, various dates. *www.ustreas.gov*

| Year | Corporate Stock Transactions | Corporate Bond Transactions |
|---|---|---|
| 1991 | $    152.6 | $    345.1 |
| 1995 | 395.8 | 927.9 |
| 2000 | 1,815.3 | 963.0 |
| 2006 | 3,742.6 | 2,024.2 |
| 2007 | 5,311.1 | 3,105.7 |
| 2008 | 5,423.0 | 2,217.7 |
| 2009 | 3,228.9 | 2,079.4 |
| 2010 | 3,734.3 | 3,704.8 |
| 2011 | 4,040.2 | 3,583.4 |
| 2012 | 3,455.2 | 3,686.8 |

**TABLE 4–11** Value of International Security Offerings (in billions of dollars)

Source: *Quarterly Review: International Banking and Financial Market Developments,* Bank for International Settlements, various issues. *www.bis.org*

| | 1995 | 2001 | 2002 | 2005 | 2006 | 2007 | 2008 | 2009 | 2010 | 2011 | 2012* |
|---|---|---|---|---|---|---|---|---|---|---|---|
| **Total International Offerings** | | | | | | | | | | | |
| Floating-rate debt | $103.0 | $ 642.7 | $ 603.3 | $1,470.7 | $2,063.9 | $2,008.1 | $2,249.9 | $1,451.6 | $1,158.8 | $1,252.5 | $ 675.1 |
| Straight debt | 394.8 | 1,590.3 | 1,454.6 | 2,323.9 | 2,763.9 | 3,301.6 | 3,040.9 | 4,261.7 | 3,689.9 | 3,698.1 | 2,673.3 |
| Convertible debt | 18.1 | 72.2 | 42.7 | 41.7 | 51.2 | 100.9 | 74.6 | 100.7 | 91.3 | 70.3 | 45.2 |
| Equity | 54.6 | 149.4 | 102.3 | 307.5 | 371.3 | 499.1 | 392.2 | 733.2 | 701.1 | 482.6 | 352.2 |
| Total offerings | $570.5 | $2,454.6 | $2,202.9 | $4,143.8 | $5,250.3 | $5,909.7 | $5,802.6 | $6,547.2 | $5,641.1 | $5,503.5 | $3,745.8 |
| **International Offerings by U.S. Issuers** | | | | | | | | | | | |
| Floating-rate debt | $ 50.9 | $ 262.3 | $ 214.4 | $ 602.4 | $ 708.8 | $ 653.3 | $ 509.4 | $ 537.2 | $ 296.3 | $ 441.1 | $ 182.8 |
| Straight debt | 115.3 | 836.1 | 755.0 | 1,454.0 | 1,202.0 | 1,482.0 | 1,294.8 | 1,866.1 | 2,002.6 | 1,899.7 | 1,310.1 |
| Convertible debt | 8.5 | 32.9 | 16.5 | 42.8 | 17.4 | 100.9 | 74.6 | 56.8 | 63.8 | 39.0 | 24.0 |
| Equity | 10.0 | 24.8 | 1.2 | 5.7 | 16.3 | 12.9 | 99.0 | 245.5 | 212.3 | 178.4 | 168.4 |
| Total offerings | $184.7 | $1,156.1 | $ 987.1 | $2,104.9 | $1,944.5 | $2,249.1 | $1,977.8 | $2,705.6 | $2,575.0 | $2,558.2 | $1,685.3 |

* Through three quarters.

institution, Mitsubishi UFJ. In March 2009, the two announced plans to form a joint venture that combined each firm's Japan-based securities business. Morgan Stanley took 40 percent ownership and managerial control of the institutional business, and Mitsubishi took the remaining ownership and control of the retail operations. This kind of arrangement provides U.S.-based investment banks with a foothold alongside a domestic firm in the foreign market. In contrast to the type of strategic alliance as that between Morgan Stanley and Mitsubishi UFJ is Citigroup, which during the financial crisis had to deal with growing U.S. government ownership, a deteriorating credit environment, and an unwieldy structure. Rather than try to compete globally in this environment, Citigroup decided to abandon several foreign markets. Citigroup sold its Japanese domestic securities unit, and its Japanese asset management unit, Nikko Asset Management, to subsidiaries of Sumitomo Mitsui Financial Group. It also sold NikkoCiti Trust and Banking Corp. to Nomura Trust & Banking Co. Moves such as the sale of international properties, originally acquired to allow the investment bank to expand globally, will likely continue to play a part in the reshaping of the global investment banking industry.

One of the more grievous actions by some global investment banks during the financial crisis was the manipulation of the LIBOR (London Interbank Offered Rate) interest rate. LIBOR is the interest rate at which banks can borrow from each other. It is also used to price, among other things, mortgage and business loans and derivative securities. LIBOR is the average of the interest rates submitted by major banks in the United States, Europe, and the United Kingdom in a variety of major currencies such as the dollar, euro, and yen. The scandal arose when it was discovered that banks had been manipulating the LIBOR rate so as to make either profits on its derivative positions (such as interest rate swaps) or to make the bank look stronger for reputational reasons. It is estimated that the banks involved made at least $75 billion on the manipulations. The After the Crisis box summarizes the allegations that several large banks tried to manipulate the LIBOR rate during the financial crisis. The scandal became widely public in June 2012 when British investment bank Barclays agreed to pay $450 million to settle allegations by U.S. and British authorities that some of its traders attempted to manipulate LIBOR rates to increase the bank's profits and reduce concerns about its stability during the financial crisis.

# After the Crisis   Traders Manipulated Key Rate, Bank Says

A group of traders and brokers successfully managed to manipulate an interest rate that affects loans around the world, one of the banks being investigated has told regulators. In a court filing in Ottawa, Canada's Competition Bureau said a bank it didn't identify has told the agency's investigators that people involved in the alleged scheme "were able to move" interest rates . . .

The Canadian regulator also sets out clearly for the first time how its investigators believe bank employees may have managed to game a system used to set costs for financial products around the world, with the alleged aim of increasing their trading profits. The yen London Interbank Offered Rate, or Libor, is calculated by Thomson Reuters under the auspices of the British Bankers' Association and is based on data submitted daily by a 16-bank panel. Around 11 a.m. London time every day, each bank submits estimates of what rates it would pay to borrow from other banks for different time periods. The top four and bottom four quotes are then discarded, and Libor is calculated using an average of the middle eight quotes. The Canadian watchdog said lawyers acting for the cooperating bank had told it that traders at six banks on the yen Libor panel... "entered into agreements to submit artificially high or artificially low" quotes, according to the court documents. The traders used emails and instant messages to tell each other whether they wanted "to see a higher or lower yen Libor [rate] to aid their

trading position(s)," according to a court filing. Each of the traders would then "communicate internally" with the person at their bank who was responsible for submitting the Libor quote, before letting each other know if this attempt to influence the quote had worked. "Not all attempts to affect Libor submissions were successful," the regulator said in the court filing.

The Canadian regulator said it is investigating whether the traders also "conspired" with individuals at interdealer broker firms, according to the documents. These brokers act as go-betweens for the different banks, advising them on the interbank borrowing rates on which Libor quotes are based. The brokers were asked by the traders "to use their influence with yen Libor submitters to affect what rates were submitted by other yen Libor panel banks," including banks that were part of the alleged conspiracy, according to a court filing . . .

The BBA has made some tweaks to how Libor is calculated, such as increasing the size of the U.S. dollar panel, since concerns about the integrity of the system were raised following the financial crisis. But the fundamental approach of calculating rates based on estimates submitted by banks remains unchanged, despite the intensifying global probe.

**Source:** *The Wall Street Journal,* February 17, 2012, by Jean Eaglesham, Paul Vieira, and David Enrich. Reprinted by permission of *The Wall Street Journal.* © 2012 Dow Jones & Company, Inc. All Rights Reserved Worldwide. *www.wsj.com*

Concerns were also raised about the failure of British and U.S. regulators to stop the manipulation of LIBOR when there was evidence that both were aware of it. In July 2012, a former trader stated that LIBOR manipulation had been occurring since at least 1991. In July 2012, the Federal Reserve Bank of New York released documents dated as far back as 2007 showing that they knew that banks were misreporting their borrowing costs when setting LIBOR. Yet, no action was taken. Similarly, documents from the Bank of England indicated that the bank knew as early as November 2007 that the LIBOR rate was being manipulated. It was not until June 2012 that Barclays became the first bank to agree to settle LIBOR manipulation allegations. In December 2012, UBS agreed to pay about $1.5 billion to settle charges that it manipulated LIBOR. In February 2013, the Royal Bank of Scotland also decided to settle at a cost of $610 million. Also in early 2013, Deutsche Bank stated that it had set aside money to cover potential fines associated with its role in the manipulation of the LIBOR.

| **Concept Questions** | 1. What have been the trends in foreign transactions in U.S. securities and U.S. transactions in foreign securities in the 1990s and 2000s? |
|---|---|
| | 2. What have been the trends in international securities offerings in the late 1990s and 2000s? |
| | 3. Why do foreign banks operating in the United States compete with both U.S. commercial banks and investment banks? |

## Summary

This chapter presented an overview of security firms (which offer largely retail services to investors) and investment banking firms (which offer largely wholesale services to corporate customers). Firms in this industry assist in getting new issues of debt and equity to the markets. Additionally, this industry facilitates trading and market making of securities after they are issued as well as corporate mergers and restructurings. We looked at the structure of the industry and changes in the degree of concentration in firm size in the industry over the last decade. We also analyzed balance sheet information which highlighted the major assets and liabilities of firms in the industry. Overall, the industry is in a period of consolidation and globalization as the array and scope of its activities expand.

## Questions and Problems

1. Explain how securities firms differ from investment banks. In what ways are they financial intermediaries?
2. In what ways have changes in the investment banking industry mirrored changes in the commercial banking industry?
3. What are the different types of firms in the securities industry and how does each type differ from the others?
4. What are the key activity areas for investment banks and securities firms? How does each activity area assist in the generation of profits and what are the major risks for each area?
5. What is the difference between an IPO and a secondary issue?
6. What is the difference between a private placement and a public offering?
7. What are the risk implications to an investment bank from underwriting on a best-efforts basis versus a firm commitment basis? If you operated a company issuing stock for the first time, which type of underwriting would you prefer? Why? What factors might cause you to choose the alternative?
8. An investment bank agrees to underwrite an issue of 15 million shares of stock for Looney Landscaping Corp.
   a. If the investment bank underwrites the stock on a firm commitment basis, it agrees to pay $12.50 per share to Looney Landscaping Corp. for the 15 million shares of stock. It can then sell those shares to the public for $13.25 per share. How much money does Looney receive? What is the profit to the investment bank? If the investment bank can sell the shares for only $11.95, how much money does Looney receive? What is the profit to the investment bank?
   b. Suppose, instead, that the investment bank agrees to underwrite the 15 million shares on a best-efforts basis. The investment bank is able to sell 13.6 million shares for $12.50 per share, and it charges Looney Landscaping Corp. $0.275 per share sold. How much money does Looney receive? What is the

profit to the investment bank? If the investment bank can sell the shares for only $11.95, how much money does Looney receive? What is the profit to the investment bank?

9. An investment bank agrees to underwrite a $500 million, 10-year, 8 percent semiannual bond issue for KDO Corporation on a firm commitment basis. The investment bank pays KDO on Thursday and plans to begin a public sale on Friday. What type of interest rate movement does the investment bank fear while holding these securities? If interest rates rise 0.05 percent, or five basis points, overnight, what will be the impact on the profits of the investment bank? What if the market interest rate falls five basis points?

10. An investment bank pays $23.50 per share for 4 million shares of JCN Company. It then sells those shares to the public for $25 per share. How much money does JCN receive? What is the profit to the investment bank? What is the stock price of JCN?

11. XYZ Inc. has issued 10 million new shares of stock. An investment bank agrees to underwrite these shares on a best-efforts basis. The investment bank is able to sell 8.4 million shares for $27 per share, and it charges XYZ $0.675 per share sold. How much money does XYZ receive? What is the profit to the investment bank? What is the stock price of XYZ?

12. What is venture capital?

13. What are the different types of venture capital firms? How do institutional venture capital firms differ from angel venture capital firms?

14. What are the advantages and disadvantages to a new or small firm of getting capital funding from a venture capital firm?

15. How do agency transactions differ from principal transactions for market makers?

16. One of the major activity areas of securities firms is trading.
    a. What is the difference between pure arbitrage and risk arbitrage?
    b. What is the difference between position trading and program trading?

17. If an investor observes that the price of a stock trading in one exchange is different from the price in another exchange, what form of arbitrage is applicable, and how can the investor participate in that arbitrage?

18. An investor notices that an ounce of gold is priced at $1,518 in London and $1,525 in New York.
    a. What action could the investor take to try to profit from the price discrepancy?
    b. Under which of the four trading activities would this action be classified?
    c. If the investor is correct in identifying the discrepancy, what pattern should the two prices take in the short term?
    d. What may be some impediments to the success of this transaction?

19. What three factors are given credit for the steady decline in brokerage commissions as a percentage of total revenues over the period beginning in 1977 and ending in 1991?

20. What factors are given credit for the resurgence of profitability in the securities industry beginning in 1991? Are firms that trade in fixed-income securities more or less likely to have volatile profits? Why?

21. Using Table 4–6, which type of security accounts for most underwriting in the United States? Which is likely to be more costly to underwrite: corporate debt or equity? Why?

22. How did the financial crisis affect the performance of securities firms and investment banks?

23. How do the operating activities, and thus the balance sheet structures, of securities firms differ from the operating activities of depository institutions? How are the balance sheet structures of securities firms similar to depository institutions?

24. Based on the data in Table 4–7, what were the largest single asset and the largest single liability of securities firms in 2012? Are these asset and liability categories related? Exactly how does a repurchase agreement work?

25. How did the National Securities Markets Improvement Act of 1996 (NSMIA) change the regulatory structure of the securities industry?

26. Identify the major regulatory organizations that are involved in the daily operations of the investment securities industry, and explain their role in providing smoothly operating markets.

27. What are the three requirements of the USA Patriot Act that financial service firms must implement after October 1, 2003?

## Web Questions

28. Go to the Securities Industry and Financial Markets Association website at **www.sifma.org** and find the most recent data on U.S. corporate underwriting activity using the following steps. Click on "Research." Click "Statistics and Data." Click on "US Key Stats." This will download an Excel file to your computer that contains the relevant data, on the page "Corporate." How has the distribution of underwriting activity changed since 2012, as reported in Table 4–6?

29. Go to the U.S. Treasury website at **www.ustreas.gov** and find the most recent data on foreign transactions in U.S. securities and U.S. transactions in foreign securities using the following steps. Under "Bureaus," click on "Financial Management Services." Under "Publications," click on "Treasury Bulletin." Click on "Capital Movements Tables (Section IV)." This will download a file onto your computer that will contain the most recent information on foreign transactions. How have these number changed since 2012, as reported in Tables 4–9 and 4–10?

# Financial Services: Mutual Funds and Hedge Funds

## INTRODUCTION

Mutual funds and hedge funds are financial institutions that pool the financial resources of individuals and companies and invest in diversified portfolios of assets. An open-ended mutual fund (the major type of mutual fund) continuously stands ready to sell new shares to investors and to redeem outstanding shares on demand at their fair market value. Thus, these funds provide opportunities for small investors to invest in financial securities and diversify risk. Mutual funds are also able to generate greater economies of scale by incurring lower transaction costs and commissions than are incurred when individual investors buy securities directly. As a result of the tremendous increase in the market value of financial assets, such as equities, in the 1990s (for example, the S&P 500 index saw a return of more than 25 percent in 1997 and 1998) and the relatively low-cost opportunity mutual funds provide to investors (particularly small investors) who want to hold such assets (through either direct mutual fund purchases or contributions to retirement funds sponsored by employers and managed by mutual funds), the mutual fund industry boomed in size and customers in the 1990s. The early 2000s and a slowdown in the U.S. economy brought an end to such a rapid pace of growth and the more severe financial crisis of 2008–09 resulted in the largest ever drop in the value of industry assets. During 2008, mutual fund losses on investments in financial securities and liquidation of mutual fund shares by investors resulted in a drop in industry assets of $2.4 trillion (or 20 percent). Further, allegations of trading abuses resulted in a loss of confidence in several mutual fund managers. Despite these issues, in 2012 more than 7,000 different stock and bond mutual companies held total assets of $10.26 trillion. If we add money market mutual funds, the number of funds rises to more than 7,600 and the 2012 value of assets under management rises to $12.87 trillion.

Hedge funds are a type of investment pool that solicit funds from (wealthy) individuals and other investors (e.g., commercial banks) and invest these funds on their behalf. Hedge funds are similar to mutual funds in that they are pooled investment vehicles that accept investors' money and generally invest it on a collective basis. Investments in hedge funds, however, are restricted to more wealthy clients.

111

In this chapter we first provide an overview of the services offered by mutual funds and highlight their rapid growth over the last twenty-five years. We look at the size, structure, and composition of the industry, highlighting historical trends in the industry, the different types of mutual funds, mutual fund objectives, investor returns from mutual fund ownership, and mutual fund costs. We also look at the industry's balance sheets and recent trends, the regulations and regulators governing the industry, and global issues for this industry. We then discuss investment pools organized as hedge funds. Because hedge funds limit investors to only the wealthiest individuals, they are examined separately from mutual funds discussed elsewhere in the chapter. Another difference between mutual funds and hedge funds is that, prior to 2010, hedge funds were generally unregulated. However, as a result of some very publicized hedge fund failures and near failures (the result of fraud by fund managers, e.g., Bernard L. Madoff Investment Securities and the financial crisis, e.g., Bear Stearns High Grade Structured Credit Strategies Fund), in 2010 federal regulators increased the oversight of hedge funds. Specifically, regulations now require that hedge funds with assets under management exceeding some threshold should be required to register with the SEC under the Investment Advisers Act of 1940 in a similar fashion to that required for mutual funds. Similarly, fund advisors are required to report financial information on the funds they manage that is sufficient to assess whether any fund poses a threat to the financial system.

# SIZE, STRUCTURE, AND COMPOSITION OF THE MUTUAL FUND INDUSTRY

### Historical Trends

The first mutual fund was founded in Boston in 1924. The industry grew very slowly at first; by 1970, 361 funds held about $50 billion in assets. Since then the number of mutual funds and the asset size of the industry have increased dramatically. This growth is attributed to the advent of money market mutual funds in 1972 (as investors looked for ways to earn market rates on short-term funds when bank deposit rates were constrained by regulatory ceilings), to tax-exempt money market mutual funds first established in 1979, and to an explosion of special-purpose equity, bond, emerging market, and derivative funds (as capital market values soared in the 1990s). Table 5–1 documents the tremendous increase from 1940 though 2007 of mutual funds. For example, total assets invested in mutual funds grew from $0.5 billion in 1940 to $12,001.46 billion in 2007 (of which $8,916.5 billion was invested in long-term funds). In addition, the number of mutual fund accounts increased from 296,000 in 1940 to 292.6 million in 2007 (253.5 million of which were long-term fund accounts), and the number of mutual funds increased from 68 in 1940 to 8,026 in 2007. The majority of this growth occurred during the bull market run in the 1990s (total assets in 1990 were $1,065.2 billion). The financial crisis and the collapse in stock and other security prices produced a sharp drop in mutual fund activity. At the end of 2008, total assets fell to $9,603.6 billion and the number of accounts to 264.6 million (of this, $5,771.3 billion and 226.5 million accounts were long-term funds). Investor demand for certain types of mutual funds plummeted, driven in large part by deteriorating financial market conditions. Equity funds suffered substantial outflows, while the inflow to U.S. government money market funds reached record highs. As the economy recovered starting in 2009, so did

**TABLE 5–1**   Growth of Mutual Fund Industry, 1940–2012

Sources: Investment Company Institute, *2006 Investment Company Fact Book* (Washington, DC: Investment Company Institute, May 2006) and *Trends in Mutual Fund Investing,* various issues. *www.ici.org*

| Year | Total Net Assets (billions) | Gross Sales (billions) | Redemptions (billions) | Net Sales (billions) | Accounts (thousands) | Number of Funds |
|------|------|------|------|------|------|------|
| 2012 | $13,045.2 | $17,020.90 | $16,618.7 | $402.2 | 264,131 | 7,596 |
| 2010 | 11,831.9 | 18,207.5 | 18,319.1 | −111.6 | 291,299 | 7,580 |
| 2009 | 11,113.0 | 20,680.0 | 20,680.2 | −0.2 | 269,450 | 7,684 |
| 2008 | 9,603.6 | 26,346.7 | 25,725.8 | 620.9 | 264,599 | 8,022 |
| 2007 | 12,001.5 | 23,471.7 | 22,353.4 | 1,118.3 | 292,555 | 8,026 |
| 2005 | 8,904.8 | 14,042.5 | 13,648.4 | 394.1 | 275,479 | 7,975 |
| 2000 | 6,964.6 | 11,109.4 | 10,586.6 | 522.8 | 244,706 | 8,155 |
| 1995 | 2,811.3 | 3,600.6 | 3,314.9 | 285.7 | 131,219 | 5,725 |
| 1990 | 1,065.2 | 1,564.8 | 1,470.8 | 94.0 | 61,948 | 3,079 |
| 1980 | 134.8 | 247.4 | 216.1 | 31.3 | 12,088 | 564 |
| 1970 | 47.6 | 4.6 | 3.0 | 1.6 | 10,690 | 361 |
| 1960 | 17.0 | 2.1 | 0.8 | 1.3 | 4,898 | 161 |
| 1950 | 2.5 | 0.5 | 0.3 | 0.2 | 939 | 98 |
| 1940 | 0.5 | N/A | N/A | N/A | 296 | 68 |

Note: Data include money market funds. Institute "gross sales" figures include the proceeds of initial fund underwritings prior to 1970.

assets invested in mutual funds, growing to $11,113.0 billion by the end of the year and to $13,045.2 billion in 2012 (finally surpassing 2007 levels). Of this, $10,351.7 billion were invested in long-term funds.

Additionally, growth has been the result of the rise in retirement funds under management by mutual funds. The retirement fund market has increased from $4 trillion in 1990 to almost $20.0 trillion in 2012. Mutual funds manage approximately one-quarter of this market and have experienced the growth along with it. Many of these retirement funds are institutional funds. *Institutional funds* are mutual funds that manage retirement plans for an institution's employees. Institutions arrange these retirement (mutual) funds for the benefit of their members. Wealthy individuals also often use institutional funds. In total, about 80 percent of all retirement plan investments are in institutional funds. Institutional funds are managed by the same companies that run mutual funds: banks, insurance companies, brokers, and mutual fund advisory companies. Costs of institutional funds are very low because there are no additional distribution fees and because the retirement plan can use its bargaining power to get the best deals. Unlike the case with traditional mutual funds, retirement plan sponsors can set out how much risk an institutional fund can take in trying to beat the market.

As can be seen in Figure 5–1, in terms of asset size, the mutual fund industry is larger than the insurance industry, but smaller than the commercial banking industry. This makes mutual funds the second most important FI group in the United States as measured by asset size. The tremendous growth in this area of FI services has not gone unnoticed by commercial banks as they have sought to directly compete by either buying existing mutual fund groups or managing mutual fund assets for a fee. Banks' share of all mutual fund assets managed was about 7 percent in 2012. Much of this growth has occurred through banks buying mutual fund companies, for example, Mellon buying Dreyfus, as well as converting internally

**FIGURE 5–1**
Assets of Major
Financial
Intermediaries,
1990, 2007, and
2012 (in trillions of
dollars)

Source: Federal Reserve
Board, "Flow of Fund
Accounts," various years.
*www.federalreserve.gov*

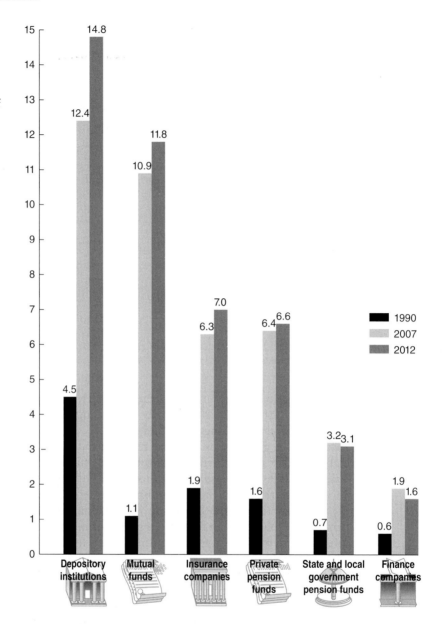

managed trust funds into open-end mutual funds. Insurance companies are also
beginning to enter this booming industry. In March 2001, for example, State Farm
began offering a family of 10 mutual funds nationwide. The funds are available
from more than 9,000 registered State Farm agents, on the Internet, or by application sent in response to phone requests made to a toll-free number. As of 2012,
insurance companies managed 5 percent of the mutual fund industry's assets.

Low barriers to entry in the U.S. mutual fund industry have allowed new
entrants to offer funds to compete for investor attention and has kept the industry
from being increasingly concentrated. As a result, the share of industry assets held
by the largest mutual fund sponsors has changed little since 1990. For example,
the largest 25 companies that sponsor mutual funds managed 73 percent of the
industry's assets in 2012, compared to 25 percent in 1990. The composition of the

list of the 25 largest fund sponsors, however, has changed, with 12 of the largest fund companies in 2012 not among the largest in 1990.

## Different Types of Mutual Funds

The mutual fund industry is usually divided into two sectors: short-term funds and long-term funds. Long-term funds include **equity funds** (comprised of common and preferred stock securities), **bond funds** (comprised of fixed-income securities with a maturity of longer than one year), and **hybrid funds** (comprised of both bond and stock securities). Short-term funds include taxable **money market mutual funds** (MMMFs) and tax-exempt money market mutual funds. Table 5–2 shows how the mix of stock, bond, hybrid, and money market fund assets changed between 1980 and 2012. As can be seen, there was a strong trend toward investing in equity mutual funds, reflecting the rise in share values during the 1990s. As a result, in 1999, 74.3 percent of all mutual fund assets were in long-term funds while the remaining funds, or 25.7 percent, were in money market mutual funds. The proportion invested in long-term versus short-term funds can vary considerably over time. For example, the share of money market funds was 44.8 percent in 1990 compared to 25.7 percent in 1999. The decline in the growth rate of short-term funds and the increase in the growth rate of long-term funds reflect the increase in equity returns during the period 1992–99 and the generally low level of short-term interest rates over the period. Notice that in the early 2000s, as interest rates rose, the U.S. economy declined, and equity returns fell, the growth in money market funds outpaced the growth in long-term funds. In 2002, the share of long-term funds fell to 62.1 percent and money market funds grew to 37.9 percent. However, in the mid-2000s, as the U.S. economy grew and stock values increased, the share of long-term funds grew (to 72.1 percent of all funds in 2007), while money market funds decreased (to 27.9 percent in 2007).

The 2008–2009 financial crisis and the collapse in stock prices produced a sharp drop in long-term mutual fund activity. Equity funds suffered substantial outflows, while inflows to U.S. government money market funds reached record highs. At the end of 2008, the share of long-term equity and bond funds plunged to 59.1 percent of all funds, while money market funds increased to 40.9 percent. As discussed below, part of the move to money market funds was the fact that during the worst of the financial crisis, the U.S. Treasury extended government insurance to all money market mutual fund accounts on a temporary basis. In 2009, as the economy and the stock market recovered, the share of long-term equity and bond funds increased back to 68.1 percent of all funds, while money market funds fell to 31.9 percent. By 2012, the share of long-term equity and bond funds was 78.7 percent of all funds, while money market funds decreased to 21.3 percent.

Money market mutual funds provide an alternative investment to interest-bearing deposits at commercial banks, which may explain the growth in MMMFs in the 1980s and late 1990s, when the spread earned on MMMF investments relative to deposits was mostly positive (see Figure 5–2). Both investments are relatively safe and earn short-term returns. The major difference between the two is that interest-bearing deposits (below $250,000 in size) are fully insured by the FDIC but due to bank regulatory costs (such as reserve requirements, capital requirements, and deposit insurance premiums) generally offer lower returns than do noninsured MMMFs.[1] Thus, the net gain in switching to MMMFs is higher returns

---

**equity funds**
Funds that contain common and preferred stock securities.

**bond funds**
Funds that contain fixed-income capital market debt securities.

**hybrid funds**
Funds that contain bond and stock securities.

**money market mutual funds**
Funds that contain various mixtures of money market securities.

---

[1] Some mutual funds are covered by private insurance and/or by implicit or explicit guarantees from mutual fund management companies.

**TABLE 5–2** Growth in Long-Term versus Short-Term Mutual Funds, 1980–2012 (in billions of dollars)

Source: Federal Reserve Bulletin, "Flow of Fund Accounts," various issues. *www.federalreserve.gov*

| | 1980 | 1990 | 1999 | 2000 | 2002 | 2004 | 2007 | 2008 | 2009 | 2012 |
|---|---|---|---|---|---|---|---|---|---|---|
| **Panel A: Equity, Hybrid, and Bond Mutual Funds** | | | | | | | | | | |
| Holdings at market value | $61.8 | $608.4 | $4,538.5 | $4,433.1 | $3,638.4 | $5,436.3 | $7,829.0 | $5,435.3 | $6,961.6 | $9,262.4 |
| Household sector | 52.1 | 511.6 | 2,894.9 | 2,704.3 | 2,218.3 | 3,417.6 | 4,832.0 | 3,442.6 | 4,161.1 | 5,542.9 |
| Nonfinancial corporate business | 1.5 | 9.7 | 127.0 | 121.9 | 95.8 | 140.5 | 217.5 | 143.3 | 161.9 | 171.4 |
| State and local governments | 0.0 | 4.8 | 33.4 | 30.8 | 24.3 | 27.5 | 34.5 | 29.8 | 37.5 | 37.1 |
| Commercial banking | 0.0 | 1.9 | 12.4 | 15.0 | 19.6 | 18.1 | 29.6 | 19.6 | 46.1 | 52.8 |
| Credit unions | 0.0 | 1.4 | 2.5 | 2.2 | 3.5 | 3.1 | 2.1 | 2.0 | 1.3 | 2.1 |
| Insurance companies | 1.1 | 30.7 | 101.4 | 99.9 | 79.6 | 119.6 | 195.2 | 125.4 | 146.1 | 165.1 |
| Private pension funds | 7.1 | 40.5 | 1,056.5 | 1,131.7 | 931.9 | 1,278.2 | 1,848.2 | 1,229.5 | 1,817.3 | 2,370.5 |
| State and local government retirement funds | 0.0 | 7.8 | 140.9 | 178.3 | 167.4 | 235.9 | 296.4 | 181.1 | 226.7 | 274.6 |
| Rest of world | 0.0 | 0.0 | 169.5 | 149.0 | 98.0 | 195.8 | 373.5 | 262.0 | 363.6 | 645.9 |
| **Panel B: Money Market Mutual Funds** | | | | | | | | | | |
| Total assets | $76.4 | $493.3 | $1,579.6 | $1,812.1 | $2,223.9 | $1,879.8 | $3,033.1 | $3,757.3 | $3,258.3 | $2,506.9 |
| Household sector | 64.3 | 389.4 | 774.2 | 937.3 | 1,071.7 | 904.1 | 1,346.6 | 1,581.9 | 1,313.1 | 1,044.5 |
| Nonfinancial corporate business | 7.0 | 19.7 | 196.8 | 213.9 | 319.7 | 299.6 | 548.5 | 710.6 | 641.7 | 427.2 |
| Nonfinancial noncorporate business | 0.0 | 6.7 | 40.7 | 49.4 | 61.3 | 66.5 | 74.3 | 75.4 | 73.7 | 70.6 |
| State and local governments | 0.0 | 0.0 | 51.2 | 53.9 | 58.7 | 78.6 | 116.6 | 113.3 | 122.0 | 126.5 |
| Insurance companies | 1.9 | 19.1 | 19.4 | 23.1 | 27.6 | 30.5 | 42.3 | 71.9 | 63.3 | 55.9 |
| Private pension funds | 2.6 | 17.8 | 76.9 | 81.1 | 84.5 | 84.9 | 93.5 | 95.7 | 96.4 | 96.1 |
| State and local government retirement funds | 0.0 | 2.8 | 11.8 | 13.2 | 15.5 | 11.6 | 12.4 | 14.3 | 14.3 | 15.1 |
| Funding corporations | 0.6 | 36.6 | 400.5 | 429.0 | 568.6 | 381.1 | 752.8 | 1,024.5 | 857.1 | 607.5 |
| Rest of world | 0.0 | 1.2 | 8.1 | 11.2 | 16.3 | 22.9 | 46.0 | 69.7 | 76.9 | 63.5 |

**FIGURE 5–2**   **Interest Rate Spread and Net New Cash Flow to Retail Money Market Funds, 1985–2012**

Source: Investment Company Institute, *Investment Company Fact Book* (Washington, DC: Investment Company Institute, various issues). *www.ici.org*

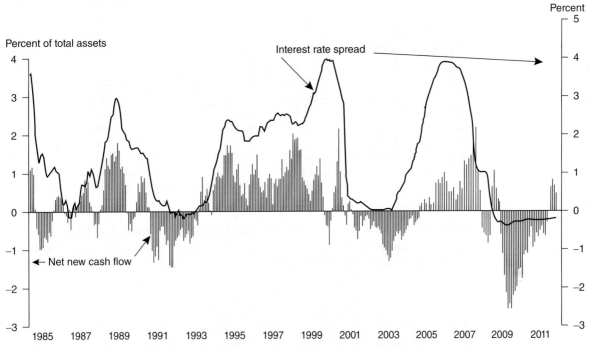

Note: Net new cash flow is a percentage of retail money market fund assets and is shown as a six-month moving average. The interest rate spread is the difference between the taxable money market fund yield and the average interest rate on savings deposits; the series is plotted with a six-month lag.

in exchange for the loss of deposit insurance coverage. Many investors appeared willing to give up insurance coverage to obtain additional returns in the 1980s and late 1990s (through 2001).

An exception occurred during the financial crisis of 2008–09. In September 2008, Reserve Primary Fund a large and reputedly conservative money market fund, had holdings of $785 million in commercial paper issued by Lehman Brothers. As a result of Lehman's failure, shares in Reserve Primary Fund "broke the buck" (i.e., fell below $1), meaning that its investors lost part of their principal investment. This was the first ever incidence of a share price dipping below a dollar for any money market mutual fund open to the general public. This type of fund had built a reputation for safe investment. Hence, exposure to Lehman's failure scared investors, leading to a broad run on all money market mutual funds. Within a few days more than $200 billion had flowed out of these funds. The U.S. Treasury stopped the run by extending government insurance to all money market mutual fund accounts held in participating money market funds as of the close of business on September 19, 2008. The insurance coverage lasted for one year (through September 18, 2009). As seen in Figure 5–2, this action is associated with a change in trend from net outflows to net inflows of funds into money market mutual funds.

Table 5–3 reports the growth in the mutual fund industry based on the number of funds in existense from 1980 through 2012. All categories of funds have generally increased in number in this time period, from a total of 564 in 1980 to 8,026 in 2007. *Tax*-exempt money market funds first became available in 1979. This was

**TABLE 5–3**
Number of Mutual
Funds, 1980–2012

Source: Investment Company Institute, *Investment Company Fact Book,* various years (Washington DC: Investment Company Institute). *www.ici.org*

| Year | Equity | Hybrid | Bond | Taxable Money Market | Tax-Exempt Money Market | Total |
|------|--------|--------|------|---------------------|------------------------|-------|
| 1980* | 288 | N/A | 170 | 96 | 10 | 564 |
| 1990 | 1,099 | 193 | 1,046 | 506 | 235 | 3,079 |
| 2000 | 4,385 | 523 | 2,208 | 703 | 336 | 8,155 |
| 2002 | 4,747 | 473 | 2,035 | 679 | 310 | 8,244 |
| 2007 | 4,763 | 489 | 1,969 | 546 | 259 | 8,026 |
| 2008 | 4,802 | 483 | 1,954 | 534 | 249 | 8,022 |
| 2009 | 4,616 | 471 | 1,893 | 476 | 228 | 7,684 |
| 2010 | 4,547 | 475 | 1,906 | 442 | 210 | 7,580 |
| 2011 | 4,581 | 495 | 1,929 | 431 | 201 | 7,637 |
| 2012 | 4,527 | 532 | 1,959 | 405 | 189 | 7,612 |

* The definition of equity, hybrid, and bond funds was reclassified in 1984. Thus, 1980 data are not directly comparable to data for other years.

the major reason for their relatively small number (10 funds) in 1980. Also, the number of equity funds has boomed, mainly in the 1990s. Equity funds numbered 4,763 in 2007, up from 1,099 in 1990, while bond funds numbered 1,969 in 2007, up from 1,046 in 1990. But again, the 2008–09 financial crisis and the collapse in financial markets produced a significant drop in the number of mutual funds. The number of equity funds fell to 4,616 and bond funds fell to 1,893 by the end of 2009. The total number of funds dropped below 8,000 for the first time since 1999. In terms of the number of funds, the industry has still not recovered from the crisis. As of 2012, the number of equity funds had fallen to 4,527 and the total number of mutual funds stood at 7,612.

Notice that in Table 5–2 households (i.e., small investors) own the majority of both long- and short-term funds: 59.8 percent for long-term mutual funds and 41.7 percent for short-term mutual funds in 2012. This is to be expected, given that the rationale for the existence of mutual funds is to achieve superior diversification through fund and risk pooling compared to what individual small investors can achieve on their own. Consider that wholesale CDs sell in minimum denominations of $100,000 each and often pay higher interest rates than passbook savings accounts or small time deposits offered by depository institutions. By pooling funds in a money market mutual fund, small investors can gain access to wholesale money markets and instruments and, therefore, to potentially higher interest rates and returns.

---

*Internet Exercise*    Go to the Federal Reserve Board's website at **www.federalreserve.gov**. Find the latest figures for the dollar value of money market and long-term mutual funds and the distribution of mutual fund investment by ownership using the following steps. Click on "Flow of Funds— Z.1." Click on the most recent date. Click on "Level tables." This downloads a file onto your computer that contains the relevant data, in Tables L.206 and L.214.

---

As of 2012, 53.8 million (44.4 percent of) U.S. households owned mutual funds. This was down from 56.3 million (52 percent) in 2001. Table 5–4 lists some characteristics of household mutual fund owners as of 2012 and 1995. Most are long-term owners, with 38 percent making their first purchases before 1990. While mutual fund

**TABLE 5–4**
Selected
Characteristics of
Household Owners
of Mutual Funds*

Source: Investment
Company Institute, *Profile
of Mutual Fund Shareholders,*
various years (Washington,
DC: Investment Company
Institute). *www.ici.org*

| | 2012 | 1995 |
|---|---|---|
| **Demographic Characteristics:** | | |
| Median age | 51 years | 44 years |
| Median household income | $ 80,000 | $ 60,000 |
| Median household financial assets | $200,000 | $ 50,000 |
| **Percent:** | | |
| Married or living with a partner | 75.0 | 71.0 |
| Employed | 72.0 | 80.0 |
| Four-year college degree or more | 48.0 | 58.0 |
| Household financial assets invested in mutual funds | 48.0 | 36.0 |
| Owning fund inside employer-sponsored retirement funds | 69.0 | 17.0 |
| Owning fund outside employer-sponsored retirement funds | 68.0 | 28.3 |
| **Mutual Fund Ownership Characteristics:** | | |
| Median mutual fund assets | $120,000 | $ 18,000 |
| Median number of funds owned | 4 | 3 |
| **Fund Types Owned (percent):** | | |
| Equity | 79 | 73 |
| Bond | 50 | 49 |
| Hybrid | 44 | N/A |
| Money market | 66 | 52 |

* Characteristics of primary financial decision maker in the household.

investors come from all age groups, ownership is concentrated among individuals in their prime saving and investing years. Two-thirds of households owning mutual funds in 2012 were headed by individuals between the ages of 35 and 64. Interestingly, the number of families headed by a person with less than a college degree investing in mutual funds is 52 percent. The bull markets of the 1990s, the low transaction costs of purchasing mutual funds shares, as well as the diversification benefits achievable through mutual fund investments are again the likely reasons for these trends. The typical fund-owning household had $120,000 invested in a median number of four mutual funds. Finally, 21 percent of investors who conducted equity fund transactions used the Internet for some or all of these transactions. This compares to 6 percent in 1998. Notice, from Table 5–4, that compared to 1995, 2012 has seen an increase in the median age of mutual fund holders (from 44 to 51 years) and a large increase in median household financial assets owned (from $50,000 to $200,000) and median mutual fund assets owned (from $18,000 to $120,000). Further, holdings of equity funds have increased from 73 to 79 percent of all households.

## Mutual Fund Objectives

Regulations require that mutual fund managers specify the investment objectives of their funds in a prospectus available to potential investors. This prospectus should include a list of the securities that the fund holds. The aggregate figures for long-term equity, bond, and hybrid funds tend to obscure the fact that there are many different funds in these groups. Every mutual fund sponsor offers multiple

**TABLE 5–5**
Total Net Asset
Value of Equity,
Hybrid, and
Bond Funds
by Investment
Classification

Source: Investment
Company Institute, *2012
Investment Company Fact Book*
(Washington, DC: Invest-
ment Company Institute,
2012). *www.ici.org*

| Classification of Fund | Combined Assets ($ billions) | Percent of Total |
|---|---|---|
| **Total net assets** | **$11,621.58** | **100.0%** |
| Capital appreciation | 2,355.66 | 20.3 |
| World equity | 1,359.35 | 11.7 |
| Total return | 1,490.09 | 12.8 |
| **Total equity funds** | **$ 5,205.10** | **44.8%** |
| **Total hybrid funds** | **$838.70** | **7.2%** |
| Corporate bond | 452.60 | 3.9 |
| High-yield bond | 212.12 | 1.8 |
| World bond | 259.51 | 2.2 |
| Government bond | 261.09 | 2.2 |
| Strategic income | 1,204.14 | 10.4 |
| State municipal | 158.91 | 1.4 |
| National municipal | 337.99 | 2.9 |
| **Total bond funds** | **$ 2,886.36** | **24.8%** |
| Taxable money market funds | 2,399.72 | 20.7 |
| Tax-exempt money market funds | 291.70 | 2.5 |
| **Total money market funds** | **$ 2,691.42** | **23.2%** |

funds of each type (e.g., long-term equity), differentiated by the securities held in the particular mutual fund as defined by the fund's objective. Table 5–5 classifies 13 major categories of investment objectives (or classifications) for mutual funds. These objectives are shown along with the assets allocated to each major category. A fund objective provides general information about the types of securities a mutual fund will hold as assets. For example, "capital appreciation" funds hold securities (mainly equities) of high-growth, high-risk firms. Again, within each of these 13 categories of mutual funds are a multitude of different funds offered by mutual fund companies (see also the mutual fund quote section below). Historically, mutual funds have had to send out lengthy prospectuses describing their objectives and investments. In 1998, the SEC adopted a new procedure in which key sections of all funds' prospectuses must be written in "plain" English instead of legal boilerplate. The idea is to increase the ability of investors to understand the risks related to the investment objectives or profile of a fund.

---

*Internet Exercise*     Go to the Vanguard Group's website at **www.vanguard.com**. Find the latest prospectus for the Vanguard 500 Index Admiral Fund using the following steps. Click on "Go to the Personal Investors site." In the box "Find a fund," enter "Vanguard 500 Index Fund Admiral Shares," and click on "Go." Click on "View prospectus and reports." Click on "Statutory Prospectus." This downloads a file onto your computer that contains the prospectus. What is listed as the primary investment objective for this fund?

---

It should be noted that, prior to 1998, the risk of returns [e.g., the fund's total return risk or even its "beta" (or systematic risk)] was rarely mentioned in prospectuses or advertisements. In 1998, the SEC adopted an initiative requiring mutual funds to disclose more information about their return risk as well as the returns

**TABLE 5–6**  Largest Mutual Funds by Assets Managed

**Sources:** *The Wall Street Journal Online*, January 18, 2013 and authors' research. Reprinted by permission of *The Wall Street Journal* © 2013 Dow Jones & Company, Inc. All Rights Reserved Worldwide. *www.wsj.com*

| Name of Fund | Objective | Total Assets (in millions) | Total Return 12 month | 5 year | 10 year | NAV | Initial Fees |
|---|---|---|---|---|---|---|---|
| Vanguard Tot Stk Inx;Inv | Growth/Income | $78,936 | 17.40% | 5.10% | 8.03% | $37.12 | 0.00% |
| Vangaurd Instl Indx:Inst | S&P 500 Index | 68,055 | 17.08 | 4.46 | 7.25 | 135.64 | 0.00 |
| Vanguard Tot Stk Idx; Adm | Growth/Income | 59,771 | 17.54 | 5.22 | 8.13 | 37.13 | 0.00 |
| Vanguard 500 Index; Adm | S&P 500 Index | 59,749 | 17.06 | 4.45 | 7.23 | 136.52 | 0.00 |
| Fidelity Contrafund | Growth | 58,819 | 17.09 | 4.95 | 10.06 | 80.20 | 0.00 |
| American Funds CIB;A | Income | 58,079 | 13.66 | 2.54 | 7.91 | 53.74 | 5.75 |
| American Funds Inc;A | Income | 57,661 | 13.41 | 4.86 | 7.94 | 18.48 | 5.75 |
| American Funds Growth;A | Growth | 55,970 | 20.07 | 3.54 | 8.33 | 35.61 | 5.75 |
| Vanguard Instl Index; InsP | S&P 500 Index | 49,286 | 17.10 | 4.48 | 7.28 | 135.65 | 0.00 |
| American Funds CWGI;A | Global | 46,651 | 19.69 | 1.45 | 10.26 | 38.33 | 5.75 |
| American Funds InvCoA | Growth/Income | 44,501 | 16.50 | 3.14 | 6.81 | 31.28 | 5.75 |
| Franklin Cust;Inc;A | Income | 42,511 | 15.12 | 5.66 | 8.81 | 2.28 | 4.25 |
| Dodge & Cox Intl Stock | International | 40,556 | 22.75 | 0.75 | 11.65 | 35.90 | 0.00 |
| Dodge & Cox Stock | Growth/Income | 39,841 | 23.16 | 2.55 | 7.54 | 128.06 | 0.00 |
| American Funds Wash;A | Growth/Income | 39,823 | 13.58 | 4.02 | 6.77 | 32.21 | 5.75 |
| Vanguard T StMk Idx; Inst | Growth/Income | 39,367 | 17.54 | 5.22 | 8.15 | 37.13 | 0.00 |
| Vanguard Wellington;Adm | Balanced | 37,959 | 13.41 | 5.93 | 8.51 | 60.16 | 0.00 |
| Vanguard Tot I Stk; Inv | International | 37,659 | 17.94 | −0.56 | 9.59 | 15.39 | 0.00 |
| American Funds Bal;A | Balanced | 34,272 | 14.72 | 5.44 | 7.17 | 21.00 | 5.75 |
| American Funds FInv;A | Growth/Income | 32,568 | 17.58 | 3.77 | 9.33 | 42.37 | 5.75 |

themselves. The SEC's rule was intended to better enable investors to compare return-risk trade-offs from investing in different mutual funds.

Table 5–6 lists the largest (in total assets held) 20 mutual funds available in January 2013, including the fund's objective; total assets; 12-month, 5-year, and 10-year returns; net asset value (discussed below); and any initial fees (discussed below). Vanguard's Total Stock Market Index Fund, Investor Class Shares (which seeks to track the performance of a benchmark index that measures the investment return of the overall stock market), was the largest fund at the time. American Funds, Vanguard, and Fidelity offered 17 of the top 20 funds measured by asset size. Many of the top funds list either growth or growth and income as the fund objective, and all of the top 20 funds performed well in 2012 as the stock market saw high returns as the economy recovered from the financial crisis. Despite a relatively small downturn in the U.S. economy from 2001 through 2002 and a severe financial crisis in 2008–09, all of the top 20 funds earned positive annual returns over the period 2002–12. Over the three time periods (12 months, 5 years, and 10 years), the S&P 500 index saw annual returns of 13.59 percent, 2.32 percent, and 5.12 percent, respectively. Of the top mutual funds, 17 outperformed the S&P 500 index over the 12-month period, 17 outperformed it over the 5-year period, and all 20 funds outperformed the S&P 500 index over the 10-year period.

A growing number of the long-term mutual funds are index funds in which fund managers buy securities in proportions similar to those included in a specified

www.americanfunds.com
www.vanguard.com
www.fidelity.com

major stock index (such as the S&P 500 index). Thus, index funds are designed to match the performance of a stock index. In 2012, 383 index funds managed total net assets of $1.1 trillion. Because little research or aggressive management is necessary for index funds, management fees (discussed later) are lower. However, returns are often higher than more actively managed funds. The difference in returns between actively managed funds and passively managed index funds can be explained. For example, from data analyzed by Morningstar and Forbes over the period 2007–2010, it was found that 18 percent of actively managed funds outperformed index fund portfolios. The overachieving, actively managed portfolios had a median outperformance of 0.4 percent annualized, while the 82 percent underperforming portfolios fell short by 1.0 percent annually.[2] Further, the average amount of expenses that an actively managed fund charges its shareholders every year is approximately 1.3 percent. Conversely, the Vanguard S&P 500 expense ratio is 0.19 percent. Finally, actively managed funds turn over their holdings rapidly. This turnover occurs at an average rate as high as 85 percent per year. The transaction costs involved in buying and selling so many shares every year result in an additional 0.7 percent of return disappearing every year.

## Investor Returns from Mutual Fund Ownership

**marked-to-market**
Adjusting asset and balance sheet values to reflect current market prices.

**NAV**
The net asset value of a mutual fund; equal to the market value of the assets in the mutual fund portfolio divided by the number of shares outstanding.

The return an investor gets from investing in mutual fund shares reflects three aspects of the underlying portfolio of mutual fund assets. First, income and dividends are earned on those assets. Second, capital gains occur when assets are sold by a mutual fund at prices higher than the purchase price. Third, capital appreciation in the underlying values of the assets held in a fund's portfolio add to the value of mutual fund shares. With respect to capital appreciation, mutual fund assets are normally **marked-to-market** daily. This means that the managers of the fund calculate the current value of each mutual fund share by computing the daily market value of the fund's total asset portfolio and then dividing this amount by the number of mutual fund shares outstanding. The resulting value is called the net asset value **(NAV)** of the fund. This is the price the investor gets when selling shares back to the fund that day or buying any new shares in the fund on that day.

---

**EXAMPLE 5–1**
*Impact of Capital Appreciation on NAV*

Suppose a mutual fund contains 2,000 shares of Sears, Roebuck currently trading at $45.50, 1,000 shares of Exxon/Mobil currently trading at $91.25, and 1,500 shares of AT&T currently trading at $33.75. The mutual fund currently has 15,000 shares outstanding held by investors. Thus, today, the NAV of the fund is calculated as:

$$NAV = [(2,000 \times \$45.50) + (1,000 \times \$91.25) + (1,500 \times \$33.75)] \div 15,000 = \$15.525$$

If next month Sears shares increase to $50, Exxon/Mobil shares increase to $95, and AT&T shares increase to $45, the NAV (assuming the same number of shares outstanding) would increase to:

$$NAV = [(2,000 \times \$50) + (1,000 \times \$95) + (1,500 \times \$45)] \div 15,000 = \$17.50$$

---

[2] *The Power of Passive Investing: More Wealth with Less Work,* Richard A. Ferri, 2011. John Wiley & Sons, Inc. Hoboken, NJ.

**open-end mutual fund**
The supply of shares in the fund is not fixed but can increase or decrease daily with purchases and redemptions of shares.

Most mutual funds are **open-end** in that the number of shares outstanding fluctuates up and down daily with the amount of share redemptions and new purchases. With open-end mutual funds, investors buy and sell shares from and to the mutual fund company. Thus, the demand for shares determines the number outstanding and the NAV of shares is determined solely by the market value of the underlying securities held in the mutual fund divided by the number of shareholders outstanding.

| **EXAMPLE 5–2** <br> *Impact of Investment Size on NAV* | Consider the mutual fund in Example 5–1, but suppose that today 1,000 additional investors buy into the mutual fund at the current NAV of $15.525. This means that the fund manager now has $15,525 in additional funds to invest. Suppose the fund manager decides to use these additional funds to buy additional shares in AT&T. At today's market price he or she can buy $15,525 ÷ $33.75 = 460 additional shares of AT&T. Thus, the mutual fund's new portfolio of shares would be 2,000 in Sears, 1,000 in Exxon/Mobil, and 1,960 in AT&T. At the end of the month the NAV of the portfolio would be: |
|---|---|

$$NAV = [(2{,}000 \times \$50) + (1{,}000 \times \$95) + (1{,}960 \times \$45)] \div 16{,}000 = \$17.70$$

given the appreciation in value of all three stocks over the month.

Note that the fund's value changed over the month due to both capital appreciation and investment size. A comparison of the NAV in Example 5–1 with the one in this example indicates that the additional shares alone enabled the fund to gain a slightly higher NAV than had the number of shares remained static ($17.70 versus $17.50).

**closed-end investment companies**
Specialized investment companies that invest in securities and assets of other firms but have a fixed supply of shares outstanding themselves.

**REIT**
A real estate investment trust. A closed-end investment company that specializes in investing in mortgages, property, or real estate company shares.

Open-end mutual funds can be compared to most regular corporations traded on stock exchanges and to **closed-end investment companies,** both of which have a fixed number of shares outstanding at any given time. For example, real estate investment trusts **(REITs)** are closed-end investment companies that specialize in investment in real estate company shares and/or in buying mortgages.[3] With closed-end funds, investors must buy and sell the investment company's shares on a stock exchange similar to the trading of corporate stock. Since the number of shares available for purchase at any moment in time is fixed, the NAV of the fund's shares is determined not only by the value of the underlying shares but also by the demand for the investment company's shares themselves. When demand is high, the shares can trade at more than the NAV of the securities held in the fund. In this case, the fund is said to be *trading at a premium,* that is, at more than the fair market value of the securities held. When the value of the closed-end fund's shares are less than the NAV of its assets, its shares are said to be *trading at a discount,* that is, at less than the fair market value of the securities held.

---

[3] The total market value of funds invested in closed-end funds was $261.3 billion at the end of 2012. This compares to $12,871.9 billion invested in open-end funds at that time.

**EXAMPLE 5–3**

*Market Value of Closed-End Mutual Fund Shares*

Because of high demand for a closed-end investment company's shares, the 50 shares ($N_S$) are trading at $20 per share ($P_S$). The market value of the equity-type securities in the fund's asset portfolio, however, is $800, or $16 ($800 ÷ 50) per share. The market value balance sheet of the fund is shown below:

| Assets | | Liabilities and Equity | |
|---|---|---|---|
| Market value of asset portfolio | $800 | Market value of closed-end fund shares ($P_S \times N_S$) | $1,000 |
| Premium | $200 | | |

The fund's shares are trading at a premium of $4 (200 ÷ 50) per share.

Because of low demand for a *second* closed-end fund, the 100 shares outstanding are trading at $25 per share. The market value of the securities in this fund's portfolio is $3,000, or each share has a NAV of $30 per share. The market value balance sheet of this fund is:

| Assets | | Liabilities and Equity | |
|---|---|---|---|
| Market value of asset portfolio | $3,000 | Market value of closed-end fund shares (100 × $25) | $2,500 |
| Discount | −$500 | | |

## Exchange Traded Funds

Similar to closed-end funds in that a fixed number of shares are outstanding at any point in time, an *exchange-traded fund* (ETF) is an investment company with shares that trade intraday on stock exchanges at market-determined prices. ETFs may be bought or sold through a broker or in a brokerage account, like trading shares of any publicly traded company. While ETFs are registered with the SEC as investment companies, they differ from traditional mutual funds both in how their shares are issued and redeemed and in how their shares or units are traded. Specifically, ETF shares are created by an institutional investor's depositing of a specified block of securities with the ETF. In return for this deposit, the institutional investor receives a fixed amount of ETF shares, some or all of which may then be sold on a stock exchange. The institutional investor may obtain its deposited securities by redeeming the same number of ETF shares it received from the ETF. Individual investors can buy and sell the ETF shares only when they are listed on an exchange. Unlike an institutional investor, a retail investor cannot purchase or redeem shares directly from the ETF, as with a traditional mutual fund.

Assets invested in the 1,193 ETFs in existence in 2012 totaled $1.29 trillion, up from $66 billion invested in a total of 80 funds in 2000. Most ETFs are long-term mutual funds that are designed to replicate a particular stock market index.[4] ETFs include funds such as SPDRs and Vanguard's Large-Cap VIPERs funds.[5] Like

[4] However, in February 2008 the SEC gave approval for the first actively managed ETF.

[5] SPDRs, Standard & Poor's Depository Receipts, hold a portfolio of the equity securities that comprise the Standard & Poor's 500 Composite Stock Price Index. SPDRs seek investment results that, before expenses, generally correspond to the price and yield performance of the Standard & Poor's 500 Composite Stock Price Index. Vanguard Large-Cap Index Participation Equity Receipts (VIPERs) seek to track the performance of a benchmark index that measures the investment return of large-capitalization stocks.

index funds, the share price of an ETF changes over time in response to a change in the stock prices underlying a stock index. Further, like index funds, most ETFs are intended to track a specific index, management of the funds is relatively simple, and management fees are lower than those for actively managed mutual funds. Unlike index funds, however, ETFs can be traded during the day, they can be purchased on margin, and they can be sold short by an investor who expects a drop in the underlying index value. Because ETFs behave like stocks, investors are subject to capital gains taxes only when they sell their shares. Thus, ETF investors can defer capital gains for as long as they hold the ETF.

Mutual fund investors can get information on the performance of mutual funds from several places. For example, for a comprehensive analysis of mutual funds, Morningstar, Inc., offers information on more than 10,000 open-end and closed-end funds. Morningstar does not own, operate, or hold an interest in any mutual fund. Similarly, Lipper Analytical services, a subsidiary of Reuters, tracks the performance of more than 115,000 funds worldwide.

www.morningstar.com

www.lipperweb.com

## Mutual Fund Costs

Mutual funds charge shareholders a price or fee for the services they provide (i.e., management of a diversified portfolio of financial securities). Two types of fees are incurred by investors: sales loads and fund operating expenses. We discuss these next. The total cost to the shareholder of investing in a mutual fund is the sum of the annualized sales load and other fees charged.

### Load versus No-Load Funds

**load fund**
A mutual fund with an up-front sales or commission charge that has to be paid by the investor.

An investor who buys a mutual fund share may be subject to a sales charge, sometimes as high as 5.75 percent. In this case, the fund is called a **load fund**.[6] Other funds that directly market shares to investors do not use sales agents working for commissions and have no up-front commission charges. These are called **no-load funds.**

**no-load fund**
A mutual fund that does not charge up-front fees or commission charges on the sale of mutual fund shares to investors.

The argument in favor of load funds is that their managers provide investors with more personal attention and advice than managers of no-load funds. However, the cost of this increased attention may not be worthwhile. For example, the last column in Table 5–6 lists initial fees for the largest U.S. stock funds in 2012. Notice that only American Funds group and Franklin Templeton Custodian Funds (Franklin Cust:Inc;A) assess a load fee on mutual fund share purchases. After adjusting for this fee, the 12-month returns on the 10 American Funds mutual funds fall from 20.07 percent to 13.41 percent (among the highest returns earned by the largest funds) to 14.32 percent to 7.66 percent (among the lowest of the returns on these funds). As Figure 5–3 indicates, investors increasingly recognized this cost disadvantage for load funds in the 1990s as stock market values increased broadly and dramatically. In 1985, load funds represented almost 70 percent of equity mutual fund sales, and no-load funds represented just over 30 percent. By 1998 new sales of no-load mutual fund shares exceeded that of load fund shares, and by 2002 total assets invested in no-load funds far exceeded those invested in load funds. Of course, because the load fee is a one-time charge, it must be converted to an annualized charge incurred by the shareholder over the life of the

---

[6] Another kind of load, called a *back-end load,* is sometimes charged when mutual fund shares are sold by investors. Back-end loads, also referred to as *deferred sales charges,* are an alternative way to compensate the fund managers or sales force for their services.

**FIGURE 5–3** Load versus No-Load Fund Assets as a Share of Fund Assets (percent)

Source: Investment Company Institute, *Investment Company Fact Book* (Washington, DC: Investment Company Institute, various issues). *www.ici.org*

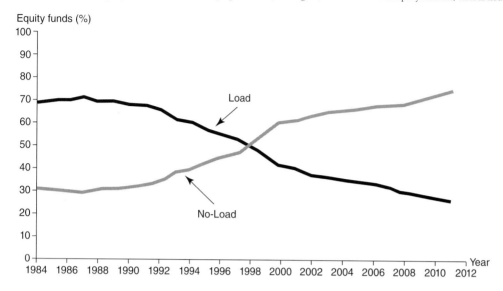

investment. If the shareholder's investment horizon is long term, the annualized load fee can end up being quite small. If the investment horizon is short, however, the load fee can leave the shareholder with little profit.

The demand for no-load funds by mutual fund investors has not gone unnoticed. Many companies, particularly discount brokers, now offer mutual fund supermarkets through which investors can buy and sell mutual fund shares, offered by several different mutual fund sponsors, through a single broker. The most important feature of a fund supermarket is its non–transaction fee program, whereby an investor may purchase mutual funds with no transaction fees from a large number of fund companies. The broker is generally paid for services from the fund's 12b–1 fees (see below). The non–transaction fee offerings at a discount broker often number in the thousands, providing an investor the convenience of purchasing no-load funds from different families at a single location.

### Fund Operating Expenses

**12b–1 fees**
Fees relating to the distribution and other operating costs of mutual fund shares.

In contrast to one-time up-front load charges on the initial investment in a mutual fund, annual fees are charged to cover all fund level expenses experienced as a percent of the fund assets. One type of fee (called a *management fee*) is charged to meet operating costs (such as administration and shareholder services). In addition, mutual funds generally require a small percentage (or fee) of investable funds to meet fund level marketing and distribution costs. Such annual fees are known as **12b–1 fees** after the SEC rule covering such charges. These annual fees cannot exceed 1 percent of a fund's average net assets per year. Marketing and servicing costs are capped at 0.25 percent per year, while management fees are capped at 0.75 percent per year, for a total maximum 12b-1 charge of 1 percent per year. Because these fees, charged to cover fund operating expenses, are paid out of the fund's assets, investors indirectly bear these expenses. These fees are generally expressed as a percentage of the average net assets invested in the fund.

**EXAMPLE 5–4**

*Calculation of Mutual Fund Costs*

The cost of mutual fund investing to a shareholder includes both the one-time sales load and any annual fees charged. Because the sales load is a one-time charge, it must be converted to an annualized payment incurred by the shareholder over the life of his or her investment. With this conversion, the total shareholder cost of investing in a fund is the sum of the annualized sales load plus any annual fees.

For example, suppose an investor purchases fund shares with a 4 percent front-end load and expects to hold the shares for 10 years. The annualized sales load[7] incurred by the investor is:

$$4\%/10 \text{ years} = 0.4\% \text{ per year}$$

Further, suppose the fund has a total fund expense ratio (including 12b–1 fees) of 1 percent per year. The annual total shareholder cost for this fund is calculated as

$$0.4\% + 1\% = 1.4\% \text{ per year}$$

Funds sold through financial professionals such as brokers have recently adopted alternative payment methods. These typically include an annual 12b–1 fee based on asset values that also may be combined with a front-end or back-end sales charge. In many cases, funds offer several different share classes (all of which invest in the same underlying portfolio of assets), but each share class may offer investors different methods of paying for broker services. Indeed, in 2010, approximately two-thirds of all mutual funds had two or more share classes, compared to 1980 when all funds had only one share class. Most funds sold in multiple classes offer investors three payment plans through three share classes (A, B, and C), each having different mixes of sales loads and management and 12b–1 fees.

Class A shares represent the traditional means for paying for investment advice. That is, class A shares carry a front-end load that is charged at the time of purchase as a percent of the sales price. The front-end load on class A shares is charged on new sales and is not generally incurred when class A shares are exchanged for another mutual fund within the same fund family. In addition to the front-end load, class A shares usually have annual management and 12b–1 fees that are used to compensate brokers and sales professionals for ongoing assistance and service provided to fund shareholders. The management and 12b–1 fees for class A shares are typically between 25 and 35 basis points of the portfolio's assets.

Unlike class A shares, class B shares are offered for sale at the NAV without a front-end load. Class B share investors pay for advice and assistance from brokers through a combination of annual management and 12b–1 fees (usually 1 percent) and a back-end load. The back-end load is charged when shares are redeemed (sold) and is typically based on the lesser of the original cost of the shares or the market value at the time of sale. After six to eight years, class B shares typically convert to class A shares, lowering the level of the annual management and 12b–1 fees from 1 percent to that of A shares.

Class C shares are offered at the NAV with no front-end load, and they typically recover distribution costs through a combination of annual management and 12b–1 fees of 1 percent and a back-end load, set at 1 percent in the first year of purchase. After the first year, no back-end load is charged on redemption. Class C shares usually do not convert to class A shares, and thus the annual

---

[7] Convention in the industry is to annualize the sales load without adjusting for the time value of money.

1 percent payment to the broker continues throughout the period of time that the shares are held.

As discussed below, the lack of complete disclosure and the inability of most mutual fund investors to understand the different fees charged for various classes of mutual fund shares came under scrutiny in the early 2000s. Indeed, the potential for overcharging fees to various classes of mutual fund shareholders led to the SEC creating new rules pertaining to these charges. Possibly as a result of these scandals and new rules, more than 850 mutual funds decreased their management fees in 2005, and over 700 lowered their fees in 2006. The average fees and expenses paid by mutual fund investors continue to fall. Investors paid 0.79 percent on the average stock fund in 2012, down from 1.98 percent in 1990 and 1.18 percent in 2004. Bond fund investors paid an average of 0.62 percent in 2009, down from 1.89 percent in 1990 and 0.92 percent in 2004.

---

| **Concept Questions** | 1. Where do mutual funds rank in terms of asset size among all FI industries? |
| --- | --- |
| | 2. Describe the difference between short-term and long-term mutual funds. |
| | 3. What have been the trends in the number of mutual funds since 1980? |
| | 4. What are the three biggest mutual fund companies? How have their funds performed in recent years? |
| | 5. Describe the difference between open-end and closed-end mutual funds. |

---

# BALANCE SHEET AND RECENT TRENDS FOR THE MUTUAL FUND INDUSTRY

## Money Market Funds

The distribution of assets of money market mutual funds from 1990 through 2012 is shown in Table 5–7. As you can see, in 2012, $2,076.9 billion (82.8 percent of total assets) was invested in short-term financial securities such as foreign deposits, domestic checkable deposits and currency, time and savings deposits, repurchase agreements (RPs), open market paper (mostly commercial paper), and U.S. government securities. This is up from 2007 (at the start of the financial crisis) when $2,094.4 billion (or 69.0 percent) of financial assets were invested in short-term securities. As financial markets tumbled in 2008, money market mutual funds moved investments out of corporate and foreign bonds (12.4 percent of the total in 2007 and 6.1 percent in 2008) into safer securities such as U.S. government securities (13.6 percent of the total investments in 2007 and 35.5 percent in 2008). Short-maturity asset holdings reflect the objective of these funds to retain the depositlike nature of the share liabilities they issue. In fact, most money market mutual fund shares have their values fixed at $1. Asset value fluctuations due to interest rate changes and capital gains or losses on assets are adjusted for by increasing or reducing the number of $1 shares owned by the investor.

In addition to these typical risks faced by fund mangers, money market mutual funds experienced unusual liquidity risk at the start of the financial crisis. On September 16, 2008 (one day after Lehman Brothers filed for bankruptcy), Reserve Primary Fund, the oldest money market fund in the United States, saw its shares fall to an equivalent of 97 cents (below the $1.00 book value) after writing off debt

**TABLE 5–7**   **Distribution of Assets in Money Market Mutual Funds, 1990–2012 (in billions of dollars)**

Source: Federal Reserve Board, "Flow of Fund Accounts," various issues. *www.federalreserve.gov*

| | 1990 | 1995 | 2000 | 2005 | 2007 | 2008 | 2010 | 2012 | Percent of Total, 2012 |
|---|---|---|---|---|---|---|---|---|---|
| Total financial assets | $493.3 | $745.3 | $1,812.1 | $2,006.9 | $3,033.1 | $3,757.3 | $2,755.3 | $2,506.9 | 100.0% |
| Foreign deposits | 26.7 | 19.7 | 91.1 | 94.7 | 127.3 | 129.3 | 105.9 | 40.2 | 1.6 |
| Checkable deposits and currency | 11.2 | −3.5 | 2.2 | −0.9 | 1.9 | 7.5 | 14.2 | 11.3 | 0.5 |
| Time and savings deposits | 21.9 | 52.3 | 142.4 | 183.0 | 270.7 | 355.2 | 468.0 | 405.3 | 16.2 |
| Security RPs | 58.2 | 87.8 | 183.0 | 346.0 | 605.9 | 542.4 | 479.3 | 513.1 | 20.5 |
| Credit market instruments | 371.3 | 545.5 | 1,290.9 | 1,340.8 | 1,936.4 | 2,675.0 | 1,621.0 | 1,471.6 | 58.6 |
| Open market paper | 204.0 | 235.5 | 608.6 | 492.2 | 674.6 | 618.5 | 394.2 | 319.4 | 12.7 |
| Treasury | 44.9 | 70.0 | 90.4 | 88.6 | 178.1 | 577.7 | 335.4 | 456.3 | 18.2 |
| Agency | 36.4 | 90.8 | 185.2 | 160.1 | 235.9 | 756.2 | 402.8 | 331.3 | 13.2 |
| Municipal securities | 84.0 | 127.7 | 244.7 | 336.7 | 471.0 | 494.6 | 334.4 | 271.6 | 10.8 |
| Corporate and foreign bonds | 2.0 | 21.5 | 161.9 | 263.2 | 376.8 | 228.0 | 154.2 | 93.0 | 3.7 |
| Miscellaneous assets | 4.0 | 43.4 | 102.5 | 43.3 | 90.9 | 47.9 | 66.9 | 65.4 | 2.6 |

issued by Lehman Brothers. Resulting investor anxiety about Reserve Primary Fund spread to other funds, and investors industrywide liquidated their MMMF shares. In just one week investors liquidated over $200 billion of the industry total $4 trillion invested in MMMFs. In response, on September 19 the federal government took steps to restore confidence in the MMMF industry. Specifically, the Department of Treasury opened the Temporary Guarantee Program for MMMFs, which provided up to $50 billion in coverage to MMMF shareholders for amounts they held in the funds as of close of business that day. The guarantee was triggered if a participating fund's net asset value fell below $0.995. The program was designed to address the severe liquidity strains in the industry and immediately stabilized the industry and stopped the outflows.

**EXAMPLE 5–5**

*Calculation of Number of Shares Outstanding in a Money Market Mutual Fund*

Due to a drop in interest rates, the market value of the assets held by a particular MMMF increases from $100 to $110. The market value balance sheet for the mutual fund before and after the drop in interest rates is:

| Assets | | Liabilities and Equity | |
|---|---|---|---|
| (a) Before the interest rate drop: Market value of MMMF assets | $100 | Market value of MMMF fund shares (100 shares × $1) | $100 |
| (b) After the interest rate drop: Market value of MMMF assets | 110 | Market value of MMMF fund shares (110 shares × $1) | 110 |

The interest rate drop results in 10 (110 − 100) new equity-type shares that are held by investors in the MMMF, reflecting the increase in the market value of the MMMF's assets of $10 (i.e., 10 new shares of $1 each).

**TABLE 5–8** Distribution of Assets in Bond, Equity, and Hybrid Mutual Funds, 1990–2012 (in billions of dollars)

Source: Federal Reserve Board, "Flow of Fund Accounts," various issues. *www.federalreserve.gov*

| | 1990 | 1995 | 2000 | 2005 | 2007 | 2008 | 2010 | 2012 | Percent of Total, 2012 |
|---|---|---|---|---|---|---|---|---|---|
| Total financial assets | $608.4 | $1,852.8 | $4,434.6 | $6,048.9 | $7,829.0 | $5,435.3 | $7,934.5 | $9,262.4 | 100.0% |
| Security RPs | 6.1 | 50.2 | 106.4 | 115.4 | 132.2 | 124.7 | 137.5 | 222.7 | 2.4 |
| Credit market instruments | 360.1 | 771.3 | 1,097.8 | 1,747.1 | 2,203.1 | 2,276.5 | 3,031.4 | 4,035.5 | 43.6 |
| Open market paper | 28.5 | 50.2 | 106.4 | 97.1 | 114.1 | 51.6 | 66.3 | 131.1 | 1.4 |
| Treasury | 111.1 | 205.3 | 123.7 | 155.7 | 179.2 | 187.9 | 297.4 | 427.6 | 4.6 |
| Agency | 48.6 | 109.9 | 275.3 | 483.4 | 565.2 | 592.7 | 791.1 | 1,066.6 | 11.5 |
| Municipal securities | 112.6 | 210.2 | 230.5 | 311.7 | 372.2 | 389.6 | 526.6 | 612.8 | 6.6 |
| Corporate and foreign bonds | 59.3 | 185.5 | 337.6 | 662.7 | 889.9 | 959.9 | 1,275.4 | 1,701.9 | 18.4 |
| Other loans and advances | 0.0 | 10.2 | 24.3 | 36.5 | 82.5 | 94.8 | 74.6 | 95.5 | 1.1 |
| Corporate equities | 233.2 | 1,024.9 | 3,226.9 | 4,175.7 | 5,476.9 | 3,014.1 | 4,762.7 | 5,004.2 | 54.0 |
| Miscellaneous assets | 8.9 | 6.3 | 3.5 | 10.7 | 16.8 | 20.0 | 2.9 | 0.0 | 0.0 |

## Long-Term Funds

Note the asset composition of long-term mutual funds shown in Table 5–8. As might be expected, it reflects the popularity of different types of bond or equity funds at any point in time. For example, underscoring the attractiveness of equity funds in 2007 was the fact that stocks comprised over 70.0 percent of total long-term mutual fund asset portfolios. Credit market instruments were the next most popular assets (28.1 percent of the asset portfolio). In contrast, look at the distribution of assets in 2008, when the equity markets were plummeting. Equities made up only 55.5 percent of the long-term mutual fund portfolios and credit market instruments were 41.9 percent of total assets. Note too that total financial assets fell from $7,829.0 billion in 2007 (before the start of the financial crisis) to just $5,435.3 billion in 2008 (at the height of the crisis), a drop of 30.6 percent. As the economy and financial markets recovered (in 2010), financial assets held by long-term mutual funds increased to $7,934.5 billion, of which only 60.0 percent were corporate equities. In 2012, long-term funds held financial assets totaling $9,262.4 billion, of which 54.0 percent were corporate equities. Thus, even four years after the start of the financial crisis, long-term funds had not switched their holdings of corporate equities back to pre-crisis levels.

| **Concept Questions** | 1. Describe the major assets held by mutual funds in the 1990s and 2000s. |
|---|---|
| | 2. How does the asset distribution differ between money market mutual funds and long-term mutual funds? |

# REGULATION OF MUTUAL FUNDS

www.sec.gov

www.nasd.com

Because mutual funds manage and invest small investors' savings, this industry is heavily regulated. Indeed, many regulations have been enacted to protect investors against possible abuses by managers of mutual funds. The SEC is the primary regulator of mutual funds. Specifically, the Securities Act of 1933 requires a mutual fund to file a registration statement with the SEC and sets rules and procedures regarding the fund's prospectus sent to investors. In addition, the Securities Exchange Act of 1934 makes the purchase and sale of mutual fund shares subject to various antifraud provisions. This regulation requires that a mutual fund furnish full and accurate information on all financial and corporate matters to prospective fund purchasers. The 1934 act also appointed the National Association of Securities Dealers (NASD) to supervise mutual fund share distributions. In 1940 Congress passed the Investment Advisers Act and the Investment Company Act. The Investment Advisers Act regulates the activities of mutual fund advisors. The Investment Company Act sets out rules to prevent conflicts of interest, fraud, and excessive fees or charges for fund shares.

More recently, the passage of the Insider Trading and Securities Fraud Enforcement Act of 1988 has required mutual funds to develop mechanisms and procedures to avoid insider trading abuses. In addition, the Market Reform Act of 1990, passed in the wake of the 1987 stock market crash, allows the SEC to introduce circuit breakers to halt trading on exchanges and to restrict program trading when it deems necessary. Finally, the National Securities Markets Improvement Act (NSMIA) of 1996 also applies to mutual fund companies. Specifically, the NSMIA exempts mutual fund sellers from oversight by state securities regulators, thus reducing their regulatory burden.

Despite the many regulations imposed on mutual fund companies, several allegations of trading abuses and improper assignment of fees were revealed and prosecuted in the early 2000s. The abusive activities fell into four general categories: market timing, late trading, directed brokerage, and improper assessment of fees to investors.

Market timing involves short-term trading of mutual funds that seeks to take advantage of short-term discrepancies between the price of a mutual fund's shares and out-of-date values on the securities in the fund's portfolio. It is especially common in international funds as traders can exploit differences in time zones. Typically, market timers hold a fund for only a few days. For example, when Asian markets close with losses, but are expected to rebound the following day, market timers can buy a U.S. mutual fund, investing in Asian securities after the loss on that day and then sell the shares for a profit the next day. This single-day investment dilutes the profits of the fund's long-term investors, while market timers profit without much risk.

Late trading allegations involved cases in which some investors were able to buy or sell mutual fund shares long after the price had been set at 4 PM eastern time each day (i.e., after the close of the NYSE and NASDAQ). Under existing rules, investors had to place an order with their broker or another FI by 4 PM. But the mutual fund company may not have received the order until much later, sometimes as late as 9 PM. However, because of this time delay, some large investors had been able to call their broker back after the market closed and alter or cancel their order.

Directed brokerage involves arrangements between mutual fund companies and brokerage houses and whether those agreements improperly influenced which funds brokers recommended to investors. The investigation examined whether some mutual fund companies agreed to direct orders for stock and bond purchases and sales to brokerage houses that agreed to promote sales of the mutual fund company's products.

Finally, regulators claimed that the disclosure of 12b–1 fees allowed some brokers to trick investors into believing they were buying no-load funds. Before 12b–1 fees, all funds sold through brokers carried front-end load fees. As discussed above, with 12b–1 fees, fund companies introduced share classes, some of which carried back-end loads that declined over time and others that charged annual fees of up to 1 percent of asset values. Funds classes that charged annual 12b–1 fees would see performance decrease by that amount and thus not perform as well as an identical fund that carried a lower 12b–1 fee. The shareholder, however, saw only the fund's raw return (before annual fees) and not the dollar amount of the fee paid. Further, regulators discovered in late 2002 that brokers often overcharged customers by failing to provide discounts to fund investors who qualified to receive them. Since discount policies differ from fund to fund, brokers did not always realize which customers qualified for them.

The result of these illegal and abusive activities was new rules and regulations imposed (in 2004 and 2005) on mutual fund companies. The rules were intended to give investors more information about conflicts of interest, improve fund governance, and close legal loopholes that some fund managers had abused. Many of these new rules involve changes to the way mutual funds operate, including requirements that funds have an independent board headed by an independent chairman. Specifically, the SEC required an increase in the percentage of independent board members to 75 percent from the previous level of 50 percent and required mutual fund companies to have independent board chairs (a move that would displace the sitting chairmen at about 80 percent of the nations mutual funds). The SEC saw independent directors as those who better serve as watchdogs guarding investors' interests. Further, the Sarbanes-Oxley Act of 2002 requires public companies, including mutual fund companies, to make sure their boards' audit committees have at least one individual who is familiar with generally accepted accounting principles and has experience with internal auditing controls, preparing or auditing financial statements of "generally comparable issuers," and applying GAAP principles for estimates, accruals, and reserves.

The SEC also took steps to close a loophole that allowed improper trading to go unnoticed at some mutual funds. Prior to the new rules, the SEC required that funds report trading by senior employees in individual stocks but not in shares of mutual funds they manage. The SEC now requires portfolio managers to report trading in funds they manage. Investment advisors also have to protect information about stock selections and client holding and transactions. The SEC and other regulators had found that advisory personnel revealed confidential information about fund portfolio holdings so that others could exploit the funds.

To address the problem of market timing, the SEC now requires funds to provide expanded disclosure of the risks of frequent trading in fund shares and of their policies and procedures regarding such activities. Mutual funds also now have to be more open about their use of fair value pricing (a practice of estimating the value of rarely traded securities or updating the values of non-U.S. securities that last traded many hours before U.S. funds calculate their share prices each day) to guard against stale share prices that could produce profits for market timers. The market timing provisions also require mutual funds to explain when they use fair value pricing. Fair value pricing is one of the most effective ways of combating the market timing that was most common in some mutual funds holding non-U.S. stocks. Many mutual funds had rarely used fair value pricing. Further, new SEC rules require brokers to tell investors about any payments, compensation, or other incentives they receive from fund companies including whether they are paid more to sell a certain fund. Conflicts would have to be disclosed before the sale is completed.

To ensure that the required rule changes take place, starting October 5, 2004, the SEC required that mutual funds hire chief compliance officers to monitor whether the mutual fund company follows the rules. The chief compliance officer reports directly to mutual fund directors, and not to executives of the fund management company. To further insulate the chief compliance officer from being bullied into keeping quiet about improper behavior, only the fund board can fire the compliance officer. Duties of the compliance officer include policing personal trading by fund managers, ensuring accuracy of information provided to regulators and investors, reviewing fund business practices such as allocating trading commissions, and reporting any wrongdoing directly to fund directors.

Finally, the new SEC rules call for shareholder reports to include the fees shareholders pay during any period covered, as well as management's discussion of the fund's performance over that period. As of September 1, 2004, mutual fund companies must provide clear information to investors on brokerage commissions and discounts, including improved disclosure on up-front sales charges for broker-sold mutual funds. Investors now get a document showing the amount they paid for a fund, the amount their broker was paid, and how the fund compares with industry averages based on fees, sales loads, and brokerage commissions. As of December 2004, mutual funds must provide to investors summary information in a fund prospectus on eligibility for breakpoint discounts and explain what records investors may need to show brokers to demonstrate they qualify for discounts.

The SEC also proposed that mutual funds or their agents receive all trading orders by 4 PM eastern time, when the fund's daily price is calculated. This "hard closing," which would require fund orders to be in the hands of the mutual fund companies by 4 PM, is intended to halt late trading abuses.

In March 2009, the SEC adopted amendments to the form used by mutual funds to register under the Investment Company Act of 1940 and to offer their securities under the Securities Act of 1933 in order to enhance the disclosures that are provided to mutual fund investors. The amendments (first proposed in November 2007) require key information to appear in plain English in a standardized order at the front of the mutual fund statutory prospectus. The amendment also includes a new option for satisfying prospectus delivery obligations with respect to mutual fund securities under the Securities Act. Under the option, key information is sent or given to investors in the form of a summary prospectus and the statutory prospectus is provided on an Internet website. The improved disclosure framework was intended to provide investors with information that is easier to use and more readily accessible, while retaining the comprehensive quality of the information that was previously available.

Finally, in a February 2013 letter sent to the Financial Stability Oversight Council (FSOC) (set up as a result of the Wall Street Reform and Consumer

Protection Act to oversee the financial system), the leaders of all 12 regional Federal Reserve banks called for a significant overhaul of the money market industry. The letter stated that even four years after the financial crisis, without reform money, market mutual fund activities could spread the risk of significant credit problems from the funds to banks to the broader financial system. New York Fed president William Dudley stated that the risk of a run on money market funds was potentially higher in 2013 than before the crisis because banks increasingly used these funds as a source of financing and because Congress blocked the Fed and Treasury from using certain emergency tools that could stabilize the funds during a market panic. A proposal released in November 2012 by the FSOC included a requirement for money market mutual funds to let fund prices adjust to changes in the net asset value of the funds' holdings, rather than fixing values at $1 a share. The logic behind the proposal is that with a floating value, investors would be less likely to rush to pull their cash out of the funds before share values "break the buck," as happened during the 2008 crisis (discussed earlier). However, little action followed the release of the proposal. The joint letter by the Fed presidents was intended to serve as impetus to renew the push for reform.

| **Concept Questions** | 1. Who is the primary regulator of mutual fund companies? |
| | 2. How did the NSMIA affect mutual funds? |

## GLOBAL ISSUES IN THE MUTUAL FUND INDUSTRY

As discussed throughout the chapter, mutual funds have been the fastest-growing sector in the U.S. financial institutions industry throughout the 1990s and into the 2000s. Only the worldwide financial crisis and the worst worldwide recession since the Great Depression curtailed the growth in this industry. Worldwide investment in mutual funds is shown in Table 5–9. Combined assets invested in non-U.S. mutual funds are approximately equal to that invested in U.S. mutual funds alone. However, recent growth in non-U.S. funds has exceeded that in U.S. funds. Worldwide (other than in the United States), investments in mutual funds have increased more than 211 percent, from $4.545 trillion in 1999 to $14.130 trillion in 2007. This compares with growth of 75 percent in U.S. funds. Likewise, non-U.S. mutual funds experienced bigger losses in total assets during the financial crisis. Worldwide funds fell to $9.316 trillion (34.1 percent) in 2008, while U.S. funds fell to $9.601 trillion (20.1 percent). By 2012, as worldwide economies improved, worldwide investments in mutual funds increased to $13.291 trillion (an increase of 42.7 percent from 2008), while U.S. investments increased to $12.754 trillion (an increase of 32.8 percent). In addition, as this industry developed in countries throughout the world, the number of mutual funds worldwide (other than in the United States) increased 46.4 percent, from 44,955 in 1999 to 65,795 in 2012. Much more established in the United States, the number of U.S. mutual funds decreased by almost 3 percent over this period. In 2012, of the total amount invested in mutual funds outside the United States, 35 percent was in equity funds, 16 percent in bond funds, 19 percent in hybrid funds, 22 percent in money market funds, and 8 percent in other funds.

**TABLE 5–9**  Worldwide Assets of Open-End Investment Companies* (in millions of dollars)

Source: Investment Company Institute, *Investment Company Fact Book* (Washington, DC: Investment Company Institute, various issues). *www.ici.org*

| Non-U.S. Countries | 1999 | 2002 | 2007 | 2008 | 2010 | 2012† |
|---|---|---|---|---|---|---|
| Argentina | $ 6,990 | $ 1,021 | $ 6,789 | $ 3,867 | $ 5,179 | $ 8,571 |
| Australia | N/A | 356,304 | 1,192,992 | 841,133 | 1,455,850 | 1,610,190 |
| Austria | 56,254 | 66,877 | 138,709 | 93,269 | 94,670 | 85,288 |
| Belgium | 65,461 | 74,983 | 149,842 | 105,057 | 96,288 | 82,499 |
| Brazil | 117,758 | 96,729 | 615,365 | 479,321 | 5,179 | 8,571 |
| Bulgaria | N/A | N/A | N/A | 226 | 302 | 296 |
| Canada | 269,825 | 248,979 | 698,397 | 416,031 | 636,947 | 840,890 |
| Chile | 4,091 | 6,705 | 24,444 | 17,587 | 38,243 | 35,040 |
| China | N/A | N/A | 434,063 | 276,303 | 364,985 | 373,519 |
| Costa Rica | N/A | 1,738 | 1,203 | 1,098 | 1,470 | 1,651 |
| Czech Republic | 1,473 | 3,297 | 7,595 | 5,260 | 5,508 | 4,657 |
| Denmark‡ | 27,558 | 40,153 | 104,082 | 65,182 | 89,800 | 98,525 |
| Finland | 10,318 | 16,516 | 81,136 | 48,750 | 71,210 | 70,483 |
| France | 656,132 | 845,147 | 1,989,690 | 1,591,082 | 1,617,176 | 1,439,987 |
| Germany | 237,312 | 209,168 | 372,072 | 237,986 | 333,713 | 314,040 |
| Greece | 36,397 | 26,621 | 29,807 | 12,189 | 8,627 | 5,001 |
| Hong Kong | 182,265 | 164,322 | 818,421 | N/A | N/A | N/A |
| Hungary | 1,725 | 3,992 | 12,577 | 9,188 | 11,532 | 8,082 |
| India | 13,065 | 20,364 | 108,582 | 62,805 | 111,421 | 110,021 |
| Ireland | 95,174 | 250,116 | 951,371 | 720,486 | 1,014,104 | 1,216,670 |
| Italy | 475,661 | 378,259 | 419,687 | 263,588 | 234,313 | 176,227 |
| Japan | 502,752 | 303,191 | 713,998 | 575,327 | 785,504 | 753,552 |
| Korea | 167,177 | 149,544 | 329,979 | 221,992 | 266,495 | 255,419 |
| Liechtenstein | N/A | 3,847 | 25,103 | 20,489 | 35,387 | 32,459 |
| Luxembourg | 661,084 | 803,869 | 2,685,065 | 1,860,763 | 2,512,874 | 2,510,001 |
| Malta | N/A | N/A | N/A | N/A | N/A | 3,002 |
| Mexico | 19,468 | 30,759 | 75,428 | 60,435 | 98,094 | 109,481 |
| Netherlands | 94,539 | 84,211 | 113,759 | 77,379 | 85,924 | 70,634 |
| New Zealand | 8,502 | 7,505 | 14,924 | 10,612 | 19,562 | 30,020 |
| Norway | 15,107 | 15,471 | 74,709 | 41,157 | 84,505 | 93,890 |
| Pakistan | N/A | N/A | 4,956 | 1,985 | 2,290 | 3,214 |
| Philippines | 117 | 474 | 2,090 | 1,263 | 2,184 | 3,210 |
| Poland | 762 | 5,468 | 45,542 | 17,782 | 25,595 | 22,554 |
| Portugal | 19,704 | 19,969 | 29,732 | 13,572 | 11,004 | 6,987 |
| Romania | N/A | 27 | 390 | 326 | 1,713 | 2,400 |
| Russia | 177 | 372 | 7,175 | 2,026 | 3,917 | N/A |
| Slovakia | N/A | N/A | 4,762 | 3,841 | 4,349 | 2,882 |
| Slovenia | N/A | N/A | 4,219 | 2,067 | 2,663 | 2,340 |
| South Africa | 18,235 | 20,983 | 95,221 | 69,417 | 141,615 | 138,283 |
| Spain | 207,603 | 179,133 | 396,354 | 270,983 | 216,915 | 188,660 |
| Sweden | 83,250 | 57,992 | 194,955 | 113,331 | 205,449 | 199,454 |
| Switzerland | 82,512 | 82,622 | 176,282 | 135,052 | 261,893 | 310,504 |
| Taiwan | 31,153 | 62,153 | 58,323 | 46,116 | 59,032 | 57,282 |
| Trinidad & Tobago | N/A | N/A | N/A | N/A | 5,812 | 6,388 |
| Turkey | N/A | 6,002 | 22,609 | 15,404 | 19,545 | 15,862 |
| United Kingdom | 375,199 | 288,887 | 897,460 | 504,681 | 854,413 | 938,832 |
| **Total non-U.S.** | **$ 4,544,799** | **$ 4,933,771** | **$14,130,041** | **$ 9,316,409** | **$12,878,305** | **$13,290,983** |
| **Total U.S.** | **$ 6,846,339** | **$ 6,390,360** | **$12,020,895** | **$ 9,601,090** | **$11,820,865** | **$12,754,273** |
| **Total world** | **$11,391,138** | **$11,324,131** | **$26,150,936** | **$18,917,499** | **$24,699,170** | **$26,045,256** |

* Funds of funds are not included. Data include home-domiciled funds, except for Hong Kong, Korea, and New Zealand.
† As of end of the third quarter.
‡ Before 2003, data include special funds reserved for institutional investors.
Note: Components may not add to total because of rounding.

As may be expected, the worldwide mutual fund market is most active in those countries with the most sophisticated securities markets (e.g., Japan, France, Australia, and the United Kingdom). However, in the late 1990s and early 2000s, the faltering Japanese economy resulted in a decrease in both the assets invested in and the number of mutual funds. Assets invested in Japanese mutual funds fell from $502.7 billion in 1999 to $303.2 billion in 2002 (a drop of 39.7 percent) and the number of funds fell from 3,444 to 2,718 (21.1 percent) over the period. Some U.S. FIs saw this decline in the Japanese market as an opportunity. U.S. FIs such as Paine Webber Group (teaming up with Yasuda Life Insurance Co.) and Merrill Lynch (buying the assets of failed Japanese brokerage firm Yamaichi Securities) entered the Japanese mutual fund market in the late 1990s and early 2000s. The U.S. FIs saw Japan as a profitable market for mutual fund sales, noting that about 60 percent of Japan's savings was in low-yielding bank deposits or government-run institutions.

Although U.S. mutual fund companies sponsor funds abroad, barriers to entry overseas are typically higher than in the United States. The U.S. mutual fund industry has worked to lower the barriers that prevent U.S. mutual fund firms from marketing their services more widely and to improve competition in the often diverse fund markets around the world. The U.S. mutual fund industry, for example, has worked to achieve a true cross-border market for mutual fund companies in Europe and to ensure that publicly offered mutual fund companies can be used as funding vehicles in the retirement fund market in Europe and Japan. The industry also has sought to reduce barriers for U.S. mutual fund sponsors seeking to offer mutual fund company products in China and other Asian countries.

| **Concept Question** | 1. What have been the trends in the assets invested in worldwide mutual funds from the 1990s through the 2000s? |
| --- | --- |

# HEDGE FUNDS

Hedge funds are a type of investment pool that solicits funds from (wealthy) individuals and other investors (e.g., commercial banks) and invests these funds on their behalf. Hedge funds are similar to mutual funds in that they are pooled investment vehicles that accept investors' money and generally invest it on a collective basis. Hedge funds are, however, not subject to the numerous regulations that apply to mutual funds for the protection of individuals, such as regulations requiring a certain degree of liquidity, regulations requiring that mutual fund shares be redeemable at any time, regulations protecting against conflicts of interest, regulations to ensure fairness in the pricing of funds shares, disclosure regulations, and regulations limiting the use of leverage. Further, hedge funds do not have to disclose their full activities to third parties. Thus, they offer a high degree of privacy for their investors. Until 2010, hedge funds were not required to register with the SEC. Thus, they were subject to virtually no regulatory oversight (e.g., by the SEC under the Securities Act and Investment Advisers Act) and generally took significant risk. Even after 2010, hedge funds offered in the United States avoid regulations by limiting the asset size of the fund (see below).

Historically, hedge funds avoided regulations by limiting the number of investors to less than 100 individuals (below that required for SEC registration), who must be deemed "accredited investors." To be accredited, an investor must have a net worth of more than $1 million or have an annual income of at least $200,000 ($300,000 if married). These stiff financial requirements allowed hedge funds to avoid regulation under the theory that individuals with such wealth should be able to evaluate the risk and return on their investments. According to the SEC, these types of investors should be expected to make more informed decisions and take on higher levels of risk. However, as a result of some heavily publicized hedge fund failures and near failures (the result of fraud by fund managers, e.g., Bernard L. Madoff Investment Securities, and the financial crisis, e.g., Bear Stearns High Grade Structured Credit Strategies Fund), in 2010 federal regulators increased the oversight of hedge funds (see below).

Even with this increased oversight, because hedge funds remain exempt from many of the rules and regulations governing mutual funds, they can use aggressive strategies that are unavailable to mutual funds, including short selling, leveraging, program trading, arbitrage, and derivatives trading. Further, since hedge funds that do not exceed $100 million in assets under management do not register with the SEC, their actual data cannot be independently tracked. Therefore, much hedge fund data are self-reported. It is estimated that in 2013 there were more than 8,000 hedge funds in the world, with managed assets estimated at $2.25 trillion. Table 5–10 lists the 10 largest hedge funds by total assets managed in 2013.

Hedge funds grew in popularity in the 1990s as investors saw returns of more than 40 percent after management fees (often more than 25 percent of the fund's profits). They came to the forefront of the news in the late 1990s when one large hedge fund, Long-Term Capital Management (LTCM), nearly collapsed. The near collapse of LTCM not only hurt its investors, but arguably came close to damaging the world's financial system. So great was the potential impact of the failure of LTCM that the Federal Reserve felt it was necessary to intervene by brokering a $3.6 billion bailout of LTCM by a consortium of some of the world's largest financial institutions.

Some hedge funds take positions (using sophisticated computer models) speculating that some prices will rise faster than others. For example, a hedge fund may buy (take a long position in) a bond expecting that its price will rise. At the

**TABLE 5–10**
**Largest Hedge Fund Firms by Assets Managed**

Source: *Institutional Investor,* January 2013. *www.institutionalinvestor.com*

| Name of Fund | Country | Total Assets (in billions) |
|---|---|---|
| Bridgewater Associates | United States | $76.1 |
| J.P. Morgan Asset Management | United States | 53.6 |
| Man Group | United Kingdom | 38.5 |
| Brevan Howard Asset Management | United Kingdom | 34.2 |
| Winton Capital Management | United Kingdom | 30.0 |
| Och-Ziff Capital Management Group | United States | 28.8 |
| BlackRock | United States | 28.8 |
| BlueCrest Capital Management | United Kingdom | 28.6 |
| Baupost Group | United States | 25.2 |
| AQR Capital Management | United States | 23.2 |

same time the fund will borrow (taking a short position) in another bond and sell it, promising to return the borrowed bond in the future. Generally, bond prices tend to move up and down together. Thus, if prices go up as expected, the hedge fund will gain on the bond it purchased while losing money on the bond it borrowed. The hedge fund will make a profit if the gain on the bond it purchased is larger than the loss on the bond it borrowed. If, contrary to expectations, bond prices fall, the hedge fund will make a profit if the gains on the bond it borrowed are greater than the losses on the bond it bought. Thus, regardless of the change in prices, the simultaneous long and short positions in bonds will minimize the risk of overall losses for the hedge fund.

## Types of Hedge Funds

Most hedge funds are highly specialized, relying on the specific expertise of the fund manager(s) to produce a profit. Hedge fund managers follow a variety of investment strategies, some of which use leverage and derivatives, while others use more conservative strategies and involve little or no leverage. Generally, hedge funds are set up with specific parameters so that investors can forecast a risk-return profile. Figure 5–4 shows the general categories of hedge funds by risk classification.

*More risky* funds are the most aggressive and may produce profits in many types of market environments. Funds in this group are classified by objectives such as aggressive growth, emerging markets, macro, market timing, and short selling. Aggressive growth funds invest in equities expected to experience acceleration in growth of earnings per share. Generally, high price-to-earnings ratio, low or no dividend companies are included. These funds hedge by shorting equities where earnings disappointment is expected or by shorting stock indexes. Emerging market funds invest in equity or debt securities of emerging markets, which tend to have higher inflation and volatile growth. Macro funds aim to profit from changes in global economies, typically brought about by shifts in government policy that impact interest rates. These funds include investments in equities, bonds, currencies, and commodities. They use leverage and derivatives to accentuate the impact of market moves. Market timing funds allocate assets among different asset classes depending on the manager's view of the economic or market outlook. Thus, portfolio emphasis may swing widely between asset classes. The unpredictability of

**FIGURE 5–4**   **Classification of Hedge Funds**

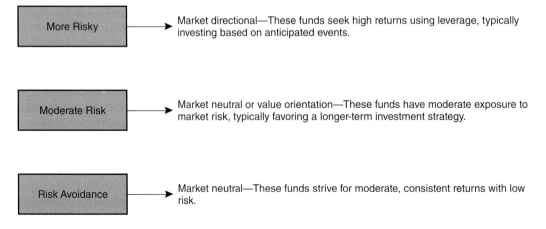

market movements and the difficulty of timing entry and exit from markets add significant risk to this strategy. Short-selling funds sell securities in anticipation of being able to buy them back in the future at a lower price based on the manager's assessment of the overvaluation of the securities or in anticipation of earnings disappointments.

*Moderate risk* funds are more traditional funds, similar to mutual funds, with only a portion of the portfolio being hedged. Funds in this group are classified by objectives such as distressed securities, fund of funds, opportunistic, multistrategy, and special situations. Distressed securities funds buy equity, debt, or trade claims, at deep discounts, of companies in or facing bankruptcy or reorganization. Profit opportunities come from the market's lack of understanding of the true value of these deep-discount securities and from the fact that the majority of institutional investors cannot own below-investment-grade securities. Funds of funds mix hedge funds and other pooled investment vehicles. This blending of different strategies and asset classes aims to provide a more stable long-term investment return than any of the individual funds. Returns and risk can be controlled by the mix of underlying strategies and funds. Capital preservation is generally an important consideration for these funds. Opportunistic funds change their investment strategy as opportunities arise to profit from events such as IPOs, sudden price changes resulting from a disappointing earnings announcement, and hostile takeover bids. These funds may utilize several investing styles at any point in time and are not restricted to any particular investment approach or asset class. Multistrategy funds take a diversified investment approach by implementing various strategies simultaneously to realize short- and long-term gains. This style of investment allows the manager to overweight or underweight different strategies to best capitalize on current investment opportunities. Special-situation funds invest in event-driven situations such as mergers, hostile takeovers, reorganizations, or leveraged buyouts. These funds may undertake the simultaneous purchase of stock in a company being acquired and sale of stock in its bidder, hoping to profit from the spread between the current market price and the final purchase price of the company.

*Risk-avoidance* funds are also more traditional funds, emphasizing consistent but moderate returns while avoiding risk. Funds in this group are classified by objectives such as income, market neutral–arbitrage, market neutral–securities hedging, and value. Income funds invest with the primary focus on yield or current income rather than solely on capital gains. These funds use leverage to buy bonds and some fixed-income derivatives, profiting from principal appreciation and interest income. Market neutral–arbitrage funds attempt to hedge market risk by taking offsetting positions, often in different securities of the same issuer, for example, long convertible bonds and short the firm's equity. Their focus is on obtaining returns with low or no correlation to both equity and bond markets. Market neutral–securities hedging funds invest equally in long and short equity portfolios in particular market sectors. Market risk is reduced, but effective stock analysis is critical to obtaining a profit. These funds use leverage to magnify their returns. They also sometimes use market index futures to hedge systematic risk. Value funds invest in securities perceived to be selling at deep discounts relative to their intrinsic values. Securities include those that may be out of favor or under-followed by analysts.

Using traditional risk-adjusted measures of performance (such as Sharpe ratios), the performance of hedge funds has been very strong compared to that

**TABLE 5–11**   Largest Hedge Funds by Fund Earnings, 2008–2009

Source: Bloomberg, 2009. *www.bloomberg.com*

| Fund, Manager Name(s) | Fund Company | 2009 Return | 2008 Return |
|---|---|---|---|
| Appaloosa Investment I, David Tepper | Appaloosa Mgmt. | 117.3% | −26.7% |
| Redwood Capital Master, Jonathan Kolatch | Redwood Captial Mgmt. | 69.1 | −33.0 |
| Glenview Institutional Partners, Larry Robbins | Glenview Capital Mgmt. | 67.1 | −49.0 |
| PARS IV, Changhong Zhu | Pacific Investment Mgmt. | 61.0 | −17.0 |
| Tennenbaum Opportunities V, TCP Investment Committee | Tennenbaum Capital Partners | 58.5 | −51.2 |
| Kensington Global Strategies, Kenneth Griffin | Citadel Investment Group | 57.0 | −55.0 |
| BlueGold Global, Pierre Andurand, Dennis Crema | BlueGold Capital Mgmt. | 54.6 | 209.4 |
| Waterstone Market Neutral Master, Shawn Bergerson | Waterstone Capital Mgmt. | 50.3 | 12.0 |
| Canyon Value Realization, Mitchell Julis, Joshua Friedman | Canyon Partners | 49.6 | −29.0 |
| Discovery Global Opportunity, Robert Citrone | Discovery Capital Mgmt. | 47.9 | −31.0 |

of traditional financial investments like stocks and bonds.[8] Many hedge funds posted strong returns during the early 2000s even as stock returns were plummeting. A few hedge funds even performed well during the financial crisis. Table 5–11 lists the top hedge fund managers and their hedge fund company by 2009 earnings. The average hedge fund lost 15.7 percent in 2008, the worst performance on record. Nearly three-quarters of all hedge funds experienced losses. Nevertheless, many funds outperformed many of the underlying markets such as the S&P 500 index. Note that two of the hedge funds listed in Table 5–11 earned positive returns for 2008 as well as 2009 and one, BlueGold Global Fund, earned 209.4 percent in 2008, a year where the S&P 500 index earned a return of −37.0 percent. Indeed, only three of the listed hedge funds performed worse during the beginning of the financial crisis than the S&P 500 index. Performance improved significantly in 2009 with the average fund earning more than 20 percent for the year, the highest level since 2003 and the second best return in 10 years. However, the 2009 return on the S&P 500 index was 26.46 percent. Note that while mutual fund performance is generally measured by returns relative to some benchmark (and therefore can perform "well" even by losing 10 percent if the benchmark loses 10.5 percent), performance of hedge funds is measured by the growth in total assets managed. Assets under management in the hedge fund industry fell by nearly 30 percent (to $1.5 trillion) in 2008. The decline was the largest on record and was attributed to a combination of negative performance, a surge in redemptions, and liquidations of funds.

Hedge fund performance continued to lag into the 2010s. In 2010, the average hedge fund earned 10.3 percent. In 2011 the average was 5.0 percent, and in 2012

---

[8] However, data deficiencies in the reporting and collection of hedge fund returns somewhat reduce confidence in all measures of hedge fund performance. Further, the inability to explain returns of individual hedge funds with standard multifactor risk models leaves open the possibility that it is not possible to properly measure the risk associated with at least some hedge fund strategies. If so, risk-adjusted returns earned by hedge funds may be overstated.

**TABLE 5–12**   Largest Hedge Funds by Fund Earnings, 2011–2012

Source: Bloomberg, 2013, *www.bloomberg.com*

| Fund, Manager Name(s) | Fund Company | 2012 Return* | 2011 Return |
|---|---|---|---|
| Metacapital Mortgage Opportunities, Deepak Narula | Metacapital Management | 37.8% | 23.6% |
| Pine River Fixed Income, Steve Kuhn | Pine River Capital Management | 32.9 | 4.8 |
| CQS Directional Opportunities, Michael Hintze | CQS | 28.9 | −10.4 |
| Pine River Liquid Mortgage, Steve Kuhn/Jiayi Chen | Pine River Capital Management | 28.0 | 7.2 |
| Omega Overseas Partners A, Leon Cooperman | Omega Advisors | 24.4 | −1.4 |
| Odey Europen, Crispin Odey | Odey Asset Management | 24.1 | −20.3 |
| Marathon Securitized Credit, Bruce Richards/ Louis Hanover | Marathon Asset Management | 24.0 | −4.2 |
| Palomino, David Tepper | Appaloosa Management | 24.0 | −3.5 |
| BTG Pactual GEMM, Team managed | BTG Pactual Global Asset Management | 23.1 | 3.4 |
| Third Point Ultra, Daniel Loeb | Third Point | 22.1 | −2.3 |

* Through three quarters.

the average was 6.2 percent. The returns on the S&P 500 Index for these three years were 15.1 percent, 2.0 percent, and 14.5 percent, respectively. As discussed later, hedge funds generally charge fees of 2 percent of the money they manage (compared to 1 percent for mutual funds) whether the fund makes money or not. Further, managers may take up to 20 percent of any profit the hedge fund earns. With performance as seen in the last four years, the question for the industry is whether investors will start to lose faith in hedge funds and start liquidating their sizable investments in these funds. In 2012, the industry saw net outflows of funds invested of $31 billion. In August 2012, Reuters reported that one hedge fund administrator's redemption indicator hit its second-highest level of the year. Also, major investors in John Paulson's prominent but struggling hedge funds (e.g., Citigroup's private bank) had requested to redeem hundreds of millions of dollars. Man Group, the world's biggest publicly traded hedge fund, has seen its stock drop by 40 percent through mid-2012 after its assets under management fell by almost a third. Table 5–12 lists the top hedge fund managers and their hedge fund company for 2012.

Despite their name, hedge funds do not always "hedge" their investments to protect the fund and its investors against market price declines and other risks. For example, while bond prices generally move in the same direction, the risk in hedge funds is that bond prices may unexpectedly move faster in some markets than others. For example, in 1997 and 1998 computer models used by LTCM detected a price discrepancy between U.S. Treasury markets and other bonds (including high yield corporate bonds, mortgaged-backed securities, and European government bonds). LTCM consequently shorted U.S. Treasury securities (betting their prices would fall) and took long positions in other types of bonds (betting their prices would rise). However, unexpectedly, in 1998 large drops in many foreign stock markets caused money to pour into the U.S. Treasury markets, driving Treasury security prices up and yields down. This drop in U.S. Treasury yields drove rates on mortgages down, which pushed down the prices of many mortgage-backed securities. Further, the flight to U.S. Treasury security markets meant a drop in funds flowing into European bond markets and high-yield corporate bond markets. With all of their positions going wrong, LTCM experienced huge losses.[9]

Similarly, the failures of two of Bear Stearns hedge funds (Bear Stearns High-Grade Structured Credit Fund and Bear Stearns High-Grade Structured Credit Enhanced Leveraged Fund) were the result of managers' failure to accurately predict how the subprime bond market would behave under extreme circumstances. The market moved against them, and their investors lost $1.6 billion when the funds, heavily invested in mortgage securities, collapsed in the summer of 2007. The failures were the first sign of the upcoming financial crisis that would eventually cripple financial markets and the overall economy.

The strategy employed by the Bear Stearns funds was quite simple. Specifically, the funds purchased collateralized debt obligations (CDOs) that paid an interest rate over and above the cost of borrowing. Thus, every incremental unit of leverage added to the hedge funds' total expected return. To capitalize on this, fund managers used as much leverage as they could raise. Because the use of leverage increased the portfolio's exposure, fund managers purchased insurance on movements in credit markets. The insurance instruments, called credit default swaps (CDSs), were designed to cover losses during times when credit concerns cause the bonds to fall in value, effectively hedging away some of the risk. In instances when credit markets (or the underling bonds' prices) remained relatively stable, or even when they behaved in line with historically based expectations, this strategy generated consistent, positive returns with very little deviation.

Unfortunately, as the problems with subprime debt began to unravel, the subprime mortgage-backed securities market behaved well outside of what the portfolio managers expected. This started a chain of events that imploded the funds. The subprime mortgage market began to see substantial increases in delinquencies from homeowners, which caused sharp decreases in the market values of these types of bonds. Since the Bear Stearns hedge fund managers failed to expect these sorts of extreme price movements, they failed to purchase sufficient credit insurance to protect against these losses. Because they had leveraged their positions substantially, the funds began to experience large losses. The large losses made the creditors who provided the debt financing uneasy. The lenders required Bear Stearns to provide additional cash on their loans because the collateral (subprime bonds) was rapidly falling in value. However, the funds had no cash holdings. Thus, fund managers needed to sell bonds in order to generate cash. Quickly, it became public knowledge that Bear Stearns was in trouble, and competing funds moved to drive the prices of subprime bonds lower to force Bear Stearns' into an asset fire-sale. As prices on bonds fell, the fund experienced losses, which caused it to sell more bonds, which lowered the prices of the bonds, which caused them to sell more bonds. It did not take long before the funds had experienced a complete loss of capital.

### Fees on Hedge Funds

Hedge fund managers generally charge two type of fees: management fees and performance fees. As with mutual funds, the management fee is computed as a

---

[9] A major reason for LTCM's large loss was that it was so highly leveraged compared to other funds. LTCM was two to four times more leveraged than the typical fund.

percentage of the total assets under management and typically runs between 1.5 and 2.0 percent. Performance fees are unique to hedge funds. Performance fees give the fund manager a share of any positive returns on a hedge fund. The average performance fee on hedge funds is approximately 20 percent but varies widely. For example, Steven Cohen's SAC Capital Partners charges a performance fee of 50 percent. Performance fees are paid to the hedge fund manager before returns are paid to the fund investors. Hedge funds often specify a *hurdle rate,* which is a minimum annualized performance benchmark that must be realized before a performance fee can be assessed. Further, a *high-water mark* is usually used for hedge funds in which the manager does not receive a performance fee unless the value of the fund exceeds the highest net asset value it has previously achieved. High-water marks are used to link the fund manager's incentives more closely to those of the fund investors and to reduce the manager's incentive to increase the risk of trades.

## Offshore Hedge Funds

Hedge funds that are organized in the United States are designated as domestic hedge funds. These funds require investors to pay income taxes on all earnings from the hedge fund. Funds located outside the United States and structured under foreign laws are designated as offshore hedge funds. Many offshore financial centers encourage hedge funds to locate in their countries. The major centers include the Cayman Islands, Bermuda, Dublin, and Luxembourg. The Cayman Islands is estimated to be the location of approximately 75 percent of all hedge funds. Offshore hedge funds are regulated in that they must obey the rules of the host country. However, the rules in most of these countries are not generally burdensome and provide anonymity to fund investors. Further, offshore hedge funds are not subject to U.S. income taxes on distributions of profit or to U.S. estate taxes on fund shares.

When compared to domestic hedge funds, offshore hedge funds have been found to trade more intensely, due to the low or zero capital gains tax for offshore funds. Further, offshore hedge funds tend to engage less often in positive feedback trading (rushing to buy when the market is booming and rushing to sell when the market is declining) than domestic hedge funds. Finally, offshore hedge funds have been found to herd (mimic each other's behavior when trading while ignoring information about the fundamentals of valuation) less than domestic hedge funds. Many hedge fund managers maintain both domestic and offshore hedge funds. Given the needs of their client investors, hedge fund managers want to have both types of funds to attract all types of investors.

## Regulation of Hedge Funds

While mutual funds are very highly regulated, hedge funds have generally been unregulated. Mutual funds in the United States are required to be registered with the SEC. Although hedge funds fall within the same statutory category as mutual funds, they operate under two exemptions from registration requirements as set forth in the Investment Company Act of 1940. First, funds are exempt if they have less than 100 investors. Second, funds are exempt if the investors are "accredited." To comply with SEC exemptions, hedge funds are also sold only via private placements. Thus, hedge funds may not be offered or advertised to the general investing public.

In 2010, the Wall Street Reform and Consumer Protection Act required hedge fund advisors with private pools of capital exceeding $100 million in assets to register with the SEC as investment advisors and become subject to all rules which apply to registered advisors by July 2011. Thus, previous exemptions from registration provided under the Investment Company Act of 1940 no longer apply to most hedge fund advisors. Under the act, hedge fund managers who have less than $100 million in assets under management will be overseen by the state where the manager is domiciled and become subject to state regulation. This registration subjects the hedge funds to periodic inspections by SEC examiners. Further, hedge funds are required to report information to the SEC about their trades and portfolios that is "necessary for the purpose of assessing systemic risk posed by a private fund." The data is kept confidential, and can be shared only with the Financial Stability Oversight Council that the legislation set up to monitor potential shocks to the economic system. Finally, should the government determine a hedge fund has grown too large or risky, the hedge fund is placed under the supervision of the Federal Reserve. Thus, while the act requires large hedge funds to be registered with the SEC, the regulations imposed on hedge funds continue to be much less onerous than those imposed on mutual funds.

Nevertheless, hedge funds are prohibited from abusive trading practices and a number got mixed up in the scandals plaguing the mutual fund industry in the 2000s. For example, Canary Capital Partners and its managers agreed to pay $30 million from its illicit profits as well as a $10 million penalty to the SEC to settle allegations that it engaged in illegal trading practices with mutual fund companies, including making deals after the market had closed and promising to make substantial investments in various funds managed by the mutual funds. In March 2007, the SEC charged 14 defendants in a scheme involving insiders at UBS Securities, Morgan Stanley, and several hedge funds and hedge fund managers. The SEC claimed that the defendants made $15 million in illicit profits through thousands of illegal trades, using inside information misappropriated from UBS. Just two months prior to this announcement, regulators announced an investigation of UBS and other banks that leased office space to hedge fund traders. Regulators stated a concern about the relationship between the banks and their hedge fund "hotel guests," looking at whether the banks might be using the real estate relationships as a way to entice hedge funds to do business with them, possibly at the expense of the funds' investors. Specifically, there was an investigation into whether hedge funds located in bank buildings were paying higher than normal trading fees to banks to compensate them for the office space and failing to disclose this expense to investors.

More recently, the late 2000s saw two highly publicized scandals associated with hedge funds. The first was that of Bernard L. Madoff Investment Securities. The Madoff investment scandal occurred after the discovery that the asset management business of former NASDAQ chairman Bernard Madoff was actually a giant "Ponzi" scheme. According to a federal criminal complaint, client statements showing $65 billion in stock holdings were fictitious, and there was no indication that any stocks were purchased since the mid-1990s. Alerted by his sons, federal authorities arrested Madoff on December 11, 2008. The firm was placed in liquidation and a trustee was appointed on December 15, 2008, after Bernard Madoff confessed to having stolen customer property over a period of many years. On March 12, 2009, Madoff pled guilty to 11 felonies and admitted to operating what has been called the largest investor fraud ever committed by an individual. On June 29, 2009, he was sentenced to 150 years in prison with restitution of $170 billion. Although Madoff did not operate as a hedge fund, he operated through various funds of hedge funds.

Second is the case of Galleon Group LLC, one of the largest hedge fund management firms in the world before announcing its closure in October 2009. The firm was at the center of a 2009 insider trading scandal that resulted in investors pulling capital from the firm rapidly. Twenty people, including Galleon Group LLC co-founder Raj Rajaratnam, were criminally charged in what federal authorities called the biggest prosecution of alleged hedge fund insider trading in the United States. Prosecutors said they had evidence from wiretaps, trading records, and cooperating witnesses to prove widespread trafficking in illegal insider information, including an insider trading operation that paid sources for nonpublic information, that netted the hedge fund more than $20 million.

| | |
|---|---|
| **Concept Questions** | 1. What is the difference between a mutual fund and a hedge fund? <br> 2. What are the performance fees charged by hedge funds? <br> 3. How is the regulatory status of hedge funds changing? |

## Summary

This chapter provided an overview of the mutual fund and hedge fund industries. Mutual funds and hedge funds pool funds from individuals and corporations and invest in diversified asset portfolios. Given the tremendous growth in the market values of financial assets—such as equities—from 1992 through 2007 and the cost-effective way in which these funds allow investors to participate in these markets, mutual funds and hedge funds have grown tremendously in size, number of funds, and number of shareholders.

## Questions and Problems

1. What is a mutual fund? In what sense is it a financial institution?
2. What are money market mutual funds? In what assets do these funds typically invest? What factors have caused the strong growth in this type of fund since the late 1970s?
3. What are long-term mutual funds? In what assets do these funds usually invest? What factors caused the strong growth in this type of fund from 1992 through 2007, the slowdown in growth in 2007, 2008, and the return to growth after 2008?
4. Using the data in Table 5–2, discuss the growth and ownership holdings over the last 32 years of long-term funds versus short-term funds.
5. Why did the proportion of equities in long-term funds increase from 38.3 percent in 1990 to more than 70 percent by 2000 and then decrease to 54 percent in 2012? How might an investor's preference for a mutual funds objective change over time?
6. How does the risk of short-term funds differ from the risk of long-term funds?
7. What are the economic reasons for the existence of mutual funds; that is, what benefits do mutual funds provide for investors? Why do individuals rather than corporations hold most mutual funds shares?
8. What are the principal demographics of household owners who own mutual funds? What are the primary reasons why household owners invest in mutual funds?
9. What change in regulatory guidelines occurred in 2009 that had the primary purpose of giving investors a better understanding of the risks and objectives of a fund?

10. What are the three possible components reflected in the return an investor receives from a mutual fund?

11. How is the net asset value (NAV) of a mutual fund determined? What is meant by the term *marked-to-market daily?*

12. Suppose today a mutual fund contains 2,000 shares of J.P. Morgan Chase, currently trading at $46.75; 1,000 shares of Walmart, currently trading at $70.10; and 2,500 shares of Pfizer, currently trading at $27.50. The mutual fund has no liabilities and 10,000 shares outstanding held by investors.
    a. What is the NAV of the fund?
    b. Calculate the change in the NAV of the fund if tomorrow J.P. Morgan's shares increase to $50, Walmart's shares increase to $73, and Pfizer's shares increase to $30.
    c. Suppose that today 1,000 additional investors buy one share each of the mutual fund at the NAV of $23.235. This means that the fund manager has $23,235 additional funds to invest. The fund manager decides to use these additional funds to buy additional shares in J.P. Morgan Chase. Calculate tomorrow's NAV given the same rise in share values as assumed in part (b).

13. A mutual fund owns 300 shares of General Electric, currently trading at $22, and 400 shares of Microsoft Inc., currently trading at $28. The fund has 1,000 shares outstanding.
    a. What is the net asset value (NAV) of the fund?
    b. If investors expect the price of General Electric shares to increase to $26 and the price of Microsoft shares to decrease to $20 by the end of the year, what is the expected NAV at the end of the year?
    c. Assume that the expected price of the General Electric shares is realized at $26. What is the maximum price decrease that can occur to the Microsoft shares to realize an end-of-year NAV equal to the NAV estimated in part (a)?

14. What is the difference between open-end and closed-end mutual funds? Which type of fund tends to be more specialized in asset selection? How does a closed-end fund provide another source of return from which an investor may either gain or lose?

15. Open-end fund A owns 165 shares of AT&T valued at $35 each and 50 shares of Toro valued at $45 each. Closed-end fund B owns 75 shares of AT&T and 120 shares of Toro. Each fund has 1,000 shares of stock outstanding.
    a. What are the NAVs of both funds using these prices?
    b. Assume that in one month the price of AT&T stock has increased to $36.25 and the price of Toro stock has decreased to $43.375. How do these changes impact the NAV of both funds? If the funds were purchased at the NAV prices in part (a) and sold at month end, what would be the realized returns on the investments?
    c. Assume that another 155 shares of AT&T are added to fund A. The funds needed to buy the new shares are obtained by selling 676 more shares in fund A. What is the effect on fund A's NAV if the stock prices remain unchanged from the original prices?

16. What is the difference between a load fund and a no-load fund? Is the argument that load funds are more closely managed and therefore have higher returns supported by the evidence presented in Table 5–6?

17. What is a 12b–1 fee? Suppose you have a choice between a load fund with no annual 12b–1 fee and a no-load fund with an annual 12b–1 fee of 25 basis points. How would the length of your expected investment horizon, or holding period, influence your choice between these two funds?

18. Suppose an individual invests $10,000 in a load mutual fund for two years. The load fee entails an up-front commission charge of 4 percent of the amount invested and is deducted from the original funds invested. In addition, annual fund operating expenses (or 12b–1 fees) are 0.85 percent. The annual fees are charged on the average net asset value invested in the fund and are recorded at the end of each year. Investments in the fund return 5 percent each year paid on the last day of the year. If the investor reinvests the annual returns paid on the investment, calculate the annual return on the mutual fund over the two-year investment period.

19. Who are the primary regulators of the mutual fund industry? How do their regulatory goals differ from those of other types of financial institutions?

20. What is a hedge fund and how is it different from a mutual fund?

21. What are the different categories of hedge funds?

22. What types of fees do hedge funds charge?

23. What is the difference between domestic hedge funds and offshore hedge funds? Describe the advantages of offshore hedge funds over domestic hedge funds.

## Web Questions

24. Go to the Fidelity Investments website and look up the annual 1-, 5-, and 10-year returns on Fidelity Select Biotechnology Fund using the following steps. The website is **www.fidelity.com**. Click on "Investment Products." Click on "Mutual Funds." Click on "Fidelity Funds." Click on "Browse all Fidelity Funds." Click on "S." Click on "Select Biotechnology Portfolio." This will bring the file onto your computer that contains the relevant data.

25. Go to the Investment Company Institute website and look up the most recent data on the asset values and number of short-term and long-term mutual funds using the following steps. The website is **www.ici.org**. Click on "Publications." Click on "Fact Books." Click on the most recent year for "XXXX Investment Company Fact Book." Go to "Data Tables." This section contains the relevant data. The data on asset values and number of mutual funds are among the first few pages. How have these values increased since those for 2012 reported in Table 5–1?

www.mhhe.com/saunders8e

# Chapter **Six**

# Financial Services: Insurance

## INTRODUCTION

Insurance services offered by FIs protect individuals and corporations (policyholders) from adverse events. By accepting premiums, FIs that offer insurance services promise policyholders compensation if certain specified events occur. These policies represent financial liabilities to the insurance company. With the premiums collected, insurance companies invest in financial securities such as corporate bonds and stocks. Insurance services are classified into two major groups: life and property–casualty. Life insurance provides protection against the possibility of untimely death, illnesses, and retirement. Property–casualty insurance protects against personal injury and liability such as accidents, theft, and fire. Many FIs (e.g., MetLife and Allstate) offer both life and property–casualty services. Further, many FIs that offer insurance services also sell a variety of investment products in a similar fashion to other financial service firms, such as mutual funds (Chapter 5) and banking services (Chapter 2).

www.metlife.com

www.allstate.com

The financial crisis showed just how much risk insurance companies can present to FIs and the global financial system. Specifically, as the subprime mortgage market began to fail in the summer of 2008, subprime mortgage pools, and the securities written on them, ended up falling precipitously in value as foreclosures and defaults rose on the underlying mortgage pools. Many credit default swaps (CDSs) were written on these subprime mortgage securities. CDS contracts offer credit protection (insurance) against default on the mortgage securities. As mortgage security losses started to rise, buyers of the CDS contracts wanted to be paid for these losses. AIG was a major writer of these CDS securities. When mortgage-backed securities started to fall in value, AIG had to make good on billions of dollars of credit default swaps. Soon it became clear that AIG was not going to be able to cover its credit default swap market losses. The result was a significant increase in the risk exposure of banks, investment banks, and insurance companies that had purchased AIG CDS insurance contracts. Indeed, the reason the federal government stepped in and bailed out AIG was that the insurer was a dominant player in the CDS market. Had AIG defaulted, every FI that had bought a CDS contract from the company would have suffered substantial losses.

www.aig.com

In this chapter we describe the main features of life insurance and property–casualty insurance companies, concentrating on (1) the size, structure, and composition of the industry in which they operate, (2) balance sheets and recent trends, and (3) regulations for each. We also look at global competition and trends in this industry.

# LIFE INSURANCE

Life insurance allows individuals and their beneficiaries to protect against losses in income through premature death or retirement. By pooling risks, life insurance transfers income-related uncertainties from the insured individual to a group.

## Size, Structure, and Composition of the Industry

In the 2010s, the United States had approximately 1,000 life insurance companies compared with more than 2,300 in 1988. The aggregate assets of life insurance companies were $5.6 trillion in 2012, compared with $1.1 trillion in 1988. The four largest life insurance companies, in terms of total assets (listed in Table 6–1) wrote 27 percent of the industry's $676.4 billion new life insurance premium business in 2011. Interestingly, many of these insurance policies were sold through commercial banks. For example, in 2012 commercial banks sold 12.8 percent of all fixed annuity insurance contracts and 12.3 percent of all variable rate insurance contracts.

Although not to the extent seen in the banking industry, the life insurance industry has seen some major mergers in recent years (e.g., SunAmerica and AIG, Prudential and Cigna, and MetLife and American Life Insurance) as competition within the industry and from other FIs has increased. In addition, many of the largest insurance companies, such as Metropolitan and Prudential, have converted to stockholder-controlled companies. In so doing, they gain access to the equity markets in order to realize additional capital for future business expansions and to compete with the rapidly consolidating banking industry. Since a mutual company is owned by its policyholders, the existing capital and reserves (equal to accumulated past profits) have to be distributed to the insurer's policyholders. Table 6–1 lists the form of ownership for the top 10 life insurers in the United States, while Figure 6–1 illustrates the difference between a mutual insurer and a stock insurance company.

While life insurance may be the core activity area, modern life insurance companies also sell annuity contracts, manage pension plans, and provide accident and health insurance (Figure 6–2 shows the distribution of premiums written for the various lines of insurance in 2011). We discuss these different activity lines in the following sections.

**TABLE 6–1**
**Biggest Life Insurers**

Sources: *Best's Review,* July 2012; and authors' research. *www.ambest.com*

| Rank | Insurance Company | Form of Ownership | Assets (billions) |
|------|-------------------|-------------------|-------------------|
| 1 | Metropolitan Life | Stock | $612.8 |
| 2 | Prudential of America | Stock | 424.1 |
| 3 | Manulife Financial | Stock | 243.3 |
| 4 | SunAmerica Financial Group | Stock | 233.9 |
| 5 | Teachers Insurance and Annuity | Stock | 229.8 |
| 6 | New York Life | Mutual | 228.3 |
| 7 | Hartford Life | Stock | 218.5 |
| 8 | Northwestern Mutual | Mutual | 189.7 |
| 9 | ING Group | Stock | 181.7 |
| 10 | Aegon USA Inc. | Stock | 180.2 |

**FIGURE 6–1**
Mutual versus
Stock Insurance
Companies

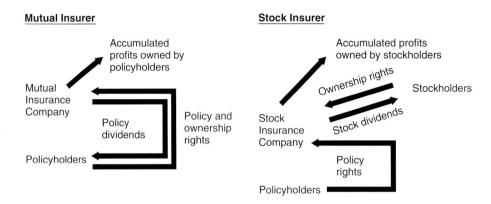

One problem that naturally faces life insurance companies (as well as property–casualty insurers) is the so-called adverse selection problem. Adverse selection is a problem in that customers who apply for insurance policies are more likely to be those most in need of insurance (i.e., someone with chronic health problems is more likely to purchase a life insurance policy than someone in perfect health). Thus, in calculating the probability of having to pay out on an insurance contract and, in turn, determining the insurance premium to charge, insurance companies' use of health (and other) statistics representing the overall population may not be appropriate (since the insurance company's pool of customers is more prone to health problems than the overall population). Insurance companies deal with the adverse selection problem by establishing different pools of the population based on health and related characteristics (such as income). By altering the pool used to determine the probability of losses to a particular customer's health characteristics, the insurance company can more accurately determine the probability of having to pay out on a policy and can adjust the insurance premium accordingly.

As the various types of insurance policies and services offered are described below, notice that some policies (such as universal life policies and annuities) provide not only insurance features but also savings components. For example, universal life policy payouts are a function of the interest earned on the investment of the policyholder's premiums.

### Types of Life Insurance
The four basic classes or lines of life insurance are distinguished by the manner in which they are sold or marketed to purchasers. These classes are (1) ordinary life, (2) group life, (3) industrial life, and (4) credit life. Among the life insurance

**FIGURE 6–2**
Distribution of
Life Insurance
Premiums Written

Source: *Best's Review,*
September 2012.
*www.ambest.com*

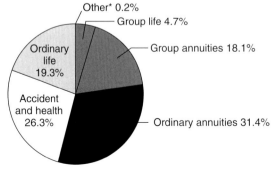

*Includes credit life and industrial life

policies in force in the United States, ordinary life accounted for approximately 79.9 percent, group life for 19.2 percent, and industrial life and credit life together for less than 1 percent of the $163.8 billion in contracts written in 2011.

*Ordinary Life*   Ordinary life insurance involves policies marketed on an individual basis, usually in units of $1,000, on which policyholders make periodic premium payments. Despite the enormous variety of contractual forms, there are essentially five basic contractual types. The first three are traditional forms of ordinary life insurance, and the last two are newer contracts that originated in the 1970s and 1980s as a result of increased competition for savings from other segments of the financial services industry. The three traditional contractual forms are term life, whole life, and endowment life. The two newer forms are variable life and universal life. The key features of each of these contractual forms are as follows:

- *Term life.* A term life policy is the closest to pure life insurance, with no savings element attached. Essentially, the individual receives a payout contingent on death during the coverage period. The term of coverage can vary from as little as 1 year to 40 years or more.

- *Whole life.* A whole life policy protects the individual over an entire lifetime. In return for periodic or level premiums, the individual's beneficiaries receive the face value of the life insurance contract on death. Thus, there is certainty that if the policyholder continues to make premium payments, the insurance company will make a payment—unlike term insurance. As a result, whole life has a savings element as well as a pure insurance element.

- *Endowment life.* An endowment life policy combines a pure (term) insurance element with a savings element. It guarantees a payout to the beneficiaries of the policy if death occurs during some endowment period (e.g., prior to reaching retirement age). An insured person who lives to the endowment date receives the face amount of the policy.

- *Variable life.* Unlike traditional policies that promise to pay the insured the fixed or face amount of a policy if a contingency arises, variable life insurance invests fixed premium payments in mutual funds of stocks, bonds, and money market instruments. Usually, policyholders can choose mutual fund investments to reflect their risk preferences. Thus, variable life provides an alternative way to build savings compared with the more traditional policies such as whole life because the value of the policy increases or decreases with the asset returns of the mutual fund in which the premiums are invested.

- *Universal life and variable universal life.* Universal life allows both the premium amounts and the maturity of the life contract to be changed by the insured, unlike traditional policies that maintain premiums at a given level over a fixed contract period. In addition, for some contracts, insurers invest premiums in money, equity, or bond mutual funds—as in variable life insurance—so that the savings or investment component of the contract reflects market returns. In this case, the policy is called variable universal life.

*Group Life Insurance*   Group life insurance covers a large number of insured persons under a single policy. Usually issued to corporate employers, these policies may be either contributory (where both the employer and employee cover a share of the employee's cost of the insurance) or noncontributory (where the employee does not contribute to the cost of the insurance) for the employees. Cost economies represent the principal advantage of group life over ordinary life policies.

Cost economies result from mass administration of plans, lower costs for evaluating individuals through medical screening and other rating systems, and reduced selling and commission costs.

*Industrial Life* Industrial life insurance currently represents a very small area of coverage. Industrial life usually involves weekly payments directly collected by representatives of the companies. To a large extent, the growth of group life insurance has led to the demise of industrial life as a major activity class.

*Credit Life* Credit life insurance is sold to protect lenders against a borrower's death prior to the repayment of a debt contract such as a mortgage or car loan. Usually, the face amount of the insurance policy reflects the outstanding principal and interest on the loan.

### Other Life Insurer Activities

Three other major activities of life insurance companies involve the sale of annuities, private pension plans, and accident and health insurance.

*Annuities* Annuities represent the reverse of life insurance activities. Whereas life insurance involves different contractual methods of *building up* a fund, annuities involve different methods of *liquidating* a fund, such as paying out a fund's proceeds. As with life insurance contracts, many different types of annuity contracts have been developed. Specifically, they can be sold to an individual or a group and on a fixed or a variable basis by being linked to the return on some underlying investment portfolio. Individuals can purchase annuities with a single payment or with payments spread over a number of years. The annuity builds up a fund whose returns are tax deferred. That is, they are not subject to capital gains taxes on their investments. Payments may be structured to start immediately, or they can be deferred (at which time taxes are paid based on the income tax rate of the annuity receiver). These payments may cease on death or continue to be paid to beneficiaries for a number of years after death.

While the traditional life insurance products described remain an important part of life insurance firm business, these lines (whether measured by premium income or by assets) are no longer the primary business of many companies in the life insurance industry. Rather, the major area of business for life insurance companies has shifted to annuities. Annuity sales in 2011 topped $334.8 billion ($212.4 billion of which were ordinary annuities), compared with $26 billion in 1996. Further, this is more than twice the $163.8 billion in sales for the traditional life insurance lines.

*Private Pension Plans* Insurance companies offer many alternative pension plans to private employers in an effort to attract this business from other financial service companies, such as commercial banks and securities firms. Some of their innovative pension plans are based on guaranteed investment contracts (GICs). This means the insurer guarantees not only the rate of interest credited to a pension plan over a given period—for example, five years—but also the annuity rates on beneficiaries' contracts. Other plans include immediate participation and separate account plans that follow more aggressive investment strategies than traditional life insurance, such as investing premiums in special-purpose equity mutual funds. In 2012, life insurance companies were managing more than $2.6 trillion in pension plan assets, equal to approximately 40 percent of all private pension plans.

*Accident and Health Insurance* While life insurance protects against mortality risk, accident and health insurance protect against morbidity, or ill health, risk. More than $177.8 billion in premiums were written by life and health companies in the accident–health area in 2011. The major activity line is group insurance, providing health insurance coverage to corporate employees. Life insurance companies write more than 50 percent of all health insurance premiums.

## Balance Sheet and Recent Trends

### Assets

Because of the long-term nature of their liabilities (as a result of the long-term nature of life insurance policyholders' claims) and the need to generate competitive returns on the savings elements of life insurance products, life insurance companies concentrate their asset investments at the longer end of the maturity spectrum (e.g., bonds, equities, and government securities). Look at Table 6–2, where we show the distribution of life insurance companies' assets.

As you can see, in 2012, 11.7 percent of assets were invested in government securities, 68.9 percent in corporate bonds and stocks, and 6.2 percent in mortgages, with other loans—including **policy loans** (loans made to policyholders using their policies as collateral)—making up the balance. While commercial banks are the major issuers of new mortgages (sometimes keeping the mortgages on their books and sometimes selling them to secondary market investors), insurance companies hold mortgages as investment securities. That is, they purchase many mortgages in the secondary markets (see Chapters 25 and 26). The major trends have been a long-term increase in the proportion of bonds and equities[1] and a decline in the

**policy loans**
Loans made by an insurance company to its policyholders using their policies as collateral.

**TABLE 6–2**   Distribution of Assets of U.S. Life Insurance Companies

Sources: American Council of Life Insurance, *Life Insurance Fact Book*, 1994; *Best's Review*, October 1996; and *Federal Reserve Bulletin*, various issues. *www.federalreserve.gov*

| Year | Total Assets (billions) | Government Securities | Corporate Securities | | Mortgages | Policy Loans | Miscellaneous U.S. Assets |
|---|---|---|---|---|---|---|---|
| | | | Bonds | Stocks | | | |
| 1917 | $    5.9 | 9.6% | 33.2% | 1.4% | 34.0% | 13.6% | 5.2% |
| 1920 | 7.3 | 18.4 | 26.7 | 1.0 | 33.4 | 11.7 | 6.5 |
| 1930 | 18.9 | 8.0 | 26.0 | 2.8 | 40.2 | 14.9 | 5.2 |
| 1940 | 30.8 | 27.5 | 28.1 | 2.0 | 19.4 | 10.0 | 6.3 |
| 1950 | 64.0 | 25.2 | 36.3 | 3.3 | 25.1 | 3.8 | 4.1 |
| 1960 | 119.6 | 9.9 | 39.1 | 4.2 | 34.9 | 4.4 | 4.4 |
| 1970 | 207.3 | 5.3 | 35.3 | 7.4 | 35.9 | 7.8 | 5.3 |
| 1980 | 479.2 | 6.9 | 37.5 | 9.9 | 27.4 | 8.6 | 6.6 |
| 1990 | 1,408.2 | 15.0 | 41.4 | 9.1 | 19.2 | 4.4 | 7.8 |
| 1995 | 2,131.9 | 18.6 | 41.4 | 17.4 | 9.9 | 4.5 | 6.3 |
| 2000 | 3,133.9 | 9.3 | 39.1 | 31.5 | 7.5 | 3.2 | 9.4 |
| 2005 | 4,350.7 | 10.6 | 44.0 | 29.2 | 6.6 | 2.5 | 7.1 |
| 2007 | 4,949.7 | 10.0 | 37.6 | 33.4 | 6.6 | 2.9 | 9.5 |
| 2008 | 4,515.5 | 11.5 | 40.3 | 24.9 | 7.6 | 3.6 | 12.1 |
| 2009 | 4,749.4 | 11.5 | 40.2 | 27.2 | 7.0 | 3.5 | 10.6 |
| 2010 | 5,176.3 | 12.5 | 39.2 | 30.1 | 6.1 | 2.7 | 9.4 |
| 2012 | 5,561.6 | 11.7 | 38.6 | 30.3 | 6.2 | 2.6 | 10.6 |

Note: Beginning with 1962, these data include the assets of separate accounts.

[1] The bull market of the 1980s and 1990s probably constitutes a major reason for the large percentage of assets invested in equities. Conversely, the large drop in equity prices during the financial crisis explains the reduction in the percentage of stocks held by insurance companies in the late 2000s.

**TABLE 6–3**
Life Insurance Industry Balance Sheet, 2012 (in billions of dollars)

Source: Reprinted with permission from *Best's Aggregates & Averages*, Life-Health, 2012, p. 2. *www.ambest.com*

| Assets | | Percent of Total Assets |
|---|---|---|
| Bonds | $2,611.5 | 47.6% |
| Preferred stock | 8.5 | 0.2 |
| Common stock | 73.5 | 1.3 |
| Mortgage loans | 332.9 | 6.1 |
| Real estate | 20.9 | 0.4 |
| Contract loans | 128.8 | 2.3 |
| Cash and short-term investments | 99.0 | 1.8 |
| Other invested assets | 184.2 | 3.4 |
| Premiums due | 24.8 | 0.5 |
| Accrued investment income | 35.1 | 0.6 |
| Separate account assets | 1,849.4 | 33.7 |
| Other assets | 114.3 | 2.1 |
| Total assets | $5,482.9 | 100.0% |
| **Liabilities and Capital/Surplus** | | |
| Net policy reserves | $2,609.3 | 47.6% |
| Deposit-type contracts | 275.3 | 5.0 |
| Policy claims | 43.6 | 0.8 |
| Other liabilities | 390.2 | 7.1 |
| Separate account business | 1,854.4 | 33.7 |
| Total capital and surplus | 319.1 | 5.8 |
| Total liabilities and capital/surplus | $5,482.9 | 100.0% |

proportion of mortgages in the balance sheet. Thus, insurance company managers must be able to measure and manage the credit risk, interest rate risk, and other risks associated with these securities.

### Liabilities

**policy reserves**
A liability item for insurers that reflects their expected payment commitment on existing policy contracts.

**surrender value of a policy**
The cash value of a policy received from the insurer if a policyholder surrenders the policy before maturity. The cash surrender value is normally only a portion of the contract's face value.

The aggregate balance sheet for the life insurance industry at the beginning of 2012 is shown in Table 6–3. Looking at the liability side of the balance sheet, we see that $2.609 trillion, or 47.6 percent, of total liabilities and capital are net **policy reserves** (the expected payment commitment on existing policy contracts). These reserves are based on actuarial assumptions regarding the insurers' expected future liability commitments to pay out on present contracts, including death benefits, matured endowments (lump sum or otherwise), and the cash **surrender values of policies** (the cash value paid to the policyholder if the policy is surrendered before it matures). Even though the actuarial assumptions underlying policy reserves are normally very conservative, unexpected fluctuations in future required payouts can occur; thus, underwriting life insurance is risky. For example, mortality rates—and life insurance payouts—might unexpectedly increase above those defined by historically based mortality tables as a result of a catastrophic epidemic illness such as AIDS or widespread influenza. To meet unexpected future losses, the life insurer holds a capital and surplus reserve fund with which to meet such losses (and reduce insolvency risk). The capital and surplus reserves of life insurers in 2012 were $319.1 billion, or 5.8 percent of total assets.[2]

---

[2] An additional line of defense against unexpected underwriting losses is the insurer's investment income from its asset portfolio plus any new premium income flows.

**separate accounts**
Annuity programs sponsored by life insurance companies in which the payoff on the policy is linked to the assets in which policy premiums are invested.

**Separate account** business represented 33.7 percent of total liabilities and capital in 2012. A separate account is a fund established and held separately from the insurance company's other funds. These funds may be invested without regard to the usual diversification restrictions; that is, they may be invested in all stocks, all bonds, and so forth. Note that these assets are also listed separately on the asset side of the balance sheet. Separate account assets are 33.7 percent of total assets. The payoff on the life insurance policy thus depends on the return on the funds in the separate account. Another important life insurer liability, GICs (5.0 percent of total liabilities and capital), are short- and medium-term debt instruments sold by insurance companies to fund their pension plan business (see deposit-type contracts in Table 6–3).

## Recent Trends

The life insurance industry was very profitable in the early and mid-2000s, with over $500 billion in premiums and annuities recorded annually in 2004 through 2009. Net income topped $34 billion in 2006, up 6.5 percent from 2005. Credit markets continued to be strong, and capital levels for the industry remained strong. However, the financial crisis took a toll on this industry. The value of stocks and bonds in insurers' asset portfolios dropped as financial markets deteriorated. Further, losses were experienced on life insurers' positions in commercial mortgage-backed securities, commercial loans, and lower-grade corporate debt as bond default rates increased and mortgage markets froze. Lower equity market values also reduced asset-based fees earned from balances on equity-linked products, such as variable annuities. As a result, life insurers with large proportions of separate-account assets were particularly hard hit with declining earnings from equities. Furthermore, as investors fled to the safety of government bonds during the financial crisis, government bond yields (which are generally a significant source of investment income for life insurers) fell. Additionally, historically low short-term interest rates prevented life insurers from lowering minimum rates on new policies, which encouraged higher surrender rates on existing policies that were already at minimum credit rates. The results were huge losses in 2008 for the industry. Realized and unrealized capital losses from bonds, preferred stocks, and common stocks topped $35 billion, representing more than an 875 percent drop from 2007. Net investment income also fell by 3.5 percent in 2008 from 2007. The result was that net after-tax income for the year was −$51.8 billion, $83.7 billion less than in 2007.

The large drop in the value of stocks and bonds that the insurers held made it harder for the companies to pay out money due to their policyholders. In late 2008/early 2009, insurance company reserves began to dwindle to dangerous levels. Further, the falling value of their assets made it harder for the insurers' to raise capital. As a result, the Treasury Department decided to extend bailout funds to a number of struggling life insurance companies, the most notable being $127 billion to AIG (including $45 billion from TARP, $77 billion to purchase collateralized debt and mortgage backed securities, and a $44 billion bridge loan). Other life insurers receiving TARP funds included Hartford Financial Services Group, Prudential Financial, Lincoln National, and Allstate. Events associated with the financial crisis continued to be felt in 2009. Premium income fell by $120 billion (19 percent) from 2008 levels, while net realized capital for the industry fell by $28.7 billion. However, late 2009 saw some improvements for the industry. Overall, the industry saw an increase in total assets of more than $200 billion and net income returned to a positive $21.1 billion. Further, the industry continued to pay dividends of $15.0 billion in 2009. Premiums continued to recover in 2010 and 2011 as annuity and most types of life insurance premiums increased. The 2011 premiums of $676.4 billion fell just short of the pre-crisis (2007) level, $677.2 billion. Further, net income increased to $28.0 billion in 2010 before dropping to $14.4 billion in 2011. The 2011 drop was the result of accounting changes and a number of one-time events involving specific companies rather than industry weakness. However, challenges remain for the industry. Interest rates remain at historical lows, which increases the risk of spread compression for existing contracts and hampers the sale of new fixed annuity and universal life insurance contracts. Further, equity markets remain volatile and new regulations (see below) could adversely affect profits.

## Regulation

**McCarran-Ferguson Act of 1945**
Legislation confirming the primacy of state over federal regulation of insurance companies.

www.naic.org

An important legislation affecting the regulation of life insurance companies is the **McCarran-Ferguson Act of 1945,** which confirms the primacy of state over federal regulation of insurance companies. Thus, unlike the depository institutions we discussed in Chapter 2, which can be chartered either at the federal or the state level, chartering of life insurers is done entirely at the state level. In addition to chartering, state insurance commissions supervise and examine insurance companies by using a coordinated examination system developed by the National Association of Insurance Commissioners (NAIC).

In 2009, the U.S. Congress considered establishing an optional federal insurance charter. The move behind such a charter picked up steam following the failure of the existing state by state regulatory system to act in preventing the problems at insurance giant AIG from becoming a systemic risk to the national economy. Those in favor of an optional federal insurance charter noted that under the current state by state system, insurers face obstacles such as inconsistent regulations, barriers to innovation, conflicting agent licensing, and education requirements. While the House version of the 2010 Financial Services Regulatory Overhaul Bill (approved in December 2009) contained no provision for federal regulation of insurance companies, Financial Services Chairman Barney Frank stated that this would still be a possibility as the bill moved through the regulatory process toward final passage.

The final version of the overhaul bill, the Wall Street Reform and Consumer Protection Act of 2010, established the Federal Insurance Office (FIO) that reports to Congress and the president on matters pertaining to the insurance industry. While the industry's main regulator continues to be the states in which firms operate, the FIO has the authority to monitor the insurance industry, identify regulatory gaps or systemic risk, deal with international insurance matters, and monitor the extent to which underserved communities have access to affordable insurance products. The Wall Street Reform and Consumer Protection Act also called for the establishment of the Financial Stability Oversight Council (FSOC), which is charged with designating any financial institution (including insurance companies) that presents a systemic risk to the economy and subjecting them to greater regulation.

**insurance guarantee funds**
Funds consisting of required contributions from within state insurance companies to compensate insurance company policyholders if there is a failure.

In addition to supervision and examination, states promote life **insurance guarantee funds.** Unlike banks and thrifts, life insurers have no access to a federal guarantee fund (although, as mentioned above, during the financial crisis the federal government took the unprecedented step of bailing out several major insurance companies). These state guarantee funds differ in a number of important ways from deposit insurance. First, although these programs are sponsored by state insurance regulators, they are actually run and administered by the (private) insurance companies themselves.

Second, unlike DIF, in which the FDIC has established a permanent reserve fund by requiring banks to pay annual premiums in excess of payouts to resolve failures (see Chapter 19), no such permanent guarantee fund exists for the insurance industry—with the sole exception of the PC and life guarantee funds in the state of New York. This means that contributions are paid into the guarantee fund by surviving firms in a state only after an insurance company has actually failed.

www.ins.state.ny.us

Third, the size of the required contributions that surviving insurers make to protect policyholders in failed insurance companies differs widely from state to state. In those states that have guarantee funds, each surviving insurer is normally levied a pro rata amount, according to the size of its statewide premium income. This amount either helps pay off small policyholders after the assets of the failed insurer have been liquidated or acts as a cash injection to make the acquisition of a failed insurer attractive. The definition of small policyholders varies among states in the range of holding policies from $100,000 to $500,000.

Finally, because no permanent fund exists and the annual pro rata payments to meet payouts to failed insurer policyholders are often legally capped, a delay usually occurs before small policyholders receive the cash surrender values of their policies or other payment obligations from the guarantee fund. This contrasts with deposit insurance, which normally provides insured depositors immediate coverage of their claims up to $250,000.

---

| **Concept Questions** | 1. What is the difference between a life insurance contract and an annuity contract? |
| | 2. Describe the different forms of ordinary life insurance. |
| | 3. Why do life insurance companies invest in long-term assets? |
| | 4. What is the major source of life insurance underwriting risk? |
| | 5. Who are the main regulators of the life insurance industry? |
| | 6. Why is traditional life insurance in decline? |

---

# PROPERTY–CASUALTY INSURANCE

Property insurance involves insurance coverages related to the loss of real and personal property. Casualty—or, perhaps more accurately, liability—insurance concerns protection against legal liability exposures. However, the distinctions between the two broad areas of property and liability insurance are increasingly becoming blurred. This is due to the tendency of property–casualty (PC) insurers to offer multiple-activity line coverages combining features of property and liability insurance into single policy packages, for example, homeowners multiple-peril insurance.

## Size, Structure, and Composition of the Industry

Currently, some 2,700 companies sell property–casualty insurance, with approximately half of these firms writing PC business in all or most of the United States. The total assets of the PC industry in 2012 were $1.6 trillion, or approximately 30 percent of the life insurance industry's assets. The U.S. PC insurance industry is quite concentrated. Collectively, the top 10 firms have a 50 percent share of the overall PC market measured by premiums written, and the top 200 firms made up 95 percent of the industry premiums written. In 2012, the top firm (State Farm) wrote 10.5 percent of all PC insurance premiums, while the second-ranked insurer (Liberty Mutual) wrote 5.3 percent (i.e., a joint total of 15.8 percent of premiums written). In contrast, in 1985, the top two firms wrote 14.5 percent of the total industry insurance premiums. Thus, the industry leaders appear to be increasing their share of this financial service sector. As with banks, much of this consolidation is coming through mergers and acquisitions.

### Types of Property–Casualty Insurance

In this section we describe the key features of the main PC lines. Note, however, that some PC activity lines are marketed as different products to both individuals and commercial firms (e.g., auto insurance), while other lines are marketed to one specific group (e.g., boiler and machinery insurance targeted at commercial purchasers). To understand the importance of each line in terms of premium income and losses incurred, look at Table 6–4. The following data show the changing

**TABLE 6–4**
**Property and Casualty Insurance Industry Underwriting by Lines, 2011**

Source: *BestWeek,* August 2012.

| | Net Premiums Written* | Losses Incurred† |
|---|---|---|
| Fire | $ 13.38 | 44.6% |
| Allied lines | 11.72 | 73.3 |
| Farm owners multiple peril (MP) | 3.18 | 87.6 |
| Multiple peril crop | 12.36 | 87.6 |
| Homeowners MP | 74.57 | 76.0 |
| Commercial MP | 33.92 | 62.5 |
| Mortgage guaranty | 4.57 | 194.6 |
| Ocean marine | 4.10 | 42.0 |
| Inland marine | 14.09 | 49.9 |
| Financial guaranty | 1.06 | 136.6 |
| Medical professional liability | 10.30 | 35.5 |
| Earthquake | 2.77 | 9.4 |
| Group accident and health | 4.72 | 62.2 |
| Individual accident and health | 3.80 | 70.6 |
| Workers' compensation | 43.99 | 70.7 |
| Other liability | 46.93 | 48.4 |
| Products liability | 2.88 | 63.7 |
| Private passenger auto liability | 103.73 | 69.7 |
| Commercial auto liability | 18.62 | 56.9 |
| Private passenger auto physical damage (PD) | 65.51 | 64.7 |
| Commercial auto PD | 5.46 | 68.3 |
| Aircraft | 1.80 | 50.2 |
| Fidelity | 1.17 | 46.0 |
| Surety | 5.15 | 13.2 |
| Burglary and theft | 0.22 | 23.8 |
| Boiler and machinery | 1.41 | 35.9 |
| Credit | 2.36 | 27.3 |
| Warranty | 2.81 | 68.5 |
| Flood | 2.80 | 62.4 |
| Other lines | 2.18 | 47.1 |
| Total | $501.56 | 65.5% |

* In billions of dollars.
† To premiums earned.

**net premiums written**
The entire amount of premiums written on insurance contracts.

composition in **net premiums written** (NPW) (the entire amount of premiums on insurance contracts written) for major PC lines over the 1960–2011 period. Important PC lines include the following:

- *Fire insurance and allied lines.* Protects against the perils of fire, lightning, and removal of property damaged in a fire (2.7 percent of all premiums written in 2011; 16.6 percent in 1960).
- *Homeowners multiple-peril (MP) insurance.* Protects against multiple perils of damage to a personal dwelling and personal property as well as provides liability coverage against the financial consequences of legal liability due to injury done to others. Thus, it combines features of both property and liability insurance (14.9 percent of all premiums written in 2011; 5.2 percent in 1960).
- *Commercial multiple-peril insurance.* Protects commercial firms against perils; similar to homeowners multiple-peril insurance (6.8 percent of all premiums written in 2011; 0.4 percent in 1960).
- *Automobile liability and physical damage (PD) insurance.* Provides protection against (1) losses resulting from legal liability due to the ownership or use of the vehicle (auto liability) and (2) theft of or damage to vehicles (auto physical damage) (38.5 percent of all premiums written in 2011; 43.0 percent in 1960).
- *Liability insurance (other than auto).* Provides either individuals or commercial firms with protection against non-automobile-related legal liability. For commercial firms, this includes protection against liabilities relating to their business operations (other than personal injury to employees covered by workers' compensation insurance) and product liability hazards (12.0 percent of all premiums written in 2011; 6.6 percent in 1960).

## Balance Sheet and Recent Trends

### The Balance Sheet and Underwriting Risk

The balance sheet of PC firms at the beginning of 2012 is shown in Table 6–5. Similar to life insurance companies, PC insurers invest the majority of their assets in long-term securities, thus subjecting them to credit and interest rate risks. Bonds ($931.1 billion), preferred stock ($11.6 billion), and common stock ($228.8 billion) constituted 72.0 percent of total assets in 2012. PC insurers hold mainly long-term securities for two reasons. First, PC insurers, like life insurers, hold long-term assets to match the maturity of their longer-term contractual liabilities. Second, PC insurers, unlike life insurers, have more uncertain payouts on their insurance contracts (i.e., they incur greater levels of liquidity risk). Thus, their asset structure includes many assets with relatively fixed returns that can be liquidated easily and at low cost. Looking at their liabilities, we can see the major component is the loss reserve and loss adjustment expenses ($632.4 billion) set aside to meet expected losses from *underwriting* and administrative expenses associated with the PC lines just described. This item constitutes 38.9 percent of total liabilities and capital. **Unearned premiums** (a reserve set-aside that contains the portion of a premium that has been paid before insurance coverage has been provided) are also a major liability, representing 15.4 percent of total liabilities and capital.

**unearned premiums**
Reserve set-aside that contains the portion of a premium that has been paid before insurance coverage has been provided.

To understand how and why a loss reserve on the liability side of the balance sheet is established, we need to understand the risks of underwriting PC insurance. In particular, PC underwriting risk results when the premiums generated on a given insurance line are insufficient to cover (1) the claims (losses) incurred

**TABLE 6–5**
Balance Sheet
for the Property–
Casualty Industry,
2012 (in billions of
dollars)

Source: Reprinted with
permission from *A.M. Best's
Aggregates and Averages*,
property–casualty, 2012, p. 1.
*www.ambest.com*

| Assets | | | | Percent of Total Assets |
|---|---|---|---|---|
| Unaffiliated investments | | $1,374.0 | | 84.5% |
| Bonds | $931.1 | | 57.2% | |
| Preferred stocks | 11.6 | | 0.7 | |
| Common stocks | 228.8 | | 14.1 | |
| Real estate investments | 15.4 | | 1.0 | |
| Cash and short-term investments | 76.3 | | 4.7 | |
| Other invested assets | 110.8 | | 6.8 | |
| Net deferred taxes | | 29.1 | | 1.8 |
| Reinsurance | | 43.1 | | 2.6 |
| Premium balances | | 128.7 | | 7.9 |
| Accrued interest | | 10.6 | | 0.7 |
| Other assets | | 41.1 | | 2.5 |
| Total assets | | $1,626.6 | | 100.0% |
| **Liabilities and Capital/Surplus** | | | | |
| Loss reserve and loss adjustment expenses | | $   632.4 | | 38.9% |
| Unearned premiums | | 251.4 | | 15.4 |
| Other liabilities | | 168.4 | | 10.4 |
| Total liabilities | | $1,052.2 | | 64.7% |
| Policyholders surplus | | $   574.4 | | 35.3% |
| Capital and assigned surplus | $248.0 | | 15.3% | |
| Surplus notes | 15.2 | | 0.9 | |
| Unassigned surplus | 311.2 | | 19.1 | |
| Total liabilities and capital/surplus | | $1,626.6 | | 100.0% |

insuring against the peril and (2) the administrative expenses of providing that insurance (legal expenses, commissions, taxes, etc.) after taking into account (3) the investment income generated between the time premiums are received and the time claims are paid. Thus, underwriting risk may result from (1) unexpected increases in loss rates, (2) unexpected increases in expenses, and/or (3) unexpected decreases in investment yields or returns. Next, we look more carefully at each of these three areas of PC underwriting risk.

*Loss Risk*   The key feature of claims loss exposure is the actuarial *predictability* of losses relative to premiums earned. This predictability depends on a number of characteristics or features of the perils insured, specifically:

- *Property versus liability.* In general, the maximum levels of losses are more predictable for property lines than for liability lines. For example, the monetary value of the loss of, or damage to, an auto is relatively easy to calculate, while the upper limit to the losses an insurer might be exposed to in a product liability line—for example, asbestos damage to workers' health under other liability insurance—may be difficult, if not impossible, to estimate.

- *Severity versus frequency.* In general, loss rates are more predictable on low severity, high-frequency lines than they are on high-severity, low-frequency lines. For example, losses in fire, auto, and homeowners peril lines tend to involve events expected to occur with a high frequency and to be independently distributed across any pool of the insured. Furthermore, the dollar loss on each event in the insured pool tends to be relatively small. Applying the law of large

**frequency of loss**
The probability that a loss will occur.

**severity of loss**
The size of the loss.

numbers, insurers can estimate the expected loss potential of such lines—the **frequency of loss** times the size of the loss (**severity of loss**)—within quite small probability bounds. Other lines, such as earthquake, hurricane, and financial guaranty insurance, tend to insure very low-probability (frequency) events. Here the probabilities are not always stationary, the individual risks in the insured pool are not independent, and the severity of the loss could be enormous. This means that estimating expected loss rates (frequency times severity) is extremely difficult in these coverage areas. For example, even with the new federal terrorism insurance program introduced in 2002, coverage for high-profile buildings in big cities, as well as other properties considered potential targets, remains expensive. Under the 2002 federal program, the government is responsible for 90 percent of insurance industry losses that arise from any future terrorist incidents that exceed a minimum amount. The government's losses are capped at $100 billion per year. Each insurer has a maximum amount it would pay before federal aid kicks in. In 2012, the amount was 15 percent of each company's commercial property–casualty premiums. The result is that in some cases, the cost of terrorism insurance has been reduced significantly since the new law took effect. But those buildings viewed as target risks will continue to have much higher premiums than properties outside of major cities. This higher uncertainty of losses forces PC firms to invest in more short-term assets and hold a larger percentage of capital and reserves than life insurance firms hold.

**long-tail loss**
A claim that is made some time after a policy was written.

- *Long tail versus short tail.* Some liability lines suffer from a long-tail risk exposure phenomenon that makes the estimation of expected losses difficult. This **long-tail loss** arises in policies in which the insured event occurs during a coverage period but a claim is not filed or reported until many years later. The delay in filing of a claim is in accordance with the terms of the insurance contract and often occurs because the detrimental consequences of the event are not known for a period of time after the event actually occurs. Losses incurred but not reported have caused insurers significant problems in lines such as medical malpractice and other liability insurance where product damage suits (e.g., the Dalkon shield case and asbestos cases) have mushroomed many years after the event occurred and the coverage period expired.[3] For example, in 2002 Halliburton, a major U.S. corporation, agreed to pay $4 billion in cash and stock, and to seek bankruptcy protection for a subsidiary, to settle more than 300,000 asbestos claims. To resolve its growing asbestos liability, Halliburton considered a novel step that put one of its biggest subsidiaries into bankruptcy courts, while allowing Halliburton to hold on to the rest of its businesses. Questions still remain about how much insurance companies will be required to reimburse Halliburton for the cost of asbestos case settlements and when. The company had only $1.6 billion of expected insurance on its books for asbestos claims. If Halliburton is successful in putting just one of its subsidiaries (and not the entire firm) into bankruptcy, it could set a precedent for many companies, such as Honeywell International and Dow Chemical, which were also trying to contain their asbestos risk in subsidiaries.

- *Product inflation versus social inflation.* Loss rates on all PC property policies are adversely affected by unexpected increases in inflation. Such increases were

---

[3] In some product liability cases, such as those involving asbestos, the nature of the risk being covered was not fully understood at the time many of the policies were written.

triggered, for example, by the oil price shocks of 1973, 1978, and 2008. However, in addition to a systematic unexpected inflation risk in each line, there may be line-specific inflation risks. The inflation risk of property lines is likely to reflect the approximate underlying inflation risk of the economy. Liability lines may be subject to social inflation, as reflected in juries' willingness to award punitive and other liability damages at rates far above the underlying rate of inflation. Such social inflation has been particularly prevalent in commercial liability and medical malpractice insurance and has been directly attributed by some analysts to faults in the U.S. civil litigation system.

*Reinsurance* An alternative to managing risk on a PC insurer's balance sheet is to purchase reinsurance from a reinsurance company. *Reinsurance* is essentially insurance for insurance companies. Note from Table 6–5 that reinsurance (the payments that may be collected under reinsurance contracts) represented 2.6 percent of total assets in 2012. Reinsurance is a way for primary insurance companies to protect against unforeseen or extraordinary losses. Depending on the contract, reinsurance can enable the insurer to improve its capital position, expand its business, limit losses, and stabilize cash flows, among other things. In addition, the reinsurer, drawing information from many primary insurers, will usually have a far larger pool of data for assessing risks. Reinsurance takes a variety of forms. It may represent a layer of risk, such as losses within certain limits, say, $5 million to $10 million, that will be paid by the reinsurer to the primary insurance company for which a premium is paid, or a sharing of both losses and profits for certain types of business. Reinsurance is an international business. About 75 percent of the reinsurance business that comes from U.S. insurance companies is written by non-U.S. reinsurers such as Munich Re. Some investment banks are now setting up reinsurers as part of a move to develop alternative risk financing deals such as catastrophe bonds.

Insurers and reinsurers also typically issue catastrophe bonds. The bonds pay high interest rates and diversify an investor's portfolio because natural disasters occur randomly and are not associated with (independent of) economic factors. Depending on how the bond is structured, if losses reach the threshold specified in the bond offering, the investor may lose all or part of the principal or interest. For example, a deep-discount or zero-coupon catastrophe bond would pay $100(1 - \alpha)$ on maturity, where $\alpha$ is the loss rate due to the catastrophe. Thus, Munich Re issued a $250 million catastrophe bond in 2012 where $\alpha$ (the loss rate) reflected losses incurred on all reinsurer policies over a 24-hour period should an event (such as a flood or hurricane) occur and losses exceed a certain threshold. The required yield on these bonds reflected the risk-free rate plus a premium reflecting investors' expectations regarding the probability of the event's occurring.

**loss ratio**
Ratio that measures pure losses incurred to premiums earned.

**premiums earned**
Premiums received and earned on insurance contracts because time has passed with no claim being filed.

*Measuring Loss Risk* The **loss ratio** measures the actual losses incurred on a line. It measures the ratio of losses incurred to **premiums earned** (premiums received and earned on insurance contracts because time has passed with no claim being filed). Thus, a loss ratio less than 100 means that premiums earned were sufficient to cover losses incurred on that line. Aggregate loss ratios for the period 1951–2012 are shown in Table 6–6. Notice the steady increase in industry loss ratios over the period, increasing from the 60 percent range in the 1950s to the 70 and 80 percent range in the 1980s into the 2010s. For example, in 2011, the aggregate loss ratio on all PC lines was 79.4. This includes, however, loss adjustment expenses (LAE)—see below—as well as (pure) losses. The (pure) loss ratio, net of LAE, in 2011 was 65.5 (see Table 6–4).

**TABLE 6–6**
Industry
Underwriting
Ratios

Source: *Best's Review,* various
issues. *www.ambest.com*

| Year | Loss Ratio* | Expense Ratio[†] | Combined Ratio | Dividends to Policyholders[‡] | Combined Ratio after Dividends |
|------|-------------|------------------|----------------|-------------------------------|--------------------------------|
| 1951 | 60.3 | 34.0 | 94.3 | 2.6 | 96.9 |
| 1960 | 63.8 | 32.2 | 96.0 | 2.2 | 98.2 |
| 1965 | 70.3 | 30.4 | 100.7 | 1.9 | 102.6 |
| 1970 | 70.8 | 27.6 | 98.4 | 1.7 | 100.1 |
| 1975 | 79.3 | 27.3 | 106.6 | 1.3 | 107.9 |
| 1980 | 74.9 | 26.5 | 101.4 | 1.7 | 103.1 |
| 1985 | 88.7 | 25.9 | 114.6 | 1.6 | 116.2 |
| 1990 | 82.3 | 26.0 | 108.3 | 1.2 | 109.6 |
| 1995 | 78.8 | 26.2 | 105.0 | 1.4 | 106.4 |
| 1997 | 72.8 | 27.1 | 99.9 | 1.7 | 101.6 |
| 2000 | 81.4 | 27.8 | 109.2 | 1.3 | 110.5 |
| 2001 | 88.4 | 26.9 | 115.3 | 0.7 | 116.0 |
| 2002 | 81.1 | 25.6 | 106.7 | 0.5 | 107.2 |
| 2003 | 74.7 | 24.9 | 99.6 | 0.5 | 100.1 |
| 2004 | 73.3 | 25.0 | 98.3 | 0.4 | 98.7 |
| 2005 | 74.8 | 25.5 | 100.3 | 0.6 | 100.9 |
| 2006 | 66.2 | 25.4 | 91.6 | 0.8 | 92.4 |
| 2007 | 68.0 | 27.1 | 95.1 | 0.5 | 95.6 |
| 2008 | 77.4 | 27.2 | 104.6 | 0.5 | 105.1 |
| 2009 | 73.2 | 27.3 | 100.5 | 0.5 | 101.0 |
| 2010 | 73.5 | 28.4 | 101.9 | 0.5 | 102.4 |
| 2011 | 79.4 | 28.4 | 107.8 | 0.4 | 108.2 |
| 2012 | 73.9 | 29.8 | 103.7 | 0.3 | 104.0 |

\* Losses and adjustment expenses incurred to premiums earned.
[†] Expenses incurred (before federal income taxes) to premiums written.
[‡] Dividends to policyholders to premiums earned.

*Expense Risk*   The two major sources of expense risk to PC insurers are (1) loss adjustment expenses (LAE) and (2) commissions and other expenses. Loss adjustment expenses relate to the costs surrounding the loss settlement process; for example, many PC insurers employ adjusters who determine the liability of the insurer and the size of the adjustment or settlement to be made. The other major area of expense occurs in the commission costs paid to insurance brokers and sales agents and other expenses related to the acquisition of business. As mentioned above, the loss ratio reported in Table 6–6 includes LAE. The expense ratio reported in Table 6–6 reflects commissions and other (non-LAE) expenses for PC insurers over the 1951–2012 period. In contrast to the increasing trend in the loss ratio, the expense ratio generally decreased over the period shown. Expenses can account for significant portions of the overall costs of operations. In 2011, for example, expenses—other than LAE—amounted to 28.4 percent of premiums written. Clearly, sharp rises in insurance broker commissions and other operating costs can rapidly render an insurance line unprofitable. One of the reasons for the secular decline in the expense ratio has been the switch in the way PC insurance has been distributed. Specifically, rather than relying on independent brokers to sell policies (the American agency method of distribution), large insurance companies are increasingly selling insurance to the public directly through their own brokers (the direct writer method of distribution).

   A common measure of the overall underwriting profitability of a line, which includes both loss and expense experience, is the **combined ratio.** Technically, the combined ratio is equal to the loss ratio plus the ratios of LAE to premiums earned, commissions and other acquisition costs and general expense costs to

**combined ratio**
Ratio that measures the overall underwriting profitability of a line; it is equal to the loss ratio plus the ratios of loss adjustment expenses to premiums earned and commission and other acquisition costs to premiums written plus any dividends paid to policyholders as a proportion of premiums earned.

premiums written, plus any dividends paid to policyholders as a proportion of premiums earned. The combined ratio after dividends adds any dividends paid to policyholders as a proportion of premiums earned to the combined ratio. If the combined ratio is less than 100, premiums alone are sufficient to cover both losses and expenses related to the line.

If premiums are insufficient and the combined ratio exceeds 100, the PC insurer must rely on investment income earned on premiums for overall profitability. For example, in 2001 the combined ratio before dividend payments was 116.0, indicating that premiums alone were insufficient to cover the costs of both losses and expenses related to writing PC insurance. Table 6–6 presents the combined ratio and its components for the PC industry for the years 1951–2012. We see that, over this period, premiums have often been unable to cover losses and expenses (i.e., combined ratios have generally been greater than 100).

*Investment Yield/Return Risk* As discussed above, when the combined ratio is more than 100, overall profitability can be ensured only by a sufficient investment return on premiums earned. That is, PC firms invest premiums in assets between the time they are received and the time they are paid out to meet claims. For example, in 2012 net investment income to premiums earned (or the PC insurers' investment yield) was 10.5 percent. As a result, the overall average profitability (or **operating ratio**) of PC insurers was 93.5. It was equal to the combined ratio after dividends (104.0) minus the investment yield 10.5. Since the operating ratio was less than 100, PC insurers were profitable in 2012. However, lower net returns on investments (e.g., 3.5 percent rather than 10.5 percent) would have meant that underwriting PC insurance was marginally unprofitable (i.e., the operating ratio of insurers in this case would have been 100.5). Thus, the effect of interest rates and default rates on PC insurers' investments is crucial to PC insurers' overall profitability. That is, measuring and managing credit and interest rate risk are key concerns of PC managers.

**operating ratio**
A measure of the overall profitability of a PC insurer; it equals the combined ratio minus the investment yield.

Consider the following example. Suppose an insurance company's projected loss ratio is 79.8 percent, its expense ratio is 27.9 percent, and it pays 2 percent of its premiums earned to policyholders as dividends. The combined ratio (after dividends) for this insurance company is equal to:

Loss ratio + Expense ratio + Dividend ratio = Combined ratio after dividends
79.8 + 27.9 + 2.0 = 109.7

Thus, expected losses on all PC lines, expenses, and dividends exceeded premiums earned by 9.7 percent.

If the company's investment portfolio, however, yielded 12 percent, the operating ratio and overall profitability of the PC insurer would be:

Operating ratio = Combined ratio after dividends − Investment yield
= 109.7 − 12.0
= 97.7 percent

and

Overall profitability = 100 − Operating ratio
= 100 − 97.7
= 2.3 percent

As can be seen, the high investment returns (12 percent) make the PC insurer profitable overall.

Given the importance of investment returns to PC insurers' profitability, we can see from the balance sheet in Table 6–5 that bonds—both Treasury and corporate—dominated the asset portfolios of PC insurers. Bonds constituted 57.2 percent of total assets and 67.8 percent of financial assets (so-called unaffiliated investments) in 2012.

Finally, if losses, expenses, and other costs are higher and investment yields are lower than expected so that operating losses are incurred, PC insurers carry a significant amount of surplus reserves (policyholder surplus) to reduce the risk of insolvency. In 2012, the ratio of policyholder surplus to assets was 35.3 percent.

### Recent Trends

**underwriting cycle**
The tendency of profits in the PC industry to follow a cyclical pattern.

While catastrophes should be random, the period 1985–2012 was characterized by a number of catastrophes of historically high severity, as shown in Figure 6–3. In the terminology of PC insurers, the industry experienced troughs of an **underwriting cycle,** or underwriting conditions were hard. These cycles are characterized by periods of rising premiums leading to increased profitability. Following a period of solid but not spectacular rates of returns, the industry enters a down phase in which premiums soften as the supply of insurance products increases. As a result, most of the period 1985–2012 was not very profitable for the PC industry. In particular, the combined ratio (the measure of loss plus expense risk) was 116.2 in 1987, 115.7 in 1992, and 116.0 in 2001. (Remember that a combined ratio higher than 100 is bad in that it means that losses, expenses, and dividends totaled *more* than premiums earned.) The major reason for these losses was a succession of catastrophes from Hurricane Hugo in 1989, the San Francisco earthquake in 1991, the Oakland fires of 1991, and the almost $20 billion in losses incurred in Florida as a result of Hurricane Andrew in 1991.

In 1993 the industry showed signs of improvement, with the combined ratio falling to 106.9. However, in 1994 that ratio rose again to 108.4, partly as a result of the Northridge earthquake with estimated losses of $7 billion to $10 billion. The industry ratio fell back down to 101.6 in 1997. However, major losses associated with El Niño (e.g., Hurricane Georges and Midwest storms) drove the combined ratio back up to 105.6 in 1998. The combined ratio increased even further to 107.9 in 1999 and 110.5 in 2000. Part of these increases is attributable to an increase in amounts paid on asbestos claims. In 1999, $3.4 billion was paid out on these claims, the largest

www.iso.com

payouts ever. The Insurance Services Office Inc. estimates that the combined ratio for 1999, 107.9, would have been one percentage point lower without these claims.

The year 2001 saw yet another blow to the insurance industry and the world with the terrorist attacks on the World Trade Center and the Pentagon. Early estimates of the costs of these attacks to insurance companies were as high as $40 billion. It was estimated that only 10 percent of the September 11 losses were reported in 2001, and yet the losses attributed to the terrorist attacks added an estimated 4 percentage points to the combined ratio after dividends of 116.0. Because of the tremendous impact these attacks had on the health of the U.S. insurance industry, the Bush administration proposed that the U.S. government pay the majority of the losses of the insurance industry due to the attacks. The proposal capped insurers' 2002 liabilities at $12 billion, 2003 liabilities at $23 billion, and 2004 liabilities at $36 billion. Despite this bailout of the industry, many insurers did not survive and those that did were forced to increase premiums significantly.

**FIGURE 6–3** U.S. Catastrophes, 1949–2012

Sources: Richard L. Sandor, Center Financial Products, 1949–1994; authors' research,1995–2012.

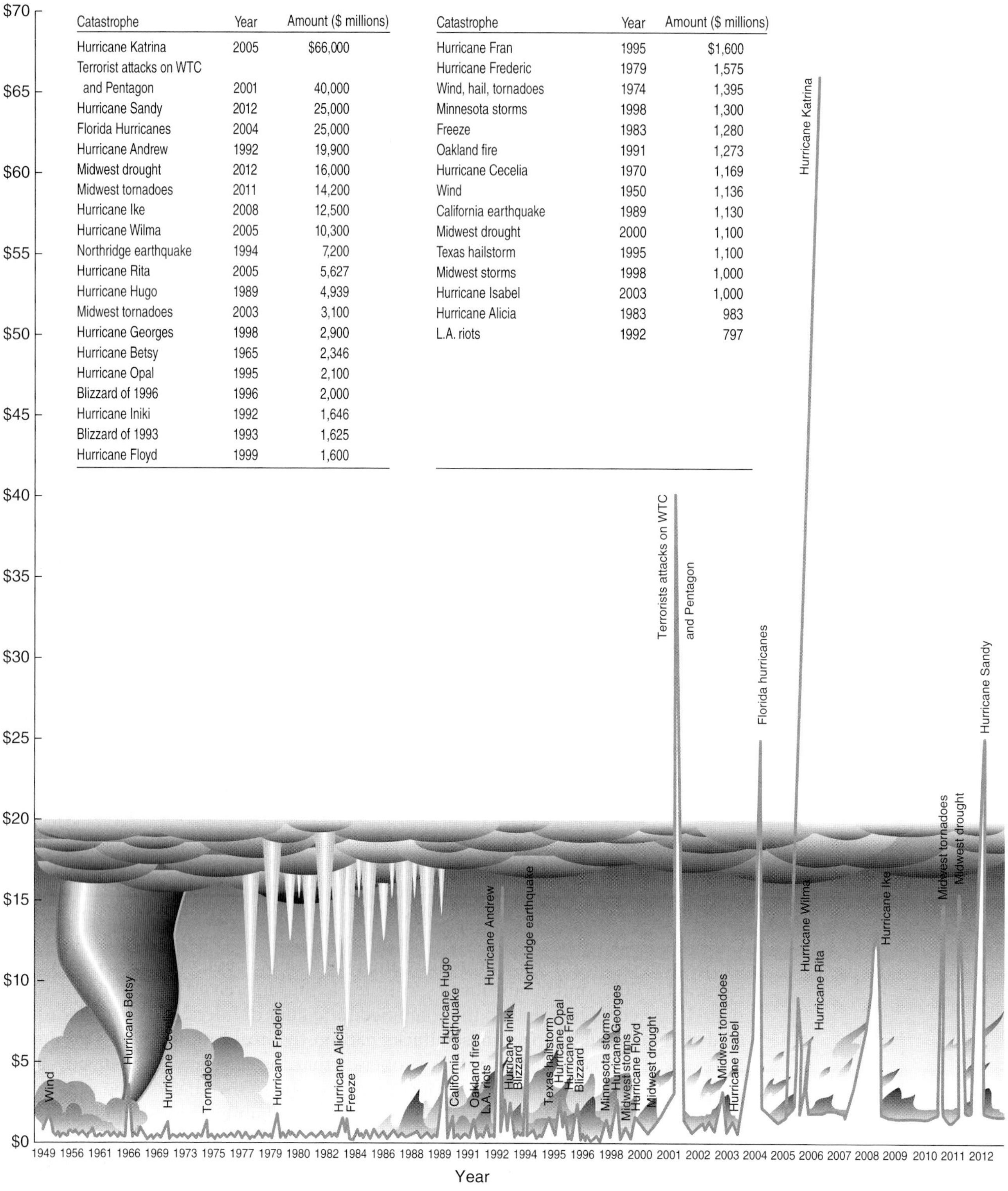

| Catastrophe | Year | Amount ($ millions) |
|---|---|---|
| Hurricane Katrina | 2005 | $66,000 |
| Terrorist attacks on WTC and Pentagon | 2001 | 40,000 |
| Hurricane Sandy | 2012 | 25,000 |
| Florida Hurricanes | 2004 | 25,000 |
| Hurricane Andrew | 1992 | 19,900 |
| Midwest drought | 2012 | 16,000 |
| Midwest tornadoes | 2011 | 14,200 |
| Hurricane Ike | 2008 | 12,500 |
| Hurricane Wilma | 2005 | 10,300 |
| Northridge earthquake | 1994 | 7,200 |
| Hurricane Rita | 2005 | 5,627 |
| Hurricane Hugo | 1989 | 4,939 |
| Midwest tornadoes | 2003 | 3,100 |
| Hurricane Georges | 1998 | 2,900 |
| Hurricane Betsy | 1965 | 2,346 |
| Hurricane Opal | 1995 | 2,100 |
| Blizzard of 1996 | 1996 | 2,000 |
| Hurricane Iniki | 1992 | 1,646 |
| Blizzard of 1993 | 1993 | 1,625 |
| Hurricane Floyd | 1999 | 1,600 |

| Catastrophe | Year | Amount ($ millions) |
|---|---|---|
| Hurricane Fran | 1995 | $1,600 |
| Hurricane Frederic | 1979 | 1,575 |
| Wind, hail, tornadoes | 1974 | 1,395 |
| Minnesota storms | 1998 | 1,300 |
| Freeze | 1983 | 1,280 |
| Oakland fire | 1991 | 1,273 |
| Hurricane Cecelia | 1970 | 1,169 |
| Wind | 1950 | 1,136 |
| California earthquake | 1989 | 1,130 |
| Midwest drought | 2000 | 1,100 |
| Texas hailstorm | 1995 | 1,100 |
| Midwest storms | 1998 | 1,000 |
| Hurricane Isabel | 2003 | 1,000 |
| Hurricane Alicia | 1983 | 983 |
| L.A. riots | 1992 | 797 |

After several tumultuous years, 2003 saw profitability in the PC industry improve. The combined ratio after dividends was 100.1, down sharply from 107.2 in 2002, and much better than most analysts and industry experts expected. The 2003 results were the best since 1979, when the combined ratio was 100.6. In 2004, Florida and the East coast were hit with several major hurricanes including Hurricanes Charley, Frances, Ivan, and Jeanne (the estimated losses from these four hurricanes were $25 billion). Yet, these were the only major catastrophes to occur in 2004. As a result, the industry saw its first overall profitable year since the 1960s. The combined ratio in 2004 was 98.7. In 2005 the PC industry reported a combined ratio of 100.9. The losses resulted from $57.7 billion in catastrophe losses primarily resulting from the record-breaking hurricane season, which included losses from Hurricanes Katrina, Wilma, and Rita. These losses added an estimated 8 points to the industry's combined ratio. If catastrophe losses are excluded, the combined ratios for 2005 and 2004 would have been 92.9 and 94.5, respectively. Losses from the record 2005 hurricane season prompted both Allstate and State Farm to stop writing new homeowner policies and drop some existing customers altogether. In 2006 and 2007 a small level of catastrophic losses, combined with a strong performance in virtually all other major lines of PC insurance, resulted in combined ratios of 92.4 (the best underwriting performance since 1936) and 95.6, respectively.

Losses rose significantly in 2008 through 2012 due to jumps in catastrophe losses (including $12.5 billion from Hurricane Ike, $25.0 billion from Hurricane Sandy, and $14.2 billion from the Midwest tornadoes) and losses in the mortgage and financial guarantee segments associated with the financial crisis. Note from Table 6–4 that these two segments experienced losses of 194.6 and 136.6 percent of premiums written, respectively, in 2012, down from 214.6 and 416.9 percent of premiums written, respectively, in 2008 at the height of the financial crisis. These losses pushed the 2008 combined ratio to 105.1 (up 9.5 points from 2007). Excluding losses from these two sectors, the industry's combined ratio would have been 101.0 for the year. Significantly, lower catastrophe losses and a recovering economy resulted in an industry combined ratio of 101.0 in 2009 and 102.4 in 2010. While 2009 saw the third straight year of negative premium growth (the first since the Great Depression), premiums written in 2010 began to recover. Further, few major catastrophes occurred during these two years. As a result, the combined ratio in 2009 and 2010 fell to 101.0 and 102.4, respectively.

The United States experienced one of the worst years ever in terms of catastrophes in 2011. Insured catastrophe losses totaled $33.6 billion, the fifth most expensive year on record for insured catastrophe losses on an inflation-adjusted basis. Overall net income after taxes fell 46 percent to $19.2 billion from $35.2 billion in 2010. Such high catastrophe losses, along with high underwriting losses in key non-catastrophe-exposed lines such as workers' compensation, pushed the industry's combined ratio to 108.2 (its highest level since 2001). As a result of large decreases in catastrophe losses and a marked acceleration in premium growth, profitability in the PC insurance industry rebounded sharply during the first nine months of 2012. Catastrophe losses fell to $16.2 billion in the first nine months of 2012 from $32.8 billion in the first nine months of 2011. However, catastrophe losses from Hurricane Sandy, which made landfall in the northeast United States in late October, totaled $25.0 billion. As a result, the industry's combined ratio fell to 100.9 in the first nine months, to 104.0 for the full year.

The federal government has gradually increased the role of providing compensation and reconstruction assistance following a variety of natural disasters such as the terrorist attacks of 9/11. Although the insurance industry has been stressed by major catastrophes, it has argued that government involvement in the market for catastrophe insurance should be minimized to avoid crowding out more efficient private market solutions, such as catastrophe bonds.

### Regulation

As with life insurance companies, PC insurers are chartered by states and regulated by state commissions. In addition, state guaranty funds provide some protection to policyholders if an insurance company fails. The National Association of Insurance Commissioners (NAIC) also provides various services to state regulatory commissions. These services include a standardized examination system called IRIS (Insurance Regulatory Information System) to identify insurers with loss, combined, and other ratios outside the normal ranges.

www.naic.org

An additional burden that PC insurers face in some activity lines—especially auto insurance and workers' compensation insurance—is rate regulation. That is, given the public utility nature of some insurance lines, state commissioners set ceilings on premiums and premium increases, usually based on specific cost of capital and line risk exposure formulas for the insurance suppliers. This had led some insurers to leave states such as New Jersey, Florida, and California, which have the most restrictive regulations.

Further, the industry came under attack for the way it handled homeowners' claims associated with Hurricane Katrina. Homeowners policies excluded damage caused by flooding. Insurers insisted the storm surge from Hurricane Katrina was classified as a flood and that damage therefore was excluded from coverage under policy forms that had been reviewed by regulators in each state and in force for years. Lawyers for policyholders of State Farm Insurance Company claimed that insurers were trying to avoid paying out on their homeowners policies by claiming the cause was a flood when it was a combination of hurricane winds and a storm surge. They claimed that the storm surge was not a flood but a direct result of the hurricane's winds, which is a covered risk. Policyholders claimed that State Farm and other insurance companies used "deceptive" sales practices to sell those hurricane policies and collected extra premiums from them. A verdict in January 2007 not only held State Farm responsible for policy limits that totaled more than $220,000 on each loss deemed to be due to storm-surge flooding but also held the company liable for punitive damages.

| **Concept Questions** | 1. Why do PC insurers hold more capital and reserves than do life insurers? |
|---|---|
| | 2. Why are life insurers' assets, on average, longer in maturity than those of PC insurers? |
| | 3. Describe the main lines of insurance offered by PC insurers. |
| | 4. What are the components of the combined ratio? |
| | 5. How does the operating ratio differ from the combined ratio? |
| | 6. Why does the combined ratio tend to behave cyclically? |

## GLOBAL ISSUES

Like the other sectors of the financial institutions industry, the insurance sector is becoming increasingly global. Table 6–7 lists the top 10 countries in terms of total premiums written in 2011 (in U.S. dollars) and their percentage share of the world market. Table 6–8 lists the top 10 insurance companies worldwide by total

**TABLE 6–7**  The World's Top Countries in Terms of Insurance Premiums Written

Source: Swiss Re, sigma No 3/2012.

| Rank | Country | Life Premiums Written (US$ billions) | Property–Casualty Premiums Written (US$ billions) | Total Premiums Written (US$ billions) | Share of World Market |
|------|---------|------|------|------|------|
| 1 | United States | $537.6 | $667.1 | $1,204.7 | 26.2% |
| 2 | Japan | 524.7 | 103.7 | 655.4 | 14.3 |
| 3 | United Kingdom | 210.1 | 109.5 | 319.6 | 7.0 |
| 4 | France | 174.8 | 98.3 | 273.1 | 5.9 |
| 5 | Germany | 113.9 | 131.3 | 245.2 | 5.3 |
| 6 | China | 134.5 | 87.3 | 221.8 | 4.8 |
| 7 | Italy | 105.1 | 55.4 | 160.5 | 3.5 |
| 8 | South Korea | 79.2 | 51.2 | 130.4 | 2.8 |
| 9 | Canada | 52.2 | 69.0 | 121.2 | 2.6 |
| 10 | Netherlands | 31.2 | 79.7 | 110.9 | 2.4 |

**TABLE 6–8**
World's Largest Insurance Companies by Total Revenues

Source: Insurance Information Institute website, 2012. *www.iii.org*

| Rank | Company | Revenues (US$ billions) | Home Country |
|------|---------|------|------|
| **Panel A: Life Insurers** | | | |
| 1 | Japan Post Holdings | $211.0 | Japan |
| 2 | AXA Group | 142.7 | France |
| 3 | Assicurazioni Generali | 112.6 | Italy |
| 4 | Nippon Life Insurance | 90.8 | Japan |
| 5 | Meiji Yasuda Life | 77.5 | Japan |
| 6 | MetLife | 70.6 | United States |
| 7 | China Life Insurance | 67.3 | China |
| 8 | Dai-ichi Mutual Life | 62.5 | Japan |
| 9 | Aviva | 61.8 | United Kingdom |
| 10 | Prudential | 58.5 | United Kingdom |
| **Panel B: Property–Casualty Insurers** | | | |
| 1 | Berkshire Hathaway | $143.7 | United States |
| 2 | Allianz | 134.2 | Germany |
| 3 | Munich Re Group | 90.1 | Germany |
| 4 | American International Group | 71.7 | United States |
| 5 | State Farm Insurance | 64.3 | United States |
| 6 | Zurich Financial Services | 53.0 | Switzerland |
| 7 | MS&AD Insurance Group | 47.7 | Japan |
| 8 | Tokio Marine | 43.3 | Japan |
| 9 | People's Insurance Co. of China | 36.5 | China |
| 10 | NKSJ Holdings | 35.3 | Japan |

revenues. While the United States, Japan, and western Europe dominate the global market, all regions are engaged in the insurance business and many insurers are engaged internationally.

Worldwide, 2011 was a bad year for life and PC insurers. Catastrophe losses were the worst on record. Japan's earthquake and tsunami (with insured losses of $40 billion), earthquakes in New Zealand (with insured losses of $13 billion), floods in Thailand (insured losses of $10 billion), and a series of severe tornadoes in the United States ($14.2 billion) all contributed to $350 billion in disaster losses. Insurance losses from these disasters would have been far greater had the central governments in these countries not picked up a large portion of the loss coverage. Worldwide insured losses in 2012 were 36 percent higher than the 10-year average ($72 billion versus $53 billion), mainly due to events in the United States (discussed above). However, except for the earthquake in Italy (with insured losses topping $1.6 billion), no major catastrophes occurred outside the United States. Insured losses in Europe, Asia, and Canada were far below their 10-year averages.

## Summary

This chapter examined the activities and regulation of insurance companies. The first part of the chapter described the various classes of life insurance and recent trends. The second part covered property–casualty companies. The various lines that make up property–casualty insurance are becoming increasingly blurred as multiple-activity line coverages are offered. Both life and property–casualty insurance companies are regulated at the state rather than the federal level. In addition, both are coming under threat from other financial service firms that offer similar or competitive products.

## Questions and Problems

1. What is the primary function of an insurance company? How does this function compare with the primary function of a depository institution?
2. What is the adverse selection problem? How does adverse selection affect the profitable management of an insurance company?
3. What are the similarities and differences among the four basic lines of life insurance products?
4. Explain how annuity activities represent the reverse of life insurance activities.
5. Explain how life insurance and annuity products can be used to create a steady stream of cash disbursements and payments to avoid paying or receiving a single lump-sum cash amount.
6. a. Calculate the annual cash flows from a $1 million, 20-year fixed-payment annuity earning a guaranteed 10 percent per year if payments are to begin at the end of the current year.
   b. Calculate the annual cash flows from a $1 million, 20-year fixed-payment annuity earning a guaranteed 10 percent per year if payments are to begin at the end of year 5.
   c. What is the amount of the annuity purchase required if you wish to receive a fixed payment of $200,000 for 20 years? Assume that the annuity will earn 10 percent per year.
7. You deposit $10,000 annually into a life insurance fund for the next 10 years, after which time you plan to retire.
   a. If the deposits are made at the beginning of the year and earn an interest rate of 8 percent, what will be the amount of retirement funds at the end of year 10?
   b. Instead of a lump sum, you wish to receive annuities for the next 20 years (years 11 through 30). What is the constant annual payment you expect to

receive at the beginning of each year if you assume an interest rate of 8 percent during the distribution period?

   c. Repeat parts (a) and (b) above assuming earning rates of 7 percent and 9 percent during the deposit period and earning rates of 7 percent and 9 percent during the distribution period. During which period does the change in the earning rate have the greatest impact?

8. You deposit $12,000 annually into a life insurance fund for the next 10 years, at which time you plan to retire. Instead of a lump sum, you wish to receive annuities for the next 20 years. What is the annual payment you expect to receive beginning in year 11 if you assume an interest rate of 6 percent for the whole time period?

9. a. Suppose a 65-year-old person wants to purchase an annuity from an insurance company that would pay $20,000 per year until the end of that person's life. The insurance company expects this person to live for 15 more years and would be willing to pay 6 percent on the annuity. How much should the insurance company ask this person to pay for the annuity?

   b. A second 65-year-old person wants the same $20,000 annuity, but this person is much healthier and is expected to live for 20 years. If the same 6 percent interest rate applies, how much should this healthier person be charged for the annuity?

   c. In each case, what is the difference in the purchase price of the annuity if the distribution payments are made at the beginning of the year?

10. Contrast the balance sheet of a life insurance company (Table 6–3) with the balance sheet of a commercial bank (Table 2–6) and with that of a savings institution (Table 2–10). Explain the balance sheet differences in terms of the differences in the primary functions of the three organizations.

11. Using the data in Table 6–2, how has the composition of assets of U.S. life insurance companies changed over time?

12. How do life insurance companies earn a profit?

13. How would the balance sheet of a life insurance company change if it offered to run a private pension fund for another company?

14. How does the regulation of insurance companies differ from the regulation of depository institutions? What are the major pieces of life insurance regulatory legislation?

15. How do state guarantee funds for life insurance companies compare with deposit insurance for depository institutions?

16. What are the two major activity lines of property–casualty insurance firms?

17. How have the product lines of property–casualty insurance companies changed over time?

18. Contrast the balance sheet of a property–casualty insurance company (Table 6–5) with the balance sheet of a commercial bank (Table 2–6). Explain the balance sheet differences in terms of the differences in the primary functions of the two organizations.

19. What are the three sources of underwriting risk in the property–casualty insurance industry?

20. How do unexpected increases in inflation affect property–casualty insurers?

21. Identify the four characteristics or features of the perils insured against by property–casualty insurance. Rank the features in terms of actuarial predictability and total loss potential.

22. Insurance companies will charge a higher premium for which of the insurance lines listed below? Why?

    a. Low-severity, high-frequency lines versus high-severity, low-frequency lines.

    b. Long-tail lines versus short-tail lines.

23. What does the loss ratio measure? What has been the long-term trend of the loss ratio? Why?

24. What does the expense ratio measure? Identify and explain the two major sources of expense risk to a property–casualty insurer. Why has the long-term trend in this ratio been decreasing?

25. How is the combined ratio defined? What does it measure?

26. What is the investment yield on premiums earned? Why has this ratio become so important to property–casualty insurers?

27. Consider the data in Table 6–6. Since 1980, what has been the necessary investment yield for the industry to enable the operating ratio to be less than 100 in each year? How is this requirement related to the interest rate risk and credit risk faced by a property–casualty insurer?

28. a. What is the combined ratio for a property insurer that has a loss ratio of 73 percent, a loss adjustment expense of 12.5 percent, and a ratio of commissions and other acquisition expenses of 18 percent?

    b. What is the combined ratio adjusted for investment yield if the company earns an investment yield of 8 percent?

29. An insurance company's projected loss ratio is 77.5 percent and its loss adjustment expense ratio is 12.9 percent. The company estimates that commission payments and dividends to policyholders will be 16 percent. What must be the minimum yield on investments to achieve a positive operating ratio?

30. An insurance company collected $3.6 million in premiums and disbursed $1.96 million in losses. Loss adjustment expenses amounted to 6.6 percent and dividends paid to policyholders totaled 1.2 percent. The total income generated from the company's investments was $170,000 after all expenses were paid. What is the net profitability in dollars?

31. A property-casualty insurer brings in $6.25 million in premiums on its homeowners' multiple peril line of insurance. The line's losses amount to $4,343,750, expenses are $1,593,750, and dividends are $156,250. The insurer earns $218,750 on the investment of its premiums. Calculate the line's loss ratio, expense ratio, dividend ratio, combined ratio, investment ratio, operating ratio, and overall profitability.

## Web Questions

32. Go to the Federal Reserve Board's website at **www.federalreserve.gov** and find the most recent distribution of life insurance industry assets for Table 6–2. Click on "Economic Research and Data." Click on "Flow of Fund Accounts of the United States." Click on the most recent date. Click on "Level tables." This will bring the file (Table L.115) onto your computer that contains the relevant data. How have the values of government securities, corporate securities, mortgages, and policy loans changed since 2012?

33. Go to the Insurance Information Institute's website at **www.iii.org** and use the following steps to find the most recent data on the largest life insurance companies by total revenue. Click on "Facts & Statistics." Click on "Life Insurance." This will bring the file onto your computer that contains the relevant data. What are total revenues and assets of the top 10 life insurance companies?

# Risks of Financial Institutions

## INTRODUCTION

A major objective of FI management is to increase the FI's returns for its owners. This often comes, however, at the cost of increased risk. This chapter overviews the various risks facing FIs: interest rate risk, credit risk, liquidity risk, foreign exchange risk, country or sovereign risk, market risk, off-balance-sheet risk, technology and operational risk, and insolvency risk. Table 7–1 presents a brief definition of each of these risks. By the end of this chapter, you will have a basic understanding of the variety and complexity of the risks facing managers of modern FIs. In the remaining chapters of the text, we look at the measurement and management of the most important of these risks in more detail. As will become

**TABLE 7–1**
**Risks Faced by Financial Intermediaries**

**Interest rate risk**   The risk incurred by an FI when the maturities of its assets and liabilities are mismatched.

**Credit risk**   The risk that promised cash flows from loans and securities held by FIs may not be paid in full.

**Liquidity risk**   The risk that a sudden surge in liability withdrawals may require an FI to liquidate assets in a very short period of time and at less than fair market prices.

**Foreign exchange risk**   The risk that exchange rate changes can affect the value of an FI's assets and liabilities denominated in nondomestic currencies.

**Country or sovereign risk**   The risk that repayments from foreign borrowers may be interrupted because of restrictions, intervention, or interference from foreign governments.

**Market risk**   The risk incurred from assets and liabilities in an FI's trading book due to changes in interest rates, exchange rates, and other prices.

**Off-balance-sheet risk**   The risk incurred by an FI as the result of activities related to its contingent assets and liabilities held off the balance sheet.

**Technology risk**   The risk incurred by an FI when its technological investments do not produce anticipated cost savings.

**Operational risk**   The risk that existing technology, auditing, monitoring, and other support systems may malfunction or break down.

**Insolvency risk**   The risk that an FI may not have enough capital to offset a sudden decline in the value of its assets.

clear, the effective management of these risks is central to an FIs performance. Indeed, it can be argued that the main business of FIs is to manage these risks.[1]

While over the past decade, U.S. financial institution profitability has generally been robust, the risks of financial intermediation have increased as the U.S. and overseas economies have become more integrated. For example, weakening economic conditions inside and outside the United States—especially in Greece, Italy, Spain, and Portugal—have presented great risks for those FIs that operate in and lend to foreign markets and customers. Even those FIs that do not have foreign customers can be exposed to foreign exchange and sovereign risk if their domestic customers have business dealings with foreign countries. As a result, FI managers must devote significant time to understanding and managing the various risks to which their FIs are exposed.

# INTEREST RATE RISK

**interest rate risk**
The risk incurred by an FI when the maturities of its assets and liabilities are mismatched.

Chapter 1 discussed asset transformation as a key special function of FIs. Asset transformation involves an FI's buying primary securities or assets and issuing secondary securities or liabilities to fund asset purchases. The primary securities purchased by FIs often have maturity and liquidity characteristics different from those of the secondary securities FIs sell. In mismatching the maturities of assets and liabilities as part of their asset-transformation function, FIs potentially expose themselves to **interest rate risk.**

**EXAMPLE 7–1**

*Impact of an Interest Rate Increase on an FI's Profits When the Maturity of Its Assets Exceeds the Maturity of Its Liabilities*

Consider an FI that issues $100 million of liabilities of one-year maturity to finance the purchase of $100 million of assets with a two-year maturity. We show this situation in the following time lines:

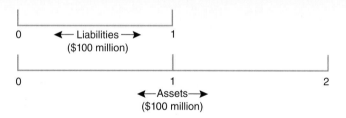

In these time lines the FI can be viewed as being "short-funded." That is, the maturity of its liabilities is less than the maturity of its assets.

Suppose the cost of funds (liabilities) for the FI is 9 percent per year and the return on assets is 10 percent per year. Over the first year the FI can lock in a profit spread of 1 percent (10 percent − 9 percent) times $100 million by borrowing short term (for one year) and lending long term (for two years). Thus, its profit is $1 million (0.01 × $100 m).

However, its profits for the second year are uncertain. If the level of interest rates does not change, the FI can *refinance* its liabilities at 9 percent and lock in a 1 percent, or $1 million, profit for the second year as well. There is always a risk, however, that interest rates will change between years 1 and 2. If interest rates were to rise and the FI can borrow new one-year liabilities only at 11 percent in the second year, its profit spread in the second year

[1] Recall that Appendix 2B at the book's website (www.mhhe.com/saunders8e) contains an overview of the evaluation of FI performance and risk exposure ("Commercial Banks' Financial Statements and Analysis"). Included are several accounting ratio–based measures of risk.

would actually be negative; that is, 10 percent − 11 percent = −1 percent, or the FI's loss is $1 million (−0.01 × $100 m). The positive spread earned in the first year by the FI from holding assets with a longer maturity than its liabilities would be offset by a negative spread in the second year. Note that if interest rates were to rise by more than 1 percent in the second year, the FI would stand to take losses over the two-year period as a whole. As a result, when an FI holds longer-term assets relative to liabilities, it potentially exposes itself to **refinancing risk.** This is the risk that the cost of rolling over or reborrowing funds could be more than the return earned on asset investments. The classic example of this type of mismatch was demonstrated by U.S. savings institutions during the 1980s (see Chapter 2).

**refinancing risk**
The risk that the cost of rolling over or reborrowing funds will rise above the returns being earned on asset investments.

---

**EXAMPLE 7–2**

*Impact of an Interest Rate Decrease When the Maturity of an FI's Liabilities Exceeds the Maturity of Its Assets*

An alternative balance sheet structure would have the FI borrowing $100 million for a longer term than the $100 million of assets in which it invests. In the time lines below the FI is "long-funded." The maturity of its liabilities is longer than the maturity of its assets. Using a similar example, suppose the FI borrows funds at 9 percent per year for two years and invests the funds in assets that yield 10 percent for one year. This situation is shown as follows:

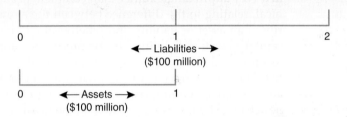

In this case, the FI is also exposed to an interest rate risk; by holding shorter-term assets relative to liabilities, it faces uncertainty about the interest rate at which it can reinvest funds in the second period. As before, the FI locks in a one-year profit spread of 1 percent, or $1 million. At the end of the first year, the assets mature and the funds that have been borrowed for two years have to be reinvested. Suppose interest rates fall between the first and second years so that in the second year the return on $100 million invested in new one-year assets is 8 percent. The FI would face a loss, or negative spread, in the second year of 1 percent (that is, 8 percent asset return minus 9 percent cost of funds), or the FI loses $1 million (−0.01 × $100 m). The positive spread earned in the first year by the FI from holding assets with a shorter maturity than its liabilities is offset by a negative spread in the second year. Thus, the FI is exposed to **reinvestment risk;** by holding shorter-term assets relative to liabilities, it faces uncertainty about the interest rate at which it can reinvest funds borrowed for a longer period. As interest rates fell in the 2000s, good examples of this exposure were provided by banks that borrowed fixed-rate deposits while investing in floating-rate loans, that is, loans whose interest rates changed or adjusted frequently.

**reinvestment risk**
The risk that the return on funds to be reinvested will fall below the cost of funds.

---

In addition to a potential refinancing or reinvestment risk that occurs when interest rates change, an FI faces *market value* risk as well. Remember that the market (or fair) value of an asset or liability is conceptually equal to the present value of current and future cash flows from that asset or liability. Therefore, rising interest rates increase the discount rate on those cash flows and reduce the market value of that asset or liability. Conversely, falling interest rates increase the market values of assets and liabilities. Moreover, mismatching maturities by holding longer-term assets than liabilities means that when interest rates rise, the market value of the FI's assets falls by a greater amount than its liabilities. This exposes the FI to the risk of economic loss and, potentially, the risk of insolvency.

If holding assets and liabilities with mismatched maturities exposes FIs to reinvestment (or refinancing) and market value risks, FIs can seek to hedge, or protect against, interest rate risk by matching the maturity of their assets and liabilities.[2] This has resulted in the general philosophy that matching maturities is somehow the best policy to hedge interest rate risk for FIs that are averse to risk. Note, however, that matching maturities is not necessarily consistent with an active asset-transformation function for FIs. That is, FIs cannot be asset transformers (e.g., transforming short-term deposits into long-term loans) and direct balance sheet matchers or hedgers at the same time. While reducing exposure to interest rate risk, matching maturities may also reduce the FI's profitability because returns from acting as specialized risk-bearing asset transformers are reduced. As a result, some FIs emphasize asset–liability maturity mismatching more than others. For example, depository institutions traditionally hold longer-term assets than liabilities, whereas life insurers tend to match the long-term nature of their liabilities with long-term assets. Finally, matching maturities hedges interest rate risk only in a very approximate rather than complete fashion. The reasons for this are technical, relating to the difference between the average life (or duration) and maturity of an asset or liability and whether the FI partly funds its assets with equity capital as well as liabilities. In the preceding simple examples, the FI financed its assets completely with borrowed funds. In the real world, FIs use a mix of liabilities and stockholders' equity to finance asset purchases. When assets and liabilities are not equal, hedging risk (i.e., insulating FI's stockholders' equity values) may be achieved by not exactly matching the maturities (or average lives) of assets and liabilities. We discuss the causes of interest rate risk and methods used to measure interest rate risk in detail in Chapters 8 and 9. We discuss the methods and instruments used to hedge interest rate risk in Chapters 22 through 24.

---

| **Concept Questions** | 1. What is refinancing risk? |
| --- | --- |
| | 2. Why does a rise in the level of interest rates adversely affect the market value of both assets and liabilities? |
| | 3. Explain the concept of maturity matching. |

---

# CREDIT RISK

**credit risk**
The risk that the promised cash flows from loans and securities held by FIs may not be paid in full.

**Credit risk** arises because of the possibility that promised cash flows on financial claims held by FIs, such as loans or bonds, will not be paid in full. Virtually all types of FIs face this risk. However, in general, FIs that make loans or buy bonds with long maturities are more exposed than are FIs that make loans or buy bonds with short maturities. This means, for example, that depository institutions and life

---

[2] This assumes that FIs can directly "control" the maturities of their assets and liabilities. As interest rates fall, many mortgage borrowers seek to "prepay" their existing loans and refinance at a lower rate. This prepayment risk—which is directly related to interest rate movements—can be viewed as a further interest rate–related risk. Prepayment risk is discussed in detail in Chapter 26.

insurers are more exposed to credit risk than are money market mutual funds and property–casualty insurers. If the principal on all financial claims held by FIs was paid in full on maturity and interest payments were made on the promised dates, FIs would always receive back the original principal lent plus an interest return. That is, they would face no credit risk. If a borrower defaults, however, both the principal loaned and the interest payments expected to be received are at risk. As a result, many financial claims issued by corporations and held by FIs promise a limited or fixed upside return (principal and interest payments to the lender) with a high probability and a large downside risk (loss of loan principal and promised interest) with a much smaller probability. Good examples of financial claims issued with these return-risk trade-offs are fixed-income coupon bonds issued by corporations and bank loans. In both cases, an FI holding these claims as assets earns the coupon on the bond or the interest promised on the loan if no borrower default occurs. In the event of default, however, the FI earns zero interest on the asset and may lose all or part of the principal lent, depending on its ability to lay claim to some of the borrower's assets through legal bankruptcy and insolvency proceedings. Accordingly, a key role of FIs involves screening and monitoring loan applicants to ensure that FIs fund the most creditworthy loans (see Chapter 10).

The effects of credit risk are evident in Figure 7–1, which shows commercial bank charge-off (or write-off) rates for various types of loans between 1984 and 2012. Notice, in particular, the high rate of charge-offs experienced on credit card loans throughout this period. Indeed, credit card charge-offs by commercial banks increased persistently from the mid-1980s until 1993 and again from 1995 through early 1998. By 1998, charge-offs leveled off, and they even declined after 1998.

**FIGURE 7–1**
**Charge-Off Rates for Commercial Bank Lending Activities, 1984–2012**

Source: FDIC, *Quarterly Banking Profile,* various issues. *www.fdic.gov*

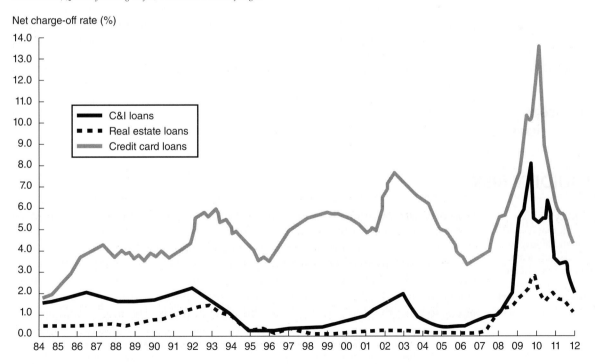

However, a weak economy and change in bankruptcy laws[3] resulted in a surge in credit card charge-offs in the early 2000s and during the recession from 2007–2010. Despite these losses, credit card loans extended by commercial banks (including unused balances) continued to grow, from $1.856 trillion in March 1997 to $4.367 trillion in September 2008. With the financial crisis, total credit card loans had fallen to $3.626 trillion in March 2009, and they remained relatively low for several years as the U.S. economy failed to show any robust growth. In March 2012, credit card loans extended by commercial banks totaled $3.289 trillion.

The potential loss an FI can experience from lending suggests that FIs need to monitor and collect information about borrowers whose assets are in their portfolios and to monitor those borrowers over time. Thus, managerial monitoring efficiency and credit risk management strategies directly affect the return and risks of the loan portfolio. Moreover, one of the advantages FIs have over individual household investors is the ability to diversify some credit risk from a single asset away by exploiting the law of large numbers in their asset investment portfolios (see Chapter 1). Diversification across assets, such as loans exposed to credit risk, reduces the overall credit risk in the asset portfolio and thus increases the probability of partial or full repayment of principal and/or interest.

FIs earn the maximum dollar return when all bonds and loans pay off interest and principal in full. In reality, some loans or bonds default on interest payments, principal payments, or both. Thus, the mean return on the asset portfolio would be less than the maximum possible. The effect of risk diversification is to truncate or limit the probabilities of the bad outcomes in the portfolio. In effect, diversification reduces individual **firm-specific credit risk,** such as the risk specific to holding the bonds or loans of General Motors, while leaving the FI still exposed to **systematic credit risk,** such as factors that simultaneously increase the default risk of all firms in the economy (e.g., an economic recession). We describe methods to measure the default risk of individual corporate claims such as bonds and loans in Chapter 10. In Chapter 11, we investigate methods of measuring the risk in portfolios of such claims. Chapter 25 discusses various methods—for example, loan sales, reschedulings, and a good bank–bad bank structure—to manage and control credit risk exposures better, while Chapters 22, 23, 24, and 26 discuss the role of the credit derivative markets in hedging credit risk.

---

**firm-specific credit risk**
The risk of default of the borrowing firm associated with the specific types of project risk taken by that firm.

**systematic credit risk**
The risk of default associated with general economywide or macro conditions affecting all borrowers.

---

| **Concept Questions** | 1. Why does credit risk exist for FIs?<br>2. How does diversification affect an FI's credit risk exposure? |
| --- | --- |

---

# LIQUIDITY RISK

**liquidity risk**
The risk that a sudden surge in liability withdrawals may leave an FI in a position of having to liquidate assets in a very short period of time and at low prices.

**Liquidity risk** arises when an FI's liability holders, such as depositors or insurance policyholders, demand immediate cash for the financial claims they hold with an FI or when holders of off-balance-sheet loan commitments (or credit lines) suddenly exercise their right to borrow (draw down their loan commitments). For example, when liability holders demand cash immediacy—that is, "put" their financial claims back to the FI—the FI must either borrow additional funds or sell assets to meet the demand for the withdrawal of funds. The most liquid asset of

---

[3] In the early 2000s, the U.S. Congress considered and passed legislation that made it more difficult for individuals to declare bankruptcy. This congressional activity brought about a rise in bankruptcy filings before changes took effect.

all is cash, which FIs can use to directly meet liability holders' demands to withdraw funds. Although FIs limit their cash asset holdings because cash earns no interest, low cash holdings are usually not a problem. Day-to-day withdrawals by liability holders are generally predictable, and FIs can normally expect to borrow additional funds to meet any sudden shortfalls of cash on the money and financial markets.

However, there are times when an FI can face a liquidity crisis. Because of a lack of confidence by liability holders in the FI or some unexpected need for cash, liability holders may demand *larger* withdrawals than normal. When all, or many, FIs face abnormally large cash demands, the cost of additional purchased or borrowed funds rises and the supply of such funds becomes restricted. As a consequence, FIs may have to sell some of their less liquid assets to meet the withdrawal demands of liability holders. This results in a more serious liquidity risk, especially as some assets with "thin" markets generate lower prices when the asset sale is immediate than when the FI has more time to negotiate the sale of an asset. As a result, the liquidation of some assets at low or fire-sale prices (the price an FI receives if an asset must be liquidated immediately at less than its fair market value) could threaten an FI's profitability and solvency. For example, in the summer of 2008 IndyMac bank failed, in part due to a bank run that con-

www.fdic.gov    tinued for several days, even after being taken over by the FDIC. The bank had announced on July 7 that, due to its deteriorating capital position, its mortgage operations would stop and it would operate only as a retail bank. News reports over the weekend highlighted the possibility that IndyMac would become the largest bank failure in over 20 years. Worried that they would not have access to their money, bank depositors rushed to withdraw money from IndyMac even though their deposits were insured up to $100,000 by the FDIC.[4] The run was so large that within a week of the original announcement, the FDIC had to step in and take over the bank.

---

**EXAMPLE 7–3**

*Impact of Liquidity Risk on an FI's Equity Value*

Consider the simple FI balance sheet in Table 7–2. Before deposit withdrawals, the FI has $10 million in cash assets and $90 million in nonliquid assets (such as small business loans). These assets were funded with $90 million in deposits and $10 million in owner's equity. Suppose that depositors unexpectedly withdrew $15 million in deposits (perhaps due to the release of negative news about the profits of the FI) and the FI receives no new deposits to replace them. To meet these deposit withdrawals, the FI first uses the $10 million it has in cash assets and then seeks to sell some of its nonliquid assets to raise an additional $5 million in cash. Assume that the FI cannot borrow any more funds in the short-term money markets, and because it cannot wait to get better prices for its assets in the future (as it needs the cash now to meet immediate depositor withdrawals), the FI has to sell any nonliquid assets at 50 cents on the dollar. Thus, to cover the remaining $5 million in deposit withdrawals, the FI must sell $10 million in nonliquid assets, incurring a loss of $5 million from the face value of those assets. The FI must then write off any such losses against its capital or equity funds. Because its capital was only $10 million before the deposit withdrawal, the loss on the fire-sale of assets of $5 million leaves the FI with only $5 million in equity.

---

[4] One reason is that, although deposits were insured up to $100,000 (since increased to $250,000), it may take some days to transfer deposits to the bank of an acquirer. IndyMac was eventually acquired by OneWest Bank Group.

**TABLE 7–2**
Adjusting to a
Deposit Withdrawal
Using Asset Sales

| *(in millions)* | | | | | | | |
|---|---|---|---|---|---|---|---|
| **Before the Withdrawal** | | | | **After the Withdrawal** | | | |
| **Assets** | | **Liabilities/Equity** | | **Assets** | | **Liabilities/Equity** | |
| Cash assets | $ 10 | Deposit | $ 90 | Cash assets | $ 0 | Deposits | $ 75 |
| Nonliquid assets | 90 | Equity | 10 | Nonliquid assets | 80 | Equity | 5 |
| | $100 | | $100 | | $80 | | $ 80 |

We examine the nature of normal, abnormal, and run-type liquidity risks and their impact on FIs in more detail in Chapter 12. In addition, we look at ways an FI can better manage liquidity and liability risk exposures in Chapter 18. Chapter 19 discusses the roles of deposit insurance and other liability guarantee schemes in deterring deposit (liability) runs.

---

**Concept Questions**

1. Why might an FI face a sudden liquidity crisis?
2. What circumstances might lead an FI to liquidate assets at fire-sale prices?

---

# FOREIGN EXCHANGE RISK

Increasingly, FIs have recognized that both direct foreign investment and foreign portfolio investments can extend the operational and financial benefits available from purely domestic investments. Thus, U.S. pension funds that held approximately 5 percent of their assets in foreign securities in the early 1990s now hold over 12 percent of their assets in foreign securities. At the same time, many large U.S. banks, investment banks, and mutual funds have become more global in their orientation. To the extent that the returns on domestic and foreign investments are imperfectly correlated, there are potential gains for an FI that expands its asset holdings and liability funding beyond the domestic borders.

The returns on domestic and foreign direct investing and portfolio investments are not perfectly correlated for two reasons. The first is that the underlying technologies of various economies differ, as do the firms in those economies. For example, one economy may be based on agriculture while another is industry based. Given different economic infrastructures, one economy could be expanding while another is contracting. In the early 2010s, for example, the U.S. economy was expanding while the European economy was recessionary. The second reason is that exchange rate changes are not perfectly correlated across countries. This means the dollar–euro exchange rate may be appreciating while the dollar–yen exchange rate may be falling.

**foreign exchange risk**
The risk that exchange rate changes can affect the value of an FI's assets and liabilities denominated in foreign currencies.

One potential benefit from an FI's becoming increasingly global in its outlook is an ability to expand abroad directly through branching or acquisitions or by developing a financial asset portfolio that includes foreign securities as well as domestic securities. Even so, foreign investment exposes an FI to **foreign exchange risk.** Foreign exchange risk is the risk that exchange rate changes can adversely affect the value of an FI's assets and liabilities denominated in foreign currencies.

To understand how foreign exchange risk arises, suppose that a U.S. FI makes a loan to a British company in pounds (£). Should the British pound depreciate in value relative to the U.S. dollar, the principal and interest payments received by U.S. investors would be devalued in dollar terms. Indeed, were the British pound to fall far enough over the investment period, when cash flows are converted back into dollars, the overall return could be negative. That is, on the conversion of principal and interest payments from pounds into dollars, foreign exchange losses can offset the promised value of local currency interest payments at the original exchange rate at which the investment occurred.

In general, an FI can hold assets denominated in a foreign currency and/or issue foreign liabilities. Consider a U.S. FI that holds £100 million in pound loans as assets and funds £80 million of them with pound certificates of deposit. The difference between the £100 million in pound loans and £80 million in pound CDs is funded by dollar CDs (i.e., £20 million worth of dollar CDs). See Figure 7–2. In this case, the U.S. FI is *net long* £20 million in pound assets; that is, it holds more foreign assets than liabilities. The U.S. FI suffers losses if the exchange rate for pounds falls or depreciates against the dollar over this period. In dollar terms, the value of the pound loan assets falls or decreases in value by more than the pound CD liabilities do. That is, the FI is exposed to the risk that its net foreign assets may have to be liquidated at an exchange rate lower than the one that existed when the FI entered into the foreign asset–liability position.

Instead, the FI could have £20 million more pound liabilities than assets; in this case, it would be holding a *net short* position in pound assets, as shown in Figure 7–3. Under this circumstance, the FI is exposed to foreign exchange risk if the pound appreciates against the dollar over the investment period. This occurs because the value of its pound liabilities in dollar terms rose faster than the return on its pound assets. Consequently, to be approximately hedged, the FI must match its assets and liabilities in each foreign currency.

Note that the FI is fully hedged only if we assume that it holds foreign assets and liabilities of exactly the same maturity.[5] Consider what happens if the FI matches the size of its foreign currency book (Pound assets = Pound liabilities = £100 million in that currency) but mismatches the maturities so that the pound assets are of

**FIGURE 7–2**
The Foreign Asset and Liability Position: Net Long Asset Position in Pounds

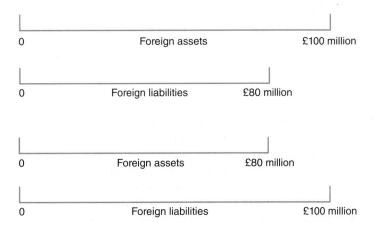

**FIGURE 7–3**
The Foreign Asset and Liability Position: Net Short Asset Position in Pounds

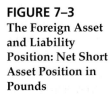

[5] Technically speaking, hedging requires matching the durations (average lives of assets and liabilities) rather than simple maturities (see Chapter 9).

six-month maturity and the liabilities are of three-month maturity. The FI would then be exposed to foreign interest rate risk—the risk that British interest rates would rise when it has to roll over its £100 million in pound CD liabilities at the end of the third month. Consequently, an FI that matches both the size and maturities of its exposure in assets and liabilities of a given currency is hedged, or immunized, against foreign currency and foreign interest rate risk. To the extent that FIs mismatch their portfolio and maturity exposures in different currency assets and liabilities, they face both foreign currency and foreign interest rate risks. As already noted, if foreign exchange rate and interest rate changes are not perfectly correlated across countries, an FI can diversify away part, if not all, of its foreign currency risk. We discuss the measurement and evaluation of an FI's foreign currency risk exposure in depth in Chapter 13.

| **Concept Questions** | 1. Explain why the returns on domestic and foreign portfolio investments are not, in general, perfectly correlated. |
|---|---|
| | 2. A U.S. bank is net long in European assets. If the euro appreciates against the dollar, will the bank gain or lose? |

## COUNTRY OR SOVEREIGN RISK

**country or sovereign risk**
The risk that repayments from foreign borrowers may be interrupted because of interference from foreign governments.

As we noted in the previous section, a globally oriented FI that mismatches the size and maturities of its foreign assets and liabilities is exposed to foreign currency and foreign interest rate risks. Even beyond these risks, and even when investing in dollars, holding assets in a foreign country can expose an FI to an additional type of foreign investment risk called **country or sovereign risk.** Country or sovereign risk is a different type of credit risk that is faced by an FI that purchases assets such as the bonds and loans of foreign corporations. For example, when a domestic corporation is unable or unwilling to repay a loan, an FI usually has recourse to the domestic bankruptcy courts and eventually may recoup at least a portion of its original investment when the assets of the defaulted firm are liquidated or restructured. By comparison, a foreign corporation may be unable to repay the principal or interest on a loan even if it would like to. Most commonly, the government of the country in which the corporation is headquartered may prohibit or limit debt payments because of foreign currency shortages and adverse political reasons.

For example, in 2001, the government of Argentina, which had pegged its peso to the dollar on a one-to-one basis since the early 1990s, had to default on its government debt largely because of an overvalued peso and the adverse effect this had on its exports and foreign currency earnings. In December 2001, Argentina ended up defaulting on $130 billion in government-issued debt and, in 2002, passed legislation that led to defaults on $30 billion of corporate debt owed to foreign creditors. Argentina's economic problems continued into the mid-2000s. In September 2003 it defaulted on a $3 billion loan repayment to the IMF and in 2005 Argentina announced that it was offering its creditors about 30 cents on the dollar from its 2001 debt restructuring of $103 billion. More recently, despite massive injections of bailout funds by the eurozone and the International Monetary Fund, in March 2012, Greek government debtholders lost 53.5 percent of their $265 billion investment as Greece restructured much of its sovereign debt. The restructuring produced the largest-ever sovereign debt default.

In the event of such restrictions, reschedulings, or outright prohibitions on the payment of debt obligations by sovereign governments, the FI claimholder has little, if any, recourse to the local bankruptcy courts or an international civil claims court. The major leverage available to an FI to ensure or increase repayment probabilities and amounts is its control over the future supply of loans or funds to the country concerned. However, such leverage may be very weak in the face of a country's collapsing currency and government. Chapter 14 discusses how country or sovereign risk is measured and considers possible financial market solutions to the country risk exposure problems of a globally oriented FI.

| **Concept Questions** | 1. Can an FI be subject to sovereign risk if it lends only to the highest-quality foreign corporations? |
| --- | --- |
| | 2. What is one major way an FI can discipline a country that threatens not to repay its loans? |

# MARKET RISK

**market risk**
The risk incurred in the trading of assets and liabilities due to changes in interest rates, exchange rates, and other asset prices.

**Market risk** arises when FIs actively trade assets and liabilities (and derivatives) rather than hold them for longer-term investment, funding, or hedging purposes. Market risk is closely related to interest rate risk, credit risk, and foreign exchange risk in that as these risks increase or decrease, the overall risk of the FI is affected. However, market risk adds another dimension resulting from its trading activity. Market risk is the incremental risk incurred by an FI when interest rate, foreign exchange, and credit risks are combined with an active trading strategy, especially one that involves short trading horizons such as a day. Conceptually, an FI's trading portfolio can be differentiated from its investment portfolio on the basis of time horizon and secondary market liquidity. The trading portfolio contains assets, liabilities, and derivative contracts that can be quickly bought or sold on organized financial markets. The investment portfolio (or in the case of banks, the so-called banking book) contains assets and liabilities that are relatively illiquid and held for longer holding periods. Table 7–3 shows a hypothetical breakdown

**TABLE 7–3**
**The Investment (Banking) Book and Trading Book of a Commercial Bank**

| | **Assets** | **Liabilities** |
| --- | --- | --- |
| Banking book | Cash | Deposits |
| | Loans | Other illiquid borrowed funds |
| | Premises and equipment | Capital |
| | Other illiquid assets | |
| Trading book | Bonds (long) | Bonds (short) |
| | Commodities (long) | Commodities (short) |
| | FX (long) | FX (short) |
| | Equities (long) | Equities (short) |
| | Derivatives* (long) | Derivatives* (short) |

*Derivatives are off-balance-sheet items (as discussed in Chapter 16).

between banking book and trading book assets and liabilities. As can be seen, the banking book contains the majority of loans and deposits plus other illiquid assets. The trading book contains long and short positions in instruments such as bonds, commodities, foreign exchange (FX), equities, and derivatives.

With the increasing securitization of bank loans (e.g., mortgages), more and more assets have become liquid and tradable. Of course, with time, every asset and liability can be sold. While bank regulators have normally viewed tradable assets as those being held for horizons of less than one year, private FIs take an even shorter-term view. In particular, FIs are concerned about the fluctuation in the value of their trading account assets and liabilities for periods as short as one day especially if such fluctuations pose a threat to their solvency.

An extreme case of the type of risk involved in active trading is, of course, the market meltdown of 2008–2009. As mortgage borrowers defaulted on their mortgages, financial institutions that held these mortgages and mortgage-backed securities started announcing huge losses on them. It is these securitized loans, and particularly securitized subprime mortgage loans, that led to huge financial losses resulting from market risk. Investment banks and securities firms were major purchasers of mortgage originators in the early 2000s, which allowed them to increase their business of packaging the loans as securities. As mortgage borrowers defaulted on their mortgages, the securitized mortgage market froze up and FIs were left to hold these "toxic" assets at deeply reduced market values. Investment banks were particularly hard hit with huge losses on the mortgages and securities backing them. On Monday, September 15, Lehman Brothers (the 158-year-old investment bank) filed for bankruptcy, Merrill Lynch was bought by Bank of America, AIG (one of the world's largest insurance companies) met with federal regulators to raise desperately needed cash, and Washington Mutual (the largest savings institution in the United States) was acquired by J.P. Morgan Chase. A sense of foreboding gripped Wall Street. The Dow fell more than 500 points, the largest drop in over seven years. World stock markets saw huge swings in value as investors tried to sort out who might survive (markets from Russia to Europe were forced to suspend trading as stock prices plunged). By mid-September, financial markets froze and banks stopped lending to each other at anything but exorbitantly high rates. Banks that were active traders faced extreme market risk.

The financial market crisis illustrates that market, or trading, risk is present whenever an FI takes an open or unhedged long (buy) or sell (short) position in bonds, equities, foreign exchange, and derivative products, and prices change in a direction opposite to that expected. As a result, the more volatile are asset prices in the markets in which these instruments trade, the greater are the market risks faced by FIs that adopt open trading positions. This requires FI management (and regulators) to establish controls to limit positions taken by traders as well as to develop models to measure the market risk exposure of an FI on a day-to-day basis. These market risk measurement models are discussed in Chapter 15.

| **Concept Questions** | 1. What is market, or trading, risk? |
| | 2. What modern conditions have led to an increase in this particular type of risk for FIs? |

# OFF-BALANCE-SHEET RISK

**off-balance-sheet risk**
The risk incurred by an FI due to activities related to contingent assets and liabilities.

One of the most striking trends for many modern FIs has been the growth in their off-balance-sheet activities and thus their **off-balance-sheet risk.** While all FIs to some extent engage in off-balance-sheet activities, most attention has been drawn to the activities of banks, especially large banks, who invest heavily in off-balance-sheet assets and liabilities, particularly derivative securities. By contrast, off-balance-sheet activities have been less of a concern to smaller depository institutions and many insurance companies, who hold relatively few off-balance-sheet securities. An off-balance-sheet activity, by definition, does not appear on an FI's current balance sheet since it does not involve holding a *current primary* claim (asset) or the issuance of a *current secondary* claim (liability). Instead, off-balance-sheet activities affect the *future* shape of an FI's balance sheet in that they involve the creation of contingent assets and liabilities that give rise to their potential (future) placement on the balance sheet. Thus, accountants place them "below the bottom line" of an FI's asset and liability balance sheet.

**letter of credit**
A credit guarantee issued by an FI for a fee on which payment is contingent on some future event occurring.

A good example of an off-balance-sheet activity is the issuance of standby **letter of credit** guarantees by insurance companies and banks to back the issuance of municipal bonds. Many state and local governments could not issue such securities without bank or insurance company *letter of credit guarantees* that promise principal and interest payments to investors should the municipality default on its future obligations. Thus, the letter of credit guarantees payment should a municipal government (e.g., New York State) face financial problems in paying the promised interest payments and/or the principal on the bonds it issues. If a municipal government's cash flow is sufficiently strong so as to pay off the principal and interest on the debt it issues, the letter of credit guarantee issued by the FI expires unused. Nothing appears on the FI's balance sheet today or in the future. However, the fee earned for issuing the letter of credit guarantee appears on the FI's income statement.

As a result, the ability to earn fee income while not loading up or expanding the balance sheet has become an important motivation for FIs to pursue off-balance-sheet business. Unfortunately, this activity is not risk free. Suppose the municipal government defaults on its bond interest and principal payments. Then the contingent liability or guaranty the FI issued becomes an actual liability that appears on the FI's balance sheet. That is, the FI has to use its own equity to compensate investors in municipal bonds.

Letters of credit are just one example of off-balance-sheet activities. Others include loan commitments by banks, mortgage servicing contracts by depository institutions, and positions in forwards, futures, swaps, and other derivative securities by almost all large FIs. While some of these activities are structured to reduce an FI's exposure to credit, interest rate, or foreign exchange risks, mismanagement or speculative use of these instruments can result in major losses to FIs. Indeed, as seen during the financial crisis of 2008–2009, significant losses in off-balance-sheet activities (e.g., credit default swaps) can cause an FI to fail, just as major losses due to balance sheet default and interest rate risks can cause an FI to fail.

We detail the specific nature of the risks of off-balance-sheet activities more fully in Chapter 16. We look at how some of these instruments (forwards, futures, options, and swaps) can be used to manage risks in Chapters 22, 23, 24, and 26.

**EXAMPLE 7–4**

*Impact of Off-Balance-Sheet Risk on an FI's Equity Value*

Consider Table 7–4. In Panel A, the value of the FI's net worth ($E$) is calculated in the traditional way as the difference between the market values of its on-balance-sheet assets ($A$) and liabilities ($L$):

$$E = A - L$$
$$10 = 100 - 90$$

Under this calculation, the market value of the stockholders' equity stake in the FI is 10 and the ratio of the FI's capital to assets is 10 percent. Regulators and FIs often use the latter ratio as a simple measure of solvency (see Chapter 20 for more details).

A more accurate picture of the FI's economic solvency should consider the market values of both its on-balance-sheet and OBS activities (Panel B of Table 7–4). Specifically, the FI manager should value contingent or future asset and liability claims as well as current assets and liabilities. In our example, the current market value of the FI's contingent assets ($CA$) is 50; the current market value of its contingent liabilities ($CL$) is 55. Since $CL$ exceed $CA$ by 5, this difference is an additional obligation, or claim, on the FI's net worth. That is, stockholders' true net worth ($E$) is really:

$$E = (A - L) + (CA - CL)$$
$$= (100 - 90) + (50 - 55) = 5$$

rather than 10 when we ignored off-balance-sheet activities. Thus, economically speaking, contingent assets and liabilities are contractual claims that directly impact the economic value of the equity holders' stake in an FI. Indeed, from both the stockholders' and regulators' perspectives, large increases in the value of OBS liabilities can render the FI economically insolvent just as effectively as losses due to mismatched interest rate gaps and default or credit losses from on-balance-sheet activities.

**TABLE 7–4**
Valuation of an FI's Net Worth with and without Consideration of Off-Balance-Sheet Activities

| Panel A: Traditional Valuation of an FI's Net Worth | | | | |
|---|---|---|---|---|
| Market value of assets ($A$) | 100 | Market value of liabilities ($L$) | | 90 |
| | | Net worth ($E$) | | 10 |
| | 100 | | | 100 |

| Panel B: Valuation of an FI's Net Worth with On- and Off-Balance-Sheet Activities Valued | | | | |
|---|---|---|---|---|
| Market value of assets ($A$) | 100 | Market value of liabilities ($L$) | | 90 |
| | | Net worth ($E$) | | 5 |
| Market value of contingent assets ($CA$) | 50 | Market value of contingent liabilities ($CL$) | | 55 |
| | 150 | | | 150 |

**Concept Questions**

1. Why are letter of credit guarantees an off-balance-sheet item?
2. Why are FIs motivated to pursue off-balance-sheet business? What are the risks?

# TECHNOLOGY AND OPERATIONAL RISKS

Technology and operational risks are closely related and in recent years have caused great concern to FI managers and regulators alike. The Bank for International Settlements (BIS), the principal organization of central banks in the major economies

www.bis.org

of the world, defines operational risk (inclusive of technological risk) as "the risk of loss resulting from inadequate or failed internal processes, people, and systems or from external events."[6] A number of FIs add reputational risk and strategic risk (e.g., due to a failed merger) as part of a broader definition of operational risk.

Technological innovation was a major growth area of FIs in the 1990s and 2000s. Banks, insurance companies, and investment companies all sought to improve operational efficiency with major investments in internal and external communications, computers, and an expanded technological infrastructure. For example, most banks provide depositors with the capabilities to check account balances, transfer funds between accounts, manage finances, pay bills, and perform other functions from their home personal computers. At the wholesale level, electronic transfer of funds through automated clearing houses (ACH) and wire transfer payment networks such as the Clearing House Interbank Payments Systems (CHIPS) have been developed. Indeed, the global financial services firm Citigroup has operations in more than 100 countries connected in real time by a proprietary-owned satellite system.

The major objectives of technological expansion are to lower operating costs, increase profits, and capture new markets for the FI. In current terminology, the objective is to allow the FI to exploit, to the fullest extent possible, better potential economies of scale and economies of scope in selling its products. **Economies of scale** refer to an FI's ability to lower its average costs of operations by expanding its output of financial services. **Economies of scope** refer to an FI's ability to generate cost synergies by producing more than one output with the same inputs. For example, an FI could use the same information on the quality of customers stored in its computers to expand the sale of both loan products and insurance products. That is, the same information (e.g., age, job, size of family, income) can identify both potential loan and life insurance customers.

**Technology risk** occurs when technological investments do not produce the anticipated cost savings in the form of economies of either scale or scope. Diseconomies of scale, for example, arise because of excess capacity, redundant technology, and/or organizational and bureaucratic inefficiencies that become worse as an FI grows in size. Diseconomies of scope arise when an FI fails to generate perceived synergies or cost savings through major new technological investments. We describe the measurement and evidence of economies of scale and scope in FIs in Chapter 17. Technological risk can result in major losses in the competitive efficiency of an FI and, ultimately, in its long-term failure. Similarly, gains from technological investments can produce performance superior to an FI's rivals as well as allow it to develop new and innovative products, enhancing its long-term survival chances.

**Operational risk** is partly related to technology risk and can arise whenever existing technology malfunctions or back-office support systems break down. For example, the biggest known theft of credit card numbers was discovered in May 2007, when, over a two-year period, as many as 200 million card numbers were stolen from TJX Company—parent company to such retail stores as Marshalls and TJ Maxx. The retailer's wireless network reportedly had less security than most home networks. Even though such computer breakdowns are rare, their occurrence can cause major dislocations in the FIs involved and potentially disrupt the financial system in general.

**economies of scale**
The degree to which an FI's average unit costs of producing financial services fall as its outputs of services increase.

**economies of scope**
The degree to which an FI can generate cost synergies by producing multiple financial service products.

**technology risk**
The risk incurred by an FI when technological investments do not produce the cost savings anticipated.

**operational risk**
The risk that existing technology or support systems may malfunction or break down.

---

[6] See Basel Committee on Bank Supervision, "Sound Practices for the Management and Supervision of Operational Risk," July 2002, p. 2, Basel, Switzerland.

Operational risk is not exclusively the result of technological failure. For example, employee fraud and errors constitute a type of operational risk that often negatively affects the reputation of an FI (see Chapter 17). A good example involves $2 billion in trading losses incurred by J.P. Morgan Chase's trader, Bruno Iksil, also known as "the London Whale," who had taken large credit default swap (CDS) positions in expectation that the financial crisis in Europe would cause anxiety in financial markets. Instead, bailouts, austerity measures, and interventions prevented any major events in Europe. To maintain the proper balance and deal with expiring contracts, Iksil needed to continually make new trades. But the CDS market was too small and the amounts Iksil was trading were too large to let J.P. Morgan operate in secrecy. Once the story got out, hedge funds traders took positions designed to gain from the trades that Iksil had to make to keep the position going. That activity negatively altered prices on the CDSs that Iksil needed. Eventually, the only choice was to close the CDS position and take the loss. These activities by employees of FIs result in an overall loss of reputation and, in turn, business for the FI employers.

---

| **Concept Questions** | 1. What is the difference between economies of scale and economies of scope? |
| | 2. How is operational risk related to technology risk? |
| | 3. How does technological expansion help an FI better exploit economies of scale and economies of scope? When might technology risk interfere with these goals? |

---

# INSOLVENCY RISK

**insolvency risk**
The risk that an FI may not have enough capital to offset a sudden decline in the value of its assets relative to its liabilities.

**Insolvency risk** is a consequence or outcome of one or more of the risks described above: interest rate, credit, liquidity, foreign exchange, sovereign, market, off-balance-sheet, and technology risks. Technically, insolvency occurs when the capital or equity resources of an FI's owners are driven to, or near to, zero because of losses incurred as the result of one or more of the risks described above. Consider the case of Washington Mutual (WaMu), which incurred heavy losses from its on- and off-balance-sheet holdings during the financial crisis. By early September 2008, WaMu's market capital was worth only $3.5 billion, down from $43 billion at the end of 2006. In September 2008, the bank was taken over by the FDIC and sold to J.P. Morgan Chase. In contrast, in March 2009, Citigroup's stock price fell to below $1 per share, and the once largest bank in the United States was near failure. Proving that some banks are too big to fail, Citigroup received a substantial government guarantee against losses (up to $306 billion) and a $20 billion injection of cash to prevent failure. Indeed, through December 2009 more than 700 banks had received a total of $205 billion in federal government funds (through the Capital Purchase Program) in an effort to prop up capital and support lending.

In general, the more equity capital to borrowed funds an FI has—that is, the lower its leverage—the better able it is to withstand losses, whether due to adverse interest rate changes, unexpected credit losses, or other reasons. Thus, both management and regulators of FIs focus on an FI's capital (and adequacy) as a key measure of its ability to remain solvent and grow in the face of a multitude of risk exposures. The issue of what is an adequate level of capital to manage an FI's overall risk exposure is discussed in Chapter 20.

| **Concept Questions** | 1. When does insolvency risk occur? |
| :--- | :--- |
| | 2. How is insolvency risk related to the other risks discussed in this chapter? |

## OTHER RISKS AND THE INTERACTION OF RISKS

In this chapter we have concentrated on 10 major risks continuously affecting an FI manager's decision-making process and risk management strategies. These risks were interest rate risk, credit risk, liquidity risk, foreign exchange risk, country or sovereign risk, market risk, off-balance-sheet risk, technology and operational risk, and insolvency risk. Even though the discussion generally described each independently, in reality, these risks are often interdependent. For example, when interest rates rise, corporations and consumers find maintaining promised payments on their debt more difficult. Thus, over some range of interest rate movements, credit, interest rate, and off-balance-sheet risks are positively correlated. Furthermore, the FI may have been counting on the funds from promised payments on its loans for liquidity management purposes. Thus, liquidity risk is also correlated with interest rate and credit risks. The inability of a customer to make promised payments also affects the FI's income and profits and, consequently, its equity or capital position. Thus, each risk and its interaction with other risks ultimately affects insolvency risk. Similarly, foreign exchange rate changes and interest rate changes are also highly correlated. When the Federal Reserve changes a key interest rate (such as the Fed funds rate) through its monetary policy actions, exchange rates are also likely to change.

Various other risks, often of a more discrete or event type, also impact an FI's profitability and risk exposure, although, as noted earlier, many view discrete or event risks as part of operational risks. Discrete risks might include events external to the FI, such as a sudden change in regulation policy. These include lifting the regulatory barriers to lending or to entry or on products offered (see Chapter 21). The 1994 regulatory change allowing interstate branching after 1997 is one example, as are the 1999 Financial Services Modernization Act and the Wall Street Reform and Consumer Protection Act of 2010. Other discrete or event risks involve sudden and unexpected changes in financial market conditions due to war, revolution, or sudden market collapse, such as the 1929 and 2008 stock market crashes or the September 2001 terrorist attacks in the United States. These can have a major impact on an FI's risk exposure. Other event risks include fraud, theft, earthquakes, storms, malfeasance, and breach of fiduciary trust; all of these can ultimately cause an FI to fail or be severely harmed. Yet each is difficult to model and predict.

Finally, more general macroeconomic or systematic risks, such as increased inflation, inflation volatility, and unemployment, can directly and indirectly impact an FI's level of interest rate, credit, and liquidity risk exposure. For example, the U.S. unemployment rate was greater than 10 percent in the fall of 2009, the highest level since September 1992. Since December 2007 (as the recession began) the U.S. economy lost some 8 million jobs, most of which were lost in the period November 2008 through June 2009. With so many people out of work, credit risk exposure of FIs increased dramatically as borrowers had trouble keeping up with their loan payments after losing their jobs.

| **Concept Questions** | 1. What is meant by the term *event risk?* |
| :--- | :--- |
| | 2. What are some examples of event and general macroeconomic risks that impact FIs? |

## Summary

This chapter provided an introductory view of 10 major risks faced by modern FIs. They face *interest rate risk* when the maturities of their assets and liabilities are mismatched. They face *credit risk* or default risk if their clients default on their loans and other obligations. They encounter *liquidity risk* as a result of excessive withdrawals or problems in refinancing liabilities. If FIs conduct foreign business, they are subject to additional risks, namely, *foreign exchange* and *sovereign risks*. They incur *market risk* on their trading assets and liabilities if adverse movements in interest rates, exchange rates, or other asset prices occur. Modern-day FIs also engage in significant off-balance-sheet activities that expose them to *off-balance-sheet risks:* contingent asset and liability risks. The advent of sophisticated technology and automation exposes FIs to both *technological* and *operational risks.* FI's face *insolvency risk* when their capital is insufficient to withstand the losses that they incur as a result of such risks. The interaction of the various risks means that FI managers face making trade-offs among them. As they take actions in an attempt to affect one type of risk, FI managers must consider the possible impact on other risks. The effective management of these risks determines a modern FI's success or failure. The chapters that follow analyze each of these risks in greater detail.

## Questions and Problems

1. What is the process of *asset transformation* performed by a financial institution? Why does this process often lead to the creation of *interest rate risk?* What is interest rate risk?

2. What is *refinancing risk?* How is refinancing risk part of interest rate risk? If an FI funds long-term assets with short-term liabilities, what will be the impact on earnings of an increase in the rate of interest? A decrease in the rate of interest?

3. What is *reinvestment risk?* How is reinvestment risk part of interest rate risk? If an FI funds short-term assets with long-term liabilities, what will be the impact on earnings of a decrease in the rate of interest? An increase in the rate of interest?

4. The sales literature of a mutual fund claims that the fund has no risk exposure since it invests exclusively in federal government securities which are free of default risk. Is this claim true? Explain why or why not.

5. How can interest rate risk adversely affect the economic or market value of an FI?

6. Consider an FI that issues $100 million of liabilities with one year to maturity to finance the purchase of $100 million of assets with a two-year maturity. Suppose that the cost of funds (liabilities) for the FI is 5 percent per year and the interest return on the assets is 8 percent per year.

   a. Calculate the FI's profit spread and dollar value of profit in year 1.

   b. Calculate the profit spread and dollar value of profit in year 2 if the FI can refinance its liabilities at 5 percent.

   c. If interest rates rise and the FI can borrow new one-year liabilities at 9 percent in the second year, calculate the FI's profit spread and dollar value of profit in year 2.

   d. If interest rates fall and the FI can borrow new one-year liabilities at 3 percent in the second year, calculate the FI's profit spread and dollar value of profit in year 2.

7. Consider an FI that issues $200 million of liabilities with two years to maturity to finance the purchase of $200 million of assets with a one year maturity. Suppose that the cost of funds (liabilities) for the FI is 5 percent per year and the interest return on the assets is 9 percent per year.

    a. Calculate the FI's profit spread and dollar value of profit in year 1.

    b. Calculate the profit spread and dollar value of profit in year 2 if the FI can reinvest its assets at 9 percent.

    c. If interest rates fall and the FI can invest in one-year assets at 6 percent in the second year, calculate the FI's profit spread and dollar value of profit in year 2.

    d. If interest rates rise and the FI can invest in one-year assets at 11 percent in the second year, calculate the FI's profit spread and dollar value of profit in year 2.

8. A financial institution has the following market value balance sheet structure:

| Assets | | Liabilities and Equity | |
|---|---|---|---|
| Cash | $ 1,000 | Certificate of deposit | $10,000 |
| Bond | 10,000 | Equity | 1,000 |
| Total assets | $11,000 | Total liabilities and equity | $11,000 |

    a. The bond has a 10-year maturity, a fixed-rate coupon of 10 percent paid at the end of each year, and a par value of $10,000. The certificate of deposit has a 1-year maturity and a 6 percent fixed rate of interest. The FI expects no additional asset growth. What will be the net interest income at the end of the first year? *Note:* Net interest income equals interest income minus interest expense.

    b. If at the end of year 1, market interest rates have increased 100 basis points (1 percent), what will be the net interest income for the second year? Is this result caused by reinvestment risk or refinancing risk?

    c. Assuming that market interest rates increase 1 percent, the bond will have a value of $9,446 at the end of year 1. What will be the market value of equity for the FI? Assume that all of the NII in part (a) is used to cover operating expenses or dividends.

    d. If market interest rates had decreased 100 basis points by the end of year 1, would the market value of equity be higher or lower than $1,000? Why?

    e. What factors have caused the changes in operating performance and market value for this firm?

9. How does a policy of matching the maturities of assets and liabilities work (a) to minimize interest rate risk and (b) against the asset-transformation function of FIs?

10. Corporate bonds usually pay interest semiannually. If a company decided to change from semiannual to annual interest payments, how would this affect the bond's interest rate risk?

11. Two 10-year bonds are being considered for an investment that may have to be liquidated before the maturity of the bonds. The first bond is a 10-year premium bond with a coupon rate higher than its required rate of return, and the second bond is a zero-coupon bond that pays only a lump-sum payment after 10 years with no interest over its life. Which bond would have more interest rate risk? That is, which bond's price would change by a larger amount for a given change in interest rates? Explain your answer.

12. Consider again the two bonds in problem 11. If the investment goal is to leave the assets untouched until maturity, such as for a child's education or for one's retirement, which of the two bonds has more interest rate risk? What is the source of this risk?

13. A money market mutual fund bought $1 million of two-year Treasury notes six months ago. During this time, the value of the securities has increased, but for tax reasons the mutual fund wants to postpone any sale for two more months. What type of risk does the mutual fund face for the next two months?

14. A bank invested $50 million in a two-year asset paying 10 percent interest per year and simultaneously issued a $50 million, one-year liability paying 8 percent interest per year. The liability will be rolled over after one year at the current market rate. What will be the impact on the bank's net interest income if at the end of the first year all interest rates have increased by 1 percent (100 basis points)?

15. What is *credit risk*? Which types of FIs are more susceptible to this type of risk? Why?

16. What is the difference between *firm-specific credit risk* and *systematic credit risk*? How can an FI alleviate firm-specific credit risk?

17. Many banks and savings institutions that failed in the 1980s had made loans to oil companies in Louisiana, Texas, and Oklahoma. When oil prices fell, these companies, the regional economy, and the banks and savings institutions all experienced financial problems. What types of risk were inherent in the loans that were made by these banks and savings institutions?

18. What is *liquidity risk*? What routine operating factors allow FIs to deal with this risk in times of normal economic activity? What market reality can create severe financial difficulty for an FI in times of extreme liquidity crises?

19. Consider the simple FI balance sheet below (in millions of dollars).

| **Before the Withdrawal** | | | |
|---|---|---|---|
| **Assets** | | **Liabilities/Equity** | |
| Cash assets | $ 20 | Deposit | $150 |
| Nonliquid Assets | 155 | Equity | 25 |
| | $175 | | $175 |

Suppose that depositors unexpectedly withdraw $50 million in deposits and the FI receives no new deposits to replace them. Assume that the FI cannot borrow any more funds in the short-term money markets, and because it cannot wait to get better prices for its assets in the future (as it needs the cash now to meet immediate depositor withdrawals), the FI has to sell any nonliquid assets at 75 cents on the dollar. Show the FI's balance sheet after adjustments are made for the $50 million of deposit withdrawals.

20. What two factors provide potential benefits to FIs that expand their asset holdings and liability funding sources beyond their domestic borders?

21. What is *foreign exchange risk*? What does it mean for an FI to be *net long* in foreign assets? What does it mean for an FI to be *net short* in foreign assets? In each case, what must happen to the foreign exchange rate to cause the FI to suffer losses?

22. If the Swiss franc is expected to depreciate in the near future, would a U.S.-based FI in Bern City prefer to be net long or net short in its asset positions? Discuss.

23. If international capital markets are well integrated and operate efficiently, will FIs be exposed to foreign exchange risk? What are the sources of foreign exchange risk for FIs?

24. If an FI has the same amount of foreign assets and foreign liabilities in the same currency, has that FI necessarily reduced the risk involved in these international transactions to zero? Explain.

25. A U.S. insurance company invests $1,000,000 in a private placement of British bonds. Each bond pays £300 in interest per year for 20 years. If the current exchange rate is £1.564/$, what is the nature of the insurance company's exchange rate risk? Specifically, what type of exchange rate movement concerns this insurance company?

26. Assume that a bank has assets located in London that are worth £150 million on which it earns an average of 8 percent per year. The bank has £100 million in liabilities on which it pays an average of 6 percent per year. The current spot exchange rate is £1.50/$.
    a. If the exchange rate at the end of the year is £2.00/$, will the dollar have appreciated or depreciated against the pound?
    b. Given the change in the exchange rate, what is the effect in dollars on the net interest income from the foreign assets and liabilities? *Note:* The net interest income is interest income minus interest expense.
    c. What is the effect of the exchange rate change on the value of assets and liabilities in dollars?

27. Six months ago, Qualitybank issued a $100 million, one-year maturity CD denominated in euros. On the same date, $60 million was invested in a €-denominated loan and $40 million was invested in a U.S. Treasury bill. The exchange rate on this date was €1.5675/$. Assume no repayment of principal and an exchange rate today of €1.2540/$.
    a. What is the current value of the CD principal (in euros and dollars)?
    b. What is the current value of the euro-denominated loan principal (in dollars and euros)?
    c. What is the current value of the U.S. Treasury bill (in euros and dollars)?
    d. What is Qualitybank's profit/loss from this transaction (in euros and dollars)?

28. Suppose you purchase a 10-year, AAA-rated Swiss bond for par that is paying an annual coupon of 6 percent. The bond has a face value of 1,000 Swiss francs (SF). The spot rate at the time of purchase is SF1.15/$. At the end of the year, the bond is downgraded to AA and the yield increases to 8 percent. In addition, the SF appreciates to SF1.05/$.
    a. What is the loss or gain to a Swiss investor who holds this bond for a year? What portion of this loss or gain is due to foreign exchange risk? What portion is due to interest rate risk?
    b. What is the loss or gain to a U.S. investor who holds this bond for a year? What portion of this loss or gain is due to foreign exchange risk? What portion is due to interest rate risk?

29. What is *country or sovereign risk?* What remedy does an FI realistically have in the event of a collapsing country or currency?

30. What is *market risk?* How does this risk affect the operating performance of financial institutions? What actions can be taken by an FI's management to minimize the effects of this risk?

www.mhhe.com/saunders8e

31. What is the nature of an off-balance-sheet activity? How does an FI benefit from such activities? Identify the various risks that these activities generate for an FI, and explain how these risks can create varying degrees of financial stress for the FI at a later time.

32. What is *technology risk?* What is the difference between *economies of scale* and *economies of scope?* How can these economies create benefits for an FI? How can these economies prove harmful to an FI?

33. What is the difference between technology risk and *operational risk?* How does internationalizing the payments system among banks increase operational risk?

34. Why can *insolvency risk* be classified as a consequence or outcome of any or all of the other types of risks?

35. Discuss the interrelationships among the different sources of FI risk exposure. Why would the construction of an FI risk management model to measure and manage only one type of risk be incomplete?

36. Characterize the risk exposure(s) of the following FI transactions by choosing one or more of the risk types listed below:
    a. Interest rate risk
    b. Credit risk
    c. Off-balance-sheet risk
    d. Technology risk
    e. Foreign exchange risk
    f. Country or sovereign risk
    (1) A bank finances a $10 million, six-year fixed-rate commercial loan by selling one-year certificates of deposit.
    (2) An insurance company invests its policy premiums in a long-term municipal bond portfolio.
    (3) A French bank sells two-year fixed-rate notes to finance a two-year fixed-rate loan to a British entrepreneur.
    (4) A Japanese bank acquires an Austrian bank to facilitate clearing operations.
    (5) A mutual fund completely hedges its interest rate risk exposure by using forward contingent contracts.
    (6) A bond dealer uses his own equity to buy Mexican debt on the less developed country (LDC) bond market.
    (7) A securities firm sells a package of mortgage loans as mortgage-backed securities.

37. Consider these four types of risks: credit, foreign exchange, market, and sovereign. These risks can be separated into two pairs of risk types in which each pair consists of two related risk types, with one being a subset of the other. How would you pair off the risk types, and which risk type could be considered a subset of the other type in the pair?

# Measuring Risk

See Appendices Online at www.mhhe.com/saunders8e
• Appendix 8A: The Maturity Model

# Interest Rate Risk I

## INTRODUCTION

**net worth**
The value of an FI to its owners; this is equal to the difference between the market value of assets and that of liabilities.

www.federalreserve.gov

In Chapter 7 we established that while performing their asset-transformation functions, FIs often mismatch the maturities of their assets and liabilities. In so doing, they expose themselves to interest rate risk. For example, in the 1980s a large number of thrifts suffered economic insolvency (i.e., the **net worth** or equity of their owners was eradicated) when interest rates unexpectedly increased. All FIs tend to mismatch their balance sheet maturities to some degree. However, measuring interest rate risk exposure by looking only at the size of the maturity mismatch can be misleading. The next two chapters present techniques used by FIs to measure their interest rate risk exposures.

This chapter begins with a discussion of the Federal Reserve's monetary policy, which is a key determinant of interest rate risk. As we discuss later, in 2008–2014, the Fed, in an effort to address the severe financial crisis and the slowly improving economy afterward, dropped its target fed funds rate to a range between zero and a quarter of 1 percent and lowered its discount window rate to half a percent. Thus, at this time interest rate risk at FIs may be relatively low. However, as the economy recovers and/or inflation arises, interest rate risk will again become a significant risk for FIs to manage.

The chapter also analyzes the simpler method used to measure an FI's interest rate risk: *the repricing model.* The repricing, or funding gap, model concentrates on the impact of interest rate changes on an FI's net interest income (NII), which is the difference between an FI's interest income and interest expense. Because of its simplicity, smaller depository institutions (the vast majority of DIs) still use this model as their primary measure of interest rate risk. Until recently, U.S. bank regulators had been content to base their evaluations of bank interest rate risk exposures on the repricing model. As explained later in this chapter, however, the repricing model has some serious weaknesses. Appendix 8A, at the book's website (**www.mhhe.com/saunders8e**), compares and contrasts this model with the market value–based maturity model. While rarely used anymore by FIs, the maturity model was a first attempt to include the impact of interest rate changes on the overall market value of an FI's assets and liabilities and, ulti-

www.bis.org   mately, its net worth. In the early 2000s, the Bank for International Settlements www.bis.org (the organization of the world's major Central Banks) issued a consultative document[1] suggesting a standardized model be used by regulators in evaluating a bank's interest rate risk exposure. The approach suggested is firmly based on market value accounting and the duration model (see Chapter 9). As regulators move to adopt these models, bigger banks (which hold the vast majority of total assets in the banking industry) have adopted them as their primary measure of interest rate risk. Moreover, where relevant, banks may be allowed to use their own market-value-based models (see Chapter 15) to assess the interest rate risk of the banking book.

Appendix 8B, at the end of this chapter, looks at the term structure of interest rates that compares the market yields or interest rates on securities, assuming that all characteristics except maturity are the same. This topic is generally covered in introductory finance courses. For students needing a review, Appendix 8B is encouraged introductory reading.

# THE LEVEL AND MOVEMENT OF INTEREST RATES

While many factors influence the level and movement of interest rates, it is the central bank's monetary policy strategy that most directly underlies the level and movement of interest rates that, in turn, affect an FI's cost of funds and return on assets. The central bank in the United States is the Federal Reserve (the Fed).

www.federalreserve.gov Through its daily open market operations, such as buying and selling Treasury bonds and Treasury bills, the Fed seeks to influence the money supply, inflation, and the level of interest rates (particularly short-term interest rates). In turn, changing interest rates impact economic decisions, such as whether to consume or save. When the Fed finds it necessary to slow down the economy, it tightens monetary policy by raising interest rates. The normal result is a decrease in business and household spending (especially that financed by credit or borrowing). Conversely, if business and household spending declines to the extent that the Fed finds it necessary to stimulate the economy, it allows interest rates to fall (an expansionary monetary policy). The drop in rates promotes borrowing and spending. For example, in December 2008, as the U.S. economy fell into its deepest depression since the Great Depression, the Fed, in a historic move, unexpectedly announced that it would drop its target fed funds rate to a range between zero and a quarter of one percent and lower its discount window rate to a half a percent, the lowest level since the 1940s. Even through January 2012, because of the economy's continued weakness, the Fed announced that it expected to keep fed fund rates below 1 percent until late 2014. Figure 8–1 shows the interest rate on U.S. three-month T-bills for the period 1965–2012. While Federal Reserve actions are targeted mostly at short-term rates (especially the federal funds rate), changes in short-term rates usually feed through to the whole term structure of interest rates. The linkages between short-term rates and long-term rates and theories of the term structure of interest rates are discussed in Appendix 8B to this chapter.

---

[1] See Basel Committee on Banking Supervision, "Principles for the Management and Supervision of Interest Rate Risk," Bank for International Settlements, Basel, Switzerland, January 2001.

**FIGURE 8–1**   Interest Rate on U.S. 91-Day Treasury Bills, 1965–2012

Source: Federal Reserve Board website, various dates. *www.federalreserve.gov*

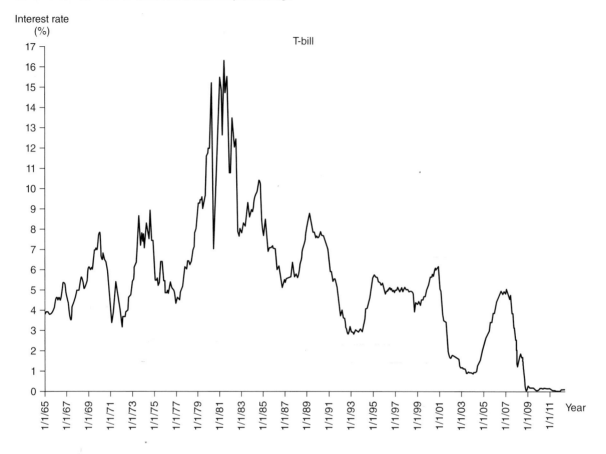

---

*Internet Exercise*   Go to the Federal Reserve Board's website at **www.federalreserve.gov** to find the latest information available on three-month Treasury bill rates using the following steps. Click on "Economic Research and Data." Click on "Selected Interest Rates—H.15." Click on "Current Release." This will download the data onto your computer that will contain the most recent information on Treasury bill rates.

---

In addition to the Fed's impact on interest rates via its monetary policy strategy, the increased level of financial market integration over the last decade has also affected interest rates. Financial market integration increases the speed with which interest rate changes and associated volatility are transmitted among countries, making the control of U.S. interest rates by the Federal Reserve more difficult and less certain than before. The increased globalization of financial market flows in recent years has made the measurement and management of interest rate risk a prominent concern facing many modern FI managers. For example, investors across the world carefully evaluate the statements made by Ben Bernanke (chairman of the Federal Reserve Board of Governors) before Congress. Even hints of changes in U.S. interest rates may have a major effect on world interest rates (as well as foreign exchange rates and stock prices).

The level and volatility of interest rates and the increase in worldwide financial market integration make the measurement and management of interest rate risk one of the key issues facing FI managers. Further, the Bank for International Settlements requires depository institutions (DIs) to have interest rate risk measurement systems that assess the effects of interest rate changes on both earnings and economic value. These systems should provide meaningful measures of a DI's current levels of interest rate risk exposure and should be capable of identifying any excessive exposures that might arise (see Chapter 20). In this chapter and in Chapter 9, we analyze the different ways an FI might measure the exposure it faces in running a mismatched maturity book (or gap) between its assets and its liabilities in a world of interest rate volatility.

In particular, we concentrate on three ways, or models, of measuring the asset–liability gap exposure of an FI:

The repricing (or funding gap) model (in Chapter 8).

The maturity model (in Appendix 8A at **www.mhhe.com/saunders8e**).

The duration model (in Chapter 9).

---

**Concept Questions**

1. How is the Federal Reserve's monetary policy linked to the degree of interest rate uncertainty faced by FIs?
2. How has financial market integration affected interest rate movements?

---

# THE REPRICING MODEL

**repricing gap**
The difference between assets whose interest rates will be repriced or changed over some future period (rate-sensitive assets) and liabilities whose interest rates will be repriced or changed over some future period (rate-sensitive liabilities).

The repricing, or funding gap, model is a simple model used by small (thus most) FIs in the United States. This model is essentially a book value accounting cash flow analysis of the **repricing gap** between the interest income earned on an FI's assets and the interest expense paid on its liabilities (or its net interest income) over a particular period of time. This contrasts with the market value–based maturity and duration models discussed in the appendix to this chapter and in Chapter 9.

Under the repricing gap approach, commercial banks report quarterly on their call reports, interest-rate sensitivity reports which show the repricing gaps for assets and liabilities with various maturities: For example,

1. One day.
2. More than one day to three months.
3. More than three months to six months.
4. More than six months to twelve months.
5. More than one year to five years.
6. More than five years.

**rate-sensitive asset or liability**
An asset or liability that is repriced at or near current market interest rates within a maturity bucket.

A bank reports the gaps in each maturity bucket by calculating the rate sensitivity of each asset (RSA) and each liability (RSL) on its balance sheet. **Rate sensitivity** here means that the asset or liability is repriced at or near current market interest rates within a certain time horizon (or maturity bucket). Repricing can be the

**TABLE 8–1**
Repricing Gap (in millions of dollars)

|  | (1) Assets | (2) Liabilities | (3) Gaps | (4) Cumulative Gap |
|---|---|---|---|---|
| 1. One day | $ 20 | $ 30 | $−10 | $−10 |
| 2. More than one day–three months | 30 | 40 | −10 | −20 |
| 3. More than three months–six months | 70 | 85 | −15 | −35 |
| 4. More than six months–twelve months | 90 | 70 | +20 | −15 |
| 5. More than one year–five years | 40 | 30 | +10 | −5 |
| 6. Over five years | 10 | 5 | +5 | 0 |
|  | $260 | $260 |  |  |

result of a rollover of an asset or liability (e.g., a loan is paid off at or prior to maturity and the funds are used to issue a new loan at current market rates), or it can occur because the asset or liability is a variable-rate instrument (e.g., a variable-rate mortgage whose interest rate is reset every quarter based on movements in a prime rate). Table 8–1 presents a simple interest rate sensitivity report showing the asset and liability repricing gaps of an FI, categorized into each of the six previously defined maturity buckets.

The advantage of the repricing model lies in its information value and its simplicity in pointing to an FI's *net interest income exposure* (or profit exposure) to interest rate changes in different maturity buckets. For example, suppose that an FI has a negative $10 million difference between its assets and liabilities being repriced in one day (one-day bucket). Assets and liabilities that are repriced each day are likely to be interbank borrowings on the federal funds or repurchase agreement market (see Chapter 2). Thus, a negative gap (RSA < RSL) exposes the FI to

**refinancing risk**
The risk that the cost of rolling over or reborrowing funds will rise above the returns being earned on asset investments.

**reinvestment risk**
The risk that the returns on funds to be reinvested will fall below the cost of the funds.

**refinancing risk,** in that a rise in these short-term rates would lower the FI's *net interest income* since the FI has more rate-sensitive liabilities than assets in this bucket. In other words, assuming equal changes in interest rates on RSAs and RSLs, interest expense will increase by more than interest revenue. Conversely, if the FI has a positive $20 million difference between its assets and liabilities being repriced in 6 months to 12 months, it has a positive gap (RSA > RSL) for this period and is exposed to **reinvestment risk,** in that a drop in rates over this period would lower the FI's net interest income; that is, interest income will decrease by more than interest expense. Specifically, let:

$\Delta NII_i$ = Change in net interest income in maturity bucket $i$

$GAP_i$ = Dollar size of the gap between the book value of rate-sensitive assets and rate-sensitive liabilities in maturity bucket $i$

$\Delta R_i$ = Change in the level of interest rates impacting assets and liabilities in the $i$th bucket

Then:

$$\Delta NII_i = (GAP_i) \Delta R_i = (RSA_i - RSL_i) \Delta R_i$$

In this first bucket, if the gap is negative $10 million and short-term interest rates (such as fed fund and/or repo rates) rise 1 percent, the annualized change in the FI's future net interest income is:

$$\Delta NII_i = (-\$10 \text{ million}) \times 0.01 = -\$100,000$$

That is, the negative gap and associated refinancing risk results in a loss of $100,000 in net interest income for the FI.

This approach is very simple and intuitive. Remember, however, from Chapter 7 and our overview of interest rate risk that capital or market value losses also occur when rates rise. The capital loss effect that is measured by both the maturity and duration models developed in Appendix A to this chapter and in Chapter 9 is not accounted for in the repricing model. The reason is that in the book value accounting world of the repricing model, asset and liability values are reported at their *historic* values or costs. Thus, interest rate changes affect only current interest income or interest expense—that is, net interest income on the FI's income statement—rather than the market value of assets and liabilities on the balance sheet.[2]

The FI manager can also estimate cumulative gaps (CGAPs) over various repricing categories or buckets. A common cumulative gap of interest is the one-year repricing gap estimated from Table 8–1 as:

$$CGAP = (-\$10) + (-\$10) + (-\$15) + \$20 = -\$15 \text{ million}$$

If $\Delta R_i$ is the average interest rate change affecting assets and liabilities that can be repriced within a year, the cumulative effect on the bank's net interest income is:[3]

$$\begin{aligned} \Delta NII_i &= (CGAP)\,\Delta R_i \\ &= (-\$15 \text{ million})\,(0.01) = -\$150,000 \end{aligned} \tag{1}$$

We can now look at how an FI manager would calculate the cumulative one-year gap from a balance sheet. Remember that the manager asks: Will or can this asset or liability have its interest rate changed within the next year? If the answer is yes, it is a rate-sensitive asset or liability. If the answer is no, it is not rate sensitive.

Consider the simplified balance sheet facing the FI manager in Table 8–2. Instead of the original maturities, the maturities are those remaining on different assets and liabilities at the time the repricing gap is estimated.

### Rate-Sensitive Assets

Looking down the asset side of the balance sheet in Table 8–2, we see the following one-year rate-sensitive assets (RSAs):

1. *Short-term consumer loans: $50 million.* These are repriced at the end of the year and just make the one-year cutoff.
2. *Three-month T-bills: $30 million.* These are repriced on maturity (rollover) every three months.
3. *Six-month T-notes: $35 million.* These are repriced on maturity (rollover) every six months.
4. *30-year floating-rate mortgages: $40 million.* These are repriced (i.e., the mortgage rate is reset) every nine months. Thus, these long-term assets are rate-sensitive assets in the context of the repricing model with a one-year repricing horizon.

---

[2] For example, a 30-year bond purchased 10 years ago when rates were 13 percent would be reported as having the same book (accounting) value as when rates are 7 percent. Using market value, gains and losses to asset and liability values would be reflected in the balance sheet as rates change.

[3] Note that a change in the dollar value and mix of rate-sensitive assets and liabilities (or a change in CGAP) also affects the FI's net income.

**TABLE 8–2**
**Simple FI Balance Sheet (in millions of dollars)**

| Assets | | Liabilities | |
|---|---|---|---|
| 1. Short-term consumer loans (one-year maturity) | $ 50 | 1. Equity capital (fixed) | $ 20 |
| 2. Long-term consumer loans (two-year maturity) | 25 | 2. Demand deposits | 40 |
| 3. Three-month Treasury bills | 30 | 3. Passbook savings | 30 |
| 4. Six-month Treasury notes | 35 | 4. Three-month CDs | 40 |
| 5. Three-year Treasury bonds | 70 | 5. Three-month bankers acceptances | 20 |
| 6. 10-year, fixed-rate mortgages | 20 | 6. Six-month commercial paper | 60 |
| 7. 30-year, floating-rate mortgages (rate adjusted every nine months) | 40 | 7. One-year time deposits | 20 |
| | | 8. Two-year time deposits | 40 |
| | $270 | | $270 |

Summing these four items produces total one-year rate-sensitive assets (RSAs) of $155 million. The remaining $115 million of assets are not rate sensitive over the one-year repricing horizon—that is, a change in the level of interest rates will not affect the size of the interest income generated by these assets over the next year.[4] Although the $115 million in long-term consumer loans, 3-year Treasury bonds, and 10-year, fixed-rate mortgages generate interest income, the size of income generated will not change over the next year, since the interest rates on these assets are not expected to change (i.e., they are fixed over the next year).

## Rate-Sensitive Liabilities

Looking down the liability side of the balance sheet in Table 8–2, we see the following liability items clearly fit the one-year rate or repricing sensitivity test:

1. *Three-month CDs: $40 million.* These mature in three months and are repriced on rollover.

2. *Three-month bankers acceptances: $20 million.* These also mature in three months and are repriced on rollover.

3. *Six-month commercial paper: $60 million.* These mature and are repriced every six months.

4. *One-year time deposits: $20 million.* These get repriced right at the end of the one-year gap horizon.

Summing these four items produces one-year rate-sensitive liabilities (RSLs) of $140 million. The remaining $130 million is not rate sensitive over the one-year period. The $20 million in equity capital and $40 million in demand deposits (see the following discussion) do not pay interest and are therefore classified as non-interest-paying. The $30 million in passbook savings (see the following discussion) and $40 million in two-year time deposits generate interest expense over the next year, but the level of the interest expense generated will not change if the general level of interest rates changes. Thus, we classify these items as rate-insensitive liabilities.

[4] We are assuming that the assets are noncallable over the year and that there will be no prepayments (runoffs, see below) on the mortgages within a year.

Note that demand deposits (or transaction accounts in general) are not included as RSLs. We can make strong arguments for and against their inclusion as rate-sensitive liabilities.

### Against Inclusion

The explicit interest rate on demand deposits is zero by regulation. Further, although explicit interest is paid on transaction accounts such as NOW accounts, the rates paid by FIs do not fluctuate directly with changes in the general level of interest rates (particularly when the general level of rates is rising). Moreover, many demand deposits act as **core deposits** for FIs, meaning they are a long-term source of funds.

### For Inclusion

Even though they pay no explicit interest, demand deposits pay implicit interest because FIs do not charge fees that fully cover their costs for checking services. Further, if interest rates rise, individuals draw down (or run off) their demand deposits, forcing the bank to replace them with higher yielding, interest bearing, rate-sensitive funds. This is most likely to occur when the interest rates on alternative instruments are high. In such an environment, the opportunity cost of holding funds in demand deposit accounts is likely to be larger than it is in a low–interest rate environment.

Similar arguments for and against inclusion of retail passbook savings accounts can be made. Although Federal Reserve Regulation Q ceilings on the maximum rates to be charged for these accounts were abolished in March 1986, banks still adjust these rates only infrequently. However, savers tend to withdraw funds from these accounts when rates rise, forcing banks into more expensive fund substitutions.[5]

The four repriced liabilities ($40 + $20 + $60 + $20) sum to $140 million, and the four repriced assets ($50 + $30 + $35 + $40) sum to $155 million. Given this, the cumulative one-year repricing gap (CGAP) for the bank is:

$$CGAP = \text{One-year rate-sensitive assets} - \text{One-year rate-sensitive liabilities}$$
$$= RSA - RSL$$
$$= \$155 \text{ million} - \$140 \text{ million} = \$15 \text{ million}$$

Often FIs express interest rate sensitivity as a percentage of assets ($A$):

$$\frac{CGAP}{A} = \frac{\$15 \text{ million}}{\$270 \text{ million}} = 0.056 = 5.6\%$$

Expressing the repricing gap in this way is useful since it tells us (1) the direction of the interest rate risk exposure (positive or negative CGAP) and (2) the scale of that exposure as indicated by dividing the gap by the asset size of the institution. In our example the FI has 5.6 percent more RSAs than RSLs in one-year-and-less buckets as a percentage of total assets. Alternatively, FIs calculate a gap ratio defined as rate-sensitive assets divided by rate-sensitive liabilities. A gap ratio

---

[5] The Federal Reserve's repricing report has traditionally viewed transaction accounts and passbook savings accounts as rate-insensitive liabilities, as we have done in this example. However, with the growth of the Internet and competition from money market mutual funds, the mobility of these funds is highly sensitive to (relative) rates paid by banks versus other nonbank FIs (such as money market mutual funds).

---

**core deposits**
Those deposits that act as an FI's long-term sources of funds.

greater than 1 indicates that there are more rate sensitive assets than liabilities (similar to a gap $> 0$). Thus, the FI is set to see increases in net interest income when interest rates increase. A gap ratio less than 1 indicates that there are more rate sensitive liabilities than assets (similar to a gap $< 0$). Thus, the FI is set to see increases in net interest income when interest rates decrease. In our example, the gap ratio is 1.107 meaning that in the one-year-and-less time bucket, the FI has $1.107 of RSAs for every $1 of RSLs. Table 8–3 shows an interest rate sensitivity report for Harleysville Savings Financial Corp. (headquartered in Harleysville, Pennsylvania) for 2011. In this report, Harleysville reports the repricing gap for periods ranging from one to five years.

The choice of time horizon used to measure interest rate risk is critical to managing this risk. An excessively long repricing period includes many securities that are repriced at different times within the repricing period. That is, it overstates the rate sensitivity of the balance sheet and leaves the FI exposed to interest rate risk. For example, consider a bank that measures interest rate risk exposure over a one-year time horizon only and has a repricing gap of $0 over the one year. However, if the bank has $50 million more RSAs than RSLs that are repriced in the first six months of the year and $50 million more liabilities than assets that are repriced over the last six months, it would be exposed to changes in interest rates occurring within the year. In its gap analysis, the bank would show a zero repricing gap for the year $[+50 + (-50) = 0]$. But the bank's assets and liabilities are *mismatched* within the bucket, and therefore, the bank is exposed to interest rate risk. Clearly, the shorter the range over which bucket gaps are calculated, the smaller is this problem. Conversely, an excessively short repricing period omits consideration of the interest rate risk exposure of assets and liabilities are that repriced in the period immediately following the end of the repricing period. That is, it understates the rate sensitivity of the balance sheet.

## Equal Changes in Rates on RSAs and RSLs

The CGAP provides a measure of an FI's interest rate sensitivity. Table 8–4 highlights the relation between CGAP and changes in NII when interest rate changes for RSAs are equal to interest rate changes for RSLs. For example, when CGAP is positive (or the FI has more RSAs than RSLs), NII will rise when interest rates rise (row 1, Table 8–4), since interest income increases more than interest expense does.

---

**EXAMPLE 8–1**

*Impact of Rate Changes on Net Interest Income When CGAP Is Positive*

Suppose that, for the FI depicted in Table 8–2, interest rates rise by 1 percent on both RSAs and RSLs. The CGAP would project the expected annual change in net interest income ($\Delta NII$) of the FI as:

$$\Delta NII = (RSA \times \Delta R) - (RSL \times \Delta R) = CGAP \times \Delta R$$
$$= (\$155 \text{ million} \times 0.01) - (\$140 \text{ million} \times 0.01) = (\$15 \text{ million}) \times 0.01$$
$$= (\$1.55 \text{ million} - \$1.40 \text{ million}) = \$150,000$$

Similarly, if interest rates fall equally for RSAs and RSLs (row 2, Table 8–4), NII will fall when CGAP is positive. As rates fall, interest income falls by more than interest expense. Thus, NII falls. Suppose that for our FI, rates fall by 1 percent. The CGAP predicts that NII will fall by:

$$\Delta NII = (\$155 \text{ million} \times (-0.01)) - (\$140 \text{ million} \times (-0.01)) = \$15 \text{ million} \times -0.01$$
$$= -\$1.55 \text{ million} - (-\$1.40 \text{ million}) = -\$150,000$$

**TABLE 8–3**   Harleysville Savings Financial Corp., Interest Rate Sensitivity Report, 2011

Source: Harleysville Savings Financial, Form 10-K, 2011.

| | 1 Year or less | 1 to 3 Years | 3 to 5 Years | Over 5 Years | Total |
|---|---|---|---|---|---|
| | | **(In Thousands)** | | | |
| **Interest-earning assets:** | | | | | |
| Mortgage loans | $ 56,557 | $ 59,050 | $ 46,569 | $180,021 | $342,197 |
| Commercial loans | 49,658 | 17,216 | 14,329 | 16,144 | 97,347 |
| Mortgage-backed securities | 55,908 | 41,406 | 23,289 | 29,944 | 150,547 |
| Consumer and other loans | 68,042 | 9,690 | 4,552 | 4,373 | 86,657 |
| Investment securities and other investments | 80,462 | 23,846 | 21,445 | 5,806 | 131,559 |
| Total interest-earning assets | 310,627 | 151,208 | 110,184 | 236,288 | 808,307 |
| **Interest-bearing liabilities:** | | | | | |
| Passbook and Club accounts | 401 | — | — | 3,793 | 4,194 |
| NOW and interest-bearing checking accounts | 6,931 | — | — | 62,379 | 69,310 |
| Consumer Money Market Deposit accounts | 53,172 | — | — | 58,021 | 111,193 |
| Business Money Market Deposit accounts | 17,563 | — | — | 5,855 | 23,418 |
| Certificate accounts | 126,177 | 124,560 | 44,713 | — | 295,450 |
| Borrowed money | 57,708 | 59,253 | 26,389 | 106,844 | 250,194 |
| Total interest-bearing liabilities | 261,952 | 183,813 | 71,102 | 236,892 | 753,759 |
| Repricing GAP during the period | $ 48,675 | $(32,605) | $ 39,082 | $    (604) | $ 54,548 |
| Cumulative GAP | $ 48,675 | $ 16,070 | $ 55,152 | $ 54,548 | |
| Ratio of GAP during the period to total assets | 5.82% | −3.90% | 4.68% | −0.07% | |
| Ratio of cumulative GAP to total assets | 5.82% | 1.92% | 6.60% | 6.53% | |

It is evident from this equation that the larger the absolute value of CGAP, the larger the expected change in NII (i.e., the larger the increase or decrease in the FI's interest income relative to interest expense). In general, when CGAP is positive, the change in NII is positively related to the change in interest rates. Thus, an FI would want its CGAP to be positive when interest rates are expected to rise. Conversely, when CGAP is negative, if interest rates rise by equal amounts for RSAs and RSLs (row 3, Table 8–4), NII will fall (since the FI has more RSLs than RSAs). If interest rates fall equally for RSAs and RSLs (row 4, Table 8–4), NII will increase when CGAP is negative. As rates fall, interest expense decreases by more than interest income. In general then, when CGAP is negative, the change in NII is negatively related to the change in interest rates. Thus, an FI would want its CGAP to be negative when interest rates are expected to fall. We refer to these relationships as **CGAP effects.**

**CGAP effects**
The relations between changes in interest rates and changes in net interest income.

## Unequal Changes in Rates on RSAs and RSLs

The previous section considered changes in net interest income as interest rates changed, assuming that the change in rates on RSAs was exactly equal to the change in rates on RSLs (in other words, assuming the interest rate spread between rates on RSAs and RSLs remained unchanged). This is not often the case. Rather, rate changes on RSAs generally differ from those on RSLs (i.e., the spread between interest rates on assets and liabilities change along with the levels of these rates). See Figure 8–2,

**TABLE 8–4**
Impact of CGAP on
the Relation between
Changes in Interest
Rates and Changes
in Net Interest
Income, Assuming
Rate Changes for
RSAs Equal Rate
Changes and RSLs

| Row | CGAP | Change in Interest Rates | Change in Interest Income | | Change in Interest Expense | Change in NII |
|---|---|---|---|---|---|---|
| 1 | >0 | ⇑ | ⇑ | > | ⇑ | ⇑ |
| 2 | >0 | ⇓ | ⇓ | > | ⇓ | ⇓ |
| 3 | <0 | ⇑ | ⇑ | < | ⇑ | ⇓ |
| 4 | <0 | ⇓ | ⇓ | < | ⇓ | ⇑ |

which plots quarterly CD rates (liabilities) and prime lending rates (assets) for the period 1990–2012. Notice that although the rates generally move in the same direction, they are not perfectly correlated. In this case, as we consider the impact of rate changes on NII, we have a spread effect in addition to the CGAP effect.

If the spread between the rate on RSAs and RSLs increases, when interest rates rise (fall), interest income increases (decreases) by more (less) than interest expense. The result is an increase in NII. Conversely, if the spread between the rates on RSAs and RSLs decreases, when interest rates rise (fall), interest income increases (decreases) less (more) than interest expense, and NII decreases. In general, the **spread effect** is such that, regardless of the direction of the change in interest rates, a positive relation exists between changes in the spread (between rates on RSAs and RSLs) and changes in NII. Whenever the spread increases (decreases), NII increases (decreases).

**spread effect**
The effect that a
change in the spread
between rates on
RSAs and RSLs has
on net interest income
as interest rates
change.

**EXAMPLE 8–2**
*Impact of Spread
Effect on Net
Interest Income*

To understand spread effect, assume for a moment that RSAs equal RSLs equal $155 million. Suppose that rates rise by 1.2 percent on RSAs and by 1 percent on RSLs (i.e., the spread between the rates on RSAs and RSLs increases by 1.2 percent −1 percent = 0.2 percent). The resulting change in NII is calculated as:

$$\Delta NII = (RSA \times \Delta R_{RSA}) - (RSL \times \Delta R_{RSL})$$
$$= \Delta \text{Interest revenue} - \Delta \text{Interest expense}$$
$$= (\$155 \text{ million} \times 1.2\%) - (\$155 \text{ million} \times 1.0\%)$$
$$= \$155 \text{ million} (1.2\% - 1.0\%)$$
$$= \$310,000 \tag{2}$$

See Table 8–5 for various combinations of CGAP and spread changes and their effects on NII. The first four rows in Table 8–5 consider an FI with a positive CGAP; the last four rows consider an FI with a negative CGAP. Notice in Table 8–5 that both the CGAP and spread effects can have the same effect on NII. For example, in row 6 of Table 8–5, if CGAP is negative and interest rates increase, the CGAP effect says NII will decrease. If, at the same time, the spread between RSAs and RSLs decreases as interest rates increase, the spread effect also says NII will decrease. In these cases, FI managers can accurately predict the direction of the change in NII as interest rates change. When the two work in opposite directions, however, the change in NII cannot be predicted without knowing the size of the CGAP and expected change in the spread. For example, in row 5 of Table 8–5, if CGAP is negative and interest rates increase, the CGAP effect says NII will decrease. If, at the same time, the spread between RSAs and RSLs increases as interest rates increase, the spread effect says NII will increase.

**FIGURE 8–2**
Three-Month CD
Rates versus Prime
Rates for 1990–2012

Source: *Federal Reserve
Bulletin,* various issues.
*www.federalreserve.gov*

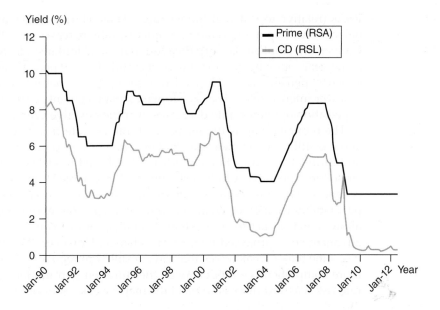

**TABLE 8–5**
Impact of CGAP
on the Relation
between Changes
in Interest Rates
and Changes
in Net Interest
Income, Allowing
for Different Rate
Changes for RSAs
and RSLs

| Row | CGAP | Change in Interest Rates | Change in Spread | NII |
|-----|------|--------------------------|------------------|-----|
| 1 | >0 | ⇑ | ⇑ | ⇑ |
| 2 | >0 | ⇑ | ⇓ | ⇑ ⇓ |
| 3 | >0 | ⇓ | ⇑ | ⇑ ⇓ |
| 4 | >0 | ⇓ | ⇓ | ⇓ |
| 5 | <0 | ⇑ | ⇑ | ⇑ ⇓ |
| 6 | <0 | ⇑ | ⇓ | ⇓ |
| 7 | <0 | ⇓ | ⇑ | ⇑ |
| 8 | <0 | ⇓ | ⇓ | ⇑ ⇓ |

**EXAMPLE 8–3**

*Combined
Impact of CGAP
and Spread Effect
on Net Interest
Income*

Suppose that for the FI in Table 8–2, interest rates fall by 1 percent on RSAs and by 1.2 percent on RSLs. Now the change in NII is calculated as:

$$\Delta NII = [\$155 \text{ million} \times (-0.01)] - [\$140 \text{ million} \times (-0.012)]$$
$$= -\$1.55 \text{ million} - (-\$1.68 \text{ million})$$
$$= \$0.13 \text{ million or } \$130,000$$

Even though the CGAP effect (i.e., RSA > RSL) is putting negative pressure on NII (in Example 8–1, the CGAP effect of a 1 percent decrease in the rate on both RSAs and RSLs produced a *decrease* in NII of $150,000), the increase in the spread, and the resulting spread effect, is so big that NII *increases* by $130,000.

Some FIs accept quite large interest rate exposures relative to their asset sizes. For example, the one-year repricing gap to total assets ratio of Harleysville Savings Financial Corporation (Harleysville, Pennsylvania) was 5.82 percent at the end of 2011 and the five-year gap to total assets ratio was 6.60 percent (i.e., it had more RSAs than RSLs). If interest rates rose in 2012, Harleysville Savings was set up to see net interest income increases due to the repricing of its large amount of

RSAs (relative to RSLs) at higher rates. Thus, Harleysville's management set its balance sheet up in expectation of interest rate increases over the next five years. Conversely, HopFed Bancorp (headquartered in Hopkinsville, Kentucky) reported a one-year repricing gap to total assets ratio of −5.69 percent and a five-year ratio of −6.98 percent. Thus, HopFed was set up to see net interest income increases at lower interest rates. That is, HopFed's management set its balance sheet up in expectation of interest rate decreases over the next five years.

The repricing gap is the measure of interest rate risk historically used by FIs, and it is still the main measure of interest rate risk used by small community banks and thrifts. In contrast to the market value–based models of interest rate risk discussed in Appendix A to this chapter and in Chapter 9, the repricing gap model is conceptually easy to understand and can easily be used to forecast changes in profitability for a given change in interest rates. The repricing gap can be used to allow an FI to structure its assets and liabilities or to go off the balance sheet to take advantage of a projected interest rate change. However, the repricing gap model has some major weaknesses that have resulted in regulators' calling for the use of more comprehensive models (e.g., the duration gap model) to measure interest rate risk. We next discuss some of the major weaknesses of the repricing model.

| Concept Questions | 1. Summarize the case for and against the inclusion of demand deposits as a rate-sensitive liability.<br>2. How can FIs change the size and the direction of their repricing gap?<br>3. Why is it useful to express the repricing gap in terms of a percentage of assets? What specific information does this provide? |
|---|---|

## WEAKNESSES OF THE REPRICING MODEL

Despite the fact that this model of interest rate risk is used by the vast majority of depository institutions in the United States, the repricing model has four major shortcomings: (1) It ignores market value effects of interest rate changes, (2) it is overaggregative, (3) it fails to deal with the problem of rate-insensitive asset and liability runoffs and prepayments, and (4) it ignores cash flows from off-balance-sheet activities. In this section we discuss each of these weaknesses in more detail.

### Market Value Effects

As was discussed in the overview of FI risks (Chapter 7), interest rate changes have a market value effect in addition to an income effect on asset and liability values. That is, the present values of the cash flows on assets and liabilities change, in addition to the immediate interest received or paid on them, as interest rates change. In fact, the present values (and where relevant, the market prices) of virtually all assets and liabilities on an FI's balance sheet change as interest rates change. The repricing model ignores the market value effect—implicitly assuming a book value accounting approach. As such, the repricing gap is only a *partial* measure of the true interest rate risk exposure of an FI. As we discuss the market value–based measures of interest rate risk (in Appendix A and in Chapter 9), we highlight the impact that ignoring the market value effect has on the ability to accurately measure the overall interest rate risk of an FI.

## Overaggregation

The problem of defining buckets over a range of maturities ignores information regarding the distribution of assets and liabilities within those buckets. For example, the dollar values of RSAs and RSLs within any maturity bucket range may be equal. However, on average, liabilities may be repriced toward the end of the bucket's range, while assets may be repriced toward the beginning, in which case a change in interest rates will have an effect on asset and liability cash flows that will not be accurately measured by the repricing gap approach.

Look at the simple example for the three-month to six-month bucket in Figure 8–3. Note that $50 million more RSAs than RSLs are repriced between months 3 and 4, while $50 million more RSLs than RSAs are repriced between months 5 and 6. The FI in its interest rate sensitivity report would show a zero repricing gap for the three-month to six-month bucket [+50 + (−50) = 0]. But as you can easily see, the FI's assets and liabilities are mismatched within the bucket. Clearly, the shorter the range over which bucket gaps are calculated, the smaller this problem is. If an FI manager calculated one-day bucket gaps out into the future, this would give a more accurate picture of the net interest income exposure to rate changes. Reportedly, many large FIs have internal systems that indicate their repricing gaps on any given day in the future (252 days' time, 1,329 days' time, etc.). This suggests that although regulators examine the reporting of repricing gaps over only relatively wide maturity bucket ranges, FI managers could set in place internal information systems to report the daily future patterns of such gaps.

## The Problem of Runoffs

In the simple repricing model discussed earlier, we assumed that all consumer loans matured in 1 year or that all conventional mortgages matured in 30 years. In reality, the FI continuously originates and retires consumer and mortgage loans as it creates and retires deposits. For example, today, some 30-year original maturity mortgages may have only 1 year left before they mature; that is, they are in their 29th year. In addition, these loans may be listed as 30-year mortgages (and included as not rate sensitive), yet they will sometimes be prepaid early as mortgage holders refinance their mortgages and/or sell their houses. Thus, the resulting proceeds will be reinvested at current market rates within the year. In addition, even if an

**FIGURE 8–3**

**The Overaggregation Problem: The Three-Month to Six-Month Bucket**

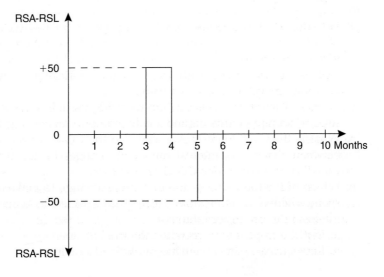

**runoff**
Periodic cash flow of interest and principal amortization payments on long-term assets, such as conventional mortgages, that can be reinvested at market rates.

asset or liability is rate insensitive, virtually all assets and liabilities (e.g., long-term mortgages) pay some principal and/or interest back to the FI in any given year. As a result, the FI receives a **runoff** cash flow from its rate-insensitive portfolio that can be reinvested at current market rates. That is, this runoff cash flow component of a rate-insensitive asset or liability is itself rate sensitive. The FI manager can deal easily with this in the repricing model by identifying for each asset and liability item the estimated dollar cash flow that will run off within the next year and adding these amounts to the value of rate sensitive assets and liabilities.

## Cash Flows from Off-Balance-Sheet Activities

The RSAs and RSLs used in the repricing model generally include only the assets and liabilities listed on the balance sheet. Changes in interest rates will affect the cash flows on many off-balance-sheet instruments as well. For example, an FI might have hedged its interest rate risk with an interest rate futures contract (see Chapter 22). As interest rates change, these futures contracts—as part of the marking-to-market process—produce a daily cash flow (either positive or negative) for the FI that may offset any on-balance-sheet gap exposure. These offsetting cash flows from futures contracts are ignored by the simple repricing model and should (and could) be included in the model.

| **Concept Questions** | 1. What are four major weaknesses of the repricing model? |
|---|---|
| | 2. What does runoff mean? |

## Summary

This chapter introduced a method of measuring an FI's interest rate risk exposure: the repricing model. The repricing model looks at the difference, or gap, between an FI's rate-sensitive assets and rate-sensitive liabilities to measure interest rate risk. The chapter showed that the repricing model has difficulty in accurately measuring the interest rate risk of an FI. In particular, the repricing model ignores the market value effects of interest rate changes. More complete and accurate measures of an FI's exposure are duration and the duration gap, which are explained in the next chapter.

## Questions and Problems

1. How do monetary policy actions made by the Federal Reserve impact interest rates?
2. How has the increased level of financial market integration affected interest rates?
3. What is the repricing gap? In using this model to evaluate interest rate risk, what is meant by rate sensitivity? On what financial performance variable does the repricing model focus? Explain.
4. What is a maturity bucket in the repricing model? Why is the length of time selected for repricing assets and liabilities important in using the repricing model?
5. What is the CGAP effect? According to the CGAP effect, what is the relation between changes in interest rates and changes in net interest income when CGAP is positive? When CGAP is negative?
6. Which of the following is an appropriate change to make on a bank's balance sheet when GAP is negative, spread is expected to remain unchanged, and interest rates are expected to rise?
   a. Replace fixed-rate loans with rate-sensitive loans.
   b. Replace marketable securities with fixed-rate loans.

    c. Replace fixed-rate CDs with rate-sensitive CDs.

    d. Replace equity with demand deposits.

    e. Replace vault cash with marketable securities.

7. If a bank manager was quite certain that interest rates were going to rise within the next six months, how should the bank manager adjust the bank's six-month repricing gap to take advantage of this anticipated rise? What if the manager believed rates would fall in the next six months?

8. Consider the following balance sheet positions for a financial institution:
   - Rate-sensitive assets = $200 million
     Rate-sensitive liabilities = $100 million
   - Rate-sensitive assets = $100 million
     Rate-sensitive liabilities = $150 million
   - Rate-sensitive assets = $150 million
     Rate-sensitive liabilities = $140 million

   a. Calculate the repricing gap and the impact on net interest income of a 1 percent increase in interest rates for each position.

   b. Calculate the impact on net interest income of each of the above situations, assuming a 1 percent decrease in interest rates.

   c. What conclusion can you draw about the repricing model from these results?

9. Consider the following balance sheet for MMC Bancorp (in millions of dollars):

| Assets | | Liabilities | |
|---|---|---|---|
| 1. Cash and due from | $  6.25 | 1. Equity capital (fixed) | $ 25.00 |
| 2. Short-term consumer loans (one-year maturity) | 62.50 | 2. Demand deposits | 50.00 |
| 3. Long-term consumer loans (two-year maturity) | 31.25 | 3. Passbook savings | 37.50 |
| 4. Three-month T-bills | 37.50 | 4. Three-month CDs | 50.00 |
| 5. Six-month T-notes | 43.75 | 5. Three-month bankers' acceptances | 25.00 |
| 6. Three-year T-bonds | 75.00 | 6. Six-month commercial paper | 75.00 |
| 7. 10-year, fixed-rate mortgages | 25.00 | 7. One-year time deposits | 25.00 |
| 8. 30-year, floating-rate mortgages | 50.00 | 8. Two-year time deposits | 50.00 |
| 9. Premises | 6.25 | | |
| | $337.50 | | $337.50 |

    a. Calculate the value of MMC's rate-sensitive assets, rate-sensitive liabilities, and repricing gap over the next year.

    b. Calculate the expected change in the net interest income for the bank if interest rates rise by 1 percent on both RSAs and RSLs. If interest rates fall by 1 percent on both RSAs and RSLs.

    c. Calculate the expected change in the net interest income for the bank if interest rates rise by 1.2 percent on RSAs and by 1 percent on RSLs. If interest rates fall by 1.2 percent on RSAs and by 1 percent on RSLs.

10. What are the reasons for not including demand deposits as rate-sensitive liabilities in the repricing analysis for a commercial bank? What is the subtle but potentially strong reason for including demand deposits in the total of rate sensitive liabilities? Can the same argument be made for passbook savings accounts?

11. What is the gap to total assets ratio? What is the value of this ratio to interest rate risk managers and regulators?
12. Which of the following assets or liabilities fit the one-year rate or repricing sensitivity test?

    3-month U.S. Treasury bills
    1-year U.S. Treasury notes
    20-year U.S. Treasury bonds
    20-year floating-rate corporate bonds with annual repricing
    30-year floating-rate mortgages with repricing every two years
    30-year floating-rate mortgages with repricing every six months
    Overnight fed funds
    9-month fixed-rate CDs
    1-year fixed-rate CDs
    5-year floating-rate CDs with annual repricing
    Common stock

13. What is the spread effect?
14. A bank manager is quite certain that interest rates are going to fall within the next six months. How should the bank manager adjust the bank's six-month repricing gap and spread to take advantage of this anticipated rise? What if the manager believes rates will rise in the next six months?
15. Consider the following balance sheet for WatchoverU Savings Inc. (in millions):

| Assets | | Liabilities and Equity | |
|---|---|---|---|
| Floating-rate mortgages (currently 10% annually) | $ 50 | 1-year time deposits (currently 6% annually) | $ 70 |
| 30-year fixed-rate loans (currently 7% annually) | 50 | 3-year time deposits (currently 7% annually) | 20 |
| | | Equity | 10 |
| Total assets | $100 | Total liabilities and equity | $100 |

   a. What is WatchoverU's expected net interest income at year-end?
   b. What will net interest income be at year-end if interest rates rise 2 percent?
   c. Using the cumulative repricing gap model, what is the expected net interest income for a 2 percent increase in interest rates?
   d. What will net interest income be at year-end if interest rates on RSAs increase by 2 percent but interest rates on RSLs increase by 1 percent? Is it reasonable for changes in interest rates on RSAs and RSLs to differ? Why?

16. Use the following information about a hypothetical government security dealer named M. P. Jorgan. Market yields are in parentheses, and amounts are in millions.

| Assets | | Liabilities and Equity | |
|---|---|---|---|
| Cash | $ 10 | Overnight repos | $170 |
| 1-month T-bills (7.05%) | 75 | Subordinated debt | 150 |
| 3-month T-bills (7.25%) | 75 | 7-year fixed rate (8.55%) | |
| 2-year T-notes (7.50%) | 50 | | |
| 8-year T-notes (8.96%) | 100 | | |
| 5-year munis (floating rate) (8.20% reset every 6 months) | 25 | Equity | 15 |
| Total assets | $335 | Total liabilities and equity | $335 |

a. What is the repricing gap if the planning period is 30 days? 3 months? 2 years? Recall that cash is a non-interest-earning asset.

b. What is the impact over the next 30 days on net interest income if interest rates increase 50 basis points? Decrease 75 basis points?

c. The following one-year runoffs are expected: $10 million for two-year T-notes and $20 million for eight-year T-notes. What is the one-year repricing gap?

d. If runoffs are considered, what is the effect on net interest income at year end if interest rates increase 50 basis points? Decrease 75 basis points?

17. A bank has the following balance sheet:

| Assets | | Avg. Rate | Liabilities/Equity | | Avg. Rate |
|---|---|---|---|---|---|
| Rate sensitive | $ 550,000 | 7.75% | Rate sensitive | $ 375,000 | 6.25% |
| Fixed rate | 755,000 | 8.75 | Fixed rate | 805,000 | 7.50 |
| Nonearning | 265,000 | | Nonpaying | 390,000 | |
| Total | $1,570,000 | | Total | $1,570,000 | |

Suppose interest rates rise such that the average yield on rate-sensitive assets increases by 45 basis points and the average yield on rate-sensitive liabilities increases by 35 basis points.

a. Calculate the bank's CGAP, gap to total assets ratio, and gap ratio.

b. Assuming the bank does not change the composition of its balance sheet, calculate the resulting change in the bank's interest income, interest expense, and net interest income.

c. Explain how the CGAP and spread effects influenced the change in net interest income.

18. A bank has the following balance sheet:

| Assets | | Avg. Rate | Liabilities/Equity | | Avg. Rate |
|---|---|---|---|---|---|
| Rate sensitive | $ 550,000 | 7.75% | Rate sensitive | $ 575,000 | 6.25% |
| Fixed rate | 755,000 | 8.75 | Fixed rate | 605,000 | 7.50 |
| Nonearning | 265,000 | | Nonpaying | 390,000 | |
| Total | $1,570,000 | | Total | $1,570,000 | |

Suppose interest rates fall such that the average yield on rate-sensitive assets decreases by 15 basis points and the average yield on rate-sensitive liabilities decreases by 5 basis points.

a. Calculate the bank's CGAP, gap to total assets ratio, and gap ratio.

b. Assuming the bank does not change the composition of its balance sheet, calculate the resulting change in the bank's interest income, interest expense, and net interest income.

c. The bank's CGAP is negative and interest rates decreased, yet net interest income decreased. Explain how the CGAP and spread effects influenced this decrease in net interest income.

19. The balance sheet of A. G. Fredwards, a government security dealer, is listed below. Market yields are in parentheses, and amounts are in millions.

| Assets | | Liabilities and Equity | |
|---|---|---|---|
| Cash | $ 20 | Overnight repos | $340 |
| 1-month T-bills (7.05%) | 150 | Subordinated debt | |
| 3-month T-bills (7.25%) | 150 | 7-year fixed rate (8.55%) | 300 |
| 2-year T-notes (7.50%) | 100 | | |
| 8-year T-notes (8.96%) | 200 | | |
| 5-year munis (floating rate) | | | |
| (8.20% reset every 6 months) | 50 | Equity | 30 |
| Total assets | $670 | Total liabilities and equity | $670 |

a. What is the repricing gap if the planning period is 30 days? 3 months? 2 years?

b. What is the impact over the next three months on net interest income if interest rates on RSAs increase 50 basis points and on RSLs increase 60 basis points?

c. What is the impact over the next two years on net interest income if interest rates on RSAs increase 50 basis points and on RSLs increase 75 basis points?

d. Explain the difference in your answers to parts (b) and (c). Why is one answer a negative change in NII, while the other is positive?

20. A bank has the following balance sheet:

| Assets | | Avg. Rate | Liabilities/Equity | | Avg. Rate |
|---|---|---|---|---|---|
| Rate sensitive | $225,000 | 6.35% | Rate sensitive | $300,000 | 4.25% |
| Fixed rate | 550,000 | 7.55 | Fixed rate | 505,000 | 6.15 |
| Nonearning | 120,000 | | Nonpaying | 90,000 | |
| Total | $895,000 | | Total | $895,000 | |

Suppose interest rates rise such that the average yield on rate-sensitive assets increases by 45 basis points and the average yield on rate-sensitive liabilities increases by 35 basis points.

a. Calculate the bank's repricing GAP.

b. Assuming the bank does not change the composition of its balance sheet, calculate the net interest income for the bank before and after the interest rate changes. What is the resulting change in net interest income?

c. Explain how the CGAP and spread effects influenced this increase in net interest income.

21. What are some of the weaknesses of the repricing model? How have large banks solved the problem of choosing the optimal time period for repricing? What is runoff cash flow, and how does this amount affect the repricing model's analysis?

The following questions and problems are based on material in Appendix 8A, located on the website (**www.mhhe.com/saunders8e**).

22. What is a maturity gap? How can the maturity model be used to immunize an FI's portfolio? What is the critical requirement that allows maturity matching to have some success in immunizing the balance sheet of an FI?

23. Nearby Bank has the following balance sheet (in millions):

| Assets | | Liabilities and Equity | |
|---|---|---|---|
| Cash | $ 60 | Demand deposits | $140 |
| 5-year Treasury notes | 60 | 1-year certificates of deposit | 160 |
| 30-year mortgages | 200 | Equity | 20 |
| Total assets | $320 | Total liabilities and equity | $320 |

What is the maturity gap for Nearby Bank? Is Nearby Bank more exposed to an increase or a decrease in interest rates? Explain why.

24. County Bank has the following market value balance sheet (in millions, all interest at annual rates). All securities are selling at par equal to book value.

| Assets | | Liabilities and Equity | |
|---|---|---|---|
| Cash | $ 20 | Demand deposits | $100 |
| 15-year commercial loan at 10% interest, balloon payment | 160 | 5-year CDs at 6% interest, balloon payment | 210 |
| 30-year mortgages at 8% interest, balloon payment | 300 | 20-year debentures at 7% interest, balloon payment | 120 |
| | | Equity | 50 |
| Total assets | $480 | Total liabilities and equity | $480 |

a. What is the maturity gap for County Bank?

b. What will be the maturity gap if the interest rates on all assets and liabilities increase 1 percent?

c. What will happen to the market value of the equity?

25. If a bank manager is certain that interest rates are going to increase within the next six months, how should the bank manager adjust the bank's maturity gap to take advantage of this anticipated increase? What if the manager believes rates will fall? Would your suggested adjustments be difficult or easy to achieve?

26. An insurance company has invested in the following fixed-income securities: (a) $10,000,000 of five-year Treasury notes paying 5 percent interest and selling at par value, (b) $5,800,000 of 10-year bonds paying 7 percent interest with a par value of $6,000,000, and (c) $6,200,000 of 20-year subordinated debentures paying 9 percent interest with a par value of $6,000,000.

a. What is the weighted-average maturity of this portfolio of assets?

b. If interest rates change so that the yields on all the securities decrease 1 percent, how does the weighted-average maturity of the portfolio change?

c. Explain the changes in the maturity values if the yields increase 1 percent.

d. Assume that the insurance company has no other assets. What will be the effect on the market value of the company's equity if the interest rate changes in (b) and (c) occur?

27. The following is a simplified FI balance sheet:

| Assets | | Liabilities and Equity | |
|---|---|---|---|
| Loans | $1,000 | Deposits | $ 850 |
| | | Equity | 150 |
| Total assets | $1,000 | Total liabilities and equity | $1,000 |

The average maturity of loans is four years and the average maturity of deposits is two years. Assume that loan and deposit balances are reported as book value, zero-coupon items.

a. Assume that the interest rate on both loans and deposits is 9 percent. What is the market value of equity?

b. What must be the interest rate on deposits to force the market value of equity to be zero? What economic market conditions must exist to make this situation possible?

c. Assume that the interest rate on both loans and deposits is 9 percent. What must be the average maturity of deposits for the market value of equity to be zero?

28. Gunnison Insurance has reported the following balance sheet (in thousands):

| Assets | | Liabilities and Equity | |
|---|---|---|---|
| 2-year Treasury note | $175 | 1-year commercial paper | $135 |
| 15-year munis | 165 | 5-year note | 160 |
| | | Equity | 45 |
| Total assets | $340 | Total liabilities and equity | $340 |

All securities are selling at par equal to book value. The two-year notes are yielding 5 percent, and the 15-year munis are yielding 9 percent. The one-year commercial paper pays 4.5 percent, and the five-year notes pay 8 percent. All instruments pay interest annually.

a. What is the weighted-average maturity of the assets for Gunnison?

b. What is the weighted-average maturity of the liabilities for Gunnison?

c. What is the maturity gap for Gunnison?

d. What does your answer to part (c) imply about the interest rate risk exposure of Gunnison Insurance?

e. Calculate the values of all four securities on Gunnison Insurance's balance sheet assuming that all interest rates increase 2 percent. What is the dollar change in the total asset and total liability values? What is the percentage change in these values?

f. What is the dollar impact on the market value of equity for Gunnison? What is the percentage change in the value of the equity?

g. What would be the impact on Gunnison's market value of equity if the liabilities paid interest semiannually instead of annually?

29. Scandia Bank has issued a one-year, $1 million CD paying 5.75 percent to fund a one-year loan paying an interest rate of 6 percent. The principal of the loan will be paid in two installments: $500,000 in six months and the balance at the end of the year.

a. What is the maturity gap of Scandia Bank? According to the maturity model, what does this maturity gap imply about the interest rate risk exposure faced by Scandia Bank?

b. Assuming no change in interest rates over the year, what is the expected net interest income at the end of the year?

c. What would be the effect on annual net interest income of a 2 percent interest rate increase that occurred immediately after the loan was made? What would be the effect of a 2 percent decrease in rates?

d. What do these results indicate about the ability of the maturity model to immunize portfolios against interest rate exposure?

30. EDF Bank has a very simple balance sheet. Assets consist of a two-year, $1 million loan that pays an interest rate of LIBOR plus 4 percent annually. The loan is funded with a two-year deposit on which the bank pays LIBOR plus 3.5 percent interest annually. LIBOR currently is 4 percent, and both the loan and the deposit principal will be paid at maturity.
    a. What is the maturity gap of this balance sheet?
    b. What is the expected net interest income in year 1 and year 2?
    c. Immediately prior to the beginning of year 2, LIBOR rates increase to 6 percent. What is the expected net interest income in year 2? What would be the effect on net interest income of a 2 percent decrease in LIBOR?
    d. What do the answers to parts (b) and (c) of this question suggest about the use of maturity gap to immunize an FI against interest rate risk?

31. What are the weaknesses of the maturity gap model?

The following questions and problems are based on material in Appendix 8B to the chapter.

32. Suppose that the current one-year rate (one-year spot rate) and expected one-year T-bill rates over the following three years (i.e., years 2, 3, and 4, respectively) are as follows:

$$_1R_1 = 6\% \quad E(_2r_1) = 7\% \quad E(_3r_1) = 7.5\% \quad E(_4r_1) = 7.85\%$$

Using the unbiased expectations theory, calculate the current (long-term) rates for one-, two-, three-, and four-year-maturity Treasury securities. Plot the resulting yield curve.

33. The current one-year Treasury bill rate is 5.2 percent, and the expected one-year rate 12 months from now is 5.8 percent. According to the unbiased expectations theory, what should be the current rate for a two-year Treasury security?

34. *The Wall Street Journal* reported interest rates of 6 percent, 6.35 percent, 6.65 percent, and 6.75 percent for three-year, four-year, five-year, and six-year Treasury notes, respectively. According to the unbiased expectations theory, what are the expected one-year rates for years 4, 5, and 6?

35. *The Wall Street Journal* reports that the rate on three-year Treasury securities is 5.60 percent and the rate on four-year Treasury securities is 5.65 percent. According to the unbiased expectations hypothesis, what does the market expect the one-year Treasury rate to be in year 4, $E(_4r_1)$?

36. How does the liquidity premium theory of the term structure of interest rates differ from the unbiased expectations theory? In a normal economic environment, that is, an upward-sloping yield curve, what is the relationship of liquidity premiums for successive years into the future? Why?

37. Based on economists' forecasts and analysis, one-year Treasury bill rates and liquidity premiums for the next four years are expected to be as follows:

$$_1R_1 = 5.65\%$$
$$E(_2r_1) = 6.75\% \quad L_2 = 0.05\%$$
$$E(_3r_1) = 6.85\% \quad L_3 = 0.10\%$$
$$E(_4r_1) = 7.15\% \quad L_4 = 0.12\%$$

Using the liquidity premium hypothesis, plot the current yield curve. Make sure you label the axes on the graph and identify the four annual rates on the curve both on the axes and on the yield curve itself.

38. *The Wall Street Journal* reports that the rate on three-year Treasury securities is 5.25 percent and the rate on four-year Treasury securities is 5.50 percent. The one-year interest rate expected in year four, $E(_4r_1)$, is 6.10 percent. According to the liquidity premium hypothesis, what is the liquidity premium on the four-year Treasury security, $L_4$?

39. You note the following yield curve in *The Wall Street Journal*. According to the unbiased expectations hypothesis, what is the one-year forward rate for the period beginning two years from today, $_2f_1$?

| Maturity | Yield |
|---|---|
| One day | 2.00% |
| One year | 5.50 |
| Two years | 6.50 |
| Three years | 9.00 |

# Integrated Mini Case

## CALCULATING AND USING THE REPRICING GAP

State Bank's balance sheet is listed below. Market yields are in parentheses, and amounts are in millions.

| Assets | | Liabilities and Equity | |
|---|---|---|---|
| Cash | $ 20 | Demand deposits | $ 250 |
| Fed funds (5.05%) | 150 | Savings accounts (1.5%) | 20 |
| 3-month T-bills (5.25%) | 150 | MMDAs (4.5%) (no minimum | |
| 2-year T-notes (6.50%) | 100 | balance requirement) | 340 |
| 8-year T-bonds (7.50%) | 200 | 3-month CDs (4.2%) | 120 |
| 5-year munis (floating rate) (8.20%, repriced | | 6-month CDs (4.3%) | 220 |
| @ 6 months) | 50 | 1-year CDs (4.5%) | 375 |
| 6-month consumer loans (6%) | 250 | 2-year CDs (5%) | 425 |
| 1-year consumer loans (5.8%) | 300 | 4-year CDs (5.5%) | 330 |
| 5-year car loans (7%) | 350 | 5-year CDs (6%) | 350 |
| 7-month C&I loans (5.8%) | 200 | Fed funds (5%) | 225 |
| 2-year C&I loans (floating rate) (5.15%, repriced | | Overnight repos (5%) | 290 |
| @ 6 months) | 275 | 6-month commercial paper (5.05%) | 300 |
| 15-year variable-rate mortgages (5.8%, repriced | | Subordinate notes: | |
| @ 6 months) | 200 | 3-year fixed rate (6.55%) | 200 |
| 15-year variable-rate mortgages (6.1%, repriced | | Subordinated debt: | |
| @ year) | 400 | 7-year fixed rate (7.25%) | 100 |
| 15-year fixed-rate mortgages (7.85%) | 300 | Total liabilities | $3,545 |
| 30-year variable-rate mortgages (6.3%, repriced | | | |
| @ quarter) | 225 | | |
| 30-year variable-rate mortgages (6.4%, repriced | | | |
| @ month) | 355 | | |
| 30-year fixed-rate mortgages (8.2%) | 400 | | |
| Premises and equipment | 20 | Equity | 400 |
| Total assets | $3,945 | Total liabilities and equity | $3,945 |

1. What is the repricing gap if the planning period is 30 days? 6 months? 1 year? 2 years? 5 years?
2. What is the impact over the next six months on net interest income if interest rates on RSAs increase 60 basis points and on RSLs increase 40 basis points?
3. What is the impact over the next year on net interest income if interest rates on RSAs increase 60 basis points and on RSLs increase 40 basis points?

## Appendix 8A: The Maturity Model

View Appendix 8A at the website for this textbook (**www.mhhe.com/saunders8e**).

## Appendix 8B

# Term Structure of Interest Rates

To explain the process of estimating the impact of an unexpected shock in short-term interest rates on the entire term structure of interest rates, FIs use the theory of the term structure of interest rates or the yield curve. The *term structure of interest rates* compares the market yields or interest rates on securities, assuming that all characteristics (default risk, coupon rate, etc.) except maturity are the same. The change in required interest rates as the maturity of a security changes is called the *maturity premium (MP)*. The MP, or the difference between the required yield on long- and short-term securities of the same characteristics except maturity, can be positive, negative, or zero. The yield curve for U.S. Treasury securities is the most commonly reported and analyzed yield curve. The shape of the yield curve on Treasury securities has taken many forms over the years, but the three most common shapes are shown in Figure 8B–1. In graph (a), the yield curve on May 29, 2012, yields rise steadily with maturity when the yield curve is upward sloping. This is the most common yield curve, so on average the MP is positive. Graph (b) shows an inverted or downward-sloping yield curve, reported on

November 24, 2000, for which yields decline as maturity increases. Inverted yield curves do not generally last very long. Finally, graph (c) shows a flat yield curve, reported on June 4, 2007, in which the yield to maturity is virtually unaffected by the term to maturity.

Note that these yield curves may reflect factors other than investors' preferences for the maturity of a security, since in reality there may be liquidity differences among the securities traded at different points along the yield curve. For example, newly issued 20-year Treasury bonds offer a rate of return less than (seasoned issues) 10-year Treasury bonds if investors prefer new ("on the run") securities to previously issued ("off the run") securities. Specifically, since the Treasury (historically) issues new 10-year notes and 20-year bonds only at the long end of the maturity spectrum, an existing 10-year Treasury bond would have to have been issued 10 years previously (i.e., it was originally a 20-year bond when it was issued 10 years previously). The increased demand for the newly issued "liquid" 20-year Treasury bonds relative to the less liquid 10-year Treasury bonds can be large enough to push the equilibrium interest rate on the

**FIGURE 8B–1** Treasury Yield Curves

Source: U.S. Treasury, "Daily Treasury Rates." *www.ustreas.gov*

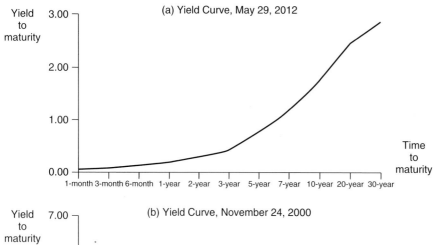

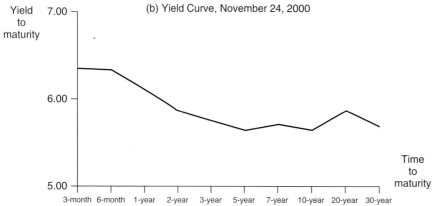

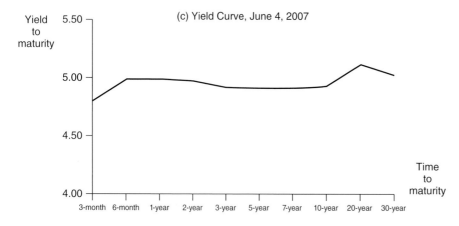

20-year Treasury bonds below that on the 10-year Treasury bonds and even below short-term rates. Explanations for the shape of the yield curve fall predominantly into three theories: the unbiased expectations theory, the liquidity premium theory, and the market segmentation theory.

# UNBIASED EXPECTATIONS THEORY

According to the unbiased expectations theory for the term structure of interest rates, at a given point in time the yield curve reflects the market's

**FIGURE 8B–2**   Unbiased Expectations Theory of the Term Structure of Interest Rates

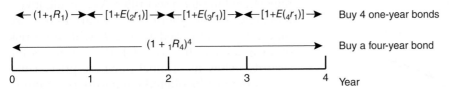

current expectations of future short-term rates. Thus, an upward-sloping yield curve reflects the market's expectation that short-term rates will rise throughout the relevant time period (e.g., the Federal Reserve is expected to tighten monetary policy in the future). Similarly, a flat yield curve reflects the expectation that short-term rates will remain constant over the relevant time period.

As illustrated in Figure 8B–2, the intuition behind the unbiased expectations theory is that if investors have a 4-year investment horizon, they either could buy a current 4-year bond and earn the current yield on a 4-year bond each year ($_1R_4$, if held to maturity) or could invest in 4 successive one-year bonds (of which they know only the current one-year rate, $_1R_1$, but form expectations of the unknown future one-year rates). In equilibrium, the return to holding a 4-year bond to maturity should equal the expected return to investing in 4 successive one-year bonds. Similarly, the return on a 3-year bond should equal the expected return on investing in 3 successive one-year bonds. If future one-year rates are expected to rise each successive year into the future, then the yield curve will slope upward. Specifically, the current 4-year T-bond rate or return will exceed the 3-year bond rate, which will exceed the 2-year bond rate, and so on. Similarly, if future one-year rates are expected to remain constant each successive year into the future, then the 4-year bond rate will be equal to the 3-year bond rate. That is, the term structure of interest rates will remain constant over the relevant time period. Specifically, the unbiased expectations theory posits that long-term rates are a geometric average of current and expected short-term interest rates. That is, the interest rate that equates the return on a series of short-term security investments with the return on a long-term security with an equivalent maturity reflects the market's forecast of future interest

rates. The mathematical equation representing this relationship is:

$$(1 + {}_1R_N)^N = (1 + {}_1R_1)[1 + E({}_2r_1)] \dots [1 + E({}_Nr_1)]$$

where

$$
\begin{aligned}
{}_1R_N &= \text{Actual } N\text{-period rate} \\
N &= \text{Term to maturity} \\
{}_1R_1 &= \text{Current one-year rate} \\
E({}_tr_1) &= \text{Expected one-year (forward) yield during period } t
\end{aligned}
$$

Notice that uppercase interest rate terms, $_1R_t$, are the actual current interest rates on securities purchased today with a maturity of $t$ years. Lowercase interest rate terms, $_tr_1$, are estimates of future one-year interest rates starting $t$ years into the future. For example, suppose the current one-year spot rate and expected one-year Treasury bill rates over the following three years (i.e., years 2, 3, and 4, respectively) are as follows:

$$
\begin{array}{ll}
{}_1R_1 = 2.94\% & E({}_2r_1) = 4.00\% \\
E({}_3r_1) = 4.74\% & E({}_4r_1) = 5.10\%
\end{array}
$$

This would be consistent with the market's expecting the Federal Reserve to increasingly tighten monetary policy. With the unbiased expectations theory, current long-term rates for one-, two-, three-, and four-year maturity Treasury securities should be:

$$
\begin{aligned}
{}_1R_1 &= 2.940\% \\
{}_1R_2 &= [(1 + 0.0294)(1 + 0.04)]^{1/2} - 1 = 3.47\% \\
{}_1R_3 &= [(1 + 0.0294)(1 + 0.04)(1 + 0.0474)]^{1/3} - 1 \\
&= 3.89\% \\
{}_1R_4 &= [(1 + 0.0294)(1 + 0.04)(1 + 0.0474) \\
&\qquad (1 + 0.051)]^{1/4} - 1 = 4.19\%
\end{aligned}
$$

And the yield curve should look like this:

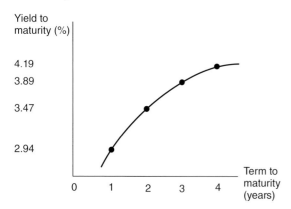

Thus, the upward-sloping yield curve reflects the market's expectation of consistently rising one-year (short-term) interest rates in the future.

## LIQUIDITY PREMIUM THEORY

The unbiased expectations theory has the shortcoming that it neglects to recognize that forward rates are not perfect predictors of future interest rates. If forward rates were perfect predictors of future interest rates, future prices of Treasury securities would be known with certainty. The return over any investment period would be certain and independent of the maturity of the instrument initially purchased and of the time at which the investor needs to liquidate the security. However, with uncertainty about future interest rates (and future monetary policy actions) and hence about future security prices, these instruments become risky in the sense that the return over a future investment period is unknown. In other words, because of future uncertainty of returns, there is a risk in holding long-term securities, and that risk increases with the security's maturity.

The liquidity premium theory of the term structure of interest rates allows for this future uncertainty. It is based on the idea that investors will hold long-term maturities only if they are offered a premium to compensate for the future uncertainty in a security's value, which increases with an asset's maturity. Specifically, in a world of uncertainty, short-term securities provide greater marketability (due to their more active secondary market) and have less price risk (due to smaller price fluctuations for a given change in interest rates) than long-term securities. As a result, investors prefer to hold shorter-term securities because they can be converted into cash with little risk of a capital loss, that is, a fall in the price of the security below its original purchase price. Thus, investors must be offered a liquidity premium to buy longer-term securities that have higher risk of capital losses. This difference in price or liquidity risk can be directly related to the fact that longer-term securities are more sensitive to interest rate changes in the market than are shorter-term securities—see Appendix 9A for a discussion on bond interest rate sensitivity and the link to a bond's maturity. Because the longer the maturity on a security the greater its risk, the liquidity premium increases as maturity increases.

The liquidity premium theory states that long-term rates are equal to the geometric average of current and expected short-term rates (as with the unbiased expectations theory) plus a liquidity or risk premium that increases with the maturity of the security. Figure 8B–3 illustrates the difference in the shape of the yield curve under the unbiased expectations theory versus the liquidity premium theory. For example, according to the liquidity premium theory, an upward-sloping yield curve may reflect the investor's expectations that future short-term rates will rise, be flat, or fall, but because the liquidity premium increases with maturity, the yield curve will nevertheless increase with the term to maturity. The liquidity premium theory may be mathematically represented as:

$$_1R_N = \{(1 + {}_1R_1)[1 + E({}_2r_1) + L_2]...[1 + E({}_Nr_1) + L_N]\}^{1/N} - 1$$

where

$L_t$ = liquidity premium for a period $t$ and $L_2 < L_3 < ... < L_N$.

For example, suppose that the current one-year rate (one-year spot rate) and expected one-year T-bill rates over the following three years (i.e., years 2, 3, and 4, respectively) are as follows:

$$_1R_1 = 2.94\% \quad E({}_2r_1) = 4.00\%$$
$$E({}_3r_1) = 4.74\%$$
$$E({}_4r_1) = 5.10\%$$

**FIGURE 8B–3**   Yield Curve under the Unbiased Expectations Theory (UET) versus the Liquidity Premium Theory (LPT)

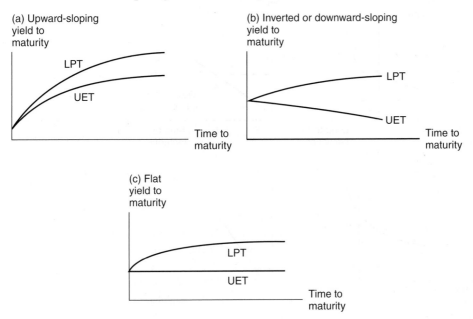

(a) Upward-sloping yield to maturity

LPT
UET
Time to maturity

(b) Inverted or downward-sloping yield to maturity

LPT
UET
Time to maturity

(c) Flat yield to maturity

LPT
UET
Time to maturity

In addition, investors charge a liquidity premium on longer-term securities such that:

$$L_2 = 0.10\% \quad L_3 = 0.20\% \quad L_4 = 0.30\%$$

Using the liquidity premium theory, current rates for one-, two-, three-, and four-year-maturity Treasury securities should be:

$$_1R_1 = 2.94\%$$

$$_1R_2 = [(1 + 0.0294)(1 + 0.04 + 0.001)]^{1/2} - 1 = 3.52\%$$

$$_1R_3 = [(1 + 0.0294)(1 + 0.04 + 0.001)(1 + 0.0474$$
$$+ 0.002)]^{1/3} - 1 = 3.99\%$$

$$_1R_4 = [(1 + 0.0294)(1 + 0.04 + 0.001)(1 + 0.0474$$
$$+ 0.002)(1 + 0.051 + 0.003)]^{1/4} - 1 = 4.34\%$$

and the current yield to maturity curve will be upward sloping as shown:

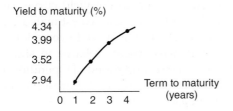

Yield to maturity (%)

4.34
3.99
3.52
2.94

Term to maturity (years)

0  1  2  3  4

Comparing the yield curves in the example above (using the unbiased expectations hypothesis) and here, notice that the liquidity premium in year 2 ($L_2 = 0.10\%$) produces a 0.05 percent premium on the yield to maturity on a two-year T-note, the liquidity premium for year 3 ($L_3 = 0.20\%$) produces a 0.10 percent premium on the yield to maturity on the three-year T-note, and the liquidity premium for year 4 ($L_4 = 0.30\%$) produces a 0.15 percent premium on the yield to maturity on the four-year T-note.

## MARKET SEGMENTATION THEORY

Market segmentation theory argues that individual investors have specific maturity preferences. Accordingly, securities with different maturities are not seen as perfect substitutes under the market segmentation theory. Instead, individual investors have preferred investment horizons dictated by the nature of the assets and liabilities they hold. For example, banks might prefer to hold relatively short-term U.S. Treasury bills because of the short-term nature of their deposit liabilities, while insurance companies might prefer to

**FIGURE 8B–4** Market Segmentation and Determination of the Slope of the Yield Curve

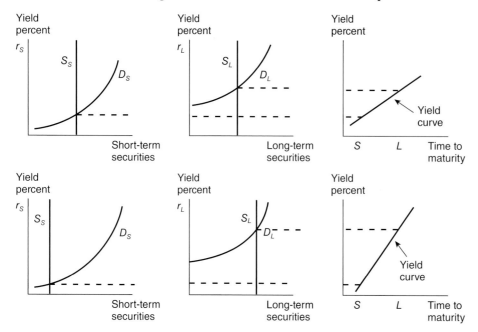

hold long-term U.S. Treasury bonds because of the long-term nature of their life insurance contractual liabilities. As a result, interest rates are determined by distinct supply and demand conditions within a particular maturity bucket or market segment (e.g., the short end and the long end of the market). The market segmentation theory assumes that neither investors nor borrowers are willing to shift from one maturity sector to another to take advantage of opportunities arising from changes in yields. Figure 8B–4 demonstrates how changes in the supply curve for short-versus long-term bonds result in changes in the shape of the yield curve. Such a change may occur if the U.S. Treasury decides to issue fewer short-term bonds and more long-term bonds (i.e., to lengthen the average maturity of government debt outstanding). Specifically in Figure 8B–4, the higher the yield on securities, the higher the demand for them.

Thus, as the supply of securities decreases in the short-term market and increases in the long-term market, the slope of the yield curve becomes steeper. If the supply of short-term securities had increased while the supply of long-term securities had decreased, the yield curve would have become flatter (and may even have sloped downward). Indeed, the large-scale repurchases of long-term Treasury bonds (i.e., reductions in supply) by the U.S. Treasury in 2000 have been viewed as the major cause of the inverted yield curve that appeared in 2000. More recently, in 2011 the Federal Reserve announced its Operation Twist in which the Fed purchased $400 billion of 15- and 20-year Treasury bonds, and at the same time, sold $400 billion of its short-term securities. The name of the plan came from what the Fed hoped the plan would do to the yield curve: flip it around, or at least flatten the curve, so that long-term rates go down and short-term rates rise. In June 2012, the Fed announced an extension of Operation Twist involving a swap of $267 billion short-term for long-term securities. Both moves did immediately flatten the yield curve. Federal Reserve Bank of San Francisco estimated that the first round of Operation Twist, lowered long-term yields by 15 basis points relative to short-term yields. With the second round of Operation Twist, the spread between long- and short-term rates fell another 11 basis points.

# FORECASTING INTEREST RATES

As interest rates change, so do the values of financial securities. Accordingly, the ability to predict or forecast interest rates is critical to the profitability of FIs. For example, if interest rates rise, the value of investment portfolios of FIs will fall, resulting in a loss of wealth. Thus, interest rate forecasts are extremely important for the financial wealth of FIs. The discussion of the unbiased expectations theory above indicates that the shape of the yield curve is determined by the market's current expectations of future short-term interest rates. For example, an upward-sloping yield curve suggests that the market expects future short-term interest rates to increase. Given that the yield curve represents the market's current expectations of future short-term interest rates, the unbiased expectations theory can be used to forecast (short-term) interest rates in the future (i.e., forward one-year interest rates). A forward rate is an expected or implied rate on a short-term security that is to be originated at some point in the future. With the equations representing the unbiased expectations theory, the market's expectation of forward rates can be derived directly from existing or actual rates on securities currently traded in the spot market.

To find an implied forward rate on a one-year security to be issued one year from today, we can rewrite the unbiased expectation theory equation as follows:

$$_1R_2 = \{(1 + {_1R_1})[1 + ({_2f_1})]\}^{1/2} - 1$$

where

$_2f_1$ = Expected one-year rate for year 2, or the implied forward one-year rate for next year

Therefore, $_2f_1$ is the market's estimate of the expected one-year rate for year 2. Solving for $_2f_1$, we get:

$$_2f_1 = \{(1 + {_1R_2})^2 / [1 + ({_1R_1})]\} - 1$$

In general, we can find the one-year forward rate for any year, $N$ years into the future, using the following equation:

$$_Nf_1 = \{(1 + {_1R_N})^N / [1 + ({_1R_{N-1}})]^{N-1}\} - 1$$

For example, on May 29, 2012, the existing or current (spot) one-year, two-year, three-year, and four-year zero-coupon Treasury security rates were as follows:

$$_1R_1 = 0.203\% \quad {_1R_2} = 0.304\%$$
$$_1R_3 = 0.439\% \quad {_1R_4} = 0.604\%$$

With the unbiased expectations theory, one-year forward rates on zero-coupon Treasury bonds for years 2, 3, and 4 as of May 29, 2012, were:

$$_2f_1 = [(1.00304)^2 / (1.00203)] - 1 = 1.004\%$$
$$_3f_1 = [(1.00439)^3 / (1.00304)^2] - 1 = 1.007\%$$
$$_4f_1 = [(1.00604)^4 / (1.00439)^3] - 1 = 1.011\%$$

Thus, the expected one-year rate one year into the future was 1.004 percent; the expected one-year rate two years into the future was 1.007 percent; and the expected one-year rate three years into the future was 1.011 percent.

See Appendices Online at www.mhhe.com/saunders8e
• Appendix 9A: The Basics of Bond Valuation

# Interest Rate Risk II

## INTRODUCTION

**book value accounting**
Accounting method in which the assets and liabilities of the FI are recorded at historic values.

**market value accounting**
Accounting method in which the assets and liabilities of the FI are revalued according to the current level of interest rates.

**mark to market**
Valuing securities at their current market price.

As mentioned in Chapter 8, a weakness of the repricing model is its reliance on book values rather than market values of assets and liabilities. Indeed, in most countries, FIs report their balance sheets by using **book value accounting.** This method records the historic values of securities purchased, loans made, and liabilities sold. For example, for U.S. banks, investment assets (i.e., those expected to be held to maturity) are recorded at book values, while those assets expected to be used for trading (trading securities or available-for-sale securities) are reported according to market value.[1] The recording of market values means that assets and liabilities are revalued to reflect current market conditions. Thus, if a fixed-coupon bond had been purchased at $100 per $100 of face value in a low-interest rate environment, a rise in current market rates reduces the present value of the cash flows from the bond to the investor. Such a rise also reduces the price—say to $97—at which the bond could be sold in the secondary market today. That is, the **market value accounting** approach reflects economic reality, or the true values of assets and liabilities if the FI's portfolio were to be liquidated at today's securities prices rather than at the prices when the assets and liabilities were originally purchased or sold. This practice of valuing securities at their market value is referred to as **marking to market.** We discuss book value versus market value accounting and the impact that the use of the alternate methods has in measuring the value of an FI in more detail in Chapter 20. Appendix 9A, located at the book's website (**www.mhhe.com/saunders8e**), presents a review of bond pricing and price volatility. This topic is generally covered in introductory finance courses. For students needing a review, Appendix 9A is encouraged reading.

In this second chapter on measuring interest rate risk, we present a market value–based model of managing interest rate risk: the duration gap model. We explain the concept of *duration* and see that duration and the duration gap are more accurate measures of an FI's interest rate risk exposure than is the repricing gap model described in Chapter 8. Unlike the repricing gap model, duration

---

[1] More accurately, they are reported at the lower of cost or current market value (LOCOM). However, both the SEC and the Financial Accounting Standards Board (FASB) have strongly advocated that FIs switch to full market value accounting in the near future. Currently, FASB 115 requires FIs to value certain bonds at market prices but not loans.

gap considers market values and the maturity distributions of an FI's assets and liabilities. Further, duration gap considers the degree of leverage on an FI's balance sheet as well as the timing of the payment or arrival of cash flows on assets and liabilities. Thus, duration gap is a more comprehensive measure of an FI's interest rate risk. As a result, regulators are increasingly focusing on this model in determining an appropriate level of capital reserves for an FI exposed to interest rate risk (see Chapter 20). We begin the chapter by presenting the basic arithmetic needed to calculate the duration of an asset or liability. Then we analyze the economic meaning of the number we calculate for duration. This number, which measures the average life of an asset or liability, also has *economic* meaning as the interest rate sensitivity (or interest elasticity) of that asset or liability's value. Next, we show how the duration measure can be used to protect an FI against interest rate risk. Finally, we examine some problems in applying the duration measure to real-world FIs' balance sheets. The more advanced issues associated with these problems are presented in Appendix 9B at the end of the chapter.

## DURATION: A SIMPLE INTRODUCTION

Duration is a more complete measure of an asset or liability's interest rate sensitivity than is maturity because duration takes into account the time of arrival (or payment) of all cash flows as well as the asset's (or liability's) maturity. Consider a loan with a 15 percent interest rate and required repayment of half the $100 in principal at the end of six months and the other half at the end of the year. The loan is financed with a one-year CD paying 15 percent interest per year. The promised cash flows (CF) received by the FI from the loan at the end of one-half year and at the end of the year appear in Figure 9–1.

$CF_{1/2}$ is the $50 promised repayment of principal plus the $7.50 promised interest payment ($100 × ½ × 15%) received after six months. $CF_1$ is the promised cash flow at the end of the year and is equal to the second $50 promised principal repayment plus $3.75 promised interest ($50 × ½ × 15%). To compare the relative sizes of these two cash flows, we should put them in the same dimensions. This is the case because $1 of principal or interest received at the end of a year is worth less to the FI in terms of the time value of money than $1 of principal or interest received at the end of six months. Assuming that the current required interest rates are 15 percent per year, we calculate the present values (PV) of the two cash flows (CF) shown in Figure 9–2 as:

$$CF_{1/2} = \$57.50 \qquad PV_{1/2} = \$57.5/(1.075) = \$53.49$$
$$CF_1 = \$53.75 \qquad PV_1 = \$53.75/(1.075)^2 = \$46.51$$
$$CF_{1/2} + CF_1 = \$111.25 \qquad PV_{1/2} + PV_1 = \$100.00$$

Note that since $CF_{1/2}$, the cash flows received at the end of one-half year, are received earlier, they are discounted at $(1 + ½R)$, where $R$ is the current annual

**FIGURE 9–1**
**Promised Cash Flows on the One-Year Loan**

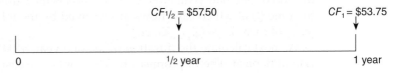

$CF_{1/2} = \$57.50$    $CF_1 = \$53.75$

0        ½ year        1 year

**FIGURE 9–2**

PV of the Cash
Flows from the
Loan

$PV_1 = \$46.51$
$PV_{1/2} = \$53.49$

$CF_{1/2} = \$57.50$

$CF_1 = \$53.75$

0  ½ year  1 year

interest rate on the loan. This is smaller than the discount rate on the cash flow received at the end of the year $(1 + \tfrac{1}{2}R)^2$. Figure 9–2 summarizes the PVs of the cash flows from the loan.

**duration**

The weighted-average time to maturity on an investment.

Technically speaking, **duration** is the *weighted-average* time to maturity on the loan using the relative present values of the cash flows as weights. On a time value of money basis, duration measures the weighted average of when cash flows are received on the loan. As Figure 9–2 shows, the FI receives some cash flows at one-half year and some at one year. Duration analysis weights the time at which cash flows are received by the relative importance in present value terms of the cash flows arriving at each point in time. In present value terms, the relative importance of the cash flows arriving at time $t = \tfrac{1}{2}$ year and time $t = 1$ year are as follows:

| Time (*t*) | Weight (*x*) | | | |
|---|---|---|---|---|
| 1/2 year | $X_{1/2} = \dfrac{PV_{1/2}}{PV_{1/2} + PV_1}$ | $= \dfrac{53.49}{100.00}$ | $= 0.5349$ | $= 53.49\%$ |
| 1 year | $X_1 = \dfrac{PV_1}{PV_{1/2} + PV_1}$ | $= \dfrac{46.51}{100.00}$ | $= 0.4651$ | $= 46.51\%$ |
| | | | 1.0 | 100% |

That is, in present value terms, the FI receives 53.49 percent of cash flows on the loan with the first payment at the end of six months ($t = \tfrac{1}{2}$) and 46.51 percent with the second payment at the end of the year ($t = 1$). By definition, the sum of the (present value) cash flow weights must equal 1:

$$X_{1/2} + X_1 = 1$$
$$0.5349 + 0.4651 = 1$$

We can now calculate the duration ($D$), or the weighted-average time to maturity, of the loan using the present value of its cash flows as weights:

$$D_1 = X_{1/2}(\tfrac{1}{2}) + X_1(1)$$
$$= 0.5349(\tfrac{1}{2}) + 0.4651(1) = 0.7326 \text{ years}$$

Thus, while the maturity of the loan is one year, its duration, or average life in a cash flow sense, is only 0.7326 years. The duration is less than the maturity of the loan because in present value terms 53.49 percent of the cash flows are received at the end of one-half year. Note that duration is measured in years since we weight the time ($t$) at which cash flows are received by the relative present value importance of cash flows ($X_{1/2}$, $X_1$, etc.).

We next calculate the duration of the one-year, $100, 15 percent interest certificate of deposit. The FI promises to make only one cash payment to depositors at

**FIGURE 9–3**
**PV of the Cash Flows of the Deposit**

$PV_1 = \$100$

$CF_1 = \$115$

0

1 year

the end of the year; that is, $CF_1 = \$115$, which is the promised principal ($100) and interest repayment ($15) to the depositor. Since weights are calculated in present value terms:

$$CF_1 = \$115, \text{ and } PV_1 = \$115/1.15 = \$100$$

We show this in Figure 9–3. Because all cash flows are received in one payment at the end of the year, $X_1 = PV_1/PV_1 = 1$, the duration of the deposit is:

$$D_D = X_1 \times 1$$
$$D_D = 1 \times 1 = 1 \text{ year}$$

Thus, only when all cash flows are limited to one payment at the end of the period with no intervening cash flows does duration equal maturity. This example also illustrates that while the maturities on the loan and the deposit are both one year (and thus the difference or gap in maturities is zero), the duration gap is negative:

$$M_L - M_D = 1 - 1 = 0$$
$$D_L - D_D = 0.7326 - 1 = -0.2674 \text{ years}$$

As will become clearer, to measure and to hedge interest rate risk, the FI needs to manage its duration gap rather than its maturity gap.

---

**Concept Questions**

1. Why is duration considered a more complete measure of an asset or liability's interest rate sensitivity than maturity?
2. When is the duration of an asset equal to its maturity?

---

## A GENERAL FORMULA FOR DURATION

You can calculate the duration (or Macaulay's duration[2]) for any fixed-income security that pays interest *annually* using the following general formula:

$$D = \frac{\displaystyle\sum_{t=1}^{N} CF_t \times DF_t \times t}{\displaystyle\sum_{t=1}^{N} CF_t \times DF_t} = \frac{\displaystyle\sum_{t=1}^{N} PV_t \times t}{\displaystyle\sum_{t=1}^{N} PV_t} \tag{1}$$

---

[2] Named after an economist who was among the first to develop the duration concept.

where

$D$ = Duration measured in years

$CF_t$ = Cash flow received on the security at end of period $t$

$N$ = Last period in which the cash flow is received

$DF_t$ = Discount factor = $1/(1 + R)^t$, where $R$ is the annual yield or current level of interest rates in the market

$\sum\limits_{t=1}^{N}$ = Summation sign for addition of all terms from $t = 1$ to $t = N$

$PV_t$ = Present value of the cash flow at the end of the period $t$, which equals $CF_t \times DF_t$

For bonds that pay interest *semiannually,* the duration equation becomes:[3]

$$D = \frac{\sum\limits_{t=1/2}^{N} \dfrac{CF_t \times t}{(1 + R/2)^{2t}}}{\sum\limits_{t=1/2}^{N} \dfrac{CF_t}{(1 + R/2)^{2t}}} \tag{2}$$

where $t = \frac{1}{2}, 1, 1\frac{1}{2}, \ldots, N$.

A key assumption of the simple Macaulay duration model is that the yield curve or the term structure of interest rates is flat and that when rates change, the yield curve shifts in a parallel fashion. Further, the simple duration equation assumes that the issuer of a security or the borrower of a loan pays the interest and principal as promised. That is, the equation assumes no default risk. As we go through the theory and analysis of the duration model and interest rate risk in the body of the chapter, we use the simple Macaulay duration model and these assumptions. In Appendix 9B, we relax these assumptions, allowing for something other than a flat yield curve and default risk. Relaxing these assumptions changes the formulas in the body of the chapter slightly. However, the intuition and general trends remain the same as those seen in the body of the chapter.

Notice that the denominator of the duration equation is the present value of the cash flows on the security (which in an efficient market will be equal to the current market price). The numerator is the present value of each cash flow received on the security multiplied or weighted by the length of time required to receive the cash flow. To help you fully understand this formula, we next look at some examples. Table 9–1 summarizes duration and its features, which we illustrate in the examples.

---

[3] In general, the duration equation is written as:

$$D = \frac{\sum\limits_{t=1/m}^{N} \dfrac{CF_t \times t}{(1 + R/m)^{mt}}}{\sum\limits_{t=1/m}^{N} \dfrac{CF_t}{(1 + R/m)^{mt}}}$$

where $m$ = number of times per year interest is paid.

**TABLE 9–1**
Duration:
Definition and
Features

**Definition of Duration**

1. The weighted-average time to maturity on a security.
2. The interest elasticity of a security's price to small interest rate changes.

**Features of Duration**

1. Duration increases with the maturity of a fixed-income security, but at a decreasing rate.
2. Duration decreases as the yield on a security increases.
3. Duration decreases as the coupon or interest payment increases.

**Risk Management with Duration**

1. Duration is equal to the maturity of an immunized security.
2. Duration gap is used by FIs to measure and manage the interest rate risk of an overall balance sheet.

## The Duration of Interest-Bearing Bonds

**EXAMPLE 9–1**
*The Duration of a Six-Year Eurobond*

Eurobonds pay coupons *annually.* Suppose a Eurobond matures in 6 years, the annual coupon is 8 percent, the face value of the bond is $1,000, and the current yield to maturity ($R$) is also 8 percent. We show the calculation of its duration in Table 9–2. Column 1 lists the time period (in years) in which a cash flow ($CF$) is received. Column 2 lists the $CF$ received in time period $t$. Column 3 lists the discount factor used to convert a future value to a present value. Column 4 is the present value of the $CF$ received in each period $t$ (Column 2 times Column 3). The sum of Column 4 is the present value of the bond: the denominator of the duration equation. Column 5 is the present value of the $CF$ received each period times the time it takes to receive the $CF$ (Column 4 times Column 1). The sum of Column 5 is the time weighted present value of the bond: the numerator of the duration equation. As the calculation indicates, the duration or weighted-average time to maturity on this bond is 4.993 years.

**TABLE 9–2**
Duration of a Six-Year Eurobond with 8 Percent Coupon and Yield

| $t$ | $CF_t$ | $DF_t$ | $CF_t \times DF_t$ | $CF_t \times DF_t \times t$ |
|---|---|---|---|---|
| 1 | 80 | 0.9259 | 74.07 | 74.07 |
| 2 | 80 | 0.8573 | 68.59 | 137.18 |
| 3 | 80 | 0.7938 | 63.51 | 190.53 |
| 4 | 80 | 0.7350 | 58.80 | 235.20 |
| 5 | 80 | 0.6806 | 54.45 | 272.25 |
| 6 | 1,080 | 0.6302 | 680.58 | 4,083.48 |
| | | | 1,000.00 | 4,992.71 |

$$D = \frac{4,992.71}{1,000} = 4.993 \text{ years}$$

**EXAMPLE 9–2**

*The Duration of a Two-Year U.S. Treasury Bond*

U.S. Treasury bonds pay coupon interest semiannually. Suppose a Treasury bond matures in two years, the annual coupon rate is 8 percent, the face value is $1,000, and the annual yield to maturity (R) is 12 percent. See Table 9–3 for the calculation of the duration of this bond. As the calculation indicates, the duration, or weighted-average time to maturity, on this bond is 1.883 years. Table 9–4 shows that if the annual coupon rate is lowered to 6 percent, duration rises to 1.909 years. Since 6 percent coupon payments are lower than 8 percent, it takes longer to recover the initial investment in the bond. In Table 9–5 duration is calculated for the original 8 percent bond, assuming that the yield to maturity increases to 16 percent. Now duration falls from 1.883 years (in Table 9–3) to 1.878 years. The higher the yield to maturity on the bond, the more the investor earns on reinvested coupons and the shorter the time to recover the initial investment. Finally, when the maturity on a bond decreases to 1 year (see Table 9–6), its duration falls to 0.980 year. Thus, the shorter the maturity on the bond, the more quickly the initial investment is recovered.

**TABLE 9–3**

Duration of a Two-Year U.S. Treasury Bond with 8 Percent Coupon and 12 Percent Yield

| $t$ | $CF_t$ | $DF_t$ | $CF_t \times DF_t$ | $CF_t \times DF_t \times t$ |
|---|---|---|---|---|
| ½ | 40 | 0.9434 | 37.74 | 18.87 |
| 1 | 40 | 0.8900 | 35.60 | 35.60 |
| 1½ | 40 | 0.8396 | 33.58 | 50.37 |
| 2 | 1,040 | 0.7921 | 823.78 | 1,647.56 |
| | | | 930.70 | 1,752.40 |

$$D = \frac{1,752.40}{930.70} = 1.883 \text{ years}$$

**TABLE 9–4**

Duration of a Two-Year U.S. Treasury Bond with 6 Percent Coupon and 12 Percent Yield

| $t$ | $CF_t$ | $DF_t$ | $CF_t \times DF_t$ | $CF_t \times DF_t \times t$ |
|---|---|---|---|---|
| ½ | 30 | 0.9434 | 28.30 | 14.15 |
| 1 | 30 | 0.8900 | 26.70 | 26.70 |
| 1½ | 30 | 0.8396 | 25.19 | 37.78 |
| 2 | 1,030 | 0.7921 | 815.86 | 1,631.71 |
| | | | 896.05 | 1,710.34 |

$$D = \frac{1,710.34}{896.05} = 1.909 \text{ years}$$

**TABLE 9–5**

Duration of a Two-Year U.S. Treasury Bond with 8 Percent Coupon and 16 Percent Yield

| $t$ | $CF_t$ | $DF_t$ | $CF_t \times DF_t$ | $CF_t \times DF_t \times t$ |
|---|---|---|---|---|
| ½ | 40 | 0.9259 | 37.04 | 18.52 |
| 1 | 40 | 0.8573 | 34.29 | 34.29 |
| 1½ | 40 | 0.7938 | 31.75 | 47.63 |
| 2 | 1,040 | 0.7350 | 764.43 | 1,528.86 |
| | | | 867.51 | 1,629.30 |

$$D = \frac{1,629.30}{867.51} = 1.878 \text{ years}$$

**TABLE 9–6**
Duration of a One-Year U.S. Treasury Bond with 8 Percent Coupon and 12 Percent Yield

| $t$ | $CF_t$ | $DF_t$ | $CF_t \times DF_t$ | $CF_t \times DF_t \times t$ |
|-----|--------|--------|---------------------|------------------------------|
| ½ | 40 | 0.9434 | 37.74 | 18.87 |
| 1 | 1,040 | 0.8900 | 925.60 | 925.60 |
| | | | 963.34 | 944.47 |

$$D = \frac{944.47}{963.34} = 0.980 \text{ year}$$

Next, we look at two other types of bonds that are useful in understanding duration.

## The Duration of Zero-Coupon Bonds

The U.S. Treasury has created zero-coupon bonds that allow securities firms and other investors to strip individual coupons and the principal from regular Treasury bonds and sell them to investors as separate securities. Elsewhere, such as in the corporate bond markets, corporations have issued discount or zero-coupon bonds directly. U.S. T-bills and commercial paper usually are issued on a discount basis and are additional examples of discount bonds. These bonds sell at a discount from face value on issue, pay the face value (e.g., $1,000) on maturity, and have no intervening cash flows, such as coupon payments, between issue and maturity. The current price an investor is willing to pay for such a bond is equal to the present value of the single, fixed (face value) payment on the bond that is received on maturity (here, $1,000), or:

$$P = \frac{1,000}{(1 + R)^N}$$

where $R$ is the required annually compounded yield to maturity, $N$ is the number of years to maturity, and $P$ is the price. Because there are no intervening cash flows such as coupons between issue and maturity, the following must be true:

$$D_B = M_B$$

That is, the duration of a zero-coupon bond equals its maturity. Note that only for zero-coupon bonds are duration and maturity equal. Indeed, for any bond that pays some cash flows prior to maturity, its duration will always be less than its maturity.

## The Duration of Consol Bonds (Perpetuities)

Although consol bonds have yet to be issued in the United States, they are of theoretical interest in exploring the differences between maturity and duration. A **consol bond** pays a fixed coupon each year. The novel feature of this bond is that it *never* matures; that is, it is a perpetuity:

**consol bond**
A bond that pays a fixed coupon each year forever.

$$M_c = \infty$$

In fact, consol bonds that were issued by the British government in the 1890s to finance the Boer Wars in South Africa are still outstanding. However, while its maturity is theoretically infinity, the formula for the duration of a consol bond is:

$$D_c = 1 + \frac{1}{R}$$

where $R$ is the required yield to maturity. Suppose that the yield curve implies $R = 5$ percent annually. Then the duration of the consol bond would be:

$$D_c = 1 + \frac{1}{0.05} = 21 \text{ years}$$

Thus, while maturity is infinite, duration is finite. Moreover, as interest rates rise, the duration of the consol bond falls. Consider the 1979–82 period, when some yields rose to around 20 percent on long-term government bonds. Then:

$$D_c = 1 + \frac{1}{0.2} = 6 \text{ years}$$

| **Concept Questions** | 1. What does the denominator of the duration equation measure? |
|---|---|
| | 2. What does the numerator of the duration equation measure? |
| | 3. Calculate the duration of a one-year, 8 percent coupon, 10 percent yield bond that pays coupons quarterly. |
| | 4. What is the duration of a zero-coupon bond? |
| | 5. What feature is unique about a consol bond compared with other bonds? |

# FEATURES OF DURATION

From the preceding examples, we derive three important features of duration relating to the maturity, yield, and coupon interest of the security being analyzed.

## Duration and Maturity

A comparison of Tables 9–6, 9–3, and 9–7 indicates that duration *increases* with the maturity of a fixed-income asset or liability, but at a *decreasing* rate:[4]

$$\frac{\partial D}{\partial M} > 0 \qquad \frac{\partial^2 D}{\partial M^2} < 0$$

To see this, look at Figure 9–4, where we plot duration against maturity for a three-year, a two-year, and a one-year U.S. Treasury bond using the *same yield of*

---

[4] This is the case for the vast majority of securities. It needs to be noted, however, that for bonds selling below par, duration increases at a decreasing rate up to a point. At long maturities (e.g., 50 years) duration starts to decline. Few bonds in the market have a maturity long enough to see this decline.

**TABLE 9–7**
Duration of a
Three-Year U.S.
Treasury Bond with
8 Percent Coupon
and 12 Percent Yield
(Coupon Interest
Paid Semiannually)

| $t$ | $CF_t$ | $DF_t$ | $CF_t \times DF_t$ | $CF_t \times DF_t \times t$ |
|---|---|---|---|---|
| ½ | 40 | 0.9434 | 37.04 | 18.87 |
| 1 | 40 | 0.8900 | 35.60 | 35.60 |
| 1½ | 40 | 0.8396 | 33.58 | 50.37 |
| 2 | 40 | 0.7921 | 31.68 | 63.36 |
| 2½ | 40 | 0.7473 | 29.89 | 74.72 |
| 3 | 1,040 | 0.7050 | 733.16 | 2,199.48 |
| | | | 901.65 | 2,442.40 |

$$D = \frac{2{,}442.40}{901.65} = 2.709 \text{ years}$$

**FIGURE 9–4**
Duration versus
Maturity

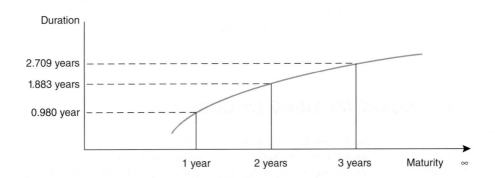

12 *percent* for all three and assuming an annual coupon of 8 percent (with semiannual payments of 4 percent) on each bond. As the maturity of the bond increases from one year to two years (Tables 9–6 and 9–3), duration increases by 0.903 year, from 0.980 year to 1.883 years. Increasing maturity an additional year, from two years to three years (Tables 9–3 and 9–7), increases duration by 0.826, from 1.883 years to 2.709 years.

### Duration and Yield

A comparison of Tables 9–3 and 9–5 indicates that duration decreases as yield increases:

$$\frac{\partial D}{\partial R} < 0$$

As the yield on the Treasury bond increases from 12 percent to 16 percent (Tables 9–3 and 9–5), the duration on the bond decreases from 1.883 years to 1.878 years. This makes sense intuitively because higher yields discount later cash flows more heavily and the relative importance, or weights, of those later cash flows decline when compared with earlier cash flows on an asset or liability.

### Duration and Coupon Interest

A comparison of Tables 9–4 and 9–3 indicates that the higher the coupon or promised interest payment on the security, the lower its duration:

$$\frac{\partial D}{\partial C} < 0$$

As the coupon rate on the U.S. Treasury bond increases from 6 percent to 8 percent in Tables 9–4 and 9–3, the duration on the bond decreases from 1.909 years to 1.883 years. This is due to the fact that the larger the coupons or promised interest payments, the more quickly cash flows are received by investors and the higher are the present value weights of those cash flows in the duration calculation. On a time value of money basis, the investor recoups the initial investment faster when coupon payments are larger.

---

| **Concept Questions** | 1. Which has the longest duration, a 30-year, 8 percent, zero-coupon or discount bond or an 8 percent infinite maturity consol bond? |
|---|---|
| | 2. What is the relationship between duration and yield to maturity on a financial security? |
| | 3. Do high-coupon bonds have high or low durations? |

## THE ECONOMIC MEANING OF DURATION

So far we have calculated duration for a number of different fixed-income assets and liabilities. Now we are ready to make the direct link between the number measured in years we call duration and the interest rate sensitivity of an asset or liability or of an FI's entire portfolio.

In addition to being a measure of the average life, in a cash flow sense, of an asset or liability, duration is also a *direct* measure of the interest rate sensitivity, or elasticity, of an asset or liability. In other words, the larger the numerical value of $D$, the more sensitive is the price of that asset or liability to changes or shocks in interest rates.

Consider the following equation showing that the current price of a bond that pays interest annually is equal to the present value of the coupons and principal payment on the bond:

$$P = \frac{C}{(1 + R)} + \frac{C}{(1 + R)^2} + \cdots + \frac{C + F}{(1 + R)^N} \tag{3}$$

where

$P$ = Price on the bond
$C$ = Coupon or interest payment (annual)
$R$ = Yield to maturity
$N$ = Number of periods to maturity
$F$ = Face value of the bond

We want to find out how the price of the bond ($P$) changes when yields ($R$) rise. We know that bond prices fall, but we want to derive a direct measure of the size of this fall (i.e., its degree of price sensitivity).

Taking the derivative of the bond's price (*P*) with respect to the yield to maturity (*R*), we can show that:[5]

$$\frac{dP}{dR} = -\frac{1}{1+R}(P \times D)$$

By cross multiplying:

$$\frac{dP}{dR} \times \frac{1+R}{P} = -D$$

or, alternatively, and recognizing that interest rate changes tend to be discrete:[6]

$$\frac{\dfrac{\Delta P}{P}}{\dfrac{\Delta R}{1+R}} = -D \qquad\qquad\textbf{(4)}$$

**interest elasticity**
The percentage change in the price of a bond for any given change in interest rates.

The economic interpretation of equation (4) is that the number *D* is the **interest elasticity,** or sensitivity, of the security's price to small interest rate changes. That is, *D*

[5] The first derivative of the bond's price in equation (3) with respect to the yield to maturity (*R*) is:

$$\frac{dP}{dR} = \frac{-C}{(1+R)^2} + \frac{-2C}{(1+R)^3} + \cdots + \frac{-N(C+F)}{(1+R)^{N+1}}$$

By rearranging, we get:

$$\frac{dP}{dR} = -\frac{1}{1+R}\left[\frac{C}{(1+R)} + \frac{2C}{(1+R)^2} + \cdots + \frac{N(C+F)}{(1+R)^N}\right] \qquad\qquad\textbf{(A)}$$

We have shown that duration (*D*) is the weighted-average time to maturity using the present value of cash flows as weights; that is, by definition:

$$D = \frac{1 \times \dfrac{C}{(1+R)} + 2 \times \dfrac{C}{(1+R)^2} + \cdots + N \times \dfrac{(C+F)}{(1+R)^N}}{\dfrac{C}{(1+R)} + \dfrac{C}{(1+R)^2} + \cdots + \dfrac{(C+F)}{(1+R)^N}}$$

Since the denominator of the duration equation is simply the price (*P*) of the bond that is equal to the present value of the cash flows on the bond, then:

$$D = \frac{1 \times \dfrac{C}{(1+R)} + 2 \times \dfrac{C}{(1+R)^2} + \cdots + N \times \dfrac{(C+F)}{(1+R)^N}}{P}$$

Multiplying both sides of this equation by *P*, we get:

$$P \times D = 1 \times \frac{C}{(1+R)} + 2 \times \frac{C}{(1+R)^2} + \cdots + N \times \frac{C+F}{(1+R)^N} \qquad\qquad\textbf{(B)}$$

The term on the right side of equation (B) is the same term as that in square brackets in equation (A). Substituting equation (B) into equation (A), we get:

$$\frac{dP}{dR} = -\frac{1}{1+R}[P \times D]$$

[6] In what follows, we use the Δ (change) notation instead of *d* (derivative notation) to recognize that interest rate changes tend to be discrete rather than infinitesimally small. For example, in real-world financial markets, the smallest observed rate change is usually one basis point, or 1/100th of 1 percent.

describes the percentage price fall of the bond ($\Delta P / P$) for any given (present value) increase in required interest rate or yield ($\Delta R / (1 + R)$).

Equation (4) can be rearranged in another useful way for interpretation regarding interest rate sensitivity. That is, the percentage change in the price of a bond for a change in interest rates can be written as:

$$\frac{\Delta P}{P} = -D\left[\frac{\Delta R}{1 + R}\right] \qquad \textbf{(5)}$$

Equation (5) shows that for small changes in interest rates, bond prices move *in an inversely proportional* fashion according to the size of *D*. Clearly, for any given change in interest rates, long duration securities suffer a larger capital loss (or receive a higher capital gain) should interest rates rise (fall) than do short-duration securities. By implication, gains and losses under the duration model are *symmetric*. That is, if we repeat the above examples but allow interest rates to *decrease* by one basis point annually (or 1/2 basis point semiannually), the percentage increase in the price of the bond ($\Delta P / P$) would be proportionate with *D*. Further, the capital gains would be a mirror image of the capital losses for an equal (small) increase in interest rates.

The duration equation can be rearranged, combining *D* and $(1 + R)$ into a single variable $D/(1 + R)$, to produce what practitioners call **modified duration** (*MD*). For annual compounding of interest:

**modified duration**
Duration divided by 1 plus the interest rate.

$$\frac{\Delta P}{P} = -MD\, dR$$

where

$$MD = \frac{D}{1 + R}$$

This form is more intuitive because we multiply *MD* by the simple change in interest rates rather than the discounted change in interest rates as in the general duration equation.

Duration is a measure of the *percentage change* in the price of a security for a 1 percent change in the return on the security. **Dollar duration** is the *dollar value change* in the price of a security to a 1 percent change in the return on the security. The dollar duration is defined as the modified duration times the price of a security:

**dollar duration**
The dollar value change in a security's price to a 1 percent change in the return on the security.

$$\text{Dollar duration} = MD \times P$$

Thus, the total dollar value of a security will change by an amount equal to the dollar duration times the change in the return on the security:

$$\Delta P = -\text{Dollar duration} \times \Delta R$$

Like the modified duration, the dollar duration is intuitively appealing in that we multiply the dollar duration by the change in the interest rate to get the actual dollar change in the value of a security to a change in interest rates.[7] Next, we use duration to measure the interest sensitivity of an asset or liability.

---

**EXAMPLE 9–3**

*The Six-Year Eurobond*

Consider Example 9–1 for the six-year Eurobond with an 8 percent coupon and 8 percent yield. We determined in Table 9–2 that its duration was approximately $D = 4.993$ years. The modified duration is:

$$MD = D/(1 + R) = 4.993/1.08 = 4.623$$

That is, the price of the bond will increase by 4.623 percent for a 1 percent decrease in the interest rate on the bond. Further, the dollar duration is:

$$\text{Dollar duration} = 4.623 \times \$1,000 = 4,623$$

or a 1 percent (or 100 basis points) change in the return on the bond would result a change of $46.23 in the price of the bond.

To see this, suppose that yields were to rise by one basis point (1/100th of 1 percent) from 8 to 8.01 percent. Then:

$$\frac{\Delta P}{P} = -(4.993)\left[\frac{0.0001}{1.08}\right]$$
$$= -0.000462 \text{ or } -0.0462\%$$

The bond price had been $1,000, which was the present value of a six-year bond with 8 percent coupons and 8 percent yield. The duration model, and specifically dollar duration, predicts that the price of the bond would fall to $999.5377 after the increase in yield by one basis point. That is, the price would change by:

$$\Delta P = -\text{Dollar duration} \times \Delta R$$
$$= -4623 \times 0.0001 = -\$0.463$$

---

**EXAMPLE 9–4**

*The Consol Bond*

Consider a consol bond with an 8 percent coupon paid annually, an 8 percent yield, and a calculated duration of 13.5 years ($D_c = 1 + 1/0.08 = 13.5$). Thus, for a one-basis-point change in the yield (from 8 percent to 8.01 percent):

$$\frac{\Delta P}{P} = -(13.5)\left[\frac{0.0001}{1.08}\right]$$
$$= -0.00125 \text{ or } -0.125\%$$

---

[7] Another measure of interest sensitivity is spread duration. Spread duration is the sensitivity of the price of a bond to a change in its option-adjusted spread (OAS). OAS, discussed in Chapter 26, is the required interest spread of a pass-through or mortgage-backed security over a Treasury rate when prepayment risk is taken into account. Since mortgage payers tend to exercise their right to prepay when it is favorable for them, buying a pass-through or mortgage-backed security partly involves selling an option. This is the source of the option-adjusted spread. Thus, spread duration is the price sensitivity of the pass-through or mortgage-backed security to a change in the OAS. A change in the OAS of a pass-through or mortgage-backed security does not affect the cash flows that the security pays to the investor. Thus, spread duration is the impact of these cash flows at varying interest rates. We discuss this in more detail in Chapter 26.

As you can see, for any given change in yields, long-duration securities suffer a greater capital loss or receive a greater capital gain than do short-duration securities.

## Semiannual Coupon Bonds

For fixed-income assets or liabilities whose interest payments are received semiannually or more frequently than annually, the formula in equation (5) has to be modified slightly. For semiannual payments the percentage change in the price of a bond for a change in interest rates is:

$$\frac{\Delta P}{P} = -D\left[\frac{\Delta R}{1 + \frac{1}{2}R}\right] \tag{6}$$

The only difference between equation (6) and equation (5) is the introduction of a ½ in the discount rate term $1 + \frac{1}{2}R$ to take into account the semiannual payments of interest.

---

**EXAMPLE 9–5**

*Semiannual Coupon, Two-Year Maturity Treasury Bonds*

Recall from Example 9–2 the two-year T-bond with semiannual coupons whose duration we derived in Table 9–3 as 1.883 years when annual yields were 12 percent. The modified duration is:

$$MD = D/(1 + R) = 1.883/1.06 = 1.776$$

That is, the price of the bond will increase by 1.776 percent for a 1 percent decrease in the interest rate on the bond. Further, the dollar duration is:

$$\text{Dollar duration} = 1.776 \times \$930.70 = 1,653$$

or a 1 percent (or 100 basis points) change in the return on the bond would result a change of $16.53 in the price of the bond.

Thus, a one-basis-point rise in interest rates would have the following predicted effect on price:

$$\frac{\Delta P}{P} = -1.883\left[\frac{0.0001}{1.06}\right]$$
$$= -0.0001776$$

or the price of the bond would fall by 0.01776 percent from $930.6979 to $930.5326. That is,

$$\Delta P = -\text{Dollar duration} \times \Delta R$$
$$= -\$16.53 \times 0.0001 = -\$0.1653$$

---

**Concept Questions**

1. What is the relation between the duration of a bond and the interest elasticity of a bond?
2. How would the formula in equation (6) have to be modified to take into account quarterly coupon payments and monthly coupon payments?

# DURATION AND INTEREST RATE RISK

So far, you have learned how to calculate duration and you understand that the duration measure has economic meaning because it indicates the interest sensitivity, or elasticity, of an asset or liability's value. For FIs, the major relevance of duration is as a measure for managing interest rate risk exposure. Also important is the role of duration in allowing the FI to reduce and even eliminate interest rate risk on its balance sheet or some subset of that balance sheet. In the following sections we consider two examples of how FIs can use the duration measure to manage interest rate risk. The first is its use by insurance company and pension fund managers to help meet promised cash flow payments to policyholders or beneficiaries at a particular time in the future. The second is its use to reduce or immunize the whole balance sheet of an FI against interest rate risk.

## Duration and Interest Rate Risk Management on a Single Security

Frequently, pension fund and life insurance company managers face the problem of structuring their asset investments so they can pay out a given cash amount to policyholders in some future period. The classic example of this is an insurance policy that pays the holder some lump sum on reaching retirement age. The risk to the life insurance company manager is that interest rates on the funds generated from investing the holder's premiums could fall. Thus, the accumulated returns on the premiums invested could not meet the target or promised amount. In effect, the insurance company would be forced to draw down its reserves and net worth to meet its payout commitments. (See Chapter 6 for a discussion of this risk.)

Suppose that we are in 2016 and the insurer has to make a guaranteed payment to a policyholder in five years, 2021. For simplicity, we assume that this target guaranteed payment is $1,469, a lump-sum policy payout on retirement, equivalent to investing $1,000 at an annually compounded rate of 8 percent over five years. Of course, realistically, this payment would be much larger, but the underlying principles of the example do not change by scaling up or down the payout amount.

To immunize, or protect, itself against interest rate risk, the insurer needs to determine which investments would produce a cash flow of exactly $1,469 in five years regardless of what happens to interest rates in the immediate future. The FI investing either in a five-year maturity and duration zero-coupon bond or in a coupon bond with a five-year duration would produce a $1,469 cash flow in five years no matter what happened to interest rates in the immediate future. Next, we consider the two strategies: buying five-year maturity (and duration) deep-discount bonds and buying five-year duration coupon bonds.

### Buy Five-Year Maturity Discount Bonds

Given a $1,000 face value, an 8 percent yield, and assuming annual compounding, the current price per five-year discount bond would be $680.58 per bond:

$$P = 680.58 = \frac{1,000}{(1.08)^5}$$

If the insurer bought 1.469 of these bonds at a total cost of $1,000 in 2016, these investments would produce exactly $1,469 on maturity in five years ($1,000 \times (1.08)^5 = $1,469). The reason is that the duration of this bond portfolio exactly matches the target horizon for the insurer's future liability to its policy-holder. Intuitively, since no intervening cash flows or coupons are paid by the issuer of the zero-coupon discount bonds, future changes in interest rates have no reinvestment income effect. Thus, the return would be unaffected by intervening interest rate changes.

### Buy a Five-Year Duration Coupon Bond

Suppose no five-year discount bonds exist. Then the portfolio manager may seek to invest in appropriate duration coupon bonds to hedge interest rate risk. In this example the appropriate investment would be in five-year duration coupon bearing bonds.

We demonstrated earlier in Table 9–2 that a six-year maturity Eurobond paying 8 percent coupons with an 8 percent yield to maturity had a duration of 4.993 years, or approximately five years. If we buy this six-year maturity, five-year duration bond in 2016 and hold it for five years, until 2021, the term exactly matches the target horizon of the insurer. The cash flows generated at the end of five years will be $1,469 whether interest rates stay at 8 percent or instantaneously (immediately) rise to 9 percent or fall to 7 percent. Thus, buying a coupon bond whose duration exactly matches the time horizon of the insurer also immunizes the insurer against interest rate changes.

---

**EXAMPLE 9–6**

*Interest Rates Remain at 8 Percent*

The cash flows received by the insurer on the bond if interest rates stay at 8 percent throughout the five years would be

| | |
|---|---:|
| 1. Coupons, 5 × $80 | $ 400 |
| 2. Reinvestment income | 69 |
| 3. Proceeds from sale of bond at end of fifth year | 1,000 |
| | $1,469 |

We calculate each of the three components of the insurer's income from the bond investment as follows:

1. *Coupons.* The $400 from coupons is simply the annual coupon of $80 received in each of the five years.
2. *Reinvestment income.* Because the coupons are received annually, they can be reinvested at 8 percent as they are received, generating an additional cash flow of $69.[8]

---

[8] Receiving annual coupons of $80 is equivalent to receiving an annuity of $80. The appropriate terminal value of receiving $1 a year for five years and reinvesting at 8 percent can be determined from the future value of an annuity (FVA) formula:

$$FVA_{n,R} = \left[\frac{(1 + R)^n - 1}{R}\right]$$

In our example:

$$FVA_{5,\,8\%} = \left[\frac{(1 + 0.08)^5 - 1}{0.08}\right] = 5.867$$

Thus, the reinvestment income for $80 of coupons per year is:

$$\text{Reinvestment income} = (80 \times 5.867) - 400 = 469 - 400 = 69$$

Note that we take away $400 since we have already counted the simple coupon income (5 × $80).

3. *Bond sale proceeds.* The proceeds from the sale are calculated by recognizing that the six year bond has just one year left to maturity when it is sold by the insurance company at the end of the fifth year. That is:

| ↓ *Sell* | | *$1,080* |
|---|---|---|
| *Year 5* | | *Year 6* |
| *(2021)* | | *(2022)* |

What fair market price can the insurer expect to get when selling the bond at the end of the fifth year with one year left to maturity? A buyer would be willing to pay the present value of the $1,080—final coupon plus face value—to be received at the end of the one remaining year (i.e., in 2022), or:

$$P_5 = \frac{1,080}{1.08} = \$1,000$$

Thus, the insurer would be able to sell the one remaining cash flow of $1,080, to be received in the bond's final year, for $1,000.

Next, we show that since this bond has a duration of five years, matching the insurer's target period, even if interest rates were to instantaneously fall to 7 percent or rise to 9 percent, the expected cash flows from the bond would still exactly sum to $1,469. That is, the coupons + reinvestment income + principal at the end of the fifth year would be immunized. In other words, the cash flows on the bond are protected against interest rate changes.

**EXAMPLE 9–7**

*Interest Rates Fall to 7 Percent*

In this example with falling interest rates, the cash flows over the five years would be:

| | |
|---|---|
| 1. Coupons, 5 × $80 | $   400 |
| 2. Reinvestment income | 60 |
| 3. Bond sale proceeds | 1,009 |
| | $1,469 |

The total proceeds over the five years are unchanged from what they were when interest rates were 8 percent. To see why this occurs, consider what happens to the three parts of the cash flow when rates fall to 7 percent:

1. *Coupons.* Are unchanged since the insurer still gets five annual coupons of $80 = $400.
2. *Reinvestment income.* The coupons can now be reinvested only at the lower rate of 7 percent. Reinvestment income is only $60, which is $9 less than it was when rates were 8 percent.[9]

---

[9] This reinvestment income is calculated as follows.

$$FVA_{5,\,7\%} = \left[ \frac{(1 + 0.07)^5 - 1}{0.07} \right] = 5.751$$

Reinvestment income = (5.751 × 80) − 400 = 60.

3. *Bond sale proceeds.* When the six-year maturity bond is sold at the end of the fifth year with one cash flow of $1,080 remaining, investors are now willing to pay more:

$$P_5 = \frac{1,080}{1.07} = 1,009$$

That is, the bond can be sold for $9 more than it could have when rates were 8 percent. The reason for this is that investors can get only 7 percent on newly issued bonds, while this older bond was issued with a higher coupon of 8 percent.

A comparison of reinvestment income with bond sale proceeds indicates that the fall in rates has produced a *gain* on the bond sale proceeds of $9. This exactly offsets the loss of reinvestment income of $9 due to reinvesting at a lower interest rate. Thus, total cash flows remain unchanged at $1,469.

---

**EXAMPLE 9–8**

*Interest Rates Rise to 9 Percent*

In this example with rising interest rates, the proceeds from the bond investment are:

| | |
|---|---:|
| 1. Coupons, 5 × $80 | $ 400 |
| 2. Reinvestment income [(5.985 × 80) − 400] | 78 |
| 3. Bond sale proceeds (1,080/1.09) | 991 |
| | $1,469 |

Notice that the rise in interest rates from 8 percent to 9 percent leaves the final terminal cash flow unaffected at $1,469. The rise in rates has generated $9 extra reinvestment income ($78 − $69), but the price at which the bond can be sold at the end of the fifth year has declined from $1,000 to $991, equal to a capital loss of $9. Thus, the gain in reinvestment income is exactly offset by the capital loss on the sale of the bond.

---

These examples demonstrate that matching the duration of a coupon bond—or any other fixed–interest rate instrument, such as a loan or mortgage—to the FI's target or investment horizon *immunizes* the FI against instantaneous shocks to interest rates. The gains or losses on reinvestment income that result from an interest rate change are exactly offset by losses or gains from the bond proceeds on sale.

## Duration and Interest Rate Risk Management on the Whole Balance Sheet of an FI

So far we have looked at the durations of individual instruments and ways to select individual fixed-income securities to protect FIs such as life insurance companies and pensions funds with precommitted liabilities such as future pension plan payouts. The duration model can also evaluate the overall interest rate exposure for an FI, that is, measure the **duration gap** on its balance sheet.

**duration gap**
A measure of overall interest rate risk exposure for an FI.

### The Duration Gap for a Financial Institution

To estimate the overall duration gap of an FI, we determine first the duration of an FI's asset portfolio ($A$) and the duration of its liability portfolio ($L$). These can be calculated as:

$$D_A = X_{1A}D_1^A + X_{2A}D_2^A + \cdots + X_{nA}D_n^A$$

and

$$D_L = X_{1L}D_1^L + X_{2L}D_2^L + \cdots + X_{nL}D_n^L$$

where

$$X_{1j} + X_{2j} + \cdots + X_{nj} = 1 \quad \text{and} \quad j = A, L$$

The $X_{ij}$'s in the equation are the market value proportions of each asset or liability held in the respective asset and liability portfolios. Thus, if new 30-year Treasury bonds were 1 percent of a life insurer's portfolio and $D_1^A$ (the duration of those bonds) was equal to 9.25 years, then $X_{1A}D_1^A = 0.01(9.25) = 0.0925$. More simply, the duration of a portfolio of assets or liabilities is a market value weighted average of the individual durations of the assets or liabilities on the FI's balance sheet.

Consider an FI's simplified market value balance sheet:

| Assets ($) | Liabilities ($) |
|---|---|
| $A = 100$ | $L = \phantom{0}90$ |
| | $E = \phantom{0}\underline{10}$ |
| $\underline{\phantom{0}}100$ | $100$ |

From the balance sheet:

$$A = L + E$$

and

$$\Delta A = \Delta L + \Delta E$$

or

$$\Delta E = \Delta A - \Delta L$$

That is, when interest rates change, the change in the FI's equity or net worth ($E$) is equal to the difference between the change in the market values of assets and liabilities on each side of the balance sheet. Since $\Delta E = \Delta A - \Delta L$, we need to determine how $\Delta A$ and $\Delta L$—the changes in the market values of assets and liabilities on the balance sheet—are related to duration.

From the duration model (assuming annual compounding of interest):

$$\frac{\Delta A}{A} = -D_A \frac{\Delta R}{(1 + R)}$$

$$\frac{\Delta L}{L} = -D_L \frac{\Delta R}{(1 + R)}$$

Here we have simply substituted $\Delta A/A$ or $\Delta L/L$, the percentage change in the market values of assets or liabilities, for $\Delta P/P$, the percentage change in any single bond's price and $D_A$ or $D_L$, the duration of the FI's asset or liability portfolio, for $D$, the duration on any given bond, deposit, or loan. The term $\Delta R/(1 + R)$ reflects the shock to interest rates as before.[10] These equations can be rewritten to show the dollar changes in assets and liabilities on an FI's balance sheet:

$$\Delta A = -D_A \times A \times \frac{\Delta R}{(1 + R)} \tag{7}$$

and

$$\Delta L = -D_L \times L \times \frac{\Delta R}{(1 + R)} \tag{8}$$

We can substitute these two expressions into the equation $\Delta E = \Delta A - \Delta L$. Rearranging and combining this equation results in a measure of the change in the market value of equity on an FI's balance sheet for a change in interest rates:

$$\Delta E = -[D_A - D_L k] \times A \times \frac{\Delta R}{1 + R} \tag{9}$$

where $k = L/A$ is a measure of the FI's leverage, that is, the amount of borrowed funds or liabilities rather than owners' equity used to fund its asset portfolio.[11] The effect of interest rate changes on the market value of an FI's equity or net worth ($\Delta E$) breaks down into three effects:

1. *The leverage adjusted duration gap* $= [D_A - D_L k]$. This gap is measured in years and reflects the degree of duration mismatch in an FI's balance sheet. Specifically, the larger this gap is *in absolute terms*, the more exposed the FI is to interest rate shocks.
2. *The size of the FI.* The term $A$ measures the size of the FI's assets. The larger the scale of the FI, the larger the dollar size of the potential net worth exposure from any given interest rate shock.
3. *The size of the interest rate shock* $= \Delta R/(1 + R)$. The larger the shock, the greater the FI's exposure.

Given this, we express the exposure of the net worth of the FI as:

$$\Delta E = -[\text{Leverage adjusted duration gap}] \times \text{Asset size} \times \text{Interest rate shock}$$

Interest rate shocks are largely external to the FI and often result from changes in the Federal Reserve's monetary policy (as discussed in the first section of Chapter 8). The size of the duration gap and the size of the FI, however, are under the control of management.

The Industry Perspectives box reports the duration gaps and the estimated changes in equity value for three financial institutions during the first quarter of 2012. Note that all three institutions had average duration gaps that were negative

---

[10] We assume that the level of rates and the expected shock to interest rates are the same for both assets and liabilities, which means that the FI's spread (the difference between the rate on earning assets and interest-bearing liabilities) is zero. However, as long as the FI has more earning assets than interest bearing liabilities, it will have a positive level for net interest income. This assumption is standard in Macaulay duration analysis. While restrictive, this assumption can be relaxed. However, if this is done, the duration measure changes, as is discussed later in Appendix 9B to this chapter.

[11] We do this as follows:

$$\Delta E = \left[ -D_A \times A \times \frac{\Delta R}{(1 + R)} \right] - \left[ -D_L \times L \times \frac{\Delta R}{(1 + R)} \right]$$

Assuming that the level of rates and the expected shock to interest rates are the same for both assets and liabilities:

$$\Delta E = [-D_A A + D_L L] \frac{\Delta R}{(1 + R)}$$

or

$$\Delta E = -[D_A A - D_L L] \frac{\Delta R}{(1 + R)}$$

To rearrange the equation in a slightly more intuitive fashion, we multiply and divide both $D_A A$ and $D_L L$ by $A$ (assets):

$$\Delta E = -\left[ D_A \frac{A}{A} - D_L \frac{L}{A} \right] \times A \times \frac{\Delta R}{(1 + R)}$$

or $\quad \Delta E = -[D_A - D_L k] \times A \times \dfrac{\Delta R}{(1 + R)}$

or zero. However, Fannie Mae's duration gaps ranged between −0.9 month and 0.4 month, while Freddie Mac's ranged between −0.3 month and 0.6 month. Even these small fluctuations exposed Fannie Mae and Freddie Mac to as much as $200 million and $379 million, respectively, in equity value losses.

# Industry Perspectives   Duration GAP for Various Financial Institutions, March 2012

## PRINCIPAL FINANCIAL GROUP

| Risk Management Strategy | March 31, 2012 | | | |
| --- | --- | --- | --- | --- |
| | Value of total assets | Duration of assets | Net duration gap | Net fair value change |
| | (in millions) | | | (in millions) |
| Primary duration-managed | $26,074.4 | 3.73 | (0.12) | $31.3 |
| Duration-monitored | 25,566.4 | 4.28 | (3.44) | 879.9 |
| Non-duration-managed | 5,253.9 | 4.19 | N/A | N/A |
| Total | $56,894.7 | | | $911.2 |

Net fair value change is based on a 100 basis point immediate, parallel increase in interest rates increases.

**Duration-Managed**

Our exposure to interest rate risk stems largely from our substantial holdings of guaranteed fixed rate liabilities in our Retirement and Investor Services segment. We actively manage the duration of assets and liabilities in these products by minimizing the difference between the two.

**Duration-Monitored**

For products such as whole life insurance and term life insurance that are less sensitive to interest rate risk, and for other products such as individual fixed deferred annuities, we manage interest rate risk based on a modeling process that considers the target average life, maturities, crediting rates, and assumptions of policyholder behavior.

**Non-Duration-Managed**

We also have a block of participating general account pension business that passes most of the actual investment performance of the assets to the customer. The investment strategy of this block is to maximize investment return to the customer on a "best efforts" basis, and there is little or no attempt to manage the duration of this portfolio since there is little or no interest rate risk.

**FANNIE MAE**

The duration gap for the three months ended March 31, 2012, averaged zero months, which is similar to the results for the three months ended March 31, 2011. Rate Slope Shock measures the change in the value of the equity for the stated change in interest rates.

| | For the Three Months Ended March 31, 2012 | | |
| --- | --- | --- | --- |
| | Duration Gap | Rate Slope Shock 25 Bps | Rate Level Shock 50 Bps |
| | | Exposure | |
| | (in months) | (dollars in billions) | |
| Average.......................... | (0.1) | $— | $— |
| Minimum ........................ | (0.9) | — | — |
| Maximum ........................ | 0.4 | 0.1 | 0.2 |
| Standard deviation................. | 0.3 | — | 0.1 |

*continued*

# Industry Perspectives *continued*

|  | For the Three Months Ended March 31, 2011 | | |
|---|---|---|---|
|  | Duration Gap | Rate Slope Shock 25 Bps | Rate Level Shock 50 Bps |
|  |  | Exposure | |
|  | (in months) | (dollars in billions) | |
| Average.......................... | 0.4 | $0.1 | $0.2 |
| Minimum ....................... | (0.4) | — | 0.1 |
| Maximum ....................... | 0.8 | 0.2 | 0.4 |
| Standard deviation................ | 0.2 | — | 0.1 |

## FREDDIE MAC

|  | Three Months Ended March 31, | | | | | |
|---|---|---|---|---|---|---|
|  | 2012 | | | 2011 | | |
|  | Duration Gap | PMVS* 25 bps | PMVS 50 bps | Duration Gap | PMVS 25 bps | PMVS 50 bps |
|  | (in months) | (dollars in millions) | | (in months) | (dollars in millions) | |
| Average..................... | 0.0 | $16 | $223 | (0.3) | $21 | $448 |
| Minimum ................... | (0.3) | $ 1 | $130 | (1.0) | $— | $280 |
| Maximum ................... | 0.6 | $57 | $379 | 0.4 | $51 | $721 |
| Standard deviation............ | 0.2 | $12 | $ 47 | 0.3 | $13 | $101 |

\* PMVS measures the change in the value of the equity for the stated change in interest rates.

Sources: Principal Financial Group, Form 10-Q, March 31, 2012; Fannie Mae, Form 10-Q, March 31, 2012; Freddie Mac, Form 10-Q, March 31, 2012.

Equation (9) and the duration model provide an FI manager with a benchmark measure of the FI's performance for various interest rate changes and therefore the extent to which the FI is exposed to interest rate risk. If, for an expected change in interest rates, managers find the change in equity will be small or negative, the duration model can be used to identify changes needed on or off the FI's balance sheet to reduce or even immunize the FI against interest rate risk. Using an example, the next section explains how a manager can use information on an FI's duration gap to restructure the balance sheet to limit losses and even immunize stockholders' net worth against interest rate risk (i.e., to set the balance sheet up *before* a change in interest rates, so that $\Delta E$ is nonnegative for an expected change in interest rates). Chapters 22, 23, and 24 look at ways a manager can use the duration gap to take off-balance-sheet positions in derivative securities to reduce or immunize the FI against interest rate risk.

**EXAMPLE 9–9**

*Duration Gap
Measurement
and Exposure*

Suppose the FI manager calculates that:

$$D_A = 5 \text{ years}$$
$$D_L = 3 \text{ years}$$

Then the manager learns from an economic forecasting unit that rates are expected to rise from 10 percent to 11 percent in the immediate future; that is:

$$\Delta R = 1\% = 0.01$$
$$1 + R = 1.10$$

The FI's initial balance sheet is assumed to be:

| Assets ($ millions) | Liabilities ($ millions) |
|---|---|
| A = 100 | L = 90 |
| | E = 10 |
| 100 | 100 |

The FI's manager calculates the potential loss to equity holders' net worth (*E*) if the forecast of rising rates proves true as follows:

$$\Delta E = -(D_A - kD_L) \times A \times \frac{\Delta R}{(1 + R)}$$
$$= -(5 - (0.9)(3)) \times \$100 \text{ million} \times \frac{0.01}{1.10} = -\$2.09 \text{ million}$$

The FI could lose $2.09 million in net worth if rates rise 1 percent. Since the FI started with $10 million in equity, the loss of $2.09 million is almost 21 percent of its initial net worth. The market value balance sheet after the rise in rates by 1 percent would look like this:[12]

| Assets ($ millions) | Liabilities ($ millions) |
|---|---|
| A = 95.45 | L = 87.54 |
| | E = 7.91 |
| 95.45 | 95.45 |

---

[12] These values are calculated as follows:

$$\Delta A/A = -5(0.01/1.10) = -0.04545 = -4.545\%$$
$$100 + (-0.04545)100 = 95.45$$

and

$$\Delta L/L = -3(0.01/1.10) = -0.02727 = -2.727\%$$
$$90 + (-0.02727)90 = 87.54$$

Even though the rise in interest rates would not push the FI into economic insolvency, it reduces the FI's net worth-to-assets ratio from 10 (10/100) to 8.29 (7.91/95.45) percent. To counter this effect, the manager might reduce the FI's duration gap. In an extreme case, the gap might be reduced to zero:

$$\Delta E = -[0] \times A \times \Delta R/(1 + R) = 0$$

To do this, the FI should not directly set $D_A = D_L$, which ignores the fact that the FI's assets ($A$) do not equal its borrowed liabilities ($L$) and that $k$ (which reflects the ratio $L/A$) is not equal to 1. To see the importance of factoring in leverage, suppose the manager increased the duration of the FI's liabilities to five years, the same as $D_A$. Then:

$$\Delta E = -[5 - (0.9)(5)] \times \$100 \text{ million} \times (0.01/1.10) = -\$0.45 \text{ million}$$

The FI is still exposed to a loss of $0.45 million if rates rise by 1 percent. An appropriate strategy would involve changing $D_L$ until:

$$D_A = kD_L = 5 \text{ years}$$

For example,

$$\Delta E = -[5 - (0.9)\,5.55] \times \$100 \text{ million} \times (0.01/1.10) = 0$$

In this case the FI manager sets $D_L = 5.55$ years, or slightly longer than $D_A = 5$ years, to compensate for the fact that only 90 percent of assets are funded by borrowed liabilities, with the other 10 percent funded by equity. Note that the FI manager has at least three other ways to reduce the duration gap to zero:

1. *Reduce $D_A$*. Reduce $D_A$ from 5 years to 2.7 years [equal to $kD_L$ or (0.9)3] such that:

$$[D_A - kD_L] = [2.7 - (0.9)(3)] = 0$$

2. *Reduce $D_A$ and increase $D_L$*. Shorten the duration of assets and lengthen the duration of liabilities at the same time. One possibility would be to *reduce $D_A$* to 4 years and to *increase $D_L$* to 4.44 years such that:

$$[D_A - kD_L] = [4 - (0.9)(4.44)] = 0$$

3. *Change $k$ and $D_L$*. Increase $k$ (leverage) from 0.9 to 0.95 and increase $D_L$ from 3 years to 5.26 years such that:

$$[D_A - kD_L] = [5 - (0.95)(5.26)] = 0$$

---

**Concept Questions**

1. Refer to the example of the insurer in Examples 9–6 through 9–8. Suppose rates fell to 6 percent. Would the FI's portfolio still be immunized? What if rates rose to 10 percent?
2. How is the overall duration gap for an FI calculated?
3. How can a manager use information on an FI's duration gap to restructure, and thereby immunize, the balance sheet against interest rate risk?
4. Suppose $D_A = 3$ years, $D_L = 6$ years, $k = 0.8$, and $A = \$100$ million. What is the effect on owners' net worth if $\Delta R/(1 + R)$ rises 1 percent? ($\Delta E = \$1,800,000$)

# IMMUNIZATION AND REGULATORY CONSIDERATIONS

In the above section we assumed that the FI manager wants to structure the duration of assets and liabilities to immunize the equity or net worth ($E$) of the FI's equity owners from interest rate shocks. However, regulators periodically monitor the solvency or capital position of FIs. As we discuss in greater detail in Chapter 20 on capital adequacy, regulators set minimum target ratios for an FI's capital (or net worth) to assets. The simplest is the ratio of FI capital to its assets, or:

$$\frac{E}{A} = \text{Capital (net worth) ratio}$$

www.sec.gov

While this target has normally been formulated in book value accounting terms for depository institutions, it is evaluated in a market value context for investment banks. Also, the SEC has long advocated a capital ratio based on market value accounting for U.S. depository institutions.

Given these regulations imposed on the minimum level of the capital ratio, if an FI's asset levels change significantly through time, FI managers may be most interested in immunizing against changes in the capital ratio ($\Delta(E/A)$) due to interest rate risk rather than changes in the level of capital ($\Delta E$). For example, suppose the FI manager is close to the minimum regulatory required $E/A$ (or capital) ratio (e.g., 4.5 percent for depository institutions) and wants to immunize the FI against any fall in this ratio if interest rates rise.[13] That is, the immunization target is no longer $\Delta E = 0$ when rates change but $\Delta(E/A) = 0$.

Obviously, immunizing $\Delta E$ against interest rate risk cannot result in the same management strategy as immunizing $\Delta(E/A)$. A portfolio constructed to immunize $\Delta E$ would have a different duration match from that required to immunize $\Delta(E/A)$. Or, more simply, the manager could satisfy either the FI's stockholders or the regulators *but not both* simultaneously. More specifically, when the objective is to immunize equity capital against interest rate risk, that is, to set $\Delta E = 0$, the FI manager should structure the balance sheet so that the leverage adjusted duration gap is zero:

$$\Delta E = 0 = D_A - kD_L$$

or set

$$D_A = kD_L$$

By comparison, to immunize the capital ratio, that is, to set $\Delta(E/A) = 0$ the manager needs to set:

$$D_A = D_L$$

In this scenario, the leverage adjustment effect ($k$) drops out. If $D_A = 5$, then immunizing the capital ratio would require setting $D_L = 5$.

---

| **Concept Question** | 1. Is immunizing a bank's net worth the same as immunizing its net worth-to-assets ratio? If not, why not? |
| --- | --- |

---

[13] In actuality, depository institutions face three required minimum capital ratios. The 4.5 percent rule used in this example is for the common equity capital ratio (see Chapter 20 for more details).

In the next section, we analyze weaknesses of the duration model. Specifically, there are several practical problems in estimating duration and duration gap for real-world FIs.

# DIFFICULTIES IN APPLYING THE DURATION MODEL

www.bis.org

Critics of the duration model have often claimed that it is difficult to apply in real world situations. However, duration measures and immunization strategies are useful in most real-world situations. In fact, the model used by the Bank for International Settlements to monitor bank interest rate risk taking is based heavily on the duration model. In this section, we look at the various criticisms of the duration model and discuss ways that an FI manager would deal with them in practice. In Appendix 9B to the chapter, we present some of the more advanced issues associated with these weaknesses.

## Duration Matching Can Be Costly

Critics charge that although in principle an FI manager can change $D_A$ and $D_L$ to immunize the FI against interest rate risk, restructuring the balance sheet of a large and complex FI can be both time-consuming and costly. While this argument may have been true historically, the growth of purchased funds, asset securitization, and loan sales markets has considerably eased the speed and lowered the transaction costs of major balance sheet restructurings. (See Chapters 25 and 26 for a discussion of these strategies.) Moreover, an FI manager could still manage risk exposure using the duration model by employing techniques other than direct portfolio rebalancing to immunize against interest rate risk. Managers can get many of the same results of direct duration matching by taking hedging positions in the markets for derivative securities, such as futures and forwards (Chapter 22); options, caps, floors, and collars (Chapter 23); and swaps (Chapter 24).

## Immunization Is a Dynamic Problem

Immunization is an aspect of the duration model that is not well understood. Let's go back to the earlier immunization example in which an insurer sought to buy bonds to provide an accumulated cash flow of $1,469 in five years no matter what happened to interest rates. We showed that buying a six-year maturity, 8 percent coupon bond with a five-year duration immunizes the insurer against an instantaneous change in interest rates. The word *instantaneous* is very important here; it means a change in interest rates immediately after purchasing the bond. However, interest rates can change at any time over the holding period. Further, the duration of a bond changes as time passes, that is, as it approaches maturity or the target horizon date. In addition, duration changes at a different rate than does real or calendar time.

To understand this time effect, consider the initially hedged position in which the insurer bought the five-year duration (six-year maturity), 8 percent coupon bond in 2016 to match its cash flow target of $1,469 in 2021. Suppose the FI manager puts the bond in the bottom drawer of a desk and does not think about it for a year, believing that the insurance company's position is fully hedged. After one year has passed (in 2017), suppose interest rates (yields) have fallen from 8 percent to 7 percent and the manager opens the drawer of the desk and finds the bond. Knowing the target date is now only four years away, the manager recalculates the duration of the bond. Imagine the manager's shock on finding that the same 8 percent coupon bond with a 7 percent yield and only five years left to maturity has a duration of 4.33 years. This means the insurance company is no longer hedged; the 4.33-year duration of this bond portfolio *exceeds* the investment horizon of four years. As a result, the manager has to restructure the bond portfolio to remain immunized. One way to do this is to sell some of the five-year bonds (4.33-year duration) and buy some bonds of shorter duration so that the overall duration of the investment portfolio is four years.

For example, suppose the insurer sold 50 percent of the five-year bonds with a 4.33-year duration and invested the proceeds in 3.67-year duration and maturity zero-coupon bonds. Because duration and maturity are the same for discount bonds, the duration of the asset portfolio is:

$$D_A = [4.33 \times 0.5] + [3.67 \times 0.5] = 4 \text{ years}$$

This simple example demonstrates that immunization based on duration is a dynamic strategy. In theory, the strategy requires the portfolio manager to rebalance the portfolio continuously to ensure that the duration of the investment portfolio exactly matches the investment horizon (i.e., the duration of liabilities). Because continuous rebalancing may not be easy to do and involves costly transaction fees, most portfolio managers seek to be only approximately dynamically immunized against interest rate changes by rebalancing at discrete intervals, such as quarterly. That is, there is a trade-off between being perfectly immunized and the transaction costs of maintaining an immunized balance sheet dynamically.

## Large Interest Rate Changes and Convexity

Duration accurately measures the price sensitivity of fixed-income securities for small changes in interest rates of the order of one basis point. But suppose interest rate shocks are much larger, of the order of 2 percent, or 200 basis points. Then duration becomes a less accurate predictor of how much the prices of securities will change and therefore a less accurate measure of interest rate sensitivity. Looking at Figure 9–5, you can see the reason for this. Note first the change in a bond's price due to yield changes according to the duration model and second, the true relationship, as calculated directly, using the exact present value calculation for bond valuation.

The duration model predicts that the relationship between interest rate shocks and bond price changes will be proportional to $D$ (duration). However, by precisely calculating the true change in bond prices, we would find that for large interest rate increases, duration overpredicts the *fall* in bond prices, while for large interest rate decreases, it underpredicts the *increase* in bond prices. That is, the duration model predicts symmetric effects for rate increases and decreases on bond prices. As Figure 9–5 shows, in actuality, for rate increases, the *capital loss effect* tends to be smaller than the *capital gain effect* is for rate decreases. This is the result of the bond price–yield relationship exhibiting a property called *convexity* rather than *linearity*, as assumed by the basic duration model.

**FIGURE 9–5**
**Duration versus**
**True Relationship**

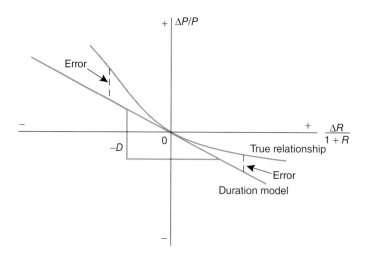

**convexity**
The degree of curvature of the price–yield curve around some interest rate level.

Note that **convexity** is a desirable feature for an FI manager to capture in a portfolio of assets. Buying a bond or a portfolio of assets that exhibits a lot of convexity, or curvature, in the price–yield curve relationship is similar to buying partial interest rate risk insurance. Specifically, high convexity means that for equally large changes of interest rates up and down (e.g., plus or minus 2 percent), the capital gain effect of a rate decrease more than offsets the capital loss effect of a rate increase. As we show in Appendix 9B to the chapter, all fixed-income assets or liabilities exhibit some convexity in their price–yield relationships.

To see the importance of accounting for the effects of convexity in assessing the impact of large rate changes on an FI's portfolio, consider the six-year Eurobond with an 8 percent coupon and yield. According to Table 9–2, its duration is 4.993 years, and its current price $P_0$ is $1,000 at a yield of 8 percent:

$$P_0 = \frac{80}{(1.08)} + \frac{80}{(1.08)^2} + \frac{80}{(1.08)^3}$$
$$+ \frac{80}{(1.08)^4} + \frac{80}{(1.08)^5} + \frac{1,080}{(1.08)^6} = \$1,000$$

This is point $A$ on the price–yield curve in Figure 9–6.

If rates rise from 8 to 10 percent, the duration model predicts that the bond price will fall by 9.2463 percent; that is:

$$\frac{\Delta P}{P} = -4.993 \left[ \frac{0.02}{1.08} \right] = -9.2463\%$$

or, from a price of $1,000 to $907.537 (see point $B$ in Figure 9–6). However, calculating the exact change in the bond's price after a rise in yield to 10 percent, we find that its true value is:

$$P_0 = \frac{80}{(1.10)} + \frac{80}{(1.10)^2} + \frac{80}{(1.10)^3}$$
$$+ \frac{80}{(1.10)^4} + \frac{80}{(1.10)^5} + \frac{1,080}{(1.10)^6} = \$912.895$$

**FIGURE 9–6**
The Price–Yield
Curve for the Six-
Year Eurobond

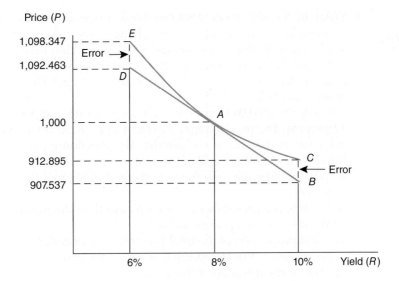

This is point *C* in Figure 9–6. As you can see, the true or actual fall in price is less than the predicted fall by $5.358. This means that there is over a 0.5 percent error using the duration model. The reason for this is the natural convexity to the price–yield curve as yields rise.

Reversing the experiment reveals that the duration model would predict the bond's price to rise by 9.2463 percent if yields fell from 8 to 6 percent, resulting in a predicted price of $1,092.463 (see point *D* in Figure 9–6). By comparison, the true or actual change in price can be computed as $1,098.347 by estimating the present value of the bond's coupons and its face value with a 6 percent yield (see point *E* in Figure 9–6). The duration model has underpredicted the bond price increase by $5.884, or by over 0.5 percent of the true price increase.

An important question for the FI manager is whether a 0.5 percent error is big enough to be concerned about. This depends on the size of the interest rate change and the size of the portfolio under management. Clearly, 0.5 percent of a large number will still be a large number!

## Summary

This chapter analyzed the duration gap model approach to measuring interest rate risk. The duration gap model is superior to the simple repricing gap model in that it incorporates the timing of cash flows as well as maturity effects into a simple measure of interest rate risk. The duration gap measure could be used to immunize a particular liability as well as the whole FI balance sheet. However, as the concluding section of the chapter indicates, a number of potential problems exist in applying the duration gap model in real-world scenarios. Despite these weaknesses, the duration gap model is fairly robust and can deal with a large number of real-world complexities, such as credit risk, convexity, floating interest rates, and uncertain maturities.

**Questions and Problems**

1. What is the difference between book value accounting and market value accounting? How do interest rate changes affect the value of bank assets and liabilities under the two methods? What is marking to market?

2. What are the two different general interpretations of the concept of duration, and what is the technical definition of this term? How does duration differ from maturity?

3. A one-year, $100,000 loan carries a coupon rate and a market interest rate of 12 percent. The loan requires payment of accrued interest and one-half of the principal at the end of six months. The remaining principal and the accrued interest are due at the end of the year.

    a. What will be the cash flows at the end of six months and at the end of the year?

    b. What is the present value of each cash flow discounted at the market rate? What is the total present value?

    c. What proportion of the total present value of cash flows occurs at the end of six months? What proportion occurs at the end of the year?

    d. What is the duration of this loan?

4. Two bonds are available for purchase in the financial markets. The first bond is a two-year, $1,000 bond that pays an annual coupon of 10 percent. The second bond is a two-year, $1,000 zero-coupon bond.

    a. What is the duration of the coupon bond if the current yield to maturity (R) is 8 percent? 10 percent? 12 percent? (*Hint:* You may wish to create a spreadsheet program to assist in the calculations.)

    b. How does the change in the yield to maturity affect the duration of this coupon bond?

    c. Calculate the duration of the zero-coupon bond with a yield to maturity of 8 percent, 10 percent, and 12 percent.

    d. How does the change in the yield to maturity affect the duration of the zero coupon bond?

    e. Why does the change in the yield to maturity affect the coupon bond differently than it affects the zero-coupon bond?

5. What is the duration of a five-year, $1,000 Treasury bond with a 10 percent semiannual coupon selling at par? Selling with a yield to maturity of 12 percent? 14 percent? What can you conclude about the relationship between duration and yield to maturity? Plot the relationship. Why does this relationship exist?

6. Consider three Treasury bonds each of which has a 10 percent semiannual coupon and trades at par.

    a. Calculate the duration for a bond that has a maturity of four years, three years, and two years.

    b. What conclusions can you reach about the relationship between duration and the time to maturity? Plot the relationship.

7. A six-year, $10,000 CD pays 6 percent interest annually and has a 6 percent yield to maturity. What is the duration of the CD? What would be the duration if interest were paid semiannually? What is the relationship of duration to the relative frequency of interest payments?

8. What is a consol bond? What is the duration of a consol bond that sells at a yield to maturity of 8 percent? 10 percent? 12 percent? Would a consol trading at a yield to maturity of 10 percent have a greater duration than a 20-year zero-coupon bond trading at the same yield to maturity? Why?

9. Maximum Pension Fund is attempting to manage one of the bond portfolios under its management. The fund has identified three bonds that have five year maturities and trade at a yield to maturity of 9 percent. The bonds differ only in that the coupons are 7 percent, 9 percent, and 11 percent.
   a. What is the duration for each bond?
   b. What is the relationship between duration and the amount of coupon interest that is paid? Plot the relationship.

10. An insurance company is analyzing three bonds and is using duration as the measure of interest rate risk. All three bonds trade at a yield to maturity of 10 percent, have $10,000 par values, and have five years to maturity. The bonds differ only in the amount of annual coupon interest they pay: 8, 10, and 12 percent.
    a. What is the duration for each five-year bond?
    b. What is the relationship between duration and the amount of coupon interest that is paid?

11. You can obtain a loan of $100,000 at a rate of 10 percent for two years. You have a choice of (i) paying the interest (10 percent) each year and the total principal at the end of the second year or (ii) amortizing the loan, that is, paying interest (10 percent) and principal in equal payments each year. The loan is priced at par.
    a. What is the duration of the loan under both methods of payment?
    b. Explain the difference in the two results.

12. How is duration related to the interest elasticity of a fixed-income security? What is the relationship between duration and the price of the fixed-income security?

13. You have discovered that the price of a bond rose from $975 to $995 when the yield to maturity fell from 9.75 percent to 9.25 percent. What is the duration of the bond?

14. A 10-year, 10 percent annual coupon, $1,000 bond trades at a yield to maturity of 8 percent. The bond has a duration of 6.994 years. What is the modified duration of this bond? What is the practical value of calculating modified duration? Does modified duration change the result of using the duration relationship to estimate price sensitivity?

15. What is dollar duration? How is dollar duration different from duration?

16. Calculate the duration of a two-year, $1,000 bond that pays an annual coupon of 10 percent and trades at a yield of 14 percent. What is the expected change in the price of the bond if interest rates fall by 0.50 percent (50 basis points)?

17. The duration of an 11-year, $1,000 Treasury bond paying a 10 percent semiannual coupon and selling at par has been estimated at 6.763 years.
    a. What is the modified duration of the bond? What is the dollar duration of the bond?
    b. What will be the estimated price change on the bond if interest rates increase 0.10 percent (10 basis points)? If rates decrease 0.20 percent (20 basis points)?
    c. What would the actual price of the bond be under each rate change situation in part (b) using the traditional present value bond pricing techniques? What is the amount of error in each case?

18. Suppose you purchase a six-year, 8 percent coupon bond (paid annually) that is priced to yield 9 percent. The face value of the bond is $1,000.
    a. Show that the duration of this bond is equal to five years.

b. Show that if interest rates rise to 10 percent within the next year and your investment horizon is five years from today, you will still earn a 9 percent yield on your investment.

c. Show that a 9 percent yield also will be earned if interest rates fall next year to 8 percent.

19. Suppose you purchase a five-year, 15 percent coupon bond (paid annually) that is priced to yield 9 percent. The face value of the bond is $1,000.

a. Show that the duration of this bond is equal to four years.

b. Show that if interest rates rise to 10 percent within the next year and your investment horizon is four years from today, you will still earn a 9 percent yield on your investment.

c. Show that a 9 percent yield also will be earned if interest rates fall next year to 8 percent.

20. Consider the case in which an investor holds a bond for a period of time longer than the duration of the bond, that is, longer than the original investment horizon.

a. If interest rates rise, will the return that is earned exceed or fall short of the original required rate of return? Explain.

b. What will happen to the realized return if interest rates decrease? Explain.

c. Recalculate parts (b) and (c) of problem 19 above, assuming that the bond is held for all five years, to verify your answers to parts (a) and (b) of this problem.

d. If either calculation in part (c) is greater than the original required rate of return, why would an investor ever try to match the duration of an asset with his or her investment horizon?

21. Two banks are being examined by regulators to determine the interest rate sensitivity of their balance sheets. Bank A has assets composed solely of a 10-year $1 million loan with a coupon rate and yield of 12 percent. The loan is financed with a 10-year $1 million CD with a coupon rate and yield of 10 percent. Bank B has assets composed solely of a 7-year, 12 percent zero-coupon bond with a current (market) value of $894,006.20 and a maturity (principal) value of $1,976,362.88. The bond is financed with a 10-year, 8.275 percent coupon $1,000,000 face value CD with a yield to maturity of 10 percent. The loan and the CDs pay interest annually, with principal due at maturity.

a. If market interest rates increase 1 percent (100 basis points), how do the market values of the assets and liabilities of each bank change? That is, what will be the net effect on the market value of the equity for each bank?

b. What accounts for the differences in the changes in the market value of equity between the two banks?

c. Verify your results above by calculating the duration for the assets and liabilities of each bank, and estimate the changes in value for the expected change in interest rates. Summarize your results.

22. If an FI uses only duration to immunize its portfolio, what three factors affect changes in the net worth of the FI when interest rates change?

23. Financial Institution XY has assets of $1 million invested in a 30-year, 10 percent semiannual coupon Treasury bond selling at par. The duration of this bond has been estimated at 9.94 years. The assets are financed with equity and a $900,000, two-year, 7.25 percent semiannual coupon capital note selling at par.

a. What is the leverage adjusted duration gap of Financial Institution XY?

b. What is the impact on equity value if the relative change in all market interest rates is a decrease of 20 basis points? *Note:* The relative change in interest rates is $\Delta R/(1 + R/2) = -0.0020$.

c. Using the information in parts (a) and (b), what can be said about the desired duration gap for the financial institution if interest rates are expected to increase or decrease.

d. Verify your answer to part (c) by calculating the change in the market value of equity assuming that the relative change in all market interest rates is an increase of 30 basis points.

e. What would the duration of the assets need to be to immunize the equity from changes in market interest rates?

24. The balance sheet for Gotbucks Bank Inc. (GBI) is presented below ($ millions).

| Assets | | Liabilities and Equity | |
|---|---|---|---|
| Cash | $ 30 | Core deposits | $ 20 |
| Federal funds | 20 | Federal funds | 50 |
| Loans (floating) | 105 | Euro CDs | 130 |
| Loans (fixed) | 65 | Equity | 20 |
| Total assets | $220 | Total liabilities and equity | $220 |

Notes to the balance sheet: The fed funds rate is 8.5 percent, the floating loan rate is LIBOR + 4 percent, and currently LIBOR is 11 percent. Fixed-rate loans have five-year maturities, are priced at par, and pay 12 percent annual interest. The principal is repaid at maturity. Core deposits are fixed rate for two years at 8 percent paid annually. The principal is repaid at maturity. Euro CDs currently yield 9 percent.

a. What is the duration of the fixed-rate loan portfolio of Gotbucks Bank?

b. If the duration of the floating-rate loans and fed funds is 0.36 year, what is the duration of GBI's assets?

c. What is the duration of the core deposits if they are priced at par?

d. If the duration of the Euro CDs and fed funds liabilities is 0.401 year, what is the duration of GBI's liabilities?

e. What is GBI's duration gap? What is its interest rate risk exposure?

f. What is the impact on the market value of equity if the relative change in all interest rates is an increase of 1 percent (100 basis points)? Note that the relative change in interest rates is $\Delta R/(1 + R) = 0.01$.

g. What is the impact on the market value of equity if the relative change in all interest rates is a decrease of 0.5 percent ($-50$ basis points)?

h. What variables are available to GBI to immunize the bank? How much would each variable need to change to get DGAP to equal zero?

25. Hands Insurance Company issued a $90 million, one-year note at 8 percent add-on annual interest (paying one coupon at the end of the year) or with an 8 percent yield. The proceeds were used to fund a $100 million, two-year commercial loan with a 10 percent coupon rate and a 10 percent yield. Immediately after these transactions were simultaneously closed, all market interest rates increased 1.5 percent (150 basis points).

a. What is the true market value of the loan investment and the liability after the change in interest rates?

b. What impact did these changes in market value have on the market value of the FI's equity?

   c. What was the duration of the loan investment and the liability at the time of issuance?

   d. Use these duration values to calculate the expected change in the value of the loan and the liability for the predicted increase of 1.5 percent in interest rates.

   e. What is the duration gap of Hands Insurance Company after the issuance of the asset and note?

   f. What is the change in equity value forecasted by this duration gap for the predicted increase in interest rates of 1.5 percent?

   g. If the interest rate prediction had been available during the time period in which the loan and the liability were being negotiated, what suggestions would you have offered to reduce the possible effect on the equity of the company? What are the difficulties in implementing your ideas?

26. The following balance sheet information is available (amounts in thousands of dollars and duration in years) for a financial institution:

| | Amount | Duration |
|---|---|---|
| T-bills | $ 90 | 0.50 |
| T-notes | 55 | 0.90 |
| T-bonds | 176 | X |
| Loans | 2,724 | 7.00 |
| Deposits | 2,092 | 1.00 |
| Federal funds | 238 | 0.01 |
| Equity | 715 | |

Treasury bonds are five-year maturities paying 6 percent semiannually and selling at par.

   a. What is the duration of the T-bond portfolio?

   b. What is the average duration of all the assets?

   c. What is the average duration of all the liabilities?

   d. What is the leverage adjusted duration gap? What is the interest rate risk exposure?

   e. What is the forecasted impact on the market value of equity caused by a relative upward shift in the entire yield curve of 0.5 percent [i.e., $\Delta R/(1 + R) = 0.0050$]?

   f. If the yield curve shifts downward 0.25 percent [i.e., $\Delta R/(1 + R) = -0.0025$], what is the forecasted impact on the market value of equity?

   g. What variables are available to the financial institution to immunize the balance sheet? How much would each variable need to change to get DGAP to equal 0?

27. Assume that a goal of the regulatory agencies of financial institutions is to immunize the ratio of equity to total assets, that is, $\Delta(E/A) = 0$. Explain how this goal changes the desired duration gap for the institution. Why does this differ from the duration gap necessary to immunize the total equity? How would your answers to part (h) in problem 24 and part (g) in problem 26 change if immunizing equity to total assets was the goal?

28. Identify and discuss three criticisms of using the duration gap model to immunize the portfolio of a financial institution.

29. In general, what changes have occurred in the financial markets that would allow financial institutions to restructure their balance sheets more rapidly and efficiently to meet desired goals? Why is it critical for an FI manager who

has a portfolio immunized to match a desired investment horizon to rebalance the portfolio periodically? What is convexity? Why is convexity a desirable feature to capture in a portfolio of assets?

30. A financial institution has an investment horizon of two years 9.33 months (or 2.777 years). The institution has converted all assets into a portfolio of 8 percent, $1,000 three-year bonds that are trading at a yield to maturity of 10 percent. The bonds pay interest annually. The portfolio manager believes that the assets are immunized against interest rate changes.
    a. Is the portfolio immunized at the time of the bond purchase? What is the duration of the bonds?
    b. Will the portfolio be immunized one year later?
    c. Assume that one-year, 8 percent zero-coupon bonds are available in one year. What proportion of the original portfolio should be placed in these bonds to rebalance the portfolio?

The following questions and problems are based on material in Appendix 9A, at the book's website (**www.mhhe.com/saunders8e**).

31. Consider a 12-year, 12 percent annual coupon bond with a required return of 10 percent. The bond has a face value of $1,000.
    a. What is the price of the bond?
    b. If interest rates rise to 11 percent, what is the price of the bond?
    c. What has been the percentage change in price?
    d. Repeat parts (a), (b), and (c) for a 16-year bond.
    e. What do the respective changes in bond prices indicate?

32. Consider a five-year, 15 percent annual coupon bond with a face value of $1,000. The bond is trading at a yield to maturity of 12 percent.
    a. What is the price of the bond?
    b. If the yield to maturity increases 1 percent, what will be the bond's new price?
    c. Using your answers to parts (a) and (b), what is the percentage change in the bond's price as a result of the 1 percent increase in interest rates?
    d. Repeat parts (b) and (c) assuming a 1 percent decrease in interest rates.
    e. What do the differences in your answers indicate about the interest rate–price relationships of fixed-rate assets?

33. Consider a $1,000 bond with a fixed-rate 10 percent annual coupon rate and a maturity (N) of 10 years. The bond currently is trading at a yield to maturity (YTM) of 10 percent.
    a. Complete the following table:

| | Change | | | | |
|---|---|---|---|---|---|
| *N* | Coupon Rate | YTM | Price | $ Change in Price from Par | % Change in Price from Par |
| 8 | 10% | 9% | | | |
| 9 | 10 | 9 | | | |
| 10 | 10 | 9 | | | |
| 10 | 10 | 10 | | | |
| 10 | 10 | 11 | | | |
| 11 | 10 | 11 | | | |
| 12 | 10 | 11 | | | |

b. Use this information to verify the principles of interest rate–price relationships for fixed-rate financial assets.

*Rule 1.* Interest rates and prices of fixed-rate financial assets move inversely.
*Rule 2.* The longer is the maturity of a fixed-income financial asset, the greater is the change in price for a given change in interest rates.
*Rule 3.* The change in value of longer-term fixed-rate financial assets increases at a decreasing rate.
*Rule 4.* Although not mentioned in Appendix 9A, for a given percentage ($\pm$) change in interest rates, the increase in price for a decrease in rates is greater than the decrease in value for an increase in rates.

The following questions and problems are based on material in Appendix 9B to the chapter.

34. MLK Bank has an asset portfolio that consists of $100 million of 30-year, 8 percent coupon, $1,000 bonds that sell at par.
    a. What will be the bonds' new prices if market yields change immediately by $+/-$ 0.10 percent? What will be the new prices if market yields change immediately by $+/-$ 2.00 percent?
    b. The duration of these bonds is 12.1608 years. What are the predicted bond prices in each of the four cases using the duration rule? What is the amount of error between the duration prediction and the actual market values?
    c. Given that convexity is 212.4, what are the bond price predictions in each of the four cases using the duration plus convexity relationship? What is the amount of error in these predictions?
    d. Diagram and label clearly the results in parts (a), (b), and (c).
35. Estimate the convexity for each of the following three bonds, all of which trade at a yield to maturity of 8 percent and have face values of $1,000.

    A 7-year, zero-coupon bond.
    A 7-year, 10 percent annual coupon bond.
    A 10-year, 10 percent annual coupon bond that has a duration value of 6.994 years (i.e., approximately 7 years).

    Rank the bonds in terms of convexity, and express the convexity relationship between zeros and coupon bonds in terms of maturity and duration equivalencies.

# Integrated Mini Case

## CALCULATING AND USING DURATION GAP

State Bank's balance sheet is listed below. Market yields and durations (in years) are in parenthesis, and amounts are in millions.

| Assets | | Liabilities and Equity | |
|---|---|---|---|
| **Assets** | | **Liabilities and Equity** | |
| Cash | $ 20 | Demand deposits | $ 250 |
| Fed funds (5.05%, 0.02) | 150 | MMDAs (4.5%, 0.50) | |
| T-bills (5.25%, 0.22) | 300 | (no minimum balance requirement) | 360 |
| T-bonds (7.50%, 7.55) | 200 | CDs (4.3%, 0.48) | 715 |

| Assets | | Liabilities and Equity | |
|---|---|---|---|
| Consumer loans (6%, 2.50) | 900 | CDs (6%, 4.45) | 1,105 |
| C&I loans (5.8%, 6.58) | 475 | Fed funds (5%, 0.02) | 515 |
| Fixed-rate mortgages (7.85%, 19.50) | 1,200 | Commercial paper (5.05%, 0.45) | 400 |
| Variable-rate mortgages, | | Subordinated debt: | |
| repriced @ quarter (6.3%, 0.25) | 580 | Fixed-rate (7.25%, 6.65) | 200 |
| Premises and equipment | 120 | Total liabilities | $3,545 |
| | | Equity | 400 |
| Total assets | $3,945 | Total liabilities and equity | $3,945 |

a. What is State Bank's duration gap?

b. Use these duration values to calculate the expected change in the value of the assets and liabilities of State Bank for a predicted increase of 1.5 percent in interest rates.

c. What is the change in equity value forecasted from the duration values for a predicted increase in interest rates of 1.5 percent?

# Integrated Mini Case: Chapters 8 and 9

## CALCULATING AND USING REPRICING AND DURATION GAP

State Bank's balance sheet is listed below. Market yields and durations (in years) are in parenthesis, and amounts are in millions.

| Assets | | Liabilities and Equity | |
|---|---|---|---|
| Cash | $   31 | Demand deposits | $ 253 |
| Fed funds (2.05%, 0.02) | 150 | Savings accounts (0.5%, 1.25) | 50 |
| 3-month T-bills (3.25%, 0.22) | 200 | MMDAs (3.5%, 0.50) | |
| 8-year T-bonds (6.50%, 7.55) | 250 | (no minimum balance requirement) | 460 |
| 5-year munis (7.20%, 4.25) | 50 | 3-month CDs (3.2%, 0.20) | 175 |
| 6-month consumer loans (5%, 0.42) | 250 | 1-year CDs (3.5%, 0.95) | 375 |
| 5-year car loans (6%, 3.78) | 350 | 5-year CDs (5%, 4.85) | 350 |
| 7-month C&I loans (4.8%, 0.55) | 200 | Fed funds (2%, 0.02) | 225 |
| 2-year C&I loans (4.15%, 1.65) | 275 | Repos (2%, 0.05) | 290 |
| Fixed-rate mortgages (5.10%, 0.48) (maturing | | 6-month commercial paper | |
| in 5 months) | 450 | (4.05%, 0.55) | 300 |
| Fixed-rate mortgages (6.85%, 0.85) (maturing | | Subordinate notes: | |
| in 1 year) | 300 | 1-year fixed rate (5.55%, 0.92) | 200 |
| Fixed-rate mortgages (5.30%, 4.45) (maturing | | Subordinated debt: | |
| in 5 years) | 275 | 7-year fixed rate (6.25%, 6.65) | 100 |
| Fixed-rate mortgages (5.40%, 18.25) (maturing | | Total liabilities | $2,778 |
| in 20 years) | 355 | | |
| Premises and equipment | 20 | | |
| Total assets | $3,156 | Equity | 3078 |
| | | Total liabilities and equity | $3,156 |

a. What is State Bank's repricing gap if the planning period is six months? one year?

b. What is State Bank's duration gap?

c. What is the impact over the next six months on net interest income if interest rates on RSAs increase 50 basis points and on RSLs increase 35 basis points? Explain the results.

d. What is the impact over the next year on net interest income if interest rates on RSAs decrease (increase) 35 basis points and on RSLs decrease (increase) 50 basis points? Explain the results.

e. Use these duration values to calculate the expected change in the value of the assets and liabilities of State Bank for a predicted decrease of 0.35 percent in interest rates on assets and 0.50 percent on liabilities.

f. What is the change in equity value forecasted from the duration values for decrease of 0.35 percent in interest rates on assets and 0.50 percent on liabilities?

g. Use the duration gap model to calculate the change in equity value if the relative change in all market interest rates is a decrease of 50 basis points.

## Appendix 9A: The Basics of Bond Valuation

View Appendix 9A at the website for this textbook (**www.mhhe.com/saunders8e**).

# Appendix 9B

# Incorporating Convexity into the Duration Model

In the main body of the chapter, we established these three characteristics of convexity:

1. *Convexity is desirable.* The greater the convexity of a security or a portfolio of securities, the more insurance or interest rate protection an FI manager has against interest rate increases and the greater the potential gains after interest rate decreases.

2. *Convexity and duration.* The larger the interest rate changes and the more convex a fixed income security or portfolio, the greater the error the FI manager faces in using just duration (and duration matching) to immunize exposure to interest rate shocks.

3. *All fixed-income securities are convex.*[1] To see this, we can take the six-year, 8 percent coupon, 8 percent yield bond and look at two extreme price–yield scenarios. What is the price on the

bond if yields falls to zero, and what is its price if yields rise to some very large number, such as infinity?

When $R = 0$:

$$P = \frac{80}{(1 + 0)} + \cdots + \frac{1,080}{(1 + 0)^6} = \$1,480$$

The price is just the simple undiscounted sum of the coupon values and the face value. Since yields can never go below zero, $1,480 is the maximum possible price for the bond.

When $R = \infty$:

$$P = \frac{80}{(1 + \infty)} + \cdots + \frac{1,080}{(1 + \infty)^6} \approx 0$$

As the yield goes to infinity, the bond price falls asymptotically toward zero, but by definition a bond's price can never be negative. Thus, zero must be the minimum bond price (see Figure 9B–1).

---

[1] This applies to fixed-income securities without special option features such as calls and puts.

**FIGURE 9B–1**
**The Natural**
**Convexity of Bonds**

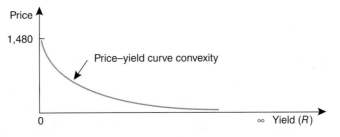

Since convexity is a desirable feature for assets, the FI manager might ask: Can we measure convexity? And can we incorporate this measurement in the duration model to adjust for or offset the error in prediction due to its presence? The answer to both questions is yes.

Theoretically speaking, duration is the slope of the price–yield curve, and convexity, or curvature, is the change in the slope of the price–yield curve. Consider the total effect of a change in interest rates on a bond's price as being broken into a number of separate effects. The precise mathematical derivation of these separate effects is based on a Taylor series expansion that you might remember from your math classes. Essentially, the first-order effect $(dP/dR)$ of an interest rate change on the bond's price is the price–yield curve slope effect, which is measured by duration. The second-order effect $(dP^2/d^2R)$ measures the change in the slope of the price–yield curve. This is the curvature, or convexity, effect. There are also third-, fourth-, and higher-order effects from the Taylor series expansion, but for all practical purposes these effects can be ignored.

We have noted that overlooking the curvature of the price–yield curve may cause errors in predicting the interest rate sensitivity of a portfolio of assets and liabilities, especially when yields change by large amounts. We can adjust for this by explicitly recognizing the second-order effect of yield changes by measuring the change in the slope of the price–yield curve around a given point. Just as $D$ (duration) measures the slope effect *(dP/dR)*, we introduce a new parameter $(CX)$ to measure the curvature effect $(dP^2/d^2R)$ of the price–yield curve.

The resulting equation, predicting the change in a security's price $(\Delta P/P)$, is:

$$\frac{\Delta P}{P} = -D\frac{\Delta R}{(1 + R)} + \frac{1}{2}CX(\Delta R)^2 \qquad \textbf{(1)}$$

or:

$$\frac{\Delta P}{P} = -MD\,\Delta R + \frac{1}{2}CX(\Delta R)^2 \qquad \textbf{(2)}$$

The first term in equation (1) is the simple duration model that over- or underpredicts price changes for large changes in interest rates. The second term is the second-order effect of interest rate changes, that is, the convexity or curvature adjustment. In equation (1), the first term $D$ can be divided by $1 + R$ to produce what we called earlier modified duration $(MD)$. You can see this in equation (2). In the convexity term, the number $1/2$ and $(\Delta R)^2$ result from the fact that the convexity effect is the second-order effect of interest rate changes, while duration is the first-order effect. The parameter $CX$ reflects the degree of curvature in the price–yield curve at the current yield level; that is, the degree to which the *capital gain effect* exceeds the *capital loss effect* for an equal change in yields up or down. At best, the FI manager can only approximate the curvature effect by using a parametric measure of $CX$. Even though calculus is based on infinitesimally small changes, in financial markets the smallest change in yields normally observed is one basis point, or a 1/100th of 1 percent change. One possible way to measure $CX$ is introduced next.

As just discussed, the convexity effect is the degree to which the capital gain effect more than offsets the capital loss effect for an equal increase and decrease in interest rates at the current interest rate level. In Figure 9B–2 we depict yields changing upward by one basis point $(R + 0.01\%)$ and downward by one basis point $(R - 0.01\%)$. Because convexity measures the curvature of the price–yield curve around the rate level $R$ percent, it intuitively measures the degree to which the capital gain effect of a small yield decrease exceeds

**FIGURE 9B–2**
Convexity and the
Price–Yield Curve

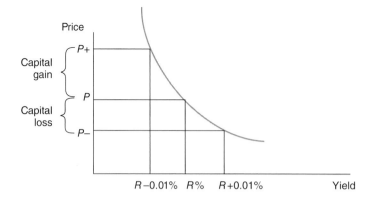

the capital loss effect of a small yield increase.
Definitionally, the $CX$ parameter equals:

$$CX = \frac{\text{Scaling}}{\text{factor}} \begin{bmatrix} \text{Capital} & \text{Capital} \\ \text{loss from a} & \text{gain from a} \\ \text{one-basis-point} + \text{one-basis-point} \\ \text{rise in yield} & \text{fall in yield} \\ (\text{negative effect}) & (\text{positive effect}) \end{bmatrix}$$

The sum of the two terms in the brackets
reflects the degree to which the capital gain effect
exceeds the capital loss effect for a small one-
basis-point interest rate change down and up. The
scaling factor normalizes this measure to account
for a larger 1 percent change in rates. Remember,
when interest rates change by a large amount, the
convexity effect is important to measure. A commonly used scaling factor is $10^8$ so that:[2]

$$CX = 10^8 \left[ \frac{\Delta P-}{P} + \frac{\Delta P+}{P} \right]$$

## Calculation of CX

To calculate the convexity of the 8 percent coupon, 8 percent yield, six-year maturity Eurobond
that had a price of $1,000:[3]

---

[2] This is consistent with the effect of a 1 percent (100 basis points) change in rates.
[3] You can easily check that $999.53785 is the price of the six-year bond when rates are 8.01 percent and $1,000.46243 is the price of the bond when rates fall to 7.99 percent. Since we are dealing in small numbers and convexity is sensitive to the number of decimal places assumed, we use at least five decimal places in calculating the capital gain or loss. In fact, the more decimal places used, the greater the accuracy of the $CX$ measure.

$$CX = 10^8 \left[ \frac{999.53785 - 1,000}{1,000} + \frac{1,000.46243 - 1,000}{1,000} \right]$$

Capital loss from     Capital gain from
a one-basis-point  +  a one-basis-point
increase in rates     decrease in rates

$$CX = 10^8 [0.00000028]$$
$$CX = 28$$

This value for $CX$ can be inserted into the bond
price prediction equation (2) with the convexity
adjustment:

$$\frac{\Delta P}{P} = -MD\,\Delta R + \frac{1}{2}(28)\Delta R^2$$

Assuming a 2 percent increase in $R$ (from 8 to
10 percent),

$$\frac{\Delta P}{P} = -\left[ \frac{4.993}{1.08} \right] 0.02 + \frac{1}{2}(28)(0.02)^2$$
$$= -0.0925 + 0.0056$$
$$= -0.0869 \text{ or } -8.69\%$$

The simple duration model (the first term)
predicts that a 2 percent rise in interest rates will
cause the bond's price to fall 9.25 percent. However, for large changes in yields, the duration
model overpredicts the price fall. The duration
model with the second-order convexity adjustment predicts a price fall of 8.69 percent; it adds
back 0.56 percent because of the convexity effect.
This is much closer to the true fall in the six-year,
8 percent coupon bond's price if we calculate this
using 10 percent to discount the coupon and face
value cash flows on the bond. The true value of

**TABLE 9B–1**   **Properties of Convexity**

| 1. Convexity Increases with Bond Maturity | | | 2. Convexity Varies with Coupon | | 3. Same Duration, Zero-Coupon Bonds Are Less Convex Than Coupon Bonds | |
| --- | --- | --- | --- | --- | --- | --- |
| Example | | | Example | | Example | |
| A | B | C | A | B | A | B |
| $N = 6$ | $N = 18$ | $N = \infty$ | $N = 6$ | $N = 6$ | $N = 6$ | $N = 5$ |
| $R = 8\%$ | $R = 8\%$ | $R = 8\%$ | $R = 8\%$ | $R = 8\%$ | $R = 8\%$ | $R = 8\%$ |
| $C = 8\%$ | $C = 8\%$ | $C = 8\%$ | $C = 8\%$ | $C = 0\%$ | $C = 8\%$ | $C = 0\%$ |
| $D = 5$ | $D = 10.12$ | $D = 13.5$ | $D = 5$ | $D = 6$ | $D = 5$ | $D = 5$ |
| $CX = 28$ | $CX = 130$ | $CX = 312$ | $CX = 28$ | $CX = 36$ | $CX = 28$ | $CX = 25.72$ |

the bond price fall is 8.71 percent. That is, using the convexity adjustment reduces the error between predicted value and true value to just a few basis points.[4]

In Table 9B–1 we calculate various properties of convexity, where

$$N = \text{Time to maturity}$$
$$R = \text{Yield to maturity}$$
$$C = \text{Annual coupon}$$
$$D = \text{Duration}$$
$$CX = \text{Convexity}$$

Part 1 of Table 9B–1 shows that as the bond's maturity ($N$) increases, so does its convexity ($CX$). As a result, long-term bonds have more convexity—which is a desirable property—than do short-term bonds. This property is similar to that possessed by duration.[5]

Part 2 of Table 9B–1 shows that coupon bonds of the same maturity ($N$) have less convexity than do zero-coupon bonds. However, for coupon bonds

and discount or zero-coupon bonds of the same duration, part 3 of the table shows that the coupon bond has more convexity. We depict the convexity of both in Figure 9B–3.

Finally, before leaving convexity, we might look at one important use of the concept by managers of insurance companies, pension funds, and mutual funds. Remembering that convexity is a desirable form of interest rate risk insurance, FI managers could structure an asset portfolio to maximize its desirable effects. Consider a pension fund manager with a 15-year payout horizon. To immunize the risk of interest rate changes, the manager purchases bonds with a 15-year duration. Consider two alternative strategies to achieve this:

Strategy 1: Invest 100 percent of resources in a 15-year deep-discount bond with an 8 percent yield.

Strategy 2: Invest 50 percent in the very short-term money market (Federal funds)[6] and 50 percent in 30-year deep-discount bonds with an 8 percent yield.

The duration ($D$) and convexities ($CX$) of these two asset portfolios are:

Strategy 1: $D = 15, CX = 206$

Strategy 2: $D = \frac{1}{2}(0) + \frac{1}{2}(30) = 15,$
$CX = \frac{1}{2}(0) + \frac{1}{2}(797) = 398.5$

---

[4] It is possible to use the third moment of the Taylor series expansion to reduce this small error (8.71 percent versus 8.69 percent) even further. In practice, few FIs do this.

[5] Note that the $CX$ measure differs according to the level of interest rates. For example, we are measuring $CX$ in Table 9B–1 when yields are 8 percent. If yields were 12 percent, the $CX$ number would change. This is intuitively reasonable, as the curvature of the price–yield curve differs at each point on the price–yield curve. Note that duration also changes with the level of interest rates.

[6] The duration and convexity of one-day federal funds are approximately zero.

**FIGURE 9B–3**
**Convexity of a Coupon versus a Discount Bond with the Same Duration**

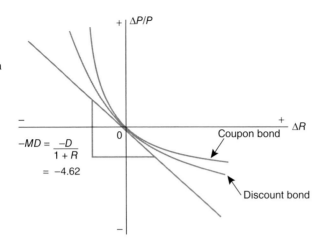

Strategies 1 and 2 have the same durations, but strategy 2 has a greater convexity. Strategy 2 is often called a barbell portfolio, as shown in Figure 9B–4 by the shaded bars.[7] Strategy 1 is the unshaded bar. To the extent that the market does not price (or fully price) convexity, the barbell strategy dominates the direct duration-matching strategy (strategy 1).[8]

More commonly, an FI manager may seek to attain greater convexity in the asset portfolio than in the liability portfolio, as shown in Figure 9B–5. As a result, both positive and negative shocks to interest rates would have beneficial effects on the FI's net worth.[9]

# THE PROBLEM OF THE FLAT TERM STRUCTURE

We have been calculating the simple, or Macaulay, duration. A key assumption of the simple duration model is that the yield curve or term structure of interest rates is flat and that when rates change, the yield curve shifts in a parallel fashion.

In the real world, the yield curve can take many shapes and at best may only approximate a flat yield curve. If the yield curve is not flat, using simple duration could be a potential source of error in predicting asset and liability interest rate sensitivities. Many models can deal with this problem. These models differ according to the shapes and shocks to the yield curve that are assumed.

Suppose the yield curve is not flat but shifts in such a manner that the yields on different maturity discount bonds change in a proportional fashion.[10] Consider calculating the duration of the six-year Eurobond when the yield curve is not flat at 8 percent. Instead, the yield curve looks like the one in Figure 9B–6.

Suppose the yield on one-year discount bonds rises. Assume also that the discounted changes in longer-maturity discount bond yields are just

---

[7] This is called a barbell because the weights are equally loaded at the extreme ends of the duration range, or bar, as in weight lifting.

[8] In a world in which convexity is priced, the long-term 30-year bond's price would rise to reflect the competition among buyers to include this more convex bond in their barbell asset portfolios. Thus, buying bond insurance—in the form of the barbell portfolio—would involve an additional cost to the FI manager. In addition, for the FI to be hedged in both a duration sense and a convexity sense, the manager should not choose the convexity of the asset portfolio without seeking to match it to the convexity of the liability portfolio.

[9] Another strategy would be for the FI to issue callable bonds as liabilities. Callable bonds have limited upside capital gains because if rates fall to a low level, then the issuer calls the bond in early (and reissues new lower coupon bonds). The effect of limited upside potential for callable bond prices is that the price–yield curve for such bonds exhibits negative convexity. Thus, if asset investments have positive convexity and liabilities negative convexity, then yield shocks (whether positive or negative) are likely to produce net worth gains for the FI.

[10] We are interested in the yield curve on discount bonds because these yields reflect the time value of money for single payments at different maturity dates. Thus, we can use these yields as discount rates for cash flows on a security to calculate appropriate present values of its cash flows and its duration.

**FIGURE 9B–4**
**Barbell Strategy**

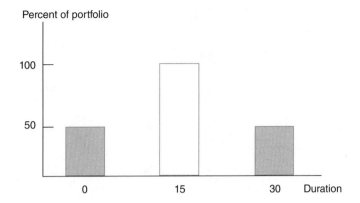

**FIGURE 9B–5**
**Assets Are More Convex Than Liabilities**

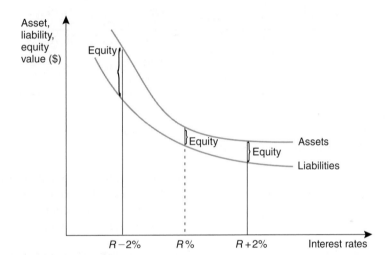

**FIGURE 9B–6**
**Nonflat Yield Curve**

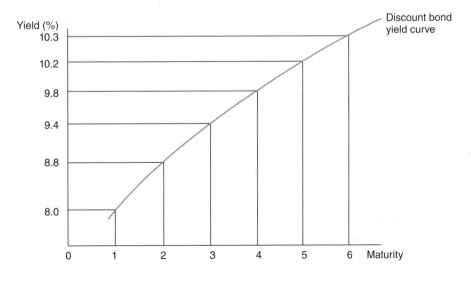

**TABLE 9B–2**
Duration with an
Upward-Sloping
Yield Curve

| t | CF | DF | CF × DF | CF × DF × t |
|---|---|---|---|---|
| 1 | 80 | $\frac{1}{(1.08)} = 0.9259$ | 74.07 | 74.07 |
| 2 | 80 | $\frac{1}{(1.088)^2} = 0.8448$ | 67.58 | 135.16 |
| 3 | 80 | $\frac{1}{(1.094)^3} = 0.7637$ | 61.10 | 183.30 |
| 4 | 80 | $\frac{1}{(1.098)^4} = 0.6880$ | 55.04 | 220.16 |
| 5 | 80 | $\frac{1}{(1.102)^5} = 0.6153$ | 49.22 | 246.10 |
| 6 | 1,080 | $\frac{1}{(1.103)^6} = 0.5553$ | 599.75 | 3,598.50 |
| | | | 906.76 | 4,457.29 |

$$D^* = \frac{4,457.29}{906.76} = 4.91562$$

proportional to the change in the one-year discount bond yield:

$$\frac{\Delta R_1}{1 + R_1} = \frac{\Delta R_2}{1 + R_2} = \cdots = \frac{\Delta R_6}{1 + R_6}$$

Given this quite restrictive assumption, it can be proved that the appropriate duration measure of the bond—call it $D^*$—can be derived by discounting the coupons and principal value of the bond by the discount rates or yields on appropriate maturity zero-coupon bonds. Given the discount bond yield curve plotted in Figure 9B–6, $D^*$ is calculated in Table 9B–2.

Notice that $D^*$ is 4.916 years, while the simple Macaulay duration (with an assumed flat 8 percent yield curve) is 4.993 years. $D^*$ and $D$ differ because, by taking into account the upward-sloping yield curve in Figure 9B–6, the later cash flows are discounted at higher rates than they are under the flat yield curve assumption underlying Macaulay's measure $D$.

With respect to the FI manager's problem, choosing to use $D^*$ instead of $D$ does not change the basic problem except for a concern with the gap between the $D^*$ on assets and leverage-weighted liabilities:

$$D^*_A - kD^*_L$$

However, remember that the $D^*$ was calculated under very restrictive assumptions about the yield curve. If we change these assumptions in any way, the measure of $D^*$ changes.

## THE PROBLEM OF DEFAULT RISK

The models and the duration calculations we have looked at assume that the issuer of bonds or the borrower of a loan pays the promised interest and principal with a probability of 1; we assume no default or delay in the payment of cash flows. In the real world, problems with principal and interest payments are common and lead to restructuring and workouts on debt contracts as bankers and bond trustees renegotiate with borrowers; that is, the borrower reschedules or recontracts interest and principal payments rather than defaulting outright. If we view default risk as synonymous with the rescheduling of cash flows to a later date, this is quite easy to deal with in duration models.

Consider the six-year, 8 percent coupon, 8 percent yield Eurobond. Suppose the issuer gets into difficulty and cannot pay the first coupon. Instead, the borrower and the FI agree that the

**TABLE 9B–3**
Duration and
Rescheduling

| t | CF | DF | CF × DF | CF × DF × t |
|---|-----|--------|---------|-------------|
| 1 | 0 | 0.9259 | 0 | 0 |
| 2 | 160 | 0.8573 | 137.17 | 274.34 |
| 3 | 80 | 0.7938 | 63.51 | 190.53 |
| 4 | 80 | 0.7350 | 58.80 | 235.21 |
| 5 | 80 | 0.6806 | 54.45 | 272.25 |
| 6 | 1,080 | 0.6302 | 680.58 | 4,083.48 |
|   |   |   | 994.51 | 5,055.81 |

$$D = \frac{5{,}055.81}{994.51} = 5.0837 \text{ years}$$

unpaid interest can be paid in year 2. This alleviates part of the cash flow pressure on the borrower while lengthening the duration of the bond from the FI's perspective (see Table 9B–3). The effect of rescheduling the first interest payment is to increase duration from approximately 5 years to 5.08 years.

More commonly, an FI manager unsure of the future cash flows because of future default risk might multiply the promised cash flow ($CF_t$) by the probability of repayment ($p_t$) in year $t$ to generate expected cash flows in year $t$—$E(CF_t)$.

$$E(CF_t) = p_t \times CF_t$$

Chapter 10 suggests a number of ways to generate these repayment probabilities. Once the cash flows have been adjusted for default risk, a duration measure can be directly calculated in the same manner as the Macaulay formula (or $D^*$) except that $E(CF_t)$ replaces $CF_t$.[11]

## FLOATING-RATE LOANS AND BONDS

The duration models we have looked at assume that the interest rates on loans or the coupons on bonds are fixed at issue and remain unchanged until maturity. However, many bonds and loans carry floating interest rates. Examples include loan rates indexed to LIBOR (London Interbank

Offered Rate) and adjustable-rate mortgages (ARMs) whose rates can be indexed to Treasury or other securities yields. Moreover, in the 1980s, many banks and security firms either issued or underwrote perpetual floating-rate notes (FRNs). These are like consol bonds in that they never mature. Unlike consols, their coupons fluctuate with market rates. The FI manager, who wants to analyze overall gap exposure, may ask: What are the durations of such floating-rate securities? The duration of a floating-rate instrument is generally the time interval between the purchase of the security and the time when the next coupon or interest payment is readjusted to reflect current interest rate conditions. We call this the *time to repricing* of the instrument.

For example, suppose the investor bought a perpetual floating-rate note. These floating-rate notes never mature. At the beginning of each year, the FI sets the coupon rate, which is paid at the end of that year. Suppose the investor buys the bond in the middle of the first year ($t = \frac{1}{2}$) rather than at the beginning (see Figure 9B–7).

The present value of the bond from time of purchase is:

$$P = \frac{C_1}{(1 + \frac{1}{2}R)} + \frac{C_2}{(1 + \frac{1}{2}R)(1 + R)}$$
$$+ \frac{C_3}{(1 + \frac{1}{2}R)(1 + R)^2} + \frac{C_4}{(1 + \frac{1}{2}R)(1 + R)^3}$$
$$+ \frac{C_5}{(1 + \frac{1}{2}R)(1 + R)^4} + \cdots$$
$$+ \frac{C_\infty}{(1 + \frac{1}{2}R)(1 + R)^{\infty - 1}}$$

[11] Alternatively, the promised cash flow could be discounted by the appropriate discount yield on a risk-free Treasury security plus an appropriate credit-risk spread; that is, $CF_t/(1 + d_t + S_t)^t$, where $CF_t$ is the promised cash flow in year $t$, $d_t$ is the yield on a $t$-period zero-coupon Treasury bond, and $S_t$ is a credit-risk premium.

**FIGURE 9B–7**
**Floating-Rate Note**

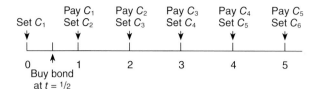

Note three important aspects of this present value equation. First, the investor has to wait only a half year to get the first coupon payment—hence, the discount rate is $(1 + \frac{1}{2}R)$. Second, the investor knows with certainty only the size of the first coupon $C_1$, which was preset at the beginning of the first coupon period to reflect interest rates at that time. The FI set the first coupon rate six months before the investor bought the bond. Third, the other coupons on the bond, $C_2, C_3, C_4, C_5, \ldots C\infty$, are unknown at the time the bond is purchased because they depend on the level of interest rates at the time they are reset (see Figure 9B–7).

To derive the duration of the bond, rewrite the cash flows at one-half year onward as:

$$P = \frac{C_1}{(1 + \frac{1}{2}R)} + \frac{1}{(1 + \frac{1}{2}R)}$$
$$\left[ \frac{C_2}{(1 + R)} + \frac{C_3}{(1 + R)^2} + \frac{C_4}{(1 + R)^3} + \right.$$
$$\left. \frac{C_5}{(1 + R)^4} + \cdots + \frac{C_\infty}{(1 + R)^{\infty - 1}} \right]$$

where $P$ is the present value of the bond (the bond price) at one-half year, the time of purchase.

The term in brackets is the present value or fair price ($P_1$) of the bond if it were sold at the end of year 1, the beginning of the second coupon period. As long as the variable coupons exactly match fluctuations in yields or interest rates, the present value of the cash flow in the square brackets is unaffected by interest rate changes. Thus,

$$P = \frac{C_1}{(1 + \frac{1}{2}R)} + \frac{P_1}{(1 + \frac{1}{2}R)}$$

Since $C_1$ is a fixed cash flow preset before the investor bought the bond and $P_1$ is a fixed cash flow

in present value terms, buying this bond is similar to buying two single-payment deep-discount bonds each with a maturity of six months. Because the duration of a deep-discount bond is the same as its maturity, this floating rate bond has:

$$D = \frac{1}{2} \text{ year}$$

As indicated earlier, a half year is exactly the interval between the time when the bond was purchased and the time when it was first repriced.

## DEMAND DEPOSITS AND PASSBOOK SAVINGS

Many banks and thrifts hold large amounts of checking and passbook savings account liabilities. This is especially true for smaller banks. The problem in assessing the duration of such claims is that their maturities are open-ended and many demand deposit accounts do not turn over very frequently. Although demand deposits allow holders to demand cash immediately— suggesting a very short maturity—many customers tend to retain demand deposit balances for lengthy periods. In the parlance of banking, they behave as if they were a bank's core deposits. One way for an FI manager to get around this problem is to analyze the runoff, or the turnover characteristics, of the FI's demand and passbook savings account deposits. For example, suppose the manager learns that on average each dollar in demand deposit accounts turns over five times a year. This suggests an average turnover or maturity per dollar of around 73 days, (i.e., 365 days/5).

A second method is to consider demand deposits as bonds that can be instantaneously put back to the bank in return for cash. As instantaneously putable bonds, the duration of demand deposits is approximately zero.

A third approach is more directly in line with the idea of duration as a measure of interest rate sensitivity. It looks at the percentage change of demand deposits ($\Delta DD/DD$) to interest rate changes ($\Delta R$). Because demand deposits and, to a lesser extent, passbook savings deposits pay either low explicit or implicit interest—where implicit interest takes forms such as subsidized checking fees—there tend to be enhanced withdrawals and switching into higher-yielding instruments as rates rise. You can use a number of quantitative techniques to test this sensitivity, including linear and nonlinear time series regression analysis.

A fourth approach is to use simulation analysis. This is based on forecasts of future interest rates and the net withdrawals by depositors from their accounts over some future time period. Taking the discounted present values of these cash flows allows a duration measure to be calculated.

## MORTGAGES AND MORTGAGE-BACKED SECURITIES

Calculating the durations of mortgages and mortgage-backed securities is difficult because of prepayment risk. Essentially, as the level of interest rates falls, mortgage holders have the option to prepay their old mortgages and refinance with a new mortgage at a lower interest rate. In the terminology of finance, fixed-rate mortgages and mortgage-backed securities contain an embedded option. Calculating duration requires projecting the future cash flows on an asset. Consequently, to calculate the duration of mortgages, we need to model the prepayment behavior of mortgage holders. Possible ways to do this are left to Chapter 26 on mortgage asset securitization.

## FUTURES, OPTIONS, SWAPS, CAPS, AND OTHER CONTINGENT CLAIMS

When interest rates change, so do the values of (off-balance-sheet) derivative instruments such as futures, options, swaps, and caps (see Chapter 16). Market value gains and losses on these instruments can also have an impact on the net worth ($E$) of an FI. The calculation of the durations of these instruments is left to Chapters 22, 23, and 24. However, it should be noted that a fully fledged duration gap model of an FI should take into account the durations of its derivatives portfolio as well as the duration of its on-balance-sheet assets and liabilities. This is especially so today as more and more FIs take positions in derivative contracts.

# Chapter Ten

See Appendices Online at www.mhhe.com/saunders8e
- Appendix 10A: Credit Analysis
- Appendix 10B: Black–Scholes Option Pricing Model

# Credit Risk: Individual Loan Risk

## INTRODUCTION

As discussed in Chapter 1, financial institutions (FIs) are special because of their ability to efficiently transform financial claims of household savers into claims issued to corporations, individuals, and governments. An FI's ability to evaluate information and to control and monitor borrowers allows it to transform these claims at the lowest possible cost to all parties. One of the specific types of financial claim transformation discussed in Chapter 1 is credit allocation. That is, FIs transform claims of household savers (in the form of deposits) into loans issued to corporations, individuals, and governments. The FI accepts the credit risk on these loans in exchange for a fair return sufficient to cover the cost of funding (e.g., covering the costs of borrowing, or issuing deposits) to household savers and the credit risk involved in lending.

In this chapter, the first of two chapters on credit risk, we discuss various approaches to analyzing and measuring the credit or default risk on *individual* loans (and bonds). In the next chapter, we consider methods for evaluating the risk of the *overall loan portfolio*, or loan concentration risk. Methods for hedging and managing an FI's credit risk, such as the use of credit derivative swaps, are left to Chapters 22 through 26. Measurement of the credit risk on individual loans or bonds is crucial if an FI manager is to (1) price a loan or value a bond correctly and (2) set appropriate limits on the amount of credit extended to any one borrower or the loss exposure it accepts from any particular counterparty.

Indeed, the default of one major borrower can have a significant impact on the value and reputation of many FIs. For example, total exposure of U.S. banks to WorldCom at the time of its bankruptcy in 2002 was over $700 million. Losses from this single failure resulted in a drop in earnings per share at J.P. Morgan Chase of 5 cents (or nearly 2 percent), at then Bank One (Bank One is now a part of J.P. Morgan Chase), of 3 cents (or 1 percent), and at Bank of America of 5 cents (or 1 percent). Similarly, a single major economic event can cause losses to many FIs' loan portfolios. For example, in 2005 Hurricanes Katrina and Rita resulted in over $1.3 billion in bad loans for major banks operating in areas hit by the storm. And, of course, the financial market crisis of the late 2000s resulted in the largest ever credit risk-related losses for U.S. financial institutions. Losses from the falling value of on- and off-balance-sheet credit instruments (e.g., mortgages, mortgage-backed securities, credit cards) topped $2.3 trillion worldwide, with $1.6 trillion coming from loans and assets originated at U.S. financial institutions. In just the first quarter of 2009, the annualized net charge-off rate on total loans and leases at U.S. banks was 1.94 percent, slightly below the 1.95 percent rate in the fourth quarter of 2008 (that was the highest quarterly net charge-off rate in the 25 years that insured institutions have reported these data). The year-over-year rise in charge-offs was led by loans to commercial and industrial (C&I) borrowers, where charge-offs increased by $4.2 billion (170 percent), then credit cards (up $3.4 billion, or 68.9 percent), real estate construction loans (up $2.9 billion, or 161.7 percent), and 1–4 family residential real estate loans (up $2.7 billion, or 64.9 percent).

Many financial institutions were unable to survive the mortgage crisis. For example, Countrywide Financial, the country's largest mortgage issuer, nearly failed in the summer of 2007 due to defaults by its subprime mortgage borrowers. Only a $2 billion equity investment by Bank of America in 2007 and then an acquisition by Bank of America in 2008 kept this thrift alive. IndyMac Bank, the ninth largest mortgage lender in the U.S. in 2007, was seized by the FDIC in July 2008. At a cost to the FDIC of between $4 billion and $8 billion, IndyMac represented the largest bank failure in more than 20 years. Overall, in 2008–2010, 322 U.S. banks failed, compared to 3 in 2005–2007. Further, the Federal Deposit Insurance Corporation reported that it had 884 banks on its list of troubled institutions at year end 2010, up from 90 in the first quarter of 2008. Most recently, bank loan portfolios were exposed to losses from the European debt crisis. In early 2012, U.S. banks had virtually no exposure to Greek debt, approximately $5.8 billion. Despite this relatively insignificant amount, the risks posed to U.S. banks and the banking system system from a Greek debt default and a contagion crisis in other Eurozone countries were huge. U.S. banks had more than $50 billion worth of debt exposure to both Spain and Ireland, $6.6 billion to Portugal, and more than $66 billion to Italy, all countries in risk of debt default in the event of a continued economic slowdown. Further, U.S. banks had even larger exposures to the larger countries in Europe and to European banks. These seemingly unending credit-related events stress that FIs need to manage their loan portfolios to protect the overall FI from failure due to credit risk.

We begin this chapter with a look at the types of loans (commercial and industrial [C&I], real estate, individual (consumer), and others) as well as the characteristics of those loans made by U.S. FIs. We then look at how both interest and fees are incorporated to calculate the return on a loan. This is followed by a discussion of how the return on a loan versus the quantity of credit made available for lending is used by FIs to make decisions on wholesale (C&I) versus retail (consumer) lending. Finally, we examine various models used to measure credit risk, including qualitative and quantitative models (credit scoring models and newer models of credit risk measurement). Indeed, technological advances have been at least one driving force behind the advances and new models of credit risk measurement and management in recent years. Appendix 10A, located at the book's website **(www.mhhe.com/saunders8e),** discusses cash flow and financial ratio analysis widely used in the credit analysis process for mortgage, consumer, and commercial loans.

# CREDIT QUALITY PROBLEMS

**junk bonds**
Bonds rated as speculative or less than investment grade by bond-rating agencies such as Moody's.

www.moodys.com
www.standardandpoors.com

Over the past three decades the credit quality of many FIs' lending and investment decisions has attracted a great deal of attention. In the 1980s there were tremendous problems with bank loans to less developed countries (LDCs) as well as with thrift and bank residential and farm mortgage loans. In the early 1990s attention switched to the problems of commercial real estate loans (to which banks, thrifts, and insurance companies were all exposed) as well as **junk bonds** (rated as speculative or less than investment grade securities by bond-rating agencies such as Moody's or Standard & Poors). In the late 1990s concerns shifted to the rapid growth in low-quality auto loans and credit cards as well as the declining quality in commercial lending standards as loan delinquencies started to increase. In the late 1990s and early 2000s, attention focused on problems with telecommunication companies, new technology companies, and a variety of sovereign countries including at various times Argentina, Brazil, Russia, and South Korea. Despite these credit concerns, the credit quality of most FIs improved throughout the 1990s. For example, for FDIC-insured commercial banks, the ratio of nonperforming loans to assets declined significantly from 1992 through 2000 (see Figure 10–1).[1]

The recession in the U.S. economy in the early 2000s led to a reversal in this trend as nonperforming loan rates increased, particularly on commercial and industrial (C&I) loans. However, the nonperformance of loans in all categories was still below that of the early 1990s. As the U.S. economy improved in the mid-2000s, nonperforming loan rates fell. However, mortgage delinquencies, particularly on subprime mortgages, surged in the last quarter of 2006 and all of 2007 as home owners who stretched themselves financially to buy a home or refinance

**FIGURE 10–1** **Nonperforming Asset Ratio for U.S. Commercial Banks**

Source: Federal Deposit Insurance Corporation, *Quarterly Banking Profile,* various issues. *www.fdic.gov*

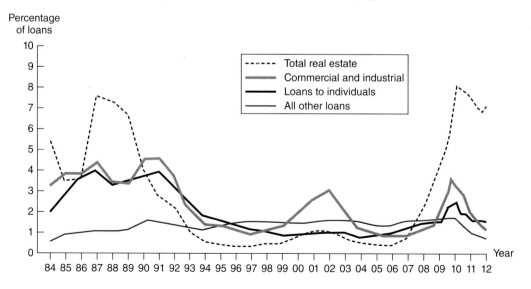

[1] Nonperforming loans are loans that are 90 days or more past due or are not accruing interest.

a mortgage in the early 2000s fell behind on their loan payments. Trouble in the mortgage markets continued to escalate as the number of foreclosures hit a record 1.5 million in the first six months of 2009. Nonperforming real estate loans reached levels higher than those seen in the 1980s. Problems in the mortgage markets spread to other sectors as well. In 2008 consumer bankruptcy filings rose to 1.06 million, up from 801,840 in 2007 and 602,000 in 2006. Business loan losses grew as well. For example, when Chrysler went into bankruptcy in May 2009, it owed banks, including Citigroup and J.P. Morgan Chase, $6.9 billion. President Obama's plan for Chrysler's bankruptcy cut that to $1 billion for a loss to banks of $5.9 billion. The banks ended up realizing 33 cents on the dollar for these loans, a loss of $4.6 billion. As the U.S. economy slowly recovered in 2010–2012, nonperforming loans rates edged downward but still remained at levels higher than those seen throughout most of the 30-year period.

| | |
|---|---|
| *Internet Exercise* | Go to the Federal Deposit Insurance Corporation website and find the latest information available for nonperforming loans at commercial banks in the United States, using the following steps: Go to the Federal Deposit Insurance Corporation website at **www.fdic.gov**. Click on "Analysts." Click on "FDIC Quarterly Banking Profile." Click on "Quarterly Banking Profile." Click on the most recent date and "Commercial Bank Section." Click on "TABLE V-A. Loan Performance." This will download a file on to your computer that will contain the most recent information as "Percent of Loans Noncurrent: Total Loans and Leases." |

Credit quality problems, in the worst case, can cause an FI to become insolvent or can result in such a significant drain on capital[2] and net worth that they adversely affect its growth prospects and ability to compete with other domestic and international FIs. However, credit risk does not apply only to traditional areas of lending and bond investing. As banks and other FIs have expanded into credit guarantees and other off-balance-sheet activities (see Chapter 16), new types of credit risk exposure have arisen, causing concern among managers and regulators. Thus, credit risk analysis is now important for a whole variety of contractual agreements between FIs and counterparties.[3]

| | |
|---|---|
| **Concept Questions** | 1. What are some of the credit quality problems faced by FIs over the last three decades? |
| | 2. What are some of the newer, nontraditional activities that create credit risk for today's FIs? |

[2] Losses drain capital through the income statement item "provision for loan losses." The provision for loan losses is a noncash, tax-deductible expense representing the FI management's prediction of loans at risk of default for the current period. As credit quality problems arise, the FI recognizes its expected bad loans by recording this expense, which reduces net income and, in turn, the FI's capital. The provision for loan losses is then allocated to the allowance for loan losses listed on the balance sheet. The allowance for loan and lease losses is a cumulative estimate by the FI's management of the gross loans (and leases) that will not be repaid to the FI. Actual losses are then deducted from, and recoveries are added to (referred to as *net write-offs),* their accumulated loans and lease loss reserve balance. See Appendix 2A, "Commercial Banks' Financial Statements and Analysis" (located at the book's website, **www.mhhe.com/saunders8e**) for a more detailed discussion of these items.

[3] This is one of the reasons for bank regulators' setting capital requirements against credit risk (see Chapter 20).

# TYPES OF LOANS

Although most FIs make loans, the types of loans made and the characteristics of those loans differ considerably. This section analyzes the major types of loans made by U.S. financial institutions. Table 10–1 shows a recent breakdown of the aggregate loan portfolio of U.S. commercial banks into four broad classes: commercial and industrial (19.6 percent of all commercial bank loans), real estate (52.9 percent), individual (17.5 percent), and all others (10.0 percent). We look briefly at each of these loan classes in turn.

## Commercial and Industrial Loans

The figures in Table 10–1 disguise a great deal of heterogeneity in the commercial and industrial loan portfolio. Indeed, commercial loans can be made for periods as short as a few weeks to as long as eight years or more. Traditionally, short-term commercial loans (those with an original maturity of one year or less) are used to finance firms' working capital needs and other short-term funding needs, while long-term commercial loans are used to finance credit needs that extend beyond one year, such as the purchase of real assets (machinery), new venture start-up costs, and permanent increases in working capital. They can be made in quite small amounts, such as $100,000, to small businesses or in packages as large as $10 million or more to major corporations. Large C&I loans are often syndicated.

**syndicated loan**
A loan provided by a group of FIs as opposed to a single lender.

A **syndicated loan** is provided by a group of FIs as opposed to a single lender. A syndicated loan is structured by the lead FI (or agent) and the borrower. Once the terms (rates, fees, and covenants) are set, pieces of the loan are sold to other FIs. In addition, C&I loans can be secured or unsecured. A **secured loan** (or asset-backed loan) is backed by specific assets of the borrower. If the borrower defaults, the lender has a first lien or claim on those assets. Secured debt is senior to an **unsecured loan** (or junior debt) that has only a general claim on the assets of the borrower if default occurs. As we explain later in this chapter, there is normally a trade-off between the security or collateral backing of a loan and the loan interest rate or risk premium charged by the lender on a loan.

**secured loan**
A loan that is backed by a first claim on certain assets (collateral) of the borrower if default occurs.

**unsecured loan**
A loan that has only a general claim to the assets of the borrower if default occurs.

In addition, commercial loans can be made at either fixed or floating rates of interest. A fixed-rate loan has the rate of interest set at the beginning of the contract period. This rate remains in force over the loan contract period no matter what happens to market rates. Suppose, for example, IBM borrowed $10 million at a fixed rate of 10 percent for one year, but the FI's cost of funds rose over the course of the year. Because this is a fixed-rate loan the FI bears all the interest rate risk. This is why many loans have floating-rate contractual terms; that is, IBM borrows $10 million at a floating rate, e.g., LIBOR + 5 percent, for one year. The loan rate can be periodically adjusted according to a formula so that the interest rate risk is

**TABLE 10–1**
**Types of U.S. Bank Loans (in billions of dollars)**

Source: Federal Reserve Board, *Assets and Liabilities of Commercial Banks*, June 2012. *www.federalreserve.gov*

|  | Amount | Percent |
|---|---|---|
| Total loans* | $6,739.8 | 100.0% |
| C&I | 1,322.1 | 19.6 |
| Real estate | 3,562.3 | 52.9 |
| Individual | 1,183.0 | 17.5 |
| Other | 672.4 | 10.0 |

*Excluding interbank loans.

transferred in large part from the FI to the borrower. As might be expected, longer-term loans are more likely to be made under floating-rate contracts than are relatively short-term loans.[4]

**spot loan**
The loan amount is withdrawn by the borrower immediately.

**loan commitment**
A credit facility with a maximum size and a maximum period of time over which the borrower can withdraw funds; a line of credit.

Finally, loans can be made either spot or under commitment. A **spot loan** is made by the FI, and the borrower uses or takes down the entire loan amount immediately. With a **loan commitment,** or line of credit, the lender makes an amount of credit available, such as $10 million. The borrower has the option to take down any amount up to the $10 million at any time over the commitment period. In a fixed-rate loan commitment, the interest rate to be paid on any takedown is established when the loan commitment contract originates. In a floating-rate commitment, the borrower pays the loan rate in force when the loan is actually taken down. For example, suppose the $10 million floating-rate IBM loan was made under a one-year loan commitment. When the loan commitment was originated (say, January 2015), IBM borrows nothing. Instead, it waits until six months have passed (say, July 2015) before it takes down the entire $10 million. Since this is a floating-rate loan commitment, IBM pays the loan rate in force as of July 2015. We discuss the special features of loan commitments more fully in Chapter 16.

To determine the basic characteristics of C&I loans, the Federal Reserve surveys more than 400 banks each quarter. Table 10–2 shows the major characteristics in a recent lending survey. As you can see, more short-term (under one year) C&I loans ($62.27 billion) than long-term loans ($3.36 billion) were reported. Also, short-term loans are less likely to be backed or secured by collateral (ranging from 27.1 percent for daily loans to 67.9 percent for zero loans) than long-term loans (80.7 percent).

**commercial paper**
Unsecured short-term debt instrument issued by corporations.

Finally, as we noted in Chapter 2, commercial loans are declining in importance in bank loan portfolios. The major reason for this has been the rise in nonbank loan substitutes, especially commercial paper. **Commercial paper** is an unsecured short-term debt instrument issued by corporations either directly or via an underwriter to purchasers in the financial markets, such as money market mutual funds.

**TABLE 10–2**   **Characteristics of Commercial Loan Portfolios, March 2012**

Source: Federal Reserve Board website, June 2012. *www.federalreserve.gov*

|  | Long-Term Loans | Short-Term Loans | | | |
|---|---|---|---|---|---|
|  |  | Zero* | Daily | 2 to 30 days | 31 to 365 days |
| Amount outstanding ($ billions) | $3.36 | $17.96 | $17.34 | $20.87 | $6.10 |
| Average size of loan ($ thousands) | $355 | $294 | $2,282 | $501 | $713 |
| Percent of which made under commitment | 88.8% | 95.9% | 31.9% | 83.5% | 89.7% |
| Percent of loans secured by collateral | 80.7% | 67.9% | 27.1% | 39.9% | 54.6% |

*Floating-rate loans that are subject to repricing at any time.

[4] However, floating-rate loans are more credit risky than fixed-rate loans, holding all other contractual features the same. This is because floating-rate loans pass the risk of all interest rate changes onto borrowers. Thus, in rising interest rate environments, floating-rate borrowers may find themselves unable to pay the interest on their loans and may be forced to default. This is what happened in the mortgage markets in the late 2000s and ignited the financial crisis. The benefit of floating-rate loans to lenders is that they better enable FIs to hedge the cost of rising interest rates on liabilities (such as deposits). This suggests that controlling interest rate risk may be at the expense of enhanced credit risk.

By using commercial paper, a corporation can sidestep banks and the loan market to raise funds often at rates below those banks charge. As of June 2012, the total commercial paper outstanding in the United States was $1,007.1 billion compared with C&I loans of $1,322.1 billion. Prior to the financial crisis, in December 2007 commercial paper outstanding was $1,788.1 billion compared to $1,445.8 billion in bank loans. Moreover, since only the largest corporations can tap the commercial paper market, banks are often left with a pool of increasingly smaller and riskier borrowers in the C&I loan market. For example, as the U.S. economy slowed in the early 2000s, noncurrent (loans that are 90 days or more past due or are not accruing interest) C&I loans increased from $14 billion (in the fourth quarter of 1999) to almost $24 billion (in the second quarter of 2003). As the economy strengthened in the mid-2000s, this amount decreased to $2.4 billion. The recession and financial crisis in the late 2000s saw noncurrent C&I loans grow again; to a high of $45 billion in the third quarter of 2009.

The commercial paper market was also hard hit by the financial crisis, but not because of nonperformance issues related to the commercial paper issuing firms. At the height of the crisis, in September 2008, money market mutual fund withdrawals skyrocketed. Fund investors pulled out a record $144.5 billion during the week ending Wednesday, September 17 (redemptions during the week of September 10 totaled just $7.1 billion), as investors worried about the safety of even these safest investments. Money market mutual funds participated heavily in the $1.7 trillion commercial paper market, which provided a bulk of the short-term funds to corporations. As investors pulled their money from these funds, the commercial paper market shrank by $52.1 billion for the week (through Wednesday). These outflows severely undermined the stability of short-term funding markets, upon which many large corporations rely heavily to meet their short-term borrowing needs. In response, businesses that had them drew down their loan commitments at FIs. Thus, C&I loans issued by commercial banks increased as the commercial paper market decreased in size.

## Real Estate Loans

Real estate loans are primarily mortgage loans and some revolving home equity loans (approximately 13 percent of the real estate loan portfolio in March 2012).[5] We show the distribution of mortgage debt for U.S. banks in 2012 in Table 10–3. For banks (as well as thrifts), residential mortgages are still the largest component of the real estate loan portfolio (63.5 percent in 2012).

**TABLE 10–3**
**Distribution of U.S. Commercial Bank Real Estate Mortgage Debt**

Source: Federal Deposit Insurance Corporation website, June 2012. *www.fdic.gov*

|  | Percent |
|---|---|
| One- to four-family residences | 63.5% |
| Multifamily residences | 5.1 |
| Commercial | 29.3 |
| Farm | 2.1 |
|  | 100.0% |

[5] Under home equity loans, borrowers use the equity they have in their homes as collateral backing for loans.

**FIGURE 10–2**  ARMs' Share of Total Loans Closed, 1987–2012

Sources: Federal Housing Finance Agency website, *www.fhfa.gov*, and Federal Reserve Board website, *www.federalreserve.gov*.

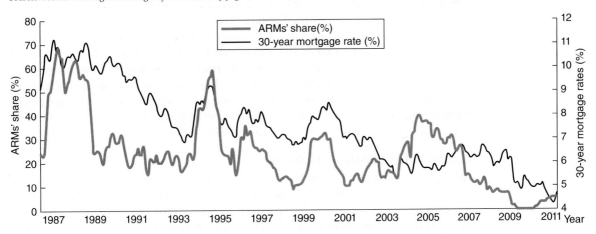

**adjustable-rate mortgage (ARM)**
A mortgage whose interest rate adjusts with movements in an underlying market index interest rate.

As with C&I loans, the characteristics of residential mortgage loans differ widely. These characteristics include the size of the loan, the ratio of the loan to the property's price (the loan price or loan value ratio), and the maturity of the mortgage. Other important characteristics are the mortgage interest (or commitment) rate and fees and charges on the loan, such as commissions, discounts, and points paid by the borrower or the seller to obtain the loan.[6] In addition, the mortgage rate differs according to whether the mortgage has a fixed rate or a floating rate, also called an adjustable rate. **Adjustable-rate mortgages (ARMs)** have their contractual rates periodically adjusted to some underlying index, such as the one-year T-bill rate. The proportion of fixed-rate mortgages to ARMs in FI portfolios varies with the interest rate cycle. In low–interest rate periods, borrowers prefer fixed-rate to adjustable-rate mortgages. As a result, the proportion of ARMs to fixed-rate mortgages can vary considerably over the rate cycle. In Figure 10–2, note the behavior of ARMs over one recent interest rate cycle—1999 to 2007— when interest rates (and ARMs) rose, then fell, and then rose and fell again. Note also that ARMs were virtually nonexistent in late 2008 and 2009 as the federal government, in an effort to stimulate the devasted housing market, took actions that lowered fixed mortgage rates to historic lows. Table 10–4 presents a summary of the major contractual terms on conventional fixed-rate mortgages as of 2012.

**TABLE 10–4**
**Contractual Terms on Conventional New Home Mortgages**

Source: *Federal Housing Finance Agency,* Mortgage Interest Rates, June 2012. *www.fhfa.gov*

| | |
|---|---|
| Purchase price ($ thousands) | $349.2 |
| Amount of loan ($ thousands) | $256.2 |
| Loan-to-value ratio (percent) | 75.3% |
| Maturity (years) | 27.3 |
| Fees and charges (percent of loan amount) | 0.90% |
| Contract rate (percent) | 3.93% |

[6] Points are a certain percentage of the face value of the loan paid up front, as a fee, by the borrower to the lender.

Home buyers raised an average of 75.3 percent of the value of their new homes by borrowing through mortgage loans. Rates charged on the average loan remained at historical lows (3.93 percent), and mortgage lenders charged an additional 0.9 percent in fees for processing the mortgages.

Residential mortgages are very long-term loans with an average maturity of 29 years. To the extent that house prices can fall below the amount of the loan outstanding—that is, the loan-to-value ratio rises—the residential mortgage portfolio can also be susceptible to default risk. For example, during the collapse in real estate prices in the late 2000s, many house prices actually fell below the prices of the mid-2000s. This led to a dramatic surge in the level of mortgage defaults and eventually foreclosures by banks and thrifts.

## Individual (Consumer) Loans

Another major type of loan is the individual, or consumer, loan, such as personal and auto loans. Commercial banks, finance companies, retailers, savings institutions, credit unions, and oil companies also provide consumer loan financing through credit cards, such as Visa, MasterCard, and proprietary credit cards issued by, for example, Sears and AT&T. Credit card transactions typically must be authorized by the cardholder's bank. Thus, verification of satisfactory credit quality occurs with each transaction. The five largest credit card issuers and their outstanding balances in 2011 are shown in Table 10–5. Together, these five credit card issuers hold more than 66 percent of all outstanding balances.

In Table 10–6 are the two major classes of consumer loans at U.S. banks. The largest class of loans is nonrevolving consumer loans (66.2 percent), which include new and used automobile loans, mobile home loans, and fixed-term consumer loans such as 24-month personal loans. The other major class of consumer loans is revolving loans (33.8 percent), such as credit card debt. With a **revolving loan,** the borrower has a credit line on which to draw as well as to repay, up to some maximum over the life of the credit contract. In recent years, bank's have faced charge-off rates between 4 and 8 percent on their credit card loans outstanding. Note particularly that in October 2005, the Bankruptcy Reform Act was signed into law.

**revolving loan**
A credit line on which a borrower can both draw and repay many times over the life of the loan contract.

**TABLE 10–5**
**Biggest Credit Card Issuers**

Source: The Nilson Report, February 2012.

| Card Issuer | Total Outstanding Balances ($ billions) | Market Share, 2011 | Market Share, 2010 |
|---|---|---|---|
| J.P. Morgan Chase | $130.02 | 18.23% | 18.64% |
| Bank of America | 112.62 | 15.79 | 17.19 |
| Citigroup | 92.33 | 12.94 | 13.34 |
| American Express | 80.25 | 11.92 | 11.28 |
| Capital One Financial | 50.88 | 7.13 | 7.05 |

**TABLE 10–6**
**Types of Consumer Loans at Commercial Banks**

Source: Federal Reserve Board website, Consumer Credit, June 2012.
*www.federalreserve.gov*

| | Percent |
|---|---|
| Revolving | 33.8% |
| Nonrevolving | 66.2 |
| | 100.0% |

**FIGURE 10–3**   **Annual Net Charge-Off Rates on Loans**

Source: Federal Deposit Insurance Corporation, *Quarterly Banking Profile*, various issues. *www.fdic.gov*

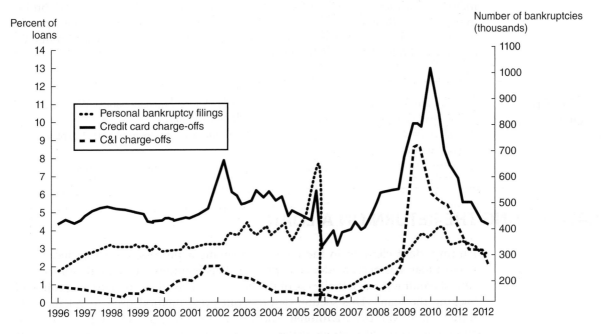

This act made it more difficult for consumers to declare bankruptcy. As a result, there was a surge in bankruptcy filings in the summer and early fall of 2005, just before the new rules went into effect. Consequently, banks saw a surge in credit card charge-offs. These charge-off rates were significantly higher than those on commercial loans (see Figure 10–3). Note also that the level of credit card charge offs rose sharply during the financial crisis (to over 13 percent), which is significantly higher than that seen on commercial loan charge offs (which peaked at 8.7 percent). Such relatively high default rates again point to the importance of risk evaluation prior to the credit decision.

In Table 10–7 we show indicative interest rates on car (5.07 percent), personal (10.88 percent), and credit card (12.34 percent) loans as of February 2012. These rates differ widely depending on features such as collateral backing, maturity, default rate experience, and non–interest rate fees. In addition, competitive conditions in each market as well as regulations such as national-, state-, or city-imposed **usury ceilings** (maximum rates FIs can charge on consumer and mortgage debt) all affect the rate structure for consumer loans. For example, in 2012 federally chartered credit unions were prohibited from charging more than 18 percent on any loan.

**usury ceilings**
National-, state-, or city-imposed ceilings on the maximum rate FIs can charge on consumer and mortgage debt.

**TABLE 10–7**
**Interest Rate Terms on Consumer Loans**

Source: Federal Reserve Board website, Consumer Credit, June 2012. *www.federalreserve.gov*

|  | Percent |
| --- | --- |
| 48-month car loan | 5.07% |
| 24-month personal loan | 10.88 |
| Credit card | 12.34 |

### Other Loans

The "other loans" category can include a wide variety of borrowers and types, including farmers, other banks, nonbank financial institutions such as broker margin loans (loans financing a percentage of an individual investment portfolio), state and local governments, foreign banks, and sovereign governments. We discuss sovereign loans in Chapter 14.

---

**Concept Questions**

1. What are the four major types of loans made by U.S. commercial banks? What are the basic distinguishing characteristics of each type of loan?
2. Will more ARMs be originated in high- or low-interest-rate environments? Explain your answer.
3. In Table 10–7, explain why credit card loan rates are much higher than car loan rates.

---

## CALCULATING THE RETURN ON A LOAN

An important element in the credit management process, once the decision to make a loan has been made, is its pricing. This includes adjustments for the perceived credit risk or default risk of the borrower as well as any fees and collateral backing the loan.[7] This section demonstrates one method used to calculate the return on a loan: the traditional *return on assets approach*. Although we demonstrate the return calculations using examples of commercial and industrial loans, the techniques can be used to calculate the return on other loans (such as credit card or mortgage loans) as well.

### The Contractually Promised Return on a Loan

The previous description of loans makes it clear that a number of factors impact the promised return an FI achieves on any given dollar loan (asset) amount. These factors include the following:

1. The interest rate on the loan.
2. Any fees relating to the loan.
3. The credit risk premium on the loan.
4. The collateral backing of the loan.
5. Other nonprice terms (especially compensating balances and reserve requirements).

First, let us consider an example of how to calculate the promised return on a C&I loan. Suppose that an FI makes a spot one-year, $1 million loan. The loan rate is set as follows:

$$\text{Base lending rate } (BR) = 12\%$$
$$+\text{Credit risk premium or margin}\,(\phi) = \underline{\phantom{xx}2\%}$$
$$BR + \phi = 14\%$$

---

[7] FIs have developed relationship pricing programs, which offer discounts on interest rates for customers based on the total amount of fee-based services used and investments held at the FI. Relationship pricing is in contrast to (the more traditional) transaction pricing, in which customers pay a stated rate for a service regardless of the total amount of other (nonloan) business conducted with the FI.

The base lending rate (*BR*) could reflect the FI's weighted-average cost of capital or its marginal cost of funds, such as the commercial paper rate, the federal funds rate, or **LIBOR**—the London Interbank Offered Rate, which is the rate for interbank dollar loans of a given maturity in the Eurodollar market. The center of the Eurodollar market is London. Initially, most variable-rate business loans were tied to the U.S. fed funds rate. However, the tremendous growth of the Eurodollar market has resulted in the LIBOR becoming the standard rate by which these loan rates are now priced. For example, the commercial paper market in the United States now quotes rates as a spread over the LIBOR rate rather than over the Treasury bill rate. Higher LIBOR rates result in higher borrowing costs for businesses while lower rates can make FIs hesitant to lend. In addition to business loans, some bonds and interest rate swaps also use LIBOR as their benchmark. The After the Crisis box looks at allegations that several large banks tried to manipulate the LIBOR rate during the financial crisis. Because of the extensive use of LIBOR as a base rate on business loans, and even mortgages and credit card rates, even a small bit of manipulation can cause massive redistribution of resources. In addition to the Canadian government, the U.S. Justice Department as well as officials in Switzerland and the United Kingdom are involved in the investigation. As stated in the box, in June 2012, the British bank Barclays agreed to pay $453 million to U.S. and British authorities to settle allegations that it manipulated the LIBOR. The Barclays settlement put increasing pressure on other banks to cooperate in the probe that could cost the financial industry billions of dollars and brought to question the use of LIBOR as the benchmark loan rate.

Alternatively, the base lending rate could reflect the **prime lending rate.** The prime rate is most commonly used in pricing longer-term loans, while the fed funds rate and LIBOR rate are most commonly used in pricing short-term loans. Traditionally, the prime rate has been the rate charged to the FI's lowest-risk customers. Now, it is more of a base rate to which positive or negative risk premiums ($\phi$) can be added. In other words, the best and largest borrowers now commonly pay below prime rate to be competitive with the commercial paper market.

Direct and indirect fees and charges relating to a loan generally fall into three categories:

1. A loan origination fee (*of*) charged to the borrower for processing the application.
2. A compensating balance requirement (*b*) to be held as (generally non-interest-bearing demand) deposits. **Compensating balances** are a percentage of a loan that a borrower cannot actively use for expenditures. Instead, these balances must be kept on deposit at the FI. For example, a borrower facing a 10 percent compensating balance requirement on a $100 loan would have to place $10 on deposit (traditionally on demand deposit) with the FI and could use only $90 of the $100 borrowed. This requirement raises the effective cost of loans for the borrower since less than the full loan amount ($90 in this case) can actually be used by the borrower and the deposit rate earned on compensating balances is less than the borrowing rate. Thus, compensating balance requirements act as an additional source of return on lending for an FI.[8]
3. A reserve requirement (*RR*) imposed by the Federal Reserve on the FI's (specifically depository institution's) demand deposits, including any compensating balances.

---

**LIBOR**
The London Interbank Offered Rate, which is the rate for interbank dollar loans of a given maturity in the offshore or Eurodollar market.

**prime lending rate**
The base lending rate periodically set by banks.

**compensating balance**
A percentage of a loan that a borrower is required to hold on deposit at the lending institution.

---

[8] They also create a more stable supply of deposits and thus mitigate liquidity problems. Further, compensating balances are sometimes used as an offset to fees charged on the loan. That is, loans with a compensating balance requirement often have lower fees than loans without a compensating balance. In this case, the additional revenue from the compensating balances is offset by the loss in fee income.

# After the Crisis    Interest Rate Probe Escalates: Barclays Agrees to Pay Record Fine; Emails Show Traders Tried to Manipulate Libor

Barclays agreed to pay $453 million in fines after admitting that traders and executives tried to manipulate benchmark interest rates tied to loans and contracts around the world . . . A series of Wall Street Journal articles in 2008 raised questions about whether global banks were manipulating the process by low-balling a key interest rate to avoid looking desperate for cash amid the financial crisis. Emails and instant messages disclosed in the bank's settlement show how Barclays's traders tried to manipulate rates to benefit their own trading positions. "This is the way you pull off deals like this chicken," one trader told another trader in March 2007, according to the U.K. regulator. "Don't tell ANYBODY.". . .

The unusually steep punishment reflected what officials said were serious and widespread efforts by traders and senior managers at Barclays to manipulate the London Interbank Offered Rate, or Libor, and the Euro Interbank Offered Rate, or Euribor. The rates are used globally to help set the price of many types of loans, from home mortgages to commercial borrowing. The bank's $200 million fine with the Commodity Futures Trading Commission was the U.S. agency's largest penalty ever . . . Other banks that have disclosed they are under investigation include Citigroup Inc., HSBC Holdings, J.P. Morgan Chase, Lloyds Banking Group, and Royal Bank of Scotland Group PLC. None of these banks have been charged with any wrongdoing in the matter by U.S. or U.K. regulators.

The CFTC filing said the wrongful conduct at Barclays lasted at least four years and "at times occurred on an almost daily basis." In an October 2006 email quoted by the U.K. regulator, an employee at another bank told a Barclays trader to try to get the benchmark rate lower, saying: "If it comes in unchanged I'm a dead man." Hours later he offered a bottle of Bollinger as thanks for the attempted manipulation: "Dude. I owe you big time!". . .

Libor is set each day in London based on estimates submitted by a panel of banks. The banks are supposed to say how much it would cost them to borrow from each other in different currencies over different time periods. The CFTC said the rates affect "enormous volumes" of financial transactions, including $360 trillion of swaps and loans, as well as futures traded on the Chicago Mercantile Exchange with a notional value in 2011 of more than $564 trillion . . . In its filing, the CFTC alleged that a senior manager at Barclays warned the bankers' association in a phone call in 2008 that the bank hadn't been submitting accurate Libor rates.

**Source:** *The Wall Street Journal,* June 28, 2012, by Jean Eaglesham and Max Colchester. Reprinted by permission of *The Wall Street Journal.* © 2012 Dow Jones & Company, Inc. All Rights Reserved Worldwide. **www.wsj.com**

While credit risk may be the most important factor ultimately affecting the return on a loan, these other factors should not be ignored by FI managers in evaluating loan profitability and risk. Indeed, FIs can compensate for high credit risk in a number of ways other than charging a higher explicit interest rate or risk premium on a loan or restricting the amount of credit available. In particular, higher fees, high compensating balances, and increased collateral backing all offer implicit and indirect methods of compensating an FI for lending risk. The contractually promised gross return on the loan, $k$, per dollar lent—or ROA per dollar lent—equals:[9]

$$1 + k = 1 + \frac{of + (BR + \phi)}{1 - [b(1 - RR)]}$$

This formula may need some explanation. The numerator is the promised gross cash inflow to the FI per dollar lent, reflecting direct fees ($of$) plus the loan interest

[9] This formula ignores present value aspects that could easily be incorporated. For example, fees are earned in up-front undiscounted dollars while interest payments and risk premiums are normally paid on loan maturity and thus should be discounted by the FI's cost of funds.

rate $(BR + \phi)$. In the denominator, for every \$1 the FI lends, it retains $b$ as non-interest-bearing compensating balances. Thus, $1 - b$ is the net proceeds of each \$1 of loans received by the borrower from the FI, ignoring reserve requirements. However, since $b$ (the compensating balance) is held by the borrower at the FI in a demand deposit account, the Federal Reserve requires depository institutions to hold non- (or low) interest-bearing reserves at the rate $RR$ against the compensating balance. Thus, the FI's net benefit from requiring compensating balances must consider the cost of holding additional reserve requirements. The net outflow by the FI per \$1 of loans is $1 - [b(1 - RR)]$, or 1 minus the reserve adjusted compensating balance requirement.

---

**EXAMPLE 10–1**

*Calculation of ROA on a Loan*

Suppose a bank does the following:

1. Sets the loan rate on a prospective loan at 10 percent (where $BR = 6\%$ and $\phi = 4\%$).
2. Charges a 1/8 percent (or 0.125 percent) loan origination fee to the borrower.
3. Imposes a 8 percent compensating balance requirement to be held as non-interest-bearing demand deposits.
4. Sets aside reserves, at a rate of 10 percent of deposits, held at the Federal Reserve (i.e., the Fed's cash-to-deposit reserve ratio is 10 percent).

Plugging the numbers from our example into the return formula, we have:[10]

$$1 + k = 1 + \frac{0.00125 + (0.06 + 0.04)}{1 - [(0.08)(0.9)]}$$

$$1 + k = 1 + \frac{0.10125}{0.928}$$

$$1 + k = 1.1091 \text{ or } k = 10.91\%$$

This is, of course, greater than the simple promised interest return on the loan, $BR + \phi = 10\%$.

---

In the special case where fees $(of)$ are zero and the compensating balance $(b)$ is zero:

$$of = 0$$
$$b = 0$$

the contractually promised return formula reduces to:

$$1 + k = 1 + (BR + \phi)$$

That is, the credit risk premium or margin $(\phi)$ is the fundamental factor driving the promised return on a loan once the base rate on the loan is set.

Note that as commercial lending markets have become more competitive, both origination fees $(of)$ and compensating balances $(b)$ are becoming less important. For example, where compensating balances are still charged, the FI may now allow them to be held as time deposits, and they earn interest. As a result, borrowers' opportunity losses from compensating balances have been reduced to

---

[10] If we take into account the present value effects on the fees and the interest payments and assume that the bank's discount rate $(d)$ was 10.5 percent, then the $BR + \phi$ term needs to be discounted by $1 + d = 1.105$, while fees (as up-front payments) are undiscounted. In this case, $k$ is 9.89 percent.

the difference between the loan rate and the compensating balance time-deposit rate.[11] Further, compensating balance requirements are very rare on international loans such as Eurodollar loans. Finally, note that for a given promised gross return on a loan, $k$, FI managers can use the pricing formula to find various combinations of fees, compensating balances, and risk premiums they may offer their customers that generate the same returns.

## The Expected Return on a Loan

**default risk**
The risk that the borrower is unable or unwilling to fulfill the terms promised under the loan contract.

The promised return on the loan $(1 + k)$ that the borrower and lender contractually agree on includes both the loan interest rate and non–interest rate features such as fees. The promised return on the loan, however, may well differ from the expected and, indeed, actual return on a loan because of default risk. **Default risk** is the risk that the borrower is unable or unwilling to fulfill the terms promised under the loan contract. Default risk is usually present to some degree in all loans. Thus, at the time the loan is made, the expected return $[E(r)]$ per dollar lent is related to the promised return as follows:

$$1 + E(r) = p(1 + k) + (1 - p)0$$

where $p$ is the probability of complete repayment of the loan (such that the FI receives the principal and interest as promised) and $(1 - p)$ is the probability of default (in which the FI receives nothing, i.e., 0). Rearranging this equation, we get:

$$E(r) = p(1 + k) - 1$$

To the extent that $p$ is less than 1, default risk is present. This means the FI manager must (1) set the risk premium $(\phi)$ sufficiently high to compensate for this risk and (2) recognize that setting high risk premiums as well as high fees and base rates may actually reduce the probability of repayment $(p)$. That is, $k$ and $p$ are not independent. Indeed, over some range, as fees and loan rates increase, the probability that the borrower pays the promised return may decrease (i.e., $k$ and $p$ may be negatively related). As a result, FIs usually have to control for credit risk along two dimensions: the price or promised return dimension $(1 + k)$ and the quantity or credit availability dimension. Further, even after adjusting the loan rate for the default risk of the borrower (by increasing the risk premium on the loan), there is no guarantee that the FI will actually receive the promised payments. The measurement and pricing approaches discussed in the chapter consider credit risk based on probabilities of receiving promised payments on the loan. The actual payment or default on a loan once it is issued may vary from the probability expected.

In general, compared with wholesale (e.g., C&I) loans, the quantity dimension controls credit risk differences on retail (e.g., consumer) loans more than the price dimension does. We discuss the reasons for this in the next section. That is followed by a section that evaluates various ways FI managers can assess the appropriate size of $\phi$, the risk premium on a loan. This is the key to pricing wholesale loan and debt risk exposures correctly.

---

[11] If compensating balances held as deposits paid interest at 2 percent ($r_d$ = 2%), then the numerator (cash flow) of the bank in the example would be reduced by $b \times r_d$, where $r_d$ = 0.02 and $b$ = 0.08. In this case, the $k$ = 10.74 percent. This assumes that the reserve requirement on compensating balances held as time deposits ($RR$) is 10 percent. However, while currently reserve requirements on demand deposits are 10 percent, the reserve requirement on time deposits is 0 percent (zero). Recalculating but assuming $RR$ = 0 and interest of 2 percent on compensating balances, we find $k$ = 10.83 percent.

| **Concept Questions** | 1. Calculate the promised return ($k$) on a loan if the base rate is 13 percent, the risk premium is 2 percent, the compensating balance requirement is 5 percent, fees are ½ percent, and reserve requirements are 10 percent. (16.23%) |
|---|---|
|  | 2. What is the expected return on this loan if the probability of default is 5 percent? (10.42%) |

# RETAIL VERSUS WHOLESALE CREDIT DECISIONS

## Retail

Because of the small dollar size of the loans in the context of an FI's overall asset portfolio and the higher costs of collecting information on household borrowers (consumer loans), most loan decisions made at the retail level tend to be accept or reject decisions. Regardless of their credit risk, borrowers who are accepted are often charged the same rate of interest and by implication the same credit risk premium. For example, a wealthy individual borrowing from a credit union to finance the purchase of a Rolls-Royce is likely to be charged the same auto loan rate as a less wealthy individual borrowing from that credit union to finance the purchase of a Honda. In the terminology of finance, retail customers (consumer loans) are more likely to be sorted or rationed by loan quantity restrictions than by price or interest rate differences.[12] That is, at the retail level an FI controls its credit risks by **credit rationing** rather than by using a range of interest rates or prices. Thus, the FI may offer the wealthy individual a loan of up to $80,000, while the same FI may offer the less wealthy individual a loan of up to $20,000, both at the same interest rate. Residential mortgage loans provide another good example. While two borrowers may be accepted for mortgage loans, an FI discriminates between them according to the loan-to-value ratio—the amount the FI is willing to lend relative to the market value of the house being acquired—rather than by setting different mortgage rates.

**credit rationing**
Restricting the quantity of loans made available to individual borrowers.

## Wholesale

In contrast to the retail level, at the wholesale (C&I) level FIs use both interest rates and credit quantity to control credit risk. Thus, when FIs quote a prime lending rate ($BR$) to C&I borrowers, lower-risk borrowers may be charged a lending rate below the prime lending rate (i.e., $\phi < 0$). Higher-risk borrowers are charged a markup on the prime rate, or a credit (default) risk premium (i.e., $\phi > 0$), to compensate the FI for the additional credit risk involved.

As long as they are compensated with sufficiently high interest rates (or credit risk premiums), over some range of credit demand, FIs may be willing to lend funds to high-risk wholesale borrowers. However, as discussed earlier, increasing loan interest rates ($k$) may decrease the probability ($p$) that a borrower will pay the promised return. For example, a borrower who is charged 15 percent for a loan—a prime rate of 6 percent plus a credit risk premium of 9 percent—may be able to make the promised payments on the loan only by using the funds to invest in high-risk investments with some small chance of a big payoff. However,

---

[12] This does not mean that rates cannot vary across FIs. For example, finance companies associated with car manufacturers (e.g., GMAC) offered 0.0 percent financing on car loans for much of the 2000s. Unrecognized by many car buyers, the lenders' costs of funds were incorporated into an increased price for the car. Depository institutions, not able to recover their costs of funds in this manner, offered varying rates in an attempt to compete with finance companies. However, for a given FI, the rate offered on car loans would be the same for all borrowers.

by definition, high-risk projects have relatively high probabilities that they will *fail* to realize the big payoff. If the big payoff does not materialize, the borrower may have to default on the loan. In an extreme case, the FI receives neither the promised interest and fees on the loan nor the original principal lent. This suggests that very high contractual interest rate charges on loans may actually reduce an FI's expected return on loans because high interest rates induce the borrower to invest in risky projects.[13] Alternatively, only borrowers that intend to use the borrowed funds to invest in high-risk projects (high-risk borrowers) may be interested in borrowing from FIs at high interest rates. Low-risk borrowers drop out of the potential borrowing pool at high-rate levels. This lowers the average quality of the pool of potential borrowers. We show these effects in Figure 10–4.

At very low contractually promised interest rates ($k$), borrowers do not need to take high risks in their use of funds and those with relatively safe investment projects use FI financing. As interest rates increase, borrowers with fairly low-risk, low-return projects no longer think it is profitable to borrow from FIs and drop out of the pool of potential borrowers. Alternatively, borrowers may switch their use of the borrowed funds to high-risk investment projects to have a (small) chance of being able to pay off the loan. In terms of Figure 10–4, when interest rates rise above $k^*$ (8 percent), the additional expected return earned by the FI through higher contractually promised interest rates ($k$) is increasingly offset by a lower probability of repayment on the loan ($p$). In other words, because of the potential increase in the probability of default when contractually promised loan rates are high, an FI charging wholesale borrowers loan rates in the 9 to 14 percent region can earn a *lower* expected return than will an FI charging 8 percent.

This relationship between contractually promised interest rates and the expected returns on loans suggests that beyond some interest rate level, it may be best for the FI to *credit ration* its wholesale loans, that is, to not make loans or to

**FIGURE 10–4**

Relationship between the Promised Loan Rate and the Expected Return on the Loan

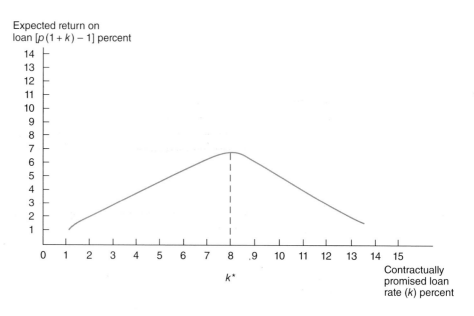

[13] In the context of the previous section, a high $k$ on the loan reflecting a high base rate ($BR$) and risk premium ($\phi$) can lead to a lower probability of repayment ($p$) and thus a lower $E(r)$ on the loan, where $E(r) = p(1 + k) - 1$. Indeed, for very high $k$, the expected return on the loan can become negative.

make fewer loans. Rather than seeking to ration by price (by charging higher and higher risk premiums to borrowers), the FI can establish an upper ceiling on the amounts it is willing to lend to maximize its expected returns on lending. In the context of Figure 10–4, borrowers may be charged interest rates up to 8 percent, with the most risky borrowers also facing more restrictive limits or ceilings on the amounts they can borrow at any given interest rate.

| **Concept Questions** | 1. Can an FI's expected return on its loan portfolio increase if it cuts its loan rates? |
|---|---|
| | 2. What might happen to the expected return on a wholesale loan if an FI eliminates its fees and compensating balances in a low–interest rate environment? |

# MEASUREMENT OF CREDIT RISK

To calibrate the default risk exposure of credit and investment decisions as well as to assess the credit risk exposure in off-balance-sheet contractual arrangements such as loan commitments, an FI manager needs to measure the probability of borrower default. The ability to do this depends largely on the amount of information the FI has about the borrower. At the retail level, much of the information needs to be collected internally or purchased from external credit agencies. At the wholesale level, these information sources are bolstered by publicly available information, such as certified accounting statements, stock and bond prices, and analysts' reports. Thus, for a publicly traded company, more information is produced and is available to an FI than is available for a small, single-proprietor corner store. The availability of more information, along with the lower average cost of collecting such information, allows FIs to use more sophisticated and usually more quantitative methods in assessing default probabilities for large borrowers compared with small borrowers. However, advances in technology and information collection are making quantitative assessments of even smaller borrowers increasingly feasible and less costly. The simpler details (such as cash flow and ratio analysis) associated with the measurement of credit risk at the retail and the wholesale levels are discussed in Appendix 10A, located at the book's website **(www.mhhe.com/saunders8e).**

In principle, FIs can use very similar methods and models to assess the probabilities of default on both bonds and loans. Even though loans tend to involve fewer lenders to any single borrower as opposed to multiple bondholders, in essence, both loans and bonds are contracts that promise fixed (or indexed) payments at regular intervals in the future. Loans and bonds stand ahead of the borrowing firm's equity holders in terms of the priority of their claims if things go wrong. Also, bonds, like loans, include **covenants** restricting or encouraging various actions to enhance the probability of repayment. Covenants can include limits on the type and amount of new debt, investments, and asset sales the borrower may undertake while the loan or bonds are outstanding. Financial covenants are also often imposed restricting changes in the borrower's financial ratios such as its leverage ratio or current ratio. For example, a common restrictive covenant included in many bond and loan contracts limits the amount of dividends a firm can pay to its equity holders. Clearly, for any given cash flow, a high dividend payout to stockholders means that less is available for repayments to bondholders and lenders. Moreover, bond yields, like wholesale loan rates, usually reflect risk premiums that vary with the perceived

**covenants**
Restrictions written into bond and loan contracts either limiting or encouraging the borrower's actions that affect the probability of repayment.

credit quality of the borrower and the collateral or security backing of the debt. Given this, FIs can use many of the following models that analyze default risk probabilities either in making lending decisions or when considering investing in corporate bonds offered either publicly or privately.

| Concept Questions | 1. Is it more costly for an FI manager to assess the default risk exposure of a publicly traded company or a small, single-proprietor firm? Explain your answer. |
|---|---|
| | 2. How do loan covenants help protect an FI against default risk? |

# DEFAULT RISK MODELS

Economists, analysts, and FI managers have employed many different models to assess the default risk on loans and bonds. These vary from relatively qualitative to the highly quantitative models. Further, these models are not mutually exclusive; an FI manager may use more than one model to reach a credit pricing or loan quantity rationing decision. As will be discussed below in more detail, a great deal of time and effort has recently been expended by FIs in building highly technical credit risk evaluation models. Many of these models use ideas and techniques similar to the market risk models discussed in Chapter 15. We analyze a number of models in two broad groups: qualitative models and quantitative models.

## Qualitative Models

In the absence of publicly available information on the quality of borrowers, the FI manager has to assemble information from private sources—such as credit and deposit files—and/or purchase such information from external sources—such as credit rating agencies. This information helps a manager make an informed judgment on the probability of default of the borrower and price the loan or debt correctly.

In general, the amount of information assembled varies with the size of the potential debt exposure and the costs of collection. However, a number of key factors enter into the credit decision. These include (1) *borrower-specific* factors, which are idiosyncratic to the individual borrower, and (2) *market-specific* factors, which have an impact on all borrowers at the time of the credit decision. The FI manager then weights these factors subjectively to come to an overall credit decision. Because of their reliance on the subjective judgment of the FI manager, these models are often called expert systems. Commonly used borrower-specific and market-specific factors are discussed next.

### Borrower-Specific Factors

*Reputation* The borrower's reputation involves the borrowing–lending history of the credit applicant. If, over time, the borrower has established a reputation for prompt and timely repayment, this enhances the applicant's attractiveness to the FI. A long-term customer relationship between a borrower and lender forms an **implicit contract** regarding borrowing and repayment that extends beyond the formal explicit legal contract on which borrower–lender relationships are based. The importance of reputation, which can be established only over time through repayment and observed behavior, works to the disadvantage of small, newer borrowers. This is one of the reasons initial public offerings of debt securities by small firms often require higher yields than do offerings of older, more seasoned firms.

**implicit contract**
Long-term customer relationship between a borrower and lender based on reputation.

**leverage**
The ratio of a borrower's debt to equity.

*Leverage*   A borrower's **leverage** or capital structure—the ratio of debt to equity—affects the probability of its default because large amounts of debt, such as bonds and loans, increase the borrower's interest charges and pose a significant claim on its cash flows. As shown in Figure 10–5, relatively low debt–equity ratios may not significantly impact the probability of debt repayment. Yet beyond some point, the risk of bankruptcy increases, as does the probability of some loss of interest or principal for the lender. Thus, highly leveraged firms may find it necessary to pay higher risk premiums on their borrowings if they are not rationed in the first place.

*Volatility of Earnings*   As with leverage, a highly volatile earnings stream increases the probability that the borrower cannot meet fixed interest and principal charges for any given capital structure. Consequently, newer firms or firms in high-tech industries with a high earnings variance over time are less attractive credit risks than are those with long and more stable earnings histories.

*Collateral*   As discussed earlier, a key feature in any lending and loan-pricing decision is the degree of collateral, or assets backing the security of the loan. Many loans and bonds are backed by specific assets should a borrower default on repayment obligations. Mortgage bonds give the bondholder first claim to some specific piece of property of the borrower, normally machinery or buildings; debentures give a bondholder a more general and more risky claim to the borrower's assets. Subordinated debentures are even riskier because their claims to the assets of a defaulting borrower are junior to those of both mortgage bondholders and debenture bondholders. Similarly, loans can be either secured (collateralized) or unsecured (uncollateralized).[14]

### Market-Specific Factors

*The Business Cycle*   The position of the economy in the business cycle phase is enormously important to an FI in assessing the probability of borrower default. For example, during recessions, firms in the consumer durable goods sector that produce autos, refrigerators, or houses do badly compared with those in the nondurable goods sector producing clothing and foods. People cut back on luxuries

**FIGURE 10–5**
Relationship between the Cost of Debt, the Probability of Default, and Leverage

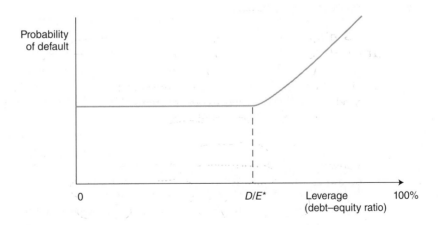

[14] However, collateralized loans are still subject to some default risk unless these loans are significantly overcollateralized; that is, assets are pledged with market values exceeding the face value of the debt instrument. There is also some controversy as to whether posting collateral signifies a high- or low-risk borrower. Arguably, the best borrowers do not need to post collateral since they are good credit risks, whereas only more risky borrowers need to post collateral. That is, posting collateral may be a signal of more rather than less credit risk.

during a recession, but are less likely to cut back on necessities such as food. Thus, corporate borrowers in the consumer durable goods sector of the economy are especially prone to default risk. Because of cyclical concerns, FIs are more likely to increase the relative degree of credit rationing in recessionary phases. This has especially adverse consequences for smaller borrowers with limited or no access to alternative credit markets such as the commercial paper market.

*The Level of Interest Rates*   High interest rates indicate restrictive monetary policy actions by the Federal Reserve. FIs not only find funds to finance their lending decisions scarcer and more expensive, but also must recognize that high interest rates are correlated with higher credit risk in general. As discussed earlier, high interest rate levels may encourage borrowers to take excessive risks and/or encourage only the most risky customers to borrow.

www.federalreserve.gov

So far, we have delineated just a few of the qualitative borrower- and economy-specific factors an FI manager may take into account in deciding on the probability of default on any loan or bond.[15] Rather than letting such factors enter into the decision process in a purely subjective fashion, the FI manager may weight these factors in a more objective or quantitative manner. We discuss quantitative models used to measure credit risk next. One frequently used source of much of this information is the Risk Management Association (RMA). RMA has become a standard reference for thousands of commercial lenders by providing average balance sheet and income data for more than 400 industries, common ratios computed for each size group and industry, five-year trend data, and financial statement data for more than 100,000 commercial borrowers.

www.rmahq.org

| **Concept Questions** | 1. Make a list of key borrower characteristics you would assess before making a mortgage loan. |
| | 2. How should the risk premium on a loan be affected if there is a reduction in a borrower's leverage? |

## Quantitative Models

### *Credit Scoring Models*

**credit scoring models**

Mathematical models that use observed loan applicant's characteristics either to calculate a score representing the applicant's probability of default or to sort borrowers into different default risk classes.

**Credit scoring models** are quantitative models that use observed borrower characteristics either to calculate a score representing the applicant's probability of default or to sort borrowers into different default risk classes. By selecting and combining different economic and financial borrower characteristics, an FI manager may be able to:

1. Numerically establish which factors are important in explaining default risk.
2. Evaluate the relative degree or importance of these factors.
3. Improve the pricing of default risk.
4. Be better able to screen out bad loan applicants.
5. Be in a better position to calculate any reserves needed to meet expected future loan losses.

The primary benefit from credit scoring is that credit lenders can more accurately predict a borrower's performance without having to use more resources.

---

[15] More generally, five Cs of credit that should be included in any subjective (qualitative) credit analysis include character (willingness to pay), capacity (cash flow), capital (wealth), collateral (security), and conditions (economic conditions). See Appendix 10A, located at the book's website (**www.mhhe.com/saunders8e**).

Using these models means fewer defaults and write-offs for lenders. Indeed, many FIs are implementing credit scoring models as a way to come in accordance with the Sarbanes–Oxley Act of 2002, which sets guidelines for corporate governance in several areas, including risk management and control assessment.

To use credit scoring models, the manager must identify objective economic and financial measures of risk for any particular class of borrower. For consumer debt, the objective characteristics in a credit scoring model might include income, assets, age, occupation, and location. For commercial debt, cash flow information and financial ratios such as the debt–equity ratio are usually key factors. After data are identified, a statistical technique quantifies, or scores, the default risk probability or default risk classification.

Credit scoring models include these three broad types: (1) linear probability models, (2) logit models, and (3) linear discriminant analysis. Appendix 10A to the chapter (located at the book's website, **www.mhhe.com/saunders8e**) looks at credit scoring models used to evaluate mortgages and consumer loans. In this section we look at credit scoring models used to evaluate commercial loans.

*Linear Probability Model and Logit Model*   The linear probability model uses past data, such as financial ratios, as inputs into a model to explain repayment experience on old loans. The relative importance of the factors used in explaining past repayment performance then forecasts repayment probabilities on new loans. That is, factors explaining past repayment performance can be used for assessing $p$, the probability of repayment discussed earlier in this chapter (a key input in setting the credit premium on a loan or determining the amount to be lent) and the probability of default (PD).

Briefly, we divide old loans into two observational groups: those that defaulted $(PD_i = 1)$ and those that did not default $(PD_i = 0)$. Then we relate these observations by linear regression to a set of $j$ causal variables $(X_{ij})$ that reflect quantitative information about the $i$th borrower, such as leverage or earnings. We estimate the model by linear regression of this form:

$$PD_i = \sum_{j=1}^{n} \beta_j X_{ij} + \text{error}$$

where $\beta_j$ is the estimated importance of the $j$th variable (e.g., leverage) in explaining past repayment experience.

If we then take these estimated $\beta_j$s and multiply them by the observed $X_{ij}$ for a prospective borrower, we can derive an expected value of $PD_i$ for the prospective borrower. That value can be interpreted as the probability of default for the borrower: $E(PD_i) = (1 - p_i) =$ expected probability of default, where $p_i$ is the probability of repayment on the loan.

| **EXAMPLE 10–2** *Estimating the Probability of Repayment on a Loan Using Linear Probability Credit Scoring Models* | Suppose there were two factors influencing the past default behavior of borrowers: the leverage or debt–equity ratio (D/E) and the sales–asset ratio (S/A). Based on past default (repayment) experience, the linear probability model is estimated as:<br><br>$$PD_i = 0.5(D/E_i) - 0.0525(S/A_i)$$<br><br>Assume a prospective borrower has a D/E = 0.3 and an S/A = 2.0. Its expected probability of default (PD_i) can then be estimated as:<br><br>$$PD_i = 0.5(0.3) - 0.0525(2.0) = 0.045 \text{ or } 4.5\%$$ |

While this technique is straightforward as long as current information on the $X_{ij}$ is available for the borrower, its major weakness is that the estimated probabilities of default can often lie outside the interval 0 to 1. The logit model overcomes this weakness by restricting the estimated range of default probabilities from the linear regression model to lie between 0 and 1. Essentially this is done by plugging the estimated value of $PD_i$ from the linear probability model (in our example, $PD_i = 0.045$) into the following formula:

$$F(PD_i) = \frac{1}{1 + e^{-PD_i}}$$

where $e$ is exponential (equal to 2.718) and $F(PD_i)$ is the logistically transformed value of $PD_i$.

*Linear Discriminant Models* While linear probability and logit models project a value for the expected probability of default if a loan is made, discriminant models divide borrowers into high or low default risk classes contingent on their observed characteristics ($X_j$). Similar to linear probability models, linear discriminant models use past data as inputs into a model to explain repayment experience on old loans. The relative importance of the factors used in explaining past repayment performance then forecasts whether the loan falls into the high or low default class.

Consider the discriminant analysis model developed by E. I. Altman for publicly traded manufacturing firms in the United States. The indicator variable $Z$ is an overall measure of the default risk classification of a commercial borrower.[16] This in turn depends on the values of various financial ratios of the borrower ($X_j$) and the weighted importance of these ratios based on the past observed experience of defaulting versus nondefaulting borrowers derived from a discriminant analysis model.[17]

Altman's discriminant function (credit-classification model) takes the form:

$$Z = 1.2X_1 + 1.4X_2 + 3.3X_3 + 0.6X_4 + 1.0X_5$$

where

$X_1 =$ Working capital[18]/total assets ratio
$X_2 =$ Retained earnings/total assets ratio
$X_3 =$ Earnings before interest and taxes/total assets ratio
$X_4 =$ Market value of equity/book value of long-term debt ratio
$X_5 =$ Sales/total assets ratio

According to Altman's credit scoring model, any firm with a Z score of less than 1.81 should be considered a high default risk firm; between 1.81 and 2.99, an indeterminant default risk firm; and greater than 2.99, a low default risk firm.

[16] The Z score is a default indicator and is not a direct probability of default (PD) measure.
[17] E. I. Altman, "Managing the Commercial Lending Process," in *Handbook of Banking Strategy,* eds. R. C. Aspinwall and R. A. Eisenbeis (New York: John Wiley & Sons, 1985), pp. 473–510.
[18] Working capital is current assets minus current liabilities.

**EXAMPLE 10–3**

*Calculation of Altman's Z Score*

Suppose that the financial ratios of a potential borrowing firm take the following values:

$X_1 = 0.2$

$X_2 = 0$

$X_3 = -0.20$

$X_4 = 0.10$

$X_5 = 2.0$

The ratio $X_2$ is zero and $X_3$ is negative, indicating that the firm has had negative earnings or losses in recent periods. Also, $X_4$ indicates that the borrower is highly leveraged. However, the working capital ratio ($X_1$) and the sales/assets ratio ($X_5$) indicate that the firm is reasonably liquid and is maintaining its sales volume. The Z score provides an overall score or indicator of the borrower's credit risk since it combines and weights these five factors according to their past importance in explaining borrower default. For the borrower in question:

$$Z = 1.2(0.2) + 1.4(0) + 3.3(-0.20) + 0.6(0.10) + 1.0(2.0)$$
$$= 0.24 + 0 - 0.66 + 0.06 + 2.0$$
$$= 1.64$$

With a Z score less than 1.81 (i.e., in the high default risk region), the FI should not make a loan to this borrower until it improves its earnings.

There are a number of problems in using the discriminant analysis model to make credit risk evaluations.[19] The first problem is that these models usually discriminate only between two extreme cases of borrower behavior: no default and default. As discussed in Chapter 7, in the real world various gradations of default exist, from nonpayment or delay of interest payments (nonperforming assets) to outright default on all promised interest and principal payments. This problem suggests that a more accurate or finely calibrated sorting among borrowers may require defining more classes in the discriminant analysis model.

The second problem is that there is no obvious economic reason to expect that the weights in the discriminant function—or, more generally, the weights in any credit scoring model—will be constant over any but very short periods. The same concern also applies to the variables ($X_j$). Specifically, because of changing real and financial market conditions, other borrower-specific financial ratios may come to be increasingly relevant in explaining default risk probabilities. Moreover, the linear discriminant model assumes that the $X_j$ variables are independent of one another.

The third problem is that these models ignore important, hard-to-quantify factors that may play a crucial role in the default or no default decision. For example, reputation of the borrower and the nature of long-term borrower–lender relationship could be important borrower-specific characteristics, as could macrofactors such as the phase of the business cycle. These variables are often ignored in credit scoring models. Moreover, traditional credit scoring models rarely use publicly available information, such as the prices of outstanding public debt and equity of the borrower.

A fourth problem relates to default records kept by FIs. Currently, no centralized database on defaulted business loans for proprietary and other reasons exists.

---

[19] Most of these criticisms also apply to the linear probability and logit models.

Some task forces set up by consortiums of commercial banks, insurance companies, and consulting firms are currently seeking to construct such databases largely in response to reforms to bank capital requirements (see Chapter 20). However, it may well be many years before they are developed. This constrains the ability of many FIs to use traditional credit scoring models (and quantitative models in general) for larger business loans—although their use for smaller consumer loans, such as credit card loans, where much better centralized databases exist, is well established.

| **Concept Questions** | 1. Suppose an estimated linear probability model looked as follows: $Z = 0.03X_1 + 0.01X_2 + $ error, where |
|---|---|
| | $X_1$ = Debt − equity ratio $\qquad$ $X_2$ = Total assets − Working capital ratio |
| | Suppose, for a prospective borrower, $X_1 = 1.5$ and $X_2 = 3.0$. What is the projected probability of default for the borrower? (7.5%) |
| | 2. Suppose $X_3 = 0.5$ in Example 10−3. Show how this would change the default risk classification of the borrower. ($Z = 3.95$) |
| | 3. What are two problems in using discriminant analysis to evaluate credit risk? |

Newer credit risk models use *financial theory* and more widely available *financial market* data to make inferences about default probabilities on debt and loan instruments. Consequently, these models are most relevant in evaluating loans to larger borrowers in the corporate sector. This is the area in which a great deal of current research is taking place by FIs, as noted in Appendixes 11A and 11B. We next consider a number of these newer approaches or models of credit risk, including:

1. Term structure of credit risk approach (also called reduced-form models).
2. Mortality rate approach.
3. RAROC models.
4. Option models (also called structural models since they are based on an economic model of why firms default).

While some of these models focus on different aspects of credit risk, they are all linked by a strong reliance on modern financial theory and financial market data.[20]

## Newer Models of Credit Risk Measurement and Pricing
### Term Structure Derivation of Credit Risk

One market-based method of assessing credit risk exposure and default probabilities is to analyze the risk premiums inherent in the current structure of yields on corporate debt or loans to similar risk-rated borrowers. Rating agencies such as Standard & Poor's (S&P) categorize corporate bond issuers into at

www.standardandpoors.com

---

[20] For further details on these newer models, see A. Saunders and L. Allen, *Credit Risk Management: In and Out of the Financial Crisis,* 3rd ed. (New York: John Wiley and Sons, 2010).

**FIGURE 10–6**
Corporate and
Treasury Discount
Bond Yield Curves

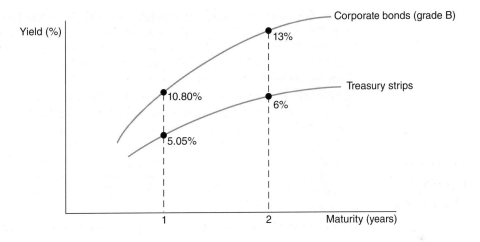

least seven major classes according to perceived credit quality.[21] The first four quality ratings—AAA, AA, A, and BBB—indicate investment-quality borrowers. The Office of the Comptroller of the Currency, which regulates national banks, restricts the ability of banks to purchase securities rated outside these classes. By comparison, insurance company regulators have permitted these FIs to purchase noninvestment-grade securities with ratings such as BB, B, and CCC, but with restrictions on the aggregate amounts they can include in their portfolios. These three classes are known as high-yield or junk bonds. Different quality ratings are reflected in the degree to which corporate bond yields exceed those implied by the Treasury (credit risk–free) yield curve.

**Treasury strips and zero-coupon corporate bonds**
Bonds that are created or issued bearing no coupons and only a face value to be paid on maturity. As such, they are issued at a large discount from face value. (Also called *deep-discount bonds*.)

Look at the spreads shown in Figure 10–6 for zero-coupon corporate (grade B) bonds over similar maturity zero-coupon Treasuries (called Treasury strips). Because **Treasury strips and zero-coupon corporate bonds** are single-payment discount bonds, it is possible to extract required credit risk premiums and implied probabilities of default from actual market data on interest rates. That is, the spreads between risk-free discount bonds issued by the Treasury and discount bonds issued by corporate borrowers of differing quality reflect perceived credit risk exposures of corporate borrowers for single payments at different times in the future. FIs can use these credit risk probabilities on existing debt to decide whether or not to issue additional debt to a particular credit risk borrower. Note that in market-based models of assessing default risk, FIs use information on credit quality processed by rating agencies rather than by the FI itself. Thus, the use of market-based models abstracts the FI's role as an information processor. Rather, the unique role played by the FI is to process market-based information to assess default probabilities.

---

[21] Rating agencies consider several factors in determining and assigning credit ratings on bond issues. For example, a financial analysis is conducted of the issuer's operations and its needs, its position in the industry, and its overall financial strength and ability to pay the required interest and principal on the bonds. Rating agencies analyze the issuer's liquidity, profitability, debt capacity, and, more recently, corporate governance structure (following the passage of the Sarbanes–Oxley Act in 2002). Then for each particular issue, rating agencies evaluate the nature and provisions of the debt issue (e.g., covenants and callability of the bond) and the protection afforded by, and relative position of, the debt issue in the event of bankruptcy, reorganization, or other arrangements under the laws of bankruptcy and other laws affecting creditors' rights.

Next, we look at the simplest case of extracting an implied probability of default for an FI considering buying one-year bonds from or making one-year loans to a risky borrower. Then, we consider multiyear loans and bonds. In each case, we show that we can extract a market view of the credit risk—the expected probability of default—of an individual borrower.

*Probability of Default on a One-Period Debt Instrument* Assume that the FI requires an expected return on a one-year (zero-coupon) corporate debt security equal to at least the risk-free return on one-year (zero-coupon) Treasury strips. Let $p$ be the probability that the corporate debt will be repaid in full; therefore, $1 - p$ is the probability of default. If the borrower defaults, the FI is (for now) assumed to get nothing (i.e., the recovery rate is zero or the loss given default is 100 percent).[22] By denoting the contractually promised return on the one-year corporate debt strip as $1 + k$ and on the credit risk–free one-year Treasury strip as $1 + i$, the FI manager would just be indifferent between corporate and Treasury securities when:[23]

$$p(1 + k) = 1 + i$$

or, the expected return on corporate securities is equal to the risk-free rate.

| | |
|---|---|
| **EXAMPLE 10–4**<br><br>*Calculating the Probability of Default on a One-Year Bond (Loan) Using Term Structure Derivation of Credit Risk* | Suppose, as shown in Figure 10–6, the interest rates in the market for one-year, zero-coupon Treasury strips and for one-year, zero-coupon grade B corporate bonds are, respectively:<br><br>$$i = 5.05\%$$<br><br>and<br><br>$$k = 10.80\%$$<br><br>This implies that the probability of repayment on the security as perceived by the market is:<br><br>$$p = \frac{1 + i}{1 + k} = \frac{1.0505}{1.1080} = 0.948$$<br><br>If the probability of repayment is 0.948, this implies a probability of default $(1 - p)$ equal to 0.052. Thus, in this simple one-period framework, a probability of default of 5.2 percent on the corporate bond (loan) requires the FI to set a risk premium $(\phi)$ of 5.75 percent.[24]<br><br>$$\phi = k - i = 5.75\%$$<br><br>Clearly, as the probability of repayment $(p)$ falls and the probability of default $(1 - p)$ increases, the required spread $\phi$ between $k$ and $i$ increases. |

[22] This is a key assumption. If the recovery rate is nonzero (which in reality is true, since in recent years banks have recovered, on average, over 80 percent of a defaulted loan and 60 percent of a senior secured bond), then the spread between the corporate bond return and the Treasury security return will reflect both the probability of default (PD) as well as the loss given default (the latter is equal to 1 minus the recovery rate). To disentangle the probability of default from the loss given default, we need to make assumptions about the size of the loss given default (LGD) or the statistical process that either the PD and/or the LGD follow, such as the Poisson process. One simple case assuming LGD is known is discussed later in this chapter.

[23] This assumes that the FI manager is not risk averse; that is, this is a risk-neutral valuation method and the probabilities so derived are called risk-neutral probabilities. In general these will differ from probabilities estimated from historic data on defaults. See Saunders and Allen, *Credit Risk Management,* chap. 5.

[24] In the real world an FI could partially capture this required spread in higher fees and compensating balances rather than only in the risk premium. In this simple example, we are assuming away compensating balances and fees. However, they could easily be built into the model.

**TABLE 10–8**
**Recovery Rates (RR) on Defaulted Debt**

Source: E. I. Altman, "Default Recovery Rates and LGD in Credit Risk Modeling and Practice," Working Paper, New York University Salomon Center, January 2012.

| Type of Debt | Recovery Rate | Number of Observations |
|---|---|---|
| Bank debt | 82.24% | 1,156 |
|    Revolving loans | 85.63 | 1,034 |
|    Term loans | 56.34 | 122 |
| Senior secured bonds | 62.00 | 320 |
| Senior unsecured bonds | 43.80 | 863 |
| Senior subordinated bonds | 30.50 | 489 |
| Subordinated bonds | 28.80 | 399 |

This analysis can easily be extended to the more realistic case in which the FI does not expect to lose all interest and all principal if the corporate borrower defaults. Realistically, the FI lender can expect to receive some partial repayment even if the borrower goes into bankruptcy. For example, Altman estimated that when firms defaulted on their bonds in 2011, the investor lost on average 63.3 cents on the dollar (i.e., recovered around 36.7 cents on the dollar).[25] Table 10–8 gives recovery rates on defaulted debt by type of debt from 1988 to 2010. As discussed earlier in this chapter, many loans and bonds are secured or collateralized by first liens on various pieces of property or real assets should a borrower default. Note that secured loans experienced the highest recovery rates among the corporate bonds listed (62.00 percent).

Let $\gamma$ be the proportion of the loan's principal and interest that is collectible on default, where in general $\gamma$ is positive. The FI manager would set the expected return on the loan to equal the risk-free rate in the following manner:

$$[(1 - p)\gamma(1 + k)] + [p(1 + k)] = 1 + i$$

The new term here is $(1 - p)\gamma(1 + k)$; this is the payoff the FI expects to get if the borrower defaults.

As might be expected, if the loan has collateral backing such that $\gamma > 0$, the required risk premium on the loan will be less for any given default risk probability $(1 - p)$. Collateral requirements are a method of controlling default risk. They act as a direct substitute for risk premiums in setting required loan rates. To see this, solve for the risk premium $\phi$ between $k$ (the required yield on risky corporate debt) and $i$ (the risk-free rate of interest):

$$k - i = \phi = \frac{(1 + i)}{(\gamma + p - p\gamma)} - (1 + i)$$

If $i = 5.05$ percent and $p = 0.948$ as before but the FI can expect to collect 90 percent of the promised proceeds if default occurs ($\gamma = 0.9$), then the required risk premium $\phi = 0.55$ percent.

Interestingly, in this simple framework, $\gamma$ and $p$ are perfect substitutes for each other. That is, a bond or loan with collateral backing of $\gamma = 0.95$ and $p = 0.9$ would have the same required risk premium as one with $\gamma = 0.9$ and $p = 0.95$. An increase in collateral $\gamma$ is a direct substitute for an increase in default risk (i.e., a decline in $p$).

[25] E. I. Altman, "Current Conditions and Outlook on Global Sovereign and Corporate Credit Markets," Working Paper, New York University Salomon Center, February 2012.

**marginal default probability**
The probability that a borrower will default in any given year.

*Probability of Default on a Multiperiod Debt Instrument* We can extend this type of analysis to derive the credit risk or default probabilities occurring in the market for longer-term loans or bonds (i.e., two-year bonds). To do this, the manager must estimate the probability that the bond will default in the second year conditional on the probability that it does not default in the first year. The probability that a bond will default in any given year is clearly conditional on the fact that the default has not occurred earlier. The probability that a bond will default in any given year, $t$, is the **marginal default probability** for that year, $1 - p_t$. However, for, say, a two-year loan, the marginal probability of default in the second year $(1 - p_2)$ can differ from the marginal probability of default in the first year $(1 - p_1)$. If we use these marginal default probabilities, the **cumulative default probability** at some time between now and the end of year 2 is:

**cumulative default probability**
The probability that a borrower will default over a specified multiyear period.

$$Cp = 1 - [(p_1)(p_2)]$$

---

**EXAMPLE 10–5**
*Calculating the Probability of Default on a Multiperiod Bond*

Suppose the FI manager wants to find out the probability of default on a two-year loan. For the one-year loan, $1 - p_1 = 0.05$ is the marginal and total or cumulative probability ($Cp$) of default in year 1. Later in this chapter we discuss ways in which $p_2$ can be estimated by the FI manager, but for the moment suppose that $1 - p_2 = 0.07$. Then:

$$1 - p_1 = .05 = \text{marginal probability of default in year 1}$$
$$1 - p_2 = .07 = \text{marginal probability of default in year 2}$$

The probability of the borrower surviving—not defaulting at any time between now (time 0) and the end of period 2—is $p_1 \times p_2 = (0.95)(0.93) = 0.8835$.

$$Cp = 1 - [(0.95)(0.93)] = 0.1165$$

There is an 11.65 percent probability of default over this period.

---

**no arbitrage**
The inability to make a profit without taking risk.

**forward rate**
A one-period rate of interest expected on a bond issued at some date in the future.

We have seen how to derive the one-year probability of default from yield spreads on one-year bonds. We now want to derive the probability of default in year 2, year 3, and so on. Look at Figure 10–6; as you can see, yield curves are rising for both Treasury issues and corporate bond issues. We want to extract from these yield curves the *market's expectation* of the multiperiod default rates for corporate borrowers classified in the grade B rating class.[26]

Look first at the Treasury yield curve. The condition of efficient markets and thus **no arbitrage** profits by investors requires that the return on buying and holding the two-year Treasury strip (T-strip) to maturity just equals the expected return from investing in the current one-year discount T-strip and reinvesting the principal and interest in a new one-year discount T-strip at the end of the first year at the expected one-year **forward rate.** That is:

$$(1 + i_2)^2 = (1 + i_1)(1 + f_1) \tag{1}$$

---

[26] To use this model, one has to place borrowers in a rating class. One way to do this for unrated firms would be to use the $Z$ score model to calculate a $Z$ ratio for this firm. E. I. Altman has shown that there is a high correlation between $Z$ scores and Standard & Poor's and Moody's bond ratings. Once a firm is placed in a bond rating group (e.g., B) by the $Z$ score model, the term structure model can be used to infer the expected (implied) probabilities of default for the borrower at different times in the future.

The term on the left side is the return from holding the two-year Treasury strip to maturity. The term on the right side results from investing in two successive one-year T-strips, where $i_1$ is the current one-year T-strips rate and $f_1$ is the expected one-year T-strip rate or forward rate next year. Since we can observe directly from the T-strip yield curve the current required yields on one- and two-year Treasuries, we can directly infer the market's expectation of the one-year Treasury strip rate next period or the one-year forward rate, $f_1$:

$$1 + f_1 = \frac{(1 + i_2)^2}{(1 + i_1)} \tag{2}$$

We can use the same type of analysis with the corporate bond yield curve to infer the one-year forward rate on corporate bonds (grade B in this example). The one-year rate expected on corporate securities ($c_1$) one year into the future reflects the market's default risk expectations for this class of borrower as well as the more general time value factors also affecting $f_1$:

$$1 + c_1 = \frac{(1 + k_2)^2}{(1 + k_1)} \tag{3}$$

The expected rates on one-year bonds can generate an estimate of the expected probability of repayment on one-year corporate bonds in one year's time, or what we have called $p_2$. Since:

$$p_2(1 + c_1) = 1 + f_1$$

then:

$$p_2 = \left[\frac{1 + f_1}{1 + c_1}\right] \tag{4}$$

Thus, the expected probability of default in year 2 is:

$$1 - p_2 \tag{5}$$

In a similar fashion, the one-year rates expected in two years' time can be derived from the Treasury and corporate term structures so as to derive $p_3$, and so on.

---

**EXAMPLE 10–6**

*Calculating the Probability of Default on a Multiperiod Bond Using Term Structure Derivation of Credit Risk*

From the Treasury strip yield curve in Figure 10–6, the current required yields on one- and two-year Treasuries are $i_1 = 5.05$ percent and $i_2 = 6$ percent, respectively. If we use equation (2), the one-year forward rate, $f_1$, is:

$$1 + f_1 = \frac{(1.06)^2}{(1.0505)} = 1.0696$$

or

$$f_1 = 6.96\%$$

The expected rise in one-year rates from 5.05 percent ($i_1$) this year to 6.96 percent ($f_1$) next year reflects investors' perceptions regarding inflation and other factors that directly affect the time value of money.

Further, the current yield curve, in Figure 10–6, indicates that appropriate one-year discount bonds are yielding $k_1 = 10.80$ percent and two-year bonds are yielding $k_2 = 13$ percent. Thus, if we use equation (3), the one-year rate expected on corporate securities, $c_1$, is:

$$1 + c_1 = \frac{(1.13)^2}{(1.1080)} = 1.1524$$

or

$$c_1 = 15.24\%$$

We summarize these calculations in Table 10–9. As you can see, the expected spread between one-year corporate bonds and Treasuries in one year's time is higher than the spread for current one-year bonds. Thus, the default risk premium increases with the maturity on the corporate (risky) bond.

From these expected rates on one-year bonds, if we use equations (4) and (5), the expected probability of repayment on one-year corporate bonds in one year's time, $p_2$, is:

$$p_2 = \frac{[1.0696]}{[1.1524]} = 0.9281$$

and the expected probability of default in year 2 is:

$$1 - p_2 = 1 - 0.9281 = 0.0719$$

or

$$7.19\%$$

The probabilities we have estimated are marginal probabilities conditional on default not occurring in a prior period. We also discussed the concept of the *cumulative probability* of default that would tell the FI the probability of a loan or bond investment defaulting over a particular time period. In the example developed earlier, the cumulative probability that corporate grade B bonds would default over the next two years is:

$$C_p = 1 - [(p_1)(p_2)]$$
$$C_p = 1 - [(0.948)(0.9281)] = 12.02\%$$

As with the credit scoring approach, this model creates some potential problems. Its principal advantages are that it is clearly forward-looking and based on market expectations. Moreover, if there are liquid markets for Treasury and corporate discount bonds—Treasury strips and corporate zero-coupon bonds—then we can easily estimate expected future default rates and use them to value and price loans. However, while the market for Treasury strips is now quite deep, the market for corporate discount bonds is quite small. Although a discount yield curve

**TABLE 10–9**
**Treasury and**
**Corporate Rates and**
**Rate Spreads**

|  | Current One-Year Rate | Expected One-Year Rate |
|---|---|---|
| Treasury | 5.05% | 6.96% |
| Corporate (B) | 10.80 | 15.24 |
| Spread | 5.75 | 8.28 |

for corporate bonds could be extracted mathematically from the corporate bond coupon yield curve, these bonds often are not very actively traded and prices are not very transparent. Given this, the FI manager might have to consider an alternative way to use bond or loan data to extract default rate probabilities for all but the very largest corporate borrowers. We consider a possible alternative next.

| **Concept Questions** | 1. What is the difference between the marginal default probability and the cumulative default probability? |
| --- | --- |
| | 2. How should the posting of collateral by a borrower affect the risk premium on a loan? |

### Mortality Rate Derivation of Credit Risk

**mortality rate**
Historic default rate experience of a bond or loan.

Rather than extracting *expected* default rates from the current term structure of interest rates, the FI manager may analyze the *historic* or past default risk experience, the **mortality rates,** of bonds and loans of a similar quality. Consider calculating $p_1$ and $p_2$ using the mortality rate model. Here $p_1$ is the probability of a grade B bond or loan surviving the first year of its issue; thus $1 - p_1$ is the **marginal mortality rate,** or the probability of the bond or loan defaulting in the first year of issue. While $p_2$ is the probability of the loan surviving in the second year given that default has not occurred during the first year, $1 - p_2$ is the marginal mortality rate for the second year. Thus, for each grade of corporate borrower quality, a marginal mortality rate (MMR) curve can show the historical default rate experience of bonds in any specific quality class in each year after issue on the bond or loan.

**marginal mortality rate**
The probability of a bond or loan defaulting in any given year after issue.

Note in Figure 10–7 that as grade B bonds age, their probability of default increases in each successive year. Of course, in reality, any shape to the mortality curve is possible. It is possible that MMRs can be flat, decline over time, or show a more complex functional form. These marginal mortality rates can be estimated from actual data on bond and loan defaults. Specifically, for grade B quality bonds (loans):

$$MMR_1 = \frac{\text{Total value of grade B bonds defaulting in year 1 of issue}}{\text{Total value of grade B bonds outstanding in year 1 of issue}}$$

$$MMR_2 = \frac{\text{Total value of grade B bonds defaulting in year 2 of issue}}{\begin{array}{c}\text{Total value of grade B bonds outstanding in year 2 of issue}\\ \text{adjusted for defaults, calls, sinking fund redemptions, and}\\ \text{maturities in the prior year}\end{array}}$$

**FIGURE 10–7**
**Hypothetical Marginal Mortality Rate Curve for Grade B Corporate Bonds**

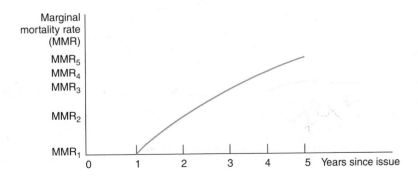

**TABLE 10–10** Mortality Rates by Original Rating—All Rated* Corporate Bonds, 1971–2011

Source: E. I. Altman and B. J. Kuehne, "Special Report on Default and Returns in the High-Yield Bond and Distressed Debt Market: The Year 2011 in Review and Outlook," New York University Salomon Center, February 2012.

| | | Years after Issuance | | | | | | | | | |
|---|---|---|---|---|---|---|---|---|---|---|---|
| | | **1** | **2** | **3** | **4** | **5** | **6** | **7** | **8** | **9** | **10** |
| AAA | Marginal | 0.00% | 0.00% | 0.00% | 0.00% | 0.02% | 0.02% | 0.01% | 0.00% | 0.00% | 0.00% |
| | Cumulative | 0.00% | 0.00% | 0.00% | 0.00% | 0.02% | 0.04% | 0.05% | 0.05% | 0.05% | 0.05% |
| AA | Marginal | 0.00% | 0.00% | 0.25% | 0.11% | 0.02% | 0.02% | 0.01% | 0.01% | 0.03% | 0.01% |
| | Cumulative | 0.00% | 0.00% | 0.25% | 0.36% | 0.38% | 0.40% | 0.41% | 0.42% | 0.45% | 0.46% |
| A | Marginal | 0.01% | 0.06% | 0.16% | 0.17% | 0.14% | 0.10% | 0.04% | 0.30% | 0.11% | 0.07% |
| | Cumulative | 0.01% | 0.07% | 0.23% | 0.40% | 0.54% | 0.64% | 0.68% | 0.98% | 1.09% | 1.15% |
| BBB | Marginal | 0.38% | 2.49% | 1.37% | 1.05% | 0.58% | 0.27% | 0.30% | 0.17% | 0.16% | 0.36% |
| | Cumulative | 0.38% | 2.86% | 4.19% | 5.20% | 5.75% | 6.00% | 6.28% | 6.44% | 6.59% | 6.93% |
| BB | Marginal | 1.01% | 2.07% | 3.95% | 2.00% | 2.42% | 1.47% | 1.51% | 1.10% | 1.50% | 3.20% |
| | Cumulative | 1.01% | 3.06% | 6.89% | 8.75% | 10.96% | 12.27% | 13.59% | 14.54% | 15.82% | 18.52% |
| B | Marginal | 2.96% | 7.86% | 7.95% | 7.93% | 5.84% | 4.58% | 3.66% | 2.15% | 1.83% | 0.82% |
| | Cumulative | 2.96% | 10.59% | 17.70% | 24.22% | 28.65% | 31.92% | 34.41% | 35.82% | 36.99% | 37.51% |
| CCC | Marginal | 8.30% | 12.65% | 18.28% | 16.35% | 4.82% | 11.78% | 5.45% | 4.95% | 0.70% | 4.41% |
| | Cumulative | 8.30% | 19.90% | 34.54% | 45.24% | 47.88% | 54.02% | 56.53% | 58.68% | 58.97% | 60.78% |

*Rated by S&P at issuance. Based on 2,644 issues.

Table 10–10 shows the estimated mortality and cumulative default rates for samples of 2,644 rated corporate bonds over the 1971–2011 period. From Table 10–10 it can be seen that mortality rates are higher the lower the rating of the bond. For example, between 1971 and 2011, there was a 1.15 percent probability that A-rated bonds would default over the 10 years after issue and a 37.51 percent probability that B-rated bonds would default over the 10 years after issue.

The mortality rate approach has a number of conceptual and applicability problems. Probably the most important of these is that, like the credit scoring model, it produces historic, or backward-looking, measures. Also, the estimates of default rates and therefore implied future default probabilities tend to be highly sensitive to the period over which the FI manager calculates the MMRs. For example, WorldCom had an S&P rating of BBB just prior to its defaulting on its debt in 2002. Note in Table 10–10 the second year's marginal mortality rate for BBB bonds (2.49 percent) is much higher than those of years 3 and 4 (1.37 percent and 1.05 percent, respectively) and is even higher than that of the second-year mortality rate for BB bonds (2.07 percent). This is primarily due to the default of World-Com in 2002. In addition, the estimates tend to be sensitive to the number of issues and the relative size of issues in each investment grade.[27]

**Concept Questions**

1. In Table 10–10, the CMR over 3 years for CCC-rated corporate bonds is 34.54 percent. Check this calculation using the individual year MMRs.
2. Why would any FI manager buy loans that have a CMR of 34.54 percent? Explain your answer.

[27] For example, even though the estimates in Table 10–10 are based on 2,644 observations of bonds, these estimates still have quite wide confidence bands. See Saunders and Allen, *Credit Risk Management*.

### RAROC Models

An increasingly popular model used to evaluate (and price) credit risk based on market data is the RAROC model. The **RAROC** (risk-adjusted return on capital) was pioneered by Bankers Trust (acquired by Deutsche Bank in 1998) and has now been adopted by virtually all the large banks in the United States and Europe, although with some significant proprietary differences between them.

**RAROC**
Risk-adjusted return on capital.

The essential idea behind RAROC is that rather than evaluating the actual or contractually promised annual ROA on a loan, as earlier in the chapter (that is, net interest and fees divided by the amount lent), the lending officer balances expected interest and fee income less the cost of funds against the loan's expected risk. Thus, the numerator of the RAROC equation is net income (accounting for the cost of funding the loan) on the loan. Further, rather than dividing annual loan income by assets lent, it is divided by some measure of asset (loan) risk or what is often called capital at risk, since (unexpected) loan losses have to be written off against an FI's capital:[28]

$$RAROC = \frac{\text{One year net income on a loan}}{\text{Loan (asset) risk or capital at risk}}$$

A loan is approved only if RAROC is sufficiently high relative to a benchmark return on capital (ROE) for the FI, where ROE measures the return stockholders require on their equity investment in the FI. The idea here is that a loan should be made only if the risk-adjusted return on the loan adds to the FI's equity value as measured by the ROE required by the FI's stockholders. Thus, for example, if an FI's ROE is 10 percent, a loan should be made only if the estimated RAROC is higher than the 10 percent required by the FI's stockholders as a reward for their investment in the FI. Alternatively, if the RAROC on an existing loan falls below an FI's RAROC benchmark, the lending officer should seek to adjust the loan's terms to make it "profitable" again. Therefore, RAROC serves as both a credit risk measure and a loan pricing tool for the FI manager.

The numerator of the RAROC equation is relatively straightforward to estimate. Specifically,

$$\text{One year net income on loan} = (\text{Spread} + \text{Fees})$$
$$\times \text{Dollar value of the loan outstanding}$$

FIs may deduct any overhead and tax expenses as well to get the one year net income on the loan. However, a more difficult problem in estimating RAROC is the measurement of loan risk (the denominator in the RAROC equation). Two methods of estimating loan risk involve the use of a duration model and the use of loan default rates.

*Using Duration to Estimate Loan Risk* Chapter 9 on duration showed that the percentage change in the market value of an asset such as a loan ($\Delta LN/LN$) is related to the duration of the loan and the size of the interest rate shock ($\Delta R/(1 + R)$), where $R$ is the base rate, $BR$, plus the credit risk premium, $\phi$:

$$\frac{\Delta LN}{LN} = -D_{LN}\frac{\Delta R}{1 + R}$$

---

[28] Traditionally, expected loan losses are covered by an FI's loss reserve (or provisions), while unexpected or extreme loan losses are being met by an FI's capital reserves.

The same concept is applied here, except that (assuming that the base rate remains constant) interest rate shocks are the consequence of credit quality (or credit risk premium) shocks (i.e., shocks to $\phi$). We can thus rewrite the duration equation with the following interpretation to estimate the loan risk or capital at risk on the loan:

$$\Delta LN \quad = \quad -D_{LN} \quad \times \quad LN \quad \times \quad (\Delta R/(1 \times R))$$

| (dollar capital risk exposure or loss amount) | (duration of the loan) | (risk amount or size of loan) | (expected maximum change in the loan rate due to a change in the credit risk premium ($\phi$) or risk factor on the loan) |
|---|---|---|---|

---

**EXAMPLE 10–7**
*Calculation of RAROC on a Loan*

Suppose an FI wants to evaluate the credit risk of a $1 million loan with a duration of 2.7 years to a AAA borrower. Assume there are currently 400 publicly traded bonds in that class (i.e., bonds issued by firms of a rating type similar to that of the borrower). The first step is to evaluate the actual changes in the credit risk premiums ($R_i - R_G$) on each of these bonds for the past year (in this example, the year 2015). These (hypothetical) changes are plotted in the frequency curve of Figure 10–8. They range from a fall in the risk premiums of negative 2 percent to an increase of 3.5 percent. Since the largest increase may be a very extreme (unrepresentative) number, the 99 percent worst-case scenario is chosen (i.e., only 4 bonds out of 400 had risk premium increases exceeding the 99 percent worst case). For the example shown in Figure 10–8 this is equal to 1.1 percent.

The estimate of loan (or capital) risk, assuming that the current average level of rates ($R$) on AAA bonds is 5 percent, is:

$$\Delta LN = -D_{LN} \times LN \times \frac{\Delta R}{1 + R}$$
$$= -(2.7)(\$1 \text{million}) \left( \frac{0.011}{1.05} \right)$$
$$= -\$28,286$$

While the market value of the loan amount is $1 million, the risk amount, or change in the loan's market value due to a decline in its credit quality, is $28,286. Thus, the denominator of the RAROC equation is this possible loss, or $28,286.

To determine whether the loan is worth making, the estimated loan risk is compared with the loan's income (spread over the FI's cost of funds plus fees on the loan). Suppose the projected (one-year) spread plus fees is as follows:

$$\text{Spread} = 0.2\% \times \$1 \text{ million} = \$2,000$$
$$\text{Fees} = 0.1\% \times \$1 \text{ million} = \underline{\$1,000}$$
$$\$3,000$$

The loan's RAROC is:

$$RAROC = \frac{\text{One year net income on loan}}{\text{Loan risk (or capital risk)}(\Delta LN)} = \frac{\$3,000}{\$28,286} = 10.61\%$$

---

Note that RAROC can be either forward looking, comparing the projected income over the next year on the loan with $\Delta LN$, or backward looking, comparing the actual income generated on the loan over the past year with $\Delta LN$. If the 10.61

**FIGURE 10–8**
Hypothetical
Frequency
Distribution of
Yield Spread
Changes for All
AAA Bonds in 2015

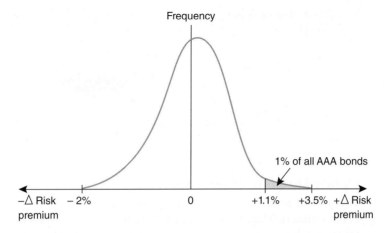

percent exceeds the FI's internal RAROC benchmark (based on its cost of capital, or ROE), the loan will be approved. If it is less, the loan will be rejected outright or the borrower will be asked to pay higher fees and/or a higher spread to increase the RAROC to acceptable levels.

While the loan's duration (2.7 years in our example) and the loan amount ($1 million) are easily estimated, it is more difficult to estimate the maximum change in the credit risk premium on the loan over the next year. Since publicly available data on loan risk premiums are scarce, we turn to publicly available corporate bond market data to estimate premiums. First, an S&P credit rating (AAA, AA, A, and so on) is assigned to a borrower. Thereafter, the available risk premium changes of all the bonds traded in that particular rating class over the last year are analyzed. The $\Delta R$ in the RAROC equation equals:

$$\Delta R = \text{Max}\,[\Delta(R_i - R_G) > 0]$$

where $\Delta(R_i - R_G)$ is the change in the yield spread between corporate bonds of credit rating class $i$ ($R_i$) and matched duration Treasury security ($R_G$) over the last year. In order to consider only the worst-case scenario, a maximum change in yield spread is chosen, as opposed to the average change. In general, it is common to pick the 1 percent worst case or 99th percentile of credit risk changes.

***Using Loan Default Rates to Estimate Loan Risk***   Other FIs have adopted different ways of calculating $\Delta LN$ in their versions of RAROC. Some FIs, usually the largest ones with very good loan default databases, divide one-year income by the product of an unexpected loss rate and the proportion of the loan lost on default, also called the loss given default. Thus:

$$RAROC = \frac{\text{One-year net income per dollar loaned}}{\text{Unexpected default rate} \times \text{Proportion of loan lost on default (loss given default)}}$$

Suppose expected income per dollar lent is 0.3 cents, or 0.003. The 99th percentile historic (extreme case) default rate for borrowers of this type is 4 percent, and the dollar proportion of loans of this type that cannot be recaptured is 80 percent. Then:[29]

$$RAROC = \frac{0.003}{(0.04)(0.8)} = \frac{0.003}{(0.032)} = 9.375\%$$

| Concept Question | 1. Describe the basic concept behind RAROC models. |
|---|---|

### Option Models of Default Risk

***Theoretical Framework*** In recent years, following the pioneering work of Nobel Prize winners Merton, Black, and Scholes, we now recognize that when a firm raises funds by issuing bonds or increasing its bank loans, it holds a very valuable default or repayment option.[30] That is, if a borrower's investment projects fail so that it cannot repay the bondholder or the bank, it has the option of defaulting on its debt repayment and turning any remaining assets over to the debtholder. Because of limited liability for equity holders, the borrower's loss is limited on the downside by the amount of equity invested in the firm. On the other hand, if things go well, the borrower can keep most of the upside returns on asset investments after the promised principal and interest on the debt have been paid. The KMV Corporation (which was purchased by Moody's in 2002 and is now part of Moody's Analytics Enterprise Risk Solutions) turned this relatively simple idea into a credit monitoring model. Many of the largest U.S. FIs are now using this model to determine the expected default risk frequency (EDF) of large corporations.[31] Before we look at the Moody's Analytics Credit Monitor model, we will take a closer look at the theory underlying the option approach to default risk estimation. Appendix 10B, located at the book's website (**www.mhhe.com/saunders8e**), reviews the Black–Scholes option pricing model.

***The Borrower's Payoff from Loans*** Look at the payoff function for the borrower in Figure 10–9, where $S$ is the size of the initial equity investment in the firm, $B$ is the value of outstanding bonds or loans (assumed for simplicity to be issued on a discount basis), and $A$ is the market value of the assets of the firm.

If the investments in Figure 10–9 turn out badly such that the firm's assets are valued at point $A_1$, the limited-liability stockholder–owners of the firm will default on the firm's debt, turn its assets (such as $A_1$) over to the debt holders, and lose only their initial stake in the firm ($S$). By contrast, if the firm does well and the

---

[29] Calculating the unexpected default rate commonly involves calculating the standard derivation ($\sigma$) of annual default rates on loans of this type and then multiplying $\sigma$ by a factor such that 99 percent (or higher) of defaults are covered by capital. For example, if the loss distribution was normally distributed, then the $\sigma$ of default rates would be multiplied by 2.33 to get the extreme 99 percent default rate. For many FIs, default rates are skewed to the right and have fat tails suggesting a multiplier much larger than 2.33. For example, to get coverage of 99.97 percent of defaults, Bank of America has historically used a multiplier of 6. Finally, the denominator can also be adjusted for the degree of correlation of the loan with the rest of the FI's portfolio.

[30] R. C. Merton, "On the Pricing of Corporate Debt: The Risk Structure of Interest Rates," *Journal of Finance* 29 (1974), pp. 449–70; and F. Black and M. Scholes, "The Pricing of Options and Corporate Liabilities," *Journal of Political Economy* 81 (1973), pp. 637–59.

[31] See KMV Corporation Credit Monitor, KMV Corporation, San Francisco, 1994; and Saunders and Allen, *Credit Risk Measurement,* chap. 4.

**FIGURE 10–9**
**Payoff Function to Corporate Borrowers (Stockholders)**

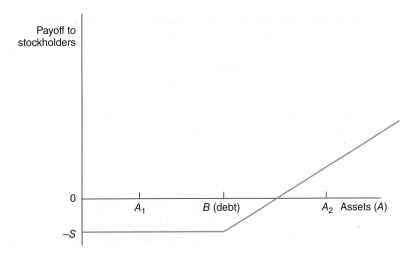

assets of the firm are valued highly ($A_2$), the firm's stockholders will pay off the firm's debt and keep the difference ($A_2 - B$). Clearly, the higher $A_2$ is relative to $B$, the better off are the firm's stockholders. Given that borrowers face only a limited downside risk of loss of their equity investment, but a very large potential upside return if things turn out well, equity is analogous to buying a call option on the assets of the firm (see also Chapter 23 on options).

*The Debt Holder's Payoff from Loans*   Consider the same loan or bond issue from the perspective of the FI or bondholder. The maximum amount the FI or bondholder can get back is $B$, the promised payment. However, the borrower who possesses the default or repayment option would rationally repay the loan only if $A > B$, that is, if the market value of assets exceeds the value of promised debt repayments. A borrower whose asset value falls below $B$ would default and turn over any remaining assets to the debt holders. The payoff function to the debt holder is shown in Figure 10–10.

After investment of the borrowed funds has taken place, if the value of the firm's assets lies to the right of $B$, the face value of the debt—such as $A_2$—the debt holder or FI will be paid off in full and receive $B$. On the other hand, if asset values fall in the region to the left of $B$—such as $A_1$—the debt holder will receive back only those assets remaining as collateral, thereby losing $B - A_1$. Thus, the value of the loan from the perspective of the lender is always the minimum of $B$ or $A$, or min $[B, A]$. That is, the payoff function to the debt holder is similar to writing a put option on the value of the borrower's assets with $B$, the face value of debt, as the *exercise price*. If $A > B$, the loan is repaid and the debt holder earns a small fixed return (similar to the premium on a put option), which is the interest rate implicit in the discount

**FIGURE 10–10**
**Payoff Function to the Debt Holder (the FI) from a Loan**

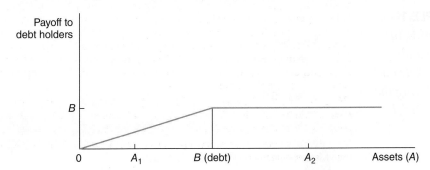

bond. If $A < B$, the borrower defaults and the debt holder stands to lose both interest and principal. In the limit, default for a firm with no assets left results in debt holders' losing all their principal and interest. In actuality, if there are also costs of bankruptcy, the debt holder can potentially lose even more than this.

*Applying the Option Valuation Model to the Calculation of Default Risk Premiums*   Merton has shown that in the context of the preceding options framework, it is quite straightforward to express the market value of a risky loan made by a lender to a borrower as:[32]

$$F(\tau) = Be^{-i\tau}[(1/d)N(h_1) + N(h_2)]$$

(6)

where

$\tau$ = Length of time remaining to loan maturity; that is, $\tau = T - t$, where $T$ is the maturity date and time $t$ is today.

$d$ = Borrower's leverage ratio measured as $Be^{-i\tau}/A$, where the market value of debt is valued at the rate $i$, the risk-free rate of interest.

$N(h)$ = Value computed from the standardized normal distribution statistical tables. This value reflects the probability that a deviation exceeding the calculated value of $h$ will occur.

$$h_1 = -\left[(\tfrac{1}{2})\sigma^2\tau - \ln(d)\right]/\sigma\sqrt{\tau}$$
$$h_2 = -\left[(\tfrac{1}{2})\sigma^2\tau + \ln(d)\right]/\sigma\sqrt{\tau}$$

$\sigma^2$ = Measures the asset risk of the borrower. Technically, it is the variance of the rate of change in the value of the underlying assets of the borrower.

Written in terms of a yield spread, $\phi$, this equation reflects an equilibrium default risk premium that the borrower should be charged:

$$\phi = k(\tau) - i = (-1/\tau)\ln[N(h_2) + (1/d)N(h_1)]$$

where

$k(\tau)$ = Required yield on risky debt (the contractually promised return from earlier)

$\ln$ = Natural logarithm

$i$ = Risk-free rate on debt of equivalent maturity (here, one period)

Thus, Merton has shown that the lender should adjust the required risk premium as $d$ and $\sigma^2$ change, that is, as leverage and asset risk change.

---

**EXAMPLE 10–8**

*Calculating the Value of and Interest Rate on a Loan Using the Option Model*

Suppose that:

$B$ = $100,000

$\tau$ = 1 year

$i$ = 5%

$d$ = 90% or 0.9

$\sigma$ = 12%

---

[32] See Merton, "On the Pricing of Corporate Debt."

That is, suppose we can measure the market value of a firm's assets (and thus $d = Be^{-i\tau}/A$) as well as the volatility of those assets ($\sigma$). Then, substituting these values into the equations for $h_1$ and $h_2$ and solving for the areas under the standardized normal distribution, we find that:

$$N(h_1) = 0.174120$$
$$N(h_2) = 0.793323$$

where

$$h_1 = \frac{-[\frac{1}{2}(0.12)^2(1) - \ln(0.9)]}{0.12} = -0.938$$

and

$$h_2 = \frac{-[\frac{1}{2}(0.12)^2(1) + \ln(0.9)]}{0.12} = +0.818$$

The current market value of the loan is:

$$
\begin{aligned}
L(t) &= Be^{-i\tau}[N(h_2) + (1/d)N(h_1)] \\
&= \frac{\$100,000}{1.05127}[0.793323 + (1.1111)(0.17412)] \\
&= \frac{\$100,000}{1.05127}[0.986788] \\
&= \$93,866.18
\end{aligned}
$$

and the required risk spread or premium, $\phi$, is:

$$
\begin{aligned}
\phi = k(\tau) - i &= \left(\frac{-1}{\tau}\right)\ln[N(h_2) + (1/d)N(h_1)] \\
&= (-1)\ln[0.986788] \\
&= 1.33\%
\end{aligned}
$$

Thus, the risky loan rate $k(\tau)$ should be set at 6.33 percent when the risk-free rate ($i$) is 5 percent.

Theoretically, this model is an elegant tool for extracting premiums and default probabilities. It also has important conceptual implications regarding which variables to focus on in credit risk evaluation [e.g., the firm's market value of assets ($A$) and asset risk ($\sigma^2$)]. Even so, this model has a number of real-world implementation problems. Probably the most significant is the fact that neither the market value of a firm's assets ($A$) nor the volatility of the firm's assets ($\sigma^2$) is directly observed.

**The Moody's Analytics Option Model and Expected Default Frequency**  The Moody's Analytics model in fact recognizes this problem by using an option pricing model (OPM) approach to extract the implied market value of assets ($A$) and the asset volatility of a given firm's assets ($\sigma^2$). The Moody's Analytics model uses the value of equity in a firm (from a stockholder's perspective) as equivalent to holding a call option on the assets of the firm (with the amount of debt borrowed acting similarly to the exercise price of the option). From this approach, and the link between the volatility of the market value of the firm's equity and that of its assets, it is possible to derive the asset volatility (risk) of any given firm ($\sigma$) and

www.moodysanalytics.com

**FIGURE 10–11**
**Expected Default Frequency Using the Moody's Analytics Model**

Source: Moody's Analytics.
*www.moodysanalytics.com*

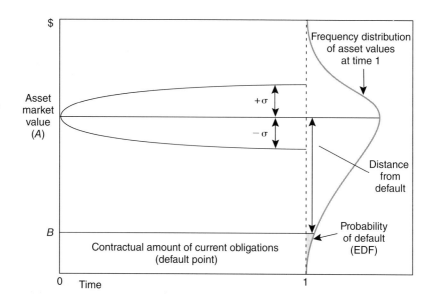

the market value of the firm's assets $(A)$.[33] Using the implied value of $\sigma$ for assets and $A$, the market value of assets, the likely distribution of possible asset values of the firm relative to its current debt obligations can be calculated over the next year. As shown in Figure 10–11, the expected default frequency (EDF) that is calculated reflects the probability that the market value of the firm's assets $(A)$ will fall below the promised repayments on its short-term debt liabilities $(B)$ in one year. If the value of a firm's assets falls below its debt liabilities, it can be viewed as being economically insolvent.

Suppose the value of the firm's assets $(A)$ at the time zero is $100 million and the value of its short-term debt is $80 million. Suppose also that the implied volatility $(\sigma)$ of asset values is estimated at $12.12 million, and it is assumed that asset-value changes are normally distributed. The firm becomes distressed only if the value of its assets falls to $80 million or below (falls by $20 million). Such a fall is equal to $1.65\sigma$, i.e., $1.65 \times \$12.12$ million $= \$20$ million. From statistics, we know that the area of the normal distribution (in each tail) lying $\pm 1.65\sigma$ from the mean is theoretically 5 percent. Thus, the Moody's Analytics model would suggest a theoretical 5 percent probability of the firm's going into distress over the next year (by time 1). However, Moody's Analytics calculates empirical EDFs, since we do not know the true distribution of asset values $(A)$ over time. Essentially, it asks this question: In practice, how many firms that started the year with asset values $1.65\sigma$ distance from default (see Figure 10–11) actually defaulted by the end of the year? This value may or may not equal 5 percent.

---

[33] More specifically, it does this by using the equity (stock market) value of the firm's shares $(E)$ and the volatility of the value of the firm's shares $(\sigma_E)$. Since equity can be viewed as a call option on the firm's assets and the volatility of a firm's equity value will reflect the leverage adjusted volatility of its underlying assets, we have in general form:

$$\bar{E} = f(A, \sigma, \bar{B}, \bar{r}, \bar{\tau})$$

and

$$\bar{\sigma}_E = g(\sigma)$$

where the bars denote values that are directly measurable. Since we have two equations and two unknowns $(A, \sigma)$, we can directly solve for both $A$ and $\sigma$ and use these, along with the firm's outstanding short-term liabilities or current liabilities, to calculate the EDF (expected default frequency).

**FIGURE 10–12**   Moody's Analytics EDF, Moody's, and S&P Ratings for AMR Corporation

Source: Moody's Analytics. *www.moodysanalytics.com*

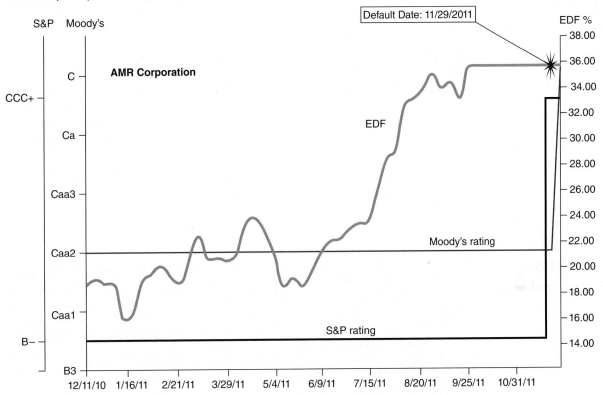

Simulations by Moody's Analytics have shown that EDF models outperform both Z score–type models and S&P rating changes as predictors of corporate failure and distress.[34] An example for AMR Corp., which filed for Chapter 11 bankruptcy protection on November 29, 2011, is shown in Figure 10–12. Note that the Moody's Analytics EDF score (expected default frequency) is rising earlier than the rating agencies are downgrading the firm's debt. Indeed, the rating agency ratings are very slow to react to, if not totally insensitive to, the increase in AMR Corp. risk. The Moody's Analytics EDF score starts to rise almost a year prior to AMR Corp. bankruptcy and suggests a C rating by July 2011. Thus, the Moody's Analytics EDF score gives a better early warning of impending default. In an effort to get control over credit rating firms, that give high-quality ratings to high-risk firms, such as AMR, in April 2009 the Credit Rating Agency Reform Act was passed. This act gave the SEC regulatory authority over credit rating firms and was intended to increase competition and oversight of credit rating firms.

| **Concept Questions** | 1. Which is the only credit risk model discussed in this section that is really forward looking?<br><br>2. How should the risk premium on a loan be affected if there is a reduction in a borrower's leverage and the underlying volatility of its earnings?<br><br>3. What is the link between the implied volatility of a firm's assets and its expected default frequency? |
|---|---|

[34] The Moody's Analytics database contains 30 years of information on more than 6,000 public and 220,000 private company default events for a total of 60,000 public and 2.8 million private companies, healthy and distressed, around the world.

## Summary

This chapter discussed different approaches to measuring credit or default risk on individual loans (bonds). The different types of loans made by FIs and some of their basic characteristics were first examined. The expected return on a loan was shown to depend on factors such as origination fees, compensating balances, interest rates, and maturity. The various models to assess default risk include both qualitative and quantitative models. The qualitative models usually contain both firm-specific factors, such as reputation and leverage, and market-specific factors, such as the business cycle and the level of interest rates. Quantitative models, such as the linear probability model, the logit model, and the linear discriminant model, were shown to provide credit scores that can rank or classify loans by expected default risk. The more rigorous of the quantitative models make use of both financial theory and financial data. These include the term structure and mortality rate models as well as the RAROC (risk-adjusted return on capital) and option-based models. In the next chapter we look at methods to evaluate the risk of loan portfolios, or loan concentration risk.

## Questions and Problems

1. Why is credit risk analysis an important component of FI risk management? What recent activities by FIs have made the task of credit risk assessment more difficult for both FI managers and regulators?
2. Differentiate between a secured loan and an unsecured loan. Who bears most of the risk in a fixed-rate loan? Why would FI managers prefer to charge floating rates, especially for longer-maturity loans?
3. How does a spot loan differ from a loan commitment? What are the advantages and disadvantages of borrowing through a loan commitment?
4. Why is commercial lending declining in importance in the United States? What effect does this decline have on overall commercial lending activities?
5. What are the primary characteristics of residential mortgage loans? Why does the ratio of adjustable-rate mortgages to fixed-rate mortgages in the economy vary over an interest rate cycle? When would the ratio be highest?
6. What are the two major classes of consumer loans at U.S. banks? How do revolving loans differ from nonrevolving loans?
7. Why are rates on credit cards generally higher than rates on car loans?
8. What are compensating balances? What is the relationship between the amount of compensating balance requirement and the return on the loan to the FI?
9. Suppose that a bank does the following:
   a. Sets a loan rate on a prospective loan at 8 percent (where BR = 5% and $\phi$ = 3%).
   b. Charges a $\frac{1}{10}$ percent (or 0.10 percent) loan origination fee to the borrower.
   c. Imposes a 5 percent compensating balance requirement to be held as noninterest-bearing demand deposits.
   d. Holds reserve requirements of 10 percent imposed by the Federal Reserve on the bank's demand deposits.

   Calculate the bank's ROA on this loan.
10. County Bank offers one-year loans with a stated rate of 9 percent but requires a compensating balance of 10 percent. What is the true cost of this loan to the borrower? How does the cost change if the compensating balance is 15 percent? If the compensating balance is 20 percent? In each case, assume origination fees and the reserve requirement are zero.

11. Metrobank offers one-year loans with a 9 percent stated or base rate, charges a 0.25 percent loan origination fee, imposes a 10 percent compensating balance requirement, and must hold a 6 percent reserve requirement at the Federal Reserve. The loans typically are repaid at maturity.
    a. If the risk premium for a given customer is 2.5 percent, what is the simple promised interest return on the loan?
    b. What is the contractually promised gross return on the loan per dollar lent?
    c. Which of the fee items has the greatest impact on the gross return?

12. Why are most retail borrowers charged the same rate of interest, implying the same risk premium or class? What is credit rationing? How is it used to control credit risks with respect to retail and wholesale loans?

13. Why could a lender's expected return be lower when the risk premium is increased on a loan? In addition to the risk premium, how can a lender increase the expected return on a wholesale loan? A retail loan?

14. What are covenants in a loan agreement? What are the objectives of covenants? How can these covenants be negative? Positive?

15. Identify and define the borrower-specific and market-specific factors that enter into the credit decision. What is the impact of each type of factor on the risk premium?
    a. Which of these factors is more likely to adversely affect small businesses rather than large businesses in the credit assessment process by lenders?
    b. How does the existence of a high debt ratio typically affect the risk of the borrower?
    c. Why is the volatility of the earnings stream of a borrower important to a lender?

16. Why is the degree of collateral as specified in the loan agreement of importance to a lender? If the book value of the collateral is greater than or equal to the amount of the loan, is the credit risk of a lender fully covered? Why or why not?

17. Why are FIs consistently interested in the expected level of economic activity in the markets in which they operate? Why is monetary policy of the Federal Reserve System important to FIs?

18. What are the purposes of credit scoring models? How do these models assist an FI manager in better administering credit?

19. Suppose there were two factors influencing the past default behavior of borrowers: the leverage or debt–assets ratio $(D/A)$ and the profit margin ratio $(PM)$. Based on past default (repayment) experience, the linear probability model is estimated as:

$$PD_i = 0.105(D/A_i) - 0.35(PM_i)$$

Prospective borrower A has a $D/A = 0.65$ and a $PM = 5\%$, and prospective borrower B has a $D/A = 0.45$ and a $PM = 1\%$. Calculate the prospective borrowers' expected probabilities of default $(PD_i)$. Which borrower is the better loan candidate? Explain your answer.

20. Suppose the estimated linear probability model used by an FI to predict business loan applicant default probabilities is $PD = 0.03X_1 + 0.02X_2 - 0.05X_3 +$ error, where $X_1$ is the borrower's debt/equity ratio, $X_2$ is the volatility of borrower earnings, and $X_3$ is the borrower's profit ratio. For a particular loan applicant, $X_1 = 0.75$, $X_2 = 0.25$, and $X_3 = 0.10$.
    a. What is the projected probability of default for the borrower?
    b. What is the projected probability of repayment if the debt/equity ratio is 2.5?
    c. What is a major weakness of the linear probability model?

21. Describe how a linear discriminant analysis model works. Identify and discuss the criticisms which have been made regarding the use of this type of model to make credit risk evaluations.

22. Suppose that the financial ratios of a potential borrowing firm take the following values:

Working capital/total assets ratio $(X_1) = 0.75$
Retained earnings/total assets ratio $(X_2) = 0.10$
Earnings before interest and taxes/total assets ratio $(X_3) = 0.05$
Market value of equity/book value of long-term debt ratio $(X_4) = 0.10$
Sales/total assets ratio $(X_5) = 0.65$

Calculate the Altman's Z-score for the borrower in question. How is this number a sign of the borrower's default risk?

23. MNO Inc., a publicly traded manufacturing firm in the United States, has provided the following financial information in its application for a loan. All numbers are in thousands of dollars.

| Assets | | Liabilities and Equity | |
|---|---|---|---|
| Cash | $ 20 | Accounts payable | $ 30 |
| Accounts receivable | 90 | Notes payable | 90 |
| Inventory | 90 | Accruals | 30 |
| | | Long-term debt | 150 |
| Plant and equipment | 500 | Equity (retained earnings = $22) | 400 |
| Total assets | $700 | Total liabilities and equity | $700 |

Also assume sales = $500,000; cost of goods sold = $360,000; and the market value of equity is equal to the book value.

a. What is the Altman discriminant function value for MNO Inc.? Recall that:
   Net working capital = Current assets − Current liabilities.
   Current assets = Cash + Accounts receivable + Inventories.
   Current liabilities = Accounts payable + Accruals + Notes payable.
   EBIT = Revenues − Cost of goods sold.

b. Based on the Altman's Z score only, should you approve MNO Inc.'s application to your bank for a $500,000 capital expansion loan?

c. If sales for MNO were $300,000, the market value of equity was only half of book value, and all other values are unchanged, would your credit decision change?

d. Would the discriminant function change for firms in different industries? Would the function be different for manufacturing firms in different geographic sections of the country? What are the implications for the use of these types of models by FIs?

24. Consider the coefficients of Altman's Z score. Can you tell by the size of the coefficients which ratio appears most important in assessing creditworthiness of a loan applicant? Explain.

25. If the rate on one-year Treasury strips currently is 6 percent, what is the repayment probability for each of the following two securities? Assume that if the loan is defaulted, no payments are expected. What is the market-determined risk premium for the corresponding probability of default for each security?

    a. One-year AA-rated zero-coupon bond yielding 9.5 percent.

    b. One-year BB-rated zero-coupon bond yielding 13.5 percent.

26. A bank has made a loan charging a base lending rate of 10 percent. It expects a probability of default of 5 percent. If the loan is defaulted, the bank expects to recover 50 percent of its money through the sale of its collateral. What is the expected return on this loan?

27. Assume that a one-year Treasury strip is currently yielding 5.5 percent and an AAA-rated discount bond with similar maturity is yielding 8.5 percent.

    a. If the expected recovery from collateral in the event of default is 50 percent of principal and interest, what is the probability of repayment of the AAA-rated bond? What is the probability of default?

    b. What is the probability of repayment of the AAA-rated bond if the expected recovery from collateral in the case of default is 94.47 percent of principal and interest? What is the probability of default?

    c. What is the relationship between the probability of default and the proportion of principal and interest that may be recovered in case of default on the loan?

28. What is meant by the phrase *marginal default probability?* How does this term differ from *cumulative default probability?* How are the two terms related?

29. Suppose an FI manager wants to find the probability of default on a two-year loan. For the one-year loan, $1 - p_1 = 0.03$ is the marginal and total or cumulative probability (Cp) of default in year 1. For the second year, suppose that $1 - p_2 = 0.05$. Calculate the cumulative probability of default over the next two years.

30. From the Treasury strip yield curve, the current required yields on one- and two-year Treasuries are $i_1 = 4.65$ percent and $i_2 = 5.50$ percent, respectively. Further, the current yield curve indicates that appropriate one-year discount bonds are yielding $k_1 = 8.5$ percent, and two-year bonds are yielding $k_2 = 10.25$ percent.

    a. Calculate the one-year forward rate on the Treasuries and the corporate bond.

    b. Using the current and forward one-year rates, calculate the marginal probability of repayment on the corporate bond in years 1 and 2, respectively.

    c. Calculate the cumulative probability of default on the corporate bond over the next two years.

31. Calculate the term structure of default probabilities over three years using the following spot rates from the Treasury strip and corporate bond (pure discount) yield curves. Be sure to calculate both the annual marginal and the cumulative default probabilities.

|                  | Spot 1 Year | Spot 2 Year | Spot 3 Year |
| ---------------- | ----------- | ----------- | ----------- |
| Treasury strip   | 5.0%        | 6.1%        | 7.0%        |
| BBB-rated bonds  | 7.0         | 8.2         | 9.3         |

32. The bond equivalent yields for U.S. Treasury and A-rated corporate bonds with maturities of 93 and 175 days are given below:

|  | 93 Days | 175 Days |
|---|---|---|
| Treasury strip | 8.07% | 8.11% |
| A-rated corporate | 8.42 | 8.66 |
| Spread | 0.35 | 0.55 |

   a. What are the implied forward rates for both an 82-day Treasury and an 82-day A-rated bond beginning in 93 days? Use daily compounding on a 365-day year basis.
   b. What is the implied probability of default on A-rated bonds over the next 93 days? Over 175 days?
   c. What is the implied default probability on an 82-day, A-rated bond to be issued in 93 days?

33. What is the mortality rate of a bond or loan? What are some of the problems with using a mortality rate approach to determine the probability of default of a given bond issue?

34. The following is a schedule of historical defaults (yearly and cumulative) experienced by an FI manager on a portfolio of commercial and mortgage loans.

| Loan Type | Years after Issuance | | | | |
|---|---|---|---|---|---|
|  | 1 Year | 2 Years | 3 Years | 4 Years | 5 Years |
| Commercial: |  |  |  |  |  |
| Annual default | 0.00% | _____ | 0.50% | _____ | 0.30% |
| Cumulative default | _____ | 0.10% | _____ | 0.80% | _____ |
| Mortgage: |  |  |  |  |  |
| Annual default | 0.10% | 0.25% | 0.60% | _____ | 0.80% |
| Cumulative default | _____ | _____ | _____ | 1.64% | _____ |

   a. Complete the blank spaces in the table.
   b. What are the probabilities that each type of loan will not be in default after five years?
   c. What is the measured difference between the cumulative default (mortality) rates for commercial and mortgage loans after four years?

35. The table below shows the dollar amounts of outstanding bonds and corresponding default amounts for every year over the past five years. Note that the default figures are in millions, while those outstanding are in billions. The outstanding figures reflect default amounts and bond redemptions.

| Loan Type | Years after Issuance | | | | |
|---|---|---|---|---|---|
|  | 1 Year | 2 Years | 3 Years | 4 Years | 5 Years |
| A-rated: Annual default (millions) | 0 | 0 | 0 | $ 1 | $ 2 |
| Outstanding (billions) | $100 | $95 | $93 | $91 | $88 |
| B-rated: Annual default (millions) | 0 | $ 1 | $ 2 | $ 3 | $ 4 |
| Outstanding (billions) | $100 | $94 | $92 | $89 | $85 |
| C-rated: Annual default (millions) | $ 1 | $ 3 | $ 5 | $ 5 | $ 6 |
| Outstanding (billions) | $100 | $97 | $90 | $85 | $79 |

What are the annual and cumulative default rates of the above bonds?

36. What is RAROC? How does this model use the concept of duration to measure the risk exposure of a loan? How is the expected change in the credit risk premium measured? What precisely is $\Delta LN$ in the RAROC equation?

37. An FI wants to evaluate the credit risk of a $5 million loan with a duration of 4.3 years to a AAA borrower. There are currently 500 publicly traded bonds in that class (i.e., bonds issued by firms with a AAA rating). The current average level of rates ($R$) on AAA bonds is 8 percent. The largest increase in credit risk premiums on AAA loans, the 99 percent worst-case scenario, over the last year was equal to 1.2 percent (i.e., only 6 bonds out of 500 had risk premium increases exceeding the 99 percent worst case). The projected (one-year) spread on the loan is 0.3 percent and the FI charges 0.25 percent of the face value of the loan in fees. Calculate the capital at risk and the RAROC on this loan.

38. A bank is planning to make a loan of $5,000,000 to a firm in the steel industry. It expects to charge a servicing fee of 50 basis points. The loan has a maturity of 8 years with a duration of 7.5 years. The cost of funds (the RAROC benchmark) for the bank is 10 percent. The bank has estimated the maximum change in the risk premium on the steel manufacturing sector to be approximately 4.2 percent, based on two years of historical data. The current market interest rate for loans in this sector is 12 percent.
    a. Using the RAROC model, determine whether the bank should make the loan.
    b. What should be the duration in order for this loan to be approved?
    c. Assuming that the duration cannot be changed, how much additional interest and fee income will be necessary to make the loan acceptable?
    d. Given the proposed income stream and the negotiated duration, what adjustment in the loan rate would be necessary to make the loan acceptable?

39. Calculate the value of and interest rate on a loan using the option model and the following information.

    Face value of loan ($B$) = $500,000
    Length of time remaining to loan maturity ($\tau$) = 4 years
    Risk-free rate ($i$) = 4%
    Borrower's leverage ratio ($d$) = 60%
    Standard deviation of the rate of change in the value of the underlying assets = 15%

40. A firm is issuing a two-year loan in the amount of $200,000. The current market value of the borrower's assets is $300,000. The risk-free rate is 4 percent and the standard deviation of the rate of change in the underlying assets of the borrower is 20 percent. Using an options framework, determine the following:
    a. The current market value of the loan.
    b. The risk premium to be charged on the loan.

41. A firm has assets of $200,000 and total debts of $175,000. With an option pricing model, the implied volatility of the value of the firm's assets is estimated at $10,730. Under the Moody's Analytic method, what is the expected default frequency (assuming a normal distribution for assets)?

42. Carman County Bank (CCB) has a $5 million face value outstanding adjustable-rate loan to a company that has a leverage ratio of 80 percent. The current risk-free rate is 6 percent and the time to maturity on the loan is exactly ½ year. The asset risk of the borrower, as measured by the standard deviation of the rate of change in the value of the underlying assets, is 12 percent. The normal density function values are given below.

| h | N(h) | h | N(h) |
|---|---|---|---|
| −2.55 | 0.0054 | 2.50 | 0.9938 |
| −2.60 | 0.0047 | 2.55 | 0.9946 |
| −2.65 | 0.0040 | 2.60 | 0.9953 |
| −2.70 | 0.0035 | 2.65 | 0.9960 |
| −2.75 | 0.0030 | 2.70 | 0.9965 |

    a. Use the Merton option valuation model to determine the market value of the loan.

    b. What should be the interest rate for the last six months of the loan?

The questions and problems that follow refer to Appendix 10A.

43. Suppose you are a loan officer at Carbondale Local Bank. Joan Doe listed the following information on her mortgage application.

| Characteristic | Value |
|---|---|
| Annual gross income | $45,000 |
| TDS | 10% |
| Relations with FI | Checking account |
| Major credit cards | 5 |
| Age | 27 |
| Residence | Own/mortgage |
| Length of residence | 2½ years |
| Job stability | 5½ years |
| Credit history | Missed 2 payments 1 year ago |

Use the information below to determine whether or not Joan Doe should be approved for a mortgage from your bank.

| Characteristic | Characteristic Values and Weights | | | | |
|---|---|---|---|---|---|
| Annual gross income | <$10,000 | $10,000–$25,000 | $25,000–$50,000 | $50,000–$100,000 | >$100,000 |
| Score | 0 | 10 | 20 | 35 | 60 |
| TDS | >50% | 35%–50% | 15%–35% | 5%–15% | <5% |
| Score | −10 | 0 | 20 | 40 | 60 |
| Relations with FI | None | Checking account | | Savings account | Both |
| Score | 0 | 10 | | 10 | 20 |
| Major credit cards | None | Between 1 and 4 | 5 or more | | |
| Score | 0 | 20 | 10 | | |
| Age | <25 | 25–60 | >60 | | |
| Score | 5 | 25 | 35 | | |
| Residence | Rent | Own with mortgage | | Own outright | |
| Score | 5 | 20 | | 50 | |
| Length of residence | <1 year | 1–5 years | | >5 years | |
| Score | 0 | 25 | | 40 | |
| Job stability | <1 year | 1–5 years | >5 years | | |
| Score | 0 | 25 | 50 | | |
| Credit history | No record | Missed a payment in last 5 years | | Met all payments | |
| Score | 0 | −15 | | 40 | |

The loan is automatically rejected if the applicant's total score is less than or equal to 120; the loan is automatically approved if the total score is greater than or equal to 190. A score between 120 and 190 (noninclusive) is reviewed by a loan committee for a final decision.

44. What are some of the special risks and considerations when lending to small businesses rather than large businesses?

45. How does ratio analysis help to answer questions about the production, management, and marketing capabilities of a prospective borrower?

46. Consider the following company balance sheet and income statement.

### Balance Sheet

| Assets | | Liabilities and Equity | |
|---|---|---|---|
| Cash | $ 4,000 | Accounts payable | $ 30,000 |
| Accounts receivable | 52,000 | Notes payable | 12,000 |
| Inventory | 40,000 | Total current liabilities | 42,000 |
| Total current assets | 96,000 | Long-term debt | 36,000 |
| Fixed assets | 44,000 | Equity | 62,000 |
| Total assets | $140,000 | Total liabilities and equity | $140,000 |

### Income Statement

| | |
|---|---|
| Sales (all on credit) | $200,000 |
| Cost of goods sold | 130,000 |
| Gross margin | 70,000 |
| Selling and administrative expenses | 20,000 |
| Depreciation | 8,000 |
| EBIT | 42,000 |
| Interest expense | 4,800 |
| Earning before tax | 37,200 |
| Taxes | 11,160 |
| Net income | $ 26,040 |

For this company, calculate the following:
   a. Current ratio.
   b. Number of days' sales in receivables.
   c. Sales to total assets.
   d. Number of days in inventory.
   e. Debt to assets ratio.
   f. Cash flow to debt ratio.
   g. Return on assets.
   h. Return on equity.

47. Industrial Corporation has an income to sales (profit margin) ratio of 0.03, a sales to assets (asset utilization) ratio of 1.5, and a debt to asset ratio of 0.66. What is Industrial's return on equity?

## Web Questions

48. Go to the Federal Reserve Board's website at **www.federalreserve.gov** and update the data in Table 10–1 using the following steps. Click on "All Statistical Releases." Click on "Assets and Liabilities of Commercial Banks in the

U.S." This downloads a file onto your computer that contains the relevant data. How has the data changed since that reported in Table 10–1 for 2012?

49. Go to the Federal Housing Finance Agency's website at **www.fhfa.gov** and find the most recent data on the percentage of conventional single-family mortgages with adjustable rates using the following steps. Under "Research & Analysis," then "Market Data," and then "Monthly Interest Rate Survey Data," click on "Historical Summary Tables." Click on "Annual, All Homes, 1963–20XX." This downloads a file onto your computer that contains the relevant data. How has this data changed since 2012?

50. Go to the Federal Reserve Board's website at **www.federalreserve.gov** and update Table 10–7 using the following steps. Click on "All Statistical Releases." Click on "Consumer Credit." This downloads a file onto your computer that contains the relevant data. How have consumer loan rates changed since 2012 as reported in Table 10–7?

# Integrated Mini Case

## LOAN ANALYSIS

As a senior loan officer at MC Bancorp, you have the following loan applications waiting for review. The bank uses Altman's $Z$ score, default probabilities, mortality rates, and RAROC to assess loan acceptability. The bank's cost of equity (the RAROC benchmark) is 9 percent. The bank's loan policy states that the maximum probability of default for loans by type is as follows:

| Loan Type and Maturity | Maximum Allowable Default Probability |
|---|---|
| AAA-rated | 0.50% |
| A-rated | 1.25 |

Which loans should be approved and which rejected?

1. An AAA-rated, one-year C&I loan from a firm with a liquidity ratio of 2.15, a debt-to-asset ratio of 45 percent, volatility in earnings of 0.13, and a profit margin of 12 percent. MC Bancorp uses a linear probability model to evaluate AAA-rated loans as follows:

$$PD = -0.08X_1 + 0.15X_2 + 1.25X_3 - 0.45X_4$$

where

$X_1$ = Liquidity ratio
$X_2$ = Debt-to-asset ratio
$X_3$ = Volatility in earnings
$X_4$ = Profit margin

2. An AA-rated, one-year C&I loan from a firm with the following financial statement information (in millions of dollars):

| Assets | | Liabilities and Equity | |
|---|---|---|---|
| Cash | $ 40 | Accounts payable | $ 55 |
| Accounts receivables | 120 | Notes payable | 60 |
| Inventory | 210 | Accruals | 70 |
| | | Long-term debt | 550 |
| Plant and equipment | 1,100 | Equity (ret. earnings = $200) | 735 |
| Total assets | $1,470 | Total liabilities and equity | $1,470 |

Also assume sales = $1,250 m, cost of goods sold = $930 m, and the market value of equity is equal to 2.2 times the book value. MC Bancorp uses the Altman's $Z$ score model to evaluate AA-rated loans.

3. An A-rated corporate loan with a maturity of three years. A-rated corporate loans are evaluated using the mortality rate approach.

A schedule of historical defaults (annual and cumulative) experienced by the bank on its A-rated corporate loans is as follows:

| Loan type | Years after Issuance | | | |
| | 1 year | 2 years | 3 years | 4 years |
| --- | --- | --- | --- | --- |
| A-rated corporate loans | | | | |
| Annual default | 0.10% | 0.25% | 0.40% | 0.65% |
| Cumulative default | 0.10 | 0.325 | 0.595 | 1.858 |

4. A $2 million, five-year loan to a BBB-rated corporation in the computer parts industry. MC Bancorp charges a servicing fee of 75 basis points. The duration on the loan is 4.5 years. The cost of funds for the bank is 8 percent.

Based on four years of historical data, the bank has estimated the maximum change in the risk premium on the computer parts industry to be approximately 5.5 percent. The current market rate for loans in this industry is 10 percent.

## Appendix 10A: Credit Analysis

View Appendix 10A at the website for this textbook (**www.mhhe.com/saunders8e**).

## Appendix 10B: Black–Scholes Option Pricing Model

View Appendix 10B at the website for this textbook (**www.mhhe.com/saunders8e**).

# Chapter **Eleven**

# Credit Risk: Loan Portfolio and Concentration Risk

## INTRODUCTION

The models discussed in the previous chapter describe alternative ways by which an FI manager can measure the default risks on *individual* debt instruments such as loans and bonds. Rather than looking at credit risk one loan at a time, this chapter concentrates on the ability of an FI manager to measure credit risk in a loan (asset) *portfolio context* and the benefit from loan (asset) portfolio diversification. We discuss and illustrate several models that are used by FI managers to assess the risk of the overall loan portfolio. The risk-return characteristics of each loan in the portfolio are a concern for the FI, but the risk-return of the overall loan portfolio, with some of the risk of the individual loans diversified, affects an FI's overall credit risk exposure. Additionally, we look at the potential use of loan portfolio models in setting maximum concentration (borrowing) limits for certain business or borrowing sectors (e.g., sectors identified by their Standard Industrial Classification [SIC] codes).

This chapter also discusses regulatory methods for measuring default risk of a portfolio. In particular, the FDIC Improvement Act of 1991 required bank regulators to incorporate credit concentration risk into their evaluation of bank insolvency risk. Moreover, a debate currently is being conducted among bankers and regulators about how this can be done. Some banks are allowed to use their own internal models, such as CreditMetrics and CreditRisk+ (discussed in the Appendices to this chapter) and Moody's Analytics Portfolio Manager (discussed later in this chapter), to calculate their capital requirements against insolvency risk from excessive loan concentrations. Further, the National Association of Insurance Commissioners (NAIC) has developed limits for different types of assets and borrowers in insurers' portfolios—a so-called pigeonhole approach.

www.naic.org

## SIMPLE MODELS OF LOAN CONCENTRATION RISK

FIs widely employ two simple models to measure credit risk concentration in the loan portfolio beyond the purely subjective model of "We have already lent too

**TABLE 11–1**
A Hypothetical
Rating Migration, or
Transition, Matrix

| | | Risk Rating at End of Year | | | |
|---|---|---|---|---|---|
| | | AAA-A | BBB-B | CCC-C | D* |
| Risk Rating at | AAA-A | 0.85 | 0.10 | 0.04 | 0.01 |
| Beginning of Year | BBB-B | 0.12 | 0.83 | 0.03 | 0.02 |
| | CCC-C | 0.03 | 0.13 | 0.80 | 0.04 |

*D = default.

**migration analysis**
A method to measure
loan concentration
risk by tracking credit
ratings of firms in
a particular sector
or ratings class for
unusual declines.

www.standardandpoors.com

www.moodys.com

**loan migration
matrix**
A measure of the
probability of a loan
being upgraded,
downgraded, or
defaulting over some
period.

much to this borrower." The first is migration analysis, where lending officers track S&P, Moody's, or their own internal credit ratings of certain pools of loans or certain sectors—for example, machine tools. If the credit ratings of a number of firms in a sector or rating class decline faster than has been historically experienced, FIs curtail lending to that sector or class.

A **loan migration matrix** (or transition matrix) seeks to reflect the historic experience of a pool of loans in terms of their credit rating migration over time. As such, it can be used as a benchmark against which the credit migration patterns of any new pool of loans can be compared. Table 11–1 shows a hypothetical credit migration matrix, or table, in which loans are assigned to one of three rating classes (most FIs use 10 to 13 rating classes). The rows in Table 11–1 list the S&P rating at which the portfolio of loans began the year and the columns list the rating at which the portfolio ended the year. The numbers in the table are called *transition probabilities,* reflecting the average experience (proportions) of loans that began the year, say, as rating BB remaining rating BB at the end of the year, being upgraded to an AA, being downgraded to a CC, or defaulting (D).

For example, for loans that began the year at rating BBB-B, historically (on average) 12 percent have been upgraded to AAA-A, 83 percent have remained at BBB-B, 3 percent have been downgraded to CCC-C, and 2 percent have defaulted by the end of the year. Suppose that the FI is evaluating the credit risk of its current portfolio of loans of borrowers rated BBB-B and that over the last few years a much higher percentage (say, 5 percent) of loans has been downgraded to CCC-C and a higher percentage (say, 3 percent) has defaulted than is implied by the historic transition matrix. The FI may then seek to restrict its supply of lower-quality loans (e.g., those rated BBB-B and CCC-C), concentrating more of its portfolio on grade AAA-A loans. At the very least, the FI should seek higher credit risk premiums on lower-quality (rated) loans. Not only is migration analysis used to evaluate commercial loan portfolios, it is widely used to analyze credit card portfolios and consumer loans as well.

**concentration limits**
External limits set
on the maximum
loan size that can be
made to an individual
borrower.

The second simple model requires management to set some firm external limit on the maximum amount of loans that will be made to an individual borrower or sector. The FI determines **concentration limits** on the proportion of the loan portfolio that can go to any single customer by assessing the borrower's current portfolio, its operating unit's business plans, its economists' economic projections, and its strategic plans. Typically, FIs set concentration limits to reduce exposures to certain industries and increase exposures to others. When two industry groups' performances are highly correlated, an FI may set an aggregate limit of less than the sum of the two individual industry limits. FIs also typically set geographic limits. They may set aggregate portfolio limits or combinations of industry and geographic limits. Bank regulators in recent years have limited loan concentrations to *individual borrowers* to a maximum of 10 percent of a bank's capital.

**EXAMPLE 11–1**
*Calculating Concentration Limits for a Loan Portfolio*

Suppose management is unwilling to permit losses exceeding 10 percent of an FI's capital to a particular sector. If management estimates that the amount lost per dollar of defaulted loans in this sector is 40 cents, the maximum loans to a single sector as a percent of capital, defined as the concentration limit, is:

$$\text{Concentration limit} = \text{Maximum loss as a percent of capital} \times \frac{1}{\text{Loss rate}}$$

$$= 10\% \times (1/0.4)$$

$$= 25\%$$

**Concept Questions**

1. In Example 11–1, what would the concentration limit be if the loss rate on bad loans is 25 cents on the dollar? (40%)
2. In Example 11–1, what would the concentration limit be if the maximum loss (as a percent of capital) is 15 percent instead of 10 percent? (60%)

Next we look at the use of more sophisticated portfolio theory–based models to set concentration limits. While these models have a great deal of potential, data availability and other implementation problems have, until recently, hindered their use. The basic idea is to select the portfolio of loans that maximizes the return on the loan portfolio for any given level of risk (or that minimizes the degree of portfolio risk for any given level of returns).

# LOAN PORTFOLIO DIVERSIFICATION AND MODERN PORTFOLIO THEORY (MPT)

To the extent that an FI manager holds widely traded loans and bonds as assets or, alternatively, can calculate loan or bond returns, portfolio diversification models can be used to measure and control the FI's aggregate credit risk exposure. Suppose the manager can estimate the expected return of each loan or bond ($R_i$) in the FI's portfolio.

After calculating the individual security return series, the FI manager can compute the expected return ($R_p$) on a portfolio of assets as:

$$R_p = \sum_{i=1}^{N} X_i R_i \tag{1}$$

In addition, the variance of returns or risk of the portfolio ($\sigma_i^2$) can be calculated as:

$$\sigma_p^2 = \sum_{i=1}^{n} X_i^2 \sigma_i^2 + \sum_{i=1}^{n} \sum_{\substack{j=1 \\ i \neq j}}^{n} X_i X_j \sigma_{ij} \tag{2}$$

or

$$\sigma_p^2 = \sum_{i=1}^{n} X_i^2 \sigma_i^2 + \sum_{i=1}^{n} \sum_{\substack{j=1 \\ i \neq j}}^{n} X_i X_j \rho_{ij} \sigma_i \sigma_j \tag{3}$$

where

$R_p$ = Expected or mean return on the asset portfolio

$\Sigma$ = Summation sign

$R_i$ = return on the $i$th asset in the portfolio

$X_i$ = Proportion of the asset portfolio invested in the $i$th asset (the desired concentration amount)

$\sigma_i^2$ = of returns on the $i$th asset

$\sigma_{ij}$ = Covariance of returns between the $i$th and $j$th assets

$\rho_{ij}$ = Correlation between the returns on the $i$th and $j$th assets[1]

The fundamental lesson of modern portfolio theory (MPT) is that by taking advantage of its size, an FI can diversify considerable amounts of credit risk as long as the returns on different assets are imperfectly correlated with respect to their default risk adjusted returns.[2]

Consider the $\sigma_p^2$ in equation (3). If many loans have negative correlations of returns ($\rho_{ij}$ are negative)—that is, when one borrower's loans do badly and another's do well—then combining loans to both borrowers may reduce the FI's overall credit risk exposure. That is, if there is negative correlation across borrower default probabilities, then a portfolio of loans may have less risk than an individual loan, all else equal. Thus, the sum of the individual credit risks of loans viewed independently overestimates the risk of the whole portfolio. Because correlation is constrained to lie between plus and minus one, we can evaluate the effect of a change in $\rho_{ij}$ on asset portfolio risk. For example, in the two-asset case, if $\rho_{ij}$ is negative, the second term in equation (3) will also be negative and will offset the first term, which will always be positive. By appropriately exploiting correlation relationships among assets, an FI can significantly reduce risk in the asset portfolio and improve the portfolio's risk-return trade-off. This is what we meant in Chapter 1 when we stated that by pooling funds, FIs can reduce risk by taking advantage of the law of large numbers in their investment decisions.

| | |
|---|---|
| **EXAMPLE 11–2** | Suppose that an FI holds two loans with the following characteristics:[3] |
| *Calculation of Return and Risk on a Two-Asset Portfolio* | |

| Loan $i$ | $X_i$ | $R_i$ | $\sigma_i$ | $\sigma_i^2$ | |
|---|---|---|---|---|---|
| 1 | 0.40 | 10% | 0.0857 | 0.007344 | $\rho_{12} = -0.84$ |
| 2 | 0.60 | 12 | 0.0980 | 0.009604 | $\sigma_{12} = -0.0070548$ |

[1] The correlation coefficient reflects the joint movement of asset returns, or default risks in the case of loans, and lies between the values $-1 \leq \rho \leq +1$, where $\rho$ is the correlation coefficient. As can be seen from equations (2) and (3), the covariance between any two assets ($\sigma_{ij}$) is related to the correlation coefficient ($\rho_{ij}$) by $\sigma_{ij} = \rho_{ij}\sigma_i\sigma_j$.

[2] One objection to using modern portfolio theory for loans is that the returns on individual loans are not normally or symmetrically distributed. In particular, most loans have limited upside returns and long-tail downside risks; see Appendix 11A and Chapter 9 in Saunders and Allen, *Credit Risk Management: In and Out of the Financial Crisis,* 3rd ed. (New York: John Wiley & Sons, 2010). Also, concerns about maintaining relationships with traditional customers may limit the ability of an FI to diversify. The relationship limit on diversification has been called the "paradox of credit." That is, leading institutions specialize in monitoring and generating information about their key customers (see Chapter 1), yet such monitoring specialization may lead to a highly concentrated loan portfolio. Relationship concerns may inhibit the loan portfolio's being managed in a fashion similar to a mutual fund's management of an equity portfolio.

[3] Note that variance ($\sigma^2$) is measured in percent squared; standard deviation ($\sigma$) is measured in percent.

The return on the loan portfolio is:

$$R_p = 0.4(10\%) + 0.6(12\%) = 11.2\%$$

while the risk of the portfolio is:

$$\sigma_p^2 = (0.4)^2(0.007344) + (0.6)^2(0.009604) + 2(0.4)(0.6)(-0.84)(0.0857)(0.0980) = 0.0012462$$

thus, $\sigma_p = \sqrt{0.0012462} = 0.0353 = 3.53\%$

Notice that the risk (or standard deviation of returns) of the portfolio, $\sigma_p$ (3.53 percent), is less than the risk of either individual asset (8.57 percent and 9.80 percent, respectively). The negative correlation between the returns of the two loans ($-0.84$) results in an overall reduction of risk when they are put together in an FI's portfolio.

To see more generally the advantages of diversification, consider Figure 11–1. Note that $A$ is an undiversified portfolio with heavy investment concentration in just a few loans or bonds. By fully exploiting diversification potential with bonds or loans whose returns are negatively correlated or that have a low positive correlation with those in the existing portfolio, the FI manager can lower the credit risk on the portfolio from $\sigma_{pA}$ to $\sigma_{pB}$ while earning the same expected return. That is, portfolio $B$ is the efficient (lowest-risk) portfolio associated with portfolio return level $R_p$. By varying the proportion of the asset portfolio invested in each asset (in other words, by varying the required portfolio return level $R_p$ up and down), the manager can identify an entire frontier of efficient portfolio mixes (weights) of loans and bonds. Each portfolio mix is efficient in the sense that it offers the lowest risk level to the FI manager at each possible level of portfolio returns. However, as you can see in Figure 11–1, of all possible efficient portfolios that can be generated, portfolio $B$ produces the lowest possible risk level for the FI manager. That is, it maximizes the gains from diversifying across all available loans and bonds so that the manager cannot reduce the risk of the portfolio below $\sigma_{pB}$. For this reason, $\sigma_{pB}$ is usually labeled the **minimum risk portfolio.**

Even though $B$ is clearly the minimum risk portfolio, it does not generate the highest returns. Consequently, portfolio $B$ may be chosen only by the most

**minimum risk portfolio**
Combination of assets that reduces the risk of portfolio returns to the lowest feasible level.

**FIGURE 11–1**
**FI Portfolio Diversification**

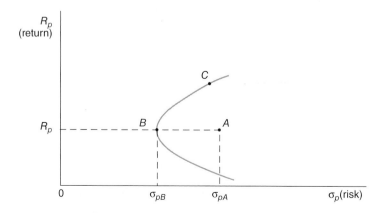

risk-averse FI managers, whose sole objective is to minimize portfolio risk regardless of the portfolio's return. Most portfolio managers have some desired return-risk trade-off in mind; they are willing to accept more risk if they are compensated with higher expected returns. One such possibility would be portfolio C in Figure 11–1. This is an efficient portfolio in that the FI manager has selected loan proportions ($X_i$) to produce a portfolio risk level that is a minimum for that higher expected return level. This portfolio dominates all other portfolios that can produce the same expected return level.[4]

Portfolio theory is a highly attractive tool. Still, over and above the intuitive concept that diversification is generally good, a question arises as to its applicability for banks, insurance companies, and thrifts. These FIs often hold significant amounts of regionally specific nontraded or infrequently traded loans and bonds.

---

**Concept Questions**

1. What is the main point in using MPT for loan portfolio risk?
2. Why would an FI not always choose to operate with a minimum risk portfolio?

---

www.moodysanalytics.com

## Moody's Analytics Portfolio Manager Model

**Moody's Analytics Portfolio Manager**
A model that applies modern portfolio theory to the loan portfolio.

Despite the nontraded aspect of many loans, a great deal of recent research has gone into developing modern portfolio theory models for loans. Below we look at one approach developed by KMV Corporation (now owned and operated by Moody's Analytics) called **Portfolio Manager.**[5] We will see that Moody's Analytics Portfolio Manager model differs from MPT in that it does not require loan returns to be normally distributed. Further, Moody's Analytics has developed a proprietary model to estimate the value of infrequently traded loans. Thus, the Moody's Analytics model is unique in the way it estimates the return, risk, and correlations between loans in an FI's loan portfolio. Once these variables are estimated in the Moody's Analytics Portfolio Manager model, they are then incorporated into the standard MPT equations to get an estimate of the risk and return of the FI's loan portfolio. The Moody's Analytics Credit Monitor model examines Moody's Analytics' method of evaluating default risk on an individual loan (so-called expected default frequency, or EDF). The Moody's Analytics Portfolio Manager model, examined in this chapter, uses the default probability on each loan in a portfolio to identify the overall risk of the portfolio.

Any model that seeks to estimate an efficient frontier for loans, as in Figure 11–1, and thus the optimal or best proportions ($X_i$) in which to hold loans made to different borrowers, needs to determine and measure three things [see equations (1), (2), and (3)]: the expected return on a loan to borrower $i$ ($R_i$), the risk of a loan to borrower $i$ ($\sigma_i$), and the correlation of default risks between loans made to borrowers $i$ and $j$ ($\rho_{ij}$). Specifically, in the Moody's Analytics Portfolio Manager model

---

[4] Rather than selecting a point on the loan efficient frontier that reflects managerial risk aversion, as in Figure 11–1, point *C*, the FI manager would pick a point that maximizes firm value. This would be the point where the return of the portfolio minus the risk-free rate divided by the standard deviation of portfolio returns is maximized, that is, the maximum of $[(R_p - R_f)/\sigma_p)]$. In MPT this is often called the *Sharpe ratio*. Diagramatically, this is a point on the efficient frontier where a straight line drawn from the vertical axis, from a point equal to $R_f$, is just tangential to the efficient frontier. At this tangency point, it is impossible to improve upon the risk-return trade-off.

[5] Other portfolio models have been developed, including CreditMetrics, CreditRisk+, and Credit Portfolio View (McKinsey and Company). See Saunders and Allen, *Credit Risk Management.*

portfolio return and risk are a function of the extent to which loan (exposure) values can change over a one-year horizon and how these value changes move together across different loans in the loan portfolio (correlations). Changes in loan values are determined by changes in the borrower's credit quality (measured as the expected default frequency [EDF], discussed in Chapter 10) and the amount of the loan not recovered (i.e., the loss given default [LGD] on the loan). To calculate correlations, Moody's Analytics considers the joint impact of 120 different systematic factors, which reflect the global economy, region, industry, and country.

In its simplest form, Moody's Analytics measures each of these as follows:

$$R_i = AIS_i - E(L_i) = AIS_i - [EDF_i \times LGD_i] \qquad \textbf{(4)}$$

$$\sigma_{i} = UL_i = \sigma_{Di} \times LGD_i = \sqrt{EDF_i(1 - EDF_i)} \times LGD_i$$

$$\rho_{ij} = \text{Correlation between the systematic return components of the asset returns of borrower } i \text{ and borrower } j \qquad \textbf{(5)}$$

Each of these needs some explanation.

### Return on the Loan ($R_i$)

The return on a loan is measured by the so-called annual all-in-spread (AIS), which measures annual fees earned on the loan by the FI plus the annual spread between the loan rate paid by the borrower and the FI's cost of funds. Deducted from this is the expected loss on the loan [$E(L_i)$]. This expected loss is equal to the product of the expected probability of the borrower defaulting over the next year, or its expected default frequency ($EDF_i$)—as discussed in Chapter 10—times the amount lost by the FI if the borrower defaults (the loss given default, or $LGD_i$). Also, if desired, the return on the loan can be expressed in excess return form by deducting the risk-free rate on a security of equivalent maturity.

We looked at Altman's estimates of recovery rates (1–LGD) on defaulted bonds in Chapter 10. Altman's research consistently finds that approximately 90 percent of bond recovery rates can be explained and estimated using regressions that include default rates on bonds, one-year changes in bond default rates, and the amount of high yield bonds outstanding in a particular year (which represents the potential supply of defaulted bonds). Macroeconomic factors are found to be insignificant in explaining recovery rates on defaulted bonds (much of this effect is captured in bonds default rates).[6] Different types of debt instruments have different recovery rates. For example, more senior securities tend to have higher recovery rates than subordinated securities, all else equal. Moody's Analytics research has found that the highest (lowest) LGD is for preferred stock and junior subordinated bonds (industrial revenue bonds, senior secured bonds, and senior secured loans). The Basel Committee assessed a fixed 45 percent LGD on secured loans if fully secured by physical, non-real estate collateral and 40 percent if fully secured by receivables. However, there is evidence suggesting that these fixed LGD rates may be too high for bank loans.

### Risk of the Loan ($\sigma_i$)

The risk of the loan reflects the volatility of the loan's default rate ($\sigma_{Di}$) around its expected value times the amount lost given default ($LGD_i$). The product of

---

[6] See E. Altman, "Loss Given Default: The Link between Default and Recovery Rates, Recovery Ratings and Recent Empirical Evidence," New York University Salomon Center Working Paper, May 2008.

**FIGURE 11–2**
Moody's Analytics
Asset Level
Correlation

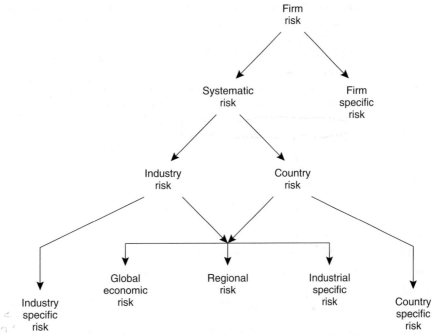

the volatility of the default rate and the *LGD* is called the unexpected loss on the loan ($UL_i$) and is a measure of the loan's risk, or $\sigma_i$. To measure the volatility of the default rate, assume that loans can either default or repay (no default). Then defaults are binomially distributed, and the standard deviation of the default rate for the *i*th borrower ($\sigma_{Di}$) is equal to the square root of the probability of default times 1 minus the probability of default [$\sqrt{(EDF)(1 - EDF)}$].

## *Correlation* ($\rho_{ij}$)

To measure the unobservable default risk correlation between any two borrowers, the Moody's Analytics Portfolio Manager model uses the systematic asset return components of the two borrowers—as discussed in Chapter 10—and calculates a correlation that is based on the historical co-movement between those returns. The model decomposes asset returns into systematic and unsystematic risk using a three-level structural model illustrated in Figure 11–2. Asset returns are extracted from equity returns using Moody's Analytics Credit Manager's approach for imputing firm asset values. Using a time series of these asset values, asset returns are calculated. Once asset returns are estimated, the first-level decomposition into risk factors is a single-index model that regresses asset returns on a composite market factor that is constructed individually for each firm. The composite market factor used in the first-level analysis is composed of a weighted sum of country and industry factors. These factors are estimated at the second level of analysis and may be correlated with each other. The second level separates out the systematic component of industry and country risk, each of which is further decomposed into three sets of independent factors at a third level. These third-level factors are: (1) two global economic factors—a market-weighted index of returns for all firms and the return index weighted by the log of market values; (2) five regional factors—Europe, North America, Japan, Southeast Asia, and Australia/New Zealand; (3) seven sector factors—interest sensitive (banks, real estate, and utilities), extraction (oil and gas, mining), consumer nondurables, consumer durables, technology, medical services, and other (materials processing, chemicals, paper, steel production).

According to Moody's Analytics, default correlations tend to be low and lie between 0.002 and 0.15. This makes intuitive sense. For example, what is the probability that both IBM and General Motors will go bankrupt at the same time? For both firms, their asset values would have to fall below their debt values at the same time over the next year. The likelihood of this is small except in a very severe or extreme recession or extremely high growth in each firm's short-term debt obligations. The generally low (positive) correlations between the default risks of borrowers is also good news for FI managers in that it implies that by spreading loans across many borrowers, they can reduce portfolio risk significantly.[7]

**EXAMPLE 11–3**
*Calculation of Return and Risk on a Two-Asset Portfolio Using Moody's Analytics Portfolio Manager*

Suppose that an FI holds two loans with the following characteristics:

| Loan $i$ | $X_i$ | Annual Spread between Loan Rate and FI's Cost of Funds | Annual Fees | Loss to FI Given Default | Expected Default Frequency | |
|---|---|---|---|---|---|---|
| 1 | 0.60 | 5.0% | 2.0% | 25% | 3% | $\rho_{12} = -0.25$ |
| 2 | 0.40 | 4.5 | 1.5 | 20 | 2 | |

The return and risk on loan 1 are:

$$R_1 = (0.05 + 0.02) - [0.03 \times 0.25] = 0.0625 \text{ or } 6.25\%$$

$$\sigma_1 = [\sqrt{0.03(0.97)}] \times 0.25 = 0.04265 \text{ or } 4.265\%$$

---

[7] The Portfolio Manager model of Moody's Analytics also can be used to assess the risk of extending more loans to any one borrower. If more loans are extended to one borrower, fewer loans can be made to others (assuming a fixed amount of loans). Technically, since the variance of the loan portfolio is:

$$UL_p^2 = \sum_{i=1}^{n} X_i^2 UL_i^2 + \sum_{i=1}^{n} \sum_{\substack{j=1 \\ i \neq j}}^{n} X_i X_j UL_i UL_j \rho_{ij}$$

The marginal risk contribution of a small amount of additional loans to borrower $i$ can be calculated as:

$$\text{Marginal risk contribution} = \frac{dUL_p}{dX_i}$$

where $UL_p$ is the standard deviation (in dollars) of the loan portfolio. Clearly, the marginal risk contribution ($dUL_p$) of an additional amount of loans to borrower $i$, ($dX_i$), will depend not just on the risk of loan $i$ on a stand-alone basis, but also on (1) the correlation of loan $i$ with $j$ other loans, (2) the risk of the $j$ other loans, and (3) where the funds to increase loan $i$ come from. In particular, if $dX_i > 0$, then the sum of the proportion of all remaining loans must decrease unless new funds are raised. Indeed, in the presence of a binding funding constraint $\sum_{i=1}^{n} dX_i < 0$ where $j \neq i$, the key insight is that a loan to a BBB-rated borrower may well be more valuable to an FI (in an MPT sense) if it has a lower correlation with other loans than a loan to an A-rated borrower. That is, it is the loan's marginal risk contribution to total portfolio risk that is important, not its stand-alone risk.

The return and risk on loan 2 are:

$$R_2 = (0.045 + 0.015) - [0.02 \times 0.20] = 0.056 \text{ or } 5.60\%$$

$$\sigma_2 = [\sqrt{0.02(0.98)}] \times 0.20 = 0.028 \text{ or } 2.80\%$$

The return and risk of the portfolio are then:

$$R_p = 0.6(6.25\%) + 0.4(5.60\%) = 5.99\%$$

$$\sigma_p^2 = (0.6)^2 (0.04265)^2 + (0.4)^2 (0.028)^2 + 2 (0.6)(0.4)(-0.25)(0.04265)(0.028) = 0.0006369$$

thus, $\sigma_p = \sqrt{0.0006369} = 0.0252 = 2.52\%$

The world's leading FIs are using the Moody's Analytics model (and other similar models) to actively measure portfolio risk and manage their loan portfolios.

---

**Concept Questions**

1. How does Moody's Analytics measure the return on a loan?
2. If $EDF$ = 0.1 percent and $LGD$ = 50 percent, what is the unexpected loss ($\sigma_i$) on the loan? (1.58%)
3. How does Moody's Analytics calculate loan default correlations?

---

## Partial Applications of Portfolio Theory
### Loan Volume–Based Models

As discussed earlier, direct application of modern portfolio theory is often difficult for FIs lacking information on market prices of assets because many of the assets—such as loans—are not bought and sold in established markets. However, sufficient loan volume data may be available to allow managers to construct a modified or partial application of MPT to analyze the overall concentration or credit risk exposure of the FI. Such loan volume data include:

www.federalreserve.gov

1. *Commercial bank call reports.* These reports to the Federal Reserve classify loans as real estate, agriculture, commercial and industrial (C&I), depository institution, individual, state and political subdivision, and international. Produced for individual banks, these data can be aggregated to estimate the notional allocation of loans among categories or types.

2. *Data on shared national credits.* This is a national database on large commercial and industrial loans that categorizes loan volume by two-digit Standard Industrial Classification (SIC) codes. For example, loans made to businesses in SIC code 49 are loans to public utilities. Because this database provides a national picture of the allocation of large loans across sectors, it is analogous to the market portfolio or basket of commercial and industrial loans.

www.loanpricing.com

3. *Commercial databases.* These are data on 100,000-plus loans by bank and by borrower on the *Loan Pricing Corporations, Dealscan* database.

These data therefore provide *market benchmarks* against which an individual FI can compare its own internal allocations of loans across major lending sectors

**TABLE 11–2**
Allocation of the
Loan Portfolio to
Different Sectors
(in percentages)

| | (1) National | (2) Bank A | (3) Bank B |
|---|---|---|---|
| Real estate | 45% | 65% | 10% |
| C&I | 30 | 20 | 25 |
| Individuals | 15 | 10 | 55 |
| Others | 10 | 5 | 10 |
| | 100% | 100% | 100% |

such as real estate and C&I. For example, the Federal Reserve's Shared National Credit (SNC) database provides a market benchmark of the allocation of loans across various industries or borrowers.

By comparing its own allocation, or the proportions $(X_{ij})$, of loans in any specific area with the national allocations across borrowers $(X_i$, where $i$ designates different loan groups), the $j$th FI can measure the extent to which its loan portfolio deviates from the market portfolio benchmark. This indicates the degree to which the FI has developed *loan concentrations* or relatively undiversified portfolios in various areas.

Consider Table 11–2. In this table we evaluate the first level of the loan asset allocation, which is the amount to be lent to each major loan sector or type. Here we show hypothetical numbers for four types of loans: real estate, commercial and industrial, individual, and others. Column (1) shows the loan allocation proportions at the national level for all banks; this is the market portfolio allocation. Column (2) lists the allocations chosen by bank A, and column (3) shows the allocations chosen by bank B.

Note that bank A has concentrated loans more heavily in real estate lending than the national average, while bank B has concentrated loans more heavily in lending to individuals. To calculate the extent to which each bank deviates from the national benchmark, we use the standard deviation of bank A's and bank B's loan allocations from the national benchmark. Of course, the national benchmark may be inappropriate as the relevant market portfolio for a very small regional bank, insurance company, or thrift. In this case, the FI could construct a regional benchmark from the call report data of banks (or similar data collected by insurance company and thrift regulators) in a given regional area, such as the American Southwest, or, alternatively, a peer group benchmark of banks of a similar asset size and location.

We calculate the relative measure of loan allocation deviation as:[8]

$$\sigma_j = \sqrt{\frac{\sum_{i=1}^{N}(X_{ij} - X_i)^2}{N}}$$

(6)

where

$\sigma_j$ = Standard deviation of bank $j$'s asset allocation proportions from the national benchmark

$X_i$ = National asset allocations

$X_{ij}$ = Asset allocation proportions of the $j$th bank

$N$ = Number of observations or loan categories, $N = 4$

[8] For small samples such as this, it may be more appropriate for the divisor of equation (6) to be $N - 1$ rather than $N$.

**EXAMPLE 11–4**

*Calculating Loan Allocation Deviation*

Refer again to Table 11–2. Applying equation (6) to bank A's loan portfolio, we get the deviation in its loan portfolio allocation as follows:

$$(X_{1A} - X_1)^2 = (0.65 - 0.45)^2 = 0.0400$$
$$(X_{2A} - X_2)^2 = (0.20 - 0.30)^2 = 0.0100$$
$$(X_{3A} - X_3)^2 = (0.10 - 0.15)^2 = 0.0025$$
$$(X_{4A} - X_4)^2 = (0.05 - 0.10)^2 = \underline{0.0025}$$

and

$$\sum_{i=1}^{4} = 0.0550$$

Therefore, $\sigma_A = (0.0550/4)^{1/2} = 11.73\%$. Repeating this process for bank B's loan portfolio, we get:

$$(X_{1B} - X_1)^2 = (0.10 - 0.45)^2 = 0.1225$$
$$(X_{2B} - X_2)^2 = (0.25 - 0.30)^2 = 0.0025$$
$$(X_{3B} - X_3)^2 = (0.55 - 0.15)^2 = 0.1600$$
$$(X_{4B} - X_4)^2 = (0.10 - 0.10)^2 = \underline{0.0000}$$

and

$$\sum_{i=1}^{4} = 0.2850$$

Therefore, $\sigma_B = (0.2850/4)^{1/2} = 26.69\%$. As you can see, bank B deviates more significantly from the national benchmark than bank A because of its heavy concentration on loans to individuals.

Deviation from the national benchmark is not necessarily bad. An FI could have comparative advantages that are not required or available to a national, well-diversified bank. For example, an FI could generate high returns by serving specialized markets or product niches that are not well diversified. An FI may specialize in this area of lending because of its comparative advantage in information collection and monitoring of personal loans (perhaps due to its size or location). Additionally, an FI could specialize in only one product, such as mortgages, but be well diversified within this product line by investing in several different types of mortgages that are distributed both nationally and internationally. This would still enable it to obtain portfolio diversification benefits that are similar to the national average. The standard deviation simply provides a manager with a measure of the degree to which an FI's loan portfolio composition deviates from the national average or benchmark. Nevertheless, to the extent that the national composition of a loan portfolio represents a more diversified market portfolio, because it aggregates across all banks, the asset proportions derived nationally (the $X_i$) are likely to be closer to the *most efficient portfolio composition* than the $X_{ij}$ of the individual bank. This partial use of modern portfolio theory provides an FI manager with a sense of the relative degree of loan concentration carried in the asset portfolio. Finally, although the preceding analysis has referred to the loan portfolio of banks, any FI can use this portfolio theory for any asset group or, indeed, the whole asset portfolio, whether the asset is traded or not. The key data needed are the allocations of a peer group of regional or national financial institutions faced with similar investment decision choices.

### Loan Loss Ratio–Based Models

**systematic loan loss risk**
A measure of the sensitivity of loan losses in a particular business sector relative to the losses in an FI's loan portfolio.

A second partial application of MPT is a model based on historic loan loss ratios. This model involves estimating the **systematic loan loss risk** of a particular (SIC) sector or industry relative to the loan loss risk of an FI's total loan portfolio. This systematic loan loss can be estimated by running a time-series regression of quarterly losses of the $i$th sector's loss rate on the quarterly loss rate of an FI's total loans:

$$\left( \frac{\text{Sectoral losses in the } i\text{th sector}}{\text{Loans to the } i\text{th sector}} \right) = \alpha + \beta_i \left( \frac{\text{Total loan losses}}{\text{Total loans}} \right)$$

where $\alpha$ measures the loan loss rate for a sector that has no sensitivity to losses on the aggregate loan portfolio (i.e., its $\beta = 0$) and $\beta_i$ measures the systematic loss sensitivity of the $i$th sector loans to total loan losses. For example, regression results showing that the consumer sector has a $\beta$ of 0.2 and the real estate sector has a $\beta$ of 1.4 suggest that loan losses in the real estate sector are systematically higher relative to the total loan losses of the FI (by definition, the loss rate $\beta$ for the whole loan portfolio is 1). Similarly, loan losses in the consumer sector are systematically lower relative to the total loan losses of the FI. Consequently, it may be prudent for the FI to maintain lower concentration limits for the real estate sector as opposed to the consumer sector, especially as the economy moves toward a recession and total loan losses start to rise. The implication of this model is that sectors with lower $\beta$s could have higher concentration limits than high $\beta$ sectors— since low $\beta$ loan sector risks (loan losses) are less systematic, that is, are more diversifiable in a portfolio sense.

**EXAMPLE 11–5**
*Calculating Loan Loss Ratios*

Over the past 10 years, a finance company has experienced the following loan losses on its C&I loans, consumer loans, and total loan portfolio.

| Year | C&I Loans | Consumer Loans | Total Loans |
| --- | --- | --- | --- |
| 2015 | 0.02175 | 0.03625 | 0.0250 |
| 2014 | 0.02318 | 0.03862 | 0.0269 |
| 2013 | 0.02340 | 0.03900 | 0.0272 |
| 2012 | 0.02535 | 0.04225 | 0.0298 |
| 2011 | 0.02437 | 0.04062 | 0.0285 |
| 2010 | 0.02415 | 0.04025 | 0.0282 |
| 2009 | 0.02400 | 0.04000 | 0.0280 |
| 2008 | 0.02370 | 0.03950 | 0.0276 |
| 2007 | 0.02325 | 0.03875 | 0.0270 |
| 2006 | 0.02212 | 0.03688 | 0.0255 |

Using regression analysis on these historical loan losses, the finance company gets the following:

$$X_{C\&I} = 0.003 + 0.75X_L \quad \text{and} \quad X_{con} = 0.005 + 1.25X_L$$

where $X_{C\&I}$ = the loss rate in the commercial and industrial loan sector, $X_{con}$ = the loss rate in the consumer loan sector, and $X_L$ = the loss rate for the finance company's loan portfolio. If the finance company's total loan loss rate increases by 15 percent, the expected loss rate increase in the commercial and industrial loan sector will be:

$$X_{C\&I} = 0.003 + 0.75(0.15) = 11.55\%$$

and in the consumer loan sector will be:

$$X_{con} = 0.005 + 1.25(0.15) = 19.25\%$$

To protect against this increase in losses, the finance company should consider reducing its concentration of consumer loans.

## Regulatory Models

www.federalreserve.gov

As noted in the introduction to this chapter, bank and insurance regulators have also been investigating ways to measure concentration risk. After examining various quantitative approaches, the Federal Reserve in 1994 issued a final ruling on its proposed measure of credit concentration risk. The method adopted is largely subjective and is based on examiner discretion. The reasons given for rejecting the more technical models were that (1) at the time, the methods for identifying concentration risk were not sufficiently advanced to justify their use and (2) insufficient data were available to estimate more quantitative-type models. This

www.bis.org

changed in June 2006 as the Bank for International Settlements released guidance on sound credit risk assessment and valuation for loans. The guidance addresses how common data and processes related to loans may be used for assessing credit risk, accounting for loan impairment, and determining regulatory capital requirements and is structured around 10 principles that fall within two broad categories: supervisory expectations concerning sound credit risk assessment and valuation for loans and supervisory evaluation of credit risk assessment for loans, controls, and capital adequacy. In Chapter 20, we look at the details of how credit risk is one component used to determine depository institutions' required level of capital.

Life and property–casualty (PC) insurance regulators have also been concerned with excessive industry sector and borrower concentrations. The Model Act estab-

www.naic.org

lished by the National Association of Insurance Commissioners (NAIC) for state regulators (remember that insurance companies are regulated at the state level—see Chapter 6) sets maximums on the investments an insurer can hold in securities or obligations of any single issuer. These so-called **general diversification limits**

**general diversification limits**

Maximums set on the amount of investments an insurer can hold in securities of any single issuer.

are set at 3 percent for life insurers and 5 percent for property–casualty insurers—implying that the minimum number of different issues is 33 for life companies and for PC companies is 20. The rationale for such a rule comes from modern portfolio theory, which shows *equal* investments across approximately 15 or more stocks can provide significant gains from diversification, thus, lowering portfolio risk or the variance of returns.

<table>
<tr><td>

**Concept Questions**

</td><td>

1. Suppose the returns on different loans are independent. Would there be any gains from loan portfolio diversification?
2. How would you find the minimum risk loan portfolio in a modern portfolio theory framework?
3. Should FI managers select the minimum risk loan portfolio? Why or why not?
4. Explain the reasoning behind the Federal Reserve's 1994 decision to rely more on a subjective rather than a quantitative approach to measuring credit concentration risk. Is that view valid today?

</td></tr>
</table>

## Summary

This chapter discussed various approaches available to an FI manager to measure credit portfolio and concentration risk. It showed how portfolio diversification can reduce the loan risk exposure of an FI. Two simple models that allow an FI to monitor and manage its loan concentration risk were also discussed: migration analysis, which relies on rating changes to provide information on desirable and undesirable loan concentrations, and a model that sets concentration limits based on an FI's capital exposure to different lending sectors. The application of the fully fledged MPT model to the credit (loan) concentration issue was also analyzed as was the Moody's Analytics Portfolio Manager model. In addition, a model that applies portfolio theory to loan loss ratios in different sectors to determine loan concentrations was discussed. Finally, the approaches of regulators to measuring loan concentrations were described.

## Questions and Problems

1. How do loan portfolio risks differ from individual loan risks?
2. What is migration analysis? How do FIs use it to measure credit risk concentration? What are its shortcomings?
3. What does loan concentration risk mean?
4. A manager decides not to lend to any firm in sectors that generate losses in excess of 5 percent of capital.
   a. If the average historical losses in the automobile sector total 8 percent, what is the maximum loan a manager can lend to firms in this sector as a percentage of total capital?
   b. If the average historical losses in the mining sector total 15 percent, what is the maximum loan a manager can make to firms in this sector as a percentage of total capital?
5. An FI has set a maximum loss of 2 percent of total capital as a basis for setting concentration limits on loans to individual firms. If it has set a concentration limit of 25 percent of capital to a firm, what is the expected loss rate for that firm?
6. Explain how modern portfolio theory can be applied to lower the credit risk of an FI's portfolio.
7. Suppose that an FI holds two loans with the following characteristics:

| Loan $i$ | $X_i$ | $R_i$ | $\sigma_i$ | $\sigma_i^2$ | |
|---|---|---|---|---|---|
| 1 | 0.55 | 8% | 8.55% | 73.1025% | $\rho_{12} = 0.24$ |
| 2 | 0.45 | 10 | 9.15 | 83.7225 | $\sigma_{12} = 18.7758$ |

Calculate the return and risk of the portfolio.

8. The Bank of Tinytown has two $20,000 loans with the following characteristics: Loan A has an expected return of 10 percent and a standard deviation of returns of 10 percent. The expected return and standard deviation of returns for loan B are 12 percent and 20 percent, respectively.

   a. If the correlation between loans A and B is 0.15, what are the expected return and the standard deviation of this portfolio?

   b. What is the standard deviation of the portfolio if the correlation is −0.15?

   c. What role does the covariance, or correlation, play in the risk reduction attributes of modern portfolio theory?

9. Why is it difficult for small banks and thrifts to measure credit risk using modern portfolio theory?

10. What is the minimum risk portfolio? Why is this portfolio usually not the portfolio chosen by FIs to optimize the return-risk trade-off?

11. The obvious benefit to holding a diversified portfolio of loans is to spread risk exposures so that a single event does not result in a great loss to an FI. Are there any benefits to not being diversified?

12. A bank vice president is attempting to rank, in terms of the risk-reward trade-off, the loan portfolios of three loan officers. Information on the portfolios is noted below. How would you rank the three portfolios?

| Portfolio | Expected Return | Standard Deviation |
|-----------|-----------------|--------------------|
| A | 10% | 8% |
| B | 12 | 9 |
| C | 11 | 10 |

13. Suppose that an FI holds two loans with the following characteristics.

| Loan | $X_i$ | Annual Spread between Loan Rate and FI's Cost of Funds | Annual Fees | Loss to FI Given Default | Expected Default Frequency | |
|------|-------|--------------------------------------------------------|-------------|--------------------------|----------------------------|---|
| 1 | 0.45 | 5.5% | 2.25% | 30% | 3.5% | $\rho_{12} = -0.15$ |
| 2 | 0.55 | 3.5 | 1.75 | 20 | 1.0 | |

Calculate the return and risk on the two-asset portfolio using Moody's Analytics Portfolio Manager.

14. CountrySide Bank uses Moody's Analytics Portfolio Manager to evaluate the risk-return characteristics of the loans in its portfolio. A specific $10 million loan earns 2 percent per year in fees and the loan is priced at a 4 percent spread over the cost of funds for the bank. Because of collateral considerations, the loss to the bank if the borrower defaults will be 20 percent of the loan's face value. The expected probability of default is 3 percent. What is the anticipated return on this loan? What is the risk of the loan?

15. Suppose that an FI holds two loans with the following characteristics.

| Loan | $X_i$ | Annual Spread between Loan Rate and FI's Cost of Funds | Annual Fees | Loss to FI Given Default | Expected Default Frequency | |
|---|---|---|---|---|---|---|
| 1 | ? | 4.0% | 1.50% | ?% | 4.0% | $\rho_{12} = -0.10$ |
| 2 | ? | 2.5 | 1.15 | ? | 1.5 | |

The return on loan 1 is $R_1 = 6.25\%$, the risk on loan 2 is $\sigma_2 = 1.8233\%$, and the return of the portfolio is $R_p = 4.555\%$. Calculate of the loss given default on loans 1 and 2, the proportions of loans 1 and 2 in the portfolio, and the risk of the portfolio, $\sigma_p$, using Moody's Analytics Portfolio Manager.

16. What databases are available that contain loan information at the national and regional levels? How can they be used to analyze credit concentration risk?

17. Information concerning the allocation of loan portfolios to different market sectors is given below.

**Allocation of Loan Portfolios in Different Sectors (%)**

| Sectors | National | Bank A | Bank B |
|---|---|---|---|
| Commercial | 30% | 50% | 10% |
| Consumer | 40 | 30 | 40 |
| Real Estate | 30 | 20 | 50 |

Bank A and Bank B would like to estimate how much their portfolios deviate from the national average.

a. Which bank is further away from the national average?

b. Is a large standard deviation necessarily bad for an FI using this model?

18. Assume that, on average, national banks engaged primarily in mortgage lending have their assets diversified in the following proportions: 60 percent residential, 15 percent commercial, 5 percent international, and 20 percent mortgage-backed securities. A local bank has the following distribution of mortgage loans: 50 percent residential, 30 percent commercial, and 20 percent international. How does the local bank differ from national banks?

19. Over the past 10 years, a bank has experienced the following loan losses on its C&I loans, consumer loans, and total loan portfolio.

| Year | C&I Loans | Consumer Loans | Total Loans |
|---|---|---|---|
| 2015 | 0.0080 | 0.0165 | 0.0075 |
| 2014 | 0.0088 | 0.0183 | 0.0085 |
| 2013 | 0.0100 | 0.0210 | 0.0100 |
| 2012 | 0.0120 | 0.0255 | 0.0125 |
| 2011 | 0.0104 | 0.0219 | 0.0105 |
| 2010 | 0.0084 | 0.0174 | 0.0080 |
| 2009 | 0.0072 | 0.0147 | 0.0065 |
| 2008 | 0.0080 | 0.0165 | 0.0075 |
| 2007 | 0.0096 | 0.0201 | 0.0095 |
| 2006 | 0.0144 | 0.0309 | 0.0155 |

Using regression analysis on these historical loan losses, the bank has estimated the following:

$$X_C = 0.002 + 0.8X_L \quad \text{and} \quad X_h = 0.003 + 1.8X_L$$

where $X_C$ = loss rate in the commercial sector, $X_h$ = loss rate in the consumer (household) sector, and $X_L$ = loss rate for its total loan portfolio.

    a. If the bank's total loan loss rates increase by 10 percent, what are the expected loss rate increases in the commercial and consumer sectors?

    b. In which sector should the bank limit its loans and why?

20. What reasons did the Federal Reserve Board offer for recommending the use of subjective evaluations of credit concentration risk instead of quantitative models? How did this change in 2006?

21. What rules on credit concentrations has the National Association of Insurance Commissioners enacted? How are they related to modern portfolio theory?

22. An FI is limited to holding no more than 8 percent of its assets in securities of a single issuer. What is the minimum number of securities it should hold to meet this requirement? What if the requirements are 2 percent, 4 percent, and 7 percent?

The questions and problems that follow refer to Appendixes 11A and 11B. Refer to the information in Appendix 11A for problems 23 through 25. Refer to Appendix 11B for problem 26.

23. From Table 11A–1, what is the probability of a loan upgrade? A loan downgrade?

    a. What is the impact of a rating upgrade or downgrade?

    b. How is the discount rate determined after a credit event has occurred?

    c. Why does the probability distribution of possible loan values have a negative skew?

    d. How do the capital requirements of the CreditMetrics approach differ from those of the BIS and the Federal Reserve System?

24. A five-year fixed-rate loan of $100 million carries a 7 percent annual interest rate. The borrower is rated BB. Based on hypothetical historical data, the probability distribution given below has been determined for various ratings upgrades, downgrades, status quo, and default possibilities over the next year. Information also is presented reflecting the forward rates of the current Treasury yield curve and the annual credit spreads of the various maturities of BBB bonds over Treasuries.

| Rating | Probability Distribution | New Loan Value plus Coupon $ | Forward Rate Spreads at Time $t$ | | |
|---|---|---|---|---|---|
| | | | $t$ | $r_t\%$ | $\phi_t\%$ |
| AAA | 0.01% | $114.82 m | 1 | 3.00% | 0.72% |
| AA | 0.31 | 114.60 m | 2 | 3.40 | 0.96 |
| A | 1.45 | 114.03 m | 3 | 3.75 | 1.16 |
| BBB | 6.05 | | 4 | 4.00 | 1.30 |
| BB | 85.48 | 108.55 m | | | |
| B | 5.60 | 98.43 m | | | |
| CCC | 0.90 | 86.82 m | | | |
| Default | 0.20 | 54.12 m | | | |

    a. What is the present value of the loan at the end of the one-year risk horizon for the case where the borrower has been upgraded from BB to BBB?

b. What is the mean (expected) value of the loan at the end of year 1?

c. What is the volatility of the loan value at the end of year 1?

d. Calculate the 5 percent and 1 percent VARs for this loan assuming a normal distribution of values.

e. Estimate the approximate 5 percent and 1 percent VARs using the actual distribution of loan values and probabilities.

f. How do the capital requirements of the 1 percent VARs calculated in parts (d) and (e) above compare with the capital requirements of the BIS and the Federal Reserve System?

25. How does the CreditRisk+ model of Credit Suisse Financial Products differ from the CreditMetrics model of J.P. Morgan Chase?

26. An FI has a loan portfolio of 10,000 loans of $10,000 each. The loans have a historical average default rate of 4 percent and the severity of loss is 40 cents per dollar.

a. Over the next year, what are the probabilities of having default rates of 2, 3, 4, 5, and 8 percent?

b. What would be the dollar loss on the portfolios with default rates of 4 and 8 percent?

c. How much capital would need to be reserved to meet the 1 percent worst-case loss scenario? What proportion of the portfolio's value would this capital reserve be?

# Integrated Mini Case

## LOAN PORTFOLIO ANALYSIS

As a senior loan officer at MC Financial Corp, you have a loan application from a firm in the biotech industry. While the loan has been approved on the basis of an individual loan, you must evaluate the loan based on its impact on the risk of the overall loan portfolio. The FI uses the following three methods to assess its loan portfolio risk.

1. Concentration Limits—The FI currently has lent an amount equal to 40 percent of its capital to the biotech industry and does not lend to a firm in any sector that generates losses in excess of 2 percent of capital. The average historical losses in the biotech industry total 5 percent.

2. Loan Volume–Based Model—National and MC Financial's loan portfolio allocations are as follows.

**Allocation of Loan Portfolios in Different Sectors (%)**

| Sectors | National | MC Financial |
|---|---|---|
| Commercial | 30% | 40% |
| Real Estate | 50% | 45% |
| Consumer | 20% | 15% |

MC Financial does not want to deviate from the national average by more than 12.25 percent.

3. Loan Loss Ratio–Based Model—Based on regression analysis on historical loan losses, the FI estimates the following loan loss ratio models:

$$X_{C\&I} = 0.001 + 0.85X_L$$
$$\text{and } X_{con} = 0.003 + .65X_L$$

where $X_{C\&I}$ = loss rate in the commercial sector, $X_{con}$ = loss rate in the consumer (household) sector, $X_L$ = loss rate for its total loan portfolio. MC Financial's total increase in the loan loss ratio is expected to be 12 percent next year.

Should MC Financial Corp. grant this loan?

## Appendix 11A

# CreditMetrics

CreditMetrics was introduced in 1997 by J.P. Morgan (**www.creditmetrics.com**) and its co-sponsors (Bank of America, Union Bank of Switzerland, et al.) as a value at risk (VAR) framework to apply to the valuation and risk of nontradable assets such as loans and privately placed bonds.[1] Thus, while RiskMetrics seeks to answer the question, "if tomorrow is a bad day, how much will I lose on tradable assets such as stocks, bonds, and equities?," CreditMetrics asks, "if next year is a bad year, how much will I lose on my loans and loan portfolio?"[2]

With RiskMetrics (see Chapter 15) we answer this question by looking at the market value or price of an asset and the volatility of that asset's price or return in order to calculate a probability (e.g., 5 percent) that the value of that asset will fall below some given value tomorrow. In the case of RiskMetrics, this involves multiplying the estimated standard deviation of returns on that asset by 1.65 and then revaluing the current market value of the position ($P$) downward by $1.65\sigma$. That is, VAR for one day is:

$$VAR = P \times 1.65 \times \sigma$$

Unfortunately, since loans are not publicly traded, we observe neither $P$ (the loan's market value) nor $\sigma$ (the volatility of loan value over the horizon of interest—assumed to be one year for loans and bonds under CreditMetrics). However, using (1) available data on a borrower's credit rating, (2) the probability of that rating changing over the next year (the rating transition matrix), (3) recovery rates on defaulted loans, and (4) yield spreads in the bond market, it is possible to calculate a hypothetical $P$ and $\sigma$ for any nontraded loan or bond and thus a VAR figure for individual loans and the loan portfolio.

Consider the example of a five-year, fixed-rate loan of $100 million made at 6 percent annual interest.[3] The borrower is rated BBB.

## RATING MIGRATION

On the basis of historical data collected by S&P, Moody's, and other bond analysts, it is estimated that the probability of a BBB borrower's staying at BBB over the next year is 86.93 percent. There is also some probability that the borrower of the loan will be upgraded (e.g., to A), and there is some probability that it will be downgraded (e.g., to CCC) or even default. Indeed, there are eight possible transitions the borrower can make over the next year, seven of which involve upgrades, downgrades, and no rating changes and one which involves default. The estimated probabilities are shown in Table 11A–1.

**TABLE 11A–1** One-Year Transition Probabilities for BBB-Rated Borrower

| Rating | Transition Probability | |
|--------|------------------------|---|
| AAA | 0.02% | |
| AA | 0.33 | |
| A | 5.95 | |
| BBB | 86.93 | ← Most likely to stay in same class |
| BB | 5.30 | |
| B | 1.17 | |
| CCC | 0.12 | |
| Default | 0.18 | |

---

[1] See CreditMetrics, *Technical Document*, New York, April 2, 1997; and Saunders and Allen, *Credit Risk Measurement*, chap. 6.

[2] In 2002, J.P. Morgan introduced a third measure of credit risk, CreditGrades. The CreditGrades model establishes a framework linking the credit and equity markets. The model employs approximations for the asset value, volatility, and drift, which are used to value credit as an exotic equity derivative. This model is similar in approach to the Moody's Analytics model described in the chapter. See "CreditGrades: Technical Documents," RiskMetrics Group, Inc., May 2002.

[3] This example is based on the one used in the CreditMetrics, *Technical Document*, April 2, 1997.

# VALUATION

The effect of rating upgrades and downgrades is to impact the required credit risk spreads or premiums on loans and thus the implied market value (or present value) of the loan. If a loan is downgraded, the required credit spread premium should rise (remember, the loan rate in our example is fixed at 6 percent) so that the present value of the loan to the FI should fall; the reverse is true for a credit rating upgrade.

Technically, since we are revaluing the five-year $100 million, 6 percent loan at the end of the first year after a credit event has occurred during that year, then (measured in millions of dollars):

$$P = \$6 \text{ m.} + \frac{\$6 \text{ m.}}{(1 + r_1 + \phi_1)} + \frac{\$6 \text{ m.}}{(1 + r_2 + \phi_2)^2} + \frac{\$6 \text{ m.}}{(1 + r_3 + \phi_3)^3} + \frac{\$106 \text{ m.}}{(1 + r_4 + \phi_4)^4}$$

where the $r_i$ are the risk-free rates on T-bonds expected to exist one year, two years, and so on, into the future (i.e., they reflect forward rates from the current Treasury yield curve—see discussion in Chapters 8 and 10) and $\phi_i$ are annual credit spreads for loans of a particular rating class of one year, two years, three years, and four years to maturity (the latter are derived from observed spreads in the corporate bond market over Treasuries). Suppose the borrower gets upgraded during the first year from BBB to A. Table 11A–2 shows the hypothetical values of $r_c$ and $\phi_c$ over the four years.

The first coupon or interest payment of $6 million in the above example is undiscounted and can be viewed as being similar to the accrued interest earned on a bond or a loan since we are revaluing the loan at the end (not the beginning) of the first

year of its life. Then the present value or market value of the loan to the FI at the end of the one-year risk horizon (in millions of dollars) is:

$$P = \$6 \text{ m.} + \frac{\$6 \text{ m.}}{(1.0372)} + \frac{\$6 \text{ m.}}{(1.0432)^2} + \frac{\$6 \text{ m.}}{(1.0493)^3} + \frac{\$106 \text{ m.}}{(1.0532)^4}$$

$$= \$108.64 \text{ m.}$$

That is, at the end of the first year, if the loan borrower is upgraded from BBB to A, the $100 million (book value) loan has a market value to the FI of $108.64 million. (This is the value the FI would theoretically be able to obtain if it "sold" the loan, with the accrued first year coupon of $6 million, to another FI at the end of year 1 horizon at the fair market price or value.) Table 11A–3 shows the value of the loan if other credit events occur. Note that the loan has a maximum market value of $109.37 million (if the borrower is upgraded to AAA) and a minimum value of $51.13 million if the borrower defaults. The minimum value is the estimated recovery value of the loan if the borrower declares bankruptcy.

The probability distribution of loan values is shown in Figure 11A–1. As can be seen, the value of the loan has a fixed upside and a long downside (i.e., a negative skew). It is clear that the value of the loan is not symmetrically (or normally) distributed. Thus CreditMetrics produces two VAR measures:

1. Based on the normal distribution of loan values.
2. Based on the actual distribution of loan values.

**TABLE 11A–2**   Risk-Free Rates on T-Bonds and Annual Credit Spreads

| Year | $r_t$ | $\phi_t$ |
|------|-------|----------|
| 1 | 3.00% | 0.72% |
| 2 | 3.57 | 0.75 |
| 3 | 4.05 | 0.88 |
| 4 | 4.40 | 0.92 |

**TABLE 11A–3**   Value of the Loan at the End of One Year under Different Ratings

| Year-End Rating | Loan Value ($) (including first-year coupon) |
|-----------------|----------------------------------------------|
| AAA | $109.37 m. |
| AA | 109.19 m. |
| A | 108.64 m. |
| BBB | 107.55 m. |
| BB | 102.02 m. |
| B | 98.10 m. |
| CCC | 83.64 m. |
| Default | 51.13 m. |

**FIGURE 11A–1** Distribution of Loan Values on a Five-Year BBB Loan at the End of Year 1

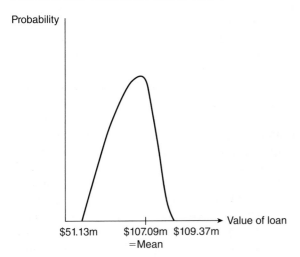

## CALCULATION OF VAR

Table 11A–4 shows the calculation of the VAR based on each approach for both the 5 percent worst-case and the 1 percent worst-case scenarios.

The first step in calculating VAR is to calculate the mean of the loan's value, or its expected value, at year 1, which is the sum of each possible loan value at the end of year 1 times its transition probability. As can be seen, the mean value of the loan is $107.09 million (also see Figure 11A–1). However, the FI is concerned about losses or volatility in value. In particular, if next year is a bad year, how much can it expect to lose? We could define a bad year as occurring once every 20 years (the 5 percent VAR) or once every 100 years (the 1 percent VAR)—this is similar to market risk VAR except that for credit risk the horizon is longer: 1 year rather than 1 day.

Assuming that loan values are normally distributed, the variance of loan value around its mean is $8.9477 million (squared) and its standard deviation or volatility is the square root of the variance equal to $2.99 million. Thus, the 5 percent VAR for the loan is $1.65 \times \$2.99$ million = $4.93 million, while the 1 percent VAR is $2.33 \times \$2.99$ million = $6.97 million. However, this is likely to underestimate the actual or true VAR

**TABLE 11A–4** VAR Calculations for the BBB Loan

| Year-End Rating | (1) Probability of State (%) | (2) New Loan Value plus Coupon (in millions $) | (3) = (1) × (2) Probability Weighted Value (in millions $) | (4) = (2) − Mean Difference of Value from Mean (in millions $) | (5) = (4)² × (1) Probability Weighted Difference Squared |
|---|---|---|---|---|---|
| AAA | 0.02% | $109.37 | $ 0.02 | $ 2.28 | 0.0010 |
| AA | 0.33 | 109.19 | 0.36 | 2.10 | 0.0146 |
| A | 5.95 | 108.64 | 6.44 | 1.55 | 0.1474 |
| BBB | 86.93 | 107.55 | 93.49 | 0.46 | 0.1853 |
| BB | 5.30 | 102.02 | 5.41 | (5.06) | 1.3592 |
| B | 1.17 | 98.10 | 1.15 | (8.99) | 0.9446 |
| CCC | 0.12 | 83.64 | 1.10 | (23.45) | 0.6598 |
| Default | 0.18 | 51.13 | 0.09 | (55.96) | 5.6358 |
| | | Mean = $107.09 m. | | | Variance = 8.94777 |
| | | | | | $\sigma$ = Standard deviation = $2.99 m. |

Assuming Normal Distribution $\begin{cases} 5\% \text{ VAR } = 1.65 \times \sigma = \$4.93 \text{ m.} \\ 1\% \text{ VAR } = 2.33 \times \sigma = \$6.97 \text{ m.} \end{cases}$

Assuming Actual Distribution* $\begin{cases} 5\% \text{ VAR } = 95\% \text{ of actual distribution} = \$107.09 \text{ m. } - \$102.02 \text{ m.} = \$5.07 \text{ m.} \\ 1\% \text{ VAR } = 99\% \text{ of actual distribution} = \$107.09 \text{ m. } - \$98.10 \text{ m.} = \$8.99 \text{ m.} \end{cases}$

* 5% VAR approximated by 6.77% VAR (i.e., 5.3% + 1.17% + 0.12% + 0.18%) and 1% VAR approximated by 1.47% VAR (i.e., 1.17% + 0.12% + 0.18%).

of the loan because, as shown in Figure 11A–1, the distribution of the loan's value is clearly non-normal. In particular, it demonstrates a negative skew or a long-tail downside risk. Using the actual distribution of loan values and probabilities, we can see from Table 11A–4 that there is a 6.77 (5.30 + 1.17 + 0.12 + 0.18) percent probability that the loan value will fall below $102.02 million, implying an approximate 5 percent actual VAR of over $107.09 million − $102.02 million = $5.07 million, and that there is a 1.47 percent probability that the loan value will fall below $98.10 million, implying an approximate 1 percent actual VAR of over $107.09 million − $98.10 million = $8.99 million. These actual VARs could be made less approximate by using linear interpolation to get the exact 5 percent and 1 percent VAR measures. For example, since the 1.47 percentile equals $98.10 million and the 0.3 percentile equals $83.64 million, then, using linear interpolation, the 1.00 percentile equals $92.29 million. This suggests an actual 1 percent VAR of $107.09 million − $92.29 million = $14.80 million.

## CAPITAL REQUIREMENTS

It is interesting to compare these VAR figures with the capital reserves against loans currently required by the Federal Reserve and the BIS. While these requirements are explained in more detail in Chapter 20, they basically amount to a requirement that a bank (or thrift) hold an 8 percent ratio of the risk-weighted book value of the loan as a capital reserve against unexpected losses. In our example of a $100 million face (book) value BBB loan, the capital requirement would be $8 million. This contrasts to the two market-based VAR measures developed above. Using the 1 percent VAR based on the normal distribution, a capital requirement of $6.97 million would be required (i.e., less than the BIS requirement), while using the 1 percent VAR based on the iterated value from the actual distribution, a $14.80 million capital requirement would be required (which is much greater than the BIS capital requirement).

It should be noted that under the CreditMetrics approach, every loan is likely to have a different VAR and thus a different implied capital requirement.

## Appendix 11B

# CreditRisk+

CreditRisk+ is a model developed by Credit Suisse Financial Products (CSFP).[1] Unlike Credit-Metrics, which seeks to develop a full VAR framework, CreditRisk+ attempts to estimate the expected loss of loans and the distribution of those losses with a focus on calculating the FI's required capital reserves to meet losses above a certain level.

The key ideas come from the insurance literature (especially fire insurance), in which the losses incurred by an insurer reflect two things: (1) the frequency of the event (e.g., the probability of a house burning down) and (2) the severity of the loss (e.g., the value of the house lost if it burns down). We can apply the idea to loans, in which the loss distribution on a portfolio of loans reflects the combination (or product) of the frequency of loan defaults and their severity. This framework is shown in Figure 11B–1.

Unlike CreditMetrics, which assumes that there is a fixed probability of a loan defaulting in the next period (defined by its historic transition probability), it is assumed in its simplest form that (1) the probability of any individual loan defaulting

**FIGURE 11B–1   CreditRisk+ Model of the Determinants of Loan Losses**

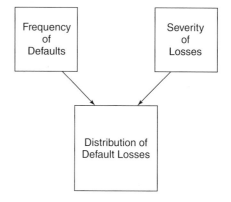

---

[1] See Credit Suisse Financial Products, "CreditRisk+; Credit Risk Management Framework," October 1997, New York/London; and Saunders and Allen, *Credit Risk Measurement*, chap. 7.

**FIGURE 11B–2**
**Frequency of Default on a Loan Assumed by CreditRisk+**

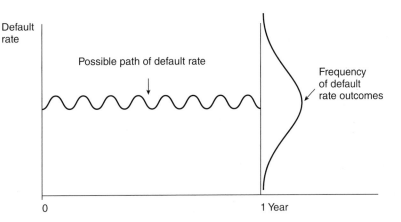

in the portfolio of loans is random and (2) the correlation between the defaults on any pair of loans is zero (i.e., individual loan default probabilities are independent). This framework is therefore most appropriate for analyzing the default risk on large portfolios of small loans (e.g., small business loans, mortgages, and consumer loans) rather than portfolios that contain a few large loans. The model's assumptions about the probability (frequency) of default are shown in Figure 11B–2.

When the probability of default on individual loans is small and this probability is independent across loans in the portfolio, the frequency distribution of default rates can be modeled by a Poisson distribution. Below we look at an example.

Assume that:

1. The FI makes 100 loans of $100,000 each.
2. Historically, 3 percent (3 of 100) of loans have defaulted on average.
3. On default, the severity of loss on each of these loans is the same, at 20 cents per $1 (or $20,000 per $100,000 loan).

## THE FREQUENCY DISTRIBUTION OF DEFAULT RATES

From the Poisson distribution, we can easily generate the probability of different numbers of defaults (in a 100-loan portfolio) occurring:

$$\text{Probability of } n \text{ defaults} = \frac{e^{-m}m^n}{n!}$$

Where $e$ is the exponential function (2.71828), $m$ is the historic average number of defaults (3 of 100, or 3 percent) for loans of this type, and

$n!$ is $n$ factorial, where $n$ is the number of loans for which we are trying to determine the probability of default.

For example, the probability of 3 of 100 loans defaulting over the next year is:

$$\frac{(2.71828)^{-3} \times 3^3}{1 \times 2 \times 3} = 0.224$$

That is, there is a 22.4 percent probability of 3 loans defaulting. We can also determine the probability of 4 of the 100 loans defaulting:

$$\frac{(2.71828)^{-3} \times 3^4}{1 \times 2 \times 3 \times 4} = 0.168$$

or 16.8 percent. The frequency distribution of default rates is shown in Figure 11B–3.

We can multiply these default numbers by loss severity to get the distribution of dollar *losses* on the loan:

$$\text{Dollar loss of 3 loans defaulting} = 3 \times 0.20 \times \$100,000$$
$$= \$60,000$$

$$\text{Dollar loss of 4 loans defaulting} = 4 \times 0.20 \times \$100,000$$
$$= \$80,000$$

The distribution of dollar losses is shown in Figure 11B–4.

As under CreditMetrics, we may ask what the 1 percent worst-case loss scenario (i.e., the 99th worst year's loss out of 100 years) is. From the Poisson distribution, the probability of having 8 losses per 100 loans is approximately 1 percent; thus, there is a 1 percent chance of losing $160,000. In the framework of CreditRisk+ the FI would

**FIGURE 11B–3**
Frequency
Distribution of
Default Rates from
Example

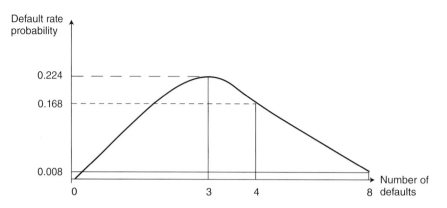

**FIGURE 11B–4**
Frequency
Distribution of
Losses on Loan
Portfolio from
Example

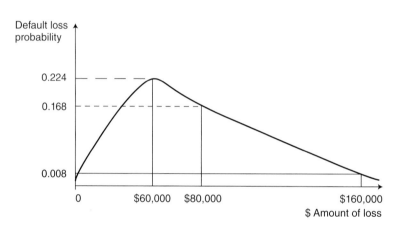

hold a capital reserve to meet the difference between the unexpected (1 percent) loss rate and the average or expected loss rate (the losses associated with three defaults), with expected losses being covered by loan loss provisions and pricing. In our example the capital reserve would be $160,000 − $60,000 = $100,000, or approximately 1 percent of the value of the portfolio. One reason capital reserves are low in this case is that the severity of loss is assumed to be low and equal in each case (i.e., only 20 percent). If, for example, each of the loans in the portfolio lost 80 cents on default, the required capital reserve would rise to 4 percent of the loan portfolio's value. Moreover, in general, the severity of the losses themselves

has a distribution. For example, if loan 1 defaults, the FI might lose 20 cents in $1, while if loan 2 defaults, it may lose 30 cents in $1, and so on. Allowing for a distribution in the severity of losses as well as in the number of defaults can easily be built into the CreditRisk+ framework, as can allowing the mean default rate itself to be variable (see the CSFP technical document for more details).[2]

----

[2] If the (variable) mean default rate is incorporated into the model, this allows the FI to analyze unexpected loan losses in recessions versus expansions. In general, allowing the mean default rate to vary over time increases unexpected losses and required capital reserves.

# Chapter Twelve

See Appendices Online at www.mhhe.com/saunders8e
- Appendix 12A: Sources and Uses of Funds Statement, Bank of America, March 2012

# Liquidity Risk

## INTRODUCTION

Chapters 10 and 11 examined how credit risk can threaten the solvency of an FI. This chapter looks at the problems created by liquidity risk. Unlike risks that threaten the very solvency of an FI, liquidity risk is a normal aspect of the everyday management of an FI. For example, DIs must manage liquidity so they can pay out cash as deposit holders request withdrawals of their funds. Only in extreme cases do liquidity risk problems develop into solvency risk problems, where an FI cannot generate sufficient cash to pay creditors as promised. This chapter identifies the causes of liquidity risk on the liability side of an FI's balance sheet as well as on the asset side. We discuss methods used to measure an FI's liquidity risk exposure and consequences of extreme liquidity risk (such as deposit or liability drains and runs) and examine regulatory mechanisms put in place to ease liquidity problems and prevent runs on FIs. Moreover, some FIs are more exposed to liquidity risk than others. At one extreme, depository institutions are highly exposed; in the middle, life insurance companies are moderately exposed; and at the other extreme, mutual funds, hedge funds, pension funds, and property–casualty insurance companies have relatively low exposure. However, these FIs are certainly exposed to some liquidity risk.

The financial crisis of 2008–2009 was, in part, due to liquidity risk. As mortgage and mortgage-backed securities markets started to experience large losses, credit markets froze and banks stopped lending to each other at anything but high over-night rates. The overnight London Interbank Offered Rate (a benchmark rate that reflects the rate at which banks lend to one another) more than doubled, rising from 2.57 percent on September 29, 2008, to an all time high of 6.88 percent on September 30, 2009. Banks generally rely on each other for cash needed to meet their daily liquidity needs. Interest rates on interbank borrowings are generally low because of confidence that financial institutions will repay each other. However, this confidence broke down in August of 2007. Without interbank funding, banks became reluctant to lend to other credit markets, resulting in a more general and widespread liquidity crisis.

# CAUSES OF LIQUIDITY RISK

Liquidity risk arises for two reasons: a liability-side reason and an asset-side reason. The liability-side reason occurs when an FI's liability holders, such as depositors or insurance policyholders, seek to cash in their financial claims immediately. When liability holders demand cash by withdrawing deposits, the FI needs to borrow additional funds or sell assets to meet the withdrawal. The most liquid asset is cash; FIs use this asset to pay claim holders who seek to withdraw funds. However, FIs tend to minimize their holdings of cash reserves as assets because those reserves pay no interest. To generate interest revenues, most FIs invest in less liquid and/or longer-maturity assets. While most assets can be turned into cash eventually, for some assets this can be done only at a high cost when the asset must be liquidated immediately. The price the asset holder must accept for immediate sale may be far less than it would receive with a longer horizon over which to negotiate a sale. Thus, some assets may be liquidated only at low **fire-sale prices,** thus threatening the solvency of the FI. Alternatively, rather than liquidating assets, an FI may seek to purchase or borrow additional funds.

**fire-sale price**
The price received for an asset that has to be liquidated (sold) immediately.

The second cause of liquidity risk is asset-side liquidity risk, such as the ability to fund the exercise of off-balance-sheet loan commitments. As we will describe in Chapter 16, a loan commitment allows a customer to borrow (take down) funds from an FI (over a commitment period) on demand. When a borrower draws on its loan commitment, the FI must fund the loan on the balance sheet immediately; this creates a demand for liquidity. As it can with liability withdrawals, an FI can meet such a liquidity need by running down its cash assets, selling off other liquid assets, or borrowing additional funds.

To analyze the differing degrees of importance of liquidity risk across FIs, we next consider liquidity risk problems faced by depository institutions, insurance companies, and mutual and pension funds.

---

**Concept Questions**

1. What are the sources of liquidity risk?
2. Why is cash more liquid than loans for an FI?

---

# LIQUIDITY RISK AT DEPOSITORY INSTITUTIONS

## Liability-Side Liquidity Risk

As discussed in Chapter 2, a depository institution's (DI's) balance sheet typically has a large amount of short-term liabilities, such as demand deposits and other transaction accounts, which fund relatively long-term assets. Demand deposit accounts, money market deposit accounts (MMDAs), and other transaction accounts are contracts that give the holders the right to put their claims back to the DI on any given day and demand immediate repayment of the face value of their deposit claims in cash.[1] Thus, an individual demand deposit account holder with

---

[1] Accounts with this type of put option include demand deposits, NOW accounts (interest bearing checking accounts with minimum balance requirements), and money market accounts (checking accounts often with minimum balance and number-of-checks-written restrictions). We describe these accounts in more detail in Chapter 18. Depository institutions typically liquidate deposit account contracts immediately upon request of the customer. Many savings account contracts, however, give a DI some powers to delay withdrawals by requiring notification of withdrawal a certain number of days before withdrawal or by imposing penalty fees such as loss of interest.

**TABLE 12–1**
Assets and
Liabilities of U.S.
Banks (in billions
of dollars)

Source: Federal Deposit
Insurance Corporation
website, July 2012.
*www.fdic.gov*

| Assets | | | Liabilities* | | |
|---|---|---|---|---|---|
| Total cash assets | $ 1,220.6 | 9.55% | Total deposits | $ 9,383.0 | 82.85% |
| Total securities | 3,798.0 | 29.72 | Borrowings | 1,598.5 | 14.11 |
| Total loans | 6,565.4 | 51.37 | Other liabilities | 344.3 | 3.04 |
| Other assets | 1,197.0 | 9.36 | Total liabilities | $11,325.8 | |
| Total assets | $12,781.0 | | | | |

*Excluding bank equity capital.

a balance of $10,000 can demand cash to be repaid immediately, as can a corporation with $100 million in its demand deposit account. In theory, at least, a DI that has 20 percent of its liabilities in demand deposits, MMDAs, and other transaction accounts must stand ready to pay out that amount by liquidating an equivalent amount of assets on any banking day. Table 12–1 shows the aggregate balance sheet of the assets and liabilities of U.S. commercial banks as of March 2012. As seen in this table, total deposits are 82.85 percent of total liabilities (with 43.94 percent demand deposits, MMDAs, and other transaction accounts). By comparison, cash assets are only 9.55 percent of total assets. Also note that borrowed funds are 14.11 percent of total liabilities.

In reality, a depository institution knows that normally only a small proportion of its deposits will be withdrawn on any given day. Most demand deposits act as consumer **core deposits** on a day-by-day basis, providing a relatively stable or long-term source of savings and time deposit funds for the DI. Moreover, deposit withdrawals may in part be offset by the inflow of new deposits (and income generated from the DI's on- and off-balance-sheet activities). The DI manager must monitor the resulting net deposit withdrawals or net deposit drains.[2] Specifically, over time, a DI manager can normally predict—with a good degree of accuracy—the probability distribution of **net deposit drains** (the difference between deposit withdrawals and deposit additions) on any given normal banking day.[3]

Consider the two possible distributions shown in Figure 12–1. In Panel (A) of Figure 12–1, the distribution is assumed to be strongly peaked at the 5 percent net deposit withdrawal level—this DI expects approximately 5 percent of its net deposit funds to be withdrawn on any given day with the highest probability. The DI in Panel (A) has a mean, or expected, net positive drain on deposits, so its new deposit funds and other cash flows are expected to be insufficient to offset deposit withdrawals. The liability side of its balance sheet is contracting. Panel A in Table 12–2 illustrates an actual 5 percent net drain of deposit accounts (or, in terms of dollars, a drain of $5 million).

**core deposits**
Those deposits that provide a DI with a long-term funding source.

**net deposit drains**
The amount by which cash withdrawals exceed additions; a net cash outflow.

---

[2] Also a part of liquidity risk (although not as likely to cause an FI to fail) is an unexpected inflow of funds. For example, in 2008 as stock prices fell, investors liquidated their stock investments and deposited these funds in their banks and credit unions. With interest rates at historic lows, depository institutions faced a problem of finding sufficiently attractive (in a return sense) loans and securities in which to invest these funds.

[3] Apart from predictable daily seasonality to deposit flows, there are other seasonal variations, many of which are, to a greater or lesser degree, predictable. For example, many retail DIs face above-average deposit outflows around the end of the year and in the summer (due to Christmas and the vacation season). Also, many rural DIs face a deposit inflow–outflow cycle that closely matches the agricultural cycle of the local crop or crops. In the planting and growing season, deposits tend to fall, while in the harvest season, deposits tend to rise (as crops are sold).

**FIGURE 12–1**
Distribution of Net
Deposit Drains

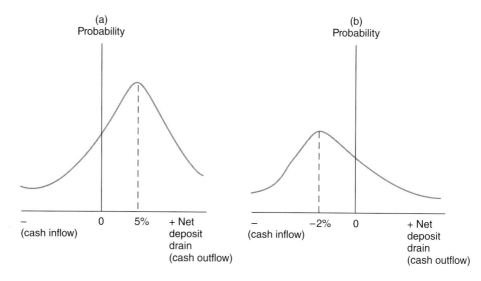

For a DI to be growing, it must have a mean or average deposit drain such that new deposit funds more than offset deposit withdrawals. Thus, the peak of the net deposit drain probability distribution would be at a point to the left of zero. See the −2 percent in Panel (B) in Figure 12–1, where the distribution of net deposit drains is peaked at −2 percent, or the FI is receiving net cash inflows with the highest probability.

A DI can manage a drain on deposits in two major ways: (1) purchased liquidity management and/or (2) stored liquidity management. Traditionally, DI managers have relied on stored liquidity management as the primary mechanism of liquidity management. Today, many DIs—especially the largest banks with access to the money market and other nondeposit markets for funds—rely on purchased liquidity (or liability) management to deal with the risk of cash shortfalls. A more extensive discussion of liability management techniques is left to Chapter 18. Here we briefly discuss the alternative methods of liquidity risk management.

**TABLE 12–2**
Effect of Net
Deposit Drain on
the Balance Sheet
(in millions of
dollars)

| Panel A: Balance Sheet Immediately before and after Deposit Drain | | | | | | | |
|---|---|---|---|---|---|---|---|
| **Before the Drain** | | | | **After the Drain** | | | |
| **Assets** | | **Liabilities** | | **Assets** | | **Liabilities** | |
| Assets | 100 | Deposits | 70 | Assets | 100 | Deposits | 65 |
| | | Borrowed funds | 10 | | | Borrowed funds | 10 |
| | | Other liabilities | 20 | | | Other liabilities | 20 |
| | 100 | | 100 | | 100 | | 95 |

| Panel B: Adjusting to a Deposit Drain through Purchased Liquidity Management | | |
|---|---|---|
| **Assets** | **Liabilities** | |
| Assets | 100 | Deposits | 65 |
| | | Borrowed funds | 15 |
| | | Other liabilities | 20 |
| | 100 | | 100 |

### Purchased Liquidity Management

A DI manager who purchases liquidity turns to the markets for purchased funds, such as the federal funds market and/or the repurchase agreement markets,[4] which are interbank markets for short-term loans. Alternatively, the DI manager could issue additional fixed-maturity wholesale certificates of deposit or even sell some notes and bonds.[5] For example, Table 12–2, Panel A shows a DI's balance sheet immediately before and after a deposit drain of $5 million. As long as the total amount of funds raised equals $5 million, the DI in Table 12–2 could fully fund its net deposit drain. However, this can be expensive for the DI since it is paying *market rates* for funds in the wholesale money market to offset net drains on low-interest-bearing deposits.[6] Thus, the higher the cost of purchased funds relative to the rates earned on assets, the less attractive this approach to liquidity management becomes. Further, since most of these funds are not covered by deposit insurance, their availability may be limited should the depository institution incur insolvency difficulties. Table 12–2, Panel B, shows the DI's balance sheet if it responds to deposit drains by using purchased liquidity management techniques.

**purchased liquidity management**
An adjustment to a deposit drain that occurs on the liability side of the balance sheet.

Note that **purchased liquidity management** has allowed the DI to maintain its overall balance sheet size of $100 million without disturbing the size and composition of the asset side of its balance sheet—that is, the complete adjustment to the deposit drain occurs on the liability side of the balance sheet. In other words, purchased liquidity management can insulate the asset side of the balance sheet from normal drains on the liability side of the balance sheet. This is one of the reasons for the enormous growth in recent years of FI purchased liquidity management techniques and associated purchased fund markets such as fed funds, repurchase agreements, and wholesale CDs. (We describe and discuss these instruments in more detail in Chapter 18.) In the early 2000s regulators expressed concerns about the increased use of these (wholesale) funding sources by DIs. Indeed, with the liquidity crunch experienced during the financial crisis, additional (wholesale) funds were hard and sometimes impossible to obtain.

### Stored Liquidity Management

**stored liquidity management**
An adjustment to a deposit drain that occurs on the asset side of the balance sheet.

Instead of meeting the net deposit drain by purchasing liquidity in the wholesale money markets, the DI could use **stored liquidity management.** That is, the FI could liquidate some of its assets, utilizing its stored liquidity. Traditionally, U.S. DIs have held stored cash reserves only at the Federal Reserve and in their vaults for this very purpose. The Federal Reserve sets minimum reserve requirements for the cash reserves banks must hold.[7] Even so, DIs still tend to hold cash reserves in excess of the minimum required to meet liquidity drains.

---

[4] Securities companies and institutional investors use the repurchase agreement market extensively for liquidity management purposes.

[5] The discount window is also a source of funds. See the section "Bank Runs, the Discount Window, and Deposit Insurance" in this chapter and Chapter 19 for more discussion of the role of the discount window.

[6] While checking accounts pay no explicit interest, other transaction accounts such as NOW and MMDAs do. However, the rates paid are normally sticky, are slow to adjust to changes in market interest rates, and lie below purchased fund rates (see Chapter 18).

[7] Currently, the Fed requires 3 percent on the first $79.5 million and 10 percent on the rest of a DI's demand deposit and transaction account holdings. The $79.5 million figure is adjusted annually along with the growth in bank deposits. The first $12.4 million of the $79.5 million is not subject to reserve requirements (the figures are as of July 2013).

**TABLE 12–3**
Composition of the
DI's Balance Sheet
(in millions of
dollars)

| Panel A: Balance Sheet Immediately before Deposit Drain | | | |
|---|---|---|---|
| **Assets** | | **Liabilities** | |
| Cash | 9 | Deposits | 70 |
| Other assets | 91 | Borrowed funds | 10 |
| | | Other liabilities | 20 |
| | 100 | | 100 |

| Panel B: Adjusting to a Deposit Drain through Stored Liquidity Management | | | |
|---|---|---|---|
| **Assets** | | **Liabilities** | |
| Cash | 4 | Deposits | 65 |
| Other assets | 91 | Borrowed funds | 10 |
| | | Other liabilities | 20 |
| | 95 | | 95 |

Suppose, in our example, that on the asset side of the balance sheet the DI normally holds $9 million of its assets in cash (of which $3 million are to meet Federal Reserve minimum reserve requirements and $6 million are in an "excess" cash reserve). We depict the situation before the net drain in liabilities in Table 12–3, Panel A. As depositors withdraw $5 million in deposits, the DI can meet this directly by using the excess cash stored in its vaults or held on deposit at other DIs or at the Federal Reserve. If the reduction of $5 million in deposit liabilities is met by a $5 million reduction in cash assets held by the DI, its balance sheet will be as shown in Table 12–3, Panel B.

When the DI uses its cash as the liquidity adjustment mechanism, both sides of its balance sheet contract. In this example, the DI's total assets and liabilities shrink from $100 to $95 million. The cost to the DI from using stored liquidity, apart from decreased asset size, is that it must hold excess low-rate assets in the form of cash on its balance sheet.[8] Thus, the cost of using cash to meet liquidity needs is the forgone return (or opportunity cost) of being unable to invest these funds in loans and other higher-income-earning assets.

Finally, note that while stored liquidity management and purchased liquidity management are alternative strategies for meeting deposit drains, a DI can combine the two methods by using some purchased liquidity management and some stored liquidity management to meet liquidity needs.

## Asset-Side Liquidity Risk

Just as deposit drains can cause a DI liquidity problems, so can loan requests and the exercise by borrowers of their loan commitments and other credit lines. In recent years, DIs, especially commercial banks, have increased their loan commitments tremendously, with the belief they would not be used. Unused loan commitments to cash grew from 529.4 percent in 1994 to 1014.6 percent in October 2008 (before falling back to 608.6 percent during the financial crisis). Table 12–4, Panel A, shows the effect of a $5 million exercise of a loan commitment by a borrower: Part (a) in Table 12–4, Panel A is the balance sheet before the commitment

[8] DIs could hold highly liquid interest-bearing assets such as T-bills, but these are still less liquid than cash and immediate liquidation may result in some small capital value losses.

**TABLE 12–4**
Effects of a Loan Commitment Exercise (in millions of dollars)

### Panel A: Balance Sheet Immediately before and after Exercise

| (a) Before Exercise | | | | (b) After Exercise | | | |
|---|---|---|---|---|---|---|---|
| Cash | 9 | Deposits | 70 | Cash | 9 | Deposits | 70 |
| Other assets | 91 | Borrowed funds | 10 | Other assets | 96 | Borrowed funds | 10 |
| | | Other liabilities | 20 | | | Other liabilities | 20 |
| | 100 | | 100 | | 105 | | 100 |

### Panel B: Adjusting the Balance Sheet to a Loan Commitment Exercise

| (a) Purchased Liquidity Management | | | | (b) Stored Liquidity Management | | | |
|---|---|---|---|---|---|---|---|
| Cash | 9 | Deposits | 70 | Cash | 4 | Deposits | 70 |
| Other assets | 96 | Borrowed funds | 15 | Other assets | 96 | Borrowed funds | 10 |
| | | Other liabilities | 20 | | | Other liabilities | 20 |
| | 105 | | 105 | | 100 | | 100 |

exercise and part (b) is the balance sheet after the exercise. The exercise of the loan commitment means that the DI needs to provide $5 million in loans immediately to the borrower (other assets rise from $91 to $96 million). This can be done either by purchased liquidity management (borrowing an additional $5 million in the money market and lending these funds to the borrower) or by stored liquidity management (decreasing the DI's excess cash assets from $9 million to $4 million). We present these two policies in Table 12–4, Panel B.

Another type of asset-side liquidity risk arises from the FI's investment portfolio. Specifically, unexpected changes in interest rates can cause investment portfolio values to fluctuate significantly. If interest rates increase, the value of the investment securities portfolio falls and large losses in portfolio value can occur (see Chapter 15 on market risk). Further, there is the risk that liquidity in a particular market will deteriorate because market traders want to sell and no one wants to buy. It has been argued that technological and other developments have led to a steady improvement in the liquidity of financial markets. However, this is questionable in that there is an increasing tendency toward "herd" behavior, where most traders want to make the same type of trade (such as a sale) at a particular time. During the sell-off, liquidity dries up and investment securities can be sold only at fire-sale prices. The result is a reduction in the value of the investment portfolio and increased liquidity risk for the FI.

In Table 12–5, Panel A shows an FI's balance sheet immediately before and after a $5 million decrease in the market value of its investment portfolio. In addition to a loss in equity value, the FI must fund the $5 million loss in value on the balance sheet such that loan requests and deposit withdrawals can be met. The FI must replace the loss in value of the investment portfolio. This can be done either by purchased liquidity management (borrowing an additional $5 million in deposits or purchased funds) or by stored liquidity management (purchasing an additional $5 million in assets).[9] Panel B of Table 12–5 shows the effect of these two strategies on the balance sheet. Notice, in both cases, that the FI has lost $5 million in equity.

---

[9] Note that the FI could raise an additional $5 million in equity, e.g., through a common stock issue. However, this is likely to be more costly than adjusting to the loss via purchased liquidity management or stored liquidity management.

**TABLE 12–5**   Effects of a Drop in the Value of the Investment Securities Portfolio (in millions of dollars)

**Panel A: Balance Sheet Immediately before and after Drop in Portfolio Value**

| Before Drop in Value | | | | After Drop in Value | | | |
|---|---|---|---|---|---|---|---|
| Cash | $ 9 | Deposits | $ 60 | Cash | $ 9 | Deposits | $60 |
| Investment portfolio | 40 | Borrowed funds | 10 | Investment portfolio | 35 | Borrowed funds | 10 |
| Other assets | 51 | Other liabilities | 20 | Other assets | 51 | Other liabilities | 20 |
| | | Equity | 10 | | | Equity | 5 |
| | $100 | | $100 | | $95 | | $95 |

**Panel B: Adjusting the Balance Sheet for a Drop in Investment Portfolio Value**

| (a) Purchased Liquidity Management | | | | (b) Stored Liquidity Management | | | |
|---|---|---|---|---|---|---|---|
| Cash | $ 9 | Deposits | $ 65 | Cash | $ 4 | Deposits | $60 |
| Investment portfolio | 40 | Borrowed funds | 10 | Investment portfolio | 40 | Borrowed funds | 10 |
| Other assets | 51 | Other liabilities | 20 | Other assets | 51 | Other liabilities | 20 |
| | | Equity | 5 | | | Equity | 5 |
| | $100 | | $100 | | $95 | | $95 |

## Measuring a DI's Liquidity Risk Exposure

### Sources and Uses of Liquidity

As discussed earlier, a DI's liquidity risk arises from ongoing conduct of business such as a withdrawal of deposits or from new loan demand, and the subsequent need to meet those demands through liquidating assets or borrowing funds. Therefore, a DI manager must be able to measure its liquidity position on a daily basis, if possible. A useful tool is a *net liquidity statement* that lists sources and uses of liquidity and thus provides a measure of a DI's net liquidity position. Such a statement for a hypothetical U.S. money center bank is presented in Table 12–6.

The DI can obtain liquid funds in three ways. First, it can sell its liquid assets such as T-bills immediately with little price risk and low transaction cost. Second, it can borrow funds in the money/purchased funds market up to a maximum amount (this is an *internal* guideline based on the manager's assessment of the credit limits that the purchased or borrowed funds market is likely to impose on the DI). Third, it can use any excess cash reserves over and above the amount held

**TABLE 12–6**
Net Liquidity
Position (in
millions of dollars)

| Sources of Liquidity | |
|---|---|
| 1. Total cash-type assets | $ 2,000 |
| 2. Maximum borrowed funds limit | 12,000 |
| 3. Excess cash reserves | 500 |
| Total | $14,500 |
| **Uses of Liquidity** | |
| 1. Funds borrowed | $ 6,000 |
| 2. Federal Reserve borrowing | 1,000 |
| Total | 7,000 |
| Total net liquidity | $ 7,500 |

to meet regulatory imposed reserve requirements. In Table 12–6 the DI's *sources* of liquidity total $14,500 million. Compare this with the DI's *uses* of liquidity, in particular the amount of borrowed or purchased funds it has already utilized (e.g., fed funds, RPs borrowed) and the amount of cash it has already borrowed from the Federal Reserve through discount window loans. These total $7,000 million. As a result, the DI has a positive net liquidity position of $7,500 million. These liquidity sources and uses can be easily tracked on a day-by-day basis.

The net liquidity position in Table 12–6 lists management's expected sources and uses of liquidity for a hypothetical money center bank. All FIs report their historical sources and uses of liquidity in their annual and quarterly reports. Appendix 12A to this chapter (located at the book's website, **www.mhhe.com/saunders8e**) presents the March 2012 Sources and Uses of Funds Statement for Bank of America. As an FI manager deals with liquidity risk, historical sources and uses of liquidity statements can assist the manager in determining where future liquidity issues may arise.

### Peer Group Ratio Comparisons

Another way to measure a DI's liquidity exposure is to compare certain key ratios and balance sheet features of the DI—such as its loans to deposits, borrowed funds to total assets, and commitments to lend to assets ratios—with those of DIs of a similar size and geographic location. A high ratio of loans to deposits and borrowed funds to total assets means that the DI relies heavily on the short-term money market rather than on core deposits to fund loans. This could mean future liquidity problems if the DI is at or near its borrowing limits in the purchased funds market. Similarly, a high ratio of loan commitments to assets indicates the need for a high degree of liquidity to fund any unexpected takedowns of these loans—high-commitment DIs often face more liquidity risk exposure than do low-commitment DIs.

Table 12–7 lists the March 2012 values of these ratios for two banks: Northern Trust Bank (NT) and Bank of America (BOA). BOA (a money center bank) relies on borrowed funds more heavily than does NT (a non–money center bank). The banks' ratios of borrowed funds to total assets were 7.48 percent for NT and 11.67 percent for BOA. Further, the ratios of loans to deposits were 38.26 percent and 71.02 percent for NT and BOA, respectively. As a major money center bank, BOA gets much more of the funding of its loans from the borrowed funds markets than from the deposit markets. Northern Trust, a smaller, non–money center bank, uses deposits much more than borrowed funds to fund its loans. The result is that BOA is subject to greater liquidity risk than NT. The banks' ratios of core deposits (the stable deposits of the FI, such as demand deposits, NOW accounts, MMDAs, other savings accounts, and retail CDs) to total assets, on the other hand, were 34.75 percent and 62.65 percent for NT and BOA, respectively. While BOA uses more borrowed funds than NT, more than half of NT's deposits are foreign accounts rather than domestic core deposits. Thus, while BOA gets more of its

**TABLE 12–7**
Liquidity Exposure Ratios for Two Banks, 2012 Values

|  | Northern Trust Bank | Bank of America |
|---|---|---|
| Borrowed funds to total assets | 7.48% | 11.67% |
| Loans to deposits | 38.26 | 71.02 |
| Core deposits to total assets | 34.75 | 62.65 |
| Commitments to lend to total assets | 36.79 | 47.17 |

liquid funds from the borrowed funds market than NT, it has a much larger supply of stable deposits to limit the DI's liquidity risk. Furthermore, NT had a ratio of loan commitments (or credit lines) to total assets of 36.79 percent, while BOA had a much greater ratio of 47.17 percent. If these commitments are "taken down" (see Chapter 16), BOA must come up with the cash to fulfill these commitments, more so than NT. Thus, BOA is exposed to substantially greater liquidity risk than NT from unexpected takedowns of loan commitments by its customers.

### *Liquidity Index*

**liquidity index**
A measure of the potential losses an FI could suffer as the result of sudden (or fire-sale) disposal of assets.

A third way to measure liquidity risk is to use a **liquidity index.** Developed by Jim Pierce at the Federal Reserve, this index measures the potential losses an FI could suffer from a sudden or fire-sale disposal of assets compared with the amount it would receive at a fair market value established under normal market (sale) conditions—which might take a lengthy period of time as a result of a careful search and bidding process. The greater the differences between immediate fire-sale asset prices ($P_i$) and fair market prices ($P_i^*$) the less liquid is the DI's portfolio of assets. Define an index $I$ such that:

$$I = \sum_{i=1}^{N} [(w_i)(P_i/P_i^*)]$$

where $w_i$ is the percent of each asset in the FI's portfolio:

$$\sum_{i=1}^{N} w_i = 1$$

The liquidity index will always lie between 0 and 1. The liquidity index for this DI could also be compared with indexes calculated for a peer group of similar DIs.

---

**EXAMPLE 12–1**

*Calculation of the Liquidity Index*

Suppose that a DI has two assets: 50 percent in one-month Treasury bills and 50 percent in real estate loans. If the DI must liquidate its T-bills today ($P_1$), it receives $99 per $100 of face value. If it can wait to liquidate them on maturity (in one month's time), it will receive $100 per $100 of face value ($P_1^*$). If the DI has to liquidate its real estate loans today, it receives $85 per $100 of face value ($P_2$). Liquidation at the end of one month (closer to maturity) will produce $92 per $100 of face value ($P_2^*$). Thus, the one-month liquidity index value for this DI's asset portfolio is:

$$I = [\tfrac{1}{2}(0.99/1.00)] + [\tfrac{1}{2}(0.85/0.92)]$$
$$= 0.495 + 0.462$$
$$= 0.957$$

Suppose, alternatively, that a slow or thin real estate market caused the DI to be able to liquidate the real estate loans at only $65 per $100 of face value ($P_2$). The one-month liquidity index for the DI's asset portfolio is:

$$I = [\tfrac{1}{2}(0.99/1.00)] + [\tfrac{1}{2}(0.65/0.92)]$$
$$= 0.495 + 0.353$$
$$= 0.848$$

The value of the one-month liquidity index decreases as a result of the larger discount on the fire-sale price—from the fair (full value) market price of real estate—over the one-month period. The larger the discount from fair value, the smaller the liquidity index or higher the liquidity risk the DI faces.

### *Financing Gap and the Financing Requirement*

A fourth way to measure liquidity risk exposure is to determine the DI's financing gap. As we discussed earlier, even though demand depositors can withdraw their funds immediately, they do not do so in normal circumstances. On average, most demand deposits stay at DIs for quite long periods—often two years or more. Thus, a DI manager often thinks of the average deposit base, including demand deposits, as a core source of funds that over time can fund a DI's average amount of loans.

**financing gap**
The difference between a DI's average loans and average (core) deposits.

We define a **financing gap** as the difference between a DI's average loans and average (core) deposits, or:

$$\text{Financing gap} = \text{Average loans} - \text{Average deposits}$$

If this financing gap is positive, the DI must fund it by using its cash and liquid assets and/or borrowing funds in the money market. Thus:

$$\text{Financing gap} = -\text{Liquid assets} + \text{Borrowed funds}$$

We can write this relationship as:

$$\text{Financing gap} + \text{Liquid assets} = \text{Financing requirement (borrowed funds)}$$

**financing requirement**
The financing gap plus a DI's liquid assets.

As expressed in this fashion, the liquidity and managerial implications of the **financing requirement** (the financing gap plus a DI's liquid assets) are that the level of core deposits and loans as well as the amount of liquid assets determines the DI's borrowing or purchased fund needs. In particular, the larger a DI's financing gap and liquid asset holdings, the larger the amount of funds it needs to borrow in the money markets and the greater is its exposure to liquidity problems from such a reliance. The balance sheet in Table 12–8 indicates the relationship between the financing gap, liquid assets, and the borrowed fund financing requirement. See also the following equation:

$$\underset{(\$5 \text{ million})}{\text{Financing gap}} + \underset{(\$5 \text{ million})}{\text{Liquid assets}} = \underset{(\$10 \text{ million})}{\text{Financing requirement}}$$

A widening financing gap can warn of future liquidity problems for a DI since it may indicate increased deposit withdrawals (core deposits falling below $20 million in Table 12–8) and increasing loans due to increased exercise of loan commitments (loans rising above $25 million). If the DI does not reduce its liquid assets—they stay at $5 million—the manager must resort to more money market borrowings. As these borrowings rise, sophisticated lenders in the money market may be concerned about the DI's creditworthiness. They may react by imposing higher risk premiums on borrowed funds or establishing stricter credit limits by not rolling over funds lent to the DI. If the DI's financing requirements exceed such limits, it may become insolvent. This possibility of insolvency also highlights the need for DI managers to engage in active liquidity planning to avoid such crises.

## New Liquidity Risk Measures Implemented by the Bank for International Settlements

During the financial crisis, many DIs struggled to maintain adequate liquidity. Indeed, extraordinary levels of liquidity assistance were required from central banks in order to maintain the financial system. Even with this extensive support, a number of DIs failed or were forced into mergers. Recognizing the need for DIs to improve their liquidity risk management and control their liquidity risk exposures,

**TABLE 12–8**
Financing Requirement of a DI (in millions of dollars)

| Assets | | Liabilities | |
|---|---|---|---|
| Loans | $25 | Core deposits | $20 |
| Liquid assets | 5 | Financing requirement (borrowed funds) | 10 |
| Total | $30 | Total | $30 |
| | | Financing gap | 5 |

the Bank for International Settlement's Basel Committee on Banking Supervision developed two new regulatory standards for liquidity risk supervision. The standards are intended to "enhance tools, metrics, and benchmarks that supervisors can use to assess the resilience of banks' liquidity cushions and constrain any weakening in liquidity maturity profiles, diversity of funding sources, and stress testing practices."[10] The two new liquidity ratios to be maintained by DIs are the liquidity coverage ratio (beginning in 2015 and to be fully implemented in 2019) and a net stable funds ratio (to be implemented in 2018).

### Liquidity Coverage Ratio

The liquidity coverage ratio (LCR) aims to ensure that a DI maintains an adequate level of high-quality assets that can be converted into cash to meet liquidity needs for a 30-day time horizon under an "acute liquidity stress scenario" specified by supervisors. The specified scenario incorporates both institution-specific and systemic shocks that are based on actual circumstances experienced in the global financial crisis. Thus, maintenance of the LCR is intended to ensure that DIs can survive a severe liquidity stress scenario for at least 30 days. The LCR will be reported to DI supervisors monthly starting in 2015.

$$\text{Liquidity coverage ratio} = \frac{\text{Stock of high-quality liquid assets}}{\text{Total net cash outflows over the next 30 calendar days}} \geq 100\%$$

The stock of high quality liquid assets (the numerator of the LCR) is defined as follows:

- Liquid assets must remain liquid in times of stress (i.e., convertible into cash at little loss of value and can be used at the central bank discount window as collateral).
- The liquid assets must be "unencumbered."
- Liquid assets are divided into level 1 and level 2. Level 1 amount has no cap, level 2 amount is capped at 40 percent of total liquid assets.

> Level 1 = Cash + Central bank reserves + Sovereign debt
>
> Level 2A = (Mortgage-backed securities that are government guaranteed) + (Corporate bonds [plain vanilla] rated at least AA−)
>
> Level 2B = (Residential mortgage-backed securities that are not government guaranteed) + (Lower-rated corporate bonds [plain vanilla]) + (Blue chip equities)

- A minimum 15 percent "haircut" has to be applied to the value of each level 2 asset.

[10] International Framework for Liquidity Risk Measurement, Standards and Monitoring, Bank for International Settlements, December 2009, **www.bis.org**.

- Level 2B assets may not account for more than 15 percent of a bank's stock of high-quality liquid assets.
- Level 2 assets may not, in aggregate, account for more than 40 percent of a bank's stock of high-quality liquid assets.

Total net cash outflows (the denominator of the ratio) is defined as:

$$\text{Total } net \text{ cash outflows over the next 30 calendar days} = \text{Outflows} - \text{Min (inflows; 75\% of outflows)}$$

where cash outflows and inflows are defined in Table 12–9. Appendix 12B to the chapter presents the template provided by the Bank for International Settlements used to calculate the LCR.

---

**EXAMPLE 12–2**

*Calculation of the Liquidity Coverage Ratio*

OneBank has the following balance sheet (in millions of dollars). Cash inflows over the next 30 days from the bank's performing assets are $5 million.

| Assets | | Liquidity Level | Liabilities and Equity | | Run-off Factor |
|---|---|---|---|---|---|
| Cash | $ 10 | Level 1 | Stable retail deposits | $ 95 | 3% |
| Deposits at the Fed | 15 | Level 1 | Less stable retail deposits | 40 | 10 |
| Treasury securities | 100 | Level 1 | Unsecured wholesale funding from: | | |
| GNMA securities | 75 | Level 2A | Stable small business deposits | 100 | 5 |
| Loans to A rated corporations | 110 | Level 2A | Less stable small business deposits | 80 | 10 |
| Loans to B rated corporations | 85 | Level 2B | Nonfinancial corporates | 50 | 75 |
| Premises | 15 | | Equity | 45 | |
| Total | $410 | | | $410 | |

The liquidity coverage ratio for OneBank is calculated as follows:

| | | |
|---|---|---|
| Level 1 assets = $10 + $15 + $100 = | | $125 |
| Level 2A assets = ($75 + $110) × 0.85 = $157.25 | Capped at 40% of Level 1 = $125 × 0.40 = | 50 |
| Level 2B assets = $85 × 0.85 = $72.25 | 40% cap on Level 2 assets already met | |
| | Stock of highly liquid assets | $175 |

Cash outflows:

| | |
|---|---|
| Stable retail deposits | $ 95 × 0.03 = $ 2.85 |
| Less stable retail deposits | $ 40 × 0.10 = 4.00 |
| Stable small business deposits | $100 × 0.05 = 5.00 |
| Less stable small business deposits | $ 80 × 0.10 = 8.00 |
| Nonfinancial corporates | $ 50 × 0.75 = 37.50 |
| Total cash outflows over next 30 days | $57.35 |
| | |
| Total cash inflows over next 30 days | 5.00 |
| Total net cash outflows over next 30 days | $52.35 |

Liquidity coverage ratio = $175m/$52.35m = 334.29%. The bank is in compliance with liquidity requirements based on the LCR.

**TABLE 12–9**  Cash Outflows and Inflows Used in the Liquidity Coverage Ratio

**Cash outflows included in the LCR:**

- Retail deposits = Stable + Less stable.
  Stable = Deposits covered by deposit insurance (receive a minimum run-off factor of 3%).
  Less stable = Deposits not covered by deposit insurance (receive a minimum run-off factor of 10%).
- Retail deposits with maturity > 30 days and no early withdrawal (0% run-off factor).
- All unsecured wholesale funds with < 30 days maturity (i.e., callable by funds provider) (100% run-off factor).
- Secured funds backed by Level 1 assets (0% run-off factor), backed by Level 2 assets (15% run-off factor).
- Loss of funding on commercial paper if maturity <30 days (100% run-off factor).
- All debt maturing within 30 days (100% run-off factor).
- Loan commitment (draw-down) factors:
  - 5% draw-downs on committed credit and liquidity facilities to retail and small business customers.
  - 10% draw-downs on committed credit facilities to nonfinancial corporate, sovereigns and central banks, public-sector entities, and multilateral development banks.
  - 30% draw-downs on committed liquidity facilities to nonfinancial corporate, sovereigns and central banks, public-sector entities, and multilateral development banks.
  - 40% draw-downs on committed credit and liquidity facilities to other legal entities. These entities include financial institutions (e.g., banks, securities firms, and insurance companies), conduits and special-purpose vehicles, and fiduciaries beneficiaries.
- Cash outflows related to operating costs (0% run-off factor).

**Cash inflows included in the LCR:**

- Only include inflows for sources where no default is expected in next 30 days.
- There is a 75% cap on inflows meeting outflows so DIs do not just rely of inflows for liquidity.
- Assume that no lines of credit on other banks can be drawn on (0% inflow).
- Assume 100% inflow received on wholesale loans and 50% inflow on retail loans from counterparties.
- 100% inflow on known derivative payments.

### Net Stable Funding Ratio

The net stable funding ratio (NSFR) takes a longer-term look at liquidity on a DI's balance sheet. The NSFR evaluates liquidity over the entire balance sheet and provides incentives for DIs to use stable sources of financing. This longer-term liquidity ratio requires a minimum amount of stable funding be held over a one-year time horizon based on liquidity risk factors assigned to liquidity exposures of on- and off-balance-sheet assets. The NSFR is intended to ensure that long-term assets are funded with a minimum amount of stable liabilities. It limits reliance on short-term wholesale funding, which was a major problem in the financial crisis. Basically, stable funding is sought for all illiquid assets and securities held, where stable funding is defined as equity and liability financing expected to be reliable sources of funds over a one-year time horizon. The NSFR ratio will be reported to DI supervisors quarterly starting in 2018.

$$\text{NSFR} = \frac{\text{Available amount of stable funding}}{\text{Required amount of stable funding}} > 100\%$$

**TABLE 12–10**  Components of Available Stable Funding and Associated ASF Factors

| ASF Factor | Components of ASF Category |
|---|---|
| 100% | • The total amount of capital, including both Tier 1 and Tier 2 as defined in existing global capital standards issued by the committee.<br>• The total amount of any preferred stock not included in Tier 2 that has an effective remaining maturity of 1 year or greater, taking into account any explicit or embedded options that would reduce the expected maturity to less than 1 year.<br>• The total amount of secured and unsecured borrowings and liabilities (including term deposits) with effective remaining maturities of 1 year or greater, excluding any instruments with explicit or embedded options that would reduce the expected maturity to less than 1 year. Such options include those exercisable at the investor's discretion within the 1-year horizon. |
| 90% | • "Stable" nonmaturity (demand) deposits and/or term deposits (as defined in the LCR) with residual maturities of less than 1 year provided by retail customers and small-business customers. |
| 80% | • "Less stable" (as defined in the LCR) nonmaturity (demand) deposits and/or term deposits with residual maturities of less than 1 year provided by retail and small-business customers. |
| 50% | • Unsecured wholesale funding, nonmaturity deposits, and/or term deposits, with a residual maturity of less than 1 year, provided by nonfinancial corporate, sovereigns, central banks, multilateral development banks and PSEs. |
| 0% | • All other liabilities and equity categories not included in the preceding categories. |

Available stable funding (the numerator of the ratio) includes:

- Bank capital.
- Preferred stock with a maturity $> 1$ year.
- Liabilities with maturities $> 1$ year.
- The portion of retail deposits and wholesale deposit expected to stay with bank during a period of idiosyncratic stress.

The available amount of stable funding (ASF) is calculated by first assigning the value of a DI's equity and liabilities to one of five categories as presented in Table 12–10. The amount assigned to each category is multiplied by an ASF factor. The total ASF is the sum of the weighted amounts.

Required stable funding (the denominator of the ratio) is measured using supervisory assumptions on the characteristics of the liquidity risk profiles of a DI's assets, off-balance sheet exposures, and other selected activities. The required amount of stable funding is calculated as the sum of the value of the on-balance-sheet assets held and funded by the DI, multiplied by a specific required stable funding (RSF) factor assigned to each particular asset type, plus the amount of off-balance-sheet (OBS) activities (or potential liquidity exposure) multiplied by the associated RSF factor. The RSF factor applied to the reported values of each asset or OBS exposure is the amount of that item that supervisors believe should be supported with stable funding. The RSF factors assigned to various types of assets are intended to approximate the amount of a particular asset that could not be sold or used as collateral in a secured borrowing during a severe liquidity event lasting one year. Table 12–11 summarizes the specific types of assets to be assigned to each asset category and their associated RSF factor.

**EXAMPLE 12–3**

*Calculation of the Net Stable Funding Ratio*

OneBank has the following balance sheet (in millions of dollars).

| Assets | | Required Stable Funding Factor | Liabilities and Equity | | Available Stable Funding Factor |
|---|---|---|---|---|---|
| Cash | $ 10 | 0% | Stable retail deposits | $ 95 | 90% |
| Deposits at the Fed | 15 | 5 | Less stable retail deposits | 40 | 80 |
| Treasury securities | 100 | 5 | Unsecured wholesale funding from: | | |
| GNMA securities | 75 | 20 | Stable small business deposits | 100 | 90 |
| Loans to A rated corporations (maturity > 1 year) | 110 | 65 | Less stable small business deposits | 80 | 80 |
| | | | Nonfinancial corporates | 50 | 50 |
| Loans to B rated corporations (maturity < 1 year) | 85 | 50 | | | |
| Premises | 15 | 100 | Equity | 45 | 100 |
| Total | $410 | | | $410 | |

The net stable funding ratio for OneBank is calculated as follows:
Available amount of stable funding =
   $45 × 1.00 + ($95 + $100) × 0.90 + ($40 + $80) × 0.80 + $50 × 0.50 = $341.5m
Required amount of stable funding =
   $10 × 0.00 + ($15 + $100) × 0.05 + $75 × 0.20 + $110 × 0.65 + $85 × 0.50
   + $15 × 1.00 = $149.75m
Net stable funding ratio = $341.5m/$149.75m = 228.05%. The bank is in compliance with liquidity requirements based on the NSFR.

**TABLE 12–11** Detailed Composition of Asset Categories and Associated RSF Factors

| Components of RSF Category | RSF Factor |
|---|---|
| • Cash immediately available to meet obligations, not currently encumbered as collateral and not held for planned use (as contingent collateral, salary payments, or for other reasons).<br>• Unencumbered short-term unsecured instruments and transactions with outstanding maturities of less than 1 year.<br>• Unencumbered securities with slated remaining maturities of less than one year with no embedded options that would increase the expected maturity to more than 1 year.<br>• Unencumbered securities held where the institution has an offsetting reverse repurchase transaction when the security on each transaction has the same unique identifier (e.g., ISN number or CUSIP).<br>• Unencumbered loans to financial entities with effective maturity of less than 1 year that are not renewable and for which the lender has an irrevocable right to call. | 0% |
| • Unencumbered marketable securities with residual maturities of 1 year or greater, representing claims on or claims guaranteed by sovereigns, central banks, BIS, IMF, EC, non-central government PSEs, or multilateral development banks that are assigned a 0% risk-weight under the Basel II standardized approach, provided that active repo or sale markets exist for these securities.<br>• Off-balance-sheet exposures require little long-term funding. Thus, revocable and irrevocable credit and liquidity facilities to any client has an RSF ratio = 5%. | 5% |

*continued*

**TABLE 12–11** *Continued*

| Components of RSF Category | RSF Factor |
|---|---|
| • Unencumbered corporate bonds or covered bonds rated AA− or higher with residual maturities of 1 year or greater satisfying all of the conditions for level 2 assets in the LCR.<br>• Unencumbered marketable securities with residual maturities of 1 year or greater representing claims on or claims guaranteed by sovereigns, central banks, or non-central government PSEs that are assigned a 20% risk-weight under the Basel II standardized approach, provided that they meet all of the conditions for Level 2 assets in the LCR. | 20% |
| • Unencumbered gold.<br>• Unencumbered equity securities, not issued by financial institutions or their affiliates, listed on a recognized exchange and included in a large cap market index.<br>• Unencumbered corporate bonds and covered bonds that satisfy all of the following conditions:<br>  − Central bank eligibility to intraday liquidity needs and overnight liquidity shortages in relevant jurisdictions.<br>  − Not issued by financial institutions or their affiliates (except in the case of covered bonds).<br>  − Not issued by the respective firm itself or its affiliates.<br>  − Low credit risk: assets have a credit assessment by a recognized rating agency of A+ to BBB−, or do not have a credit assessment by a recognized rating agency and are internally rated as having a PD corresponding to a credit assessment of A+ to BBB−.<br>  − Traded in large, deep, and active markets characterized by a low level of concentration.<br>• Unencumbered loans to nonfinancial corporate clients, sovereigns, central banks, and PSEs having a remaining maturity of less than 1 year. | 50% |
| • Unencumbered residential mortgages of any maturity that would qualify for the 35% or lower risk weight under Basel II Standardized Approach for credit risk.<br>• Other unencumbered loans, excluding loans to financial institutions, with a remaining maturity of 1 year or greater, that would qualify for the 35% or lower risk weight under Basel II Standardized Approach for credit risk. | 65% |
| • Unencumbered loans to retail customers (i.e., natural persons) and small-business customers (as defined in the LCR) having a remaining maturity of less than 1 year (other than those that qualify for the 65% RSF). | 85% |
| • All other assets not included in the preceding categories. | 100% |

## Other Liquidity Risk Control Measures

In addition to the LCR and NSFR, regulators will monitor several additional DI and systemwide trends. These additional metrics capture specific information related to a bank's cash flows, balance sheet structure, available unencumbered collateral, and certain market indicators. The additional monitoring measures include the following:

*Contractual maturity mismatch:* Compare assets with liabilities in time bands based on maturity (e.g., overnight, 7 and 14 days, 1, 2, 3, 4, and 9 months, 1, 2, 3, 5 years, and beyond). Data on maturity mismatches are to be provided to DI supervisors on a frequent basis.

*Concentration of funding:* Identify those sources of wholesale funding that are of such significance that withdrawal of these funds could trigger liquidity problems.

*Available unencumbered asset:* Identify the quantity and key characteristics, including currency denomination and location, of banks' available unencumbered assets. These assets have the potential to be used as collateral to raise additional secured funding in secondary markets and/or are eligible at central banks and, as such, may potentially be additional sources of liquidity for the bank.

*LCR by significant currency:* Monitor the LCR in significant currencies. This will allow DIs and supervisors to track potential currency mismatch issues that could arise.

*Market-related monitoring tools:* Monitor high-frequency market data (including marketwide data and information on the financial sector) with little or no time lag. These measures can be used as early warning indicators in monitoring potential liquidity difficulties at banks.

## Liquidity Risk, Unexpected Deposit Drains, and Bank Runs

Under normal conditions and with appropriate management planning, neither net deposit withdrawals nor the exercise of loan commitments poses significant liquidity problems for DIs because borrowed funds availability or excess cash reserves are adequate to meet anticipated needs. For example, even in December and the summer vacation season, when net deposit withdrawals are high, DIs anticipate these *seasonal* effects by holding larger than normal excess cash reserves or borrowing more than normal on the wholesale money markets.

Major liquidity problems can arise, however, if deposit drains are abnormally *large* and unexpected. Abnormal deposit drains (shocks) may occur for a number of reasons, including:

1. Concerns about a DI's solvency relative to those of other DIs.
2. Failure of a related DI leading to heightened depositor concerns about the solvency of other DIs (the contagion effect).
3. Sudden changes in investor preferences regarding holding nonbank financial assets (such as T-bills or mutual fund shares) relative to deposits.

**bank run**
A sudden and unexpected increase in deposit withdrawals from a DI.

In such cases, any sudden and unexpected surges in net deposit withdrawals risk triggering a **bank run** that could eventually force a bank into insolvency.

### *Deposit Drains and Bank Run Liquidity Risk*

At the core of bank run liquidity risk is the fundamental and unique nature of the *demand deposit contract.* Specifically, demand deposit contracts are first-come, first-served contracts in the sense that a depositor's place in line determines the amount he or she will be able to withdraw from a DI. In particular, a depositor either gets paid in full or gets nothing.[11] Because demand deposit contracts pay in full only a certain proportion of depositors when a DI's assets are valued at less than its deposits—and because depositors realize this—any line outside a DI encourages other depositors to join the line immediately even if they do not need cash today for normal consumption purposes. Thus, even the DI's core depositors, who do not really need to withdraw deposits for consumption needs, rationally seek to withdraw their funds immediately when they observe a sudden increase in the lines at their DI.

As a bank run develops, the demand for net deposit withdrawals grows. The DI may initially meet this by decreasing its cash reserves, selling off liquid or readily marketable assets such as T-bills and T-bonds, and seeking to borrow in the money markets. As a bank run increases in intensity, more depositors join the withdrawal line, and a liquidity crisis develops. Specifically, the DI finds it

---

[11] We are assuming no deposit insurance exists that guarantees payments of deposits and no discount window borrowing is available to fund a temporary liquidity need for funds. The presence of deposit insurance and the discount window alters the incentives to engage in a bank run, as we describe later in this chapter and in Chapter 19.

difficult, if not impossible, to borrow in the money markets at virtually any price. Also, it has sold all its liquid assets, cash, and bonds as well as any salable loans (see Chapter 25). The DI is likely to have left only relatively illiquid loans on the asset side of the balance sheet to meet depositor claims for cash. However, these loans can be sold or liquidated only at very large discounts from face value. A DI needing to liquidate long-term assets at fire-sale prices to meet continuing deposit drains faces the strong possibility that the proceeds from such asset sales are insufficient to meet depositors' cash demands. The DI's liquidity problem then turns into a solvency problem; that is, the DI must close its doors.

The incentives for depositors to run first and ask questions later creates a fundamental instability in the banking system in that an otherwise sound DI can be pushed into insolvency and failure by unexpectedly large depositor drains and liquidity demands. This is especially so in periods of contagious runs, or **bank panics,** when depositors lose faith in the banking system as a whole and engage in a run on all DIs by not materially discriminating among them according to their asset qualities.

**bank panic**
A systemic or contagious run on the deposits of the banking industry as a whole.

## Bank Runs, the Discount Window, and Deposit Insurance

Regulators have recognized the inherent instability of the banking system due to the all-or-nothing payoff features of the deposit contract. As a result, regulatory mechanisms are in place to ease DIs' liquidity problems and to deter bank runs and panics. The two major liquidity risk insulation devices are *deposit insurance* and the *discount window.* Because of the serious social welfare effects that a contagious run on DIs could have, government regulators of depository institutions have established guarantee programs offering deposit holders varying degrees of insurance protection to deter runs. For example, during the financial crisis of 2008–2009, in an attempt to provide stability to the U.S. banking system, the Troubled Asset Relief Program (or TARP) that gave the U.S. Treasury funds to buy "toxic" mortgages and other securities from financial institutions also called for the FDIC to increase deposit insurance to $250,000 from $100,000 per person per institution. If a deposit holder believes a claim is totally secure, even if the DI is in trouble, the holder has no incentive to run. The deposit holder's place in line no longer affects his or her ability to obtain the funds. Deposit insurance deters runs as well as contagious runs and panics. However, knowing that (because their deposits are insured) deposit holders are less likely to run or panic if there is a perceived bank solvency problem, deposit insurance creates a situation in which DIs are more likely to increase the liquidity risk on their balance sheets.

www.fdic.gov

www.federalreserve.gov

Three lending programs are offered through the Fed's discount window. Primary credit is available to generally sound depository institutions on a very short-term basis, typically overnight, at a rate above the Federal Open Market Committee's (FOMC's) target rate for federal funds. Secondary credit is available to depository institutions that are not eligible for primary credit. It is extended on a very short-term basis, typically overnight, at a rate that is above the primary credit rate. The Federal Reserve's seasonal credit program is designed to assist small depository institutions in managing significant seasonal swings in their loans and deposits. Seasonal credit is available to depository institutions that can demonstrate a clear pattern of recurring intrayearly swings in funding needs. Eligible institutions are usually located in agricultural or tourist areas. We discuss these in detail in Chapter 19. As we describe there, deposit insurance has effectively deterred bank panics since 1933, although the provision of deposit insurance has not been without other costs.

<table>
<tr><td>Concept<br>Questions</td><td>1. List two benefits and two costs of using (a) purchased liquidity management and (b) stored liquidity management to meet a deposit drain.<br>2. What are the three major sources of DI liquidity? What are the two major uses?<br>3. What are the measures of liquidity risk used by FIs?</td></tr>
</table>

## LIQUIDITY RISK AND LIFE INSURANCE COMPANIES

**surrender value**
The amount received by an insurance policyholder when cashing in a policy early.

Depository institutions are not the only FIs exposed to liquidity risk or run problems. Like DIs, life insurance companies hold cash reserves and other liquid assets to meet policy cancelations (surrenders) and other working capital needs that arise in the course of writing insurance. The early cancelation of an insurance policy results in the insurer's having to pay the insured the **surrender value** of that policy.[12] In the normal course of business, premium income and returns on an insurer's asset portfolio are sufficient to meet the cash outflows required when policyholders cash in or surrender their policies early. As with DIs, the distribution or pattern of premium income minus policyholder liquidations is normally predicable. When premium income is insufficient to meet surrenders, however, a life insurer can sell some of its relatively liquid assets, such as government bonds. In this case, bonds act as a buffer or reserve asset source of liquidity for the insurer.

Nevertheless, concerns about the solvency of an insurer can result in a run in which new premium income dries up and existing policyholders seek to cancel their policies by cashing them in early. To meet exceptional demands for cash, a life insurer could be forced to liquidate the other assets in its portfolio, such as commercial mortgage loans and other securities, potentially at fire-sale prices.[13] As with DIs, forced asset liquidations can push an insurer into insolvency.[14]

<table>
<tr><td>Concept<br>Questions</td><td>1. What is likely to be a life insurance company's first source of liquidity when premium income is insufficient?<br>2. Can a life insurance company be subjected to a run? If so, why?</td></tr>
</table>

## LIQUIDITY RISK AND PROPERTY–CASUALTY INSURERS

As discussed in Chapter 3, property–casualty (PC) insurers sell policies insuring against certain contingencies impacting either real property or individuals. Unlike those of life insurers, PC contingencies (and policy coverages) are relatively short term, often one to three years. With the help of mortality tables, claims on life

---

[12] A surrender value is usually some proportion or percent less than 100 percent of the face value of the insurance contract. The surrender value continues to grow as funds invested in the policy earn interest (returns). Earnings to the policyholder are taxed if and when the policy is actually surrendered or cashed in before the policy matures.

[13] Life insurers also provide a considerable amount of loan commitments, especially in the commercial property area. As a result, they face asset-side loan commitment liquidity risk in a fashion similar to that of DIs.

[14] State guaranty schemes deter policyholder runs. In general, the level of coverage and the value of the guarantees are less than deposit insurance. We discuss these guaranty schemes in Chapter 19.

insurance policies are generally predictable. PC claims (such as those associated with natural disasters), however, are virtually impossible to predict. As a result, PC insurers' assets tend to be shorter term and more liquid than those of life insurers. PC insurers' contracts and premium-setting intervals are usually relatively short term as well, so problems caused by policy surrenders are less severe. PC insurers' greatest liquidity exposure occurs when policyholders cancel or fail to renew policies with an insurer because of insolvency risk, pricing, or competitive reasons. This may cause an insurer's premium cash inflow, when added to its investment returns, to be insufficient to meet policyholders' claims.

Alternatively, large unexpected claims may materialize and exceed the flow of premium income and income returns from assets. Disasters such as Hurricane Andrew in 1991 and Hurricane Katrina in 2005 have caused severe liquidity crises and failures among smaller PC insurers.[15] More recent is the near failure of insurance giant AIG, which in late summer 2008 was hit by $18 billion in losses from guarantees (credit default swaps (CDS)) it wrote on mortgage derivatives. As the mortgage debt securities' values declined, AIG was forced to post more collateral to signal to CDS contract counterparties that it could pay off the mortgage guarantees it wrote. Despite these actions by AIG, Standard & Poor's announced that it would downgrade AIG's credit rating. The rating downgrade required AIG to post up to an additional $14.5 billion in collateral, funds which it did not have. AIG made an unprecedented approach to the Federal Reserve seeking $40 billion in short-term financing. The company announced that a financing entity—funded by the Federal Reserve Bank of New York and AIG—had purchased $46.1 billion in the complex debt securities insured by AIG. The deal also included a broader restructuring of the federal government's bailout of AIG, which originally included an $85 billion bridge loan and $37.8 billion in Fed financing.

| **Concept Questions** | 1. What is the greatest cause of liquidity exposure faced by property–casualty insurers? |
|---|---|
| | 2. Is the liquidity risk of property–casualty insurers in general greater or less than that of life insurers? |

# INVESTMENT FUNDS

**closed-end fund**
An investment fund that sells a fixed number of shares in the fund to outside investors.

**open-end fund**
An investment fund that sells an elastic or nonfixed number of shares in the fund to outside investors.

Investment funds such as mutual funds and hedge funds sell shares as liabilities to investors and invest the proceeds in assets such as bonds and equities. These funds are open-end or closed-end. **Closed-end funds** issue a fixed number of shares as liabilities. Unless the issuing fund chooses to repurchase them, the number of outstanding shares does not change. As discussed in Chapter 5, by far the majority of U.S. investment funds are **open-end funds;** that is, they can issue an unlimited supply of shares to investors. Open-end funds must also stand ready to buy back previously issued shares from investors at the current market price for the fund's shares. Thus, at a given market price, $P$, the supply of open-end fund shares is perfectly elastic. The price at which an open-end investment fund stands ready to sell new shares or redeem existing shares is the

---

[15] Also, claims may arise in long-tail lines where a contingency takes place during the policy period but a claim is not lodged until many years later. As mentioned in Chapter 6, one example is the claims regarding damage caused by asbestos contacts.

**net asset value**
The price at which investment fund shares are sold (or can be redeemed). It equals the total market value of the assets of the fund divided by the number of shares in the funds.

net asset value (NAV) of the fund. NAV is the current or market value of the fund's assets divided by the number of shares in the fund. An investment fund's willingness to provide instant liquidity to shareholders while it invests funds in equities, bonds, and other long-term instruments could expose it to liquidity problems similar to those banks, thrifts, and life insurance companies face when the number of withdrawals (or mutual fund shares cashed in) rises to abnormally and unexpectedly high levels. Indeed, investment funds can be subject to dramatic liquidity runs if investors become nervous about the NAV of the mutual funds' assets. However, the fundamental difference in the way investment fund contracts are valued compared with the valuation of DI deposit and insurance policy contracts mitigates the incentives for fund shareholders to engage in runs. Specifically, if an investment fund were to be liquidated, its assets would be distributed to fund shareholders on a pro rata basis rather than the first-come, first-served basis employed under deposit and insurance contracts.

To illustrate this difference, we can directly compare the incentives for investment fund investors to engage in a run with those of DI depositors. Table 12–12 shows a simple balance sheet of an open-end mutual fund and a DI. When they perceive that a DI's assets are valued below its liabilities, depositors have an incentive to engage in a run on the DI to be first in line to withdraw. In the example in Table 12–12, only the first 90 depositors would receive \$1 back for each \$1 deposited. The last 10 would receive nothing at all.

Now consider the mutual fund with 100 shareholders who invested \$1 each for a total of \$100, but whose assets are worth \$90. If these shareholders tried to cash in their shares, *none* would receive \$1. Instead, a mutual fund values its balance sheet liabilities on a market value basis; the price of any share liquidated by an investor is:

$$P = \frac{\text{Value of assets}}{\text{Shares outstanding}} = \text{NAV (net asset value)}$$

Thus, unlike deposit contracts that have fixed face values of \$1, the value of a mutual fund's shares reflects the changing value of its assets divided by the number of shares outstanding.

In Table 12–12, the value of each shareholder's claim is:

$$P = \frac{\$90}{100} = \$0.90$$

That is, each mutual fund shareholder participates in the fund's loss of asset value on a *pro rata,* or proportional, basis. Technically, whether first or last in line, each mutual fund shareholder who cashes in shares on any given day receives the same net asset value per share of the mutual fund. In this case, it is 90 cents, representing a loss of 10 cents per share. All mutual fund shareholders realize this and know that investors share asset losses on a pro rata basis. Being the first in line to withdraw has no overall advantage as it has at DIs.

**TABLE 12–12**
**Run Incentives of DI Depositors versus Investment Fund Investors**

| Depository Institution | | Mutual Fund | |
|---|---|---|---|
| **Assets** | **Liabilities** | **Assets** | **Liabilities** |
| Assets        \$90 | \$100 Deposits (100 depositors with \$1 deposits) | Assets        \$90 | \$100 Shares (100 shareholders with \$1 shares) |

This is not to say that mutual funds bear no liquidity risk. Money market mutual funds (MMMFs) experienced tremendous liquidity risk at the start of the financial crisis. On September 16, 2008 (one day after Lehman Brothers filed for bankruptcy), Reserve Primary Fund, the oldest money market fund in the United States saw its shares fall to 97 cents (below the $1.00 book value) after writing off debt issued by Lehman Brothers. Resulting investor anxiety about Reserve Primary Fund spread to other funds, and investors industrywide liquidated their MMMF shares. In just one week investors liquidated $170 billion of the industry total $4 trillion invested in MMMFs. In response, on September 19 the federal government took steps to restore confidence in the MMMF industry. Specifically, the Department of Treasury opened the Temporary Guarantee Program for MMMFs, which provided up to $50 billion in coverage to MMMF shareholders for amounts they held in the funds as of close of business that day. The guarantee was triggered if a participating fund's net asset value fell below $0.995. The program was designed to address the severe liquidity strains in the industry and immediately stabilized the industry and stopped the outflows.

Some of the biggest liquidity crises experienced by FIs recently have occurred with hedge funds, which are highly specialized investment funds with a limited number of wealthy investors, usually 100 or less. For example, in the summer of 2007, two Bear Stearns hedge funds suffered heavy losses on investments in the subprime mortgage market. The two funds filed for bankruptcy in the fall of 2007. Bear Stearns' market value was hurt badly from these losses. The losses became so great that by March 2008 Bear Stearns was struggling to finance its day-to-day operations. Rumors of Bear Stearns' liquidity crisis became a reality as investors began quickly selling off their stock and draining what little liquid assets the firm had left; the first major run on a U.S. FI since the Great Depression. Bear Stearns had no choice but to basically sell themselves to the highest bidder to avoid declaring bankruptcy or completely closing down and leaving investors totally empty handed. J.P. Morgan Chase purchased the company for $236 million; Bear Stearns' skyscraper in New York was worth over $2 billion alone.

Despite these recent crises, the incentives for mutual fund shareholders to engage in runs that produce the extreme form of liquidity problems faced by DIs and life insurance companies are generally absent. This situation has led some academics to argue for deposit contracts to be restructured in a form more similar to mutual fund or equity contracts. This might also obviate the need for deposit insurance to deter bank runs.[16]

---

| **Concept Questions** | 1. What would be the impact on their liquidity needs if DIs offered deposit contracts of an open-end mutual fund type rather than the traditional all-or-nothing demand deposit contract? |
| | 2. How do the incentives of mutual fund investors to engage in runs compare with the incentives of DI depositors? |

---

[16] A common argument against this is that since deposits are money and money is the unit of account in the economy, equity-type contracts could pose a problem if the value of a deposit were to fluctuate from day to day. However, note that money market mutual funds offer depositlike contracts as well. As their NAV varies, they solve the fluctuating share value problem by setting the value of each share at $1 but allowing the number of shares an individual holds to fluctuate so that the value of the individual's overall holdings moves in line with asset values, while the price of each money market mutual fund share remains at $1. A similar policy could be adopted for deposits at DIs.

## Summary

Liquidity risk, as a result of heavier-than-anticipated liability withdrawals or loan commitment exercise, is a common problem faced by FI managers. Well-developed policies for holding liquid assets or having access to markets for purchased funds are normally adequate to meet liability withdrawals. However, very large withdrawals can cause asset liquidity problems that can be compounded by incentives for liability claim holders to engage in runs at the first sign of a liquidity problem. These incentives for depositors and life insurance policyholders to engage in runs can push normally sound FIs into insolvency. Mutual funds are generally able to avoid runs because liabilities are marked to market so that losses are shared equally among liability holders. Since such insolvencies have costs to society as well as to private shareholders, regulators have developed mechanisms such as deposit insurance and the discount window to alleviate liquidity problems. We discuss these mechanisms in detail in Chapter 19.

## Questions and Problems

1. How does the degree of liquidity risk differ for different types of financial institutions?

2. What are the two reasons liquidity risk arises? How does liquidity risk arising from the liability side of the balance sheet differ from liquidity risk arising from the asset side of the balance sheet? What is meant by fire-sale prices?

3. What are core deposits? What role do core deposits play in predicting the probability distribution of net deposit drains?

4. The probability distribution of the net deposit drains of a DI has been estimated to have a mean of 2 percent and a standard deviation of 1 percent. Is this DI increasing or decreasing in size? Explain.

5. How is a DI's distribution pattern of net deposit drains affected by the following?
   a. The holiday season.
   b. Summer vacations.
   c. A severe economic recession.
   d. Double-digit inflation.

6. What are two ways a DI can offset the liquidity effects of a net deposit drain of funds? How do the two methods differ? What are the operational benefits and costs of each method?

7. What are two ways a DI can offset the effects of asset-side liquidity risk such as the drawing down of a loan commitment?

8. A DI with the following balance sheet (in millions) expects a net deposit drain of $15 million.

| Assets | | Liabilities and Equity | |
|---|---|---|---|
| Cash | $10 | Deposits | $68 |
| Loans | 50 | Equity | 7 |
| Securities | 15 | | |
| Total assets | $75 | Total liabilities and equity | $75 |

Show the DI's balance sheet if the following conditions occur:
a. The DI purchases liabilities to offset this expected drain.
b. The stored liquidity management method is used to meet the expected drain.

9. AllStarBank has the following balance sheet (in millions):

| Assets | | Liabilities and Equity | |
|---|---|---|---|
| Cash | $ 30 | Deposits | $110 |
| Loans | 90 | Borrowed funds | 40 |
| Securities | 50 | Equity | 20 |
| Total assets | $170 | Total liabilities and equity | $170 |

AllStarBank's largest customer decides to exercise a $15 million loan commitment. How will the new balance sheet appear if AllStar uses the following liquidity risk strategies?

a. Stored liquidity management.

b. Purchased liquidity management.

10. A DI has assets of $10 million consisting of $1 million in cash and $9 million in loans. The DI has core deposits of $6 million, subordinated debt of $2 million, and equity of $2 million. Increases in interest rates are expected to cause a net drain of $2 million in core deposits over the year.

a. The average cost of deposits is 6 percent and the average yield on loans is 8 percent. The DI decides to reduce its loan portfolio to offset this expected decline in deposits. What will be the effect on net interest income and the size of the DI after the implementation of this strategy?

b. If the interest cost of issuing new short-term debt is expected to be 7.5 percent, what would be the effect on net interest income of offsetting the expected deposit drain with an increase in interest-bearing liabilities?

c. What will be the size of the DI after the drain if the DI uses this strategy?

d. What dynamic aspects of DI management would support a strategy of replacing the deposit drain with interest-bearing liabilities?

11. Define each of the following four measures of liquidity risk. Explain how each measure would be implemented and utilized by a DI.

a. Sources and uses of liquidity.

b. Peer group ratio comparisons.

c. Liquidity index.

d. Financing gap and financing requirement.

12. A DI has $10 million in T-bills, a $5 million line of credit to borrow in the repo market, and $5 million in excess cash reserves (above reserve requirements) with the Fed. The DI currently has borrowed $6 million in fed funds and $2 million from the Fed's discount window to meet seasonal demands.

a. What is the DI's total available (sources of) liquidity?

b. What is the DI's current total uses of liquidity?

c. What is the net liquidity of the DI?

d. What conclusions can you derive from the result?

13. A DI has the following assets in its portfolio: $10 million in cash reserves with the Fed, $25 million in T-bills, and $65 million in mortgage loans. If the DI has to liquidate the assets today, it will receive only $98 per $100 of face value of the T-bills and $90 per $100 of face value of the mortgage loans. Liquidation at the end of one month (closer to maturity) will produce $100 per $100 of face value of the T-bills and $97 per $100 of face value of the mortgage. Calculate the one-month liquidity index for this DI using the preceding information.

14. A DI has the following assets in its portfolio: $20 million in cash reserves with the Fed, $20 million in T-bills, and $50 million in mortgage loans. If the assets

need to be liquidated at short notice, the DI will receive only 99 percent of the fair market value of the T-bills and 90 percent of the fair market value of the mortgage loans. Liquidation at the end of one month (closer to maturity) will produce $100 per $100 of face value of the T-bills and the mortgage loans. Calculate the liquidity index using the above information.

15. Conglomerate Corporation has acquired Acme Corporation. To help finance the takeover, Conglomerate will liquidate the overfunded portion of Acme's pension fund. The face values and current and one-year future liquidation values of the assets that will be liquidated are given below.

| | Liquidation Values | | |
| --- | --- | --- | --- |
| **Asset** | **Face Value** | $t = 0$ | $t = 1$ year |
| IBM stock | $10,000 | $9,900 | $10,500 |
| GE bonds | 5,000 | 4,000 | 4,500 |
| Treasury securities | 15,000 | 13,000 | 14,000 |

Calculate the one-year liquidity index for these securities.

16. Plainbank has $10 million in cash and equivalents, $30 million in loans, and $15 million in core deposits.
    a. Calculate the financing gap.
    b. What is the financing requirement?
    c. How can the financing gap be used in the day-to-day liquidity management of the bank?

17. How can an FI's liquidity plan help reduce the effects of liquidity shortages? What are the components of a liquidity plan?

18. Central Bank has the following balance sheet (in millions of dollars).

| Assets | | Liabilities and Equity | |
| --- | --- | --- | --- |
| Cash | $ 20 | Stable retail deposits | $ 190 |
| Deposits at the Fed | 30 | Less stable retail deposits | 70 |
| Treasury bonds | 145 | CDs maturing in 6 months | 100 |
| Qualifying marketable securities | 50 | Unsecured wholesale funding from: | |
| GNMA bonds | 60 | Stable small business deposits | 125 |
| Loans to AA– rated corporations | 540 | Less stable small business deposits | 100 |
| Mortgages | 285 | Nonfinancial corporates | 450 |
| Premises | 35 | Equity | 130 |
| Total | $1,165 | Total | $1,165 |

Cash inflows over the next 30 days from the bank's performing assets are $7.5 million. Calculate the LCR for Central Bank.

19. WallsFarther Bank has the following balance sheet (in millions of dollars).

| Assets | | Liabilities and Equity | |
| --- | --- | --- | --- |
| Cash | $ 12 | Stable retail deposits | $ 55 |
| Deposits at the Fed | 19 | Less stable retail deposits | 20 |
| Treasury securities | 125 | Unsecured wholesale funding from: | |
| GNMA securities | 94 | Stable small business deposits | 80 |
| Loans to AA rated corporations | 138 | Less stable small business deposits | 49 |
| Loans to BB rated corporations | 106 | Nonfinancial corporates | 250 |
| Premises | 20 | Equity | 60 |
| Total | $514 | Total | $514 |

Cash inflows over the next 30 days from the bank's performing assets are $5.5 million. Calculate the LCR for WallsFarther Bank.

20. FirstBank has the following balance sheet (in millions of dollars).

| Assets | | Liabilities and Equity | |
|---|---|---|---|
| Cash | $ 12 | Stable retail deposits | $ 55 |
| Deposits at the Fed | 19 | Less stable retail deposits | 20 |
| Treasury securities | 125 | Unsecured wholesale funding from: | |
| GNMA securities | 94 | Stable small business deposits | 80 |
| Loans to A rated corporations | 138 | Less stable small business deposits | 49 |
| (maturity > 1 year) | | Nonfinancial corporates | 250 |
| Loans to B rated corporations | 106 | Equity | 60 |
| (maturity < 1 year) | | Total | $514 |
| Premises | 20 | | |
| Total | $514 | | |

Calculate the NSFR for FirstBank.

21. BancTwo has the following balance sheet (in millions of dollars).

| Assets | | Liabilities and Equity | |
|---|---|---|---|
| Cash | $ 20 | Stable retail deposits | $ 190 |
| Deposits at the Fed | 30 | Less stable retail deposits | 70 |
| Treasury bonds | 145 | CDs maturing in 6 months | 100 |
| Qualifying marketable securities | 50 | Unsecured wholesale funding from: | |
| (maturity < 1 year) | | Stable small business deposits | 125 |
| FNMA bonds | 60 | Less stable small business deposits | 100 |
| Loans to AA− rated corpora- | 540 | Nonfinancial corporates | 450 |
| tions (maturity > 1 year) | | Equity | 130 |
| Mortgages (unencumbered) | 285 | Total | $1,165 |
| Premises | 35 | | |
| Total | $1,165 | | |

Calculate the NSFR for BancTwo.

22. What is a bank run? What are some possible withdrawal shocks that could initiate a bank run? What feature of the demand deposit contract provides deposit withdrawal momentum that can result in a bank run?

23. The following is the balance sheet of a DI (in millions):

| Assets | | Liabilities and Equity | |
|---|---|---|---|
| Cash | $ 2 | Demand deposits | $50 |
| Loans | 50 | | |
| Premises and equipment | 3 | Equity | 5 |
| Total | $55 | Total | $55 |

The asset–liability management committee has estimated that the loans, whose average interest rate is 6 percent and whose average life is three years, will have to be discounted at 10 percent if they are to be sold in less than two days. If they can be sold in four days, they will have to be discounted at 8 percent. If they can be sold later than a week, the DI will receive the full market value. Loans are not amortized; that is, the principal is paid at maturity.

    a. What will be the price received by the DI for the loans if they have to be sold in two days? In four days?

    b. In a crisis, if depositors all demand payment on the first day, what amount will they receive? What will they receive if they demand to be paid within the week? Assume no deposit insurance.

24. What government safeguards are in place to reduce liquidity risk for DIs?

25. What are the levels of defense against liquidity risk for a life insurance company? How does liquidity risk for a property–casualty insurer differ from that for a life insurance company?

26. How is the liquidity problem faced by investment funds different from that faced by DIs and insurance companies? How does the liquidity risk of an open-end mutual fund compare with that of a closed-end fund?

27. A mutual fund has the following assets in its portfolio: $40 million in fixed-income securities and $40 million in stocks at current market values. In the event of a liquidity crisis, the fund can sell the assets at 96 percent of market value if they are disposed of in two days. The fund will receive 98 percent if the assets are disposed of in four days. Two shareholders, A and B, own 5 percent and 7 percent of equity (shares), respectively.

    a. Market uncertainty has caused shareholders to sell their shares back to the fund. What will the two shareholders receive if the mutual fund must sell all the assets in two days? In four days?

    b. How does this situation differ from a bank run? How have bank regulators mitigated the problem of bank runs?

28. A mutual fund has $1 million in cash and $9 million invested in securities. It currently has 1 million shares outstanding.

    a. What is the net asset value (NAV) of this fund?

    b. Assume that some of the shareholders decide to cash in their shares of the fund. How many shares at its current NAV can the fund take back without resorting to a sale of assets?

    c. As a result of anticipated heavy withdrawals, the fund sells 10,000 shares of IBM stock currently valued at $40. Unfortunately, it receives only $35 per share. What is the net asset value after the sale? What are the cash assets of the fund after the sale?

    d. Assume that after the sale of IBM shares, 100,000 shares are sold back to the fund. What is the current NAV? Is there a need to sell more securities to meet this redemption?

## Web Question

29. Go to the Federal Deposit Insurance Corporation's website (**www.fdic.gov**) and Click on "Analysts." Click on "Statistics on Banking." Click on "Assets and Liabilities," and then "Run Report." Using information in this file update Table 12–1. How have the assets and liabilities of U.S. banks increased since March 2012?

# Integrated Mini Case

## MEASURING LIQUIDITY RISK

A DI has the following balance sheet (in millions):

| Assets | | Liabilities and Equity | |
|---|---|---|---|
| Cash | $ 9 | Deposits | $ 75 |
| Loans | 95 | Purchased funds | 40 |
| Securities | 26 | Equity | 15 |
| Total assets | $130 | Total liabilities and equity | $130 |

The DI's securities portfolio includes $16 million in T-bills and $10 million in GNMA securities. The DI has a $20 million line of credit to borrow in the repo market and $5 million in excess cash reserves (above reserve requirements) with the Fed. The DI currently has borrowed $22 million in Fed funds and $18 million from the Fed discount window to meet seasonal demands.

1. What is the DI's total available (sources of) liquidity?
2. What is the DI's current total uses of liquidity?
3. What is the net liquidity of the DI?
4. Calculate the financing gap.
5. What is the financing requirement?

6. The DI expects a net deposit drain of $20 million. Show the DI's balance sheet if the following conditions occur:
   a. The DI purchases liabilities to offset this expected drain.
   b. The stored liquidity management method is used to meet the expected drain (the DI does not want the cash balance to fall below $5 million, and securities can be sold at their fair value).

7. In the event of an unexpected and severe drain on deposits in the next 3 days, and 10 days, the DI will liquidate assets in the following manner:

| Liquidation Values ($ millions) | | | |
|---|---|---|---|
| Asset | Fair Value | *t* = 3 days | *t* = 10 days |
| Cash | $ 9 | $ 9 | $ 9 |
| Treasury bills | 16 | 14 | 15.5 |
| GNMAs | 10 | 8 | 9 |
| Loans | 95 | 65 | 75 |

Calculate the 3-day and 10-day liquidity index for the DI.

---

## Appendix 12A: Sources and Uses of Funds Statement, Bank of America, March 2012

View Appendix 12A at the website for this textbook (**www.mhhe.com/saunders8e**).

## Appendix 12B

# Illustrative Template for the LCR

| Item | Factor (to be multiplied against total amount) |
|---|---|
| **Stock of High-Quality Liquid Assets** | |
| **A. Level 1 Assets:** | |
| Cash | 100% |
| Qualifying marketable securities from sovereigns, central banks, public-sector entities, and multilateral development banks | 100% |
| Qualifying central bank reserves | 100% |
| Domestic sovereign or central bank debt in domestic currency | 100% |
| Domestic sovereign debt for non-0% risk-weighted sovereigns, issued in foreign currency | 100% |
| **B. Level 2 Assets:** | |
| Sovereign, central bank, and PSE assets qualifying for 20% risk weighting | 85% |
| Qualifying corporate bonds rated AA- or higher | 85% |
| Qualifying covered bonds rated AA- or higher | 85% |
| *Calculation of 40% cap of liquid assets* | Maximum of 2/3 of adjusted Level 1 assets that would exist after an unwind of all secured funding transactions. |
| **Total value of stock of highly liquid assets** | |
| **Cash Outflows** | |
| **A. Retail Deposits:** | |
| Demand deposit and qualifying term deposits with residual maturity or notice period within 30 days | |
| • Stable deposits | Minimum 5% (additional categories to be determined by jurisdiction) |
| • Less stable retail deposits | Minimum 10% (additional categories to be determined by jurisdiction) |
| Term deposit with residual maturity greater than 30 days with a withdrawal with a significant penalty, or no legal right to withdraw | 0% (or higher rate to be determined by jurisdictions) |
| **B. Unsecured Wholesale Funding:** | |
| Funding from: | |
| Stable small-business customers | Minimum 5% (additional categories to be determined by jursidiction) |
| Less stable small-business customers | Minimum 10% (additional categories to be determined by jurisdiction) |
| Legal entities with operational relationships | 25% of deposits needed for operational purposes |

| Item | Factor (to be multiplied against total amount) |
|---|---|
| • Portion of corporate deposits with operational relationships covered by deposit insurance—same treatment as for retail demand deposits | |
| Cooperative banks in an institutional network | 25% of the qualifying deposits with the centralized institution |
| Nonfinancial corporates, sovereigns, central banks, and PSEs | 75% |
| Other legal entity customers | 100% |

### C. Secured Funding:

| | |
|---|---|
| Secured funding transactions backed by Level 1 assets, with any counterparty | 0% |
| Secured funding transactions backed by Level 2 assets, with any counterparty | 15% |
| Secured funding transactions backed by assets that are not eligible for the stock of highly liquid assets, with domestic sovereigns, domestic central banks, or domestic public-sector entities as a counterparty | 25% |
| All other secured funding transactions | 100% |

### D. Additional Requirements:

| | |
|---|---|
| Liabilities related to derivative collateral calls related to a downgrade of up to 3 notches | 100% of collateral that would be required to cover the contracts in case of up to a 3-notch downgrade |
| Market valuation changes on derivatives transactions | Treatment determined by supervisors in each jurisdiction |
| Valuation changes on posted collateral securing derivative transactions that is comprised of non-level 1 assets | 20% |
| ABCP, SIVs, conduits, etc.: | |
| Liabilities from maturing ABCP, SIVs, SPVs, etc. | 100% of maturing amounts and 100% of returnable assets |
| Asset-backed securities (including covered bonds) | 100% of maturing amounts |
| Currently undrawn portion of committed credit and liquidity facilities to: | |
| • Retail and small-business clients | 5% of outstanding credit and liquidity lines |
| • Nonfinancial corporates, sovereigns and central banks, and PSEs; credit facilities | 10% of outstanding credit lines |
| • Nonfinancial corporates, sovereigns and central banks, and PSEs; liquidity facilities | 100% of outstanding liquidity lines |
| • Other legal entity customers, credit and liquidity facilites | 100% of outstanding credit and liquidity lines |
| Other contingent funding liabilities (such as guarantees, letters of credit, revocable credit and liquidity facilities, derivative valuations) | Treatment determined by supervisors in each jurisdiction |
| Any additional contractual outflows | 100% |
| Net derivative payables | 100% |
| Any other contractual cash outflows | 100% |

### Total Cash Outflows

| Item | Factor (to be multiplied against total amount) |
|---|---|
| **Cash Inflows** | |
| Reverse repos and securities borrowing, with the following as collateral: | |
| • Level 1 assets | 0% |
| • Level 2 assets | 15% |
| • All other assets | 100% |
| Credit or liquidity facilities | 0% |
| Operational deposits held at other financial institutions | 0% |
| • Deposits held at centralized insitution of a network of cooperative banks | 0% of the qualifying deposits with the centralized insitution |
| Other inflows by counterparty: | |
| • Amounts receivable from retail counterparties | 50% |
| • Amounts receivable from nonfinancial wholesale counterparties, from transactions other than those listed in the inflow categories | 50% |
| • Amounts receivable from financial institutions, from transactions other than those listed in the inflow categories | 100% |
| Net derivative receivables | 100% |
| Other contractual cash inflows | Treatment determined by supervisors in each jurisdiction |
| **Total Cash Inflows** | |
| **Total net cash outflows = Total cash outflows − Min [Total cash inflows, 75% of gross outflows]** | |
| **LCR (= Total value of stock of high-quality liquid assets/ Net cash outflows)** | |

# Chapter Thirteen

# Foreign Exchange Risk

## INTRODUCTION

The globalization of the U.S. financial services industry has meant that FIs are increasingly exposed to foreign exchange (FX) risk. FX risk can occur as a result of trading in foreign currencies, making foreign currency loans (such as a loan in pounds to a corporation), buying foreign-issued securities (U.K. pound–denominated gilt-edged bonds or German euro–government bonds), or issuing foreign currency–denominated debt (pound certificates of deposit) as a source of funds. Extreme foreign exchange risk at a single FI was evident in 2002 when a single trader at Allfirst Bank covered up $700 million in losses from foreign currency trading. After five years in which these losses were successfully hidden, the activities were discovered in 2002. More recently, in 2012 a strengthening dollar reduced profits for internationally active firms. For example, IBM experienced a drop in revenue of 3 percent due to foreign exchange trends. Similarly, Coca-Cola, which gets the majority of its sales from outside the United States, saw 2012 revenues decrease by approximately 5 percent as the U.S. dollar strengthened relative to foreign currencies.

This chapter looks at how FIs evaluate and measure the risks faced when their assets and liabilities are denominated in foreign (as well as in domestic) currencies and when they take major positions as traders in the spot and forward foreign currency markets.

## FOREIGN EXCHANGE RATES AND TRANSACTIONS

### Foreign Exchange Rates

**direct quote**
U.S. dollars received for one unit of the foreign currency exchanged.

**indirect quote**
Foreign currency received for each U.S. dollar exchanged.

A foreign exchange rate is the price at which one currency (e.g., the U.S. dollar) can be exchanged for another currency (e.g., the Swiss franc). Table 13–1 lists the exchange rates between the U.S. dollar and other currencies as of 4 PM eastern standard time on July 4, 2012. Foreign exchange rates are listed in two ways: U.S. dollars received for one unit of the foreign currency exchanged, or a **direct quote** (in US$), and foreign currency received for each U.S. dollar exchanged, or an **indirect quote** (per US$). For example, the exchange rate of U.S. dollars for Canadian dollars on July 4, 2012, was 0.9870 (US$/C$), or $0.9870 could be received for each Canadian dollar exchanged. Conversely, the exchange rate of Canadian dollars for U.S. dollars was 1.0131 (C$/US$), or 1.0131 Canadian dollars could be received for each U.S. dollar exchanged.

**TABLE 13–1**   Foreign Currency Exchange Rates

Source: *The Wall Street Journal Online*, July 5, 2012. Reprinted by permission of *The Wall Street Journal*. © 2012 Dow Jones & Company Inc. All rights reserved worldwide. *www.wsj.com*

# Currencies

U.S.-dollar foreign-exchange rates in late New York trading

| Country/currency | Wed in US$ | Wed per US$ | US$ ys, YTD chg (%) | Country/currency | Wed in US$ | Wed per US$ | US$ ys, YTD chg (%) |
|---|---|---|---|---|---|---|---|
| **Americas** | | | | **Europe** | | | |
| Argentina peso* | .2211 | 4.5234 | 5.0 | Czech. Rep. koruna** | .04907 | 20.378 | 3.2 |
| Brazil real | .4932 | 2.0278 | 8.7 | Denmark krone | .1684 | 5.9367 | 3.5 |
| Canada dollar | .9870 | 1.0131 | −0.8 | Euro area euro | 1.2527 | .7983 | 3.5 |
| Chile peso | .002015 | 496.40 | −4.5 | Hungary forint | .004378 | 228.41 | −6.1 |
| Colombia peso | .0005650 | 1770.00 | −8.8 | Norway krone | .1670 | 5.9891 | 0.2 |
| Ecuador US dollar | 1 | 1 | unch | Poland zloty | .2971 | 3.3656 | −2.4 |
| Mexico peso* | .0750 | 13.3339 | −4.4 | Russia ruble‡ | .03093 | 32.331 | 0.6 |
| Peru new sol | .3785 | 2.642 | −2.0 | Sweden krona | .1447 | 6.9106 | 0.4 |
| Uraguay peso† | .04597 | 21.7520 | 9.8 | Switzerland franc | 1.0428 | .9589 | 2.3 |
| Venezuela b.fuerte | .229885 | 4.3500 | unch | 1-month forward | 1.0436 | .9582 | 2.2 |
| | | | | 3-months forward | 1.0455 | .9565 | 2.2 |
| **Asia-Pacific** | | | | 6-months forward | 1.0483 | .9539 | 2.2 |
| Australian dollar | 1.0277 | .9731 | −0.7 | Turkey lira** | .5533 | 1.8073 | −5.7 |
| 1-month forward | 1.0254 | .9761 | −0.7 | U.K. pound | 1.5591 | .6414 | −0.3 |
| 3-months forward | 1.0186 | .9817 | −0.8 | 1-month forward | 1.5590 | .6414 | −0.3 |
| 6-months forward | 1.0110 | .9891 | −0.9 | 3-months forward | 1.5588 | .6415 | −0.4 |
| China yuan | .1575 | 6.3486 | 0.5 | 6-months forward | 1.5584 | .6417 | −0.5 |
| Hong Kong dollar | .1289 | 7.7551 | −0.2 | | | | |
| India rupee | .01833 | 54.545 | 2.9 | **Middle East/Africa** | | | |
| Indonesia rupiah | .0001070 | 9343 | 3.4 | Bahrain dinar | 2.6528 | .3770 | unch |
| Japan yen | .012520 | 79.87 | 3.8 | Egypt pound* | .1650 | 6.0610 | 0.2 |
| 1-month forward | .012524 | 79.84 | 3.7 | Israel shekel | .2550 | 3.9220 | 2.9 |
| 3-months forward | .012535 | 79.78 | 3.8 | Jordan dinar | 1.4119 | .7083 | −0.2 |
| 6-months forward | .012553 | 79.66 | 3.8 | Kuwait dinar | 3.5632 | .2806 | 0.9 |
| Malaysia ringgit | .3171 | 3.1538 | −0.7 | Lebanon pound | .0006641 | 1505.70 | unch |
| New Zealand dollar | .8037 | 1.2443 | −3.2 | Saudi Arabia riyal | .2667 | 3.7501 | unch |
| Pakistan rupee | .01058 | 94.500 | 5.2 | South Africa rand | .1229 | 8.1386 | 0.6 |
| Philippines peso | .0240 | 41.654 | −5.0 | UAE dirham | .2723 | 3.6730 | unch |
| Singapore dollar | .7897 | 1.2661 | −2.3 | | | | |
| South Korea won | .0008793 | 1137.30 | −2.0 | | | | |

*Floating rate    †Financial    ‡Russian Central Bank rate    **Rebased as of Jan 1, 2005
Note: Based on trading among banks of $1 milliion and more, as quoted at 4p.m. ET by Reuters.

## Foreign Exchange Transactions

**spot foreign exchange transaction**
A foreign exchange transaction involving the immediate exchange of currencies at the current (or spot) exchange rate.

There are two basic types of foreign exchange rates and foreign exchange transactions: spot and forward. **Spot foreign exchange transactions** involve the immediate exchange of currencies at the current (or spot) exchange rate (see Figure 13–1). Spot transactions can be conducted through the foreign exchange division of commercial banks or a nonbank foreign currency dealer. For example, a U.S. investor wanting to buy British pounds through a local bank on July 4, 2012, essentially has the dollars transferred from his or her bank account to the dollar account of a pound seller at a rate of $1 per 0.6414 pound (or $1.5591 per pound).[1] Simultaneously, pounds are transferred from the seller's account into

[1] In actual practice, settlement—exchange of currencies—occurs normally two days after a transaction.

**FIGURE 13–1**

Spot versus Forward Foreign Exchange Transaction

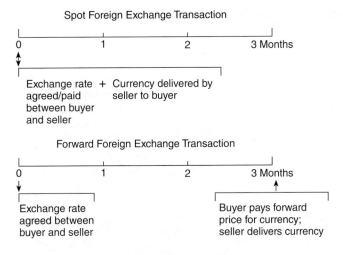

an account designated by the U.S. investor. If the dollar depreciates in value relative to the pound (e.g., $1 per 0.6360 pound or $1.5723 per pound), the value of the pound investment, if converted back into U.S. dollars, increases. If the dollar appreciates in value relative to the pound (e.g., $1 per 0.6433 pound or $1.5545 per pound), the value of the pound investment, if converted back into U.S. dollars, decreases.

The exchange rates listed in Table 13–1 all involve the exchange of U.S. dollars for the foreign currency, or vice versa. Historically, the exchange of a sum of money into a different currency required a trader to first convert the money into U.S. dollars and then convert it into the desired currency. More recently, cross-currency trades allow currency traders to bypass this step of initially converting into U.S. dollars. Cross-currency trades are a pair of currencies traded in foreign exchange markets that do not involve the U.S. dollar. For example, GBP/JPY cross-exchange trading was created to allow individuals in the United Kingdom and Japan who wanted to convert their money into the other currency to do so without having to bear the cost of having to first convert into U.S. dollars. Cross-currency exchange rates for eight major countries are listed at Bloomberg's website: **www.bloomberg.com/ markets/currencies/fxc.html**.

The appreciation of a country's currency (or a rise in its value relative to other currencies) means that the country's goods are more expensive for foreign buyers and that foreign goods are cheaper for foreign sellers (all else constant). Thus, when a country's currency appreciates, domestic manufacturers find it harder to sell their goods abroad and foreign manufacturers find it easier to sell their goods to domestic purchasers. Conversely, depreciation of a country's currency (or a fall in its value relative to other currencies) means the country's goods become cheaper for foreign buyers and foreign goods become more expensive for foreign sellers. Figure 13–2 shows the pattern of exchange rates between the U.S. dollar and several foreign currencies from 2003 through June 2012. Notice the significant swings in the exchange rates of foreign currencies relative to the U.S. dollar during the financial crisis. Between September 2008 and mid-2010, exchange rates went through three trends. During the first phase, from September 2008 to March 2009, the U.S. dollar appreciated relative to most foreign currencies (or, foreign currencies depreciated relative to the dollar) as investors sought a safe haven

**FIGURE 13–2    Exchange Rate of U.S. Dollars with Various Foreign Currencies**

in U.S. Treasury securities. During the second phase, from March 2009 through November 2009, much of the appreciation of the dollar relative to foreign currencies was reversed as worldwide confidence returned. Between November 2009 and June 2010, countries (particularly those in the eurozone) began to see depreciation relative to the dollar resume (the dollar appreciated relative to the euro) amid concerns about the euro, due to problems in various EU countries (such as Portugal, Ireland, Iceland, Greece, and Spain, the so-called PIIGS). From June 2010 through August 2011, worries about Europe subsided somewhat, and the U.S. government struggled to pass legislation allowing an increase in the national debt ceiling that would allow the country to avoid a potential default on U.S. sovereign debt. The dollar depreciated against many foreign currencies until a debt ceiling increase was passed on August 2, 2011. Despite a downgrade in the rating on the U.S. debt by Standard & Poor's on August 5, 2011 (resulting from the inability of the U.S. Congress to work to stabilize the U.S. debt deficit situation in the long term), the dollar again appreciated relative to most foreign currencies in the period after August 2011 as fears of escalating problems in Europe, including a possible dissolution of the euro, led investors to again seek safe haven in U.S. Treasury securities.

**forward foreign exchange transaction**
The exchange of currencies at a specified exchange rate (or forward exchange rate) at some specified date in the future.

A **forward foreign exchange transaction** is the exchange of currencies at a specified exchange rate (or forward exchange rate) at some specified date in the future, as illustrated in Figure 13–1. An example is an agreement today (at time 0) to exchange dollars for pounds at a given (forward) exchange rate three months in the future. Forward contracts are typically written for one-, three-, or six-month periods, but in practice they can be written over any given length of time.

| **Concept Question** | 1. What is the difference between a spot and a forward foreign exchange market transaction? |
|---|---|

# SOURCES OF FOREIGN EXCHANGE RISK EXPOSURE

The nation's largest commercial banks are major players in foreign currency trading and dealing, with large money center banks such as Citigroup and J.P. Morgan Chase also taking significant positions in foreign currency assets and liabilities (see also Chapter 15 on market risk, where we look at methods of calculating the risk on foreign exchange contracts). Table 13–2 shows the outstanding dollar value of U.S. banks' foreign assets and liabilities for the period 1994 to March 2012. The 2012 figure for foreign assets (claims) was $319.4 billion, with foreign liabilities of $235.3 billion. As you can see, both foreign currency liabilities and assets were growing until 1997 and then fell from 1998 through 2000. The financial crises in Asia and Russia in 1997 and 1998 and in Argentina in the early 2000s are likely reasons for the decrease in foreign assets and liabilities during this period. After this period, growth accelerated rapidly as the world economy recovered. While the growth of liability and asset claims on foreigners slowed during the financial crisis, levels remained stable as U.S. FIs were seen as some of the safest FIs during the crisis. Further, in 1994 through 2000, U.S. banks had more liabilities to than claims (assets) on foreigners. Thus, if the dollar depreciates relative to foreign currencies, more dollars (converted into foreign currencies) would be needed to pay off the liabilities and U.S. banks experience a loss due to foreign exchange risk. However, the reverse was true in 2005 through 2012; that is, as the dollar depreciates relative to foreign currencies, U.S. banks experience a gain from their foreign exchange exposures.

Table 13–3 gives the categories of foreign currency positions (or investments) of all U.S. banks in major currencies as of June 2012. Columns (1) and (2) refer to the assets and liabilities denominated in foreign currencies that are held in the

**TABLE 13–2   Liabilities to and Claims on Foreigners Reported by Banks in the United States, Payable in Foreign Currencies (in millions of dollars, end of period)**

Source: *Federal Reserve Bulletin*, Table 3.16, various issues. *www.federalreserve.gov*

| Item | 1994 | 1995 | 1997 | 1998 | 2000 | 2005 | 2008 | 2009 | 2012* |
|---|---|---|---|---|---|---|---|---|---|
| Banks' liabilities | $89,284 | $109,713 | $117,524 | $101,125 | $76,120 | $85,841 | $290,467 | $215,883 | $235,300 |
| Banks' claims | 60,689 | 74,016 | 83,038 | 78,162 | 56,867 | 93,290 | 324,230 | 333,622 | 319,401 |
| Deposits | 19,661 | 22,696 | 28,661 | 45,985 | 22,907 | 43,868 | 108,417 | 97,822 | 135,211 |
| Other claims | 41,028 | 51,320 | 54,377 | 32,177 | 33,960 | 49,422 | 215,813 | 237,649 | 184,190 |
| Claims of banks' domestic customers† | 10,878 | 6,145 | 8,191 | 20,718 | 29,782 | 54,698 | 42,208 | 47,236 | 45,386 |

Note: Data on claims exclude foreign currencies held by U.S. monetary authorities.

* 2012 data are for end of March.

† Assets owned by customers of the reporting bank located in the United States that represent claims on foreigners held by reporting banks for the accounts of the domestic customers.

**TABLE 13–3**   Monthly U.S. Bank Positions in Foreign Currencies and Foreign Assets and Liabilities, March 2012 (in currency of denomination)

Source: *Treasury Bulletin*, June 2012, pp. 89–99. *www.treas.gov*

|  | (1) Assets | (2) Liabilities | (3) FX Bought* | (4) FX Sold* | (5) Net Position† |
|---|---|---|---|---|---|
| Canadian dollars (millions of C$) | 158,058 | 149,893 | 901,521 | 934,328 | −24,642 |
| Japanese yen (billions of ¥) | 59,620 | 54,591 | 471,248 | 481,227 | −4,950 |
| Swiss francs (millions of SF) | 142,614 | 105,387 | 1,091,408 | 1,132,886 | −4,251 |
| British pounds (millions of £) | 621,761 | 516,453 | 1,579,274 | 1,626,368 | 58,214 |
| Euros (millions of €) | 2,278,375 | 2,212,581 | 6,816,463 | 6,840,067 | 42,190 |

* Includes spot, future, and forward contracts.
† Net position = (Assets − Liabilities) + (FX bought − FX sold).

**spot market for FX**
The market in which foreign currency is traded for immediate delivery.

**forward market for FX**
The market in which foreign currency is traded for future delivery.

**net exposure**
The degree to which an FI is net long (positive) or net short (negative) in a given currency.

portfolios at U.S. banks. Columns (3) and (4) refer to trading in foreign currency markets (the **spot** market and **forward market for foreign exchange** in which contracts are bought—a long position—and sold—a short position—in each major currency). Foreign currency trading dominates direct portfolio investments. Even though the aggregate trading positions appear very large—for example, U.S. banks bought ¥471,248 billion—their overall or net exposure positions can be relatively small (e.g., the net position in yen was −¥4,950 billion).

An FI's overall FX exposure in any given currency can be measured by the **net position exposure,** which is measured in local currency and reported in column (5) of Table 13–3 as:

$$\text{Net exposure}_i = (\text{FX assets}_i - \text{FX liabilities}_i) + (\text{FX bought}_i - \text{FX sold}_i)$$
$$= \text{Net foreign assets}_i + \text{Net FX bought}_i$$

where

$i = i$th currency.

Clearly, an FI could match its foreign currency assets to its liabilities in a given currency and match buys and sells in its trading book in that foreign currency to reduce its foreign exchange net exposure to zero and thus avoid FX risk. It could also offset an imbalance in its foreign asset–liability portfolio by an opposing imbalance in its trading book so that its net exposure position in that currency would be zero. Further, financial holding companies can aggregate their foreign exchange exposure even more. Financial holding companies might have a commercial bank, an insurance company, and a pension fund all under one umbrella that allows them to reduce their net foreign exchange exposure across all units. For example, in March 2012, Citigroup held over $5.84 trillion in foreign exchange derivative securities off the balance sheet. Yet the company estimated the value at risk from its foreign exchange exposure was $145 million, or 0.001 percent.

Notice in Table 13–3 that U.S. banks had positive net FX exposures in two of the five major currencies in March 2012. A *positive* net exposure position implies a U.S. FI is overall **net long in a currency** (i.e., the FI has bought more foreign currency than it has sold) and faces the risk that the foreign currency will fall in value against the U.S. dollar, the domestic currency. A *negative* net exposure position implies that a U.S. FI is **net short in a foreign currency** (i.e., the FI has sold

**net long (short) in a currency**
Holding more (fewer) assets than liabilities in a given currency.

more foreign currency than it has purchased) and faces the risk that the foreign currency could rise in value against the dollar. Thus, failure to maintain a fully balanced position in any given currency exposes a U.S. FI to fluctuations in the FX rate of that currency against the dollar. Indeed, the greater the volatility of foreign exchange rates given any net exposure position, the greater the fluctuations in value of an FI's foreign exchange portfolio (see Chapter 15, where we discuss market risk).

We have given the FX exposures for U.S. banks only, but most large nonbank FIs also have some FX exposure either through asset–liability holdings or currency trading. The absolute sizes of these exposures are smaller than those for major U.S. money center banks. The reasons for this are threefold: smaller asset sizes, prudent person concerns,[2] and regulations.[3] For example, U.S. pension funds invest approximately 5 percent of their asset portfolios in foreign securities, and U.S. life insurance companies generally hold less than 10 percent of their assets in foreign securities. Interestingly, U.S. FIs' holdings of overseas assets are less than those of FIs in Japan and Britain. For example, in Britain, pension funds have traditionally invested more than 20 percent of their funds in foreign assets.

## Foreign Exchange Rate Volatility and FX Exposure

We can measure the potential size of an FI's FX exposure by analyzing the asset, liability, and currency trading mismatches on its balance sheet and the underlying volatility of exchange rate movements (see also Chapter 15 on market risk). Specifically, we can use the following equation:

$$\text{Dollar loss/gain in currency } i = [\text{Net exposure in foreign currency } i \text{ measured in U.S. dollars}] \times \text{Shock (volatility) to the }\$/\text{foreign currency } i \text{ exchange rate}$$

The larger the FI's net exposure in a foreign currency and the larger the foreign currency's exchange rate volatility, the larger is the potential dollar loss or gain to an FI's earnings. As we discuss in more detail later in the chapter, the underlying causes of FX volatility reflect fluctuations in the demand for and supply of a country's currency. That is, conceptually, an FX rate is like the price of any good and will appreciate in value relative to other currencies when demand is high or supply is low and will depreciate in value when demand is low or supply is high. For example, during the summer of 2011, as the magnitude of the European crisis became apparent and the United States grappled with a looming debt default, Switzerland was one of the few countries with a safe and robust financial system and secure fiscal conditions. Investors bought Swiss francs as a safe haven currency. The purchases led to large appreciation of the currency: From September 2010 to September 2011, the Swiss franc appreciated by 14.8 percent against the U.S. dollar, 7.7 percent against the euro, 20.7 percent against the Japanese yen, and 14.8 percent against British pound (see Figure 13–2).

---

[2] Prudent person concerns are especially important for pension funds.

[3] For example, New York State restricts foreign asset holdings of New York–based life insurance companies to less than 10 percent of their assets.

**TABLE 13–4**
Top Currency Traders by Percent of Overall Volume

| Rank | Name | Market Share |
|------|------|--------------|
| 1 | Deutsche Bank | 14.57% |
| 2 | Citigroup | 12.26 |
| 3 | Barclays | 10.95 |
| 4 | UBS | 10.48 |
| 5 | HSBC | 6.72 |
| 6 | J.P. Morgan Chase | 6.60 |
| 7 | RBS | 5.86 |
| 8 | Credit Suisse | 4.68 |
| 9 | Morgan Stanley | 3.52 |
| 10 | Goldman Sachs | 3.12 |

**Concept Questions**

1. How is the net foreign currency exposure of an FI measured?
2. If a bank is long in British pounds (£), does it gain or lose if the dollar appreciates in value against the pound?
3. A bank has £10 million in assets and £7 million in liabilities. It has also bought £52 million in foreign currency trading. What is its net exposure in pounds? (£55 million)

# FOREIGN CURRENCY TRADING

The FX markets of the world have become one of the largest of all financial markets. Trading turnover averaged as high as $4.7 trillion a day in recent years, 70 times the daily trading volume on the New York Stock Exchange. Of the $4.7 trillion in average daily trading volume in the foreign exchange markets in 2011, $1.57 trillion (33.5 percent) involved spot transactions, while $3.13 trillion (66.5 percent) involved forward and other transactions. This compares to 1989 where average daily trading volume was $590 billion; $317 billion (53.7 percent) of which was spot foreign exchange transactions and $273 billion (46.3 percent) forward and other foreign exchange transactions. The main reason for this increase in the use of forward relative to spot foreign exchange transactions is the increased ability to hedge foreign exchange risk with forward foreign exchange contracts (discussed later). Indeed, foreign exchange trading has continued to be one of the few sources of steady income for global banks during the late 2000s and early 2010s.

London continues to be the largest FX trading market, followed by New York and Tokyo.[4] Table 13–4 lists the top foreign currency traders as of June 2012. The top four banks operating in these markets, Deutsche Bank (14.57 percent), Citigroup (12.26 percent), Barclays (10.95 percent), and UBS (10.48 percent), comprise almost half of all foreign currency trading. Foreign exchange trading has been called the fairest market in the world because of its immense volume and the fact that no single institution can control the market's direction. Although professionals refer to global foreign exchange trading as a market, it is not really one in the traditional sense of the word. There is no central location where foreign exchange trading takes place. Moreover, the FX market is essentially a 24-hour market,

---

[4] On a global basis, approximately 34 percent of trading in FX occurs in London, 17 percent in New York, and 6 percent in Tokyo. The remainder is spread throughout the world.

moving among Tokyo, London, and New York throughout the day. Therefore, fluctuations in exchange rates and thus FX trading risk exposure continues into the night even when other FI operations are closed. This clearly adds to the risk from holding mismatched FX positions. Most of the volume is traded among the top international banks, which process currency transactions for everyone from large corporations to governments around the world. Online foreign exchange trading is increasing. Electronic foreign exchange trading volume tops 60 percent of overall global foreign exchange trading. The transnational nature of the electronic exchange of funds makes secure, Internet-based trading an ideal platform. Online trading portals—terminals where currency transactions are being executed—are a low-cost way of conducting spot and forward foreign exchange transactions.

## FX Trading Activities

An FI's position in the FX markets generally reflects four trading activities:

1. The purchase and sale of foreign currencies to allow customers to partake in and complete international commercial trade transactions.
2. The purchase and sale of foreign currencies to allow customers (or the FI itself) to take positions in foreign real and financial investments.
3. The purchase and sale of foreign currencies for hedging purposes to offset customer (or FI) exposure in any given currency.
4. The purchase and sale of foreign currencies for speculative purposes through forecasting or anticipating future movements in FX rates.

In the first two activities, the FI normally acts as an *agent of* its customers for a fee but does not assume the FX risk itself. Citigroup is the dominant supplier of FX to retail customers in the United States and worldwide. As of 2012, the aggregate value of Citigroup's principal amount of foreign exchange contracts totaled $5.8 trillion. In the third activity, the FI acts defensively as a hedger to reduce FX exposure. For example, an FI may take a short (sell) position in the foreign exchange of a country to offset a long (buy) position in the foreign exchange of that same country. Thus, FX risk exposure essentially relates to **open positions** taken as a principal by the FI for speculative purposes, the fourth activity. An FI usually creates an open position by taking an unhedged position in a foreign currency in its FX trading with other FIs.

**open position**
An unhedged position in a particular currency.

The Federal Reserve estimates that 200 FIs are active market makers in foreign currencies in the U.S. foreign exchange market with about 25 commercial and investment banks making a market in the five major currencies. FIs can make speculative trades directly with other FIs or arrange them through specialist FX brokers. The Federal Reserve Bank of New York estimates that approximately 45 percent of speculative or open position trades are accomplished through specialized brokers who receive a fee for arranging trades between FIs. Speculative trades can be instituted through a variety of FX instruments. Spot currency trades are the most common, with FIs seeking to make a profit on the difference between buy and sell prices (i.e., on movements in the bid–ask prices over time). However, FIs can also take speculative positions in foreign exchange forward contracts, futures, and options.

Most profits or losses on foreign trading come from taking an open position or speculating in currencies. Revenues from market making—the bid–ask spread—or from acting as agents for retail or wholesale customers generally provide only

**TABLE 13–5**
Foreign Exchange Trading Income of Major U.S. Banks (in millions of dollars)

Source: FDIC, *Statistics on Depository Institutions,* various dates. *www.fdic.gov*

| | 1995 | 2000 | 2005 | 2008 | 2009 | 2011 |
|---|---|---|---|---|---|---|
| Bank of America | $ 303.0 | $ 524.0 | $ 769.8 | $ 1,772.8 | $ 833.2 | $1,391.3 |
| Bank of New York Mellon | 42.0 | 261.0 | 266.0 | 1,181.5 | 832.3 | 727.0 |
| Citigroup | 1,053.0 | 1,243.0 | 2,519.0 | 2,590.0 | 1,855.0 | 1,871.0 |
| Fifth Third | 0.0 | 0.0 | 51.7 | 105.6 | 76.3 | 63.4 |
| HSBC North America | 0.0 | 6.5 | 133.9 | 643.8 | 915.2 | 164.7 |
| J.P. Morgan Chase | 253.0 | 1,456.0 | 997.0 | 1,844.0 | 2,541.0 | 1,043.0 |
| KeyCorp | 8.0 | 19.6 | 38.6 | 63.0 | 47.1 | 42.9 |
| Northern Trust | 54.8 | 142.0 | 180.2 | 616.2 | 445.7 | 382.2 |
| PNC | 4.5 | 22.3 | 38.3 | 74.0 | 79.7 | 89.2 |
| State Street B&TC | 140.7 | 386.5 | 468.5 | 1,066.4 | 679.9 | 685.1 |
| Suntrust | 0.0 | 16.9 | 5.7 | 35.7 | 37.6 | 44.2 |
| U.S. Bancorp | 7.3 | 22.4 | 30.9 | 68.2 | 67.0 | 76.0 |
| Wells Fargo | 14.7 | 191.9 | 350.0 | 392.4 | 516.2 | 524.0 |
| Total | 1,881.0 | $4,292.1 | $5,849.6 | $10,453.6 | $8,926.2 | $7,104.0 |

www.citigroup.com
www.bankofamerica.com
www.jpmorganchase.com

a secondary or supplementary revenue source. Note the trading income from FX trading for some large U.S. banks in Table 13–5. The dominant FX trading banks in the United States are Citigroup, Bank of America, and J.P. Morgan Chase. As can be seen, total trading income grew steadily in the years prior to the financial crises. For just these 13 FIs, income from trading activities increased from $1,881.0 million in 1995 to $10,453.6 million in 2008, a 456 percent increase over the 13-year period. Income from foreign exchange trading activities, however, fell during the financial crisis, to $8,923.2 million in 2009, and had yet to recover by 2011, falling further to $7,104.0 million.

**Concept Questions**

1. What are the four major FX trading activities?
2. In which trades do FIs normally act as agents, and in which trades as principals?
3. What is the source of most profits or losses on foreign exchange trading? What foreign currency activities provide a secondary source of revenue?

## FOREIGN ASSET AND LIABILITY POSITIONS

The second dimension of an FI's FX exposure results from any mismatches between its foreign financial asset and foreign financial liability portfolios. As discussed earlier, an FI is long a foreign currency if its assets in that currency exceed its liabilities, while it is short a foreign currency if its liabilities in that currency exceed its assets. Foreign financial assets might include Swiss franc–denominated bonds, British pound–denominated gilt-edged securities, or peso-denominated Mexican bonds. Foreign financial liabilities might include issuing British pound CDs or a yen-denominated bond in the Euromarkets to raise yen funds. The globalization of financial markets has created an enormous range of possibilities for raising funds in currencies other than the home currency. This is important for

FIs that wish to not only diversify their sources and uses of funds but also exploit imperfections in foreign banking markets that create opportunities for higher returns on assets or lower funding costs.

## The Return and Risk of Foreign Investments

This section discusses the extra dimensions of return and risk from adding foreign currency assets and liabilities to an FI's portfolio. Like domestic assets and liabilities, profits (returns) result from the difference between contractual income from and costs paid on a security. With foreign assets and liabilities, however, profits (returns) are also affected by changes in foreign exchange rates.

**EXAMPLE 13–1**

*Calculating the Return on Foreign Exchange Transactions of a U.S. FI*

Suppose that an FI has the following assets and liabilities:

| Assets | Liabilities |
|---|---|
| $100 million U.S. loans (1 year) in dollars | $200 million U.S. CDs (1 year) in dollars |
| $100 million equivalent U.K. loans (1 year) (loans made in pounds) | |

The U.S. FI is raising all of its $200 million liabilities in dollars (one-year CDs) but investing 50 percent in U.S. dollar assets (one-year maturity loans) and 50 percent in U.K. pound assets (one-year maturity loans).[5] In this example, the FI has matched the duration of its assets and liabilities ($D_A = D_L = 1$ year), but has mismatched the currency composition of its asset and liability portfolios. Suppose the promised one-year U.S. CD rate is 8 percent, to be paid in dollars at the end of the year, and that one-year, default risk–free loans in the United States are yielding 9 percent. The FI would have a positive spread of 1 percent from investing domestically. Suppose, however, that default risk–free, one-year loans are yielding 15 percent in the United Kingdom.

To invest in the United Kingdom, the FI decides to take 50 percent of its $200 million in funds and make one-year maturity U.K. pound loans while keeping 50 percent of its funds to make U.S. dollar loans. To invest $100 million (of the $200 million in CDs issued) in one-year loans in the United Kingdom, the U.S. FI engages in the following transactions [illustrated in panel (a) of Figure 13–3].

1. At the beginning of the year, sells $100 million for pounds on the spot currency markets. If the exchange rate is $1.60 to £1, this translates into $100 million/1.6 = £62.5 million.
2. Takes the £62.5 million and makes one-year U.K. loans at a 15 percent interest rate.
3. At the end of the year, pound revenue from these loans will be £62.5(1.15) = £71.875 million.
4. Repatriates these funds back to the United States at the end of the year. That is, the U.S. FI sells the £71.875 million in the foreign exchange market at the spot exchange rate that exists at that time, the end of the year spot rate.

Suppose the spot foreign exchange rate has not changed over the year; it remains fixed at $1.60/£1. Then the dollar proceeds from the U.K. investment will be:

$$£71.875 \text{ million} \times \$1.60/£1 = \$115 \text{ million}$$

---

[5] For simplicity, we ignore the leverage or net worth aspects of the FI's portfolio.

or, as a return,

$$\frac{\$115\text{ million} - \$100\text{ million}}{\$100\text{ million}} = 15\%$$

Given this, the weighted return on the bank's portfolio of investments would be:

$$(0.5)(0.09) + (0.5)(0.15) = 0.12 \text{ or } 12\%$$

This exceeds the cost of the FI's CDs by 4 percent (12% − 8%).

Suppose, however, that at the end of the year the British pound falls in value relative to the dollar, or the U.S. dollar appreciates in value relative to the pound. The return on the U.K. loans could be far less than 15 percent even in the absence of interest rate or credit risk. For example, suppose the exchange rate falls from $1.60/£1 at the beginning of the year to $1.45/£1 at the end of the year when the FI needs to repatriate the principal and interest on the loan. At an exchange rate of $1.45/£1, the pound loan revenues at the end of the year translate into:

$$£71.875\text{ million} \times \$1.45/£1 = \$104.22\text{ million}$$

or as a return on the original dollar investment of:

$$\frac{\$104.22 - \$100}{\$100} = 0.0422 = 4.22\%$$

The weighted return on the FI's asset portfolio would be:

$$(0.5)(0.09) + (0.5)(0.0422) = 0.0661 = 6.61\%$$

In this case, the FI actually has a loss or has a negative interest margin (6.61% − 8% = −1.39%) on its balance sheet investments.

**FIGURE 13–3**
**Time Line for a Foreign Exchange Transaction**

(a) Unhedged Foreign Exchange Transaction

FI lends $100 million for pounds at $1.6/£1

FI receives £62.5(1.15) for dollars at $?/£1

|————————————————————————|
0                                              1 year

(b) Foreign Exchange Transaction Hedged on the Balance Sheet

FI lends $100 million for pounds at $1.6/£1

FI receives £62.5(1.15) for dollars at $?/£1

FI receives (from a CD) $100 million for pounds at $1.6/£1

FI pays £62.5(1.11) with dollars at $?/£1

|————————————————————————|
0                                              1 year

(c) Foreign Exchange Transaction Hedged with Forwards

FI lends $100 million for pounds at $1.6/£1

FI sells a 1-year pounds-for-dollars forward contract with a stated forward rate of $1.55/£1 and nominal value of £62.5(1.15)

FI receives £62.5(1.15) from borrower and delivers funds to forward buyer receiving £62.5 × (1.15) × 1.55 guaranteed.

|————————————————————————|
0                                              1 year

The reason for the loss is that the depreciation of the pound from $1.60 to $1.45 has offset the attractive high yield on British pound loans relative to domestic U.S. loans. If the pound had instead appreciated (risen in value) against the dollar over the year—say, to $1.70/£1—then the U.S. FI would have generated a dollar return from its U.K. loans of:

$$£71.875 \times \$1.70 = \$122.188 \text{ million}$$

or a percentage return of 22.188 percent. Then the U.S. FI would receive a double benefit from investing in the United Kingdom: a high yield on the domestic British loans plus an appreciation in pounds over the one-year investment period.

## Risk and Hedging

Since a manager cannot know in advance what the pound/dollar spot exchange rate will be at the end of the year, a portfolio imbalance or investment strategy in which the FI is *net long* $100 million in pounds (or £62.5 million) is risky. As we discussed, the British loans would generate a return of 22.188 percent if the pound appreciated from $1.60/£1 to $1.70/£1, but would produce a return of only 4.22 percent if the pound depreciated in value against the dollar to $1.45/£1.

In principle, an FI manager can better control the scale of its FX exposure in two major ways: on-balance-sheet hedging and off-balance-sheet hedging. On-balance-sheet hedging involves making changes in the on-balance-sheet assets and liabilities to protect FI profits from FX risk. Off-balance-sheet hedging involves no on-balance-sheet changes, but rather involves taking a position in forward or other derivative securities to hedge FX risk.

### *On-Balance-Sheet Hedging*

The following example illustrates how an FI manager can control FX exposure by making changes on the balance sheet.

**EXAMPLE 13–2**
*Hedging on the Balance Sheet*

Suppose that instead of funding the $100 million investment in 15 percent British loans with U.S. CDs, the FI manager funds the British loans with $100 million equivalent one-year pound CDs at a rate of 11 percent [as illustrated in panel (b) of Figure 13–3]. Now the balance sheet of the bank would look like this:

| Assets | Liabilities |
|---|---|
| $100 million<br>U.S. loans (9%) | $100 million<br>U.S. CDs (8%) |
| $100 million<br>U.K. loans (15%)<br>    (loans made in pounds) | $100 million<br>U.K. CDs (11%)<br>    (deposits raised in pounds) |

In this situation, the FI has both a matched maturity and currency foreign asset–liability book. We might now consider the FI's profitability or spread between the return on assets and the cost of funds under two scenarios: first, when the pound depreciates in value against the dollar over the year from $1.60/£1 to $1.45/£1 and second, when the pound appreciates in value over the year from $1.60/£1 to $1.70/£1.

### The Depreciating Pound

When the pound falls in value to $1.45/£1, the return on the British loan portfolio is 4.22 percent. Consider now what happens to the cost of $100 million in pound liabilities in dollar terms:

1. At the beginning of the year, the FI borrows $100 million equivalent in pound CDs for one year at a promised interest rate of 11 percent. At an exchange rate of $1.60£, this is a pound equivalent amount of borrowing of $100 million/1.6 = £62.5 million.
2. At the end of the year, the bank has to pay back the pound CD holders their principal and interest, £62.5 million(1.11) = £69.375 million.
3. If the pound depreciates to $1.45/£1 over the year, the repayment in dollar terms would be £69.375 million × $1.45/£1 = $100.59 million, or a dollar cost of funds of 0.59 percent.

Thus, at the end of the year the following occurs:

*Average return on assets:*

$$(0.5)(0.09) + (0.5)(0.0422) = 0.0661 = 6.61\%$$
$$\text{U.S. asset return} + \text{U.K. asset return} = \text{Overall return}$$

*Average cost of funds:*

$$(0.5)(0.08) + (0.5)(0.0059) = 0.04295 = 4.295\%$$
$$\text{U.S. cost of funds} + \text{U.K. cost of funds} = \text{Overall cost}$$

*Net return:*

$$\text{Average return on assets} - \text{Average cost of funds}$$
$$6.61\% - 4.295\% = 2.315\%$$

### The Appreciating Pound

When the pound appreciates over the year from $1.60/£1 to $1.70/£1, the return on British loans is equal to 22.188. Now consider the dollar cost of British one-year CDs at the end of the year when the U.S. FI has to pay the principal and interest to the CD holder:

$$£69.375 \text{ million} × \$1.70/£1 = \$117.9375 \text{ million}$$

or a dollar cost of funds of 17.9375 percent. Thus, at the end of the year:

*Average return on assets:*

$$(0.5)(0.09) + (0.5)(0.22188) = 0.15594 \text{ or } 15.594\%$$

*Average cost of funds:*

$$(0.5)(0.08) + (0.5)(0.179375) = 0.12969 \text{ or } 12.969\%$$

*Net return:*

$$15.594 - 12.969 = 2.625\%$$

Note that even though the FI locked in a positive return when setting the net foreign exchange exposure on the balance sheet to zero, net return is still volatile. Thus, the FI is still exposed to foreign exchange risk. However, by directly matching its foreign asset and liability book, an FI can lock in a positive return or profit spread whichever direction exchange rates change over the investment period. For example, even if domestic U.S. banking is a relatively low profit activity (i.e., there is a low spread between the return on assets and the cost of funds), the FI could be quite profitable overall. Specifically, it could lock in a large positive spread—if it exists—between deposit rates and loan rates in foreign markets. In our example, a 4 percent positive spread existed between British one-year loan rates and deposit rates compared with only a 1 percent spread domestically.

Note that for such imbalances in domestic spreads and foreign spreads to continue over long periods of time, financial service firms would have to face significant barriers to entry in foreign markets. Specifically, if real and financial capital is free to move, FIs would increasingly withdraw from the U.S. market and reorient their operations toward the United Kingdom. Reduced competition would widen loan deposit interest spreads in the United States, and increased competition would contract U.K. spreads, until the profit opportunities from foreign activities disappears. We discuss FIs' abilities, and limits on their abilities, to engage in cross-border financial and real investments further in Chapter 21.[6]

### Hedging with Forwards

Instead of matching its $100 million foreign asset position with $100 million of foreign liabilities, the FI might have chosen to remain unhedged on the balance sheet. As a lower-cost alternative, it could hedge by taking a position in the forward market for foreign currencies—for example, the one-year forward market for selling pounds for dollars.[7] We discuss the nature and use of forward contracts by FI managers more extensively in Chapter 22. However, here we introduce them to show how they can insulate the FX risk of the FI in our example. Any forward position taken would not appear on the balance sheet. It would appear as a contingent off-balance-sheet claim, which we described in Chapter 16 as an item below the bottom line. The role of the forward FX contract is to offset the uncertainty regarding the future spot rate on pounds at the end of the one-year investment horizon. Instead of waiting until the end of the year to transfer pounds back into dollars at an unknown spot rate, the FI can enter into a contract to sell forward its *expected* principal and interest earnings on the loan, at today's known **forward exchange rate** for dollars/pounds, with delivery of pound funds to the buyer of the forward contract taking place at the end of the year. Essentially, by selling the expected proceeds on the pound loan forward, at a known (forward FX) exchange rate today, the FI removes the future spot exchange rate uncertainty and thus the uncertainty relating to investment returns on the British loan.

**forward exchange rate**
The exchange rate agreed to today for future (forward) delivery of a currency.

---

[6] In the background of the previous example was the implicit assumption that the FI was also matching the durations of its foreign assets and liabilities. In our example, it was issuing one-year duration pound CDs to fund one-year duration pound loans. Suppose instead that it still had a matched book in size ($100 million) but funded the one-year 15 percent British loans with three-month 11 percent pound CDs.

$$D_{£A} - D_{£L} = 1 - 0.25 = 0.75 \text{ year}$$

Thus, pound assets have a longer duration than do pound liabilities.

If British interest rates were to change over the year, the market value of pound assets would change by more than the market value of pound liabilities. This effect should be familiar from Chapter 9. More importantly, the FI would no longer be locking in a fixed return by matching in the size of its foreign currency book since it would have to take into account its potential exposure to capital gains and losses on its pound assets and liabilities due to shocks to British interest rates. In essence, an FI is hedged against both foreign exchange rate risk and foreign interest rate risk only if it matches both the size and the durations of its foreign assets and liabilities in a specific currency.

[7] An FI could also hedge its on-balance-sheet FX risk by taking off-balance-sheet positions in futures, swaps, and options on foreign currencies. Such strategies are discussed in detail in Chapters 22, 23, and 24.

**EXAMPLE 13–3**

*Hedging with Forwards*

Consider the following transactional steps when the FI hedges its FX risk immediately by selling its expected one-year pound loan proceeds in the forward FX market [illustrated in panel (c) of Figure 13–3].

1. The U.S. FI sells $100 million for pounds at the *spot* exchange rate *today* and receives $100 million/1.6 = £62.5 million.
2. The FI then immediately lends the £62.5 million to a British customer at 15 percent for one year.
3. The FI also sells the expected principal and interest proceeds from the pound loan forward for dollars at today's forward rate for one-year delivery. Let the current forward one-year exchange rate between dollars and pounds stand at $1.55/£1, or at a 5 cent discount to the spot pound; as a percentage discount:

$$(\$1.55 - \$1.60)/\$1.6 = -3.125\%$$

This means that the forward buyer of pounds promises to pay:

$$£62.5 \text{ million} (1.15) \times \$1.55/£1 = £71.875 \text{ million} \times \$1.55/£1 = \$111.406 \text{ million}$$

to the FI (the forward seller) in one year when the FI delivers the £71.875 million proceeds of the loan to the forward buyer.

4. In one year, the British borrower repays the loan to the FI plus interest in pounds (£71.875 million).
5. The FI delivers the £71.875 million to the buyer of the one-year forward contract and receives the promised $111.406 million.

Barring the pound borrower's default on the loan or the forward buyer's reneging on the forward contract, the FI knows from the very beginning of the investment period that it has locked in a guaranteed return on the British loan of:

$$\frac{\$111.406 - \$100}{\$100} = 0.11406 = 11.406\%$$

Specifically, this return is fully hedged against any dollar/pound exchange rate changes over the one-year holding period of the loan investment. Given this return on British loans, *the overall expected return* on the FI's asset portfolio is:

$$(0.5)(0.09) + (0.5)(0.11406) = 0.10203 \text{ or } 10.203\%$$

Since the cost of funds for the FI's $200 million U.S. CDs is an assumed 8 percent, it has been able to lock in a risk-free return spread over the year of 2.203 percent regardless of spot exchange rate fluctuations between the initial foreign (loan) investment and repatriation of the foreign loan proceeds one year later.

In the preceding example, it is profitable for the FI to increasingly drop domestic U.S. loans and invest in hedged foreign U.K. loans, since the hedged dollar return on foreign loans of 11.406 percent is so much higher than 9 percent domestic loans. As the FI seeks to invest more in British loans, it needs to buy more spot pounds. This drives up the spot price of pounds in dollar terms to more than $1.60/£1. In addition, the FI would need to sell more pounds forward (the proceeds of these pound loans) for dollars, driving the forward rate to below $1.55/£1. The outcome would widen the dollar forward–spot exchange rate spread on pounds, making forward hedged pound investments less attractive than before. This process would continue until the U.S. cost of FI funds just equals the forward hedged return on British loans. That is, the FI could make no further profits by borrowing in U.S. dollars and making forward contract–hedged investments in U.K. loans (see also the discussion below on the interest rate parity theorem).

## Multicurrency Foreign Asset–Liability Positions

So far, we have used a one-currency example of a matched or mismatched foreign asset–liability portfolio. Many FIs, including banks, mutual funds, and pension funds, hold multicurrency asset–liability positions. As for multicurrency trading portfolios, diversification across many asset and liability markets can potentially reduce the risk of portfolio returns and the cost of funds. To the extent that domestic and foreign interest rates or stock returns for equities do not move closely together over time, potential gains from asset–liability portfolio diversification can offset the risk of mismatching individual currency asset–liability positions.

**real interest rate**
The difference between a nominal interest rate and the expected rate of inflation.

Theoretically speaking, the one-period nominal interest rate ($r_i$) on fixed-income securities in any particular country has two major components. First, the **real interest rate** reflects underlying real sector demand and supply for funds in that currency. Second, the *expected inflation rate* reflects an extra amount of interest lenders demand from borrowers to compensate the lenders for the erosion in the principal (or real) value of the funds they lend due to inflation in goods prices expected over the period of the loan. Formally:[8]

$$r_i = rr_i + i_i^e$$

where

$r_i$ = Nominal interest rate in country $i$

$rr_i$ = Real interest rate in country $i$

$i_i^e$ = Expected one-period inflation rate in country $i$

If real savings and investment demand and supply pressures, as well as inflationary expectations, are closely linked or economic integration across countries exists, we expect to find that nominal interest rates are highly correlated across financial markets. For example, if, as the result of a strong demand for investment funds, German real interest rates rise, there may be a capital outflow from other countries toward Germany. This may lead to rising real and nominal interest rates in other countries as policymakers and borrowers try to mitigate the size of their capital outflows. On the other hand, if the world capital market is not very well integrated, quite significant nominal and real interest deviations may exist before equilibrating international flows of funds materialize. Foreign asset or liability returns are likely to be relatively weakly correlated and significant diversification opportunities exist.

Table 13–6 lists the correlations among the returns in major stock indices before and during the financial crisis. Looking at correlations between foreign stock market returns and U.S. stock market returns, you can see that all are positive. Further, relative to the pre-crisis period, stock market return correlations increased during the financial crisis. In the pre-crisis period, correlations across markets vary from a high of 0.778 between the United Kingdom and Germany to a low of 0.131

---

[8] This equation is often called the *Fisher equation* after the economist who first publicized this hypothesized relationship among nominal rates, real rates, and expected inflation. As shown, we ignore the small cross-product term between the real rate and the expected inflation rate.

**TABLE 13–6**
Correlation of Returns on Stock Markets before and during the Financial Crisis

Source: R. Horvath and P. Poldauf, "International Stock Market Comovements: What Happened During the Financial Crisis?" *Global Economy Journal*, March 2012.

| Panel A: Pre-crisis, December 19, 2000–September 12, 2008 | | | | |
|---|---|---|---|---|
| | United States | United Kingdom | Japan | Hong Kong |
| United States | 1.000 | 0.456 | 0.132 | 0.135 |
| United Kingdom | 0.456 | 1.000 | 0.294 | 0.302 |
| Japan | 0.131 | 0.294 | 1.000 | 0.506 |
| Hong Kong | 0.135 | 0.302 | 0.506 | 1.000 |
| Australia | 0.085 | 0.281 | 0.488 | 0.500 |
| Brazil | 0.553 | 0.354 | 0.132 | 0.174 |
| Canada | 0.663 | 0.460 | 0.176 | 0.220 |
| Germany | 0.538 | 0.778 | 0.283 | 0.285 |

| Panel B: Crisis, September 15, 2008–December 15, 2010 | | | | |
|---|---|---|---|---|
| | United States | United Kingdom | Japan | Hong Kong |
| United States | 1.000 | 0.631 | 0.138 | 0.216 |
| United Kingdom | 0.631 | 1.000 | 0.273 | 0.351 |
| Japan | 0.138 | 0.273 | 1.000 | 0.573 |
| Hong Kong | 0.216 | 0.351 | 0.573 | 1.000 |
| Australia | 0.160 | 0.340 | 0.640 | 0.611 |
| Brazil | 0.702 | 0.514 | 0.112 | 0.301 |
| Canada | 0.777 | 0.574 | 0.213 | 0.302 |
| Germany | 0.663 | 0.865 | 0.271 | 0.327 |

between the United States and Japan. In the crisis period, correlations across markets vary from a high of 0.865 between the United Kingdom and Germany to a low of 0.112 between Japan and Brazil.[9]

**Concept Questions**

1. The cost of one-year U.S. dollar CDs is 8 percent, one-year U.S. dollar loans yield 10 percent, and U.K. pound loans yield 15 percent. The dollar/pound spot exchange rate is $1.50/£1, and the one-year forward exchange rate is $1.48/£1. Are one-year U.S. dollar loans more or less attractive than U.K. pound loans?
2. What are two ways an FI manager can control FX exposure?

# INTERACTION OF INTEREST RATES, INFLATION, AND EXCHANGE RATES

As global financial markets have become increasingly interlinked, so have interest rates, inflation, and foreign exchange rates. For example, higher domestic interest rates may attract foreign financial investment and impact the value of the domestic currency. In this section, we look at the effect that inflation in one country has on its foreign currency exchange rates—purchasing power parity (PPP). We also examine the links between domestic and foreign interest rates and spot and forward foreign exchange rates—interest rate parity (IRP).

---

[9] From the Fisher relationship, high correlations may be due to high correlations of real interest rates over time and/or inflation expectations.

## Purchasing Power Parity

One factor affecting a country's foreign currency exchange rate with another country is the relative inflation rate in each country (which, as shown below, is directly related to the relative interest rates in these countries). Specifically:

$$r_{US} = i_{US} + rr_{US}$$

and

$$r_S = i_S + rr_S$$

where

$r_{US}$ = Interest rate in the United States
$r_S$ = Interest rate in Switzerland (or another foreign country)
$i_{US}$ = Inflation rate in the United States
$i_S$ = Inflation rate in Switzerland (or another foreign country)
$rr_{US}$ = Real rate of interest in the United States
$rr_S$ = Real rate of interest in Switzerland (or another foreign country)

Assuming real rates of interest (or rates of time preference) are equal across countries:

$$rr_{US} = rr_S$$

Then

$$r_{US} - r_S = i_{US} - i_S$$

The (nominal) interest rate spread between the United States and Switzerland reflects the difference in inflation rates between the two countries.

As relative inflation rates (and interest rates) change, foreign currency exchange rates that are not constrained by government regulation should also adjust to account for relative differences in the price levels (inflation rates) between the two countries. One theory that explains how this adjustment takes place is the theory of **purchasing power parity (PPP).** According to PPP, foreign currency exchange rates between two countries adjust to reflect changes in each country's price levels (or inflation rates and, implicitly, interest rates) as consumers and importers switch their demands for goods from relatively high inflation (interest) rate countries to low inflation (interest) rate countries. Specifically, the PPP theorem states that the change in the exchange rate between two countries' currencies is proportional to the difference in the inflation rates in the two countries. That is:

$$i_{Domestic} - i_{Foreign} = \Delta S_{Domestic/Foreign} / S_{Domestic/Foreign}$$

**purchasing power parity (PPP)**
The theory explaining the change in foreign currency exchange rates as inflation rates in the countries change.

where

$S_{Domestic/Foreign}$ = Spot exchange rate of the domestic currency for the foreign currency (e.g., U.S. dollars for Swiss francs)
$\Delta S_{Domestic/Foreign}$ = Change in the one-period spot foreign exchange rate

Thus, according to PPP, the most important factor determining exchange rates is the fact that in open economies, differences in prices (and, by implication, price level changes with inflation) drive trade flows and thus demand for and supplies of currencies.

**EXAMPLE 13–4**

*Application of Purchasing Power Parity*

Suppose that the current spot exchange rate of U.S. dollars for Russian rubles, $S_{US/R}$, is 0.17 (i.e., 0.17 dollar, or 17 cents, can be received for 1 ruble). The price of Russian-produced goods increases by 10 percent (i.e., inflation in Russia, $i_R$, is 10 percent), and the U.S. price index increases by 4 percent (i.e., inflation in the United States, $i_{US}$, is 4 percent). According to PPP, the 10 percent rise in the price of Russian goods relative to the 4 percent rise in the price of U.S. goods results in a depreciation of the Russian ruble (by 6 percent). Specifically, the exchange rate of Russian rubles to U.S. dollars should fall, so that:[10]

$$\frac{\text{U.S. inflation rate} - \text{Russian inflation rate}}{\text{Initial spot exchange rate of U.S. dollars for Russian rubles}} = \text{Change in spot exchange rate of U.S. dollars for Russian rubles}$$

or

$$i_{US} - i_R = \Delta S_{US/R} / S_{US/R}$$

Plugging in the inflation and exchange rates, we get:

$$0.04 - 0.10 = \Delta S_{US/R} / S_{US/R} = \Delta S_{US/R} / 0.17$$

or

$$-0.06 = \Delta S_{US/R} / 0.17$$

and

$$\Delta S_{US/R} = -0.06 \times 0.17 = -0.0102$$

Thus, it costs 1.02 cents less to receive a ruble (i.e., 1 ruble costs 15.98 cents: 17 cents − 1.02 cents), or 0.1598 of $1 can be received for 1 ruble. The Russian ruble depreciates in value by 6 percent against the U.S. dollar as a result of its higher inflation rate.[11]

## Interest Rate Parity Theorem

**interest rate parity theorem**
Relationship in which the discounted spread between domestic and foreign interest rates equals the percentage spread between forward and spot exchange rates.

We discussed above that foreign exchange spot market risk can be reduced by entering into forward foreign exchange contracts. In general, spot rates and forward rates for a given currency differ. For example, the spot exchange rate between the British pound and the U.S. dollar was 1.5591 on July 4, 2012, meaning that 1 pound could be exchanged on that day for 1.5591 U.S. dollars. The three-month forward rate between the two currencies, however, was 1.5590 on July 4, 2012. This forward exchange rate is determined by the spot exchange rate and the interest rate differential between the two countries. The specific relationship that links spot exchange rates, interest rates, and forward exchange rates is described as the **interest rate parity theorem** (IRPT). Intuitively, the IRPT implies that by hedging in the forward exchange rate market, an investor realizes the same returns whether investing domestically or in a foreign country. This is a so-called no-arbitrage relationship in the sense that the investor cannot make a risk-free

[10] This is the relative version of the PPP theorem. There are other versions of the theory (such as absolute PPP and the law of one price). However, the version shown here is the one most commonly used.

[11] A 6 percent fall in the ruble's value translates into a new exchange rate of 0.1598 dollar per ruble if the original exchange rate between dollars and rubles was 0.17.

return by taking offsetting positions in the domestic and foreign markets. That is, the hedged dollar return on foreign investments just equals the return on domestic investments. The eventual equality between the cost of domestic funds and the hedged return on foreign assets, or the IRPT, can be expressed as:

$$1 + r_{ust}^D = \frac{1}{S_t} \times [1 + r_{ukt}^L] \times F_t$$

Rate on U.S. investment = Hedged return on foreign (U.K.) investment

where

$$1 + r_{ust}^D = 1 \text{ plus the interest rate on U.S. CDs for the FI at time } t$$
$$S_t = \$/£ \text{ spot exchange rate at time } t$$
$$1 + r_{ukt}^L = 1 \text{ plus the interest rate on UK CDs at time } t$$
$$F_t = \$/£ \text{ forward exchange at time } t$$

---

**EXAMPLE 13–5**

*An Application of Interest Rate Parity Theorem*

Suppose $r_{ust}^D = 8$ percent and $r_{ukt}^L = 11$ percent, as in our preceding example. As the FI moves into more British CDs, suppose the spot exchange rate for buying pounds rises from \$1.60/£1 to \$1.63/£1. In equilibrium, the forward exchange rate would have to fall to \$1.5859/£1 to eliminate completely the attractiveness of British investments to the U.S. FI manager. That is:

$$(1.08) = \left(\frac{1}{1.63}\right)[1.11](1.5859)$$

This is a *no-arbitrage* relationship in the sense that the hedged dollar return on foreign investments just equals the FI's dollar cost of domestic CDs. Rearranging, the IRPT can be expressed as:

$$\frac{r_{ust}^D - r_{ukt}^L}{1 + r_{ukt}^L} \approx \frac{F_t - S_t}{S_t}$$
$$\frac{0.08 - 0.11}{1.11} \approx \frac{1.5859 - 1.63}{1.63}$$
$$-0.0270 \approx -0.0270$$

That is, the discounted spread between domestic and foreign interest rates is approximately equal to ($\approx$) the percentage spread between forward and spot exchange rates.

---

Suppose that in the preceding example, the annual rate on U.S. time deposits is 8.1 percent (rather than 8 percent). In this case, it would be profitable for the investor to put excess funds in the U.S. rather than the UK deposits. The arbitrage opportunity that exists results in a flow of funds out of UK time deposits into U.S. time deposits. According to the IRPT, this flow of funds would quickly drive up the U.S. dollar–British pound exchange rate until the potential profit opportunities from U.S. deposits are eliminated. The implication of IRPT is that in a competitive market for deposits, loans, and foreign exchange, the potential profit opportunities from overseas investment for the FI manager are likely to be small and fleeting. Long-term violations of IRPT are likely to occur only if there are major imperfections in international deposit, loan, and other financial markets, including barriers to cross-border financial flows.

## Summary

This chapter analyzed the sources of FX risk faced by FI managers. Such risks arise through mismatching foreign currency trading and/or foreign asset–liability positions in individual currencies. While such mismatches can be profitable if FX forecasts prove correct, unexpected outcomes and volatility can impose significant losses on an FI. They threaten its profitability and, ultimately, its solvency in a fashion similar to interest rate and liquidity risks. This chapter discussed possible ways to mitigate such risks, including direct hedging through matched foreign asset–liability books, hedging through forward contracts, and hedging through foreign asset and liability portfolio diversification.

## Questions and Problems

1. What are four FX risks faced by FIs?
2. What is the spot market for FX? What is the forward market for FX? What is the position of being net long in a currency?
3. Refer to Table 13–1.
   a. What was the spot exchange rate of Canadian dollars for U.S. dollars on July 4, 2012?
   b. What was the six-month forward exchange rate of Japanese yen for U.S. dollars on July 4, 2012?
   c. What was the three-month forward exchange rate of U.S. dollars for Swiss francs on July 4, 2012?
4. Refer to Table 13–1.
   a. On June 4, 2012, you purchased a British pound–denominated CD by converting $1 million to pounds at a rate of 0.6435 pound for U.S. dollars. It is now July 4, 2012. Has the U.S. dollar appreciated or depreciated in value relative to the pound?
   b. Using the information in part (a), what is your gain or loss on the investment in the CD? Assume no interest has been paid on the CD.
5. On July 4, 2012, you convert $500,000 U.S. dollars to Japanese yen in the spot foreign exchange market and purchase a one-month forward contract to convert yen into dollars. How much will you receive in U.S. dollars at the end of the month? Use the data in Table 13–1 for this problem.
6. X-IM Bank has ¥14 million in assets and ¥23 million in liabilities and has sold ¥8 million in foreign currency trading. What is the net exposure for X-IM? For what type of exchange rate movement does this exposure put the bank at risk?
7. What two factors directly affect the profitability of an FI's position in a foreign currency?

8. The following are the foreign currency positions of an FI, expressed in the foreign currency:

| Currency | Assets | Liabilities | FX Bought | FX Sold |
|---|---|---|---|---|
| Swiss francs (SF) | SF 134,394 | SF 53,758 | SF 10,752 | SF 16,127 |
| British pound (£) | £ 30,488 | £ 13,415 | £ 9,146 | £ 12,195 |
| Japanese yen (¥) | ¥ 7,075,472 | ¥ 2,830,189 | ¥ 1,132,075 | ¥ 8,301,887 |

The exchange rate of dollars per SF is 0.9301, dollars per British pounds is 1.6400, and dollars per yen is 0.010600. The following are the foreign currency positions converted to dollars.

| Currency | Assets | Liabilities | FX Bought | FX Sold |
|---|---|---|---|---|
| Swiss francs (SF) | $125,000 | $50,000 | $10,000 | $15,000 |
| British pound (£) | $50,000 | $22,001 | $14,999 | $20,000 |
| Japanese yen (¥) | $75,000 | $30,000 | $12,000 | $88,000 |

   a. What is the FI's net exposure in Swiss francs stated in SF and $s?

   b. What is the FI's net exposure in British pounds stated in £ and $s?

   c. What is the FI's net exposure in Japanese yen stated in ¥ and $s?

   d. What is the expected loss or gain if the SF exchange rate appreciates by 1 percent? State your answers in SFs and $s.

   e. What is the expected loss or gain if the £ exchange rate appreciates by 1 percent? State your answers in £s and $s.

   f. What is the expected loss or gain if the ¥ exchange rate appreciates by 2 percent? State your answers in ¥s and $s.

9. What are the four FX trading activities undertaken by FIs? How do FIs profit from these activities?

10. City Bank issued $200 million of one-year CDs in the United States at a rate of 6.50 percent. It invested part of this money, $100 million, in the purchase of a one-year bond issued by a U.S. firm at an annual rate of 7 percent. The remaining $100 million was invested in a one-year Brazilian government bond paying an annual interest rate of 8 percent. The exchange rate at the time of the transactions was Brazilian real 0.50/$.

   a. What will be the net return on this $200 million investment in bonds if the exchange rate between the Brazilian real and the U.S. dollar remains the same?

   b. What will be the net return on this $200 million investment if the exchange rate changes to real 0.4167/$?

   c. What will the net return on this $200 million investment be if the exchange rate changes to real 0.625/$1?

11. Sun Bank USA has purchased a 16 million one-year euro loan that pays 12 percent interest annually. The spot rate of U.S. dollars per euro is 1.25. Sun Bank has funded this loan by accepting a British pound–denominated deposit for the equivalent amount and maturity at an annual rate of 10 percent. The current spot rate of U.S. dollars per British pound is 1.60.

   a. What is the net interest income earned in dollars on this one-year transaction if the spot rates of U.S. dollars per euro and U.S. dollars per British pound at the end of the year are 1.35 and 1.70?

b. What should be the spot rate of U.S. dollars per British pound at the end of the year in order for the bank to earn a net interest margin of 4 percent?

c. Does your answer to part (b) imply that the dollar should appreciate or depreciate against the pound?

d. What is the total effect on net interest income and principal of this transaction given the end-of-year spot rates in part (a)?

12. Bank USA just made a one-year $10 million loan that pays 10 percent interest annually. The loan was funded with a Swiss franc–denominated one-year deposit at an annual rate of 6 percent. The current spot rate is SF 1.05/$1.

a. What will be the net interest income in dollars on the one-year loan if the spot rate at the end of the year is SF 1.03/$1?

b. What will be the net interest return on assets?

c. What is the total effect on net interest income and principal of this transaction given the end-of-year spot rates in part (a)?

d. How far can the SF/$ appreciate before the transaction will result in a loss for Bank USA?

13. What motivates FIs to hedge foreign currency exposures? What are the limitations to hedging foreign currency exposures?

14. What are the two primary methods of hedging FX risk for an FI? What two conditions are necessary to achieve a perfect hedge through on-balance-sheet hedging? What are the advantages and disadvantages of off-balance-sheet hedging in comparison to on-balance-sheet hedging?

15. Suppose that a U.S. FI has the following assets and liabilities:

| Assets | Liabilities |
|---|---|
| $100 million U.S. loans (one year) in dollars | $200 million U.S. CDs (one year) in dollars |
| $100 million equivalent U.K. loans (one year) (loans made in pounds) | |

The promised one-year U.S. CD rate is 5 percent, to be paid in dollars at the end of the year; the one-year, default risk–free loans in the United States are yielding 6 percent; and default risk–free one-year loans are yielding 12 percent in the United Kingdom. The exchange rate of dollars for pounds at the beginning of the year is $1.6/£1.

a. Calculate the dollar proceeds from the UK investment at the end of the year, the return on the FI's investment portfolio, and the net interest margin for the FI if the spot foreign exchange rate has not changed over the year.

b. Calculate the dollar proceeds from the UK investment at the end of the year, the return on the FI's investment portfolio, and the net interest margin for the FI if the spot foreign exchange rate falls to $1.45/£1 over the year.

c. Calculate the dollar proceeds from the UK investment at the end of the year, the return on the FI's investment portfolio, and the net interest margin for the FI if the spot foreign exchange rate rises to $1.70/£1 over the year.

16. Suppose that instead of funding the $100 million investment in 12 percent British loans with U.S. CDs, the FI manager in problem 15 funds the British

loans with $100 million equivalent one-year pound CDs at a rate of 8 percent. Now the balance sheet of the FI would be as follows:

| Assets | Liabilities |
|---|---|
| $100 million<br>U.S. loans (6%) | $100 million<br>U.S. CDs (5%) |
| $100 million<br>U.K. loans (12%)<br>(loans made in pounds) | $100 million<br>U.K. CDs (8%)<br>(deposits raised in pounds) |

a. Calculate the return on the FI's investment portfolio, the average cost of funds, and the net interest margin for the FI if the spot foreign exchange rate falls to $1.45/£1 over the year.

b. Calculate the return on the FI's investment portfolio, the average cost of funds, and the net interest margin for the FI if the spot foreign exchange rate rises to $1.70/£1 over the year.

17. Suppose that instead of funding the $100 million investment in 12 percent British loans with CDs issued in the United Kingdom, the FI manager in problem 16 hedges the foreign exchange risk on the British loans by immediately selling its expected one-year pound loan proceeds in the forward FX market. The current forward one-year exchange rate between dollars and pounds is $1.50/£1, or at a 5 cent discount to the spot pound.

a. Calculate the return on the FI's investment portfolio (including the hedge) and the net interest margin for the FI over the year.

b. Will the net return be affected by changes in the dollar for pound spot foreign exchange rate at the end of the year?

18. Suppose that a U.S. FI has the following assets and liabilities:

| Assets | Liabilities |
|---|---|
| $300 million<br>U.S. loans (one year)<br>in dollars | $500 million<br>U.S. CDs (one year)<br>in dollars |
| $200 million equivalent<br>German loans (one year)<br>(loans made in euros) | |

The promised one-year U.S. CD rate is 4 percent, to be paid in dollars at the end of the year; the one-year, default risk–free loans in the United States are yielding 6 percent; and default risk–free one-year loans are yielding 10 percent in Germany. The exchange rate of dollars to euros at the beginning of the year is $1.25/€1.

a. Calculate the dollar proceeds from the German loan at the end of the year, the return on the FI's investment portfolio, and the net interest margin for the FI if the spot foreign exchange rate has not changed over the year.

b. Calculate the dollar proceeds from the German loan at the end of the year, the return on the FI's investment portfolio, and the net interest margin for the FI if the spot foreign exchange rate falls to $1.15/€1 over the year.

c. Calculate the dollar proceeds from the German loan at the end of the year, the return on the FI's investment portfolio, and the net interest margin for the FI if the spot foreign exchange rate rises to $1.35/€1 over the year.

19. Suppose that instead of funding the $200 million investment in 10 percent German loans with U.S. CDs, the FI manager in problem 18 funds the German loans with $200 million equivalent one-year euro CDs at a rate of 7 percent. Now the balance sheet of the FI would be as follows:

| Assets | Liabilities |
|---|---|
| $300 million | $300 million |
| U.S. loans (6%) | U.S. CDs (4%) |
| | |
| $200 million | $200 million |
| German loans (10%) | German CDs (7%) |
| (loans made in euros) | (deposits raised in euros) |

   a. Calculate the return on the FI's investment portfolio, the average cost of funds, and the net interest margin for the FI if the spot foreign exchange rate falls to $1.15/€1 over the year.

   b. Calculate the return on the FI's investment portfolio, the average cost of funds, and the net interest margin for the FI if the spot foreign exchange rate rises to $1.35/€1 over the year.

20. Suppose that instead of funding the $200 million investment in 10 percent German loans with CDs issued in Germany, the FI manager in problem 19 hedges the foreign exchange risk on the German loans by immediately selling its expected one-year euro loan proceeds in the forward FX market. The current forward one-year exchange rate between dollars and euros is $1.20/€1.

   a. Calculate the return on the FI's investment portfolio (including the hedge) and the net interest margin for the FI over the year.

   b. Will the net return be affected by changes in the dollar for euro spot foreign exchange rate at the end of the year?

21. North Bank has been borrowing in the U.S. markets and lending abroad, thus incurring foreign exchange risk. In a recent transaction, it issued a one-year, $2 million CD at 6 percent and funded a loan in euros at 8 percent. The spot rate for the euro was €1.45/$1 at the time of the transaction.

   a. Information received immediately after the transaction closing indicated that the euro will change to €1.47/$1 by year-end. If the information is correct, what will be the realized spread on the loan inclusive of principal? What should have been the bank interest rate on the loan to maintain the 2 percent spread?

   b. The bank had an opportunity to sell one-year forward euros at €1.46/$1. What would have been the spread on the loan if the bank had hedged forward its foreign exchange exposure?

   c. What would have been an appropriate change in loan rates to maintain the 2 percent spread if the bank intended to hedge its exposure using forward contracts?

22. A bank purchases a six-month, $1 million Eurodollar deposit at an annual interest rate of 6.5 percent. It invests the funds in a six-month Swedish krone AA-rated bond paying 7.5 percent per year. The current spot rate is $0.18/SK1.

   a. The six-month forward rate on the Swedish krone is being quoted at $0.1810/SK1. What is the net spread earned on this investment if the bank covers its foreign exchange exposure using the forward market?

b. What forward rate will cause the spread to be only 1 percent per year?

c. Explain how forward and spot rates will both change in response to the increased spread.

d. Why will a bank still be able to earn a spread of 1 percent knowing that interest rate parity usually eliminates arbitrage opportunities created by differential rates?

23. How does the lack of perfect correlation of economic returns between international financial markets affect the risk-return opportunities for FIs holding multicurrency assets and liabilities? Refer to Table 13–6. Which country pairings seem to have the highest correlation of stock returns before and during the financial crisis?

24. What is the purchasing power parity theorem?

25. Suppose that the current spot exchange rate of U.S. dollars for Australian dollars, $S_{US\$/A\$}$, is 1.0277 (i.e., $1.0277 can be received for 1 Australian dollar). The price of Australian-produced goods increases by 5 percent (i.e., inflation in Australia, $i_A$, is 5 percent), and the U.S. price index increases by 3 percent (i.e., inflation in the United States, $i_{US}$, is 3 percent). Calculate the new spot exchange rate of U.S. dollars for Australian dollars that should result from the differences in inflation rates.

26. Explain the concept of interest rate parity. What does this concept imply about the long-run profit opportunities from investing in international markets? What market conditions must prevail for the concept to be valid?

27. Assume that annual interest rates are 8 percent in the United States and 4 percent in Japan. An FI can borrow (by issuing CDs) or lend (by purchasing CDs) at these rates. The spot rate is $0.0125/¥.

a. If the forward rate is $0.0135/¥, how could the FI arbitrage using a sum of $1 million? What is the expected spread?

b. What forward rate will prevent an arbitrage opportunity?

28. What is the relationship between the real interest rate, the expected inflation rate, and the nominal interest rate on fixed-income securities in any particular country? What factors may be the reasons for the relatively high correlation coefficients?

29. What is economic integration? What impact does the extent of economic integration of international markets have on the investment opportunities for FIs?

30. An FI has $100,000 of net positions outstanding in British pounds (£) and −$30,000 in Swiss francs (SF). The standard deviation of the net positions as a result of exchange rate changes is 1 percent for the SF and 1.3 percent for the £. The correlation coefficient between the changes in exchange rates of the £ and the SF is 0.80.

a. What is the risk exposure to the FI of fluctuations in the £/$ rate?

b. What is the risk exposure to the FI of fluctuations in the SF/$ rate?

c. What is the risk exposure if both the £ and the SF positions are combined?

31. A money market mutual fund manager is looking for some profitable investment opportunities and observes the following one-year interest rates on government securities and exchange rates: $r_{US} = 12\%$, $r_{UK} = 9\%$, $S = \$1.50/£1$, $F = \$1.60/£1$, where $S$ is the spot exchange rate and F is the forward exchange rate. Which of the two types of government securities would constitute a better investment?

## Web Questions

32. Go to the website of the U.S. Treasury at **www.treas.gov** and update Table 13–3 using the following steps. Under "Bureaus," click on "Financial Management Service." Under "Reports," click on "Treasury Bulletin." Click on "Foreign Currency Positions." This will bring the file onto your computer that contains the relevant data. Which countries have positive versus negative net exposures in foreign currencies?

33. Go to the FDIC website at **www.fdic.gov** and find the most recent values for foreign exchange trading revenue at J.P. Morgan Chase and Citigroup using the following steps. Click on "Analysts." Click on "Statistics on Depository Institutions (SDI)." Click on "ID Home." Click on "Bank Holding Cos." At "BHC Name:," enter "Citigroup" then click on "find." Under "BHC ID," click on "1951350." Under "ID Report Selections:" select "Income and Expenses," then click on "Generate Report." Click on "Trading account gains & fees." This will bring the file onto your computer that contains revenue from foreign exchange exposures. Repeat this process for J.P. Morgan Chase and BHC ID 1039502.

# Integrated Mini Case

# Foreign Exchange Risk Exposure

Suppose that a U.S. FI has the following assets and liabilities:

| Assets | Liabilities |
|---|---|
| $500 million<br>U.S. loans (one year)<br>in dollars | $1,000 million<br>U.S. CDs (one year)<br>in dollars |
| $300 million equivalent<br>U.K. loans (one year)<br>(loans made in pounds) | |
| $200 million equivalent<br>Turkish loans (one year)<br>(loans made in Turkish lira) | |

The promised one-year U.S. CD rate is 4 percent, to be paid in dollars at the end of the year; the one-year, default risk–free loans in the United States are yielding 6 percent; default risk–free one-year loans are yielding 8 percent in the United Kingdom; and default risk–free one-year loans are yielding 10 percent in Turkey. The exchange rate of dollars for pounds at the beginning of the year is $1.6/£1, and the exchange rate of dollars for Turkish lira at the beginning of the year is $0.5533/TRY1.

1. Calculate the dollar proceeds from the FI's loan portfolio at the end of the year, the return on the FI's loan portfolio, and the net interest margin for the FI if the spot foreign exchange rate has not changed over the year.

2. Calculate the dollar proceeds from the FI's loan portfolio at the end of the year, the return on the FI's loan portfolio, and the net interest margin for the FI if the pound spot foreign exchange rate falls to $1.45/£1 and the lira spot foreign exchange rate falls to $0.52/TRY1 over the year.

3. Calculate the dollar proceeds from the FI's loan portfolio at the end of the year, the return on the FI's loan portfolio, and the net interest margin for the FI if the pound spot foreign exchange rate rises to $1.70/£1 and the lira spot foreign exchange rate rises to $0.58/TRY1 over the year.

4. Suppose that instead of funding the $300 million investment in 8 percent British loans with U.S. CDs, the FI manager funds the British loans with $300 million equivalent one-year pound CDs at a rate of 5 percent and that instead of funding the $200 million investment in 10 percent Turkish loans with U.S. CDs, the FI manager funds the Turkish loans with $200 million

equivalent one-year Turkish lira CDs at a rate of 6 percent. What will the FI's balance sheet look like after these changes have been made?

5. Using the information in part 4, calculate the return on the FI's loan portfolio, the average cost of funds, and the net interest margin for the FI if the pound spot foreign exchange rate falls to $1.45/£1 and the lira spot foreign exchange rate falls to $0.52/TRY1 over the year.

6. Using the information in part 4, calculate the return on the FI's loan portfolio, the average cost of funds, and the net interest margin for the FI if the pound spot foreign exchange rate rises to $1.70/£1 and the lira spot foreign exchange rate falls to $0.58/TRY1 over the year.

7. Suppose that instead of funding the $300 million investment in 8 percent British loans with CDs issued in the United Kingdom, the FI manager hedges the foreign exchange risk on the British loans by immediately selling its expected one-year pound loan proceeds in the forward FX market. The current forward one-year exchange rate between dollars and pounds is $1.53/£1. Additionally, instead of funding the $200 million investment in 10 percent Turkish loans with CDs issued in the Turkey, the FI manager hedges the foreign exchange risk on the Turkish loans by immediately selling its expected one-year lira loan proceeds in the forward FX market. The current forward one-year exchange rate between dollars and Turkish lira is $0.5486/TRY1. Calculate the return on the FI's investment portfolio (including the hedge) and the net interest margin for the FI over the year.

# Chapter **Fourteen**

See Appendices Online at www.mhhe.com/saunders8e
• Appendix 14A: Mechanisms for Dealing with Sovereign Risk Exposure

# Sovereign Risk

## INTRODUCTION

www.worldbank.org

www.imf.org

In the 1970s, commercial banks in the United States and other countries rapidly expanded their loans to Eastern European, Latin American, and other emerging markets and less developed countries (LDCs). This was largely to meet these countries' demand for funds beyond those provided by the World Bank and the International Monetary Fund (IMF) to aid their development, and to allow commercial banks to recycle petrodollar funds from huge dollar holders such as Saudi Arabia. In many cases, these loans appear to have been made with little judgment regarding the credit quality of the sovereign country in which the borrower resided or whether that body was a government-sponsored organization (such as Pemex) or a private corporation.

**debt moratoria**
Delay in repaying interest and/or principal on debt.

**loan loss reserves**
Special reserves created on the balance sheet against which to write off bad loans.

Due to rapidly deteriorating macroeconomic conditions, in the fall of 1982 Mexican and Brazilian governments announced **debt moratoria** (a delay in repaying interest and/or principal on debt) that had a major and long-lasting impact on commercial banks' balance sheets and profits. Indeed, at the time of the 1982 moratoria, the 10 largest U.S. money center banks had overall sovereign risk exposure of $56 billion, 80 percent of which was to Latin America. As a result, large banks such as Citicorp (now Citigroup) had to make provisions to their **loan loss reserves** because they had to write down the value of these loans in their portfolios. For example, in 1987, more than 20 U.S. banks announced major additions to their loan loss reserves, with Citicorp alone setting aside $3 billion.

Notwithstanding their experience with LDC lending, U.S. and other FIs began once again to invest considerable amounts in emerging market countries in the late 1980s to early 1990s. However, emerging markets in Asia faltered in 1997 when an economic and financial crisis in Thailand, a relatively small country in terms of financial markets, produced worldwide reactions. In early July, the devaluation of the Thai baht resulted in contagious devaluations of currencies throughout Southeast Asia (including those of Indonesia, Singapore, Malaysia, and South Korea) and the devaluations eventually spread to South America and Russia.

Possibly as a reaction to the events (losses) experienced with the Latin American countries in the 1980s or to improved sovereign risk assessment techniques (see later discussion), U.S. FIs held their exposure in Asia (in the mid- and late 1990s) to approximately one-third of the investment made by Japanese and European banks. However, they still experienced losses from these sovereign risks. For example, in November 1997, Chase Manhattan Corp. announced losses from emerging market securities holdings in the $150 million to $200 million range. This was followed by a similar announcement of poor earnings by J.P. Morgan. Then in 1999, U.S. banks such as Bank of America, Republic New York Corp. (now a part of HSBC Holdings), and Chase Manhattan (now J.P. Morgan Chase) wrote off hundreds of millions of dollars in losses as they accepted a payoff of less than five cents on the dollar for Russian securities.

More recently, in the early 2000s, concerns were raised about the ability of Argentina and Turkey to meet their debt obligations and the effects this would have on other emerging market countries. For example, in December 2001, Argentina defaulted on $130 billion in government-issued debt, and in 2002, passed legislation that led to defaults on $30 billion of corporate debt owed to foreign creditors. The situation continued to deteriorate, and in November 2002 Argentina's government paid only $79.5 million of an $805 million repayment (that had become more than 30 days delinquent) due to the World Bank.

Finally, in the late 2000s economies plummeted worldwide as a result of the global financial crisis. The annualized gross domestic product in the first quarter of 2009 fell by 21.5 percent in Mexico, 15.2 percent in Japan, and 14.4 percent in Germany. The United Kingdom's economy saw its worst drop in GDP in 30 years, 7.6 percent. The value of German exports fell by 20.7 percent, and Spain's jobless rate soared to 17.3 percent. Globally, manufacturing output fell by 2.9 percent and world trade by nearly 10 percent from 2008 to 2009. GDP in developing countries fell sharply from 5.9 percent in 2008 to 1.2 percent in 2009. The World Bank projected that developing countries were likely to face a dramatic decrease in private capital flows, and many of these countries would find it difficult to meet their external financing needs, estimated to be $2 trillion. International organizations, such as the World Bank and IMF, and national governments worldwide took steps to avoid debt moritia seen in the 1980s, 1990s, and early 2000s. Table 14–1 lists some of the actions taken by governments in developed countries to shore up their countries' banking systems. Further, the IMF pledged to inject $250 billion into the global economy to bolster countries' reserves, $100 billion of which would be allocated to emerging market and developing countries. Additionally, the World Bank committed $58.8 billion in fiscal year 2009 to help countries struggling amid the global economic crisis. Despite these efforts, in November 2009, Dubai World, the finance arm of Dubai, asked creditors for a six month delay on interest payments due on $60 billion of the country's debt. In the mid- and late 2000s, Dubai became a center of investment and development, much of it funded by burgeoning oil wealth from neighboring countries. But during the financial crisis, the Middle East nation was hard hit by a falling real estate market.

While much of the world slowly recovered from the financial crisis, throughout 2009–12 Greece struggled with a severe debt crisis. Early on, some of the healthier European countries tried to step in and assist the debt ridden country. Specifically, in March 2010 a plan led by Germany and France to bail out Greece with as much as $41 billion in aid began to take shape. However, in late April Greek bond prices dropped dramatically as traders began betting a debt default was inevitable, even if the country received a massive bailout. The selloff was the result of still more bad news for Greece, which showed that the 2009 budget deficit was worse than had been previously reported, and as a result politicians in Germany began to voice opposition to a Greek bailout. Further, Moody's Investors Service downgraded Greece's debt rating and warned that additional cuts could be on the way. The

**TABLE 14–1**
Elements of
Banking System
Rescue Plans
in Developed
Economies

Source: *BIS Quarterly Review,*
Bank for International Settle-
ments, Basle, Switzerland,
December 2008.

| Country | Expansion of Retail Deposit Insurance | Guarantee of Wholesale Liabilities* | | Capital Injections† | Asset Purchases |
| | | New Debt | Existing Debt | | |
|---|:---:|:---:|:---:|:---:|:---:|
| Australia | ✓ | ✓ | ✓ | | ✓ |
| Austria | ✓ | ✓ | | ✓ | |
| Belgium | ✓ | ✓ | | | |
| Canada | | ✓ | | | ✓ |
| Denmark | ✓ | ✓ | ✓ | | |
| Finland | ✓ | | | | |
| France | | ✓ | | ✓ | |
| Germany | ✓ | ✓ | | ✓ | ✓ |
| Greece | ✓ | ✓ | | ✓ | |
| Ireland | ✓ | ✓ | ✓ | | |
| Italy | | ✓ | | ✓ | |
| Netherlands | ✓ | ✓ | | ✓ | |
| New Zealand | ✓ | | | | |
| Norway | | | | | ✓ |
| Portugal | ✓ | ✓ | | | |
| Spain | ✓ | ✓ | | ✓ | ✓ |
| Sweden | ✓ | ✓ | | ✓ | |
| Switzerland | | | | ✓ | ✓ |
| United Kingdom | ✓ | ✓ | | ✓ | |
| United States | ✓ | ✓ | | ✓ | ✓ |

\* Includes bond issuance, interbank lending, and other wholesale liabilities. Coverage of the guarantee on these items varies across countries.
† Refers to announced programs only (excluding standalone actions).

problems in the Greek bond market then spread to other European nations with fiscal problems, such as Portugal, Spain, and Italy. As a result, in May euro-zone countries and the International Monetary Fund, seeking to halt a widening European debt crisis that had now threatened the stability of the euro, agreed to extend Greece an unprecedented $147 billion rescue in return for huge budget cuts.

Additional rescue packages and promises of further austerity measures intended to cut the burgeoning Greek deficit occurred through 2012. Yet the European debt crisis continued. While Greece had not yet missed a bond payment, in March the International Swaps and Derivatives Association (ISDA)[1] declared that Greece had undergone a "restructuring credit event," which triggered insurance policy payments. The restructuring event was a forced swap of old debt held by some of its private bondholders for new debt. The swap forced a 74 percent haircut on those creditors that held out, triggering the effective default. At one point, Greece seemed unable to form a government, and the leader of one party rejected the country's bailout commitments. It seemed increasingly conceivable that Greece might have to leave the eurozone. Yet, the leaders of EU countries, particularly Germany and France, continued to work to keep Greek reform on

[1] The ISDA is the trade group that oversees the market for credit default swaps. Credit default swaps are essentially insurance policies against bond defaults (see Chapter 24).

**TABLE 14–2**  Foreign Exposures to Greece, Ireland, Portugal, and Spain, End of Third Quarter, 2010 (in billions of $s)

Source: *BIS Quarterly Review,* March 2011, Bank of International Settlements. *www.bis.org*

| Exposure to | Germany | Spain | France | Italy | Other Euro Area | United Kingdom | United States | Rest of World | Total |
|---|---|---|---|---|---|---|---|---|---|
| Greece | $ 69.4 | $ 1.5 | $ 92.0 | $ 6.5 | $ 33.5 | $ 20.4 | $ 43.1 | $ 11.5 | $ 277.9 |
| Ireland | 208.3 | 17.5 | 78.1 | 24.4 | 67.2 | 224.6 | 113.9 | 79.8 | 813.8 |
| Portugal | 48.5 | 108.6 | 45.5 | 7.9 | 21.9 | 33.7 | 47.1 | 8.6 | 321.8 |
| Spain | 242.3 | – | 224.7 | 41.8 | 179.6 | 152.4 | 187.5 | 70.5 | 1,098.8 |
| Total | $568.5 | $127.6 | $440.3 | $80.6 | $302.2 | $431.1 | $391.6 | $170.4 | $2,512.3 |

track and the EU together. Through June 2012, the cost of bailouts required to do so totaled more than $480 billion and, while calmer, the crisis in the EU was not over as Spain and Italy required bailouts as well. Fear arose that keeping the European Union together and the euro intact might actually draw sound countries into a crisis as they bailed out unhealthy countries to prevent them from defaulting on their sovereign debt and from leaving the currency union.

The risks posed to U.S. banks and the banking system from a Greek debt default and a contagion crisis in other eurozone countries were huge. In late 2010, the United States had sovereign risk exposure to Greece totaling $43.1 billion. In addition, exposures to Ireland totaled $113.9 billion, to Portugal totaled $47.1 billion, and to Spain $187.5 billion. Worldwide, bank exposure to these four countries totaled $2,512.3 billion. Table 14–2 shows the foreign exposure to these four countries by bank nationality. As the European debt crisis progressed, banks reduced their Greek exposure significantly. For example, in early 2012, U.S. banks had virtually no exposure to Greek debt, approximately $5.8 billion. However, U.S. banks had more than $50 billion worth of debt exposure to both Spain and Ireland, $6.6 billion to Portugal, and more than $66 billion to Italy—all countries in risk of debt default in the event of a continued economic slowdown.

U.S. banks would also feel the impact of the Greek debt crisis as it impacted the overall U.S. economy. Nearly 13 percent of all U.S. exports, more than $49 billion, were to the 17 countries in the eurozone. A Greek debt default, and the events that would follow, would mean a reduction in the size of these exports (at a time when the U.S. economy was growing, but slowly). Further, a freeze of financial markets resulting from a Greek default on its debt could lead to a worldwide credit freeze and, in turn, a drop in worldwide equity prices, similar to that after the Lehman Brothers bankruptcy in September 2008. Thus, banks, in their role as lenders to businesses and as investors in securities issued by eurozone countries and worldwide, would feel the effects of changes in economic conditions due to the Greek debt crisis from multiple fronts.

These recurring experiences confirm the importance of assessing the country or sovereign risk of a borrowing country before making lending or other investment decisions such as buying foreign bonds or equities. In this chapter, we first define sovereign or country risk. We next look at measures of sovereign risk that FI managers can use as screening devices before making loans or other investment decisions. Appendix 14A, on the text's website, looks at ways FIs have managed sovereign risk problems, including entering into **multiyear restructuring agreements (MYRAs),** debt–equity swaps, loan sales, and bond-for-loan swaps.

**multiyear restructuring agreements (MYRAs)**
The official terminology for a sovereign loan rescheduling.

# CREDIT RISK VERSUS SOVEREIGN RISK

**rescheduling**
Changing the contractual terms of a loan, such as its maturity and interest payments.

To understand the difference between the sovereign risk and the credit risk on a loan or a bond, consider what happens to a domestic firm that refuses to repay, or is unable to repay, its loans. The lender would probably seek to work out the loan with the borrower by **rescheduling** its promised interest and principal payments on the loan into the future. Ultimately, continued inability or unwillingness to pay would likely result in bankruptcy proceedings and eventual liquidation of the firm's assets. Consider next a dollar loan made by a U.S. FI to a private Greek corporation. Suppose that this first-class corporation always maintained its debt repayments in the past. However, the Greek economy and the Greek government's dollar reserve position are now in bad shape. As a result, the Greek government refuses to allow any further debt repayment to be made in dollars to outside creditors. This puts the Greek borrower automatically into default even though, when viewed on its own, the company is a good credit risk. The Greek government's decision is a *sovereign* or *country risk event* in large part independent of the credit standing of the individual loan to the borrower. Further, unlike the situation in the United States, where the lender might seek a legal remedy in the local bankruptcy courts, there is no international bankruptcy court to which the lender can take the Greek government. That is, the lenders' legal remedies to offset a sovereign country's default or moratoria decisions are very limited. For example, lenders can and have sought legal remedies in U.S. courts, but such decisions pertain only to Greek government or Greek corporate assets held in the United States itself.

This situation suggests that making a lending decision to a party residing in a foreign country is a *two-step* decision. First, lenders must assess the underlying *credit quality* of the borrower, as they would do for a normal domestic loan, including setting an appropriate credit risk premium or credit limits (see Chapter 10). Second, lenders must assess the *sovereign risk quality* of the country in which the borrower resides. Should the credit risk or quality of the borrower be assessed as good but the sovereign risk be assessed as bad, the lender should not make the loan. When making international lending or foreign bond investment decisions, an FI manager should consider sovereign risk above considerations of private credit risk.

| **Concept Questions** | 1. What is the difference between credit risk and sovereign risk? |
|---|---|
| | 2. In deciding to lend to a party residing in a foreign country, what two considerations must an FI weigh? |

# DEBT REPUDIATION VERSUS DEBT RESCHEDULING

**repudiation**
Outright cancelation of all current and future debt obligations by a borrower.

A good deal of misunderstanding exists regarding the nature of a sovereign risk event. In general, a sovereign country's (negative) decisions on its debt obligations or the obligations of its public and private organizations may take two forms: repudiation and rescheduling.

• *Debt repudiation.* **Repudiation** is an outright cancelation of all a borrower's current and future foreign debt and equity obligations. Since World War II, only China (1949), Cuba (1961), and North Korea (1964) have followed this course.

www.worldbank.org

www.imf.org

The low level of repudiations partly reflects recent international policy toward the poorest countries in the world. Specifically, in the fall of 1996, the World Bank, the International Monetary Fund, and major governments around the world agreed to forgive the external debt of the world's poorest, most heavily indebted poor countries (HIPCs). The HIPC initiative broke new ground by removing debt obligations from countries that pursue economic and social reform targeted at measurable poverty reduction. By 2012, 36 countries had received irrevocable debt relief under the HIPC initiative, 30 of them in Africa. Together, these countries had their outstanding debt reduced by $76 billion. Repudiations on debt obligations were far more common before World War II, as we discuss later in this chapter.

- *Debt rescheduling.* Rescheduling has been the most common form of sovereign risk event. Specifically, a country (or a group of creditors in that country) declares a moratorium or delay on its current and future debt obligations and then seeks to ease credit terms through a rescheduling of the contractual terms, such as debt maturity and/or interest rates. Such delays may relate to the principal and/or the interest on the debt (South Korea in January 1998, Argentina in 2001, and Greece in 2011–12 are recent examples of debt reschedulings).

One of the interesting questions in the provision of international financial services is why we have generally witnessed international debtor problems (of other than the poorest highly indebted countries) being met by reschedulings in the post–World War II period, whereas a large proportion of debt problems were met with repudiations before World War II. A fundamental reason given for this difference in behavior is that until recently, most postwar international debt has been in *bank loans,* while before the war it was mostly in the form of *foreign bonds.*

International loan rather than bond financing makes rescheduling more likely for reasons related to the inherent nature of international loan versus bond contracts. First, there are generally fewer FIs in any international lending syndicate compared with thousands of geographically dispersed bondholders. The relatively small number of lending parties makes renegotiation or rescheduling easier and less costly than when a borrower or a bond trustee has to get thousands of bondholders to agree to changes in the contractual terms on a bond.

Second, many international loan syndicates comprise the same groups of FIs, which adds to FI cohesiveness in loan renegotiations and increases the probability of consensus being reached. For example, Citigroup was chosen the lead bank negotiator by other banks in five major loan reschedulings in the 1980s, as well as in both the Mexican and South Korean reschedulings, while J.P. Morgan Chase was the lead bank involved in the loan reschedulings of Argentina.

Third, many international loan contracts contain cross-default provisions that state that if a country were to default on just one of its loans, all the other loans it has outstanding would automatically be put into default as well. Cross-default clauses prevent a country from selecting a group of weak lenders for special default treatment and make the outcome of any individual loan default decision potentially very costly for the borrower.

A further set of reasons rescheduling is likely to occur on loans relates to the behavior of governments and regulators in lending countries. One of the overwhelming public policy goals in recent years has been to prevent large FI failures in countries such as the United States, Japan, Germany, and the United Kingdom. Thus, government-organized rescue packages for LDCs arranged either directly or indirectly via World Bank/IMF guarantees are ways of subsidizing large FIs and/or reducing the incentives for LDCs to default on their loans. To the extent that banks are viewed as special (see Chapter 1), domestic governments may seek political and economic avenues to reduce the probability of foreign sovereign borrowers defaulting on or repudiating their debt contracts. Governments and regulators appear to view the social costs of default on international bonds as less worrisome than those on loans. The reason is that bond defaults are likely to be more geographically and numerically dispersed in their effects, and bondholders do not play a key role in the provision of liquidity services to the domestic and world economy. It should also be noted that the tendency of the IMF/governments to bail out countries and thus, indirectly, FI lenders such as the major U.S., Japanese, and European FIs has not gone without criticism. Specifically, it has been argued that unless FIs and countries are ultimately punished, they will have no incentives to avoid similar risks in the future. This is one reason sovereign debt crises keep recurring.

---

| **Concept Questions** | 1. What is the difference between debt repudiation and debt rescheduling? |
| | 2. Provide four reasons we see sovereign loans being rescheduled rather than repudiated. |

---

# COUNTRY RISK EVALUATION

In evaluating sovereign risk, an FI can use alternative methods, varying from the highly quantitative to the very qualitative. Moreover, as in domestic credit analysis, an FI may rely on outside evaluation services or develop its own internal evaluation or sovereign risk models. Of course, to make a final assessment, an FI may use many models and sources together because different measures of country risk are not mutually exclusive.

We begin by looking at three country risk assessment services available to outside investors and FIs: the *Euromoney Country Risk Index*, the *Economist Intelligence Unit*, and the *Institutional Investor Index*. We then look at ways an FI manager might make internal risk assessments regarding sovereign risk.

## Outside Evaluation Models

### The Euromoney Country Risk Index

The Euromoney Country Risk (ECR) index rates sovereign risk of more than 180 countries based on the opinions of a global network of economists and policy analysts. The index is based on a large number of economic and political factors, including a country's economic characteristics, political characteristics, structural characteristics, access to capital and credit ratings, and debt indicators. ECR scores are scaled from 0 to 100 (0 = maximum risk, 100 = no risk) and are put into one of five tiers that are updated quarterly. ECR tier 1 countries have a score between 80 and 100, which can be equated to a credit rating of AA and above; tier 2 countries have a score between 65 and 79.9, which can be equated with a credit rating of A− to AA; tier 3 countries have a score between 50 and 64.9, translated to a credit rating of BB+ to A−; tier 4 countries have a score between 36 and 49.9, equivalent to a credit rating of B− to BB+; and tier 5 countries have a score between 0 and 35.9,

**TABLE 14–3**
**Euromoney Country Risk Ratings, April 2012**

Source: Euromoney Country Risk, *Euromoney*, April 2012. *www.euromoneycountryrisk.com*

| Country | Tier | Score |
|---|---|---|
| Norway | 1 | 90.69 |
| Switzerland | 1 | 89.12 |
| Sweden | 1 | 85.12 |
| Canada | 1 | 84.57 |
| Australia | 1 | 82.25 |
| United States | 2 | 75.66 |
| United Kingdom | 2 | 75.64 |
| France | 2 | 75.05 |
| Italy | 3 | 63.19 |
| Spain | 3 | 61.83 |
| Ireland | 3 | 57.28 |
| Turkey | 3 | 57.12 |
| Portugal | 3 | 52.17 |
| Venezuela | 5 | 35.12 |
| Greece | 5 | 33.00 |
| Iraq | 5 | 29.85 |
| Sudan | 5 | 26.98 |
| Iran | 5 | 26.40 |
| Syria | 5 | 24.27 |
| Libya | 5 | 24.07 |
| Zimbabwe | 5 | 16.87 |
| Somalia | 5 | 13.85 |

equivalent to a credit rating of D to B−. Table 14–3 reports ECR scores for several countries as of April 2012. As can be seen in this table, ECR ratings assess Norway as the country with the least chance of default and Somalia as the country with the highest chance of default.

### The Economist Intelligence Unit

www.economist.com

A sister firm to *The Economist,* the Economist Intelligence Unit (EIU) rates country risk by combined economic and political risk on a 100-point (maximum) scale. The higher the number, the worse the sovereign risk rating of the country. The EIU country risk ratings reported as of 2012 are presented in Figure 14–1.

### The Institutional Investor Index

Normally published twice a year, this index is based on surveys of the loan officers of major multinational banks. These officers give subjective scores regarding the credit quality of given countries. Originally, the score was based on 10, but since 1980 it has been based on 100, with a score of 0 indicating certainty of default and 100 indicating no possibility of default. The *Institutional Investor* then weighs the scores received from the officers surveyed by the exposure of each bank to the country in question. For a sampling of the *Institutional Investor*'s country credit ratings as of March 2012, see Table 14–4. For example, in March 2012, loan officers around the world assessed Norway as the country with the least chance of default, while they assessed Somalia as the country with the highest chance of default.

**FIGURE 14–1**

*The Economist* **Intelligence Unit Country Risk Ratings**

Source: "Country Risk Service Risk Ratings," 2012, *The Economist. www.eiu.com*

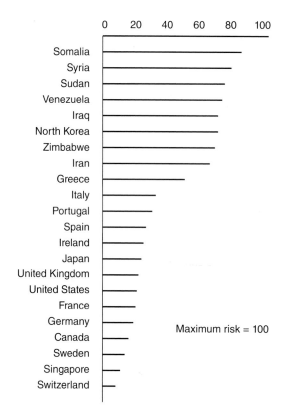

## Internal Evaluation Models
### *Statistical Models*

By far, the most common approach to evaluating sovereign country risk among large FIs has been to develop sovereign country risk-scoring models based on key economic ratios for each country, similar to the domestic credit risk–scoring models discussed in Chapter 10.

An FI analyst begins by selecting a set of macro- and microeconomic variables and ratios that might be important in explaining a country's probability of rescheduling. Then the analyst uses past data on rescheduling and nonrescheduling countries to see which variables best discriminate between those countries that rescheduled their debt and those that did not. This helps the analyst identify a set of key variables that best explain rescheduling and a group of weights indicating the relative importance of these variables. For example, domestic credit risk analysis can employ discriminant analysis to calculate a Z-score rating of the probability of corporate bankruptcy. Similarly, in sovereign risk analysis we can develop a Z-score to measure the probability that a country will reschedule (see Chapter 10 for discussion of the Z-score model).[2]

The first step in this country risk analysis (CRA) is to pick a set of variables that may be important in explaining rescheduling probabilities. In many cases analysts select more than 40 variables. Here we identify the variables most commonly included in sovereign risk probability models.

---

[2] Alternatively, analysts could employ linear probability, logit, or probit models.

**TABLE 14–4**
*Institutional Investor's 2012 Country Credit Ratings*

Source: *Institutional Investor,* March 2012. *www.institutional-investor.com*

| March 2012 | September 2011 | Country | Institutional Investor Rank | Six-Month Change | One-Year Change |
|---|---|---|---|---|---|
| 1 | 1 | Norway | 94.8 | −0.7 | −0.4 |
| 2 | 2 | Switzerland | 94.1 | −0.8 | 0.0 |
| 3 | 7 | Canada | 93.1 | 0.7 | 0.0 |
| 4 | 4 | Sweden | 92.9 | −0.4 | 0.3 |
| 5 | 5 | Finland | 92.5 | −0.5 | 0.0 |
| 6 | 8 | Singapore | 92.4 | 0.2 | −0.3 |
| 7 | 3 | Luxembourg | 91.6 | −2.5 | −0.9 |
| 8 | 9 | Netherlands | 90.8 | −0.7 | −0.2 |
| 9 | 6 | Germany | 89.8 | −2.8 | −3.5 |
| 10 | 11 | Australia | 89.7 | −0.9 | −1.2 |
| 11 | 12 | United States | 89.4 | −1.1 | −2.0 |
| 12 | 10 | Denmark | 89.1 | −1.7 | −2.1 |
| 13 | 13 | Austria | 88.2 | −1.5 | −1.9 |
| 14 | 16 | Hong Kong | 85.6 | 0.2 | 0.1 |
| 15 | 17 | United Kingdom | 85.6 | 0.8 | −2.2 |
| 16 | 15 | New Zealand | 85.2 | −1.1 | −2.0 |
| 17 | 14 | France | 85.2 | −2.7 | −4.5 |
| 18 | 19 | Chile | 82.1 | −0.5 | 2.6 |
| 19 | 18 | Japan | 81.1 | −1.9 | −4.2 |
| 20 | 25 | Qatar | 80.2 | 2.3 | 1.2 |
| 42 | 34 | Italy | 66.5 | −5.9 | −9.9 |
| 43 | 42 | Spain | 64.7 | −2.6 | −7.3 |
| 68 | 75 | Ireland | 51.9 | 2.9 | −9.1 |
| 75 | 72 | Portugal | 46.5 | −3.4 | −18.9 |
| 151 | 131 | Greece | 19.6 | −7.6 | −27.3 |
| 160 | 149 | Tonga | 16.3 | −5.3 | −16.3 |
| 161 | 165 | Liberia | 16.3 | 0.4 | 2.0 |
| 162 | 155 | Sao Tome & Principe | 16.1 | −3.2 | −4.3 |
| 163 | 163 | Chad | 15.7 | −0.8 | −2.0 |
| 164 | 171 | Eritrea | 15.0 | 2.3 | 1.4 |
| 165 | 161 | Cuba | 14.1 | −2.9 | −1.0 |
| 166 | 168 | Guinea-Bissau | 13.0 | −1.9 | 1.0 |
| 167 | 162 | Haiti | 12.6 | −4.0 | −1.4 |
| 168 | 170 | Burundi | 12.6 | −1.7 | −3.2 |
| 169 | 167 | Comoros | 12.5 | −2.7 | −2.3 |
| 170 | 173 | Central African Rep. | 12.4 | 0.4 | 0.8 |
| 171 | 169 | Dem. Rep. of Congo | 11.9 | −2.4 | −1.8 |
| 172 | 166 | Guinea | 11.8 | −3.7 | −0.3 |
| 173 | 172 | Afghanistan | 11.4 | −1.1 | −1.5 |
| 174 | 174 | Sudan | 10.4 | −1.4 | 0.5 |
| 175 | – | South Sudan | 10.0 | – | – |
| 176 | 175 | Myanmar | 9.9 | 0.0 | −2.7 |
| 177 | 178 | North Korea | 6.0 | 1.6 | 0.3 |
| 178 | 177 | Zimbabwe | 5.3 | 0.3 | −0.5 |
| 179 | 176 | Somalia | 5.2 | −0.7 | 1.3 |
| | | Global average rating | 44.1 | −1.6 | −2.2 |

### Debt Service Ratio (DSR)

$$DSR = \frac{\text{Interest plus amortization on debt}}{\text{Exports}}$$

A country's exports are its primary way of generating dollars and other hard currencies. The larger the debt repayments in hard currencies are in relation to export revenues, the greater the probability that the country will have to reschedule its debt. Thus, there should be a *positive* relationship between the size of the **debt service ratio** and the probability of rescheduling. Table 14–5 shows the scheduled debt service ratios of various countries. Note that Latvia is servicing debt obligations at almost a third the level of its exports (e.g., Latvia's debt service ratio is 30.81 percent).

**debt service ratio**
The ratio of a country's interest and amortization obligations to the value of its exports.

### Import Ratio (IR)

$$IR = \frac{\text{Total imports}}{\text{Total foreign exchange reserves}}$$

Many countries must import manufactured goods since their infrastructure limits their domestic production. In times of famine, even food becomes a vital import. To pay for imports, the country must run down its stock of hard currencies—its foreign exchange reserves. The greater its need for imports—especially vital imports—the quicker a country can be expected to deplete its foreign exchange reserves. For example, Greece's import ratio was 1377.91 in 2011, implying that Greece imported more goods and services than it had foreign reserves to pay for them. In contrast, China's import ratio was 58.52 percent in 2011, implying that China imported fewer goods and services than it had foreign reserves to pay for them. Since the first use of reserves is to buy vital imports, the larger the ratio of imports to foreign exchange reserves, the higher the probability that the country will have to reschedule its debt repayments. This is so because these countries generally view repaying foreign debtholders as being less important than supplying

**TABLE 14–5**
**Debt Service Ratio for Various Countries**

Source: "2012 Data By Topic," World Bank website. *www.worldbank.org*

| Country | Debt Service Ratio |
|---|---|
| Argentina | 3.62% |
| Armenia | 23.29 |
| Brazil | 5.71 |
| Bulgaria | 22.32 |
| Chile | 11.20 |
| China | 1.17 |
| Colombia | 4.58 |
| El Salvador | 14.76 |
| Latvia | 30.81 |
| Mexico | 1.60 |
| Nicaragua | 10.02 |
| Romania | 15.28 |
| Russia | 8.07 |
| Serbia | 23.96 |
| Turkey | 18.28 |
| Ukraine | 19.52 |
| United States | 15.98 |

**import ratio**
The ratio of a country's imports to its total foreign currency reserves.

vital goods to the domestic population. Thus, the **import ratio** and the probability of rescheduling should be *positively* related.

### Investment Ratio (INVR)

$$INVR = \frac{\text{Real investment}}{\text{GNP}}$$

**investment ratio**
The ratio of a country's real investment to its GNP.

The **investment ratio** measures the degree to which a country is allocating resources to real investment in factories, machines, and so on, rather than to consumption. The higher this ratio, the more productive the economy should be in the future and the lower the probability that the country would need to reschedule its debt. This implies a *negative* relationship between INVR and the probability of rescheduling. An opposing view is that a higher investment ratio allows a country to build up its investment infrastructure. The higher ratio puts it in a stronger bargaining position with external creditors since the country would rely less on funds in the future and would be less concerned about future threats of credit rationing by FIs should it request a rescheduling. This view argues for a *positive* relationship between the investment ratio and the probability of rescheduling, especially if the country invests heavily in import competing industries. Just before the collapse of their economies (in 2007), investment ratios in Greece, Italy, and Portugal were 25.69, 22.12, and 22.83 percent, respectively. By 2011, the values had fallen to 14.53, 19.63, and 17.43 percent, respectively. In contrast, China's investment ratio was 41.74 percent in 2007 and 46.78 percent in 2011.

### Variance of Export Revenue (VAREX)

$$VAREX = \sigma^2_{ER}$$

A country's export revenues may be highly variable as a result of two risk factors. *Quantity risk* means that the production of the raw commodities the country sells abroad—for example, coffee or sugar—is subject to periodic gluts and shortages. *Price risk* means that the international dollar prices at which the country can sell its exportable commodities are subject to high volatility as world demand for and supply of a commodity, such as copper, vary. The more volatile a country's export earnings, the less certain creditors can be that at any time in the future it will be able to meet its repayment commitments. That is, there should be a *positive* relationship between $\sigma^2_{ER}$ and the probability of rescheduling.

### Domestic Money Supply Growth (MG)

$$MG = \frac{\Delta M}{M}$$

The faster the domestic growth rate of a country's money supply [$\Delta M / M$, which measures the change in the money supply ($\Delta M$) over its initial level ($M$)], the higher the domestic inflation rate and the weaker that country's currency becomes in domestic and international markets.[3] When a country's currency loses credibility as a medium of exchange, real output is often adversely impacted, and the country must increasingly rely on hard currencies for both domestic and international

[3] The purchasing power parity (PPP) theorem argues that high relative inflation rates lead to a country's currency depreciating in value against other currencies (see Chapter 13).

payments, a recent case being Venezuela in 2011, where money supply growth was 54.40 percent and inflation was 26.09 percent. These inflation, output, and payment effects suggest a *positive* relationship between domestic money supply growth and the probability of rescheduling.

We can summarize the expected relationships among these five key economic variables and the probability of rescheduling ($p$) for any country as:

$$p = f(DSR, IR, INVR, VAREX, MG \dots)$$
$$+ \quad + \ + \text{ or } - \quad + \quad +$$

After selecting the key variables, the FI manager normally places countries into two groups or populations:

$P_1$ = Bad (reschedulers)

$P_2$ = Good (nonreschedulers)

Then the manager uses a statistical methodology such as discriminant analysis (see Chapter 10) to identify which of these variables best discriminates between the population of rescheduling borrowers and that of nonrescheduling borrowers. Once the key variables and their relative importance or weights have been identified, the discriminant function can classify as good or bad current sovereign loans or sovereign loan applicants using currently observed values for the *DSR*, *IR*, and so on. Again, the methodology is very similar to the credit scoring models discussed in Chapter 10.

### Problems with Statistical CRA Models

Even though this methodology has been one of the most common forms of CRA used by FIs, it is fraught with problems. This section discusses six major problems in using traditional CRA models and techniques. We do not imply in any way that these techniques should not be used, but instead indicate that FI managers should be aware of the potential pitfalls in using such models.

*Measurement of Key Variables* Very often the FI manager's information on a country's DSR or IR is out of date because of delays in collection of data and errors in measurement. For example, the Bank for International Settlements (BIS) collects aggregate loan volume data for countries. Frequently, this information is six months old or more before it is published. This example illustrates the problem: Citigroup may know today the current amount of its outstanding loans to Indonesia, but it is unlikely to know with any great degree of accuracy Indonesia's total outstanding external loans and debt with every other lender in the world.

www.bis.org

Moreover, these measurement problems are compounded by forecast errors when managers use these statistical models to predict the probabilities of rescheduling with future or projected values of key variables such as *DSR* and *IR*.

*Population Groups* Usually, analysts seek to find variables that distinguish between only two possible outcomes: reschedulers and nonreschedulers. In actuality, a finer distinction may be necessary—for example, a distinction between those countries announcing a moratorium on only interest payments and those announcing a moratorium on both interest and principal payments. Thus, Greece, which in 2011 forced a 74 percent haircut on debt to private debtholders, should be viewed as a higher-risk country than a country, such as Dubai, that delayed the interest payments on its debt for a few months in 2009 because of short-term foreign exchange shortages.

*Political Risk Factors*  Traditionally, CRA statistical credit-scoring models incorporate only economic variables. While there may be a strong correlation between an economic variable such as money supply growth and rescheduling, the model may not capture very well purely political risk events such as *strikes, elections, corruption,* and *revolutions.* For example, the election of a strongly nationalist politician may reduce the probability of repayment and increase the probability of rescheduling. A considerable part of the debt repayment and banking crisis problems in Southeast Asia was attributed to cronyism and corruption.

www.heritage.org

Since 1995, the Index of Economic Freedom (compiled by the Heritage Foundation) has provided a measure that summarizes the economic freedom of over 180 countries in the world. The Heritage Foundation defines economic freedom as "the absence of government coercion or constraint on the production, distribution, or consumption of goods and services beyond the extent necessary for citizens to protect and maintain liberty itself."[4] The index includes measures of trade policy, fiscal burden of government, government intervention in the economy, monetary policy, capital flows and foreign investment, banking and finance, wages and prices, prosperity rights, regulation, and black market activities. Each country is assigned a score ranging from 0 to 100 for each of the 10 individual factors as well as an overall score based on the average of these factors. A score of 100 signifies the maximum economic freedom. Table 14–6 lists the economic freedom index for the 10 highest and lowest-rated countries as of 2012.

www.transperancy.org

An alternative quantitative measure of country risk is the Corruption Perceptions Index produced by Transparency International. Figure 14–2 shows the corruption index for 22 out of 182 countries covered for 2012. The least corrupt countries are assigned a score of 10, while the most corrupt countries are assigned a score of 0.

**TABLE 14–6**
**Economic Freedom Index for Various Countries**

Source: The Heritage Foundation website, July 2012. *www.heritage.org*

| Country | Overall Economic Freedom Index |
|---|---|
| Hong Kong | 89.9 |
| Singapore | 87.5 |
| Australia | 83.1 |
| New Zealand | 82.1 |
| Switzerland | 81.1 |
| Canada | 79.9 |
| Chile | 78.3 |
| Mauritius | 77.0 |
| Ireland | 76.9 |
| United States | 76.3 |
| Equatorial Guinea | 42.8 |
| Iran | 42.3 |
| Congo | 41.1 |
| Burma | 38.7 |
| Venezuela | 38.1 |
| Eritrea | 36.2 |
| Libya | 35.9 |
| Cuba | 28.3 |
| Zimbabwe | 26.3 |
| North Korea | 1.0 |

[4] See *2012 Index of Economic Freedom* (Washington, DC: Heritage Foundation, 2012), **www.heritage.org**.

**FIGURE 14–2**
Corruption
Perceptions Index,
2012

Source: Transparency International, July 2012.
*www.transparency.org*

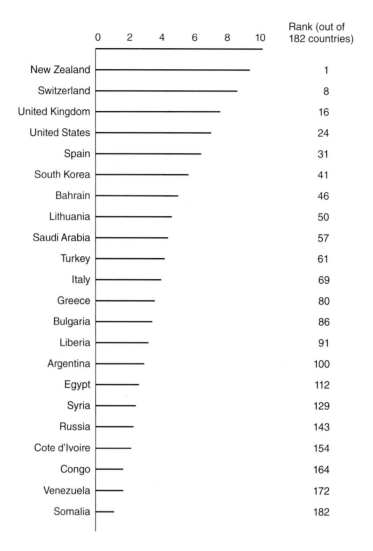

Rank (out of
182 countries)

| Country | Rank |
| --- | --- |
| New Zealand | 1 |
| Switzerland | 8 |
| United Kingdom | 16 |
| United States | 24 |
| Spain | 31 |
| South Korea | 41 |
| Bahrain | 46 |
| Lithuania | 50 |
| Saudi Arabia | 57 |
| Turkey | 61 |
| Italy | 69 |
| Greece | 80 |
| Bulgaria | 86 |
| Liberia | 91 |
| Argentina | 100 |
| Egypt | 112 |
| Syria | 129 |
| Russia | 143 |
| Cote d'Ivoire | 154 |
| Congo | 164 |
| Venezuela | 172 |
| Somalia | 182 |

***Portfolio Aspects*** Traditional CRA considers each country separately. However, many large FIs with sovereign risk exposures hold a portfolio of loans. In a portfolio context, the risk of holding a well-diversified portfolio of sovereign loans may be smaller than that of having a portfolio heavily concentrated in non-oil-producing sovereign loans. In particular, the lender may distinguish between those key risk indicator variables having a *systematic* effect on the probability of repayment across a large number of sovereign countries and those variables having an *unsystematic* effect by impacting only one or a few countries.

One way to address this problem is to employ a portfolio framework such as those discussed in Chapter 11 for sovereign risk analysis. Such an analysis would identify those indicator variables that have a *systematic* impact across all borrowers' probability of repayment and those that tend to be country specific (or *unsystematic*). The indicator variables that the FI manager should really be concerned with are the *systematic* variables since they cannot be diversified away in a multi-sovereign loan portfolio. By comparison, unsystematic, or country-specific, risks can be diversified away. Consider the following model (see Chapters 10 and 11 for a discussion of the construction of these models):

$$X_i = a_i + b_i \bar{X} + e_i$$

where

$X_i$ = Key variable or country risk indicator for country $i$ (e.g., the DSR for country $i$)

$\bar{X}$ = index of this key risk indicator across all countries to which the lender makes loans (e.g., the DSR for each country weighted by the shares of loans for each country in the FI's portfolio)

$e_i$ = Other factors impacting $X_i$ for any given country

Expressing this equation in variance terms, we get:

$$VAR(X_i) = b_i^2 VAR(\bar{X}) + VAR(e_i)$$

Total risk = Systematic risk + Unsystematic risk

From this equation, you can see that the total risk or variability of any given risk indicator for a country, such as the DSR for Poland, can be divided into a nondiversifiable *systematic* risk element that measures the extent to which that country's DSR moves in line with the DSRs of all other debtor countries and an unsystematic risk element that impacts the DSR for Poland independently. The greater the size of the *unsystematic* element relative to the systematic risk element, the less important this variable is to the lender since it can be diversified away by holding a broad array of LDC loans.

---

**EXAMPLE 14–1**

*Calculating Sovereign Risk for an FI's Portfolio*

The average $\sigma^2_{INVR}$ (or *INVR* = investment ratio) of a group of countries has been estimated at 20 percent. The individual INVRs of two countries in an FI's portfolio, Belgium and Hong Kong, have been estimated at 10 percent and 20 percent, respectively. The regression of individual country INVR on average INVR provides the following beta coefficient estimates:

$$\beta_B = \text{Beta of Belgium} = 0.75$$
$$\beta_{HK} = \text{Beta of Hong Kong} = 0.60$$

Based only on the INVR estimates, Hong Kong should be charged a higher risk premium because its INVR (20 percent) is higher than is Belgium's (10 percent). However, if the FI includes systematic risk in its estimation of risk premiums, the addition of loans to Hong Kong will reduce the overall systematic risk of the FI's foreign loan portfolio. In this case, it benefits the FI to add Hong Kong to its list of countries because its unsystematic risk can be diversified away.

---

Past research has found that the DSR has a high systematic element across countries, as does export revenue variance (VAREX). This implies that when one LDC country is experiencing a growing debt burden relative to its exports, so are all others. Similarly, when commodity prices or world demand collapses for one debtor country's commodity exports, the same occurs for other debtor countries as well. A possible reason for the high systematic risk of the DSR is the sensitivity of this ratio to rising nominal and real interest rates in the developed (or lending) countries. As we discussed in Chapter 13, international interest rates tend to be positively correlated over time. A possible reason for the high systematic risk of the export variance is the tendency of prices and world demands for commodities to reflect simultaneously economic conditions such as recessions and expansions in developed countries.

By comparison, money supply growth ($\Delta M/M$) and the import ratio appear to have low systematic elements. This is not surprising since control over the money supply and the use of domestic reserves are relatively discretionary variables for governments. Thus, while Argentina may choose a money supply growth rate of 50 percent per year, the Chilean government may choose a target rate of 10 percent per year. Similarly, the Argentinian and Chilean economies may have very different demands for imports, and the scale of vital imports may differ quite widely across countries. Using this type of analysis allows an FI manager to focus on relatively few variables such as the *DSR*s and export variances that affect the risk of the sovereign loan portfolio.

*Incentive Aspects* CRA statistical models often identify variables based on rather loose or often nonexistent analyses of the borrower or lender's incentives to reschedule. Rarely are the following questions asked: What are the *incentives* or *net benefits* to a country seeking a rescheduling? What are the incentives or net benefits to an FI that grants a rescheduling? That is, what determines the demand for rescheduling by countries and the supply of rescheduling by FIs? Presumably, only when the benefits outweigh the costs for both parties does rescheduling occur. Consider the following benefits and costs of rescheduling for borrowers on the one hand and FIs on the other.

### Borrowers

*Benefits*

- By rescheduling its debt, the borrower lowers the present value of its future payments in hard currencies to outside lenders. This allows it to increase its consumption of foreign imports and/or increase the rate of its domestic investment.

*Costs*

- By rescheduling now, the borrower may close itself out of the market for loans in the future. As a result, even if the borrower encounters high-growth investment opportunities in the future, it may be difficult or impossible to finance them.

- Rescheduling may result in significant interference with the borrower's international trade since it would be difficult to gain access to instruments such as letters of credit, without which trade may be more costly.

### Lenders (FIs)

*Benefits*

- Once a loan has been made, a rescheduling is much better than a borrower default. With a rescheduling, the FI lender may anticipate some present value loss of principal and interest on the loan. With an outright default, the FI stands to lose all its principal and future interest repayments.

- The FI can renegotiate fees and various other collateral and option features into a rescheduled loan.

- There may be tax benefits to an FI's taking a recognized write-down or loss in value on a rescheduled LDC loan portfolio.

*Costs*

- Through rescheduling, loans become similar to long-term bonds or even equity, and the FI often becomes locked into a particular loan portfolio structure.
- Those FIs with large amounts of rescheduled loans are subject to greater regulatory attention. For example, in the United States, such FIs may be placed on the regulators' problem list of FIs.

All these relevant economic incentive considerations go into the demand for and the supply of rescheduling. However, it is far from clear how the simple statistical models just described incorporate this complex array of incentives. At a very minimum, statistical models should clearly reflect the underlying theory of rescheduling.

*Stability*   A final problem with simple statistical CRA models is that of stability. The fact that certain key variables may have explained rescheduling in the past does not mean that they will perform or predict well in the future. Over time, new variables and incentives affect rescheduling decisions, and the relative weights on the key variables change. This suggests that the FI manager must continuously update the CRA model to incorporate all currently available information and ensure the best predictive power possible. This is particularly true in today's new global environment of enhanced trade and competition with major changes in production technology taking place in countries such as China and India.

## Using Market Data to Measure Risk: The Secondary Market for LDC and Emerging Market Debt

Since the mid-1980s, shortly after the beginning of the debt crisis in Latin America, the LDC debt secondary market began to develop among large commercial banks in New York and London. Trading volume was initially small, around $2 billion per year. However, trading volume increased significantly in late 1980s as several LDC countries adopted debt-for-equity swap programs to restructure their debt, and implementation of programs that allowed for sovereign debt restructuring and trading of existing and proposed new debt. What started as a market of highly individualized loans sales transactions between a limited number of FIs developed into a large and sophisticated trading market, which become known in the early 1990s as the emerging market (EM). By the mid-1990s, trading volume had topped $4.5 billion. Trading declined to $4.2 billion in 1998 after the Russian debt defaults and again in 1999 after Ecuador's failure to pay interest on its already restructured bonds. Trading has also been adversely affected by schemes of the more successful emerging market countries to get investors to swap restructured bonds for domestic government bonds (see below). The early 2000s were characterized by increasing trading activity and growing investor confidence in emerging markets, sparked in large part by Brazil's rapid economic recovery, Mexico's upgraded credit rating to investment grade, and Russia's successful debt restructuring. By 2007, secondary market LDC and EM trading volumes had grown to $6.5 trillion. With the onset of the financial crisis and the worldwide recession, investors turned to more conservative, less risky investments. LDC and EM trading volume fell to $4.173 trillion in 2008, the lowest level since 2003 ($3.973 trillion). However, as worldwide economic conditions improved, trading volumes rebounded to $6.765 trillion in 2010 and $6.5 trillion in 2011.

### The Structure of the Market

This secondary market in LDC and EM debt has considerably enhanced the liquidity of LDC and EM loans on bank and other FI balance sheets. The following are the market players that sell and buy LDC and EM loans and debt instruments.

**Sellers**

- Large FIs willing to accept write-downs of loans on their balance sheets.
- Small FIs wishing to disengage themselves from the LDC and EM loan market.
- FIs willing to swap one country's LDC and EM debt for another's to rearrange their portfolios of country risk exposures.

**Buyers**

- Wealthy investors, hedge funds (see Chapter 5), FIs, and corporations seeking to engage in debt-for-equity swaps or speculative investments.
- FIs seeking to rearrange their LDC and EM balance sheets by reorienting their LDC and EM debt concentrations.

### The Early Market for Sovereign Debt

Consider the quote sheet from Salomon Brothers, in Table 14–7, for May 2, 1988—a relatively early stage of LDC loan market development. As indicated in Table 14–7, FIs such as investment banks and major commercial banks act as market makers, quoting two-way bid–ask prices for LDC debt.[5] Thus, an FI or an investor could have bought $100 of Peruvian loans from Salomon for $9 in May 1988, or at a 91 percent discount from face value. However, in selling the same loans to Salomon, the investor would have received only $7 per $100, or a 93 percent discount. The bid–ask spreads for certain countries were very large in this period; for example, Sudan's $2 bid and $10 ask exemplified a serious lack of market demand for the sovereign loans of many countries.

### Today's Market for Sovereign Debt

In recent years there have been a large number of changes in the structure of the market. Now there are three market segments: sovereign bonds, performing loans, and nonperforming loans.[6]

*Sovereign Bonds*   The first segment of the LDC and EM debt market is that for sovereign bonds, i.e., government issued debt. Sovereign bonds have historically been issued in foreign currencies, either U.S. dollars or euros. LDC and EM

---

[5] Major market makers include the Dutch ING bank, as well as Citigroup, J.P. Morgan, and Merrill Lynch.

[6] A fourth, but now very small market is that for Brady bonds. Brady bonds reflect programs under which the U.S. and other FIs exchanged their dollar loans for dollar bonds issued by the relevant less developed countries (LDCs). These bonds have a much longer maturity than that promised on the original loans and a lower promised original coupon (yield) than the interest rate on the original loan. However, the principal has usually been collateralized through the issuing country's purchasing U.S. Treasury bonds and holding them in a special-purpose escrow account. Should that country default on its Brady bonds the buyers of the bonds could access the dollar bonds held as collateral. These loan-for-bond restructuring programs, also called *debt-for-debt swaps,* were developed under the auspices of the U.S. Treasury's 1989 Brady Plan and international organizations such as the IMF. Once loans were swapped for bonds by banks and other FIs, they could be sold on the secondary market. The Brady bond process ended in the 1990s. Yet a small amount of these bonds still exist and trade.

**TABLE 14–7**
**Indicative Prices
for Less Developed
Country Bank
Loans**

Source: Salomon Brothers
Inc., May 2, 1988.

| Country | Indicative Cash Prices Bid | Offer | Trading Commentary |
|---|---|---|---|
| Algeria | $91.00 | $93.00 | Longer-dated paper resurfacing as cash substitute in swaps. |
| Argentina | 29.00 | 30.00 | Less volume this period; consolidation exercise slows note trades. |
| Bolivia | 10.00 | 13.00 | Minimal current activity. |
| Brazil | 53.00 | 54.00 | Rally topping out as supply catches up with auction interest. |
| Chile | 60.50 | 61.50 | Market firm and rising as deal calendar fills. |
| Colombia | 67.00 | 68.00 | Resurgence of interest as high-quality exists. |
| Costa Rica | 13.00 | 16.00 | Market building reserves of patience to deal with this name again. |
| Dominican Republic | 17.00 | 20.00 | Trading picks up at lower levels. |
| Ecuador | 31.00 | 33.00 | Occasional swaps surfacing. |
| Honduras | 25.00 | 28.00 | Viewed as expensive on a relative value basis. |
| Ivory Coast | 30.00 | 33.00 | Newly sighted by fee swappers. |
| Jamaica | 33.00 | 36.00 | Slow but serious inquiry continues. |
| Mexico | 52.50 | 53.50 | Prices continue upward drift on lower, lumpy flow. |
| Morocco | 50.00 | 51.00 | Fee swappers oblige sellers by jumping into the wider breach versus Latins. |
| Nicaragua | 3.00 | 4.00 | Avoided by the surviving court testers. |
| Nigeria | 28.50 | 30.50 | Retail stonewalls dealer interest. |
| Panama | 20.00 | 23.00 | Recent bidding stirs the mud. |
| Peru | 7.00 | 9.00 | Debt-for-debt workouts and debt-for-goods deals continue. |
| Philippines | 52.00 | 53.00 | Prices drift higher with good interest in non-CB names. |
| Poland | 43.25 | 44.50 | Somewhat slower trading this period. |
| Romania | 82.00 | 84.00 | Bidding improves on expectations of 1988 principal payments. |
| Senegal | 40.00 | 45.00 | Trading talk more serious. |
| Sudan | 2.00 | 10.00 | Still on the mat. |
| Turkey | 97.50 | 99.00 | CTLDs remain well bid. |
| Uruguay | 59.50 | 61.50 | Remains a patience-trying market. |
| Venezuela | 55.00 | 55.75 | Trading stronger as uptick in Chile brings swaps back into range. |
| Yugoslavia | 45.50 | 47.00 | More frequent trading. |
| Zaire | 19.00 | 23.00 | New interest develops. |

sovereign debt tends to have lower credit ratings than other sovereign debt because of the increased economic and political risks. Where most developed countries are either AAA or AA-rated, most LDC issuance is rated below investment grade. Further, sovereign bonds are uncollateralized and their price or value reflects the credit risk rating of the country issuing the bonds. For example, the

$2.8 billion June 1997 issue by Brazil of 30-year dollar denominated bonds (rated BB grade by Standard & Poor's) was sold at a yield spread of nearly 4 percent over U.S. Treasuries at the time of issue. In July 2001, Argentinian sovereign bonds were trading at spreads of over 15 percent above U.S. Treasury rates, with the J.P. Morgan Emerging Market Bond Index showing a spread of nearly 10 percent over U.S. Treasuries. This reflected the serious economic problems in Argentina and the contagious effects these were having on other sovereign bond markets. More recently, in September 2008, fears of the global economic crisis and falling commodity prices hit emerging markets particularly hard: Mexico's sovereign debt spread jumped from 165bps to over 587bps, Brazil's from 200bps to over 586bps, Chile's from 69bps to over 322bps, Colombia's from over 29bps to more than 600bps, and Argentina's and Venezuela's spreads went from 942bps and 873bps to over 4,019bps and 2,325bps, respectively. By the week of October 24, spreads had tripled since early August 2008. However, it should also be noted that credit default spreads on 10-year U.S. Treasury debt rose to a record 29.2bps: developed countries were not immune to the crisis.

Under the doctrine of sovereign-immunity, the repayment of sovereign debt cannot be forced by the creditors and it is thus subject to compulsory rescheduling, interest rate reduction, or even repudiation. The only protection available to the creditors is threat of the loss of credibility and lowering of the international standing (the sovereign debt rating of the country, which may make it much more difficult to borrow in the future).

*Performing Loans* The second segment of the LDC and EM debt market is that for performing loans. Performing loans are original or restructured outstanding sovereign loans on which the sovereign country is currently maintaining promised payments to lenders or debt holders. Any discounts from 100 percent reflect expectations that these countries may face repayment problems in the future. Table 14–8 reports external bank loans outstanding for several countries in 2003 through 2011. Note the increase in bank loans outstanding throughout the period.

**TABLE 14–8**
**Bank Loans Outstanding, 2003 through 2012 (in billions of dollars)**

Source: World Bank website, January 2004, November 2006, August 2009, and July 2012. *www.worldbank.org*

| Country | 2003 | 2006 | 2009 | 2011 |
|---|---|---|---|---|
| Argentina | $ 25.0 | $ 10.5 | $ 14.0 | $ 3.9 |
| Brazil | 58.2 | 57.5 | 92.8 | 138.2 |
| Bulgaria | 0.8 | 3.9 | 18.7 | 7.3 |
| Costa Rica | 3.0 | 2.9 | 5.5 | 2.3 |
| Ecuador | 1.8 | 2.2 | 2.1 | 1.0 |
| Greece | 35.4 | 90.4 | 162.6 | 118.0 |
| Ireland | 388.3 | 888.8 | 952.4 | 479.2 |
| Italy | 460.5 | 789.1 | 867.5 | 712.4 |
| Mexico | 45.7 | 38.9 | 72.9 | 22.0 |
| Peru | 4.2 | 4.7 | 12.5 | 10.3 |
| Philippines | 12.2 | 17.2 | 13.0 | 7.8 |
| Poland | 16.8 | 23.4 | 69.9 | 66.0 |
| Portugal | 479.2 | 820.3 | 1,127.8 | 927.0 |
| Russia | 35.3 | 87.6 | 147.7 | 160.7 |
| Spain | 155.8 | 202.1 | 269.7 | 174.4 |

*Nonperforming Loans*   The third segment of the LDC and EM market is that for nonperforming loans. Nonperforming loans reflect the secondary market prices for the sovereign loans of countries where there are no interest or principal payments currently being made. These are normally traded at very deep discounts from 100 percent.

| | |
|---|---|
| **Concept Questions** | 1. Are the credit ratings of countries in the *Institutional Investor* rating scheme forward looking or backward looking?<br>2. What variables are most commonly included in country risk analysis models? What does each one measure?<br>3. What are the major problems involved with using traditional CRA models and techniques?<br>4. Which sovereign risk indicators are the most important for a large FI, those with a high or those with a low systematic element? |

---

**Summary**

This chapter reviewed the problems FIs face from sovereign or country risk exposures. Sovereign risk is the risk of a foreign government's limiting or preventing domestic borrowers in its jurisdiction from repaying the principal and interest on debt owned to external lenders. In recent years this risk has caused enormous problems for U.S. banks lending to LDCs, and Latin American, Asian, and even European countries. We reviewed various models for country risk analysis (CRA), including those produced by external monitoring agencies such as Euromoney, the Economist Intelligence Unit, and the *Institutional Investor* and those that could be constructed by an FI manager for internal evaluation purposes. Such statistical CRA models have problems and pitfalls. An alternative approach using secondary market prices on LDC and EM loans and bonds was also described. In Appendix 14A, we analyze the advantages and disadvantages of using four alternative mechanisms for dealing with problem sovereign credits from the perspective of the lender: debt–equity swaps, MYRAs, loan sales, and bond-for-loan swaps.

**Questions and Problems**

1. What risks are incurred in making loans to borrowers based in foreign countries? Explain.
2. What is the difference between debt rescheduling and debt repudiation?
3. Identify and explain at least four reasons that rescheduling debt in the form of loans is easier than rescheduling debt in the form of bonds.
4. What three country risk assessment models are available to investors? How is each model compiled?
5. What types of variables normally are used in a CRA Z-score model? Define the following ratios and explain how each is interpreted in assessing the probability of rescheduling.
   a. Debt service ratio.
   b. Import ratio.
   c. Investment ratio.
   d. Variance of export revenue.
   e. Domestic money supply growth.

6. An FI manager has calculated the following values and weights to assess the credit risk and likelihood of having to reschedule a loan. From the Z-score calculated using these weights and values, is the manager likely to approve the loan? Validation tests of the Z-score model indicated that scores below 0.500 were likely to be nonreschedulers, while scores above 0.700 indicated a likelihood of rescheduling. Scores between 0.500 and 0.700 do not predict well.

| Variable | Country Value | Weight |
| --- | --- | --- |
| DSR | 1.25 | 0.05 |
| IR | 1.60 | 0.10 |
| INVR | 0.60 | 0.35 |
| VAREX | 0.15 | 0.35 |
| MG | 0.02 | 0.15 |

7. Countries A and B have exports of $2 billion and $6 billion, respectively. The total interest and amortization on foreign loans for both countries are $1 billion and $2 billion, respectively.
   a. What is the debt service ratio (DSR) for each country?
   b. Based only on this ratio, to which country should lenders charge a higher risk premium?
   c. What are the shortcomings of using only these ratios to determine your answer in part (b)?

8. How do price and quantity risks affect the variability of a country's export revenue?

9. Explain the following relation:

$$p = f(IR, INVR)$$
$$+, + \text{ or } -$$

where

$$p = \text{Probability of rescheduling}$$
$$IR = \text{Total imports/Total foreign exchange reserves}$$
$$INVR = \text{Real investment/GNP}$$

10. What shortcomings are introduced by using traditional CRA models and techniques? In each case, what adjustments are made in the estimation techniques to compensate for the problems?

11. What is systematic risk in terms of sovereign risk? Which of the variables often used in statistical models tend to have high systematic risk? Which variables tend to have low systematic risk?

12. The average $\sigma_{ER}^2$ (or $VAREX$ = variance of export revenue) of a group of countries has been estimated at 20 percent. The individual VAREXes of two countries in the group, the Netherlands and Singapore, have been estimated at 15 percent and 28 percent, respectively. The regression of individual country VAREX on average VAREX provides the following beta (coefficient) estimates:

$$\beta_N = \text{Beta of the Netherlands} = 0.80$$
$$\beta_S = \text{Beta of Singapore} = 0.20$$

a. Based only on the VAREX estimates, which country should be charged a higher risk premium? Explain.

b. If FIs include systematic risk in their estimation of risk premiums, how would your conclusions to (a) be affected? Explain.

13. What are the benefits and costs of rescheduling to the following?
  a. A borrower.
  b. A lender.

14. Who are the primary sellers of LDC and EM debt? Who are the buyers? Why are FIs often both sellers and buyers of LDC and EM debt in the secondary markets?

15. Identify and describe the three market segments of the secondary market for LDC and EM debt.

The following questions and problems are based on material presented in Appendix 14A.

16. What are the risks to an investing company participating in a debt-for-equity swap?

17. Chase Bank holds a $200 million loan to Argentina. The loans are being traded at bid–offer prices of 91–93 per 100 in the London secondary market.
  a. If Chase has an opportunity to sell this loan to an investment bank at a 7 percent discount, what are the savings after taxes compared with the revenue from selling the loan in the secondary market? Assume the tax rate is 40 percent.
  b. The investment bank in turn sells the debt at a 6 percent discount to a real estate company planning to build apartment complexes in Argentina. What is the profit after taxes to the investment bank?
  c. The real estate company converts this loan into pesos under a debt-for-equity swap organized by the Argentinian government. The official rate for dollar to peso conversion is P1.05/$1. The free market rate is P1.10/$1. How much did the real estate company save by investing in Argentina through the debt-for-equity swap program as opposed to directly investing $200 million using the free market rates?
  d. How much would Chase benefit from doing a local currency debt-for-equity swap itself? Why does the bank not do this swap?

18. Zlick Company plans to invest $20 million in Chile to expand its subsidiary's manufacturing output. Zlick has two options. It can convert the $20 million at the current exchange rate of 410 pesos to a dollar (i.e., P410/$1), or it can engage in a debt-for-equity swap with its bank, City Bank, by purchasing Chilean debt and then swapping that debt into Chilean equity investments.
  a. If City Bank quotes bid–offer prices of 94–96 for Chilean loans, what is the bank expecting to receive from Zlick Corporation (ignore taxes)? Why would City Bank want to dispose of this loan?
  b. If Zlick decides to purchase the debt from City Bank and convert it to equity, it will have to exchange it at the official rate of P400/$1. Is this option better than investing directly in Chile at the free market rate of P410/$1?
  c. What official exchange rate will cause Zlick to be indifferent between the two options?

19. What is concessionality in the process of rescheduling a loan?

20. Which variables typically are negotiation points in a multiyear restructuring agreement (MYRA)? How do changes in these variables provide benefits to the borrower and to the lender?

21. How would the restructuring, such as rescheduling, of sovereign bonds affect the interest rate risk of the bonds? Is it possible that such restructuring would cause the FI's cost of capital not to change? Explain.

22. A bank is in the process of renegotiating a sovereign loan. The principal outstanding is $50 million and is to be paid back in two installments of $25 million each, plus interest of 8 percent. The new terms will stretch the loan out to five years with only interest payments of 6 percent, no principal payments, for the first three years. The principal will be paid in the last two years in payments of $25 million along with the interest. The cost of funds for the bank is 6 percent for both the old loan and the renegotiated loan. An up-front fee of 1 percent is to be included for the renegotiated loan.
    a. What is the present value of the existing loan for the bank?
    b. What is the present value of the rescheduled loan for the bank?
    c. Is the concessionality positive or negative for the bank?

23. A bank is in the process of renegotiating a three-year nonamortizing loan to Greece. The principal outstanding is $20 million, and the interest rate is 8 percent. The new terms will extend the loan to 10 years at a new interest rate of 6 percent. The cost of funds for the bank is 7 percent for both the old loan and the renegotiated loan. An up-front fee of 50 basis points is to be included for the renegotiated loan.
    a. What is the present value of the existing loan for the bank?
    b. What is the present value of the rescheduled loan for the bank?
    c. What is the concessionality for the bank?
    d. What should be the up-front fee to make the concessionality zero?

24. A $20 million loan outstanding to the Nigerian government is currently in arrears with City Bank. After extensive negotiations, City Bank agrees to reduce the interest rate from 10 percent to 6 percent and to lengthen the maturity of the loan to 10 years from the present 5 years remaining to maturity. The principal of the loan is to be paid at maturity. There will be no grace period and the first interest payment is expected at the end of the year.
    a. If the cost of funds is 5 percent for the bank, what is the present value of the loan prior to the rescheduling?
    b. What is the present value of the rescheduled loan to the bank?
    c. What is the concessionality of the rescheduled loan if the cost of funds remains at 5 percent and an up-front fee of 5 percent is charged?
    d. What up-front fee should the bank charge to make the concessionality equal zero?

25. A bank was expecting to receive $100,000 from a loan issued to the Spanish government. Since Spain has problems repaying the loan immediately, the bank extends the loan for another year at the same interest rate of 10 percent. However, in the rescheduling agreement, the bank reserves the right to exercise an option for receiving the payment in euros, equal to €87,813 converted at the exchange rate of €0.7983.
    a. If the cost of funds to the bank is also assumed to be 10 percent, what is the value of this option built into the agreement if only two possible exchange rates are expected at the end of the year, €0.8467/$ or €0.7499/$, with equal probability?
    b. How would your answer differ if the probability of the exchange rate being €0.8467/$ is 70 percent and that of €0.7499/$ is 30 percent?
    c. Does the currency option have more or less value as the volatility of the exchange rate increases?

26. What are the major benefits and costs of loan sales to an FI?
27. What are the major costs and benefits of converting loans to bonds for an FI?

## Web Questions

28. Go to the Heritage Foundation website at **www.heritage.org/index** and find the most recent Economic Freedom Index for the United States using the following steps. Click on "Explore the data." This will bring the file onto your computer that contains the relevant data. What factors led to this rating?
29. Go to the World Bank website at **www.worldbank.org** and find the amount of bank loans currently outstanding in Brazil using the following steps. Click on "Research." Under "Key Statistics," click on "Online Data Bases." Click on "GO." Click on "Quarterly External Debt Statistics/SDDS" and "Next >>." In the "Country" tab, click on "Brazil" and then "Select." In the "Series" tab, click on "027_T1_Banks" and then "Select." In the "Time" tab, click on the most recent year end quarter, i.e., "20XXQ4," and then "Select." Click on "Next >>." Click on "View Data." This will bring the file onto your computer that contains the relevant data.

## Appendix 14A: Mechanisms for Dealing with Sovereign Risk Exposure

View Appendix 14A at the website for this textbook (**www.mhhe.com/saunders8e**).

# Chapter Fifteen

# Market Risk

## INTRODUCTION

**market risk**
Risk related to the
uncertainty of an FI's
earnings on its trad-
ing portfolio caused
by changes in market
conditions.

**Market risk** can be defined as the risk related to the uncertainty of an FI's earnings on its trading portfolio caused by changes, and particularly extreme changes,
in market conditions such as the price of an asset, interest rates, market volatility, and market liquidity.[1] Thus, risks such as interest rate risk (discussed in
Chapters 8 and 9), credit risk (including credit risk from sovereign debt exposure,
discussed in Chapters 10, 11, and 14), liquidity risk (discussed in Chapter 12),
and foreign exchange risk (discussed in Chapter 13) affect market risk. However,
market risk emphasizes the risks to FIs that actively trade assets and liabilities
(and derivatives) rather than hold them for longer-term investment, funding, or
hedging purposes.

Indeed, market risk was at the heart of much of the losses associated with the
financial crisis. Signs of significant problems in the U.S. economy first arose in
late 2006 and the first half of 2007 when home prices plummeted and defaults
by subprime mortgage borrowers began to affect the mortgage lending industry
as a whole, as well as other parts of the economy, noticeably. As mortgage borrowers defaulted on their mortgages, financial institutions that held and actively
traded these mortgages and mortgage-backed securities started announcing huge
losses on them. Losses from the falling value of subprime mortgages and securities backed by these mortgages reached more than $1 trillion worldwide through
mid-2009. Investment banks and securities firms were major traders of mortgage-
backed securities. As mortgage borrowers defaulted on their mortgages, investment banks were particularly hard hit with huge losses on the mortgages and
securities backing them.

A prime example of the losses incurred is that of Bear Stearns. In the summer of
2007, two Bear Stearns hedge funds suffered heavy market risk related losses on
investments in the subprime mortgage market. The two funds filed for bankruptcy
in the fall of 2007. Bear Stearns' market value was hurt badly from these losses.
The losses became so great that in March 2008 J.P. Morgan Chase and the Federal
Reserve stepped in to rescue the then fifth largest investment bank in the United
States before it failed or was sold piecemeal to various financial institutions. The
market risk meltdown continued through the summer and fall of 2008. On Monday,
September 15, Lehman Brothers (the 158-year-old investment bank) filed for bank-
ruptcy, Merrill Lynch was bought by Bank of America, AIG (one of the world's

---

[1] Market risk used by FI managers and regulators is not synonymous with systematic market risk analyzed
by investors in securities markets. Systematic (market) risk reflects the co-movement of a security with
the market portfolio (reflected by the security's beta), although beta is used to measure the market risk of
equities, as noted below.

largest insurance companies) met with federal regulators to raise desperately needed cash, and Washington Mutual (the largest savings institution in the United States) was acquired by J.P. Morgan Chase. As news spread that Lehman Brothers would not survive, financial institutions moved to disentangle trades made with Lehman. The Dow fell more than 500 points, the largest drop in over seven years. Also by Wednesday, tension mounted around the world. Stock markets saw huge swings in value as investors tried to sort out who might survive (markets from Russia to Europe were forced to suspend trading as stock prices plunged). By mid-September, financial markets froze and banks stopped lending to each other at anything but exorbitantly high rates. Market risk was the root cause of much of this market failure and substantial losses incurred by financial institutions.

Conceptually, an FI's trading portfolio can be differentiated from its investment portfolio on the basis of time horizon and liquidity. The trading portfolio contains assets, liabilities, and derivative contracts that can be quickly bought or sold on organized financial markets (such as long and short positions in bonds, commodities, foreign exchange, equity securities, interest rate swaps, and options). Further, with the increasing securitization of bank loans (e.g., mortgages), more and more assets have become liquid and tradable (e.g., mortgage-backed securities). Additionally, many large syndicated loans are often partly sold off (participations in loans, see Chapter 25). The lead bank usually retains a percentage (normally 15 to 30 percent). These syndicated loans can be viewed as held for sale and thus part of the trading book. The investment portfolio (or, in the case of banks, the so-called banking book) contains assets and liabilities that are relatively illiquid and held for longer holding periods (such as consumer and commercial loans, retail deposits, and branches). Table 15–1 shows a hypothetical breakdown between banking book and trading book assets and liabilities. Note that capital produces a cushion against losses on either the banking or trading books—see Chapter 20.

Income from trading activities is increasingly replacing income from traditional FI activities of deposit taking and lending. The resulting earnings uncertainty, or market risk, can be measured over periods as short as a day or as long as a year. While bank regulators have normally viewed tradable assets as those being held for horizons of less than one year, private FIs take an even shorter-term view. In particular, FIs are concerned about the fluctuation in value—or value at risk (VAR)—of their trading account assets and liabilities for periods as short as one day—especially if such fluctuations pose a threat to their solvency. Moreover, market risk can be defined in absolute terms as a *dollar* exposure amount or as a

**TABLE 15–1**
The Investment (Banking) Book and Trading Book of a Commercial Bank

| | Assets | Liabilities |
|---|---|---|
| **Banking Book** | Cash<br>Loans<br>Premises and equipment<br>Other illiquid assets | Deposits<br>Other illiquid borrowed funds<br>Capital |
| **Trading Book** | Bonds (long)<br>Commodities (long)<br>FX (long)<br>Equities (long)<br>Mortgage-backed securities (long) | Bonds (short)<br>Commodities (short)<br>FX (short)<br>Equities (short) |
| | Derivatives* (long) | Derivatives* (short) |

* Derivatives are off-balance-sheet (as discussed in Chapter 6).

relative amount against some benchmark. For example, Bank of America's 2011 Annual Report (p. 114) states, "To evaluate risk in our trading activities, we focus on the actual and potential volatility of individual positions as well as portfolios. VAR is the key statistic used to measure market risk. In order to manage day-to-day risks, VAR is subject to trading limits both for our overall trading portfolio and within individual businesses." In recent years, market risk of FIs has raised considerable concern among regulators as well. So important is market risk in determining the viability of an FI that since 1998, U.S. regulators have included market risk in determining the required level of capital an FI must hold.

Further, part of the Wall Street Reform and Consumer Protection Act, passed in 2010 in response to the financial crisis, is the Volker Rule (to be implemented by banks by July 2014 at the earliest). The Volcker Rule prohibits U.S. depository institutions (DIs) from engaging in proprietary trading (i.e., any transaction to purchase or sell as a principal for the trading account of the bank) and from investing in hedge funds or private equity funds. However, a DI may organize and offer a hedge fund or private equity fund if it does not have an ownership interest in the fund except for a seed investment that is limited to no more than 3 percent of total ownership interest of the fund within one year after the date of establishment of the fund. Additionally, the DI's overall investment in hedge funds or private equity funds may not exceed 3 percent of the DI's tier 1 capital. The rule was named after former Federal Reserve Chairman Paul Volcker, who had been outspoken in his claims that such activities played a major part in the financial crisis. The Volker Rule is intended to restrict speculative trades made by depository institutions with their own money and, thus, is intended to reduce market risk at depository institutions. However, some have said the new rules are anti–bank specialness. This argument stems from the fact that the new rules on FIs' trading portfolios virtually force FIs to hold a matched maturity book. This limits the traditional specialness in bank maturity intermediation—that is, borrow in the short-term funds market to lend in the long-term market.

Table 15–2 summarizes several benefits of measuring market risk, including providing management with information on the extent of market risk exposure, market risk limits, resource allocation, and performance evaluation, as well as providing regulators with information on how to protect banks and the financial system against failure due to extreme market risk. The sections that follow concentrate on absolute dollar measures of market risk. We look at three major approaches that are being used to measure market risk: RiskMetrics, historic or back simulation, and Monte Carlo simulation. The link between market risk and required capital levels is also discussed in the chapter.

# CALCULATING MARKET RISK EXPOSURE

Large commercial banks, investment banks, insurance companies, and mutual funds have all developed market risk models. In the development of these models, four major approaches have been followed:

- RiskMetrics (or the variance/covariance approach).
- Historic or back simulation.
- Monte Carlo simulation.
- Expected shortfall.

**TABLE 15–2**
Benefits of Market
Risk Measurement
(MRM)

1. *Management information.* MRM provides senior management with information on the risk exposure taken by FI traders. Management can then compare this risk exposure to the FI's capital resources.
2. *Setting limits.* MRM considers the market risk of traders' portfolios, which will lead to the establishment of economically logical position limits per trader in each area of trading.
3. *Resource allocation.* MRM involves the comparison of returns to market risks in different areas of trading, which may allow for the identification of areas with the greatest potential return per unit of risk into which more capital and resources can be directed.
4. *Performance evaluation.* MRM considers the return-risk ratio of traders, which may allow a more rational bonus (compensation) system to be put in place. That is, those traders with the highest returns may simply be the ones who have taken the largest risks. It is not clear that they should receive higher compensation than traders with lower returns and lower risk exposures.
5. *Regulation.* With the Bank for International Settlements (BIS) and Federal Reserve currently regulating market risk through capital requirements (discussed later in this chapter), private sector benchmarks are important, since it is possible that regulators will overprice some risks. MRM conducted by the FI can be used to point to potential misallocations of resources as a result of prudential regulation. As a result, in certain cases regulators are allowing banks to use their own (internal) models to calculate their capital requirements.

The first three models offer different methods used to calculate value at risk. We consider RiskMetrics first and then compare it with other internal model approaches, such as historic or back simulation. The expected shortfall model (also called the conditional value at risk) is an alternative to the traditional value at risk measure that is more sensitive to the shape of the loss tail of the probability distribution of returns. Starting in January 2013, regulators have replaced value at risk with the expected shortfall measure as the main measure of market risk.

# THE RISKMETRICS MODEL

The ultimate objective of market risk measurement models can best be seen from the following question from an FI manager: "I am X% sure that the FI will not lose more than $VAR in the next T days." In a nutshell, the FI manager wants a single *dollar* number that tells him the FI's market risk exposure over the next days—especially if those days turn out to be extremely "bad" days.

This can be nontrivial, given the extent of a large or even mid-sized FI's trading business. When JPM developed its RiskMetrics model in 1994 it had 14 active trading locations with 120 independent units trading fixed-income securities, foreign exchange, commodities, derivatives, emerging-market securities, and proprietary assets.[2] In 2011, J.P. Morgan Chase operated worldwide and held a trading portfolio worth over more than $444 billion. This scale and variety of activities is typical of the major money center banks, large overseas banks (e.g., Deutsche Bank and Barclays), and major insurance companies and investment banks.

---

[2] J.P. Morgan (JPM) first developed RiskMetrics in 1994. In 1998 the Corporate Risk Management Department that operated RiskMetrics was spun off from J.P. Morgan and became known as RiskMetrics Group. The company went public in January 2008 and was subsequently acquired, in June 2010, by MSCI. The material presented in this chapter is an overview of the RiskMetrics model. The details, additional discussion, and examples are found in "Return to RiskMetrics: The Evolution of a Standard," April 2001, available at the J.P. Morgan Chase website, **www.jpmorganchase.com**, or **www.riskmetrics.com**.

Here, we will concentrate on measuring the market risk exposure of a major FI on a daily basis using the RiskMetrics approach. As will be discussed later, measuring the risk exposure for periods longer than a day (e.g., five days) is under certain assumptions a simple transformation of the daily risk exposure number. Essentially, the FI is concerned with how to preserve equity if market conditions move adversely tomorrow; that is:

Market risk = Estimated potential loss under adverse circumstances

**daily earnings at risk (DEAR)**
Market risk exposure over the next 24 hours.

More specifically, the market risk is measured in terms of the FI's **daily earnings at risk (DEAR)** and has three components:

$$\begin{array}{c}\text{Daily earnings}\\\text{at risk}\end{array} = \left(\begin{array}{c}\text{Dollar market}\\\text{value of}\\\text{the position}\end{array}\right) \times \left(\begin{array}{c}\text{Price}\\\text{sensitivity of}\\\text{the position}\end{array}\right) \times \left(\begin{array}{c}\text{Potential}\\\text{adverse move}\\\text{in yield}\end{array}\right)$$

Since price sensitivity multiplied by adverse yield move measures the degree of price volatility of an asset, we can also write this equation as:

$$\begin{array}{c}\text{Daily earnings}\\\text{at risk}\end{array} = \left(\begin{array}{c}\text{Dollar market}\\\text{value of}\\\text{the position}\end{array}\right) \times \left(\begin{array}{c}\text{Price}\\\text{volatility}\end{array}\right) \tag{1}$$

How price sensitivity and an adverse yield move will be measured depends on the FI and its choice of a price-sensitivity model as well as its view of what exactly is a potentially adverse price (yield) move.

We concentrate on how the RiskMetrics model calculates daily earnings at risk in three trading areas—fixed income, foreign exchange (FX), and equities—and then on how it estimates the aggregate risk of the entire trading portfolio to meet an FI manager's objective of a single aggregate dollar exposure measure across the whole bank on a given day.

## The Market Risk of Fixed-Income Securities

Suppose an FI has a $1 million market value position in zero-coupon bonds of seven years to maturity with a face value of $1,631,483. Today's yield on these bonds is 7.243 percent per year.[3] These bonds are held as part of the trading portfolio. Thus,

Dollar market value of position = $1 million

The FI manager wants to know the potential exposure the FI faces should interest rates move against the FI as the result of an adverse or reasonably bad market

---

[3] The face value of the bonds is $1,631,483—that is, $1,631,483/(1.07243)^7 = $1,000,000 market value. In the original model, prices were determined using a discrete rate of return, $R_j$. In the April 2001 document "Return to RiskMetrics: The Evolution of a Standard," prices are determined using a continuously compounded return, $e^{-rt}$. The change was implemented because continuous compounding has properties that facilitate mathematical treatment. For example, the logarithmic return on a zero-coupon bond equals the difference of interest rates multiplied by the maturity of the bond. That is:

$$\ln\left(\frac{e^{-\tilde{r}t}}{e^{-rt}}\right) = -(\tilde{r} - r)t$$

where $\tilde{r}$ is the expected return.

move the next day. How much the FI will lose depends on the bond's price volatility. From the duration model in Chapter 9 we know that:

Daily price volatility = (Price sensitivity to a small change in yield)

$$\times \text{ (Adverse daily yield move)} \qquad \textbf{(2)}$$

$$= (MD) \times \text{ (Adverse daily yield move)}$$

The modified duration (MD) of this bond is:[4]

$$MD = \frac{D}{1 + R} = \frac{7}{(1.07243)} = 6.527$$

given that the yield on the bond is $R = 7.243$ percent. To estimate price volatility, multiply the bond's MD by the expected adverse daily yield move.

| | |
|---|---|
| **EXAMPLE 15–1**<br><br>*Daily Earnings at Risk on Fixed-Income Securities* | Suppose we define bad yield changes such that there is only a 1 percent chance that the yield changes will exceed this amount in either direction—or, since we are concerned only with bad outcomes, and we are long in bonds, that there is 1 chance in 100 (or a 1 percent chance) that the next day's yield increase (or shock) will exceed this given adverse move.<br><br>If we assume that yield changes are normally distributed,[5] we can fit a normal distribution to the histogram of recent past changes in seven-year zero-coupon interest rates (yields) to get an estimate of the size of this adverse rate move. From statistics, we know that (the middle) 98 percent of the area under the normal distribution is to be found within $\pm 2.33$ standard deviations ($\sigma$) from the mean—that is, $2.33\sigma$—and 2 percent of the area under the normal distribution is found beyond $\pm 2.33\sigma$ (1 percent under each tail, $-2.33\sigma$ and $+2.33\sigma$, respectively).[6] Suppose that during the last year the mean change in daily yields on seven-year zero-coupon bonds was 0 percent,[7] while the standard deviation was 10 basis points (or 0.001). Thus, $2.33\sigma$ is 23.3 basis points (bp).[8] In other words, over the last year, daily yields on seven-year, zero-coupon bonds have fluctuated (either positively or negatively) by more than 23.3 bp 2 percent of the time. Adverse moves in yields are those that decrease the value of the security (i.e., the yield increases). These occurred 1 percent of the time, or 1 in 100 days. This is shown in Figure 15–1. |

[4] Assuming annual compounding for simplicity.

[5] In reality, many asset return distributions—such as exchange rates and interest rates—have "fat tails." Thus, the normal distribution will tend to underestimate extreme outcomes. This is a major criticism of the RiskMetrics modeling approach and a major reason for regulators' move to the use of expected shortfall from the traditional value at risk measure of market risk. Further, the original CreditMetrics calculation of DEAR incorporated a 5 percent chance that the next day's yield increase will exceed this given adverse move. The use of 1 percent to measure adverse moves produces a more conservative estimate of an FI's value at risk.

[6] For 95 percent of the area under the normal distribution (2.5 percent under each tail), we use $\pm 1.96$, and for 90 percent of the area (5 percent under each tail) we use $\pm 1.65$. CreditMetrics originally used the 90 percent confidence level.

[7] If the mean were nonzero (e.g., $-1$ basis point), this could be added to the 23.3 bp (i.e., 22.3 bp) to project the yield shock.

[8] RiskMetrics weights more recent observations more highly than past observations (this is called *exponential weighting*). This allows more recent news to be more heavily reflected in the calculation of $\sigma$. Regular $\sigma$ calculations put an equal weight on all past observations.

We can now calculate the potential daily price volatility on seven-year discount bonds using equation (2) as:

$$\text{Price volatility} = (MD) \times (\text{Potential adverse move in yield})$$
$$= (6.527) \times (0.00233)$$
$$= 0.01521 \text{ or } 1.521\%$$

Given this price volatility and the initial market value of the seven-year bond portfolio, then equation (1) can be used to calculate the daily earnings at risk as:[9]

$$\text{Daily earnings at risk} = (\text{Dollar market value of position}) \times (\text{Price volatility})$$
$$= (\$1,000,000) \times (0.01521)$$
$$= \$15,210$$

That is, the potential daily loss in earnings on the $1 million position is $15,210 if the 1 bad day in 100 occurs tomorrow.

We can extend this analysis to calculate the potential loss over 2, 3, . . . N days. If we assume that yield shocks are independent and daily volatility is approximately constant,[10] and that the FI is locked in to holding this asset for N number

**FIGURE 15–1**
**Adverse Rate Move,**
**Seven-Year Rates**

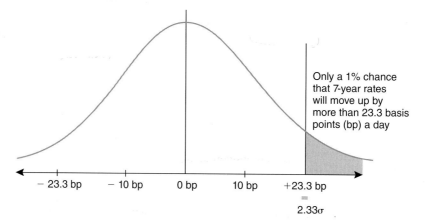

Only a 1% chance that 7-year rates will move up by more than 23.3 basis points (bp) a day

− 23.3 bp  − 10 bp  0 bp  10 bp  +23.3 bp
=
2.33σ

[9] Since we are calculating loss, we drop the minus sign here.

[10] The assumptions that daily volatility is constant and that there is no autocorrelation in yield shocks are strong assumptions. Much recent literature suggests that shocks are autocorrelated in many asset markets over relatively long horizons. To understand why we take the square root of N, consider a five-day holding period. The $\sigma_5^2$, or five-day variance of asset returns, will equal the current one-day variance, $\sigma_1^2$, times 5 under the assumptions of constant daily variance and no autocorrelation in shocks, or:

$$\sigma_5^2 = \sigma_1^2 \times 5$$

The standard deviation of this equation is:

$$\sigma_5 = \sigma_1 \times \sqrt{5}$$

or since DEAR is measured in the same dimensions as a standard deviation ($\sigma$), in the terminology of Risk-Metrics, the five-day value at risk is:

$$\text{5-day } VAR = DEAR \times \sqrt{5}$$

of days, then the N-day market value at risk (VAR) is related to daily earnings at risk (DEAR) by:

$$N\text{-day } VAR = DEAR \times \sqrt{N} \qquad (3)$$

That is, the earnings the FI has at risk, should interest rate yields move against the FI, are a function of the value or earnings at risk for one day (DEAR) and the (square root of the) number of days that the FI is forced to hold the securities because of an illiquid market. Specifically, DEAR assumes that the FI can sell all the bonds tomorrow, even at the new lower price. In reality, it may take many days for the FI to unload its position. This relative illiquidity of a market exposes the FI to magnified losses (measured by the square root of N).[11] If N is five days, then:

$$5\text{-day } VAR = \$15,210 \times \sqrt{5} = \$34,011$$

If N is 10 days, then:[12]

$$10\text{-day } VAR = \$15,210 \times \sqrt{10} = \$48,098$$

In the preceding calculations, we estimated price sensitivity using modified duration. However, the RiskMetrics model generally prefers using the present value of cash flow changes as the price-sensitivity weights over modified durations. Essentially, each cash flow is discounted by the appropriate zero-coupon rate to generate the daily earnings at risk measure. If we used the direct cash flow calculation in this case, the loss would be $15,209.63.[13] The estimates in this case are very close.

## Foreign Exchange

Large FIs also actively trade in foreign exchange (FX). Remember that:

$$DEAR = (\text{Dollar value of position}) \times (\text{Price volatility})$$

**EXAMPLE 15–2**
*Daily Earnings at Risk of Foreign Exchange Contracts*

Suppose the FI had a €800,000 trading position in spot euros at the close of business on a particular day. The FI wants to calculate the daily earnings at risk from this position (i.e., the risk exposure on this position should the next day be a bad day in the FX markets with respect to the value of the euro against the dollar).

The first step is to calculate the dollar value of the position:

Dollar equivalent value of position = (FX position) × ($ per unit of foreign currency)

Suppose for simplicity that the exchange rate is €0.8000/$1 or $1.25/€ at the daily close; then:

Dollar value of position = €800,000 × $1.25/€
= $ 1 million

[11] In practice, a number of FIs calculate N internally by dividing the position held in a security by the median daily volume of trading of that security over recent days. Thus, if trading volume is low because of a "one-way market," in that most people are seeking to sell rather than buy, then N can rise substantially; that is, N = ($ position in security/median daily $ volume of trading).

[12] Under the BIS market risk capital requirements, a 10-day holding period (N = 10) is assumed to measure exposure.

[13] The initial market value of the seven-year zero was $1,000,000, or $1,631,483/(1.07243)[7]. The (loss) effect on each $1 (market value) invested in the bond of a rise in rates by 1 bp from 7.243 percent to 7.253 percent is 0.00065277. However, the adverse rate move is 23.3 bp. Thus:

$$DEAR = (\$1 \text{ million}) \times (0.00065277) \times (23.3) = \$15,210$$

Suppose that, looking back at the €/$ exchange rate over the past year, we find that the volatility, or standard deviation ($\sigma$), of daily percentage changes in the spot exchange rate was 56.5 bp. However, suppose that the FI is interested in adverse moves—that is, bad moves that will not occur more than 1 percent of the time, or 1 day in every 100. Statistically speaking, if changes in exchange rates are historically "normally" distributed, the exchange rate must change in the adverse direction by $2.33\sigma$ ($2.33 \times 56.5$ bp) for this change to be viewed as likely to occur only 1 day in every 100 days:[14]

$$\text{FX volatility} = 2.33 \times 56.5 \text{ bp} = 131.645 \text{ bp}$$

In other words, during the last year, the euro declined in value against the dollar by 131.645 bp 1 percent of the time. As a result:

$$
\begin{aligned}
DEAR &= (\text{Dollar value of position}) \times (\text{FX volatility}) \\
&= (\$1 \text{ million}) \times (0.0131645) \\
&= \$13,164
\end{aligned}
$$

This is the potential daily earnings exposure to adverse euro to dollar exchange rate changes for the FI from the €1.4 million spot currency holdings.

## Equities

Many large FIs also take positions in equities. As is well known from the Capital Asset Pricing Model (CAPM), there are two types of risk to an equity position in an individual stock *i*:

$$
\begin{aligned}
\text{Total risk} &= \text{Systematic risk} + \text{Unsystematic risk} \\
(\sigma_{it}^2) &= (\beta_i^2 \sigma_{mt}^2) + (\sigma_{eit}^2)
\end{aligned}
\tag{4}
$$

**beta**
Systematic (undiversifiable) risk reflecting the co-movement of the returns on a specific stock with returns on the market portfolio.

Systematic risk reflects the co-movement of that stock with the market portfolio reflected by the stock's **beta** ($\beta_i$) and the volatility of the market portfolio ($\sigma_{mt}$), while unsystematic risk is specific to the firm itself ($\sigma_{eit}$).

In a very well diversified portfolio, unsystematic risk ($\sigma_{eit}^2$) can be largely diversified away (i.e., will equal zero), leaving behind systematic (undiversifiable) market risk ($\beta_i^2 \sigma_{mt}^2$). If the FI's trading portfolio follows (replicates) the returns on the stock market index, the $\beta$ of that portfolio will be 1, since the movement of returns on the FI's portfolio will be one to one with the market,[15] and the standard deviation of the portfolio, $\sigma_{it}$, will be equal to the standard deviation of the stock market index, $\sigma_{mt}$.

---

[14] Technically, 98 percent of the area under a normal distribution lies between $+/- 2.33\sigma$ from the mean. This means that 1 percent of the time, daily exchange rate changes will increase by more than $2.33\sigma$, and 1 percent of the time, will decrease by $2.33\sigma$. This case concerns only adverse moves in the exchange rate of euros to dollars (i.e., a depreciation of $2.33\sigma$).

[15] If $\beta \neq 1$, as in the case of most individual stocks, $DEAR = $ dollar value of position $\times \beta_i \times 2.33\sigma_m$, where $\beta_i$ is the systematic risk of the *i*th stock.

**EXAMPLE 15–3**

*Daily Earnings at Risk on Equities*

Suppose the FI holds a $1 million trading position in stocks that reflect a U.S. stock market index (e.g., the Wilshire 5000). Then $\beta = 1$ and the DEAR for equities is:

$$DEAR = \text{(Dollar market value of position)} \times \text{(Stock market return volatility)}$$
$$= (\$1,000,000) \times (2.33\,\sigma_m)$$

If, over the last year, the $\sigma_m$ of the daily returns on the stock market index was 200 bp, then $2.33\sigma_m = 466$ bp (i.e., the adverse change or decline in the daily return on the stock market exceeded 466 bp only 1 percent of the time). In this case:

$$DEAR = (\$1,000,000) \times (0.0466)$$
$$= \$46,600$$

That is, the FI stands to lose at least $46,600 in earnings if adverse stock market returns materialize tomorrow.[16]

In less well diversified portfolios or portfolios of individual stocks, the effect of unsystematic risk $\sigma_{eit}$ on the value of the trading position would need to be added. Moreover, if the CAPM does not offer a good explanation of asset pricing compared with, say, multi-index arbitrage pricing theory (APT), a degree of error will be built into the DEAR calculation.[17]

## Portfolio Aggregation

The preceding sections analyzed the daily earnings at risk of individual trading positions. The examples considered a seven-year, zero-coupon, fixed-income security ($1 million market value); a position in spot euros ($1 million market value); and a position in the U.S. stock market index ($1 million market value). The individual DEARs were:

1. Seven-year, zero-coupon bonds = $15,210
2. Euro spot = $13,164
3. U.S. equities = $46,600

However, senior management wants to know the aggregate risk of the entire trading position. To calculate this, we *cannot* simply sum the three DEARs—$15,210 + $13,164 + $46,600 = $74,974—because that ignores any degree of offsetting covariance or correlation among the fixed-income, FX, and equity trading positions. In particular, some of these asset shocks (adverse moves) may be negatively correlated. As is well known from modern portfolio theory, anything but perfect positive correlations among asset shocks will reduce the degree of portfolio risk.

[16] If we consider a single equity security with a beta ($\beta$) = 1.25 (i.e., one that is more sensitive than the market, such that as market returns increase [decrease] by 1 percent, the security's return increases [decreases] by 1.25 percent), then with a $1 million investment and the same (assumed) volatility ($\sigma$) of 2 percent, the FI would stand to lose at least $58,250 in daily earnings if adverse stock returns materialize (i.e., $DEAR = \$1,000,000 \times 1.25 \times 2.33 \times 0.02 = \$58,250$).

[17] As noted in the introduction, derivatives are also used for trading purposes. In the calculation of its DEAR, a derivative has to be converted into a position in the underlying asset (e.g., bond, FX, or equity).

**EXAMPLE 15–4**
*Calculation of the DEAR of a Portfolio*

Table 15–3 shows a hypothetical correlation matrix between daily seven-year, zero-coupon bond yield changes, €/$ spot exchange rate changes, and changes in daily returns on a U.S. stock market index (Wilshire 5000). From Table 15–3, the correlation between the seven-year, zero-coupon bonds and €/$ exchange rates, $\rho_{z,\epsilon}$, is negative ($-0.2$), while U.S. stock return changes with, respectively, seven-year, zero coupon yields, $\rho_{z,U.S.}$ (0.4) and €/$ shocks, $\rho_{U.S.,\epsilon}$, (0.1) are positively correlated.

Using this correlation matrix along with the individual asset DEARs, we can calculate the risk or standard deviation of the whole (three-asset) trading portfolio as:[18]

$$DEAR \text{ portfolio} = \begin{bmatrix} [(DEAR_z)^2 + (DEAR_\epsilon)^2 + (DEAR_{U.S.})^2 \\ + (2 \times \rho_{z,\epsilon} \times DEAR_z \times DEAR_\epsilon) \\ + (2 \times \rho_{z,U.S.} \times DEAR_z \times DEAR_{U.S.}) \\ + (2 \times \rho_{U.S.,\epsilon} \times DEAR_{U.S.} \times DEAR_\epsilon)] \end{bmatrix}^{1/2} \quad (5)$$

This is a direct application of modern portfolio theory (MPT) since DEARs are directly similar to standard deviations. Substituting into equation (5) the calculated individual DEARs, we get:

$$DEAR \text{ portfolio} = \begin{bmatrix} [(15,210)^2 + (13,164)^2 + (46,600)^2 + 2(-0.2)(15,210)(13,164) \\ + 2(0.4)(15,210)(46,600) + 2(0.1)(13,164)(46,600)] \end{bmatrix}^{1/2}$$

$$= \$56,443$$

The equation indicates that considering the risk of each trading position as well as the correlation structure among those positions' returns results in a lower measure of portfolio trading risk ($56,443) than when risks of the underlying trading positions (the sum of which was $74,974) are added. A quick check will reveal that had we assumed that all three assets were perfectly positively correlated (i.e., $\rho_{ij} = 1$), DEAR for the portfolio would have been $74,974 (i.e., equal to the sum of the three DEARs). Clearly, even in abnormal market conditions, assuming that asset returns are perfectly correlated will exaggerate the degree of actual trading risk exposure.

Table 15–4 shows the type of spreadsheet used by FIs to calculate DEAR. As you can see, in this example, positions are taken in 13 different country (currency) bonds in eight different maturity buckets.[19] There is also a column for FX risk (and, if necessary, equity risk) in these different country markets, although in this example, the FI has no FX risk exposure (all the cells are empty).

[18] This is a standard relationship from modern portfolio theory in which the standard deviation or risk of a portfolio of three assets is equal to the square root of the sum of the variances of returns on each of the three assets individually plus two times the covariances among each pair of these assets. With three assets there are three covariances. Here we use the fact that a correlation coefficient times the standard deviations on each pair of assets equals the covariance between each pair of assets. Note that DEAR is measured in dollars and has the same dimensions as a standard deviation. We discussed modern portfolio theory in more detail in Chapter 11.

[19] Bonds held with different maturity dates (e.g., six years) are split into two and allocated to the nearest two of the eight maturity buckets (here, five years and seven years) using three criteria: (1) The sum of the current market *value* of the two resulting cash flows must be identical to the market value of the original cash flow; (2) the market *risk* of the portfolio of two cash flows must be identical to the overall market risk of the original cash flow; and (3) the two cash flows have the same *sign* as the original cash flow. See J.P. Morgan, "RiskMetrics—Technical Document," November 1994, and "Return to RiskMetrics: The Evolution of a Standard," April 2001, **www.msci.com**.

**TABLE 15–3**
Correlations ($\rho_{ij}$) among Assets

|  | 7-Year Zero | €/$1 | U.S. Stock Index |
|---|---|---|---|
| 7-year zero | — | −0.2 | .4 |
| €/$1 |  | — | .1 |
| U.S. stock index |  |  | — |

**TABLE 15–4**  **Portfolio DEAR Spreadsheet**

| | Interest Rate Risk Notional Amounts (US$ millions equivalents) | | | | | | | | Interest | FX Risk | | Total | |
|---|---|---|---|---|---|---|---|---|---|---|---|---|---|
| | 1 Month | 1 Year | 2 Years | 3 Years | 4 Years | 5 Years | 7 Years | 10 Years | DEAR ($000s) | Spot FX | FX DEAR | Portfolio Effect | Total DEAR |
| Australia | | | | | | | | | | AUD | | | |
| Brazil | | | | | | | | | | BRL | | | |
| Canada | | | | | | | | | | CAD | | | |
| Denmark | 19 | | | −30 | | | | 11 | 48 | DKK | | | 48 |
| European Union | −19 | | | 30 | | | | −11 | 27 | EUR | | | 27 |
| Hong Kong | | | | | | | | | | HKD | | | |
| Japan | | | | | | | | | | YEN | | | |
| Mexico | | | | | | | | | | MXN | | | |
| Singapore | | | | | | | | | | SGD | | | |
| Sweden | | | | | | | | | | SEK | | | |
| Switzerland | | | | | | | | | | CHF | | | |
| United Kingdom | | | | | | | | | | GBP | | | |
| United States | | | | | 10 | | | 10 | 76 | USD | | | 76 |
| Total | | | | | 10 | | | 10 | 151 | | | | 151 |
| | | | | | Portfolio effect | | | | (62) | | | | (62) |
| RISK | DATA | PRINT | CLOSE | | Total DEAR ($000s) | | | | 89 | | | | 89 |

In the example in Table 15–4, while the FI is holding offsetting long and short positions in both Danish bonds and Eurobonds, it is still exposed to trading risks of $48,000 and $27,000, respectively (see the column Interest DEAR). This happens because the European Union yield curve is more volatile than the Danish and shocks at different maturity buckets are not equal. The DEAR figure for a U.S. bond position of long $20 million is $76,000. Adding these three positions yields a DEAR of $151,000. However, this ignores the fact that Danish, European Union, and U.S. yield shocks are not perfectly correlated. Allowing for diversification effects (the portfolio effect) results in a total DEAR of only $89,000. This would be the number reported to the FI's senior management. Most financial institutions establish limits for value at risk, daily earnings at risk, position limits, and dollar trading loss limits for their trading portfolios. Actual activity compared with these limits is then monitored daily. Should a risk exposure level exceed approved limit levels, management must provide a strategy for bringing risk levels within approved limits. Table 15–5 reports the average, minimum, and maximum daily earnings at risk for several large U.S. commercial banks in 2005 and 2011. Note the increase in market risk for all of these FIs over this period. For example, Citigroup was exposed to an average DEAR of $109 million in 2005 and $153 million in 2011. Currently, the number of markets covered by Citigroup's traders and the number of correlations among those markets require the daily production and updating of over 250,000 volatility estimates ($\sigma$) and correlations ($\rho$). These data are updated daily.

**TABLE 15–5**
Daily Earnings at Risk for Large U.S. Commercial Banks, 2005 and 2011* (in millions of dollars)

Source: Year 2011 and 2005 10-K reports for the respective companies.

| Name | Average DEAR for the year | Minimum DEAR during the year | Maximum DEAR during the year |
|---|---|---|---|
| **2011:** | | | |
| Bank of America | $167 | $ 75 | $319 |
| Citigroup | 153 | 104 | 205 |
| J.P. Morgan Chase | 101 | 67 | 147 |
| KeyCorp | 2 | 1 | 2 |
| Wells Fargo | 29 | 19 | 42 |
| Sun Trust | 5 | 3 | 7 |
| **2005:** | | | |
| Bank of America | $ 62 | $ 38 | $ 92 |
| Citigroup | 109 | 78 | 157 |
| J.P. Morgan Chase | 86 | 53 | 130 |
| KeyCorp | 2 | 1 | 5 |
| Wells Fargo | 18 | 11 | 24 |
| Sun Trust | 4 | 2 | 6 |

* The figures are based on these banks' internal models, i.e., they may be based on methodologies other than RiskMetrics.

---

**Concept Questions**

1. What is the ultimate objective of market risk measurement models?
2. Refer to Example 15–1. What is the DEAR for this bond if $\sigma$ is 15 bp?
3. Refer to Example 15–4. What is the DEAR of the portfolio if the returns on the three assets are independent of each other?

---

# HISTORIC (BACK SIMULATION) APPROACH

A major criticism of RiskMetrics is the need to assume a symmetric (normal) distribution for all asset returns.[20] Clearly, for some assets, such as options and short-term securities (bonds), this is highly questionable. For example, the most an investor can lose if he or she buys a call option on an equity is the call premium.

[20] Another criticism is that VAR models like RiskMetrics ignore the (risk in the) payments of accrued interest on an FI's debt securities. Thus, VAR models will underestimate the true probability of default and the appropriate level of capital to be held against this risk. Also, because of the distributional assumptions, while RiskMetrics produces reasonable estimates of downside risk for FIs with highly diversified portfolios, FIs with small, undiversified portfolios will significantly underestimate their true risk exposure using RiskMetrics. Further, a number of authors have argued that many asset distributions have "fat tails" and that RiskMetrics, by assuming the normal distribution, underestimates the risk of extreme losses. One alternative approach to dealing with the "fat-tail" problem is extreme value theory. Simply put, one can view an asset distribution as being explained by two distributions. For example, a normal distribution may explain returns up to the 95 percent threshold, but for losses beyond that threshold another distribution, such as the generalized Pareto distribution, may provide a better explanation of loss outcomes such as the 99 percent level and beyond. In short, the normal distribution is likely to underestimate the importance and size of observations in the tail of the distribution, which is, after all, what value at risk models are meant to be measuring. Finally, VAR models by definition concern themselves with risk rather than return. It should be noted that minimizing risk may be highly costly in terms of the return the FI gives up. Indeed, there may be many more return–risk combinations preferable to that achieved at the minimum risk point in the trading portfolio. Recent upgrades to RiskMetrics (see the RiskMetrics Web site at **www.msci.com**) allow management to incorporate a return dimension to VAR analysis so that management can evaluate how trading portfolio returns differ as VAR changes.

However, the investor's potential upside returns are unlimited. In a statistical sense, the returns on call options are nonnormal since they exhibit a positive skew.[21]

Because of these and other considerations discussed herein, many FIs that have developed market risk models have employed a historic or back simulation approach. The advantages of this approach are that (1) it is simple, (2) it does not require that asset returns be normally distributed, and (3) it does not require that the correlations or standard deviations of asset returns be calculated.

The essential idea is to take the current market portfolio of assets (FX, bonds, equities, etc.) and revalue them on the basis of the actual prices (returns) that existed on those assets yesterday, the day before that, and so on. Frequently, the FI will calculate the market or value risk of its current portfolio on the basis of prices (returns) that existed for those assets on each of the last 500 days. It will then calculate the 1 percent worst case—the portfolio value that has the 5th lowest value out of 500. That is, on only 5 days out of 500, or 1 percent of the time, would the value of the portfolio fall below this number based on recent historic experience of exchange rate changes, equity price changes, interest rate changes, and so on.

Consider the following simple example in Table 15–6, where a U.S. FI is trading two currencies: the Japanese yen and the Swiss franc. At the close of trading on December 1, 2015, it has a long position in Japanese yen of 500 million and a long position in Swiss francs of 20 million. It wants to assess its VAR. That is, if tomorrow is that 1 bad day in 100 (the 1 percent worst case), how much does it stand to lose on its total foreign currency position? As shown in Table 15–6, six steps are required to calculate the VAR of its currency portfolio. It should be noted that the same methodological approach would be followed to calculate the VAR of any asset, liability, or derivative (bonds, options, etc.) as long as market prices were available on those assets over a sufficiently long historic time period.

- *Step 1: Measure exposures.* Convert today's foreign currency positions into dollar equivalents using today's exchange rates. Thus, an evaluation of the FX position of the FI on December 1, 2015, indicates that it has a long position of $5,000,000 (¥500,000,000/(¥100/$1)) in yen and $18,181,818 (SF20,000,000/(SF1.1/$1)) in Swiss francs.

- *Step 2: Measure sensitivity.* Measure the sensitivity of each FX position by calculating its delta, where delta measures the change in the dollar value of each FX position if the yen or the Swiss franc depreciates (declines in value) by 1 percent against the dollar.[22] As can be seen from Table 15–6, line 6, the delta for the Japanese yen position is −$49,505 (or, (¥500,000,000/(¥101/$1) − ¥500,000,000/(¥100/$1)), and for the Swiss franc position, it is −$180,018 (or (SF20,000,000/(SF1.111/$1) − SF20,000,000/(SF1.1/$1)).

- *Step 3: Measure risk.* Look at the actual percentage changes in exchange rates, ¥/$ and SF/$, on each of the past 500 days. Thus, on November 30, 2015, the yen declined in value against the dollar over the day by 0.5 percent while the Swiss franc declined in value against the dollar by 0.2 percent. (It might be noted that if the currencies were to appreciate in value against the dollar, the sign against the number in row 7 of Table 15–6 would be negative; that is, it

---

[21] For a normal distribution, its skew (which is the third moment of a distribution) is zero.

[22] That is, in the case of FX, delta measures the dollar change in FX holdings for a 1 percent change in the foreign exchange rate. In the case of equities, it would measure the change in the value of those securities for a 1 percent change in price, while for bonds, it measures the change in value for a 1 percent change in the yield on the bond (note that delta measures sensitivity of a bond's value to a change in yield, not price).

**TABLE 15–6**   Hypothetical Example of the Historic, or Back Simulation, Approach Using Two Currencies, as of December 1, 2015

| | Yen | Swiss Franc |
|---|---|---|
| **Step 1. Measure exposures** | | |
| 1. Closing position on December 1, 2015 | ¥500,000,000 | SF20,000,000 |
| 2. Exchange rate on December 1, 2015 | ¥100/$1 | SF1.1/$1 |
| 3. U.S. $ equivalent position on December 1, 2015 | $5,000,000 | $18,181,818 |
| **Step 2. Measure sensitivity** | | |
| 4. 1.01 × current exchange rate *decline* | ¥101/$1 | SF1.111/$1 |
| 5. Revalued position in $s | $4,950,495 | $18,001,800 |
| 6. Delta of position ($s) (measure of sensitivity to a 1% adverse change in exchange rate, or row 5 minus row 3) | −$49,505 | −$180,018 |
| **Step 3. Measure risk of December 1, 2015, closing position using exchange rates that existed on each of the last 500 days** | | |

| **November 30, 2015** | *decline* | Yen | Swiss Franc |
|---|---|---|---|
| 7. Change in exchange rate (%) on November 30, 2015 | | 0.5% | 0.2% |
| 8. Risk (<u>delta × change in exchange rate</u>) | | −$24,752.5 | −$36,003.6 |
| 9. Sum of risks = <u>−$60,756.1</u> | | | |

**Step 4. Repeat step 3 for each of the remaining 499 days**

November 29, 2015
⋮

April 15, 2014
⋮

November 30, 2013
⋮

**Step 5. Rank days by risk from worst to best**

| Date | Risk ($) |
|---|---|
| 1. May 6, 2014 | −$119,096 |
| 2. Jan 27, 2015 | −$116,703 |
| 3. Dec 1, 2013 | −$104,366 |
| 4. Sept 14, 2013 | −100,248 |
| 5. Aug 8, 2014 | −97,210 |
| ⋮ | ⋮ |
| 25. Nov 30, 2015 | −$60,756.1 |
| ⋮ | ⋮ |
| 499. April 8, 2015 | +$112,260 |
| 500. July 28, 2014 | +$121,803 |

**Step 6. VAR (5th worst day out of last 500)**

VAR = −97,210 (August 8, 2014)

takes fewer units of foreign currency to buy a dollar than it did the day before). As can be seen in row 8, combining the delta and the actual percentage change in each FX rate means a total loss of $60,756.1 if the FI had held the current ¥500,000,000 and SF20,000,000 positions on that day (November 30, 2015).

- *Step 4: Repeat step 3.* Step 4 repeats the same exercise for the yen and Swiss franc positions but uses actual exchange rate changes on November 29, 2015; November 28, 2015; and so on. That is, we calculate the FX losses and/or gains on each of the past 500 trading days, excluding weekends and holidays, when the FX market is closed. This amounts to going back in time over two years. For each of these days the actual change in exchange rates is calculated (row 7) and multiplied by the deltas of each position (the numbers in row 6 of Table 15–6). These two numbers are summed to attain total risk measures for each of the past 500 days.

- *Step 5: Rank days by risk from worst to best.* These risk measures can then be ranked from worst to best. Clearly the worst-case loss would have occurred on this position on May 6, 2014, with a total loss of $119,096. While this worst case scenario is of interest to FI managers, we are interested in the 1 percent worst case, that is, a loss that does not occur more than 5 days out of the 500 days ($5 \div 500 = 1$ percent). As can be seen, in our example, the 5th worst loss out of 500 occurred on August 8, 2014. This loss amounted to $97,210.

- *Step 6: VAR.* If it is assumed that the recent past distribution of exchange rates is an accurate reflection of the likely distribution of FX rate changes in the future — that exchange rate changes have a stationary distribution—then the $97,210 can be viewed as the FX value at risk (VAR) exposure of the FI on December 1, 2015. That is, if tomorrow (in our case, December 2, 2015) is a bad day in the FX markets, and given the FI's position of long yen 500 million and long Swiss francs 20 million, the FI can expect to lose $97,210 (or more) with a 1 percent probability. This VAR measure can then be updated every day as the FX position changes and the delta changes. For example, given the nature of FX trading, the positions held on December 5, 2015, could be very different from those held on December 1, 2015.[23]

## The Historic (Back Simulation) Model versus RiskMetrics

One obvious benefit of the historic, or back simulation, approach is that we do not need to calculate standard deviations and correlations (or assume normal distributions for asset returns) to calculate the portfolio risk figures in row 9 of Table 15–6.[24] A second advantage is that it directly provides a worst-case scenario number, in our example, a loss of $119,096—see step 5. RiskMetrics, since it assumes asset returns are normally distributed (that returns can go to plus and minus infinity), provides no such worst-case scenario number.[25]

The disadvantage of the back simulation approach is the degree of confidence we have in the 1 percent VAR number based on 500 observations. Statistically speaking, 500 observations are not very many, so there will be a very wide confidence

---

[23] As in RiskMetrics, an adjustment can be made for illiquidity of the market, in this case, by assuming the FI is locked into longer holding periods. For example, if it is estimated that it will take five days for the FI to sell its FX position, then the FI will be interested in the weekly (i.e., five trading days) changes in FX rates in the past. One immediate problem is that with 500 past trading days, only 100 weekly periods would be available, which reduces the statistical power of the VAR estimate (see below).

[24] The reason is that the historic, or back simulation, approach uses actual exchange rates on each day that explicitly include correlations or comovements with other exchange rates and asset returns on that day.

[25] The 1 percent number in RiskMetrics tells us that we will lose more than this amount on 1 day out of every 100. It does not tell us the maximum amount we can lose. As noted in the text, theoretically, with a normal distribution, this could be an infinite amount.

band (or standard error) around the estimated number ($97,210 in our example). One possible solution to the problem is to go back in time more than 500 days and estimate the 1 percent VAR based on 1,000 past daily observations (the 10th worst case) or even 10,000 past observations (the 100th worst case). The problem is that as one goes back farther in time, past observations may become decreasingly relevant in predicting VAR in the future. For example, 10,000 observations may require the FI to analyze FX data going back 40 years. Over this period we have moved through many very different FX regimes: from relatively fixed exchange rates in the 1950–70 period, to relatively floating exchange rates in the 1970s, to more managed floating rates in the 1980s and 1990s, to the abolition of exchange rates and the introduction of the euro in January 2002, to large fluctuations in exchange rates during the financial crisis of 2008–2009. Clearly, exchange rate behavior and risk in a fixed–exchange rate regime will have little relevance to an FX trader or market risk manager operating and analyzing risk in a floating–exchange rate regime.

This seems to confront the market risk manager with a difficult modeling problem. There are, however, at least two approaches to this problem. The first is to weight past observations in the back simulation unequally, giving a higher weight to the more recent past observations. The second is to use a Monte Carlo simulation approach, which generates additional observations that are consistent with recent historic experience. The latter approach, in effect, amounts to simulating or creating artificial trading days and FX rate changes.

## The Monte Carlo Simulation Approach

To overcome the problems imposed by a limited number of actual observations, we can generate additional observations (in our example, FX changes). Normally, the simulation or generation of these additional observations is structured using a Monte Carlo simulation approach so that returns or rates generated reflect the probability with which they have occurred in recent historic time periods. The first step is to calculate the historic variance–covariance matrix ($\Sigma$) of FX changes. This matrix is then decomposed into two symmetric matrices, $A$ and $A'$.[26] This allows the FI to generate scenarios for the FX position by multiplying the $A'$ matrix, which reflects the historic volatilities and correlations among FX rates, by a random number vector $z$:[27] 10,000 random values of $z$ are drawn for each FX exchange rate.[28] This simulation approach results in realistic FX scenarios being generated as historic volatilities and correlations among FX rates are multiplied by the randomly drawn values of $z$. The VAR of the current position is then calculated as in Table 15–6, except that in the Monte Carlo approach, the VAR is the 100th worst simulated loss out of 10,000.

Monte Carlo simulation is, therefore, a tool for considering portfolio valuation under all possible combinations of factors that determine a security's value. The model generates random market values drawn from the multivariate normal distributions representing each variable. The Industry Perspectives box outlines the process Citigroup follows in estimating VAR using the Monte Carlo simulation approach and gives more detail on its 2011 VARs.

---

[26] The only difference between $A$ and $A'$ is that the numbers in the rows of $A$ become the numbers in the columns of $A'$. The technical term for this procedure is the Cholesky decomposition, where $\Sigma = AA'$.

[27] Where $z$ is assumed to be normally distributed with a mean of zero and a standard deviation of 1 or $z \sim N(0, 1)$.

[28] Technically, let $y$ be an FX scenario; then $y = A'z$. For each FX rate, 10,000 values of $z$ are randomly generated to produce 10,000 values of $y$. The $y$ values are then used to revalue the FX position and calculate gains and losses.

# Industry Perspectives    Citigroup—Value at Risk

Value at risk (VAR) estimates, at a 99 percent confidence level, the potential decline in the value of a position or a portfolio under normal market conditions. VAR statistics can be materially different across firms due to differences in portfolio composition, differences in VAR methodologies, and differences in model parameters. Citi believes VAR statistics can be used more effectively as indicators of trends in risk taking within a firm, rather than as a basis for inferring differences in risk taking across firms.

Citi uses Monte Carlo simulation, which it believes is conservatively calibrated to incorporate the greater of short-term (most recent month) and long-term (three years) market volatility. The Monte Carlo simulation involves approximately 300,000 market factors, making use of 180,000 time series, with market factors updated daily and model parameters updated weekly.

The conservative features of the VAR calibration contribute approximately 20 percent add-on to what would be a VAR estimated under the assumption of stable and perfectly normally distributed markets. Under normal and stable market conditions, Citi would thus expect the number of days where trading losses exceed its VAR to be less than two or three exceptions per year. Periods of unstable market conditions could increase the number of these exceptions. During the last four quarters, there was one back-testing exception where trading losses exceeded the VAR estimate at the Citigroup level (back-testing is the process in which the daily VAR of a portfolio is compared to the actual daily change in the market value of transactions). This occurred on August 8, 2011, after the U.S. government rating was downgraded by S&P.

The accompanying table summarizes VAR for Citi-wide trading portfolios at and during 2011 and 2010, including quarterly averages. Historically, Citi included only the hedges associated with the CVA (credit valuation adjustment) of its derivative transactions in its VAR calculations and disclosures (these hedges were, and continue to be, included within the relevant risk type e.g., interest rate, foreign exchange, equity). However, Citi now includes both the hedges associated with the CVA of its derivatives and the CVA on the derivative counterparty exposure (included in the line "Incremental Impact of Derivative CVA"). The inclusion of the CVA on derivative counterparty exposure reduces Citi's total trading VAR; Citi believes this calculation and presentation reflect a more complete and accurate view of its mark-to-market risk profile as it incorporates both the CVA underlying derivative transactions and related hedges.

| In Millions of Dollars | Dec. 31, 2011 | 2011 Average | Dec. 31, 2010 | 2010 Average |
|---|---|---|---|---|
| Interest rate | $250 | $246 | $235 | $234 |
| Foreign exchange | 51 | 61 | 52 | 61 |
| Equity | 36 | 46 | 56 | 59 |
| Commodity | 16 | 22 | 19 | 23 |
| Covariance adjustment[1] | (118) | (162) | (171) | (172) |
| Total Trading VAR—all market risk factors, including general and specific risk (excluding derivative CVA) | $235 | $213 | $191 | $205 |
| Specific risk-only component[2] | $ 14 | $ 22 | $  8 | $ 18 |
| **Total—general market factors only** | $221 | $191 | $183 | $187 |
| Incremental impact of derivative CVA | $ (52) | $ (24) | $  (5) | N/A |
| **Total Trading and CVA VAR** | $183 | $189 | $186 | N/A |

(1) Covariance adjustment (also known as diversification benefit) equals the difference between the total VAR and the sum of the VARs tied to each individual risk type. The benefit reflects the fact that the risks within each and across risk types are not perfectly correlated and, consequently, the total VAR on a given day will be lower than the sum of the VARs relating to each individual risk type. The determination of the primary drivers of changes to the covariance adjustment is made by an examination of the impact of both model parameter and position changes.

(2) The specific risk-only component represents the level of equity and fixed income issuer-specific risk embedded in VAR.

N/A Not available

**Source:** *Citigroup 2011 10-k Report,* March 2012, p. 98.

**EXAMPLE 15–5**

*Calculating Value at Risk Using Monte Carlo Simulation*

Consider an FI with a long position in a one-year, zero-coupon €1,000,000 bond. The current one year interest rate on the Eurobond is 10 percent. So, the present value of the one-year, €1m notional Eurobond is €909,091. The current $/€ exchange rate is 0.65 (i.e., the €/$ exchange rate is 1.538461). Thus, the FI has a long position of $590,909 in the Eurobond. The FI wants to evaluate the value at risk for this bond based on changes in interest rates and FX rates over the next 10 days.

The two underlying bond characteristics to be simulated are the $/€ exchange rate and the one year Eurobond price for changes in one year interest rates. Historical daily volatilities of the $/€ exchange rate and the bond price are such that $\sigma_{FX} = 0.0042$ and $\sigma_B = 0.0008$. The historic correlation between the two is $\rho_{FX,B} = -0.17$. To generate one thousand scenarios for values of the two underlying assets in 10 days, Monte Carlo analysis first generates one thousand pairs of standard normal variates whose correlation is $\rho_{FX,B} = -0.17$. Label each pair $z_{FX}$ and $z_B$. Histograms for the results are shown in Figure 15–2. Note that the distributions are essentially the same.

Next, Monte Carlo simulation creates the actual scenarios for the variables, FX and *B*. That is, for each pair $z_{FX}$ and $z_B$ future values are created by applying

$$P_{FX} = 0.65e^{0.0042 \times \sqrt{5} \times z_{FX}} \qquad \text{(6)}$$

and

$$P_B = €909,091e^{0.0008 \times \sqrt{5} \times z_B} \qquad \text{(7)}$$

To express the bond price in dollars (accounting for both the exchange rate and interest rate risk for the bond), it is necessary to multiply the simulated bond price by the exchange rate in each scenario. Figures 15–3 and 15–4 show the distributions of future values, $P_{FX}$ and $P_B$, respectively, obtained by one thousand simulations. Note that the distributions are no longer normal, and for the bond price, the distribution shows a marked asymmetry. This is due to the transformation made from normal to lognormal variates by applying Equations (6) and (7). Table 15–7 lists the first ten scenarios generated from Monte Carlo analysis. The process would be repeated until the 10,000 random observations are generated. Then with the observations rank ordered from worst (biggest loss) to best (biggest gain), the VAR is the 100th worst estimate out of 10,000.

**FIGURE 15–2**

**Frequency Distribution for $Z_{FX}$ and $Z_B$ (1000 trials)**

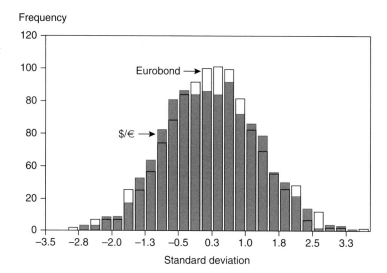

**FIGURE 15–3**
**Frequency Distribution for Eurobond Price (1000 trials)**

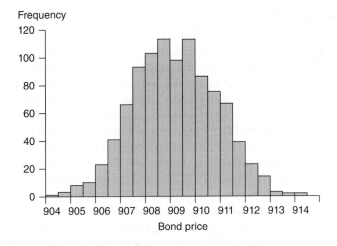

**FIGURE 15–4**
**Frequency Distribution for $/€ Exchange Rate (1000 trials)**

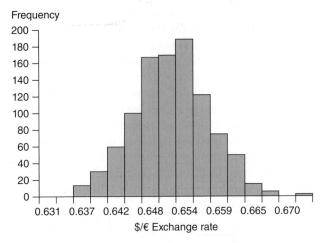

**TABLE 15–7**
**Monte Carlo Scenarios (1000 trials)**

| $/€ | PV of Cash Flow (in €s) | PV of Cash Flow (in $s) |
| --- | --- | --- |
| 0.6500 | €906,663 | $589,350 |
| 0.6540 | 907,898 | 593,742 |
| 0.6606 | 911,214 | 601,935 |
| 0.6513 | 908,004 | 591,399 |
| 0.6707 | 910,074 | 610,430 |
| 0.6444 | 908,478 | 585,460 |
| 0.6569 | 908,860 | 597,053 |
| 0.6559 | 906,797 | 594,789 |
| 0.6530 | 906,931 | 592,267 |
| 0.6625 | 920,768 | 603,348 |

**Concept Questions**

1. What are the advantages of the historic, or back simulation, approach over RiskMetrics to measure market risk?

2. What are the steps involved with the historic, or back simulation, approach to measuring market risk?

3. What is the Monte Carlo simulation approach to measuring market risk?

## Expected Shortfall

As mentioned earlier, a criticism of VAR is that it tells the FI manager the level of possible losses that might occur with a given confidence level—that is, the 99th percentile—assuming a normally shaped return distribution. Expected shortfall (ES), also referred to as conditional VAR and expected tail loss, tells us the average of the losses in the tail of the distribution beyond the 99th percentile—that is, if 1 in every 100 days there is a loss, ES tells us the average of those 1 in 100 day losses. For example, in Table 15–6, the FI's 99 percent confidence level VAR is $97,210. Thus, if tomorrow is a bad day, there is a 1 percent probability that the FI's losses will exceed $97,210 assuming a normal probability distribution. However, many return distributions have "fat tails." Consider Figure 15–5. The VAR of the probability distribution is $97,210— that is, assuming a normal probability distribution, there is a 1 in 100 chance that the FI will lose $97,210. However, clearly the probability distribution is not normal, but has a fat-tail loss. Thus, the average of the 1 in 100 day losses will be larger than $97,210.

VAR corresponds to a specific point of loss on the probability distribution. It does not provide information about the potential size of the loss that exceeds it— that is, VAR completely ignores the patterns and the severity of the losses in the extreme tail. Thus, VAR gives only partial information about the extent of possible losses, particularly when probability distributions are non-normal. The drawbacks of VAR became painfully evident during the financial crisis as asset returns plummeted into the fat-tail region of non-normally shaped distributions. FI managers and regulators were forced to recognize that VAR projections of possible losses far underestimated actual losses on extreme bad days.

ES is a measure of market risk that estimates the expected value of losses beyond a given confidence level—that is, it is the average of VARs beyond a given confidence level. Specifically, for a confidence level $c$, ES can be solved using the following formula for a continuous probability distribution:

$$ES(c) = \frac{1}{1 - c} \int_c^1 Var(u) \, du$$

That is, for a confidence level of, say, 99 percent (i.e., $c$), we measure the area under the probability distribution from the 99th to 100th percentile.

**FIGURE 15–5**
**Probability Distribution of Returns for a Security**

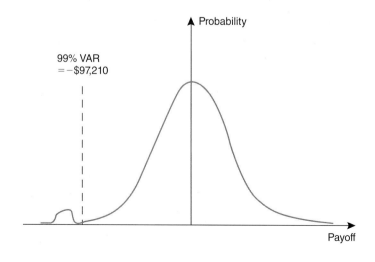

For a discrete distribution,

$$ES = -E(\Delta V \,|\, \Delta V < -\text{Var})$$

That is, for a confidence level of, say, 99 percent, we sum the weighted value of any observation in the discrete probability distribution from the 99th to 100th percentile.

In Figure 15–5, VAR tells the FI manager the loss at a particular point, *c*, on the probability distribution (i.e., 99th percentile). It, however, fails to incorporate information regarding the shape of the probability distribution below that particular point. Expected shortfall is the average VAR to the left of the 99 percent confidence level. Thus, VAR is identical for both probability distributions. However, ES, which incorporates points to the left of VAR, is larger when the probability distribution exhibits fat-tail losses. Accordingly, ES provides more information about possible market risk losses than VAR. For situations in which probability distributions exhibit fat-tail losses, VAR may look relatively small, but ES may be very large.

| **EXAMPLE 15–6** *Simple Example of VAR versus ES* | Consider the following discrete probability distribution of payoffs for two securities, A and B, held in the trading portfolio of an FI: |
|---|---|

| Probability | A | Probability | B |
|---|---|---|---|
| 50.00% | $100 m | 50.00% | $100 m |
| 49.00 | 80 m | 49.00 | 92 m |
| 1.00 | −920 m | 0.25 | −920 m |
| | | 0.75 | −1,704 m |

The FI wants to estimate which of the two securities will add more market risk to its trading portfolio according to both the VAR and ES measures.

Expected return on security A = 0.50($100 m) + 0.49($80 m) + 0.01(−$920 m) = $80 m

Expected return on security B = 0.50($100 m) + 0.49($92 m) + 0.0025(−$920 m)
                                              + 0.0075(−$1,704 m) = $80 m

For a 99 percent confidence level,

$$VAR_A = VAR_B = -\$920\ m$$

Yet, for a 99 percent confidence level,

$$ES_A = -\$920\ m, \text{ while } ES_B = 0.25(-\$920\ m) + 0.75(-\$1,704\ m) = -\$1,508\ m$$

Thus, while the VAR is identical for both securities, the ES finds that security B has the potential to subject the FI to much greater losses than security A. Specifically, if tomorrow is a bad day, VAR finds that there is a 1 percent probability that the FI's losses will exceed $920 million on either security. However, if tomorrow is a bad day, ES finds that there is a 1 percent probability that the FI's losses will exceed $920 million if security A is in its trading portfolio, but losses will exceed $1,508 million if security B is in its trading portfolio.

For continuous probability distributions ES uses a scaling factor based on a fat-tailed student's t distribution.[29] Thus, while the scaling factors for VAR are 2.33 for a 1 percent confidence level (and 1.65 for a 5 percent confidence level), ES scales up the risk factor to account for fat tails in the probability distribution, using 2.665 for a 1 percent confidence level (and 2.063 for a 5 percent confidence level).

---

**EXAMPLE 15–7**

*Estimating VAR and ES of Trading Portfolio Securities*

An FI has €1 million in its trading portfolio on the close of business on a particular day. The FI wants to calculate the one-day VAR and ES from this position. The first step is to calculate the dollar value position:

Suppose the current exchange rate of euros for dollars is €0.7983/$, or dollars for euros is $1.2527, at the daily close. So,

$$\text{Dollar value of position} = €1 \text{ million} \times 1.2527 = \$1,252,700$$

Suppose also that looking back at the daily percentage changes in the €/$ exchange rate over the past year, we find that the volatility, or standard deviation ($\sigma$), of daily percentage changes in the spot exchange rate was 44.3 bp. However, the FI is interested in adverse moves—bad moves that will not occur more than 1 percent of the time, or 1 day in every 100.

**Value at Risk**

Using VAR, which assumes that changes in exchange rates are normally distributed, the exchange rate must change in the adverse direction by $2.33\sigma$ (2.33 × 44.3 bp) for this change to be viewed as likely to occur only 1 day in every 100 days:

$$\text{FX volatility} = 2.33 \times 44.3 \text{ bp} = 103.219 \text{ bp}$$

In other words, using VAR during the last year the euro declined in value against the dollar by 103.219 bp 1 percent of the time. As a result, the one-day VAR is:

$$\text{VAR} = \$1,252,700 \times 0.0103219 = \$12,930$$

**Expected Shortfall**

Using ES, which assumes that changes in exchange rates are normally distributed but with fat tails, the exchange rate must change in the adverse direction by $2.665\sigma$ (2.665 × 44.3 bp) for this change to be viewed as likely to occur only 1 day in every 100 days:

$$\text{FX volatility} = 2.665 \times 44.3 \text{ bp} = 118.0595 \text{ bp}$$

In other words, using ES during the last year the euro declined in value against the dollar by 118.0595 bp 1 percent of the time. As a result, the one-day ES is:

$$\text{ES} = \$1,252,700 \times 0.01180595 = \$14,798$$

The potential loss exposure to adverse euro to dollar exchange rate changes for the FI from the €1 million spot currency holdings are higher using the ES measure of market risk. ES estimates potential losses that are $1,868 higher than VAR. This is because VAR focuses on the location of the extreme tail of the probability distribution. ES also considers the shape of the probability distribution once VAR is exceeded.

---

[29] Specifically,

$$\text{ES} = \text{Scale}^{ES} \times \sigma \times X$$

where,

$$\text{Scale}^{ES} = -\frac{N^{pdf}\left(N^{-1}(1-c)\right)}{1-c}$$

| **Concept Questions** | 1. What is the difference between VAR and ES? |
| | 2. Why is ES superior to VAR as a measure of market risk? |

# REGULATORY MODELS: THE BIS STANDARDIZED FRAMEWORK

www.bis.org

www.federalreserve.gov

The development of internal market risk models by FIs such as J.P. Morgan Chase was partly in response to proposals by the Bank for International Settlements (BIS) in 1993 to measure and regulate the market risk exposures of banks by imposing capital requirements on their trading portfolios.[30] As noted in Chapter 7, the BIS is an organization encompassing the largest central banks in the world. After refining these proposals over a number of years, most recently in 2013, the BIS (including the Federal Reserve) decided on a final approach to measuring market risk and the capital reserves necessary for an FI to hold to withstand and survive market risk losses. These required levels of capital held to protect against market risk exposure are in addition to the minimum level of capital banks are required to hold for credit risk purposes (see Chapter 20). Since January 1998 banks in the countries that are members of the BIS can calculate their market risk exposures in one of two ways. The first is to use a simple standardized framework (to be discussed below). The second, with regulatory approval, is to use their own internal models, which are similar to the models described above. However, if an internal model is approved for use in calculating capital requirements for the FI, it is subject to regulatory audit and certain constraints. Before looking at these constraints, we examine the BIS standardized framework. Additional details of this model can be found at the BIS website, **www.bis.org**.[31]

The financial crisis exposed a number of shortcomings in the way market risk was being measured in accordance with Basel II rules. Although the crisis largely exposed problems with the large-bank internal models approach to measuring market risk, the BIS also identified shortcomings with the standardized approach. These included a lack of risk sensitivity, a very limited recognition of hedging and diversification benefits, and an inability to sufficiently capture risks associated with more complex instruments. To address shortcomings of the standardized approach to measuring market risk, Basel III proposes a "partial risk factor" approach as a revised standardized approach. Basel III also introduces a "fuller risk factor" approach as an alternative to the revised partial risk factor standardized approach.

## Partial Risk Factor Approach

The partial risk factor approach applies risk weights to the market values of trading portfolio securities, with enhancements to prudently reflect hedging of and diversification across securities. Particularly, the partial risk factor approach requires the following process be followed by FIs to determine capital requirements:

1. *Assign instruments to asset "buckets."* Instruments are placed in one of 20 asset buckets across each of five risk classes according to their risk similarity. The five

---

[30] BIS, Basel Committee on Banking Supervision, "The Supervisory Treatment of Market Risks," Basel, Switzerland, April 1993; "The New Basel Capital Accord: Third Consultative Paper," Basel, Switzerland, April 2003; and Revisions to Basel II Market Risk Framework, Basel, Switzerland, January 2009.

[31] Specifically, Basel 2.5 and Basel 3 changes are discussed in "Fundamental Review of the Trading Book," BIS Basel Committee on Banking Supervision, May 2012.

risk classes include FX, interest rates, equities, credit (including securitizations), and commodities.

2. *Calculate each bucket's risk measure.* A risk measure is calculated for each bucket using a regulator-specified formula based on ES estimates. The market values of the assets in each bucket are then multiplied by the risk weight.

3. *Aggregate the buckets.* The risk measures of the individual asset buckets are aggregated to obtain the capital requirement for the trading portfolio. The formula used to aggregate is:

$$\text{Capital} = \sqrt{\sum_{b=1}^{B} K_b^2 + \sum_{b=1}^{B} \sum_{c \neq b} \gamma_{bc} S_b S_c}$$

where $S_b = \sum_{i \neq b} RW_i MV_i$, and $\gamma_{bc}$ is correlation parameter between buckets $b$ and $c$, defined by regulators. The first term in this formula aggregates risk across buckets without considering cross-bucket diversification (the "sum of squares"). The second term adjusts for the "same direction" correlation between the asset types in $b$ and $c$ (i.e., long/long or short/short), $\gamma_{bc}$.

## Fuller Risk Factor Approach

The fuller risk factor approach maps each trading portfolio security to a set of risk factors and associated shocks that explain the variation in the security values. The set of risk factors and shocks to the risk factors are established by regulators. The risk factors are organized in a hierarchy. Those risk factors listed at the top of the hierarchy affect the largest number of securities. Risk factors listed further down in the hierarchy are more specific in nature. Thus, changes in these risk factors would impact a smaller number of instruments. Finally, risk factors listed at the bottom of the hierarchy are nonhedgeable risk factors (i.e., risk that cannot easily be hedged in period of financial stress). Table 15–8 provides an illustration of the

**TABLE 15–8**   **Hierarchy of Hedgeable Risk Factors under the Standardized Model Fuller Risk Factor Approach**

Source: "Fundamental Review of the Trading Book," BIS Basel Committee on Banking Supervision, May 2012.

| Level | FX Risk | Interest Rate Risk | Equity Risk | Credit Risk | Commodity Risk |
|---|---|---|---|---|---|
| I | Exchange rate of domestic currency to worldwide currency basket | Worldwide interest rate index | Worldwide equity index | Worldwide credit spread index | Commodity price index |
| II | Exchange rate of worldwide currency basket to respective foreign currency | Level of money market/swap rate curve in respective currency | Equity index by broad industry category | Credit spread index by industry category | Price index for commodity type |
| III | | Slope of money market/swap rate curve in respective currency | Price of individual equity | Credit spread for individual issuer | Price index for physical type of commodity |
| IV | | Money market/swap rate between vertex points in respective currency (residual) | | | |

order of risk factors proposed by the BIS for Basel III. FIs then apply BIS empirically estimated standard deviations of shocks to these underlying risk factors. The capital charge is then determined by converting the risk position to an expected shortfall (ES) similar to that described in the previous section. The fuller risk factor approach requires the following process be followed by FIs to determine capital requirements:

1. *Assign each instrument to applicable risk factors.* The BIS defines a set of risk factors and associated shocks that explain the variation in the value of an FI's trading portfolio securities. Using a BIS-provided description of the mapping of securities to each risk factor, FIs determine which risk factors influence the value of their trading portfolio securities.

2. *Determine the size of the net risk position in each risk factor.* Once the FI determines the risk factors that apply to each of its trading portfolio securities, it uses a pricing model to determine the size of the risk positions from each security with respect to the applicable risk factors. The size of the risk positions is based on the sensitivity of the instruments to the prescribed risk factors. The FI then aggregates all negative and positive gross risk positions to determine the net risk position. For nonhedgeable risk factors, the gross risk position would equal the net risk position.

3. *Aggregate overall risk position across risk factors.* To compute the overall capital requirement for each risk factor class, the net risk positions determined in step 2 are aggregated. Regulators specify the distribution of the risk factors (i.e., the standard deviations to apply against each of the risk factors). One option offered by the BIS is to assume that all risk factors of the same risk factor class are independently distributed.[32] Thus, the overall portfolio standard deviation is calculated using a sum of squares multiplied by a scalar that approximates the average across the loss tail of the portfolio distribution (i.e., the ES). The ES scalar factor implemented by regulators in Basel III is four. Thus, the overall capital requirement is four times the overall portfolio standard deviation.

The following example is the BIS illustration of the fuller risk factor approach of the standardized model.[33]

| | |
|---|---|
| **EXAMPLE 15–8**<br><br>*Calculating Market Risk Capital Requirement Using the Fuller Risk Factor Approach* | In its trading portfolio, an FI holds 1,000 Daimler shares at a share price of €101 and has sold 500 Volkswagen shares under a forward contract that matures in one year. The current share price for Volkswagen is €20. To calculate the market risk capital charge on these securities, the FI proceeds as follows.<br><br>**Step 1. Assign each instrument to applicable risk factors**<br>From Table 15–8, hedgeable risk factors for these equities include level I movements in global equity markets (worldwide equity index), level II movements in sectoral equity indices (equity index by broad industry category), and level III movements in the prices of individual equity. Daimler and Volkswagen have the same hedgeable risk factors at levels I and II (i.e., global and industry specific equity indices). However, movements in the prices of the two firms are unique. Thus, they do not have the same risk factor at level III, and as a result, they are |

[32] The BIS stated that to recognize diversification it would be necessary to impose a distribution on the risk factors. However, specifying a distribution of risk factors, with appropriate pairwise correlations between risk factors, is likely to be a burdensome and complex task for regulators and would also complicate FIs' calculations considerably. Thus, the BIS decided that the computationally simplest approach is to treat all risk factors of the same risk factor class as independently distributed.

[33] See "Fundamental Review of the Trading Book," BIS Basel Committee on Banking Supervision, May 2012.

mapped to different individual equity risk factors.[34] There is also a nonhedgeable risk factor for the Volkswagen equity price to capture basis risk from the forward contract.

### Step 2. Determine the size of the net risk position in each risk factor

For each risk factor, the FI determines a net risk position, calculated as the sum of gross risk positions for all instruments that are subject to that risk factor.[35] Table 15–9 shows the gross and net positions for Daimler and Volkswagen equities for the equity risk factor. The size of the gross position in Daimler for the three applicable risk factors is €101,000 (1,000 shares × €101) and for the short position in Volkswagen is −€10,000 (500 shares × €20). Note again that the two securities do not have the same risk factor at level III. Thus, they are mapped to different individual equity risk factors. Further, to capture basis risk from the forward contract, there is a nonhedgeable risk factor for the Volkswagen equity price, −€10,000. The net risk position of the two securities for each risk factor, listed in the last column of Table 15–9, is the sum of the gross risk factors for the securities at each level—that is, €91,000 for levels I and II, €101,000 and −€10,000, respectively, for level III, and −€10,000 for nonhedgeable risk.

### Step 3. Aggregate overall risk position across risk factors

The net risk positions is then converted into a capital charge by multiplying by regulator specified standard deviations (i.e., shift risk factors). Table 15–10 shows the calculations of the capital charge for market risk. The net risk positions (listed in column 3 for each risk level) are multiplied by the standard deviations assigned for each level (column 4) to produce the standard deviations of the net risk position (column 5). For example, the standard deviation of the net risk position for the level I worldwide equity index is equal to the net risk (€91,000) times the regulator set shift risk factor (5 percent) to give the standard deviation associated with level I risk factor (€4,550). The square of the standard deviation (the variance) is then listed in column 6 (i.e., €20,702,500 for level I). Summing the squared standard deviations gives the portfolio variance (€164,289,400) and taking the square root of this gives the portfolio standard deviation (€12,818). Finally, this portfolio standard deviation is multiplied by a scalar (currently set at 4) to achieve the overall expected shortfall for the portfolio.

**TABLE 15–9**    Calculation of Gross and Net Risk Position

| Level | Equity Risk | Daimler Gross Risk Position | Volkswagen Gross Risk Position | Total Size of Net Risk Position |
|---|---|---|---|---|
| I | Worldwide equity index | €101,000 | −€10,000 | €91,000 |
| II | Industry equity index | €101,000 | −€10,000 | €91,000 |
| III | Daimler share price | €101,000 | — | €101,000 |
| | Volkswagen share price | — | −€10,000 | −€10,000 |
| N-h* | Volkswagen share price | — | −€10,000 | −€10,000 |

\* Nonhedgeable risk factor.

[34] However, these risk factors can be hedged with other positions that shared this risk factor, such as Daimler equity options.

[35] For equities, this is equivalent to assuming that equity betas are homogeneous and equal to one. For FX, the size of the gross risk position is the market value of the instrument converted to the reporting currency of the FI. For linear interest rate risk and credit risk–related instruments, the size of the gross risk position is determined by applying a small shift to the respective risk factor and determining the value change of the instrument in relation to the shift applied.

**TABLE 15–10**  Calculation of Market Risk Capital Charge

| Level | Equity Risk: Portfolio | Net Risk Position (EUR) | Standard Deviation (i.e., shift of risk factor) | Standard Deviation of Net Risk Position | Square the Standard Deviation of the Net Risk Position (i.e, variance) |
|---|---|---|---|---|---|
| I | Worldwide equity index | €91,000 | 5% | €4,550 | €20,702,500 |
| II | Industry equity index | 91,000 | 7% | 6,370 | 40,576,900 |
| III | Daimler share price | 101,000 | 10% | 10,100 | 102,010,000 |
|  | Volkswagen share price | −10,000 | −10% | 1,000 | 1,000,000 |
| N-h* | Volkswagen share price | −10,000 | 1% | 100 | 10,000 |
| Portfolio | Sum the squared standard deviations (portfolio variance) | | | | €164,289,400 |
| Portfolio | Take the square root (portfolio standard deviation) | | | | €12,818 |
| Portfolio | Multiply by scalar to obtain expected shortfall | | | | €51,270 |

\* Nonhedgeable risk factor.

**Notes:** ES scalar factor decided by regulators = 4 × standard deviation. Correlation (ρ) between stocks = 0 is assumed by the model.

# THE BIS REGULATIONS AND LARGE-BANK INTERNAL MODELS

As discussed above, the BIS capital requirement for market risk exposure introduced in January 1998 allows large banks (subject to regulatory permission) to use their own internal models to calculate market risk instead of the standardized framework. The initial market risk capital requirements were included as part of what became known as Basel I capital rules. However, details of the capital calculations have been refined and revised over the years. Today, FIs' internal models are governed by Basel 2.5 (implemented in 2012) and Basel III (being phased in between 2013 and 2019) versions of the rules for adequate capital at FIs. (We examine the initiatives taken by the BIS and the major central banks, e.g., the Federal Reserve, in controlling bank risk exposure through capital requirements in greater detail in Chapter 20.)

During the financial crisis, losses due to market risk were significantly higher than the minimum market risk capital requirements under BIS Basel I and Basel II rules. As a result, in July 2009 the BIS announced Basel 2.5, a final version of revised rules for market risk capital requirements. Specifically, in addition to the risk capital charge already in place (steps 1 and 2 listed below), an incremental capital charge is assessed which includes a "stressed value at risk" capital requirement taking into account a one-year observation period of significant financial stress relevant to the FI's portfolio (step 3 listed below). The introduction of stressed VAR in Basel 2.5 is intended to reduce the cyclicality of the VAR measure and alleviate the problem of market stress periods dropping out of the data period used to calculate VAR after some time. Basel 2.5 requires the following process be followed by large FIs using internal models to calculate the market risk capital charge.

1. In calculating DEAR, the FI must define an adverse change in rates as being in the 99th percentile (multiply $\sigma$ by 2.33).
2. The FI must assume the minimum holding period to be 10 days (this means that daily DEAR would have to be multiplied by $\sqrt{10}$).
3. The FI must add to this a "stressed VAR" that is intended to replicate a VAR calculation that would be generated on the FI's trading portfolio if the relevant

market factors were experiencing a period of stress. The stressed VAR is based on the 10-day, 99th percentile VAR of the trading portfolio, with model inputs incorporating historical data from a one-year period of significant financial stress. The period used must be approved by the supervisor and regularly reviewed. For example, a 12-month period relating to significant losses during the financial crisis would adequately reflect a period of such stress.

The FI must consider its proposed capital charge or requirement as the sum of:

1. The higher of the previous day's VAR (value at risk or $DEAR \times \sqrt{10}$) and the average daily VAR over the previous 60 business days times a multiplication factor with a minimum value of 3, i.e., capital charge $= DEAR \times \sqrt{10} \times 3$ (in general, the multiplication factor makes required capital significantly higher than VAR produced from private models), plus
2. The higher of its latest available stressed VAR and an average of the stressed VAR over the preceding 60 business days times a multiplication factor with a minimum value of 3 and a maximum of 4.

From this,

Capital charge for market risk $= (\text{VAR} \times \sqrt{10} \times 3) + (\text{Stressed VAR} \times \sqrt{10} \times 3)$

For example, suppose an FI's portfolio VAR over the previous 60 days was $10 million and stressed VAR over the previous 60 days was $25 million using the 1 percent worst case (or 99th percentile). The minimum capital charge would be:[36]

$$\text{Capital charge} = (\$10 \text{ million} \times \sqrt{10} \times 3) + (\$25 \text{ million} \times \sqrt{10} \times 3)$$
$$= \$332.04 \text{ million}$$

Basel III proposes to replace VAR models with those based on extreme value theory and expected shortfall (ES). As discussed earlier, the ES measure analyzes the size and likelihood of losses above the 99th percentile in a crisis period for a traded asset and thus measures "tail risk" more precisely. Thus, ES is a risk measure that considers a more comprehensive set of potential outcomes than VAR. The BIS change to ES highlights the importance of maintaining sufficient regulatory capital not only in stable market conditions, but also in periods of significant financial stress. Indeed, it is precisely during periods of stress that capital is vital for absorbing losses and safeguarding the stability of the banking system. Accordingly, the committee intends to move to a framework that is calibrated to a period of significant financial stress.

Two methods of identifying the stress period and calculating capital requirements under the internal models are the direct method and the indirect method. The direct method is based on the approach used in the Basel 2.5 stressed VAR. The FI would search the entire historical period and identify the period that produces

---

[36] The idea of a minimum multiplication factor of 3 is to create a scheme that is "incentive compatible." Specifically, if FIs using internal models constantly underestimate the amount of capital they need to meet their market risk exposures, regulators can punish those FIs by raising the multiplication factor to as high as 4. Such a response may effectively put the FI out of the trading business. The degree to which the multiplication factor is raised above 3 depends on the number of days an FI's model underestimates its market risk over the preceding year. For example, an underestimation error that occurs on more than 10 days out of the past 250 days will result in the multiplication factor's being raised to 4.

**TABLE 15–11**
Ratio of Market Risk to Total Risk-Based Capital for Bank Holding Companies Using Internal Models

Source: Federal Reserve Board, FR Y-9C Reports, 2011.

| Name | Market Risk to Total Risk-Based Capital (%) |
|---|---|
| Bank of America | 2.34% |
| Citigroup | 0.81 |
| J.P. Morgan Chase | 4.42 |
| HSBC North America | 1.48 |
| KeyCorp | 0.67 |
| Suntrust | 0.45 |
| Wells Fargo | 0.80 |
| Bank of New York Mellon | 1.13 |
| PNC Financial | 0.81 |
| US Bancorp | 0.10 |

the highest ES result when all risk factors are included. However, Basel III would require the FI to determine the stressed period on the basis of a reduced set of risk factors. Once the FI has identified the stressed period, it must then determine the ES for the full set of risk factors for the stress period. The indirect method identifies the relevant historical period of stress by using a reduced set of risk factors. However, instead of calculating the full ES model to that period, the FI calculates a loss based on the reduced set of risk factors. This loss is then scaled using the ratio of the full ES model using current market data to the full ES model using the reduced set of risk factors using current market data.

Finally, it should be noted that the market risk framework discussed earlier is based on an assumption that an FI's trading book positions are liquid—that is, that FIs can exit or hedge the trading book positions over a 10-day horizon. The financial crisis proved this to be false. Thus, under the new liquidity risk measures the 10-day liquidity metric as used in the VAR calculations (i.e., VAR $\times \sqrt{10}$) are replaced with liquidity horizons based on a set of quantitative and qualitative criteria that allow for changes in market liquidity conditions. Specifically, FIs' exposures would be assigned to one of five liquidity horizon categories, ranging from 10 days to one year based on the time required to exit or hedge a risk position in a stressed market environment. Further, capital add-ons are included for jumps in liquidity premia. These add-ons would apply only to instruments that could become particularly illiquid to the extent that the market risk measures, even with extended liquidity horizons, would not sufficiently capture the risk to FI solvency from large fluctuations in liquidity premia on these securities.

Table 15–11 lists the market risk to the total risk-based capital for several large U.S. bank holding companies in 2011. Notice how small the market risk capital is relative to the total risk-based capital for these banks. Only J.P. Morgan Chase has a ratio greater than 4 percent. The average ratio of market risk capital to total risk-based capital required for the 10 bank holding companies is only 1.30 percent. Moreover, very few banks, other than the very largest (above), report market risk exposures at all.

| **Concept Questions** | 1. What is the BIS standardized framework for measuring market risk? |
|---|---|
| | 2. What is the effect of using the 99th percentile (1 percent worst case) rather than the 95th percentile (5 percent worst case) on the measured size of an FI's market risk exposures? |

## Summary

In this chapter we analyzed the importance of measuring an FI's market risk exposure. This risk is likely to continue to grow in importance as more and more loans and previously illiquid assets become marketable and as the traditional franchises of commercial banks, insurance companies, and investment banks shrink. Given the risks involved, both private FI management and regulators are investing increasing resources in models to measure and track market risk exposures. We analyzed in detail four approaches FIs have used to measure market risk: RiskMetrics, the historic (or back simulation) approach, the Monte Carlo simulation approach, and the expected shortfall (ES) approach. The four approaches were also compared in terms of simplicity and accuracy. Market risk is also of concern to regulators. Beginning in January 1998, banks in the United States have had to hold a capital requirement against the risk of their trading positions. The novel feature of the regulation of market risk is that the Federal Reserve and other central banks (subject to regulatory approval) have given large FIs the option to calculate capital requirements based on their own internal models rather than the regulatory model.

## Questions and Problems

1. What is meant by *market risk*?
2. Why is the measurement of market risk important to the manager of a financial institution?
3. What is meant by *daily earnings at risk* (DEAR)? What are the three measurable components? What is the price volatility component?
4. Follow Bank has a $1 million position in a five-year, zero-coupon bond with a face value of $1,402,552. The bond is trading at a yield to maturity of 7.00 percent. The historical mean change in daily yields is 0.0 percent and the standard deviation is 12 basis points.
   a. What is the modified duration of the bond?
   b. What is the maximum adverse daily yield move given that we desire no more than a 1 percent chance that yield changes will be greater than this maximum?
   c. What is the price volatility of this bond?
   d. What is the daily earnings at risk for this bond?
5. How can DEAR be adjusted to account for potential losses over multiple days? What would be the VAR for the bond in problem 4 for a 10-day period? What statistical assumption is needed for this calculation? Could this treatment be critical?
6. The DEAR for a bank is $8,500. What is the VAR for a 10-day period? A 20-day period? Why is the VAR for a 20-day period not twice as much as that for a 10-day period?
7. The mean change in the daily yields of a 15-year, zero-coupon bond has been five basis points (bp) over the past year with a standard deviation of 15 bp. Use these data and assume that the yield changes are normally distributed.
   a. What is the highest yield change expected if a 99 percent confidence limit is required; that is, adverse moves will not occur more than 1 day in 100?
   b. What is the highest yield change expected if a 95 percent confidence limit is required; adverse moves will not occur more than 1 day in 20?
8. In what sense is duration a measure of market risk?

9. Bank Alpha has an inventory of AAA-rated, 15–year zero-coupon bonds with a face value of $400 million. The bonds currently are yielding 9.5 percent in the over-the-counter market.
   a. What is the modified duration of these bonds?
   b. What is the price volatility if the potential adverse move in yields is 25 basis points?
   c. What is the DEAR?
   d. If the price volatility is based on a 99 percent confidence limit and a mean historical change in daily yields of 0.0 percent, what is the implied standard deviation of daily yield changes?

10. Bank Beta has an inventory of AAA-rated, 10-year zero-coupon bonds with a face value of $100 million. The modified duration of these bonds is 12.5 years, the DEAR is $2,150,000, and the potential adverse move in yields is 35 basis points. What is the market value of the bonds, the yield on the bonds, and the duration of the bonds?

11. Bank Two has a portfolio of bonds with a market value of $200 million. The bonds have an estimated price volatility of 0.95 percent. What are the DEAR and the 10-day VAR for these bonds?

12. Suppose that an FI has a €1.6 million long trading position in spot euros at the close of business on a particular day. Looking back at the daily percentage changes in the exchange rate of the €/$ for the past year, the volatility or standard deviation ($\sigma$) of daily percentage changes in the €/$ spot exchange rate was 62.5 basis points (bp). Calculate the FI's daily earnings at risk from this position (i.e., adverse moves in the FX markets with respect to the value of the euro against the dollar will not occur more than 1 percent of the time, or 1 day in every 100 days) if the spot exchange rate is €0.80/$1, or $1.25/€, at the daily close.

13. Bank of Southern Vermont has determined that its inventory of 20 million euros (€) and 25 million British pounds (£) is subject to market risk. The spot exchange rates are $0.40/€ and $1.28/£, respectively. The $\sigma$'s of the spot exchange rates of the € and £, based on the daily changes of spot rates over the past six months, are 65 bp and 45 bp, respectively. Determine the bank's 10-day VAR for both currencies. Use adverse rate changes in the 99th percentile.

14. Bank of Bentley has determined that its inventory of yen (¥) and Swiss franc (SF) denominated securities is subject to market risk. The spot exchange rates are ¥80.00/$ and SF0.9600/$, respectively. The $\sigma$'s of the spot exchange rates of the ¥ and SF, based on the daily changes of spot rates over the past six months, are 75 bp and 55 bp, respectively. Using adverse rate changes in the 99th percentile, the 10-day VARs for the two currencies, ¥ and SF, are $350,000 and $500,000, respectively. Calculate the yen and Swiss franc-denominated value positions for Bank of Bentley.

15. Suppose that an FI holds a $15 million trading position in stocks that reflect the U.S. stock market index (e.g., the S&P 500). Over the last year, the $\sigma_m$ of the daily returns on the stock market index was 156 bp. Calculate the VAR for this portfolio of stocks using a 99 percent confidence limit.

16. Bank of Alaska's stock portfolio has a market value of $10 million. The beta of the portfolio approximates the market portfolio, whose standard deviation ($\sigma_m$) has been estimated at 1.5 percent. What is the five-day VAR of this portfolio using adverse rate changes in the 99th percentile?

17. Jeff Resnick, vice president of operations at Choice Bank, is estimating the aggregate DEAR of the bank's portfolio of assets consisting of loans (L), foreign currencies (FX), and common stock (EQ). The individual DEARs are $300,700; $274,000; and $126,700, respectively. If the correlation coefficients ($\rho_{ij}$) between L and FX, L and EQ, and FX and EQ are 0.3, 0.7, and 0.0, respectively, what is the DEAR of the aggregate portfolio?

18. Calculate the DEAR for the following portfolio with the correlation coefficients and then with perfect positive correlation between various asset groups.

| Assets | Estimated DEAR | $(\rho_{S,FX})$ | $(\rho_{S,B})$ | $(\rho_{FX,B})$ |
|---|---|---|---|---|
| Stocks (S) | $300,000 | −0.10 | 0.75 | 0.20 |
| Foreign Exchange (FX) | 200,000 | | | |
| Bonds (B) | 250,000 | | | |

What is the amount of risk reduction resulting from the lack of perfect positive correlation between the various asset groups?

19. What are the advantages of using the back simulation approach to estimate market risk? Explain how this approach would be implemented.

20. Export Bank has a trading position in Japanese yen and Swiss francs. At the close of business on February 4, the bank had ¥300 million and SF10 million. The exchange rates for the most recent six days are given below.

| | Exchange Rates per U.S. Dollar at the Close of Business | | | | | |
|---|---|---|---|---|---|---|
| | 2/4 | 2/3 | 2/2 | 2/1 | 1/29 | 1/28 |
| Japanese yen | 80.13 | 80.84 | 80.14 | 83.05 | 84.35 | 84.32 |
| Swiss francs | 0.9540 | 0.9575 | 0.9533 | 0.9617 | 0.9557 | 0.9523 |

a. What is the foreign exchange (FX) position in dollar equivalents using the FX rates on February 4?

b. What is the definition of delta as it relates to the FX position?

c. What is the sensitivity of each FX position; that is, what is the value of delta for each currency on February 4?

d. What is the daily percentage change in exchange rates for each currency over the five-day period?

e. What is the total risk faced by the bank on each day? What is the worst-case day? What is the best-case day?

f. Assume that you have data for the 500 trading days preceding February 4. Explain how you would identify the worst-case scenario with a 99 percent degree of confidence.

g. Explain how the 1 percent value at risk (VAR) position would be interpreted for business on February 5.

h. How would the simulation change at the end of the day on February 5? What variables and/or processes in the analysis may change? What variables and/or processes will not change?

21. Export Bank has a trading position in euros and Australian dollars. At the close of business on October 20, the bank had €20 million and A$30 million. The exchange rates for the most recent six days are given below:

### Exchange Rates per U.S. Dollar at the Close of Business

|  | 10/20 | 10/19 | 10/18 | 10/17 | 10/16 | 10/15 |
|---|---|---|---|---|---|---|
| Euros | 0.8000 | 0.7970 | o.7775 | 0.7875 | 0.7950 | 0.8115 |
| Australian $s | 0.9700 | 0.9550 | 0.9800 | 0.9655 | 0.9505 | 0.9460 |

    a. What is the foreign exchange (FX) position in dollar equivalents using the FX rates on October 20?

    b. What is the sensitivity of each FX position; that is, what is the value of delta for each currency on October 20?

    c. What is the daily percentage change in exchange rates for each currency over the five-day period?

    d. What is the total risk faced by the bank on each day? What is the worst-case day? What is the best-case day?

22. What is the primary disadvantage of the back simulation approach in measuring market risk? What effect does the inclusion of more observation days have as a remedy for this disadvantage? What other remedies can be used to deal with the disadvantage?

23. How is Monte Carlo simulation useful in addressing the disadvantages of back simulation? What is the primary statistical assumption underlying its use?

24. What is the difference between VAR and expected shortfall (ES) as measure of market risk?

25. Consider the following discrete probability distribution of payoffs for two securities, A and B, held in the trading portfolio of an FI:

| Probability | A | Probability | B |
|---|---|---|---|
| 50.00% | $80m | 50.00% | $80m |
| 49.00 | 60m | 49.00 | 68m |
| 1.00 | −740m | 0.40 | −740m |
|  |  | 0.60 | −1,393m |

Which of the two securities will add more market risk to the FI's trading portfolio according to the VAR and ES measures?

26. Consider the following discrete probability distribution of payoffs for two securities, A and B, held in the trading portfolio of an FI:

| Probability | A | Probability | B |
|---|---|---|---|
| 55.00% | $120m | 55.00% | $120m |
| 44.00 | 95m | 44.00 | 100m |
| 1.00 | −1,100m | 0.30 | −1,100m |
|  |  | 0.70 | −1,414m |

Which of the two securities will add more market risk to the FI's trading portfolio according to the VAR and ES measures?

27. An FI has £5 million in its trading portfolio on the close of business on a particular day. The current exchange rate of pounds for dollars is £0.6400/$, or dollars for pounds is $1.5625, at the daily close. The volatility, or standard deviation ($\sigma$), of daily percentage changes in the spot £/$ exchange rate over the past year was 58.5 bp. The FI is interested in adverse moves–bad moves that will not occur more than 1 percent of the time, or 1 day in every 100. Calculate the one-day VAR and ES from this position.

28. An FI has ¥500 million in its trading portfolio on the close of business on a particular day. The current exchange rate of yen for dollars is ¥80.00/$, or dollars for yen is $0.0125, at the daily close. The volatility, or standard deviation ($\sigma$), of daily percentage changes in the spot ¥/$ exchange rate over the past year was 121.6 bp. The FI is interested in adverse moves–bad moves that will not occur more than 1 percent of the time, or 1 day in every 100. Calculate the one-day VAR and ES from this position.

29. Bank of Hawaii's stock portfolio has a market value of $250 million. The beta of the portfolio approximates the market portfolio, whose standard deviation ($\sigma_m$) has been estimated at 2.25 percent. What are the five-day VAR and ES of this portfolio using adverse rate changes in the 99th percentile?

30. Despite the fact that market risk capital requirements have been imposed on FIs since the 1990s, huge losses in value were recorded from losses incurred in FIs' trading portfolios. Why did this happen? What changes to capital requirements did regulators propose to prevent such losses from reoccurring?

31. In its trading portfolio, an FI holds 10,000 ExxonMobil (XOM) shares at a share price of $86.50 and has sold 5,000 General Electric (GE) shares under a forward contract that matures in one year. The current share price for GE is $20.50. The shift risk factor (i.e., standard deviation) for level 1 risk factor is 4 percent, for level II risk factor is 6 percent, for level III long positions is 9 percent, for level III short positions is −9 percent, and for nonhedgeable risk is 1 percent. Using the risk factors listed in Table 15–8, calculate the market risk capital charge on these securities.

32. In its trading portfolio, a U.S. FI is long £20 million worth of pound FX forward contracts and has sold €40 million of euro FX forward contracts that mature in one year. The current exchange rate of dollars for pounds is $1.5625 and the exchange rate of euros for pounds is $1.25 at the daily close. The shift risk factor (i.e., standard deviation) for level 1 risk factor is 5 percent, for level II risk factor for pounds is 8 percent, and for level II risk factors for euros is 12 percent. Using the risk factors listed in Table 15–8, calculate the market risk capital charge on these securities.

33. Suppose an FI's portfolio VAR for the previous 60 days was $3 million and stressed VAR for the previous 60 days was $8 million using the 1 percent worst case (or 99th percentile). Calculate the minimum capital charge for market risk for this FI.

# Integrated Mini Case

## CALCULATING DEAR ON AN FI'S TRADING PORTFOLIO

An FI wants to obtain the DEAR on its trading portfolio. The portfolio consists of the following securities.

*Fixed-income securities:*
(i) The FI has a $1 million position in a six-year, zero-coupon bond with a face value of $1,543,302. The bond is trading at a yield to maturity of 7.50 percent. The historical mean change in daily yields is 0.0 percent, and the standard deviation is 22 basis points.
(ii) The FI also holds a 12-year, zero-coupon bond with a face value of $1,000,000. The bond is trading at a yield to maturity of 6.75 percent. The price volatility if the potential adverse move in yields is 65 basis points.

*Foreign exchange contracts:*
The FI has a €2.0 million long trading position in spot euros at the close of business on a particular day. The exchange rate is €0.80/$1, or $1.25/€, at the daily close. Looking back at the daily percentage changes in the exchange rate of the euro to dollars for the past year, the FI finds that the volatility or standard deviation ($\sigma$) of the spot exchange rate was 55.5 basis points (bp).

*Equities:*
The FI holds a $2.5 million trading position in stocks that reflect the U.S. stock market index (e.g., the S&P 500). The $\beta = 1$. Over the last year, the standard deviation of the stock market index was 175 basis points. Correlations ($\rho_{ij}$) among assets are as follows:

|  | Six-Year, Zero-Coupon | 12-Year, Zero-Coupon | €/$ | U.S. Stock Index |
|---|---|---|---|---|
| Six-year, zero-coupon | – | 0.75 | −0.2 | 0.40 |
| 12-year, zero-coupon | – | – | −0.3 | 0.45 |
| €/$ | – | – | – | 0.25 |
| U.S. stock index | – | – | – | – |

Calculate the DEAR of this trading portfolio.

# Chapter **Sixteen**

**See Appendices Online at www.mhhe.com/saunders8e**
• Appendix 16A: A Letter of Credit Transaction

# Off-Balance-Sheet Risk

## INTRODUCTION

**contingent assets and liabilities**
Assets and liabilities off the balance sheet that potentially can produce positive or negative future cash flows for an FI.

One of the most important choices facing an FI manager is the relative scale of an FI's on- and off-balance-sheet (OBS) activities. Most of us are aware of on-balance-sheet activities because they appear on an FI's published asset and liability balance sheets. For example, an FI's deposits and holdings of bonds and loans are on-balance-sheet activities. By comparison, off-balance-sheet activities are less obvious and often are invisible to all but the best-informed investor or regulator. In accounting terms, *off-balance-sheet items* usually appear "below the bottom line," frequently just as footnotes to financial statements. In economic terms, however, off-balance-sheet items are **contingent assets and liabilities** that affect the future, rather than the current, shape of an FI's balance sheet. As such, they have a direct impact on the FI's future profitability and performance. Consequently, efficient management of these OBS items is central to controlling overall risk exposure in a modern FI.

From a valuation perspective, OBS assets and liabilities have the potential to produce positive or negative *future* cash flows. Fees from OBS activities provide a key source of noninterest income for many FIs, especially the largest and most creditworthy ones.[1] For example, in just the first quarter of 2012, derivative securities trading revenues earned by commercial banks topped $7.0 billion, compared to $1.9 billion in the first quarter of 1996, and up from a disastrous fourth quarter 2008 loss (at the height of the financial crisis) of $9.2 billion. FIs use some OBS activities (especially forwards, futures, options, and swaps) to reduce or manage their interest rate risk (see Chapters 8 and 9), foreign exchange risk (see Chapter 13), and credit risk (see Chapters 10 and 11) exposures in a manner superior to what would exist without these activities. However, OBS activities can

---

[1] This fee income can have both direct (e.g., a fee from the sale of a letter of credit) and indirect (through improved customer relationships) effects that have a positive income impact in other product areas. In cases where customers feel aggrieved with respect to derivatives purchased from a dealer FI, off-balance-sheet activities can have important negative reputational effects that have an adverse impact on the future flow of fees and other income.

**TABLE 16–1**
Major Types of
Off-Balance-Sheet
Activities

**Schedule L Activities***

**Loan commitment**   Contractual commitment to make a loan up to a stated amount at a given interest rate in the future.

**Letters of credit**   Contingent guarantees sold by an FI to underwrite the performance of the buyer of the guaranty.

**Derivative contract**   Agreement between two parties to exchange a standard quantity of an asset at a predetermined price at a specified date in the future.

**When-issued trading**   Trading in securities prior to their actual issue.

**Loans sold**   Loans originated by an FI and then sold to other investors that (in some cases) can be returned to the originating institution in the future if the credit quality of the loans deteriorates.

**Non–Schedule L Activities***

**Settlement risk**   Intraday credit risk, such as that associated with CHIPS wire transfer activities.

**Affiliate risk**   Risk imposed on one holding company affiliate as a result of the potential failure of the other holding company affiliates.

* As discussed later in the chapter, Schedule L activities are those that banks have to report to the Federal Reserve as part of their quarterly Call Reports. Non–Schedule L activities are those not subject to this requirement.

involve risks that add to an FI's overall risk exposure. Indeed, at the very heart of the financial crisis were losses associated with off-balance-sheet mortgage-backed securities created and held by FIs. Losses resulted in the failure, acquisition, or bailout of some of the largest FIs and a near meltdown of the world's financial and economic systems. As a result, the true value of an FI's capital or net worth is not simply the difference between the market value of assets and liabilities on its balance sheet, but also reflects the difference between the current market value of its off-balance-sheet or contingent assets and liabilities.

This chapter examines the various OBS activities (listed in Table 16–1) of FIs. We first discuss the effect of OBS activities on an FI's risk exposure, return performance, and solvency. We then describe the different types of OBS activities and the risks associated with each. Because OBS activities create solvency risk exposure, regulators impose capital requirements on these activities. These capital requirements are described in Chapter 20. While the discussion emphasizes that these activities may add to an FI's riskiness, the chapter concludes with a discussion of the role of OBS activities in reducing the risk of an FI.

# OFF-BALANCE-SHEET ACTIVITIES AND FI SOLVENCY

**off-balance-sheet asset**
An item or activity that, when a contingent event occurs, moves onto the asset side of the balance sheet.

An item or activity is an **off-balance-sheet asset** if, when a contingent event occurs, the item or activity moves onto the asset side of the balance sheet. Conversely, an item or activity is an **OBS liability** if, when the contingent event occurs, the item or activity moves onto the liability side of the balance sheet. For example, as we discuss in more detail later, FIs sell various performance guarantees, especially guarantees that their customers will not default on their financial and other obligations. Examples of such guarantees include letters of credit and standby letters of credit. Should a customer default occur, the FI's contingent liability (its guaranty) becomes an actual liability and it moves onto the liability side of the balance sheet. Indeed, FI managers and regulators are just beginning

**off-balance-sheet liability**
An item or activity that, when a contingent event occurs, moves onto the liability side of the balance sheet.

to recognize and measure the risk of OBS activities and their impact on the FI's value. While some part of OBS risk is related to interest rate risk, credit risk, and other risks, these items also introduce unique risks that must be managed by FIs. Indeed, the failure or near failure of some of the largest U.S. financial institutions during the financial crisis can be attributed to risks associated with OBS activities (e.g., investment banks—Lehman Brothers, Bear Stearns, and Merrill Lynch; savings institution—Washington Mutual; insurance company—AIG; commercial bank—Citigroup; finance company—CIT Group; and government sponsored agencies—Fannie Mae and Freddie Mac). Losses from the falling value of subprime mortgages and OBS securities backed by these mortgages reached over $1 trillion worldwide through mid-2009. As we discuss later in the chapter, FI OBS holdings and the collapse of the mortgage market in the mid and late-2000s resulted in changes in the regulation of OBS activities at FIs. Table 16–2 lists some other notable losses for FIs from trading in derivatives. (Derivative securities [futures, forwards, options, and swaps] are examined in detail in Chapters 22, 23 and 24 and defined in Table 16–3.)

**TABLE 16–2** Some Big Losses on Derivatives

Sources: Dan Atkinson, "UBS Pledged Derivatives Explanation," *Manchester Guardian*, 1998; and update by author.

- September–October 1994: Bankers Trust is sued by Gibson Greeting and Procter & Gamble over derivative losses which amounted to $21 million for Gibson and a $200 million settlement for Procter & Gamble.
- February 1995: Barings, Britain's oldest investment bank, announces a loss, which ultimately totals $1.38 billion, related to derivatives trading in Singapore by trader Nicholas Leeson.
- December 1996: NatWest Bank finds losses of £77 million caused by mispricing of derivatives in its investment-banking arm. Former trader Kyriacos Papouis was blamed for the loss, caused by two years of unauthorized trading by him, but NatWest Markets chief Martin Owen resigned over the incident.
- March 1997: Damian Cope, a former trader at Midland Bank's New York branch, was banned by the Federal Reserve Board over the falsification of books and records relating to his interest-rate derivatives trading activities. Midland parent HSBC said the amount of money involved was not significant.
- November 1997: Chase Manhattan was found to have lost up to $200 million on trading emerging-market debt; part of the problem was reportedly due to debt; part of the problem was reportedly due to exposure to emerging markets through complex derivatives products.
- January 1998: Union Bank of Switzerland was reported sitting on unquantified derivatives losses; UBS pledged full disclosure at a later date.

- August–September 1998: Long-Term Capital Management, a hedge fund with an exposure exceeding $1.25 trillion in derivatives and other securities, had to be rescued by a consortium of commercial and investment banks that infused an additional $3.65 billion of equity into the fund.
- July 2001: J.P. Morgan Chase and Citigroup exposed to $2.25 billion in losses on credit derivatives issued to a failing Enron.
- December 2001–January 2002: Allied Irish Banks incurs a $750 million loss from foreign exchange trades by rogue trader John Rusnak.
- September 2006: Amaranth Advisors loses $6 billion on investments in natural gas futures. Total assets before loss were $9 billion.
- September 2007: Calyon Securities' Richard Bierbaum unauthorized trading of credit derivatives caused his company $353 million in losses.
- February 2008: Société Générale's Jerome Kerviel used futures on the European stock indexes to place huge bets that European markets would continue to rise. At the beginning of 2008 the market turned against him and European markets fell sharply and amounted to the largest market risk related loss ever of $7.2 billion. He was able to circumvent any controls the bank had because he had worked in the "back office" and knew how trades were processed.
- February 2008: MF Global loses $141 million as rogue trader Evan Dooley made unauthorized trades in wheat futures.

**TABLE 16–2**   *(continued)*

| |
|---|
| • June 2008: Morgan Stanley loses $120 million as Matt Piper, a trader in credit default swaps and credit index options, inflates the value of his work in an attempt to boost his pay packet. |

- June 2008: Morgan Stanley loses $120 million as Matt Piper, a trader in credit default swaps and credit index options, inflates the value of his work in an attempt to boost his pay packet.
- April 2011: Morgan Stanley loses $1.75 billion after a series of poorly hedged bets on to interest rate and foreign exchange swaps racked up trading losses for the January–March period.
- September 2011: UBS AG loses $2 billion from unauthorized derivatives trading by a rogue trader, Kweku Adoboli. The UBS statement claimed Mr. Adoboli had conducted legitimate derivative transactions, giving the bank heavy exposure to various stock market indexes. But he had then entered "fictitious" hedges against these positions into UBS's risk management system, while in reality he had no hedge in place and was breaching the risk limits that the bank required him to work within.
- May 2012: J.P. Morgan Chase loses more than $2 billion in trading by Bruno Iksil, also known as "the London Whale," who had taken large credit default swap (CDS) positions in expectation that the financial crisis in Europe would cause anxiety in financial markets. Instead, bailouts, austerity measures, and interventions prevented any major events in Europe.

**TABLE 16–3**   **Derivative Securities Held Off the Balance Sheet of FIs**

**Forward contract**   An agreement between a buyer and a seller at time 0 to exchange a nonstandardized asset for cash at some future date. The details of the asset and the price to be paid at the forward contract expiration date are set at time 0. The price of the forward contract is fixed over the life of the contract.

**Futures contract**   An agreement between a buyer and a seller at time 0 to exchange a standardized asset for cash at some future date. Each contract has a standardized expiration and transactions occur in a centralized market. The price of the futures contract changes daily as the market value of the asset underlying the futures fluctuates.

**Option**   A contract that gives the holder the right, but not the obligation, to buy or sell the underlying asset at a specified price within a specified period of time.

**Swap**   An agreement between two parties to exchange assets or a series of cash flows for a specific period of time at a specified interval.

**delta of an option**
The change in the value of an option for a unit change in the price of the underlying security.

**notional value of an OBS item**
The face value of an OBS item.

Since off-balance-sheet items are contingent assets and liabilities and move onto the balance sheet with a probability less than 1, their valuation is difficult and often highly complex. Because many off-balance-sheet items involve option features, the most common methodology has been to apply contingent claims/option pricing theory models of finance. For example, one relatively simple way to estimate the value of an OBS position in options is by calculating the **delta of an option**—the sensitivity of an option's value to a unit change in the price of the underlying security, which is then multiplied by the notional value of the option's position. (The delta of an option lies between 0 and 1.) Thus, suppose an FI has bought call options on bonds (i.e., it has an OBS asset) with a face or **notional value** of $100 million and the delta is calculated at 0.25.[2] Then the contingent asset value of this option position would be $25 million:

$$d = \text{Delta of an option} = \frac{\text{Change in the option's price}}{\text{Change in price of underlying security}} = \frac{dO}{dS} = 0.25$$

$$F = \text{Notional or face value of options} = \$100 \text{ million}$$

---

[2] A 1-cent change in the price of the bonds underlying the call option leads to a 0.25 cent (or quarter-cent) change in the price of the option.

The delta equivalent or contingent asset value = delta × face value of option = 0.25 × $100 million = $25 million. Of course, to figure the value of delta for the option, one needs an option pricing model such as Black–Scholes or a binomial model. (We provide a review of these models in Appendix 10B, located at the book's website [**www.mhhe.com/saunders8e**].) In general, the delta of the option varies with the level of the price of the underlying security as it moves in and out of the money;[3] that is, $0 < d < 1$.[4] Note that if the FI sold options, they would be valued as a contingent liability.

Loan commitments and letters of credit are also off-balance-sheet activities that have option features. Specifically, the holder of a loan commitment or credit line who decides to draw on that credit line is exercising an *option to borrow*. When the buyer of a guaranty defaults, this buyer is exercising a *default* option. Similarly, when the counterparty to a derivatives transaction is unable or unwilling to meet its obligation to pay (e.g., in a swap), this is considered an exercise of a default option.

With respect to swaps, futures, and forwards, a common approach is to convert these positions into an equivalent value of the underlying assets. For example, a $20 million, 10-year, fixed–floating interest rate swap in which an FI receives 20 semiannual fixed–interest rate payments of 8 percent per year (i.e., 4 percent per half year) and pays floating-rate payments every half year, indexed to LIBOR, can be viewed as the equivalent, in terms of valuation, of an on-balance-sheet position in two $20 million bonds. That is, the FI can be viewed as being long $20 million (holding an asset) in a 10-year bond with an annual coupon of 8 percent per year and short $20 million (holding a liability) in a floating-rate bond of 10 years' maturity whose rate is adjusted every six months. The market value of the swap can be viewed as the present value of the difference between the cash flows on the fixed-rate bond and the expected cash flows on the floating-rate bond. This market value is usually a very small percent of the notional value of the swap. In our example of a $20 million swap, the market value is about 3 percent of this figure, or $600,000. The Bank for International Settlements reported the total notional value of OTC derivative securities was $647.8 billion in 2012, and the market value of these securities was $27.3 billion (or 4.2 percent of notional value). In December 2008 (after the start of the financial crisis), the notional value was $591.96 billion (the first ever decrease) and market value was $33.89 billion (5.7 percent).

www.bis.org

Given these valuation models, we can calculate, in an approximate sense, the current or market value of each OBS asset and liability and its effect on an FI's solvency. Indeed, from both the stockholders' and regulators' perspectives, large increases in the value of OBS liabilities can render an FI economically insolvent

---

[3] For example, for an in-the-money call option the price of the underlying security exceeds the option's exercise price. For an out-of-the money call option, the price of the underlying security is less than the option's exercise price. In general, the relationship between the value of an option and the underlying value of a security is nonlinear. Thus, using the delta method to derive the market value of an option is at best an approximation. To deal with the nonlinearity of payoffs on options, some analysts take into account the gamma as well as the delta of the option (gamma measures the change in delta as the underlying security price varies). For example, the standardized model of the BIS used to calculate the market risk of options incorporates an option's delta, its gamma, and its vega (a measure of volatility risk).

[4] In the context of the Black–Scholes model, the value of the delta on a call option is $d = N(d_1)$, where $N(.)$ is the cumulative normal distribution function and $d_1 = [ln(S/X) + (r + \sigma^2/2)T]/\sigma \sqrt{T}$ (see Chapter 10).

just as effectively as can losses due to mismatched interest rate gaps and default or credit losses from on-balance-sheet activities. For example, during the financial crisis losses on OBS collateralized debt obligations linked to U.S. mortgages reached $260 billion.

| **Concept Questions** | 1. Define a contingent asset and a contingent liability. |
| --- | --- |
| | 2. How can option pricing theory be used to price OBS assets and liabilities? |

## RETURNS AND RISKS OF OFF-BALANCE-SHEET ACTIVITIES

In the 1980s, rising losses on loans to less developed and Eastern European countries, increased interest rate volatility, and squeezed interest margins for on-balance-sheet lending due to nonbank competition induced many large commercial banks to seek profitable OBS activities. By moving activities off the balance sheet, banks hoped to earn more fee income to offset declining margins or spreads on their traditional lending business. At the same time, they could avoid regulatory costs or taxes, since reserve requirements, deposit insurance premiums, and capital adequacy requirements were not levied on off-balance-sheet activities. Thus, banks had both earnings and regulatory tax-avoidance incentives to move activities off their balance sheets.[5]

www.federalreserve.gov

The dramatic growth in OBS activities caused the Federal Reserve to introduce a tracking scheme in 1983. As part of their quarterly Call Reports, banks and savings institutions began submitting Schedule L on which they listed the notional size and variety of their OBS activities. We show these off-balance-sheet activities for U.S. commercial banks and savings institutions for 1992 and first quarter 2012 in Table 16–4. We also show the 2012 distribution of OBS activities for J.P. Morgan Chase in Table 16–4.

In Table 16–4 notice the relative growth of off-balance-sheet activities. In 1992, the notional or face value of OBS activities was $10,358.9 billion compared with $3,506.2 billion in on-balance-sheet activities. By the first quarter of 2012, the notional value of these OBS activities was $237,377.6 billion (an increase of 2,192 percent in just over 21 years) compared with $12,781.0 billion of on-balance-sheet activities (an increase of 265 percent). Likewise, in 2012 J.P. Morgan Chase alone had total OBS activities of $73,646.3 billion ($72,236.7 billion of which were derivative contracts [futures, forwards, swaps, options, and credit derivatives]) compared with on-balance-sheet assets of $1,975.7 billion. Table 16–5 shows that much of the growth in OBS activities during the period 1992–2012 was due to derivative contracts. Holdings of these contracts increased 2,501 percent, from $8,765 billion in 1992 to $227,982 billion in the first quarter of 2012. The vast majority of these OBS activities are conducted by just a few banks. For example, in 2012 approximately 1,291 of the over 7,307 U.S. banks and savings institutions held the OBS derivatives reported in Table 16–5, and the largest 25 banks held 99.8 percent

---

[5] Chapter 25 goes into further details on incentives relating to loan sales.

**TABLE 16–4** Aggregate Volume of Off-Balance-Sheet Commitments and Contingencies by U.S. Commercial Banks and Savings Institutions (in billions of dollars)

Source: FDIC, *Statistics on Banking*, various issues. *www.fdic.gov*

| | 1992 | 2012* | Distribution 2012 | J.P. Morgan Chase 2012* |
|---|---|---|---|---|
| Commitments to lend | $ 1,281.1 | $ 5,287.8 | 2.2% | $ 878.5 |
| Future and forward contracts (excludes FX) | | | | |
| On commodities and equities | 26.3 | 307.1 | 0.1 | 193.2 |
| On interest rates | 1,738.1 | 27,240.3 | 11.5 | 8,863.0 |
| Notional amount of credit derivatives | | | | |
| Bank is guarantor | 0.0 | 7,003.2 | 2.9 | 3,157.4 |
| Bank is beneficiary | 0.0 | 7,047.2 | 3.0 | 3,008.4 |
| Standby contracts and other option contracts | | | | |
| Written option contracts on interest rates | 504.7 | 13,656.3 | 5.8 | 3,999.5 |
| Purchased option contracts on interest rates | 508.0 | 14,214.6 | 6.0 | 4,102.3 |
| Written option contracts on foreign exchange | 245.7 | 2,232.6 | 0.9 | 711.4 |
| Purchased option contracts on foreign exchange | 249.1 | 2,249.4 | 1.0 | 721.3 |
| Written option contracts on commodities and equities | 30.9 | 1,197.8 | 0.5 | 850.5 |
| Purchased option contracts on commodities and equities | 29.4 | 1,074.6 | 0.5 | 762.3 |
| Commitments to buy FX (includes US$), spot, and forward | 3,015.5 | 15,430.1 | 6.5 | 4,723.2 |
| Standby LCs and foreign office guarantees | 162.5 | 515.1 | 0.2 | 125.1 |
| (amount of these items sold to others via participations) | (14.9) | (81.3) | | (18.8) |
| Commercial LCs | 28.1 | 25.9 | 0.0 | 6.1 |
| Participations in acceptances bought from others | 0.2 | 4.3 | 0.0 | 0.0 |
| Securities lent | 96.4 | 1,025.9 | 0.4 | 225.4 |
| Other significant commitments and contingencies | 8.7 | 236.1 | 0.1 | 174.5 |
| Notional value of all outstanding interest rate, FX, and commodity swaps | 2,417.2 | 138,629.0 | 58.4 | 41,144.2 |
| Mortgages or small business loans sold, with recourse | | | | |
| Outstanding principal balance of loans sold or swapped | 10.7 | 0.2 | 0.0 | 0.0 |
| Amount of recourse exposure on these loans | 6.3 | 0.1 | 0.0 | 0.0 |
| Total | $10,358.9 | $237,377.6 | 100.0% | $73,646.3 |
| Total assets (on-balance-sheet items) | $ 3,506.2 | $ 12,781.0 | | $ 1,975.7 |

FX = foreign exchange, LC = letter of credit.
\* First quarter.

**TABLE 16–5**
**Derivative Contracts Held by Commercial Banks, by Contract Product (in billions of dollars)\***

Source: Office of the Comptroller of the Currency website, various dates. *www.occ.treas.gov*

| | 1992 | 1996 | 2000 | 2004 | 2008 | 2012 (first quarter) |
|---|---|---|---|---|---|---|
| Futures and forwards | $4,780 | $ 8,041 | $ 9,877 | $11,343 | $ 22,512 | $ 40,604 |
| Swaps | 2,417 | 7,601 | 21,949 | 56,411 | 131,706 | 138,671 |
| Options | 1,568 | 4,393 | 8,292 | 17,750 | 30,267 | 34,656 |
| Credit derivatives | — | — | 426 | 2,347 | 15,897 | 14,051 |
| Total | $8,765 | $20,035 | $40,544 | $87,880 | $200,382 | $227,982 |

\* Credit derivatives were reported for the first time in the first quarter of 1997.

of the derivatives outstanding. While, as noted above, the notional value of OBS items overestimates their current market or contingent claims values, the growth of these activities is still nothing short of phenomenal. Indeed, this phenomenal increase has pushed regulators to impose capital requirements on such activities and to explicitly recognize FIs' solvency risk exposure from pursuing such activities. These capital requirements came into affect on January 1, 1993; we describe them in Chapter 20.

From Tables 16–4 and 16–5, the major types of OBS activities for U.S. banks are:

- Loan commitments
- Standby letters of credit and letters of credit
- Futures, forward contracts, swaps, and options
- When-issued securities
- Loans sold

Insurance companies engage in most of these OBS activities as well.

The next section analyzes these OBS activities in more detail and pays particular attention to the types of risk exposure an FI faces when engaging in such activities. As we discussed earlier, precise market valuation of these contingent assets and liabilities can be extremely difficult because of their complex contingent claim features and option aspects. At a very minimum, FI managers should understand not only the general features of the risk exposure associated with each major OBS asset and liability but also how each one can impact the return and profitability of an FI.

## Loan Commitments

**loan commitment agreement**
A contractual commitment to make a loan up to a stated amount at a given interest rate in the future.

These days, most commercial and industrial loans are made by firms that take down (or borrow against) prenegotiated lines of credit or loan commitments rather than borrow spot loans (see Chapter 10's discussion on C&I loans). In May 2012 over 93.0 percent of all one month to one year maturity and over 91.7 percent of greater than one year maturity C&I loans were made under commitment contracts.[6] A **loan commitment agreement** is a contractual commitment by an FI to lend to a firm a certain maximum amount (say, $10 million) at given interest rate terms (say, 12 percent). The loan commitment agreement also defines the length of time over which the borrower has the option to take down this loan. In return for making this loan commitment, the FI may charge an **up-front fee** (or facility fee) of, say, $\frac{1}{8}$ percent of the commitment size, or $12,500 in this example. In addition, the FI must stand ready to supply the full $10 million at any time over the commitment period—say, one year. Meanwhile, the borrower has a valuable option to take down any amount between $0 and $10 million. The FI also may charge the borrower a **back-end fee** (or commitment fee) on any unused balances in the commitment line at the end of the period. In this example, if the borrower takes down only $8 million in funds over the year and the fee on *unused* commitments is ¼ percent, the FI will generate additional revenue of ¼ percent times $2 million, or $5,000. Figure 16–1 presents a summary of the structure of this loan commitment.

**up-front fee**
The fee charged for making funds available through a loan commitment.

**back-end fee**
The fee imposed on the unused balance of a loan commitment.

[6] See Board of Governors of the Federal Reserve website, "Survey of Terms of Business Lending," www.federalreserve.gov, August 2012.

**FIGURE 16–1**
**Structure of a Loan Commitment**

Up-front fee of 1/8% on whole line

Back-end fee of 1/4% on unused portion

0 ◄─── 1 year $10 million commitment ───► 1

**EXAMPLE 16–1**

*Calculation of the Promised Return on a Loan Commitment*

It is quite easy to show how the unique features of loan commitments affect the promised return $(1 + k)$ on a loan. In Chapter 10 we developed a model for determining $(1 + k)$ on a spot loan. This can be extended by allowing for partial takedown and the up-front and back-end fees commonly found in loan commitments. For a one-year loan commitment, let:

$BR$ = FI's base Interest on the loans = 12%

$\phi$ = Risk premium on loan commitment = 2%

$f_1$ = Up-front fee on the whole commitment = $\frac{1}{8}$%

$f_2$ = Back-end fee on the unused commitment = $\frac{1}{4}$%

$b$ = Compensating balance on loans = 10%

$RR$ = Reserve requirements = 10%

$td$ = Expected (average) takedown rate $(0 < td < 1)$ on the loan commitment = 75%

Then the general formula for the promised return $(1 + k)$ of the loan commitment is:[7]

$$1 + k = 1 + \frac{f_1 + f_2(1 - td) + (BR + \phi)td}{td - [b(td)(1 - RR)]}$$

$$1 + k = 1 + \frac{0.00125 + 0.0025(0.25) + (0.12 + 0.02)0.75}{0.75 - [(0.10)(0.75)(0.9)]}$$

$$1 + k = 1 + \frac{0.106875}{0.682500} = 1.1566 \text{ or } k = 15.66\%$$

Note that only when the borrower actually draws on the commitment do the loans made under the commitment appear on the balance sheet. Thus, only when the $8 million loan is taken down does the balance sheet show a new $8 million loan being created. When the $10 million commitment is made at time 0, nothing shows on the balance sheet. Nevertheless, the FI must stand ready to make the full $10 million in loans on any day within the one-year commitment period; that is, at time 0 a new contingent claim on the resources of the FI was created.

This raises the question: What contingent risks are created by the loan commitment provision? At least four types of risk are associated with the extension of loan commitments: interest rate risk, takedown risk, credit risk, and aggregate funding risk.

---

[7] Note that for simplicity we have used undiscounted cash flows. Taking into account the time value of money means that we would need to discount both $f_2$ and $BR + m$ since they are paid at the end of the period. If the discount factor (cost of funds) is $d = 10$ percent, then $k = 14.25$ percent.

## Interest Rate Risk

*Interest rate risk* is a contingent risk emanating from the fact that the FI precommits to make loans available to a borrower over the commitment period at either (1) some fixed interest rate as a fixed-rate loan commitment or (2) some variable rate as a variable-rate loan commitment. Suppose the FI precommits to lend a maximum of $10 million at a fixed rate of 12 percent over the year and its cost of funds rises. The cost of funds may well rise to a level that makes the spread between the 12 percent commitment rate and the FI's cost of funds negative or very small. Moreover, 12 percent may be much less than the rate the customer would have to pay if forced to borrow on the spot loan market under current interest rate conditions. When rates do rise over the commitment period, the FI stands to lose on its portfolio of fixed-rate loan commitments as borrowers exercise to the full amount their valuable options to borrow at below-market rates.[8]

One way the FI can control this risk is by making commitment rates float with spot loan rates, for example, by indexing loan commitments to the prime rate. If the prime rate rises during the commitment period, so does the cost of commitment loans to the borrower—the borrower pays the market rate in effect when the commitment is drawn on. Nevertheless, this fixed formula rate solution does not totally eradicate interest rate risk on loan commitments. For example, suppose that the prime rate rises 1 percent but the cost of funds rises 1.25 percent; the spread between the indexed commitment loan and the cost of funds narrows by 0.25 percent. This spread risk is often called **basis risk.**[9]

**basis risk**
The variable spread between a lending rate and a borrowing rate or between any two interest rates or prices.

## Takedown Risk

Another contingent risk is **takedown risk.** Specifically, in making the loan commitment, the FI must always stand ready to provide the maximum of the commitment line—$10 million in our example. The borrower has the flexible option to borrow anything between $0 and the $10 million ceiling on any business day in the commitment period. This exposes the FI to a degree of future liquidity risk or uncertainty (see Chapter 13). The FI can never be absolutely sure when, during the commitment period, the borrower will demand the full $10 million or some proportion thereof in cash. Indeed, the borrower could come to the bank and borrow different amounts over the period ($1 million in month 1, $2 million in month 2, etc.). The only constraint is the $10 million ceiling.

**takedown risk**
The uncertainty involved with the timing of the takedown on a loan commitment.

In mid-September 2008, the net asset value of a prominent money market mutual fund fell below $1 per share, a rare event that had not occurred in many years. Investors responded with massive withdrawals from prime money market mutual funds, which hold substantial amounts of commercial paper. These outflows severely undermined the stability of short-term funding markets, upon which many large corporations rely heavily to meet their short-term borrowing needs. As a result, many financial and nonfinancial firms turned to their backup lines of credit at commercial banks for funding. For example, in June 2008, General Motors Corp. had more than $22 billion in bank credit lines available from

---

[8] In an options sense, the loans are in the money to the borrower.

[9] Basis risk arises because loan rates and deposit rates are not perfectly correlated in their movements over time.

FIs such as Bank of America and Citigroup. By the end of the year, with worries of the firm's bankruptcy limiting the availability of any nonpublic funding, General Motors had exhausted its available credit lines, taking down the full amount available to them. The Federal Reserve reported that banks' unused commitments to fund construction of both commercial and residential properties fell about 30 percent in 2008. Further, in the fourth quarter of 2008, nearly 45 percent of banks reported an increase in the dollar amount of C&I loans drawn under preexisting commitments over the previous three months. To some extent, at least, the back-end fee on unused amounts is designed to create incentives for the borrower to take down lines in full to avoid paying this fee. However, in actuality, many lines are only partially drawn upon.

### Credit Risk

FIs also face a degree of contingent credit risk in setting the interest rate on a loan commitment. Specifically, the FI often adds a risk premium based on its current assessment of the creditworthiness of the borrower. For example, the borrower may be judged as an AA credit risk paying 1 percent above prime rate. However, suppose that over the one-year commitment period the borrowing firm gets into difficulty; its earnings decline so that its creditworthiness is downgraded to BBB. The FI's problem is that the credit risk premium on the commitment had been preset to the AA level for the one-year commitment period.

To avoid being exposed to dramatic declines in borrower creditworthiness over the commitment period, most FIs include an *adverse material change in conditions clause* by which the FI can cancel or reprice a loan commitment. For example, because of the deteriorating credit quality of business and household borrowers in late 2008, banks reduced or canceled lines of credit to businesses and households, as well as unused commitments to fund loans contracted. However, exercising such a clause is really a last resort tactic for an FI because it may put the borrower out of business and result in costly legal claims for breach of contract.[10]

### Aggregate Funding Risk

Many large borrowing firms, such as Home Depot, Ford, and IBM, take out multiple commitment or credit lines with many FIs as insurance against future credit crunches. In a credit crunch, the supply of spot loans to borrowers is restricted, possibly as a result of restrictive monetary policy actions of the Federal Reserve. Another cause is an FI's increased aversion toward lending, such as seen during the financial crisis when banks were unwilling to lend to any but the most creditworthy loan applicants.

In such credit crunches, borrowers with long-standing loan commitments are unlikely to be as credit constrained as those without loan commitments. However, this also implies that borrowers' aggregate demand to take down loan commitments is likely to be greatest when the FI's borrowing and funding conditions are most costly and difficult. In difficult credit conditions, this aggregate commitment takedown effect can increase the cost of funds above normal levels while many FIs scramble for funds to meet their commitments to customers. For example in mid-September 2008, financial markets had frozen and banks stopped lending to each

---

[10] Potential damage claims can be enormous if the borrower goes out of business and attributes this to the cancelation of loans under the commitment contract. There are also important reputational costs to take into account in canceling a commitment to lend.

other at anything but exorbitantly high rates. The overnight London Interbank Offered Rate (a benchmark rate that reflects the rate at which banks lend to one another) more than doubled. Banks generally rely on each other for cash needed to meet their daily needs. Interest rates on this interbank borrowing are generally low because of the confidence that the financial institutions will pay each other back. But confidence had broken down since August of 2007 and had not been completely restored. This is similar to the *externality effect* common in many markets when all participants simultaneously act together and adversely affect the costs of each individual participant.

The four contingent risk effects just identified—interest rate risk, takedown risk, credit risk, and aggregate funding risk—appear to imply that loan commitment activities increase the insolvency exposure of FIs that engage in such activities. However, an opposing view holds that loan commitment contracts may make an FI less risky than had it not engaged in them. This view maintains that to be able to charge fees and sell loan commitments or equivalent credit insurance, the FI must convince borrowers that it will still be around to provide the credit needed in the *future.* To convince borrowers that an FI will be around to meet its future commitments, managers may have to adopt *lower*-risk portfolios *today* than would otherwise be the case. By adopting lower-risk portfolios, managers increase the probability that the FI will be able to meet all its long-term on- and off-balance-sheet obligations. Interestingly, empirical studies have confirmed that banks making more loan commitments have lower on-balance-sheet portfolio risk characteristics than those with relatively low levels of commitments; that is, safer banks have a greater tendency to make loan commitments.

## Commercial Letters of Credit and Standby Letters of Credit

**commercial letters of credit**

Contingent guarantees sold by an FI to underwrite the trade or commercial performance of the buyer of the guaranty.

**standby letters of credit**

Guarantees issued to cover contingencies that are potentially more severe and less predictable than contingencies covered under trade-related or commercial letters of credit.

In selling **commercial letters of credit** (LCs) and **standby letters of credit** (SLCs) for fees, FIs add to their contingent future liabilities. Both LCs and SLCs are essentially *guarantees* sold by an FI to underwrite the *performance* of the buyer of the guaranty (such as a corporation). In economic terms, the FI that sells LCs and SLCs is selling insurance against the frequency or severity of some particular future occurrence. Further, similar to the different lines of insurance sold by property–casualty insurers, LC and SLC contracts differ as to the severity and frequency of their risk exposures. We look next at an FI's risk exposure from engaging in LC and SLC off-balance-sheet activities.

### Commercial Letters of Credit

Commercial letters of credit are widely used in both domestic and international trade. For example, they ease the shipment of grain between a farmer in Iowa and a purchaser in New Orleans or the shipment of goods between a U.S. importer and a foreign exporter. The FI's role is to provide a formal guaranty that payment for goods shipped or sold will be forthcoming regardless of whether the buyer of the goods defaults on payment. We show a very simple LC example in Figure 16–2 for an international transaction between a U.S. importer and a German exporter.

Suppose the U.S. importer sent an order for $10 million worth of machinery to a German exporter, as shown by arrow 1 in Figure 16–2. However, the German exporter may be reluctant to send the goods without some assurance or guaranty of being paid once the goods are shipped. The U.S. importer may promise to pay for the goods in 90 days, but the German exporter may feel insecure either because

**FIGURE 16–2**
Simple Letter of
Credit Transaction

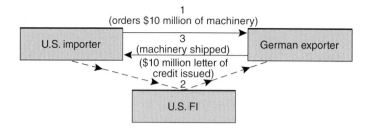

it knows little about the creditworthiness of the U.S. importer or because the U.S. importer has a low credit rating (say, B or BB). To persuade the German exporter to ship the goods, the U.S. importer may have to turn to a large U.S. FI with which it has developed a long-term customer relationship. In its role as a lender and monitor, the U.S. FI can better appraise the U.S. importer's creditworthiness. The U.S. FI can issue a contingent payment guaranty—that is, an LC to the German exporter on the importer's behalf—in return for an LC fee paid by the U.S. importer.[11] In our example, the FI would send to the German exporter an LC guaranteeing payment for the goods in 90 days regardless of whether the importer defaults on its obligation to the German exporter (see arrow 2 in Figure 16–2). Implicitly, the FI is replacing the U.S. importer's credit risk with its own credit risk guaranty. For this substitution to work effectively, in guaranteeing payment, the FI must have a higher credit standing or better credit quality reputation than the U.S. importer. Once the FI issues the LC and sends it to the German exporter, the exporter ships the goods to the U.S. importer, as shown by arrow 3. The probability is very high that in 90 days' time, the U.S. importer will pay the German exporter for the goods sent and the FI keeps the LC fee as profit. The fee is, perhaps, 10 basis points of the face value of the letter of credit, or $10,000 in this example. A more detailed version of an LC transaction is presented in Appendix 16A, located at the book's website (**www.mhhe.com/saunders8e**).

### Standby Letters of Credit

Standby letters of credit perform an insurance function similar to that of commercial letters of credit. However, the structure and type of risks covered are different. FIs may issue SLCs to cover contingencies that are potentially more *severe*, less *predictable* or frequent, and not necessarily trade related. These contingencies include

---

[11] The FI subsequently notifies the German exporter that, upon meeting the delivery requirements, the exporter is entitled to draw a time draft against the letter of credit at the importer's FI (i.e., withdraw money) for the amount of the transaction. After the export order is shipped, the German exporter presents the time draft and the shipping papers to its own (foreign) FI, who forwards these to the U.S. importer's U.S. FI. The U.S. FI stamps the time draft as accepted and the draft becomes a banker's acceptance listed *on the balance sheet*. At this point, the U.S. FI either returns the stamped time draft (now a banker's acceptance) to the German exporter's FI and payment is made on the maturity date (e.g., in 90 days), or the U.S. FI immediately pays the foreign FI (and implicitly the exporter) the discounted value of the banker's acceptance. In either case, the foreign FI pays the German exporter for the goods. When the banker's acceptance matures, the U.S. importer must pay its U.S. FI for the purchases, and the U.S. FI sends the U.S. importer the shipping papers.

performance bond guarantees whereby an FI may guarantee that a real estate development will be completed in some interval of time. Alternatively, the FI may offer default guarantees to back an issue of commercial paper (CP) or municipal revenue bonds to allow issuers to achieve a higher credit rating and a lower funding cost than would otherwise be the case.

Without credit enhancements, for example, many firms would be unable to borrow in the CP market or would have to borrow at a higher funding cost. P1 borrowers, who offer the highest-quality commercial paper, normally pay 40 basis points less than P2 borrowers, the next quality grade. By paying a fee of perhaps 25 basis points to an FI, the FI guarantees to pay CP purchasers' principal and interest on maturity should the issuing firm itself be unable to pay. The SLC backing of CP issues normally results in the paper's placement in the lowest default risk class (P1) and the issuer's savings of up to 15 basis points on issuing costs— 40 basis points (the P2–P1 spread) minus the 25-basis-point SLC fee equals 15 basis points.

Note that in selling the SLCs, FIs are competing directly with another of their OBS products, loan commitments. Rather than buying an SLC from an FI to back a CP issue, the issuing firm might pay a fee to an FI to supply a loan commitment. This loan commitment would match the size and maturity of the CP issue, for example, a $100 million ceiling and 45 days maturity. If, on maturity, the CP issuer has insufficient funds to repay the CP holders, the issuer has the right to take down the $100 million loan commitment and to use those funds to meet CP repayments. Often, the up-front fees on such loan commitments are less than those on SLCs. Therefore, many CP-issuing firms prefer to use loan commitments.

It needs to be stressed that U.S. banks are not the only issuers of SLCs. Not surprisingly, performance bonds and financial guarantees are an important business line of property–casualty insurers. The growth in these lines for property–casualty insurers has come at the expense of U.S. banks. Moreover, foreign banks increasingly are taking a share of the U.S. market in SLCs. The reason for the loss in this business line by U.S. banks is that to sell guarantees such as SLCs credibly, the seller must have a better credit rating than the customer. In recent years, few U.S. banks or their parent holding companies have had AA ratings. Other domestic FIs and foreign banks, on the other hand, have more often had AA ratings. High credit ratings not only make the guarantor more attractive from the buyer's perspective but also make the guarantor more competitive because its cost of funds is lower than that of less creditworthy FIs.

### Risks Associated with Letters of Credit

The risk to an FI in selling a letter of credit is that the buyer of the LC may fail to perform as promised under a contractual obligation. For example, with the commercial LC described above, there exists a small probability that the U.S. importer will be unable to pay the $10 million in 90 days and will default. Then the FI would be obliged to make good on its guaranty that the contractual obligation will be fulfilled. The cost of such a default would mean that the guaranteeing FI must pay $10 million to the exporter, although it would have a creditor's claim against the importer's assets to offset this loss. Likewise, for the SLC, there is a small probability that the CP issuer will be unable to pay the CP holders the $100 million as promised at maturity. The FI would then be obligated to pay $100 million to the CP holders (investors) on the issuer's behalf. Clearly, the fee on letters of credit should exceed the expected default risk on the LC or SLC, which is equal to the probability of a default by a counterparty times the expected net payout on the letter of credit, after adjusting for the FI's ability to reclaim assets from the defaulting importer/CP issuer and any monitoring costs.

During the financial crisis, many firms were unable to pay their maturing commercial paper obligations. The amount of potential defaults would have crippled already liquidity strapped FIs that had written standby letters of credit backing the commercial paper. In response, the Federal Reserve Board announced the creation of the Commercial Paper Funding Facility (CPFF), a facility that complemented the Federal Reserve's existing credit facilities to help provide liquidity to short-term funding markets. Under the plan, the Federal Reserve stepped in to purchase commercial paper and other short-term debt that financed companies' day-to-day operations. Thus, rather than having to draw on bank letters of credit to pay the commercial paper liabilities, the federal government bailed out these securities and the FIs backing them.

## Derivative Contracts: Futures, Forwards, Swaps, and Options

FIs can be either users of derivative contracts for hedging (see Chapters 22, 23, and 24) and other purposes or dealers that act as counterparties in trades with customers for a fee. In 2012, more than 1,291 U.S. banks and savings institutions were users of derivatives, with three big dealer banks (J.P. Morgan Chase, Citigroup, and Bank of America) accounting for some 75 percent of the $227,982 billion derivatives held and reported in Table 16–5. In the first quarter of 2012 these 1,291 FIs earned over $7.0 billion in trading revenue from their derivatives portfolios. However, as highlighted in Table 16–2 and the discussion throughout the chapter, risk on these securities can lead to large losses and even firm failure.

www.jpmorganchase.com
www.citigroup.com
www.bankofamerica.com

Contingent credit risk is likely to be present when FIs expand their positions in forwards, futures, swaps, and option contracts. This risk relates to the fact that the counterparty to one of these contracts may default on payment obligations, leaving the FI unhedged and having to replace the contract at today's interest rates, prices, or exchange rates. Further, such defaults are most likely to occur when the counterparty is losing heavily on the contract and the FI is in the money on the contract. This type of default risk is much more serious for forward (and swap) contracts than for futures contracts. This is so because **forward contracts** are nonstandard contracts entered into bilaterally by negotiating parties such as two FIs, and all cash flows are required to be paid at one time (on contract maturity). Thus, they are essentially over-the-counter (OTC) arrangements with no external guarantees should one or the other party default on the contract. For example, the contract seller might default on a forward foreign exchange contract that promises to deliver £10 million in three months' time at the exchange rate of $1.40 to £1 if the cost to purchase £1 for delivery is $1.60 when the forward contract matures. By contrast, **futures contracts** are standardized contracts guaranteed by organized exchanges such as the New York Futures Exchange (NYFE), a part of ICE Futures US (formerly the New York Board of Trade (NYBOT)). Futures contracts, like forward contracts, are commitments to deliver foreign exchange (or some other asset) at some future date. If a counterparty defaults on a futures contract, however, the exchange assumes the defaulting party's position and the payment obligations.

**forward contracts**
Nonstandard contracts between two parties to deliver and pay for an asset in the future.

**futures contracts**
Standardized contract guaranteed by organized exchanges to deliver and pay for an asset in the future.

www.theice.com Thus, unless a systematic financial market collapse threatens the exchange itself, futures are essentially default risk free.[12] In addition, default risk is reduced by the daily marking to market of contracts. This prevents the accumulation of losses and gains that occurs with forward contracts. These differences are discussed in more detail in Chapter 22.

An option is a contract that gives the holder the right, but not the obligation, to buy (a call option) or sell (a put option) an underlying asset at a prespecified price for a specified time period. Option contracts can also be purchased or sold by an FI, trading either over the counter (OTC) or bought/sold on organized exchanges. If the options are standardized options traded on exchanges, such as bond options, they are virtually default risk free.[13] If they are specialized options purchased OTC such as interest rate caps (see Chapter 23), some element of default risk exists.[14]

A swap is an agreement between two parties (called *counterparties*) to exchange specified periodic cash flows in the future based on some underlying instrument or price (e.g., a fixed or floating rate on a bond or note).[15] Similar to options, swaps are OTC instruments normally susceptible to counterparty risk (see Chapter 24). If interest rates (or foreign exchange rates) move a lot, one party can be faced with considerable future loss exposure, creating incentives to default.

The credit derivative market has grown exponentially over the past few years. As shown in Table 16–5, commercial banks had over $14,051 billion of notional value in credit derivatives outstanding in 2012. The emergence of these new derivatives is important since more FIs fail as a result of credit risk exposures than either interest rate or FX risk exposures. Credit derivatives (including forwards, options, and swaps) allow FIs to hedge their credit risk. They can be used to hedge the credit risk on individual loans or bonds or portfolios of loans and bonds. For example, if a borrower files for bankruptcy, the FI can exercise its right to exchange its loan with the credit derivative seller for par, thereby protecting the FI from a loss on the notional amount. In return, the FI pays the seller an up-front fee as well as periodic payments to maintain the derivative protection (see Chapters 22, 23, and 24).

Many of the financial institutions that hold large amounts of credit derivatives hold them in what is known as special purpose vehicles (SPV) or special investment vehicles (SIV), also known as shadow banks (see Chapter 21). SIVs and SPVs are fully described in Chapter 26. While SIVs are closely related to SPVs, they differ in the crucial extent of the mismatching of maturities of their liabilities (short-term commercial paper) and assets (long-term loans, mortgages, etc.). By contrast, SPVs generally match the maturities of their liabilities (bonds) to those of their assets (mortgages, long-term loans).

---

[12] More specifically, there are at least four reasons why the default risk of a futures contract is less than that of a forward contract: (1) daily marking to market of futures, (2) margin requirements on futures that act as a security bond, (3) price limits that spread out over extreme price fluctuations, and (4) default guarantees by the futures exchange itself.

[13] Note that the options can still be subject to interest rate risk; see our earlier discussion of the delta on a bond option.

[14] Under an interest rate cap, in return for a fee, the seller promises to compensate the buyer if interest rates rise above a certain level. If rates rise a lot more than expected, the cap seller may have an incentive to default to truncate the losses. Thus, selling a cap is similar to an FI selling interest rate risk insurance (see Chapter 23 for more details).

[15] Conceptually, a swap contract can be viewed as a succession of forward contracts.

An SPV purchases the assets (newly originated loans) from the originating bank for cash generated from the sale of asset-backed securities. The SPV sells the newly created asset-backed securities (credit derivatives) to investors such as insurance companies and pension funds, earning a fee for the services. An SIV is a structured operating company that invests in assets that are designed to generate higher returns than the SIV's cost of funds. Rather than selling the asset-backed securities directly to investors in order to raise cash (as do SPVs), an SIV sells bonds or commercial paper to investors in order to raise the cash to purchase the bank's assets. The SIV then holds the loans purchased from the banks on its own balance sheet until maturity. These loan assets held by the SIV back the debt instruments issued by the SIV to investors. The SIV pays a lower interest rate on the short-term debt that it issues than it earns on the mortgages and other long-term assets in which it invests. However, the SIVs' short-term funding must be rolled over fairly frequently to continue the financing of the SIV. This subjects the SIV to both a liquidity risk (failure to rollover liabilities) as well as an interest rate risk (due to the mismatch of the durations of their assets and liabilities).

The organization of an SIV as a separate entity appears to provide bankruptcy remoteness from the seller of the assets (often the bank). However, during the financial crisis, liquidity shortages made it virtually impossible for SIVs to roll over their commercial paper and fund their assets. Since these SIVs had back-up lines of credit from the sponsoring bank (e.g., Citibank provided a line of credit to its off-balance-sheet SIV), these lines were drawn down to prevent the SIV from becoming insolvent. However, in effect the SIV was re-intermediated back into the bank and effectively, what was an "off-balance-sheet bank," the SIV, became an "on-balance-sheet bank."[16]

### Credit Risk Concerns with Derivative Securities

In general, default (or credit) risk on OTC contracts increases with the time to maturity of the contract and the fluctuation of underlying prices, interest rates, or exchange rates.[17] Most empirical evidence suggests that derivative contracts have generally reduced FI risk or left it unaffected. However, the financial crisis clearly illustrates the magnitude of the risk that derivatives can impose on an FI and even the world's financial system.

Credit risk occurs because of the potential for the counterparty to default on its payment obligations under a derivative contract, a situation that would require the FI to replace the contract at the current market price and rate potentially at a loss.[18]

---

[16] In June 1998, the Financial Accounting Standards Board (FASB) issued FAS 133 that requires companies to reflect all assets and liabilities on their balance sheets at their fair value. The purpose of this standard was to prevent significant hedging losses involving derivatives. However, FIN 46, issued in 2003, and FIN46R, issued in 2008, allow FIs to avoid these requirements on of off-balance-sheet entities such as SIVs and SPVs, so-called variable interest entity (VIE) companies. Many critics have argued that SIVs should be regulated just like banks since they have a similar short-term/long-term asset-liability structure. Indeed, SIVs are virtual "off-balance-sheet banks."

[17] Reputational considerations and the need for future access to markets for hedging deter the incentive to default (see Chapter 24 as well).

[18] For instance, if the new replacement contract has a less favorable price (e.g., the replacement interest rate swap requires the bank to pay a fixed rate of 10 percent to receive a floating-rate payment based on LIBOR rates) than, say, 8 percent before the counterparty (the original floating-rate payer) defaulted. See Chapter 24 on swaps for more details.

This risk is most prevalent in OTC rather than exchange-traded derivative contracts, e.g., collateralized debt obligations (CDOs or CMOs). OTC contracts typically are nonstandardized or unique contracts that do not have external guarantees from an organized exchange. Defaults on these contracts usually occur when the FI stands to gain and the counterparty stands to lose. Such was the case in the late 2000s.

Mortgage delinquencies, particularly on subprime mortgages, surged in the last quarter of 2006 through 2008, as home owners who stretched themselves financially to buy a home or refinance a mortgage in the early 2000s fell behind on their loan payments. As mortgage borrowers defaulted on their mortgages, financial institutions that held these mortgages and credit derivatives (in the form of mortgage backed securities) started announcing huge losses on them. A prime example of the losses incurred is that of Bear Stearns. In the summer of 2007, two Bear Stearns funds suffered heavy losses on investments in the subprime mortgage backed securities market. The two funds filed for bankruptcy in the fall of 2007. The losses became so great that in March 2008 J.P. Morgan Chase and the Federal Reserve stepped in to rescue the then fifth largest investment bank in the United States before it failed. Then on Monday, September 15, Lehman Brothers (the 158-year-old investment bank) filed for bankruptcy, Merrill Lynch was bought by Bank of America, AIG (one of the world's largest insurance companies) met with federal regulators to raise desperately needed cash, and Washington Mutual (the largest savings institution in the United States) was looking for a buyer to save it from failing. A financial crisis was on hand, a big part of which was the result of FIs' dealings in OBS derivative securities.

In an attempt to unfreeze credit markets, then Treasury Secretary Henry Paulson met with congressional leaders to devise a plan to get bad mortgage loans and mortgage backed securities off balance sheets of financial institutions. After two weeks of debate (and one failed vote for passage), a $700 billion rescue plan was passed and signed into law by then President Bush on October 3, 2008. The bill established the Troubled Asset Relief Program (or TARP), that gave the U.S. Treasury funds to buy "toxic" mortgages and other securities such as credit derivatives from financial institutions. The TARP plan was slow to be instituted and not all FIs chose to participate in the program. Better capitalized FIs wanted to hold on to their troubled OBS securities rather than sell them and record losses.

The growth of the derivative securities markets was one of the major factors underlying the imposition of the BIS risk-based capital requirements in January 1993 (see Chapter 20). The fear then was that in a long-term derivative security contract, an out-of-the-money counterparty—that is, a counterparty that is currently at a disadvantage in terms of cash flows—would have incentives to default on such contracts to deter current and future losses. Consequently, the BIS imposed a required capital ratio for depository institutions against their holdings of derivative securities. As discussed above, these capital requirements were not sufficient to insure solvency of some FIs against extreme losses experienced during the financial crisis.

www.bis.org

## Forward Purchases and Sales of When-Issued Securities

**when-issued (WI) trading**
Trading in securities prior to their actual issue.

Very often banks and other FIs—especially investment banks—enter into commitments to buy and sell securities before issue. This is called **when-issued (WI) trading.** These OBS commitments can expose an FI to future or contingent interest rate risk. Commercial banks often include these securities as a part of their holdings of forward contracts.

**FIGURE 16–3**
**T-Bill Auction Time Line**

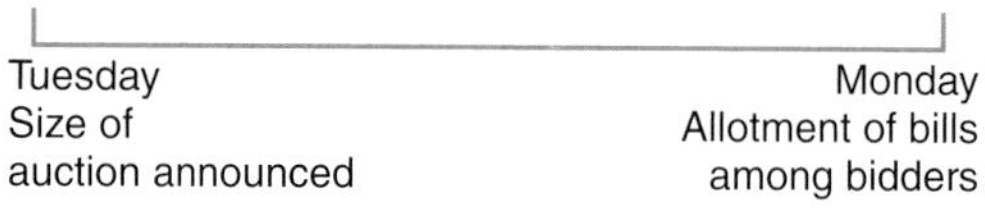

Tuesday
Size of
auction announced

Monday
Allotment of bills
among bidders

Good examples of WI commitments are those taken on with new T-bills in the week prior to the announcement of T-bill auction results. Every Tuesday the Federal Reserve, on behalf of the Treasury, announces the auction size of new three- and six-month bills to be allotted the following Monday (see Figure 16–3). Between the announcement of the total auction size on Tuesday and the announcement of the winning bill allotments on the following Monday, major T-bill dealers sell WI contracts.

### Risks Associated with When-Issued Securities

Normally, large investment banks and commercial banks are major WI T-bill dealers (currently, approximately 20 such banks). They sell the yet-to-be-issued T-bills for forward delivery to customers in the secondary market at a small margin above the price they expect to pay at the primary auction. This can be profitable if the primary dealer gets all the bills needed at the auction at the appropriate price or interest rate to fulfill these forward WI contracts. A primary dealer that makes a mistake regarding the tenor of the auction (i.e., the level of interest rates) faces the risk that the commitments entered into to deliver T-bills in the WI market can be met only at a loss. When an FI purchases T-bills on behalf of a customer prior to the actual weekly auctioning of securities, it incurs the risk of underpricing the security. On the day the T-bills are allotted, it is possible that because of high demand, prices are much higher than were forecast. The FI may then be forced to purchase the T-bills at higher prices, and thus sustain a loss on its WI forward commitments to deliver T-bills. For example, an overcommitted dealer may have to buy T-bills from other dealers at a loss right after the auction results are announced to meet the WI T-bill delivery commitments made to its customers.[19]

## Loans Sold

Increasingly, banks and other FIs originate loans on their balance sheets, but rather than holding them to maturity, they quickly sell them to outside investors. These outside investors include other banks, insurance companies, mutual funds, and even corporations. In acting as loan originators and loan sellers, FIs are operating more in the fashion of loan brokers than as traditional asset transformers (see Chapter 1). We discuss in more detail in Chapter 25 the types of loans FIs sell, their incentives to sell, and the way they can be sold.

**recourse**
The ability to put an asset or loan back to the seller if the credit quality of that asset deteriorates.

When an outside party buys a loan with absolutsely no **recourse** to the seller of the loan should the loan eventually go bad, loan sales have no OBS contingent

---

[19] This problem occurred when Salomon Brothers cornered or squeezed the market for new two-year Treasury bonds in 1990. Under the auction rules, no bidder could bid for or attain more than 35 percent of an issue. However, by bidding using customers' names (without their knowledge) in addition to bidding under its own name, Salomon vastly exceeded the 35 percent limit. This put extreme pressure on other dealers, who were unable to meet their selling commitments.

liability implications for FIs. Specifically, *no recourse* means that if the loan the FI sells goes bad, the buyer of the loan must bear the full risk of loss. In particular, the buyer cannot put the bad loan back to the seller or originating bank.

### Risks Associated with Loan Sales

Suppose the loan is sold with recourse. Then, loan sales present a long-term contingent credit risk to the seller. Essentially, the buyer of the loan holds a long-term option to put the loan back to the seller, which the buyer can exercise should the credit quality of the purchased loan deteriorate. In reality, the recourse or nonrecourse nature of loan sales is often ambiguous. For example, some have argued that FIs generally are willing to repurchase bad no-recourse loans to preserve their reputations with their customers. Obviously, reputational concerns may extend the size of a selling FI's contingent liabilities for OBS activities.

<table>
<tr><td>Concept<br>Questions</td><td>1. What are the four risks related to loan commitments?<br>2. What is the major difference between a commercial letter of credit and a standby letter of credit?<br>3. What is meant by counterparty risk in a forward contract?<br>4. Which is more risky for an FI, loan sales with recourse or loan sales without recourse?</td></tr>
</table>

## NON–SCHEDULE L OFF-BALANCE-SHEET RISKS

So far we have looked at five different OBS activities that banks and thrifts have to report to the Federal Reserve each quarter as part of their Schedule L section of the Call Report. Insurance companies, and investment banks also engage in futures, forwards, swaps, and options transactions of varying forms. Life insurers are heavily engaged in making loan commitments in commercial mortgages, property–casualty companies underwrite large amounts of financial guarantees, and investment banks engage in when-issued securities trading. The five activities just discussed are not the only OBS activities that can create contingent liabilities or risks for an FI. Next, we briefly introduce two other activities that can create them; we discuss the activities at greater length in later chapters.

### Settlement Risk

www.federalreserve.gov

www.chips.org

FIs send the bulk of their wholesale dollar payments along wire transfer systems such as Fedwire and the Clearing House InterBank Payments System (CHIPS). The Federal Reserve owns Fedwire, a domestic wire transfer network. CHIPS is an international and private network owned by 50 or so participating or member banks. Currently, these two networks transfer more than $2.6 trillion a day.

Unlike the domestic Fedwire system, a small portion of funds or payment messages sent on the CHIPS network *within* the day are provisional messages that become final and are settled only at the *end* of the day. For example, bank X sends a fund transfer payment message to bank Z at 11 AM EST. The actual cash settlement and the physical transfer of funds between X and Z take place at the end of the day, normally by transferring cash held in reserve accounts at the Federal Reserve banks. Because the transfer of funds is not finalized until the end of the day, bank Z—the message-receiving bank—faces an *intraday,* or within-day, **settlement risk.** Specifically, bank Z assumes that the funds message received at 11 AM from bank X will result in the actual delivery of the funds at the end of the day and may lend them to bank Y at 11:15 AM. However, if bank X does not deliver (settle) the promised funds at the end of the day, bank Z may be pushed into a serious net funds deficit position and may therefore be unable to meet its payment commitment to bank Y. Conceivably, bank Z's net debtor position may be large enough to exceed its capital and reserves, rendering it technically insolvent. Such a disruption can occur only if a major fraud were discovered in bank X's books during the day and bank regulators closed it the same day. That situation would make payment to bank Z impossible to complete at the end of the day. Alternatively, bank X might transmit funds it does not have in the hope of keeping its "name in the market" to be able to raise funds later in the day. However, other banks may revise their credit limits for this bank during the day, making bank X unable to deliver all the funds it promised to bank Z.

> **settlement risk**
> Intraday credit risk associated with CHIPS wire transfer activities.

The essential feature of settlement risk is that an FI is exposed to a within-day, or intraday, credit risk that does not appear on its balance sheet. The balance sheet at best summarizes only the end-of-day closing position or book of an FI. Thus, intraday settlement risk is an additional form of OBS risk that FIs participating on private wholesale wire transfer system networks face. (See Chapter 17 for a more detailed analysis of this risk and recent policy changes designed to reduce this risk.)

## Affiliate Risk

Many FIs operate as holding companies. A *holding company* is a corporation that owns the shares (normally more than 25 percent) of other corporations. For example, Citigroup is a one-bank holding company (OBHC) that owns all the shares of Citibank. Citigroup engages in certain permitted nonbank activities such as data processing through separately capitalized affiliates or companies that it owns. Similarly, a number of other holding companies are multibank holding companies (MBHCs) that own shares in a number of different banks. J.P. Morgan Chase is an MBHC that holds shares in banks nationwide. The organizational structures for these two holding companies are presented in Figure 16–4.

Legally, in the context of OBHCs, the bank and the nonbank affiliate are separate companies, as are bank 1 and bank 2 in the context of MBHCs. Thus, in Figure 16–4, the failure of the nonbank affiliate and/or bank 2 should have no effect on the financial resources of the bank in the OBHC or on bank 1 in the MBHC. This is the essence of the principle of corporate separateness underlying a legal corporation's

**FIGURE 16–4**
**One-Bank and Multibank Holding Company Structures**

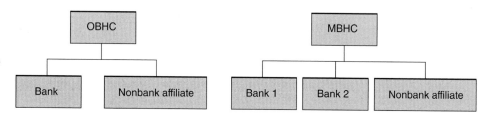

**affiliate risk**
Risk imposed on one holding company affiliate due to the potential failure of the other holding company affiliates.

limited liability in the United States. In reality, the failure of an affiliated firm or bank imposes **affiliate risk** on another bank in a holding company structure in a number of ways. We discuss two ways next.

First, *creditors* of the failed affiliate may lay claim to the surviving bank's resources on the grounds that operationally, in name or in activity, the bank is not really a separate company from its failed affiliate. This "estoppel argument" made under the law is based on the idea that the customers of the failed institution are relatively unsophisticated in their financial affairs. They probably cannot distinguish between the failing corporation and its surviving affiliate because of name similarity or some similar reason.[20] Second, *regulators* have tried to enforce a source of strength doctrine in recent years for large MBHC failures. Under this doctrine, which directly challenges the principle of corporate separateness, the resources of sound banks may be used to support failing banks. While regulators have tried to implement this principle, the courts have generally prevented this.

If either of these breaches of corporate separateness are legally supported, the risks related to the activities of the nonbank affiliate or an affiliated bank's activities impose an additional contingent OBS liability on a healthy bank. This is true for banks and potentially true for many other FIs, such as insurance companies, investment banks, and financial service conglomerates that adopt holding company organizational structures in which corporate separateness is in doubt.

In 1999, the U.S. Congress passed the Financial Services Modernization Act (FSMA, see Chapter 21). This act, viewed as the biggest change in the regulation of financial institutions in nearly 70 years, allowed the creation of a "financial services holding company" that could engage in banking activities *and* securities underwriting *and* insurance activities. Prior to the passage of the act, such combinations of commercial banks and other FI activities were highly restricted. One result of the act has been an increase in the formation of full-service financial institutions, and thus, by implication, an increase in affiliate risk. As of 2012, approximately 470 financial institutions (such as Bank of America, PNC Financial Morgan Stanley, and Goldman Sachs) have elected to become financial services holding companies. Certainly, not all of these are currently undertaking the full spectrum of financial activities allowed with FSMA, but with the new framework, all are sure to explore the opportunities available.

| Concept Questions | 1. What is the source of settlement risk on the CHIPS payments system? |
|---|---|
| | 2. What are two major sources of affiliate risk? |

# THE ROLE OF OBS ACTIVITIES IN REDUCING RISK

This chapter has emphasized that OBS activities may add to the riskiness of an FI's activities. Indeed, most contingent assets and liabilities have various characteristics that may accentuate an FI's default and/or interest rate risk exposures. Even

---

[20] For example, suppose the failing nonbank affiliate was called Town Data Processing and the affiliated bank was called Town Bank.

so, FIs use some OBS instruments—especially forwards, futures, options, and swaps—to reduce or manage their interest rate risk, foreign exchange risk, and credit risk exposures in a manner superior to what would exist in their absence. When used to hedge on-balance-sheet interest rate, foreign exchange, and credit risks, these instruments can actually work to reduce FIs' overall insolvency risk. Although we do not fully describe the role of these instruments as hedging vehicles in reducing an FI's insolvency exposure until Chapters 22, 23, and 24, you can now recognize the inherent danger in the overregulation of OBS activities and instruments. For example, the risk that a counterparty might default on a forward foreign exchange contract risk is very small. It is probably much lower than the insolvency risk an FI faces if it does not use forward contracts to hedge its foreign exchange assets against undesirable fluctuations in exchange rates. (See Chapters 13 and 22 for some examples of this.)

Despite the risk-reducing attributes of OBS derivative securities held by FIs, the expanded use of derivatives has caused many regulators to focus on the risk-increasing attributes of these securities and the possible detrimental effect the risk may have on global financial markets. The result has been an increase in the amount of regulation imposed on these activities. For example, the Derivatives Safety and Soundness Supervision Act (DSSSA) of 1994 mandated increased regulatory oversight for FIs holding derivative securities, including increased regulation of capital, disclosure, and accountability; enhanced supervision of risk management processes; and additional reporting requirements. Also in 1994, the General Accounting Office (GAO) released a report to Congress on derivative use by FIs and the regulatory actions needed to ensure the integrity of the financial system. The GAO specifically recommended that derivative activities of unregulated securities and insurance firm affiliates of banking organizations be brought under the purview of one or more existing regulatory bodies. Despite these rules and regulations passed in the early 1990s, huge losses on derivative securities by FIs before and especially during the financial crisis have resulted in the call for additional regulation.

As a result of the role derivatives—especially credit default swaps (CDS)—played in the financial crisis, in 2009 regulators revamped the U.S. financial regulatory system, extending regulatory oversight to unregulated OTC derivative securities.[21] The new regulation of derivatives markets involves reporting requirements on the issuers of asset-backed securities; elimination of regulators' reliance on credit-rating agencies; requirements that big banks and other financial institutions submit certain derivatives contracts to regulated clearinghouses, which serve as a backstop in case one party in the trade defaults; and requirements that the originator, sponsor, or broker of a securitized asset retain a financial interest in its performance. The regulation requires that all derivatives contracts be subject to regulation, all derivatives dealers subject to supervision, and regulators be empowered to enforce rules against manipulation and abuse. The increased regulation of the derivatives markets was intended to achieve four broad objectives: (1) prevent activities in those markets from posing risk to the financial system; (2) promote the efficiency and transparency of those markets; (3) prevent market manipulation, fraud, and other market abuses; and (4) ensure that OTC derivatives are not marketed inappropriately to unsophisticated parties.

---

[21] More details on CDS and their risks are discussed in Chapter 26.

Despite their risk by allowing risk-averse managers to hedge risk, derivatives may induce the managers to follow more value-maximizing investment strategies. That is, derivatives may allow manager–stockholder agency conflicts over the level of risk taking to be reduced. In addition, fees from OBS activities provide a key source of noninterest income for many FIs, especially the largest and most creditworthy ones. The importance of noninterest incomes for large banks is shown in Table 17–1 in Chapter 17. Thus, if managed carefully, increased OBS earnings can potentially compensate for increased OBS risk exposure and actually reduce the probability of insolvency for some FIs.

| | |
|---|---|
| **Concept Questions** | 1. While recognizing that OBS instruments may add to the riskiness of an FI's activities, explain how they also work to reduce the overall insolvency risk of FIs. |
| | 2. Other than hedging and speculation, what reasons do FIs have for engaging in OBS activities? |

**Summary**

This chapter showed that an FI's net worth or economic value is linked not only to the value of its traditional on-balance-sheet activities but also to the contingent asset and liability values of its off-balance-sheet activities. The risks and returns of several off-balance-sheet items were discussed in detail: loan commitments; commercial and standby letters of credit; derivative contracts such as futures, options, and swaps; forward purchases; sales of when-issued securities; and loans sold. In all cases, it is clear that these instruments have a major impact on the future profitability and risk of an FI. Two other risks associated with off-balance-sheet activities—settlement risk and affiliate risk—were also discussed. The chapter concluded by pointing out that although off-balance-sheet activities can be risk increasing, they can also be used to hedge on-balance-sheet exposures, resulting in lower risks as well as generating fee income to the FI.

**Questions and Problems**

1. Classify the following items as (1) on-balance-sheet assets, (2) on-balance-sheet liabilities, (3) off-balance-sheet assets, (4) off-balance-sheet liabilities, or (5) capital account.
   a. Loan commitments.
   b. Loan loss reserves.
   c. Letter of credit.
   d. Bankers' acceptance.
   e. Rediscounted bankers' acceptance.
   f. Loan sales without recourse.
   g. Loan sales with recourse.
   h. Forward contracts to purchase.
   i. Forward contracts to sell.
   j. Swaps.
   k. Loan participations.

      l. Securities borrowed.

      m. Securities lent.

      n. Loss adjustment expense account (PC insurers).

      o. Net policy reserves.

2. How does one distinguish between an off-balance-sheet asset and an off-balance-sheet liability?

3. Contingent Bank has the following balance sheet in market value terms (in millions of dollars).

| Assets | | Liabilities and Equity | |
|---|---|---|---|
| Cash | $ 20 | Deposits | $220 |
| Mortgages | 220 | Equity | 20 |
| Total assets | $240 | Total liabilities and equity | $240 |

In addition, the bank has contingent assets with $100 million market value and contingent liabilities with $80 million market value. What is the true stockholder net worth? What does the term *contingent* mean?

4. Why are contingent assets and liabilities like options? What is meant by the delta of an option? What is meant by the term *notional value?*

5. An FI has purchased options on bonds with a notional value of $500 million and has sold options on bonds with a notional value of $400 million. The purchased options have a delta of 0.25 and the sold options have a delta of 0.30. What is (a) the contingent asset value of this position, (b) the contingent liability value of this position, and (c) the contingent market value of net worth?

6. What factors explain the growth of off-balance-sheet activities in the 1980s through the 2000s among U.S. FIs?

7. What role does Schedule L play in reporting off-balance-sheet activities? Refer to Table 16–4. What was the annual growth rate over the 21-year period 1992–2012 in the notional value of off-balance-sheet items compared with on-balance-sheet items? Which contingencies have exhibited the most rapid growth?

8. What are the characteristics of a loan commitment that an FI may make to a customer? In what manner and to whom is the commitment an option? What are the various possible pieces of the option premium? When does the option or commitment become an on-balance-sheet item for the FI and the borrower?

9. An FI makes a loan commitment of $2.5 million with an up-front fee of 50 basis points and a back-end fee of 25 basis points on the unused portion of the loan. The takedown on the loan is 50 percent and takedown occurs at the beginning of the year.

    a. What total fees does the FI earn when the loan commitment is negotiated?

    b. What are the total fees earned by the FI at the end of the year, that is, in future value terms? Assume the cost of capital for the FI is 6 percent.

10. Use the following information on a one-year loan commitment to calculate the return on the loan commitment.

$BR$ = FI's base interest on the loans = 8%

$\phi$ = Risk premium on loan commitment = 2.5%

$f_1$ = Up-front fee on the whole commitment = 25 basis points

$f_2$ = Back-end fee on the unused commitment = 50 basis points

$b$ = Compensating balance on loans = 10%
$RR$ = Reserve requirements = 8%
$td$ = Expected (average) takedown rate on the loan commitment = 70%

11. An FI has issued a one-year loan commitment of $2 million for an up-front fee of 25 basis points. The back-end fee on the unused portion of the commitment is 10 basis points. The FI's base rate on loans is 7.5 percent and loans to this customer carry a risk premium of 2.5 percent. The FI requires a compensating balance on loans of 5 percent in the form of demand deposits. Reserve requirements on demand deposits are 8 percent. The customer is expected to draw down 80 percent of the commitment at the beginning of the year.
    a. What is the expected return on the loan without taking future values into consideration?
    b. What is the expected return using future values? That is, the net fee and interest income are evaluated at the end of the year when the loan is due.
    c. How is the expected return in part (b) affected if the reserve requirements on demand deposits are zero?
    d. How is the expected return in part (b) affected if compensating balances are paid a nominal interest rate of 2.5 percent?
    e. What is the expected return using future values, but with the compensating balance placed in certificates of deposit that have an interest rate of 5.5 percent and no reserve requirements, rather than in demand deposits?

12. Suburb Bank has issued a one-year loan commitment of $10 million for an up-front fee of 50 basis points. The back-end fee on the unused portion of the commitment is 20 basis points. The bank's base rate on loans is 7 percent, and loans to this customer carry a risk premium of 2 percent. The bank requires a compensating balance of 10 percent to be placed in demand deposits and must maintain reserve requirements on demand deposits of 10 percent. The customer is expected to draw down 60 percent of the commitment at the beginning of the year.
    a. What is the expected return on this loan?
    b. What is the expected annual return on the loan if the draw-down on the commitment does not occur until the end of six months?

13. How is an FI exposed to interest rate risk when it makes loan commitments? In what way can an FI control for this risk? How does basis risk affect the implementation of the control for interest rate risk?

14. How is an FI exposed to credit risk when it makes loan commitments? How is credit risk related to interest rate risk? What control measure is available to an FI for the purpose of protecting against credit risk? What is the realistic opportunity to implement this control feature?

15. How is an FI exposed to takedown risk and aggregate funding risk? How are these two contingent risks related?

16. Do the contingent risks of interest rate, takedown, credit, and aggregate funding tend to increase the insolvency risk of an FI? Why or why not?

17. What is a letter of credit? How is a letter of credit like an insurance contract?

18. A German bank issues a three-month letter of credit on behalf of its German customer, who is planning to import $100,000 worth of goods from the United States. The bank charges an up-front fee of 100 basis points.
    a. What up-front fee does the bank earn? How is this fee recorded on the bank's income statement?

b. If the U.S. exporter decides to discount this letter of credit after it has been accepted by the German bank, how much will the exporter receive, assuming that the interest rate currently is 5 percent and that 90 days remain before maturity? (*Hint:* To discount a security, use the time value of money formula, $PV = FV[1 - (\text{interest rate} \times (\text{days to maturity}/365))]$.)

c. What risk does the German bank incur by issuing this letter of credit?

19. How do standby letters of credit differ from commercial letters of credit? With what other types of FI products do SLCs compete? What types of FIs can issue SLCs?

20. A corporation is planning to issue $1 million of 270-day commercial paper for an effective annual yield of 5 percent. The corporation expects to save 30 basis points on the interest rate by using either an SLC or a loan commitment as collateral for the issue.

a. What are the net savings to the corporation if a bank agrees to provide a 270-day SLC for an up-front fee of 20 basis points (of the face value of the loan commitment) to back the commercial paper issue?

b. What are the net savings to the corporation if a bank agrees to provide a 270-day loan commitment to back the issue? The bank will charge 10 basis points for an up-front fee and 10 basis points for a back-end fee for any unused portion of the loan. Assume the loan is not needed and that the fees are on the face value of the loan commitment.

c. Should the corporation be indifferent to the two alternative collateral methods at the time the commercial paper is issued?

21. Explain how the use of derivative contracts such as forwards, futures, swaps, and options creates contingent credit risk for an FI. Why do OTC contracts carry more contingent credit risk than do exchange-traded contracts? How is the default risk of OTC contracts related to the time to maturity and the price and rate volatilities of the underlying assets?

22. What is meant by when-issued trading? Explain how forward purchases of when-issued government T-bills can expose FIs to contingent interest rate risk.

23. Distinguish between loan sales with and without recourse. Why would FIs want to sell loans with recourse? Explain how loan sales can leave FIs exposed to contingent interest rate risks.

24. The manager of Shakey Bank sends a $2 million funds transfer payment message via CHIPS to the Trust Bank at 10 AM. Trust Bank sends a $2 million funds transfer message via CHIPS to Hope Bank later that same day. What type of risk is inherent in this transaction? How will the risk become reality?

25. Explain how settlement risk is incurred in the interbank payment mechanism and how it is another form of off-balance-sheet risk.

26. What is the difference between a one-bank holding company and a multibank holding company? How does the principle of corporate separateness ensure that a bank is safe from the failure of its affiliates?

27. Discuss how the failure of an affiliate can affect the holding company or its affiliates even if the affiliates are structured separately.

28. Defend the statement that although off-balance-sheet activities expose FIs to several forms of risks, they also can alleviate the risks of FIs.

## Web Questions

29. Go to the FDIC website at **www.fdic.gov** and find the total amount of unused commitments and letters of credit and the notional value of interest rate swaps of FDIC-insured commercial banks for the most recent quarter available using the following steps. Click on "Analysts." From there click on "Statistics on Banking." Next click on "Assets and Liabilities" and "Run Report." Select "Total Unused Commitments," then "Letters of Credit," and finally "Derivatives" to get the relevant data. This will bring the three files onto your computer that contain the relevant data. What is the dollar value increase in these amounts over the first-quarter 2012 values reported in Table 16–4?

30. Go to the website of the Office of the Comptroller of the Currency at **www.occ.treas.gov** and update Table 16–5 using the following steps. Click on "Publications." Click on "Quarterly Report on Bank Derivatives Activities." Click on the most recent date. Under "Bookmarks," click on "Tables." This will bring the file onto your computer that contains the relevant data. What is the dollar value increase in these values over those reported in Table 16–5?

# Integrated Mini Case

## CALCULATING INCOME ON OFF-BALANCE-SHEET ACTIVITIES

Dudley National has issued the following off-balance-sheet items:

- A one-year loan commitment of $1 million with an up-front fee of 40 basis points. The back-end fee on the unused portion of the commitment is 55 basis points. The bank's base rate on loans is 8 percent, and loans to this customer carry a risk premium of 2 percent. The bank requires a compensating balance on this loan of 10 percent to be placed in demand deposits and must maintain reserve requirements on demand deposits of 8 percent. The customer is expected to draw down 75 percent of the commitment at the beginning of the year.

- A one-year loan commitment of $500,000 with an up-front fee of 25 basis points. The back-end fee on the unused portion of the commitment is 30 basis points. Loans to this customer carry a risk premium of 2.5 percent. The bank will

not require a compensating balance on this loan. The customer is expected to draw down 90 percent of the commitment at the beginning of the year.

- A three-month commercial letter of credit on behalf of one of its AA-rated customers who is planning to import $400,000 worth of goods from the Germany. The bank charges an up-front fee of 75 basis points on commercial letters of credit to AA-rated customers.

- A standby letter of credit to one its A-rated customers who is planning to issue $5 million of 270-day commercial paper for an effective yield of 5 percent. The corporation expects to save 50 basis points on the interest rate by using the SLC. The bank charges an up-front fee of 40 basis points on SLCs to A-rated customers to back the commercial paper issue.

www.mhhe.com/saunders8e

a. What up-front fees does the bank earn on each of these?
b. What other income does the bank earn on these off-balance-sheet activities?
c. Calculate the returns on each of the off-balance-sheet activities assuming that the takedowns on the loan commitments are at the expected percentage and the customers holding the letters of credit do not default on their obligations.

## Appendix 16A: A Letter of Credit Transaction

View Appendix 16A at the website for this textbook (**www.mhhe.com/saunders8e**).

# Technology and Other Operational Risks

## INTRODUCTION

Chapters 7 through 16 concentrated on the financial risks that arise as FIs perform their asset-transformation and/or brokerage functions on or off the balance sheet. However, financial risk is only one part of a modern FI's risk profile. As with regular corporations, FIs have a real or production side to their operations that results in additional costs and revenues. This chapter focuses on (1) factors that impact the operational returns and risks of FIs (with an emphasis on technology) and (2) on the importance of optimal management and control of labor, capital, and other input sources and their costs. In particular, well-managed FIs can use operational cost savings to increase profits and thus reduce the probability of insolvency.

Central to FIs' decision-making processes is the cost of inputs, or factors used to produce services both on and off the balance sheet. Two important factors are labor (tellers, credit officers) and capital (buildings, machinery, furniture). Crucial to the efficient management and combination of these inputs (which result in financial outputs at the lowest cost) is technology. Technological innovation has been a major concern of FIs in recent years. Since the 1980s, banks, insurance companies, and investment companies have sought to improve operational efficiency with major investments in internal and external communications, computers, and an expanded technological infrastructure. Internet and mobile communications technologies are having a profound effect on financial services. These technologies are more than just new distribution channels—they are a completely different way of providing financial services. Indeed, a global financial service firm such as Citigroup has operations in more than 100 countries connected in real time by a proprietary-owned satellite system. Operational risk is partly related to technology risk and can arise when existing technology malfunctions or back-office support systems break down. Further, back-office support systems combine labor and technology to provide clearance, settlement, and other services to back FIs' underlying on- and off-balance-sheet transactions.

According to Hitachi Data Systems, back-office system failures usually occur four times per year in the average firm. Recovery time from system failures averages 12 hours. The terrorist attacks on the World Trade Center and the Pentagon created back-office system failures of an unforeseen magnitude. For example, over a week after the attacks, Bank of New York was still having trouble with some crucial communications links, such as its connection to the Government Securities Clearing Corp., a central part of the government bond market. Though trades were eventually posted, Bank of New York clients were deprived of instantaneous reports on their positions. More recently, on May 6, 2010, FIs saw huge swings in the market values of their investment portfolios as financial markets experienced a brief but severe drop in prices, falling 998 points (more than 5 percent) in a matter of minutes, only to recover a short time later. The "flash crash" was attributed to trading by a little-known mutual fund—Asset Strategy Fund—located in Kansas City. A fund trader triggered the fall with the sale of $4.1 billion of futures contracts linked to the S&P 500 Index. The trader used a computer algorithm that tied the sale to the market's overall volume. Trading volume soared on May 6 and the sell order was executed. While similar trades had taken several hours to execute, this trade was executed in 20 minutes. The initial trade triggered a pyramiding effect from FIs' computerized trading programs designed to sell when the market moves lower.

On a smaller, but more typical scale, in August 2012 a computer malfunction caused by just one junior technician in India at the Royal Bank of Scotland (RBS) left 17 million customers unable to access their accounts. The inexperienced technician accidentally wiped out account information during a routine software upgrade. Deleted information had to be painstakingly re-keyed into the bank's computer system. The error created a backlog of more than 100 million transactions that were not paid in or out of customer accounts as they should have been. RBS reimbursed affected customers for the cost of any fines or late payment fees incurred from delays. It was estimated that the cost to RBS of dealing with the technology failure was likely between $75 million and $150 million. Also in August 2012, a software glitch at Knight Capital Group almost forced the company to close. Knight Capital Group Inc. was holding about $7 billion of stocks at one point as a result of errant trades made when a computer software program failed. Knight's traders worked frantically to sell shares while trying to minimize losses due to the software problem. By the end of the day, the position was down to $4.6 billion. However, the $4.6 billion position would have prevented Knight from opening for business the next day because the brokerage firm would have lacked the capital required by regulators to offset risks from holding the stocks. Knight avoided closure by agreeing to sell the portfolio to Goldman Sachs Group Inc. However, Knight ended up with a $440 million loss.

As should already be apparent, technology and operational risks are closely related and in recent years have caused great concern to FI managers and regulators alike. The Bank for International Settlements (BIS), the principal organization of central banks in the major economies of the world, has defined operational risk (inclusive of technological risk) as "the risk of losses resulting from inadequate or failed internal processes, people, and systems or from external events."[1] A number of FIs add reputational risk and strategic risk (e.g., due to a failed merger) as part of a broader definition of operational risk. Indeed, so significant has operational risk become that the BIS stated that, as of 2006, banks should be made to carry a capital cushion against losses from this risk. We discuss these requirements briefly in this chapter and in more detail in Chapter 20.

www.bis.org

---

[1] See Basel Committee on Bank Supervision, "Overview of the New Basel Capital Accord," Bank for International Settlements, April 2003, p.120.

# WHAT ARE THE SOURCES OF OPERATIONAL RISK?

Controlling and reducing operational risks improves the operational efficiency of the FI. As seen in the following section, improvements in operational efficiency lead to increases in net income, return on assets, and other quantitative measures of FI performance. However, as we see throughout the chapter, operational risk is much less tangible and is often hard to quantify. There are at least five sources of operational risk:

1. Technology (e.g., technological failure and deteriorating systems).
2. Employees (e.g., human error and internal fraud).
3. Customer relationships (e.g., contractual disputes).
4. Capital assets (e.g., destruction by fire or other catastrophes).
5. External (e.g., external fraud).

Items 1 through 4 are internally controllable for an FI, while item 5 is external, event-type risk which is relatively uncontrollable for an FI. A good example of internal operational risk (item 2) is Bernie Madoff, who lost $65 billion in client funds as part of a giant Ponzi scheme, the largest fraud ever committed by an individual. Madoff pleaded guilty to 11 felony counts of fraud in the operations of his hedge fund business, Madoff Investment Securities. In the summer of 2009, Madoff was sentenced to 150 years in prison with restitution of $170 billion. Another, more recent example of internal operational risk is Barclays PLC, which admitted to, on numerous occasions over a four-year period between 2005 and 2009, manipulating and making false reports concerning the LIBOR to benefit its derivatives trading positions. Barclays made false LIBOR reports at the direction of members of senior management to protect its reputation during the global financial crisis. In addition, attempts to manipulate LIBOR included Barclays' traders asking other banks to assist in manipulating the global benchmark interest rate. As a result of the actions, Barclays was ordered to pay $455 million in fines, cease and desist from further violations as charged, and take specified steps to ensure the integrity and reliability of its LIBOR submissions. Further, senior executives and traders involved with the manipulation resigned or were suspended and faced criminal charges.

# TECHNOLOGICAL INNOVATION AND PROFITABILITY

**technology**
Computers, audio and visual communication systems, and other information systems which can be applied to an FI's production of services.

Increasingly important to the profitability and riskiness of modern FIs has been item 1: technology. Broadly defined, **technology** includes computers, visual and audio communication systems, and other information technology (IT). In recent years U.S. banks alone have spent $50 billion per year in technology-related expenditures.[2]

---

[2] A 2011 survey by CEB Tower Group found that more than half of banking executives expected technology investment over the next two years to increase by more than 6 percent, with 15 percent expecting greater than 20 percent increases. Only 6 percent expected IT investment to decline. The survey found that for commercial banking in particular, the increase in technology spending was driven as much by the goal to reduce the long-term operating costs and maintaining outdated and duplicative systems as it was to meet regulatory requirements and client demands for enhanced solutions.

An efficient technological base for an FI can result in:

1. Lower costs, by combining labor and capital in a more efficient mix.
2. Increased revenues, by allowing a wider array of financial services to be produced or innovated and sold to customers.

The importance of an FI's operating costs and the efficient use of technology impacting these costs is clearly demonstrated by this simplified profit function:

$$\text{Earnings or profit before taxes} = (\text{Interest income} - \text{Interest expense})$$
$$+ (\text{Noninterest income} - \text{Noninterest expense}) - \text{Provision for loan losses}$$

Table 17–1 breaks down the profit data for U.S. banks over the 1991–2012 period into the different components impacting profits. For example, through the first quarter of 2012, interest income of $113,295 million and interest expense of $15,351 million produced net interest income of $97,944 million. However, U.S. banks also had total noninterest income of $58,342 million (including service charges on deposits of $8,019 million) and noninterest expenses of $98,601 million (including salaries and employee benefits of $44,697 million and premises and equipment expenses of $10,259 million). Thus, banks' net noninterest income was −$40,259. After considering provisions for loan losses of $13,016 million, net securities gains ($1,746 million), extraordinary and other gains ($152 million), and taxes ($13,863 million), after-tax net profits were $32,704 million. Underscoring the importance of operating costs is the fact that noninterest expenses amounted to 642 percent of interest expense and were 3 times net profits in the first three months of 2012.

*Internet Exercise*  Go to the Federal Deposit Insurance Corporation's website, and find the latest information available for earnings at U.S. commercial banks using the following steps. Go to the Federal Deposit Insurance Corporation's website at **www.fdic.gov**. Click on "Analysts." Click on "Statistics on Banking." Select "o Income and Expense" and click on "Run Report." This will download a file onto your computer that will contain the most recent information.

**TABLE 17–1**  **Earnings and Other Data for All Insured Banks (in millions of dollars)**

Source: Federal Deposit Insurance Corporation website, various dates. *www.fdic.gov*

| Financial Data | 1991 | 1995 | 2000 | 2005 | 2008 | 2010 | 2012* |
|---|---|---|---|---|---|---|---|
| Interest income | $289,166 | $302,663 | $427,985 | $434,501 | $530,477 | $481,521 | $113,295 |
| Interest expense | −167,265 | −148,441 | −224,195 | −165,143 | −210,564 | −89,396 | −15,351 |
| Net interest income | 121,901 | 154,222 | 203,790 | 269,357 | 319,913 | 392,125 | 97,944 |
| Provision for loan losses | −34,274 | −12,550 | −29,254 | −26,607 | −152,192 | −146,884 | −13,016 |
| Noninterest income | 59,703 | 82,440 | 152,751 | 201,328 | 193,820 | 216,574 | 58,342 |
| Noninterest expenses | −124,651 | −149,671 | −215,753 | −276,239 | −330,545 | −357,835 | −98,601 |
| Net securities gains or losses | 2,966 | 545 | −2,285 | −158 | −14,234 | 8,291 | 1,746 |
| Extraordinary and other items | 687 | 26 | −30 | 241 | 5,446 | −565 | 152 |
| Taxes | −8,285 | −26,176 | −38,043 | −53,888 | −6,204 | −33,694 | −13,863 |
| Net earnings | $ 18,047 | $ 48,836 | $ 71,176 | $114,034 | $ 16,004 | $ 78,012 | $ 32,704 |
| Total assets ($ billion) | $ 3,430.1 | $ 4,312.7 | $ 6,238.7 | $ 9,039.4 | $12,310.9 | $12,065.5 | $12,781.0 |
| Return on assets (%) | 0.53% | 1.13% | 1.14% | 1.26% | 0.13% | 0.65% | 1.02%** |

* As of the first quarter.
** Annualized.

Technology is important because well-chosen technological investments have the potential to increase both the FI's net interest margin, or the difference between interest income and interest expense, and net noninterest income. Therefore, technology can directly improve profitability, as the following examples show:

1. *Interest income* can increase if the FI sells a broader array of financial services as a result of technological developments. These may include cross-selling financial products by having the computer identify customers and then having the FI telemarket financial service products such as life insurance and bank products directly and over the Internet.[3] Additionally, the promise of additional revenue from investment in technology encourages an increase in the rate of innovation of new products and supports improvements in service quality and convenience. Many FIs use high-tech efforts to determine how they can reach more customers with more products. As marketing lines are identified and defined, new product ideas emerge that further the usefulness of FI products to customers.

2. *Interest expense* can be reduced if access to markets for liabilities is directly dependent on the FI's technological capability. For example, Fedwire and CHIPS (two wire transfer systems discussed later in the chapter) link the domestic and international interbank lending markets; they are based on interlocking computer network systems. Moreover, an FI's ability to originate and sell commercial paper is increasingly computer driven. Thus, failure to invest in the appropriate technology may lock an FI out of a lower-cost funding market.[4]

3. *Other income* increases when fees for FI services, especially those from off-balance-sheet activities, are linked to the quality of the FI's technology. For example, letters of credit are now commonly originated electronically by customers; swaps, caps, options, and other complex derivatives are usually traded, tracked, and valued using high-powered computers and algorithms. FIs could not offer innovative derivative products to customers without investments in suitable IT. Further, new technology has resulted in an evolution of the U.S. (and international) payment systems (see below), which has increased the amount of fee income (noninterest income) as a percent of total operating income (interest income plus noninterest income) for FIs. For example, referring again to Table 17–1, we see that noninterest income as a percent of total operating income was 17.11 percent in 1991 and increased to 33.99 percent by 2012.

4. *Noninterest expenses* can be reduced if the collection and storage of customer information as well as the processing and settlement of numerous financial products are computer based rather than paper based. This is particularly true of security-related back-office activities.

---

| **Concept Questions** | 1. What are some of the advantages of an efficient technological base for an FI? How can technology be used to directly improve profitability? |
|---|---|
| | 2. Looking at Table 17–1, determine if noninterest expenses and noninterest income have been increasing or decreasing as a percent of total bank costs over the 1991–2012 period. |

---

[3] The Financial Services Modernization Act of 1999 requires FIs to notify customers and allow them to opt out of the sharing of nonpublic personal information between an FI's affiliates or third parties (see Chapter 21).

[4] Not only manufacturing corporations sell commercial paper. In recent years approximately 75 percent of all commercial paper has been sold by financial firms such as bank holding companies, investment banks, and finance companies. Thus, commercial paper is now an important source of funds for many FIs.

# THE IMPACT OF TECHNOLOGY ON WHOLESALE AND RETAIL FINANCIAL SERVICE PRODUCTION

The previous discussion established that technology has the potential to directly affect all FI's profit-producing areas. The following discussion focuses on some specific technology-based products found in retail and wholesale financial institutions. Note that this is far from a complete list.

## Wholesale Financial Services

Probably the most important area in which technology has had an impact on wholesale or corporate customer services is an FI's ability to provide cash management or working capital services. Cash management services include services designed to collect, disburse and transfer funds—on a local, regional, national, or international basis—and to provide information about the location and status of those funds. Cash management service needs have largely resulted from (1) corporate recognition that excess cash balances result in a significant opportunity cost due to lost or forgone interest and (2) corporate need to know cash or working capital position on a real-time basis. More recently, FIs have used their own technological investments to help corporate customers improve the efficiency with which they incorporate technology into their business. Among the services FIs provide to improve the efficiency with which corporate clients manage their financial positions are the following:

1. *Controlled disbursement accounts.* An account feature that establishes in the morning almost all payments to be made by the customer in a given day. The FI informs the corporate client of the total funds it needs to meet disbursements, and the client wire transfers the amount needed. These checking accounts are debited early each day so that corporations can obtain an early insight into their net cash positions.

2. *Account reconciliation.* A checking feature that records which of the firm's checks have been paid by the FI.[5]

**float**

The interval between the deposit of a check and when funds become available for depositor use; that is, the time is takes a check to clear.

3. *Wholesale and electronic lockbox.* A centralized or online collection service for corporate payments used to reduce the delay in check clearing, or the **float.** In a typical lockbox arrangement, a local FI sets up a lockbox at the post office for a corporate client located outside the area. Local customers mail payments to the lockbox rather than to the out-of-town corporate headquarters. The FI collects these checks several times per day and deposits them directly into the customer's account. Details of the transaction are wired to the corporate client. With electronic lockboxes, the FI receives online payments for public utilities and similar corporate clients.

4. *Funds concentration.* Redirects funds from accounts in a large number of FIs or branches to a few centralized accounts at one FI.

5. *Electronic funds transfer.* Includes overnight payments via CHIPS or Fedwire, automated payment of payrolls or dividends via automated clearinghouses (ACHs), and automated transmission of payments messages by SWIFT, an international electronic message service owned and operated by U.S. and European FIs that instructs FIs to make specific payments.

[5] The Check Clearing for the 21st Century Act, passed by Congress in 2003, allows FIs to replace the delivery of an original, paper-based check back to deposit customers with electronically transmitted copies of the checks. In doing so, check processing time and handling costs can be reduced significantly for FIs.

6. *Check deposit services.* Encoding, endorsing, microfilming, and handling customers' checks.

7. *Electronic initiation of letters of credit.* Allows customers in a network to access FI computers to initiate letters of credit.

8. *Treasury management software.* Allows efficient management of multiple currency and security portfolios for trading and investment purposes.

9. *Electronic data interchange.* The exchange of structured information from one computer application to another by electronic means and with a minimum of human intervention. An electronic data exchange allows businesses to transfer and transact invoices, purchase orders, and shipping notices automatically, using FIs as clearinghouses.

10. *Electronic billing.* Provides the presentment and collection services for companies that send out substantial volumes of recurring bills. FIs combine the e-mail capability of the Internet to send out bills with their ability to process payments electronically through the interbank payment networks.

11. *Verification of identities.* Using encryption technology, FIs certify the identities of its own account holders and serve as the intermediary through which its business customers can verify the identities of account holders at other FIs. After the September 11, 2001 terrorist attacks, some legislators called for restrictions on encryption technology unless it permits law enforcement access to otherwise coded data.

12. *Assistance to small businesses entering into e-commerce.* Help to smaller firms in setting up the infrastructure—interactive website and payment capabilities—for engaging in e-commerce.

13. *Online customer-facing technologies.* Technologies that allow an FI's business clients to reach their customers more individually and efficiently across online channels, for example, give business customers the technology to scan checks and deposit images online, or the ability to provide online and mobile applications.

14. *Cloud computing.* Technologies that allow business clients to log into an FI provided web-based service which hosts all software the business client needs, from e-mail to word processing to complex data analysis programs.[6]

15. *Facilitation of business-to-business e-commerce.* A few of the largest FIs have begun to offer firms the technology for electronic business-to-business commerce. The FIs are essentially undertaking automation of the entire information flow associated with the procurement and distribution of goods and services among businesses.

## Retail Financial Services

Retail customers have demanded efficiency and flexibility in their financial transactions. Using only checks or holding cash is often more expensive and time-consuming than using retail-oriented electronic payments technology and, increasingly, the Internet. Further, securities trading is increasingly moving toward electronic platforms not tied to any specific location. Electronic trading networks

---

[6] Cloud computing differs from traditional hosting in that it is sold on demand rather than prearranged. It is variable in that the business client uses as little or as much of a service as they need at any given time; and the service is fully managed by the FI, so the business client needs only computer and Internet access to access the cloud.

have lowered the costs of trading and allowed for better price determination. For example, with a single click of a mouse, Bank of America Merrill Lynch customers can obtain information on all research (conducted by Bank of America Merrill Lynch) on a company. Another click gives the customer information on the best terms available on a trade, and a final click executes a customer's trade. A typical customer transaction through a branch or phone call costs a customer about $1, while a similar online transaction costs just $0.02. Some of the most important retail customer product innovations include:

1. *Automated teller machines (ATMs).* Allows customers 24-hour access to their deposit accounts. They can pay bills as well as withdraw cash from these machines. In addition, if the FI's ATMs are part of a bank network (such as CIRRUS), retail depositors can gain direct nationwide—and in many cases international—access to their deposit accounts by using the ATMs of other banks in the network to draw on their accounts.[7]

2. *Point-of-sale (POS) debit cards.* Allows customers who choose not to use cash, checks, or credit cards for purchases to buy merchandise using debit card/point-of-sale (POS) terminals. The merchant avoids the check float and any delay in payment associated with credit card receivables since the FI offers the debit card/POS service immediately and transfers funds directly from the customer's deposit account to the merchant's deposit account at the time of card use. Unlike check or credit card transactions, the use of a debit card results in an immediate transfer of funds from the customer's account to the merchant's account.[8] Moreover, the customer never runs up a debit to the card issuer as is common with a credit card.

3. *Preauthorized debits/credits.* Includes direct deposits of payroll checks into bank accounts as well as direct payments of mortgage and utility bills.

4. *Smart cards (store-value cards).* Allows the customer to store and spend money for various transactions using a card that has a chip storage device, usually in the form of a strip. These have become increasingly popular at universities.

5. *Online banking.* Allows customers to conduct retail banking and investment services offered via the Internet. In 2008, the top 10 online banks (as rated by comScore Online Bank Benchmarker) had more than 51 million online banking customers.

6. *Mobile banking.* Allows customers to acquire banking apps through Apple and Android marketplaces and/or by scanning promotional QR codes. Services provided over mobile devices include remote deposit capture and digital wallets in which bank customers can pay for items using smartphone apps.

7. *Tablet banking.* Similar to mobile banking, but allows customers access to bank services through the tablet format.

8. *FI social media sites.* Allows customers to comment, see promotional advertisements, and request services through the FI's social media site (e.g., Facebook).

9. *Integration of online, offline, and mobile channels.* Allows a customer to start a loan application online and later finish the application at a branch without having to start the process over.

---

[7] Using another bank's ATM usually results in an access fee to the customer that averages $1 but can be as high as $5.

[8] In the case of bank-supplied credit cards, the merchant normally gets compensated very quickly but not instantaneously by the credit card issuer (usually one or two days). The bank then holds an account receivable against the card user. However, even a short delay can represent an opportunity cost for the merchant.

10. *Financial planning services.* Allow customers to manage their finances and monitor spending through online, mobile, and tablet services.

11. *Instant "micro mobile loans."* Allows customers to apply for, get approval on, and receive disbursement of a loan via a mobile or tablet device.

12. *Loyalty programs.* Allow customers to receive benefits from retail, entertainment, travel, and vacation services through mobile and tablet devices.

## Advanced Technology Requirements

The services just mentioned require FIs to continuously update and integrate their technology infrastructure. Some of the specific technological advances FIs must deal with include the following:

1. *Integration of online, mobile, and tablet technologies.* As revenue generators, FIs are welcoming the mobile and tablet channels of attracting and serving customers, while at the same time continuing to support the older technology of online banking. However, FIs have not fully integrated technologies used for the various e-banking methods. Advanced technology requires FIs to develop a single technology on which to run all of these e-banking channels. An interconnected set of technologies will make mobile and tablet applications and online development easier for banks to manage and will lower the cost of their operation for FIs.

2. *Provision of integrated, multichannel business information.* To increase efficiency, lower operating costs, and satisfy regulations, FIs need advanced technologies that allow for enhanced methods of gathering and reporting data. Most FIs operate using multiple back-office systems that are not integrated. In fact, customer data across FIs are often managed and serviced by multiple business units with the FI or even by outside data managers. Advanced technology requires the integration of multiple sales channels and customer services into a single business process that allows for the sharing and collaboration of information across all organizational units within the FI. Data integration helps FIs obtain a more accurate picture of their customers, allowing them to break through data "silos" to look at all data on its customers to get a more complete view of consumers' habits. Advanced technology in banking also provides FI employees with organized and timely access to information they need to effectively and efficiently perform their jobs. While costly, this type of integrated and multichannel data organization would increase revenues by targeting banking products and services to customers based on an analysis of their individual characteristics, needs, and activities. This process requires technology that provides data mining and analytical capabilities.

3. *Cloud computing.* Just as FIs provide cloud computing for their business customers, FIs use cloud computing to support their own business activities. Rather than run software applications on in-house computers with the staff to support them, they are run on a network of computers that constitute the cloud. Cloud computing systems allow for significant reductions in technology-related employee workloads and operating expenses; the FI needs only a computer that has interface software allowing access to the cloud, which can be as simple as a web browser.

4. *Increased reliance on message centers to replace e-mail communication.* FIs have virtually abandoned e-mail for any customer communication containing sensitive or private information. Replacing e-mail is the message center. These message centers are dedicated web portals set up for secure communication between an FI and its customers. The increased incidence of e-mail phishing scams targeting FI customers made it difficult for FI customers to differentiate between a legitimate e-mail from

their FI and a phishing e-mail. Similarly, FI employees became the target of advanced attackers using phishing scams to compromise the FI. To avoid this security issue, FIs employ message center technology to communicate with customers.

5. *Technology used for security issues.* The use of advanced technology brings with it increased potential for and more complex forms of fraud. Thus, FIs have an ever-greater need for technology-based risk management systems. Such technology helps increase the efficiency and effectiveness of security monitoring efforts, using computers, rather than time and labor intensive manual processes, to detect theft, fraud, and other illegal activities. By electronically capturing and recording data across the FI, an automated technological approach to security issues can alert an FI to threats more quickly. Such a system can also track a trail of flagged activity to simplify the investigation process and reduce losses. The use of technology to identify security issues can also enable an FI to assess risk more comprehensively, across the entire FI and in an integrated manner. Such a process promotes close operational synergy between the risk and finance functions of the FI.

A specific security issue arises as more FI customers conduct their banking on mobile and tablet devices. Mobile and tablet devices are more prone to security breaches because they are a relatively new technology. Further, mobile and tablet users do not always exercise the security precautions they would with their laptop computers. Thus, the increased use of these devices, particularly at Wi-Fi hotspots, has become the growing focus of hackers. FIs face an additional security threat as employees bring their own technology to work. FI employees who use tablet computers or other mobile devices for work purposes expose the FI to security breaches when they do not use the proper security precautions with the devices.

6. *Data backup and disaster recovery.* The extensive use of advanced technology by FIs creates a need for data backup systems used to save copies of all important data at least daily. By backing up its data, an FI can recover data virtually completely and quickly in the event of a disaster, data deletion, corruption, or fraud. Data backup systems allow an FI to upload as least one copy of files and data to a remote server, which is stored and accessed online and safeguarded from anything that could compromise these files. The backed-up files are generally kept in a secret location far from the FI's branch or business locations. Thus, if a disaster happens in one part of the world, the FI has its data in a location that is unaffected. For large FIs, data backup storage requirements are substantial. Thus, organization of storage space and managing the backup process is a complicated activity.

---

| **Concept Questions** | 1. Describe some of the wholesale financial services provided to corporate customers that have been improved by technology. |
|---|---|
| | 2. Describe some of the automated retail payment products available today. What advantages do these products offer the retail customer? |

---

# THE EFFECT OF TECHNOLOGY ON REVENUES AND COSTS

The previous section presented an extensive yet partial list of current products or services being offered by FIs that are built around a strong technological base and, increasingly, the Internet. Technological advances allow an FI to offer such products to its customers and potentially to earn higher profits. The investment of resources in many of these products is risky, however, because product innovations may fail to attract sufficient business relative to the initial cash outlay and the future costs related to these investments once they are in place. In the terminology of finance, a number of technologically based product innovations may turn out to be *negative* net present value projects because of uncertainties over revenues and costs and how quickly rivals will mimic or copy any innovation. Another factor is agency conflicts, in which managers undertake growth-oriented investments to increase an FI's size. Such investments may be inconsistent with stockholders' value-maximizing objectives. As a result, losses on technological innovations and new technology can weaken an FI because scarce capital resources are invested in value-decreasing products.

Standard capital budgeting techniques can be applied to technological innovations and new FI products. Let:

$I_0$ = Initial capital outlay for developing an innovation or product at time 0

$R_i$ = Expected net revenues or cash flows from product sales in future years $i$, $i = 1 \ldots N$

$d$ = FI's discount rate reflecting its risk-adjusted cost of capital

Thus, a negative net present value (NPV) project would result if:

$$I_0 > \frac{R_1}{(1 + d)} + \cdots + \frac{R_N}{(1 + d)^N}$$

Clearly, the profitability of any product innovation is negatively related to the size of the initial setup and development costs ($I_0$) and the FI's cost of capital ($d$), and positively related to the size of the stream of expected net cash flows ($R_i$) from selling the services.

This leads one to consider whether direct or indirect evidence is available that indicates whether technology investments to update the operational structure of FIs have increased revenues or decreased costs. Most of the direct or indirect evidence has concerned the effects of size on financial firms' operating costs. Indeed, it is the largest FIs that appear to be investing most in IT and other technological innovations.

We first discuss the evidence on the product revenue side and then discuss the evidence on the operating cost side. However, before looking at these revenue and cost aspects, we should stress that the success of technologically related innovation cannot be evaluated independently from regulation and regulatory changes. To a large extent, the growth and success of the retail and wholesale cash management products described above depend on trends in FI consolidation and interstate banking (see Chapter 21). Historically, restrictions on U.S. banks' ability to branch across state lines created problems for large corporations with national and international franchises. These firms needed to consolidate and centralize their deposit funds for working capital purposes. Innovations such as wholesale lockboxes and funds concentration eased these problems. It is more than coincidence that cash management services did not attract customers in Europe to the degree that they had in the United States. One reason is that in European countries, nationwide branching and banking was far more prevalent and interregional banking restrictions notably absent. The 1997 introduction of full interstate banking for banks in the United States, as well as the rapid consolidation in the U.S. financial services industry (e.g., as a result of mergers of large banks and the development of national branch systems), has reduced the demand for such services.

## Technology and Revenues

One potential benefit of technology is that it allows an FI to cross-market both new and existing products to customers. Such joint selling does not require the FI to produce all the services sold within the same branch or financial services outlet.[9] As a result, interest and non-interest income per dollar of assets increases and return on assets increases. For example, a commercial bank may link up with an insurance company to jointly market each other's loan, credit card, and insurance products. This arrangement has proved popular in Germany, where some of the largest banks have developed sophisticated cross-marketing arrangements with large insurance companies. In the United States, Citicorp's merger with Travelers Group to create Citigroup was explicitly designed to cross-market banking, insurance, and securities products in more than 100 countries. However, Citigroup management admitted after the completion of the merger that it would take 10 or more years to integrate computer systems to a sufficient degree to achieve this objective. Indeed, by 2005 Citigroup decided to sell its life insurance underwriting division to MetLife. Reasons cited for this divestiture included earnings on insurance underwriting being more seasonal and vulnerable to large disasters. Further, it was also difficult to sell this kind of insurance directly to customers since most industrial customers are accustomed to purchasing insurance through a broker. Citigroup still heavily sells all forms of insurance, but it no longer manufactures (i.e., underwrites) insurance.

Technology also increases the rate of innovation of new financial products. In recent years, many notable failures as well as successes have occurred. For example, despite large investments by banks, product innovations such as POS/debit cards were initially slow to gain a sufficiently large market in the United States. On the other hand, electronic securities trading, bill paying via the Internet, and using preauthorized debits and credits, including direct payroll systems, have proved to be high-growth areas in FIs.

Finally, we cannot ignore the issue of *service quality* and convenience. For example, while ATMs and Internet banking may potentially lower FI operating costs compared with employing full-service tellers, the inability of machines to address customers' concerns and questions flexibly may drive retail customers away; revenue losses may counteract any cost-savings effects. Customers still want to interact with a person for many transactions. For example, a survey of the home buying and mortgage process by Mortgagebot (in 2010) found that, while home buyers used the Internet to obtain information on mortgage interest rates, only 4 percent applied for a mortgage via the Internet. The survival of small banks in the face of growing nationwide branching may well be due in part to customers' belief that overall service quality is higher with tellers who provide a human touch rather than the Internet banking and ATMs more common at bigger banks. Even Internet-only banks are recognizing this as "virtual" FIs such as ING Direct operate branch offices (called "cafés") in several states. Further, a new type of customer service will be needed; customers require prompt, well-informed support on technical issues as they increasingly conduct their financial business electronically. FI customers may be driven away if they receive poor service quality from call center staff rather than being able to contact a branch executive directly.

www.mortgagebot.com

---

[9] Title V of the Financial Services Modernization Act of 1999, however, allows FI customers to opt out of any nonpublic personal information sharing with nonaffiliated third parties. The act also requires FIs to disclose their privacy policies regarding the sharing of nonpublic personal information with both affiliates and third parties.

## Technology and Costs

Traditionally, FIs have considered the major benefits of technological advances to be on the cost side rather than the revenue side. After a theoretical look at how technology favorably or unfavorably affects an FI's costs, we look at the direct and indirect evidence of technology-based cost savings for FIs. In general, technology may favorably affect an FI's cost structure by allowing it to exploit either economies of scale or economies of scope.

### *Economies of Scale*

**economy of scale**
A drop in the average costs of production as the output of an FI increases.

As financial firms become larger, the potential scale and array of the technology in which they can invest generally expands.[10] As noted above, the largest FIs make the largest expenditures on technology-related innovations. For example, the Tower Group (a consulting firm specializing in information technology) estimated that U.S. bank technology spending in 2012–13 would increase by greater than 6 percent, and 15 percent of those surveyed expected the increase to be greater than 20 percent from the $51 billion spent in 2010. Survey participants stated that the increase in technology spending is driven by a need to reduce the long-term operating costs, maintain outdated and duplicative systems, meet regulatory requirements, and meet client demands for enhanced solutions. If enhanced or improved technology lowers an FI's average costs of financial service production, larger FIs may have an **economy of scale** advantage over smaller financial firms. Economies of scale imply that the unit or average cost of producing FI services in aggregate (or some specific service such as deposits or loans) falls as the size of the FI expands. Thus, noninterest expense per dollar of assets falls and return on assets increases.

Figure 17–1 shows economies of scale for three different-sized FIs. The average cost of producing an FI's output of financial services is measured as:

$$AC_i = \frac{TC_i}{S_i}$$

where

$AC_i$ = Average costs of the $i$th FI

$TC_i$ = Total costs of the $i$th FI

$S_i$ = Size of the FI measured by on and off-balance-sheet assets, deposits, or loans

The largest FI in Figure 17–1 (of size $S_C$) has a lower average cost of producing financial services than do smaller firms B and A. This means that at any given price for financial service firm products, firm C can make a bigger profit than either B or A. Alternatively, firm C can undercut B and A in price and potentially gain a larger market share. For example, PNC Financial's $3.62 billion acquisition of RBC's U.S. retail banking unit and credit card assets in 2012 was billed as a cost-saving acquisition. The combined company expected to realize $230 million in annual cost savings (about 27 percent of RBC's noninterest expense) through operational and administrative efficiency improvements. Cost cutting was expected to come mainly from back-office positions in departments such as accounting,

---

[10] Economies of scale and scope can result from a variety of factors other than technology (e.g., interstate bank expansion). In this section, however, we demonstrate these economies using a framework of technological investments.

**FIGURE 17–1**
**Economies of Scale in FIs**

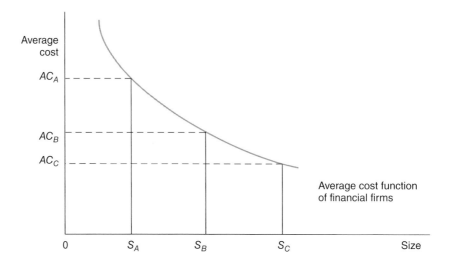

public relations, and data processing. In the framework of Figure 17–1, RBC, firm A, might be operating at $AC_A$ and PNC Financial might be represented as firm B operating at $AC_B$. The consolidation of overlapping activities would lower the average costs for the combined (larger) bank C in Figure 17–1, operating at $AC_C$.

The long-run implication of economies of scale on the FI sector is that the larger and most cost-efficient FIs will drive out smaller FIs, leading to increased large-firm dominance and concentration in financial services production. Such an implication is reinforced if time-related operating or technological improvements increasingly benefit larger FIs more than smaller FIs. For example, satellite technology and supercomputers, in which enormous technological advances are being made, may be available to only the largest FIs. The effect of improving technology over time, which is biased toward larger projects, is to shift the $AC$ curve downward over time but with a larger downward shift for large FIs (see Figure 17–2). In Figure 17–2, $AC_1$ is the hypothetical $AC$ curve prior to cost-reducing technological innovations. $AC_2$ reflects the cost-lowering effects of technology on FIs of all sizes but with the greatest benefit accruing to those of the largest size.

**FIGURE 17–2**
**Effects of Technological Improvement**

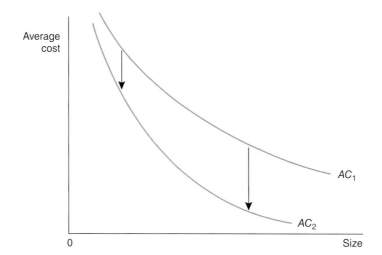

As noted earlier, technological investments are risky. If their future revenues do not cover their costs of development, they reduce the value of the FI and its net worth to the FI's owners. On the cost side, large-scale investments may result in excess capacity problems and integration problems as well as cost overruns and cost control problems. Then small FIs with simple and easily managed computer systems and/or those leasing time on large FIs' computers without bearing the fixed costs of installation and maintenance may have an average cost advantage. In this case, technological investments of large-sized FIs result in higher average costs of financial service production, causing the industry to operate under conditions of **diseconomies of scale.** Diseconomies of scale imply that small FIs are more cost efficient than large FIs and that in a freely competitive environment for financial services, small FIs prosper.

**diseconomies of scale**
Increase in the average costs of production as the output of an FI increases.

### Economies of Scope

While technological investments may have positive or negative effects on FIs in general and these effects may well differ across FIs of different size, technology tends to be applied more in some product areas than in others. That is, FIs are multiproduct firms producing services involving different technological needs. Moreover, technological improvements or investments in one financial service area (such as lending) may have incidental and synergistic benefits in lowering the costs of producing financial services in other areas (such as securities underwriting and brokerage). Specifically, computerization allows the storage and joint use of important information on customers and their needs. The simple *economy of scale* concept ignores these interrelationships among products and the "jointness" in the costs of producing financial products. In particular, FIs' abilities to generate synergistic cost savings through joint use of inputs in producing multiple products is called *economies of scope* as opposed to economies of scale.

Technology may allow two FIs to jointly use their input resources, such as capital and labor, to produce a set of financial services at a lower cost than if financial service products were produced independently of one another. Specifically, let $X_1$ and $X_2$ be two financial products; each is produced by one firm as a specialized producer. That is, firm A produces only $X_1$ and no $X_2$, and firm B produces only $X_2$ and no $X_1$. The average cost functions ($AC$) of these firms are:

$$AC_A[X_1, 0] \text{ and } AC_B[0, X_2]$$

**economies of scope**
The ability of FIs to generate synergistic cost savings through joint use of inputs in producing multiple products.

**Economies of scope** exist if these firms merge and jointly produce $X_1$ and $X_2$, resulting in:

$$AC_{A+B}[X_1, X_2] < AC_A[X_1, 0] + AC_B[0, X_2]$$

That is, the cost of joint production via cost synergies is less than the separate and independent production of these services.

---

**EXAMPLE 17–1**

*Calculation of Average Costs*

Let $TC_B$ be a specialized commercial bank's total cost of producing lending services to a corporate client. Suppose that the total operating costs of producing these services is $50,000 for a loan volume ($L_B$) of $10 million. Such costs include information collection and monitoring as well as account maintenance and processing. Thus, the average cost ($AC_B$) of loan production for the bank is:

$$AC_B = \frac{TC_B}{L_B} = \frac{\$50,000}{\$10,000,000} = 0.005 = 0.5\%$$

At the same time, a specialized investment bank is selling commercial paper for the same corporate customer. The investment bank's total cost ($TC_S$) of running the commercial paper operation is $10,000 for a $1 million issue ($P_S$). These costs include the cost of underwriting the issue as well as placing the issue with outside buyers. Thus:

$$AC_S = \frac{TC_S}{P_S} = \frac{\$10,000}{\$1,000,000} = 0.01 = 1\%$$

Consequently, the total average cost ($TAC$) of separately producing the loan services through the commercial bank and the commercial paper issuance through the investment bank is:

$$TAC = \frac{\$60,000}{\$11,000,000} = 0.54\%$$

Suppose, instead, a single FI produces both $10 million of lending services and $1 million commercial paper issuance services for the same customer (i.e., $P_{FS} = \$11$ million). Loans and commercial paper are substitute sources of funds for corporate customers. For an FI to originate a loan and commercial paper requires very similar expertise both in funding that issue and in credit risk assessment and monitoring. Common technologies in the loan and commercial paper production functions suggest that a single FI simultaneously (or jointly) producing both loan and commercial paper services for the same client at a total cost $TC_{FS}$ should be able to do this at a lower average cost than could the specialized FIs that separately produce these services. That is, the single FI should be able to produce the $11 million ($P_{FS}$) of financial services at a lower cost (say, $TC_{FS} = \$51,000$) than should two specialized FIs. Accordingly:

$$AC_{FS} = \frac{TC_{FS}}{P_{FS}} = \frac{\$51,000}{\$11,000,000} = 0.46\% < 0.54\%$$

Formally, if $AC_{FS}$ is the total average cost of a nonspecialized financial services firm, then economies of scope imply that:

$$AC_{FS} < TAC$$

**diseconomies of scope**
The costs of joint production of FI services are higher than they would be if they were produced independently.

Nevertheless, **diseconomies of scope** may occur instead. FIs may find costs actually higher from joint production of services than if they were produced independently. For example, suppose an FI purchases some very specialized information-based technology to ease the loan production and processing function. The FI could use any excess capacity this system has in other service areas. However, this process could be a relatively inefficient technology for other service areas and could add to the overall costs of production compared with using a specialized technology for each service or product area. Indeed, most studies find that cost-based economies of scope are negligible, although revenue-based economies of scope may arise for the largest FIs. It is unclear whether technological advances will make the production of financial services more efficient as financial service companies offer one-stop shopping to customers.

# TESTING FOR ECONOMIES OF SCALE AND ECONOMIES OF SCOPE

To test for economies of scale and economies of scope, FIs must clearly specify both the inputs to their production process and the cost of those inputs.[11] Basically, the two approaches to analyzing the cost functions of FIs are the production and the intermediation approaches.

## The Production Approach

The production approach views FIs' outputs of services as having two underlying inputs: labor and capital. If $w$ = wage costs of labor, $r$ = rental costs of capital, and $y$ = output of services, the total cost function ($C$) for the FI is:

$$C = f(y, w, r)$$

## The Intermediation Approach

The intermediation approach views the output of financial services as being produced by labor and capital as well as funds the intermediary uses to produce intermediated services. Thus, deposit costs would be an input in the banking and thrift industries, while premiums or reserves would be inputs in the insurance industry, and:

$$C = f(y, w, r, k)$$

where $k$ reflects the cost of funds for the FI.

---

[11] Three major production function forms have been tested: the Cobb-Douglas, the trans-log, and the Box-Cox flexible functional form.

# EMPIRICAL FINDINGS ON COST ECONOMIES OF SCALE AND SCOPE AND IMPLICATIONS FOR TECHNOLOGY EXPENDITURES

A large number of studies have examined economies of scale and scope in different financial service industry sectors. With respect to banks, most of the early studies failed to find economies of scale for any but the smallest banks.[12] More recently, better data sets and improved methodologies have suggested that economies of scale may exist for banks up to the $10 billion to $25 billion size range. Many large regional and super regional banks fall in this size range. With respect to economies of scope either among deposits, loans, and other traditional banking product areas or between on-balance-sheet products and off-balance-sheet products such as loan sales, the evidence that cost synergies exist is at best very weak. Similarly, the smaller number of studies involving nonbank financial service firms such as thrifts, insurance companies, and securities firms almost always report neither economies of scale nor economies of scope.[13]

## Economies of Scale and Scope and X-Inefficiencies

A number of studies have looked at the *dispersion* of costs in any given FI size class rather than the shape of the average cost functions. These efficiency studies find quite dramatic cost differences of 20 percent or more among banks, thrifts, and insurance companies in any given size class ($100 million asset size class, $200 million asset size class, etc.). Moreover, these studies find that only a small part of the cost differences among FIs in any size class can be attributed to economies of scale or scope.[14] This suggests that cost inefficiencies related to managerial performance and other hard-to-quantify factors (so-called *X-inefficiencies*) may better explain cost differences and operating cost efficiencies among financial firms than technology-related investments per se.[15]

There is little strong, direct evidence that larger multiproduct financial service firms enjoy cost advantages over smaller, more specialized financial firms. Nor do economies of scope and scale explain many of the cost differences among FIs of

---

[12] Good reviews are found in A. Berger, W. C. Hunter, and S. B. Timme, "The Efficiency of Financial Institutions: A Review and Preview of Research Past, Present and Future," *Journal of Banking and Finance* 17 (1993), pp. 221–49; R. DeYoung, "Learning-by-Doing, Scale Efficiencies, and Financial Performance at Internet-Only Banks," Federal Reserve Bank of Chicago Working Paper, June 2002; A. Berger, D. Humphrey, and L. B. Pulley, "Do Consumers Pay for One-Stop Banking? Evidence from an Alternative Revenue Function," *Journal of Banking and Finance* 20 (1996), pp. 1601–21, which looks at revenue economies of scope (rather than cost economies of scope) between loans and deposits over the 1978–90 period and find no evidence of revenue economies of scope; and A. Berger and R. DeYoung, "Technological Progress and the Geographic Expansion of the Banking Industry," *Journal of Money, Credit, and Banking,* September 2006, pp. 1483–1513.

[13] J. D. Cummins, S. Tennyson, and M. A. Weiss, "Consolidation and Efficiency in the U.S. Life Insurance Industry," *Journal of Banking and Finance* 23 (1999), pp. 325–57, find that mergers and acquisitions in the insurance industry do produce economies of scale, while efficiency gains are significantly smaller in non-M&A life insurers.

[14] See K. Mukherjee, S. C. Ray, and S. M. Miller, "Productivity Growth in Large U.S. Commercial Banks: The Initial Post-Deregulation Experience," *Journal of Banking and Finance* 25 (2001), pp. 913–39; and A. Akhigbe and J. E. McNulty, "The Profit Efficiency of Small U.S. Commercial Banks," *Journal of Banking and Finance* 27 (2003), pp. 307–25.

[15] See, for example, T. T. Milbourn, A. W. A. Boot, and A. V. Thakor, "Megamergers and Expanded Scope: Theories of Bank Size and Activity Diversity," *Journal of Banking and Finance* 23 (1999), pp. 195–214.

the same size. These empirical findings raise questions about the benefits of technology investments and technological innovation. While a majority of the studies tested for economies of scope and scale rather than the benefits of technology, these results are consistent with the relatively low payoff from technological innovation. To the extent that large FIs obtain benefits, they may well be on the revenue generation/new product innovation side rather than on the cost side. Indeed, recent studies looking at output and input efficiencies for banks and insurance companies derived from revenue and profit functions found that large FIs tend to be more efficient in revenue generation than smaller FIs and that such efficiencies may well offset scope and scale cost inefficiencies related to size.[16]

Early studies using data from the 1980s failed to find scale economies in any except very small banks. However, more recent studies, using data from the 1990s and 2000s and more modern methods for modeling bank technology, find significant scale economies at banks of all sizes. The difference in results between the earlier versus the more recent studies reflects improvements in the methods researchers used for measuring scale economies; geographic deregulation, which has led to larger efficient scale of banking production; and to a change in bank technology, such as the use of information technologies.[17]

The real benefits of technological innovation may be long term and dynamic, related to the evolution of the U.S. payments system away from cash and checks and toward electronic means of payment. Such benefits are difficult to obtain in traditional economy of scale and scope studies, which are largely static and ignore the more dynamic aspects of efficiency gains. This dynamic technological evolution not only has affected the fundamental role of FIs in the financial system but also has generated some new and subtle types of risks for FIs and their regulators. In the next section we take a closer look at the effects of technology on the payments system.

| **Concept Questions** | 1. What does the empirical evidence reveal about economies of scale and scope? |
| | 2. What conclusion is suggested by recent studies that have focused on the dispersion of costs across banks of a given asset size? |

[16] See A. N. Berger and L. J. Mester, "Inside the Black-Box"; J. Cummins, S. Tennyson, and M. A. Weiss, "Efficiency, Scale Economies and Consolidation in the U.S. Life Insurance Industry," *Journal of Banking and Finance*, February 1999, pp. 325–57; and R. DeYoung and K. P. Roland, "Product Mix and Earnings Volatility at Commercial Banks: Evidence from a Degree of Total Leverage Model," *Journal of Financial Intermediation* 10 (2001), pp. 54–84.

[17] See J. P. Hughes and L. J. Mester, "Efficiency in Banking: Theory, Practice, and Evidence," in *The Oxford Handbook of Banking*, A. N. Berger, P. Molyneux, and J. Wilson (eds.), New York: Oxford University Press, 2010; J. P. Hughes, W. Lang, L. J. Mester, and C.-G. Moon, "Efficient Banking Under Interstate Branching," *Journal of Money, Credit, and Banking* 28 (1996), pp. 1045–171; J. P. Hughes and L. J. Mester, "Bank Capitalization and Cost: Evidence of Scale Economies in Risk Management and Signaling," *Review of Economics and Statistics* 80 (1998), pp. 314–25; J. P. Hughes and L. J. Mester, "Who Said Large Banks Don't Experience Scale Economies? Evidence from a Risk-Return-Driven Cost Function," working paper, July 2011; D. C. Wheelock and P. W. Wilson, "Are U.S. Banks Too Large?" Working Paper 2009-054B, Federal Reserve Bank of St. Louis, December 2009; and J. P. Hughes, L. J. Mester, and C.-G. Moon, "Are Scale Economies in Banking Elusive or Illusive? Evidence Obtained by Incorporating Capital Structure and Risk-Taking into Models of Bank Production," *Journal of Banking and Finance* 25 (2001), pp. 2169–208.

# TECHNOLOGY AND THE EVOLUTION OF THE PAYMENTS SYSTEM

To better understand the changing nature of the U.S. payments system, look at Tables 17–2 and 17–3. In the United States, checks account for 21.5 percent of noncash transactions. This represents 40.7 percent of the dollar *value* of noncash transactions. Debit and credit transfers represent 10.3 percent and 6.9 percent, respectively, of noncash transactions and 21.6 percent and 32.5 percent, respectively, of the dollar value of these transactions. Credit cards entail 61.3 percent of all transactions, but only 5.2 percent of the dollar value of noncash transactions.

As can be seen from Tables 17–2 and 17–3, the use of electronic methods of payment is far higher in major developed countries other than the United States. Checks account for only 13.6 percent of noncash transactions worldwide, representing 10.5 percent of the dollar value of these transactions. Credit transfers are 17.9 percent of the transactions, representing 73.1 percent of the dollar value. Debit transfers are used in 14.9 percent of the transactions, representing 8.0 percent of the total dollar value. Credit cards are used in 52.5 percent of noncash worldwide transactions but represented only 1.7 percent of the dollar value. Finally, e-money payments, virtually nonexistent in the United States, represents 1.1 percent of noncash transactions worldwide.

Check writing lays the foundation of e-money. When a check is written and given to a person with an account at a different bank, the banks do not transfer currency. Rather, the banks use an electronic funds transfer. E-money removes the middleman. Instead of requesting that the bank transfer funds, the e-money user transfers the money from his or her bank account to the account of the funds' receiver. The primary function of e-money is to facilitate transactions on the Internet. Many of these transactions may be small in value and would not be cost efficient through other payment mediums such as credit cards. Further, e-money globalizes the economy, since money can be loaded into a cyber-wallet in any currency desired. A merchant can accept any amount and currency and convert it to local currency when the cyber-cash is uploaded to a bank account. If a user wants e-money offline, all that is necessary is smart card technology. The money is loaded onto the smart card, and electronic wallets are used to offload the money onto other smart cards or directly to an online system. In essence, e-money

**TABLE 17–2**
U.S. Cashless Payments System: Volume, Value, and Average Transaction Amount

Source: Bank for International Settlements, *Statistics on Payment Systems in Selected Countries*, Basel, Switzerland, January 2012. *www.bis.org*

| | Volume | | Value | | Transaction Average Value |
| --- | --- | --- | --- | --- | --- |
| | **Billions** | **Percent** | **$ Billions** | **Percent** | **$ Billions** |
| Check | 22.8 | 21.5% | $28,955 | 40.7% | $1,268 |
| Card payment | 65.2 | 61.3 | 3,696 | 5.2 | 57 |
| Debit function | 43.8 | 41.2 | 1,649 | 2.3 | 37 |
| Credit function | 21.4 | 20.1 | 2,047 | 2.9 | 95 |
| Debit transfer | 11.0 | 10.3 | 15,336 | 21.6 | 1,330 |
| Credit transfer | 7.3 | 6.9 | 23,065 | 32.5 | 3,026 |
| E-money payment | 0.0 | 0.0 | 0 | 0.0 | 0 |
| | 106.3 | | $71,052 | | |

**TABLE 17–3**
Worldwide Cash-
less Payment
Systems: Volume,
Value, and Average
Transaction Amount

Source: Bank for Interna-
tional Settlements, *Statistics
on Payment Systems in
Selected Countries*, Basel,
Switzerland, January 2012.
*www.bis.org*

| | Volume | | Value | | Transaction Average Value |
|---|---|---|---|---|---|
| | **Billions** | **Percent** | **$ Billions** | **Percent** | **$ Billions** |
| Check | 34.0 | 13.6 | $ 93,573 | 10.5 | $2,756 |
| Card payment | 131.7 | 52.5 | 9,499 | 1.7 | 72 |
| Debit function | 86.2 | 34.4 | 4,778 | 0.9 | 55 |
| Credit function | 45.5 | 18.1 | 4,721 | 0.8 | 104 |
| Debit transfer | 37.3 | 14.9 | 43,749 | 8.0 | 1,172 |
| Credit transfer | 45.0 | 17.9 | 399,938 | 73.1 | 8,876 |
| E-money payment | 2.9 | 1.1 | 18 | 0.0 | 6 |
| | 250.9 | | $546,777 | | |

transfers combine the benefits of other transaction methods. They are similar to debit/credit cards, but allow individuals to conduct transactions directly with each other. Like personal checks, they are feasible for very small transactions. However, unlike deposits that are insured by the U.S. government, money stored in e-money accounts and cards is not covered by deposit insurance.

To some extent, the United States is only now starting to catch up with other countries in its use of electronic payment method. Part of the reason for this involves culture and tradition in the United States. For example, checks have been obsolete in Germany for some time, but in the United States people still prefer to write checks. As a result, U.S. FIs have been slow in adopting and using online banking and electronic payment methods extensively. The speed with which this electronic payments gap will be closed will in large part depend on two factors: the speed with which the trend toward consolidation and automated banking continues and the degree and speed of technological innovation.

*www.chips.org*
*www.federalreserve.gov*

The two wire transfer systems that dominate the U.S. payments system are Fedwire and the Clearing House Interbank Payments System (CHIPS). Fedwire is a wire transfer network linking approximately 9,300 domestic FIs with the Federal Reserve System. Banks use this network to make deposit and loan payments, to transfer book entry securities among themselves, and to act as payment agents on behalf of large corporate customers, including other financial service firms. CHIPS is a privately operated payments network. At the core of the CHIPS system are approximately 50 large U.S. and foreign banks acting as correspondent banks for a larger number of domestic and international banks in clearing mostly international payments (such as foreign exchange, Eurodollar loans, certificates of deposit).

Together, these two wire transfer networks have been growing at around 10 percent per year. Indeed, in 2012 the combined value of payments sent over these two networks often exceeded $5.0 trillion a day.[18] According to data in Table 17–4, the United States is not the only country in which wholesale wire transfer systems have come to dominate the payment systems. The European Union, the Netherlands, Switzerland, Hong Kong, and Germany also have very large wire transfer

[18] In 2012, the average daily Fedwire funds volume was $1.1 trillion and the average daily CHIPS volume was $1.5 trillion. Volume on Fedwire averaged 84,000 transactions and on CHIPS, 375,000 transactions.

**TABLE 17–4**
Wholesale Wire Transfer Systems in Selected Countries

Source: Bank for International Settlements, *Statistics on Payment Systems in Selected Countries*, Basel, Switzerland, January 2012. *www.bis.org*

| | Number of Transactions (millions) | Annual Value of Transactions (US$ billions) | Ratio of Transactions Value to GDP (at annual rate) |
|---|---|---|---|
| **France** | | | |
| TARGET | 8.2 | $124,465 | 4,867.1% |
| CORE | 12,816.6 | 6,773 | 264.9 |
| **Germany** | | | |
| TARGET | 43.8 | 342,119 | 10,440.1 |
| RPS | 2,662.9 | 3,043 | 92.9 |
| **Hong Kong** | | | |
| HKD CHATS | 5.4 | 17,452 | 7,775.9 |
| USD CHATS | 3.1 | 2,725 | 1,214.0 |
| **Japan** | | | |
| FXYCS | 6.4 | 32,859 | 601.4 |
| BOJ-NET | 12.4 | 291,496 | 5,335.3 |
| Zengin System | 1,380.4 | 28,267 | 517.4 |
| **Netherlands** | | | |
| TARGET | 8.6 | 102,476 | 13,164.0 |
| Equens | 4,449.1 | 2,652 | 340.7 |
| **Switzerland** | | | |
| SIC | 394.7 | 49,702 | 9,411.9 |
| **United Kingdom** | | | |
| CHAPS-Sterling | 32.1 | 87,561 | 3,882.7 |
| BACS | 2,443.2 | 6,266 | 277.9 |
| **United States** | | | |
| Fedwire | 125.1 | 608,326 | 4,187.7 |
| CHIPS | 90.9 | 365,096 | 2,513.3 |
| **European Union** | | | |
| TARGET | 87.4 | 838,540 | 9,595.6 |
| Euro 1 | 59.4 | 82,300 | 1,386.2 |

systems measured as a percentage of local gross domestic product (GDP). In 2001 as a result of the single currency (the euro) and the European Monetary Union, a single wholesale wire transfer system for Europe fully emerged, linking all countries that are members of the European Monetary Union. The transactional system is called TARGET (Trans-European Automated Real-Time Gross-Settlement Express Transfer).

## Risks That Arise in an Electronic Transfer Payment System

At least six important risks have arisen along with the growth of wire transfer systems. We mentioned some of these while discussing off-balance-sheet activities in Chapter 16. Here, we go into more detail.

### Daylight Overdraft Risk

Some analysts and regulators view settlement, or daylight, overdraft risk as one of the greatest potential sources of instability in the financial markets today. To understand daylight overdrafts better, look at Figure 17–3. It shows a typical

**FIGURE 17–3**
Daylight Overdrafts
on Fedwire

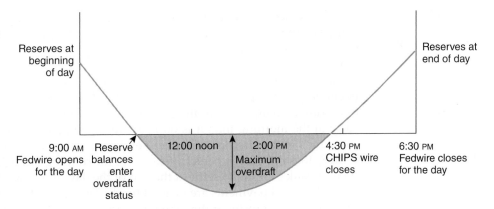

daily pattern of net wire payment transfers—payment messages sent (debits) minus payment messages received (credits)—for a large money center bank using Fedwire (the Federal Reserve's wire transfer network).

Under the Federal Reserve Act, banks must maintain cash reserves on deposit at the Fed; Fedwire settlement occurs at the end of the banking day at 6:30 PM EST. At that time, the Fed adjusts each member bank's reserve account to reflect its net debit (credit) position with other banks.[19] Under current regulations, the member bank's end-of-day reserve position cannot be negative. However, what is true at the end of the day is not true during the day; that is, the Fed allows banks to run real-time **daylight overdrafts** (or negative intraday balances) on their reserve accounts. These negative reserve balances occur under the current payments system because large banks and their customers often send payment messages repaying overnight loans and making interest payments at the beginning of the banking day and borrow funds and receive payment messages toward the end of the banking day. For periods during the day, banks frequently run daylight overdrafts on their reserve accounts at the Fed by having their payment outflow messages exceed their payment inflow messages (see Figure 17–3).

In effect, the Fed is implicitly lending banks within-day reserves. This process involves two other important institutional factors. First, until 1993, the Fed did not charge banks an explicit interest rate or fee for these daylight overdrafts. As a result, neither banks nor their large corporate customers had any incentive to economize on these transactions. Daylight Fedwire overdrafts were effectively free and therefore oversupplied. The current daylight overdraft fee is 50 basis points, quoted as an annual rate on the basis of a 24-hour day.[20] Second, under Regulation J, the Fed guarantees payment finality for every wire transfer message. Therefore, if the representative bank in Figure 17–3 were to fail at 12:00 noon, the Fed would be liable for all of the bank's Fedwire transactions made that day by that bank until 12 noon. This eliminates any risk that a payment message–receiving bank

**daylight overdraft**
A bank's negative intraday balance in its reserve account at the Fed.

[19] CHIPS transactions settle on Fedwire by 4:30 PM, before Fedwire closes.

[20] The annual rate is converted to an effective annual rate by multiplying it by the fraction of the day that Fedwire is scheduled to be open, currently 21.5 hours out of 24, or 21.5/24. Thus, the current effective annual rate charged for overdrafts is 44.79 basis points (50 basis points × 21.5/24 hours). The effective annual rate is converted to an effective daily rate by multiplying it by 1/360. See "Guide to the Federal Reserve's Payments System Risk Policy on Daylight Credit," Federal Reserve System, July 2012.

or its customers would be left short of funds at the end of the day. Essentially, the Fed bears the Fedwire credit risk of bank failures by granting overdrafts without charging a market interest rate.

On CHIPS, net payment flows often reflect a daily pattern similar to that in Figure 17–3 except that, as a privately owned pure net settlement system, the beginning-of-day position must be zero for all banks. As on Fedwire, big banks often run a daylight overdraft, but this is generally larger and more pronounced early in the morning than it is on Fedwire. Again, large banks then seek to borrow funds in the afternoon to cover net debit positions created earlier in the day. CHIPS does not charge banks explicit fees for running daylight overdrafts, but it treats a bank's failure to settle at the end of the day differently than does Fedwire. On Fedwire, all payments are in good funds. That is, the Fed guarantees the finality of any wire transfer at the time it is made. By contrast, on CHIPS, $3 billion in funds are made available to cover each day's payment transactions. These idle funds permit some 97 percent of CHIPS payments to be finally settled in real time and released to customers as no net debit is created. The 3 percent of payments that cannot be immediately settled are not released to customers until they are settled at the end of the day. Unlike previous arrangements used by CHIPS, because payments are not now released to receiving banks until adequate funds are in the sending bank's CHIPS account, there is no contractual provision for a payments unwind. However, there can be and has been a refusal of payment request on CHIPS. This last occurred in the wake of the 2001 terrorist attack in New York when some bank payment requests were not made because of insufficient funds (and the payment request was returned to the requesting bank).

Because of these concerns, the FDIC Improvement Act, passed in 1991, required the Federal Reserve to implement Regulation F, under which banks, thrifts, and foreign banks must develop internal procedures or benchmarks to limit their settlement and other credit exposures to depository institutions with which they do business (so-called correspondent banks). Accordingly, since December 1992, banks have been required to limit their exposure to an individual correspondent to no more than 25 percent of the correspondent bank's capital. However, for adequately capitalized banks, this can be raised to 50 percent, while no set benchmark is required for well-capitalized banks. Thus, it is now easier for the most solvent banks to transact on the wire transfer networks and run daylight overdrafts than for less well-capitalized banks. In addition, as long as the benchmarks are adhered to, regulators' exposure to settlement risk is reduced.

### International Technology Transfer Risk

In recent years the United States has been at the forefront in making technology investments and financial service innovations in the payments system. Indeed, the world looks to American innovation and entrepreneurship in building new banking technology and service (two areas in which the United States leads the world) to attract new customers. This suggests that U.S. financial service firms have often been unable to transfer profitably their domestic technological innovations to international markets to gain competitive advantage, at least in the short term. In contrast, foreign financial service firms entering the U.S. market gain direct access to, and knowledge of, U.S. technology–based products at a very low cost. For example, since the passage of the International Banking Act in 1978, foreign banks have had direct access to U.S. Fedwire.

## Crime and Fraud Risk

The increased replacement of checks and cash by wire transfers as methods of payment or exchange has resulted in an increase in the efficiency of the execution of transactions, but it has also resulted in new problems regarding theft, data snooping, and white-collar crime. Because huge sums are transferred across wire networks each day and some bank employees have specialized knowledge of personal identification numbers (PINS) and other entry codes, the incentive for white-collar crime appears to have increased. For example, a manager at the Sri Lankan branch of the now defunct BCCI reportedly stole a computer chip from a telex machine in the bank's Oman branch and used it to transfer $10 million from three banks in the United States and Japan to his own account in Switzerland.

Moreover, as discussed earlier in the chapter, considerable security problems exist in trying to develop the Internet as a form of electronic payment system. Indeed, cybercrime has surpassed trafficking in illegal drugs in dollar value. Financial institutions are accordingly concerned about open credit or debit card details on the Internet. Any version of electronic payment via the Internet must not only meet the requirements of recognition and acceptability associated with physical cash, but also provide the same high level of security that is demanded of cash payments but which the Internet itself cannot guarantee.

Further, penalties for cybercrimes are on the rise, and regulatory and legal requirements on data protection and data security at FIs are emerging. Government organizations are also becoming increasingly involved in cyber warfare. After the terrorist attacks on September 11, 2001, the U.S. Congress passed the USA Patriot Act of 2001. The act contains a number of specific amendments to existing criminal laws designed to streamline early detection and investigation of suspected terrorist activity conducted through financial institutions. For example, in accordance with the Patriot Act, in April 2004 the FBI and federal regulators began a probe into large cash withdrawals from Riggs National Bank by Saudi Arabian citizens/customers and accused Riggs of failing to alert regulators of suspicious transactions. The Office of the Comptroller of the Currency (OCC) also classified Riggs as a "troubled institution" for failing to adequately tighten its money laundering controls despite an order from the OCC to do so. Regulators also pursued a second line of inquiry into whether Riggs violated "know your customer" record keeping laws in its dealings with foreign customers. Treasury Department investigators were looking into the relationship between Riggs and high-risk foreign customers.

More recently, in November 2009, the FBI successfully concluded an investigation of the simultaneous theft of money from more than 2,100 ATM machines in 280 different cities on three continents. The crime came about when a 28-year-old Moldovan man discovered a vulnerable computer network of an Atlanta-based major credit card processing company. He passed the information to a hacker in Estonia. The Estonian verified the network vulnerability and shared the information with a hacker in Russia. The Russian, with the help of the three other hackers, penetrated the electronic network, reverse-engineered the PIN codes from the encrypted system, and raised the limits on the amount of money that could be withdrawn from the prepaid payroll debit cards. Another hacker organized a network of thieves around the world, who used a total of 44 counterfeit cards to withdrawal the $9 million within 12 hours. With international cooperation, the FBI was able to identify and charge all involved with the cybercrime.

In the future, greater bank and regulatory resources will have to be spent on surveillance and employee monitoring as well as on developing fail-safe and unbreakable entry codes to wire transfer accounts, especially as a number of countries have passed data privacy laws.

### Regulatory Risk

**usury ceilings**
Caps or ceilings on consumer and mortgage interest rates imposed by state governments.

The improvement in FIs' computer and telecommunications networks also enhances the power of FIs' vis-à-vis regulators, effectively aiding regulatory avoidance. Thus, as implied earlier, regulation not only can affect the profitability of technological innovations, but also can spur or hinder the rate and types of innovation. For example, many states in the United States impose usury ceilings on FIs. **Usury ceilings** place caps and controls on the fees and interest rates that many FIs can charge on credit cards, consumer loans, and residential mortgages. Because credit card operations are heavily communications based and do not need to be located directly in an FI's market, the two states that now dominate the credit card market are South Dakota and Delaware. These two states are among the most liberal regarding credit card fee and interest rate usury regulations. For example, Citigroup, the U.S. financial services firm with the largest credit card franchise, has located its credit card operations in South Dakota.

As a result of regulation in the United States, banking in the relatively unregulated Cayman Islands has experienced considerable growth. The 500 or more FIs located there do most of their business via public and private telecommunications networks. A major reason for the growth in Cayman Islands banking was the desire of large U.S. banks to avoid or reduce the cost of the Federal Reserve's low-interest-bearing reserve requirements. Many attribute its current popularity to drug- or crime-related secret money transactions. The use of telecommunications networks and technological improvements has changed, perhaps irreversibly, the balance of power between large multinational FIs and governments—both local and national—in favor of the former. Such a shift in power may create incentives for countries to lower their regulations to attract entrants; that is, the shift may increase the incentives for competitive deregulation. This trend may be potentially destabilizing to the market in financial services, with the weakest regulators attracting the most entrants.

### Tax Avoidance

The development of international wire networks as well as international financial service firm networks has enabled FIs to shift funds and profits by using internal pricing mechanisms, thereby minimizing their overall U.S. tax burden and maximizing their foreign tax credits. For example, prior to 1986, many large U.S. banks paid almost no corporate income taxes, despite large reported profits, by rapidly moving profits and funds across different tax regimes. This raised considerable public policy concerns and was a major reason underlying the 1986 tax reforms in the United States. These reforms imposed a minimum corporate income tax rate of 20 percent on U.S. banks and limited their ability to use foreign tax credits to offset their domestic income tax burdens.

In the late 2000s, the U.S. government, including the IRS, took steps to get client names from foreign FIs. These client lists contained names of U.S. individuals and business that "hid" income in the foreign FIs to intentionally avoid paying U.S. taxes. In one case, UBS AG helped individuals hide income to avoid taxes. The tax scheme relied in part on channeling funds to a Swiss UBS account held in the name of a Hong Kong entity. The Hong Kong link was important because the Justice

Department and Internal Revenue Service used that as a clue of wrongdoing as they investigated some 250 names that UBS turned over to the U.S. government.

### Competition Risk

As financial services become more technologically based, they are increasingly competing with nontraditional financial service suppliers. For example, in addition to offering its own enhanced credit card in competition with bank-supplied credit cards, AT&T owns a finance company. Also, once established, nonfinancial firms can easily purchase financial services technology. For example, General Motors has established a credit card operation linked to the purchase of its vehicles at a discount. Currently, banks issue less than half of all new credit cards; much of the new business is going to nontraditional firms such as AT&T and General Motors.

Another example is the dramatic rise in industrial loan corporations (ILCs) in Utah, owned by nonbanking companies such as AMEX, General Electric, and Pitney Bowes. ILCs provide loans to low-quality, high–interest rate corporations that banks avoid. The deposits of these ILCs are insured by the FDIC, yet ILCs are regulated by neither the Federal Reserve nor the Office of the Comptroller of the Currency. While being based in Utah (where the regulatory environment is favorable), technology has helped ILCs expand their services nationwide. As a result, assets under management grew from $2.9 billion at the end of 1995 to $232 billion in 2009. This can be compared with total C&I loans at commercial banks of $1,357 billion. Thus, technology exposes existing FIs to the increased risk of erosion of their franchises as costs of entry fall and the competitive landscape changes. The Obama administration's 2009 proposed overhaul of financial institution regulation included a provision that would mean greater oversight of ILCs and could lead to some of them being shut down by the nonfinancial companies that operate them. The overhaul included a provision that would require ILCs to register as bank holding companies with the U.S. Federal Reserve. That would subject companies that operate ILCs to greater government oversight and put them in the same category as most large U.S. banks. While the provision was not included in the final bill, possibly because of this increased attention and possible scrutiny, assets under management at ILCs fell to $155 billion in 2012.[21]

| | |
|---|---|
| **Concept Questions** | 1. Describe the six risks faced by FIs with the growth of wire transfer payment systems. |
| | 2. Why do daylight overdrafts create more of a risk problem for banks on CHIPS than on Fedwire? |
| | 3. What steps have the members of CHIPS taken to lower settlement, or daylight overdraft, risk? |

## OTHER OPERATIONAL RISKS

While technology risk has become increasingly important to the profitability and riskiness of FIs, it is not the sole source of operational risk. Indeed, studies have found that the impact of an operational risk crisis (such as embezzlement and loan

[21]At the height of the financial crisis, GMAC, one of the largest ILCs with more than $33 billion in assets, was converted to a bank holding company. GMAC's precarious financial position caused the Fed to expedite the conversion of the ILC to a bank without the usual public notice of the move.

# Industry Perspectives   Goldman Code Thief Gets 8 Years

A former Goldman Sachs Group Inc. computer programmer was sentenced to eight years and one month in prison Friday for stealing the confidential source code of the investment bank's high-speed trading system. Federal prosecutors in Manhattan had alleged that Sergey Aleynikov, 41 years old, secretly copied Goldman Sachs's confidential source code in his last days at the investment bank and intended to use it to build a similar trading platform at his new employer. "I very much regret the foolish decision to download information, part of this information was proprietary to Goldman," Mr. Aleynikov said before sentencing. "I never meant to cause Goldman any harm. I did not intend to harm anyone." However, U.S. District Judge Denise Cote in Manhattan didn't agree. "He knew that what he was doing would harm Goldman Sachs. There is no other impact," she said. . . . Mr. Aleynikov was convicted of theft of trade secrets and transportation of stolen property in December. Kevin Marino, Mr. Aleynikov's lawyer, had previously argued that Mr. Aleynikov

only intended to use portions of the downloaded code that were "open source," or freely available . . .

Mr. Aleynikov is the second person to be convicted in recent months of stealing proprietary computer code related to an investment bank's high-frequency trading business. Samarth Agrawal, a former Société Générale SA trader, was sentenced to three years in prison in February for the theft of the French investment bank's computer code. He was convicted in November of theft of trade secrets and transportation of stolen property. Late last month, a federal judge ordered that Mr. Aleynikov be jailed pending sentencing after prosecutors claimed he was an increased risk of flight in part because of the lengthy sentence he faces and his connections to his family in the U.S. are strained. Mr. Aleynikov holds dual Russian and U.S. citizenship and is separated from his wife.

**Source:** *The Wall Street Journal*, March 19, 2012, p. B5, by Chad Bray. Reprinted by permission of *The Wall Street Journal*. © 2012 Dow Jones & Company, Inc. All rights Reserved Worldwide. *www.wsj.com*

fraud) on the market value of a firm far exceeds (as much as 12 times) the actual cost. Early in the chapter we listed four other sources of operational risk. These are employees, customer relationships, capital assets, and external risks. For example, employee risk includes employee turnover, theft, and fraud, as well as programming errors by employees. (The Industry Perspectives box examines an alleged theft of trading program codes by an ex-Goldman Sachs computer programmer).

Table 17–5 lists a summary of the problems these sources of operational risk can create, including how the other sources of operational risk interact with technology risk. For example, in 2011 several banks announced their plan to institute a fee for debit card usage; the most notable among these was Bank of America, which announced a $5 per month fee. Bank of America said the fees were a consequence of the Durbin Amendment to the Dodd-Frank reform bill capping the amount banks can charge retailers for debit card purchases. Bank of America estimated it would lose $2 billion per year from the regulation. The banks saw the debit card fee as a way to offset the losses. However, customers rejected the fee vehemently. The announcement produced a consumer backlash leading to a boycott of the bank, customer petitions of the bank, and customer mobilization to close their accounts at Bank of America and take their business elsewhere. Stating that customer opinions were important, Bank of America (as well as other banks that had announced the institution of a debit card fee) rescinded the fee change.

Like technology risk, these other sources of operational risk can result in direct costs (e.g., loss of income), indirect costs (e.g., client withdrawals and legal costs), and opportunity costs (e.g., forgone business opportunities) for an FI that reduce profitability and value. To offset these costs, FI managers spend considerable effort

**TABLE 17–5   A Summary of Operational Risks Faced by FIs**

Source: C. Marshall, *Measuring and Managing Operational Risks in Financial Institutions: Tools, Techniques and Other Resources* (Singapore: John Wiley and Sons, 2001).

| Source of Risk | Specific Problem | Source of Risk | Specific Problem |
|---|---|---|---|
| **Employee risk** | Employee turnover | **Customer risk** | Contractual disagreement |
| | Key personnel risk | | Dissatisfaction |
| | Fraud risk | | Default |
| | Error | **Capital asset risk** | Safety |
| | Rogue trading | | Security |
| | Money laundering | | Operating costs |
| | Confidentiality breach | | Fire/flood |
| **Technology risk** | Programming error | **External risk** | External fraud |
| | Model risk | | Taxation risk |
| | Mark-to-market error | | Legal risk |
| | Management information | | War |
| | IT systems outage | | Collapse of markets |
| | Telecommunications failure | | Reputation risk |
| | Technology provider failure | | Relationship risk |
| | Contingency planning | | |

and resources to prevent, control, finance, and insulate the FI from losses due to operational risk. These efforts include:

1. *Loss prevention.* Training, development, and review of employees.
2. *Loss control.* Planning, organization, backup (e.g., computer systems).
3. *Loss financing.* External insurance (e.g., catastrophe insurance).
4. *Loss insulation.* FI capital.

Risk management efforts, of course, come at a cost to the FI. The greater the commitment of resources to risk management efforts, the lower the costs resulting from operational risks. However, the resources spent in preventing costs of operational risk may, at some point, be greater than the cost of the risk itself. In maximizing profits and value, FIs will invest in these risk management efforts until the costs of such efforts just offset operating losses from not undertaking such efforts.

| | |
|---|---|
| **Concept Questions** | 1. What are some examples of operational risk coming from employees, customer relationships, capital assets, and external risk? |
| | 2. What risk management efforts are involved in controlling operational risk? |

# REGULATORY ISSUES AND TECHNOLOGY AND OPERATIONAL RISKS

As stated earlier, operational risk is the risk of direct or indirect loss resulting from inadequate or failed internal processes, people, or systems, and from external events. Certainly, as FIs' use of technology increases, operational risk increases as well. However, little has been done to oversee or regulate these increasing risks. In this section, we look at two areas that have been directly impacted by the increase in operational risk.

1. *Operational Risk and FI Insolvency.* Research by Operational Research Inc., an operational risk consultancy firm, estimates that in the 1980s and 1990s, FIs lost over $200 billion due to operational risk.[22] Regulators recognized the significance of operational risk for FIs. Specifically, in 1999 the Basel Committee (of the BIS) on Banking Supervision said that operational risks "are sufficiently important for banks to devote necessary resources to quantify the level of such risks and to incorporate them (along with market and credit risk) into their assessment of their overall capital adequacy."[23] In its follow-up consultative documents released in January 2001 and April 2003, the Basel Committee proposed three specific methods by which depository institutions (DIs) could calculate the required capital to protect themselves against operational risk. These methods are the Basic Indicator Approach, the Standardized Approach, and the Advanced Measurement Approach.[24] These methods were first implemented in 2006. Banks are encouraged to move along the spectrum of available approaches as they develop more sophisticated operational risk measurement systems and practices. Internationally active banks and banks with significant operational risk exposures (such as specialized processing banks) are expected to use an approach that is more sophisticated than the Basic Indicator Approach and that is appropriate for the risk profile of the institution. A bank can be allowed to use the Basic Indicator or Standardized Approach for some parts of its operations and an Advanced Measurement Approach for others provided certain minimum criteria are met. A bank is not allowed to choose to revert to a simpler approach once it has been approved for a more advanced approach without supervisor approval. Research has found that the amount of capital held for operational risk according to these models will often exceed capital held for market risk and that the largest banks could choose to allocate several billion dollars in capital to operational risk. We discuss each of the methods in more detail in Chapter 20.

2. *Consumer Protection.* A KPMG Information Security Survey 2000 reported that business customers hesitate to put their personal and financial information on the Internet for two reasons. First, they are worried about who has access to this information and how it will be used. Second, they worry that credit card or account details will be stolen or used fraudulently. These worries are well founded. For example, in 2009 a 28-year-old American, Albert Gonzalez, along with two Russian accomplices, were indicted for what prosecutors believed was one of the nation's largest hacking and identity-theft crimes. Federal prosecutors alleged the three devised a global scheme to hack into the computer systems of five major companies, including Hannaford Brothers supermarkets, 7-Eleven, and Heartland Payment Systems Inc., to steal data from more than 130 million credit and

---

[22] See C. Smithson, "Measuring Operational Risk," *Risk,* March 2000, pp. 58–59.

[23] See "Basel Committee on Banking Supervision, 1999; A New Capital Adequacy Framework," Bank for International Settlements, Basel, Switzerland, June 1999, p. 50.

[24] See "Basel Committee on Banking Supervision, 2001; The New Basel Capital Accord," January 2001, and "Overview of The New Basel Capital Accord," April 2003, Bank for International Settlements, Basel, Switzerland (www.bis.org). The Advanced Measurement Approach offers three alternative methodologies for capital reserve calculations for the most sophisticated and largest banks in the world.

debit cards. Gonzalez and his co-conspirators committed the crime on a network of computers located from New Jersey to California to Illinois, Latvia, the Netherlands, and Ukraine. The group was able to infiltrate the computer networks of the victim companies, access credit and debit card numbers, and install so-called back doors in victims' computer networks that enabled them to steal more data in the future. They also installed "sniffer" programs to capture card data and send it to the hacker. The hackers made extensive efforts to conceal their activities, including registering the computers they used under false names and communicating online under a variety of screen names.

The advent of electronic banking is making consumer protection an increasingly important responsibility for regulators of FIs. As mentioned earlier, the 1999 Financial Services Modernization Act allows FI customers to opt out of any private information sharing an FI may want to pursue. Thus, FI customers have some control over who will see and have access to their private information. This regulation does not include the sharing of information by nonfinancial firms that have entered the financial services industry.

However, the Dodd-Frank Wall Street Reform and Consumer Protection Act of 2010 created and authorized the Consumer Financial Protection Bureau (CFPB) to supervise nonbanks in the specific markets of residential mortgage, payday, and private education lending. The CFPB also regulates a wide range of financial products and services, including credit counseling, payday loans, mortgages, credit cards, and other bank products. Further, as of 2011 the CFPB supervises larger consumer reporting agencies. This is the first time these companies have been supervised at the federal level. The CFPB announced its first enforcement action in July 2012 against Capital One Bank. Capital One was discovered to be lying to consumers about its products. Third-party call centers hired by Capital One were using high-pressure sales tactics to sell consumers add-on features to their credit cards but misleading them about the benefits. The agency said consumers were sometimes even led to believe that the product would improve their credit scores and help them increase the credit limit on their Capital One credit cards. The CFPB ordered Capital One Bank to refund approximately $150 million to 2 million customers and pay an additional $60 million in penalties.

As mentioned earlier in the chapter, with respect to security risk, because Internet transactions involve open systems, they are susceptible to interception and fraud. Cryptographic techniques for ensuring transaction security are rapidly improving and are almost fully secure for consumer transactions. Further, technological developments are soon expected that will provide protection needed for large transactions as well. Availability of these technologies does not ensure that FIs will use them (especially if their costs are high). Consequently, regulators may need to oversee (or even mandate) the implementation of these technologies if FIs are slow to use them operationally.

| **Concept Questions** | 1. What are the three approaches proposed by the Basel Committee on Banking Supervision for measuring capital requirements associated with operational risk? |
| | 2. What steps have been or are being taken to ensure privacy and protection against fraud in the use of personal and financial consumer information placed on the Internet? |

## Summary

This chapter analyzed the operating cost side of FIs' activities, including the effects of the growth of technology-based innovations. The impact of technology was first examined separately for wholesale and retail services before an analysis was presented of its impact on costs and revenues. Technology-based investments can potentially result in new product innovations and lower costs, but the evidence for such cost savings is mixed. Moreover, new and different risks appear to have been created by modern technology. These include settlement or daylight overdraft risk, international technology transfer risk, crime or fraud risk, regulatory avoidances risk, taxation avoidance risk, and competition risk. Nevertheless, although the chapter focuses on the cost and benefits of technology to an FI, a more fundamental issue may not be technology's costs and benefits but the need to invest in technology to survive as a modern full-service FI.

## Questions and Problems

1. Explain how technological improvements can increase an FI's interest and non-interest income and reduce interest and noninterest expenses. Use some specific examples.

2. Table 17–1 shows data on earnings, expenses, and assets for all insured banks. Calculate the annual growth rates in the various income, expense, earnings, and asset categories from 1991 to 2010. If part of the growth rates in assets, earnings, and expenses can be attributed to technological change, in what areas of operating performance has technological change appeared to have the greatest impact? What growth rates are more likely to be caused by economywide economic activity?

3. Compare the effects of technology on an FI's wholesale operations with the effects of technology on an FI's retail operations. Give some specific examples.

4. What are some of the risks inherent in being the first to introduce a financial innovation?

5. The operations department of a major FI is planning to reorganize several of its back-office functions. Its current operating expense is $1.5 million, of which $1 million is for staff expenses. The FI uses a 12 percent cost of capital to evaluate cost-saving projects.

   a. One way of reorganizing is to outsource a portion of its data entry functions. This will require an initial investment of approximately $500,000 after taxes. The FI expects to save $150,000 in annual operating expenses after taxes for the next seven years. Should it undertake this project?

   b. Another option is to automate the entire process by installing new state-of-the-art computers and software. The FI expects to realize more than $500,000 per year in after-tax savings, but the initial investment will be approximately $3 million. In addition, the life of this project is limited to seven years, at which time new computers and software will need to be installed. Using this seven-year planning horizon, should the FI invest in this project? What level of after-tax savings would be necessary to make this plan comparable in value creation to the plan in part (a)?

6. City Bank upgrades its computer equipment every five years to keep up with changes in technology. Its next upgrade is two years from today and is budgeted to cost $1 million. Management is considering moving up the date by two years

to install some new computers with breakthrough software that could generate significant cost savings. The cost for this new equipment also is $1 million. What should be the savings per year to justify moving up the planned upgrade by two years? Assume a cost of capital of 15 percent.

7. Identify and discuss three benefits of technology in generating revenue for FIs.

8. Distinguish between economies of scale and economies of scope.

9. What information on the operating costs of FIs does the measurement of economies of scale provide? If economies of scale exist, what implications do they have for regulators?

10. What are diseconomies of scale? What are the risks of large-scale technological investments, especially to large FIs? Why are small FIs willing to outsource production to large FIs against which they are competing? Why are large FIs willing to accept outsourced production from smaller FI competition?

11. What information on the operating costs of FIs is provided by the measurement of economies of scope? What implications do economies of scope have for regulators?

12. Buy Bank had $130 million in assets and $20 million in expenses before the acquisition of Sell Bank, which had assets of $50 million and expenses of $10 million. After the merger, the bank had $180 million in assets and $35 million in costs. Did this acquisition generate either economies of scale or economies of scope for Buy Bank?

13. A commercial bank with assets of $2 billion and costs of $200 million has acquired an investment banking firm subsidiary with assets of $40 million and expenses of $15 million. After the acquisition, the costs of the bank are $180 million and the costs of the subsidiary are $20 million. Does the resulting merger reflect economies of scale or economies of scope?

14. What are diseconomies of scope? How could diseconomies of scope occur?

15. A survey of a local market has provided the following average cost data: Mortgage Bank A (MBA) has assets of $3 million and an average cost of 20 percent. Life Insurance Company B (LICB) has assets of $4 million and an average cost of 30 percent. Corporate Pension Fund C (CPFC) has assets of $4 million and an average cost of 25 percent. For each firm, average costs are measured as a proportion of assets. MBA is planning to acquire LICB and CPFC with the expectation of reducing overall average costs by eliminating the duplication of services.

    a. What should be the average cost after acquisition for the bank to justify this merger?

    b. If MBA plans to reduce operating costs by $500,000 after the merger, what will be the average cost of the new firm?

16. What is the difference between the production approach and the intermediation approach to estimating cost functions of FIs?

17. What are some of the conclusions of empirical studies on economies of scale and scope? How important is the impact of cost reductions on total average costs? What are X-inefficiencies? What role do these factors play in explaining cost differences among FIs?

18. Why does the United States lag behind most other industrialized countries in the proportion of annual electronic noncash transactions per capita? What factors probably will be important in causing the gap to decrease?

19. What are the differences between the Fedwire and CHIPS payment systems?

20. What is a daylight overdraft? How do an FI's overdraft risks incurred during the day differ for each of the two competing electronic payment systems, Fedwire and CHIPS? What provision has been taken by the members of CHIPS to introduce an element of insurance against the settlement risk problem?
21. How does Regulation F of the 1991 FDICIA reduce the problem of daylight overdraft risk?
22. Why do FIs in the United States face a higher degree of international technology risk than do the FIs in other countries?
23. What has been the impact of rapid technological improvements in the electronic payment systems on crime and fraud risk?
24. What are usury ceilings? How does technology create regulatory risk?
25. How has technology altered the competition risk of FIs?
26. What actions has the BIS taken to protect depository institutions from insolvency due to operational risk?

## Web Questions

27. Go to the BIS website at **www.bis.org** and find the most recent data on the volume and value of payment system transactions in the United States (Table 17–2) using the following steps. Under "Statistics," click on "Payment Systems." Click on "Statistics." Click on the most recent document "Statistics on payment, clearing and settlement systems in the CPSS countries—Figures for 20XX." Click on "Full Publication." Under Bookmarks, click on "United States." This will bring the file onto your computer that contains the relevant data. How have these numbers changed since 2010 as reported in Table 17–2?
28. Go to the BIS website at **www.bis.org** and find the most recent data on the volume and value of worldwide wire transfer systems (Table 17–4). Under "Statistics," click on "Payment systems." Click on "Statistics." Click on the most recent document "Statistics on payment, clearing and settlement systems in the CPSS countries—Figures for 20XX." Click on "Comparative tables only." This will bring the file onto your computer that contains the relevant data. How have these numbers changed since 2010 as reported in Table 17–4?

# Managing Risk

See Appendices Online at www.mhhe.com/saunders8e
- Appendix 18A: Federal Reserve Requirement Accounting
- Appendix 18B: Bankers' Acceptances and Commercial Paper as Sources of Financing

# Liability and Liquidity Management

## INTRODUCTION

Depository institutions as well as life insurance companies are especially exposed to liquidity risk (see Chapter 12). The essential feature of this risk is that an FI's assets are relatively illiquid when liquid claims are suddenly withdrawn (or not renewed). The classic case is a bank run in which depositors demand cash as they withdraw their claims from a bank and the bank is unable to meet those demands because of the relatively illiquid nature of its assets. For example, the bank could have a large portfolio of nonmarketable small business or real estate loans.

To reduce the risk of a liquidity crisis, FIs can insulate their balance sheets from liquidity risk by efficiently managing their liquid asset positions or managing the liability structure of their portfolios. In reality, an FI manager can optimize over both liquid asset and liability structures to insulate the FI against liquidity risk. This chapter discusses the various liquid assets and liabilities an FI might use and the risk-return trade-offs across these assets. In addition to ensuring that FIs can meet expected and unexpected liability withdrawals, two additional motives exist for holding liquid assets: monetary policy implementations and taxation reasons. The chapter concludes with a look at specific issues associated with liability and liquidity risk management in depository institutions, insurance companies, and other FIs.

## LIQUID ASSET MANAGEMENT

A liquid asset can be turned into cash quickly and at a low transaction cost with little or no loss in principal value (see the discussion in Chapter 12 on the liquidity index). Specifically, a liquid asset is traded in an active market so that even large transactions in that asset do not move the market price or move it very little. Good examples of liquid assets are newly issued T-bills, T-notes, and T-bonds. The ultimate liquid asset is, of course, cash. While it is obvious that an FI's liquidity risk can be reduced by holding large amounts of assets such as cash, T-bills, and T-bonds, FIs usually face a return or interest earnings penalty from doing this. Because of their high liquidity and low default risks, such assets often bear low returns that reflect their essentially risk-free nature. By contrast, nonliquid assets often must promise additional returns or liquidity risk premiums to compensate an FI for the relative lack of marketability and often greater default risk of the instrument.

Holding relatively small amounts of liquid assets exposes an FI to enhanced illiquidity risk and, ultimately, risk of a run. Excessive illiquidity can result in an FI's inability to meet required payments on liability claims and, at the extreme, in insolvency. It can even lead to contagious effects that negatively impact other FIs (see Chapter 12). Consequently, regulators have often imposed minimum liquid asset reserve requirements on FIs. In general, these requirements differ in nature and scope for various FIs and even according to country. The requirements depend on the liquidity risk exposure perceived for the FI's type and other regulatory objectives that relate to minimum liquid asset requirements. Further, regulators often set minimum liquid asset requirements for at least two other reasons than simply ensuring that FIs can meet expected and unexpected liability withdrawals. The other two reasons are monetary policy implementation and taxation. We discuss these two reasons next.

## Monetary Policy Implementation Reasons

Many countries set minimum liquid asset reserve requirements to strengthen their monetary policy. Specifically, setting a minimum ratio of liquid reserve assets to deposits limits the ability of depository institutions (DIs) to expand lending and enhances the central bank's ability to control the money supply.

A decrease in the reserve requirement ratio means that depository institutions may hold fewer reserves (vault cash plus reserve deposits at the Fed) against their transaction accounts (deposits). Consequently, they are able to lend out a greater percentage of their deposits, thus increasing credit availability in the economy. As new loans are issued and used to finance consumption and investment expenditures, some of these funds will return to depository institutions as new deposits by those receiving them, in return for supplying consumer and investment goods to DI borrowers. In turn, after deducting the appropriate reserve requirement, these new deposits can be used by DIs to create additional loans, and so on. This process continues until the DIs' deposits have grown sufficiently large that the DI willingly holds its *current* reserve balance at the new lower reserve ratio. Thus, a decrease in the reserve requirement results in a multiplier effect on the supply of DI deposits and thus the money supply.

Conversely, an increase in the reserve requirement ratio means that depository institutions must hold more reserves against the transaction accounts (deposits) on their balance sheets. Consequently, they are only able to lend out a smaller percentage of their deposits than before, thus decreasing credit availability and lending, and eventually, leading to a multiple contraction in deposits and a decrease in the money supply. In this context, requiring depository institutions to hold minimum ratios of liquid assets to deposits allows the central bank to gain greater control over deposit growth and thus over the money supply (of which bank deposits are a significant portion) as part of its overall macroeconomic objectives. Appendix 18A to the chapter (located at the book's website, **www.mhhe.com/saunders8e**) describes the accounting treatment of the reserve ratio regime imposed by the U.S. Federal Reserve.

## Taxation Reasons

Another reason for minimum requirements on DI liquid asset holdings is to force DIs to invest in government financial claims rather than private sector financial

**reserve requirement "tax"**
The cost of holding reserves that pay no or little interest at the central bank. This cost is increased further if inflation erodes the purchasing power value of these reserve balances.

claims. That is, a minimum required liquid asset reserve requirement is an indirect way for governments to raise additional "taxes" from DIs. While these reserves are not official government taxes, having DIs hold cash in the vault or cash reserves at the central bank (when there is only a small interest rate compensation paid)[1] requires DIs to transfer a resource to the central bank. In fact, the profitability of many central banks is contingent on the size of the **reserve requirement "tax,"** which can be viewed as the equivalent of a levy on DIs under their jurisdiction. The tax or cost effect of low-interest reserve requirements is increased if inflation erodes the purchasing power value of those balances.

---

**Concept Questions**

1. Why do regulators set minimum liquid asset requirements for FIs?
2. Can we view reserve requirements as a tax when the consumer price index (CPI) is falling?

---

# THE COMPOSITION OF THE LIQUID ASSET PORTFOLIO

**liquid assets ratio**
A minimum ratio of liquid assets to total assets set by the central bank.

**secondary or buffer reserves**
Nonreserve assets that can be quickly turned into cash.

The composition of an FI's liquid asset portfolio, especially cash and government securities, is determined partly by earnings considerations and partly by the type of minimum liquid asset reserve requirements the central bank imposes. In many countries, such as the United Kingdom, reserve ratios have historically been imposed to encompass both cash and liquid government securities such as T-bills.[2] Thus, a 20 percent **liquid assets ratio** requires a DI to hold $1 of cash plus government securities for every $5 of assets. Many states in the United States impose liquid asset ratios on life insurance companies that require minimum cash and government securities holdings in their balance sheets. By contrast, the minimum liquid asset requirements on DIs in the United States have been cash based and have excluded government securities. As a result, government securities are less useful because they are not counted as part of reserves held by DIs and at the same time yield lower promised returns than loans. Nevertheless, many DIs view government securities holdings as performing a useful **secondary or buffer reserve** function. In times of a liquidity crisis, when significant drains on cash reserves occur, these securities can be turned into cash quickly and with very little loss of principal value because of the deep nature of the markets in which these assets are traded.

---

**Concept Question**

1. In general, would it be better to hold three-month T-bills or 10-year T-notes as buffer assets? Explain.

---

[1] The Financial Services Regulatory Relief Act of 2006 originally authorized the Federal Reserve to begin paying interest on reserve balances held by DIs beginning October 1, 2011. The Emergency Economic Stabilization Act of 2008 changed the effective date to October 1, 2008.

[2] The United Kingdom no longer imposes minimum reserve requirements on banks.

# RETURN-RISK TRADE-OFF FOR LIQUID ASSETS

In optimizing its holdings of liquid assets, an FI must trade the benefit of cash immediacy for lower returns. In addition, the FI manager's choice is one of *constrained optimization* in the sense that liquid asset reserve requirements imposed by regulators set a minimum bound on the level to which liquid reserve assets can fall on the balance sheet. Thus, an FI facing little risk of liquidity withdrawals and holding only a small amount of liquid assets for prudential reasons finds that it is forced to hold more than is privately optimal as a result of minimum reserve restrictions imposed by regulators.

## The Liquid Asset Reserve Management Problem for U.S. Depository Institutions

This section examines the risk-return trade-off in running a liquid asset position and the constraints imposed on this position. We present a detailed example of U.S. DIs liquidity management under the current minimum reserve requirements imposed by the Federal Reserve. However, many of the issues and trade-offs are readily generalizable to any FI facing liability withdrawal risk under conditions in which regulators impose minimum liquid asset reserve ratios.

**cash reserves**
Vault cash and cash deposits held at the Federal Reserve.

www.federalreserve.gov

The issues involved in the optimal management of a liquid asset portfolio are illustrated by the problems faced by the money desk manager in charge of a U.S. DI's reserve position. In the context of U.S. DI regulation, we concentrate on a DI's management of its **cash reserves,** defined as vault cash (currency and coin used to meet depositor withdrawals) and cash deposits held by the DI at the Federal Reserve. As of August 2012, in accordance with Regulation D of the Securities Act of 1933, depository institutions in the United States are required to hold the following "target" minimum cash reserves against net transaction accounts:[3]

| | |
|---|---|
| < $11.5 million | 0% |
| $11.5 million − $71.0 million | 3 |
| > $71.0 million | 10 |

**transaction accounts**
Deposits that permit the account holder to make multiple withdrawals.

**Transaction accounts** include all deposits on which an account holder may make withdrawals by negotiable or transferable instruments and may make more than three monthly telephone or preauthorized fund transfers for the purpose of making payments to third parties (i.e., demand deposits, NOW accounts, and share draft accounts—offered by credit unions). Transaction account balances are reduced by demand balances due from U.S. depository institutions and cash items in process of collection.

To calculate the target amount of reserves and to determine whether the DI is holding too many or too few reserves, the DI reserve manager requires two additional pieces of information to manage the position. First, over what period's deposits does the manager compute the DI's reserve requirement? Second, for which period or periods must the DI maintain the target reserve requirement just

---

[3] The Garn-St. Germain Depository Institutions Act of 1982 (Public Law 97-320) required that $2 million of reservable liabilities of each depository institution be subject to a 0 percent reserve requirement. Each year the Federal Reserve adjusts the amount subject to this 0 percent reserve requirement for the succeeding calendar year by 80 percent of the percentage increase in the total reservable liabilities of all depository institutions, measured on an annual basis as of June 30. In 2012 this figure was $11.5 million. The reserve was also reduced from 12 to 10 percent for transaction accounts in April 1992.

computed? The U.S. system is complicated by the fact that the period for which the DI manager computes the required reserve target differs from the period during which the reserve target is maintained or achieved. We describe the computation and maintenance periods for DI reserves next.

**reserve
computation period**
Period over which
required reserves are
calculated.

## Computation Period

For the purpose of reserve management, a U.S. DI reserve manager must think of time as being divided into two-week periods. The **reserve computation period** always begins on a Tuesday and ends on a Monday 14 days later.

---

**EXAMPLE 18–1**
*Computation of
Daily Average
Required
Reserves*

Consider ABC Bank's reserve manager, who wants to assess the bank's minimum cash reserve requirement target. The manager knows the bank's net transaction accounts balance at the close of the banking day on each of the 14 days over the period Tuesday, June 30, to Monday, July 13. Of course, in reality, the manager knows these deposit positions with certainty only at the very end of the two-week period. Consider the realized net transaction account positions of ABC Bank in Table 18–1.

The minimum daily average reserves that a bank must maintain are computed as a percentage of the daily average net transaction accounts held by the bank over the two-week reserve computation period, where Friday's balances are carried over for Saturday and Sunday. The minimum daily average for ABC Bank to hold against the daily average of $1,350.7 million in its net transaction accounts is calculated as follows (amounts in millions):

Daily average net transaction accounts × Reserve percentage = Daily average reserves required

| | | |
|---|---|---|
| $11.5 m | 0% | $  0.000 |
| $71.0 m − $11.5 m | 3 | 1.785 m |
| $1,350.7 m − $71.0 m | 10 | 127.970 m |
| Minimum average reserves to be held | | $129.755 m |

---

Note that the daily average target in Example 18–1 is calculated by taking the 14-day average of net transaction accounts, even though the DI is closed for 4 of the 14 days (two Saturdays and two Sundays). Effectively, Friday's deposit figures count three times compared with those of other days in the business week. This means that a DI manager who can engage in a strategy whereby deposits are lower on Fridays can, on average, lower the DI's reserve requirements. This may be important if required liquid asset reserve holdings are above the optimal level from the DI's perspective to handle liquidity drains due to expected and unexpected deposit withdrawals.

One strategy employed is for a DI to send deposits out of the country (i.e., transfer them to a foreign subsidiary) on a Friday, when a reduction in deposits effectively counts for $3/14$ of the two-week period, and to bring them back on the following Monday, when an increase counts for just $1/14$ of the two-week period. This action effectively reduces the average demand deposits on the balance sheet of the DI over the 14-day period by $2/14$ times the amount sent out of the country and thus, reduces the amount of reserves it needs to hold. Analysts term this the **weekend game.**

**weekend game**
Lowering deposit balances on Fridays since that day's figures count three times for reserve accounting purposes.

**TABLE 18–1**   Net Transaction Accounts and Vault Cash Balances of ABC Bank (in millions of dollars)

| | Transaction Accounts | Less Demand Balances Due from U.S. Depository Institutions | Less Cash Items in Process of Collection | Net Transaction Accounts | Vault Cash |
|---|---|---|---|---|---|
| Tuesday, June 30 | $ 1,850 | $ 240 | $ 140 | $ 1,470 | $ 30 |
| Wednesday, July 1 | 1,820 | 235 | 135 | 1,450 | 28 |
| Thursday, July 2 | 1,770 | 250 | 120 | 1,400 | 24 |
| Friday, July 3 | 1,610 | 260 | 100 | 1,250 | 21 |
| Saturday, July 4 | 1,610 | 260 | 100 | 1,250 | 21 |
| Sunday, July 5 | 1,610 | 260 | 100 | 1,250 | 21 |
| Monday, July 6 | 1,655 | 250 | 125 | 1,280 | 24 |
| Tuesday, July 7 | 1,650 | 230 | 130 | 1,290 | 26 |
| Wednesday, July 8 | 1,690 | 240 | 130 | 1,320 | 25 |
| Thursday, July 9 | 1,770 | 275 | 135 | 1,360 | 25 |
| Friday, July 10 | 1,820 | 280 | 140 | 1,400 | 27 |
| Saturday, July 11 | 1,820 | 280 | 140 | 1,400 | 27 |
| Sunday, July 12 | 1,820 | 280 | 140 | 1,400 | 27 |
| Monday, July 13 | 1,785 | 260 | 135 | 1,390 | 29 |
| Total | $24,280 | $3,600 | $1,770 | $18,910 | $355 |
| Daily average net transaction accounts | | | | $ 1,350.7 | $ 25.357 |

A second strategy is for the DI to offer its customers "sweep accounts," in which high reserve ratio demand deposits are automatically transferred, or "swept," out of customers' accounts on Friday into higher-interest-bearing savings accounts. On Monday (or in many cases when the depositor needs funds in his or her checking account) these funds are swept back. The effective result is lower average balances in a DI's demand deposit accounts and thus lower required reserve holdings at the Federal Reserve.

Note that the $129.755 million figure is a minimum reserve target. The DI manager may hold excess cash reserves above this minimum level if the privately optimal or prudential level for the DI exceeds the regulatory specified minimum level because this DI is especially exposed to deposit withdrawal risk. In addition, the DI manager may hold some buffer reserves in the form of government securities that can be turned into cash quickly if deposit withdrawals are unusually high or to preempt the early stages of a bank run.

### Maintenance Period

We have computed a daily average minimum cash reserve requirement for ABC Bank but have yet to delineate the exact period over which the bank manager has to maintain this $129.755 million daily average reserve target. Reserves may be held either as vault cash or as deposits held (by the DI) at the Federal Reserve. Under the current set of regulations, the average daily vault cash held during the reserve computation period (June 30 through July 13 in our example) is deducted from the institution's required reserves to determine the reserve balance to be maintained at the Federal Reserve. In addition, a lag of 30 days exists between the beginning of the reserve computation period and the beginning of the **reserve maintenance period** (over which deposits at the Federal Reserve Bank must meet or exceed

**reserve maintenance period**
Period over which actual reserves have to meet or exceed the required reserve target.

**FIGURE 18–1**
Lagged Reserve
Requirements

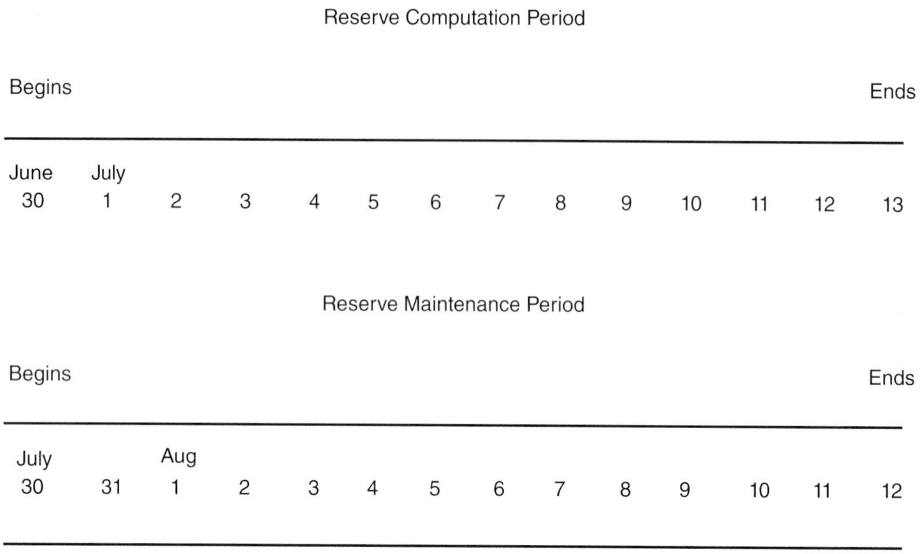

Reserve Computation Period

Begins                                                                                    Ends

| June | July | | | | | | | | | | | | |
|---|---|---|---|---|---|---|---|---|---|---|---|---|---|
| 30 | 1 | 2 | 3 | 4 | 5 | 6 | 7 | 8 | 9 | 10 | 11 | 12 | 13 |

Reserve Maintenance Period

Begins                                                                                    Ends

| July | | Aug | | | | | | | | | | | |
|---|---|---|---|---|---|---|---|---|---|---|---|---|---|
| 30 | 31 | 1 | 2 | 3 | 4 | 5 | 6 | 7 | 8 | 9 | 10 | 11 | 12 |

the required reserve target). For ABC Bank, this reserve maintenance period is from July 30 through August 12 (see Figure 18–1). Thus, the bank's reserve manager knows the value of the target reserves with perfect certainty throughout the reserve maintenance period. However, the manager still has a challenge in maintaining sufficient deposits on reserve at the Fed to hit the reserve target without holding too large an excess reserve balance (since this bears a low interest return).

The reserve manager knows the vault cash component of the reserve target, since this is based on the average vault cash held by the bank over the reserve computation period, as reported in Table 18–1. The daily balances in deposits at the Federal Reserve for ABC Bank for the 14-day reserve maintenance period from July 30 through August 12 are shown in Table 18–2. Since the average daily balance in vault cash is shown (in Table 18–1) at $25.357 million, the average daily target balance for deposits at the Federal Reserve is $104.398 million (i.e., $25.357 million + $104.398 million = $129.755 million). Essentially, since the vault cash component of the reserve target is based on vault cash held over the reserve computation 14-day period, the bank's active target during the maintenance period itself is its reserve position at the Fed (in this case, it seeks to hold an average deposit balance of $104.398 million per day at the Fed over the 14-day maintenance period).

**lagged reserve accounting system**
An accounting system in which the reserve computation and reserve maintenance periods do not overlap.

As discussed above, currently, the reserve maintenance period for meeting the reserve target begins 30 days after the start of the reserve computation period. Given that the computation period is two weeks, the reserve maintenance period does not begin until 17 days after the *end* of the computation period. Regulators introduced this **lagged reserve accounting system** to make it easier for bank reserve managers to calculate their required reserve balances and to increase the accuracy of information on aggregate required reserve balances. Prior to July 1998, regulators used a **contemporaneous reserve accounting system,** in which the two-week reserve maintenance period for meeting the reserve target began only two days (as opposed to the current 30 days) after the start of the computation period. This contemporaneous reserve system resulted in only a two-day window during which required

**contemporaneous reserve accounting system**
An accounting system in which the reserve computation and reserve maintenance periods overlap.

**TABLE 18–2**
ABC Bank's Daily Reserve Position over the July 30–August 12 Reserve Maintenance Period (in millions of dollars)

| Date | Deposits at the Federal Reserve |
|------|--------------------------------|
| Thursday, July 30 | $ 98.050 |
| Friday, July 31 | 100.000 |
| Saturday, August 1 | 100.000 |
| Sunday, August 2 | 100.000 |
| Monday, August 3 | 98.004 |
| Tuesday, August 4 | 91.000 |
| Wednesday, August 5 | 102.050 |
| Thursday, August 6 | 101.000 |
| Friday, August 7 | 99.000 |
| Saturday, August 8 | 99.000 |
| Sunday, August 9 | 99.000 |
| Monday, August 10 | 107.050 |
| Tuesday, August 11 | 154.000 |
| Wednesday, August 12 | 113.418 |
| Total | $1,461.572 |
| Daily average | 104.398 |

reserves were known with certainty.[4] In the above example, the reserve maintenance period would have been from Thursday, July 2, through Wednesday, July 15, for a reserve computation period beginning Tuesday, June 30, and ending Monday, July 13.

## Undershooting/Overshooting of the Reserve Target

### Undershooting

What happens if, at the end of the reserve maintenance period (on August 12 from the previous example) the DI *undershoots* the regulatory required daily minimum reserve ratio—that is, holds less than the required amount ($129.755 daily average million in our example)? The Federal Reserve allows the DI to make up to a 4 percent daily average error without penalty. Thus, if the DI is 4 percent in the red on its reserve target to the tune of 4 percent × $129.755 million = $5.190 million, it must make this up in the next two-week reserve maintenance period that runs from August 13 to August 26.[5]

When a DI holds a deficit in its required reserves in a given two-week period, it *must* hold a surplus amount of reserves in the subsequent two-week period. If the reserve shortfall exceeds 4 percent, the DI is liable to explicit and implicit penalty charges from the Federal Reserve. The explicit charges include the imposition of a penalty interest rate charge equal to the central bank's discount rate plus a 2 percent markup. The implicit charges can include more frequent monitoring, examinations, and surveillance if DI regulators view the undershooting of the reserve requirements as a reflection of an unsafe and unsound practice by the DI's manager. Such a view is likely to be taken only if the DI consistently undershoots its reserve targets.

[4] One result of this system was that DIs tended to hold more reserves during the last few days of each reserve maintenance period, when the opportunity cost of holding reserves was typically the highest. Uncertainty over reserve needs and the small cost of trading induced DIs to hold reserves when they had the most accurate information on their reserve needs—the last two days of the reserve maintenance period.

[5] This means that the allowable deficiency over the full 14 days would be:

$$\$129.755 \text{ million} \times 0.04 \times 14 = \$72.663 \text{ million}$$

**EXAMPLE 18–2**

*Undershooting/
Overshooting a
Reserve Target*

A bank has an average balance of transactions accounts, August 10 to 23, of $933.34 million. The average balance in the cash account is $32.214 million over this period. The bank is carrying forward a deficit of $2.276 million from the last reserve period. Calculate the net reserve requirement for the reserve maintenance period from September 9 to 22. Calculate the minimum reserves that may be maintained and the maximum reserves that will count toward the next reserve maintenance period, September 23 to October 6.

| | |
|---|---:|
| $11.5 m at 0% | $     0 |
| $71.0 m − $11.5 m at 3% | 1.785 m |
| $933.34 m − $71.0 m at 10% | 86.234 m |
| Gross reserve requirement | $88.019 m |
| Daily average vault cash, Aug. 10–23 | 32.214 m |
| Net reserve requirement | $55.805 m |
| Reserve carry forward from last period daily average | |
| amount = $2.276 m | 2.276 m |
| **Reserves to be maintained with Fed** | $58.081 m |
| **Minimum reserves to be maintained** | |
| −0.04(88.019 m) = −3.521 m | $54.560 m |
| **Maximum reserves to be maintained** | |
| +0.04(88.019 m) = +3.521 m | $61.602 m |

If over the first 12 days of the current reserve maintenance period the average daily reserves held were $57 million (or 12 × $57 m = $684 m cumulative total over the 12 days), what does the bank need to hold as reserves over the last two days to (1) exactly meet the reserve requirement, (2) meet the minimum reserve, and (3) meet the maximum reserve?

1. *To meet the reserve requirement:* Over the first 12 days the bank should have held a cumulative reserve of $58.081 m × 12 = $696.972 m. The bank is running a shortfall of $696.972 m − $684 m = $12.972 m. Thus, the *cumulative balance over the last two days,* September 21 and 22, needs to be:

$$\$58.081 \text{ m} + \$58.081 \text{ m} + \$12.972 \text{ m} = \$129.134 \text{ m}$$

2. *To hit the minimum cumulative balance:* Over the first 12 days the bank should have held a cumulative reserve of $54.560 m × 12 = $654.720 m. The bank is running a surplus of $654.720 m − $684 m = −$29.280 m. Thus, the *cumulative balance over the last two days,* September 21 and 22, needs to be:

$$\$54.560 \text{ m} + \$54.560 \text{ m} - \$29.280 \text{ m} = \$79.840 \text{ m}$$

3. *To hit the maximum cumulative balance:* Over the first 12 days the bank should have held a cumulative reserve of $61.602 m × 12 = $739.224 m. The bank is running a shortfall of $739.224 m − $684 m = $55.224 m. Thus, the *cumulative balance over the last two days,* September 21 and 22, needs to be:

$$\$61.602 \text{ m} + \$61.602 \text{ m} + \$55.224 \text{ m} = \$178.428 \text{ m}$$

Or the bank must run a reserve balance between $79.840 million and $178.428 million over the two days, September 21 and 22.

In undershooting the target, the DI manager must weigh the explicit and implicit costs of undershooting against any potential benefits. Specifically, it may be beneficial to undershoot if the privately optimal or prudential reserve position of the DI is less than the regulatory set minimum and/or there are very high opportunity costs of meeting the reserve requirement targets. There may be high opportunity costs of meeting reserve targets if interest rates and loan demands are high so that the cost of forgone loans on future profits may be significant.

A DI that undershoots the reserve target has two principal ways to build up reserves to meet the target as the reserve maintenance period comes to an end: It can (1) liquidate assets (e.g., by selling off some buffer assets such as Treasury bills) or (2) borrow in the interbank market for reserves, especially in the fed funds and repurchase agreement markets described later. The DI manager is likely to choose the least costly method to meet any reserve deficiency, such as borrowing fed funds if this rate is less than the cost of selling off liquid assets. The manager may be reluctant to fund the entire reserve deficiency in this manner, however, if the costs of adjusting to a deficiency are high and the privately optimal amount of reserves is less than the regulatory required minimum amount.

www.federalreserve.gov

Such cost considerations lead some DI managers to use the Federal Reserve's discount window to borrow the required funds to meet temporary reserve shortfalls because the cost of borrowing from the discount window is the discount rate, an administered rate set by the Federal Reserve. The discount window rate was historically set below fed funds and government security rates and offered a very attractive borrowing cost to a DI with deficient reserves as the reserve maintenance period came to an end. However, discount window loans were meant to be used by DIs on a need rather than a profit basis—that is, by DIs that were solvent but faced sudden liquidity crises due to deposit withdrawals caused by seasonality in deposit flows or some other similar lender of last resort need. In January 2003, the Fed implemented changes to its discount window lending that increased the cost of borrowing but eased the terms. Through the Fed's primary credit program, discount window loans are available to generally sound depository institutions on a very short-term basis, typically overnight, at a rate above the Federal Open Market Committee's (FOMC) target rate for federal funds. Primary credit may be used for any purpose, including financing the sale of fed funds. Primary credit may be extended for periods of up to a few weeks to depository institutions in generally sound financial condition that cannot obtain temporary funds in the financial markets at reasonable terms. We discuss the role of the discount window, and particularly the limits on its use as a source of funds during periods of economic distress, in more detail in Chapter 19.

### Overshooting

The cost of *overshooting,* or holding cash reserves in excess of the minimum required level, depends on whether the DI perceives its prudent level of reserves to meet expected and unexpected deposit withdrawals to be higher or lower than the regulatory imposed minimum reserve requirement.

If its required minimum reserves are higher than the amount managers perceive to be optimal, the first 4 percent of excess reserves can be carried forward to the next reserve period. The Federal Reserve allows this amount to count toward meeting the reserve requirement in the next two-week maintenance period. After that, any reserves held above the required minimum plus 4 percent constitute a drag on DI earnings since every dollar that is held as excess reserves—either in cash or on deposit at the central bank—earns little interest[6] and could have been lent out at the DI lending rate. In contrast, if the DI manager perceives that the regulatory required minimum level of reserves is lower than what it needs for expected and unexpected deposit withdrawal exposure, the DI overshoots the required minimum reserve target. This policy maintains the DI's liquidity position at a prudently adequate level. In choosing to overshoot the target, the manager must consider the least-cost instrument in which to hold such reserves.

While some excess reserves might be held in highly liquid (non-interest-bearing) cash form, at least part of any excess reserve position might be held in buffer assets such as short-term securities or Treasury bills that earn interest but are not quite as liquid as cash. The proportion between cash and Treasury bills held depends in large part on yield spreads. For example, suppose the loan rate is 9 percent, the T-bill rate is 4 percent, and the interest earned on excess cash holdings is 0 percent. The opportunity cost of a forgone return to the DI from holding excess reserves in cash form or T-bill form is:

$$\text{Opportunity cost cash} = 9\% - 0\% = 9\%$$

$$\text{Opportunity cost T-bills} = 9\% - 4\% = 5\%$$

Thus, T-bills have a significantly lower opportunity cost than cash, and the manager must weigh the 4 percent net opportunity cost savings of holding excess reserves in T-bill form against the ease with which such instruments can be sold and turned into cash to meet liability withdrawals or liquidity crunches. Table 18–3 shows excess cash reserves of U.S. DIs between 1990 and August 2012. Because of their opportunity cost, excess reserves are generally kept at very low levels. This was 4.34 percent of total reserves in August 2008.

Note the huge rise in excess reserves in November 2008 and August 2009 (91.65 and 91.71 percent of total reserves, respectively). The Federal Reserve sets the fed funds rate at a level it believes will foster financial and monetary conditions consistent with achieving its monetary policy objectives, and it adjusts that target in line with evolving economic developments. In September 2008, the Federal Reserve implemented several measures to provide liquidity to financial markets. The liquidity facilities introduced by the Federal Reserve in response to the financial crisis created a large quantity of reserves at DIs. Some observers claim that the large increase in excess reserves implied that many of the policies introduced by the Federal Reserve in response to the financial crisis were ineffective. Rather than promoting the flow of credit to firms and households, it was argued that the increase in excess reserves indicated that the money lent to banks and other FIs by the Federal Reserve in late 2008 and early 2009 was simply sitting idle in banks' reserve accounts. Many asked why banks were choosing to hold so many reserves instead of lending them out, and some claimed that banks' lending of their excess reserves was crucial for resolving the credit crisis. However, remember that the Federal Reserve began paying interest on reserves, for the first time, in October 2008. During the financial crisis, the Fed set the interest rate it paid on reserves equal to its target for the market interest rate. This policy essentially removed the opportunity cost of holding reserves. That is, the interest banks earned by holding of excess reserves was approximately equal to what was previously earned by lending to other FIs. As a result, banks had no incentive to change their pattern

---

[6] The interest rate paid on required and excess reserve balances is set by the Federal Open Market Committee over each reserve maintenance period. The rate paid as of August 2012 was 25 basis points.

**TABLE 18–3** Reserves and Excess Reserves of U.S. Depository Institutions (in millions of dollars)

Source: Federal Reserve Board website, various dates. *www.federalreserve.gov*

|  | December 1990 | December 2000 | December 2005 | August 2008 | November 2008 | August 2009 | August 2012 |
|---|---|---|---|---|---|---|---|
| Total reserves | $59,120 | $38,537 | $45,312 | $45,458 | $609,939 | $772,576 | $1,605,410 |
| Required reserves | 57,456 | 37,110 | 43,403 | 43,486 | 50,901 | 64,076 | 102,806 |
| Excess reserves | 1,664 | 1,427 | 1,909 | 1,972 | 559,038 | 708,500 | 1,502,604 |

of lending to firms and households. In this case, the Fed's lending policy generated a large quantity of excess reserves without changing DIs' incentives to lend to firms and households. Thus, the total level of reserves in the banking system is determined almost entirely by the actions of the central bank and is not necessarily affected by private banks' lending decisions. Notice that the level of excess reserves remained high even into August 2012, 93.60 percent of total reserve. The slow economic recovery from the financial crisis of 2008–09 meant that the Fed kept interest rates low well into the 2010s. Thus, excess reserves continued to offer rates that were approximately equal to what could be earned by lending to customers.

*Internet Exercise*   Go to the website of the Board of Governors of the Federal Reserve at **www.federalreserve. gov.** and find the latest information available for reserves and excess reserves of U.S. depository institutions using the following steps. Click on "Economic Research and Data." Click on "View All." Click on "Aggregate Reserves of Depository Institutions and the Monetary Base." This will download a file onto your computer that will contain the most recent information.

## Managing Liquid Assets Other than Cash

Chapter 12 discussed several models FIs use to measure liquidity risk, including models used to determine the FI's liquid asset needs over a future period of time. Reserve requirements establish the minimum level of cash an FI must hold to meet liquidity needs (due to deposit withdrawals). However, since cash is a nonearning asset, an FI will hold as little cash as possible to meet its liquid asset needs. The remaining liquid assets are generally stored in the FI's security portfolio (e.g., holding Treasury bills).

Managing the securities portfolio is an integral part of liquidity management for financial institutions. FI managers must determine the optimal combination of lower-yielding, liquid assets versus higher-yielding, less liquid assets. Short-term marketable securities that are not pledged for public deposits (such as Treasury securities) are held for immediate liquidity needs, and mortgage securities and other longer-term securities are held and can be sold if liquidity needs are larger than expected. Indeed, as discussed in Chapter 1, FIs are special in that they can mismatch the maturity of their assets and liabilities (issuing short-term deposits to fund long-term assets). FIs profit by performing this "special" service. However, during a liquidity crisis, such as that during the financial crisis of 2008–09, the ability to liquidate these less liquid assets may be severely constrained and may even affect the very solvency of the FI. In this respect, liquidity risk is related to operational risk (see Chapter 17); that is, external liquidity events that are unforeseen and uncontrollable by the FI can affect the FI's ability to operate. Other ways of maintaining liquidity are securitization and loan sales (see Chapters 25 and 26). Briefly, FIs can sell loans (or securitize loans) for liquidity to long-term investors, such as insurance companies. These loan sales provide a stream of liquidity that can be used to fund new loan demand or deposit withdrawals. However, as seen during the financial crisis, these securities, like other long-term securities, may have to be liquidated at fire-sale prices. In addition, if the FI removes loans from its balance sheet, it can use the funds received from the sale of loans to pay off depositors (i.e., shrinking the size of the FI). This reduces the FI's deposits and, hence, its reserve requirement—which, as noted earlier, can be viewed as a regulatory tax. With fewer assets, the FI's required capital (under capital requirements such as the 8 percent risk-based rate; see Chapter 20) can be reduced.

### Liquidity Management as a Knife-Edge Management Problem

The management of a DI's liquidity position is something of a knife-edge situation because holding too many liquid assets penalizes a DI's earnings and, thus, its stockholders. A DI manager who holds excessive amounts of liquid assets is unlikely to survive long. Similarly, a manager who excessively undershoots the reserve target faces enhanced risks of liquidity crises and regulatory intervention. Again, such a manager's tenure at the DI may be relatively short.

| Concept Questions | |
|---|---|
| | 1. In addition to the target reserve ratio, what other pieces of information does a DI reserve manager require to manage the DI's reserve requirement position? |
| | 2. For a DI that undershoots its reserve target, what ways are available to a reserve manager to build up reserves to meet the target? |
| | 3. Since 1998, U.S. DIs have operated under a lagged reserve accounting system in which the reserve computation period ends 17 days before the reserve maintenance period begins. Does the reserve manager face any uncertainty at all in managing a DI's reserve position? Explain your answer. |
| | 4. What explains the decline in the level of required reserves held by DIs between 1990 and August 2008 and the rise in August of 2009 (see Table 18–3)? |

## LIABILITY MANAGEMENT

Liquidity and liability management are closely related. One aspect of liquidity risk control is the buildup of a prudential level of liquid assets. Another aspect is the management of the DI's liability structure to reduce the need for large amounts of liquid assets to meet liability withdrawals. However, excessive use of purchased funds in the liability structure can result in a liquidity crisis if investors lose confidence in the DI and refuse to roll over such funds.

As discussed in Chapter 17, improvements in technology and demand for efficiency and flexibility in the financial transactions of wholesale and retail customers have lowered the costs of holding deposits and changed the way FIs manage liquidity risk. Technologically oriented services (such as home banking) connect customers to their deposit and brokerage accounts via personal computers and mobile devices. These technologies also provide other services such as electronic securities trading and

**FIGURE 18–2**
**Funding Risk versus Cost**

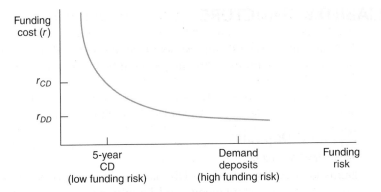

bill paying. Likewise, preauthorized debits of payroll checks get cash into FIs' deposit accounts faster and with more predictability. Finally, the Check Clearing for the 21st Century Act allows FIs to provide deposit customers with electronically transmitted copies of their checks rather than returning the original, paper checks. In doing so, check processing time and handling costs can be reduced significantly for FIs. These types of services have changed the way liquidity management is viewed by FIs.

## Funding Risk and Cost

Unfortunately, constructing a low-cost, low-withdrawal-risk liability portfolio is more difficult than it sounds. This is true because those liabilities, or sources of DI funds, that are the most subject to withdrawal risk are often the least costly to the DI. That is, a DI must trade off the benefits of attracting liabilities at a low funding cost with a high chance of withdrawal against liabilities with a high funding cost and low liquidity. For example, demand deposits are relatively low funding cost vehicles for DIs but can be withdrawn without notice.[7] By contrast, a five-year, fixed-term certificate of deposit may have a relatively high funding cost but can be withdrawn before the five-year maturity is up only after the deposit holder pays a substantial interest rate penalty. Thus, in structuring the liability, or funding, side of the balance sheet, the DI manager faces a trade-off along the lines suggested in Figure 18–2. That is, funding costs are generally inversely related to the period of time the liability is likely to remain on the DI's balance sheet (i.e., to funding risk).

Although we have discussed depository institutions' funding risk, other FIs face a similar trade-off. For example, investment banks can finance through overnight funds (repurchase agreements and brokered deposits) or longer-term sources such as notes and bonds. Finance companies have a choice between commercial paper and longer-term notes and bonds.

The next section looks at the spectrum of liabilities available to a DI manager in seeking to actively impact liquidity risk exposure through the choice of liability structure.

| **Concept Questions** | 1. How are liquidity and liability management related? |
|---|---|
| | 2. Describe the trade-off faced by an FI manager in structuring the liability side of the balance sheet. |

---

[7] Depositors do not always exercise this option. Therefore, some demand deposits behave like longer-term core deposits.

# CHOICE OF LIABILITY STRUCTURE

This section considers in more detail the withdrawal (or funding) risk and funding cost characteristics of the major liabilities available to a modern DI manager. Table 18–4 lists the March 2012 amount and distributions of the major liability categories for two banks: Bank of America (one of the largest banks in the United States) and Bank of Carbondale (a small regional bank).

## Demand Deposits

### *Withdrawal Risk*

Demand deposits issued by DIs have a high degree of withdrawal risk. Withdrawals can be instantaneous and largely expected by the DI manager, such as pre-weekend cash withdrawals, or unexpected, as occur during economic crisis situations (so-called bank runs; see Chapter 12). Bank of America draws 10.6 percent of its deposits and other borrowings from demand deposits, while Bank of Carbondale, a small ($184 million in assets in March of 2012) community bank located in Carbondale, Illinois, draws 10.1 percent.

### *Costs*

In the United States, demand deposits have paid zero explicit interest since the 1930s by law. This does not mean that they are a costless source of funds for DIs or that DIs have no price or interest mechanisms available to partially control the withdrawal risk associated with these contracts. Despite the zero explicit interest paid on demand deposit accounts, competition among DIs and other FIs (e.g., money market mutual funds) has resulted in the payment of implicit interest, or payments of interest-in-kind, on these accounts. Specifically, in providing demand deposits that are checkable accounts, a DI must provide a whole set of associated services from providing checkbooks, to clearing of checks, to sending out statements. Because such services absorb real resources of labor and capital, they are costly for DIs to provide. DIs can recapture these costs by charging fees, such as 10 cents per check cleared. To the extent that these fees do not fully cover the DI's cost of providing such services, the depositor receives a subsidy or an implicit interest payment.

---

**EXAMPLE 18–3**

*Calculation of Average Implicit Interest Rate*

Suppose a DI pays 15 cents to clear a check but charges a fee of only 10 cents per check cleared. The customer receives a 5-cent subsidy per check. We can calculate implicit yields for each service, or an average implicit interest rate, for each demand deposit account. For example, an average implicit interest rate for a DI's demand deposits might be calculated as:

$$\text{Average implicit interest rate (IIR)} = \frac{\text{DI's average management costs per account per year} - \text{Average fees earned per account per year}}{\text{Average annual size of account}}$$

Suppose that:

$$\text{DI's average management costs per account per year} = \$150$$
$$\text{Average fees earned per account per year} = \$100$$
$$\text{Average annual size of account} = \$1,200$$

Then:

$$IIR = \frac{\$150 - \$100}{\$1,200} = 4.166\%$$

**TABLE 18–4**
**Distribution of Deposits and Other Borrowing for Two DIs**

Source: Federal Deposit Insurance Corporation website, August 2012. *www. fdic.gov*

| | Bank of America | | Bank of Carbondale | |
|---|---|---|---|---|
| Demand deposits | $ 146.8 b | 10.6% | $ 18.5 m | 10.1% |
| NOW accounts | 25.9 b | 1.9 | 54.2 m | 29.6 |
| Passbook savings | 391.1 b | 28.3 | 18.8 m | 10.3 |
| MMDAs | 426.8 b | 30.9 | 36.4 m | 19.9 |
| Retail time deposits and CDs | 60.2 b | 4.4 | 33.2 m | 18.2 |
| Core deposits | $1,050.8 b | 76.1 | $161.1 m | 88.1 |
| Wholesale CDs | 170.2 b | 12.3 | 16.8 m | 9.2 |
| Fed funds and RPs | 51.5 b | 3.7 | 0.0 m | 0.0 |
| Other borrowings | 108.3 b | 7.9 | 4.9 m | 2.7 |
| Total | $1,380.8 b | | $182.8 m | |

The payment of implicit interest means that the DI manager is not absolutely powerless to mitigate deposit withdrawals, especially if rates on competing instruments are rising. In particular, the DI could lower check-clearing fees, which in turn raises implicit interest payments to depositors. Such payments are *payments in kind* or *subsidies* that are not paid in actual dollars and cents as is interest earned on competing instruments. Nevertheless, implicit payments of interest are tax free to the depositor, but explicit interest payments are taxable. Finally, demand deposits have an additional cost in the form of non-interest-bearing reserve requirements the DI must hold at the Federal Reserve.

## Interest-Bearing Checking (NOW) Accounts

### Withdrawal Risk

**NOW account**
Negotiable order of withdrawal account that is like a demand deposit account but has a minimum balance requirement, and, when the minimum balance is maintained, pays interest.

Since 1980 banks in the United States have been able to offer checkable deposits that pay interest and are withdrawable on demand; they are called negotiable order of withdrawal accounts or **NOW accounts.**[8] The major distinction between these instruments and traditional demand deposits is that these instruments require the depositor to maintain a minimum account balance to earn interest. If the minimum balance falls below some level, such as $500, the account formally converts to a status equivalent to demand deposits and earns no interest. The payment of explicit interest and the existence of minimum balance requirements make NOW accounts potentially less prone to withdrawal risk than demand deposits. Nevertheless, NOW accounts are still highly liquid instruments from the depositor's perspective. Bank of America has 1.9 percent of its deposits and other borrowings in the form of NOW accounts; Bank of Carbondale has 29.6 percent.

### Costs

As with demand deposits, the DI can influence the potential withdrawability of NOW accounts by paying implicit interest or fee subsidies such as not charging the full cost of check clearance. However, the manager has two other ways to impact the yield paid to the depositor. The first is by varying the minimum balance requirement. If the minimum balance requirement is lowered—say, from $500 to $250—a larger portion of a NOW account becomes subject to interest payments and thus the explicit return and attractiveness of these accounts increases. The second is to vary the explicit interest rate payment itself, such as increasing it from 1 to 1¼ percent. Thus, the DI manager has three pricing mechanisms to increase or decrease the attractiveness, and therefore impact the withdrawal rate,

---

[8] There are also Super-NOW accounts that have very similar features to NOW accounts but require a larger minimum balance.

of NOW accounts: implicit interest payments, minimum balance requirements, and explicit interest payments.[9]

---

**EXAMPLE 18–4**

*Gross Interest Return*

Consider a depositor who holds on average $250 per month for the first three months of the year, $500 per month for the next three months, and $1,000 per month for the final six months of the year in a NOW account. The NOW account pays 5 percent per year if the minimum balance is $500 or more and it pays no interest if the account falls below $500. The depositor writes an average of 50 checks per month and pays a service fee of 10 cents for each check although it costs the bank 15 cents to process each check. The account holder's gross interest return, consisting of implicit plus explicit interest, is:

$$\text{Gross interest return} = \text{Explicit interest} + \text{Implicit interest} = \$500\,(0.05)(0.25)$$
$$+ \$1,000\,(0.05)(0.5) + (\$0.15 - \$0.10)(50)(12)$$
$$= \$6.25 + \$25 + \$30 = \$61.25$$

Suppose the minimum balance was lowered from $500 to $250 and check service fees were lowered from 10 cents to 5 cents per check. Then:

$$\text{Gross interest return} = \$250(0.05)(0.25) + \$500(0.05)(0.25) + \$1,000(0.05)(0.5)$$
$$+ (\$0.15 - \$0.05)(50)(12)$$
$$= \$3.125 + \$6.25 + \$25 + \$60$$
$$= \$94.375$$

---

## Passbook Savings

### *Withdrawal Risk*

Passbook savings are generally less liquid than demand deposits and NOW accounts for two reasons. First, they are noncheckable and usually involve physical presence at the institution for withdrawal. Second, the DI has the legal power to delay payment or withdrawal requests for as long as one month. This is rarely done and DIs normally meet withdrawal requests with immediate cash payment, but they have the legal right to delay, which provides important withdrawal risk control to DI managers. For Bank of America, passbook savings are 28.3 percent of deposits and other borrowings; for Bank of Carbondale they are 10.3 percent.

### *Costs*

Since these accounts are noncheckable, any implicit interest rate payments are likely to be small. Thus, the principal costs to the DI are the explicit interest payments on these accounts. In recent years, DIs have normally paid slightly higher explicit rates on passbook savings than on NOW accounts.

## Money Market Deposit Accounts (MMDAs)

### *Withdrawal Risk*

Under the Garn-St. Germain Act, introduced in 1982, DIs can use money market deposit accounts (MMDAs) as an additional liability instrument to control their

---

[9] As transactions accounts, these deposits are also subject to reserve requirements at the same rate as on demand deposits as well as deposit insurance premiums (see Chapter 19). Using a 5 percent NOW account interest rate, a 10 percent reserve ratio ($R$), and a 27-basis-point deposit insurance premium (Premium) and ignoring implicit interest, the effective cost of the marginal dollar of NOW accounts to the issuing DI is:

$$\text{Effective cost} = [r_{NOW} / (1 - R)] + \text{Premium} = [0.05/0.90] + 0.0027 = 0.0583 \text{ or } 5.83\%$$

overall withdrawal risk—in particular, the risk of funds' disintermediating from DIs and flowing to money market mutual funds (MMMFs) (see Chapter 5). If DIs are to be competitive with the money market mutual funds offered by groups such as Vanguard and Fidelity, the **MMDAs** they offer must be liquid, but not as liquid as demand deposits and NOW accounts. In the United States, MMDAs are checkable but subject to restrictions on the number of checks written on each account per month, the number of preauthorized automatic transfers per month, and the minimum denomination of the amount of each check. For example, one DI may allow a customer with an MMDA to make a maximum of six preauthorized transfers, of which no more than three can be checks of at least $500 each. In addition, MMDAs impose minimum balance requirements on depositors. The Federal Reserve does not require DIs to hold reserves against MMDAs. Accordingly, DIs generally pay higher rates on MMDAs than on NOW accounts. Bank of America has 30.9 percent MMDAs to deposits and other borrowings; Bank of Carbondale has 19.9 percent.

**MMDAs**
Money market deposit accounts; retail savings accounts with some limited checking account features.

### Costs

The explicit interest paid to depositors is the major cost of MMDAs; it is also the pricing mechanism DIs use to control withdrawal risk. Since MMDAs are in direct competition with MMMFs, the DI manager can influence their net withdrawal rate by varying the rate the DI pays on such accounts. In particular, while the rate that MMMFs pay on their shares directly reflects the rates earned on the underlying money market assets in which the portfolio manager invests, such as commercial paper, bankers' acceptances, repurchase agreements, and T-bills, the rates that DI managers pay on MMDAs are not based directly on any underlying portfolio of money market assets. In general, DI managers have considerable discretion to alter the rates paid on MMDAs and thus the spread on MMMF–MMDA accounts. This can directly impact the rate of withdrawals and withdrawal risk on such accounts. Allowing MMDA rates to have a large negative spread with MMMFs increases the net withdrawal rate on such accounts.

## Retail Time Deposits and CDs
### Withdrawal Risk

**Retail CDs** are fixed-maturity instruments with face values under $100,000. By contractual design, time deposits and retail certificates of deposit (CDs) reduce the withdrawal risk to issuers. Small time deposits carry early withdrawal penalties. Although the size, maturity, and rate on these CDs are negotiable, most DIs issue standardized retail CDs. In a world of no early withdrawal requests, the DI knows the exact scheduling of interest and principal payments to depositors holding such deposit claims, since these payments are contractually specified. As such, the DI manager can directly control fund inflows and outflows by varying the maturities of the time deposits and CDs it offers to the public. In general, DIs offer time deposits and CDs with maturities varying from two weeks to eight years.

**retail CDs**
Time deposits with a face value below $100,000.

When depositors wish to withdraw before the maturity of a time deposit or CD contract, regulation empowers DIs to impose penalties on a withdrawing depositor, such as the loss of a certain number of months' interest depending on the maturity of the deposit. While this does impose a friction or transaction cost on withdrawals, it is unlikely to stop withdrawals when the depositor has exceptional liquidity needs. Also, withdrawals may increase if depositors perceive the DI to be insolvent, despite interest penalties and deposit insurance coverage up to \$250,000. Nevertheless, under normal conditions, these instruments have relatively low withdrawal risk compared with transaction accounts such as demand deposits and NOW accounts and can be used as an important liability management tool to control withdrawal/liquidity risk. Retail time deposits and CDs are 4.4 percent of deposits and other borrowings at Bank of America and 18.2 percent at Bank of Carbondale.

### Costs

Similar to those of passbook savings, the major costs of these accounts are explicit interest payments. Short-term CDs are often competitive with T-bills, and their rates are set with the T-bill rate in mind. Note that depositors who buy CDs are subject to state and local taxes on their interest payments, whereas T-bill investors do not pay state and local taxes on T-bill interest income.[10] Finally, time deposits and CDs do not at present require the bank to hold low-interest-bearing reserves at the central bank.

## Wholesale CDs

### *Withdrawal Risk*

**wholesale CDs**
Time deposits with a face value above \$100,000.

**negotiable instrument**
An instrument whose ownership can be transferred in the secondary market.

**Wholesale CDs** were innovated by banks in the early 1960s as a contractual mechanism to allow depositors to liquidate their positions in these CDs by selling them in the secondary market rather than settling up with the DI. As a result, a depositor can sell a relatively liquid instrument without causing adverse liquidity risk exposure for the DI. The unique feature of these wholesale CDs is not so much their large minimum denomination size of \$100,000 or more, but the fact that they are **negotiable instruments.** That is, they can be resold by title assignment in a secondary market to other investors. This means, for example, that if IBM bought a \$1 million three-month CD from Citibank but for unexpected liquidity reasons needs funds after only one month has passed, it could sell this CD to another outside investor in the secondary market. This does not impose any obligation on Citibank in terms of an early funds withdrawal request. Thus, a depositor can sell a relatively liquid instrument without causing adverse withdrawal risk exposure for the DI. Essentially, the only withdrawal risk (which can be substantial) is that these wholesale CDs are not rolled over and reinvested by the holder of the deposit claim on maturity. Wholesale CDs are 12.3 percent of deposits and other borrowings at Bank of America and 9.2 percent at Bank of Carbondale.

### Costs

The rates that DIs pay on these instruments are competitive with other wholesale money market rates, especially those on commercial paper and T-bills. This competitive rate aspect is enhanced by the highly sophisticated nature of investors in such CDs, such as money market mutual fund managers, and the fact that these deposits are not covered by explicit deposit insurance guarantees. Only the first

---

[10] Thus, the marginal investor is indifferent between Treasury bills and insured bank CDs when:

$$r_{TB} = r_{CD}(1 - T_L)$$

where $r_{TB}$ is the rate on T-bills, $r_{CD}$ is the CD rate, and $T_L$ is the local income tax rate. Suppose the average local tax rate is 8 percent. Then, if the T-bill rate is 3 percent, insured CDs must pay:

$$r_{CD} = r_{TB}/(1 - T_L) = 3.00\%(1 - 0.08) = 3.26\%$$

$250,000 invested in these CDs (per investor, per institution) is covered by insurance. To the extent that these CDs are most often offered by large DIs perceived as being too big to fail, the required credit risk premium on CDs is less than that required for similar-quality instruments issued by the nonbank private sector (e.g., commercial paper). In addition, required interest yields on CDs reflect investors' perceptions of the depth of the secondary market for CDs. In recent years, the liquidity of the secondary market in CDs has diminished as dealers have withdrawn. This has increased DIs' relative cost of issuing such instruments.[11]

## Federal Funds

### Withdrawal Risk

The liabilities just described are all deposit liabilities, reflecting deposit contracts issued by DIs in return for cash. However, DIs not only fund their assets by issuing deposits but also can borrow in various markets for purchased funds. Since the funds generated from these purchases are borrowed funds, not deposits, they are subject to neither reserve requirements (as with demand deposits and NOW accounts) nor deposit insurance premium payments to the FDIC (as with all the domestic deposits described earlier).[12] The largest market available for purchased funds is the federal funds market. While DIs with excess cash reserves can invest some of this excess in interest-earning liquid assets such as T-bills and short-term securities, an alternative is to lend excess reserves for short intervals to other DIs seeking increased short-term funding. The interbank market for excess cash reserves is called the federal funds (fed funds) market. In the United States, **federal funds** are short-term uncollateralized loans made by one DI to another; more than 90 percent of such transactions have maturities of one day. The DI that purchases funds shows them as a liability on its balance sheet, while the DI that sells them shows them as an asset. Fed funds and repurchase agreements (see below) are 3.7 percent of deposits and other borrowings at Bank of America and 0.0 percent at Bank of Carbondale.

For the liability-funding DIs, there is no risk that the fed funds they have borrowed can be withdrawn within the day, although there is settlement risk at the end of each day (see Chapter 17). However, there is some risk that fed funds will not be rolled over by the lending DI the next day if rollover is desired by the borrowing DI. In reality, this has occurred only in periods of extreme crisis, such as the case for many DIs during the financial crisis of 2008–09. Nevertheless, since fed funds are uncollateralized loans, institutions selling fed funds normally impose maximum bilateral limits or credit caps on borrowing institutions. This

**federal funds**
Short-term uncollateralized loans made by one DI to another.

---

[11] In addition, for all the liability instruments considered so far, the DI may have to pay an FDIC insurance premium depending on its perceived riskiness (see Chapter 19). For example, consider a bank issuing CDs at 3.26 percent, at which rate a depositor might just be indifferent to holding T-bills at 3.00 percent, given a local tax rate of 8 percent. However, the cost to the bank of the CD issue is not 3.26 percent but:

$$\text{Effective CD cost} = 3.26\% + \text{Insurance premium} = 3.26\% + 0.27\% = 3.53\%$$

where 27 basis points is the assumed size of the deposit insurance premium. Thus, deposit insurance premiums add to the cost of deposits as a source of funds.

[12] Foreign deposits are not subject to deposit insurance premiums. However, in the exceptional event of a very large failure in which all deposits are protected, under the 1991 FDICIA, the FDIC is required to levy a charge on surviving large DIs proportional to their total asset size. To the extent that assets are partially funded by foreign liabilities, this is an implied premium on foreign deposits.

may constrain the ability of a bank to expand its federal funds–borrowing position very rapidly if this is part of its overall liability management strategy.

### Costs

The cost of fed funds for the purchasing institution is the federal funds rate. The federal funds rate is set by DIs (mostly banks) that trade in the fed funds market and can vary considerably both within the day and across days—although rate variability has fallen since the introduction of lagged reserve accounting in July 1998.

## Repurchase Agreements (RPs)

### Withdrawal Risk

**repurchase agreements**
Agreements involving the sale of securities (i.e., for fed funds) by one party (i.e., a DI) to another with a promise to repurchase the securities (with fed funds) at a specified date and price in the future.

**Repurchase agreements** (RPs or repos) can be viewed as collateralized federal funds transactions. In a federal funds transaction, the DI with excess reserves sells fed funds for one day to the purchasing DI. The next day, the purchasing DI returns the fed funds plus one day's interest reflecting the fed funds rate. Since a credit risk exposure exists for the selling DI because the purchasing DI may be unable to repay the fed funds the next day, the seller may seek collateral backing for the one-day loan of fed funds. In an RP transaction, the funds-selling DI receives government securities as collateral from the funds-purchasing DI. That is, the funds-purchasing DI temporarily exchanges securities for cash.[13] The next day, this transaction is reversed. The funds-purchasing DI sends back the fed funds it borrowed plus interest (the RP rate). It receives in return (or repurchases) its securities used as collateral in the transaction.

As with the fed funds market, the RP market is a highly liquid and flexible source of funds for DIs needing to increase their liabilities and to offset deposit withdrawals. Moreover, like fed funds, these transactions can be rolled over each day. The major liability management flexibility difference between fed funds and RPs is that a fed funds transaction can be entered into at any time in the business day as long as the Fedwire is open (see Chapter 17).[14] In general, it is difficult to transact an RP borrowing late in the day since the DI sending the fed funds must be satisfied with the type and quality of the securities collateral proposed by the borrowing institution. This collateral is normally in the form of T-bills, T-notes, T-bonds, and mortgage-backed securities, but their maturities and other features, such as callability and coupons, may be unattractive to the funds seller. Negotiations over the collateral package can delay RP transactions and make them more difficult to arrange than simple uncollateralized fed fund loans.

### Costs

Because of their collateralized nature, RP rates normally lie below federal funds rates. Also, RP rates generally show less interday fluctuation than do fed funds rates. This is partly due to the lesser intraday flexibility of RPs relative to fed fund transactions.

## Other Borrowings

While fed funds and RPs have been the major sources of borrowed funds, DIs have utilized a host of other borrowing sources to supplement their liability management flexibility. We describe these briefly in the following sections. Other

---

[13] Since Treasury securities are of a book-entry form, the title to ownership is transferred along a securities Fedwire, in a manner similar to cash transfers.

[14] Normally, Fedwire closes at 6:30 PM EST.

borrowings are 7.9 percent of deposits and other borrowings at Bank of America and 2.7 percent at Bank of Carbondale.

### Bankers' Acceptances

Banks often convert off-balance-sheet letters of credit into on-balance-sheet bankers' acceptances (BAs) by discounting the letter of credit the holder presents for acceptance (see Chapter 16). Further, these BAs may then be resold to money market investors. Thus, BA sales to the secondary market are an additional funding source. We describe BAs in more detail in Appendix 18B to the chapter (located at the book's website, **www.mhhe.com/saunders8e**).

### Commercial Paper

Commercial paper is an unsecured short-term promissory note issued by a corporation to raise short-term cash. Commercial paper is one of the largest (in terms of dollar value outstanding) of the money market instruments, with $1 trillion outstanding in 2012. One reason for such large amounts of commercial paper outstanding is that companies with strong credit ratings can generally borrow money at a lower interest rate by issuing commercial paper than by directly borrowing from other sources such as commercial banks. The principal reason for this is that bank lending rates have to reflect the cost to the bank of reserve capital and other regulatory requirements in addition to the cost of funds. By contrast, commercial paper is a security directly issued to the money market. Commercial paper generally has a maturity of less than 270 days. Most commercial paper is held to maturity since the secondary market for commercial paper is somewhat limited compared with T-bills.[15] However, growth of money market mutual funds has resulted in a more liquid commercial paper market.

Although a DI subsidiary itself cannot issue commercial paper, its parent holding company can. That is, Citigroup can issue commercial paper but Citibank cannot. This provides DIs owned by holding companies—most of the largest DIs in the United States—with an additional funding source. Specifically, when the DI subsidiary itself finds funding tight, it can utilize the funds downstreamed from its holding company's issue of commercial paper. Indeed, Citigroup is one of the largest issuers of commercial paper in the United States. Note that funds downstreamed to an affiliated DI are subject to reserve requirements, detracting from the attractiveness of this mechanism as a regular funding source. We discuss commercial paper in more detail in Appendix 18B to the chapter (located at the book's website, **www.mhhe.com/saunders8e**).

### Medium-Term Notes

A number of DIs in search of more stable sources of funds with low withdrawal risk have begun to issue medium-term notes, often in the five- to seven-year range. These notes are additionally attractive because they are subject to neither reserve requirements nor deposit insurance premiums.

### Discount Window Loans

As discussed earlier, DIs facing temporary liquidity crunches can borrow from the central bank's discount window at the discount rate. We discuss discount window loans in detail in Chapter 19.

---

[15] In general, an investor can sell commercial paper only back to the dealer/underwriter who issued the paper on behalf of a firm.

| Concept Questions | 1. Describe the withdrawal risk and funding cost characteristics of some of the major liabilities available to a modern DI manager. |
|---|---|
| | 2. Since transaction accounts are subject to both reserve requirements and deposit insurance premiums, whereas fed funds are not, why should a DI not fund all its assets through fed funds? Explain your answer. |
| | 3. What are the major differences between fed funds and repurchase agreements? |

# LIQUIDITY AND LIABILITY STRUCTURES FOR U.S. DEPOSITORY INSTITUTIONS

We summarize the preceding discussion by considering some balance sheet data for U.S. banks. Table 18–5 shows the liquid asset–nonliquid asset composition of insured U.S. banks in March 2012 versus 1960. We use 1960 as a benchmark year since the next year (1961) is widely viewed as the date when banks first began to actively manage their liabilities—with Citibank's innovation of wholesale CDs.

Clearly, the ratio of traditional liquid to illiquid assets has declined since 1960, with cash plus government and agency securities in 2012 constituting 22.67 percent of the asset balance sheet of insured banks versus 44 percent in 1960. However, it may be argued that such a comparison misrepresents and overstates the fall in bank asset liquidity, since bank loans themselves became significantly more liquid over this 50-year period. As we discuss in Chapters 25 and 26, DI loans are increasingly being securitized and/or sold in secondary markets. This has fundamentally altered the illiquidity of bank loan portfolios and has made them more similar to securities than in the past. The more liquid the loan portfolio, the less the need for large amounts of traditional liquid assets, such as cash and securities, to act as buffer reserves against unexpected liability withdrawals.

Notice also from Table 18–5 that in 2012 liquid asset holdings were higher at small banks, 25.48 percent, than large banks, 22.37 percent. Large banks' relatively easier access to purchased funds and capital markets compared with small banks' access is the main reason for this difference.

Table 18–6 presents the liability composition of banks in 1960 and March 2012. The most striking feature of Table 18–6 is the shift by banks from funds sources with relative high withdrawal risk—transaction accounts (demand deposits and NOW

**TABLE 18–5**
**Liquid Assets versus Nonliquid Assets for Insured Commercial Banks, 1960 and 2012\* (in percentages)**

Source: Federal Deposit Insurance Corporation website. *www.fdic.gov*

| | | | 2012 | |
|---|---|---|---|---|
| **Assets** | **1960** | **All Banks** | **Large Banks\*\*** | **Small Banks\*\*** |
| Cash | 20% | 9.55% | 9.54% | 9.62% |
| Government and agency securities | 24 | 13.12 | 12.83 | 15.86 |
| Other securities[†] | 8 | 16.60 | 17.38 | 8.98 |
| Loans[‡] | 46 | 51.37 | 50.53 | 59.60 |
| Other assets | 2 | 9.36 | 9.72 | 5.94 |
| | 100% | 100% | 100% | 100% |

\* As of March 2012.
[†] Other securities = state and local, mortgage-backed, plus others.
[‡] Loans = C&I, mortgage, consumer, and others.
\*\* Large banks are those 525 banks with total assets greater than $1 billion. Small banks are those 5,738 banks with total assets of $1 billion or less.

**TABLE 18–6**
**Liability Structure of Insured Commercial Banks, 1960 and 2012\* (in percentages)**

Source: Federal Deposit Insurance Corporation website. *www.fdic.gov*

| | | 2012 | | |
|---|---|---|---|---|
| Liabilities | 1960 | All Banks | Large Banks\*\* | Small Banks\*\* |
| Transaction accounts | 61% | 9.85% | 8.76% | 20.56% |
| Retail CDs and savings deposits | 29 | 46.58 | 46.46 | 47.74 |
| Wholesale CDs | 0 | 16.98 | 17.07 | 16.11 |
| Borrowings and other liabilities | 2 | 15.20 | 16.25 | 4.97 |
| Bank capital | 8 | 11.39 | 11.46 | 10.62 |
| | 100% | 100% | 100% | 100% |

\* As of March 2012.
\*\* Large banks are those with total assets greater than $1 billion. Small banks are those with total assets of $1 billion or less.

accounts) and retail savings and time deposit accounts—to accounts or instruments over which the banks have greater potential control concerning the supply—for example, liability managed accounts. Specifically, the sum of transaction and retail savings and time deposit accounts fell from 90 percent in 1960 to 56.43 percent in March 2012. By contrast, wholesale CDs plus borrowed funds (fed funds, RPs, plus other borrowed funds) increased from 2 percent in 1960 to 32.18 percent in 2012. As discussed in Chapters 2 through 6 of this textbook, the increased competition among banks and other FIs for funds over this period certainly contributed to the change in the composition of the liabilities presented in Table 18–6. DIs have intentionally managed liabilities, however, to reduce withdrawal risk. As implied in Figure 18–2, there is often a trade-off between withdrawal risk and funding cost. DIs' attempts to reduce their withdrawal risk by relying more on borrowed and wholesale funds have added to their interest expense.

Notice too that in 2012, small banks used many more transaction accounts plus retail CDs and savings deposits, 68.30 percent, than large banks, 55.22 percent. Similar to the case with liquid asset management, small banks' relative inability to purchase funds and access the capital markets (compared with that of large banks) means these DIs must hold more deposit liabilities on their balance sheets. Note Table 18–4, which reports that Bank of America had 76.1 percent of its deposits and other borrowings as core deposits compared to 88.1 percent at Bank of Carbondale.

Finally, it should be noted that too heavy a reliance on borrowed funds can be a risky strategy in itself. Even though withdrawal risk may be reduced if lenders in the market for borrowed funds have confidence in the borrowing DI, perceptions that the DI is risky can lead to sudden nonrenewals of fed fund and RP loans and the nonrollover of wholesale CDs and other purchased funds as they mature. A good example of a DI's failure as a result of excessive reliance on large CDs and purchased funds was Continental Illinois in 1984, with more than 80 percent of its funds borrowed from wholesale lenders. Consequently, excessive reliance on borrowed funds may be as bad an overall liability management strategy as excessive reliance on transaction accounts and passbook savings. Thus, a well-diversified portfolio of liabilities may be the best strategy to balance withdrawal risk and funding cost considerations.

**Concept Questions**

1. Look at Table 18–5. How has the ratio of traditional liquid to illiquid assets changed over the 1960–2012 period?
2. Look at Table 18–6. How has the liability composition of banks changed over the 1960–2012 period?

# LIABILITY AND LIQUIDITY RISK MANAGEMENT IN INSURANCE COMPANIES

Insurance companies use a variety of sources to meet liquidity needs. As discussed in Chapters 6 and 12, liquidity is required to meet claims on the insurance policies these FIs have written as well as unexpected surrenders of those policies. These contracts therefore represent a potential future liability to the insurance company. Ideally, liquidity management in insurance companies is conducted so that funds needed to meet claims on insurance contracts written can be met with premiums received on new and existing contracts. However, a high frequency of claims at a single point in time (e.g., an unexpectedly severe hurricane season) could force insurers to liquidate assets at something less than their fair market value.

Insurance companies can reduce their exposure to liquidity risk by diversifying the distribution of risk in the contracts they write. For example, property–casualty insurers can diversify across the types of disasters they cover (e.g., in the 2010s the top two property–casualty insurance companies [in terms of premiums sold] held policies for more than 30 different lines—from auto physical damage, for which they wrote 29.9 percent of all industry premiums, to homeowners multiple peril, for which they wrote 15.8 percent of all industry premiums).[16]

Alternatively, insurance companies can meet liquidity needs by holding relatively marketable assets to cover claim payments. Assets such as government and corporate bonds and corporate stock usually can be liquidated quickly at close to their fair market values in financial markets to pay claims on insurance policies when premium income is insufficient. For example, in 2012, life and property–casualty insurance companies held approximately 80 percent of their assets in the form of government securities and corporate securities (see Chapter 6).

| **Concept Questions** | 1. Discuss two strategies insurance companies can use to reduce liquidity risk. |
|---|---|
| | 2. Why would property–casualty insurers hold more short-term liquid assets to manage liquidity risk than life insurers hold? |

# LIABILITY AND LIQUIDITY RISK MANAGEMENT IN OTHER FINANCIAL INSTITUTIONS

Other FIs, such as securities firms, investment banks, and finance companies, may experience liquidity risk if they rely on short-term financing (such as commercial paper or bank loans) and investors become reluctant to roll those funds over. Remember from Chapter 4 that the main sources of funding for securities firms are repurchase agreements, bank call loans,[17] and short positions in securities. Liquidity management for these FIs requires the ability to have sufficient cash and other liquid resources at hand to underwrite (purchase) new securities from quality issuers before reselling these securities to other investors. Liability

---

[16] See *Best's Review,* August 2012.

[17] A bank call loan means that a lending bank can call in the loan from an investment bank with very little notice.

management also requires an investment bank or securities firm to be able to act as a market maker, which requires the firm to finance an inventory of securities in its portfolio. As discussed in Chapter 3, finance companies fund assets mainly with commercial paper and long-term debt. Liquidity management for these FIs requires the ability to fund loan requests and loan commitments of sufficient quality without delay.

| **Concept Questions** | 1. What are the main sources of funding for securities firms?<br>2. Give two reasons an investment bank needs liquidity. |
| --- | --- |

**Summary**

Liquidity and liability management issues are intimately linked for the modern FI. Many factors, both cost and regulatory, impact an FI manager's choice of the amount of liquid assets to hold. An FI's choice of liquidity is something of a knife edge situation, trading off the costs and benefits of undershooting or overshooting regulatory specified (and prudentially specified) reserve asset targets. An FI can manage its liabilities in a fashion that affects the overall withdrawal risk of its funding portfolio and therefore the need for liquid assets to meet such withdrawals. However, reducing withdrawal risk often comes at a cost because liability sources that are easier to control from a withdrawal risk perspective are often more costly for the FI to utilize.

**Questions and Problems**

1. What are the benefits and costs to an FI of holding large amounts of liquid assets? Why are Treasury securities considered good examples of liquid assets?
2. How is an FI's liability and liquidity risk management problem related to the maturity of its assets relative to its liabilities?
3. Consider the assets (in millions) of two banks, A and B. Both banks are funded by $120 million in deposits and $20 million in equity. Which bank has the stronger liquidity position? Which bank probably has a higher profit?

| Bank A Assets | | Bank B Assets | |
| --- | --- | --- | --- |
| Cash | $ 10 | Cash | $ 20 |
| Treasury securities | 40 | Consumer loans | 30 |
| Commercial loans | 90 | Commercial loans | 90 |
| Total assets | $140 | Total assets | $140 |

4. What concerns motivate regulators to require DIs to hold minimum amounts of liquid assets?
5. How do liquid asset reserve requirements enhance the implementation of monetary policy? How are reserve requirements a tax on DIs?
6. Rank these financial assets according to their liquidity: cash, corporate bonds, NYSE-traded stocks, and T-bills.
7. Define the reserve computation period, the reserve maintenance period, and the lagged reserve accounting system.

8. City Bank has estimated that its average daily net transaction accounts balance over the recent 14-day reserve computation period was $225 million. The average daily balance with the Fed over the 14-day maintenance period was $9 million, and the average daily balance of vault cash over the two-week reserve computation period was $7.5 million.

    a. Under the rules effective in 2012, what is the amount of average daily reserves required to be held during the reserve maintenance period for these net transaction accounts balances?

    b. What is the average daily balance of reserves held by the bank over the maintenance period? By what amount were the average reserves held higher or lower than the required reserves?

    c. If the bank had transferred $20 million of its deposits every Friday over the two-week computation period to one of its offshore facilities, what would be the revised average daily reserve requirement?

9. Assume that the 14-day reserve computation period for problem 8 above extended from May 18 through May 31.

    a. What is the corresponding reserve maintenance period under the rules effective in 2012?

    b. Given your answers to parts (a) and (b) of problem 8, what would be the average required reserves need to be for the maintenance period for the bank to be in reserve compliance?

10. The average daily net transaction accounts balance of a local bank during the most recent reserve computation period is $325 million. The amount of average daily reserves at the Fed during the reserve maintenance period is $24.6 million, and the average daily vault cash corresponding to the computation period is $4.3 million.

    a. What is the average daily reserve balance required to be held by the bank during the maintenance period?

    b. Is the bank in compliance with the reserve requirements?

    c. What amount of reserves can be carried over to the next maintenance period either as excess or as shortfall?

    d. If the local bank has an opportunity cost of 6 percent and deposits at the Fed pay 0.5 percent, what is the effect on the income statement from this reserve period?

11. The following net transaction accounts and cash reserves at the Fed have been documented by a bank for computation of its reserve requirements (in millions) under lagged reserve accounting.

| April | Monday 10th | Tuesday 11th | Wednesday 12th | Thursday 13th | Friday 14th |
|---|---|---|---|---|---|
| Net transaction accounts | $200 | $300 | $250 | $280 | $260 |
| Reserves at Fed | 20 | 22 | 21 | 18 | 27 |

| | Monday 17th | Tuesday 18th | Wednesday 19th | Thursday 20th | Friday 21st |
|---|---|---|---|---|---|
| Net transaction accounts | $280 | $300 | $270 | $260 | $250 |
| Reserves at Fed | 20 | 35 | 21 | 18 | 28 |

|  | Monday 24th | Tuesday 25th | Wednesday 26th | Thursday 27th | Friday 28th |
|---|---|---|---|---|---|
| Net transaction accounts | $240 | $230 | $250 | $260 | $270 |
| Reserves at Fed | 19 | 19 | 21 | 19 | 24 |

| May | Monday 1st | Tuesday 2nd | Wednesday 3rd | Thursday 4th | Friday 5th |
|---|---|---|---|---|---|
| Net transaction accounts | $200 | $300 | $250 | $280 | $260 |
| Reserves at Fed | 20 | 22 | 21 | 18 | 27 |

|  | Monday 8th | Tuesday 9th | Wednesday 10th | Thursday 11th | Friday 12th |
|---|---|---|---|---|---|
| Net transaction accounts | $280 | $300 | $270 | $260 | $250 |
| Reserves at Fed | 20 | 35 | 21 | 18 | 27 |

|  | Monday 15th | Tuesday 16th | Wednesday 17th | Thursday 18th | Friday 19th |
|---|---|---|---|---|---|
| Net transaction accounts | $240 | $230 | $250 | $260 | $270 |
| Reserves at Fed | 20 | 35 | 21 | 18 | 28 |

|  | Monday 22nd | Tuesday 23rd | Wednesday 24th | Thursday 25th | Friday 26th |
|---|---|---|---|---|---|
| Net transaction accounts | $200 | $300 | $250 | $280 | $260 |
| Reserves at Fed | 19 | 19 | 21 | 19 | 24 |

The average vault cash for the computation period has been estimated to be $1 million per day.

   a. What level of average daily reserves is required to be held by the bank during the maintenance period, May 11–24?

   b. Is the bank in compliance with the requirements?

   c. What amount of required reserves can be carried over to the following computation period?

   d. If the average cost of funds to the bank is 8 percent per year and deposits at the Fed pay 0.5 percent, what is the effect on the income statement for this bank for this reserve period?

12. In July 1998 the lagged reserve accounting (LRA) system replaced a contemporaneous reserve accounting (CRA) system as the method of reserve calculation for DIs.

   a. Contrast a contemporaneous reserve accounting (CRA) system with a lagged reserve accounting (LRA) system.

   b. Under which accounting system, CRA or LRA, are DI reserves higher? Why?

   c. Under which accounting system, CRA or LRA, is DI uncertainty higher? Why?

13. What is the "weekend game"? Contrast the DI's ability and incentive to play the weekend game under LRA as opposed to CRA.

14. Under CRA, when is the uncertainty about the reserve requirement resolved? Discuss the feasibility of making large reserve adjustments during this period of complete information.

15. What is the relationship between funding cost and funding or withdrawal risk?

16. An FI has estimated the following annual costs for its demand deposits: management cost per account = $140, average account size = $1,500, average number of checks processed per account per month = 75, cost of clearing a check = $0.10, fees charged to customer per check = $0.05, and average fee charged per customer per month = $8.

    a. What is the implicit interest cost of demand deposits for the FI?

    b. If the FI has to keep an average of 8 percent of demand deposits as required reserves with the Fed paying no interest, what is the implicit interest cost of demand deposits for the FI?

    c. What should be the per-check fee charged to customers to reduce the implicit interest cost to 3 percent? Ignore the reserve requirements.

17. A NOW account requires a minimum balance of $750 for interest to be earned at an annual rate of 4 percent. An account holder has maintained an average balance of $500 for the first six months and $1,000 for the remaining six months. The account holder writes an average of 60 checks per month and pays $0.02 per check, although it costs the bank $0.05 to clear a check.

    a. What average return does the account holder earn on the account?

    b. What is the average return if the bank lowers the minimum balance to $400?

    c. What is the average return if the bank pays interest only on the amount in excess of $400? Assume that the minimum required balance is $400.

    d. How much should the bank increase its check fee to the account holder to ensure that the average interest it pays on this account is 5 percent? Assume that the minimum required balance is $750.

18. Rank the following liabilities with respect, first, to funding risk and, second, to funding cost.

    a. Money market deposit account.

    b. Demand deposits.

    c. Certificates of deposit.

    d. Federal funds.

    e. Bankers' acceptances.

    f. Eurodollar deposits.

    g. NOW accounts.

    h. Wholesale CDs.

    i. Passbook savings.

    j. Repos.

    k. Commercial paper.

19. How is the withdrawal risk different for federal funds and repurchase agreements?

20. How does the cash balance, or liquidity, of an FI determine the types of repurchase agreements into which it will enter?

21. How does the cost of MMMFs differ from the cost of MMDAs? How is the spread useful in managing the withdrawal risk of MMDAs?

22. Why do wholesale CDs have minimal withdrawal risk to the issuing FI?

23. What characteristics of fed funds may constrain a DI's ability to use fed funds to expand its liquidity quickly?

24. What does a low fed funds rate indicate about the level of DI reserves? Why does the fed funds rate have higher-than-normal variability around the last two days in the reserve maintenance period?
25. What trends have been observed between 1960 and 2012 in regard to liquidity and liability structures of commercial banks? What changes have occurred in the management of assets that may cause the measured trends to be overstated?
26. What are the primary methods that insurance companies can use to reduce their exposure to liquidity risk?

## Web Question

27. Go to the Federal Deposit Insurance Corporation's website at **www.fdic.gov** and update Tables 18–5 and 18–6 using the following steps. Click on "Analysts." Click on "Statistics on Banking." Click on "Assets and Liabilities." Click on "Run Report." How have the assets and liabilities of commercial banks changed since March 2012?

## Appendix 18A: Federal Reserve Requirement Accounting

View Appendix 18A at the website for this textbook (**www.mhhe.com/saunders8e**).

## Appendix 18B: Bankers' Acceptances and Commercial Paper as Sources of Financing

View Appendix 18B at the website for this textbook (**www.mhhe.com/saunders8e**).

www.mhhe.com/saunders8e

# Chapter Nineteen

See Appendices Online at www.mhhe.com/saunders8e
- Appendix 19B: FDIC Press Releases of Bank Failures
- Appendix 19C: Deposit Insurance Coverage for Commercial Banks in Various Countries

# Deposit Insurance and Other Liability Guarantees

## INTRODUCTION

Chapter 12 discussed the liquidity risks faced by FIs and Chapter 18 described ways FIs can better manage that risk. Because of concerns about the asset quality or solvency of an FI, liability holders such as depositors and life insurance policyholders (and to a lesser extent, mutual fund shareholders) have incentives to engage in runs, that is, to withdraw all their funds from an FI. As we discussed in Chapter 12, the incentive to run is accentuated in banks, thrifts, and insurance companies by the sequential servicing rule used to meet liability withdrawals. As a result, deposit and liability holders who are first in line to withdraw funds get preference over those last in line.

While a run on an unhealthy FI is not necessarily a bad thing—it can discipline the performance of managers and owners—there is a risk that runs on bad FIs can become contagious and spread to good or well-run FIs. In contagious run or panic conditions, liability holders do not bother to distinguish between good and bad FIs but instead seek to turn their liabilities into cash or safe securities as quickly as possible. Contagious runs can have a major contractionary effect on the supply of credit as well as the money supply regionally, nationally, or even internationally. Indeed, the run on Bear Stearns in March 2008 is seen by many as the initial step into the worldwide financial market collapse.

Moreover, a contagious run on FIs can have serious social welfare effects. For example, a major run on banks can have an adverse effect on the level of savings in all types of FIs and therefore can inhibit the ability of individuals to transfer wealth through time to protect themselves against major risks such as future ill health and falling income in old age.

Because of such wealth, money supply, and credit supply effects, government regulators of financial service firms have introduced guaranty programs to deter runs by offering liability holders varying degrees of failure protection. Specifically, if a liability holder believes a claim is totally secure even if the FI is in trouble, there is no incentive to run. The liability holder's place in line no longer affects getting his or her funds back. Regulatory guaranty or insurance programs for liability holders deter runs and thus deter contagious runs and panics.

Federally backed insurance programs include the Federal Deposit Insurance Corporation (FDIC) (created in 1933) for banks and thrifts, the Securities Investors Protection Corporation (SIPC) (created in 1970) for securities firms, and the Pension Benefit Guaranty Corporation (PBGC) (created in 1974) for private pension funds. In addition, because of their state rather than federal regulation, state-organized guaranty funds back up most life and property–casualty insurance companies.

This chapter discusses federal deposit insurance funds for banks and thrifts, beginning with the history of these insurance or guaranty funds and including the problems (and in one case, failure) experienced by these funds. We then analyze methods available to reduce DI risk taking, thus reducing the probability that deposit holders must be paid off with deposit insurance. We also look at the Federal Reserve's discount window as a (limited) alternative to deposit insurance. Other guarantee programs, including those for insurance companies, securities firms, and pension funds are also analyzed.

# BANK AND THRIFT GUARANTY FUNDS

www.fdic.gov    The FDIC was created in 1933 in the wake of the banking panics of 1930–33, when some 10,000 commercial banks failed. The original level of individual depositor insurance coverage at commercial banks was $2,500, which was increased (six times since 1934), to $100,000 in 1980, and to $250,000 in October 2008. Between 1945 and 1980, commercial bank deposit insurance clearly worked; there were no runs or panics, and the number of individual bank failures was very small (see Figure 19–1). Beginning in 1980, however, bank failures accelerated, with more than 1,039 failures in the decade ending in 1990, peaking at 221 in 1988. This number of failures was actually larger than that for the entire 1933–79 period. Moreover, the costs of each of these failures to the FDIC were often larger than the total costs for the mainly small bank failures in 1933–79. As the number and costs of these closures mounted in the 1980s, the FDIC fund, built up from premiums paid by banks (and the reinvestment income from those premiums), was rapidly drained. Any insurance fund becomes insolvent if the premiums collected and the reserves built up from investing premiums are insufficient to offset the cost of failure claims. The FDIC's resources were virtually depleted by early 1991, when it was given permission to borrow $30 billion from the U.S. Treasury. Even then, it ended 1991 with a deficit of $7 billion. In response to this crisis, Congress passed the FDIC Improvement Act (FDICIA) in December 1991 to restructure the bank insurance fund and prevent its potential insolvency.

After 1991 there was a dramatic turnaround in the fund's finances and a drop in DI failures—partially in response to record profit levels in banks. Specifically, as of March 2008, the FDIC's Deposit Insurance Fund (DIF) had reserves of $52.8 billion. The reserves to insured deposits ratio was 1.19 percent. In 2007 there were 3 DI failures; in 2005 and 2006 there were no DI failures. However, the financial market crisis hit the banking industry very badly. In 2008, 26 DIs failed (at a cost to the FDIC of $20 billion); in 2009, 140 additional failures occurred (at a cost of over $36 billion); and in 2010, 157 failures occurred (at a cost of $22.73 billion).

**FIGURE 19–1**   **Number of Failed Banks by Year, 1934–2012**

Source: FDIC annual reports and statistics on banking. *www.fdic.gov*

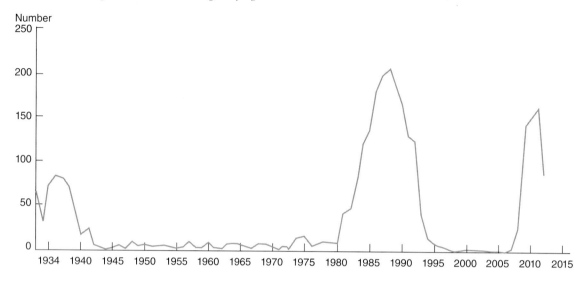

In total, during the worst of the financial crisis, 323 banks failed at a total cost to the FDIC of $78.73 billion. By September 2009, the FDIC's DIF reserves had fallen to −$8.24 billion, less than zero for only the second time since its founding in 1933. The deficit peaked in the first quarter of 2010 at −$20.86 billion. However, unlike the near bankruptcy of the FDIC in 1991, the negative balance in the FDIC's DI insurance fund did not result in talk of the insurer's possible failure. Rather, the FDIC and the federal government took several steps to ensure the fund would have sufficient resources to deal with any and all DI failures. To address the falling balance in the fund, the FDIC levied one special assessment in early 2009 and a second in the fall of 2009, in addition to raising the rates banks were charged for deposit insurance (see below). Further, the agency took the unprecedented step of requiring banks to prepay $45 billion of insurance premiums by the end of 2009. The premiums covered the fourth quarter of 2009 and all of 2010 through 2012. Finally, the FDIC was also given approval to tap $500 billion in additional funding from the Treasury Department through the end of 2010. The Notable Events from the Financial Crisis box describes other actions taken by the FDIC to reduce losses associated with bank failures during the financial crisis. The actions of regulators (and the end of the crisis) proved successful as only 92 banks failed in 2011 (costing $6.89 billion) and 12 banks failed through August 2012 (at a cost of $2.08 billion). Further, FDIC reserves became positive ($3.9 billion) in the first quarter of 2011 and rose to $11.8 billion by March 2012.

In addition to the FDIC, the Federal Savings and Loan Insurance Corporation (FSLIC) originally was established to cover deposits at savings associations (formerly called S&Ls); other thrifts, such as mutual savings banks, often chose to be insured under the FDIC rather than the FSLIC.[1] Like the FDIC, this insurance

---

[1] As we discussed in Chapter 2, credit union depositors enjoy a degree of coverage similar to that of bank, savings association, and savings bank depositors via coverage through the National Credit Union Insurance Fund (established in 1971).

# Notable Events from the Financial Crisis

## RAFT OF DEALS FOR FAILED BANKS PUTS U.S. ON HOOK FOR BILLIONS

. . . To encourage banks to pick through the wreckage of their collapsed competitors, the Federal Deposit Insurance Corp. has agreed to assume most of the risk on $80 billion in loans and other assets. The agency expects it will eventually have to cover $14 billion in future losses on deals cut so far. The initiative amounts to a subsidy for dozens of hand-picked banks. Through more than 50 deals known as "loss shares," the FDIC has agreed to absorb losses on the detritus of the financial crisis . . . The agency's total exposure is about six times the amount remaining in its fund that guarantees consumers' deposits, exposing taxpayers to a big, new risk. As financial markets heal and the economy appears to be pulling out of recession, the federal government is shifting from crisis to cleanup mode. But as the loss-share deals show, its potential financial burden isn't receding. So far, the FDIC has paid out $300 million to a handful of banks under the loss-share agreements. The practice is largely a response to the number of bank failures of the past 18 months, which has stretched the FDIC's financial and logistical resources . . .

Loss-share agreements made a brief appearance in the early 1990s during the savings-and-loan crisis, but haven't been used this extensively before. The FDIC sees the deals as a way to keep bank loans and other assets in the private sector. More importantly, it believes such deals mitigate the cost of cleaning up the industry. The FDIC contends it would cost the agency considerably more to simply liquidate the assets of failed banks, especially with the current crop of troubled institutions and their portfolios of loans on misbegotten real estate. The FDIC's premise is that banks that take on the troubled assets will work to improve their value over time. The agency estimates the loss-share deals cut will cost it $11 billion less than if the agency seized the assets and sold them at fair-market value . . . By potentially mitigating losses—or at least stretching them out over time—the deals provide some protection for the agency's insurance fund. "It's a great opportunity for banks," says James Wigand, deputy director of the FDIC's division of resolutions and receiverships. "It's a great opportunity for us." . . .

The FDIC wouldn't have to resort to such deals if it could easily sell the assets of failed banks. But last year, most healthy banks refused to bite. In 20 of 2008's 25 failures, banks acquired less than 30% of the assets of the failed banks.

**Source:** *The Wall Street Journal*, August 31, 2009, p. A1, by Damian Paletta. Reprinted by permission of *The Wall Street Journal*. © 2009 Dow Jones & Company, Inc. All rights Reserved Worldwide. *www.wsj.com*

fund was in relatively good shape until the end of the 1970s. Beginning in 1980, the fund's resources were rapidly depleted as more and more thrifts failed and had to be closed or merged. In August 1989, Congress passed the Financial Institutions Reform, Recovery, and Enforcement Act (FIRREA), largely in response to the deepening crisis in the thrift industry and the growing insolvency of the FSLIC. This act completely restructured the savings association fund and transferred its management to the FDIC.[2] At the same time, the restructured savings association insurance fund became the Savings Association Insurance Fund (SAIF). The FDIC managed the SAIF separately from the commercial bank fund, which was called the Bank Insurance Fund (BIF). In March 2006, the FDIC merged the BIF and the SAIF to form the Deposit Insurance Fund (DIF). In Figure 19–2, we present the organizational structure of the FDIC and the DIF (including the number of commercial banks and savings institutions insured and the dollar value of insured deposits) as of March 2012.

---

[2] At that time, the FSLIC ceased to exist.

**FIGURE 19–2**
FDIC DIF-Insured
Institutions

Source: FDIC, *Quarterly
Banking Profile,* First Quarter,
2012. *www.fdic.gov*

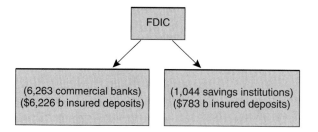

*Internet Exercise*   Go to the Federal Deposit Insurance Corporation website at **www.fdic.gov** and find the latest information available for the number of depository institutions insured by the FDIC and the dollar value of insured deposits using the following steps. Click on "Analysts." Click on "FDIC Quarterly Banking Profile." Click on "Quarterly Banking Profile." Click on "Deposit Insurance Fund Trends." Click on "Table III-B. Estimated FDIC Insured Deposits by Type of Institution." This will download a file onto your computer that will contain the most recent information on the number of and dollar value of insured deposits at depository institutions insured by DIF.

**Concept
Questions**

1. What events led to Congress's passing of the FDIC Improvement Act (FDICIA)?
2. What events brought about the demise of the FSLIC?

# THE CAUSES OF THE DEPOSITORY FUND INSOLVENCIES

There are at least two, not necessarily independent, views as to why depository institution insurance funds became economically insolvent. In addition, some factors offer better explanations of the FSLIC insolvency in the 1980s than of the FDIC's near insolvencies, especially since the FSLIC insolvency was far worse than the financial problems of the FDIC.

## The Financial Environment

One view of the cause of insolvency is that a number of external events or shocks adversely impacted U.S. banks and thrifts. In the 1980s, the first was the dramatic rise in interest rates in the 1979–82 period. This rise in rates had a major negative effect on those thrifts funding long-term, fixed-rate mortgages with short-term deposits. The second event was the collapse in oil, real estate, and other commodity prices, which particularly harmed oil, gas, and agricultural loans in the southwestern United States. The third event was increased financial service firm competition at home and abroad, which eroded the value of bank and thrift charters during the 1980s (see Chapter 21).[3] In the late 2000s, the collapse of the housing market, and the resulting increase in the number of mortgage defaults, led to sharp declines in values of on- and off-balance-sheet assets held by FIs and an increase in their liabilities. These losses drove a few high profile FIs (e.g., Bear

---

[3] The value of a bank or thrift charter is the present value of expected profits from operating in the industry. As expected profits fall, so does the value of a bank or thrift charter.

Stearns, AIG, Lehman Brothers) into (near) bankruptcy, which sent financial markets into steady declines and eventually sent the world economy into the worst recession since the Great Depression. DIs, holding loans to and securities of these failed FIs, experienced large losses. Further, the rise in unemployment that accompanied the recession meant consumer loan defaults rose significantly as well. Eventually, what began as a burst in the housing bubble resulted in large increases in the number of insolvent DIs.

## Moral Hazard

A second view is that these financial environment effects are catalysts for, rather than the causes of, a crisis. At the heart of a crisis is deposit insurance itself, especially some of its contractual features. Although deposit insurance deters depositors and other liability holders from engaging in runs, in so doing it also removes or reduces depositor discipline. Deposit insurance allows DIs to borrow at rates close to the risk-free rate and, if they choose, to undertake high-risk asset investments. DI owners and managers know that insured depositors have little incentive to restrict such behavior, either through fund withdrawals or by requiring risk premiums on deposit rates, since they are insured by the FDIC if a DI fails. Given this scenario, losses on oil, gas, and real estate loans in the 1980s and real estate loans and mortgage-backed securities in the 2000s are viewed as the outcome of bankers' exploiting underpriced or mispriced risk under the deposit insurance contract. The provision of insurance that encourages rather than discourages risk taking is called **moral hazard.**[4] This is because, with deposit insurance, a highly leveraged DI whose debt holders need not monitor the DI's (borrower's) actions has a strong incentive to undertake excessively risky investment decisions, such as in its loan-generating activities.

**moral hazard**
The loss exposure faced by an insurer when the provision of insurance encourages the insured to take more risks.

**implicit premiums**
Deposit insurance premiums or costs imposed on a DI through activity constraints rather than direct monetary charges.

In the absence of depositor discipline (as will be explained below), regulators can price risk taking by DIs either through charging explicit deposit insurance premiums linked to DI risk taking or by charging **implicit premiums** through restricting and monitoring the risky activities of DIs. This can potentially substitute for depositor discipline; those DIs that take more risk would pay directly or indirectly for this risk-taking behavior. However, from 1933 until January 1, 1993, regulators based deposit insurance premiums on a DI's deposit size rather than on its risk, and the deposit insurance scheme implemented in 1993 did not impose a fee that fully covered a DI's risk. Further, the 1980s and (to some extent) 2000s were periods of deregulation, increased risk taking, and capital adequacy forbearance rather than stringent activity regulation and tough capital requirements. Moreover, for the FSLIC, the number of bank examinations and examiners actually fell between 1981 and 1984. Finally, prompt corrective action and closure for severely undercapitalized banks did not begin until the end of 1992 (see Chapter 20).

| **Concept Questions** | 1. What two basic views are offered to explain why depository institution insurance funds become insolvent? |
|---|---|
| | 2. Why was interest rate risk less of a problem for banks than for thrifts in the early 1980s? |

---

[4] The precise definition of moral hazard is the loss exposure of an insurer (the FDIC) that results from the character or circumstances of the insured (here, the DI).

# PANIC PREVENTION VERSUS MORAL HAZARD

A great deal of attention has focused on the moral hazard reason for the collapse of the bank and thrift insurance funds. The less DI owners have to lose from taking risks, the greater are their incentives to take excessively risky asset positions. When asset investment risks or gambles pay off, DI owners make windfall gains in profits. If they fail, however, the FDIC, as the insurer, bears most of the costs, given that owners of DIs—like owners of regular corporations—have limited liability. It's a "heads I win, tails I don't lose (much)" situation.

Note that even without deposit insurance, the limited liability of DI owners or stockholders always creates incentives to take risk at the expense of fixed claimants such as depositors and debt holders. The difference between DIs and other firms is risk-taking incentives induced by mispriced deposit insurance. That is, when risk taking is not **actuarially fairly priced** in deposit insurance premiums, this adds to the incentives of DI stockholders to take additional risks.

**actuarially fairly priced insurance**
Insurance pricing based on the perceived risk of the insured.

Nevertheless, even though mispriced deposit insurance potentially accentuates DI risk taking, deposit insurance effectively deterred DI panics and runs of the 1930–33 kind in the postwar period. That is, deposit insurance has ensured a good deal of stability in the credit and monetary system. Indeed, during the financial crisis of 2008–09, DI deposits actually grew as risk averse investors liquidated alternative investments and deposited the funds at DIs, which were seen as a relatively safe haven.

This suggests that, ideally, regulators should design the deposit insurance contract with the trade-off between moral hazard risk and DI panic or run risk in mind. For example, by providing 100 percent coverage of all depositors and reducing the probability of runs to zero, the insurer may be encouraging certain DIs to take a significant degree of moral hazard risk-taking behavior. On the other hand, a very limited degree of deposit insurance coverage might encourage runs and panics, although moral hazard behavior itself would be less evident.

In the 1980s and late 2000s, extensive insurance coverage for deposit holders and the resulting lack of incentive for deposit holders to monitor and restrict DI owners' and managers' risk taking resulted in small levels of DI run risk but high levels of moral hazard risk.[5] By restructuring the deposit insurance contract, it is possible to reduce moral hazard risk quite a bit without a very large increase in DI run risk. To some extent, these were the objectives behind the passage of the FDIC Improvement Act (FDICIA) of 1991 and the depositor preference legislation contained in the Omnibus Budget Reconciliation Act of 1993, discussed later in this chapter.

| Concept Question | 1. Historically, what effect has deposit insurance had on DI panics and runs? |
| --- | --- |

[5] At this point, note that managers may not have the same risk-taking incentives as owners. This is especially true if managers are compensated through wage and salary contracts rather than through shares and share option programs. When managers are on fixed-wage contracts, their preferences in regard to risk lean toward being risk averse. That is, they are unlikely to exploit the same type of moral hazard incentives that stock owner–controlled DIs would. This is because managers have little to gain if their DIs do exceptionally well (their salaries are fixed), but probably will lose their jobs and human capital investments in a DI if they fail.

# CONTROLLING DEPOSITORY INSTITUTION RISK TAKING

There are three ways deposit insurance can be structured to reduce moral hazard behavior:

1. Increase stockholder discipline.
2. Increase depositor discipline.
3. Increase regulator discipline.

Specifically, redesigning the features of the insurance contract can either directly or indirectly impact DI owners' and stockholders' risk-taking incentives by altering the behavior of depositors and regulators. In the wake of the solvency problems of the FDIC, in 1991 FDICIA was passed with the objective of increasing discipline in all three areas.

## Stockholder Discipline

### Insurance Premiums

One approach toward making stockholders' risk taking more expensive is to link FDIC insurance premiums to the risk profile of the DI. Below we look at ways this might be done, including the risk-based premium scheme adopted by the FDIC in 1993 and revised in April 2009 and 2011.

*Theory*   A major feature of the pre-1993 FDIC deposit insurance contract was the flat deposit insurance premium levied on banks and thrifts. Specifically, each year a DI paid a given sum or premium to the FDIC based on a fixed proportion of its domestic deposits.[6] Until 1989, the premium was 8.33 cents per $100 in domestic deposits. As the FDIC fund became increasingly depleted, the level of the premium was raised several times, but its risk-insensitive nature was left unaltered. By 1993, the premiums DIs had to pay had risen to 23 cents per $100 of their domestic deposits, almost a tripling of their premiums since 1988.

To see why a flat or size-based premium schedule does not discipline a DI's risk taking, consider two banks of the same domestic deposit size, as shown in Table 19–1. Banks A and B have domestic deposits of $100 million and (in 1993) would pay the same premium to the FDIC (0.0023 × $100 million = $230,000 per year). However, their risk-taking behavior is completely different. Bank A is excessively risky, investing all its assets in real estate loans. Bank B is almost risk free, investing all its assets in government T-bills. We graph the insurance premium rates paid by the two banks compared with their asset risk in Figure 19–3.

In Figure 19–3, note that under the pre-1993 flat premium schedule, banks A and B would have been charged the same deposit insurance premium based on the bank's domestic deposit size. Critics of flat premiums argued that the FDIC should act more like a private property–casualty insurer. Under normal property–casualty insurance premium-setting principles, insurers charge those with higher risks higher premiums. That is, low-risk parties (such as bank B) do not generally subsidize high-risk parties (such as bank A) as they did under the pre-1993 FDIC premium-pricing scheme. If premiums increased as DI risk increased, DIs would have reduced incentives to take risks. Therefore, the ultimate goal might be to price risk in an actuarially fair fashion, similar to the process used by a private property–casualty insurer, so that premiums reflect the expected private costs or losses to the insurer from the provision of deposit insurance.

---

[6] In actual practice, premiums are levied and paid semiannually.

**TABLE 19–1**
Flat Deposit
Insurance
Premiums and Risk
Taking

| | Bank A | | Bank B | |
|---|---|---|---|---|
| | **Assets** | **Liabilities** | **Assets** | **Liabilities** |
| | Real estate loans 100 m | Domestic deposits 100 m | T-bills 100 m | Domestic deposits 100 m |

Note that there are arguments against imposing an actuarially fair risk-based premium schedule. If the deposit insurer's mandate is not to act as if it were a private cost-minimizing insurer such as a PC insurance company because of social welfare considerations, some type of subsidy to banks and thrifts can be justified. Remember that the FDIC is a quasi-government agency, and broader banking market stability concerns and savers' welfare concerns might arguably override private cost-minimizing concerns and require subsidies. Others have argued that if an actuarially fair premium is imposed on a banking system that is fully competitive, banking itself cannot be profitable. That is, some subsidy is needed for DIs to exist profitably. However, while U.S. banking is competitive, it probably deviates somewhat from the perfectly competitive model.

*Calculating the Actuarially Fair Premium* Economists have suggested a number of approaches for calculating the fair deposit insurance premium that a cost–minimizing insurer such as the FDIC should charge. One approach would be to set the premium equal to the expected severity of loss times the frequency of losses due to DI failure plus some load or markup factor. This would exactly mimic the approach toward premium setting in the property–casualty industry. However, the most common approach, the **option pricing model of deposit insurance** (OPM), has been to view the FDIC's provision of deposit insurance as virtually identical to the FDIC's writing a put option on the assets of the DI that buys the deposit insurance. We depict the conceptual idea underlying the option pricing model approach in Figure 19–4.

**option pricing model of deposit insurance**
A model for calculating deposit insurance as a put option on the DI's assets.

In this framework, the FDIC charges the DI a premium $P$ to insure the DI's deposits ($D$). If the DI does well and the market value of the DI's assets is greater than $D$, its net worth is positive and it can continue in business. The FDIC would face no charge against its resources and would keep the premium paid to it by the DI ($P$). If the DI is insolvent, possibly because of a bad or risky asset portfolio, such that the value of the DI's assets falls below $D$ (say to $A$), and its net worth is negative, the DI owners will "put the bank" back to the FDIC. If this happens, the FDIC will pay out to the insured depositors an amount $D$ and will liquidate the DI's assets ($A$). As a result, the FDIC bears the cost of the insolvency (or negative net worth) equal to ($D - A$) less the insurance premiums paid by the DI ($P$).

**FIGURE 19–3**
**Premium Schedules Relative to Risk**

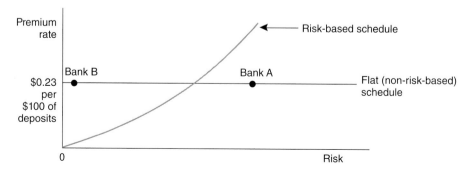

**FIGURE 19–4**

Deposit Insurance
as a Put Option
(*D* = DI's deposits;
*A* = DI's assets;
*P* = premium paid
by DI)

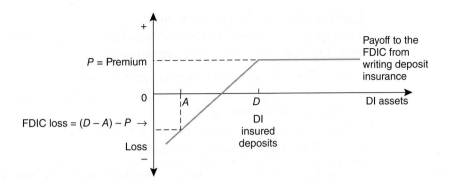

When valued in this fashion as a simple European put option, the FDIC's cost of providing deposit insurance increases with the level of asset risk ($\sigma_A^2$) and with the DI's leverage (*D/A*). That is, the actuarially fair premium (*P*) is equivalent to the premium on a put option and as such should be positively related to both asset risk ($\sigma_A^2$) and leverage risk (*D/A*). The value of a deposit insurance guaranty is the same as the Black-Scholes model for a European put option of maturity *T* (where *T* is the time period until the next premium assessment):

$$P(T) = De^{-rT}\phi(X_2) - A\phi(X_1)$$

where

$$X_1 = [\log(D/A) - (r + \sigma_A^2/2)T]/\sigma_A\sqrt{T}$$
$$X_2 = X_1 + \sigma_A\sqrt{T}$$

and $\phi$ is the standard normal distribution.

Even though the option pricing model is a conceptually and theoretically elegant tool, it is difficult to apply in practice—especially because a DI's asset value (*A*) and its asset risks ($\sigma_A^2$) are not directly observable. While values of these variables can be extracted from the equity value and the volatility of equity value of the DI (see the discussion on the Moody's Analytics model in Chapter 10), only 600 DIs have their stocks traded on the three major exchanges (AMEX, NASDAQ, and NYSE), and there are approximately 7,300 DIs (6,263 DIF-insured commercial banks and 1,044 DIF-insured savings institutions). Even so, the option model framework is useful because it indicates that both leverage and asset quality (or risk) are important elements that should enter into any deposit insurance pricing model.

Next, we look at the risk-based deposit insurance premium scheme introduced by the FDIC in January 1993; it is directly linked to both bank leverage and asset quality.

**Concept Questions**

1. Bank A has a ratio of deposits to assets of 90 percent and a variance of asset returns of 10 percent. Bank B has a ratio of deposits to assets of 85 percent and a variance of asset returns of 5 percent. Which bank should pay the higher insurance premium?
2. If deposit insurance is similar to a put option, who exercises that option?

## Implementing Risk-Based Premiums

The FDICIA required the FDIC to establish risk-based premiums by January 1, 1994. The FDIC now has to base premiums on:

1. Different categories and concentrations of assets.
2. Different categories and concentrations of liabilities—insured, uninsured, contingent, and noncontingent.
3. Other factors that affect the probability of loss.
4. The deposit insurer's revenue needs.[7]

**FDIC risk-based deposit insurance program**
A program that assesses insurance premiums on the basis of capital adequacy and supervisory judgments on DI quality.

The FDIC first introduced a **risk-based deposit insurance program** on January 1, 1993. Under this program, which applied equally to all depository-insured institutions, a bank or thrift's risk would be ranked along a capital adequacy dimension and a supervisory dimension. That is, rankings are partly based on regulators' judgments regarding asset quality, loan underwriting standards, and other operating risks. Each dimension was split into three categories, so a bank or thrift was placed in one of nine cells. See Table 19–2, Panel A, for the original structure of premiums.

The best DIs, those in Column (2) that were well capitalized and healthy, paid an annual insurance premium of 23 cents per $100 of deposits, while the worst DIs paid 31 cents. Although the 8-cent differential in insurance premiums between the safest and the riskiest DIs was a first step in risk-based pricing, it was widely considered so small that it did not effectively price insurance according to DI risk exposures. At the time of the risk-based premiums' introduction, the FDIC estimated

**TABLE 19–2** Shifting the Deposit Insurance Burden

Source: Office of the Comptroller of the Currency, January 1993 and January 1997.

| | Supervisory Groups—Premiums | | |
|---|---|---|---|
| **(1)** | **(2)** | **(3)** | **(4)** |
| **Capital Category** | **Healthy**[1] | **Supervisory Concern**[2] | **Substantial Supervisory Concern**[3] |
| **Panel A: The Fee Structure for Deposit Insurance, Effective January 1, 1993** | | | |
| Well capitalized[4] | 23 cents per $100 | 26 cents per $100 | 29 cents per $100 |
| Adequately capitalized[5] | 26 cents per $100 | 29 cents per $100 | 30 cents per $100 |
| Undercapitalized[6] | 29 cents per $100 | 30 cents per $100 | 31 cents per $100 |
| **Panel B: The Fee Structure for Deposit Insurance, Effective January 1, 1997** | | | |
| Well capitalized[4] | 0 cents per $100 | 3 cents per $100 | 17 cents per $100 |
| Adequately capitalized[5] | 3 cents per $100 | 10 cents per $100 | 24 cents per $100 |
| Undercapitalized[6] | 10 cents per $100 | 24 cents per $100 | 27 cents per $100 |

[1] Financially sound and only a few weaknesses.
[2] Weaknesses that if not corrected could result in significant risk to the fund.
[3] Substantial probability of loss to the fund unless effective corrective action is taken.
[4] Total risk based ≥ 10 percent, Tier 1 risk based ≥ 6 percent, Tier 1 leverage ≥ 5 percent.
[5] Total risk based ≥ 8 percent, Tier 1 risk based ≥ 4 percent, Tier 1 leverage ≥ 4 percent.
[6] Does not meet the capital criteria for well- or adequately capitalized depository institutions.

[7] In particular, the FDIC sets premiums so that the deposit reserve ratio is within a range of 1.15 percent to 1.50 percent of estimated insured deposits.

that about 75 percent of the over 12,000 insured commercial banks and savings banks (with 51 percent of the bank deposit base) and 60 percent of the 2,300 insured thrifts (with approximately 43 percent of the thrift deposit base) were in the group paying the lowest premium. Only about 220 banks (2 percent of all insured commercial and savings banks) and 160 thrifts (7 percent of all insured thrifts) were in the group paying the highest insurance premiums of 31 cents. The average assessment rate in 1993 was 23.2 cents per $100 of deposits. However, the improving solvency position of the FDIC (and of the banks and thrifts it insures) resulted in a considerable reduction in insurance premiums. In 1996 (for BIF-insured DIs) and 1997 (for SAIF-insured DIs) the fee structure for deposit insurance was changed to that in Panel B of Table 19–2. By December 2005, 94.6 percent of all BIF-insured DIs and 93.4 percent of all SAIF-insured DIs paid the statutory minimum premium (which had fallen to zero) and the average assessment rate was equal to 0.05 cent per $100 of deposits.

*Federal Deposit Insurance Reform Act of 2005*   In the early 2000s, the FDIC identified several weaknesses with the existing system of deposit insurance that it felt needed to be corrected. Among these was that the system did not effectively price risk. At the time, regulations restricted the FDIC from charging premiums to well-capitalized and highly rated DIs as long as the insurance fund reserves were above 1.25 percent of insured deposits—this was called the designated reserve ratio (DRR). As a result, (as noted above) more than 90 percent of all insured DIs did not pay deposit insurance premiums in the late 1990s and early 2000s. The FDIC argued that it should charge regular premiums for risk regardless of the reserve levels of the fund. Beginning in January 2007, the FDIC began calculating deposit insurance premiums based on a more aggressively risk-based system. Under the FDIC Reform Act, if the reserve ratio drops below 1.15 percent—or if the FDIC expects it to do so within six months—the FDIC must, within 90 days, establish and implement a plan to restore the DIF to 1.15 percent within five years. Such was the case in March 2008 when the FDIC reserve ratio dropped to 1.19 percent. At this point the FDIC was certain that the reserve ratio would drop below 1.15 by the end of the next quarter. Accordingly, the FDIC developed and implemented (on April 1, 2009) a restoration plan for the DIF that would restore the DIF reserve ratio to 1.15 percent. The details of the approach, including the 2009 restoration plan and the 2011 adjustment to the plan, are described in Appendix 19A to this chapter.

### Increased Capital Requirements and Stricter Closure Rules

A second way to reduce stockholders' incentives to take excessive risks is to (1) require higher capital—lower leverage—ratios (so that stockholders have more at stake in taking risky investments) and (2) impose stricter DI closure rules. The moral hazard risk-taking incentives of DI owners increase as their capital or net worth approaches zero and their leverage increases. For those thrifts allowed to operate in the 1980s with virtually no book equity capital and with negative net worth, the risk-taking incentives of their owners were enormous.

By failing to close such DIs, regulators exhibited excessive **capital forbearance.** In the short term, forbearance may save the insurance fund some liquidation costs. In the long run, owners of bad banks or thrifts have continuing incentives to grow and take additional risks in the hope of a large payoff that could turn the institution around. This strategy potentially adds to the future liabilities of the insurance fund and to the costs of DI liquidation. We now know that huge additional

**capital forbearance**
Regulators' policy of allowing an FI to continue operating even when its capital funds are fully depleted.

costs were the actual outcome of the regulators' policy of capital forbearance in the thrift industry in the 1980s.

As we discuss in Chapter 20, a system of risk-based capital requirements mandates that those banks and thrifts taking greater on- and off-balance-sheet, market, credit, operating, and interest rate risks must hold more capital. Thus, risk-based capital supports risk-based deposit insurance premiums by increasing the cost of risk taking for DI stockholders.[8] In addition, the 1991 FDIC Improvement Act sought to increase significantly the degree of regulatory discipline over DI stockholders by introducing a **prompt corrective action** program. This has imposed five capital zones for banks and thrifts, with progressively harsher mandatory actions being taken by regulators as capital ratios fall. Under this carrot-and-stick approach, a bank or thrift is placed into receivership within 90 days of the time when its capital falls below some positive book value level, that is, when it is critically undercapitalized (currently 2 percent of assets for DIs). To the extent that the book value of capital approximates true net worth or the market value of capital, this enhances stockholder discipline by imposing additional costs on DI owners for risk taking. It also increases the degree of coinsurance, in regard to risks taken, between DI owners and regulators such as the FDIC.

**prompt corrective action**
Mandatory actions that have to be taken by regulators as a DI's capital ratio falls.

---

| **Concept Questions** | 1. If you are managing a DI that is technically insolvent but has not yet been closed by the regulators, would you invest in Treasury bonds or real estate development loans? Explain your answer. |
| --- | --- |
| | 2. Do we need both risk-based capital requirements and risk-based insurance premiums to discipline shareholders? |

---

## Depositor Discipline

An alternative, more indirect route to disciplining riskier DIs is to create conditions for a greater degree of depositor discipline. Depositors could either require higher interest rates and risk premiums on deposits or ration the amount of deposits they are willing to hold in riskier DIs.

Critics argue that under the current deposit insurance regulations, neither insured depositors nor uninsured depositors have sufficient incentives to discipline riskier DIs. To understand these arguments, we consider the risk exposure of both insured and uninsured depositors under the current deposit insurance system.

### Insured Depositors

When the deposit insurance contract was introduced in 1933, the level of coverage per depositor was $2,500. This coverage cap gradually rose through the years, reaching $100,000 in 1980. The Federal Deposit Insurance Reform Act of 2005 left the deposit insurance cap at $100,000 per person per account. However, the act increased deposit insurance coverage for retirement accounts from $100,000 to $250,000. During the financial crisis of 2008–09, in an attempt to provide stability to the U.S. banking system, the Troubled Asset Relief Program (or TARP) called for the FDIC to increase the deposit insurance limit to $250,000 from $100,000 per person per institution.

---

[8] On the assumption that new equity is more costly to raise than deposits for banks.

The $250,000 cap concerns a depositor's beneficial interest and ownership of deposited funds. In actuality, by structuring deposit funds in a bank or thrift in a particular fashion, a depositor can achieve many times the $250,000 coverage cap on deposits. To see this, consider the different categories of deposit fund ownership available to an individual, shown in Table 19–3. Each of these categories represents a distinct accumulation of funds toward the deposit insurance cap, the coverage ceiling per bank. Note that this coverage ceiling is *per bank or thrift*; wealthy and institutional investors can employ **deposit brokers** to spread their funds over many DIs up to the permitted cap. In this way, all their deposits become explicitly insured. For example, a wealthy individual with $1 million in deposits could hire a deposit broker such as Bank of America Merrill Lynch to split the $1 million into 4 parcels of $250,000 and deposit those funds at 4 different banks. We give an example of how depositors can raise the coverage level by adopting certain strategies.

**deposit brokers**
Brokers who break up large deposits into smaller units at different banks to ensure full coverage by deposit insurance.

**EXAMPLE 19–1**
*Calculation of Insured Deposits*

On June 30, 2015 a married couple with one daughter, where both husband and wife had **individual retirement accounts (IRAs)** and **Keogh** private pension plans at the bank, could accrue a total coverage cap of $2.0 million as a family: $250,000 each for his individual deposit account, her individual deposit account, their joint deposit account, and their daughter's deposit account held in trust; and $250,000 each for his IRA account, his Keogh account, her IRA account, and her Keogh account. When the range of ownership is expanded in this fashion, the coverage cap for a family can rapidly approach $1 million or more.

**IRAs and Keogh accounts**
Private pension plans held by individuals with banks or other FIs.

The FDIC Improvement Act and the Federal Deposit Insurance Reform Act of 2005 initially left the insured depositor coverage cap unchanged at $100,000. While raising the coverage cap would decrease the incentives of depositors to monitor and run from more risky DIs, it would also decrease the number of DI failures and the probability of panics. Thus, the losses to the FDIC from covering a larger dollar amount of deposits per head would be weighed against the

**TABLE 19–3**
**Deposit Ownership Categories**

Source: U.S. Department of the Treasury, "Modernizing the Financial System: Recommendations for Safer More Competitive Banks," Washington, DC, February 1991.

Individual ownership, such as a simple checking account.
Joint ownership, such as the savings account of a husband and wife.
Revocable trusts, in which the beneficiary is a qualified relative of the settlor, and the settlor has the ability to alter or eliminate the trust.
Irrevocable trusts, where the beneficial interest is not subject to being altered or eliminated.
Interests in employee benefit plans where the interests are vested and thus are not subject to being altered or eliminated.
Public units, that is, accounts of federal, state, and municipal governments.
Corporations and partnerships.
Unincorporated businesses and associations.
Individual retirement accounts (IRAs).
Keogh accounts.
Executor or administrator accounts.
Accounts held by banks in an agency or fiduciary capacity.

possibility of fewer failures, with their attendant liquidation costs. This reasoning was employed in 2009 when the deposit insurance cap was raised to $250,000. At this time, the FDIC was more concerned about the possibility of contagious runs as a few major DIs (e.g., Washington Mutual) failed or nearly failed. At this point, the FDIC wanted to instill confidence in the banking system and made the change to avoid massive depositor runs from many of the troubled (and even safer) DIs, more DI failures, and an even larger collapse of the financial system. This suggests that setting the optimal level of the insurance cap per depositor per DI is a far from easy problem.

### Uninsured Depositors

The primary intention of deposit insurance is to deter DI runs and panics. A secondary and related objective has been to protect the smaller, less informed saver against the reduction in wealth that would occur if that person were last in line when a DI fails. Under the current deposit insurance contract, the small, less informed depositor is defined by the $250,000 ceiling. Theoretically at least, larger, more informed depositors with more than $250,000 on deposit are at risk if a DI fails. As a result, these large uninsured depositors should be sensitive to DI risk and seek to discipline more risky DIs by demanding higher interest rates on their deposits or withdrawing their deposits completely. Until recently, the manner in which DI failures have been resolved meant that both large and small depositors were often fully protected against losses. This was especially so where large banks got into trouble and were viewed as **too-big-to-fail.** That is, they were too big to be liquidated by regulators either because of the draining effects on the resources of the insurance fund or for fear of contagious or systemic runs spreading to other major banks. Thus, although uninsured depositors tended to lose in thrift and small-bank failures, in large-bank failures the failure resolution methods employed by regulators usually resulted in implicit 100 percent deposit insurance. As a result, for large banks in particular, neither small nor large depositors had sufficient incentives to impose market discipline on riskier banks.

*Failure Resolution Policies Post-FDICIA*   In the wake of the FDIC's growing deficit, the 1991 FDICIA sought to pass more of the costs of insured DI failures on to uninsured depositors, thereby enhancing their incentives to monitor DIs and to control risk through requiring higher deposit rates and/or through their deposit placement decisions. The FDICIA required that a **least-cost resolution** (LCR) strategy be put in place by the FDIC. In applying the LCR strategy, the FDIC evaluates failure resolution alternatives on a present value basis and documents their assumptions in deciding which method to use (see Table 19–4). These decisions can be audited by the General Accounting Office, the government's audit watchdog.

However, there was a very important and controversial exemption to using least-cost resolution in all cases. Specifically, a *systemic risk* exemption applies

**too-big-to-fail banks**
Banks that are viewed by regulators as being too big to be closed and liquidated without imposing a systemic risk to the banking and financial system.

**least-cost resolution**
Policy requiring that the lowest-cost method of closure be used for failing DIs.

**TABLE 19–4**
**Least-Cost Resolution (LCR) Requirements under FDICIA**

Source: GAO, 1992 Bank Resolutions, GAO/GGD-94-197, p. 14.

| The FDIC must: |
| --- |
| • Consider and evaluate all possible resolution alternatives by computing and comparing their costs on a present value basis, using realistic discount rates. |
| • Select the least costly alternative based on the evaluation. |
| • Document the evaluation and the assumption on which it is based, including any assumptions with regard to interest rates, asset recovery rates, asset holding costs, and contingent liabilities. |
| • Retain documentation for at least five years. |

where a large DI failure could cause a threat to the whole financial system. Then methods that could involve the full protection of uninsured depositors as well as insured depositors could be used. This appears to allow the too-big-to-fail guaranty to large DI uninsured depositors prevalent in the pre-1991 system to carry over after the passage of the FDICIA. However, the act has restricted the circumstances under which this systemic risk exemption can be used. Such an exemption is allowed only if a two-thirds majority of the boards of the Federal Reserve and the FDIC recommend it to the secretary of the Treasury and if the secretary of the Treasury, in consultation with the President of the United States, agrees. Further, any cost of such a bailout of a big DI would have to be shared among all other DIs by charging them an additional deposit insurance premium based on their size as measured by their average total assets minus average tangible equity. Because large DIs have more assets minus equity, they will have to make bigger contributions (per dollar of assets) than smaller DIs to any future bailout of a large DI.

Nevertheless, some concern has been raised about the continuance of the too-big-to-fail (TBTF) guarantee even in its more restricted form. With the growing wave of bank and financial service firm mergers, it is argued that more and more FIs are likely to be covered by TBTF guarantees. Indeed, during the financial crisis of 2008–2009, the Federal Reserve's rescue of FIs such as Bear Stearns, AIG, and Citigroup and the $200 billion invested in over 630 banks through the Treasury Department's Capital Purchase Program (CPP) demonstrated that the TBTF bailouts reached much further than anyone would have predicted, including FIs other than commercial banks and commercial bank deposits.[9]

**insured depositor transfer**
Method of resolution in which uninsured depositors take a loss, or haircut, on failure equal to the difference between their deposit claims and the estimated value of the failed DI's assets minus insured deposits.

With the exception of the systemic risk exemption, the least-cost resolution strategy requires the FDIC to employ the method that imposes most failure costs on the uninsured depositors. To this end, the FDIC has been increasingly using an **insured depositor transfer** (IDT), or "haircut," method to resolve a number of post-1991 failures. Under the IDT method of resolution, the insured deposits of a closed DI are usually transferred in full to another local DI in the community to conduct a direct payoff of the depositors for the FDIC. By contrast, uninsured depositors must file a claim against the receiver of the failed DI and share with the FDIC in any receivership distributions from the liquidation of the closed DI's assets. This usually results in a loss for uninsured depositors (a so-called haircut). For example, in 25 out of 323 failures in 2008–10, the FDIC imposed initial losses, or haircuts, on uninsured depositors. The size of the haircut depends mostly on the FDIC-estimated value of the failed DI's assets. The FDIC press release announcing the payoff of insured depositors only of the failed First Arizona Savings in October 2010 is presented in Appendix 19B to the chapter (located at the book's website, **www.mhhe.com/saunders8e**).

During the financial crisis, to avoid an even larger collapse of the financial system, uninsured deposits were covered in over 90 percent of the DI failures. However, the uninsured deposits were not paid off by the FDIC. Rather, the FDIC worked to have uninsured deposits transferred as part of the failure resolution. Further, the increase in the deposit insurance cap to $250,000 in 2009 meant that most deposits were insured. Thus, few uninsured deposits existed at many of the smaller failed banks, and the cost of covering them in the event of a failure was comparatively small.

---

[9] As of July 2012, 34 banks had paid back more than $192 billion of the $205 billion lent out through the CPP, plus an additional $12 billion in interest and dividends on the money.

Additionally, in November 2008, the FDIC enacted the Temporary Liquidity Guarantee Program to strengthen confidence and encourage liquidity in the banking system. Part of this program was the Debt Guarantee, which provided government backing of newly issued senior unsecured debt, including promissory notes, commercial paper, interbank funding, and any unsecured portion of secured debt issued by eligible institutions on or before June 30, 2009 as well as secured debt issued from January 2009 through June 30, 2010. As a result of this guarantee, the unpaid principal and contract interest of an entity's newly issued senior unsecured debt would be paid by the FDIC if the issuing insured depository institution failed to make a promised payment on the debt. As of June 2012, there was $304.1 billion in FDIC-backed debt outstanding, the agency had collected $10.4 billion in fees from banks that had participated, and the FDIC had not faced any guarantee payouts.

We describe a simplified form of the IDT, or haircut, method next.

---

**EXAMPLE 19–2**

*Liquidation and Payoff of a Failed Bank Using the Insured Deposit Transfer (IDT) Method*

In Table 19–5, a failed bank in part (a) has only $80 million in good assets to meet the $50 million in deposit claims of insured depositors and the $50 million in claims of the uninsured depositors. That is, it has $20 million negative net worth. Under an IDT, in part (b), the FDIC would transfer the $80 million in assets to an acquiring bank along with the full $50 million in small insured deposits, but only $30 million of the $50 million in uninsured deposits. Notice that the uninsured depositors get protection against losses only up to the difference between the estimated value of the failed bank's assets and its insured deposits. In effect, the uninsured depositors are subject to a haircut to their original deposit claims of $20 million (or, as a percentage, 40 percent of the value of their deposit claims on the failed bank). After the IDT, the uninsured depositors own $30 million in deposits in the acquiring bank and $20 million in receivership claims on the bad assets of the failed bank. Only if the FDIC as a receiver can recover some value from the $20 million in bad assets will the loss to the uninsured be less than $20 million.

To summarize the losses of the three parties under the IDT:

| | | Loss ($ millions) |
|---|---|---|
| Insured depositors | = | 0 |
| FDIC | = | 0 |
| Uninsured depositors | = | $20 |

---

As is seen from this simple example, the uninsured depositors bear all the losses and now have a much stronger incentive than before to monitor and control the actions of DI owners through imposing market discipline via interest rates and the amount of funds deposited.

**TABLE 19–5** Insured Depositor Transfer Resolution (in millions of dollars)

| (a) Failed | | | | (b) Insured Depositor Transfer | | | | |
|---|---|---|---|---|---|---|---|---|
| **Assets** | | **Liabilities** | | **Assets** | | **Liabilities** | | |
| Good assets | $80 | Insured deposits | $ 50 | Good assets | $80 | Insured deposits | $50 | Merger → with good bank |
| | | Uninsured deposits | 50 | | | Uninsured deposits | 30 | |
| | $80 | | $100 | | $80 | | $80 | |

| **Concept Questions** | 1. Under current deposit insurance rules, how can DI depositors achieve many times the $250,000 coverage cap on deposits? |
| :--- | :--- |
| | 2. Why do uninsured depositors benefit from a too-big-to-fail policy followed by regulators? |
| | 3. Make up a simple balance sheet example to show a case where the FDIC can lose even when it uses an IDT to resolve a failed DI. |

## Regulatory Discipline

In the event that stockholder and deposit holder discipline does not reduce moral hazard–induced risk taking by banks and thrifts, regulations can require regulators to act promptly and in a more consistent and predictable fashion to restrain DI risk-taking behavior. To bolster increased stockholder and depositor discipline, the FDICIA perceived two areas of regulatory weakness: (1) the frequency and thoroughness of examinations and (2) the forbearance shown to weakly capitalized DIs. The FDICIA included key provisions to address these weaknesses.

### Examinations

First, the FDICIA required improved accounting standards for DIs, including working toward the market valuation of balance sheet assets and liabilities. This improves the ability of examiners to monitor DIs' net worth positions off-site and is consistent with monitoring the true net worth of the DI (see Chapters 8 and 9). Second, beginning in December 1992, FDICIA required an annual on-site examination of every DI. Third, private accountants were given a greater role in monitoring a DI's performance, with independent audits being mandated.

After the financial crisis of 2008–09, the Federal Reserve Bank of New York and the Office of the Comptroller of the Currency increased the number of examiners "embedded" in the big FIs that they regulate (e.g., Bank of New York Mellon, Citigroup, J.P. Morgan Chase). About 2,500 bank examiners work on location at these FIs, up almost 40 percent from 2006. In addition to policing the FIs for their maintenance of regulations, the examiners are charged with identifying vulnerabilities in the FIs early enough to head off major problems. However, it should be noted that despite the presence of embedded examiners, J.P. Morgan Chase still managed to suffer more than $5 billion in losses in the bank's trading portfolio as certain credit risk limits were breached. Examiners failed to notice the complacency, poor judgment, and faulty risk controls of the bank as it tried to avoid showing the full amount of losses during the first quarter of 2012 by placing inaccurate prices on their positions.

### Capital Forbearance

The introduction of prompt corrective action capital zones (see Chapter 20), along with the mandatory actions required of regulators in each of those zones (including closure), is symptomatic of a movement toward a regulatory policy based on rules rather than discretion. Such rules clearly direct regulators to act in a certain manner even if they are reluctant to do so out of self-interest or for other reasons. The weakness of such rules is that if a policy is bad, then bad policy becomes more effective.

| **Concept Question** | 1. What measures were mandated by the FDICIA to bolster regulator discipline? |
|---|---|

# NON-U.S. DEPOSIT INSURANCE SYSTEMS

Deposit insurance systems are increasingly being adopted worldwide. See Appendix 19C (located at the book's website, **www.mhhe.com/saunders8e**) for a description of deposit insurance coverage in various countries before versus after the start of the financial crisis in September 2008. Many of these countries offer quite different degrees of protection to depositors compared with systems in the United States. For example, in response to the single banking and capital market in Europe, the EC established (at the end of 1999) a single deposit insurance system covering all European Community–located banks. This directive requires the insurance of deposit accounts in EC countries of at least 20,000 ECUs. This was increased to at least 50,000 ECUs in October 2008. However, depositors are subject to a 10 percent deductible in order to create incentives for them to monitor banks. The idea underlying the EC plan is to create a level playing field for banks across all European Community countries.

Japan has a deposit insurance system that was established in 1971. In the late 1990s and early 2000s, the Japanese banking system was going through an experience similar to that of U.S. banks and thrifts in the 1930s and 1980s, with record bad debts and bank failures. Over the decade 1992–2002, Japanese banks had written off over $650 billion in nonperforming loans. As of 2003, these banks still had over $400 billion in bad loans on their balance sheets. The effect on Japan's deposit insurance fund was similar to that of the United States in the 1980s, with a rapidly declining reserve fund that limited its ability to deal with the crisis. These problems led to a government "bailout" to the tune of over $500 billion and blanket protection, until April 2005, of all bank deposits. As of April 2005, deposits under full coverage have been limited to only those used for payment and settlement purposes that satisfy all the following three conditions: deposits bearing no interest, being redeemable on demand, and providing normally required payment and settlement services. All other deposits (e.g., time and savings) are insured up to a maximum principal of ¥10 million ($108,000) per account. Negotiable certificates of deposit have no insurance protection.

As early as 2000, China had proposed a deposit insurance system. It was shelved at the time because most local banks were state owned. Government-backed credit assured depositors that their savings would be protected from potential bankruptcies. In the mid-2000s, improved local financial conditions and fewer risks led the Peoples Bank of China to reinitiate its consideration of the system. Further, a growing number of small financial institutions were established to serve the small enterprises, rural areas, and the midwest region. These institutions needed a deposit insurance system to avoid risks for the entire financial industry. In late 2009, China was preparing a system to formally insure bank deposits. Officials of the China Banking Regulatory Commission planned to introduce a system like the FDIC that protects American depositors in case of a bank failure. A plan to insure about 98 percent of bank deposits in China has been submitted. The scheme would require financial institutions to buy deposit insurance from the Central Deposit Insurance Corp., which would have the right to borrow from the central bank and Ministry of Finance. The plan would be financed by participating banks. In the event of an insured institution failing, the insurance corporation would compensate depositors. However, as of September 2012, no plan had been implemented. China had $27.9 trillion in yuan-denominated deposits in 2012. More than 98 percent of deposit accounts were less than 200,000 yuan ($31,400), indicating the ceiling for the deposit insurance could be no more than 200,000 yuan.

# THE DISCOUNT WINDOW

## Deposit Insurance versus the Discount Window

The previous sections have described how a well-designed deposit insurance system might impose stockholder, depositor, and regulator discipline. Such a system can potentially stop runs on DIs and extreme liquidity problems arising in the banking system without introducing significant amounts of moral hazard risk-taking behavior among insured institutions. Whether the FDICIA (and the depositor preference legislation) has priced risk accurately enough to stop all but the most egregious cases of moral hazard, only time will tell. However, the fact that only 13 of almost 8,000 DIs failed in 2001 and 2002 (during and after a relatively small recession of the U.S. economy) and 323 DIs failed in 2008–10 (during the steepest recession since the Great Depression) is a first indication that the regulations work. The FDICIA has certainly increased the incentives of DI owners, uninsured depositors, and regulators to monitor and control DI risk. As such, changes made under the FDICIA are improvements over the old deposit insurance system. However, deposit insurance is not the only mechanism by which regulators mitigate DI liquidity risk. A second mechanism has been the central banks' provision of a lender of last resort facility through the discount window.

## The Discount Window

www.federalreserve.gov

**discount window**
Central bank lender of last resort facility.

Traditionally, central banks such as the Federal Reserve have provided a **discount window** facility to meet the short-term, nonpermanent liquidity needs of DIs. For example, suppose a DI has an unexpected deposit drain close to the end of a reserve requirement period and cannot meet its reserve target. It can seek to borrow from the central bank's discount window facility. Alternatively, short-term seasonal liquidity needs due to crop planting cycles can also be met through discount window loans. Normally, such loans are obtained by a DI's discounting short-term high-quality paper such as Treasury bills and bankers' acceptances with the central bank. The interest rate at which such securities are discounted is called the *discount rate* and is set by the central bank.

In the United States the Federal Reserve had historically set the discount rate below market rates, such as the overnight federal funds rates (see Table 19–6). The volume of outstanding discount loans was ordinarily small, however, because the Fed prohibited DIs from using discount window loans to finance sales of fed funds or to finance asset expansion. In January 2003, the Fed implemented changes to its discount window lending that increased the cost of borrowing but eased the terms. Specifically, three lending programs are now offered through the Fed's discount window. *Primary credit* is available to generally sound depository institutions on a very short-term basis, typically overnight, at a rate above the Federal Open Market Committee's (FOMC) target rate for federal funds. Primary credit may be used

**TABLE 19–6** Spread between the Discount Rate and the Fed Funds Rate

Source: Federal Reserve Board website, various dates. *www.federalreserve.gov*

|  | 1990 | 1994 | 2000 | 2003 | September 2007 | December 2008 | August 2012 |
|---|---|---|---|---|---|---|---|
| Federal funds | 8.10% | 4.21% | 6.40% | 0.94% | 5.26% | 0.16% | 0.13% |
| Discount window | 6.98 | 3.60 | 5.73 | 2.00 | 6.25 | 0.86 | 0.75 |

for any purpose, including financing the sale of fed funds. Primary credit may be extended for periods of up to a few weeks to depository institutions in generally sound financial condition. *Secondary credit* is available to depository institutions that are not eligible for primary credit. It is extended on a very short-term basis, typically overnight, at a rate that is above the primary credit rate. Secondary credit is available to meet backup liquidity needs when its use is consistent with a timely return to a reliance on market sources of funding or the orderly resolution of a troubled institution. Secondary credit may not be used to fund an expansion of the borrower's assets. The Federal Reserve's seasonal credit program is designed to assist small depository institutions in managing significant seasonal swings in their loans and deposits. *Seasonal credit* is available to depository institutions that can demonstrate a clear pattern of recurring intrayearly swings in funding needs. Eligible institutions are usually located in agricultural or tourist areas. Under the seasonal program, borrowers may obtain longer-term funds from the discount window during periods of seasonal need so that they can carry fewer liquid assets during the rest of the year and make more funds available for local lending.

With the changes, discount window loans to healthy banks would be priced at 1 percent above (rather than below) the fed funds rate. Loans to troubled banks would cost 1.5 percent above the fed funds rate. The changes were not intended to change the Fed's use of the discount window to implement monetary policy, but to significantly increase the discount rate while making it easier to get a discount window loan. By increasing banks' use of the discount window as a source of funding, the Fed hopes to reduce volatility in the fed funds market as well. The changes also allow healthy banks to borrow from the Fed regardless of the availability of private funds. Previously, the Fed required borrowers to prove they could not get funds from the private sector, which put a stigma on discount window borrowing. With the changes, the Fed will lend to all banks, but the subsidy will be gone.

In the wake of the terrorist attacks of September 11, 2001, the Federal Reserve's discount window supplied funds to the banking system in unprecedented amounts. The magnitude of destruction resulting from the attacks caused severe disruptions to the U.S. banking system, particularly in DIs' abilities to send payments. The physical disruptions caused by the attacks included outages of telephone switching equipment in Lower Manhattan's financial district, impaired records processing and communications systems at individual banks, the evacuation of buildings that were the sites for the payment operations of several large DIs, and the suspended delivery of checks by air couriers. These disruptions left some DIs unable to execute payments to other DIs through the Fed's Fedwire system (see Chapter 17), which in turn resulted in an unexpected shortfall for other DIs. The Federal Reserve took several steps to address the problems in the payments system on and after September 11, 2001. Around noon on the 11th, the Board of Governors of the Fed released a statement saying that the Fed was open and operating, and that the discount window was available to meet liquidity needs of all DIs. The Fed staff also contacted DIs often during the next few days, encouraging them to make payments and to consider the use of the discount window to cover unexpected shortfalls that the DIs might encounter. Thus, the Fed's discount window was a primary tool used to restore payments coordination during this period.

The Fed took additional unprecedented steps, expanding the usual function of the discount window, to address the financial crisis. While the discount window had traditionally been available to DIs, in March of 2008 (as Bear Stearns nearly failed) investment banks gained access to the discount window through the Primary Dealer Credit Facility (PDCF). In the first three days, securities firms borrowed an average of $31.3 billion per day from the Fed. The largest expansion of the discount window's availability to all FIs occurred in the wake of the Lehman Brothers failure, as a series of actions were taken in response to the increasingly fragile state of financial markets. In the fall of 2008, several new broad-based lending programs were implemented, providing funding to a wide array of new parties, including U.S. money market mutual funds, commercial paper issuers, insurance companies, and others. These programs rapidly expanded the current lending programs offered via the Fed.

Also, in response to a weakening economy and a growing financial crisis, the Fed significantly reduced the level of short-term interest rates by lowering its target federal funds rate to near zero, down from 5.26 percent in September 2007 (see Table 19–6). It also significantly reduced the spread (premium) between the discount rate and the federal funds target to just a quarter of a point, bringing the discount rate down to a half percent. With lower rates at the Fed's discount window and interbank liquidity scarce as many lenders cut back their lending, more financial institutions chose to borrow at the window. The magnitude and diversity of nontraditional lending programs and initiatives developed during the crisis were unprecedented in Federal Reserve history. The lending programs were all designed to "unfreeze" and stabilize various parts of the credit markets, with the overall goal that parties receiving credit via these new Fed programs would, in turn, provide funding to creditworthy individuals and firms.

Despite the recent changes in the Fed's policy regarding discount window lending, there are a number of reasons why DI access to the discount window is unlikely to deter DI runs and panics to the extent deposit insurance does. The first reason is that to borrow from the discount window, a DI generally needs high-quality liquid assets to pledge as collateral. Failing, highly illiquid DIs are unlikely to have such assets available to discount. The second reason is that discount window borrowing, unlike deposit insurance coverage, is not automatic. That is, discount window loans are made at the discretion of the central bank. Third, discount window loans are meant to provide temporary liquidity for inherently solvent DIs, not permanent long-term support for otherwise insolvent DIs.[10] Specifically, discount window loans are limited to no more than 60 days in any 120-day period unless both the FDIC and the institution's primary regulator certify that the DI is viable. Additional extensions of up to 60 days are allowed subject to regulator certification. Finally, any discount window advances to undercapitalized DIs that eventually fail would require the Federal Reserve to compensate the FDIC

---

[10] Note that all three of these reasons are the result of regulations set by U.S. regulators. If regulators and politicians want to use the discount window as a substitute for deposit insurance, it is within their jurisdiction to alleviate these barriers.

for incremental losses caused by the delay in keeping the troubled DI open longer than necessary.[11] Consequently, the discount window is a partial but not a full substitute for deposit insurance as a liquidity stabilizing mechanism.

| Concept Question | 1. Is a DI's access to the discount window as effective as deposit insurance in deterring bank runs and panics? Why or why not? |
| --- | --- |

# OTHER GUARANTY PROGRAMS

As discussed in Chapter 12, other FIs are also subject to liquidity crises and liability holder runs. To deter such runs and protect small claim holders, guaranty programs have appeared in other sectors of the financial services industry. We describe these programs and their similarities to and differences from deposit insurance next.

### National Credit Union Administration

www.ncua.gov
The National Credit Union Administration (NCUA) is an independent federal agency that charters, supervises, examines, and insures the nation's 7,100 credit unions (see Chapter 2). Through its insurance fund, the National Credit Union Share Insurance Fund (NCUSIF) the NCUA provides deposit insurance guarantees of up to $250,000 for insured credit unions. The fund's reserves come entirely from premiums paid by member credit unions. Insurance coverage and premiums are generally identical to those assessed by the FDIC. Indeed, changes to insurance coverage and premiums listed in the Federal Deposit Insurance Reform Act of 2005 apply to NCUSIF-insured credit unions as well.

Because credit unions hold almost 30 percent of their assets in government securities and hold relatively small amounts of residential mortgages, they have been less affected by the crises experienced by other thrifts such as savings associations. In addition, more than 40 percent of credit union assets are in small consumer loans, often for amounts less than $10,000. Thus, credit unions have a significant degree of credit risk diversification, which also lowers their risk of insolvency.

### Property–Casualty and Life Insurance Companies

Both life insurance companies and property–casualty (PC) insurance companies are regulated at the state level (see Chapter 3). Unlike banks and thrifts, no federal guaranty fund exists for either life or PC insurers. Beginning in the 1960s, most states began to sponsor state guaranty funds for firms selling insurance in that state. By 1991 all states had established such funds. These state guaranty funds have a number of important differences from deposit insurance. First, while these programs are sponsored by state insurance regulators, they are actually run and administered by the private insurance companies themselves.

Second, unlike the DIF, in which the FDIC established a permanent reserve fund by requiring DIs to pay annual premiums in excess of payouts to resolve failures, no such permanent guaranty fund exists for the insurance industry, with the sole exception of the PC and life guaranty funds for the state of New York. This

---

[11] In practice, the Fed would be penalized by a loss in the interest income on discount window loans made to banks that eventually fail.

means that contributions are paid into the guaranty fund by surviving firms only after an insurance company has failed.

Third, the size of the required contributions that surviving insurers make to protect policyholders in failed insurance companies differs widely across states. In those states that have no permanent guaranty fund, each surviving insurer is normally levied a pro rata amount, according to the size of its statewide premium income. This amount either helps pay off small policyholders after the assets of the failed insurer have been liquidated or acts as a cash injection to make the acquisition of a failed insurer attractive. The definition of small policyholders generally varies across states from $100,000 to $500,000.[12]

Finally, because no permanent fund exists and the annual pro rata contributions are often legally capped (often at 2 percent of premium income), there is usually a delay before small policyholders get the cash surrender values of their policies, or other payment obligations are met from the guaranty fund. This contrasts with deposit insurance, where insured depositors normally receive immediate coverage of their claims. For example, in May 1999, Martin Frankel fled to Italy after he allegedly stole $215 million from seven insurance companies he controlled. While Frankel was eventually found and extradited to the United States for trial, at year-end 2003 insurance commissioners in the five states involved were still trying to compensate policyholders, stating that some policyholders would not receive their full payment. The private nature of insurance industry guaranty funds, their lack of permanent reserves, and low caps on annual contributions mean that they provide less credible protection to claimants than do the bank and thrift insurance funds. As a result, the incentives for insurance policyholders to engage in a run if they perceive that an insurer has asset quality problems or insurance underwriting problems is quite strong even in the presence of such guaranty funds.

## The Securities Investor Protection Corporation

www.sipc.org

Since the passage of the Securities Investor Protection Act in 1970 and the creation of the Securities Investor Protection Corporation (SIPC), securities firm customers have been given specific, but limited, protection against insolvencies. Basically, customers receive pro rata shares of a liquidated securities firm's assets, with SIPC satisfying remaining claims up to a maximum of $500,000 per individual. Since its inception, the SIPC has had to intervene in approximately 1 percent of the 37,800 security dealers–brokers that have been SIPC members. Through 2008, the SIPC had advanced more than $520 million in order to make possible the recovery of over $160 billion in assets. Then in 2009 alone, the SIPC agreed to pay out an advance of $534 million on $4.44 billion in losses to some 5,000 victims of Bernie Madoff's investment fund; an amount exceeding the total of all premium payouts since its inception in 1970. Despite this record payout, compared with those of banking and insurance funds, SIPC losses have been very small. Through December 2011, the SIPC has advanced $1.8 billion in order to make possible the recovery of $117.5 billion in assets for an estimated 767,000 investors. Criminal action has been initiated in 130 of the 324 SIPC proceedings commenced since 1970. A total of 312 indictments have been returned in federal or state courts, resulting in 271 convictions to date.

---

[12] Since insurance industry guaranty fund premiums are size based, they are similar to the pre-1993 flat insurance premiums under deposit insurance. Indeed, similar types of moral hazard behavior (related to fixed-premium, risk-insensitive insurance) have been found for property–casualty companies.

# Notable Events from the Financial Crisis

## TWO UNPRECEDENTED SIPC PROCEEDINGS IN 2008

In 2007, SIPC recorded its first year without the need for initiating any customer protection proceedings whatsoever. In 2008, SIPC initiated three small liquidation proceedings, and two proceedings of unprecedented size and scope.

## LEHMAN BROTHERS INC.

The Lehman Brothers Inc. ("LBI") liquidation was preceded by the Chapter 11 filing of Lehman Brothers Holdings Inc. on September 15, 2008. The Holding Company owned a SIPC member brokerage firm, LBI, which in turn held securities customer accounts. In order to facilitate the sale of brokerage assets, SIPC initiated a customer protection proceeding on Friday, September 19th. On application by SIPC to the United States District Court for the Southern District of New York, LBI was placed in liquidation under the Securities Investor Protection Act ("SIPA"), and a trustee was appointed to oversee the liquidation of the firm. That day, upon removal of the proceeding by the District Court, the United States Bankruptcy Court for the Southern District of New York held an extended hearing and approved the sale of assets of LBI to Barclays Bank. In a matter of weeks, the trustee for LBI transferred more than 135,000 customer accounts, which contained more than $140 billion in customer assets, to two broker-dealers, one of which was the brokerage arm of Barclays. As a result, many of the customers of the defunct firm were able to exercise control over their respective portfolios in a seamless way. In addition, over $2 billion of property was returned to scores of prime brokerage accountholders. While much

remains to be done in every aspect of the LBI matter, the initial stages have proceeded very well.

## BERNARD L. MADOFF INVESTMENT SECURITIES LLC

The failure of Lehman Brothers Inc. was linked to the subprime mortgage situation and the accompanying broader financial turmoil. The failure of Bernard L. Madoff Investment Securities LLC, a registered securities broker-dealer and SIPC member, involved a very different problem: the theft of customer assets on an unprecedented scale. The firm was placed in SIPA liquidation and a trustee was appointed on December 15, 2008, after the principal of the firm, Bernard Madoff, confessed to having stolen customer property over a period of many years. Unlike the LBI case, where customer records were accurate, it became apparent very early in the Madoff case that the customer statements Mr. Madoff had been sending to investors bore little or no relation to reality. The statements sent to customers were inaccurate when compared to the inventory of securities actually held by the brokerage firm. For that reason, it was not possible to transfer all or part of any customer's account to another, solvent brokerage firm. Instead, pursuant to SIPA, the trustee sought and received authority from the United States Bankruptcy Court for the Southern District of New York to publish a notice to customers and creditors, and to mail claim forms to them. This was accomplished on January 2, 2009. As this Annual Report goes to press, the trustee in the Madoff case has begun to satisfy customer claims with SIPC's funds.

**Source:** 2008 Annual Report: Securities Investor Protection Corporation, SIPC, Washington, D.C., *www.sipc.org.*

Under extreme circumstances, SIPC guarantees can also be supplemented by other departments of the federal government. For example, on September 16, 2008, (one day after Lehman Brothers filed for bankruptcy) Reserve Primary Fund, the oldest money market fund in the United States, saw its shares fall to 97 cents (below the $1.00 book value) after writing off debt issued by Lehman Brothers. Resulting investor anxiety about Reserve Primary Fund spread to other funds and investors industrywide liquidated their MMMF shares. In just one week, investors liquidated $170 billion of the industry total $4 trillion invested in MMMFs. In response, on September 19 the federal government took steps to restore confidence in the MMMF industry. Specifically, the Department of Treasury opened the Temporary Guarantee Program for MMMFs which provided up to $50 billion in coverage to MMMF shareholders for amounts they held in the funds as of close of business that day.

In 2012, the fund's reserves stood at $1.43 billion. Prior to 2009, the SIPC charged a flat premium rate of $150 per member. Effective April 1, 2009, the SIPC moved to a more variable-rate method in which each member's premium rate was set at 0.25 percent of net operating revenues from the securities business. The Notable Events from the Financial Crisis box highlights two notable securities firm failures covered by the SIPC: Lehman Brothers Inc. and Bernard L. Madoff Investment Securities.

## The Pension Benefit Guaranty Corporation

www.pbgc.gov

In 1974, the Employee Retirement Income Security Act (ERISA) established the Pension Benefit Guaranty Corporation (PBGC). Currently, the PBGC protects the retirement benefits of nearly 44 million workers and has 26,500 insured pension plan sponsors. Prior to 1974, an employee's pension benefits with a private corporation had very limited backing from that firm's assets. The establishment of the PBGC insured pension benefits against the underfunding of plans by corporations.

When the PBGC was created in 1974, the single-employer premium was a flat-rate $1 per plan participant. Congress raised the premium to $2.60 in 1979 and to $8.50 in 1986. In 1987, the basic premium was raised to $16 and an additional variable-rate premium was imposed on underfunded plans up to a maximum of $50. In 1991, Congress set the maximum at $72 per participant for underfunded plans and $19 per participant for fully funded plans.

Despite these premiums, the PBGC entered into a deficit of $2.7 billion at the end of 1992. This reflects the fact that unlike the FDIC, the PBGC has little regulatory power over the pension plans it insures. Thus, it cannot use portfolio restrictions or on-site supervision to restrict the risk taking of plan managers. Partly in response to the growing PBGC deficit, the 1994 Retirement Protection Act was passed. Under the act (in 1997), the $72 premium cap was phased out (80 percent of underfunded plans were at the cap in 1997). Thus, underfunded programs are now subjected to even higher premiums (some as high as several hundred dollars per participant).[13] As a result of these changes (as of 1999), the PBGC's insurance fund operated at a record surplus of $5 billion. Thus, like the FDIC in 1993, the PBGC changed to a more overtly risk-based premium plan.

Despite risk-based premiums, however, in the early 2000s, falling stock market values, low interest rates, and rising employer bankruptcies (particularly in the steel and airline industries) forced the PBGC to assume billions of dollars worth of pension fund debt. As a result, the PBGC suffered a net loss of $7.6 billion in 2003. At year-end 2003, the long-term deficit of the insurance fund rose to $11.2 billion, three times larger than any previously recorded deficit. This compares with a surplus of $5 billion in 1999.

To address the growing deficit and the growing trend by large companies to abandon their pensions, the Deficit Reduction Act of 2005, enacted in February 2006, increased the PBGC's flat-rate premium of 2006 to $30 per participant for single-employer plans and $8 per participant for multi-employer plans. The act also called for the 2007 flat-rate premium for single employers to increase to $31 per participant and for multi-employer plans to remain at $8 per participant. (By 2012 the inflation adjusted fees were $35 for single employer plans and $9

---

[13] Underfunded plans pay a surcharge of $9 per participant per $1,000 of underfunding.

for multi-employer plans.) The Pension Protection Act of 2006, enacted in August 2006, made the PBGC's variable-rate premium payable by all underfunded plans, reformed the pension funding rules, imposed benefit restrictions on underfunded plans, established new limits on PBGC's guarantee, provided funding relief to certain companies (particularly those in the airline industry), and imposed new reporting and disclosure requirements.

Despite these changes, the numerous bankruptcies during the financial crisis took a further toll on the PBGC. By September 2009, the fund's deficit stood at $21.95 billion, up from $11.15 billion in September 2008. The agency assumed pension liabilities from collapsed investment bank Lehman Brothers, retailer Circuit City, plastics company Milacron, and auto supplier Delphi Corp. (where it assumed $6.2 billion in pension liabilities, the second largest amount ever behind United Airlines's $7.5 billion in 2005). However, the PBGC stated that, despite the deficit, the agency had sufficient funds to meet its obligations for many years because benefits are paid out over the benficiaries' lifetime and not in one lump sum. The PBGC also recognized that over the long term, the deficit needed to be addressed. However, by year-end 2011 the deficit had grown to $26 billion.

The problems of the PBGC are similar to those facing the FSLIC in the 1980s. As discussed earlier, a principal cause of the crisis of savings institutions in the 1980s was an asset–liability mismatch that was not recognized early enough by regulators. Similarly, the PBGC seems to be making some of the same mistakes as regulators of those savings institutions. That is, there is a belief that because pension funds have long time horizons, the risk of investing in equities is negligible, which is not true. Further, this risk is magnified by moral hazard and adverse selection problems. Companies nearing failure have an incentive to underfund their pension plans and to adopt risky investment strategies, which, if they fail, will be covered by the PBGC. Further, healthy companies have an incentive to terminate their plans and leave the system completely.

**Concept Questions**

1. How do state-sponsored guaranty funds for insurance companies differ from deposit insurance?
2. What specific protection against insolvencies does the Securities Investor Protection Corporation provide to securities firm customers?

## Summary

A contagious run on FIs can have serious social welfare effects. Because of adverse wealth, money supply, and credit supply effects, regulators of FIs have introduced guaranty programs to deter runs by offering liability holders varying degrees of failure protection. Mispriced insurance or guarantee programs, however, can lead to moral hazard behavior by FI owners. That is, since insurance guarantees result in little risk to FI owners with limited liability, they have an incentive to take excessively risky asset positions.

In the late 1980s and 2000s, DI and other financial industry guaranty programs have weakened and in some cases have been rendered insolvent. This chapter looked at the causes of the deposit insurance fund insolvencies in the late 1980s, as well as problems in the late 2000s, including external economic events and moral hazard behavior induced by the structure of the insurance plan itself. The failure of the FSLIC led to a major restructuring of the FDIC and deposit guarantees in general. We discussed the post-1991 restructuring of deposit insurance, including the introduction of risk-related premiums, risk-based capital, and increased market and regulatory discipline on DI owners and liability holders. As a result, the provision and cost of deposit insurance is currently more sensitive to a DI's risk exposure than prior to 1991. This chapter also examined liability guaranty programs for other FIs, including the credit unions, securities firms, pension plans, and life and PC insurance firms.

## Questions and Problems

1. What is a contagious run? What are some of the potentially serious adverse social welfare effects of a contagious run? Do all types of FIs face the same risk of contagious runs?

2. How does federal deposit insurance help mitigate the problem of bank runs? What other elements of the safety net are available to DIs in the United States?

3. What major changes did the Financial Institutions Reform, Recovery, and Enforcement Act of 1989 make to the FDIC and the FSLIC?

4. Contrast the two views on, or reasons why, depository institution insurance funds can become insolvent.

5. What is moral hazard? How did the fixed-rate deposit insurance program of the FDIC contribute to the moral hazard problem of the savings association industry? What other changes in the savings association environment during the 1980s encouraged the developing instability of that industry?

6. How does a risk-based insurance program solve the moral hazard problem of excessive risk taking by FIs? Is an actuarially fair premium for deposit insurance always consistent with a competitive banking system?

7. What are three suggested ways a deposit insurance contract could be structured to reduce moral hazard behavior?

8. What are some ways of imposing stockholder discipline to prevent FI managers from engaging in excessive risk taking?

9. How is the provision of deposit insurance by the FDIC similar to the FDIC's writing a put option on the assets of a DI that buys the insurance? What two factors drive the premium of the option?

10. What four factors were provided by FDICIA as guidelines to assist the FDIC in the establishment of risk-based deposit insurance premiums? What happened to the level of deposit insurance premiums in the late 1990s and 2000s? Why?

11. What is capital forbearance? How does a policy of forbearance potentially increase the costs of financial distress to the insurance fund as well as the stockholders?

12. Under what conditions may the implementation of minimum capital guidelines, either risk-based or non-risk-based, fail to impose stockholder discipline as desired by regulators?

13. Why did the fixed-rate deposit insurance system fail to induce insured and uninsured depositors to impose discipline on risky DIs in the United States in the 1980s?

    a. How is it possible to structure deposits in a DI to reduce the effects of the insured ceiling?

b. What are brokered deposits? Why are brokered deposits considered more risky than nonbrokered deposits by DI regulators?

c. What trade-offs were weighed in the decision to leave the deposit insurance ceiling at $100,000 in 2005 and then to increase the ceiling to $250,000 in 2009?

14. What changes did the Federal Deposit Insurance Reform Act of 2005 make to the deposit insurance cap?

15. What is the too-big-to-fail doctrine? What factors caused regulators to act in a way that caused this doctrine to evolve?

16. What are some of the essential features of the FDICIA of 1991 with regard to the resolution of failing DIs?

a. What is the least-cost resolution (LCR) strategy?

b. When can the systemic risk exemption be used as an exception to the LCR policy of DI closure methods?

c. What procedural steps must be taken to gain approval for using the systemic risk exemption?

d. What are the implications to the other DIs in the economy of the implementation of this exemption?

17. What is the primary goal of the FDIC in employing the LCR strategy?

a. How is the insured depositor transfer method implemented in the process of failure resolution?

b. Why does this method of failure resolution encourage uninsured depositors to more closely monitor the strategies of DI managers?

18. The following is a balance sheet of a commercial bank (in millions of dollars):

| Assets | | Liabilities and Equity | |
|---|---|---|---|
| Cash | $ 5 | Insured deposits | $30 |
| Loans | 40 | Uninsured deposits | 10 |
| | | Equity | 5 |
| Total assets | $45 | Total liabilities and equity | $45 |

The bank experiences a run on its deposits after it declares that it will write off $10 million of its loans as a result of nonpayment. The bank has the option of meeting the withdrawals by first drawing down its cash and then selling off its loans. A fire sale of the remaining loans in one day can be accomplished at a 10 percent discount. They can be sold at a 5 percent discount if they are sold in two days. The full market value will be obtained if they are sold after two days.

a. What is the amount of loss to the insured depositors if a run on the bank occurs on the first day? On the second day?

b. What amount do the uninsured depositors lose if the FDIC uses the insured depositor transfer method to close the bank immediately? The assets will be sold in two days.

19. A bank with insured deposits of $55 million and uninsured deposits of $45 million has assets valued at only $75 million. What is the cost of failure resolution to insured depositors, uninsured depositors, and the FDIC if an insured depositor transfer method is used?

20. A commercial bank has $150 million in assets at book value. The insured and uninsured deposits are valued at $75 million and $50 million, respectively,

and the book value of equity is $25 million. As a result of loan defaults, the market value of the assets has decreased to $120 million. What is the cost of failure resolution to insured depositors, uninsured depositors, shareholders, and the FDIC if an insured depositor transfer method is used?

21. In what ways did FDICIA enhance the regulatory discipline to help reduce moral hazard behavior? What has the operational impact of these directives been?

22. Match the following policies with their intended consequences:
    *Policies:*
    a. Lower FDIC insurance levels
    b. Stricter reporting standards
    c. Risk-based deposit insurance
    *Consequences:*
    1. Increased stockholder discipline
    2. Increased depositor discipline
    3. Increased regulator discipline

23. How does the Federal Reserve's discount window serve as an alternative to deposit insurance as a lender of last resort facility to financial institutions? What changes occurred in 2008 that expanded the scope of coverage for the Fed's discount window?

24. Why is access to the discount window of the Fed less of a deterrent to DI runs than deposit insurance?

25. How do insurance guaranty funds differ from deposit insurance? What impact do these differences have on the incentive for insurance policyholders to engage in a contagious run on an insurance company?

26. What was the purpose of the establishment of the Pension Benefit Guaranty Corporation (PBGC)?
    a. How does the PBGC differ from the FDIC in its ability to control risk?
    b. How were the 1994 Retirement Protection Act and the Deficit Reduction Act of 2005 expected to reduce the deficits experienced by the PBGC?

The following questions and problems are based on material in Appendix 19A to the chapter.

27. What changes did the Federal Deposit Insurance Reform Act of 2005 make to the deposit insurance assessment scheme for DIs?

28. Under the Federal Deposit Insurance Reform Act of 2005, how is a Category I deposit insurance premium determined?

29. Webb Bank has a composite CAMELS rating of 2, a total risk-based capital ratio of 10.2 percent, a Tier 1 risk-based capital ratio of 5.2 percent, and a Tier I leverage ratio of 4.8 percent. What deposit insurance risk category does the bank fall into, and what is the bank's deposit insurance assessment rate?

30. Million Bank has a composite CAMELS rating of 2, a total risk-based capital ratio of 9.8 percent, a Tier I risk-based capital ratio of 5.8 percent, and a Tier I leverage ratio of 4.9 percent. The average total assets of the bank equal $500 million and average Tier I equity equal $24.5 million. What deposit insurance risk category does the bank fall into? What is the bank's deposit insurance assessment rate and the dollar value of deposit insurance premiums?

31. Two depository institutions have composite CAMELS ratings of 1 or 2 and are "well capitalized." Thus, each institution falls into the FDIC Risk Category I

deposit insurance assessment scheme. Further, the institutions have the following financial ratios and CAMELS ratings:

|  | Institution A | Institution B |
|---|---|---|
| Tier I leverage ratio (%) | 8.62 | 7.75 |
| Loans past due 30–89 days/ gross assets (%) | 0.45 | 0.56 |
| Nonperforming assets/gross assets (%) | 0.35 | 0.50 |
| Net loan charge-offs/gross assets (%) | 0.28 | 0.32 |
| Net income before taxes/risk-weighted assets (%) | 2.15 | 1.86 |
| Adjusted brokered deposits ratio (%) | 0.00 | 15.56 |
| *CAMELS Components:* |  |  |
| C | 1 | 1 |
| A | 2 | 2 |
| M | 1 | 2 |
| E | 2 | 3 |
| L | 1 | 1 |
| S | 2 | 1 |

Calculate the initial deposit insurance assessment for each institution.

32. Two depository institutions have composite CAMELS ratings of 1 or 2 and are "well capitalized." Thus, each institution falls into the FDIC Risk Category I deposit insurance assessment scheme. Institution A has average total assets of $750 million and average Tier I equity of $75 million. Institution B has average total assets of $1 billion and average Tier I equity of $110 million. Institution A has no unsecured debt or brokered deposits. Institution B has no unsecured debt and an asset growth rate over the last four years of 8 percent. Further, the institutions have the following financial ratios and CAMELS ratings:

|  | Institution A | Institution B |
|---|---|---|
| Tier I leverage ratio (%) | 10.25 | 7.00 |
| Loans past due 30–89 days/ gross assets (%) | 0.60 | 0.82 |
| Nonperforming assets/gross assets (%) | 0.45 | 0.90 |
| Net loan charge-offs/gross assets (%) | 0.08 | 0.25 |
| Net income before taxes/ risk-weighted assets (%) | 2.40 | 1.65 |
| Adjusted brokered deposits ratio (%) | 0.00 | 25.89 |
| *CAMELS Components:* |  |  |
| C | 1 | 2 |
| A | 1 | 1 |
| M | 1 | 1 |
| E | 2 | 1 |
| L | 1 | 3 |
| S | 2 | 3 |

Calculate the initial deposit insurance assessment and the dollar value of the deposit insurance premium for each institution.

## Web Questions

33. Go to the FDIC website at **www.fdic.gov**. Click on "Analysts." Click on "FDIC Quarterly Banking Profile." Click on "Quarterly Banking Profile." Click on "Deposit Insurance Fund Trends." Click on "Table II-B. Failed/Assisted Institutions." In this file find the most recent information on failed banks and thrifts. How has the number of depository institution failures changed since 2012?
34. Go to the Federal Reserve Board's website at **www.federalreserve.gov** and click on "Economic Research and Data." Click on "Selected Interest Rate." Click on the most recent date. In this file find the most recent values for the fed funds rate and the discount window rate. What is the percentage increase or decrease in these rates since 2012?

## Appendix   19A

# Calculation of Deposit Insurance Premiums

The Federal Deposit Insurance Reform Act of 2005 instituted a deposit insurance premium scheme, effective January 1, 2007 and revised in April 2009 and April 2011, that combined examination ratings, financial ratios, and, for large banks (with total assets greater than $10 billion), long-term debt issuer ratings. The new rules consolidate the existing nine risk categories into four, named Risk Categories I through IV, as listed in Table 19A–1. Risk Category I contains all well-capitalized institutions in Supervisory Group A (generally those with CAMELS composite ratings of 1 or 2). Risk Category II contains all institutions in Supervisory Groups A and B (generally those with CAMELS composite ratings of 1, 2, or 3), except those in Risk Category I and undercapitalized institutions. Risk Category III contains all undercapitalized institutions in Supervisory Groups A and B and institutions in Supervisory Group C (generally those with CAMELS composite ratings of 4 or 5) that are not undercapitalized. Risk Category IV contains all undercapitalized institutions in Supervisory Group C. Once a risk category is determined, the assessment rate for the category is multiplied by the institution's assessment base. The assessment base is the FI's average consolidated total assets less the average tangible equity (Tier I capital).

A well-capitalized institution is one that satisfies each of the following capital ratio standards: total risk-based ratio, 10 percent or greater; Tier I risk-based ratio, 6 percent or greater and Tier I leverage ratio, 5 percent or greater (as defined in Chapter 20). An adequately capitalized institution is one that does not satisfy the standards of well capitalized but satisfies each of the following capital ratio standards: total risk-based ratio, 8 percent or greater; Tier I risk-based ratio, 4 percent or greater; and Tier I leverage ratio, 4 percent or greater. An undercapitalized institution is one that does not qualify as either well capitalized or adequately capitalized.

Within Risk Category I, the final rule combines CAMELS component ratings with financial ratios to determine an institution's assessment rate. For large institutions that have long-term debt issuer ratings, the final rule differentiates risk by combining CAMELS component ratings with these debt ratings. For Risk Category I institutions, each of six financial ratio component ratings will be multiplied by a corresponding pricing multiplier, as listed in Table 19A–2. The six financial ratios are Tier I leverage ratio, loans past due 30–89 days/gross assets, nonperforming assets/gross assets, net loan charge-offs/gross assets, net income before taxes/risk-weighted assets, and adjusted

**TABLE 19A–1**
New Risk Categories and Initial Assessment Rates for FDIC Insurance (assessment rates are in basis points)

Source: FDIC, *Federal Registar,* February 25, 2011. *www.fdic.gov*

| Panel A: Risk Category | | | |
|---|---|---|---|
| | **Supervisory Group** | | |
| **Capital Group** | **A** | **B** | **C** |
| Well capitalized | I | II | III |
| Adequately capitalized | II | II | III |
| Undercapitalized | III | III | IV |

| Panel B: Assessment Rate | | | | | |
|---|---|---|---|---|---|
| | **Risk Category** | | | | |
| | I | | | | |
| | **Minimum** | **Maximum** | **II** | **III** | **IV** |
| Annual rates | 5 | 9 | 14 | 23 | 35 |

**TABLE 19A–2**
FDIC Insurance Premium Price Multipliers for Financial Ratios

Source: FDIC, *Federal Register,* February 25, 2011. *www.fdic.gov*

| Risk Measures* | Pricing Multipliers† |
|---|---|
| Tier I leverage ratio | (0.056) |
| Loans past due 30–89 days/gross assets | 0.575 |
| Nonperforming assets/gross assets | 1.074 |
| Net loan charge-offs/gross assets | 1.210 |
| Net income before taxes/risk-weighted assets | (0.764) |
| Adjusted brokered deposit ratio | 0.065 |
| Weighted-average CAMELS component rating | 1.095 |

\* Ratios are expressed in percentages.
† Multipliers are rounded to three decimal places.

brokered deposits ratio. The weighted average of CAMELS component ratings is created by multiplying each component by a stated percentage, as listed in Table 19A–3, and adding the products. As of April 2009, the adjusted brokered deposit ratio was added to the list of financial ratios to measure the extent to which brokered deposits fund rapid asset growth. The ratio is equal to brokered deposits (less reciprocal brokered deposits) divided by domestic deposits less 0.10 multiplied by the asset growth rate factor (four-year cumulative asset growth rate [expressed as a number rather than as a percentage] multiplied by $3\frac{1}{3}$ and then reduced by $1\frac{1}{3}$).[1] Table 19A–4 shows examples of how the adjusted brokered deposit ratio would be calculated. The sum of these products will be added to

**TABLE 19A–3**
**CAMELS Component Weights**

Source: FDIC, *Federal Register,* February 25, 2011. *www.fdic.gov*

| CAMELS Component | Weight |
|---|---|
| C | 25% |
| A | 20 |
| M | 25 |
| E | 10 |
| L | 10 |
| S | 10 |

or subtracted from a uniform amount, set at 4.861 as of April 1, 2011.[2] The resulting sum will equal an institution's initial assessment rate.

Large and highly complex institutions have a slightly different numeric used to calculate the assessment rates. The score card for these institutions focuses more on the risk of the institution and differentiates risk during periods of good economic conditions and during periods of stress and downturns. The models also better take into account the losses the FDIC may incur if a large institution fails. A large institution is an institution with assets of at least $10 billion as of December 2006 and not classified as a highly complex institution (approximately 50 of the more than 7,300 institutions in 2012). A highly complex institution (approximately 40 institutions in 2012) is defined

[1] If an institution's ratio of brokered deposits to domestic deposits is 10 percent *or* less or if the institution's asset growth over the previous four years is less than 40 percent, the adjusted brokered deposit ratio will be zero and will have no effect on the institution's assessment rate. If an institution's ratio of brokered deposits to domestic deposits exceeds 10 percent, and its asset growth over the previous four years is more than 70, the adjusted brokered deposit ratio will equal the institution's ratio of brokered deposits to domestic deposits less the 10 percent threshold. If an institution's ratio of brokered deposits to domestic deposits exceeds 10 percent but its asset growth over the previous four years is between 40 percent and 70 percent, overall asset growth rates will be converted into an asset growth rate factor ranging between 0 and 1, so that the adjusted brokered deposit ratio will equal a gradually increasing fraction of the ratio of brokered deposits to domestic deposits (minus the 10 percent threshold). The asset growth rate factor is derived by multiplying by $3\frac{1}{3}$ an amount equal to the overall rate of growth (e.g., 55.0%) minus 40 percent (e.g., 15%) and expressing the result as a decimal fraction rather than as a percentage (so that, for example, $3\frac{1}{3}$ times 15 percent equals 0.500). The adjusted brokered deposit ratio will never be less than zero.

[2] The uniform amount is set based on the size of the FDIC reserve ratio. When the reserve ratio is equal to or less than 1.15 percent, the uniform amount is set at 4.861. As the reserve ratio increases above 1.15, the uniform amount decreases.

**TABLE 19A–4**
Adjusted Brokered Deposit Ratio

| A Example | B Ratio of Brokered Deposits to Domestic Deposits | C Ratio of Brokered Deposits to Domestic Deposits minus 10 Percent Threshold (Column B minus 10 Percent) | D Cumulative Asset Growth Rate over Four Years | E Asset Growth Rate Factor | F Adjusted Brokered Deposit Ratio (Column C times Column E) |
|---|---|---|---|---|---|
| 1 | 5.0% | 0.0% | 5.0% | — | 0.0% |
| 2 | 15.0% | 5.0% | 5.0% | — | 0.0% |
| 3 | 5.0% | 0.0% | 35.0% | — | 0.0% |
| 4 | 35.0% | 25.0% | 55.0% | 0.500 | 12.5% |
| 5 | 25.0% | 15.0% | 80.0% | 1.000 | 15.0% |

by the FDIC as (1) an insured depository institution (excluding a credit card bank) with greater than $50 billion in total assets that is wholly owned by a parent company with more than $500 billion in total assets, or wholly owned by one or more intermediate parent companies that are wholly owned by a holding company with more than $500 billion in assets, or (2) a processing bank and trust company with greater than $10 billion in total assets, provided that the information required to calculate assessment rates as a highly complex institution is readily available to the FDIC.

After applying all possible adjustments, minimum and maximum total base assessment rates for each risk category are set as listed in Table 19A–5. The unsecured debt adjustment is determined by multiplying an institution's unsecured debt as a percent of domestic deposits. The base assessment may also increase, depending on its ratio of secured liabilities to domestic deposits (secured liability adjustment). Finally, for institutions in Categories II, III, and IV, the assessment rate may increase based on the amount of brokered deposits to domestic deposits.

**TABLE 19A–5**
Total Base Assessment Rates

| | Risk Category I | Risk Category II | Risk Category III | Risk Category IV |
|---|---|---|---|---|
| Initial base assessment rate | 5–9 | 14 | 23 | 35 |
| Unsecured debt adjustment | −4.5–0 | −5–0 | −5–0 | −5–0 |
| Brokered deposit adjustment | | 0–10 | 0–10 | 0–10 |
| Total base assessment rate | 2.5–9 | 9–24 | 18–33 | 30–45 |

* All amounts for all risk categories are in basis points annually. Total base rates that are not the minimum or maximum rate will vary between these rates.

**EXAMPLE 19A–1**

*Calculating Insurance Assessment Rates for Depository Institutions*

Three depository institutions have composite CAMELS ratings of 1 or 2 and are "well capitalized." Thus, each institution falls into the FDIC Risk Category I deposit insurance assessment scheme. Further, the three institutions have the following financial ratios and CAMELS ratings:

|  | Institution A | Institution B | Institution C |
|---|---|---|---|
| Tier I leverage ratio (%) | 9.590 | 8.570 | 7.500 |
| Loans past due 30–89 days/gross assets (%) | 0.400 | 0.600 | 1.000 |
| Nonperforming assets/gross assets (%) | 0.200 | 0.400 | 1.500 |
| Net loan charge-offs/ gross assets (%) | 0.147 | 0.079 | 0.300 |
| Net income before taxes/risk-weighted assets (%) | 2.500 | 1.951 | 0.518 |
| Adjusted brokered deposit ratio (%) | 0.000 | 12.827 | 24.355 |
| Weighted-average CAMELS component ratings | 1.200 | 1.450 | 2.100 |

To determine the deposit insurance initial assessment for each institution, we set up the following table:

**Initial Base Assessment Rates for Three Institutions**

| (1) | (2) | Institution A | | Institution B | | Institution C | |
|---|---|---|---|---|---|---|---|
|  |  | (3) | (4) | (5) | (6) | (7) | (8) |
|  | Pricing Multiplier | Risk Measure Value | Contribution to Assessment Rate | Risk Measure Value | Contribution to Assessment Rate | Risk Measure Value | Contribution to Assessment Rate |
| Uniform amount | 4.861 |  | 4.861 |  | 4.861 |  | 4.861 |
| Tier I leverage ratio (%) | (0.056) | 9.590 | (0.537) | 8.570 | (0.480) | 7.500 | (0.420) |
| Loans past due 30–89 days/gross assets (%) | 0.575 | 0.400 | 0.230 | 0.600 | 0.345 | 1.000 | 0.575 |
| Nonperforming assets/ gross assets (%) | 1.074 | 0.200 | 0.215 | 0.400 | 0.430 | 1.500 | 1.611 |
| Net loan charge-offs/ gross assets (%) | 1.210 | 0.147 | 0.177 | 0.079 | 0.096 | 0.300 | 0.363 |
| Net income before taxes/risk-weighted assets (%) | (0.764) | 2.500 | (1.910) | 1.951 | (1.491) | 0.518 | (0.396) |
| Adjusted brokered deposits ratio (%) | 0.065 | 0.000 | 0.000 | 12.827 | 0.834 | 24.355 | 1.583 |
| Weighted-average CAMELS component rating | 1.095 | 1.200 | 1.314 | 1.450 | 1.588 | 2.100 | 2.300 |
| Sum of contributions |  |  | 4.350 |  | 6.18 |  | 10.480 |
| Assessment rate |  |  | 5.000 |  | 6.18 |  | 9.000 |

The initial assessment rate for the three institutions in the table is calculated by multiplying the pricing multipliers [see column (2)] by the risk measure values [column (3), (5), or (7)] to produce each measure's contribution to the assessment rate. The sum of the products [column (4), (6), or (8)] plus the uniform amount, 4.861, gives the initial assessment rate. For institution A, this sum is 4.35. However, the table lists the minimum assessment rate for Category I banks of 5 basis points. For institution C, the sum is 10.48. However, the table lists the maximum assessment rate of 9 basis points.

## Appendix 19B: FDIC Press Release of Bank Failures

View Appendix 19B at the website for this textbook (www.mhhe.com/saunders8e).

## Appendix 19C: Deposit Insurance Coverage for Commercial Banks in Various Countries

View Appendix 19C at the website for this textbook (www.mhhe.com/saunders8e).

# Chapter **Twenty**

See Appendices Online at www.mhhe.com/saunders8e
- Appendix 20B: Methodology Used to Determine G-SIBs' Capital Surcharge

# Capital Adequacy

## INTRODUCTION

Chapters 7 through 17 examined the major areas of risk exposure facing an FI manager. These risks can emanate from both on- and off-balance-sheet (OBS) activities and can be either domestic or international in source. To ensure survival, an FI manager needs to protect the institution against the risk of insolvency, that is, shield it from risks sufficiently large to cause the institution to fail. The primary means of protection against the risk of insolvency and failure is an FI's capital. This leads to the first function of capital, namely:

1. To absorb unanticipated losses with enough margin to inspire confidence and enable the FI to continue as a going concern.

   In addition, capital protects nonequity liability holders—especially those uninsured by an external guarantor such as the FDIC—against losses. This leads to the second function of capital:

2. To protect uninsured depositors, bondholders, and creditors in the event of insolvency, and liquidation.

   When FIs fail, regulators such as the FDIC have to intervene to protect insured claimants (see Chapter 19). The capital of an FI offers protection to insurance funds and ultimately the taxpayers who bear the cost of insurance fund insolvency. This leads to the third function of capital:

3. To protect FI insurance funds and the taxpayers.

   During the financial crisis, the FDIC's DIF incurred losses to the extent that the fund's balance was negative. As a result, the FDIC imposed a special assessment fee on the FIs it insured and required them to prepay 13 quarters worth of deposit insurance premiums. By holding capital and reducing the risk of insolvency, an FI protects the industry from larger insurance premiums. Such premiums are paid out of the net profits of the FI. Thus, a fourth function of capital is as follows:

4. To protect the FI owners against increases in insurance premiums.

   Finally, just as for any other firm, equity or capital is an important source of financing for an FI. In particular, subject to regulatory constraints, FIs have a choice between debt and equity to finance new projects and business expansion. Thus, the traditional factors that affect a business firm's choice of a capital structure—for instance, the tax deductibility of the interest on debt or the private costs of failure or insolvency—also interpose on the FI's capital decision. This leads to a fifth function of capital:

5. To fund the branch and other real investments necessary to provide financial services.[1]

Part of the TARP program of 2008–09 was the Capital Purchase Program intended to encourage U.S. financial institutions to build capital needed to increase the flow of financing to U.S. businesses and consumers and to support the U.S. economy. Under the program, the Treasury purchased more than $200 billion of preferred equity securities issued by FIs. The senior preferred shares qualified as Tier I capital and ranked senior to common stock. Financial institutions had to meet certain standards, including: (1) ensuring that incentive compensation for senior executives did not encourage unnecessary and excessive risks that threatened the value of the financial institution; (2) required payback of any bonus or incentive compensation paid to a senior executive based on statements of earnings, gains, or other criteria that were later proven to be materially inaccurate; (3) prohibition on the financial institution from making any golden parachute payment to a senior executive based on the Internal Revenue Code provision; and (4) agreement not to deduct for tax purposes executive compensation in excess of $500,000 for each senior executive. In addition to capital injections received as part of the Capital Purchase Program, TARP provided additional emergency funding to Citigroup ($25 billion) and Bank of America ($20 billion). Through August 2012, $245 billion of TARP capital injections had been allocated to DIs, of which $234 billion had been paid back plus a return of $26.25 billion in dividends and assessments.

In the following sections, we focus on the first four functions concerning the role of capital in reducing insolvency risk and in particular the adequacy of capital in attaining these functional objectives. Specifically, we examine the different measures of capital adequacy used by FI owners, managers, and regulators, and the argument for and against each. We then look at capital adequacy requirements for depository institutions, securities firms, and insurance companies set by U.S. (and, in some cases, international) regulators such as the Bank for International Settlements (BIS). Appendix 20A to the chapter describes the foundations and advanced approaches used to calculate adequate capital according to internal ratings–based models of measuring credit risk that are currently used by the BIS for banks.

www.bis.org

# CAPITAL AND INSOLVENCY RISK

## Capital

**net worth**
A measure of an FI's capital that is equal to the difference between the market value of its assets and the market value of its liabilities.

To see how capital protects an FI against insolvency risk, we must define *capital* more precisely. The problem is that there are many definitions of capital: an economist's definition of capital may differ from an accountant's definition, which, in turn, may differ from the definition used by regulators. Specifically, the economist's definition of an FI's capital or owners' equity stake in an FI is the difference between the market values of its assets and its liabilities. This is also called the **net worth** of an FI. While this is the *economic* meaning of capital, regulators have found it necessary to adopt definitions of capital that depart by a greater or lesser degree from

---

[1] A sixth function might be added. This would focus on the role of capital regulation in restraining the rate of asset growth.

economic net worth. The concept of an FI's economic net worth is really a *market value accounting concept.* With the exception of the investment banking industry, regulatory-defined capital and required capital ratios are based in whole or in part on historical or **book value** accounting concepts.

**book value**
Historical cost basis for asset and liability values.

We begin by looking at the role of economic capital or net worth as an insulation device against a major type of risk: credit risk. We then compare this market value concept with the book value concept of capital. Because it can actually distort the true solvency position of an FI, the book value of capital concept can be misleading to managers, owners, liability holders, and regulators. We also examine some possible reasons why FI regulators continue to rely on book value concepts in light of such economic value transparency problems and rulings by the Financial Accounting Standards Board (such as *FASB Statement No. 115*).

## The Market Value of Capital

**market value or mark-to-market basis**
Allowing balance sheet values to reflect current rather than historical prices.

To see how economic net worth or equity insulates an FI against risk, consider the following example. Panel A of Table 20–1 presents a simple balance sheet where all the assets and liabilities of an FI are valued in **market value** terms at current prices on a **mark-to-market basis** (see Chapter 8). On a mark-to-market or market value basis, the economic value of the FI's equity is $10 million, which is the difference between the market value of its assets and liabilities. On a market value basis, the FI is economically solvent and imposes no failure costs on depositors or regulators if it were liquidated today. Let's consider the impact of a classic type of FI risk on this FI's net worth: credit risk.

### Market Value of Capital and Credit Risk

In Panel A of Table 20–1, an FI has $20 million in long-term loans. (For simplicity, we drop the $ sign and "million" notation in the rest of the example.) Suppose that, because of a recession, a number of these borrowers get into cash flow problems and are unable to keep up their promised loan repayment schedules. A decline in the current and expected future cash flows on loans lowers the market value of the loan portfolio held by the FI below 20. Suppose that loans are really worth only 8 (the price the FI would receive if it could sell these loans in a secondary market at today's prices). This means the market value of the loan portfolio has fallen from 20 to 8. Look at the revised market value balance sheet in Panel B of Table 20–1.

**TABLE 20–1**
**An FI's Market Value Balance Sheet (in millions of dollars)**

| Panel A: Beginning Market Value Balance Sheet | | | |
|---|---|---|---|
| **Assets** | | **Liabilities** | |
| Long-term securities | $ 80 | Liabilities (short-term, floating-rate deposits) | $ 90 |
| Long-term loans | 20 | Net worth | 10 |
| | $100 | | $100 |
| **Panel B: Market Value Balance Sheet after a $12 Million Decline in Loan Portfolio Value** | | | |
| Long-term securities | $80 | Liabilities | $90 |
| Long-term loans | 8 | Net worth | −2 |
| | $88 | | $88 |

This loss renders the FI insolvent; the market value of its assets (88) is less than the value of its liabilities (90). The owners' net worth stake has been completely wiped out (reduced from 10 to −2), making net worth negative. As a result, liability holders are hurt, but only a bit. Specifically, the first 10 of the 12 loss in value of the loan portfolio is borne by the equity holders. Only after the equity holders are wiped out do the liability holders begin to lose. In this example, the economic value of their claims on the FI has fallen from 90 to 88, or a loss of 2. Note here that we are ignoring deposit insurance.[2]

This example clearly demonstrates the concept of net worth or capital as an insurance fund protecting liability holders, such as depositors, against insolvency risk. The larger the FI's net worth relative to the size of its assets, the more insolvency protection or insurance there is for liability holders and liability guarantors such as the FDIC. This is why regulators focus on capital requirements such as the ratio of net worth to assets in assessing the insolvency risk exposure of an FI and in setting risk-based deposit insurance premiums (see Chapter 19).

## The Book Value of Capital

We contrast market value or economic net worth with book value of capital or net worth. As we discuss in later sections, book value capital and capital rules based on book values are most commonly used by FI regulators. In Table 20–2, we use the same initial balance sheet we used in Table 20–1 but assume that assets and liabilities are now valued at their historical book values. That is, they reflect the values when the loans were made, the securities were purchased, and the liabilities were issued which may have been many years ago. The net worth or equity is now the book value of the stockholders' claims rather than the market value of those claims.

As the example in Table 20–2 is constructed, the book value of capital equals 10. However, invariably, the *book value of equity does not equal the market value of equity* (the difference between the market value of assets and that of liabilities). This inequality in book and market value of equity can be understood by examining the effects of the same credit risk shocks on the FI's capital position, but assuming book value accounting methods.

### Book Value of Capital and Credit Risk

Suppose that some of the 20 in loans are in difficulty regarding repayment schedules. We assumed in Panel B of Table 20–1 that the revaluation of cash flows leads to an immediate downward adjustment of the loan portfolio's market value from 20 to 8, a market value loss of 12. By contrast, under historic book value accounting methods such as generally accepted accounting principles (GAAP), FIs have

**TABLE 20–2**
Book Value of an FI's Assets and Liabilities (in millions of dollars)

| Beginning Book Value Balance Sheet | | | |
|---|---|---|---|
| **Assets** | | **Liabilities** | |
| Long-term securities | $ 80 | Short-term liabilities | $ 90 |
| Long-term loans | 20 | Net worth | 10 |
| | $100 | | $100 |

[2] In the presence of deposit insurance, the insurer, such as the FDIC, would bear some of the depositors' losses; for details, see Chapter 19.

greater discretion in reflecting or timing problem loan loss recognition on their balance sheets and thus on the impact of such losses on capital. The market value balance sheet is reflected in Panel B of Table 20–1, and the book value balance sheet is reflected in Table 20–2. Notice the book value balance sheet continues to list 10 as the value of net worth, yet the true value is −2.

## The Discrepancy between the Market and Book Values of Equity

These preceding examples show that market valuation of the balance sheet produces a more economically accurate picture of the net worth than book value accounting, and thus, the solvency position of an FI. Credit risk (and interest rate risk) shocks that result in losses in the market value of assets are borne directly by the equity holders in the sense that such losses are charges against the value of their ownership claims in the FI. As long as the owners' capital or equity stake is adequate, or sufficiently large, liability holders (and, implicitly, regulators that back the claims of liability holders) are protected against insolvency risk. That is, if an FI were closed by regulators before its economic net worth became zero, neither liability holders nor those regulators guaranteeing the claims of liability holders would stand to lose. Thus, many academics and analysts have advocated the use of market value accounting and market value of capital closure rules for all FIs.

The Financial Accounting Standards Board *FASB Statement No. 115* (effective in 1993) technically requires securities classified as "available for sale" to be marked to market. By comparison, no similar marked-to-market requirement exists on the liabilities side of the balance sheet. In 2007, FAS 157 went into effect, which mandated that assets be measured at fair value. For DIs, this meant that securities and loans held on the balance sheets had to be valued and reported according to prices being paid for similar instruments on the market. During the financial crisis, FASB clarified its position on the application of market value accounting where there are limited or no observable inputs for marking certain assets to market, as was the case with many of the mortgage-backed securities at the center of the crisis. Specifically, FASB set its guidelines to allow for the valuation of assets to be based on a price that would be received in an orderly market rather than a forced liquidation. For DIs, this meant that some asset classes, such as derivatives and marketable equity securities, are required to be carried at fair value. Valuation of other types of assets, such as loans and debt securities, depends on whether the assets are held for trading or for investment. All trading assets are carried at fair value. Loans and debt securities that are held for investment or to maturity are carried at amortized cost. The guidance did not eliminate market value accounting, but it did provide management with much more discretion with respect to applying the convention when pricing illiquid assets. This discretion included ability to use internal assumptions with respect to future cash flows, which would mean employing generally more benign estimates than what the "market" is currently imposing. The guidance specifically allows management to use internal cash flow models and assumptions to estimate fair value when there is limited market data available.

## Arguments against Market Value Accounting

The first argument against market value (MV) accounting is that it is difficult to implement. This may be especially true for small commercial banks and thrifts with large amounts of nontraded assets such as small loans on their balance sheets. When it is impossible to determine accurate market prices or values for assets, marking to market may be done only with error. A counterargument to this is that the error resulting from the use of market valuation of nontraded assets is still likely to be less than that resulting from the use of original book or historical valuation since the market value approach does not require all assets and liabilities to be traded. As long as current and expected cash flows on an asset or liability and an appropriate discount rate can be specified, approximate market values can always be imputed (see CreditMetrics, described in Appendix 11A). Further, with the growth of loan sales and asset securitization (see Chapters 25 and 26), indicative market prices are available on an increasing variety of loans.

The second argument against market value accounting is that it introduces an unnecessary degree of variability into an FI's earnings—and thus net worth—because paper capital gains and losses on assets are passed through the FI's income statement. Critics argue that reporting unrealized capital gains and losses is distortionary if the FI actually plans to hold these assets to maturity. FI managers argue that in many cases they do hold loans and other assets to maturity and, therefore, never actually realize capital gains or losses. Further, regulators have argued that they may be forced to close banks too early under the prompt corrective action requirements imposed by the FDICIA (discussed later in this chapter)—especially if an interest rate spike is only temporary and capital losses on securities can be quickly turned into capital gains as rates fall again (e.g., if interest rates are mean reverting, as much empirical evidence shows). Consistent with these arguments, and as mentioned above, in April 2009 the Financial Accounting Standards Board eased its stance on marking to market such that DIs (as well as any firm) would lessen the need to take earnings hits when asset markets are flawed. Specifically, the new FASB ruling allows DIs to avoid market losses by stating that they intend to hold the asset for the long term. The counterargument is that FIs are increasingly trading, selling, and securitizing assets rather than holding them to maturity.

The third argument against market value accounting is that FIs are less willing to accept longer-term asset exposures, such as mortgage loans and C&I loans, if these assets have to be continuously marked to market to reflect changing credit quality and interest rates. For example, as shown in Chapter 8, long-term assets are more interest rate sensitive than are short-term assets. The concern is that market value accounting may interfere with FIs' special functions as lenders and monitors (see Chapter 1) and may even result in (or accentuate) a major credit crunch. Of the three arguments against market value accounting, this one is probably the most persuasive to regulators concerned about small business finance and economic growth.

Having discussed the advantages and disadvantages of book- and market-based measures of an FI's capital, we should note that most FI regulators have chosen some form of book value accounting standard to measure an FI's capital www.sec.gov adequacy. The major exception is the Securities and Exchange Commission (SEC). Along with the NYSE and other major stock exchanges, the SEC imposes on securities firms, retail brokers, and specialists a capital or net worth rule that is, for all intents and purposes, a market value accounting rule.

Next, we examine the capital adequacy rules imposed in key FI sectors: (1) commercial banks and thrifts, (2) securities firms, (3) life insurers, and (4) PC insurers. Because many of the capital adequacy rules currently differ considerably across these sectors, the current wave of consolidation in the U.S. financial industry into financial conglomerates (or universal banks) is likely to be more difficult than it would be if market value accounting rules were adopted across all sectors. Nevertheless, there is a clear trend toward similar risk-based capital rules in the banking, thrift, and insurance (both PC and life) industries. We discuss this trend in more detail in the remainder of the chapter.

| **Concept Questions** | 1. Why is an FI economically insolvent when its net worth is negative? |
|---|---|
| | 2. Why does market value accounting produce a more accurate picture of a DI's net worth than book value accounting? |
| | 3. What are the arguments against the use of market value accounting for DIs? |

# CAPITAL ADEQUACY IN THE COMMERCIAL BANKING AND THRIFT INDUSTRY

*www.bis.org*

**Basel Agreement**
The requirement to impose risk-based capital ratios on banks in major industrialized countries.

The FDIC Improvement Act (FDICIA) of 1991 required that banks and thrifts adopt risk-based capital requirements. Consistent with this act, U.S. DI regulators formally agreed with other member countries of the Bank for International Settlements (BIS) to implement new risk-based capital ratios for all depository institutions under their jurisdiction. The BIS phased in and fully implemented these risk-based capital ratios on January 1, 1993, under what has become known as the **Basel** (or Basle) **Agreement** (now called *Basel I*). The 1993 Basel Agreement explicitly incorporated the different credit risks of assets (both on and off the balance sheet) into capital adequacy measures. This was followed with a revision in 1998 in which market risk was incorporated into risk-based capital in the form of an add-on to the 8 percent ratio for credit risk exposure (see Chapter 10). In 2001, the BIS issued a Consultative Document, "The New Basel Capital Accord," that proposed the incorporation of operational risk into capital requirements (see Chapter 17 and below) and updated the credit risk assessments in the 1993 agreement.

The new Basel Accord or Agreement (called *Basel II*) of 2006 consisted of three mutually reinforcing pillars (illustrated in Figure 20–1), which together contribute to the safety and soundness of the financial system. Pillar 1 covered regulatory minimum capital requirements for credit, market, and operational risk. The measurement of market risk did not change from that adopted in 1998. In the 2006 Accord, the BIS allowed for a range of options for addressing both credit and operational risk.[3] Two options were for the measurement of credit risk. The first is the Standardized Approach and the second is an Internal Ratings–Based (IRB) Approach. The Standardized Approach was similar to that of the 1993 agreement, but was more risk sensitive. Under the IRB Approach, DIs were allowed to use their internal estimates of borrower creditworthiness to assess credit risk in their portfolios (using their own internal rating systems and credit scoring models) subject to strict methodological and disclosure standards, as well as explicit approval by the DI's supervising regulator. Three different options were available to measure operational risk: the Basic Indicator, Standardized, and Advanced Measurement approaches. We discussed these briefly in Chapter 17 and will do so in more detail below.

---

[3] See Basel Committee on Banking Supervision, "The New Basel Capital Accord," January 2001; and "International Convergence of Capital Measurement and Capital Standards," June 2006. **www.bis.org**

**FIGURE 20–1**

Basel II and Basel III
Pillars of Capital
Regulation

**Basel II:**

| Pillar 1 | Pillar 2 | Pillar 3 |
|---|---|---|
| Calculation of regulatory minimum capital requirements | Regulatory supervisory review so as to complement and enforce minimum capital requirements calculated under Pillar 1 | Requirements on rules for disclosure of capital structure, risk exposures, and capital adequacy so as to increase FI transparency and enhance market/investor discipline |

1. Credit risk: on-balance-sheet and off-balance-sheet (Standardized vs. Internal Ratings–Based Approach)

2. Market risk (Standardized vs. Internal Ratings–Based Approach)

3. Operational risk (Basic Indicator vs. Standardized vs. Advanced Measurement Approach)

**Basel III:**

| | | |
|---|---|---|
| Enhanced minimum capital and liquidity requirements | Enhanced supervisory review for firmwide risk management and capital planning | Enhanced risk disclosure and market discipline |

1. Liquidity risk

In Pillar 2, the BIS stressed the importance of the regulatory supervisory review process as a critical complement to minimum capital requirements. Specifically, Basel II created procedures through which regulators ensure that each DI has sound internal processes in place to assess the adequacy of its capital and set targets for capital that are commensurate with the DI's specific risk profile and control environment. In Pillar 3, the BIS sought to encourage market discipline by developing a set of requirements on the disclosure of capital structure, risk exposures, and capital adequacy. Such disclosure requirements allow market participants to assess critical information describing the risk profile and capital adequacy of DIs.

The financial crisis of 2008–09 revealed weaknesses with Basel II. For example, ratings of credit risk on various securities, such as credit default swaps, were conducted by private companies without the supervision or review by official regulatory agencies. Further, the Basel II capital adequacy formula for credit risk was procyclical. Thus, as the financial crisis developed, the probability of borrower default and loss on default both increased, which meant that regulatory capital requirements increased. However, during the crisis, banks were unable to raise the required capital and thus had to turn to central banks for capital injections and liquidity support.

In response to these issues, Basel 2.5 was passed in 2009 (effective in 2013) and Basel III was passed in 2010 (fully effective in 2019). Basel 2.5 updates capital requirements on market risk from banks' trading operations (discussed in Chapter 15).

The goal of Basel III is to raise the quality, consistency, and transparency of the capital base of banks to withstand credit risk and to strengthen the risk coverage of the capital framework. Specifically, as shown in Figure 20–1, Pillar 1 of Basel III calls for enhancements to both the Standardized Approach, discussed below, and the IRB Approach, discussed in Appendix 20A to this chapter, to calculating adequate capital. Changes to Pillar I include a greater focus on common equity, the inclusion of new capital conservation and countercyclical buffers (discussed below) to the minimum level of capital, significantly higher capital requirements for trading and derivatives activities, and a substantial strengthening of counterparty credit risk calculations in determining required minimum capital. Pillar 2 calls for enhanced bankwide governance and risk management to be put in place, such as enhanced incentives for banks to better manage risk and returns over the long term, more stress testing, and implementation of sound compensation practices. Pillar 3 calls for the enhanced disclosure of risks, such as those relating to securitization exposures and sponsorship of off-balance-sheet vehicles.

Basel III is applicable to all U.S. national banks, state member and nonmember banks, state and federal savings associations, state and federal credit unions, all U.S. bank holding companies except those with less than $500 million in total consolidated assets (although the rules apply to the subsidiary banks of these small holding companies), and all U.S. savings association holding companies. Advanced (IRB) approaches may be used by institutions with consolidated assets of $250 billion or more or with consolidated on-balance-sheet foreign exposures of $10 billion or more (approximately 20 of the largest U.S. banking organizations). All other depository institutions use the Standardized Approach for calculating capital adequacy. Under Basel III, depository institutions must calculate and monitor four capital ratios: common equity Tier I (CET1) risk-based capital ratio, Tier I risk-based capital ratio, total risk-based capital ratio, and Tier I leverage ratio. U.S. regulators currently are phasing in the Basel III capital ratios and they will be fully implemented by 2019 (see Table 20–3). The calculation of these capital adequacy measures is quite complex. Their major innovation is to distinguish among the different credit risks of assets on the balance sheet and to identify the credit risk inherent in instruments off the balance sheet by using a risk-adjusted assets denominator in these capital adequacy ratios. In a very rough fashion, these capital ratios mark to market a DI's on- and off-balance-sheet positions to reflect its credit risk. Further, additional capital charges must be held against market risk and operational risk.

Since the passage of the FDICIA in 1991, a DI's capital adequacy is assessed according to where its capital ratios place in one of the five target zones listed in Table 20–4. Under Basel III, the capital ratios used include:

**common equity Tier I risk-based capital ratio**
The ratio of the common equity Tier I capital to the risk-adjusted assets of the DI.

**Tier I risk-based capital ratio**
The ratio of the Tier I capital to the risk-adjusted assets of the DI.

**total risk-based capital ratio**
The ratio of the total capital to the risk-adjusted assets of the DI.

$$\text{Common equity Tier I risk-based capital ratio} = \text{Common equity Tier I capital}/\text{Credit risk-adjusted assets}$$

$$\text{Tier I risk-based capital ratio} = \text{Tier I capital (Common equity Tier I capital + Additional Tier I capital)}/\text{Credit risk-adjusted assets}$$

$$\text{Total risk-based capital ratio} = \text{Total capital (Tier I + Tier II)}/\text{Credit risk-adjusted assets}$$

$$\text{Tier I leverage ratio} = \text{Tier I capital}/\text{Total exposure.}$$

Once the ratios are fully phased in (in 2019, see Table 20–3), to be adequately capitalized, a DI must hold a minimum ratio of common equity Tier I capital to

**TABLE 20–3** Phase-in of Basel III Capital Levels

| | 2011 2012 | 2013 | 2014 | 2015 | 2016 | 2017 | 2018 | As of 1 January 2019 |
|---|---|---|---|---|---|---|---|---|
| Leverage ratio | Supervisory monitoring | Parallel run January 1, 2013–January 1, 2017. Disclosure starts January 1, 2015 | | | | | Migration to Pillar 1 | |
| Minimum CET1 capital ratio | | 3.5% | 4.0% | 4.5% | 4.5% | 4.5% | 4.5% | **4.5%** |
| Capital conservation buffer | | | | | 0.625 | 1.25 | 1.875 | **2.50** |
| Minimum CET1 plus capital conservation buffer | | 3.5 | 4.0 | 4.5 | 5.125 | 5.75 | 6.375 | **7.0** |
| Minimum Tier I capital | | 4.5 | 5.5 | 6.0 | 6.0 | 6.0 | 6.0 | **6.0** |
| Minimum Tier I plus capital conservation buffer | | 4.5 | 5.5 | 6.0 | 6.625 | 7.25 | 7.875 | **8.50** |
| Minimum total capital | | 8.0 | 8.0 | 8.0 | 8.0 | 8.0 | 8.0 | **8.0** |
| Minimum total capital plus conservation buffer | | 8.0 | 8.0 | 8.0 | 8.625 | 9.25 | 9.875 | **10.5** |
| Maximum potential countercyclical capital buffer | | | | | 0.625 | 1.25 | 1.875 | **2.50** |

**TABLE 20–4** Specifications of Capital Categories for Prompt Corrective Action

| Zone | (1) Common Equity Tier I Risk-Based Ratio | | (2) Tier I Risk-Based Ratio | | (3) Total Risk-Based Ratio | | (4) Leverage Ratio | | Capital Directive/ Other |
|---|---|---|---|---|---|---|---|---|---|
| 1. Well capitalized | 6.5% or above | and | 8% or above | and | 10% or above | and | 5% or above | and | Not subject to a capital directive to meet a specific level for any capital measure |
| 2. Adequately capitalized | 4.5% or above | and | 6% or above | and | 8% or above | and | 4% or above | and | Does not meet the definition of well capitalized |
| 3. Undercapitalized | Under 4.5% | or | Under 6% | or | Under 8% | or | Under 4% | | |
| 4. Significantly undercapitalized | Under 3% | or | Under 4% | or | Under 6% | or | Under 3% | | |
| 5. Critically undercapitalized | Tangible equity/Total assets ≤ 2% | | | | | | | | |

credit risk-adjusted assets of 4.5 percent, Tier I capital to credit risk-adjusted assets of 6 percent, total capital to credit risk-adjusted assets of 8 percent, and Tier I capital to total exposure of 4 percent.

In addition to their use in defining adequately capitalized DIs, these capital ratios also define well capitalized, undercapitalized, significantly undercapitalized, and critically undercapitalized as part of the prompt corrective action program under the FDICIA. These five zones—specified in Table 20–4—assess capital adequacy and the actions regulators are mandated to take and those they have the discretion to take. Since December 18, 1992, under the FDICIA legislation, regulators must take specific actions—**prompt corrective action (PCA)**—when a DI falls outside the zone 1, or well-capitalized, category. Table 20–5 summarizes these regulatory actions. Most important, a receiver must be appointed when a DIs tangible equity (Tier I + Non-Tier I perpetual preferred stock) to total assets ratio falls to 2 percent or less. That is, receivership is mandatory even before the book value ratio falls to 0 percent. Between 1994 and June 2008, less than 0.5 percent of depository institution industry assets were classified as critically undercapitalized. This compares with 31.3 percent critically undercapitalized in the fourth quarter of 1990 (i.e., during the 1989–91 recession) and 2.25 percent in June 2009 (during the much deeper recession in the late 2000s).

The idea behind the mandatory and discretionary set of actions to be taken by regulators for each of the capital adequacy zones is to enforce minimum capital requirements and limit the ability of regulators to show forbearance to the worst

**prompt corrective action**
Mandatory actions that have to be taken by regulators as a DI's capital ratio falls.

**TABLE 20–5**   **Summary of Prompt Corrective Action Provisions**

| Zone | Mandatory Provisions | Discretionary Provisions |
|---|---|---|
| 1. Well capitalized | | |
| 2. Adequately capitalized | 1. No brokered deposits except with FDIC approval | |
| 3. Undercapitalized | 1. Suspend dividends and management fees | 1. Order recapitalization |
| | 2. Require capital restoration plan | 2. Restrict interaffiliate transactions |
| | 3. Restrict asset growth | 3. Restrict deposit interest rates |
| | 4. Approval required for acquisitions, branching, and new activities | 4. Restrict certain other activities |
| | 5. No brokered deposits | 5. Any other action that would better carry out prompt corrective action |
| 4. Significantly undercapitalized | 1. Same as for Zone 3 | 1. Any Zone 3 discretionary actions |
| | 2. Order recapitalization* | 2. Conservatorship or receivership if fails to submit or implement plan or recapitalize pursuant to order |
| | 3. Restrict interaffiliate transactions* | 3. Any other Zone 5 provisions if such action is necessary to carry out prompt corrective action |
| | 4. Restrict deposit interest rates* | |
| | 5. Pay of officers restricted | |
| 5. Critically undercapitalized | 1. Same as for Zone 4 | |
| | 2. Receiver/conservator within 90 days* | |
| | 3. Receiver if still in Zone 5 four quarters after becoming critically undercapitalized | |
| | 4. Suspend payments on subordinated debt* | |
| | 5. Restrict certain other activities | |

\* Not required if primary supervisor determines action would not serve purpose of prompt corrective action or if certain other conditions are met.

capitalized DIs. Analysts blame such forbearance and regulator discretion for the size of the losses born by taxpayers due to the widespread collapse of thrifts and the Federal Savings and Loan Insurance Corporation (FSLIC) in the 1980s and the technical insolvency of the FDIC in 1991 (see Chapter 19). In contrast to the forbearance seen in the 1980s, regulators acted quickly to ensure the largest DIs had sufficient capital to withstand large losses during the financial crisis of 2008–09. In late February 2009, the Obama administration announced that it would conduct a "stress test" of the 19 largest U.S. FIs that would measure the ability of these FIs to withstand a protracted economic slump: unemployment rate above 10 percent and home prices dropping another 25 percent. (This stress test focused more on leverage and tangible capital than on risk-based capital, discussed below.) Results of the stress test (reported in Table 20–6) showed that 10 of the 19 FIs needed to raise a total of $74.6 billion in capital. Within a month of the May 7, 2009, release of the results, the FIs had raised $149.45 billion of capital.

In addition to this initial stress test, as part of the 2010 Wall Street Reform and Consumer Protection Act, the largest banks are subject to annual stress tests, designed to ensure that the banks are properly capitalized. Scenarios used as part of the stress test range from mild to calamitous, with the most extreme including a 5 percent decline in gross domestic product, an unemployment rate of 12 percent, and a volatile stock market which loses half its value. As part of the 2013 stress tests, the worst-case scenarios include international events, i.e., the eurozone plunges into recession and a sharp slowdown in China spills into neighboring countries.

**TABLE 20–6**  Stress Test Results for the 19 Largest U.S FIs, May 2009 ($ values in billions)

| Bank | Total Assets | Worst-Case Loss Estimate | Capital Needed | Capital Raised* |
|---|---|---|---|---|
| Bank of America | $1,600.0 | $136.6 | $33.90 | $30.30 |
| Wells Fargo | 1,100.0 | 86.1 | 13.70 | 8.60 |
| GMAC | 172.7 | 9.2 | 11.50 | 3.50 |
| Citigroup | 996.2 | 104.7 | 5.50 | 70.00 |
| Regions Financial | 116.3 | 9.2 | 2.50 | 2.09 |
| SunTrust | 162.0 | 11.8 | 2.20 | 2.08 |
| Morgan Stanley | 310.6 | 19.7 | 1.80 | 8.00 |
| KeyCorp | 106.7 | 6.7 | 1.80 | 1.30 |
| Fifth Third Bancorp | 112.6 | 9.1 | 1.10 | 0.75 |
| PNC | 250.9 | 18.8 | 0.60 | 0.60 |
| J.P. Morgan Chase | 1,300.0 | 97.4 | 0.00 | 5.00 |
| Goldman Sachs | 444.8 | 17.8 | 0.00 | 7.65 |
| MetLife | 326.4 | 9.6 | 0.00 | 0.00 |
| U.S. Bancorp | 230.6 | 15.7 | 0.00 | 2.40 |
| Bank of New York Mellon | 115.8 | 5.4 | 0.00 | 1.20 |
| State Street | 69.6 | 8.2 | 0.00 | 2.23 |
| Capital One Financial | 131.8 | 13.4 | 0.00 | 1.55 |
| BB&T | 109.8 | 8.7 | 0.00 | 1.70 |
| American Express | 104.4 | 11.2 | 0.00 | 0.50 |

* As of June 4, 2009.

## Capital

In the measurement of a DI's capital adequacy, its capital is the standard by which each of these risks is measured. Under Basel III, a DI's capital is divided into common equity Tier I (CET1), additional Tier I, and Tier II. CET1 is primary or core capital of the DI; Tier I capital is the primary capital of the DI plus additional capital elements; Tier II capital is supplementary capital. The total capital that the DI holds is defined as the sum of Tier I and Tier II capitals. The definitions of CET1, additional Tier I capital, and Tier II supplementary capital are listed in Table 20–7.

### *Tier I Capital*

Common equity Tier I capital is closely linked to a DI's book value of equity, reflecting the concept of the core capital contribution of a DI's owners.[4] CET1

**TABLE 20–7**   **Summary Definition of Qualifying Capital for Depository Institutions**

Source: "Basel III: A Global Regulatory Framework for More Resilient Banks and Banking Systems," Bank for International Settlements, June 2011, *www.bis.org*

### *Common Equity Tier I Capital (CET1)*

- Common shares issued by the bank and stock surplus that meets the criteria for classification as common shares for regulatory purposes.
- Retained earnings.
- Accumulated other comprehensive income and other disclosed reserves.*
- Common shares issued by consolidated subsidiaries of the bank and held by third parties (i.e., minority interest) that meet the criteria for inclusion in common equity Tier I capital.
- Less goodwill.
- Regulatory adjustments applied in the calculation of common equity Tier I.

### *Additional Tier I Capital*

- Instruments with no maturity dates or incentives to redeem, but may be callable by issuer after 5 years only if replace instrument with "better" capital.
- Noncumulative perpetual preferred stock and related surplus.
- Tier I minority interest, not included in the banking organization's common equity Tier I capital.
- Instruments that currently qualify as Tier I capital under the agencies' general risk-based capital rules and that were issued under the Small Business Jobs Act of 2010, or, prior to October 4, 2010, under the Emergency Economic Stabilization Act of 2008.
- Regulatory adjustments applied in the calculation of additional Tier I capital.

### *Tier II Capital*

- Instruments subordinated to depositors and general creditors of the bank.
- Subordinated debt and preferred stock.
- Total capital minority interest, not included in the banking organization's Tier I capital.
- Allowance for loan and lease losses not exceeding 1.25 percent of the banking organization's total risk-weighted assets.
- Instruments that currently qualify as Tier II capital under the agencies' general risk-based capital rules and that were issued under the Small Business Jobs Act of 2010, or, prior to October 4, 2010, under the Emergency Economic Stabilization Act of 2008.
- Regulatory adjustments applied in the calculation of Tier II capital.

* For example, unrealized gains on AFS equity securities, losses related to defined benefit pension obligations.

[4] However, loan loss reserves are assigned to Tier II capital because they often reflect losses that have already occurred rather than losses or insolvency risks that may occur in the future.

capital consists of the equity funds available to absorb losses. Basically, it includes the book value of common equity plus minority equity interests held by the DI in subsidiaries minus goodwill. Goodwill is an accounting item that reflects the amount a DI pays above market value when it purchases or acquires other DIs or subsidiaries.

### Tier I Capital

Tier I capital is the sum of CET1 capital and additional Tier I capital. Included in additional Tier I capital are other options available to absorb losses of the bank beyond common equity. These consist of instruments with no maturity dates or incentives to redeem, for example, noncumulative perpetual preferred stock. These instruments may be callable by the issuer after 5 years only if they are replaced with "better" capital.

### Tier II Capital

Tier II capital is a broad array of secondary "equity-like" capital resources. It includes a DI's loan loss reserves plus various convertible and subordinated debt instruments with maximum caps.

We first look at how this capital is used as a cushion against credit risk using the BIS Standardized Approach described in Basel III.

## Credit Risk–Adjusted Assets

**credit risk–adjusted assets**
On- and off-balance-sheet assets whose values are adjusted for approximate credit risk.

Under Basel III capital adequacy rules, risk-adjusted assets represent the denominator of the risk-based capital ratios. Two components make up **credit risk–adjusted assets:** (1) credit risk–adjusted on-balance-sheet assets, and (2) credit risk–adjusted off-balance-sheet assets.

## Calculating Risk-Based Capital Ratios

### Credit Risk–Adjusted On-Balance-Sheet Assets under Basel III

A major criticism of the original Basel Agreement was that individual risk weights depended on the broad categories of borrowers (i.e., sovereigns, banks, or corporates). For example, under Basel I all sovereign loans had a risk weight of 100 percent regardless of the borrowing country's credit risk. The Basel II and III Standardized. Approach aligns regulatory capital requirements more closely with the key elements of DIs risk by introducing a wider differentiation of credit risk weights. The Standardized Approach of Basel III includes a greater number of exposure categories for purposes of calculating total risk-weighted assets than Basel II, provides for greater recognition of financial collateral, and permits a wider range of eligible guarantors. Accordingly, compared with Basel I and II, the Standardized Approach of Basel III should produce capital ratios more in line with the actual economic risks that DIs are facing.

Under the Basel III risk-based capital plan, each DI assigns its assets to one of several categories of credit risk exposure. Table 20–8 lists the key categories and assets in these categories. The main features are that cash assets; cash, U.S. T-bills, notes, and bonds of all maturities; and GNMA (Ginnie Mae) mortgage-backed securities (mortgage securitization packages backed by a government agency) are all zero risk based. In the 20 percent class are U.S. agency–backed securities, municipal issued general obligation bonds, FHLMC and FNMA mortgage-backed securities, and interbank deposits.[5] In the 50 percent class are multifamily mortgage

---

[5] The Federal Home Loan Mortgage Corporation (FHLMC) and the Federal National Mortgage Association (FNMA) are government-managed mortgage securitization agencies. (See Chapter 26 for more details on these agencies.)

loans and other municipal (revenue) bonds. Most other on-balance-sheet assets, such as commercial loans, consumer loans, premises, and other assets, are in the 100 percent risk category.

**TABLE 20–8** Summary of the Risk-Based Capital Standards for On-Balance-Sheet Items under Basel II

Sources: "Regulatory Capital Rules: Standardized Approach for Risk-Weighted Assets; Market Discipline and Disclosure Requirements," Office of the Comptroller of the Currency, Treasury, June 2012, *www.occ.gov*; Board of Governors of the Federal Reserve System, June 2012, *www.federalreserve.gov*; and the Federal Deposit Insurance Corporation, *www.fdic.gov*, June 2012.

### Category 1 (0% weight)

Cash; gold bullion; Federal Reserve Bank balances; direct and unconditional claims on the U.S. government, its central bank, or a U.S. government agency; exposures unconditionally guaranteed by the U.S. government, its central bank, or a U.S. government agency; claims on certain supranational entities (such as the International Monetary Fund) and certain multilateral development banking organizations; claims on and exposures unconditionally guaranteed by sovereign entities that meet certain criteria (as discussed below).

### Category 2 (20% weight)

Cash items in the process of collection; exposures conditionally guaranteed by the U.S. government, its central bank, or a U.S. government agency; claims on government-sponsored entities (GSEs); claims on U.S. depository institutions and NCUA-insured credit unions; general obligation claims on, and claims guaranteed by the full faith and credit of state and local governments (and any other public sector entity, as defined in the proposal) in the United States; claims on and exposures guaranteed by foreign banks and public sector entities if the sovereign of incorporation of the foreign bank or public sector entity meets certain criteria (as described below).

### Category 3 (35% weight)

1–4 family residential mortgages (as described below).

### Category 4 (50% weight)

"Statutory" multifamily mortgage loans meeting certain criteria; presold residential construction loans meeting certain criteria; revenue bonds issued by state and local governments in the United States; claims on and exposures guaranteed by sovereign entities, foreign banks, and foreign public sector entities that meet certain criteria (as described below); 1–4 family residential mortgages (as described below).

### Category 5 (75% weight)

1–4 family residential mortgages (as described below).

### Category 6 (100% weight)

Commercial loans; consumer loans; claims on and exposures guaranteed by sovereign entities, foreign banks, and foreign public sector entities that meet certain criteria (as described below); all other on-balance-sheet assets not listed above, including real assets, premises, fixed assets, and other real estate owned; 1–4 family residential mortgages (as described below).

### Category 7 (150% weight)

Loans and other exposures that are 90 days or more past due; high volatility commercial real estate loans; 1–4 family residential mortgages (as described below).

### Category 8 (200% weight)

1–4 family residential mortgages (as described below).

### Category 9 (1250% weight)

Securitization exposures.

*continued*

**TABLE 20–8**   *(continued)*

### Risk Weights for Equities

Most publicly traded equity exposures: 300%
Equity exposures that are not publicly traded: 400%
Equity exposures in investment funds: 600%

### Risk Weights for 1–4 Family Residential Mortgages

| Loan-to-Value Ratio | Risk Weight for Category 1 Mortgages | Risk Weight for Category 2 Mortgages |
|---|---|---|
| ≤ 60% | 35% | 100% |
| > 60% and ≤ 80% | 50 | 100 |
| > 80% and ≤ 90% | 75 | 150 |
| > 90% | 100 | 200 |

### Risk Weights for Sovereign Exposures

| | | Risk Weight |
|---|---|---|
| | 0–1 | 0% |
| | 2 | 20 |
| Sovereign CRC | 3 | 50 |
| | 4–6 | 100 |
| | 7 | 150 |
| No CRC | | 100 |
| Sovereign default | | 150 |

### Risk Weights for Foreign Banks

| | | Risk Weight |
|---|---|---|
| | 0–1 | 0% |
| | 2 | 20 |
| Sovereign CRC | 3 | 50 |
| | 4–7 | 150 |
| No CRC | | 100 |
| Sovereign default | | 150 |

Residential 1–4 family mortgages would be separated into two risk categories (category 1 residential mortgage exposures and category 2 residential mortgage exposures). Category 1 residential mortgages include traditional, first-lien, prudently underwritten mortgage loans. Category 2 residential mortgages include junior liens and nontraditional mortgage products. The risk weight assigned to the residential mortgage exposure then depends on the mortgage's loan-to-value ratio (as listed in Table 20–8). For example, category 1 mortgages with a loan-to-value ratio of less than 60 percent have a risk weight of 35 percent; category 2 mortgages with a loan-to-value ratio of greater than 90 percent have a risk weight of 200 percent. Mortgages more than 90 days past due are assigned a risk weight of 150 percent.

Risk weights for sovereign exposures are determined using OECD country risk classifications (CRCs).[6] A sovereign is a central government (including the

[6] See OECD, "Country Risk Classification,"
www.oecd.org/document/49/0,3746,en_2649_34169_1901105_1_1_1_1,00.html.

U.S. government) or an agency, department, ministry, or central bank of a central government. The OECD's CRCs assess a country's credit risk using two basic components: the country risk assessment model (CRAM)—an econometric model that produces a quantitative assessment of country credit risk—and the qualitative assessment of the CRAM results—which integrates political risk and other risk factors not fully captured by the CRAM. The two components are combined and classified into one of eight risk categories (0–7). Countries assigned to categories 0–1 have the lowest possible risk assessment and are assigned a risk weight of 0 percent, while countries assigned to category 7 having the highest possible risk assessment and are assigned a risk weight of 150 percent (see Table 20–8).[7] The OECD provides CRCs for more than 150 countries. Assessments are publicly available on the OECD website.[8] Countries with no CRC assessments are assigned a credit risk weight of 100 percent. A 150 percent risk weight is assigned to sovereign exposures immediately upon determining that an event of sovereign default has occurred or if a sovereign default has occurred during the previous five years.

Risk weights on exposures to foreign banks would also be based on the CRC assessment for the bank's home country (see Table 20–8). Banks located in countries assigned to the 0–1 category having the lowest possible risk assessment and are assigned a risk weight of 0 percent, while countries assigned to the 4–7 category having the highest possible risk assessment and are assigned a risk weight of 150 percent. Banks located in countries with no CRC assessments are assigned a credit risk weight of 100 percent; 150 percent risk weight is assigned to sovereign exposures immediately upon determining that an event of sovereign default has occurred or if a sovereign default has occurred during the previous five years.

To figure the credit risk–adjusted assets , the DI multiplies the dollar amount of assets it has in each category by the appropriate risk weight.

---

| **EXAMPLE 20–1** | Consider the bank's balance sheet in Table 20–9, categorized according to the risk weights of Basel III. Under Basel III, the credit risk–adjusted value of the bank's on-balance-sheet assets would be: |
|---|---|
| *Calculation of On-Balance-Sheet Credit Risk–Adjusted Assets under Basel III* | $$\text{Credit risk-adjusted on-balance-sheet assets} = 0(8\,m + 13\,m + 60\,m + 50\,m + 42\,m)$$ $$+ \ 0.2(10\,m + 10m + 20\,m + 55\,m + 10\,m) + 0.5(34\,m + 308\,m + 75\,m)$$ $$+ \ 1(390\,m + 108\,m + 22\,m) + 1.5\,(10\,m) = \$764.5 \text{ million}$$ |

The simple book value of on-balance-sheet assets is $1,215 million; its credit risk–adjusted value under Basel III is $764.5 million.

---

[7] Basel II used credit rating agencies' (e.g., S&P) credit ratings to assess the credit risk of sovereign exposure as well as commercial loans. However, during the financial crisis, the U.S. Congress characterized credit rating agencies as organizations whose activities are fundamentally commercial in character. Credit rating agencies played a critical "gatekeeper" role in the debt markets and performed evaluative and analytical services on behalf of clients. There were conflicts of interest of credit rating agencies in providing credit ratings to their clients. Further, by having these credit rating incorporated into federal regulations, there was a perceived government "sanctioning" of the credit rating agencies' credit ratings. Thus, Basel III no longer uses credit rating agencies' credit ratings. The OECD is a noncommercial entity that does not produce credit assessments for fee-paying clients, nor does it provide the sort of evaluative and analytical services as credit rating agencies.

[8] www.oecd.org/document/49/0,2340,en_2649_34171_1901105_1_1_1_1,00.html.

**TABLE 20–9**   Bank's Balance Sheet under Basel III (in millions of dollars)

| Weight | Assets | | Liabilities/Equity | | Capital Class |
|---|---|---|---|---|---|
| 0% | Cash | $   8 | Demand deposits | $  150 | |
| | Balances due from Fed | 13 | MMDAs deposits | 500 | |
| | Treasury bills | 60 | CDs | 380 | |
| | Long-term Treasury securities | 50 | Fed funds purchased | 80 | |
| | Long-term government agencies (GNMAs) | 42 | | | |
| 20 | Items in process of collection | 10 | Convertible bonds | 10 | Tier II |
| | Long-term government agencies (FNMAs) | 10 | Subordinated bonds | 10 | Tier II |
| | Munis (general obligation) | 20 | | | |
| | Loans to countries with OECD CRC rating of 2 | 55 | | | |
| | Loans to foreign banks in country with OECD CRC rating of 2 | 10 | Perpetual preferred stock (nonqualifying) | 5 | Tier II |
| 50 | University dorm bonds (revenue) | 34 | | | |
| | Residential 1–4 family mortgages, Category 1, loan-to-value ratio between 60% and 80% | 308 | Retained earnings | 40 | CET1 |
| | Loans to foreign banks in country with OECD CRC rating of 3 | 75 | Common stock | 30 | CET1 |
| 100 | Commercial loans | 390 | Noncumulative | | |
| | Consumer loans | 108 | perpetual preferred | | Additional |
| | Premises, equipment | 22 | stock (qualifying) | 10 | Tier I |
| 150 | Loans to countries with OECD CRC rating of 7 | 10 | | $1,215 | |
| N/A | Reserve for loan losses | (10) | | | Tier II |
| | Total assets | $1,215 | | | |

**Off-Balance-Sheet Items:**

$80 m in two-year loan commitments to a U.S. corporation
$10 m direct credit substitute standby letters of credit issued to a U.S. corporation
$50 m in commercial letters of credit issued to a U.S. corporation

One fixed–floating interest rate swap for four years with notional dollar value of $100 m and replacement cost of $3 m
One 2-year Euro$ contract for $40 m with a replacement cost of −$1 m

## Credit Risk–Adjusted Off-Balance-Sheet Activities

The credit risk–adjusted value of on-balance-sheet assets is only one component of the capital ratio denominator. The other is the credit risk–adjusted value of the DI's off-balance-sheet (OBS) activities. These OBS activities represent contingent rather than actual claims against depository institutions (see Chapter 16). Thus, regulations require that capital be held not against the full face value of these items, but against an amount equivalent to any eventual on-balance-sheet credit risk these securities might create for a depository institution. Therefore, in calculating the credit risk–adjusted asset values of these OBS items we must first convert them into **credit equivalent amounts**—amounts equivalent to an on-balance-sheet item. Further, the calculation of the credit risk–adjusted values of the off-balance-sheet activities involves some initial segregation of these activities. In particular,

**credit equivalent amount**
The on-balance-sheet equivalent credit risk exposure of an off-balance-sheet item.

**TABLE 20–10**
**Conversion Factors for Off-Balance-Sheet Contingent or Guaranty Contracts, Basel III**

Sources: "Regulatory Capital Rules: Standardized Approach for Risk-Weighted Assets; Market Discipline and Disclosure Requirements," Office of the Comptroller of the Currency, Treasury, June 2012, *www.occ.gov*; Board of Governors of the Federal Reserve System, June 2012, *www.federalreserve.gov*; and the Federal Deposit Insurance Corporation, *www.fdic .gov.*, June 2012.

Sale and repurchase agreements and assets sold with recourse that are not included on the balance sheet (100%)
Direct-credit substitute standby letters of credit (100%)
Performance-related standby letters of credit (50%)
Unused portion of loan commitments with original maturity of *one year or less* (20%)
Unused portion of loan commitments with original maturity of *more than one year* (50%)
Commercial letters of credit (20%)
Bankers' acceptances conveyed (20%)
Other loan commitments (10%)

the calculation of the credit risk exposure or the credit risk–adjusted asset amounts of contingent or guaranty contracts such as letters of credit differs from the calculation of the credit risk–adjusted asset amounts for foreign exchange and interest rate forward, option, and swap contracts. We first consider the credit risk–adjusted asset value of OBS guaranty-type contracts and contingent contracts and then derivative or market contracts.

*The Credit Risk–Adjusted Asset Value of Off-Balance-Sheet Contingent Guaranty Contracts*   Consider the appropriate conversion factors in Table 20–10. Note that under Basel III, direct credit substitute standby letter of credit guarantees issued by DIs have a 100 percent conversion factor rating, or credit equivalent amount. Similarly, sale and repurchase agreements and assets sold with recourse are also given a 100 percent conversion factor rating. Future performance-related SLCs and unused loan commitments of more that one year have a 50 percent conversion factor. Other loan commitments, those with one year or less to maturity, have a 20 percent credit conversion factor. Standard trade-related commercial letters of credit and bankers' acceptances sold have a 20 percent conversion factor. Under Basel III, risk weights assigned to OBS contingent guaranty contracts are the same as if the DI had entered into the transactions as a principal. Thus, the credit ratings used to assign a credit risk weight for on-balance-sheet assets (listed in Table 20–8) are also used to assign credit risk weights on these OBS activities (e.g., issuing a two-year loan commitment to a foreign bank located in a country with an OECD CRC assessment of 4 would result in a risk weight of 150 percent).

**EXAMPLE 20–2**
*Calculating Off-Balance-Sheet Contingent or Guaranty Contracts' Credit Risk–Adjusted Assets*

To see how OBS activities are incorporated into the risk-based ratio, we can extend Example 20–1 for the bank in Table 20–9. Notice that in addition to having $764.5 million in credit risk–adjusted assets on its balance sheet, the bank also has the following off-balance-sheet contingencies or guarantees:

1. $80 million two-year loan commitments to a U.S. corporations.
2. $10 million direct credit substitute standby letters of credit issued to a U.S. corporation.
3. $50 million commercial letters of credit issued to a U.S. corporation.

To find the risk-adjusted asset value for these OBS items, we follow a two-step process.

**Step 1. Convert OBS Values into On-Balance-Sheet Credit Equivalent Amounts**
In the first step we multiply the dollar amount outstanding of these items to derive the credit equivalent amounts using the conversion factors (CFs) listed in Table 20–10.

| OBS Item | Face Value | | Conversion Factor | | Credit Equivalent Amount |
|---|---|---|---|---|---|
| Two-year loan commitment | $80 m | × | 0.5 | = | $40 m |
| Standby letter of credit | 10 m | × | 1.0 | = | 10 m |
| Commercial letter of credit | 50 m | × | 0.2 | = | 10 m |

Thus, the credit equivalent amounts of loan commitments, standby letters of credit, and commercial letters of credit are, respectively, $40, $10, and $10 million. These conversion factors convert an OBS item into an equivalent credit or on-balance-sheet item.

### Step 2. Assign the OBS Credit Equivalent Amount to a Risk Category

In the second step we multiply these credit equivalent amounts by their appropriate risk weights. In our example, because each of the contingent guaranty contracts involves a U.S. corporation, each is assigned a risk weight of 100 percent.

| OBS Item | Credit Equivalent Amount | | Risk Weight $(w_i)$ | | Risk-Adjusted Asset Amount |
|---|---|---|---|---|---|
| Two-year loan commitment | $40 m | × | 1.0 | = | $40 m |
| Standby letter of credit | 10 m | × | 1.0 | = | 10 m |
| Commercial letter of credit | 10 m | × | 1.0 | = | 10 m |
| | | | | | $60 m |

Thus, the bank's credit risk–adjusted asset value of its OBS contingencies and guarantees is $60 million.

*The Credit Risk–Adjusted Asset Value of Off-Balance-Sheet Market Contracts or Derivative Instruments* In addition to having OBS contingencies and guarantees, FIs engage heavily in buying and selling OBS futures, options, forwards, swaps, caps, and other derivative securities contracts for interest rate risk, credit risk, and foreign exchange risk management and hedging reasons, as well as buying and selling such products on behalf of their customers (see Chapter 16). Each of these positions potentially exposes DIs to **counterparty credit risk,** that is, the risk that the counterparty (or other side of a contract) will default when suffering large actual or potential losses on its position. Such defaults mean that a DI would have to go back to the market to replace such contracts at (potentially) less favorable terms.

**counterparty credit risk**
The risk that the other side of a contract will default on payment obligations.

Under the risk-based capital ratio rules, a major distinction is made between exchange-traded derivative security contracts (e.g., Chicago Board of Trade's exchange-traded options) and over-the-counter–traded instruments (e.g., forwards, swaps, caps, and floors). The credit or default risk of exchange-traded derivatives is approximately zero because when a counterparty defaults on its obligations, the exchange itself adopts the counterparty's obligations in full. However, no such guarantees exist for bilaterally agreed, over-the-counter contracts originated and traded outside organized exchanges. Under Basel III, banks must hold capital equal to 2 percent times the margin requirement on exchange-traded derivatives. The nominal 2 percent risk weighting is intended to reflect the fact that the risk of default on an exchange traded derivative security is assumed to be very low. Hence, most OBS futures and options positions have virtually no capital requirements for a DI, while most forwards, swaps, caps, and floors do.[9]

As with contingent or guaranty contracts, the calculation of the risk-adjusted asset values of OBS market contracts requires a two-step approach. First, we calculate a conversion factor to create credit equivalent amounts. Second, we multiply the credit equivalent amounts by the appropriate risk weights.

**Step 1. Convert OBS Values into On-Balance-Sheet Credit Equivalent Amounts.** We first convert the notional or face values of all non-exchange-traded swap, forward, and other derivative contracts into credit equivalent amounts. The credit equivalent amount itself is divided into a *potential exposure* element and a *current exposure* element. That is:

$$\begin{array}{l} \text{Credit equivalent amount} \\ \text{of OBS derivative} \\ \text{security items (\$)} \end{array} = \text{Potential exposure (\$)} + \text{Current exposure (\$)}$$

**potential exposure**
The risk that a counterparty to a derivative securities contract will default in the future.

The **potential exposure** component reflects the risk if the counterparty to the contract defaults in the *future*. The probability of such an occurrence depends on the future volatility of interest rates for an interest rate contract, credit risk for a credit contract, or exchange rates for an exchange rate contract. Thus, the potential exposure conversion factors in Table 20–11 are larger for credit contracts than for interest rate contracts. Also, note the larger potential exposure risk for longer-term contracts of both types.

**current exposure**
The cost of replacing a derivative securities contract at today's prices.

In addition to calculating the potential exposure of an OBS market instrument, a DI must calculate its **current exposure** with the instrument. This reflects the cost of replacing a contract if a counterparty defaults *today*. The DI calculates this *replacement cost* or *current exposure* by replacing the rate or price initially in the contract with the current rate or price for a similar contract and recalculates all the current and future cash flows that would have been generated under current rate

**TABLE 20–11** Credit Conversion Factors for OBS Derivative Contracts Used in Calculating Potential Exposure

Sources: "Regulatory Capital Rules: Standardized Approach for Risk-Weighted Assets; Market Discipline and Disclosure Requirements," Office of the Comptroller of the Currency, Treasury, June 2012, *www.occ.gov*; Board of Governors of the Federal Reserve System, June 2012, *www.federalreserve.gov*; and the Federal Deposit Insurance Corporation, *www.fdic.gov*, June 2012.

| Remaining Maturity | (1) Interest Rate Contracts | (2) Exchange Rate Contracts | (3) Credit Contracts (Investment Grade) | (4) Credit Contracts (Non-Investment Grade) | (5) Equity Contracts | (6) Precious Metals Contracts | (7) Other |
|---|---|---|---|---|---|---|---|
| 1. Less than one year | 0% | 1.0% | 5.0% | 10.0% | 6.0% | 7.0% | 10.0% |
| 2. One to five years | 0.5 | 5.0 | 5.0 | 10.0 | 8.0 | 7.0 | 12.0 |
| 3. Over five years | 1.5 | 7.5 | 5.0 | 10.0 | 10.0 | 8.0 | 15.0 |

[9] This may create some degree of preference among DIs for using exchange-traded hedging instruments rather than over-the-counter instruments, because using the former may save a DI costly capital resources.

or price terms.[10] The DI discounts any future cash flows to give a current present value measure of the contract's replacement cost. If the contract's replacement cost is negative (i.e., the DI profits on the replacement of the contract if the counterparty defaults), regulations require the replacement cost (current exposure) to be set to zero. If the replacement cost is positive (i.e., the DI loses on the replacement of the contract if the counterparty defaults), this value is used as the measure of current exposure. Since each swap or forward is in some sense unique, calculating current exposure involves a considerable computer processing task for the DI's management information systems. Indeed, specialized service firms are likely to perform this task for smaller DIs.

**Step 2. Assign the OBS Credit Equivalent Amount to a Risk Category.** Once the current and potential exposure amounts are summed to produce the credit equivalent amount for each contract, we multiply this dollar number by a risk weight to produce the final credit risk–adjusted asset amount for OBS market contracts.

Under Basel III, the appropriate risk weight is generally 1.0, or 100 percent. That is:

$$\begin{array}{l}\text{Credit risk-adjusted} \\ \quad \text{value of OBS} \\ \quad \text{market contracts}\end{array} = \text{Total credit equivalent amount} \times 1.0 \text{ (risk weight)}$$

| **EXAMPLE 20–3** *Calculating Off-Balance-Sheet Market Contract Credit Risk–Adjusted Assets* | The bank in Examples 20–1 and 20–2 has taken one interest rate hedging position in the fixed–floating interest rate swap market for four years with a notional dollar amount of $100 million and one 2-year forward foreign exchange contract for $40 million (see Table 20–9). |
|---|---|

**Step 1**

We calculate the credit equivalent amount for each item or contract as:

| | | **Potential Exposure** + **Current Exposure** | | | | | |
|---|---|---|---|---|---|---|---|
| **Type of Contract (remaining maturity)** | **Notional Principal** × | **Potential Exposure Conversion Factor** = | **Potential Exposure** | **Replacement Cost** | **Current Exposure** = | **Credit Equivalent Amount** |
| Four-year fixed–floating interest rate swap | $100 m × | 0.005 = | **$0.5 m** | $3 m | **$3 m** | **$3.5 m** |
| Two-year forward foreign exchange contract | $ 40 m × | 0.050 = | **$2 m** | −$1 m | **$0** | **$2 m** |

For the four-year, fixed–floating interest rate swap, the notional value (contract face value) of the swap is $100 million. Since this is a long-term (one to five years to maturity) interest rate

[10] For example, suppose a £1 million two-year forward foreign exchange contract was entered into in January 2015 at $1.55/£. In January 2016, the bank has to evaluate the credit risk of the contract, which now has one year remaining. To do this, it replaces the agreed forward rate $1.55/£ with the forward rate on current one-year forward contracts, e.g., $1.65/£. It then recalculates its net gain or loss on the contract if it had to be replaced at this price. If the spot rate in January 2016 is $1.64/£, then the replacement cost on this contract is ($1.65 − $1.55) × £1 m × $1.64 = $164,000.

market contract, its face value is multiplied by 0.005 to get a potential exposure or credit risk equivalent value of $0.5 million (see row 2 of Table 20–11). We add this potential exposure to the replacement cost (current exposure) of this contract to the bank. The replacement cost reflects the cost of having to enter into a new four-year, fixed–floating swap agreement at today's interest rates for the remaining life of the swap should the counterparty default. Assuming that interest rates today are less favorable, on a present value basis, the cost of replacing the existing contract for its remaining life would be $3 million. Thus, the total credit equivalent amount—current plus potential exposures—for the interest rate swap is $3.5 million.

Next, look at the foreign exchange two-year forward contract of $40 million face value. Since this is a foreign exchange contract with a maturity of one to five years, the potential (future) credit risk is $40 million × 0.05, or $2 million (see row 2 in Table 20–11). However, its replacement cost is *minus* $1 million. That is, in this example our bank actually stands to gain if the counterparty defaults. Exactly why the counterparty would do this when it is in the money is unclear. However, regulators cannot permit a DI to gain from a default by a counterparty since this might produce all types of perverse risk-taking incentives. Consequently, as in our example, current exposure has to be set equal to zero (as shown). Thus, the sum of potential exposure ($2 million) and current exposure ($0) produces a total credit equivalent amount of $2 million for this contract. Since the bank has just two OBS derivative contracts, summing the two credit equivalent amounts produces a total credit equivalent amount of $3.5 m + $2 m = $5.5 million for the bank's OBS market contracts.

**Step 2**

The next step is to multiply this credit equivalent amount by the appropriate risk weight. Specifically, to calculate the risk-adjusted asset value for the bank's OBS derivative or market contracts, we multiply the credit equivalent amount by the appropriate risk weight, which is generally 1.0, or 100 percent:

$$\begin{array}{ccccc} \text{Credit risk-adjusted} & = & \$5.5 \text{ million} & \times & 1.0 & = & \$5.5 \text{ million} \\ \text{asset value of} & & \text{(credit equivalent} & & \text{(risk weight)} \\ \text{OBS derivatives} & & \text{amount)} \end{array}$$

### Total Credit Risk-Adjusted Assets under Basel II

Under Basel III, the total credit risk-adjusted assets are $830 million ($764.5 million from on-balance-sheet activities, plus $60 million for the risk-adjusted value of OBS contingencies and guarantees, plus $5.5 million for the risk-adjusted value of OBS derivatives).

### Calculating the Overall Risk-Based Capital Position

After calculating the risk-weighted assets for a depository institution, the final step is to calculate the Tier I and total risk-based capital ratios.

**EXAMPLE 20–4**
*Calculating the Overall Risk-Based Capital Position of a Bank*

From Table 20–9, the bank's CET1 capital (common stock and retained earnings) totals $70 million; additional Tier I capital (qualifying perpetual preferred stock) totals $10 million; and Tier II capital (convertible bonds, subordinate bonds, nonqualifying perpetual preferred stock, and reserve for loan losses) totals $35 million.

We can now calculate our bank's capital adequacy under the Basel III risk-based capital requirements as:

$$\text{CET1 risk-based ratio} = \frac{\$70\,m}{\$830.0\,m} = 8.43\%$$

$$\text{Tier I risk-based capital ratio} = \frac{\$70\,m + \$10\,m}{\$830.0\,m} = 9.64\%$$

and

$$\text{Total risk-based capital ratio} = \frac{\$70\text{ m} + \$10\text{ m} + \$35\text{ m}}{\$830.0\text{ m}} = 13.86\%$$

To be adequately capitalized, the minimum CET1 risk-based capital ratio is 4.5 percent (see Table 20–4), the minimum Tier I capital ratio is 6 percent, and the minimum total risk-based capital ratio required is 8 percent. Thus, the bank in our example has more than adequate capital under all three capital requirement formulas.

### Capital Conservations Buffer

In addition to revising the minimum capital ratio requirements for credit risk, Basel III introduced a capital conservation buffer designed to ensure that DIs build up a capital surplus, or buffer, outside periods of financial stress that can be drawn down as losses are incurred during periods of financial stress. The buffer requirements provide incentives for DIs to build up a capital surplus [e.g., by reducing discretionary distributions of earnings (reduced dividends, share buy-backs, and staff bonuses)] to reduce the risk that their capital levels would fall below the minimum requirements during periods of stress. The capital conservation buffer must be composed of CET1 capital and is held separately from the minimum risk-based capital requirements.

Under Basel III, a DI would need to hold a capital conservation buffer of greater than 2.5 percent of total risk-weighted assets (the capital buffer is being phased in between 2016 and 2019, when it will be set a 2.5 percent, see Table 20–3) to avoid being subject to limitations on capital distributions and discretionary bonus payments to executive officers. If a DI's capital buffer falls below 2.5 percent constraints on earnings payouts e.g., *dividends, share buy-backs,* and *"bonus" payments* will be imposed. Table 20–12 lists the maximum dividend payout ratio allowed as the conservation buffer falls below 2.5 percent. As can be seen, the smaller the conservation buffer, the greater the constraint on a DI's discretionary payout of earnings. For example, a DI with a capital conservation buffer between 1.875 and 2.5 percent (e.g., a CET1 capital ratio of 6.75 percent, a Tier I capital ratio of 8.2 percent, or a total capital ratio of 10.2 percent) at the end of the previous calendar quarter would be allowed to distribute no more than 60 percent of its eligible retained income in the form of capital distributions or discretionary bonus payments during the current calendar quarter. Rather, the DI would need to conserve at least 40 percent of its eligible retained income during the current calendar quarter, using these earnings to build up its capital conservation buffer.

**TABLE 20–12** Capital Conservation Buffer, Capital Ratio Levels, and Maximum Payout Ratios

| Capital Conservation Buffer (%) | Common Equity Tier I Capital Ratio (%) | Tier I Capital Ratio (%) | Total Capital Ratio (%) | Maximum Payout Ratios (expressed as a percentage of earnings) |
|---|---|---|---|---|
| 0–0.625 | 4.5–5.125 | 6.0–6.625 | 8.0–8.625 | 0% |
| >0.625–1.25 | >5.125–5.75 | >6.625–7.25 | >8.625–9.25 | 20 |
| >1.25–1.875 | >5.75–6.375 | >7.25–7.875 | >9.25–9.875 | 40 |
| >1.875–2.5 | >6.375–7.0 | >7.875–8.5 | >9.875–10.5 | 60 |
| >2.5 | >7.0 | >8.5 | >10.5 | No payout ratio limitation |

### Countercyclical Capital Buffer

Basel III also introduced a countercyclical capital buffer that may be declared by any country experiencing excess aggregate credit growth. The countercyclical capital buffer can vary between 0 percent and 2.5 percent of risk-weighted assets (the countercyclical buffer is being phased in between 2016 and 2019, when it will be set at a maximum of 2.5 percent, see Table 20–3). This buffer must be met with CET1 capital, and DIs are given 12 months to adjust to the buffer level. Like the capital conservation buffer, if a DI's capital levels fall below the set countercyclical capital buffer, restrictions on earnings payouts are applied. Table 20–13 lists these restrictions. International banks will pay a weighted average buffer charge based on their credit exposures to each country. Thus, if a bank has 60 percent of its assets in country A with an imposed countercyclical buffer of 2 percent and 40 percent of its assets in country B with a countercyclical buffer requirement of 1 percent the countercyclical buffer for the bank is 1.6 percent [(0.60 × 2%) + (0.40 × 1%)].

The countercyclical capital buffer aims to protect the banking system and reduce systemic exposures to economic downturns. Losses can be particularly large when a downturn is preceded by a period of excess credit growth. The accumulation of a capital buffer during an expansionary phase would increase the ability of the banking system to remain healthy during periods of declining asset prices and losses from weakening credit conditions. By assessing a countercyclical buffer when credit markets are overheated, accumulated capital buffers can absorb any abnormal losses that a DI might experience when the credit cycle turns. Consequently, even after these losses are realized, DIs would remain healthy and able to access funding, meet obligations, and continue to serve as credit intermediaries.

### Global Systemically Important Banks

As part of Basel III, the BIS imposed an additional common equity Tier I surcharge ("loss absorbency requirement") on global systemically important banks (G-SIBs): banking groups whose distress or disorderly failure would cause significant disruption to the wider financial system and economic activity. The basic idea is that because G-SIBs are too-big-to-fail banks (that would have to be bailed out by central governments and taxpayers), they need to lower their risk by increasing their tangible capital requirements even more than other banks. The surcharge ranges from 1 percent to 3.5 percent to be held over and above the 7 percent minimum CET1 plus conservation buffer requirement. The purpose of the additional capital requirement is twofold: (1) to reduce the probability of failure of a G-SIB by

**TABLE 20–13**   Countercyclical Buffer, Capital Ratio Levels, and Maximum Payout Ratios

| Capital Conservation Plus Countercyclical Buffer (%) | Common Equity Tier I Capital Ratio (%) | Tier I Capital Ratio (%) | Total Capital Ratio (%) | Maximum Payout Ratios (expressed as a percentage of earnings) |
|---|---|---|---|---|
| 0–1.25 | 4.5–5.75 | 6.0–7.25 | 8.0–9.25 | 0% |
| >1.25–2.5 | >5.75–7.0 | >7.25–8.5 | >9.25–10.5 | 20 |
| >2.5–3.75 | >7.0–8.25 | >8.5–9.75 | >10.5–11.75 | 40 |
| >3.75–5.0 | >8.25–9.5 | >9.75–11.0 | >11.75–13.0 | 60 |
| >5.0 | >9.5 | >11.0 | >13.0 | No payout ratio limitation |

increasing its going-concern loss absorbency and (2) to reduce the extent or impact of the failure of a G-SIB on the financial system by improving global recovery and resolution frameworks.

G-SIBs are identified using a methodology developed by the BIS based on an indicator measurement approach that identifies factors that cause international contagion. The indicators were selected to capture the systemic impact of a bank's failure, rather than the probability that the bank will fail. The indicators include bank size, interconnectedness, cross-jurisdictional (global) activity, the lack of substitutes for their services, and complexity to rank their global systemic importance (see Appendix 20B to the chapter, located at the book's website **www.mhhe.com/saunders8e**). Using this methodology on an initial sample of 73 of the world's largest banks and year-end 2009 data for each indicator, the BIS designated 27 banks as G-SIBs. Two additional banks were added to this initial list based on the home supervisor's judgment, resulting in 29 G-SIBs headquartered in 12 countries. Table 20–14 provides the initial list of 29 G-SIBs. The number of G-SIBs can change over time, reflecting changes in the systemic importance of banks. The sample of banks to be assessed will be reviewed every three years, and the BIS also anticipates eventually expanding the surcharge to a wider group of financial institutions, including insurance companies and other nonbank financial institutions.[11]

The exact amount of the surcharge depends on a bank's placement in one of five "buckets" (requiring a 1, 1.5, 2, 2.5, and 3.5 percent surcharge, respectively) based on the bank's score from the indicator measurement approach and may be met with CET1 capital only. The surcharge requirement will be phased-in with the Basel III capital conservation and countercyclical capital buffers, beginning in 2016 and becoming fully effective in 2019.

### Leverage Ratio

One of the features of the financial crisis of 2008–09 was the accumulation of extreme on- and off-balance-sheet leverage throughout the banking system. During the worst of the crisis, DIs were forced by the market to reduce leverage to an extent

**TABLE 20–14**
Global Systematically Important Banks

| Bank | Country | Bank | Country |
|------|---------|------|---------|
| Dexia | Belgium | Bank of China | China |
| Banque Populaire CdE | France | BNP Paribas | France |
| Crédit Agricole Groupe | France | Société Générale | France |
| Commerzbank | Germany | Deutsche Bank | Germany |
| Unicredit Group | Italy | Mitsubishi UFJ FG | Japan |
| Mizuho FG | Japan | Sumitomo Mitsui FG | Japan |
| ING Bank | Netherlands | Santander | Spain |
| Nordea | Sweden | Credit Suisse | Switzerland |
| UBS | Switzerland | Barclays | United Kingdom |
| HSBC | United Kingdom | Lloyds Banking Group | United Kingdom |
| Royal Bank of Scotland | United Kingdom | Bank of America | United States |
| Bank of New York Mellon | United States | Citigroup | United States |
| Goldman Sachs | United States | J.P. Morgan Chase | United States |
| Morgan Stanley | United States | State Street Bank | United States |
| Wells Fargo | United States | | |

[11] For example, in June 2013, the U.S. Financial Stability Oversight Council proposed the designation of nonbanks AIG, Prudential Financial, and General Electric Capital Corp. as systemically important FIs.

that intensified falling asset prices and intensified DI losses, declines in DI capital, and the reduction in credit availability. To prevent this cycle from reoccurring, Basel III introduced a leverage ratio requirement that is intended to discourage the use of excess leverage and to act as a backstop to the risk-based capital requirements described earlier.

Under the Standardized Approach, the Basel III leverage ratio is defined as the ratio of Tier I capital to on-balance-sheet assets. Once Basel III is fully phased in (in 2019, see Table 20–3), to be well capitalized, a DI must hold a minimum leverage ratio of 5 percent; to be adequately capitalized, a DI must hold a minimum leverage ratio of 4 percent. Under the Advanced Approach, Basel III leverage ratio is defined as the ratio of Tier I capital to a combination of on- and off-balance sheet assets:

$$\text{Leverage ratio} = \frac{\text{Tier I capital}}{\text{Total exposure (on + off balance sheet)}}$$

Total exposure is equal to the DI's total assets plus off-balance-sheet exposure. For derivative securities, off-balance-sheet exposure is current exposure plus potential exposure as described earlier. For off-balance-sheet credit (loan) commitments, a conversion factor of 100 percent is applied unless the commitments are immediately cancelable. In this case, a conversion factor of 10 percent is used.

### Interest Rate Risk, Market Risk, and Risk-Based Capital

From a regulatory perspective, a credit risk–based capital ratio is adequate only as long as a depository institution is not exposed to undue interest rate or market risk. The reason is that the risk-based capital ratio takes into account only the adequacy of a DI's capital to meet both its on- and off-balance-sheet credit risks. Not explicitly accounted for is the insolvency risk emanating from interest rate risk (duration mismatches) and market (trading) risk.

www.federalreserve.gov

To meet these criticisms, in 1993 the Federal Reserve (along with the Bank for International Settlements) developed additional capital requirement proposals for interest rate risk (see Chapter 9) and market risk (see Chapter 15). As is discussed in Chapter 15, since 1998 DIs have had to calculate an add-on to the 8 percent risk-based capital ratio to reflect their exposure to market risk. There were two approaches available to DIs to calculate the size of this add-on: (1) the standardized model proposed by regulators and (2) the DI's own internal market risk model.

www.bis.org

As discussed in Chapter 15, the financial crisis exposed a number of shortcomings in the way market risk was being measured in accordance with Basel II rules. Although the crisis largely exposed problems with the large-bank internal models approach to measuring market risk, the BIS also identified shortcomings with the standardized approach. These included a lack of risk sensitivity, a very limited recognition of hedging and diversification benefits, and an inability to sufficiently capture risks associated with more complex instruments. To address shortcomings of the standardized approach to measuring market risk, Basel III proposes a "partial risk factor" approach as a revised standardized approach. Basel III also introduces a "fuller risk factor" approach as an alternative to the revised partial risk factor standardized approach. Both models are discussed and illustrated in Chapter 15. In addition, for large banks, which rely on internal-based models to measure regulatory capital for market risk, a great reliance is place on the expected shortfall of capital that would likely result from a major shock rather than value-at-risk (VAR) (see Chapter 15). Moreover, the illiquidity measures to be used in internal model based calculations are to be significantly increased.

To date, no formal add-on has been required for interest rate risk, although Basel II suggests a framework for a future capital ratio for interest rate risk similar to the original 1993 proposal. Specifically, Basel II states that DIs should have interest rate risk measurement systems that assess the effects of interest rate changes on both earnings and economic value. These systems should provide meaningful measures of a DI's current levels of interest rate risk exposure, and should be capable of identifying any excessive exposures that might arise.[12]

### Operational Risk and Risk-Based Capital

Basel II implemented an additional add-on to capital for operational risk. Prior to this proposal, the BIS had argued that the operational risk exposures of DIs were adequately taken care of by the 8 percent credit risk–adjusted ratio. But increased visibility of operational risks in recent years (see Chapter 17) has induced regulators to propose a separate capital requirement for credit and operational risks. As noted above, the BIS now believes that operational risks are sufficiently important for DIs to devote resources to quantify such risks and to incorporate them separately into their assessment of their overall capital adequacy. In the 2001 and 2003 Consultative Documents the Basel Committee outlined three specific methods by which depository institutions can calculate capital to protect against operational risk: the Basic Indicator Approach, the Standardized Approach, and the Advanced Measurement Approach.[13] Basel III continued the use of these methods.

The Basic Indicator Approach is structured so that DIs, on average, will hold 12 percent of their total regulatory capital for operational risk. This 12 percent target was based on a widespread survey conducted internationally of current practices by large DIs. To achieve this target, the Basic Indicator Approach focuses on the gross income of the DI, that is, its net profits. This equals a DI's net interest income plus net noninterest income:

$$\text{Gross income} = \text{Net interest income} + \text{Net noninterest income}$$

According to BIS calculations, a DI that holds a fraction (alpha) of its gross income for operational risk capital, where alpha ($\alpha$) is set at 15 percent, will generate enough capital for operational risk such that this amount will be 12 percent of its total regulatory capital holdings against all risks (i.e., credit, market, and operational risks). For example, under the Basic Indicator Approach:

$$\text{Operational capital} = \alpha \times \text{Gross income}$$

or

$$= 0.15 \times \text{Gross income}$$

The problem with the Basic Indicator Approach is that it is too aggregative, or "top-down," and does not differentiate at all among different areas in which operational risks may differ (e.g., Payment and Settlement may have a very different operational risk profile from Retail Brokerage).[14]

---

[12] See Basel Committee on Banking Supervision, "Principles for the Management and Supervision of Interest Rate Risk," January 2001. www.bis.org

[13] See Basel Committee on Banking Supervision, "International Convergence of Capital Measurement and Capital Standards," June 2006. www.bis.org

[14] A second issue is that the $\alpha$ term implies operational risk that is proportional to gross income. This ignores possible economies-of-scale effects that would make this relationship nonlinear (nonproportional); that is, $\alpha$ might fall as DI profits and/or size grows.

**TABLE 20–15**
**BIS Standardized Approach Business Units and Lines**

Source: Bank for International Settlements, "International Convergence of Capital Measurement and Capital Standards," June 2006. *www.bis.org*

| Business Line | Indicator | Capital Factors |
|---|---|---|
| Corporate finance | Gross income* | $\beta_1 = 18\%$ |
| Trading and sales | Gross income | $\beta_2 = 18\%$ |
| Retail banking | Gross income | $\beta_3 = 12\%$ |
| Commercial banking | Gross income | $\beta_4 = 15\%$ |
| Payment and settlement | Gross income | $\beta_5 = 18\%$ |
| Agency services and custody | Gross income | $\beta_6 = 15\%$ |
| Retail brokerage | Gross income | $\beta_7 = 12\%$ |
| Asset management | Gross income | $\beta_8 = 12\%$ |

* The indicator relates to gross income reported for the particular line of business.

In an attempt to provide a finer differentiation of operational risks in a DI across different activity lines while still retaining a basically top-down approach, the BIS offers a second method for operational capital calculation. The second method, the Standardized Approach, divides activities into eight major business units and lines (shown in Table 20–15). Within each business line, there is a specified broad indicator (defined as beta, $\beta$) that reflects the scale or volume of a DI's activities in that area. The indicator relates to the gross income reported for a particular line of business. It serves as a rough proxy for the amount of operational risk within each of these lines. A capital charge is calculated by multiplying the $\beta$ for each line by the indicator assigned to the line and then summing these components. The $\beta$s reflect the importance of each activity in the average DI. The $\beta$s are set by regulators and are calculated from average industry figures from a selected sample of DIs.

Suppose the industry $\beta$ for Corporate Finance is 18 percent and gross income from the Corporate Finance line of business (the activity indicator) is $30 million for the DI. Then, the regulatory capital charge for this line for this year is:

$$\text{Capital}_{\text{Corporate Finance}} = \beta \times \text{Gross income from the Corporate Finance line of}$$
$$\text{business for the DI}$$
$$= 18\% \times \$30 \text{ million}$$
$$= \$5,400,000$$

The total capital charge is calculated as the three-year average of the simple summation of the regulatory capital charge across each of the eight business lines.

The third method, the Advanced Measurement Approach, allows individual DIs to rely on internal data for regulatory capital purposes subject to supervisory approval. Under the Advanced Measurement Approach, supervisors require the DI to calculate its regulatory capital requirement as the sum of the expected loss (EL) and unexpected loss (UL) for each event type, as listed in Table 20–16. Internally generated operational risk measures used for regulatory capital purposes must be based on a minimum three-year observation period of internal loss data, whether the internal loss data are used directly to build the loss measure or to validate it. A DI's internal loss data must be comprehensive in that the data capture all material activities and exposures from all appropriate subsystems and geographic locations. Risk measures for different operational risk estimates are added for purposes of calculating the regulatory minimum capital requirement.

**TABLE 20–16**
Operational Risk
Loss Event Types

**Internal fraud**   Losses due to acts of a type intended to defraud, misappropriate property, or circumvent regulations, the law, or company policy, excluding diversity/discrimination events, which involve at least one internal party.

**External fraud**   Losses due to third-party acts of a type intended to defraud, misappropriate property, or circumvent the law.

**Employment practices and workplace safety**   Losses arising from acts inconsistent with employment, health, or safety laws or agreements, from payment of personal injury claims, or from diversity/discrimination events.

**Clients, products, and business practices**   Losses arising from an unintentional or negligent failure to meet a professional obligation to specific clients (including fiduciary and suitability requirements) or from the nature or design of a product.

**Damage to physical assets**   Losses arising from loss or damage to physical assets from natural disaster or other events.

**Business disruption and system failures**   Losses arising from disruption of business or system failures.

**Execution, delivery, and process management**   Losses from failed transaction processing or process management or from relations with trade counterparties and vendors.

## Criticisms of the Risk-Based Capital Ratio

The risk-based capital requirement seeks to (1) incorporate credit, market, and operational risks into the determination of capital adequacy; (2) more systematically account for credit risk differences among assets; (3) incorporate off-balance-sheet risk exposures; and (4) apply a similar capital requirement across all the major DIs in the world. Unfortunately, the requirements have a number of conceptual and applicability weaknesses in achieving these objectives:

1. *Risk weights.* It is unclear how closely the risk weight categories in Basel III reflect true credit risk. For example, residential mortgage loans have risk weights between 35 and 200 percent under Basel III. Taken literally, these relative weights imply that some residential mortgage loans are 5.7 times as risky as other loans. Further, under Basel III all business loans are given a single 100 percent risk weight regardless of the risk of the business. Thus, loans made to AAA-rated companies are assigned a credit risk weight of 1, as are loans made to CCC-rated companies. That is, within a broad risk weight class, such as commercial loans, credit risk quality differences are not recognized. This may create perverse incentives for DIs to pursue lower-quality customers, thereby increasing the risk of the DI.[15]

2. *Risk weights based on OECD country risk classifications.* While the change to the use of OECD country risk classifications (CRCs) in Basel III removed the problems associated with the use of a noncommercial entity (e.g., S&P) to assign credit risk to sovereign loans and foreign bank loans, OECD country risk ratings have problems of their own. As they were developed, in 1999, CRC ratings were not intended to reflect the probability of sovereign defaults. Rather, CRCs were intended to measure the minimum risk premiums for use in the market for export credits. They are

---

[15] Indeed, Basel I introduced in 1992, was heavily criticized for having a single risk weight on loans and creating incentives for banks to shift to more risky loans that had the same capital requirement as relatively safe loans.

not sovereign ratings such as those described in Chapter 14. Individual CRCs are estimated by economists using a quantitative country risk assessment model, as well as qualitative input. Countries that are classified with a zero CRC rating are not subject to the quantitative model and review. Instead, OECD rules state that in these circumstances, pricing on export credits should not be less than the risk premium available in the wider market. Thus, when a country has a CRC rating of zero, it does not mean the country should have zero country risk premiums. For example, CRC ratings for Greece, Portugal, and Italy would be zero—corresponding to a zero risk weight and zero capital to be held against those countries' debts. Regulators respond to this argument by pointing out that under the new rules, a sovereign that has defaulted or restructured its debt over the previous five years would receive a risk weighting factor of 150 percent. However, countries near, but not yet at, default would still be misrepresented under this classification method.

3. *Portfolio aspects.* The BIS plans largely ignore credit risk portfolio diversification opportunities. As we discussed in Chapter 11, when returns on assets have negative or less than perfectly positive correlations, a DI may lower its portfolio risk through diversification. As constructed, Basel III (standardized model) capital adequacy plans are essentially linear risk measures that ignore correlations or covariances among assets and asset group credit risks—such as between residential mortgages and commercial loans. That is, the DI manager weights each asset separately by the appropriate risk weight and then sums those numbers to get an overall measure of credit risk. No account is taken of the covariances among asset risks between different counterparties (or risk weights).[16]

4. *Excessive complexity.* Basel III will greatly raise the cost of regulation by adding new levels of complexity. The cost of developing and implementing new risk management systems will clearly be significant, and the benefits may turn out to be small. Indeed, Andrew Haldane, executive director for financial stability at the Bank of England, pointed out that risk models have grown so complex that to have statistical confidence that a given set of formulas have captured true risks, you need 400 to 1,000 years of data.

5. *Loan-to-value ratio used for residential mortgages.* Basel III places a great reliance on the loan-to-value ratio for residential mortgages. During the financial crisis, property values used by DIs were inflated by real estate appraisers. If this were to happen again, insufficient capital would be held against these mortgages.

6. *Pillar 2 may ask too much of regulators.* Pillar 2 of Basel III requires lots of very sensitive judgment calls from regulators (such as the determination of the adequacy of internal bank models) who may be ill-equipped to make them. This will particularly be a problem for developing-country regulators. If Pillar 2 is taken seriously, supervisors may be exposed to a lot of criticism that most would rather avoid.

7. *Leverage, liquidity, and specialness.* Reducing bank leverage levels (through increased capital) will reduce DIs' ROEs and make it harder for them to generate additional capital. Indeed, rather than earning traditional ROEs of more than 15 percent, many DIs will see ROEs in the range of 8 to 10 percent post–Basel III. When added to the two new liquidity ratios introduced under Basel III (discussed

---

[16] However, the more advanced internal ratings–based approach (IRB—see Appendix 20A to this chapter) assesses correlations for borrower exposures. Currently, it is estimated that only approximately 20 (the biggest) U.S. banks use the IRB approach.

in Chapter 12) that force DIs to more closely match maturities of assets and liabilities rather than "borrowing short" and "lending long" as has traditionally been a special feature of DIs, the special features of banking discussed in Chapter 1 will be reduced.

---

**Concept Questions**

1. What are the major strengths of the risk-based capital ratios?
2. You are a DI manager with a total risk-based capital ratio of 6 percent. Discuss four strategies to meet the required 8 percent ratio in a short period of time without raising new capital.
3. Why isn't a capital requirement levied on exchange-traded derivative contracts?
4. What is the difference between Tier I capital and Tier II capital?
5. Identify one asset in each of the credit risk weight categories.

---

# CAPITAL REQUIREMENTS FOR OTHER FINANCIAL INSTITUTIONS

### Securities Firms

Unlike the book value capital rules employed by bank and thrift regulators, the capital requirements for broker–dealers set by the SEC's Rule 15C 3–1 in 1975 are close to a market value accounting rule. Essentially, broker–dealers must calculate a market value for their net worth on a day-to-day basis and ensure that their net worth–assets ratio exceeds 2 percent:

$$\frac{\text{Net worth}}{\text{Assets}} \geq 2\%$$

The essential idea is that if a broker–dealer has to liquidate all assets at near market values, a capital cushion of 2 percent should be sufficient to satisfy all customer liabilities, such as brokerage accounts held with the firm.[17]

Specifically, to compute net capital, the broker–dealer calculates book capital or net worth—the difference between the book values of assets and liabilities—and then makes a number of adjustments: subtracting (1) all assets such as fixed assets not readily convertible into cash and (2) securities that cannot be publicly offered or sold. Moreover, the dealer must make other deductions, or haircuts, reflecting potential market value fluctuations in assets. For example, the net capital rule requires haircuts on illiquid equities of up to 40 percent and on debt securities generally between 0 and 9 percent. Finally, other adjustments must reflect unrealized profits and losses, subordinated liabilities, contractual commitments, deferred taxes, options, commodities and commodity futures, and certain collateralized liabilities. Thus, broker–dealers must make significant adjustments to the book value of net worth to reach an approximate market value net worth figure. This figure must exceed 2 percent of assets.

### Life Insurance

In 1993 the life insurance industry adopted a model risk-based capital scheme. The most recent revision of the scheme occurred in 2011. Although similar in nature to that adopted by banks and thrifts, it is more extensive in that it also covers

---

[17] If a broker–dealer fails with negative net worth, the SIPC provides guarantees of up to $500,000 per customer (see Chapter 19).

www.naic.org other types of risk. Although capital requirements are imposed at the state level, they are heavily influenced by recommendations from the National Association of Insurance Commissioners (NAIC). We describe the NAIC model next.

The model begins by identifying five risks faced by the life insurer:

C0 = Asset risk—affiliate

C1 = Asset risk—other

C2 = Insurance risk

C3 = Interest rate, credit, and market risk

C4 = Business risk

### C0: Asset Risk—Affiliate

Asset risk—affiliate is the risk of default of assets for affiliated investments. The risk-based capital (RBC) requirement of insurance subsidiaries owned by the insurer is calculated based on the total risk-based capital of the subsidiary and then prorated based on the percent of ownership. The RBC requirement for other subsidiaries is calculated based on a set factor. The parent company is required to hold an equivalent amount of risk-based capital to protect against financial downturns of affiliates.

### C1: Asset Risk—Other

Asset risk—other reflects the riskiness of the asset portfolio of the life insurer. It is similar in spirit to the credit risk–adjusted asset calculations for DIs in that a credit risk weight is multiplied by the dollar or face value of the assets on the balance sheet. Table 20–17 shows the relative asset risk weights for life and PC insurers. Thus, an insurer with $100 million in common stocks would have a risk-based capital requirement of $30 million, while for one with $100 million in BBB corporate bonds, only $1 million would be required.

**TABLE 20–17**
**Risk-Based Capital (RBC) Factors for Selected Assets**

| Asset | Insurer | |
|---|---|---|
| | Life | Property–Casualty |
| Bonds: | | |
| U.S. government | 0.0% | 0.0% |
| NAIC 1: AAA–A* | 0.3 | 0.3 |
| NAIC 2: BBB | 1.0 | 1.0 |
| NAIC 3: BB | 4.0 | 2.0 |
| NAIC 4: B | 9.0 | 4.5 |
| NAIC 5: CCC | 20.0 | 10.0 |
| NAIC 6: In or near default | 30.0 | 30.0 |
| Residential mortgages (whole loans) | 0.5[†] | 5.0 |
| Commercial mortgages | 3.0[†] | 5.0 |
| Common stock | 30.0 | 15.0 |
| Preferred stock–bond factor for same NAIC category plus: | 2.0 | 2.0 |

* Includes agencies and most collateralized mortgage obligations.
† Mortgage factors are for loans in good standing. These factors will be adjusted for a company's default experience relative to the industry.

### C2: Insurance Risk

**mortality risk**
The risk of death.

**morbidity risk**
The risk of ill health.

Insurance risk captures the risk of adverse changes in **mortality risk** and **morbidity risk.** As we discussed in Chapter 6, mortality tables give life insurers an extremely accurate idea of the probability that an insured will die in any given year. However, epidemics such as AIDS or H1N1 flu can upset these predictions drastically. As a result, insurers adjust insurance in force for the current level of reserves and multiply the resulting number by an insurance risk factor. Similar calculations are carried out for accident and health insurance, which covers morbidity (ill health) risk.

### C3: Interest Rate, Credit, and Market Risk

Interest rate, credit, and market risk in part reflects the liquidity of liabilities and their probability or ease of withdrawal as interest rates, credit quality, and market risk change. For example, insurance company–issued guaranteed investment contracts (GICs) have characteristics similar to those of long-term, fixed-rate bank deposits and are often highly sensitive to interest rate movements. As we also discuss in Chapter 12, illiquidity problems have led to a number of insurer insolvencies in past years. With respect to interest rate, credit, and market risk, insurers must divide liabilities into three risk classes: low risk (0.5 percent risk-based capital requirement), medium risk (1 percent capital requirement), and high risk (2 percent capital requirement).

### C4: Business Risk

As we discuss in Chapter 19, states have organized guaranty funds that partially pay for insurer insolvencies by levying a charge on surviving firms. Thus, the capital requirement for business risk is set to equal the maximum potential assessment by state guaranty funds (2 percent for life and annuity premiums and 0.5 percent for health premiums for each surviving insurer). Also, company-specific fraud and litigation risks may require an additional capital charge.

After calculating C0, C1, C2, C3, and C4, the life insurance manager computes a risk-based capital measure (RBC) based on the following equation:

$$RBC = C0 + C4 + \sqrt{(C1 + C3)^2 + C2^2 + C3^2 + C4^2}$$

As calculated, the RBC is the minimum required capital for the life insurer. The insurer compares this risk-based capital measure to the actual capital and surplus (total capital) held:

$$\frac{\text{Total surplus and capital}}{\text{Risk-based capital (RBC)}}$$

If this ratio is greater than 1, the life insurance manager is meeting or is above the minimum capital requirements. If the ratio falls below 1, the manager will be subject to regulatory scrutiny.

## Property–Casualty Insurance

Capital requirements for property–casualty (PC) insurers are quite similar to the life insurance industry's RBC—introduced by the NAIC in 1993 and revised most recently in 2011—except that there are six (instead of five) risk categories, including three separate asset risk categories. The risk weights in some areas—especially common stock—are lower than those for life insurers because of the relatively smaller exposures of PC companies to this type of asset risk. The six different types of risk and the calculation of RBC (to be compared with a PC insurer's total capital and surplus) are shown in Table 20–18.

**TABLE 20–18**
Calculation of Total
Risk–Based Capital
(RBC)

| Risk | Type | Description |
|------|------|-------------|
| R0 | Asset | RBC for investments (common and preferred) in property–casualty affiliates |
| R1 | Asset | RBC for fixed income |
| R2 | Asset | RBC for equity—includes common and preferred stocks (other than in property–casualty affiliates) and real estate |
| R3 | Credit | RBC for reinsurance recoverables and other receivables |
| R4 | Underwriting | RBC for loss and loss adjustment expense (LAE) reserves plus growth surcharges |
| R5 | Underwriting | RBC for written premiums plus growth surcharges |

$$RBC = R0 + \sqrt{R1^2 + R2^2 + R3^2 + R4^2 + R5^2}$$

**TABLE 20–19**
Risk-Based Capital
(RBC) Charges for
Typical Company

| Risk | Description | RBC Charge (millions) |
|------|-------------|----------------------|
| R0 | Affiliated property–casualty | $ 10 |
| R1 | Fixed income | 5 |
| R2 | Common stock | 10 |
| R3 | Credit | 10 |
| R4 | Reserve | 40 |
| R5 | Premium | 25 |
| Total charges before covariance | | $100 |

$$RBC = 10 + \sqrt{5^2 + 10^2 + 10^2 + 40^2 + 25^2} = \$59.50$$

The calculation of RBC assumes that risks $R1$ to $R5$ are independent of each other—that is, have a zero correlation coefficient, whereas investments in PC affiliates (risk $R0$) are assumed to be perfectly correlated with the net risk of the $R1$ to $R5$ components. If the total capital and surplus of a PC insurer exceed the calculated RBC, the insurer is viewed as being adequately capitalized. For example, suppose a PC insurer had total capital and surplus of $60 million and its RBC charge is calculated as $59.5 million (as shown in Table 20–19); it has a capital to RBC ratio exceeding 1 (i.e., 60/59.5 = 1.008) and is adequately capitalized.

**Concept Questions**

1. How do the capital requirements for securities firms differ from the book value capital rules employed by DI regulators?
2. What types of risks are included by the NAIC in estimating the RBC of life insurance firms?
3. How does the NAIC's model of risk-based capital requirements for PC insurers differ from the life insurance industry's RBC?

**Summary**

This chapter reviewed the role of an FI's capital in insulating it against credit, interest rate, and other risks. According to economic theory, capital or net worth should be measured on a market value basis as the difference between the market values of assets and liabilities. In actuality, regulators use book value accounting rules. While a book value capital adequacy rule accounts for credit risk exposure in a rough fashion, it overlooks the effects of interest rate changes and interest rate exposure on net worth. We analyzed the specific and proposed capital rules adopted by the regulators of banks and thrifts, insurance companies, and securities firms and discussed their problems and weaknesses. In particular, we looked at how bank, thrift, PC, and life insurance regulators are now adjusting book value–based capital rules to account for different types of risk as part of their imposition of risk-based capital adequacy ratios. As a result, actual capital requirements in banks, life insurance companies, PC insurance companies, and thrifts are moving closer to the market value–based net worth requirements of broker–dealers.

## Questions and Problems

1. Identify and briefly discuss the importance of the five functions of an FI's capital.
2. Why are regulators concerned with the levels of capital held by an FI compared with those held by a nonfinancial institution?
3. What is the difference between the economic definition of capital and the book value definition of capital?
   a. How does economic value accounting recognize the adverse effects of credit risk?
   b. How does book value accounting recognize the adverse effects of credit risk?
4. Why is the market value of equity a better measure of an FI's ability to absorb losses than book value of equity?
5. State Bank has the following year-end balance sheet (in millions):

| Assets | | Liabilities and Equity | |
|---|---|---|---|
| Cash | $ 10 | Deposits | $ 90 |
| Loans | 90 | Equity | 10 |
| Total assets | $100 | Total liabilities and equity | $100 |

The loans primarily are fixed-rate, medium-term loans, while the deposits are either short-term or variable-rate deposits. Rising interest rates have caused the failure of a key industrial company, and as a result, 3 percent of the loans are considered uncollectable and thus have no economic value. One-third of these uncollectable loans will be charged off. Further, the increase in interest rates has caused a 5 percent decrease in the market value of the remaining loans. What is the impact on the balance sheet after the necessary adjustments are made according to book value accounting? According to market value accounting?

6. What are the arguments for and against the use of market value accounting for DIs?
7. What is the significance of prompt corrective action as specified by the FDICIA legislation?
8. What is the Basel Agreement?
9. What are the major features of the Basel III capital requirements?
10. What are the definitional differences between CET1, Tier I, and Tier II capital?
11. Under Basel III, what four capital ratios must DIs calculate and monitor?

12. What are the credit risk-adjusted assets in the denominator of the common equity Tier I (CET1) risk-based capital ratio, the Tier I risk-based capital ratio, and the total risk-based capital ratio?
13. How is the leverage ratio for a DI defined?
14. Identify the five zones of capital adequacy and explain the mandatory regulatory actions corresponding to each zone.
15. Explain the process of calculating credit risk-adjusted on-balance-sheet assets.
16. Under Basel III, how are residential 1–4 family mortgages assigned to a credit risk class?
17. Under Basel III, how are risk weights for sovereign exposures are determined?
18. National Bank has the following balance sheet (in millions) and has no off-balance-sheet activities.

| Assets | | Liabilities and Equity | |
|---|---|---|---|
| Cash | $ 20 | Deposits | $ 980 |
| Treasury bills | 40 | Subordinated debentures | 25 |
| Residential mortgages | 600 | Common stock | 45 |
| (category 1, loan-to-value | | Retained earnings | 40 |
| ratio = 70%) | | Total liabilities and equity | $1,090 |
| Business loans | 430 | | |
| Total assets | $1,090 | | |

   a. What is the CET1, risk-based ratio?
   b. What is the Tier I risk-based capital ratio?
   c. What is the total risk–based capital ratio?
   d. What is the leverage ratio?
   e. In what capital category would the bank be placed?
19. What is the capital conservation buffer? How would this buffer affect your answers to question 18?
20. What is the countercylical capital buffer? If the home country set a countercyclical capital buffer of 1.5 percent, how would this buffer affect your answers to question 18?
21. Onshore Bank has $20 million in assets, with risk-adjusted assets of $10 million. CET1 capital is $500,000, additional Tier I capital is $50,000, and Tier II capital is $400,000. How will each of the following transactions affect the value of the CET1, Tier I, and total capital ratios? What will the new values of each ratio be?
   a. The bank repurchases $100,000 of common stock with cash.
   b. The bank issues $2 million of CDs and uses the proceeds to issue category 1 mortgage loans with a loan-to-value ratio of 80 percent.
   c. The bank receives $500,000 in deposits and invests them in T-bills.
   d. The bank issues $800,000 in common stock and lends it to help finance a new shopping mall.
   e. The bank issues $1 million in nonqualifying perpetual preferred stock and purchases general obligation municipal bonds.
   f. Homeowners pay back $4 million of category 1 mortgages with a loan-to-value ratio of 40 percent and the bank uses the proceeds to build new ATMs.

22. Explain the process of calculating risk-adjusted off-balance-sheet contingent guaranty contracts.
    a. What is the basis for differentiating the credit equivalent amounts of contingent guaranty contracts?
    b. On what basis are the risk weights for the credit equivalent amounts differentiated?
23. Explain how off-balance-sheet market contracts, or derivative instruments, differ from contingent guaranty contracts.
    a. What is counterparty credit risk?
    b. Why do exchange-traded derivative security contracts have no capital requirements?
    c. What is the difference between the potential exposure and the current exposure of over-the-counter derivative contracts?
    d. Why are the credit conversion factors for the potential exposure of foreign exchange contracts greater than they are for interest rate contracts?
    e. Why do regulators not allow DIs to benefit from positive current exposure values?
24. What are G-SIBs? How do capital ratio requirements differ for these FIs?
25. Identify and discuss the problems in the risk-based capital approach to measuring capital adequacy.
26. What is the contribution to the credit risk–adjusted asset base of the following items under the Basel III requirements?
    a. $10 million cash reserves.
    b. $50 million 91-day U.S. Treasury bills.
    c. $25 million cash items in the process of collection.
    d. $5 million U.K. government bonds, OECD CRC rated 1.
    e. $5 million French short-term government bonds, OECD CRC rated 2.
    f. $1 million general obligation municipal bonds.
    g. $40 million repurchase agreements (against U.S. Treasuries).
    h. $2 million loan to foreign banks, OECD CRC rated 3.
    i. $500 million 1–4-family home mortgages, category 1, loan-to-value ratio 80%.
    j. $10 million 1–4-family home mortgages, category 2, loan-to-value ratio 95%.
    k. $5 million 1–4-family home mortgages, 100 days past due.
    l. $500 million commercial and industrial loans, AAA rated.
    m. $500 million commercial and industrial loans, B-rated.
    n. $100,000 performance-related standby letters of credit to an AAA rated corporation.
    o. $100,000 performance-related standby letters of credit to a municipality issuing general obligation bonds.
    p. $7 million commercial letter of credit to a foreign bank, OECD CRC rated 2.
    q. $3 million five-year loan commitment to foreign government, OECD CRC rated 1.
    r. $8 million bankers' acceptance conveyed to a U.S., AA rated corporation.
    s. $17 million three-year loan commitment to a private agent.
    t. $17 million three-month loan commitment to a private agent.
    u. $30 million standby letter of credit to back an A rated corporate issue of commercial paper.
    v. $4 million five-year interest rate swap with no current exposure.
    w. $6 million two-year currency swap with $500,000 current exposure.

27. How does the leverage ratio test impact the stringency of regulatory monitoring of DI capital positions?
28. Third Bank has the following balance sheet (in millions), with the risk weights in parentheses.

| Assets | | Liabilities and Equity | |
|---|---|---|---|
| Cash (0%) | $ 21 | Deposits | $176 |
| OECD interbank deposits (20%) | 25 | Subordinated debt (5 years) | 2 |
| Mortgage loans (50%) | 70 | Cumulative preferred stock | 2 |
| Consumer loans (100%) | 70 | Equity | 5 |
| Resesrve for loan losses | (1) | Total liabilities and equity | $185 |
| Total assets | $185 | | |

The cumulative preferred stock is qualifying and perpetual. In addition, the bank has $30 million in performance-related standby letters of credit (SLCs) to a public corporation, $40 million in two-year forward FX contracts that are currently in the money by $1 million, and $300 million in six-year interest rate swaps that are currently out of the money by $2 million. Credit conversion factors follow:

| | |
|---|---|
| Performance-related standby LCs | 50% |
| 1- to 5-year foreign exchange contracts | 5% |
| 1- to 5-year interest rate swaps | 0.5% |
| 5- to 10-year interest rate swaps | 1.5% |

a. What are the risk-adjusted on-balance-sheet assets of the bank as defined under the Basel Accord?
b. To be adequately capitalized, what are the CET1, Tier I, and total capital required for both off- and on-balance-sheet assets?
c. Disregarding the capital conservation buffer, does the bank have enough capital to meet the Basel requirements? If not, what minimum, CET1, additional Tier I, or total capital does it need to meet the requirement?
d. Does the bank have enough capital to meet the Basel requirements, including the capital conservation buffer requirement? If not, what minimum CET1, additional Tier I, or total capital does it need to meet the requirement?
29. Third Fifth Bank has the following balance sheet (in millions), with the risk weights in parentheses.

| Assets | | Liabilities and Equity | |
|---|---|---|---|
| Cash (0%) | $ 21 | Deposits | $133 |
| Mortgage loans (50%) | 50 | Subordinated debt (>5 years) | 1 |
| Consumer loans (100%) | 70 | Equity | 6 |
| Reserve for loan losses | (1) | Total liabilities and equity | $140 |
| Total assets | $140 | | |

In addition, the bank has $20 million in commercial direct-credit substitute standby letters of credit to a public corporation and $40 million in 10-year FX forward contracts that are in the money by $1 million.

a. What are the risk-adjusted on-balance-sheet assets of the bank as defined under Basel III?

b. What is the CET1, Tier I, and total capital required for both off- and on-balance-sheet assets?

c. Disregarding the capital conservation buffer, does the bank have sufficient capital to meet the Basel requirements? How much in excess? How much short?

d. Does the bank have enough capital to meet the Basel requirements, including the capital conservation buffer requirement? If not, what minimum CET1, additional Tier I, or total capital does it need to meet the requirement?

30. According to SEC Rule 15C 3–1, what adjustments must securities firms make in the calculation of the book value of net worth?

31. A securities firm has the following balance sheet (in millions):

| Assets | | Liabilities and Equity | |
|---|---|---|---|
| Cash | $ 40 | Five-day commercial paper | $ 20 |
| Debt securities | 300 | Bonds | 550 |
| Equity securities | 500 | Debentures | 300 |
| Other assets | 60 | Equity | 30 |
| Total assets | $900 | Total liabilities and equity | $900 |

The debt securities have a coupon rate of 6 percent, 20 years remaining until maturity, and trade at a yield of 8 percent. The equity securities have a market value equal to book value, and the other assets represent building and equipment that was recently appraised at $80 million. The company has 1 million shares of stock outstanding and its price is $35 per share. Is this company in compliance with SEC Rule 15C 3–1?

32. An investment bank specializing in fixed-income assets has the following balance sheet (in millions). Amounts are in market values and all interest rates are annual unless indicated otherwise.

| Assets | | Liabilities and Equity | |
|---|---|---|---|
| Cash | $ 0.5 | 5% 1-year Eurodollar deposits | $ 5.0 |
| 8% 10-year Treasury notes | | 6% 2-year subordinated debt | |
| semiannual (par = $16.0) | 15.0 | (par = $10.0) | 10.0 |
| | | Equity | 0.5 |
| Total assets | $15.5 | Total liabilities and equity | $15.5 |

Assume that the haircut for all assets is 15 basis points and for all liabilities, 25 basis points (per year).

a. Does the investment bank have sufficient liquid capital to cushion any unexpected losses per the net capital rule?

b. What should the FI do to maintain the net minimum required liquidity?

c. How does the net capital rule for investment banks differ from the capital requirements imposed on depository institutions?

33. Identify and define the five risk categories incorporated into the life insurance risk-based capital model.

34. A life insurance company has estimated capital requirements for each of the following risk classes: asset risk-affiliate (C0) = $2 million, asset risk-other (C1) = $5 million, insurance risk (C2) = $4 million, interest rate risk (C3) = $1 million, and business risk (C4) = $3 million.
    a. What is the required risk-based capital for the life insurance company?
    b. If the total surplus and capital held by the company is $11.34 million, does it meet the minimum requirements?
    c. How much capital must be raised to meet the minimum requirements?

35. How do the risk categories in the risk-based capital model for property–casualty insurance companies differ from those for life insurance companies? What are the assumed relationships between the risk categories in the model?

36. A property–casualty insurance company has estimated the following required charges for its various risk classes (in millions):

| Risk | Description | RBC Charge |
|------|-------------|-----------|
| R0 | Affiliated P/C | $ 2 |
| R1 | Fixed income | 3 |
| R2 | Common stock | 4 |
| R3 | Reinsurance | 3 |
| R4 | Loss adjustment expense | 2 |
| R5 | Written premiums | 3 |
| Total | | $17 |

    a. What is the RBC charge per the model recommended by the NAIC?
    b. If the firm currently has $7 million in capital, what should be its surplus to meet the minimum capital requirement?

## Web Question

37. Go to the website of the Bank for International Settlements at **www.bis.org.** Under "Basel Committee on Bank Supervision," click on "Basel III." This will download a file onto your computer that contains information on the most recent set of capital requirements for depository institutions. How have these changed since 2013?

# Integrated Mini Case

## CALCULATING CAPITAL REQUIREMENTS

A bank's balance sheet information is listed below (in $000).

1. What is the bank's risk-adjusted asset base under Basel III?

2. To be adequately capitalized, what are the bank's CET1, Tier I, and total risk–based capital requirements under Basel II?

3. Using the leverage ratio requirement, what is the minimum regulatory capital required to keep the bank in the well-capitalized zone?

4. Disregarding the capital conservation buffer, what is the bank's capital adequacy level (under Basel III) if the par value of its equity is $225,000, surplus value of equity is $200,000, qualifying perpetual preferred stock is $50,000, subordinated debt is $50,000, and loan loss reserve is $85,000? Does the bank meet Basel

(CET1, Tier I, and total) adequate capital standards? Does the bank comply with the well-capitalized leverage ratio requirement?

5. Does the bank have enough capital to meet the Basel requirements, including the capital conservation buffer requirement?

6. The bank's various lines of business produced the following gross income:

| Retail banking | $40,000 |
| Commercial banking | 50,000 |
| Payment and settlement | 15,000 |
| Trading and sales | 5,000 |
| Asset management | 10,000 |

What is the add-on to capital for operational risk? Does the bank have sufficient capital to cover this add-on and remain adequately capitalized, while meeting the capital conservation buffer?

| On-Balance-Sheet Items | Face Value |
| --- | --- |
| Cash | $ 121,600 |
| Short-term government securities ($<$92 days) | 5,400 |
| Long-term government securities ($>$92 days) | 414,400 |
| Federal Reserve stock | 9,800 |
| Repos secured by federal agencies | 159,000 |
| Claims on U.S. depository institutions | 937,900 |
| Loans to foreign banks, OECD CRC rated 2 | 1,640,000 |
| General obligation municipals | 170,000 |
| Claims on or guaranteed by federal agencies | 26,500 |
| Municipal revenue bonds | 112,900 |
| Residential mortgages category 1, loan-to-value ratio 75% | 5,000,000 |
| Commercial loans. | 4,667,669 |
| Loans to sovereigns, OECD CRC rated 3 | 11,600 |
| Premises and equipment | 455,000 |

| Off-Balance-Sheet Items | Conversion Factor | Face Value |
| --- | --- | --- |
| **U.S. Government Counterparty** | | |
| Loan commitments: | | |
| $<$1 year | 20% | $ 300 |
| 1–5 years | 50% | 1,140 |
| Standby letters of credit: | | |
| Performance-related | 50% | 200 |
| Direct-credit substitute | 100% | 100 |
| **U.S. Depository Institutions Counterparty** | | |
| Loan commitments: | | |
| $<$1 year | 20% | 100 |
| $>$1 year | 50% | 3,000 |
| Standby letters of credit: | | |
| Performance-related | 50% | 200 |
| Direct-credit substitute | 100% | 56,400 |
| Commercial letters of credit: | 20% | 400 |

| Off-Balance-Sheet Items | Conversion Factor | Face Value |
|---|---|---|
| **State and Local Governments Counterparty (revenue municipals)** | | |
| Loan commitments: | | |
| >1 year | 50% | 100 |
| Standby letters of credit: | | |
| Performance-related | 50% | 135,400 |
| **Corporate Customers Counterparty** | | |
| Loan commitments: | | |
| <1 year | 20% | 3,212,400 |
| >1 year | 50% | 3,046,278 |
| Standby letters of credit: | | |
| Performance-related | 50% | 101,543 |
| Direct-credit substitute | 100% | 490,900 |
| Commercial letters of credit: | 20% | 78,978 |
| **Sovereign Counterparty** | | |
| Loan commitments, OECD CRC rated 1: | | |
| <1 year | 20% | 110,500 |
| >1 year | 50% | 1,225,400 |
| **Sovereign Counterparty** | | |
| Loan commitments, OECD CRC rated 2: | | |
| <1 year | 20% | 85,000 |
| >1 year | 50% | 115,500 |
| **Sovereign Counterparty** | | |
| Loan commitments, OECD CRC rated 7: | | |
| >1 year | 50% | 30,000 |
| Interest rate market contracts (current exposure assumed to be zero): | | |
| <1 year (notional amount) | 0% | 2,000 |
| >1–5 years (notional amount) | 0.5% | 5,000 |

## Appendix 20A

# Internal Ratings-Based Approach to Measuring Credit Risk-Adjusted Assets

The main body of this chapter described the Standardized Approach to measuring credit risk–adjusted asset values for DIs under Basel III. Rather than using the Standardized Approach, DIs with a sufficient number of internal credit risk rating grades for loans may (with regulatory approval) adopt one of two Internal Ratings–Based (IRB) approaches to calculating credit risk–adjusted assets for capital requirements: the *Foundations Approach* and the *Advanced Approach.* The IRB results in an individualized capital requirement for each asset depending on five key variables. That is, in general, for asset *i*:

$$\text{Capital requirement}_i = f(PD_i, LGD_i, R_i, EAD_i, M_i)$$

where

$PD_i$ = One-year probability of default of the *i*th borrower

$LGD_i$ = Loss given default of the *i*th borrower

$R_i$ = Correlation of the *i*th borrower with the rest of the economy

$EAD_i$ = Amount (in dollars) of exposure at default

$M_i$ = Maturity of the loan

Under the Foundations Approach to corporate, bank, and sovereign exposures, a DI internally estimates the one-year probability of default (PD) associated with a borrower class, as well as its exposure at default (EAD) to the borrower, while relying on supervisory rules for the estimation of the three other risk components (LGD, *R*, and *M*). With regulatory approval, DIs may use the Advanced Approach, in which DIs use internal estimates of two additional risk measures: loss given default (LGD) and maturity (*M*). For both models, *R* (the correlation of the borrower's risk with the economy) is set by the regulator.

Under these models a distinction is made between capital that is held to meet unexpected losses (UL) and loss reserves that are held to meet expected losses (EL). The distinction is shown in Figure 20A–1, which shows the probability of loss on a given loan. For simplicity (and as assumed by the Basel III model), this is normally distributed.

As can be seen, a DI's loss reserve is meant to cover losses up to the expected loss on the loan, which is simply the probability of default (PD) on a loan times its loss given default (LGD) or $EL = PD \times LGD$. However, a DI's capital is meant to protect it against unexpected losses, that is, losses *beyond* those that are expected. Indeed, under Basel III, the capital reserves and loss reserves together are meant to be sufficiently large to protect the DI against failure (i.e., losses exceeding the two reserves held by the DI) in all but 1 year in 1,000, or 99.9 percent of the time. In Figure 20A–1, the required capital for unexpected loss is shown as the distance between the expected losses and the 99.9 percent loss point, where there is only a 0.1 percent chance of losses exceeding this amount.

If we call the *whole* loss distribution up to the 99.9 percent point the *value at risk* (VAR) on the loan, then:

$$VAR_{loan} = EL_{loan} + UL_{loan} = \text{Loan loss reserves} + \text{Capital reserves}$$

This can be rewritten as:

$$\text{Capital reserves} = VAR_{loan} - EL_{loan} \quad (UL)$$

Next, assume that the loss given default is constant over time (this is an assumption of the Basel III model).[1] However, the probability of default (PD) will be higher in bad economic conditions than in average conditions. Call the probability of default in unexpectedly adverse conditions the conditional probability of default (PD conditional) and that in average conditions the average probability of default (PD average).

Under Basel III the amount of capital the bank needs to hold is thus:

$$\begin{aligned} \text{Capital reserves} &= VAR_{loan} - EL_{loan} \\ &= (LGD \times PD_{conditional}) - (LGD \times PD) \end{aligned}$$

---

[1] In practice DIs are meant to calculate an LGD in down-market conditions.

**FIGURE 20A–1**
**Probability of Loss on a Given Loan**

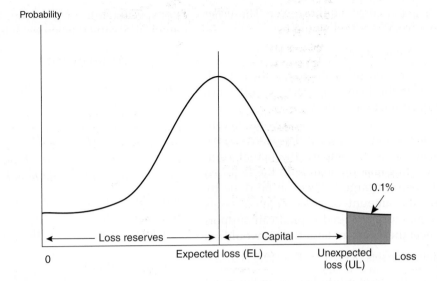

Under Basel III the conditional probability of default is a correlation ($R$) weighted average of the average probability of default and the 99.9 percent probability of default. Technically:

$$PD_{conditional} = N\,[(1 - R)^{-0.5} \times G\,(PD)$$
$$+ (R / 1 - R)^{0.5} \times G\,(0.999)]$$

or

$$PD_{conditional} = N\,[w_1 G\,(PD_{avg}) + w_2 G\,(0.999)]$$

where $N[\cdot]$ is the area under the normal distribution, $G[\cdot]$ is the inverse of the area under the normal distribution,[2] and $w_i$ is the correlation weight. Since it has been shown that the longer the maturity of the loan the more likely it is to default, the Basel III model requires that the basic amount of capital computed above be multiplied by a maturity adjustment factor. Thus:

$$\text{Capital reserves} = [VAR_{loss} - \text{Expected loss}]$$
$$(\text{UL}) \qquad \times \text{Maturity adjustment}$$

Technically:

$$\text{Maturity adjustment} = (1 - 1.5 \times b)^{-1}$$
$$\times [1 + (M - 2.5) \times b]$$

where

$$b = [0.11852 - 0.05478 \times \ln (PD)]^2$$

[2] According to the BIS, the functions $N$ and $G$ are generally available in spreadsheet and statistical packages. For both functions, the mean should be set equal to zero and the standard deviation should be set equal to 1.

Intuitively, $b$ is similar to the slope of a regression line, reflecting the degree to which default risk increases with the maturity of the loan.

If we now put together the basic capital requirement ($VAR_{loss}$ − Expected loss) and the maturity adjustment, then we have the full Basel III capital requirement under the IRB models (i.e., both Foundations and Advanced). This is:

Capital requirement ($k$)

$$=[VAR_{loss}-\text{Expected loss}] \times \text{Maturity adjustment}$$

or

$$\text{Capital requirement } (k) = [LGD \times N[(1 - R)^{-0.5}$$
$$\times G(PD) + (R / (1 - R))^{0.5} \times G(0.999)]$$
$$- (PD \times LGD)] \times (1 - 1.5 \times b)^{-1}$$
$$\times [1 + (M - 2.5) \times b]$$

where $R$ is the correlation coefficient on the loan (with the economy) and is set by the regulator to lie between 0.12 and 0.24 (for both the Foundations and the Advanced models) according to the probability of default on the loan (PD). That is:

$$\text{Correlation}(R) = 1.25 \times [0.12 \times [1 - EXP(-50 \times PD)]$$
$$/[1 - EXP(-50)] + 0.24 \times \{1 - [1 - EXP(-50 \times PD)] / [1 - EXP(-50)]\}]$$

The correlation ($R$) is assumed to be inversely related to the PD on the loan. The above formula shows the amount of capital required per $1 of loans to a given corporate borrower. The *dollar* amount of capital required would be:

$$\text{Dollar capital} = K \times EAD$$

where EAD, or exposure at default, is the net dollar amount of the loan (adjusted for collateral) outstanding at the time of default.

Alternatively, since the Basel III model is calibrated to achieving an overall 8 percent capital requirement, we can compare the actual capital being held against the loan with the required amount (8 percent target). This can be done by computing the amount of risk-weighted assets that the regulatory required capital can support (so as to meet the 8 percent target). This would be:

$$\text{Risk-weighted assets} (RWA) = K \times 12.5 \times EAD$$

where 12.5 is the asset multiplier for an 8 percent capital ratio (i.e., $1/0.08 = 12.5$).

The issue for capital adequacy is whether:

$$\frac{\text{Actual capital}}{RWA} \geq 8\%$$

where actual capital reflects the amount of capital currently being held by the DI against an unexpected loss of the loan, that is, $K_{actual}$, the amount of capital held per dollar, times EAD.

$$\text{Actual capital} = K_{actual} \times EAD$$

Thus, the acid test is whether:

$$\frac{\text{Actual capital}}{RWA} = \frac{(K_{actual} \times EAD)}{(K \times 12.5 \times EAD)}$$
$$= \frac{K_{actual}}{K \times 12.5} \geq 8\%$$

where $K$ is the required regulatory capital determined above.

Clearly if $K_{actual} = K$, then the 8 percent target is reached; that is, $\dfrac{K_{actual}}{K = 12.5} = 8\%$. This can be seen because the $K$'s cancel, leaving $\dfrac{1}{12.5} = 0.08$ or 8%. If $K_{actual}$ exceeds $K$, then the 8 percent target is exceeded, and if $K_{actual} < K$, then the DI will be capital deficient. In this latter situation, the DI would have to either cut back its loans to the borrower or increase its capital.

# Appendix 20B: Methodology Used to Determine G-SIBs' Capital Surcharge

View Appendix 20B at the website for this textbook (**www.mhhe.com/saunders8e**).

# Chapter Twenty-One

**See Appendices Online at www.mhhe.com/saunders8e**

• Appendix 21A: EU and G-10 Countries: Regulatory Treatment of the Mixing of Banking, Securities, and Insurance Activities and the Mixing of Banking and Commerce

# Product and Geographic Expansion

## INTRODUCTION

**universal FI**
An FI that can engage in a broad range of financial service activities.

The U.S. financial system has traditionally been structured along separatist or segmented product lines. Regulatory barriers and restrictions have often inhibited the ability of an FI operating in one area of the financial services industry to expand its product set into other areas. This might be compared with FIs operating in Germany, Switzerland, and the United Kingdom, where a more **universal FI** structure allows individual financial services organizations to offer a far broader range of banking, insurance, securities, and other financial services products. Just as product expansion has traditionally been restricted for U.S. banks, so has geographic expansion. Geographic expansions can have a number of dimensions. In particular, they can be either domestic, within a state or region, or international, by participating in a foreign market. Many FIs can diversify domestically, but only the very largest can aspire to diversify beyond national frontiers. Expansions can also be effected through opening a new office or branch or by acquiring another FI.

The merger between Citicorp and Travelers to create Citigroup, the then third-largest universal bank or financial conglomerate in the world, was a sign that the importance of regulatory barriers in the United States was receding. Moreover, the passage of the Riegle-Neal Interstate Banking and Branching Efficiency Act of 1994 and the Financial Services Modernization Act of 1999 (discussed below) has accelerated the reduction in the barriers among financial service firms. Indeed, as consolidation in the U.S. and global financial services industry proceeds, we are likely to see an acceleration in the creation of very large, globally oriented, multiproduct financial service firms that will operate with a new set of risks and management strategies to handle these risks. Table 21–1 shows the largest financial service firms in the world (measured by assets) as of 2012. Note that these banks are headquartered throughout the world, and the United States is headquarters to only 2 of the top 10 financial service firms worldwide.

**TABLE 21–1**
The 10 Largest Banks in the World (in billions of dollars)

Source: *The Banker,* July 2012. *www.thebanker.com*

| | Total Assets |
|---|---|
| Deutsche Bank (Germany) | $2,800.1 |
| Mitsubishi UFJ Financial Group (Japan) | 2,664.2 |
| HSBC Holdings (United Kingdom) | 2,555.6 |
| BNP Paribas (France) | 2,542.9 |
| ICBC (China) | 2,456.3 |
| Crédit Agricole Groupe (France) | 2,431.9 |
| Barclays Bank (United Kingdom) | 2,417.4 |
| Royal Bank of Scotland (United Kingdom) | 2,329.8 |
| J.P. Morgan Chase (United States) | 2,265.8 |
| Bank of America (United States) | 2,136.6 |

This chapter first examines product diversification. We analyze the problems and risks that can arise, and have arisen historically, for U.S. FIs constrained to limited financial service sectors or franchises as well as the potential benefits from greater product expansion of the Citigroup kind; the laws and regulations that have restricted product expansions for banks, insurance companies, and securities firms in the United States and elsewhere, as well as the recent modifications of many of these laws and regulations; barriers to product expansion between the financial sector and the real or commercial sector of the economy; and the advantages and disadvantages of allowing U.S. FIs to adopt more universal franchises, as appears to be the current trend. Second, we examine the potential benefits and costs to the risk management strategies considered by FI managers from domestic and international geographic expansion—especially through mergers and acquisitions. In particular, we examine the potential return-risk advantages and disadvantages of such expansions. We also present some evidence on the cost and revenue synergies as well as other market and firm-specific factors impacting geographic expansion.

## PRODUCT DIVERSIFICATION

**money market mutual funds (MMMFs)**
Mutual funds that offer high liquidity, check-writing ability, and a money market return to smaller individual investors.

Historically, many U.S. financial service firms have faced return and risk problems due to constraints on product diversification. Arguably, product expansion restrictions have affected commercial banks the most. For example, to the extent that regulations have limited the franchise of banks to traditional areas such as deposit taking and commercial lending, banks have been increasingly susceptible to nonbank or shadow bank competition on both the liability and asset sides of their balance sheets. Specifically, the growth of **money market mutual funds (MMMFs)** that offer checking account–like deposit services with high liquidity, stability of value, and an attractive return has proven to be very strong competition for bank deposit and transaction account products. From virtually no assets in 1972, MMMFs had grown to more than $2.5 trillion by June 2012, compared to money market deposit accounts of $3.8 trillion in commercial banks. In addition, until recently banks have been threatened by the growth of annuities offered by the life insurance industry. Annuities are a savings product that have many of the same features as bank CDs. In 2012, fixed and variable annuities held in U.S. retirement funds totaled $1.7 trillion.

On the asset side of the balance sheet, the commercial and industrial (C&I) loans of banks have faced increased competition from the dynamic growth of the commercial paper market as an alternative source of short-term financing for large- and middle-sized corporations. For example, in January 1988, C&I loans outstanding were $565 billion versus $380 billion of commercial paper; in June 2012, C&I loans were $1.37 trillion versus $1.00 trillion of commercial paper outstanding. In addition, relatively unregulated finance companies are taking an increasing share of the business credit market. In June 2012, the ratio of finance company business credit to bank C&I loans was approximately 31 percent.

These trends mean that the economic value of narrowly defined bank franchises has declined. In particular, product line restrictions inhibit the ability of an FI to optimize the set of financial services it can offer, potentially forcing it to adopt a more risky set of activities than it would adopt if it could fully diversify.

Product restrictions also limit the ability of FI managers to adjust flexibly to shifts in the demand for financial products by consumers and to shifts in costs due to technology and related innovations. We analyze the advantages and disadvantages of increased product line diversification in more detail after we look more closely at the major laws and regulations segmenting the U.S. financial services industry and ways in which U.S. FIs have tried to overcome the effects of such regulations.

| **Concept Questions** | 1. Offer support for the claim that product expansion restrictions have affected commercial banks more than any other type of financial services firm. |
|---|---|
| | 2. What sources of competition have had an impact on the asset side of banks' balance sheets? |

# SEGMENTATION IN THE U.S. FINANCIAL SERVICES INDUSTRY

## Commercial and Investment Banking Activities

**commercial banking**
Banking activity of deposit taking and lending.

**investment banking**
Banking activity of underwriting, issuing, and distributing securities.

The United States has experienced several phases in regulating the links between the commercial and investment banking industries. Simply defined, **commercial banking** is the activity of deposit taking and commercial lending; **investment banking** is the activity of underwriting, issuing, and distributing securities.

After the 1929 stock market crash, the United States entered a major recession and some 10,000 banks failed between 1930 and 1933. A commission of inquiry (the Pecora Commission), established in 1932, began looking into the causes of the crash. The commission pointed to banks' securities activities and the inherent abuses and conflicts of interest that arise when commercial and investment banking activities were mixed as major causes. The findings resulted in new legislation, the 1933 Banking Act, or the Glass-Steagall Act. The Glass-Steagall Act sought to impose a rigid separation between commercial banking—taking deposits and making commercial loans—and investment banking—underwriting, issuing, and distributing stocks, bonds, and other securities. Specifically, the act limited the ability of banks and securities firms to engage directly in each other's activities and also limited the ability of banks and securities firms to engage indirectly in such activities through separately established affiliates.

For most of the 1933–63 period, commercial banks and investment banks generally appeared to be willing to abide by the letter and spirit of the Glass-Steagall Act. However, between 1963 and 1987, banks challenged restrictions on municipal revenue bond underwriting, commercial paper underwriting, discount brokerage, managing and advising of open- and closed-end mutual funds, underwriting of mortgage-backed securities, and selling annuities. In most cases, the courts eventually upheld these activities.

With this onslaught and de facto erosion of the Glass-Steagall Act by legal interpretation, in April 1987 the Federal Reserve Board allowed commercial bank holding companies—such as Citicorp, the then-parent of Citibank—to establish separate **Section 20 affiliates** as investment banks. Through these Section 20 affiliates, bank holding companies began to conduct all their ineligible or gray area securities activities, such as commercial paper underwriting, mortgage-backed securities underwriting, and municipal revenue bond underwriting.[1] Note the organizational structure of Bank of America Corp., its bank, and the Section 20 subsidiary (or investment bank) in Figure 21–1.

**Section 20 affiliate**
A securities subsidiary of a bank holding company through which a banking organization engages in investment banking activities.

Legally, these Section 20 subsidiaries did not violate Section 20 of the Glass-Steagall Act, which restricts bank–securities firm affiliations as long as the revenue generated from the securities underwriting activities restricted under the act amounted to less than 50 percent of the total revenues they generated; that is, a majority of a Section 20 subsidiary's revenue does *not* come from ineligible security activities.

Significant changes occurred in 1997 as the Federal Reserve and the Office of the Comptroller of the Currency (OCC) took actions to expand bank holding companies' permitted activities. In particular, the Federal Reserve allowed commercial banks to acquire directly existing investment banks rather than establish completely new Section 20 investment banking subsidiaries. The result was a number of mergers and acquisitions between commercial and investment banks in 1997 through 2000. Indeed, the largest FI merger prior to those completed during the financial crisis (see below) was Citicorp's $83 billion merger with Travelers Group in April 1998. The FIs stated that one motivation for the acquisition was the desire to establish a presence in the securities business as laws separating investment banking and commercial banking were changing. Also noted as a motivation in the merger was the opportunity to expand business lines, taking advantage of economies of scale and scope to reduce overall costs and merge the customer bases of the respective FIs involved in the acquisitions.

The erosion of the product barriers between the commercial and investment banking industries was not one way. Large investment banks such as Merrill Lynch increasingly sought to offer banking products. For example, in the late

**FIGURE 21–1**
**A Bank Holding Company and Its Bank and Section 20 Subsidiary**

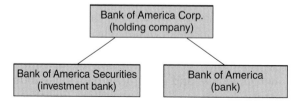

---

[1] In 1989 corporate bond underwriting and in 1990 corporate equities underwriting were added to the permitted list.

1970s, Merrill Lynch introduced the cash management account (CMA), which allowed investors to own a money market mutual fund with check-writing privileges into which bond and stock sale proceeds could be swept on a daily basis. This account allowed the investor to earn interest on cash held in a brokerage account. In addition, many investment banks acted as deposit brokers. As we discussed in Chapter 18, deposit brokers charge a fee to break large deposits into $100,000 deposit units and place them in banks across the country. Further, investment banks have been major participants as traders and investors in the secondary market for LDC and other loans (see Chapters 14 and 25).

In recognition of the years of "homemade" deregulation by banks and securities firms described above, the U.S. Congress passed the Financial Services Modernization Act (FSMA), which repealed the Glass-Steagall barriers between commercial banking and investment banking.[2] The bill, promoted as the biggest change in the regulation of financial institutions in nearly 70 years, allowed for the creation of "financial services holding companies" that could engage in banking activities *and* securities activities through a Section 4(k)(4)(E) securities subsidiary (replacing the Section 20 subsidiary). The bill also allowed large national banks to place certain activities, including some securities underwritings, in direct bank subsidiaries regulated by the Office of the Comptroller of the Currency. Thus, after nearly 70 years of partial or complete separation between investment banking and commercial banking, the Financial Services Modernization Act of 1999 opened the door for the creation of full-service financial institutions in the United States similar to those that existed before 1933 and that exist in many other countries today.

After the passage of FSMA, the two industries came together to a degree. Commercial banks like Bank of America and Wachovia tried to build up their own investment-banking operations, but they did not have much success in eating into the core franchises of the five big independent investment banks: Merrill Lynch, Goldman Sachs, Morgan Stanley, Lehman Brothers, and Bear Stearns. Generally, the investment banks, which were not subject to regulation by the Federal Reserve and did not have to adhere to as strict capital requirements, remained the major investment banking financial institutions. However, the financial crisis changed the landscape dramatically. In March 2008, the Federal Reserve helped J.P. Morgan acquire Bear Stearns as the investment bank faced bankruptcy. This was seen as a controversial decision and cost the Federal Reserve $30 billion. However, the Fed defended the move as essential. In September 2008, Lehman Brothers was allowed to fail and Merrill Lynch was purchased by Bank of America.

Of the five major independent investment banks that existed a year earlier, only two—Goldman Sachs and Morgan Stanley—remained. However, these two FIs were facing severe liquidity crises during the weekend of September 20–21, 2008. To address the crises, one week after the closure of Lehman Brothers and the sale of Merrill Lynch to Bank of America, the Federal Reserve granted a request by the investment banks to change their status to bank holding companies. By becoming bank holding companies, the firms agreed to significantly tighter regulations and much closer supervision by bank examiners from several government agencies rather than only the Securities and Exchange Commission. With the conversion, the investment banks would look more like commercial banks, with more disclosure, higher capital reserves and less risk taking. In exchange for subjecting

---

[2] The Financial Services Modernization Act also reduced the barriers between commercial banking and insurance.

themselves to more regulation, the companies would have access to the full array of the Federal Reserve's lending facilities. For example, as bank holding companies, Morgan and Goldman now have greater access to the discount window of the Federal Reserve, which banks can use to borrow money from the central bank. These events on Wall Street—the failure or sale of three of the five largest independent investment banks and the conversion of the two remaining firms from investment banks to commercial banks—effectively turned back the clock to the 1920s, when investment banks and commercial banks functioned under the same corporate umbrella.

As part of the increased authority given to the Federal Reserve in the 2010 Wall Street Reform and Consumer Protection Act, the Fed proposed in late 2011 that net credit exposures between any two of the nation's six largest financial firms would be limited to 10 percent of the company's regulatory capital. Other financial firms would be subject to a 25 percent limit, which was required by the 2010 act. The proposed Fed rule aims to reduce the interconnectedness of financial institutions in the U.S. financial system and reduce the ability of any single financial firm to damage the financial system and the broader economy—as happened when Lehman Brothers was allowed to fail. The result of the new rules is that big U.S. banks could be forced to return to a more traditional banking model that revolves around deposit taking and making loans. This could result in smaller capital markets and less securities lending.

## Banking and Insurance

Certain types of insurance—for example, credit life insurance, mortgage insurance, and auto insurance—tend to have natural synergistic links to bank lending products. Moreover, we must make a distinction between a bank selling insurance as an agent by selling other FIs' policies for a fee and a bank acting as an insurance underwriter and bearing the direct risk of underwriting losses. In general, the risks of insurance agency activities are quite low in loss potential compared to insurance underwriting.

Prior to the Financial Services Modernization Act of 1999, banks were under very stringent restrictions when selling and underwriting almost every type of insurance. For example, national banks were restricted to offering credit-related life, accident, health, or unemployment insurance. Moreover, they could act as insurance agents only in small towns of less than 5,000 people (although they could sell insurance from these offices anywhere in the United States). Further, the Bank Holding Company Act of 1956 (and its 1970 amendments) and the Garn-St. Germain Depository Institutions Act of 1982 placed severe restrictions on bank holding companies establishing separately capitalized insurance affiliates and on insurance companies acquiring banks. Most states also took quite restrictive actions regarding the insurance activities of state-chartered banks. A few states—most notably Delaware—passed liberal laws allowing state-chartered banks to underwrite and broker various types of property–casualty and life insurance. This encouraged large bank holding companies such as Chase to enter Delaware and establish state-chartered banking subsidiaries with their own insurance affiliates.

**nonbank bank**
A bank divested of its commercial loans and/or demand deposits.

Beginning in the early 1980s, several insurance companies and commercial firms found indirect ways to engage in banking activities. This was through the organizational mechanism of establishing **nonbank bank** subsidiaries. The 1956 Bank Holding Company Act legally defined a bank as an organization that both accepts demand deposits and makes commercial and industrial loans and severely limited the ability of an insurance company or commercial firm to acquire such a bank. An insurance company could get around this restrictive provision by buying a full-service bank and then divesting its demand deposits or commercial loans. This converted the bank into a nonbank bank. In 1987, Congress passed the Competitive Equality Banking Act (CEBA), blocking the nonbank bank loophole. This essentially prevented the creation of any new nonbank banks by redefining a bank as any institution that accepts and is accepted for deposit insurance coverage.

A great challenge to the Bank Holding Company Act and CEBA came from the 1998 merger between Citicorp and Travelers to create the largest financial services conglomerate in the United States. The primary activity of Travelers was insurance (life and property–casualty), while the primary activity of Citicorp was banking (both also were engaged in securities activities: Citicorp through its Section 20 subsidiary and Travelers through its earlier acquisition of Smith Barney and Salomon Brothers). Under the Bank Holding Company Act, the Federal Reserve had up to five years to formally approve the merger. The Federal Reserve gave initial approval in September 1998.

The Financial Services Modernization Act of 1999 completely changed the landscape for insurance activities (and implicitly ratified the Citicorp-Travelers merger) as it allowed bank holding companies to open insurance underwriting affiliates and insurance companies to open commercial bank as well as securities firm affiliates through the creation of financial service holding companies (FSHC). With the passage of this act, banks no longer have to fight legal battles to overcome restrictions on their ability to sell insurance. Indeed, just two years after passage of the FSMA more than 50 percent of all U.S. banks sold insurance products, totaling a record $3.49 billion in insurance commissions and premium income.

The insurance industry applauded the act, as it forced banks that underwrite and sell insurance to operate under the same set of state regulations (pertaining to their insurance lines) as insurance companies. Under the new act, a financial services holding company that engages in commercial banking, investment banking, and insurance activities is functionally regulated. This means that the holding company's banking activities are regulated by bank regulators (such as the Federal Reserve, FDIC, OCC), its securities activities are regulated by the SEC, and its insurance activities are regulated by up to 50 state insurance regulators (since insurance is not regulated at the federal level—see Chapter 6). Further, in March 2008, then Treasury Secretary Henry Paulson's plan to overhaul the regulation of financial institutions included a proposal of a dual state–federal regulatory system for the insurance industry similar to the dual system for banks. The plan proposed an optional federal insurance charter for insurance companies. However, this change in the chartering of insurance companies did not make it into the final version of the regulation.

## Commercial Banking and Commerce

While the direct holding of equity by national banks has been constrained since 1863, restrictions on the commercial activities of bank holding companies are more recent phenomena. In particular, the 1970 amendments to the 1956 Bank Holding Company Act required bank holding companies to divest themselves of nonbank-related subsidiaries over a 10-year period following the amendment.

When Congress passed the amendments, bank holding companies owned some 3,500 commercial sector subsidiaries ranging from public utilities to transportation and manufacturing firms. Nevertheless, prior to late 1999 bank holding companies could hold up to 4.9 percent of the voting shares in any commercial firm without regulatory approval.[3]

The FSMA of 1999 changed restrictions on ownership limits imposed on financial services holding companies. Commercial banks belonging to a financial service holding company can now take a controlling interest in a nonfinancial enterprise provided that two conditions are met. First, the investment cannot be made for an indefinite period of time. The act did not provide an explicit time limit and simply states that the investment can be "held for a period of time to enable the sale or disposition thereof on a reasonable basis consistent with the financial viability of the [investment]." Second, the bank cannot become actively involved in the management of the corporation in which it invests. Nevertheless, corporate stocks or equities are still conspicuously absent from most bank balance sheets (see Chapter 2).

## Nonbank Financial Service Firms and Banking

In comparison with the barriers separating banking and securities, insurance, or commercial-sector activities, the barriers among nonbank financial service firms and banking are generally much weaker. Indeed, as mentioned earlier, the erosion of product barriers between commercial banks and other financial institution services firms has not been all one way. Nonbank financial service firms increasingly offer traditional banking services. For example, money market mutual funds offer checking-account-like deposit services; annuities are financial products issued by insurance companies that offer many of the features of CD; and finance companies and industrial loan corporations (see below) provide commercial, real estate, and consumer loans that compete directly with the same services offered by commercial banks. These financial institutions provide credit, maturity, and liquidity intermediation without access to central bank liquidity provisions or deposit insurance.[4] Their activities occur beyond the reach of existing state and federal monitoring and regulation.

**shadow banking**
Activities of nonfinancial service firms that perform banking services.

More recently activities of nonfinancial service firms that perform banking services has been termed **shadow banking.**[5] Beyond the examples listed previously, new participants in the shadow banking system include structured investment vehicles (SIVs), special-purpose vehicles (SPVs), asset-backed paper vehicles, credit hedge funds, asset-backed commercial paper (ABCP) conduits, limited-purpose finance companies, and credit hedge funds. As of the end of 2011, worldwide total assets managed by the shadow banking system totaled $67 trillion. In the shadow banking system, savers place their funds with money market mutual and similar funds, which invest these funds in the liabilities of shadow banks. Borrowers get loans and leases from shadow banks such as finance companies rather than from

[3] Under the Bank Holding Company Act, *control* is defined as when a holding company has an equity stake exceeding 25 percent in a subsidiary bank or affiliate.

[4] However, to show the banking-like nature of money market mutual funds deposits, the government gave a 100 percent guarantee on the safety of those deposits for one year following the Lehman Brothers failure in the fall of 2008.

[5] The term "shadow banking system" is attributed to Paul McCulley, "Teton Reflections," *PIMCO Global Central Bank Focus* (2007), Federal Reserve Bank of Kansas City's Jackson Hole economic symposium.

banks. Like the traditional banking system, the shadow banking system intermediates the flow of funds between net savers and net borrowers. However, instead of the bank serving as the middleman, it is the nonbank financial service firm, or shadow bank, that intermediates. Further, unlike the traditional banking system, where the complete credit intermediation is performed by a single bank, in the shadow banking system it is performed through a series of steps involving many nonbank financial service firms. For example and as discussed in more detail in Chapter 26, the lending process might involve (1) loan originations performed by a finance company, (2) purchase and warehousing of these loans conducted by single and multiple SIVs funded through asset–backed commercial paper (ABCP), and (3) purchase of ABCP by money market mutual funds. Thus, the shadow banking system decomposes the traditional process of deposit-funded, hold-to-maturity lending conducted by banks, into a more complex, wholesale-funded, securitization-based lending process that involves multiple shadow banks that are not regulated by a specific regulatory body.

Because of the specialized nature involved in the credit intermediation process performed by shadow banks, these nonbank financial service firms can often perform the process more cost efficiently than traditional banks. Further, because of the lower costs and lack of regulatory controls, shadow banks can take on risks that traditional banks either cannot or are unwilling to take. Thus, the shadow banking system allows credit to be available that might not otherwise have been generated through the traditional banking system. Moreover, because commercial banks and shadow banks are interrelated through the credit intermediation system, problems that arise in the shadow banking system can quickly spread to the traditional banking system. Indeed, by transforming the way the credit intermediation process works—from the traditional banking method to the multilayered process used by shadow banks—shadow banks fueled much of the unprecedented growth in the real estate markets in the mid-2000s that eventually crashed and led to the financial crisis.

While as of late 2012, these shadow banks are unregulated by the federal government, the 2010 Wall Street Reform and Consumer Protection Act called for regulators to be given broad authority to monitor and regulate nonbank financial firms that pose risks to the financial system. As of the fall of 2012, U.S. regulators had outlined a process to identify nonbank financial services firms that should receive increased oversight. In the first stage of a proposed three-step process, regulators identify any nonbank financial service firm that has at least $50 billion in assets and also meets one of five "quantitative" thresholds relating to interconnectedness, leverage, outstanding debt, and other risk factors that will be considered for increased scrutiny. In the second stage, regulators evaluate individual firms' potential riskiness using a variety of metrics. In the third stage, with a two-thirds vote, the Financial Stability Oversight Council (created as part of the 2010 act) can designate an individual firm as one that will receive additional regulation and monitoring. Regulators may also designate any nonbank bank that would not be captured by the three-step process as one that poses risks to the financial system and should receive additional regulatory oversight. The designated firms come under the supervision of the Federal Reserve and must comply with new rules, such as more stringent capital, risk management, and leverage standards. When implemented, the process is one tool by which the 2010 act will enable regulators to extend oversight and regulation to the shadow banking system.

### Nonbank Financial Service Firms and Commerce

In recent years, nonbank financial service firms and commercial firms have faced few barriers to entering into and exiting from various areas of nonbank financial service activity. For example, Travelers Group acquired Salomon Brothers in 1997, one year after acquiring Smith Barney. Various other major nonbank financial service acquisitions and divestitures have occurred, many involving commercial firms such as Sears Roebuck, Xerox, and Gulf and Western.

Importantly, however, the passage of the FSMA of 1999 standardized the relationship among financial service sectors (commercial banking, insurance, investment banking) and commerce. Specifically, a financial services holding company is now defined as holding a minimum of 85 percent of its assets in financial assets (i.e., a maximum of 15 percent in commercial sector or real assets). Any nonfinancial assets (activities) exceeding the maximum are grandfathered for at least 10 years (with a possible additional 5-year extension). Nevertheless, eventually, many financial service firms may well have to sell off (divest) some of their real sector assets and activities.

---

| **Concept Questions** | 1. What was the rationale for the passage of the Glass-Steagall Act in 1933? What permissible underwriting activities did it identify for commercial banks? |
|---|---|
| | 2. Does a bank that currently specializes in making consumer loans but makes no commercial loans qualify as a nonbank bank? |
| | 3. How has the Financial Services Modernization Act of 1999 opened the doors for the establishment of full-service financial institutions in the United States? |

---

## ACTIVITY RESTRICTIONS IN THE UNITED STATES VERSUS OTHER COUNTRIES

We have just described the barriers to product expansion and financial conglomeration in the United States. Although many of the barriers have been eroded, those that remain fall most heavily on this nation's commercial banks. This is shown in Appendix 21A located at the book's website (**www.mhhe.com/saunders8e**), which compares the range of activities permitted to U.S. commercial banks with the range of product activities permitted to banks in other major industrialized countries and financial centers. Universal banks offer not just investment banking services, but also commercial lending, foreign exchange, and custody and cash management services. Universal banks include Citigroup, J.P. Morgan Chase, UBS, Deutsche Bank, Credit Suisse First Boston, and to a lesser extent Bank of America. However, with the possible exception of Japan, U.S. banks are still among the most constrained of all the major industrialized countries in terms of the range of nonbank product activities permitted. This has created continuing pressure on Congress to bring U.S. banks' activity powers in line with those of their global competitors and counterparts such as those in the EU and Switzerland.

In the next section, we look at the issues that have been raised and will continue to be raised whenever the question of expanded product (or more universal) powers for banks and other FIs arise.

| Concept Questions | 1. How does the range of product activities permitted for U.S. commercial banks compare to that of banks in other major industrialized countries? |
| --- | --- |
| | 2. How are the product activities of U.S. commercial banks likely to change in the future? |

# ISSUES INVOLVED IN THE DIVERSIFICATION OF PRODUCT OFFERINGS

Whether the debate concerns existing or expanded bank expansion into securities activities, insurance, or commerce, or nonbank financial service firm expansion into banking or commerce, similar issues arise. These include:

1. Safety and soundness issues.
2. Economy of scale and scope issues.
3. Conflict of interest issues.
4. Deposit insurance issues.
5. Regulatory oversight issues.
6. Competition issues.

This section evaluates these issues with a main focus on banks entering into securities activities.

## Safety and Soundness Concerns

With respect to the securities activities of commercial banks and the possible effects on their safety and soundness, two key questions arise: How risky is securities underwriting? And, if losses occur for a securities subsidiary, can this cause the affiliated bank to fail?

### The Risk of Securities Underwriting

To understand the risk of securities underwriting, you must understand the mechanics of a best-efforts versus a firm commitment offering. With best-efforts offerings, investment bankers act as *agents* on a fee basis related to their success in placing the issue. In a **firm commitment offering,** the underwriter purchases securities directly from the issuing firm (say, at $99 per share) and then reoffers them to the public or the market at large at a slightly higher price, say, $99.50. The difference between the underwriter's buy price ($99) and the public offer price ($99.50) is the spread that compensates the underwriter for accepting the principal risk of placing the securities with outside investors as well as any administrative and distribution costs associated with the underwriting. In our simple example of a $0.50 spread, the maximum revenue the underwriter can gain from underwriting the issue is $0.50 times the number of shares issued. Thus, if 1 million shares were offered, the maximum gross revenue for the underwriting would be $0.50 times 1,000,000, or $500,000. Note that once the public offering has been made and the price specified in the prospectus, the underwriter cannot raise the price over the offering period even if they find the market values the shares more highly.

The upside return from firm commitment underwriting is normally capped, but the downside risk is not, and can be very large. The downside risk arises if the underwriter overprices the public offering, setting the public offer price higher

**firm commitment offering**
Securities offered from the issuing firm, purchased by an underwriter.

**FIGURE 21–2**
The Role of
Firewalls in
Protecting Banks

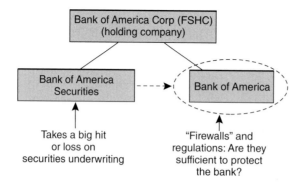

than outside investors' valuations. As a result, the underwriter will be unable
to sell the shares during the public offering period and will have to lower the
price to get rid of the inventory of unsold shares. In our example, suppose that
the issue can be placed only at $97; the underwriter's losses will be $2 times
1,000,000 shares, or $2 million.

### If Underwriting Losses Occur for the Securities Affiliate, Can This Cause a Bank to Fail?

In a financial services holding company structure, the bank is legally a separate
corporation from the securities affiliate. As shown in Figure 21–2, its only link to
the securities affiliate is indirect, through the holding company that owns a controlling equity stake in both the bank and securities affiliate. However, even this
indirect link raises the concern that the effects of losses by the securities affiliate
could threaten the safety of the bank unless firewalls or regulatory barriers are
introduced to insulate the bank against such losses (see Figure 21–2).

There are at least three ways a bank could be harmed by losses of a securities affiliate in a holding company structure. First, a holding company might be
tempted to drain capital and funds from the bank by requiring excessive dividends and fees from the bank (this is called *upstreaming*). The holding company
could then *downstream* these funds to protect the failing securities affiliate from
insolvency. As a result, the bank would be weakened at the expense (or because)
of the securities affiliate.

A second way in which a bank could be harmed is through interaffiliate loans.
For example, the holding company may induce the bank to extend loans to the
securities affiliate to keep it afloat even though such loans are excessively risky.
To prevent this, the Federal Reserve Act limits bank loans to any single nonbank
affiliate to 10 percent of a bank's capital. If bank capital is approximately 10 percent of bank assets, this limits loans to an affiliate to 0.1 × 0.1 of bank assets, or
1 percent of bank assets.

The third way in which a bank may be affected is through a contagious confidence problem. Specifically, difficulty of a securities firm subsidiary may result in
a negative information signal to financial service consumers and investors regarding the quality of the management of the holding company and its bank affiliate.
Such negative information can create incentives for large depositors and investors
to withdraw their money from the bank in the manner described in Chapter 19.
This bank run possibility seems more likely to occur if the bank and its securities
affiliate share similar names and logos, which in general they do.

Recognizing that allowing banking organizations to expand their securities activities may lead to more risk in the banking system, the FSMA of 1999 explicitly incorporated provisions regarding the way the new financial services holding companies would be regulated. For example, the act streamlines bank holding company supervisions by clarifying the regulatory roles of the Federal Reserve as the umbrella holding company supervisor and of the state and federal financial regulators that "functionally" regulate various affiliates. It provides for federal bank regulators to prescribe prudential safeguards for bank organizations engaging in new financial activities. It provides for state regulation of insurance, subject to a standard that no state may discriminate against persons affiliated with a bank. Finally, the act prohibits FDIC assistance to affiliates and subsidiaries of banks and savings institutions. However, FDIC "bailouts" to failing bank holding companies during the financial crisis provided indirect assistance to their affiliates and subsidiaries. As discussed below, the Wall Street Reform and Consumer Protection Act calls for the Federal Reserve to receive new oversight powers and to impose conditions designed to discourage any type of financial institution from posing extensive risk to the overall financial system.

Obviously, a big hit taken by the securities subsidiary can potentially threaten the safety and solvency of the affiliated bank, especially through the confidence effect. However, at least one countervailing risk-reducing effect may enhance the safety and soundness of a bank indirectly linked to a securities subsidiary in a holding company framework. This effect is a **product diversification benefit.** A well-diversified financial services firm (financial services holding company) potentially enjoys a far more stable earnings and profit stream over time than does a product-specialized bank. As demand and cost shifts reduce earnings in one activity area, such as banking, offsetting demand and cost shifts may take place in other activity areas, such as securities or insurance, increasing the holding company's earnings. A more stable and diversified earnings stream for the holding company enables it to act as a source of strength in keeping the affiliated bank well capitalized, and thus reduces its bankruptcy risk.

**product diversification benefit**
Stabilization of earnings and profits resulting from a well-diversified financial services holding company.

## Economies of Scale and Scope

A second issue concerning the expansion of banks into securities and other nonbank activities is the potential for additional economies of scale and scope. As financial firms become larger, the potential scale can lower an FI's average costs of financial service production. Thus, larger financial services holding companies may have an economy of scale advantage over smaller financial firms. Further, financial services holding companies' abilities to generate synergistic cost savings through joint use of inputs in producing multiple financial products create economies of scope.

As we discussed in Chapter 17, there appear to be economy of scale opportunities for financial firms of all asset sizes. However, most studies find cost-based economies of scope are negligible, although revenue-based economies of scope may arise for the largest FIs. Arguably, the pre-1997 restrictions between banks and their Section 20 investment banking affiliates covering finance, management and cross-marketing severely limited economies of scope and related revenue and cost synergies. Post-1997 and, more so, post-1999 U.S. financial service firms may realize greater economies of scope as restrictions were removed and the FSHCs became more universal in product scope.

## Conflicts of Interest

A third issue—the potential for conflicts of interest—lies at the very heart of opposition to an expansion of banking powers into other financial service areas. Indeed, concerns regarding conflicts of interest provided the main foundation for the passage of the Glass-Steagall Act in 1933. The two principal questions that arise are (1) the potential conflicts of interest arising from the expansion of banks' securities activities and (2) the type of incentive structures that change *potential* conflicts into *actual* conflicts.

### Six Potential Conflicts of Interest

Conflicts of interest that arise when commercial banks, investment banks, and insurance companies combine operations have been prominent in U.S. financial markets throughout the 2000s. Several high-profile legal violations as well as a loss of investor confidence rocked Wall Street and the financial services industry. In this section, we discuss the six most common potential conflicts of interest identified by regulators and academics.

*Salesperson's Stake*   Critics argue that when banks have the power to sell non-bank products, bank employees no longer dispense dispassionate advice to their customers about which product to buy. Instead, they have a salesperson's stake in pushing the bank's own products, often to the disadvantage of the customer.

*Stuffing Fiduciary Accounts*   Suppose a bank is acting as a securities underwriter and is unable to place these securities in a public offering. To avoid being exposed to potential losses, the bank may "stuff" these unwanted securities in accounts managed by its own trust department and over which it has discretionary investment powers. For example, a federal judge threw money manager Alan Bond, CIO of Albriond Capital, in jail after he was convicted on charges of allocating winning trades to his own brokerage account and saddling his clients' accounts with losers.

*Bankruptcy Risk Transference*   Assume that a bank has a loan outstanding to a firm whose credit or bankruptcy risk has increased to the private knowledge of the banker. With this private knowledge, the banker may have an incentive to induce the firm to issue bonds underwritten by the bank's securities affiliate to an unsuspecting public. The proceeds of this bond issue could then be used to pay down the bank loan. As a result, the bank would have transferred the borrowing firm's credit risk from itself to less informed outside investors, while the securities affiliate also earned an underwriting fee. For example, in 2002 J.P. Morgan Chase and Citigroup faced several investor lawsuits over funding deals for high-profile bankruptcies such as Enron and WorldCom. Investors say that because of their lending relationships, the banks knew or should have known of the problems at these companies when they sold the firms' bonds to the public.

   More recent is the 2010 case of investment banks' sales of mortgage-backed securities. A hearing of the U.S. Senate Permanent Subcommittee on Investigations (created with the broad mandate to determine whether any changes are required in U.S. law to better protect the public) focused on the role of investment banks in contributing to the financial crisis. Investment banks frequently bundled toxic mortgages into complex financial instruments—many of which were rated AAA by credit rating agencies—and sold them to investors. Some of these banks, in an attempt to manage their own risk on these securities, reportedly shorted the mortgage market, setting themselves up for gains that would offset losses on the mortgage securities.

*Third-Party Loans*   To ensure that an underwriting goes well, a bank may make cheap loans to third-party investors on the implicit condition that this loan is used to purchase securities underwritten by its securities affiliate.

*Tie-Ins*   A bank may use its lending powers to coerce or "tie in" a customer to the products sold by its securities affiliate. For example, the bank may threaten to ration credit unless the customer agrees to let the bank's securities affiliate do its securities underwritings. In the early 2000s, J.P. Morgan Chase poured money into the telecommunications and cable businesses, not expecting to make much money on the loans themselves. Rather, it anticipated a huge payback from investment banking business these firms would send its way.

*Information Transfer*   In acting as a lender, the bank may become privy to certain inside information about its customers or rivals that it can use to set the prices, or help the distribution of securities offerings by its affiliate. This information could also flow from the securities affiliate to the bank. Such conflicts are potentially present when M&A activity is involved along with new security issues and loan originations. The reverse was the case with J.P. Morgan Chase and Citigroup, FIs involved as lead advisors *and* lead bankers in Enron's failed merger attempt with Dynegy in 2001. The two FIs had large balance sheets and boasted of their ability to provide both loans and advice in the merger. However, the FIs lost their bragging rights for pulling off a difficult deal as Dynegy pulled out of the merger. The FIs attempted to preserve their reputations after the deal failed, stating they were deprived of enough information on the deal and then learning that Enron had been hiding billions of dollars in debt and had been reporting exaggerated profits for years. Enron ended up declaring bankruptcy in December 2001 and J.P. Morgan Chase and Citigroup ended up losing between $800 and $900 million each on loans to Enron.

### *Potential Conflicts of Interest and Their Actual Exploitation*

On their own, and unquestionably accepted, these conflicts appear to be extremely troublesome. Remember, however, that specific and general checks and balances limit their exploitation. Many of these conflicts are likely to remain potential rather than become actual conflicts of interest. Specifically, many of these conflicts, such as tie-ins and third-party loans, breach existing bank regulations and laws. Also, internal barriers or **Chinese walls** in most banks prohibit internal information transfers when they potentially conflict with the best interests of the customer. Further, sales of debt issues to a less informed public to pay down bank loans may result in future lawsuits against the underwriter once investors discover their losses.[6]

> **Chinese wall**
> An internally imposed barrier within an organization that limits the flow of confidential client information among departments or areas.

More generally, conflicts of interest are exploitable only under three conditions. First, markets for bank services are uncompetitive so that banks have monopoly power over their customers, for example, in making loans. Second, information flows between the customer and the bank are imperfect or asymmetric so that the bank possesses an information advantage over its customers. Third, the bank places a relatively low value on its reputation. The discovery of having exploited a conflict can result in considerable market and regulatory penalties.

### Deposit Insurance

A traditional argument against expanded powers is that the explicit and implicit protection given to banks by deposit insurance coverage give banks a competitive advantage over other financial service firms (see Chapter 19). For example,

---

[6] In particular, the underwriter may be accused of lack of due diligence in not disclosing information in the new issue's prospectus.

because bank deposits up to $250,000 are covered by explicit deposit insurance, banks are able to raise funds at subsidized, lower-cost rates than are available to other financial services firms. This may allow them to pass on these lower costs in cheaper loans to their affiliates. However, since the FSMA allowed other financial service firms to establish banks that offer deposit insurance coverage, this explicit subsidy advantage has been lessened.

## Regulatory Oversight

Currently, most bank holding companies with extensive nonbank subsidiaries face a diffuse and multilayered regulatory structure that would potentially hinder the monitoring and control of conflicts of interest abuses and excessive risk taking as banks are allowed to expand their securities activities further. Specifically, for a financial services holding company such as J.P. Morgan Chase, the Federal Reserve is the primary regulator. For its bank subsidiary, the Office of the Comptroller of the Currency, which is the charterer of national banks, shares regulatory oversight with the Federal Reserve and the FDIC. For its securities subsidiary, the primary regulator is the SEC, although the Federal Reserve also has some oversight powers. Likewise, the Fed coordinates its supervisory responsibilities with the state insurance authority when the bank holding company operates an insurance company subsidiary.

www.federalreserve.gov
www.occ.treas.gov

www.fdic.gov
www.sec.gov

The Fed's role as the supervisor of a bank holding company is to review and assess the consolidated organization's operations, risk management systems, and capital adequacy to ensure that the holding company and its nonbank subsidiaries do not threaten the financial stability of the company's depository institutions. In this role, the Fed serves as the umbrella supervisor of the consolidated organization. In fulfilling this role, the Fed relies to the fullest extent possible on information and analysis provided by the appropriate supervisory authority of the company's bank, securities, or insurance subsidiaries.

The 2010 Wall Street Reform and Consumer Protection Act calls for the Federal Reserve to receive new oversight powers. The proposals put the Federal Reserve in charge of monitoring the country's biggest financial firms—those considered critical to the health of the system as a whole. Those firms would also face new, stiffer requirements on how much capital and liquidity they keep in reserve. The overhaul also provides unprecedented powers to the Fed to step into any financial institutions—such as insurance giant AIG (whose main regulators include the New York State Department of Insurance and the Office of the Comptroller of the Currency)—that are facing imminent collapse, in order to force an orderly bankruptcy that would protect the wider economy.

## Competition

The final issue concerns the effects of bank activity expansions on competition in investment banking product lines. In securities underwriting, there are three primary factors for believing that bank expansions would enhance competition. One factor is cited as a reason that it would do the reverse.

### Procompetitive Effects

The three factors supporting a procompetitive effect of banks' expansion of their securities activities are in the following sections.

*Increased Capital Market Access for Small Firms* Most large investment banks are headquartered in New York and the Northeast. As a result, small U.S. firms based in the Midwest and Southwest have often had a more difficult time accessing national capital markets than have firms of a similar size in the Northeast. Consequently, the entry of regional and superregional banks into securities underwriting through securities affiliates could potentially expand the national capital market access of smaller firms.

*Lower Commissions and Fees* Increased competition for securities underwritings should reduce the underwriter's spread. That is, it should reduce the spread between the new issue bid price paid to the issuing firm and the offer price at which those securities are resold to the market. This potentially raises the amount of new issue proceeds for the issuing firm by raising the underwriter's bid price.

*Reduce the Degree of Underpricing of New Issues* The greatest risk to the underwriter is to price a new issue too high relative to the market's valuation of that security. That is, underwriters stand to lose when they overprice new issues. Given this, underwriters have an incentive to underprice new issues by setting the public offer price (OP) below the price established for the security in the secondary market once trading begins (P). The investment bank stands to gain by underpricing as it increases the demand for the shares by investors and the probability of selling the whole issue to the public very quickly. Both the underwriter and the outside investor may benefit from underpricing. The loser is the firm issuing the securities because it obtains lower proceeds than if the offer price had been set at a higher price reflecting a more accurate market valuation.

If a major cause of IPO underpricing is a lack of competition among existing investment banks, then bank entry and competition should lower the degree of underpricing and increase the new issue proceeds for firms. Nevertheless, many economists argue that monopoly power is not the primary reason for the underpricing of new issues. In their view, underpricing reflects a risk premium that must be paid to investors and investment bankers for information imperfections. That is, underpricing is a risk premium for the information advantage possessed by issuers who better know the true quality of their firm's securities and its assets. If this is so, bank entry into securities underwriting may reduce the degree of underpricing only to the extent that it reduces the degree of information imperfection among issuers and investors. This might reasonably be expected given the specialized role of banks as delegated monitors (see Chapter 1).

## Anticompetitive Effects

While bank entry may be procompetitive in the short term, there still exists considerable concern about potential anticompetitive behavior in the long term. The biggest banking organizations, measured by either capital or assets, are many times larger than the biggest securities firms—or insurance firms, for that matter (see Table 21–1). The largest bank organizations may aggressively compete for business in the short run, trying to force traditional investment banks out of business. If successful, they would assume quasi-oligopoly positions, market concentration may rise, and in the long run prices for investment banking services would rise rather than fall. Such a long-run outcome would outweigh any short-term procompetitive benefits.

| Concept Questions | 1. What are some of the issues that tend to arise in response to bank expansion into securities, insurance, and commercial activities? |
| --- | --- |
| | 2. Describe three ways in which the losses of a securities affiliate in a holding company structure could be transmitted to a bank. |
| | 3. In addition to the six potential conflicts of interest discussed in this section, can you think of any additional possible conflicts that might arise if commercial banks were allowed to expand their investment banking activities? |
| | 4. What are three potential procompetitive effects cited in support of banks' expansion into securities activities? What reason is given to support the opposite claim (i.e., that bank expansion would not enhance competition)? |

# DOMESTIC GEOGRAPHIC EXPANSION

**de novo office**
A newly established office.

In the United States, the ability of FIs to expand domestically has historically been constrained by regulation. By comparison, no special regulations have inhibited the ability of commercial firms such as General Motors, IBM, and Walmart from establishing new or **de novo offices,** factories, or stores anywhere in the country. Nor have commercial firms been prohibited from acquiring other firms—as long as they are not banks. While securities firms and insurance companies have faced relatively few restrictions in expanding their business domestically, other FIs, especially banks, have faced a complex and changing network of rules and regulations. While such regulations may inhibit expansions, they also create potential opportunities to increase an FI's returns. In particular, regulations may create locally uncompetitive markets with monopoly economic rents that new entrants can potentially exploit. Thus, for the most innovative FIs, regulation can provide profit opportunities as well as costs. As a result, regulation both inhibits and creates incentives to engage in geographic expansions. One result of the extensive regulatory review on bank geographic expansion is that it is rare that we see a hostile takeover or unfriendly merger in banking. Unlike the case of a merger or acquisition of commercial firms, the extensive review by regulators virtually forces the two parties in a bank merger to work together so that they can get through the review process successfully.

The economic factors that impact commercial firm expansion and acquisition decisions are likely to impact the decisions of FIs as well. Two major groups of factors are cost and revenue synergies and firm- or market-specific attractions, such as the specialized skills of an acquired firm's employees and the markets of the firm to be acquired. Thus, the attractiveness of a geographic expansion, whether through acquisition, branching, or opening a new office, depends on a broad set of factors encompassing:

1. Regulation and the regulatory framework.
2. Cost and revenue synergies.
3. Firm- or market-specific factors.

We start by considering how the first factor—regulation—impacts a U.S.-based FI's geographic expansion decision. Specifically, we briefly discuss the restrictions applying to insurance companies and thrifts. Then we look in more detail at regulations affecting commercial banks.

| Concept Questions | 1. Explain why regulation both inhibits and provides incentives to an FI to engage in geographic expansion. |
|---|---|
| | 2. What three basic factors influence the attractiveness of geographic expansion to an FI? |

# REGULATORY FACTORS AFFECTING GEOGRAPHIC EXPANSION

## Insurance Companies

As discussed in Chapter 6, insurance companies are state-regulated firms. By establishing a subsidiary in one state, an insurance company normally has the opportunity to sell insurance anywhere in that state and often to market the product nationally by Internet marketing, telemarketing, and direct sales. To deliver a financial service effectively, however, it is often necessary to establish a physical presence in a local market. To do this, insurance companies establish subsidiaries and offices in other states. This is usually easy since the initial capital requirement for establishing a new subsidiary is set at a relatively low level by state regulators. Thus, most large insurance companies have a physical presence in virtually every state in the union.

## Thrifts

www.ots.treas.gov

Between 1989 and October 2011, the ability to branch was under the power of the Office of Thrift Supervision (OTS) as part of the 1989 FIRREA legislation (see Chapter 19). Historically, the policy was that a federally chartered thrift could not branch across state lines. In the 1980s, a considerable loosening of these restrictions occurred. Both the Garn-St. Germain Act of 1982 and the Financial Institutions Reform, Recovery, and Enforcement Act (FIRREA) of 1989 allowed sound banks and thrifts to acquire failing thrifts across state lines and to either run them as separate subsidiaries or convert them into branches. Finally, in 1992 the OTS announced that it was willing to allow interstate branching for all federally chartered savings institutions. By 1993 interstate savings institutions controlled 25 percent of all savings institutions' assets and had established over 1,200 branches across state lines. By 2009, almost 500 institutions had branches in two or more states. The 2010 Wall Street Reform and Consumer Protection Act called for the closure of the OTS. As a result, the OTS was closed on October 19, 2011. Most of its duties were taken over by the Office of the Comptroller of the Currency.

## Commercial Banks

### Restrictions on Intrastate Banking

**unit bank**
A bank with a single office.

For most of the 1900s, most U.S. banks were **unit banks** with a single office. Improving communications and customer needs resulted in a rush to branching in the first two decades of the 20th century. Increasingly, this movement ran into opposition from the smallest unit banks and the largest money center banks. The smallest unit banks perceived a competitive threat to their retail business from the larger branching banks. Money center banks feared a loss of valuable correspondent business such as check clearing and other payment services. As a result, several states restricted the ability of banks to branch within the state. Indeed, some states prohibited intrastate branching per se, effectively constraining a bank to unit status. Over the years and in a very piecemeal fashion, states liberalized their restrictions on within-state branching. By 1994 (prior to the passage of the Riegle-Neal Act) only one state (Iowa) had not deregulated intrastate banking.

### Restrictions on Interstate Banking

The defining piece of legislation affecting interstate branching until 1994 was the McFadden Act, passed in 1927 and amended in 1933. The McFadden Act and its amendments restricted nationally chartered banks' branching abilities to the same extent allowed to state-chartered banks. Because states prohibit interstate banking for state-chartered banks in general, nationally chartered banks were similarly prohibited.

**multibank holding company (MBHC)**
A parent banking organization that owns a number of individual bank subsidiaries.

Between 1927 and 1997, given the McFadden prohibition on interstate branching, bank organizations expanding across state lines largely relied on establishing subsidiaries rather than branches. Some of the biggest banking organizations established **multibank holding companies** for that purpose. A multibank holding company (MBHC) is a parent company that acquires more than one bank as a direct subsidiary. While MBHCs had been around in the early part of the 20th century, the 1927 restrictions on interstate branching gave the bank acquisition movement an added impetus. By 1956, some 47 multibank holding companies were established, many owning banks in two or more states.

In 1956, Congress recognized the potential loophole to interstate banking posed by the MBHC movement and passed the Douglas amendment to the Bank Holding Company Act. This act permitted MBHCs to acquire bank subsidiaries only to the extent allowed by the laws of the state in which the proposed bank target resided. Because states prohibited out-of-state bank acquisitions, this temporarily curtailed the growth of the MBHC movement.

**regional or interstate banking pact**
An agreement among states describing the conditions for entrance of out-of-state banks by acquisition.

Maine took the first step in eroding interstate banking restrictions in 1978 by passing a law that exploited a loophole in the Douglas amendments of 1956. To increase employment in and growth of its financial services industry, Maine passed a law allowing banks from any other state to enter and acquire local banks even if the banks in Maine could not engage in such acquisitions in other states. This nationwide nonreciprocal bank acquisition law led to a rapid acquisition of Maine's banking assets by out-of-state bank holding companies. Indeed, by 1988, some 85 percent of bank assets in Maine were held by out-of-state banking organizations such as Citicorp (now Citigroup). In the early 1980s other states in New England sought to follow Maine's example by enacting their own **interstate banking pacts.** By 1994, all states but Hawaii had passed some form of interstate banking law or pact.

*Riegle-Neal Interstate Banking and Branching Efficiency Act of 1994*   It had long been recognized that nationwide banking expansion through multibank holding companies was potentially far more expensive than through branching. Separate corporations and boards of directors must be established for each bank in an MBHC, and it is hard to achieve the same level of economic and financial integration as with branches. Moreover, most of the major banking competitor countries, such as Japan, Germany, France, and the United Kingdom, had nationwide branching.

In the fall of 1994, the U.S. Congress passed the Riegle-Neal Interstate Banking and Branching Efficiency Act that allows U.S. and nondomestic banks to branch interstate by consolidating out-of-state bank subsidiaries into a branch network and/or acquiring banks or individual branches of banks by merger and acquisition. (The effective date for these new branching powers was June 1, 1997.) While the act is silent on the ability of banks to establish de novo (new) branches in other states—essentially leaving it to individual states to pass laws allowing de novo branching—it became possible under the new law for a New York bank such as Citibank to purchase a single branch of a California bank such as a branch of Bank of America in San Francisco.

The implication of the Riegle-Neal Act is that full interstate banking—with the exception of de novo branching—became a reality in the United States in 1997.[7] The relaxation of the branching restrictions, along with recognition of the potential cost, revenue, and risk benefits from geographic expansions (discussed next), set off a wave of consolidation in the U.S. banking system. This consolidation trend has been particularly evident among the largest U.S. banks in a wave of "megamergers." Figure 21–3 shows some of the biggest mergers between 1995 and 2012 that are reshaping the U.S. banking industry into a nationwide banking system along European and Canadian lines. Note that as a result of merges and acquisitions, 25 major U.S. banks in existence in 1995 have become 4 by 2009.

*Nonbank Banks*   Another way interstate banking barriers were eroded came through the establishment of nonbank banks (described above). Until 1987, a large U.S. bank could acquire a full-service out-of-state bank, divest it of its commercial loans, and legally operate it as a nonbank bank specializing in consumer

**FIGURE 21–3**   **The New Shape of U.S. Banking Major Mergers, 1995–2012 (in millions of dollars)**

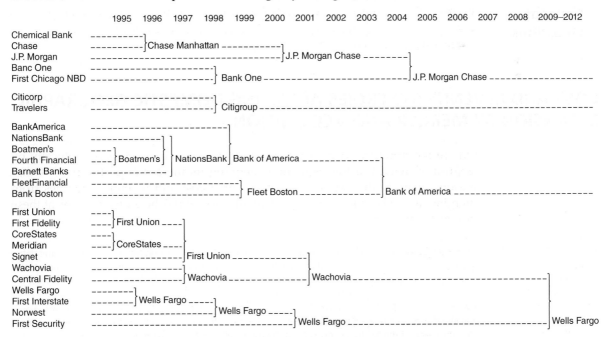

[7] The reason for the restriction on de novo branching is to protect smaller community banks' franchise values. If you can branch only by acquisition, the franchise values of small banks will be greater than when larger banks have the alternative of branching de novo.

finance.[8] However, the Competitive Equality Banking Act (CEBA) effectively put an end to this loophole in 1987, although it grandfathered existing nonbank banks.

Also exempted from the CEBA legislation were industrial loan corporations (ILCs). ILCs, owned by nonbanking companies such as Target, Harley Davidson, and Pitney Bowes,[9] provide loans to low-quality, high-interest-rate corporations that banks avoid. While only seven states grant ILC charters, ILCs can operate in nearly all 50 states by direct mail and other electronic means. ILCs are regulated at the state level, and deposits of ILCs are insured by the Federal Deposit Insurance Corporation. Yet ILCs are regulated by neither the Federal Reserve nor the Office of the Comptroller of the Currency. By operating in Utah, nonbank companies can behave like commercial banks without being regulated like them. As a result, assets under management in ILCs grew from $2.9 billion at the end of 1995 to $232 billion in 2009 (held by 45 ILCs). This compares to total commercial and industrial loans at commercial banks of $1,357 billion.

The Obama administration's 2009 proposed overhaul of financial institution regulation included a provision that would have meant greater oversight of ILCs and could have led to some of them being shut down by the nonfinancial companies that operate them. The proposed overhaul would have required ILCs to register as bank holding companies with the U.S. Federal Reserve. That would have subjected companies that operate ILCs to greater government oversight and put them in the same category as most large U.S. banks. While the final version of the bill failed to include this increase in ILC regulation, the possibility of increased regulation of the industry may have had some effect on the industry. By year-end 2011, there were only 34 ILCs still in existence, managing $102.4 billion in assets.

| | |
|---|---|
| **Concept Questions** | 1. What are some of the ways in which interstate banking barriers have been eroded? |
| | 2. What were the main features of the Riegle-Neal Interstate Banking and Branching Efficiency Act of 1994? |

## COST AND REVENUE SYNERGIES AFFECTING DOMESTIC GEOGRAPHIC EXPANSION BY MERGER AND ACQUISITION

One reason for an FI deciding to expand (or not to expand) geographically by acquisition relates to the regulations defining its merger opportunities.[10] Other reasons relate to the exploitation of potential cost and revenue synergies from merging (as well as the associated diversification of risk benefits). We look at these potential gains next.

---

[8] For the purposes of the 1956 Bank Holding Company Act's restrictions on MBHC acquisitions, the definition of a bank was an institution that accepted demand deposits and made commercial and industrial loans. By stripping a bank of its commercial loans, it turned into a nonbank bank that was not subject to restrictions on interstate banking.

[9] At the height of the financial crisis, GMAC, one of the largest ILCs with over $33 billion in assets, was converted to a bank holding company. GMAC's precarious financial position caused the Fed to expedite the conversion of the ILC to a bank without the usual public notice of the move.

[10] It should be noted that expansion via de novo entry is a possible method of geographic expansion as well as M&A. However, de novo entry generally involves small banks that can be financially fragile and the degree to which they are reliable long-run sources of expansion depends on whether they can survive to financial maturity.

## Cost Synergies

**X-efficiency**
Cost savings due to the greater managerial efficiency of the acquiring bank.

A common reason given for bank mergers is the potential cost synergies that may result from economies of scale, economies of scope, or managerial efficiency sources (often called **X-efficiencies**[11] because they are difficult to pin down in a quantitative fashion). For example, in 1996, Chase Manhattan and Chemical Bank merged, creating the (then) largest banking organization in the United States, with assets of $300 billion. It was estimated that annual cost savings from the merger would be $1.5 billion, to be achieved by consolidating certain operations and eliminating redundant costs, including the elimination of some 12,000 positions from a combined staff of 75,000 in 39 states and 51 countries. Similarly, Region Financial's $10 billion merger with AmSouth Bancorp in 2007 was expected to reduce costs by $400 million annually (an amount equivalent to more than 20 percent of their combined net income). The merger created the then ninth-largest bank in the United States. Savings were expected to come through cutting as many as 4,000 of the 37,000 employees and consolidating some 150 of the almost 2,000 branches of the two Birmingham, Alabama-based institutions.

**megamerger**
The merger of two large banks.

While the mergers discussed above are interesting examples of **megamergers,** they are still essentially mergers in the same or closely related banking markets. By comparison, mergers such as Bank of America and FleetBoston and J.P. Morgan Chase and Bank One are clearly a geographic extension merger between two banks with little or no geographic overlap. By acquiring FleetBoston in 2003 for $43 billion, Bank of America added nearly 1,500 branches and 3,400 ATM machines in the New England area. The combined banks projected annual cost savings to be $1.1 billion, including consolidation of redundant technology systems. This was followed in 2004 by J.P. Morgan Chase's $60 billion merger with Bank One to form the second-largest bank in the United States. With this merger J.P. Morgan Chase (which had been operating in only four states) acquired Bank One's First USA credit card operations and a massive retail network of about 1,800 branches concentrated in the Midwest. Together the merged bank would hold about $125 billion in credit card balances, giving the combined company an almost 20 percent share of the credit card market. Further, the combined bank was projecting before-tax savings of $2.2 billion in the three years after the merger with job cuts estimated to total 10,000 of a combined 140,000 workers.

In a recent study of nine megamergers by Steve Rhoades (seven of the nine occurring since 1990), large cost savings were found. Specifically, four of the nine mergers showed significant cost efficiency gains relative to a peer group of non-merged banks and seven of the nine showed a significant improvement in their return on assets. In addition to cutting duplicate back-office operations, larger banks can also take more advantage of outsourcing these operations locally or abroad. It is estimated that in 2011, 77 percent of retail banks outsourced at least one part of their business, reducing bank costs of these services between 20 and 40 percent. Larger banks find it more cost effective to outsource a larger number of services and, therefore, experience the bigger costs savings from outsourcing. Interestingly, where cost efficiency gains were *not* realized, the major problems came from integrating data processing and operating systems.

---

[11] X-efficiencies are those cost savings not directly due to economies of scope or economies of scale. As such, they are usually attributed to superior management skills and other difficult-to-measure managerial factors. To date, the explicit identification of what composes these efficiencies remains to be established in the empirical banking literature.

## Revenue Synergies

The revenue synergies argument has three dimensions. First, revenues may be enhanced by acquiring a bank in a growing market. For example, the 2009 merger of Wells Fargo and Wachovia was estimated to produce cost savings of $5 billion per year. However, the success of the merger was attributed to revenue growth and synergies. By late 2009, the merged companies announced that business and revenue synergies were ahead of expectations and on track to realize annual revenue growth of $5 billion upon full integration. The merged banks recorded broad-based revenue contribution from diverse businesses, with particular strength in regional banking, commercial banking, mortgage banking, investment banking, asset-based lending, auto lending, student lending, debit card, merchant card, wealth management, securities brokerage retirement services, and international operations. Shortly after the merger, over 40 percent of legacy Wells Fargo retail households had purchased over six Wachovia based products, and one of every four retail households had at least eight products with the merged banks.

Second, the acquiring bank's revenue stream may become more stable if the asset and liability portfolio of the target institution exhibits different credit, interest rate, and liquidity risk characteristics from the acquirer. For example, real estate loan portfolios showed very strong regional cycles in the 1980s. Specifically, U.S. real estate declined in value in the Southwest, then in the Northeast, and then in California with a long and variable lag. Thus, a geographically diversified real estate portfolio may be far less risky than one in which both acquirer and target specialize in a single region. Studies confirm risk diversification gains from geographic expansions.

Third, there is an opportunity for revenue enhancement by expanding into markets that are less than fully competitive. That is, banks may be able to identify and expand geographically into those markets where *economic rents* potentially exist, but where such entry will not be viewed as being potentially anticompetitive by regulators. Arguably, one of the great potential benefits of the J.P. Morgan Chase and Bank One merger was the potential for enhanced revenue diversification due to the lack of overlap of the branch networks of the two systems due to the merger. The new bank had a branching presence in 17 states and an 8.3 percent share of federally insured banking deposits (see Figure 21–4).

## Merger Guidelines for Acceptability

www.usdoj.gov

To the extent that geographic expansions of the J.P. Morgan Chase–Bank One kind are viewed as enhancing the monopoly power of an FI, regulators may act to prevent a merger unless the merger produces potential efficiency gains that cannot be reasonably achieved by other means. In recent years, the ultimate enforcement of antimonopoly laws and guidelines has fallen to the U.S. Department of Justice. In particular, the Department of Justice has laid down guidelines regarding the acceptability or unacceptability of acquisitions based on the potential increase in concentration in the market in which an acquisition takes place, with the cost efficiency exception just noted.[12]

---

[12] U.S. Department of Justice, "Horizontal Merger Guidelines," April 2, 1982. It should also be added that the Riegle-Neal Act of 1994 placed a maximum 10 percent cap on the market share of the national (insured) deposit base held by any bank.

**FIGURE 21–4**
The Branching Presence of J.P. Morgan Chase as a Result of Its Merger with Bank One

Source: Federal Deposit Insurance Corporation. *www.fdic.gov*

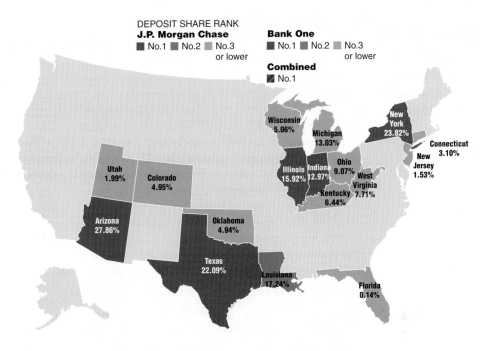

**HHI**
An index or measure of market concentration based on the squared market shares of market participants.

These merger guidelines are based on a measure of market concentration called the Herfindahl-Hirschman Index **(HHI).** This index is created by taking the percentage market shares of each firm in a market, squaring them, and then adding these squared shares. Thus, in a market where a single firm had a 100 percent market share, the HHI would be:

$$HHI = (100)^2 = 10,000$$

Alternatively, in a market in which there were an infinitely large number of firms of equal size, then:

$$HHI = 0$$

Thus, the HHI must lie between 0 and 10,000.

Whether a merger will be challenged under the Department of Justice guidelines depends on the postmerger HHI level.[13] As you can see in Table 21–2, the Department of Justice defines a *concentrated* market as having a postmerger HHI ratio of greater than 2,500, a moderately concentrated market as having a ratio of 1,500 to 2,500, and an unconcentrated market as having a ratio of less than 1,500. In a highly concentrated (moderately concentrated) market, postmerger HHI increases of 200 (100) or more may be challenged.

There are two problems of interpretation of the HHI in the context of banking and financial services. First, what is the relevant geographic scope of the market

---

[13] The Federal Reserve also has the power to approve or disapprove mergers among state member banks and bank holding companies. The Comptroller of the Currency has similar powers over nationally chartered banks. The Federal Reserve's criteria are similar to those of the Department of Justice in that they take into account the HHI (market concentration index). However, it also evaluates the risk effects of the merger. The Department of Justice has powers to review the decisions made by the bank regulatory agencies.

**EXAMPLE 21–1**

*Calculation of Change in the HHI Associated with a Merger*

Consider a market that has three banks with the following market shares:

Bank A = 50%

Bank B = 46%

Bank C = 4%

The premerger HHI for the market is:

$$HHI = (50)^2 + (46)^2 + (4)^2 = 2,500 + 2,116 + 16 = 4,632$$

Thus, the market is highly concentrated according to the Department of Justice guidelines.

Suppose Bank A wants to acquire Bank C so that the post-acquisition market would exhibit the following shares:[14]

$$A + C = 54\%$$
$$B = 46\%$$

The postmerger HHI would be:

$$HHI = (54)^2 + (46)^2 = 2,916 + 2,116 = 5,032$$

Thus, the increase or change in the HHI ($\Delta$HHI) postmerger is:

$$\Delta HHI = 5,032 - 4,632 = 400$$

Since the increase is 400 points, which is more than the 200-point benchmark defined in the Department of Justice guidelines, the market is heavily concentrated and the merger could be challenged.

for financial services—national, regional, or city? Second, once that market is defined, do we view banks, thrifts, and insurance companies as separate or unique lines of business, or are they competing in the same financial market? That is, what defines the institutional scope of the market? In the case of financial services, it has been traditional to define markets on functional, or line of business, criteria, so that commercial banking is a separate market from savings (thrift) banking and other financial services. Further, the relevant market area has usually been

**TABLE 21–2**

**Department of Justice Horizontal Merger Guidelines**

Source: Department of Justice, Merger Guidelines, 2010.

| Postmerger Market Concentration | Level of Herfindahl-Hirschman Index | Change in Herfindahl-Hirschman Index and Likelihood of a Challenged Merger |
|---|---|---|
| Highly concentrated | Greater than 1,800 | Greater than 100—likely to be challenged<br>50 to 100—depends on other factors*<br>Less than 50—unlikely to be challenged |
| Moderately concentrated | 1,000–1,800 | Greater than 100—likely to be challenged; other factors considered*<br>Less than or equal to 100—unlikely to be challenged |
| Unconcentrated | Less than 1,000 | Any increase—unlikely to be challenged |

* In addition to the postmerger concentration of the market and the size of the resulting increase in concentration, the department will consider the presence of the following factors in deciding whether to challenge a merger: ease of entry; the nature of the product and its terms of sale; market information about specific transactions; buyer market characteristics; conduct of firms in the market; and market performance.

[14] Here we consider the effect on the HHI of a within-market acquisition. Similar calculations can be carried out for between-market acquisitions.

**TABLE 21–3**   U.S. Bank Asset Concentration, 1984 versus 2012

Sources: General Accounting Office, *Interstate Banking*, GAO/GGD, 95-35, December 1994, p. 101; and *FDIC Quarterly Banking Profile*, June 2012.

| | 2012 | | | | 1984 | | | |
| --- | --- | --- | --- | --- | --- | --- | --- | --- |
| | Number | Percent of Total | Assets ($ billions) | Percent of Total | Number | Percent of Total | Assets ($ billions) | Percent of Total |
| **All FDIC-insured commercial banks** | 6,222 | | $12,889.8 | | 14,483 | | $2,508.9 | |
| 1. Under $100 million | 2,085 | 33.5% | 121.0 | 0.9% | 12,044 | 83.2% | 404.2 | 16.1% |
| 2. $100 million–$1 billion | 3,614 | 58.1 | 1,057.1 | 8.2 | 2,161 | 14.9 | 513.9 | 20.5 |
| 3. $1–$10 billion | 435 | 7.0 | 1,132.0 | 8.8 | 254 | 1.7 | 725.9 | 28.9 |
| 4. $10 billion or more | 88 | 1.4 | 10,579.8 | 82.1 | 24 | 0.2 | 864.8 | 34.5 |

defined as highly localized: the standard metropolitan statistical areas (SMSAs) or rural areas (non-SMSAs). Unfortunately, such definitions become increasingly irrelevant in a world of greater geographic and product expansions. Indeed, the use of HHIs should increasingly be based on regional or national market lines and include a broad financial service firm definition of the marketplace. Consequently, in recent years the Federal Reserve has often included one-half of thrift deposits in calculating bank market HHIs.

Interestingly, comparing asset concentrations by bank size, the merger wave in banking appears to have decreased the national asset share of the very smallest banks (under $100 million) from 16.1 percent in 1984 to 0.9 percent in 2012, while the relative size of the very biggest banks (over $10 billion) has increased from 34.5 percent in 1984 to 82.1 percent in 2012. The relative market shares of intermediate-sized banks ($100 million to $10 billion) have decreased as well, falling from 49.4 percent in 1984 to 17.0 percent in 2012 (see Table 21–3). However, even though the degree of concentration of assets among the largest banks has increased, the percentage share exhibited by the largest U.S. banks is still well below the shares attained by the largest Canadian and European banks in their domestic markets. Thus, mergers involving the largest U.S. banks will likely continue to be approved by the Department of Justice as well as other regulatory bodies.

| **Concept Questions** | 1. What recent bank mergers have been motivated by cost synergies? |
| --- | --- |
| | 2. What are the three dimensions of revenue synergy gains? |
| | 3. Suppose each of five firms in a banking market has a 20 percent share. What is the HHI? |

# OTHER MARKET- AND FIRM-SPECIFIC FACTORS AFFECTING DOMESTIC GEOGRAPHIC EXPANSION DECISIONS

In addition to regulation and cost and revenue synergies, other factors may impact a decision to expand geographically. For example, an acquiring FI may be concerned about the solvency and asset quality of a potential target FI in another region. Thus, important factors influencing the acquisition decision may include the target FI's leverage or capital ratio, its loss reserves, and the amount of nonperforming loans in its portfolio.

**merger bid premium**
The ratio of the purchase price of a target bank's equity to its book value.

In a review of a number of studies that analyzed the determinants of **merger bid premiums** (the ratio of the purchase price of a target bank's equity to its book value), Darius Palia found that premiums are higher (1) in states with the most restrictive regulations and (2) for target banks with high-quality loan portfolios. Palia also concludes that the growth rate of the target bank has little effect on bid premiums, while the results for the effects on bid premiums of target bank profitability and capital adequacy are rather mixed. More recently, Brewer, Jackson, Jagtiani, and Nguyen find that, in the 1990s, higher performing targets (as measured by both return on equity and return on assets) receive higher bids; the lower the capital-to-deposit ratio, the larger the bid the acquiring bank is willing to offer; larger targets' loan-to-assets ratios and bank size are positively related to bid premiums; and higher prices occurred in the post–Riegle-Neal environment.[15]

---

**Concept Questions**

1. Suppose you are a manager of an FI looking at another FI as a target for acquisition. What three characteristics of the target FI would most attract you?
2. Given the same scenario as in question 1, what three characteristics would most discourage you?

---

## GLOBAL AND INTERNATIONAL EXPANSIONS

www.bis.org

Total assets of banks that report data to the Bank for International Settlements were $33.8 trillion in 2012. Only 10.5 percent of this amount was assets of U.S. banks. Thus, the international banking market presents an opportunity for geographic expansion beyond what an FI can achieve domestically. There are at least three ways an FI can establish a global or international presence: (1) selling financial services from its domestic offices to foreign customers, such as a loan originated in the New York office of J.P. Morgan Chase made to a Brazilian manufacturer; (2) selling financial services through a branch, agency, or representative office established in the foreign customer's country, such as making a loan to the Brazilian customer through J.P. Morgan Chase's branch in Brazil; and (3) selling financial services to a foreign customer through subsidiary companies in the foreign customer's country, such as J.P. Morgan Chase buying a Brazilian bank and using that wholly owned bank to make loans to the Brazilian customer. Note that these three methods of global activity expansion are not mutually exclusive; an FI could use all three simultaneously to expand the scale and scope of its operations.

U.S. banks, insurance companies, and securities firms have all expanded abroad in recent years, often through branches and subsidiaries. This has been reciprocated by the entrance and growth, until recently, of foreign FIs in U.S. financial service markets. In the late 2000s, several banks in the world had more than 25 percent

---

[15] D. Palia, "Recent Evidence of Bank Mergers," *Financial Markets, Instruments, and Institutions* 3, no. 5 (1994), pp. 36–59; and E. Brewer II, W. E. Jackson III, J. A. Jagtiani, and T. Nguyen, "The Price of Bank Mergers in the 1990s," Federal Reserve Bank of Chicago, *Economic Perspectives* 24, no. 1 (2000), pp. 2–24.

of their bank assets held in foreign countries. For example, HSBC Holdings PLC, headquartered in London, holds 28.8 percent of its customer accounts outside the United Kingdom. This next section concentrates on the growth of global banking. It begins with U.S. bank expansions into foreign countries and the factors motivating these expansions and then discusses foreign bank expansions into the United States.

## U.S. Banks Abroad

While some U.S. banks, such as J.P. Morgan Chase, have had offices abroad since the beginning of the twentieth century, the major phase of growth began in the early 1960s after the passage of the Overseas Direct Investment Control Act of 1964. This law restricted domestic U.S. banks' ability to lend to U.S. corporations that wanted to make foreign investments. The law was eventually repealed, but it created incentives for U.S. banks to establish foreign offices to service the funding and other business needs of their U.S. clients in other countries. This offshore funding and lending in dollars created the beginning of a market we now call the *Eurodollar market*. The term **Eurodollar transaction** denotes any transaction involving dollars that takes place outside the United States. For example, a banking transaction booked externally to the boundaries of the United States, often through an overseas branch or subsidiary, qualifies as a Eurodollar.[16]

**Eurodollar transaction**
Any transaction involving dollars that takes place outside the United States.

Table 21–4 shows the aggregate size of U.S. bank activities abroad between 1980 and 2012. Assets in U.S. bank foreign offices increased from $353.8 billion in 1980 to $1,542.6 billion in 2008, then decreased to $1,440.5 billion by March 2009 during the financial crisis. However, as a percent of these banks' total assets, assets in foreign offices fell from 32.4 percent in 1980 to 16.8 percent in 2008 and 16.2 percent in 2009. By March 2012, assets in foreign offices had risen back to $1,578.8 billion. However, as a percent of total assets, assets in foreign offices remained at financial crisis levels, 16.2 percent.

### Factors Encouraging U.S. Bank Expansions Abroad

While regulation of foreign lending was the original impetus for the early growth of the Eurodollar market and the associated establishment of U.S. branches and subsidiaries outside the United States, other regulatory and economic factors also have impacted the growth of U.S. offshore banking. These factors are discussed next.

**TABLE 21–4**  Assets of U.S. Banks with Foreign Offices, 1980–2012 (in billions of dollars)

Source: *Federal Reserve Bulletin,* various issues, Table 4–20.

|                 | 1980      | 1990      | 1995      | 2000      | 2005      | 2008      | 2009      | 2010      | 2012*     |
|-----------------|-----------|-----------|-----------|-----------|-----------|-----------|-----------|-----------|-----------|
| Total assets    | $1,091.4  | $1,901.5  | $2,530.1  | $4,311.4  | $6,101.0  | $9,207.5  | $8,869.3  | $9,184.2  | $9,738.1  |
| Domestic assets | 768.7     | 1,559.3   | 1,962.8   | 3,576.3   | 5,088.0   | 7,664.9   | 7,428.8   | 7,659.6   | 8,159.3   |
| Foreign assets  | 353.8     | 410.7     | 666.3     | 735.1     | 1,013.0   | 1,542.6   | 1,440.5   | 1,524.6   | 1,578.8   |

* As of March.

[16] That is, the definition of a Eurodollar transaction is more general than "a transaction booked in Europe." In fact, any deposit in dollars taken externally to the United States normally qualifies that transaction as a Eurodollar transaction.

*The Dollar as an International Medium of Exchange*   The growth of international trade after World War II and the use of the dollar as an international medium of exchange encouraged foreign corporations and investors to demand dollars. A convenient way to do this was by using U.S. banks' foreign offices to intermediate such fund flows between the United States and foreigners wishing to hold dollars. Today, trade-related transactions underlie much of the activity in the Eurodollar market.

*Political Risk Concerns*   Political risk concerns among savers in emerging market countries have led to enormous outflows of dollars from those countries, often to U.S. branches and subsidiaries in the Cayman Islands and the Bahamas, where there are very stringent bank secrecy rules. Because of the secrecy rules in some foreign countries and the possibility that these rules may result in money laundering and the financing of terrorist activities, the U.S. government enacted the USA Patriot Act of 2001. The act prohibits U.S. banks from providing banking services to foreign banks that have no physical presence in any country (so-called shell banks). The bill also added foreign corruption offenses to the list of crimes that can trigger a U.S. money-laundering prosecution. Also, federal authorities have the power to subpoena the records of a foreign bank's U.S. correspondent account. Further, the bill makes a depositor's funds in a foreign bank's U.S. correspondent account subject to the same civil forfeiture rules that apply to depositors' funds in other U.S. accounts. Finally, the act requires U.S. banks to improve their due diligence reviews in order to guard against money laundering.

*Domestic Regulatory Restrictions/Foreign Regulatory Relaxations*   As discussed earlier in the chapter, prior to the 1999 Financial Services Modernization Act, U.S. banks faced considerable activity restrictions at home regarding their securities, insurance, and commercial activities. However, with certain exceptions, Federal Reserve regulations have allowed U.S. banking offices in other countries to engage in the permitted banking activities of the foreign country even if such activities were not permitted in the United States. For example, U.S. banks setting up foreign subsidiaries can lease real property, act as general insurance agents, and underwrite and deal in foreign corporate securities (up to a maximum commitment of $2 million). Foreign activity regulations also encourage U. S. bank expansion abroad. For example, in the 2000s the Chinese Banking Regulatory Commission signaled a shift in policy away from restricting overseas competition to one of cautiously embracing it when it announced a comprehensive plan to overhaul the country's shaky banking system. Subsequently, U.S. banks began to enter the Chinese market. In late 2004, Goldman Sachs was one of the first financial firms to enter China. It was six years later, however, before another U.S. firm was awarded approval to enter China. In January 2011, J.P. Morgan Chase and Morgan Stanley won approval for securities joint ventures in mainland China.

*Technology and Communications Improvements*   The improvements in telecommunications and other communications technologies such as CHIPS (the international payment system, see Chapter 17) and the development of proprietary communication networks by large FIs have allowed U.S. parent FIs to extend and maintain real-time control over their foreign operations at a decreasing cost. The decreasing operating costs of such expansions have made it feasible to locate offices in an even wider array of international locations.

### Factors Deterring U.S. Expansions Abroad

A number of potential factors deter international expansion, as discussed next.

*Capital Constraints*  The Basel II and III reforms of the Bank for International Settlements (BIS) capital requirements raised the required capital needed to back loans to sovereign countries outside of the OECD. Under Basel III (see Chapter 20), risk weights for sovereign exposures are determined using OECD country risk classifications (CRCs), which assign countries to one of eight risk categories (0–7). Countries assigned to categories 0–1 have the lowest possible risk assessment and are assigned a risk weight of 0 percent, while countries assigned to category 7 having the highest possible risk assessment and are assigned a risk weight of 150 percent (see Chapter 20).

*Emerging and European Market Problems*  The problems of other emerging market countries, such as Korea, Thailand, and Indonesia in 1997 and 1998 and more recently (in the early 2000s) in Argentina, have made many U.S. banks more cautious in expanding outside traditional foreign markets. This is despite the existence of increasingly favorable regulatory environments. For example, the 1994 **NAFTA** agreement has given U.S. (and Canadian) banks greater powers to expand into Mexico. The December 1997 agreement by 100 countries, reached under the auspices of the World Trade Organization (WTO), is also an important step toward dismantling the regulatory barriers inhibiting the entry of U.S. FIs into emerging market countries.

The financial crisis spread to emerging markets in 2008 and 2009 and again led U.S. banks to be cautious about expansion into these areas. Even with the perceptions that emerging market economies were delinked from events in the Developed World, in Eastern Europe, Latin America, and Asia, the financial collapse was evident. Even China, the country most immune to contagion, saw its growth decline from 12 percent to 9 percent. Panic in global financial markets compelled the International Monetary Fund (IMF) to reinstate programs of lending and financial rescue. The IMF engaged in talks with Hungary, Iceland, Ukraine, Pakistan, and other countries. Further, the United States and its European partners began discussions about stepping in with credit lifelines to middle income developing countries in need of dollar loans to avoid default.

Throughout the spring of 2010, Greece struggled with a severe debt crisis. Early on, some of the healthier European countries tried to step in and assist the debt-ridden country. However, in late April, Greek bond prices dropped dramatically as traders began betting a debt default was inevitable, even if the country received a massive bailout. The problems in the Greek bond market then spread to other European nations with fiscal problems, such as Portugal, Spain, and Italy. The risks posed to U.S. banks and the banking system from a Greek debt default and a contagion crisis in other eurozone countries were significantly large. In late 2010, the United States had sovereign risk exposure to Greece totaling $43.1 billion. In addition, exposures to Ireland totaled $113.9 billion, to Portugal totaled $47.1 billion, and to Spain $187.5 billion. As the European debt crisis progressed, banks reduced their Greek exposure dramatically. For example, in early 2012, U.S. banks had cut their exposure to Greek debt to approximately $5.8 billion, exposure to both Spain and Ireland had been cut to $50 billion, and exposure to Portugal's debt had been cut to $6.6 billion.

*Competition*  U.S. banks face extensive competition from foreign banks for overseas business. For example, aiding the competitive position of European banks

**NAFTA**
The North American Free Trade Agreement.

has been the passage of the European Community (EC) Second Banking Directive, which has created a single banking market in Europe as well as the introduction of a single currency for much of Europe (the euro). Under the directive, European banks are allowed to branch and acquire banks throughout the European Community—that is, they have a single EC passport. While the Second Banking Directive did not come fully into effect until the end of 1992, it had been announced as early as 1988. As a result, there has been a cross-border merger wave among European banks that has paralleled the U.S. domestic merger and acquisition wave that followed the dismantling of interstate branching restrictions after the passage and implementation of the Riegle-Neal Act in 1994. In addition, a number of European banks have formed strategic alliances that enable retail bank customers to open new accounts, access account information, and make payments to third parties through any of the branches of the member banks in the alliance. This greater consolidation in European banking has created more intense competition for U.S. and other foreign banks in European wholesale markets and has made it more difficult for them to penetrate European retail markets.

### Foreign Banks in the United States

Just as U.S. banks can profitably expand into foreign markets, foreign banks have historically viewed the United States as an attractive market for entry. Table 21–5 shows the expansion of foreign banks in the United States between 1980 and 2012. In 1980 foreign banks had $166.7 billion in assets held in the U.S. (10.8 percent of the size of total U.S. bank assets). This activity grew through 1992, when foreign banks had $514.3 billion in assets (16.4 percent of the size of U.S. assets). In the mid-1990s, there was a modest retrenchment in the asset share of foreign banks in the United States. In 1994, their U.S. assets totaled $471.1 billion (13.8 percent of the size of U.S. assets). This retrenchment reflected a number of factors, including the highly competitive market for wholesale banking in the United States, a decline in average U.S. loan quality, capital constraints on Japanese banks at home, and their poor lending performance at home, and the introduction of the Foreign Bank Supervision and Enhancement Act (FBSEA) of 1991, which tightened regulations on foreign banks in the United States (discussed below).

**TABLE 21–5**
U.S. and Foreign Bank Assets, 1980–2012

Source: "Assets and Liabilities of Commercial Banks in the United States," Federal Reserve Board website, various dates. *www.federalreserve.gov*

| | Bank Assets Held in United States ($ billions) | |
| --- | --- | --- |
| | U.S.-Owned | Foreign-Owned |
| 1980 | $ 1,537.0 | $ 166.7 |
| 1985 | 2,284.8 | 175.5 |
| 1990 | 3,010.3 | 389.6 |
| 1992 | 3,138.4 | 514.3 |
| 1994 | 3,409.9 | 471.1 |
| 1995 | 3,660.6 | 530.1 |
| 2000 | 5,366.0 | 863.9 |
| 2005 | 7,738.1 | 938.5 |
| 2008 (June) | 10,689.6 | 1,333.8 |
| 2009 (September) | 10,400.7 | 1,369.0 |
| 2010 | 10,417.4 | 1,539.9 |
| 2012 (September) | 11,049.5 | 1,967.7 |

However, as foreign banks adjusted to these developments and because of the strong U.S. economy in the late 1990s, activity of foreign banks in the United States grew, reaching 16.1 percent in 2000. The worldwide economic recession in the early 2000s again depressed the level of international activity in the United States. As the economic situation improved, the level of international activity in the United States accelerated. In September 2009 (late in the financial crisis), foreign bank assets in the U.S. were 13.2 percent the size of domestic bank assets. At year-end 2010, they were 14.8 percent the size of domestic assets and, most recently, in September 2012, foreign bank assets in the United States were 17.8 percent the size of domestic assets.

### Regulation of Foreign Banks in the United States

Before 1978, foreign branches and agencies entering the United States were licensed mostly at the state level. As such, their entry, regulation, and oversight were almost totally confined to the state level. Beginning in 1978 with the passage of the International Banking Act (IBA) and the more recent passage of the Foreign Bank Supervision Enhancement Act (FBSEA), Title II of the FDICIA of December 1991, federal regulators have exerted increasing control over foreign banks operating in the United States.

**The International Banking Act of 1978** Before the passage in 1978 of the IBA, foreign agencies and branches entering the United States with state licenses had some competitive advantages and disadvantages relative to most domestic banks. The unequal treatment of domestic and foreign banks regarding federal regulation and lobbying by domestic banks regarding the unfairness of this situation provided the impetus for Congress to pass the International Banking Act in 1978. The fundamental regulatory philosophy underlying the IBA was one of **national treatment,** a philosophy that attempted to create a level playing field for both domestic and foreign banks in U.S. banking markets. As a result of this act, foreign banks were required to hold Federal Reserve–specified reserve requirements if their worldwide assets exceeded $1 billion, were subjected to Federal Reserve examinations, and were subjected to both the McFadden and Glass-Steagall Acts.

**national treatment**
Regulating foreign banks in the same fashion as domestic banks or creating a level playing field.

**The Foreign Bank Supervision Enhancement Act (FBSEA) of 1991** Along with the growth of foreign bank assets in the United States came concerns about foreign banks' rapidly increasing share of U.S. banking markets as well as about the weakness of regulatory oversight of many of these institutions. Three events focused attention on the weaknesses of foreign bank regulation. The first event was the collapse of the Bank of Credit and Commerce International (BCCI), which had a highly complex international organizational structure based in the Middle East, the Cayman Islands, and Luxembourg and had undisclosed ownership stakes in two large U.S. banks. BCCI was not subject to any consolidated supervision by a home country regulator. This quickly became apparent after its collapse, when massive fraud, insider lending abuses, and money-laundering operations were discovered. The second event was the issuance of more than $1 billion in unauthorized letters of credit to Saddam Hussein's Iraq by the Atlanta agency of the Italian Banca Nazionale del Lavoro. The third event was the unauthorized taking of deposit funds by the U.S. representative office of the Greek National Mortgage Bank of New York.

These events and related concerns led to the passage of the FBSEA of 1991. The objective of this act was to extend federal regulatory authority over foreign banking organizations in the United States, especially where these organizations have entered using state licenses. The act's five main features have significantly enhanced the powers of federal bank regulators over foreign banks in the United States.

1. *Entry.* Under FBSEA, a foreign banking organization must now have the Fed's approval to establish a subsidiary, branch, agency, or representative office in the United States. The approval applies to both a new entry and an entry by acquisition. To get Fed approval, the organization must meet a number of standards, two of which are mandatory. First, the foreign bank must be subject to comprehensive supervision on a consolidated basis by a home country regulator. Second, that regulator must furnish all the information needed by the Federal Reserve to evaluate the application.

2. *Closure.* The act also gives the Federal Reserve authority to close a foreign bank if its home country supervision is inadequate, if it violates U.S. laws, or if it engages in unsound and unsafe banking practices.

3. *Examination.* The Federal Reserve has the authority to examine each office of a foreign bank, including its representative offices. Further, each branch or agency must be examined at least once a year.

4. *Deposit taking.* Only foreign subsidiaries with access to FDIC insurance can take retail deposits under $250,000. This effectively rolls back the provision of the IBA that gave foreign branches and agencies access to FDIC insurance.

5. *Activity powers.* Beginning on December 19, 1992, state-licensed branches and agencies of foreign banks could not engage in any activity that was not permitted to a federal branch.

| **Concept Questions** | 1. What regulatory and economic factors have encouraged the growth of U.S. offshore banking? What factors have deterred U.S. offshore banking? |
|---|---|
| | 2. What were the major policy changes pertaining to bank expansion introduced by NAFTA? |
| | 3. How did the IBA of 1978 and the FBSEA of 1991 affect foreign banks operating in the United States? |

# ADVANTAGES AND DISADVANTAGES OF INTERNATIONAL EXPANSION

Historical and recent trends affecting the geographic expansion of FIs both into and outside the United States have been discussed above. Here we summarize the advantages and disadvantages of international expansions to the individual FI seeking to generate additional returns or better diversify its risk.

## Advantages

Below are the six major advantages of international expansion.

### Revenue and Risk Diversification

As with domestic geographic expansions, an FI's international activities potentially enhance its opportunity to diversify the risk of its revenue flows. Often, domestic revenue flows from financial services are strongly linked to the state of that economy. Therefore, the less integrated the economies of the world are, the greater is the potential for revenue diversification through international expansions.

### Economies of Scale

To the extent that economies of scale exist, an FI can potentially lower its average operating costs by expanding its activities beyond domestic boundaries.

### Innovations

An FI can generate extra returns from new product innovations if it can sell such services internationally rather than just domestically. For example, consider complex financial innovations, such as securitization, caps, floors, and options, that FIs have innovated in the United States and sold to new foreign markets with, until recently, few domestic competitors.

### Funds Source

International expansion allows an FI to search for the cheapest and most available sources of funds. This is extremely important given the very thin profit margins in domestic and international wholesale banking. Also, it reduces the risk of fund shortages (credit rationing) in any one market.

### Customer Relationships

International expansions also allow an FI to maintain contact with and service the needs of domestic multinational corporations. Indeed, one of the fundamental factors determining the growth of FIs in foreign countries has been the parallel growth of foreign direct investment and foreign trade by globally oriented multinational corporations from the FI's home country.

### Regulatory Avoidance

To the extent that domestic regulations such as activity restrictions and reserve requirements impose constraints or taxes on the operations of an FI, seeking out low regulatory tax countries can allow an FI to lower its net regulatory burden and to increase its potential net profitability.

## Disadvantages

Below are the three major disadvantages of international expansion.

### Information/Monitoring Costs

While global expansions give an FI the potential to better diversify its geographic risk, the absolute level of exposure in certain areas such as lending can be high, especially if the FI fails to diversify in an optimal fashion. For example, the FI may fail to choose a loan portfolio combination on the efficient lending frontier (see Chapter 11). Foreign activities may also be riskier for the simple reason that monitoring and information collection costs are often higher in foreign markets. For example, Japanese and German accounting standards differ significantly from the generally accepted accounting principles (GAAP) used by U.S. firms. In addition, language, legal, and cultural issues can impose additional transaction costs on international activities. Finally, because the regulatory environment is controlled locally and regulation imposes a different array of net costs in each market, a truly global FI must master the various rules and regulations in each market.

### Nationalization/Expropriation

To the extent that an FI expands by establishing a local presence through investing in fixed assets such as branches or subsidiaries, it faces the political risk that a change in government may lead to the nationalization of those fixed assets.[18] Further, if foreign FI depositors take losses following a nationalization, they may seek legal recourse from the FI in U.S. courts rather than from the nationalizing government. For example, it took many years to resolve the outstanding claims of depositors in Citicorp's branches in Vietnam following the Communist takeover and expropriation of those branches.

### Fixed Costs

The fixed costs of establishing foreign organizations may be extremely high. For example, a U.S. FI seeking an organizational presence in the Tokyo banking market faces real estate prices significantly higher than those in New York. Such relative costs can be even higher if an FI chooses to enter by buying an existing Japanese bank rather than establishing a new operation because of the considerable cost of acquiring Japanese equities measured by price-earnings ratios. These relative cost considerations become even more important if there is uncertainty about the expected volume of business to be generated and thus revenue flows from foreign entry.

| **Concept Questions** | 1. What are the major advantages of international expansion to an FI? |
| | 2. What are the major disadvantages of international expansion to an FI? |
| | 3. Comparing the advantages and disadvantages discussed above, why do you think so few U.S. banks have established branches in the Ukraine? |

## Summary

Traditionally, the U.S. financial system has been structured on segmented product lines. Unlike most other countries, until 1999 commercial banking, investment banking, and insurance activities have been separated by several legislative acts, including the Glass-Steagall Act of 1933 and the Bank Holding Company Act of 1956. These restrictions on product or activity expansion have had some significant costs. Most important has been the loss of potential risk-reducing gains that arise from both regional and product diversification, as well as gains from the potential generation of cost and revenue synergies. Nevertheless, in recent years, there has been a dramatic breakdown in many of the regulatory barriers to financial service conglomeration culminating with the Financial Services Modernization Act of 1999. The act allowed the creation of a financial service holding company that could engage in banking activities *and* securities underwriting and insurance. As a result, the U.S. financial system is rapidly converging toward a "universal banking"–type system. In such a system, bank, insurance, and securities products are increasingly cross-sold by large conglomerate (universal) financial service firms with the objective of maximizing revenue and cost synergies and reducing risk through diversification.

Domestic and international expansions are another way in which an FI can improve its risk-return performance. While regulatory considerations and costs

---

[18] Such nationalizations have occurred with some frequency in African countries.

are fundamental to geographic expansion decisions, several other economic factors play an important role in the net return or benefit-cost analysis for any given FI. For example, considerations such as earnings diversification, economies of scale and scope, extension of customer relationships, and better exploiting of financial service innovations add to the potential benefits from geographic expansions. However, there are also costs or risks of such expansions such as monitoring costs, expropriation of assets, and the fixed costs of market entry. Managers need to carefully weigh each of these factors before making a geographic expansion decision, whether international or domestic.

**Questions and Problems**

1. How does product segmentation reduce the profitability and risk of FIs? How does it increase the profitability and risk of FIs?
2. What general prohibition regarding the activities of commercial banking and investment banking did the Glass-Steagall Act impose?
3. What restrictions were placed on Section 20 subsidiaries of U.S. commercial banks that made investment banking activities other than those permitted by the Glass-Steagall Act less attractive? How did this differ from banking activities in other countries?
4. Explain in general terms what impact the Financial Services Modernization Act of 1999 should have on the strategic implementation of Section 20 activities.
5. What types of insurance products were commercial banks permitted to offer before 1999? How did the Financial Services Modernization Act of 1999 change this? How have nonbanks managed to exploit the loophole in the Bank Holding Company Act of 1956 and engage in banking activities? What law closed this loophole? How did insurance companies circumvent this law?
6. The Financial Services Modernization Act of 1999 allows banks to own controlling interests in nonfinancial companies. What are the two restrictions on such ownership?
7. What is shadow banking? How does the shadow banking system differ from the traditional banking system?
8. What are the differences in the risk implications of a firm commitment securities offering versus a best-efforts offering?
9. An FI is underwriting the sale of 1 million shares of Ultrasonics, Inc., and is quoting a bid–ask price of $6.00–$6.50.
   a. What are the fees earned by the FI if a firm commitment method is used to underwrite the securities?
   b. What are the fees if the FI uses the best-efforts method and a commission of 50 basis points is charged?
   c. How would your answer be affected if the FI manages to sell the shares only at $5.50 using the firm commitment method? The commission for best efforts is still 50 basis points.
10. A Section 20 affiliate agrees to underwrite a debt issue for one of its clients. It has suggested a firm commitment offering for issuing 100,000 shares of stock. The FI quotes a bid–ask spread of $97–$97.50 to its customer on the issue date.

    a. What are the total underwriting fees generated if all the issue is sold? If only 60 percent is sold?

    b. Instead of taking a chance that only 60 percent of the shares will be sold on the issue date, the FI suggests a price of $95 to the issuing firm. The FI quotes a bid–ask spread of $95–$95.40 and sells 100 percent of the issue. From the FI's perspective, which price is better if it expects to sell the remaining 40 percent at the bid price of $97 under the first quote?

11. What are three ways that the failure of a securities affiliate in a holding company organizational form could negatively affect a bank affiliate? How has the Fed attempted to prevent a breakdown of the firewalls between bank and nonbank affiliates in these situations?

12. What role does bank activity diversification play in the ability of a bank to exploit economies of scale and scope? What remains as the limitation to creating potentially greater benefits?

13. What six conflicts of interest have been identified as potential roadblocks to the expansion of banking powers into the financial services area?

14. Under what circumstances could the existence of deposit insurance provide an advantage to banks in competing with other traditional securities firms?

15. In what ways does the current regulatory structure argue against providing additional securities powers to the banking industry? Does this issue just concern banks?

16. How do limitations on domestic geographic diversification affect an FI's profitability?

17. How are insurance companies able to offer services in states beyond their state of incorporation?

18. In what way did the Garn-St. Germain Act and FIRREA provide incentives for the expansion of interstate branching?

19. What is an interstate banking pact?

20. How did the provisions of the Riegle-Neal Interstate Banking and Branching Efficiency Act of 1994 allow for full interstate banking? What are the expected profit performance effects of interstate banking? What has been the impact on the structure of the banking and financial services industry?

21. What cost synergies may be obtained by an FI from domestic geographic expansion?

22. What are the three revenue synergies that may be obtained by an FI from domestic geographic expansion?

23. What is the Herfindahl-Hirschman Index? How is it calculated and interpreted?

24. City Bank currently has a 60 percent market share in banking services, followed by NationsBank with 20 percent and State Bank with 20 percent.

    a. What is the concentration ratio as measured by the Herfindahl-Hirschman Index (HHI)?

    b. If City Bank acquires State Bank, what will be the new HHI?

    c. Assume that the Justice Department will allow mergers as long as the changes in HHI do not exceed 1,400. What is the minimum amount of assets that City Bank will have to divest after it merges with State Bank?

25. The Justice Department has been asked to review a merger request for a market with the following four FIs:

| Bank | Assets |
|------|--------|
| A | $ 12 million |
| B | 25 million |
| C | 102 million |
| D | 3 million |

    a. What is the HHI for the existing market?
    b. If bank A acquires bank D, what will be the impact on the market's level of concentration?
    c. If bank C acquires bank D, what will be the impact on the market's level of concentration?
    d. What is likely to be the Justice Department's response to the two merger applications?

26. What factors other than market concentration does the Justice Department consider in determining the acceptability of a merger?

27. What are some plausible reasons for the percentage of assets of small and intermediate sized banks decreasing and the percentage of assets of large banks increasing since 1984?

28. What are some of the benefits for banks engaging in domestic geographic expansion?

29. How did the Overseas Direct Investment Control Act of 1964 assist in the growth of global banking activities? How much growth in foreign assets occurred from 1980 to 2012?

30. Identify and explain the impact of at least four factors that have encouraged global U.S. bank expansion.

31. What is the expected impact of the implementation of the Basel III risk-based capital requirements on the international activities of some major U.S. banks?

32. What effect have the problems of emerging market economies in the late 1990s and 2000s had on the global expansion of traditional banking activities by U.S. banks?

33. What is the European Community (EC) Second Banking Directive? What impact has the Second Banking Directive had on the competitive banking environment in Europe?

34. What factors affected the proportion of U.S. banking assets that were controlled by foreign banks during the 1990s through 2012?

35. What was the fundamental philosophical focus of the International Banking Act (IBA) of 1978?

36. What events led to the passage of the Foreign Bank Supervision Enhancement Act (FBSEA) of 1991? What was the main objective of this legislation?

37. What were the main features of FBSEA? How did FBSEA encourage cooperation with the home country regulator? What was the effect of the FBSEA on the Federal Reserve and on foreign banks?

38. What are the major advantages of international expansion to FIs? Explain how each advantage can affect the operating performance of FIs.

39. What are the difficulties of expanding globally? How can each of these difficulties create negative effects on the operating performance of FIs?

## Web Question

40. Go to the FDIC website at **www.fdic.gov**. Find the most recent breakdown of bank holding company deposit share for the State of New York using the following steps. Click on "Analysts." From there click on "Summary of Deposits" and then click on "Deposit Market Share" Under "State- > County- > City- > Zip." Click on "Submit." Under "State," select "New York," and then click on "Continue." Click on "Continue." Click on "Run Report." This will download files onto your computer that contain the relevant data. What banks are the top deposit holders in the state?

## Appendix 21A: EU and G-10 Countries: Regulatory Treatment of the Mixing of Banking, Securities, and Insurance Activities and the Mixing of Banking and Commerce

View Appendix 21A at the website for this textbook (**www.mhhe.com/saunders8e**).

**See Appendices Online at www.mhhe.com/saunders8e**
• Appendix 22A: Microhedging with Futures

# Futures and Forwards

## INTRODUCTION

Chapter 16 describes the growth in FIs' off-balance-sheet activities. A major component of this growth has been in derivative contracts such as futures and forwards. While a significant amount of derivatives reflect the trading activity of large banks and other FIs, FIs of all sizes have used these instruments to hedge their asset–liability risk exposures and thus reduce the value of their net worth at risk due to adverse events. Derivative securities generally involve an agreement between two parties to exchange a standard quantity of an asset or cash flow at a predetermined price and at a specified date in the future. As the value of the underlying security to be exchanged changes, the value of the derivative security changes. Derivatives involve the buying and selling, or transference, of risk. As such they can involve profits and losses if a position is unhedged.

Table 22–1 lists the derivative contract holdings of all commercial banks, and specifically the 25 largest U.S. banks, as of June 2012. The table shows notional (dollar) contract volumes for these 25 banks exceeding $220 trillion, while the other 1,332 bank and trust companies with derivatives activity report notional contract volumes of $522 billion. This compares to a total of $17 trillion outstanding in December 1995. Table 22–1 also shows the breakdown of the positions into futures and forwards, swaps, options, and credit derivatives. As can be seen, swaps ($134.5 trillion) are the largest group of derivatives, followed by futures and forwards ($40.7 trillion), options ($33.6 trillion), and credit derivatives ($13.6 trillion). The current credit risk (exposure) of these derivative contracts for the top 25 derivative users is reported at $399 billion, while total credit exposure is $1,092 billion (or 129 percent of the capital of these banks).[1] Not only do FIs hold these contracts to hedge their own risk (interest rate, credit, etc.), but FIs also serve as the counterparty (for a fee) in these contracts for other (financial and nonfinancial) firms wanting to hedge risks on their balance sheets.

---

[1] See Chapter 20 for a discussion of how the credit exposure of derivatives is calculated for regulatory reporting.

**TABLE 22–1** Derivative Contracts: Notional Amount and Credit Equivalent Exposure of the 25 Commercial Banks and Trust Companies with the Most Derivative Contracts, June 2012 (in millions of dollars)

Source: Office of the Comptroller of the Currency website, October 2012. www.occ.gov

| Rank | Bank Name | Total Assets | Derivative Contracts | | | | | Current Credit Exposure | Potential Future Exposure | Credit Exposure from All Contracts | Credit Exposure to Capital Ratio |
| | | | Futures & Forwards | Total Swaps | Total Options | Credit Derivatives | Total Derivatives | | | | |
|---|---|---|---|---|---|---|---|---|---|---|---|
| 1. | J.P. Morgan Chase Bank | $ 1,812,837 | $13,242,193 | $ 38,953,299 | $11,025,862 | $ 6,016,995 | $ 69,238,349 | $162,867 | $181,892 | $ 344,759 | 246 |
| 2. | Citibank NA | 1,347,841 | 7,129,350 | 32,630,778 | 9,344,370 | 3,046,472 | 52,150,970 | 72,809 | 164,919 | 237,728 | 174 |
| 3. | Bank of America NA | 1,445,093 | 11,440,172 | 26,283,299 | 3,291,616 | 3,390,285 | 44,405,372 | 66,064 | 139,939 | 206,003 | 141 |
| 4. | Goldman Sachs Bank | 114,693 | 4,478,725 | 28,810,776 | 7,809,128 | 481,766 | 41,508,395 | 27,757 | 119,715 | 147,472 | 738 |
| 5. | HSBC Bank USA | 193,995 | 896,034 | 2,793,846 | 270,043 | 575,870 | 4,535,794 | 7,015 | 30,086 | 37,101 | 172 |
| 6. | Wells Fargo Bank NA | 1,180,190 | 1,096,881 | 1,914,889 | 512,720 | 66,360 | 3,590,850 | 29,613 | 19,656 | 49,269 | 42 |
| 7. | Morgan Stanley Bank NA | 69,390 | 454,621 | 1,285,759 | 720,259 | 20,982 | 2,481,621 | 350 | 14,179 | 14,529 | 135 |
| 8. | Bank of New York Mellon | 259,069 | 373,852 | 677,825 | 244,115 | 221 | 1,296,013 | 6,490 | 5,257 | 11,747 | 87 |
| 9. | State Street Bank & TC | 196,960 | 795,187 | 2,930 | 69,005 | 28 | 867,150 | 4,821 | 7,374 | 12,195 | 90 |
| 10. | PNC Bank NA | 291,824 | 82,410 | 224,863 | 81,543 | 3,415 | 392,231 | 3,304 | 850 | 4,154 | 12 |
| 11. | SunTrust Bank | 172,028 | 43,307 | 161,771 | 64,398 | 4,507 | 273,983 | 2,868 | 1,539 | 4,407 | 25 |
| 12. | Northern Trust Co | 94,216 | 215,280 | 10,310 | 104 | 76 | 225,770 | 2,462 | 2,322 | 4,785 | 61 |
| 13. | Standard Chartered Bank | 48,377 | 134,888 | 2,566 | 7,930 | 0 | 145,384 | 0 | 0 | 0 | 0 |
| 14. | U.S. Bank National Assn | 342,823 | 54,616 | 49,489 | 13,921 | 3,048 | 121,074 | 1,373 | 245 | 1,617 | 5 |
| 15. | Regions Bank | 121,330 | 57,424 | 59,687 | 3,083 | 739 | 120,933 | 948 | 235 | 1,183 | 8 |
| 16. | Keybank National Assn | 83,966 | 17,185 | 55,688 | 5,675 | 2,613 | 81,161 | 1,066 | 136 | 1,202 | 11 |
| 17. | Branch Banking and Trust | 173,678 | 17,029 | 39,015 | 20,968 | 0 | 77,013 | 1,569 | 402 | 1,971 | 12 |
| 18. | Fifth Third Bank | 115,041 | 14,586 | 33,068 | 23,527 | 1,317 | 72,498 | 1,714 | 711 | 2,425 | 17 |
| 19. | TD Bank National Assn | 195,943 | 9,633 | 57,714 | 1,594 | 740 | 69,680 | 2,575 | 754 | 3,329 | 23 |
| 20. | Union Bank National Assn | 87,275 | 7,384 | 36,655 | 14,715 | 35 | 58,790 | 1,036 | 525 | 1,561 | 15 |
| 21. | RBS Citizens National Assn | 106,894 | 7,573 | 25,984 | 2,122 | 887 | 36,567 | 1,122 | 284 | 1,406 | 13 |
| 22. | Bank of Oklahoma NA | 25,415 | 28,748 | 3,139 | 3,282 | 0 | 35,168 | 235 | 242 | 477 | 20 |
| 23. | Capital One NA | 158,240 | 825 | 31,735 | 44 | 705 | 33,310 | 657 | 270 | 927 | 6 |
| 24. | BMO Harris Bank NA | 92,222 | 1,294 | 26,670 | 2,905 | 90 | 30,959 | 621 | 318 | 939 | 9 |
| 25. | Ally Bank | 87,336 | 8,239 | 13,216 | 7,383 | 0 | 28,838 | 139 | 177 | 316 | 2 |
| | **Total 25 commercial banks** | $ 8,816,679 | $40,607,436 | $134,184,972 | $33,540,312 | $13,617,151 | $221,949,873 | $399,474 | $692,028 | $1,091,501 | 129[a] |
| | **Other 1,332 commercial banks** | $ 3,525,137 | $ 141,054 | $ 297,514 | $ 75,475 | $ 7,622 | $ 521,665 | $ 10,240 | $ 3,847 | $ 14,087 | 4 |
| | **Total for all banks** | $12,341,817 | $40,748,491 | $134,482,486 | $33,615,787 | $13,624,773 | $222,471,538 | $409,714 | $695,875 | $1,105,589 | 90 |

[a] Average.

The rapid growth of derivatives use by both FIs and nonfinancial firms has been controversial. In the 1990s and 2000s, critics charged that derivatives contracts contain potential losses that can materialize to haunt their holders, particularly banks and insurance companies that deal heavily in these instruments. As will be discussed in this chapter and the following two chapters, when employed appropriately, derivatives can be used to hedge (or reduce an FI's risk). However, when misused, derivatives can increase the risk of an FI's insolvency. In the 1990s, a number of scandals involving FIs, firms, and municipalities (such as Bankers Trust and the Allied Irish Bank) led to a tightening of the accounting (reporting) requirements for derivative contracts. Specifically, beginning in 2000, the Financial Accounting Standards Board (FASB) required all derivatives to be marked to market and mandated that losses and gains be immediately transparent on FIs' and other firms' financial statements. Then in the late 2000s, billions of dollars of losses on derivative securities and the near collapse of the world's financial markets led to a call for major regulations imposed on the trading of derivative securities. The regulations intended to bring the many over-the-counter derivative contracts made between financial institutions under federal regulation and empower securities and commodities regulators to police them.

www.fasb.org

In this chapter, we look at the role futures and forward contracts play in managing an FI's interest rate, FX, and credit risk exposures as well as their role in hedging natural catastrophes. We start with a comparison of forward and futures contracts to spot contracts. We then examine how forwards and futures can be used to hedge interest rate risk, FX risk, credit risk, and catastrophe risk. We look at option-type derivatives and swaps in Chapters 23 and 24.

# FORWARD AND FUTURES CONTRACTS

To understand the essential nature and characteristics of forward and futures contracts, we can compare them with spot contracts. We show appropriate time lines for each of the three contracts using a bond as the underlying financial security to the derivative contract in Figure 22–1.

## Spot Contracts

**spot contract**
An agreement involving the immediate exchange of an asset for cash.

A **spot contract** is an agreement between a buyer and a seller at time 0, when the seller of the asset agrees to deliver it immediately and the buyer of the asset agrees to pay for that asset immediately.[2] Thus, the unique feature of a spot market contract is the immediate and simultaneous exchange of cash for securities, or what is often called *delivery versus payment*. A spot bond quote of $97 for a 20-year maturity bond is the price the buyer must pay the seller, per $100 of face value, for immediate (time 0) delivery of the 20-year bond.

## Forward Contracts

**forward contract**
An agreement involving the exchange of an asset for cash at a fixed price in the future.

A **forward contract** is a contractual agreement between a buyer and a seller at time 0 to exchange a prespecified asset for cash at a later date. For example, in a three month forward contract to deliver 20-year bonds, the buyer and seller agree on a price and quantity today (time 0) but the delivery (or exchange) of the 20-year

---

[2] Technically, physical settlement and delivery may take place one or two days after the contractual spot agreement in bond markets. In equity markets, delivery and cash settlement normally occur three business days after the spot contract agreement.

**FIGURE 22–1**
**Contract Time Lines**

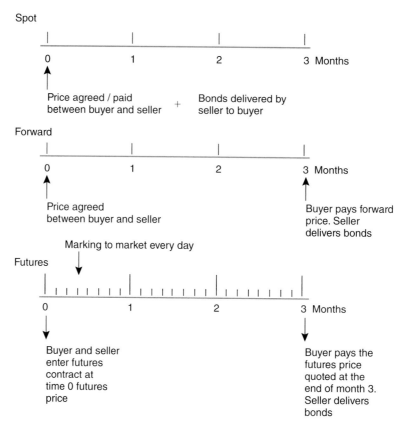

bond for cash does not occur until three months hence. If the forward price agreed to at time 0 was $97 per $100 of face value, in three months' time the seller delivers $100 of 20-year bonds and receives $97 from the buyer. This is the price the buyer must pay and the seller must accept no matter what happened to the spot price of 20-year bonds during the three months between the time the contract was entered into and the time the bonds are delivered for payment.

Commercial banks, investment banks, and broker–dealers are the major forward market participants, acting as both principals and agents. These financial institutions make a profit on the spread between the prices at which they buy and sell the asset underlying the forward contracts. Each forward contract is originally negotiated between the financial institution and the customer, and therefore the details of each (e.g., price, expiration, size, delivery date) can be unique. As the forward market has grown over the last decade, however, traders have begun making secondary markets in some forward contracts, communicating the buy and sell prices on the contracts over computer networks. As of June 2012, U.S. commercial banks held over $36.0 trillion of forward contracts that were listed for trading in the over-the-counter markets.

## Futures Contracts

**futures contract**
An agreement involving the future exchange of an asset for cash at a price that is determined daily.

A **futures contract** is normally arranged through an organized exchange. It is an agreement between a buyer and a seller at time 0 to exchange a standardized, prespecified asset for cash at a later date. As such, a futures contract is very similar to a forward contract. However, there are four major differences between a futures and a forward contract. The first difference relates to the price, which in a

**marking to market**
The process by which the prices on outstanding futures contracts are adjusted each day to reflect current futures market conditions.

forward contract is fixed over the life of the contract ($97 per $100 of face value for three months), but in a futures contract is **marked to market** daily. This means the contract's price is adjusted each day as the futures price for the contract changes. Therefore, actual daily cash settlements occur between the buyer and seller in response to this marking-to-market process. This can be compared to a forward contract, where the whole cash payment from buyer to seller occurs at the end of the contract period. As of June 2012, U.S. commercial banks held over $4.7 trillion of futures contracts that were listed for trading.

A second difference between futures and forward contracts is that forwards are tailor-made contracts that are negotiated between two parties, while futures contracts are standardized because they are offered by and traded on an exchange. Third, as exchange-traded securities (see below), the exchange itself guarantees the performance of the futures contract. Thus, the risk of default by either party is minimized since the exchange will step in and take over the defaulting counterparty's position. No such guarantee exists for a forward contract. Finally, delivery of the underlying asset almost always occurs for forward contracts, but seldom occurs for futures contracts. Instead, an offsetting or reverse futures transaction occurs through the exchange prior to the maturity of the contract.

www.cmegroup.com

www.cftc.gov

Futures trading occurs on organized exchanges—for example, the Chicago Board of Trade (CBT) and the Chicago Mercantile Exchange (CME) (both part of the CME Group). Financial futures market trading was introduced in 1972 with the establishment of foreign exchange future contracts on the International Money Market (IMM). By the mid-1990s, five major exchanges existed in the United States,[3] and several exchanges existed abroad.[4] The terms of futures contracts (e.g., contract size, delivery month, trading hours, minimum price fluctuation, daily price limits, and process used for delivery) traded in the United States are set by the exchange and are subject to the approval of the Commodity Futures Trading Commission (CFTC), the principal regulator of futures markets. In recent years, "off-market" trading systems have sprung up in which institutional investors and money managers can continue to trade during, as well as after, futures exchange operating hours. Indeed, it is estimated that trading volume in off-market currencies, interest rate swaps, and Eurodollars has grown 3 to 10 times faster than trading volume on futures exchanges.

| **Concept Questions** | 1. What is the difference between a futures contract and a forward contract? |
|---|---|
| | 2. What are the major differences between a spot contract and a forward contract? |

# FORWARD CONTRACTS AND HEDGING INTEREST RATE RISK

**naive hedge**
When a cash asset is hedged on a direct dollar-for-dollar basis with a forward or futures contract.

To see the usefulness of forward contracts in hedging the interest rate risk of an FI, consider a simple example of a **naive hedge** (the hedge of a cash asset on a direct dollar-for-dollar basis with a forward or futures contract). Suppose an FI portfolio manager holds a 20-year, $1 million face value bond on the balance sheet. At time 0, these bonds are valued by the market at $97 per $100 face value, or $970,000

---

[3] These include the Chicago Board of Trade, the Chicago Mercantile Exchange, the Intercontinental Exchange, and the Kansas City Board of Trade. The CBT and the CME merged in 2007 to become the CME Group.

[4] These include the London International Financial Futures Exchange (LIFFE) part of NYSE Euronext, the Singapore Exchange Limited, and the Montreal Exchange.

in total. Assume the manager receives a forecast that interest rates are expected to rise by 2 percent from their current level of 8 to 10 percent over the next three months. Knowing that rising interest rates mean that bond prices will fall, the manager stands to make a capital loss on the bond portfolio. Having read Chapters 8 and 9, the manager is an expert in duration and has calculated the 20-year maturity bonds' duration to be exactly 9 years. Thus, the manager can predict a capital loss, or change in bond values ($\Delta P$), from the duration equation of Chapter 9:[5]

$$\frac{\Delta P}{P} = -D \times \frac{\Delta R}{1 + R}$$

where

$\Delta P$ = Capital loss on bonds = ?
$P$ = Initial value of bond position = \$970,000
$D$ = Duration of the bonds = 9 years
$\Delta R$ = Change in forecast yield = 0.02
$1 + R$ = 1 plus the current yield on 20-year bonds = 1.08

$$\frac{\Delta P}{\$970,000} = -9 \times \left[\frac{0.02}{1.08}\right]$$

$$\Delta P = -9 \times \$970,000 \times \left[\frac{0.02}{1.08}\right] = -\$161,667$$

As a result, the FI portfolio manager expects to incur a capital loss on the bond portfolio of \$161,667 (as a percentage loss ($\Delta P/P$) = 16.67%), or as a drop in price from \$97 per \$100 face value to \$80.833 per \$100 face value. To offset this loss—in fact, to reduce the risk of capital loss to zero—the manager may hedge this position by taking an off-balance-sheet hedge, such as selling \$1 million face value of 20-year bonds for forward delivery in three months' time.[6] Suppose at time 0 the portfolio manager can find a buyer willing to pay \$97 for every \$100 of 20-year bonds delivered in three months' time.

Now consider what happens to the FI portfolio manager if the gloomy forecast of a 2 percent rise in interest rates proves to be true. The portfolio manager's bond position has fallen in value by 16.67 percent, equal to a capital loss of \$161,667. After the rise in interest rates, the manager can buy \$1 million face value of 20-year bonds in the spot market at \$80.833 per \$100 of face value, a total cost of \$808,333, and deliver these bonds to the forward contract buyer. Remember that the forward contract buyer agreed to pay \$97 per \$100 of face value for the \$1 million of face value bonds delivered, or \$970,000. As a result, the portfolio manager makes a profit on the forward transaction of:

$$
\underset{\substack{\text{(price paid by} \\ \text{forward buyer to} \\ \text{forward seller)}}}{\$970,000} \quad - \quad \underset{\substack{\text{(cost of purchasing} \\ \text{bonds in the spot market} \\ \text{at } t = \text{month 3 for delivery} \\ \text{to the forward buyer)}}}{\$808,333} \quad = \quad \$161,667
$$

[5] For simplicity, we ignore issues relating to convexity here.

[6] Since a forward contract involves delivery of bonds in a future time period, it does not appear on the balance sheet, which records only current and past transactions. Thus, forwards are one example of off-balance-sheet items (see Chapter 16).

**immunized**

Describes an FI that is fully hedged or protected against adverse movements in interest rates (or other asset prices).

As you can see, the on-balance-sheet loss of $161,667 is exactly offset by the off-balance-sheet gain of $161,667 from selling the forward contract. In fact, for any change in interest rates, a loss (gain) on the balance sheet is offset by a gain (loss) on the forward contract. Indeed, the success of a hedge does not hinge on the manager's ability to accurately forecast interest rates. Rather, the reason for the hedge is the lack of ability to perfectly predict interest rate changes. The hedge allows the FI manager to protect against interest rate changes even if they are unpredictable. Thus, the FI's net interest rate exposure is zero; it has **immunized** its assets against interest rate risk.

---

| **Concept Questions** | 1. Explain how a naive hedge works. |
| | 2. What does it mean to say that an FI has immunized its portfolio against a particular risk? |

---

# HEDGING INTEREST RATE RISK WITH FUTURES CONTRACTS

Even though some hedging of interest rate risk does take place using forward contracts—such as forward rate agreements commonly used by insurance companies and banks prior to mortgage loan originations—most FIs hedge interest rate risk either at the micro level (called *microhedging*) or at the macro level (called *macrohedging*) using futures contracts. Before looking at futures contracts, we explain the difference between microhedging and macrohedging and between routine hedging and selective hedging.

## Microhedging

**microhedging**

Using a futures (forward) contract to hedge a specific asset or liability.

An FI is **microhedging** when it employs a futures or a forward contract to hedge a particular asset or liability risk. For example, earlier we considered a simple example of microhedging asset-side portfolio risk, where an FI manager wanted to insulate the value of the institution's bond portfolio fully against a rise in interest rates. An example of microhedging on the liability side of the balance sheet occurs when an FI, attempting to lock in a cost of funds to protect itself against a possible rise in short-term interest rates, takes a short (sell) position in futures contracts on CDs or T-bills. In microhedging, the FI manager often tries to pick a futures or forward contract whose underlying deliverable asset is closely matched to the asset (or liability) position being hedged. The earlier example, where we had an exact matching of the asset in the portfolio with the deliverable security underlying the forward contract (20-year bonds) was unrealistic. Such exact matching cannot be achieved often, and this produces a residual unhedgable risk termed **basis risk.** We discuss basis risk in detail later in this chapter. It arises mainly because the prices of the assets or liabilities that an FI wishes to hedge are imperfectly correlated over time with the prices on the futures or forward contract used to hedge risk.

**basis risk**

A residual risk that arises because the movement in a spot (cash) asset's price is not perfectly correlated with the movement in the price of the asset delivered under a futures or forward contract.

## Macrohedging

**macrohedging**

Hedging the entire duration gap of an FI.

**Macrohedging** occurs when an FI manager wishes to use futures or other derivative securities to hedge the entire balance sheet duration gap. This contrasts to microhedging, where an FI manager identifies specific assets and liabilities and seeks individual futures and other derivative contracts to hedge those individual risks. Note that macrohedging and microhedging can lead to quite different hedging strategies and results. In particular, a macrohedge takes a whole portfolio view and allows for individual asset and liability interest sensitivities or durations to net each other out. This can result in a very different aggregate futures position than when an FI manager disregards this netting or portfolio effect and hedges individual asset and liability positions on a one-to-one basis.

## Routine Hedging versus Selective Hedging

**routine hedging**
Seeking to hedge all interest rate risk exposure.

**Routine hedging** occurs when an FI reduces its interest rate or other risk exposure to the lowest possible level by selling sufficient futures to offset the interest rate risk exposure of its whole balance sheet or cash positions in each asset and liability. For example, this might be achieved by macrohedging the duration gap, as described next. However, since the reduction of risk generally results in a reduction of expected return and thus shareholder wealth, not all FI managers seek to do this. Indeed, a manager would follow this strategy only if the direction and size of interest rate changes are extremely unpredictable to the extent that the manager is willing to forgo return to hedge this risk. Figure 22–2 shows the trade-off between expected return and risk and the minimum-risk fully hedged portfolio.[7]

**hedging selectively**
Only partially hedging the gap or individual assets and liabilities.

Rather than a fully hedged position, most FIs choose to bear some interest rate risk as well as credit and FX risks because of their comparative advantage as FIs (see Chapter 1). One possibility is that an FI may choose to **hedge selectively** its portfolio. For example, an FI manager may generate expectations regarding future interest rates before deciding on a futures position. As a result, the manager may selectively hedge only a proportion of its balance sheet position. Alternatively, the FI manager may decide to remain unhedged or even to overhedge by selling more futures than required by the cash position, although regulators may view this as speculative. Thus, the fully hedged position—and the minimum risk portfolio—becomes one of several choices depending, in part, on managerial interest rate expectations, managerial objectives, and the nature of the return-risk trade-off from hedging. Finally, an FI may selectively hedge in an attempt to arbitrage profits between a spot asset's price movements and movements in a futures price.

## Macrohedging with Futures

The number of futures contracts that an FI should buy or sell in a macrohedge depends on the size and direction of its interest rate risk exposure and the return risk trade-off from fully or selectively hedging that risk. Chapter 9 showed that an

**FIGURE 22–2**
**The Effects of Hedging on Risk and Expected Return**

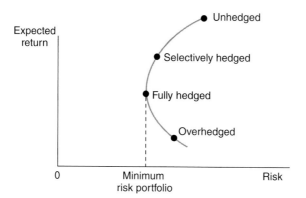

[7] The minimum-risk portfolio is not shown as zero here because of basis risk (discussed below) that prevents perfect hedging. In the absence of basis risk, a zero-risk position becomes possible.

FI's net worth exposure to interest rate shocks was directly related to its leverage adjusted duration gap as well as its asset size. Again, this is:

$$\Delta E = -[D_A - kD_L] \times A \times \frac{\Delta R}{1 + R}$$

where

$\Delta E$ = Change in an FI's net worth

$D_A$ = Duration of its asset portfolio

$D_L$ = Duration of its liability portfolio

$k$ = Ratio of an FI's liabilities to assets ($L/A$)

$A$ = Size of an FI's asset portfolio

$\dfrac{\Delta R}{1 + R}$ = Shock to interest rates

**EXAMPLE 22–1**
*Calculation of Change in FI Net Worth as Interest Rates Rise*

To see how futures might fully hedge a positive or negative portfolio duration gap, consider the following FI where:

$$D_A = 5 \text{ years}$$
$$D_L = 3 \text{ years}$$

Suppose the FI manager receives information from an economic forecasting unit that interest rates are expected to rise from 10 percent to 11 percent over the next year. That is:

$$\Delta R = 1\% = 0.01$$
$$1 + R = 1.10$$

The FI's initial balance sheet is:

| Assets (in millions) | Liabilities (in millions) |
|---|---|
| $A = \$100$ | $L = \$\ 90$ |
|  | $E = \underline{\ \ \ 10}$ |
| $\overline{\$100}$ | $\$100$ |

so that $k$ equals $L/A$ equals 90/100 equals 0.9.

The FI manager wants to calculate the potential loss to the FI's net worth ($E$) if the forecast of rising rates proves to be true. As we showed in Chapter 9:

$$\Delta E = -(D_A - kD_L) \times A \times \frac{\Delta R}{1 + R}$$

so that

$$\Delta E = -[5 - (0.9)(3)] \times \$100 \times \frac{0.01}{1.1} = -\$2.091 \text{ million}$$

The FI could expect to lose $2.091 million in net worth if the interest rate forecast turns out to be correct. Since the FI started with a net worth of $10 million, the loss of $2.091 million is almost 21 percent of its initial net worth position. Clearly, as this example illustrates, the impact of the rise in interest rates could be quite threatening to the FI and its insolvency risk exposure.

### The Risk-Minimizing Futures Position

The FI manager's objective to fully hedge the balance sheet exposure would be fulfilled by constructing a futures position such that if interest rates do rise by 1 percent to 11 percent, as in the prior example, the FI will make a gain on the futures position that just offsets the loss of balance sheet net worth of $2.091 million.

When interest rates rise, the price of a futures contract falls since its price reflects the value of the underlying bond that is deliverable against the contract. The amount by which a bond price falls when interest rates rise depends on its duration. Thus, we expect the price of the 20-year T-bond futures contract to be more sensitive to interest rate changes than the price of the 3-month T-bill futures contract since the former futures price reflects the price of the 20-year T-bond deliverable on contract maturity. Thus, the sensitivity of the price of a futures contract depends on the duration of the deliverable bond underlying the contract, or:

$$\frac{\Delta F}{F} = -D_F \frac{\Delta R}{1 + R}$$

where

$\Delta F$ = Change in dollar value of futures contracts

$F$ = Dollar value of the initial futures contracts

$D_F$ = Duration of the bond to be delivered against the futures contracts such as a 20-year, 8 percent coupon T-bond

$\Delta R$ = Expected shock to interest rates

$1 + R$ = 1 plus the current level of interest rates

This can be rewritten as:

$$\Delta F = -D_F \times F \times \frac{\Delta R}{1 + R}$$

The left side of this expression ($\Delta F$) shows the dollar gain or loss on a futures position when interest rates change.

To see this dollar gain or loss more clearly, we can decompose the initial dollar value position in futures contracts, $F$, into its two component parts:

$$F = N_F \times P_F$$

The dollar value of the outstanding futures position depends on the number of contracts bought or sold ($N_F$) and the price of each contract ($P_F$). $N_F$ is positive when the futures contracts are bought and is assigned a negative value when contracts are sold.

Futures contracts are homogeneous in size. Thus, futures exchanges sell T-bond futures in minimum units of $100,000 of face value; that is, one T-bond future ($N_F = 1$) equals $100,000. T-bill futures are sold in larger minimum units: one T-bill future ($N_F = 1$) equals $1,000,000. The quote for each contract reported in the newspaper is the price per $100 of face value for delivering the underlying bond. *The Wall Street Journal Online* reports the most recent quotes for each type of interest rate futures contract. See, for example, part of an interest rate futures quote retrieved from the website on September 21, 2012, listed in Figure 22–3. Looking at Figure 22–3, a closing price quote, SETTLE, of $146\frac{28}{32}$ on September 21, 2012, for the T-bond futures contract maturing in December 2012 means that the buyer locks in a purchase price for the underlying T-bonds of $146,875 for one contract. That is, at maturity (in December 2012), the futures buyer would pay $146,875 to

**FIGURE 22–3**   **Futures Contracts on Interest Rates**

Source: *The Wall Street Journal Online*, September 21, 2012. Reprinted by permission of the Wall Street Journal, © 2012 Dow Jones & Company, Inc. All Rights Reserved Worldwide. *www.wsj.com*

**Interest Rate Futures** | Index | Agricultural | Currency | Metals & Petroleum

Friday, September 21, 2012                                                                 Find Historical Data  ⬛ | WHATS THIS?

**Treasury Bonds** (CBT)-$100,000; pts 32nds of 100%

| | OPEN | HIGH | LOW | SETTLE | CHG | LIFETIME HIGH | (▲▼) | LOW | OPEN INT |
|---|---|---|---|---|---|---|---|---|---|
| Dec 12 | 146–270 | 147–040 | 146–100 | 146–280 | +5.0 | 154–170 | | 133–200 | 544,847 |
| Mar 13 | 145–060 | 145–210 | 145–060 | 145–190 | +1.0 | 152–000 | | 143–080 | 88 |

Est vol 277,007; vol n.a.n.a.; open Int. 544,935,n.a..
Sources: Thomson Reuters; WSJ Market Data Group

**Eurodollar** (CME)-$1,000,000; pts of 100%

| | OPEN | HIGH | LOW | SETTLE | CHG | LIFETIME HIGH | (▲▼) | LOW | OPEN INT |
|---|---|---|---|---|---|---|---|---|---|
| Oct 12 | 96.6575 | 99.6650 | 96.6575 | 99.6625 | +.0050 | 99.6800 | | 99.3300 | 43,053 |
| Nov 12 | 99.6600 | 99.6750 | 99.6600 | 99.6700 | +.0050 | 99.6850 | | 99.4350 | 6,159 |
| Dec 12 | 99.6600 | 99.6800 | 99.6500 | 99.6750 | +.0150 | 99.7100 | | 99.2300 | 975,691 |
| Mar 12 | 99.6500 | 99.6650 | 99.6400 | 99.6600 | +.0100 | 99.7100 | | 99.2350 | 843,769 |
| Jun 13 | 99.6350 | 99.6450 | 99.6250 | 99.6350 | ... | 99.6900 | | 99.2250 | 716,912 |
| Sep 13 | 99.6200 | 99.6300 | 99.6100 | 99.6200 | ... | 99.6700 | | 99.1700 | 646,903 |
| Dec 13 | 99.5950 | 99.6050 | 99.5850 | 99.5950 | ... | 99.6450 | | 99.0500 | 689,197 |
| Mar 14 | 99.5700 | 99.5800 | 99.5600 | 99.5750 | +.0050 | 99.6200 | | 98.9300 | 618,685 |
| Jun 14 | 99.5300 | 99.5400 | 99.5150 | 99.5350 | +.0050 | 99.5750 | | 98.7950 | 479,843 |
| Sep 14 | 99.4800 | 99.5000 | 99.4650 | 99.4900 | +.0050 | 99.5250 | | 98.6350 | 420,306 |
| Dec 14 | 99.4200 | 99.4400 | 99.4050 | 99.4350 | +.0100 | 99.4650 | | 98.4400 | 421,721 |
| Mar 15 | 99.3650 | 99.3900 | 99.3500 | 99.3800 | +.0100 | 99.4150 | | 98.2450 | 399,149 |
| Jun 15 | 99.2850 | 99.3100 | 99.2650 | 99.3050 | +.0150 | 99.3350 | | 98.0350 | 499,138 |

**Eurodollar** (CME)-$1,000,000; pts of 100%

| | OPEN | HIGH | LOW | SETTLE | CHG | LIFETIME HIGH | (▲▼) | LOW | OPEN INT |
|---|---|---|---|---|---|---|---|---|---|
| Sep 15 | 99.1750 | 99.2100 | 99.1450 | 99.2000 | +.0200 | 99.2350 | | 97.8400 | 315,681 |
| Dec 15 | 99.0400 | 99.0800 | 99.0150 | 99.0650 | +.0200 | 99.1050 | | 97.6550 | 251,377 |
| Mar 16 | 98.9000 | 98.9500 | 98.8800 | 98.9300 | +.0200 | 98.9800 | | 97.4400 | 178,599 |
| Jun 16 | 98.7450 | 98.7950 | 98.7150 | 98.7800 | +.0250 | 98.8350 | | 97.3250 | 132,677 |
| Sep 16 | 98.5850 | 98.6350 | 98.5550 | 98.6200 | +.0300 | 98.6800 | | 97.1700 | 114,475 |
| Dec 16 | 98.4100 | 98.4650 | 98.3850 | 98.4500 | +.0300 | 98.5350 | | 97.0050 | 94,904 |
| Mar 17 | 98.2600 | 98.3150 | 98.2250 | 98.2950 | +.0300 | 98.4200 | | 96.8700 | 75,633 |
| Jun 17 | 98.1050 | 98.1550 | 98.0650 | 98.1350 | +.0300 | 98.3050 | | 96.7700 | 45,180 |
| Sep 17 | 97.9550 | 98.0050 | 97.9200 | 97.9850 | +.0250 | 98.1800 | | 96.6250 | 28,478 |
| Dec 17 | 97.8050 | 97.8500 | 97.7650 | 97.8300 | +.0200 | 98.0600 | | 96.5100 | 14,887 |

Est vol 1,231,726;vol n.a. n.a.;open int,8,067,463, n.a..
Sources: Thomson Reuters; WSJ Market Data Group

the futures seller and the futures seller would deliver one $100,000, 20-year, 8 percent T-bond to the futures buyer.[8] The subsequent profit or loss from a position in the December 2012 T-bond taken on September 21, 2012, is graphically described in Figure 22–4. A short position in the futures contract will produce a profit when interest rates rise (meaning that the value of the underlying T-bond decreases). Therefore, a short position in the futures market is the appropriate hedge when the FI stands to lose on the balance sheet if interest rates are expected to rise (e.g., the FI has a positive duration gap). A long position in the futures market

**FIGURE 22–4**
**Profit or Loss on a Futures Position in Treasury Bonds Taken on September 21, 2012**

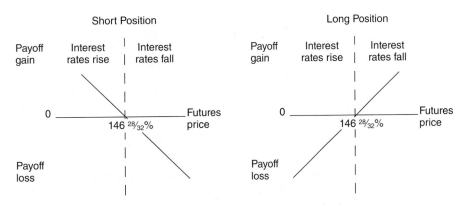

[8] In practice, the futures price changes day to day and gains or losses would be generated for the seller/buyer over the period between when the contract is entered into and when it matures. See our later discussion of this unique marking-to-market feature. Note that the FI could sell contracts in T-bonds maturing at later dates. However, while contracts exist for up to two years into the future, longer-term contracts tend to be infrequently traded and therefore relatively illiquid.

produces a profit when interest rates fall (meaning that the value of the underlying T-bond increases).[9] Therefore, a long position is the appropriate hedge when the FI stands to lose on the balance sheet if interest rates are expected to fall (e.g., has a negative duration gap).

In actuality, the seller of the futures contract has a number of alternatives other than an 8 percent coupon 20-year bond that can be delivered against the T-bond futures contract. If only one type of bond could be delivered, a shortage or squeeze might develop, making it very hard for the short side or seller to deliver. In fact, the seller has quite flexible delivery options. Apart from delivering the 20-year, 8 percent coupon bond, the seller can deliver bonds that range in maturity from 15 years upward. Often, up to 25 different bonds may qualify for delivery. When a bond other than the 20-year benchmark bond is delivered, the buyer pays a different invoice price for the futures contract based on a **conversion factor** that calculates the price of the deliverable bond if it were to yield 8 percent divided by face value. Suppose $100,000 worth of 18-year, 6 percent semiannual coupon Treasury bonds were valued at a yield of 5.5 percent. This would produce a fair present value of the bond of approximately $105,667. The conversion factor for the bond would be 1.057 (or $105,667/$100,000). This means the buyer would have to pay the seller the conversion factor of 1.057 times the published futures price of $146,875. That is, the futures price would be $155,198.41.[10]

We can now solve for the number of futures contracts to buy or sell to fully macrohedge an FI's on-balance-sheet interest rate risk exposure. We have shown that:

**conversion factor**
A factor used to figure the invoice price on a futures contract when a bond other than the benchmark bond is delivered to the buyer.

1. *Loss on balance sheet.* The loss of net worth for an FI when rates rise is equal to:

$$\Delta E = -(D_A - kD_L)A\frac{\Delta R}{1 + R}$$

2. *Gain off balance sheet on futures.* The gain off balance sheet from selling futures is equal to:[11]

$$\Delta F = -D_F(N_F \times P_F)\frac{\Delta R}{1 + R}$$

Fully hedging can be defined as buying or selling a sufficient number of futures contracts $(N_F)$ so that the loss of net worth on the balance sheet $(\Delta E)$ when interest rates change is just offset by the gain from off-balance-sheet buying or selling of futures $(\Delta F)$, or:

$$\Delta F + \Delta E = 0$$

Substituting in the appropriate expressions for each:

$$\left[-D_F(N_F \times P_F)\frac{\Delta R}{1 + R}\right] + \left[-(D_A - kD_L)A\frac{\Delta R}{1 + R}\right] = 0$$

[9] Notice that if rates move in an opposite direction from that expected, losses are incurred on the futures position. That is, if rates rise and futures prices drop, the long hedger loses. Similarly, if rates fall and futures prices rise, the short hedger loses. However, such losses are offset by gains on their cash market positions. Thus, the hedger is still protected.

[10] In practice, the seller exploits the delivery option by choosing the cheapest bond to deliver, that is, bonds whose conversion factor is most favorable (being based on an 8 percent yield) relative to the true price of the bond to be delivered (which reflects the actual level of yields).

[11] When futures prices fall, the buyer of the contract compensates the seller, here the FI. Thus, the FI gains when the prices of futures fall.

Canceling $\Delta R/(1 + R)$ and multiplying by $-1$ on both sides gives:[12]

$$D_F(N_F \times P_F) + (D_A - kD_L)A = 0$$

Solving for $N_F$ (the number of futures to sell):

$$N_F = \frac{-(D_A - kD_L)A}{D_F \times P_F}$$

For a microhedge, this equation becomes:

$$N_F = \frac{-D \times P}{D_F \times P_F}$$

where $P$ is the price of the asset or liability being hedged and $D$ is its duration. Appendix 22A (located at the book's website, **www.mhhe.com/saunders8e**) derives the equation and provides an example for the number of futures contracts to buy or sell for a microhedge.

### Short Hedge

An FI takes a short position in (i.e., sells) a futures contract when rates are expected to rise; that is, the FI loses net worth on its balance sheet if rates rise, so it seeks to hedge the value of its net worth by selling an appropriate number of futures contracts.

---

**EXAMPLE 22–2**

*Macrohedge of Interest Rate Risk Using a Short Hedge*

From the equation for $N_F$, we can now solve for the correct number of futures positions to sell ($N_F$) in the context of Example 22–1, where the FI was exposed to a balance sheet loss of net worth ($\Delta E$) amounting to $2.091 million when interest rates rose. In that example:

$D_A = 5$ years
$D_L = 3$ years
$k = 0.9$
$A = \$100$ million

Suppose the current futures price quote is $97 per $100 of face value for the benchmark 20-year, 8 percent coupon bond underlying the nearby futures contract, the minimum contract size is $100,000, and the duration of the deliverable bond is 9.5 years. That is:

$D_F = 9.5$ years
$P_F = \$97,000$

Inserting these numbers into the expression for $N_F$, we can now solve for the number of futures contracts:[13]

$$N_F = \frac{-[5 - (0.9)(3)] \times \$100,000,000}{9.5 \times \$97,000}$$

$$= \frac{-\$230,000,000}{\$921,500}$$

$$= -249.59 \text{ contracts}$$

When $N_F < 0$ then contracts should be shorted, or sold.

---

[12] This amounts to assuming that the interest changes of the cash asset position match those of the futures position; that is, there is no basis risk. This assumption is relaxed later.

[13] Also note that if the FI intends to deliver any bond other than the 20-year benchmark bond, the $P_F$ has to be multiplied by the appropriate conversion factor ($c$). If $c = 1.19$, then $P_F = 97 \times 1.19 = \$115.43$ per $100 of face value and the invoice price per contract would be $115,430.

Since the FI cannot sell a part of a contract, the number of contracts should be rounded down to the nearest whole number, or 249 contracts.[14] Note that the hedging formula simply gives the number of futures contract to use in the hedge. If the FI is hedging a loss on the balance sheet as interest rates rise, the futures position to take is a short one (i.e., $N_F$ is $<0$). As interest rates rise (and losses occur on the balance sheet), the value of the futures contracts falls and the FI makes a profit on the short position to offset the on-balance-sheet losses. If the FI is hedging a loss on the balance sheet as interest rates fall, the futures position to take is a long one (i.e., $N_F$ is $>0$). As interest rates fall (and losses occur on the balance sheet), the value of the futures contracts rise, and the FI makes a profit on the long position to offset the on-balance-sheet losses.

Next, we verify that selling 249 T-bond futures contracts will indeed hedge the FI against a sudden increase in interest rates from 10 to 11 percent, or a 1 percent interest rate shock.

### On-Balance-Sheet

As shown above, when interest rates rise by 1 percent, the FI loses $2.091 million in net worth ($\Delta E$) on the balance sheet:

$$\Delta E = -(D_A - kD_L)A \frac{\Delta R}{1 + R}$$

$$-\$2,091,000 = -[5 - (0.9)(3)] \times \$100,000,000 \times \left(\frac{0.01}{1.1}\right)$$

### Off-Balance-Sheet

When interest rates rise by 1 percent, the change in the value of the futures position is:

$$\Delta F = -D_F(N_F \times P_F) \frac{\Delta R}{1 + R}$$

$$= -9.5 (-249 \times \$97,000) \left(\frac{0.01}{1.1}\right)$$

$$= \$2.086 \text{ million}$$

The value of the off-balance-sheet futures position ($\Delta F$) falls by $2.086 million when the FI sells 249 futures contracts in the T-bond futures market. Such a fall in value of the futures contracts means a positive cash flow to the futures seller as the buyer compensates the seller for a lower futures price through the marking-to-market process. This requires a cash flow from the buyer's margin account to the seller's margin account as the price of a futures contract falls.[15] Thus, as the seller of the futures, the FI makes a gain of $2.086 million. As a result, the net gain/loss on and off the balance sheet is

$$\Delta E + \Delta F = -\$2.091\,m + \$2.086\,m = -\$0.005 \text{ million}$$

[14] The reason for rounding down rather than rounding up is technical. The target number of contracts to sell is that which minimizes interest rate risk exposure. By slightly underhedging rather than overhedging, the FI can generate the same risk exposure level but the underhedging policy produces a slightly higher return (see Figure 22–2).

[15] An example of marking to market might clarify how the seller gains when the price of the futures contract falls. Suppose on day 1 the seller entered into a 90-day contract to deliver 20-year T-bonds at $P = \$97$. The next day, because of a rise in interest rates, the futures contract, which now has 89 days to maturity, is trading at $96 when the market closes. Marking to market requires the prices on all contracts entered into on the previous day(s) to be marked to market at each night's closing (settlement) price. As a result, the price of the contract is lowered to $96 per $100 of face value, but in return for this lowering of the price from $97 to $96, the buyer has to compensate the seller to the tune of $1 per $100 of face value. Thus, given a $100,000 contract, there is a cash flow payment of $1,000 on that day from the buyer to the seller. Note that if the price had risen to $98, the seller would have had to compensate the buyer $1,000. The marking-to-market process goes on until the futures contract matures. If, over the period, futures prices have mostly fallen, then the seller accumulates positive cash flows on the futures position. It is this accumulation of cash flows that can be set off against losses in net worth on the balance sheet.

This small remaining net loss of $0.005 million to equity or net worth reflects the fact that the FI could not achieve the perfect hedge—even in the absence of basis risk—as it needed to round down the number of futures to the nearest whole contract from 249.59 to 249 contracts. Table 22–2 summarizes the key features of the hedge (assuming no rounding of futures contracts).

Suppose instead of using the 20-year T-bond futures to hedge, it had used the three-month Eurodollar futures. We can use the same formula to solve for $N_F$ in the case of Eurodollar futures:

$$N_F = \frac{-(D_A - kD_L)A}{D_F \times P_F}$$

$$= \frac{-[5 - (0.9)(3)]\,\$100,000,000}{D_F \times P_F}$$

Assume that $P_F = \$97$ per $100 of face value or $970,000 per contract (the minimum contract size of a Eurodollar future is $1,000,000) and $D_F = 0.25$ (the duration of a three-month Eurodollar deposit that is the discount instrument deliverable under the contract).[16] Then:

$$N_F = \frac{-[5 - (0.9)(3)]\,\$100,000,000}{0.25 \times \$970,000} = \frac{-\$230,000,000}{\$242,500}$$

$$N_F = -948.45 \text{ contracts, or sell } 948.45 \text{ contracts}$$

Rounding down to the nearest whole contract, $N_F = 948$.

As this example illustrates, we can hedge an FI's on-balance-sheet interest rate risk when its $D_A > kD_L$ by shorting or selling either T-bond or Eurodollar futures. In general, fewer T-bond than Eurodollar contracts need to be sold—in our case, 948 Eurodollar versus 249 T-bond contracts. This suggests that on a simple transaction cost basis, the FI might normally prefer to use T-bond futures. However, other considerations can be important, especially if the FI holds the futures contracts until the delivery date. The FI needs to be concerned about the availability

**TABLE 22–2** **On- and Off-Balance-Sheet Effects of a Macrohedge Hedge**

| | On-Balance-Sheet | Off-Balance-Sheet |
|---|---|---|
| Begin hedge $t = 0$ | Equity value of $10 million exposed to impact of rise in interest rates. | Sell 249.59 T-bond futures contracts at $97,000. Underlying T-bond coupon rate is 8%. |
| End hedge $t = 1$ day | Interest rates rise on assets and liabilities by 1%. Opportunity loss on-balance-sheet: $$\Delta E = -[5 - 0.9(3)] \times \$100,000,000 \times \frac{0.01}{1.1}$$ $$= -\$2.091 \text{ million}$$ | Buy 249.59 T-bond futures (closes out futures position). Real gain on futures hedge: $$\Delta F = -9.5 \times (-249.59 \times \$97,000) \times \frac{0.01}{1.1}^*$$ $$= \$2.091 \text{ million}$$ |

\* Assuming no basis risk and no contract "rounding."

[16] We assume the same futures price ($97) here for purposes of comparison. Of course, the actual prices of the two futures contracts are very different (see Figure 22–3).

of the deliverable set of securities and any possible supply shortages or squeezes. Such liquidity concerns may favor Eurodollars.[17]

## The Problem of Basis Risk

Because spot bonds and futures on bonds are traded in different markets, the shift in yields, $\Delta R/(1 + R)$, affecting the values of the on-balance-sheet cash portfolio may differ from the shift in yields, $\Delta R_F/(1 + R_F)$, affecting the value of the underlying bond in the futures contract; that is, changes in spot and futures prices or values are not perfectly correlated. This lack of perfect correlation is called *basis risk*. In the previous section, we assumed a simple world of no basis risk in which $\Delta R/(1 + R) = \Delta R_F/(1 + R_F)$.

Basis risk occurs for two reasons. First, the balance sheet asset or liability being hedged is not the same as the underlying security on the futures contract. For instance, in Example 22–2 we hedged interest rate changes on the FI's entire balance sheet with T-bond futures contracts written on 20-year maturity bonds with a duration of 9.5 years. The interest rates on the various assets and liabilities on the FI's balance sheet and the interest rates on 20-year T-bonds do not move in a perfectly correlated (or one-to-one) manner. The second source of basis risk comes from the difference in movements in spot rates versus futures rates. Because spot securities (e.g., government bonds) and futures contracts (e.g., on the same bonds) are traded in different markets, the shift in spot rates may differ from the shift in futures rates (i.e., they are not perfectly correlated).

To solve for the risk-minimizing number of futures contracts to buy or sell, $N_F$, while accounting for greater or less rate volatility and hence price volatility in the futures market relative to the spot or cash market, we look again at the FI's on-balance-sheet interest rate exposure:

$$\Delta E = -(D_A - kD_L) \times A \times \Delta R/(1 + R)$$

and its off-balance-sheet futures position:

$$\Delta F = -D_F(N_F \times P_F) \times \Delta R_F/(1 + R_F)$$

Setting:

$$\Delta E = \Delta F = 0$$

and solving for $N_F$, we have:

$$N_F = \frac{-(D_A - kD_L) \times A \times \Delta R/(1 + R)}{D_F \times P_F \times \Delta R_F/(1 + R_F)}$$

Let *br* reflect the relative sensitivity of rates underlying the bond in the futures market relative to interest rates on assets and liabilities in the spot market, that is, $br = [\Delta R_F/(1 + R_F)]/[\Delta R/(1 + R)]$. Then the number of futures contracts to buy or sell is:

$$N_F = \frac{-(D_A - kD_L)A}{D_F \times P_F \times br}$$

[17] However, when rates change, the loss of net worth on the balance sheet and the gain on selling the futures are instantaneous. Therefore, delivery need not be a concern. Indeed, because of the daily marking-to-market process, an FI manager can close out a futures position by taking an exactly offsetting position. That is, a manager who had originally sold 100 futures contracts could close out a position on any day by buying 100 contracts. Because of the unique marking-to-market feature, the marked-to market price of the contracts sold equals the price of any new contracts bought on that day.

The only difference between this and the previous formula is an adjustment for basis risk (*br*), which measures the degree to which the futures price (yield) moves more or less than spot bond price (yield).

---

**EXAMPLE 22–3**

*Macrohedging Interest Rate Risk When Basis Risk Exists*

From Example 22–2, let $br = 1.1$. This means that for every 1 percent change in discounted spot rates [$\Delta R/(1 + R)$], the implied rate on the deliverable bond in the futures market moves by 1.1 percent. That is, futures prices are more sensitive to interest rate shocks than are spot market prices. Solving for $N_F$ we have:

$$N_F = \frac{-[5 - (0.9)(3)]\ \$100,000,000}{9.5 \times \$97,000 \times 1.1}$$

$$= -226.9 \text{ contracts, or sell } 226.9 \text{ contracts}$$

or 226 contracts, rounding down. This compares to 249 when we assumed equal rate shocks in both the cash and futures markets [$\Delta R/(1 + R) = \Delta R_F/(1 + R_F)$]. Here we need fewer futures contracts than was the case when we ignored basis risk because futures rates and prices are more volatile then spot rates and prices, so that selling fewer futures would be sufficient to provide the same change in $\Delta F$ (the value of the futures position) than before when we implicitly assumed $br = 1$. Note that if futures rates or prices had been less volatile than spot rates or prices, we would have had to sell more than 249 contracts to get the same dollar gain in the futures position as was lost in net worth on the balance sheet so that $\Delta E + \Delta F = 0$.

---

An important issue FIs must deal with in hedging interest rate and other risks is how to estimate the basis risk adjustment in the preceding formula. One method is to look at the ratio between $\Delta R/(1 + R)$ and $\Delta R_F/(1 + R_F)$ today. Since this is only one observation, the FI might better analyze the relationship between the two interest rates by investigating their relative behavior in the recent past. We can do this by running an ordinary least squares linear regression of implied futures rate changes on spot rate changes with the slope coefficient of this regression giving an estimate of the degree of comovement of the two rates over time. We discuss this regression procedure in greater detail next in connection with calculating basis risk when hedging with FX futures.[18]

---

**Concept Questions**

1. What is the difference between microhedging and macrohedging and between routine hedging and selective hedging?
2. In Example 22–2, suppose the FI had the reverse duration gap; that is, the duration of its assets was shorter ($D_A = 3$) than the duration of its liabilities ($D_A = 5$). (This might be the case of a bank that borrows with long-term notes or time deposits to finance floating-rate loans.) How should it hedge using futures?
3. In Example 22–3, how many futures contracts should have been sold using the 20-year bond futures contracts if the basis risk measure $br = 0.8$?

---

[18] Another problem with the simple duration gap approach to determining $N_F$ is that it is assumes that yield curves are flat. This could be relaxed by using duration measures that allow for nonflat yield curves (see Chapter 9).

# HEDGING FOREIGN EXCHANGE RISK

Just as forwards and futures can hedge an FI against losses due to interest rate changes, they also can hedge against foreign exchange risk.

## Forwards

Chapter 13 analyzed how an FI uses forward contracts to reduce the risks due to FX fluctuations when it mismatches the sizes of its foreign asset and liability portfolios. That chapter considered the simple case of an FI that raised all its liabilities in dollars while investing half of its assets in British pound–denominated loans and the other half in dollar-denominated loans. Its balance sheet looks as follows:

| Assets | Liabilities |
|---|---|
| U.S. loans ($) $100 million<br>U.K. loans (£) $100 million | U.S. CDs $200 million |

All assets and liabilities are of a one-year maturity and duration. Because the FI is net long in pound assets, it faces the risk that over the period of the loan, the pound will depreciate against the dollar so that the proceeds of the pound loan (along with the dollar loan) will be insufficient to meet the required payments on the maturing dollar CDs. Then the FI will have to meet such losses out of its net worth; that is, its insolvency risk will increase.

Chapter 13 showed that by selling both the pound loan principal and interest forward one year at the known forward exchange rate at the beginning of the year, the FI could hedge itself against losses on its pound loan position due to changes in the dollar–pound exchange rate over the succeeding year. Note the strategy for hedging (£100 million) of British pound loans with forwards in Figure 22–5.

## Futures

Instead of using FX forward contracts to hedge foreign exchange risk, the FI could use FX futures contracts. Consider a U.S.-based FI wishing to hedge a one-year British pound loan of £100 million principal plus £15 million interest (or £115 million) against the risk of the pound falling in value against the dollar over the succeeding year. Suppose the FI wished to hedge this loan position on September 24, 2012, via the futures markets. How many futures should it sell? The answer to this question is that it should sell the amount that produces a sufficient profit on the

**FIGURE 22–5**
Hedging a Long
Position in Pound
Assets through Sale
of Pound Forwards

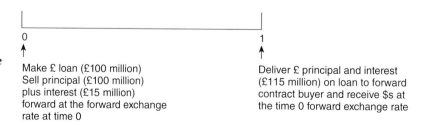

pound futures contracts to just offset any exchange rate losses on the pound loan portfolio should the pound fall in value relative to the dollar. There are two cases to consider:

1. The futures dollar–pound price is expected to change in exactly the same fashion as the spot dollar–pound price over the course of the year. That is, futures and spot price changes are perfectly correlated; there is no basis risk.
2. Futures and spot prices, while expected to change in the same direction, are not perfectly correlated (there is basis risk).

---

**EXAMPLE 22–4**

*Hedging Foreign Exchange Risk Assuming Perfect Correlation between Spot and Futures Prices*

On September 24, 2012, *The Wall Street Journal* reported:

$S_t$ = Spot exchange rate ($/£): $1.6230 per £1
$f_t$ = Futures price ($/£) for the contract expiring in September 2013 (in approximately one year): $1.6215 per £1

Suppose the FI made a £100 million loan at 15 percent interest and wished to hedge fully the risk that the dollar value of the proceeds would be eroded by a declining British pound over the year. Also suppose that the FI manager receives a forecast that in one year's time the spot and futures will be:

$S_{t+1}$ = $1.5730 per £1
$f_{t+1}$ = $1.5715 per £1

so that over the year:

$\Delta S_t$ = −5 cents
$\Delta f_t$ = −5 cents

For a manager who believes this forecast of a depreciating pound against the dollar, the correct full-hedge strategy is to cover the £115 million of expected earnings on the British loan by selling, or shorting, £115 million of British pound futures contracts on September 24, 2012. We assume here that the FI manager will get out of futures on September 24, 2013.

The size of each British pound futures contract is £62,500. Therefore, the number ($N_F$) of futures to be sold is:

$$N_F = \frac{£115,000,000}{£62,500} = \frac{\text{Size of long position}}{\text{Size of a pound futures contract}}$$

$$= 1,840 \text{ contracts to be sold}$$

Next, we consider whether losses on the long asset position (the British loan) would just offset gains on the futures should the FI sell 1,840 British pound futures contracts should spot and futures prices change in the direction and amount expected.

**Loss on British Pound Loan**
The loss on the British pound loan in dollars would be:

$$(\text{£ Principal} + \text{Interest}) \times \Delta S_t$$

$$(£115,000,000) \times (\$1.6230/£ - \$1.5730/£) = \$5.75 \text{ million}$$

That is, the dollar value of the British pound loan proceeds would be $5.75 million less should the pound depreciate from $1.6230/£ to $1.5730/£ in the spot market over the year.

**Gain on Futures Contracts**

The gain on the futures contracts would be:

$$(N_F \times £62{,}500) \times \Delta f_t$$
$$(1{,}840 \times £62{,}500) \times (\$1.6215/£ - \$1.5715/£) = \$5.75 \text{ million}$$

By selling 1,840 futures contracts of 62,500 each, the seller makes $5.75 million as the futures price falls from $1.6215/£ at the contract initiation on September 24, 2012, to $1.5715/£ at the futures position termination on September 24, 2013. This cash flow of $5.75 million results from the marking to market of the futures contract. As the futures price falls, due to the daily marking to market, the pound futures contract buyer has the contract repriced to a lower level in dollars to be paid per pound. But the seller must be compensated from the buyer's margin account for the difference between the original contract price and the new lower marked-to-market contract price. Thus, over the one year, the buyer compensates the seller by a net of 5 cents per £1 of futures purchased: that is, $1.6215/£1 minus $1.5715/£1 as the futures price falls, or a total of 5 cents $\times$ the number of contracts (1,840) $\times$ the pound size of each contract (62,500). Note that on September 24, 2013, when the principal and interest on the pound loan are paid by the borrower, the FI seller of the pound futures terminates its position in 1,840 short contracts by taking an opposing position of 1,840 long in the same contract. This effectively ends any net cash flow implications from futures positions beyond this date.

**tail the hedge**
Reducing the number of futures contracts that are needed to hedge a cash position because of the interest income that is generated from reinvesting the marked-to-market cash flows generated by the futures contract.

Finally, in this example we have ignored the interest income effects of marking to market. In reality, the $5.75 million from the futures position would be received by the FI seller over the course of the year. As a result, this cash flow can be reinvested at the current short-term dollar interest rate to generate a cash flow of more than $5.75 million. Given this, an FI hedger can sell slightly fewer contracts in anticipation of this interest income. The number of futures contracts that could be sold, below the 1,840 suggested, would depend on the level and pattern of short-term rates over the hedging horizon as well as the precise expected pattern of cash flows from marking to market. In general, the higher the level of short-term interest, the more an FI manager could **tail the hedge** in this fashion.[19]

**EXAMPLE 22–5**

*Hedging Foreign Exchange Risk Assuming Imperfect Correlation between Spot and Futures Prices (Basis Risk)*

Suppose, instead, the FI manager did not believe that the spot exchange rate and futures price on the dollar/pound contract would fall by exactly the same amount. Instead, let the forecast for one year's time be:

$$S_{t+1} = 1.5730/£1$$
$$f_{t+1} = \$1.5915/£1$$

Thus, in expectation, over the succeeding year:

$$\Delta S_t = -5 \text{ cents}$$
$$\Delta f_t = -3 \text{ cents}$$

This means that the dollar–pound futures price is expected to depreciate less than the dollar–pound spot price. This basis risk arises because spot and futures contracts are traded in different markets with different demand and supply functions. Given this, even though futures and spot prices are normally highly correlated, this correlation is often less than 1.

[19] One way to do this is to discount the calculated hedge ratio (the optimal number of futures to sell per $1 of cash position) by a short-term interest rate such as the federal funds rate.

Because futures prices and spot prices do not always move exactly together, this can create a problem for an FI manager seeking to hedge the long position of £115 million with pound futures. Suppose the FI manager ignored the fact that the spot pound is expected to depreciate faster against the dollar than the futures price for pounds and continued to believe that selling 1,840 contracts would be the best hedge. That manager could be in for a big (and nasty) surprise in one year's time. To see this, consider the loss on the cash asset position and the gain on the futures position under a new scenario where the dollar–pound spot rate falls by 2 cents more than the dollar–pound futures rate over the year.

### Loss on British Pound Loan

The expected fall in the spot value of the pound by 5 cents over the year results in a loss of:

$$(£115,000,000) \times (\$1.6230/£ - \$1.5730/£) = \$5.75 \text{ million}$$

### Gain on Futures Position

The expected gain on the futures position is:

$$(1,840 \times £62,500) \times (\$1.6215/£ - \$1.5915/£) = \$3.45 \text{ million}$$

Thus, the net loss to the FI is:

$$\text{Net loss} = \text{Loss on British pound loan} - \text{Gain on British pound futures}$$
$$= \$5.75 - \$3.45$$
$$= \$2.3 \text{ million}$$

Such a loss would have to be charged against the FI's profits and implicitly its net worth or equity. As a result, the FI manager needs to take into account the lower sensitivity of futures prices relative to spot exchange rate changes by selling more than 1,840 futures contracts to hedge fully the British pound loan risk.

To see how many more contracts are required, we need to know how much more sensitive spot exchange rates are relative to futures rates. Let $h$ be the ratio of $\Delta S_t$ to $\Delta f_t$:

$$h = \frac{\Delta S_t}{\Delta f_t}$$

Then, in our example:

$$h = \frac{\$0.05}{\$0.03} = 1.66$$

That is, spot rates are 66 percent more sensitive than futures prices, or—put slightly differently—for every 1 percent change in futures prices, spot rates change by 1.66 percent.[20]

**hedge ratio**
The dollar value of futures contracts that should be sold per dollar of cash position exposure.

An FI manager could use this ratio, $h$, as a **hedge ratio** to solve the question of how many futures should be sold to hedge the long position in the British pound when the spot and futures prices are imperfectly correlated. Specifically, the value of $h$ means that for every £1 in the long asset position, £1.66 futures contracts should be sold. To see this, look at the FI's losses on its long asset position in pound loans relative to the gains on its selling pound futures.

### Loss on British Pound Loans

As before, its losses are:

$$(£115,000,000) \times (\$1.6230/£ - \$1.5730/£) = \$5.75 \text{ million}$$

---

[20]Of course, this can always be expressed the other way around: a 1 percent change in spot prices leads, on average, to only a 0.6 percent change in futures prices.

### Gains on British Pound Futures Position

Taking into account the degree to which spot exchange rates are more sensitive than futures prices—the hedge ratio ($h$)—we can solve for the number of futures ($N_F$) to sell as:

$$N_F = \frac{\text{Long asset position} \times h}{\text{Size of one futures contract}}$$

$$= \frac{£115,000,000 \times 1.66}{£62,500} = 3,054.4 \text{ contracts}$$

or, rounding down to the nearest whole contract, 3,054 contracts. Selling 3,054 British pound futures results in expected profits of:

$$(3,054 \times £62,500) \times (\$1.6215/£ - \$1.5915/£) = \$5.73 \text{ million}$$

The difference of \$0.02 million between the loss on British pound loans and the gain on the pound futures is due to rounding.

## Estimating the Hedge Ratio

The previous example showed that the number of FX futures that should be sold to hedge fully foreign exchange rate risk exposure depends crucially on expectations regarding the correlation between the change in the dollar–pound spot rate ($\Delta S_t$) and the change in its futures rate ($\Delta f_t$). When:

$$h = \frac{\Delta S_t}{\Delta f_t} = \frac{\$0.05}{\$0.05} = 1$$

there is no basis risk. Both the spot and futures exchange rates are expected to change together by the same absolute amount, and the FX risk of the cash position should be hedged dollar for dollar by selling FX futures. When basis risk is present, the spot and future exchange rates are expected to move imperfectly together:

$$h = \frac{\Delta S_t}{\Delta f_t} = \frac{\$0.05}{\$0.03} = 1.66$$

The FI must sell a greater number of futures than it has to when basis risk is absent.

Unfortunately, without perfect foresight, we cannot know exactly how exchange rates and futures prices will change over some future time period. If we did, we would have no need to hedge in the first place! Thus, a common method to calculate $h$ is to look at the behavior of $\Delta S_t$ relative to $\Delta f_t$ over the *recent past* and to use this past behavior as a prediction of the appropriate value of $h$ in the future. One way to estimate this past relationship is to run an ordinary least squares regression of recent changes in spot prices on recent changes in futures prices.[21]

Consider Figure 22–6, where we plot hypothetical monthly changes in the pound–dollar spot exchange rate ($\Delta S_t$) against monthly changes in the pound–dollar futures exchange rate ($\Delta f_t$) for the year 20XX. Thus, we have 12 observations from January through December. For information purposes, the first observation

---

[21] When we calculate $h$ (the hedge ratio), we could use the ratio of the most recent spot and futures price changes. However, this would amount to basing our hedge ratio estimate on *one* observation of the change in $S_t$ and $f_t$. This is why the regression model, which uses many past observations, is usually preferred by market participants.

**FIGURE 22–6**
**Monthly Changes in $\Delta S_t$ and $\Delta f_t$ in 20XX**

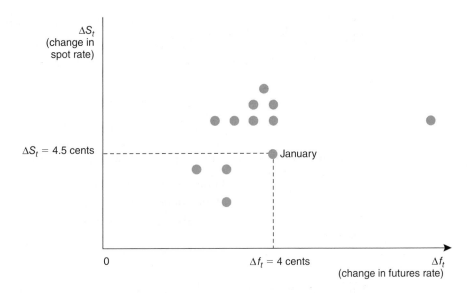

(January) is labeled in Figure 22–6. In January, the dollar–pound spot rate rose by 4.5 cents and the dollar–pound futures rate rose by 4 cents. Thus, the pound appreciated in value over the month of January but the spot exchange rate rose by more than the futures rate did. In some other months, as implied by the scatter of points in Figure 22–6, the futures rate rose by more than the spot rate did.

An ordinary least squares (OLS) regression fits a line of best fit to these monthly observations such that the sum of the squared deviations between the observed values of $\Delta S_t$ and its predicted values (as given by the line of best fit) is minimized. This line of best fit reflects an intercept term and a slope coefficient β. That is:

$$\Delta S_t = \alpha + \beta\,\Delta f_t + u_t$$

where the $u_t$ are the regression's residuals (the differences between actual values of $\Delta S_t$ and its predicted values based on the line of best fit).

Definitionally, β, or the slope coefficient, of the regression equation is equal to:

$$\beta = \frac{\text{Cov}\,(\Delta S_t,\,\Delta f_t)}{\text{Var}\,(\Delta f_t)}$$

that is, the covariance between the change in spot rates and change in futures rate divided by the variance of the change in futures rates. Suppose $\Delta S_t$ and $\Delta f_t$ moved perfectly together over time. Then:

$$\text{Cov}\,(\Delta S_t,\,\Delta f_t) = \text{Var}\,(\Delta f_t)\text{ and }\beta = 1$$

If spot rate changes are greater than futures rate changes, then $\text{Cov}\,(\Delta S_t, \Delta f_t) > \text{Var}\,(\Delta f_t)$ and β > 1. Conversely, if spot rate changes are less sensitive than futures rate changes over time, then $\text{Cov}\,(\Delta S_t, \Delta f_t) < \text{Var}\,(\Delta f_t)$ and β < 1.

Moreover, the value of β, or the estimated slope of the regression line, has theoretical meaning as the hedge ratio ($h$) that minimizes the risk of a portfolio of spot assets and futures contracts. Put more simply, we can use the estimate of β from the regression model as the appropriate measure of $h$ (the hedge ratio) to be used by the FI manager. For example, suppose we used the 12 observations on $\Delta S_t$ and

$\Delta f_t$ in 20XX to estimate an OLS regression equation (the equation of the line of best fit in Figure 22–6). This regression equation takes the form:

$$\Delta S_t = 0.15 + 1.2\, \Delta f_t$$

Thus:

$$\alpha = 0.15 \qquad \beta = 1.2$$

Using $\beta = 1.2$ as the appropriate risk minimizing hedge ratio $h$ for the portfolio manager, we can solve our earlier problem of determining the number of futures contracts to sell to protect the FI from FX losses on its £115 million loan:

$$N_F = \frac{\text{Long position in £ assets} \times \beta \text{ (estimated value of hedge ratio } h \text{ using past data)}}{\text{Size of one £ futures contract}}$$

$$= \frac{£115{,}000{,}000 \times 1.2}{£62{,}500} = 2{,}208 \text{ contracts}$$

Thus, using the past relationship between $\Delta S_t$ and $\Delta f_t$ as the best predictor of their future relationship over the succeeding year dictates that the FI manager sell 2,208 contracts.

The degree of confidence the FI manager may have in using such a method to determine the appropriate hedge ratio depends on how well the regression line fits the scatter of observations. The standard measure of the goodness of fit of a regression line is the $R^2$ of the equation, where the $R^2$ is the square of the correlation coefficient between $\Delta S_t$ and $\Delta f_t$:

$$R^2 = \rho^2 = \left[ \frac{\text{Cov}\,(\Delta S_t, \Delta f_t)}{\sigma_{\Delta St} \times \sigma_{\Delta ft}} \right]^2$$

The term in brackets is the statistical definition of a correlation coefficient. If changes in the spot rate ($\Delta S_t$) and changes in the futures rate ($\Delta f_t$) are perfectly correlated, then:

$$R^2 = \rho^2 = (1)^2 = 1$$

and all observations between $\Delta S_t$ and $\Delta f_t$ lie on a straight line. By comparison, an $R^2 = 0$ indicates that there is no statistical association at all between $\Delta S_t$ and $\Delta f_t$.

**hedging effectiveness**
The (squared) correlation between past changes in spot asset prices and futures prices.

Since we are using futures contracts to hedge the risk of loss on spot asset positions, the $R^2$ of the regression measures the degree of **hedging effectiveness** of the futures contract. A low $R^2$ means that we might have little confidence that the slope coefficient $\beta$ from the regression is actually the true hedge ratio. As the $R^2$ approaches 1, the degree of confidence increases in the use of futures contracts, with a given hedge ratio ($h$) estimate, to hedge our cash asset-risk position.

---

**Concept Questions**

1. Circle an observation in Figure 22–6 that shows futures price changes exceeding spot price changes.
2. Suppose that $R^2 = 0$ in a regression of $\Delta S_t$ on $\Delta f_t$. Would you still use futures contracts to hedge? Explain your answer.
3. In running a regression of $\Delta S_t$ on $\Delta f_t$, the regression equation is $\Delta S_t = 0.51 + 0.95\, \Delta f_t$ and $R^2 = 72$ percent. What is the hedge ratio? What is the measure of hedging effectiveness?

# HEDGING CREDIT RISK WITH FUTURES AND FORWARDS

Chapter 11 demonstrated that by diversifying their loan portfolios across different borrowers, sectors, and regions, FIs can diversify away much of the borrower specific or unsystematic risk of the loan portfolio. Of course, the ability of an FI manager to diversify sufficiently depends in part on the size of the loan portfolio under management. Thus, the potential ability to diversify away borrower-specific risk increases with the size of the FI.

In recent years, however, new types of derivative instruments have been developed (including forwards, options, and swaps) to better allow FIs to hedge their credit risk. Credit derivatives can be used to hedge the credit risk on individual loans or bonds or on portfolios of loans and bonds. The credit derivative market, while still relatively young, is one of the largest derivatives securities markets. As shown in Table 22–1, commercial banks had over $13.6 trillion of notional value in credit derivatives outstanding in June 2012, and there were an estimated $24.9 trillion outstanding worldwide. This is down from the $54.6 trillion in credit derivatives outstanding in July 2008, just before the worst of the financial crisis.

The emergence of these new derivatives is important since more FIs fail due to credit risk exposures than to either interest rate or FX risk exposures. Credit derivatives, such as credit default swaps, allow FIs to separate the credit risk exposure from the lending process itself. That is, FIs can assess the creditworthiness of loan applicants, originate loans, fund loans, and even monitor and service loans without retaining exposure to loss from credit events, such as default or missed payments. This decoupling of the risk from the lending activity allows the market to efficiently transfer risk across counterparties. However, it also loosens the incentives to carefully perform each of the steps of the lending process and can result in poor loan underwriting, shoddy documentation and due diligence, failure to monitor borrower activity, and fraudulent activity on the part of both lenders and borrowers. This loosening of incentives was an important factor leading to the global financial crisis of 2008–2009. Further, although the credit protection buyer hedges exposure to default risk, there is still counterparty credit risk in the event that the seller fails to perform their obligations under the terms of the contract (as was the concern in September 2008 with regard to AIG, an active credit default swap seller).[22]

Typically, banks, securities firms, and corporates are net buyers of credit protection, whereas insurance companies, hedge funds, mutual funds, and pension funds are net sellers. However, some financial firms are market makers in the market for credit derivatives, and therefore take both long and short positions. We discuss credit forward contracts below (less than 1 percent of all credit derivatives outstanding). In Chapter 23 we discuss credit options (less than 0.02 percent of all credit derivatives outstanding), and in Chapter 24 we discuss credit swaps (over 98 percent of all credit derivatives outstanding).

---

[22]Indeed, under the U.S. government's bailout of AIG, the largest component was to satisfy counterparty claims in AIG credit default swaps (CDS). Under AIG CDS programs if AIG was downgraded (e.g., from AAA to BB), then the CDS contracts had to be marked to market. Any marking to market losses of AIG had to be paid to the CDS counterparties. Since AIG was close to insolvent, these losses were borne by the U.S. government as part of the AIG bailout.

## Credit Forward Contracts and Credit Risk Hedging

**credit forward**
An agreement that hedges against an increase in default risk on a loan after the loan terms have been determined and the loan has been issued.

A **credit forward** is a forward agreement that hedges against an increase in default risk on a loan (a decline in the credit quality of a borrower) after the loan rate is determined and the loan is issued. Common buyers of credit forwards are insurance companies and common sellers are banks. The credit forward agreement specifies a credit spread (a risk premium above the risk-free rate to compensate for default risk) on a benchmark bond issued by an FI borrower. For example, suppose the benchmark bond of a bank borrower was rated BBB at the time a loan was originated. Further, at the time the loan was issued, the benchmark bonds had a 2 percent interest rate or credit spread (representing default risk on the BBB bonds) over a U.S. Treasury bond of the same maturity. To hedge against an increase in the credit risk of the borrower, the bank enters into (sells) a credit forward contract when the loan is issued. We define $\phi_F$ as the credit spread over the U.S. Treasury rate on which the credit forward contract is written (equals 2 percent in this example). Table 22–3 illustrates the payment pattern resulting from this credit forward. In Table 22–3, $\phi_T$ is the actual credit spread on the bond when the credit forward matures, for example, one year after the loan was originated and the credit forward contract was entered into, $MD$ is the modified duration on the benchmark BBB bond, and $A$ is the principal amount of the forward agreement.

From the payment pattern established in the credit forward agreement, Table 22–3 shows that the credit forward buyer (an insurance company) bears the risk of an increase in default risk on the benchmark bond of the borrowing firm, while the credit forward seller (the bank lender) hedges itself against an increase in the borrower's default risk. That is, if the borrower's default risk increases so that when the forward agreement matures the market requires a higher credit spread on the borrower's benchmark bond, $\phi_T$, than that originally agreed to in the forward contract, $\phi_F$ (i.e., $\phi_T > \phi_F$), the credit forward buyer pays the credit forward seller, which is the bank, $(\phi_T - \phi_F) \times MD \times A$. For example, suppose the credit spread between BBB bonds and U.S. Treasury bonds widened to 3 percent from 2 percent over the year, the modified duration ($MD$) of the benchmark BBB bond was five years, and the size of the forward contract $A$ was $10 million. Then the gain on the credit forward contract to the seller (the bank) would be $500,000 [(3% − 2%) × 5 × $10,000,000]. This amount could be used to offset the loss in market value of the loan due to the rise in the borrower's default risk. However, if the borrower's default risk and credit spread decrease over the year, the credit forward seller pays the credit forward buyer $(\phi_F - \phi_T) \times MD \times A$. [However, the maximum loss on the forward contract (to the bank seller) is limited, as will be explained below.]

**TABLE 22–3**  Payment Pattern on a Credit Forward

| Credit Spread at End of Forward Agreement | Credit Spread Seller (Bank) | Credit Spread Buyer (Counterparty) |
|---|---|---|
| $\phi_T > \phi_F$ | Receives $(\phi_T - \phi_F) \times MD \times A$ | Pays $(\phi_T - \phi_F) \times MD \times A$ |
| $\phi_F > \phi_T$ | Pays $(\phi_F - \phi_T) \times MD \times A$ | Receives $(\phi_F - \phi_T) \times MD \times A$ |

**FIGURE 22–7**

**Impact on a Bank of Hedging a Loan with a Credit Forward Contract**

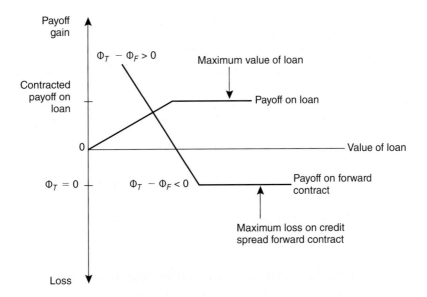

Figure 22–7 illustrates the impact on the bank from hedging the loan. If the default risk on the loan increases, the market or present value of the loan falls below its value at the beginning of the hedge period. However, the bank hedged the change in default risk by selling a credit forward contract. Assuming the credit spread on the borrower's benchmark bond also increases (so that $\phi_T > \phi_F$), the bank receives $(\phi_T - \phi_F) \times MD \times A$ on the forward contract. If the characteristics of the benchmark bond (i.e., change in credit spread, modified duration, and principal value) are the same as those of the bank's loan to the borrower, the loss on the balance sheet is offset completely by the gain (off the balance sheet) from the credit forward (i.e., in our example a $500,000 market value loss in the loan would be offset by a $500,000 gain from selling the credit forward contract).

If the default risk does not increase or decreases (so that $\phi_T < \phi_F$), the bank selling the forward contract will pay $(\phi_F - \phi_T) \times MD \times A$ to the credit forward buyer (the insurance company). However, importantly, this payout by the bank is limited to a maximum. This is when $\phi_T$ falls to zero, that is, the default spread on BBB bonds falls to zero or the original BBB bonds of the borrower are viewed as having the same default risk as Treasury bonds (in other words, the credit spread or rate on the benchmark bond cannot fall below the risk-free rate). In this case the maximum loss on the credit forward $[\phi_F - (0)] \times MD \times A$ mirrors (offsets) the maximum and limited upside gain (return) on the loan. Anyone familiar with options will recognize that (as was discussed in Chapter 10) when the bank makes a loan, it is similar to writing a put option. In selling a credit forward, the payoff is similar to buying a put option (see Chapter 23 as well).

**EXAMPLE 22–6**

*Hedging Credit Risk with Credit Spread Forward Contract*

A bank issues a $5 million loan to a firm with an A− credit rating. The modified duration on the loan is 4.5 years. At the time of issue, the credit spread between A− bonds and U.S. Treasury bonds is 2 percent ($\phi_F$). The bank believes that the borrower's credit rating may fall during the period of the loan. To hedge this credit risk, the bank enters (or sells) a $5 million credit spread forward contract. Subsequently, at the end of the forward period, the borrower's credit rating does indeed drop, to BB ($\phi_T$). The credit spread between BB rated bonds and U.S. Treasury bonds is 5 percent (or $\phi_T > \phi_F$). Thus, the change in the market value of the loan to the bank, from the duration model, is:

$$\Delta L = L \times D \times [\Delta R_L / (1 + R_L)] = L \times D / (1 + R_L) \times \Delta R_L = L \times MD \times \Delta R_L$$

or:

$$\Delta L = \$5,000,000 \times 4.5 \times (0.03) = \$675,000$$

However, the bank hedged this risk with a credit spread forward and receives, from the credit spread buyer:

$$(5\% - 2\%) \times 4.5 \times \$5,000,000 = \$675,000$$

Thus, the loss in the value of the loan due to a drop in the credit rating of the borrower is completely offset with the gain from the credit spread forward contract.

## Futures Contracts and Catastrophe Risk

www.cmegroup.com

In recent years, the Chicago Board of Trade (CBOT) of the CME Group has introduced futures and options for catastrophe insurance. This chapter discusses catastrophe insurance futures, and the next chapter discusses catastrophe insurance options. The essential idea of catastrophe futures is to allow property–casualty insurers to hedge the extreme losses that occur after major hurricanes, such as the series of hurricanes that hit the east coast in October 2012 (which resulted in damage of over $65 billion on the properties directly affected) or Hurricane Katrina in 2005 (which resulted in losses exceeding $200 billion). Since in a catastrophe the ratio of insured losses to premiums rises (i.e., the so-called loss ratio increases), the payoff on a catastrophe futures contract is directly linked to the loss ratio. Specifically, on settlement, the payoff to the buyer of the futures is equal to the nominal value of the futures contract (which is $25,000) times the actual loss ratio incurred by insurers. Suppose that on maturity of the futures contract the loss ratio was 1.5. This means that the payoff to the insurance company futures hedger would be $1.5 \times \$25,000 = \$37,500$. Also suppose that three months earlier (before the catastrophe occurred) the market expected the loss ratio to be only 0.8. Thus, the insurer would have been able to pay $0.8 \times \$25,000 = \$20,000$ to buy the futures contract. Because actual losses exceeded expected losses, the insurer makes a profit of $\$37,500 - \$20,000 = \$17,500$ on each contract. These profits on futures contracts can be used to help offset the huge payouts on hurricane insurance contracts.

| **Concept Questions** | 1. Why are credit forwards useful for hedging the credit risk of an FI's portfolio? |
| --- | --- |
| | 2. What are some of the practical problems an FI manager may face when using catastrophe futures to hedge losses on insurance lines? |

# REGULATION OF DERIVATIVE SECURITIES

Derivatives are subject to three levels of institutional regulation. First, regulators of derivatives specify "permissible activities" that institutions may engage in. Second, once permissible activities have been specified, institutions engaging in those activities are subjected to supervisory oversight. Third, regulators attempt to judge the overall integrity of each institution engaging in derivative activities by assessing the capital adequacy of the institutions and by enforcing regulations to ensure compliance with those capital requirements. The Securities and Exchange Commission (SEC) and the Commodities Futures Trading Commission (CFTC) are often viewed as "functional" regulators. The SEC regulates all securities traded on national securities exchanges, including several derivatives. The SEC's regulation of derivatives includes price reporting requirements, antimanipulation regulations, position limits, audit trail requirements, and margin requirements. The CFTC has exclusive jurisdiction over all exchange-traded derivative securities. It therefore regulates all national futures exchanges, as well as all futures and options on futures. The CFTC's regulations include minimum capital requirements for traders, reporting and transparency requirements, antifraud and antimanipulation regulations, and minimum standards for clearinghouse organizations.

www.sec.gov
www.cftc.gov

www.federalreserve.gov
www.fdic.gov
www.occ.treas.gov

The main bank regulators—the Federal Reserve, the FDIC, and the Comptroller of the Currency—also have issued uniform guidelines for banks that trade in futures and forwards. These guidelines require a bank to (1) establish internal guidelines regarding its hedging activity, (2) establish trading limits, and (3) disclose large contract positions that materially affect bank risk to shareholders and outside investors. Overall, the policy of regulators is to encourage the use of futures for hedging and discourage their use for speculation, although on a practical basis it is often difficult to distinguish between the two.

www.fasb.org

Since January 1, 2000, the main regulator of accounting standards (the FASB) has required all FIs (and nonfinancial firms) to reflect the mark-to-market value of their derivative positions in their financial statements. This means that FIs must immediately recognize all gains and losses on such contracts and disclose those gains and losses to shareholders and regulators. Further, firms must show whether they are using derivatives to hedge risks connected to their business or whether they are just taking an open (risky) position. Finally, as noted in Chapter 20, exchange-traded derivative securities such as futures contracts are subject to nominal risk-based capital requirements. This is because the credit or default risk of exchange-traded derivatives is approximately zero: when a counterparty defaults on its obligations, the exchange itself adopts the counterparty's obligations in full. By contrast, no such guarantees exist for bilaterally agreed, over-the-counter contracts originated and traded outside organized exchanges. Thus, OTC derivative securities such as forward contracts are potentially subject to capital requirements. Other things being equal, the risk-based capital requirements favor the use of futures over forwards.

Because of their lack of regulation and because of the significant negative role that over-the-counter (OTC) derivative securities played during the financial crisis, the Wall Street Reform and Consumer Protection Act of 2010 included a plan to regulate OTC derivatives. The plan, first, called for most of the OTC derivatives to trade on regulated exchanges which would guarantee trades and help cushion against potential defaults. This change makes it easier for participants to see market prices of these securities and make the markets more transparent. Second, like exchanged traded derivatives, the previous OTC traded securities now come under the authority of the SEC and the CFTC, while bank regulators oversee banks that deal in derivatives. Thus, the changes result in OTC derivative securities being regulated in a similar fashion as exchange traded securities. While proposed in July 2010, as of July 2013 no plan has been implemented.

| **Summary** | This chapter analyzed the risk-management role of futures and forwards. We saw that while they are close substitutes, they are not perfect substitutes. A number of characteristics, such as maturity, liquidity, flexibility, marking to market, and capital requirements, differentiate these products and make one or the other more attractive to any given FI manager. These products might be used to partially or fully hedge at least four types of risk commonly faced by an FI: interest rate risk, foreign exchange risk, credit risk, and catastrophe risk. An FI can engage in micro-hedging or macrohedging as well as engage in selective or routine hedging. In all cases, perfect hedging is shown to be difficult because of basis risk. |

**Questions and Problems**

1. What are derivative contracts? What is the value of derivative contracts to the managers of FIs? Which type of derivative contracts had the highest notional value outstanding among all U.S. banks as of June 2012?

2. What are some of the major differences between futures and forward contracts? How do these contracts differ from spot contracts?

3. What is a naive hedge? How does a naive hedge protect an FI from risk?

4. An FI holds a 15-year, $10 million par value bond that is priced at 104 with a yield to maturity of 7 percent. The bond has a duration of eight years, and the FI plans to sell it after two months. The FI's market analyst predicts that interest rates will be 8 percent at the time of the desired sale. Because most other analysts are predicting no change in rates, two-month forward contracts for 15-year bonds are available at 104. The FI would like to hedge against the expected change in interest rates with an appropriate position in a forward contract. What will this position be? Show that if rates rise 1 percent as forecast, the hedge will protect the FI from loss.

5. Contrast the position of being short with that of being long in futures contracts.

6. Suppose an FI purchases a Treasury bond futures contract at 95.
   a. What is the FI's obligation at the time the futures contract is purchased?
   b. If an FI purchases this contract, in what kind of hedge is it engaged?
   c. Assume that the Treasury bond futures price falls to 94. What is the loss or gain?
   d. Assume that the Treasury bond futures price rises to 97. Mark to market the position.

7. Long Bank has assets that consist mostly of 30-year mortgages and liabilities that are short-term demand and time deposits. Will an interest rate futures contract the bank buys add to or subtract from the bank's risk?

8. In each of the following cases, indicate whether it would be appropriate for an FI to buy or sell a forward contract to hedge the appropriate risk.
   a. A commercial bank plans to issue CDs in three months.
   b. An insurance company plans to buy bonds in two months.
   c. A savings bank is going to sell Treasury securities it holds in its investment portfolio next month.
   d. A U.S. bank lends to a French company. The loan is payable in euros.
   e. A finance company has assets with a duration of six years and liabilities with a duration of 13 years.

9. The duration of a 20-year, 8 percent coupon Treasury bond selling at par is 10.292 years. The bond's interest is paid semiannually, and the bond qualifies for delivery against the Treasury bond futures contract.
   a. What is the modified duration of this bond?
   b. What is the impact on the Treasury bond price if market interest rates increase 50 basis points?
   c. If you sold a Treasury bond futures contract at 95 and interest rates rose 50 basis points, what would be the change in the value of your futures position?
   d. If you purchased the bond at par and sold the futures contract, what would be the net value of your hedge after the increase in interest rates?
10. What are the differences between a microhedge and a macrohedge for an FI? Why is it generally more efficient for FIs to employ a macrohedge than a series of microhedges?
11. What are the reasons why an FI may choose to hedge selectively its portfolio?
12. Hedge Row Bank has the following balance sheet (in millions):

| Assets | $150 | Liabilities | $135 |
|--------|------|-------------|------|
|        |      | Equity      | 15   |
| Total  | $150 | Total       | $150 |

The duration of the assets is six years and the duration of the liabilities is four years. The bank is expecting interest rates to fall from 10 percent to 9 percent over the next year.
   a. What is the duration gap for Hedge Row Bank?
   b. What is the expected change in net worth for Hedge Row Bank if the forecast is accurate?
   c. What will be the effect on net worth if interest rates increase 110 basis points?
   d. If the existing interest rate on the liabilities is 6 percent, what will be the effect on net worth of a 1 percent increase in interest rates?
13. For a given change in interest rates, why is the sensitivity of the price of a Treasury bond futures contract greater than the sensitivity of the price of a Treasury bill futures contract?
14. What is the meaning of the Treasury bond futures price quote 101–130?
15. What is meant by fully hedging the balance sheet of an FI?
16. Tree Row Bank has assets of $150 million, liabilities of $135 million, and equity of $15 million. The asset duration is six years and the duration of the liabilities is four years. Market interest rates are 10 percent. Tree Row Bank wishes to hedge the balance sheet with Eurodollar futures contracts, which currently have a price quote of $96 per $100 face value for the benchmark three-month Eurodollar CD underlying the contract. The current rate on three-month Eurodollar CDs is 4.0 percent and the duration of these contracts is 0.25 year.
   a. Should the bank go short or long on the futures contracts to establish the correct macrohedge?
   b. Assuming no basis risk, how many contracts are necessary to fully hedge the bank?
   c. Verify that the change in the futures position will offset the change in the cash balance sheet position for a change in market interest rates of plus 100 basis points and minus 50 basis points.

d. If the bank had hedged with Treasury bond futures contracts that had a market value of $95 per $100 of face value, a yield of 8.5295 percent, and a duration of 10.3725 years, how many futures contracts would have been necessary to fully hedge the balance sheet? Assume no basis risk.

e. What additional issues should be considered by the bank in choosing between Eurodollar and T-bond futures contracts?

17. What is basis risk? What are the sources of basis risk?

18. How would your answer for part (b) in problem 16 change if the relationship of the price sensitivity of futures contracts to the price sensitivity of underlying bonds were $br = 0.92$?

19. Reconsider Tree Row Bank in problem 16 but assume that the cost rate on the liabilities is 6 percent. On-balance-sheet rates are expected to increase by 100 basis points. Further, assume there is basis risk such that rates on 3-month Eurodollar CDs are expected to change by 0.10 times the rate change on assets and liabilities. That is, $\Delta R_F = 0.10 \times \Delta R$.

a. How many contracts are necessary to fully hedge the bank?

b. Verify that the change in the futures position will offset the change in the cash balance sheet position for a change in market interest rates of plus 100 basis points and minus 50 basis points.

c. If the bank had hedged with Treasury bond futures contracts that had a market value of $95 per $100 of face value, a yield of 8.5295 percent, and a duration of 10.3725 years, how many futures contracts would have been necessary to fully hedge the balance sheet? Assume there is basis risk such that rates on T-bonds are expected to change by 0.75 times the rate change on assets and liabilities. That is, $\Delta R_F = 0.75 \times \Delta R$.

20. A mutual fund plans to purchase $500,000 of 30-year Treasury bonds in four months. These bonds have a duration of 12 years and are priced at 96.25 (percent of face value). The mutual fund is concerned about interest rates changing over the next four months and is considering a hedge with T-bond futures contracts that mature in six months. The T-bond futures contracts are selling for 98–24 (32nds) and have a duration of 8.5 years.

a. If interest rate changes in the spot market exactly match those in the futures market, what type of futures position should the mutual fund create?

b. How many contracts should be used?

c. If the implied rate on the deliverable bond in the futures market moves 12 percent more than the change in the discounted spot rate, how many futures contracts should be used to hedge the portfolio?

d. What causes futures contracts to have a different price sensitivity than assets in the spot markets?

21. Consider the following balance sheet (in millions) for an FI:

| Assets | | Liabilities | |
|---|---|---|---|
| Duration = 10 years | $950 | Duration = 2 years | $860 |
| | | Equity | 90 |

a. What is the FI's duration gap?

b. What is the FI's interest rate risk exposure?

c. How can the FI use futures and forward contracts to put on a macrohedge?

d. What is the impact on the FI's equity value if the relative change in interest rates is an increase of 1 percent? That is, $\Delta R/(1 + R) = 0.01$.

e. Suppose that the FI macrohedges using Treasury bond futures that are currently priced at 96. What is the impact on the FI's futures position if the relative change in all interest rates is an increase of 1 percent? That is, $\Delta R/(1 + R) = 0.01$. Assume that the deliverable Treasury bond has a duration of nine years.

f. If the FI wants to macrohedge, how many Treasury bond futures contracts does it need?

22. Refer again to problem 21. How does consideration of basis risk change your answers to problem 21?

   a. Compute the number of futures contracts required to construct a macrohedge if

$$[\Delta R_f/(1 + R_f) \: / \: \Delta R/(1 + R)] = br = 0.90$$

   b. Explain what is meant by $br = 0.90$.

   c. If $br = 0.90$, what information does this provide on the number of futures contracts needed to construct a macrohedge?

23. An FI is planning to hedge its $100 million bond instruments with a cross hedge using Eurodollar interest rate futures. How would the FI estimate

$$br = [\Delta R_f/(1 + R_f) \: / \: \Delta R/(1 + R)]$$

to determine the exact number of Eurodollar futures contracts to hedge?

24. Village Bank has $240 million worth of assets with a duration of 14 years and liabilities worth $210 million with a duration of 4 years. In the interest of hedging interest rate risk, Village Bank is contemplating a macrohedge with interest rate T-bond futures contracts now selling for 102–21 (32nds). The T-bond underlying the futures contract has a duration of nine years. If the spot and futures interest rates move together, how many futures contracts must Village Bank sell to fully hedge the balance sheet?

25. Assume that an FI has assets of $250 million and liabilities of $200 million. The duration of the assets is six years and the duration of the liabilities is three years. The price of the futures contract is $115,000 and its duration is 5.5 years.

   a. What number of futures contracts is needed to construct a perfect hedge if $br = 1.10$?

   b. If $\Delta R_f/(1 + R_f) = 0.0990$, what is the expected $\Delta R/(1 + R)$?

26. Suppose an FI purchases a $1 million 91-day (360-day year) Eurodollar futures contract trading at 98.50.

   a. If the contract is reversed two days later by selling the contract at 98.60, what is the net profit?

   b. What is the loss or gain if the price at reversal is 98.40?

27. Dudley Hill Bank has the following balance sheet:

| Assets (in millions) | | Liabilities and Equity (in millions) | |
|---|---|---|---|
| A | $425 | L | $380 |
|  |  | E | 45 |
|  | $425 |  | $425 |

Further,

$$D_A = 6 \text{ years}$$
$$D_L = 2 \text{ years}$$

The bank manager receives information from an economic forecasting unit that interest rates are expected to rise from 8 to 9 percent over the next six months.

a. Calculate the potential loss to Dudley Hill's net worth ($E$) if the forecast of rising rates proves to be true.

b. Suppose the manager of Dudley Hill Bank wants to hedge this interest rate risk with T-bond futures contracts. The current futures price quote is 122.03125 per 100 of face value for the benchmark 20-year, and the minimum contract size is 100,000, so $P_F$ equals 122,031.25. The duration of the deliverable bond is 14.5 years. That is, $D_F = 14.5$ years. How many futures contracts will be needed? Should the manager buy or sell these contracts? Assume no basis risk.

c. Verify that selling T-bond futures contracts will indeed hedge the FI against a sudden increase in interest rates from 8 to 9 percent, a 1 percent interest rate shock.

d. If the bank had hedged with Eurodollar futures contracts that had a market value of $98 *per* $100 of face value, how many futures contracts would have been necessary to hedge fully the balance sheet?

e. How would your answer for part (b) change if the relationship of the price sensitivity of futures contracts to the price sensitivity of underlying bonds were $br = 1.15$?

f. Verify that selling T-bond futures contracts will indeed hedge the FI against a sudden increase in interest rates from 8 to 9 percent, a 1 percent interest rate shock. Assume the yield on the T-bond underlying the futures contract is 8.45 percent as the bank enters the hedge, and rates rise by 1.154792 percent.

28. An FI has an asset investment in euros. The FI expects the exchange rate of $/€ to increase by the maturity of the asset.

a. Is the dollar appreciating or depreciating against the euro?

b. To fully hedge the investment, should the FI buy or sell euro futures contracts?

c. If there is perfect correlation between changes in the spot and futures contracts, how should the FI determine the number of contracts necessary to hedge the investment fully?

29. What is meant by tailing the hedge? What factors allow an FI manager to tail the hedge effectively?

30. What does the hedge ratio measure? Under what conditions is this ratio valuable in determining the number of futures contracts necessary to hedge fully an investment in another currency?

31. What technique is commonly used to estimate the hedge ratio? What statistical measure is an indicator of the confidence that should be placed in the estimated hedge ratio? What is the interpretation if the estimated hedge ratio is greater than 1? Less than 1?

32. An FI has assets denominated in British pounds of $125 million and pound liabilities of $100 million. The exchange rate of pounds for dollars is currently $1.60/£.

a. What is the FI's net FX exposure?

b. Is the FI exposed to a dollar appreciation or depreciation?

c. How can the FI use futures or forward contracts to hedge its FX rate risk?

d.  If a futures contract is currently trading at $1.55/£, what is the number of futures contracts that must be utilized to fully hedge the FI's currency risk exposure? Assume the contract size on the British pound futures contract is £62,500.

e.  If the British pound exchange rate falls from $1.60/£ to $1.50/£, what will be the impact on the FI's cash position?

f.  If the British pound futures exchange rate falls from $1.55/£ to $1.45/£, what will be the impact on the FI's futures position?

g.  Using the information in parts (e) and (f), what can you conclude about basis risk?

33.  An FI is planning to hedge its one-year, 100 million Swiss francs (SF)–denominated loan against exchange rate risk. The current spot rate is $0.60/SF. A 1-year SF futures contract is currently trading at $0.58/SF. SF futures are sold in standardized units of SF125,000.

a.  Should the FI be worried about the SF appreciating or depreciating?

b.  Should the FI buy or sell futures to hedge against exchange rate risk exposure?

c.  How many futures contracts should the FI buy or sell if a regression of past changes in the spot exchange rate on changes in the future exchange rate generates an estimated slope of 1.4?

d.  Show exactly how the FI is hedged if it repatriates its principal of SF100 million at year end, the spot exchange rate of SF at year end is $0.55/SF, and the forward exchange rate is $0.5443/SF.

34.  A U.S. FI has a long position in £75,500,000 assets funded with U.S. dollar denominated liabilities. The FI manager is concerned about the £ appreciating relative to the dollar and is considering a hedge of this FX risk using £ futures contracts. The manager has regressed recent changes in the spot £ exchange rate on changes in £ futures contracts. The resulting regression equation is: $\Delta S_T = 0.09 + 1.5\Delta F_t$. Further, the $Cov(\Delta S_t, \Delta F_t)$ was found to be 0.06844, $\sigma_{\Delta S_t} = 0.3234$, and $\sigma_{\Delta F_t} = 0.2279$. Pound futures contracts are sold in standardized units of £62,500. Calculate the number of futures contracts needed to hedge the risk of the £75,500,000 asset. Calculate the hedging effectiveness of these futures contracts. To what extent can the manager have confidence that the correct hedge ratio is being used to hedge the FI's FX risk position?

35.  An FI has made a loan commitment of SF10 million that is likely to be taken down in six months. The current spot rate is $0.60/SF.

a.  Is the FI exposed to the dollar's depreciating or appreciating relative to the SF? Why?

b.  If the spot rate six months from today is $0.64/SF, what amount of dollars is needed if the loan is taken down and the FI is unhedged?

c.  If the FI decides to hedge using SF futures, should it buy or sell SF futures?

d.  A six-month SF futures contract is available for $0.61/SF. What net amount would be needed to fund the loan at the end of six months if the FI had hedged using the SF10 million futures contract? Assume that futures prices are equal to spot prices at the time of payment (i.e., at maturity).

36.  A U.S. FI has assets denominated in Swiss francs (SF) of 75 million and liabilities of 125 million. The spot rate is $0.6667/SF, and one-year futures are available for $0.6579/SF.

a.  What is the FI's net exposure?

b.  Is the FI exposed to dollar appreciation or depreciation relative to the SF?

    c. If the SF spot rate changes from $0.6667/SF to $0.6897/SF, how will this impact the FI's currency exposure? Assume no hedging.

    d. What is the number of futures contracts necessary to fully hedge the currency risk exposure of the FI? The contract size is SF125,000 per contract.

    e. If the SF futures exchange rate falls from $0.6579/SF to $0.6349/SF, what will be the impact on the FI's futures position?

37. What is a credit forward? How is it structured?

38. What is the gain on the purchase of a $20 million credit forward contract with a modified duration of seven years if the credit spread between a benchmark Treasury bond and a borrowing firm's debt decreases 50 basis points?

39. How is selling a credit forward similar to buying a put option?

40. A property–casualty (PC) insurance company purchased catastrophe futures contracts to hedge against losses during the hurricane season. At the time of purchase, the market expected a loss ratio of 0.75. After processing claims from a severe hurricane, the PC actually incurred a loss ratio of 1.35. What amount of profit did the PC make on each $25,000 futures contract?

41. What is the primary goal of regulators in regard to the use of futures by FIs? What guidelines have regulators given to banks for trading in futures and forwards?

## Web Question

42. Go to the Office of the Comptroller of the Currency website at **www.occ.treas. gov**. Find the most recent levels of futures, forwards, options, swaps, and credit derivatives using the following steps. Click on "Publications." From there click on "Quarterly Report on Bank Derivatives Activities." Click on the most recent date. This will download files onto your computer that contain the relevant data. The tables containing the data are at the bottom of this document. How have these values increased since June 2012 (as reported in Table 22–1)?

## Integrated Mini Case

## HEDGING INTEREST RATE RISK WITH FUTURES CONTRACTS

Use the following December 31, 2014, market value balance sheet for Bank One to answer the questions below.

| Assets (in thousands of $s) | | | Liabilities/Equity (in thousands of $s) | | |
|---|---|---|---|---|---|
| | **Value** | **Duration** | | **Value** | **Duration** |
| T-bills | $ 1,500 | 0.75 | NOW accounts | $6,250 | 0.50 |
| T-bonds | 4,250 | 9.50 | CDs | 7,500 | 7.55 |
| Loans | 15,500 | 12.50 | Federal funds | 5,500 | 0.10 |
| | | | Equity | 2,000 | |

The bank's manager thinks rates will increase by 0.50 percent in the next 3 months. To hedge this interest rate risk the manager will use June T-bond futures contracts. The T-bonds underlying the futures contracts have a maturity = 15 years, a duration = 14.25 years, and a price = 108−10 or $108,312.50. Assume that interest rate changes in the futures market relative to the cash market are such that $br = 0.885$.

1. Calculate the leverage adjusted duration gap (DGAP) for Bank One.

2. Using the DGAP model, if interest rates on assets and liabilities increase such that $\Delta R_A/(1 + R_A) = \Delta R_L/(1 + R_L) = 0.0075$, calculate the *change* in the value of assets and liabilities and the *new* value of the assets and liabilities for Bank One.

3. Calculate the change in the market value of equity for Bank One if rates increase such that $\Delta R/(1 + R) = 0.0075$.

4. Calculate the correct number of futures contracts needed to hedge the bank's interest rate risk (do not round to the nearest whole contract). Make sure you specify whether you should enter the hedge with a short or long futures position.

5. Calculate the change in the bank's market value of equity and the change in the value of the T-bond futures position for the bank if interest rates increase by 0.55 percent from the current rate of 6 percent on the T-bond and increase 0.65 percent from the current rate of 8 percent on the balance sheet assets and liabilities.

## Appendix 22A: Microhedging with Futures

View Appendix 22A at the website for this textbook (**www.mhhe.com/saunders8e**).

See Appendices Online at www.mhhe.com/saunders8e
• Appendix 23A: Microhedging with Options

# Options, Caps, Floors, and Collars

## INTRODUCTION

Just as there is a wide variety of forward and futures contracts available for an FI to use in hedging, there is an even wider array of option products, including exchange-traded options, over-the-counter options, options embedded in securities, and caps, collars, and floors. As we saw with futures contracts (in Chapter 22), the use of options can protect an FI against a loss of net worth due to unexpected changes in interest rates, credit risk, foreign exchange risk, and so forth. Not only has the range of option products increased in recent years, but the use of options has increased as well. However, like fowards, futures, and swaps, options can also lead to huge losses for FIs.

This chapter starts with a review of the four basic options strategies: buying a call, writing a call, buying a put, and writing a put. We then look at economic and regulatory reasons FIs choose to buy versus write (sell) options. The chapter then concentrates on the use of fixed-income or interest rate options to hedge interest rate risk. We also discuss the role of options in hedging foreign exchange and credit risks as well as catastrophe risk. The chapter concludes with an examination of caps, floors, and collars. As with futures and forwards, discussed in Chapter 22, options, caps, floors, and collars are held by FIs not only to hedge their own risk, but also to serve as counterparties (for a fee) for other (financial and nonfinancial) firms wanting to hedge risk on their own balance sheets.

## BASIC FEATURES OF OPTIONS

**option**
A contract that gives the holder the right, but not the obligation, to buy or sell the underlying asset at a specified price within a specified period of time.

An **option** is a contract that gives the holder the right, but not the obligation, to buy or sell an underlying asset at a prespecified price for a specified time period. Options are classified as either call options or put options. We discuss both of these below, highlighting their profits in terms of price movements on the underlying asset. The Chicago Board of Options Exchange (CBOE), opened in 1973, was the first exchange devoted solely to the trading of (stock) options. In 1982, financial futures options contracts (options on financial futures contracts, e.g., Treasury bond futures contracts) started trading. Options markets have grown rapidly since the mid-1980s. As of June 2012, U.S. commercial banks held over $33.6 trillion of option contracts that were listed for trading.

The trading process for options is the same as that for futures contracts. An FI desiring to take an option position places an order to buy or sell a stated number of call or put option contracts with a stated expiration date and exercise price. The order is directed to a representative on the appropriate exchange for execution. Trading on the largest exchanges such as the CBOE takes place in trading pits, where traders for each delivery date on an option contract informally group together. As with futures contracts, options trading often occurs using an open-outcry auction method. Once an option price is agreed on in a trading pit, the two parties send the details of the trade to the option clearinghouse (the Options Clearing Corporation), which breaks up trades into buy and sell transactions and takes the opposite side of each transaction—becoming the seller for every option contract buyer and the buyer for every option contract seller. The broker on the floor of the options exchange confirms the transaction with the investor's broker.

In the early 2000s, the CBOE increased the speed at which orders can be placed, executed, and filled by equipping floor brokers with handheld touch-screen computers that allow them to route and execute orders more easily and efficiently. For example, when a broker selects an order from the workstation, an electronic trading card appears on his or her computer screen. The electronic card allows the broker to work the order and enter necessary trade information (e.g., volume, price, opposing market makers). When the card (details of the transaction) is complete, the broker can execute the trade with the touch of a finger. Once the broker has submitted the trade, the system simultaneously sends a "fill" report to the customer and instantaneously transmits this data to traders worldwide.

In describing the features of the four basic option strategies FIs might employ to hedge interest rate risk, we discuss their return payoffs in terms of interest rate movements. Specifically, we consider bond options whose payoff values are inversely linked to interest rate movements in a manner similar to bond prices and interest rates in general (see Chapter 8).

**call option**
Gives a purchaser the right (but not the obligation) to buy the underlying security from the writer of the option at a prespecified exercise price on a prespecified date.

## Buying a Call Option on a Bond

The first strategy of buying (or taking a long position in) a call option on a bond is shown in Figure 23–1. A **call option** gives the purchaser the right (but not the obligation) to buy the underlying security—a bond—at a prespecified *exercise* or *strike price* (X). In return, the buyer of the call option must pay the writer or seller an upfront fee known as a *call premium* (C). This premium is an immediate negative cash flow for the buyer of the call, who potentially stands to make a profit if

**FIGURE 23–1**
**Profit Function for the Buyer of a Call Option on a Bond**

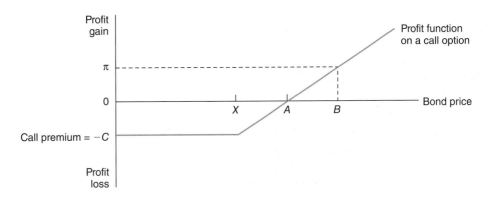

the underlying bond's price rises above the exercise price by an amount exceeding the premium. If the price of the bond never rises above $X$, the buyer of the call never exercises the option (i.e., buying the bond at $X$ when its market value is less than $X$). In this case, the option matures unexercised. The call buyer incurs a cost, $C$, for the option, and no other cash flows result.

As shown in Figure 23–1, if the price of the bond underlying the option rises to price $B$, the buyer makes a profit of $\pi$, which is the difference between the bond price ($B$) and the exercise price of the option ($X$) minus the call premium ($C$). If the bond price rises to $A$, the buyer of the call has broken even in that the profit from exercising the call ($A - X$) just equals the premium payment for the call ($C$).

Notice two important things about bond call options in Figure 23–1:

1. As interest rates fall, bond prices rise and the call option buyer has large profit potential. The more that rates fall, the higher bond prices rise and the larger the profit on the exercise of the option.

2. As interest rates rise, bond prices fall and the potential for a negative profit (loss) for the buyer of the call option increases. If rates rise so that bond prices fall below the exercise price $X$, the call buyer is not obliged to exercise the option. Thus, the losses of the buyer are truncated by the amount of the up-front premium payment ($C$) made to purchase the call option.

Thus, buying a call option is a strategy to take when interest rates are expected to fall. Notice that unlike interest rate futures, whose prices and profit move symmetrically with changes in the level of rates, the profit on bond call options moves asymmetrically with interest rates.

## Writing a Call Option on a Bond

The second strategy is writing (or taking a short position in) a call option on a bond. In writing a call option on a bond, the writer or seller receives an up-front fee or premium ($C$) and must stand ready to sell the underlying bond to the purchaser of the option at the exercise price, $X$. Note the profit from writing a call option on a bond in Figure 23–2.

There are two important things to notice about this profit function:

1. When interest rates rise and bond prices fall, there is an increased potential for the writer of the call to receive a positive profit. The call buyer is less likely to exercise the option, which would force the option writer to sell the underlying bond at the exercise price. However, this profit has a maximum equal to the call premium ($C$) charged up front to the buyer of the option.

**FIGURE 23–2**

**Profit Function for the Writer of a Call Option on a Bond**

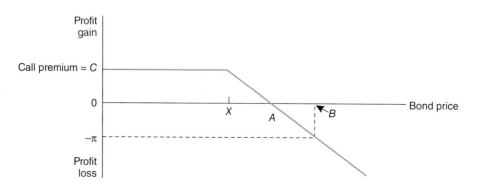

2. When interest rates fall and bond prices rise, the writer has an increased potential to take a loss. The call buyer will exercise the option, forcing the option writer to sell the underlying bonds. Since bond prices can rise to equal the sum of the interest and principal payments on the bond, these losses could be very large.

Thus, writing a call option is a strategy to take when interest rates are expected to rise. Caution is warranted, however, because profits are limited but losses are potentially large if rates fall. In Figure 23–2, a fall in interest rates and a rise in bond prices to $B$ results in the writer of the option losing $\pi$.

### Buying a Put Option on a Bond

**put option**
Gives a purchaser the right (but not the obligation) to sell the underlying security to the writer of the option at a prespecified exercise price on a prespecified date.

The third strategy is buying (or taking a long position in) a put option on a bond. The buyer of a **put option** on a bond has the right (but not the obligation) to sell the underlying bond to the writer of the option at the agreed exercise price ($X$). In return for this option, the buyer of the put option pays a premium ($P$) to the writer. We show the potential profits to the buyer of the put option in Figure 23–3. Note that:

1. When interest rates rise and bond prices fall, the buyer of the put has an increased probability of making a profit from exercising the option. Thus, if bond prices fall to $D$, the buyer of the put option can purchase bonds in the bond market at that price and put them (sell them) back to the writer of the put at the higher exercise price ($X$). As a result, the buyer makes a profit, after deducting the cost of the put premium ($P$), of $\pi p$ in Figure 23–3.

2. When interest rates fall and bond prices rise, the probability that the buyer of a put will lose increases. If rates fall so that bond prices rise above the exercise price $X$, the put buyer does not have to exercise the option. Thus, the maximum loss is limited to the size of the up-front put premium ($P$).

Thus, buying a put option is a strategy to take when interest rates are expected to rise.

### Writing a Put Option on a Bond

The fourth strategy is writing (or taking a short position in) a put option on a bond. In writing a put option on a bond, the writer or seller receives a fee or premium ($P$) in return for standing ready to buy bonds at the exercise price ($X$) if the buyer of the put chooses to exercise the option to sell. See the profit function for writing a put option on a bond in Figure 23–4. Note that:

1. If interest rates fall and bond prices rise, the writer has an enhanced probability of making a profit. The put buyer is less likely to exercise the option, which

**FIGURE 23–3**
**Profit Function for the Buyer of a Put Option on a Bond**

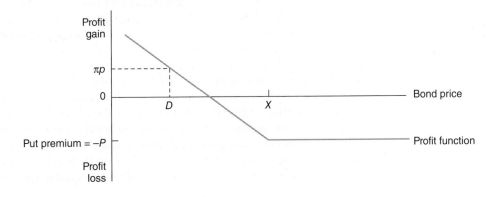

**FIGURE 23–4**
Profit Function for
the Writer of a Put
Option on a Bond

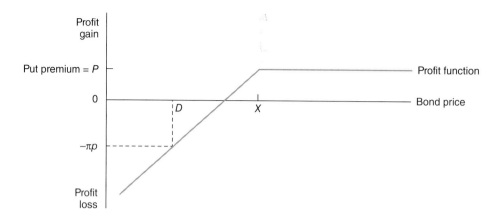

would force the option writer to buy the underlying bond. However, the writer's maximum profit is constrained to be equal to the put premium ($P$).

2. If interest rates rise and bond prices fall, the writer of the put is exposed to potentially large losses (e.g., $-\pi p$, if bond prices fall to $D$ in Figure 23–4).

Thus, writing a put option is a strategy to take when interest rates are expected to fall. However, profits are limited and losses are potentially unlimited.

---

**Concept Questions**

1. How do interest rate increases affect the payoff from buying a call option on a bond? How do they affect the profit from writing a call option on a bond?
2. How do interest rate increases affect the payoff from buying a put option on a bond? How do they affect the profit from writing a put option on a bond?

---

# WRITING VERSUS BUYING OPTIONS

Many small FIs are restricted to buying rather than writing options. There are two reasons for this, one economic and the other regulatory. However, as we note later, large FIs such as money center banks often both write and buy options, including caps, floors, and collars, which are complex forms of interest rate options.

## Economic Reasons for Not Writing Options

In writing an option, the upside profit potential is truncated, but the downside losses are not. While such risks may be offset by writing a large number of options at different exercise prices and/or hedging an underlying portfolio of bonds, the downside risk exposure of the writer may still be significant. To see this, look at Figure 23–5, where an FI is long in a bond in its portfolio and seeks to hedge the interest rate risk on that bond by writing a bond call option.

Figure 23–6 shows the net profit, or the difference between the bond and option payoff. Note that writing the call may hedge the FI when rates fall and bond prices rise. That is, the increase in the value of the bond is offset by losses on the written call. When the reverse occurs and interest rates rise, the FI's profits from writing the call may be insufficient to offset the loss on its bonds. This occurs because the upside profit (per call written) is truncated and is equal to the premium income ($C$).

**FIGURE 23–5**
Writing a Call
Option to Hedge
the Interest Rate
Risk on a Bond

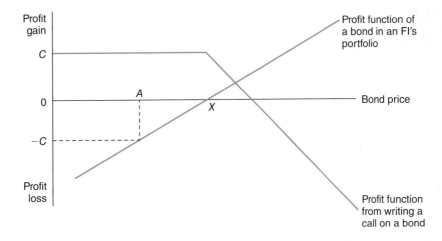

**FIGURE 23–6**
Net Profit from
Writing a Call
Option and
Investing in a Bond

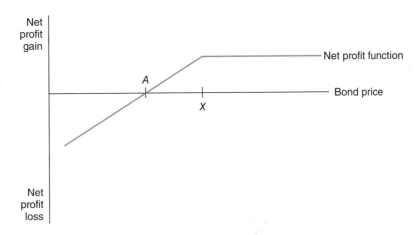

If the decrease in the bond value is larger than the premium income (to the left of point *A* in Figure 23–5), the FI is unable to offset the associated capital value loss on the bond with profits from writing options.

By contrast, hedging the FI's risk by buying a put option on a bond offers the manager a much more attractive alternative. Figure 23–7 shows the gross profit from the bond and the profit from buying a put option on a bond. In this case, any losses on the bond (as rates rise and bond values fall) are offset with profits from the put option that was bought (points to the left of point *X* in Figure 23–7). If rates fall, the bond value increases. Yet the accompanying losses on the purchased put option positions are limited to the option premiums paid (points to the right of point *X*). Figure 23–8 shows the net profit or the difference between the bond and option payoff.

Note that:

1. Buying a put option truncates the downside losses on the bond following interest rate rises to some maximum amount and scales down the upside profits by the cost of bond price risk insurance—the put premium—leaving some positive upside profit potential.

2. The combination of being long in the bond and buying a put option on a bond mimics the profit function of buying a call option (compare Figures 23–1 and 23–8).

**FIGURE 23–7**
**Buying a Put Option to Hedge the Interest Rate Risk on a Bond**

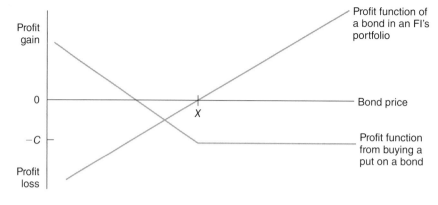

**FIGURE 23–8**
**Net Profit from Buying a Bond Put and Investing in a Bond**

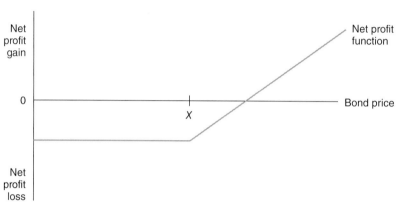

## Regulatory Reasons

**naked options**
Option positions that do not identifiably hedge an underlying asset or liability.

There are also regulatory reasons why FIs buy options rather than write options. Regulators view writing options, especially **naked options** that do not identifiably hedge an underlying asset or liability position, to be risky because of the large loss potential. Indeed, bank regulators prohibit banks from writing puts or calls in certain areas of risk management.

## Futures versus Options Hedging

To understand the differences between using futures versus options contracts to hedge interest rate risk, compare the profit gains illustrated in Figure 23–9 (for futures contracts) with those in Figure 23–7 (for buying put option contracts). A hedge with futures contracts reduces volatility in profit gains on both the upside and downside of interest rate movements. That is, if the FI in Figure 23–9 loses value on the bond resulting from an interest rate increase (to the left of point $X$), a gain on the futures contract offsets the loss. If the FI gains value on the bond due to an interest rate decrease (to the right of point $X$), however, a loss on the futures contract offsets the gain.

In comparison, the hedge with the put option contract completely offsets losses but only partly offsets gains. That is, in Figure 23–7, if the FI loses value on the bond due to an interest rate increase (to the left of point $X$), a gain on the put option contract offsets the loss. However, if the FI gains value on the bond due to an interest rate decrease (to the right of point $X$), the gain is offset only to the extent that the FI loses the put option premium (because it never exercises the option).

**FIGURE 23–9**
**Buying a Futures Contract to Hedge the Interest Rate Risk on a Bond**

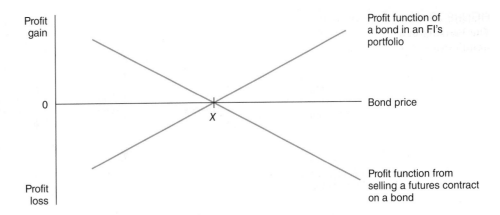

Thus, the put option hedge protects the FI against value losses when interest rates move against the on-balance-sheet securities but, unlike futures hedging, does not reduce value when interest rates move in favor of on-balance-sheet securities.

| Concept Questions | 1. What are some of the economic reasons for an FI not to write options? |
|---|---|
| | 2. What are some regulatory reasons why an FI might choose to buy options rather than write options? |

## THE MECHANICS OF HEDGING A BOND OR BOND PORTFOLIO

You have seen how buying a put option on a bond can potentially hedge the interest rate risk exposure of an FI that holds bonds as part of its investment portfolio. In this section, we use a simple example to demonstrate the mechanics of buying a put option as a hedging device and how an FI manager can calculate the fair premium value for a put option on a bond.

In calculating the fair value of an option, two alternative models can be used: the binomial model and the Black-Scholes model. The Black-Scholes model produces a closed-form solution to the valuation of call and put options.[1] Appendix 10B (located

[1] The Black-Scholes formulas for a put and a call are:

$$P = Xe^{-rT}N[-D + \sigma\sqrt{T}] - SN[-D]$$
$$C = SN[D] - Xe^{-rT}N[D - \sigma\sqrt{T}]$$

where

$S$ = Price of the underlying asset
$X$ = Exercise price
$T$ = Time to option expiration
$r$ = Instantaneous riskless interest rate

$$D = \frac{ln(S/X) + (r + \sigma^2/2)T}{\sigma\sqrt{T}}$$

$ln[.]$ = Natural logarithm
$\sigma$ = Volatility of the underlying asset
$N[.]$ = Cumulative normal distribution function, that is, the probability of observing a value less than the value in brackets when drawing randomly from a standardized normal distribution

**FIGURE 23–10**
The Variance of a
Bond's Price

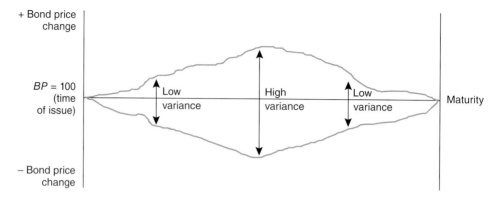

at the book's website, **www.mhhe.com/saunders8e**) shows the basic structural and pricing concepts of an option using the Black-Scholes model. Although it works well for stocks, the Black-Scholes model has two major problems when employed to value bond options. First, it assumes that short-term interest rates are constant, which they generally are not. Second, it assumes a constant variance of returns on the underlying asset. The application of the Black-Scholes formula to bonds is problematic because of the way bond prices behave between issuance and maturity. This is shown in Figure 23–10, where a bond is issued at par, that is, the price of the bond is 100 percent times its face value at time of issue. If interest rates fall, its price may rise above 100 percent, and if interest rates rise, its price may fall below 100 percent. However, as the bond approaches maturity, all price paths must lead to 100 percent of the face value of the bond or principal paid by the issuer on maturity.[2] Because of this **pull-to-par,** the variance of bond prices is nonconstant over time, rising at first and then falling as the bond approaches maturity. We evaluate the mechanics of hedging using bond put options in a simple binomial framework next.

**pull-to-par**
The tendency of the variance of a bond's price or return to decrease as maturity approaches.

## Hedging with Bond Options Using the Binomial Model

Suppose that an FI manager has purchased a $100 zero-coupon bond with exactly two years to maturity. A zero-coupon bond, if held to maturity, pays its face value of $100 on maturity in two years. Assume that the FI manager pays $80.44 per $100 of face value for this zero-coupon bond. This means that if held to maturity, the FI's annual yield to maturity ($R_2$) from this investment would be:

$$BP_2 = \frac{100}{(1 + R_2)^2}$$

$$80.44 = \frac{100}{(1 + R_2)^2}$$

Solving for $R_2$,   $R_2 = \sqrt{\dfrac{100}{80.44}} - 1 = 0.115 = 11.5\%$

---

[2] There are models that modify Black-Scholes to allow for nonconstant variance. These include Merton, who allows variance to be time dependent; Ball and Tourous, who allow bond prices to change as a stochastic process with a variance that first increases and then decreases (the Brownian bridge process); and the Schaefer-Schwartz model, which assumes that the standard deviation of returns is proportional to a bond's duration. See R. C. Merton, "On the Pricing of Corporate Debt: The Risk Structure of Interest Rates," *Journal of Finance* 29 (1974), pp. 449–70; C. Ball and W. N. Tourous, "Bond Price Dynamics and Options," *Journal of Financial and Quantitative Analysis* 18 (1983), pp. 517–31; and S. Schaefer and E. S. Schwartz, "Time Dependent Variance and the Pricing of Bond Options," *Journal of Finance* 42 (1987), pp. 1113–28.

Suppose also that, at the end of the first year, interest rates rise unexpectedly. As a result, depositors, seeking higher returns on their funds, withdraw deposits. To meet these unexpected deposit withdrawals, the FI manager is forced to liquidate (sell) the two-year bond before maturity, at the end of year 1. Because of the unexpected rise in interest rates at the end of year 1, the FI manager must sell the bond at a low price.

Assume when the bond is purchased, the current yield on one-year discount bonds $(R_1)$ is $R_1 = 10$ percent. Also, assume that at the end of year one, the one year interest rate $(r_1)$ is forecasted to rise to either 13.82 percent or 12.18 percent. If one-year interest rates rise from $R_1 = 10$ percent when the bond is purchased to $r_1 = 13.82$ percent at the end of year 1, the FI manager will be able to sell the zero-coupon bond with one year remaining to maturity for a bond price, $BP$, of:

$$BP_1 = \frac{100}{(1 + r_1)} = \frac{100}{(1.1382)} = \$87.86$$

If, on the other hand, one-year interest rates rise to 12.18 percent, the manager can sell the bond with one year remaining to maturity for:

$$BP_1 = \frac{100}{(1 + r_1)} = \frac{100}{(1.1218)} = \$89.14$$

In these equations, $r_1$ stands for the two possible one-year rates that might arise one year into the future.[3] That is:

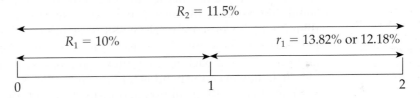

Assume the manager believes that one-year rates $(r_1)$ one year from today will be 13.82 percent or 12.18 percent with an equal probability. This means that the expected one-year rate one year from today would be:

$$E(r_1) = 0.5(0.1382) + 0.5(0.1218) = 0.13 = 13\%$$

Thus, the expected price if the bond has to be sold at the end of the first year is:[4]

$$E(P_1) = \frac{100}{(1.13)} = \$88.50$$

---

[3] If one-year bond rates next year equaled the one-year bond rate this year, $R_1 = r_1 = 10$ percent, then the bond could be sold for $BP_1 = \$90.91$.

[4] The interest rates assumed in this example are consistent with arbitrage-free pricing under current term structure conditions. That is, the expectations theory of interest rates implies that the following relationship must hold:

$$(1 + R_2)^2 = (1 + R_1) \times (1 + E(r_1))$$

As you can easily see, when the interest rates from our example are inserted, $R_1 = 10\%$, $R_2 = 11.5\%$, $E(r_1) = 13\%$, this equation holds. Also, the two interest rates (prices) imply that the current volatility of one-year interest rates is 6.3 percent. That is, from the binomial model, $\sigma = \frac{1}{2}ln[r_u/r_d]$, such that $\sigma = \frac{1}{2}ln[13.82/12.18] = 0.063$ or 6.3%.

**FIGURE 23–11**
Binomial Model of
Bond Prices: Two-
Year Zero-Coupon
Bond

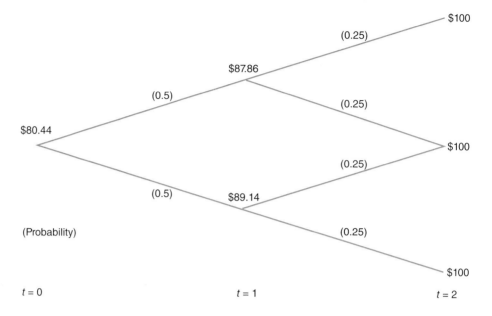

Assume that the FI manager wants to ensure that the bond sale produces at least $88.50 per $100; otherwise, the FI has to find alternative and very costly sources of liquidity (for example, the FI might have to borrow from the central bank's discount window and incur the direct and indirect penalty costs involved; see Chapter 19). One way for the FI to ensure that it receives at least $88.50 on selling the bond at the end of the year is to buy a put option on the bond at time 0 with an exercise price of $88.50 at time (year) 1. If the bond is trading below $88.50 at the end of the year—say, at $87.86—the FI can exercise its option and put the bond back to the writer of the option, who will have to pay the FI $88.50. If, however, the bond is trading above $88.50—say, at $89.14—the FI does not have to exercise its option and instead can sell the bond in the open market for $89.14.

The FI manager will want to recalculate the fair premium to pay for buying this put option or bond insurance at time 0. Figure 23–11 shows the possible paths (i.e., the binomial tree or lattice) of the zero-coupon bond's price from purchase to maturity over the two-year period. The FI manager purchased the bond at $80.44 with two years to maturity. Given expectations of rising rates, there is a 50 percent probability that the bond with one year left to maturity will trade at $87.86 and a 50 percent probability that it will trade at $89.14. Note that between $t = 1$, or one year left to maturity, and maturity ($t = 2$), there must be a pull to par on the bond. That is, all paths must lead to a price of $100 on maturity.

The value of the option is shown in Figure 23–12. The option in Figure 23–12 can be exercised only at the end of year 1 ($t = 1$). If the zero-coupon bond with one year left to maturity trades at $87.86, the option is worth $88.50 − $87.86 in time 1 dollars, or $0.64. If the bond trades at $89.14, the option has no value since the bond could be sold at a higher value than the exercise price of $88.50 on the open market. This suggests that in time 1 dollars, the option is worth:

$$0.5(0.64) + 0.5(0) = \$0.32$$

**FIGURE 23–12**

The Value of a Put Option on the Two-Year Zero-Coupon Bond

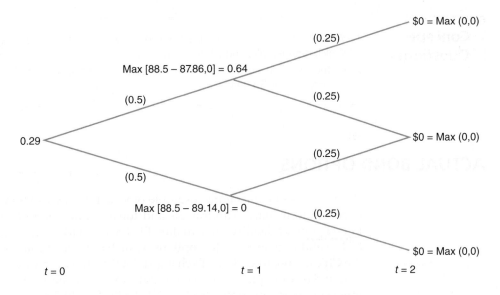

However, the FI is evaluating the option and paying the put premium at time $t = 0$, that is, one year before the date when the option might be exercised. Thus, the fair value of the put premium ($P$) the FI manager should be willing to pay is the discounted present value of the expected payoff from buying the option. Since one-year interest rates ($R_1$) are currently 10 percent, this implies:

$$P = \frac{\$0.32}{1 + R_1} = \frac{\$0.32}{(1.1)} = \$0.29$$

or a premium, $P$, of approximately 29 cents per $100 bond option purchased.

Further, as you can easily see, the option becomes increasingly valuable as the variability of interest rates increases. Conceptually, the branches of the binomial tree diagram become more widely dispersed as variability increases. For example, suppose one-year interest rates on the upper branch were expected to be 14.82 percent instead of 13.82 percent. Then, the price on a one-year, zero-coupon bond associated with a one-year yield of 14.82 percent is $87.09 and the option is worth $88.50 − $87.09 in time 1 dollars, or $1.41. Thus, the value of the put option ($P$) with the same exercise price of $88.50 is:

$$P = \frac{0.5(1.41) + 0.5(0)}{1.1} = \$0.64$$

Notice the familiar result from option pricing theory holds:

$$\frac{\delta P}{\delta \sigma} > 0$$

That is, the value of the put option increases with an increase in underlying variance of asset returns.

<table>
<tr><td>

**Concept Questions**

</td><td>

1. What are two common models used to calculate the fair value of a bond option? Which is preferable, and why?

2. In the example above, calculate the value of the option if the exercise price (*X*) = $88. (*P* = $0.064)

</td></tr>
</table>

# ACTUAL BOND OPTIONS

www.cboe.com

We have presented a simple example of how FIs may use bond options to hedge exposure to liability withdrawals and forced liquidation of assets in a world of interest rate variability. In actuality, FIs have a wide variety of over-the-counter (OTC) and exchange-traded options available. Interest rate options are listed on the Chicago Board Options Exchange (CBOE). However, these contracts are rarely traded. For example, in September 2012 there was no trading of any of the four interest rate option contracts (13-week T-bill, T-yield 5 years, 10-year T-notes, and T-yield 30 year). In actual practice, most pure bond options trade over-the-counter. This is not because interest rate or bond options are not used, although the open interest is relatively small, but because the preferred method of hedging is an option on an interest rate futures contract.

**futures option**
An option contract that, when exercised, results in the delivery of a futures contract as the underlying asset.

A **futures option** is a contract in which the underlying asset is a futures contract (e.g., $100,000 Treasury bond futures). The buyer of a call (put) option on a futures contract has the right to buy (sell) the underlying futures contract before expiration (i.e., an American option). The seller of a call (put) option on a futures contract creates the obligation to sell (buy) the underlying futures contract on exercise by the option buyer. If exercised, a call (put) option holder can buy (sell) the underlying futures contract at the exercise price. Options on futures can be more attractive to FIs than options on an underlying asset when it is cheaper or more convenient to deliver futures contracts on the asset rather than the actual asset. For example, trading options on T-bond futures contracts rather than options on T-bonds ensures that a highly liquid asset will be delivered and that problems associated with accrued interest and the determination of which long-term bond to deliver are avoided. Another advantage is that price information about futures contracts (the underlying asset on the option) is generally more readily available than price information on the T-bonds themselves (T-bond price information can be obtained only by surveying bond dealers).

Finally, bond or interest rate futures options are generally preferred to options on the underlying bond because they combine the favorable liquidity, credit risk, homogeneity, and marking-to-market features of futures with the same asymmetric payoff functions as regular puts and calls. Figure 23–13 lists settle prices for some of the futures options (i.e., an option contract that, when exercised, results in the delivery of a futures contract as the underlying asset) on bonds trading on September 21, 2012.

When the FI hedges by buying put options on bond futures, if interest rates rise and bond prices fall, the exercise of the put causes the FI to deliver a bond futures contract to the writer at an exercise price higher than the cost of the bond future currently trading on the futures exchange. The futures price itself reflects the price of the underlying deliverable bond such as a 15-year, 8 percent coupon

## FIGURE 23–13   Futures Options on Interest Rates, September 21, 2012

Source: *The Wall Street Journal Online,* September 21, 2012. Reprinted by permission of *The Wall Street Journal,* © 2012 Dow Jones & Company, Inc. All Rights Reserved Worldwide. *www.wsj.com*

### Interest Rate Futures Options

For Friday, September 21, 2012
All prices are settlement prices. Open interest is from the previous trading day. Source: AP

**US Treasury Bonds** (CBOT)
$100,000, pts & 64ths of 100 pct

| STRIKE PRICE | OCT | DEC | MAR | OCT | DEC | MAR |
|---|---|---|---|---|---|---|
| | CALLS | | | PUTS | | |
| 14100 | 5-57 | 6-37 | 6-53 | 0-01 | 0-46 | 2-16 |
| 14200 | 4-57 | 5-50 | 6-10 | 0-01 | 0-58 | 2-37 |
| 14300 | 3-57 | 5-01 | 5-33 | 0-01 | 1-09 | 2-60 |
| 14400 | 2-57 | 4-19 | 4-59 | 0-01 | 1-27 | 3-21 |
| →14500 | 1-57 | 3-41 | 4-22 | 0-01 | 1-49 | 3-48 |
| 14600 | 0-57 | 3-03 | 3-52 | 0-01 | 2-11 | 4-14 |
| 14700 | 0-01 | 2-33 | 3-21 | 0-09 | 2-41 | 4-47 |
| 14800 | 0-01 | 2-03 | 2-57 | 1-09 | 3-11 | 5-18 |
| 14900 | 0-01 | 1-41 | 2-32 | 2-09 | 3-49 | 5-57 |
| 15000 | 0-01 | 1-20 | 2-09 | 3-09 | 4-28 | 6-34 |

Open Interest          calls   259,217   Puts   297,542

**10 Yr. Treasury** (CBOT)
$100,000 prin, pts & 64ths of 100 pct

| STRIKE PRICE | OCT | DEC | MAR | OCT | DEC | MAR |
|---|---|---|---|---|---|---|
| 15000 | 0-01 | 0-01 | 0-01 | 17-22 | 17-21 | 17-58 |
| 15050 | 0-01 | 0-01 | 0-01 | 17-54 | 17-53 | 18-26 |
| 15100 | 0-01 | 0-01 | 0-01 | 18-22 | 18-21 | 18-58 |
| 15150 | 0-01 | 0-01 | 0-01 | 18-54 | 18-35 | 19-26 |
| 15200 | 0-01 | 0-01 | 0-01 | 19-22 | 19-21 | 19-58 |
| 15250 | 0-01 | 0-01 | 0-01 | 19-54 | 19-53 | 20-26 |
| 15300 | 0-01 | 0-01 | 0-01 | 20-22 | 20-21 | 20-58 |
| 15350 | 0-01 | 0-01 | 0-01 | 20-54 | 20-53 | 21-26 |

Open Interest          calls   775,688   Puts   1,037,195

**Eurodollars** (CME)
$1 million, pts of 100 pct

| STRIKE PRICE | OCT | DEC | MAR | OCT | DEC | MAR |
|---|---|---|---|---|---|---|
| 981250 | 155.00 | 155.00 | 153.75 | — | 0.25 | 0.25 |
| 982500 | 142.50 | 142.50 | 141.25 | — | 0.25 | 0.25 |
| 983750 | 130.00 | 130.00 | 128.75 | — | 0.25 | 0.25 |
| 985000 | 117.50 | 117.50 | 116.25 | — | 0.25 | 0.25 |
| 986250 | 105.00 | 105.00 | 104.00 | — | 0.25 | 0.50 |
| 987500 | 92.50 | 92.50 | 91.50 | 0.25 | 0.25 | 0.50 |
| 988750 | 80.00 | 80.00 | 79.25 | 0.25 | 0.25 | 0.75 |
| 990000 | 67.50 | 67.50 | 66.75 | 0.25 | 0.25 | 0.75 |
| 991250 | 55.00 | 55.00 | 54.50 | 0.25 | 0.25 | 1.00 |
| 992500 | 42.50 | 42.75 | 42.25 | 0.25 | 0.25 | 1.25 |
| 993750 | 30.00 | 30.25 | 30.25 | 0.25 | 0.25 | 1.75 |
| 995000 | 17.50 | 18.00 | 18.50 | 0.25 | 0.50 | 2.50 |
| 996250 | 5.25 | 7.00 | 8.25 | 0.25 | 2.00 | 4.75 |
| 997500 | 0.25 | 1.00 | 2.00 | 7.75 | 8.50 | 11.00 |
| 998750 | 0.25 | 0.25 | 0.50 | 20.00 | 20.00 | 22.00 |
| 1000000 | — | 0.25 | 0.25 | 32.50 | 32.50 | 34.00 |
| 1001250 | — | — | — | 45.00 | 45.00 | 46.50 |
| 1002500 | — | — | — | 57.50 | 57.50 | 59.00 |

Open Interest          Calls   2,086,816   Puts   3,843,362

### Currency Futures Options

For Friday, September 21, 2012
All prices are settlement prices. Open interest is from the previous trading day. Source: AP

**Japanese Yen** (CME)
12,500,000 yen, cents per 100 yen

| STRIKE PRICE | OCT | DEC | MAR | OCT | DEC | MAR |
|---|---|---|---|---|---|---|
| | CALLS | | | PUTS | | |
| 1260 | 1.17 | 2.11 | 3.20 | 0.04 | 0.94 | 1.89 |
| 1265 | 0.67 | 1.80 | 2.91 | 0.09 | 1.13 | 2.10 |
| 1270 | 0.17 | 1.52 | 2.64 | 0.19 | 1.35 | 2.33 |
| 1275 | 0.36 | 1.27 | 2.38 | 0.33 | 1.60 | 2.57 |
| 1280 | 0.16 | 1.04 | 2.14 | 0.83 | 1.87 | 2.83 |
| 1285 | 0.06 | 0.84 | 1.93 | 1.33 | 2.17 | 3.12 |
| 1290 | 0.01 | 0.67 | 1.73 | 1.83 | 2.50 | 3.41 |

Open Interest          Calls   26,801   Puts   44,440

**Canadian Dollar** (CME)
100,000 dollars, cents per dollar

| STRIKE PRICE | OCT | DEC | MAR | OCT | DEC | MAR |
|---|---|---|---|---|---|---|
| 1000 | 1.98 | 2.47 | 2.97 | — | 0.49 | 1.23 |
| 1005 | 1.48 | 2.09 | 2.65 | 0.02 | 0.61 | 1.40 |
| 1010 | 0.98 | 1.74 | 2.33 | 0.06 | 0.76 | 1.58 |
| →1015 | 0.48 | 1.42 | 2.03 | 0.17 | 0.94 | 1.78 |
| 1020 | 0.18 | 1.14 | 1.76 | 0.02 | 1.16 | 2.01 |
| 1025 | 0.05 | 0.89 | 1.51 | 0.52 | 1.41 | 2.26 |
| 1030 | 0.01 | 0.68 | 1.29 | 1.02 | 1.70 | 2.54 |

Open Interest          Calls   30,756   Puts   40,678

**British Pound** (CME)
62,500 pounds, cents per pound

| STRIKE PRICE | OCT | DEC | MAR | OCT | DEC | MAR |
|---|---|---|---|---|---|---|
| 1580 | 3.38 | 3.97 | 4.90 | 0.01 | 0.60 | 1.57 |
| 1590 | 2.38 | 3.20 | 4.21 | 0.01 | 0.82 | 1.88 |
| 1600 | 1.38 | 2.50 | 3.56 | 0.02 | 1.12 | 2.23 |
| 1610 | 0.38 | 1.89 | 2.98 | 0.11 | 1.51 | 2.64 |
| 1620 | 0.29 | 1.38 | 2.45 | 0.62 | 2.00 | 3.11 |
| 1630 | 0.06 | 0.96 | 2.00 | 1.62 | 2.58 | 3.65 |
| 1640 | 0.01 | 0.66 | 1.60 | 2.62 | 3.28 | 4.25 |

Open Interest          Calls   23,236   Puts   23,592

**Swiss Franc** (CME)
125,000 francs, cents per franc

| STRIKE PRICE | OCT | DEC | MAR | OCT | DEC | MAR |
|---|---|---|---|---|---|---|
| 1060 | 1.71 | 2.56 | 3.58 | 0.01 | 0.85 | 1.70 |
| 1065 | 1.21 | 2.22 | 3.26 | 0.04 | 1.01 | 1.88 |
| 1070 | 0.71 | 1.91 | 2.97 | 0.12 | 1.20 | 2.08 |
| 1075 | 0.21 | 1.62 | 2.68 | 0.29 | 1.41 | 2.29 |
| 1080 | 0.17 | 1.36 | 2.41 | 0.29 | 1.65 | 2.52 |
| 1085 | 0.06 | 1.13 | 2.17 | 0.79 | 1.92 | 2.78 |
| 1090 | 0.02 | 0.93 | 1.94 | 1.29 | 2.22 | 3.05 |

Open Interest          Calls   2,381   Puts   1,786

T-bond; see Figure 23–13. As a result, a profit on futures options may be made to offset the loss on the market value of bonds held directly in the FI's portfolio. If interest rates fall and bond and futures prices rise, the buyer of the futures option will not exercise the put, and the losses on the futures put option are limited to the put premium. Thus, if on September 21, 2012, the FI had bought one $100,000

December 2012 T-bond futures put option at a strike price of $145.00 but did not exercise the option, the FI's loss equals the put premium of $7\frac{57}{64}$ per $100, or $1,890.625 per $100,000 contract. Offsetting these losses, however, would be an increase in the market value of the FI's underlying bond portfolio. Unlike futures positions in Chapter 22, an upside profit potential remains when interest rates fall and FIs use put options on futures to hedge interest rate risk. We show this in the next section.

---

**Concept Questions**

1. Why are bond or interest rate futures options generally preferred to options on the underlying bond?
2. If an FI hedges by buying put options on futures and interest rates rise (i.e., bond prices fall), what is the outcome?

---

## USING OPTIONS TO HEDGE INTEREST RATE RISK ON THE BALANCE SHEET

Our previous simple example showed how a bond option could hedge the interest rate risk on an underlying bond position in the asset portfolio. Next, we determine the put option position that can hedge the interest rate risk of the overall balance sheet. That is, we analyze macrohedging rather than microhedging.

Chapter 8 showed that an FI's net worth exposure to an interest rate shock could be represented as:

$$\Delta E = -(D_A - kD_L) \times A \times \frac{\Delta R}{1 + R}$$

where

$$\Delta E = \text{Change in the FI's net worth}$$
$$(D_A - kD_L) = \text{FI's duration gap}$$
$$A = \text{Size of the FI's assets}$$
$$\frac{\Delta R}{1 + R} = \text{Size of the interest rate shock}$$
$$k = \text{FI's leverage ratio } (L/A)$$

Suppose the FI manager wishes to determine the optimal number of put options to buy to insulate the FI against rising rates. An FI with a positive duration gap (see Figure 23–14) would lose on-balance-sheet net worth when interest rates rise. In this case, the FI manager would buy put options.[5] That is, the FI manager wants to adopt a put option position to generate profits that just offset the loss in net worth due to an interest rate shock (where $E_0$ is the FI's initial equity (net worth) position in Figure 23–14).

---

[5] Conversely, an FI with a negative duration gap would lose on-balance-sheet net worth when interest rates fall. In this case, the FI manager wants to buy call options to generate profits to offset the loss in net worth due to an interest rate shock.

**FIGURE 23–14**
**Buying Put Options to Hedge the Interest Rate Risk Exposure of the FI**

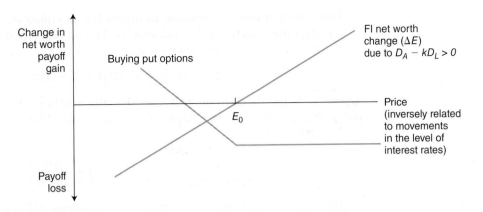

Let $\Delta P$ be the total change in the value of the put option position in T-bonds. This can be decomposed into:

$$\Delta P = (N_p \times \Delta p) \tag{1}$$

where $N_p$ is the number of \$100,000 put options on T-bond contracts to be purchased (the number for which we are solving) and $\Delta p$ is the change in the dollar value for each \$100,000 face value T-bond put option contract.

The change in the dollar value of each contract ($\Delta p$) can be further decomposed into:

$$\Delta p = \frac{dp}{dB} \times \frac{dB}{dR} \times \Delta R \tag{2}$$

This decomposition needs some explanation. The first term ($dp/dB$) shows the change in the value of a put option for each \$1 change in the underlying bond. This is called the *delta of an option* ($\delta$), and its absolute value lies between 0 and 1. For put options, the delta has a negative sign since the value of the put option falls when bond prices rise.[6] The second term ($dB/dR$) shows how the market value of a bond changes if interest rates rise by one basis point. This value of one basis point term can be linked to duration. Specifically, we know from Chapter 9 that:

$$\frac{dB}{B} = -MD \times dR \tag{3}$$

That is, the percentage change in the bond's price for a small change in interest rates is proportional to the bond's modified duration ($MD$). Equation (3) can be rearranged by cross multiplying as:

$$\frac{dB}{dR} = -MD \times B \tag{4}$$

---

[6] For call options, the delta has a positive sign since the value of the call rises when bond prices rise. As we proceed with the derivation, we examine only the case of a hedge using a put option contract (i.e., the FI has a positive duration gap and expects interest rates to rise). For a hedge with a call option contract (i.e., the FI has a negative duration gap), the derivation below changes only in that the sign on the delta is reversed (from negative to positive).

Thus, the term $dB/dR$ is equal to minus the modified duration on the bond ($MD$) times the current market value of the T-bond ($B$) underlying the put option contract. As a result, we can rewrite equation (2) as:

$$\Delta p = [(-\delta) \times (-MD) \times B \times \Delta R] \tag{5}$$

where $\Delta R$ is the shock to interest rates (i.e., the number of basis points by which rates change). Since from Chapter 9 we know that $MD = D/(1 + R)$, we can rewrite equation (5) as:

$$\Delta p = \left[(-\delta) \times (-D) \times B \times \frac{\Delta R}{1 + R}\right] \tag{6}$$

Thus, the change in the total value of a put position[7] ($\Delta P$) is:

$$\Delta P = N_p \times \left[\delta \times D \times B \times \frac{\Delta R}{1 + R}\right] \tag{7}$$

The term in brackets is the change in the value of one \$100,000 face-value T-bond put option as rates change, and $N_p$ is the number of put option contracts.

To hedge net worth exposure, we require the profit on the off-balance-sheet put options ($\Delta P$) to just offset the loss of on-balance-sheet net worth ($\Delta E$) when interest rates rise (and thus, bond prices fall). That is:

$$\Delta P + \Delta E = 0$$

$$N_p \times \left[\delta \times D \times B \times \frac{\Delta R}{1 + R}\right] + \left[-[D_A - kD_L] \times A \times \frac{\Delta R}{1 + R}\right] = 0$$

Canceling $\Delta R/(1 + R)$ on both sides, we get:

$$N_p \times [\delta \times D \times B] - [D_A - kD_L] \times A = 0$$

Solving for $N_p$—the number of put options to buy—we have:[8]

$$N_p = \frac{[D_A - kD_L] \times A}{[\delta \times D \times B]}$$

Appendix 23A (located at the book's website, **www.mhhe.com/saunders8e**) derives the equation for the number of option contracts to buy or sell for a microhedge.[9]

---

[7] Note that since both the delta and $D$ of the put option and bond have negative signs, their product will be positive. Thus, these negative signs are not shown in the equation to calculate $N_p$.

[8] For a hedge involving a call option, the formula is:

$$N_C = \frac{[D_A - kD_L] \times A}{-[\delta \times D \times B]}$$

[9] For a microhedge, this equation becomes:

$$N_o = \frac{D \times P}{\delta \times D \times B}$$

where $P$ is the price of the asset or liability being hedged and $D$ is its duration.

**EXAMPLE 23–1**

*Macrohedge of Interest Rate Risk Using a Put Option*

Suppose, as in Chapter 22, an FI's balance sheet is such that $D_A = 5$, $D_L = 3$, $k = 0.9$, and $A = \$100$ million. Rates are expected to rise from 10 to 11 percent over the next six months, which would result in a $2.09 million loss in net worth to the FI. Suppose also that $\delta$ of the put option is 0.5, which indicates that the option is close to being in the money, $D = 8.82$ for the bond underlying the put option contract, and the current market value of $100,000 face value of long-term Treasury bonds underlying the option contract, $B$, equals $97,000. Solving for $N_p$, the number of put option contracts to buy:

$$N_p = \frac{[5 - 0.9 \times 3] \times 100m}{[0.5 \times 8.82 \times \$97,000]} = \frac{\$230,000,000}{\$427,770}$$

$$= 537.672 \text{ contracts}$$

If the FI slightly underhedges, this will be rounded down to 537 contracts. If rates increase from 10 to 11 percent, the value of the FI's put options will change by:

$$\Delta P = 537 \times \left[ 0.5 \times 8.82 \times \$97,000 \times \frac{0.01}{1.1} \right] = \$2.09 \text{ million}$$

just offsetting the loss in net worth on the balance sheet.

The total premium cost to the FI of buying these puts is the price (premium) of each put times the number of puts:

$$\text{Cost} = N_p \times \text{Put premium per contract}$$

Suppose that T-bond put option premiums are quoted at $2½ per $100 of face value for the nearby contract or $2,500 per $100,000 put contract. Then the cost of macrohedging the gap with put options will be:

$$\text{Cost} = 537 \times \$2,500 = \$1,342,500$$

or just over $1.3 million. Remember, the total assets of the FI were assumed to be $100 million.

Figure 23–15 summarizes the change in the FI's overall value from a 1 percent increase in interest rates and the offsetting change in value from the hedge in the put option market. If rates increase as predicted, the FI's gap exposure results in a decrease in net worth of $2.09 million. This decrease is offset with a $2.09 million

**FIGURE 23–15**
**Buying Put Options to Hedge an FI's Interest Rate Gap Risk Exposure**

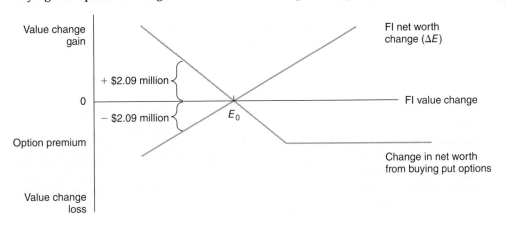

gain on the put option position held by the FI. Should rates decrease, however, the resulting increase in net worth is not offset by a decrease in an out-of-the-money put option.

Appendix 23B to this chapter (located at the book's website, **www.mhhe.com/saunders8e**) illustrates how these options can be used to microhedge a specific asset or liability on an FI's balance sheet against interest rate risk.

### Basis Risk

It is again important to recognize that in the previous examples, the FI hedged interest rate risk exposure perfectly because basis risk was assumed to be zero. That is, we assumed the change in interest rates on the balance sheet is equal to the change in the interest rate on the bond underlying the option contract [i.e., $\Delta R / (1 + R) = \Delta R_b/(1 + R_b)$]. As discussed in Chapter 22, the introduction of basis risk means that the FI must adjust the number of option contracts it holds to account for the degree to which the rate on the option's underlying security (i.e., T-bond) moves relative to the spot rate on the asset or liability the FI is hedging.

Allowing basis risk to exist, the equation used to determine the number of put options to buy to hedge interest rate risk becomes:

$$N_p = \frac{(D_A - kD_L) \times A}{\delta \times D \times B \times br}$$

where $br$ is a measure of the volatility of interest rates ($R_b$) on the bond underlying the options contract relative to the interest rate that impacts the bond on the FI's balance sheet ($R$). That is:

$$br = \frac{\dfrac{\Delta R_b}{1 + R_b}}{\dfrac{\Delta R}{1 + R}}$$

---

**EXAMPLE 23–2**

*Put Option Macrohedge with Basis Risk*

Refer to Example 23–1. Suppose that basis risk, $br$, is 0.92 (i.e., the rate on the option's underlying bond changes by 92 percent of the spot rate change on the balance sheet being hedged). In Example 23–1, with no basis risk, the number of options needed to hedge interest rate risk on the bond position is 537.672 put option contracts. Introducing basis risk, $br = 0.92$:

$$N_p = \frac{\$230,000,000}{0.5 \times 8.82 \text{ years} \times \$97,000 \times 0.92} = 584.4262 \text{ put option contracts}$$

Additional put option contracts are needed to hedge interest rate risk because interest rates on the bond underlying the option contract do not move as much as interest rates on the balance sheet.

---

As described in Chapter 22, the FI can analyze the relationship between interest rates on the security underlying the futures option contract (e.g., T-bond) and the security being hedged on the FI's balance sheet by investigating their relative behavior in the recent past. This can be done by running an ordinary least squares linear regression of T-bond rate changes on spot rate changes with the slope coefficient of this regression giving an estimate of the degree of co-movement of the two rates over time, or basis risk.

| Concept Questions | 1. If interest rates fall, are you better off purchasing call or put options on T-bonds, and why? |
|---|---|
| | 2. In the example above, what number of put options should you purchase if $\delta = 0.25$ and $D = 6$? ($N_p = 1,718.213$) |

# USING OPTIONS TO HEDGE FOREIGN EXCHANGE RISK

Just as an FI can hedge a long position in bonds against interest rate risk through bond options or futures options on bonds, a similar opportunity is available to micro-hedge long or short positions in a foreign currency asset against foreign exchange rate risk. To see this, suppose that an FI bought, or is long in, a Canadian dollar (C$) asset in September 2012. This C$ asset is a two-month T-bill paying C$100 million in December 2012. Since the FI's liabilities are in U.S. dollars, it may wish to hedge the FX risk that the Canadian dollar will depreciate over the two months. Suppose that if the C$ were to fall from the current exchange rate of $1.0217/C$1, the FI would take a loss on its Canadian T-bill investment when measured in U.S. dollar terms. For example, if the C$ depreciated from $1.0217/C$ in September 2012 to $1.0037/C$1 in December 2012, the C$100 million asset would be worth only $100.37 million on maturity instead of the expected $102.17 million when it was purchased in September. If the foreign exchange rate depreciation is sufficiently severe, the FI might be unable to meet its dollar liability commitments used to fund the T-bill purchase. To offset this exposure, the FI may buy three month put options on Canadian dollars at an exercise price of $1.015/C1$. Thus, if the exchange rate does fall to $100.37/C$1 at the end of three months, the FI manager can put the C$100 million proceeds from the T-bill on maturity to the writer of the option. Then the FI receives $101.5 million instead of the $100.37 million if the Canadian dollars were sold at the open market spot exchange rate at the end of the two months. If the C$ actually appreciates in value, or does not depreciate below $1.015/C$1, the option expires unexercised and the proceeds of the C$100 million asset will be realized by the FI manager by a sale of Canadian dollars for U.S. dollars in the spot foreign exchange market two months into the future (see Figure 23–16).

As with bonds, the FI can buy put options on foreign currency futures contracts to hedge this currency risk. The futures option contracts for foreign currencies traded on the Chicago Mercantile Exchange (CME) are shown in Figure 23–13.

www.cmegroup.com

**FIGURE 23–16**
**Hedging FX Risk by Buying a Put Option on Canadian Dollars**

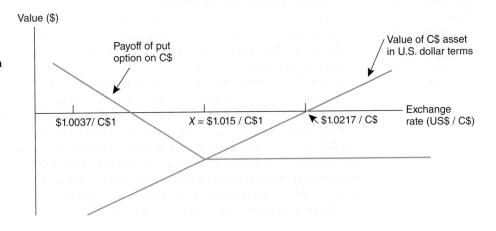

A put position in one foreign currency futures contract with expiration in December 2012 and exercise price of $1.015/C$1 would have cost the FI a premium of $0.0094 per C$1 on September 21, 2012. Since each Canadian dollar futures option contract is C$100,000 in size, the cost would have been $940 per contract. If we ignore the question of basis risk—that is, the imperfect correlation between the U.S.$/C$ exchange rate on the spot and futures in options markets—the optimal number of futures options purchased would be:

$$\frac{\text{C\$100,000,000}}{\text{C\$100,000}} = 1,000 \text{ contracts}$$

with a total premium cost of $940,000.

---

**Concept Questions**

1. What is the difference between options on foreign currency and options on foreign currency futures?
2. If an FI has to hedge a $5 million liability exposure in Swiss francs (SF), what options should it purchase to hedge this position? Using Figure 23–13, how many contracts of Swiss franc futures options should it purchase (assuming no basis risk) if it wants to hedge against the SF falling in value against the dollar given a current exchange rate of $1.0755/SF1 (or 0.9298 SF/$1). (Buy 37.192 call options on SF futures.)

---

# HEDGING CREDIT RISK WITH OPTIONS

Options also have a potential use in hedging the credit risk of an FI. Relative to their use in hedging interest rate risk, option use to hedge credit risk is a relatively new phenomenon. In June 2012, commercial bank holdings of credit options totaled $118 billion, which represented less than 0.9 percent of all credit derivatives outstanding. Although FIs are always likely to be willing to bear some credit risk as part of the intermediation process (i.e., exploit their comparative advantage to bear such risk), options may allow them to modify that level of exposure selectively. In Chapter 22 we stated that an FI could seek an appropriate credit risk hedge by selling credit forward contracts. Rather than using credit forwards to hedge, an FI has at least two alternative credit option derivatives with which it can hedge its on-balance-sheet credit risk.

**credit spread call option**
A call option whose payoff increases as a yield spread increases above some stated exercise spread.

A **credit spread call option** is a call option whose payoff increases as the (default) risk premium or yield spread on a specified benchmark bond of the borrower increases above some exercise spread, *S*. An FI concerned that the risk on a loan to that borrower will increase can purchase a credit spread call option to hedge the increased credit risk.

Figure 23–17 illustrates the change in the FI's capital value and its payoffs from the credit spread call option as a function of the credit spread. As the credit spread increases on an FI's loan to a borrower, the value of the loan, and consequently the FI's net worth, decreases. However, if the credit risk characteristics of the benchmark bond (i.e., change in credit spread) are the same as those on the FI's loan, the loss of net worth on the balance sheet is offset with a gain from the credit spread call option. If the required credit spread on the FI's loan decreases (perhaps because the credit quality of the borrower improves over the loan period), the value of the FI's loan and net worth increases (up to some maximum value), but

**FIGURE 23–17**
**Buying Credit**
**Spread Call Options**
**to Hedge Credit**
**Risk**

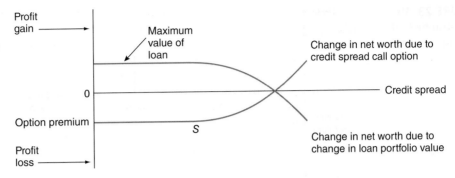

**FIGURE 23–18**
**Buying a Digital**
**Default Option to**
**Hedge Credit Risk**

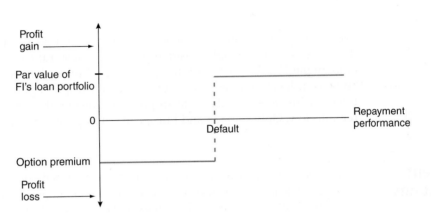

the credit spread call option will expire out of the money. As a result, the FI will suffer a maximum loss equal to the required (call) premium on the credit option, which will be offset by the market value gain of the loan in the portfolio (which is reflected in a positive increase in the FI's net worth).

**digital default**
**option**
An option that pays
the par value of a
loan in the event of
default.

A **digital default option** is an option that pays a stated amount in the event of a loan default (the extreme case of increased credit risk). As shown in Figure 23–18, the FI can purchase a default option covering the par value of a loan (or loans) in its portfolio. In the event of a loan default, the option writer pays the FI the par value of the defaulted loans. If the loans are paid off in accordance with the loan agreement, however, the default option expires unexercised. As a result, the FI will suffer a maximum loss on the option equal to the premium (cost) of buying the default option from the writer (seller).

## HEDGING CATASTROPHE RISK WITH CALL SPREAD OPTIONS

www.cmegroup.com

**catastrophe (CAT)**
**call spread**
A call option on the
loss ratio incurred in
writing catastrophe
insurance with a
capped (or maximum)
payout.

In 1993 the Chicago Board of Trade (CBOT) introduced **catastrophe (CAT) call spread** options to hedge the risk of unexpectedly high losses being incurred by property–casualty insurers as a result of catastrophes such as hurricanes. The basic idea can be seen in Figure 23–19. For an option premium, the insurer can hedge a range of loss ratios that may occur (remember that the loss ratio is the ratio of losses incurred divided by premiums written). In Figure 23–19, the insurer buys a call spread to hedge the risk that the loss ratio on its catastrophe insurance may be anywhere between 50 percent and 80 percent. If the loss ratio ends up below 50 percent (perhaps because of a mild hurricane season), the insurance company

**FIGURE 23–19**
**Catastrophe Call**
**Spread Options**

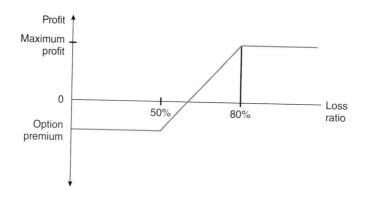

loses the option premium. For loss ratios between 50 percent and 80 percent, it receives an increasingly positive payoff. For loss ratios above 80 percent, the amount paid by the writers of the option to the buyer (the insurer) is capped at the 80 percent level. Studies have found that catastrophe options can be used effectively by insurers to hedge catastrophe risk. Despite this, trading in CAT options remains low. Only Canada and European CAT options still trade on the CBOT.

| | |
|---|---|
| **Concept Questions** | 1. What is the difference between a credit spread call option and a digital default option? |
| | 2. What is the difference between the payoff on the catastrophe call spread option in Figure 23–19 and the payoff of a standard call option on a stock? |

# CAPS, FLOORS, AND COLLARS

**cap**
A call option on interest rates, often with multiple exercise dates.

**floor**
A put option on interest rates, often with multiple exercise dates.

**collar**
A position taken simultaneously in a cap and a floor.

Caps, floors, and collars are derivative securities that have many uses, especially in helping an FI hedge interest rate risk exposure as well as risk unique to its individual customers. Buying a **cap** means buying a call option or a succession of call options on interest rates. Specifically, if interest rates rise above the cap rate, the seller of the cap—usually a bank—compensates the buyer—for example, another FI—in return for an up-front premium. As a result, buying an interest rate cap is like buying insurance against an (excessive) increase in interest rates. A cap agreement can have one or many exercise dates.

Buying a **floor** means buying a put option on interest rates. If interest rates fall below the floor rate, the seller of the floor compensates the buyer in return for an up-front premium. As with caps, floor agreements can have one or many exercise dates.

A **collar** occurs when an FI takes a simultaneous position in a cap and a floor, such as buying a cap and selling a floor. The idea here is that the FI wants to hedge itself against rising rates but wants to finance the cost of the cap. One way to do this is to sell a floor and use the premiums on the floor to pay the premium on the purchase of the cap. Thus, these three over-the-counter instruments are special cases of options; FI managers use them like bond options and bond futures options to hedge the interest rate risk of an FI's portfolios.

In general, FIs purchase interest rate caps if they are exposed to losses when interest rates rise. Usually, this happens if they are funding assets with floating-rate liabilities such as notes indexed to LIBOR (or some other cost of funds) and they have fixed-rate assets or they are net long in bonds, or—in a macrohedging context—their duration gap is $D_A - kD_L > 0$. By contrast, FIs purchase floors when they have fixed costs of debt and have variable rates (returns) on assets, are net short in bonds, or $D_A - kD_L < 0$. Finally, FIs purchase collars when they are concerned about excessive volatility of interest rates and to finance cap or floor positions.

## Caps

Under a cap agreement, in return for paying an up-front premium, the seller of the cap stands ready to compensate the buying FI whenever the interest rate index defined under the agreement is above the cap rate on the dates specified under the cap agreement. This effectively converts the cost of the FI's floating-rate liabilities into fixed-rate liabilities.

| | |
|---|---|
| **EXAMPLE 23–3**<br><br>*Illustration of a Cap Used to Hedge Interest Rate Risk* | Assume that an FI buys a 9 percent cap at time 0 from another FI with a notional face value of $100 million. The cap agreement specifies exercise dates at the end of the second year and the end of the third year. That is, the cap has a three-year maturity from initiation until the final exercise dates, with exercise dates at the end of year 2 and year 3.[10]<br><br>Thus, the buyer of the cap would demand two cash payments from the seller of the cap if rates lie above 9 percent at the end of the second year and at the end of the third year on the cap exercise dates. In practice, cap exercise dates usually closely correspond to payment dates on liabilities, for example, coupon dates on floating-rate notes. Consider one possible scenario in Figure 23–20.<br><br>In Figure 23–20, the seller of the cap has to pay the buyer of the cap the amount shown in Table 23–1. In this scenario, the cap-buying FI would receive $3 million (undiscounted) over the life of the cap to offset any rise in the cost of liability funding or market value losses on its bond/asset portfolio. However, the interest rates in Figure 23–20 are only one possible scenario. Consider the possible path to interest rates in Figure 23–21. In this interest scenario, rates fall below 9 percent by the end of the second year to 8 percent and by the end of the third year to 7 percent on the cap exercise dates. Thus, the cap seller makes no payments. |

**FIGURE 23–20**
**Hypothetical Path of Interest Rates**

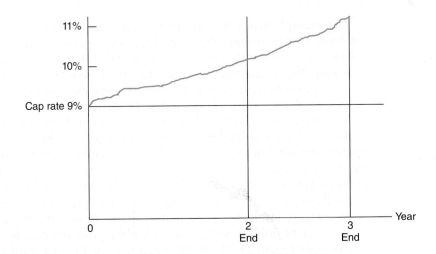

[10] There is no point exercising the option at the end of year 1 (i.e., having three exercise dates) since interest rates for year 1 are set at the beginning of that year and are contractually set throughout. As a result, the FI does not bear interest rate uncertainty until the end of year 1 (i.e., interest uncertainty exists only in years 2 and 3).

**TABLE 23–1**
Payments under
the Cap

| End of Year | Cap Rate | Actual Interest Rate | Interest Differential | Payment by Seller to Buyer |
|---|---|---|---|---|
| 2 | 9% | 10% | 1% | $1 million |
| 3 | 9 | 11 | 2 | $2 million |
| Total | | | | $3 million |

**FIGURE 23–21**
Hypothetical Path
of Interest Rates

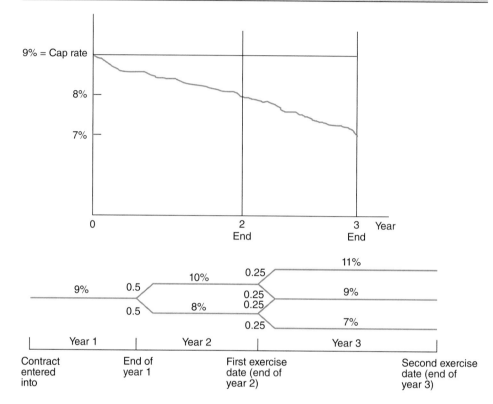

**FIGURE 23–22**
Interest Rate Cap
with a 9 Percent
Cap Rate

This example makes it clear that buying a cap is similar to buying a call option on interest rates in that when the option expires out of the money, because the interest rate is below the cap level, the cap seller makes no payments to the buyer. Conceptually, buying this cap is like buying a complex call option on an interest rate or a put option on a bond price with a single exercise price or interest rate and two exercise dates: the end of year 2 and the end of year 3.

The problem for the FI manager is to calculate the fair value of this 9 percent cap in the face of interest rate uncertainty. In particular, the FI manager does not know whether interest rates will be 10 percent at the end of year 2 or 8 percent. Similarly, the manager does not know whether interest rates will be 11 percent or 7 percent at the end of year 3. Nevertheless, to buy interest rate risk insurance in the form of a cap, the manager has to pay an up-front fee or premium to the seller of the cap. Next, we solve for the fair value of the cap premium in the framework of the binomial model introduced earlier to calculate the premium on a bond option.

Consider Figure 23–22, the binomial tree for the cap contract entered into at time 0 (the beginning of year 1). The cap can be exercised at the end of the second year and the end of the third year.[11] The current (time 0) value of the cap or the

[11] Interest rates are normally set at the *beginning* of each period and paid at the *end* of each period.

fair cap premium is the sum of the present value of the cap option exercised at the end of year 2 plus the present value of the cap option exercised at the end of year 3:

$$\text{Fair premium} = P = PV \text{ of year 2 option} + PV \text{ of year 3 option}$$

**EXAMPLE 23–4**

*Calculating the Premium on an Interest Rate Cap*

**PV of Year 3 Option**

In year 3, there are three possible interest rate scenarios: 11 percent, 9 percent, and 7 percent. With a cap exercise price of 9 percent and the 9 percent or 7 percent scenarios realized, the cap would have no value to the buyer. In other words, it would expire out of the money. The only interest rate scenario where the cap has exercise value to the buyer at the end of the third year is if rates rise to 11 percent. With rates at 11 percent, the interest differential would be 11 percent minus 9 percent, or 2 percent. But since there is only a 25 percent probability that interest rates will rise to 11 percent in the third year, the expected value of this interest differential is:

$$0.25 \times 2\% = 0.5\%$$

With a $100 million cap, therefore, the expected cash payment at the end of year 3 would be $0.5 million. However, to calculate the fair value of the cap premium in current dollars, the expected cash flow at the end of year 3 has to be discounted back to the present (time 0):

$$PV_2 = \frac{0.5}{(1.09)(1.1)(1.11)} = 0.3757$$

where 9 percent, 10 percent, and 11 percent are the appropriate one-year discount rates for payments in years 1, 2, and 3. Thus, the fair present value of the option at the end of year 3 is 0.3757, or $375,700, given the $100 million face value of the cap.

**PV of Year 2 Option**

In year 2, there are two interest rate scenarios: Interest rates could rise to 10 percent or fall to 8 percent. If rates fall to 8 percent, the 9 percent cap has no value to the buyer. However, if rates rise to 10 percent, this results in a positive interest differential of 1 percent at the end of year 2. However, the expected interest differential is only 0.5 of 1 percent since this is the probability that rates will rise from 9 percent to 10 percent in year 2:

$$0.5 \times 1\% = 0.5\%$$

In dollar terms, with a $100 million cap, the expected value of the cap at the end of year 2 is $0.5 million. To evaluate the time 0 or present value of a cap exercised at the end of time period 2, this expected cash flow has to be discounted back to time 0 using the appropriate one-year discount rates. That is:

$$PV_1 = \frac{0.5}{(1.09)(1.1)} = 0.417$$

or $417,000, given the $100 million face value of the cap. As a result, the fair value of the premium the FI should be willing to pay for this cap is:

$$\begin{aligned} \text{Cap premium} &= PV_2 + PV_3 \\ &= \$417,000 + \$375,700 \\ &= \$792,700 \end{aligned}$$

That is, under the interest rate scenarios implied by this simple binomial model, the FI should pay no more than $792,700, or 0.7927 percent of notional face value, in buying the cap from the seller.

## Floors

A floor is a put option or a collection of put options on interest rates. Here the FI manager who buys a floor is concerned about falling interest rates. Perhaps the FI is funding liabilities at fixed rates and has floating-rate assets, or maybe it is short in some bond position and will lose if it has to cover the position with higher priced bonds after interest rates fall. In a macrohedging sense, the FI could face a duration gap where the duration of assets is less than the leverage-adjusted duration of liabilities ($D_A - kD_L > 0$).

---

**EXAMPLE 23–5**

*Illustration of a Floor Used to Hedge Interest Rate Risk*

Consider the profit from buying a floor depicted in Figure 23–23. In this simple example, the floor is set at 4 percent and the buyer pays an up-front premium to the seller of the floor. While caps can be viewed as buying a complex call option on interest rates, a floor can be viewed as buying a complex put option on interest rates. In our example, the floor has two exercise dates: the end of year 2 and the end of year 3.

If the interest scenario in Figure 23–23 is the actual interest rate path, the payments from the seller to the buyer would be as shown in Table 23–2.

---

Since the buyer of the floor is uncertain about the actual path of interest rates—rates could rise and not fall—such profits are only probabilistic. That is, the buyer would have to use a model similar to the binomial model for caps to calculate the fair up-front premium to be paid for the floor at time 0.

**FIGURE 23–23**
**Interest Rate Floor with a 4 Percent Floor Rate**

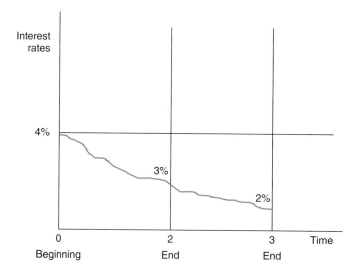

**TABLE 23–2**
**Hypothetical Floor Payments**

| End of Year | Cap Rate | Actual Interest Rate | Interest Differential | Payment by Seller to Buyer |
|---|---|---|---|---|
| 2 | 4% | 3% | 1% | $1 million |
| 3 | 4 | 2 | 2 | $2 million |
| Total | | | | $3 million |

## Collars

FI managers who are very risk averse and overly concerned about the exposure of their portfolios to increased interest rate volatility may seek to protect the FI against such increases. One method of hedging this risk is through buying a cap and a floor together. This is usually called a *collar*. Figure 23–24 illustrates the essential risk-protection features of a collar when an FI buys a 9 percent cap and a 4 percent floor.

The shaded areas in Figure 23–24 show the interest rate payment regions (>9 percent or <4 percent) where the cap or floor is in the money and the buyer potentially receives either a cap or a floor payment from the seller. If interest rates stay in the 4 through 9 percent range, the buyer of the collar receives no compensation from the seller. In addition, the buyer has to pay two up-front premiums: one for the cap and one for the floor to the cap and floor sellers. As is clear, buying a collar is similar to simultaneously buying a complex put and call bond option, or straddle.

An alternative and more common use of a collar is to finance the cost of purchasing a cap. In our earlier example of the $100 million cap, the fair cap premium (*pc*) was $792,700, or 0.7927 percent of the notional face value ($NV_c$) of the cap. That is, the cost (*C*) of the cap is:

$$C = NV_c \times pc$$
$$= \$100,000,000 \times 0.007927$$
$$= \$792,700$$

To purchase the cap, the FI must pay this premium to the cap seller in up-front dollars.

Many large FIs, more exposed to rising interest rates than falling interest rates—perhaps because they are heavily reliant on interest-sensitive sources of liabilities—seek to finance a cap by selling a floor at the same time.[12] In so doing, they generate up-front revenues; this floor premium can finance the cost of the cap

**FIGURE 23–24**
**Payoffs from a Collar**

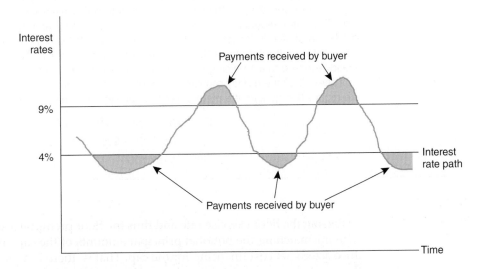

---

[12] In this context, the sale of the floor is like the sale of any revenue-generating product.

purchase or the cap premium. Nevertheless, they give up potential profits if rates fall rather than rise. Indeed, when rates fall, the floor is more likely to be triggered and the FI must compensate the buyer of the floor.

After an FI buys a cap and sells a floor, its net cost of the cap is:

$$C = (NV_c \times pc) - (NV_f \times pf)$$

$$= \text{Cost of cap} - \text{Revenue on floor}$$

where

$NV_f$ = Notional principal of the floor
$pf$ = Premium rate on the floor

---

**EXAMPLE 23–6**

*Calculating the Cost of a Collar*

Suppose that, in Example 23–3, while buying the cap the FI sold a two-year $100 million notional face value floor at a premium of 0.75 percent. The net up-front cost of purchasing the cap is reduced to:

$$C = (\$100,000,000 \times 0.007927) - (\$100,000,000 \times 0.0075) = \$42,700$$

Note that if the FI is willing to raise the floor exercise interest rate, thereby exposing itself to increasing losses if rates fall, it can generate higher premiums on the floor it sells. Like any option, as the exercise price or rate moves from being out of the money, when current rates are above the floor, to being in the money, when current rates are below the floor, the floor buyer would be willing to pay a higher premium to the writer (the FI). Given this, the buyer of the cap could set the floor rate with notional face values of $100 million each so that the floor premium earned by the FI just equals the cap premium paid:

$$C = (\$100,000,000 \times 0.007927) - (\$100,000,000 \times 0.007927)$$

$$= 0$$

When $pc = pf$, the cap buyer–floor seller can reduce the cap's net cost of purchase to zero.

Indeed, if the cap buyer bought a very out-of-the-money cap and sold a very in-the-money floor, as shown in Figure 23–25, the net cost of the cap purchase could actually be negative. In Figure 23–25, the current interest rate is 6 percent while the cap rate is 9 percent. Thus, rates would have to rise at least 3 percent for the cap buyer to receive a payment at the end of year 2. By contrast, the 7 percent floor is already 1 percent above the current 6 percent rate. If rates stay at 6 percent until the end of year 2, the FI seller of the floor is already exposed to a 1 percent notional face value loss in writing the floor.

If the out-of-the-money cap can be bought at a premium of 0.7927 percent, but the in-the-money floor is sold at a premium of 0.95 percent, the (net) cost of the cap purchase is:

$$C = (NV_c \times pc) - (NV_f \times pf)$$

$$= \$792,700 - \$950,000$$

$$= -\$157,300$$

---

Raising the floor exercise rate and thus the floor premium also can be combined with mismatching the notional principal amounts of the cap and the floor to produce a zero net cost financing for the cap. That is, there is no reason why both the floor and cap agreements have to be written against the same notional face values ($NV_c - NV_f = \$100$ million).

**FIGURE 23–25**

In-the-Money Floor and Out-of-the-Money Cap

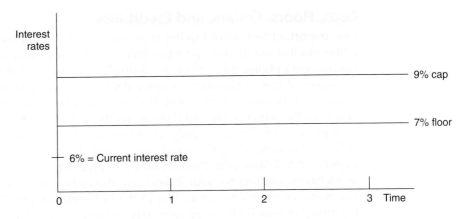

Suppose the out-of-the-money cap can be bought at a premium of 0.7927 percent and the in-the-money floor can be sold at a 0.95 percent premium. An FI manager might want to know what notional principal on the floor (or contract size) is necessary to finance a $100 million cap purchase at zero net up-front cost. That is,

$$C = (NV_c \times pc) - (NV_f \times pf) = 0$$
$$= (\$100,000,000 \times 0.007927) - (NV_f \times 0.0095) = 0$$

Solving for $NV_f$:

$$NV_f = \frac{(\$100,000,000 \times 0.007927)}{0.0095} = \frac{(NV_c \times pc)}{pf}$$
$$= \$83.44 \text{ million}$$

Clearly, the higher premium rate on the floor requires a lower notional face value floor amount to generate sufficient premium income up-front to finance the cap's purchase. In general, to fund fully the cap purchase ($C = 0$), the relationship between premium rates and notional value should be:[13]

$$\frac{NV_f}{NV_c} = \frac{pc}{pf}$$

---

[13] As shown earlier in this chapter, it is possible to macrohedge a gap position of an FI using put options. A cap is economically equivalent to a call option on an interest rate or a put option on a bond. However, the major difference is that the cap is a complex option in that there are multiple exercise dates. For example, in our simple model of the determination of the fair cap premium, there were two exercise dates: the end of year 2 and the end of year 3. However, we showed that we could decompose the value of the cap as a whole into the value of the (end of) year 2 option and the value of the (end of) year 3 option. Both of these options would have their own deltas ($\delta$) because of the different maturity of these options. Thus, the change in the total value of the cap ($\Delta C$) position would equal:

$$\Delta C = N_c \times \{[\delta_1 \times (D_1 \times B)] + [\delta_2 \times (D_2 \times B)]\} \times \Delta R/(1 + R)$$

where $N_c$—the number of $100,000 cap contracts—is calculated by solving:

$$N_c = \frac{[D_A - kD_L] \times S}{\{[\delta_1 \times (D_1 \times B)] + [\delta_2 \times (D_2 \times B)]\}}$$

## Caps, Floors, Collars, and Credit Risk

One important feature of buying caps, collars, and floors for hedging purposes is the implied credit risk exposure involved that is absent for exchange-traded futures and options. Since these are multiple exercise over-the-counter contracts, the buyer of these instruments faces a degree of counterparty credit risk. To see this, consider the cap example just discussed. Suppose, at the beginning of the second year, the writer of the cap defaults on the $1 million due if interest rates rose to 10 percent. The buyer not only would fail to collect on this in-the-money option at the end of year 2, but also would lose a potential payment at the end of year 3. In general, a default year 2 would mean that the cap buyer would have to find a replacement contract for year 2 (and any succeeding years thereafter) at the cap rate terms or premiums prevailing at the beginning of year 2 rather than at the beginning of year 1. These cap rates may be far less favorable than those under the original cap contract (reflecting the higher interest rate levels of year 2). In addition, the buyer could incur further transaction and contracting costs in replacing the original contract. Because of the often long-term nature of cap agreements, occasionally extending up to 10 years, only FIs that are the most creditworthy are likely to be able to write and run a large cap/floor book without the backing of external guarantees such as standby letters of credit. As we discuss in the next chapter, swaps have similar credit risk exposures due to their long-run contractual nature and their OTC origination.

| | |
|---|---|
| **Concept Questions** | 1. In Example 23–4 suppose that in year 3 the highest and lowest rates were 12 percent and 6 percent instead of 11 percent and 7 percent. Calculate the fair premium on the cap. ($975,515) |
| | 2. Assume two exercise dates at the end of year 2 and the end of year 3. Suppose the FI buys a floor of 4 percent at time 0. The binomial tree suggests that rates at the end of year 2 could be 3 percent ($p = 0.5$) or 5 percent ($p = 0.5$) and at the end of year 3 rates could be 2 percent ($p = 0.25$), 4 percent ($p = 0.5$), or 6 percent ($p = 0.25$). Calculate the fair value of the floor premium. Assume the notional face value of the floor is $100 million. ($924,400) |
| | 3. An FI buys a $100 million cap at a premium of 0.75 percent and sells a floor at a 0.85 percent premium. What size floor should be sold so that the net cost of the cap purchase is zero? ($88,235,294) |
| | 4. Why are only the most creditworthy FIs able to write a large cap/floor book without external guarantees? |

## Summary

In this chapter we evaluated a wide range of option-type contracts that are available to FI managers to hedge the risk exposures of individual assets, portfolios of assets, and the balance sheet gap itself. We illustrated how these options—some of which are exchange traded and some of which are sold OTC—can hedge the interest rate, credit, FX, and catastrophe risks of FIs. In particular, we described how the unique nature of the asymmetric payoff function of option-type contracts often makes them more attractive to FIs than other hedging instruments, such as forwards and futures.

**Questions and Problems**

1. How does using options differ from using forward or futures contracts?
2. What is a call option?
3. What must happen to interest rates for the purchaser of a call option on a bond to make money? How does the writer of the call option make money?
4. What is a put option?
5. What must happen to interest rates for the purchaser of a put option on a bond to make money? How does the writer of the put option make money?
6. Consider the following:
   a. What are the two ways to use call and put options on T-bonds to generate positive cash flows when interest rates decline? Verify your answer with a diagram.
   b. Under what balance sheet conditions would an FI use options on T-bonds to hedge its assets and/or liabilities against interest rate declines?
   c. Is it more appropriate for FIs to hedge against a decline in interest rates with long calls or short puts?
7. In each of the following cases, identify what risk the manager of an FI faces and whether that risk should be hedged by buying a put or a call option.
   a. A commercial bank plans to issue CDs in three months.
   b. An insurance company plans to buy bonds in two months.
   c. A thrift plans to sell Treasury securities next month.
   d. A U.S. bank lends to a French company with the loan payable in euros.
   e. A mutual fund plans to sell its holding of stock in a British company.
   f. A finance company has assets with a duration of six years and liabilities with a duration of 13 years.
8. Consider an FI that wishes to use bond options to hedge the interest rate risk in the bond portfolio.
   a. How does writing call options hedge the risk when interest rates decrease?
   b. Will writing call options fully hedge the risk when interest rates increase? Explain.
   c. How does buying put options reduce the losses on the bond portfolio when interest rates rise?
   d. Diagram the purchase of a bond call option against the combination of a bond investment and the purchase of a bond put option.
9. What are the regulatory reasons why FIs seldom write options?
10. What are the problems of using the Black-Scholes option pricing model to value bond options? What is meant by the term *pull-to-par?*
11. An FI has purchased a two-year, $1,000 par value zero-coupon bond for $867.43. The FI will hold the bond to maturity unless it needs to sell the bond at the end of one year for liquidity purposes. The current one-year interest rate is 7 percent and the one-year rate in one year is forecast to be either 8.04 percent or 7.44 percent with equal likelihood. The FI wishes to buy a put option to protect itself against a capital loss if the bond needs to be sold in one year.
    a. What is the yield on the bond at the time of purchase?
    b. What is the market-determined, implied one-year rate one year before maturity?
    c. What is the expected sale price if the bond has to be sold at the end of one year?
    d. Diagram the bond prices over the two-year horizon.
    e. If the FI buys a put option with an exercise price equal to your answer in part (c), what will be its value at the end of one year?

f. What should be the premium on the put option today?

g. Diagram the value of the put option on the two-year, zero-coupon bond.

h. What would have been the premium on the option if the one-year interest rates at the end of one year were expected to be 8.14 percent and 7.34 percent?

12. A pension fund manager anticipates the purchase of a 20-year, 8 percent coupon Treasury bond at the end of two years. Interest rates are assumed to change only once every year at year-end, with an equal probability of a 1 percent increase or a 1 percent decrease. The Treasury bond, when purchased in two years, will pay interest semiannually. Currently the Treasury bond is selling at par.

a. What is the pension fund manager's interest rate risk exposure?

b. How can the pension fund manager use options to hedge this interest rate risk exposure?

c. What prices are possible on the 20-year T-bonds at the end of year 1 and year 2?

d. Diagram the prices over the two-year period.

e. If options on $100,000, 20-year, 8 percent coupon Treasury bonds (both puts and calls) have a strike price of 101, what are the possible (intrinsic) values of the option position at the end of year 1 and year 2?

f. Diagram the possible option values.

g. What is the option premium? (Use an 8 percent discount factor.)

13. Why are options on interest rate futures contracts preferred to options on cash instruments in hedging interest rate risk?

14. Consider Figure 23–13. What are the prices paid for the following futures option?

a. March T-bond calls at $143.00.

b. March 10-year T-note puts at $151.50.

c. December Eurodollar puts at 99.50 percent.

15. Consider Figure 23–13 again. What happens to the option price of the following?

a. A call when the exercise price increases.

b. A call when the time until expiration increases.

c. A put when the exercise price increases.

d. A put when the time to expiration increases.

16. An FI manager writes a call option on a T-bond futures contract with an exercise price of 11400 at a quoted price of 0–55.

a. What type of opportunities or obligations does the manager have?

b. In what direction must interest rates move to encourage the call buyer to exercise the option?

17. What is the delta of an option ($\delta$)?

18. An FI has a $100 million portfolio of six-year Eurodollar bonds that have an 8 percent coupon. The bonds are trading at par and have a duration of five years. The FI wishes to hedge the portfolio with T-bond options that have a delta of $-0.625$. The underlying long-term Treasury bonds for the option have a duration of 10.1 years and trade at a market value of $96,157 per $100,000 of par value. Each put option has a premium of $3.25 per $100 of face value.

a. How many bond put options are necessary to hedge the bond portfolio?

b. If interest rates increase 100 basis points, what is the expected gain or loss on the put option hedge?

c. What is the expected change in market value on the bond portfolio?

d. What is the total cost of placing the hedge?

e. Diagram the payoff possibilities.

f. How far must interest rates move before the payoff on the hedge will exactly offset the cost of placing the hedge?

g. How far must interest rates move before the gain on the bond portfolio will exactly offset the cost of placing the hedge?

h. Summarize the gain, loss, and cost conditions of the hedge on the bond portfolio in terms of changes in interest rates.

19. Corporate Bank has $840 million of assets with a duration of 12 years and liabilities worth $720 million with a duration of seven years. Assets and liabilities are yielding 7.56 percent. The bank is concerned about preserving the value of its equity in the event of an increase in interest rates and is contemplating a macrohedge with interest rate options. The call and put options have a delta ($\delta$) of 0.4 and $-0.4$, respectively. The price of an underlying T-bond is 104.53125 (104 (104 $^{34}\!/_{64}$)), its duration is 8.17 years, and its yield to maturity is 7.56 percent.

a. What type of option should Corporate Bank use for the macrohedge?

b. How many options should be purchased?

c. What is the effect on the economic value of the equity if interest rates rise 50 basis points?

d. What will be the effect on the hedge if interest rates rise 50 basis points?

e. What will be the cost of the hedge if each option has a premium of $0.875 per $100 of face value?

f. Diagram the economic conditions of the hedge.

g. How much must interest rates move against the hedge for the increased value of the bank to offset the cost of the hedge?

h. How much must interest rates move in favor of the hedge, or against the balance sheet, before the payoff from the hedge will exactly cover the cost of the hedge?

i. Formulate a management decision rule regarding the implementation of the hedge.

20. An FI has a $200 million asset portfolio that has an average duration of 6.5 years. The average duration of its $160 million in liabilities is 4.5 years. Assets and liabilities are yielding 10 percent. The FI uses put options on T-bonds to hedge against unexpected interest rate increases. The average delta ($\delta$) of the put options has been estimated at $-0.3$ and the average duration of the T-bonds is seven years. The current market value of the T-bonds is $96,000.

a. What is the modified duration of the T-bonds if the current level of interest rates is 10 percent?

b. How many put option contracts should the FI purchase to hedge its exposure against rising interest rates? The face value of the T-bonds is $100,000.

c. If interest rates increase 50 basis points, what will be the change in value of the equity of the FI?

d. What will be the change in value of the T-bond option hedge position?

e. If put options on T-bonds are selling at a premium of $1.25 per face value of $100, what is the total cost of hedging using options on T-bonds?

f. Diagram the spot market conditions of the equity and the option hedge.

g. What must be the change in interest rates before the change in value of the balance sheet (equity) will offset the cost of placing the hedge?

h. How much must interest rates change before the profit on the hedge will exactly cover the cost of placing the hedge?

i. Given your answer in part (g), what will be the net gain or loss to the FI?

21. A mutual fund plans to purchase $10 million of 20-year T-bonds in two months. The bonds are yielding 7.68 percent. These bonds have a duration of 11 years. The mutual fund is concerned about interest rates changing over the next two months and is considering a hedge with a two-month option on a T-bond futures contract. Two-month calls with a strike price of 105 are priced at 1–25, and puts of the same maturity and exercise price are quoted at 2–09. The delta of the call is 0.5 and the delta of the put is −0.7. The current price of a deliverable T-bond is $103.2500 per $100 of face value, its duration is nine years, and its yield to maturity is 7.68 percent.

   a. What type of option should the mutual fund purchase?

   b. How many options should it purchase?

   c. What is the cost of those options?

   d. If rates change +/− 50 basis points, what will be the impact on the price of the desired T-bonds?

   e. What will be the effect on the value of the hedge if rates change +/−50 basis points?

   f. Diagram the effects of the hedge and the spot market value of the desired T-bonds.

   g. What must be the change in interest rates to cause the change in value of the purchased T-bonds to exactly offset the cost of placing the hedge?

22. An FI must make a single payment of 500,000 Swiss francs in six months at the maturity of a CD. The FI's in-house analyst expects the spot price of the franc to remain stable at the current $0.80/SF. But as a precaution, the analyst is concerned that it could rise as high as $0.85/SF or fall as low as $0.75/SF. Because of this uncertainty, the analyst recommends that the FI hedge the CD payment using either options or futures. Six-month call and put options on the Swiss franc with an exercise price of $0.80/SF are trading at 4 cents and 2 cents per SF, respectively. A six-month futures contract on the Swiss franc is trading at $0.80/SF.

   a. Should the analyst be worried about the dollar depreciating or appreciating?

   b. If the FI decides to hedge using options, should the FI buy put or call options to hedge the CD payment? Why?

   c. If futures are used to hedge, should the FI buy or sell Swiss franc futures to hedge the payment? Why?

   d. What will be the net payment on the CD if the selected call or put options are used to hedge the payment? Assume the following three scenarios: the spot price in six months will be $0.75, $0.80, or $0.85/SF. Also assume that the options will be exercised.

   e. What will be the net payment if futures had been used to hedge the CD payment? Use the same three scenarios as in part (d).

   f. Which method of hedging is preferable after the fact?

23. An American insurance company issued $10 million of one-year, zero-coupon GICs (guaranteed investment contracts) denominated in Swiss francs at a rate of 5 percent. The insurance company holds no SF-denominated assets and has neither bought nor sold francs in the foreign exchange market.

   a. What is the insurance company's net exposure in Swiss francs?

   b. What is the insurance company's risk exposure to foreign exchange rate fluctuations?

c. How can the insurance company use futures to hedge the risk exposure in part (b)? How can it use options to hedge?

d. If the strike price on SF options is $0.6667/SF and the spot exchange rate is $0.6452/SF, what is the intrinsic value (on expiration) of a call option on Swiss francs? What is the intrinsic value (on expiration) of a Swiss franc put option? (*Note:* Swiss franc futures options traded on the Chicago Mercantile Exchange are set at SF125,000 per contract.)

e. If the June delivery call option premium is 0.32 cent per franc and the June delivery put option is 10.7 cents per franc, what is the dollar premium cost per contract? Assume that today's date is April 15.

f. Why is the call option premium lower than the put option premium?

24. An FI has made a loan commitment of SF10 million that is likely to be taken down in six months. The current spot exchange rate is $0.60/SF.

a. Is the FI exposed to the dollar depreciating or the dollar appreciating? Why?

b. If the FI decides to hedge using SF futures, should it buy or sell SF futures?

c. If the spot rate six months from today is $0.64/SF, what dollar amount is needed in six months if the loan is drawn?

d. A six-month SF futures contract is available for $0.61/SF. What is the net amount needed at the end of six months if the FI has hedged using the SF10 million of futures contracts? Assume that futures prices are equal to spot prices at the time of payment, that is, at maturity.

e. If the FI decides to use options to hedge, should it purchase call or put options?

f. Call and put options with an exercise price of $0.61/SF are selling for $0.02 and $0.03 per SF, respectively. What would be the net amount needed by the FI at the end of six months if it had used options instead of futures to hedge this exposure?

25. What is a credit spread call option?

26. What is a digital default option?

27. How do the cash flows to the lender for a credit spread call option hedge differ from the cash flows for a digital default option?

28. What is a catastrophe call spread option? How do the cash flows of this option affect the buyer of the option?

29. What are caps? Under what circumstances would the buyer of a cap receive a payoff?

30. What are floors? Under what circumstances would the buyer of a floor receive a payoff?

31. What are collars? Under what circumstances would an FI use a collar?

32. How is buying a cap similar to buying a call option on interest rates?

33. Under what balance sheet circumstances would it be desirable to sell a floor to help finance a cap? When would it be desirable to sell a cap to help finance a floor?

34. Use the following information to price a three-year collar by purchasing an in-the-money cap and writing an out-of-the-money floor. Assume a binomial options pricing model with an equal probability of interest rates increasing 2 percent or decreasing 2 percent per year. Current rates are 7 percent, the cap rate is 7 percent, and the floor rate is 4 percent. The notional value is $1 million. All interest payments are annual payments as a percent of notional value, and all payments are made at the end of year 2 and the end of year 3.

35. Use the following information to price a three-year collar by purchasing an out-of-the-money cap and writing an in-the-money floor. Assume a binomial options pricing model with an equal probability of interest rates increasing 2 percent or decreasing 2 percent per year. Current rates are 4 percent, the cap rate is 7 percent, and the floor rate is 4 percent. The notional value is $1 million. All interest payments are annual payments as a percent of notional value, and all payments are made at the end of year 2 and the end of year 3.

36. Contrast the total cash flows associated with the collar position in question 34 against the collar in question 35. Do the goals of FIs that utilize the collar in question 34 differ from those that put on the collar in question 35? If so, how?

37. An FI has purchased a $200 million cap of 9 percent at a premium of 0.65 percent of face value. A $200 million floor of 4 percent is also available at a premium of 0.69 percent of face value.
    a. If interest rates rise to 10 percent, what is the amount received by the FI? What are the net savings after deducting the premium?
    b. If the FI also purchases a floor, what are the net savings if interest rates rise to 11 percent? What are the net savings if interest rates fall to 3 percent?
    c. If, instead, the FI sells (writes) the floor, what are the net savings if interest rates rise to 11 percent? What if they fall to 3 percent?
    d. What amount of floors should the FI sell to compensate for its purchase of caps, given the above premiums?

38. What credit risk exposure is involved in buying caps, floors, and collars for hedging purposes?

## Web Question

39. Go to *The Wall Street Journal*'s website at **www.wsj.com**. Find the most recent quote for options on U.S. Treasury futures contracts using the following steps. Click on "Market Data," then under the section titled "COMMODITIES AND FUTURES," click on "Futures Options." Click on "INTEREST RATE" to get closing quotes for options on U.S. Treasury futures contracts. What is the reported level of trading for calls and puts on these options?

# Integrated Mini Case

## HEDGING INTEREST RATE RISK WITH FUTURES VERSUS OPTIONS

On January 4, 2015, an FI has the following balance sheet (rates = 10 percent):

| Assets | | | Liabilities/Equity | | |
|---|---|---|---|---|---|
| A | 200 m | $D_A$ = 6 years | L | 170 m | $D_L$ = 4 years |
| | | | E | 30 m | |

DGAP = $[6 - (170/200)4] = 2.6$ years $> 0$

The FI manager thinks rates will increase by 0.75 percent in the next three months. If this happens, the equity value will change by:

$$\Delta E = -[6 - \frac{170}{200}(4)]200m\frac{0.0075}{1.10} = -\$3,545,455$$

The FI manager will hedge this interest rate risk with either futures contracts or option contracts. If the FI uses futures, it will select June T-bonds to hedge. The duration on the T-bonds underlying the contract is 14.5 years, and the T-bonds are selling at a price of $114.34375 per $100 or $114,343.75. T-bond futures rates, currently 9 percent, are expected to increase by 1.25 percent over the next three months.

If the FI uses options, it will buy puts on 15-year T-bonds with a June maturity, an exercise price of 113, and an option premium of $1^{36}\!/_{64}$ percent. The spot price on the T-bond underlying the option is $135.71875 per $100. The duration on the T-bonds underlying the options is 14.5 years, and the delta of the put options is $-0.75$. Managers expect these T-bond rates to increase by 1.24 percent from 7.875 percent in the next three months.

If by April 4, 2015, balance sheet rates increase by 0.8 percent, futures rates by 1.4 percent, and T-bond rates underlying the option contract by 1.30 percent, would the FI have been better off using the futures contract or the option contract as its hedge instrument?

If by April 4, 2015, balance sheet rates actually fall by 0.75 percent, futures rates fall by 1.05 percent, and T-bond rates underlying the option contract fall by 1.24 percent, would the FI have been better off using the futures contract or the option contract as its hedge instrument?

## Appendix 23A: Microhedging with Options

View Appendix 23A at the website for this textbook (**www.mhhe.com/saunders8e**).

# Swaps

## INTRODUCTION

**swap**
An agreement
between two parties
to exchange assets or
a series of cash flows
for a specific period
of time at a specified
interval.

A **swap** is an agreement between two parties (called *counterparties*) to exchange specified periodic cash flows in the future based on some underlying instrument or price (e.g., a fixed or floating rate on a bond or note). Like forward, futures, and option contracts, swaps allow firms to better manage their interest rate, foreign exchange, and credit risks. However, swaps can also result in large losses. At the heart of the financial crisis in 2008–09 were derivative securities, mainly credit swaps, held by financial institutions. Losses on these derivatives led to the failure or near failure of some of the largest FIs in the United States (e.g., Lehman Brothers, Washington Mutual, and Merrill Lynch), the federal takeover of mortgage giants Fannie Mae and Freddie Mac and insurance giant AIG, and the near collapse of the world's financial system. More recently, in 2012 J.P. Morgan lost $5 billion on credit default swap contracts it held in its trading portfolio. Using the credit default swap (CDS) contracts as a bet that the U.S. economy would improve, the massive losses occurred when the markets moved against this bet.

Swaps were first introduced in the early 1980s, and the market for swaps has grown enormously. The notional value of swap contracts outstanding of U.S. commercial banks was $134.5 trillion in 2012 (see Chapter 22), and worldwide over $454.0 trillion in swap contracts were outstanding. Commercial banks and investment banks are major participants in the market as dealers, traders, and users for proprietary hedging purposes. Insurance companies have more recently adopted hedging strategies using swaps, and their interest in this market is growing quickly. A swap dealer can act as an intermediary or third party by putting a swap together and/or creating an over-the-counter (OTC) secondary market for swaps for a fee.

Even before the financial crisis, the massive growth of the swap market raised regulatory concerns regarding the credit risk exposures of banks engaging in this market. This growth was one of the motivations behind the introduction of the Bank for International Settlements (BIS)–sponsored risk-based capital adequacy reforms described in Chapter 20. In addition, the enormous sums of money in the swap markets means that large events such as problems in the credit default swap markets can have implications for the global financial system. For example, in the late 2000s, FIs such as Lehman Brothers and AIG had written and (in the case of AIG) insured billions of dollars of CDS contracts. When mortgages underlying these contracts fell drastically in value, CDS writers found themselves unable to make good on their promised payments to CDS holders. The result was a significant increase in risk and decrease in profits for the FIs that had purchased these CDS contracts. To prevent a massive collapse of the financial system, the federal government had to step in and bail out several of these FIs. The CDS case demonstrates the potentially devastating problems the swap market can create for FIs as well as the financial system as a whole.

The five generic types of swaps, in order of their quantitative importance, are interest rate swaps, currency swaps, credit swaps, commodity swaps, and equity swaps.[1] While the instrument underlying the swap may change, the basic principle of a swap agreement is the same in that there is a restructuring of asset or liability cash flows in a preferred direction by the transacting parties. Next, we consider the role of the two major generic types of swaps—interest rate and currency—in hedging FI risk. We then go on to examine the newest and fastest growing type of swap: the credit swap.

# SWAP MARKETS

In some ways a swap is similar to a forward or futures contract. That is, a forward or futures contract requires delivery or taking delivery of some commodity or financial security at a specified time in the future at a price specified at the time of origination. In a swap, each party promises to deliver and/or receive a prespecified series of payments at specific intervals over a specified time horizon. In this way, a swap can be considered to be the same as a series of forward or futures contracts. Although similar in many ways, swaps are different from other derivative securities. First, a swap can be viewed as a portfolio of forward contracts with different maturity dates. Since cash flows on forward contracts are symmetric, the same can be said of swaps. This is in contrast to options, whose cash flows are asymmetric (truncated either on the positive or negative side depending upon the position). Second, the introduction of a swap dealer or intermediary—which stands between the two swap parties—can reduce the credit risk exposure and the information and monitoring costs that are associated with a portfolio of individual forward contracts. Indeed, most swaps are intermediated through a third-party dealer. Third, while futures and options are marked to market continuously and swaps are marked to market at coupon payment dates, forward contracts are settled only upon delivery (at maturity). Therefore, the credit risk exposure is greatest under a forward contract, where no third party guarantor exists as in options (the options clearing corporation for exchange-traded options) and swaps (the swap intermediary). Fourth, transactions costs are highest for the option (the nonrefundable option premium), next for the swap (the swap intermediary's fee), and finally for the forward (which has no up-front payment). Finally, swaps have a longer maturity than any other derivative instruments and provide an additional opportunity for FIs to hedge longer-term positions at lower cost.

Swap transactions are generally heterogeneous in terms of maturities, indexes used to determine payments, and timing of payments—there is no standardized contract. Commercial and investment banks have evolved as the major swap dealers, mainly because of their close ties to the financial markets and their specialized skills in assessing credit risk. Each swap market dealer manages a portfolio of swaps and, as a result, can diversify some of the swap risk exposure away. Swap dealers exist to serve the function of keeping the swap market liquid by locating

---

[1] There are also *swaptions,* which are options to enter into a swap agreement at some preagreed contract terms (e.g., a fixed rate of 10 percent) at some time in the future in return for the payment of an up-front premium.

or matching counterparties or, in many cases, taking one side of the swap themselves. In a direct swap between two counterparties, each party must find another party having a mirror image financing requirement—for example, a financial institution in need of swapping fixed-rate payments (for floating-rate payments), made quarterly for the next 10 years on $25 million in liabilities must find a counterparty in need of swapping $25 million in floating-rate payments (for fixed-rate payments) made quarterly for the next 10 years. Without swap dealers, the search costs of finding such counterparties to a swap can be significant.

Swap dealers also generally guarantee swap payments over the life of the contract. If one of the counterparties defaults on a direct swap, the other counterparty is no longer adequately hedged against risk and may have to replace the defaulted swap with a new swap at less favorable terms (so-called replacement risk). By booking or engaging in a swap through a swap dealer as the intermediary, a default by one counterparty will generally not affect the other counterparty since the swap dealer incurs any costs associated with the default by replacing the defaulting party on the same terms as the original swap.[2] However, if an extreme amount of defaults occurs such that the swap dealer cannot honor the terms of the swap agreement, both counterparties are exposed to risk. Such was the case with credit default swaps written by AIG in 2008. At the time, AIG had more than $440 billion in CDS contracts outstanding. FIs all over the world bought CDS protection from AIG. A major customer included Lehman Brothers. When Lehman declared bankruptcy on September 15, 2008, AIG was exposed to $9 billion in losses on CDS contracts with Lehman. This exposure was so large that AIG could not cover or meet all of the CDS obligations, and many FIs had to buy replacement coverage at dramatically higher swap rates.

# INTEREST RATE SWAPS

**interest rate swap**
An exchange of fixed interest payments for floating interest payments by two counterparties.

By far the largest segment of the global swap market is comprised of **interest rate swaps.** Conceptually, an interest rate swap is a succession of forward contracts on interest rates arranged by two parties.[3] As such, it allows an FI to put in place a long-term hedge sometimes for as long as 15 years. This hedge reduces the need to roll over contracts if reliance had been placed on futures or forward contracts to achieve such long-term hedges.

**swap buyer**
By convention, makes the fixed-rate payments in an interest rate swap transaction.

In a swap, the **swap buyer** agrees to make a number of fixed interest rate payments on periodic settlement dates to the **swap seller.** The seller of the swap in turn agrees to make floating-rate payments to the swap buyer on the same periodic settlement dates. The fixed-rate side—by convention, the swap buyer—generally has a comparative advantage in making fixed-rate payments, while the floating-rate side—by convention, the swap seller—generally has a comparative advantage in making variable or floating-rate payments. In undertaking this transaction, the FI that is the fixed-rate payer is seeking to transform the variable-rate nature of its liabilities into fixed-rate liabilities to better match the fixed returns earned on its assets. Meanwhile, the FI that is the variable-rate payer seeks to turn its fixed-rate liabilities into variable-rate liabilities to better match the variable returns on its assets.

**swap seller**
By convention, makes the floating-rate payments in an interest rate swap.

---

[2] The fee or spread charged by the swap dealer to each party in a swap incorporates this credit risk.
[3] For example, a four-year swap with annual swap dates involves four net cash flows between the parties to a swap. This is essentially similar to arranging four forward contracts: a one-year, a two-year, a three-year, and a four-year contract.

**TABLE 24–1**
Balance Sheets of
Swap Participants

| Assets | | Liabilities | |
|---|---|---|---|
| **Panel A: Money Center Bank's Balance Sheet (Swap Seller)** | | | |
| C&I loans (rate indexed to LIBOR) = | $100 million | Medium-term notes (coupons fixed) = | $100 million |
| **Panel B: Savings Bank's Balance Sheet (Swap Buyer)** | | | |
| Fixed-rate mortgages = | $100 million | Short-term CDs (one year) = | $100 million |

To explain the role of a swap transaction in hedging FI interest rate risk, we use a simple example. Consider two FIs: The first is a money center bank that has raised $100 million of its funds by issuing four-year, medium-term notes with 10 percent annual fixed coupons rather than relying on short-term deposits to raise funds (see Panel A of Table 24–1). On the asset side of its portfolio, the bank makes commercial and industrial (C&I) loans whose rates are indexed to annual changes in the London Interbank Offered Rate (LIBOR). As we discussed in Chapter 10, FIs currently index most large commercial and industrial loans to either LIBOR or the federal funds rate in the money market.

As a result of having floating-rate loans and fixed-rate liabilities in its asset–liability structure, the money center bank has a negative duration gap: the duration of its assets is shorter than that of its liabilities.

$$D_A - kD_L < 0$$

One way for the bank to hedge this exposure is to shorten the duration or interest rate sensitivity of its liabilities by transforming them into short-term floating-rate liabilities that better match the duration characteristics of its asset portfolio. The bank can make changes either on or off the balance sheet. On the balance sheet, the bank could attract an additional $100 million in short-term deposits that are indexed to the LIBOR rate (say, LIBOR plus 2.5 percent) in a manner similar to its loans. The proceeds of these deposits can be used to pay off the medium-term notes. This reduces the duration gap between the bank's assets and liabilities. Alternatively, the bank could go off the balance sheet and sell an interest rate swap—that is, enter into a swap agreement to make the floating-rate payment side of a swap agreement.

The second party in the swap is a savings bank that has invested $100 million in fixed-rate residential mortgages of long duration. To finance this residential mortgage portfolio, the savings bank has had to rely on short-term certificates of deposit with an average duration of one year (see Panel B of Table 24–1). On maturity, these CDs have to be rolled over at the current market rate.

Consequently, the savings bank's asset-liability balance sheet structure is the reverse of the money center bank's. That is:

$$D_A - kD_L > 0$$

The savings bank could hedge its interest rate risk exposure by transforming the short-term floating-rate nature of its liabilities into fixed-rate liabilities that better match the long-term maturity/duration structure of its assets. On the balance sheet, the savings bank could issue long-term notes with a maturity equal or close to that on the mortgages (at, say, 12 percent). The proceeds of the sale of the notes can be used to pay off the CDs and reduce the duration gap. Alternatively, the savings bank can buy a swap—take the fixed payment side of a swap agreement.

The opposing balance sheet and interest rate risk exposures of the money center bank and the savings bank provide the necessary conditions for an interest rate swap agreement between the two parties. This swap agreement can be arranged directly between the parties. However, it is likely that an FI—another bank or an investment bank—would act as either a broker or an agent, receiving a fee for bringing the two parties together or intermediating fully by accepting the credit risk exposure and guaranteeing the cash flows underlying the swap contract. By acting as a principal as well as an agent, the FI can add a credit risk premium to the fee. However, the credit risk exposure of a swap to an FI is somewhat less than that on a loan (this is discussed later in this chapter). Conceptually, when a third-party FI fully intermediates the swap, that FI is really entering into two separate swap agreements: one with the money center bank and one with the savings banks.

**plain vanilla**
Standard agreement without any special features.

For simplicity, we consider a **plain vanilla** fixed-floating-rate swap where a third-party intermediary acts as a simple broker or agent by bringing together two FIs with opposing interest rate risk exposures to enter into a swap agreement or contract.

---

**EXAMPLE 24–1**

*Expected Cash Flows on an Interest Rate Swap*

Suppose the notional value of a swap is $100 million—equal to the size of the money center bank's medium-term note issue—and the maturity of four years is equal to the maturity of the bank's note liabilities. The annual coupon cost of these note liabilities is 10 percent, and the money center bank's problem is that the variable return on its assets may be insufficient to cover the cost of meeting these coupon payments if market interest rates, and therefore asset returns, *fall*. By comparison, the fixed returns on the savings bank's mortgage asset portfolio may be insufficient to cover the interest cost of its CDs if market rates *rise*. As a result, a feasible swap agreement might dictate that the savings bank send fixed payments of 10 percent per year of the notional $100 million value of the swap to the money center bank to allow the bank to cover fully the coupon interest payments on its note issue. In return, the money center bank sends annual payments indexed to one-year LIBOR to help the savings bank cover the cost of refinancing its one-year renewable CDs. Suppose that one-year LIBOR is currently 8 percent and the money center bank agrees to send annual payments at the end of each year equal to one-year LIBOR plus 2 percent to the savings bank.[4] We depict this fixed-floating-rate swap transaction in Figure 24–1; the expected net financing costs for the FIs are listed in Table 24–2.

As a result of the swap, the money center bank has transformed its four-year, fixed-rate interest payments into variable-rate payments, matching the variability of returns on its assets. Further, through the interest rate swap, the money center bank effectively pays LIBOR plus 2 percent for its financing. Had it gone to the debt market, we assumed that the money center bank would pay LIBOR plus 2.5 percent (a savings of 0.5 percent with the swap). Further, the savings bank has transformed its variable-rate interest payments into fixed-rate payments, plus a "small" variable component (CD rate − LIBOR), similar to those received on its assets. Had it gone to the debt market, we assumed that the savings bank would pay 12 percent (a savings of 4 percent + CD rate − LIBOR with the swap).

---

Note in Example 24–1 that in the absence of default/credit risk, only the money center bank is really fully hedged. This happens because the annual 10 percent payments it receives from the savings bank at the end of each year allow it to meet the promised 10 percent coupon rate payments to its note holders regardless of the

---

[4] These rates implicitly assume that this is the cheapest way each party can hedge its interest rate exposure. For example, LIBOR + 2 percent is the lowest-cost way in which the money center bank can transform its fixed-rate liabilities into floating-rate liabilities.

**FIGURE 24–1**
Fixed-Floating-Rate
Swap

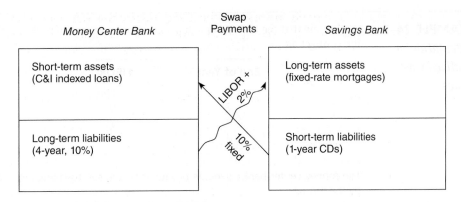

return it receives on its variable-rate assets. By contrast, the savings bank receives variable-rate payments based on LIBOR plus 2 percent. However, it is quite possible that the CD rate the savings bank has to pay on its deposit liabilities does not exactly track the LIBOR-indexed payments sent by the money center bank. That is, the savings bank is subject to basis risk exposure on the swap contract. There are two possible sources of this basis risk. First, movements in CD rates do not exactly match the movements of LIBOR rates over time since the former are determined in the domestic money market and the latter in the Eurodollar market. Second, the credit/default risk premium on the savings bank's CDs may increase over time. Thus, the +2 percent add-on to LIBOR may be insufficient to hedge the savings bank's cost of funds. The savings bank might be better hedged by requiring the money center bank to send it floating payments based on U.S. domestic CD rates rather than LIBOR. To do this, the money center bank would probably require additional compensation since it would then be bearing basis risk. Its asset returns would be sensitive to LIBOR movements, while its swap payments were indexed to U.S. CD rates.

In analyzing this swap, one has to distinguish between how rates should be set at time 0 (now) [that is, how the exchange rate of fixed (10 percent) for floating (LIBOR + 2 percent) is set when the swap agreement is initiated] and the actual realized cash flows on the swap. As we discuss in Appendix 24A to this chapter, the fixed and floating rates set on initiation of the swap depend on the market's expectations of future short-term rates, while realized cash flows on the swap depend on the actual market rates (here, LIBOR) that materialized over the life of the swap contract.

**TABLE 24–2**
**Financing Cost Resulting from Interest Rate Swap (in millions of dollars)**

|  | Money Center Bank | Savings Bank |
|---|---|---|
| Cash outflows from balance sheet financing | $-10\% \times \$100$ | $-(CD) \times \$100$ |
| Cash inflows from swap | $10\% \times \$100$ | $(LIBOR + 2\%) \times \$100$ |
| Cash outflows from swap | $-(LIBOR + 2\%) \times \$100$ | $-10\% \times \$100$ |
| Net cash flows | $-(LIBOR + 2\%) \times \$100$ | $-(8\% + CD\ rate - LIBOR) \times \$100$ |
| Rate available on: |  |  |
| Variable-rate debt | $LIBOR + 2\frac{1}{2}\%$ |  |
| Fixed-rate debt |  | 12% |

**EXAMPLE 24–2**
*Calculation of Realized Cash Flows*

We assume that the realized or actual path of interest rates (LIBOR) over the four-year life of the contract are:

| End of Year | LIBOR |
|:-----------:|:-----:|
| 1 | 9% |
| 2 | 9 |
| 3 | 7 |
| 4 | 6 |

The money center bank's variable payments to the savings bank are indexed to these rates by the formula:

$$(LIBOR + 2\%) \times \$100 \text{ million}$$

By contrast, the fixed annual payments the savings bank makes to the money center bank are the same each year: 10 percent × $100 million. We summarize the actual or realized cash flows among the two parties over the four years in Table 24–3. The savings bank's net gains from the swap in years 1 and 2 are $1 million per year. The enhanced cash flow offsets the increased cost of refinancing its CDs in a higher interest rate environment—that is, the savings bank is hedged against rising rates. By contrast, the money center bank makes net gains on the swap in years 3 and 4 when rates fall. Thus, it is hedged against falling rates. The positive cash flow from the swap offsets the decline in the variable returns on the money center bank's asset portfolio. Overall, the money center bank makes a net dollar gain of $1 million in nominal dollars. Its true realized gain is the present value of this amount.

## Realized Cash Flows on an Interest Rate Swap

**off-market swaps**
Swaps that have nonstandard terms that require one party to compensate another.

Swaps can always be molded or tailored to the needs of the transacting parties as long as one party is willing to compensate the other party for accepting nonstandard terms or **off-market swap** arrangements, usually in the form of an up-front fee or payments. Relaxing a standardized swap can include special interest rate terms and indexes as well as allowing for varying notional values underlying the swap.

**fully amortized mortgages**
Mortgage portfolio cash flows that have a constant payment.

For example, in the case we just considered, the notional value of the swap was fixed at $100 million for each of the four annual swap dates. However, swap notional values can be allowed either to decrease or to increase over a swap contract's life. This flexibility is useful when one of the parties has heavy investments in mortgages (in our example, the savings bank) and the mortgages are **fully amortized,** meaning that the annual and monthly cash flows on the mortgage portfolio reflect repayments of both principal and interest such

**TABLE 24–3**
**Realized Cash Flows on the Swap Agreement (in millions of dollars)**

| End of Year | 1-Year LIBOR | 1-Year LIBOR + 2% | Cash Payment by MCB | Cash Payment by Savings Bank | Net Payment Made by MCB |
|:-----------:|:------------:|:-----------------:|:-------------------:|:----------------------------:|:-----------------------:|
| 1 | 9% | 11% | $11 | $10 | $+1 |
| 2 | 9 | 11 | 11 | 10 | +1 |
| 3 | 7 | 9 | 9 | 10 | −1 |
| 4 | 6 | 8 | 8 | 10 | −2 |
| Total | | | $39 | $40 | $−1 |

that the periodic payment is kept constant. Fixed-rate mortgages normally have larger payments of interest than principal in the early years, with the interest component falling as mortgages approach maturity. One possibility is for the savings bank to enter into a mortgage swap to hedge the amortizing nature of the mortgage portfolio or alternatively to allow the notional value of the swap to decline at a rate similar to the decline in the principal component of the mortgage portfolio.

Another example of a special type of interest rate swap is the inverse floater swap, which was engineered by major FIs as part of structured note financing deals to lower the cost of financing to various government agencies. Such arrangements have resulted in enormous problems for investor groups such as municipal authorities and corporations that are part of the overall swap deal.

A structured note–inverse floater swap arrangement is shown in Figure 24–2. In this arrangement, a government agency issues notes (say, $100 million) to investors with a coupon that is equal to 7 percent minus LIBOR—that is, a (inverse) floating coupon. The novel feature of this coupon is that when market rates fall (and thus LIBOR is low), the coupon received by the investor is large. The government agency then converts this spread liability (7 percent − LIBOR) into a LIBOR liability by entering into a swap with an FI dealer (e.g., J.P. Morgan Chase). In effect, the cost of the $100 million note issue is LIBOR to the agency plus any fees relating to the swap.

The risk of these notes to the investor is very clear. If LIBOR is 2 percent, then the investor will receive coupons of 7 percent − 2 percent = 5 percent, which is an excellent spread return if the investor can borrow at close to LIBOR (or 2 percent in this case). However, consider what happens if interest rates rise. If LIBOR rises from 2 percent to 8 percent, the promised coupon becomes 7 percent − 8 percent = −1 percent. Since negative coupons cannot be paid, the actual coupon paid to the investor is 0 percent. However, if the investor borrowed funds to buy the notes at LIBOR, the cost of funds is 8 percent in this case. Thus, the investor is facing an extremely large negative spread and loss.

## Macrohedging with Swaps

The duration model shown in Chapters 22 and 23 to estimate the optimal number of futures and options contracts to hedge an FI's duration gap also can be applied to estimate the optimal number of swap contracts. For example, an FI manager might wish to know how many 10-year (or 5-year) swap contracts are needed to hedge its overall risk exposure. The optimal notional value of swap contracts should be set so that the gain on swap contracts entered into off the balance sheet just offsets any loss in net worth on the balance sheet when interest rates change.

Assume that an FI (such as a savings bank) has a positive duration gap so that it has positive net worth exposure to rising interest rates:

$$\Delta E = -(D_A - kD_L)A\frac{\Delta R}{1 + R} > 0$$

**FIGURE 24–2**
**Inverse Floater Swap-Structured Note**

As discussed above, the savings bank can seek to hedge by paying fixed and receiving floating payments through an interest rate swap. However, many different maturity swaps are available. As will be shown below, the size of the notional value of the interest rate swaps entered into will depend on the maturity (duration) of the swap contract. Suppose the FI manager chooses to hedge with 10-year swaps.

In terms of valuation, a 10-year swap arrangement can be considered in terms of bond equivalent valuation. That is, the fixed-rate payments on a 10-year swap are formally equivalent to the fixed payments on a 10-year T-bond. Similarly, the floating-rate payments on a 10-year swap with *annual* payments can be viewed as equivalent to floating coupons on a bond where coupons are repriced (to LIBOR) every year. That is, the change in the value of the swap ($\Delta S$) when interest rates rise [$\Delta R/(1 + R)$] will depend on the relative interest sensitivity of 10-year bonds to 1-year bonds, or in duration terms ($D_{10} - D_1$).[5] In general:

$$\Delta S = (D_{fixed} - D_{float}) \times N_S \times \frac{\Delta R}{1 + R}$$

where

$$\Delta S = \text{Change in the market value of the swap contract}$$

$(D_{fixed} - D_{float}) =$ Difference in durations between a government bond that has the same maturity and coupon as the fixed-payment side of the swap and a government bond that has the same duration as the swap-payment interval (e.g., annual floating payments)

$$N_S = \text{Notional value of swap contracts}$$

$$\frac{\Delta R}{1 + R} = \text{Shock to interest rates}$$

Note that as long as $D_{fixed} > D_{float}$, when interest rates rise, the market (present) value of fixed-rate payments will fall by more than the market (present) value of floating-rate payments. In market (or present) value terms, the fixed-rate payers gain when rates rise and lose when rates fall.

To solve for the optimal notional value of swap contracts,[6] we set:

$$\Delta S + \Delta E = 0$$

The gain on swap contracts entered into off the balance sheet just offsets the loss in net worth on the balance sheet when rates rise. Substituting values for $\Delta S$ and $\Delta E$:

$$\left[(D_{fixed} - D_{float}) \times N_S \times \frac{\Delta R}{1 + R}\right] + \left[-(D_A - kD_L) \times A \times \frac{\Delta R}{1 + R}\right] = 0$$

Canceling out the common terms:

$$\left[(D_{fixed} - D_{float}) \times N_S\right] + \left[-(D_A - kD_L) \times A\right] = 0$$

---

[5] Although principal payments on bonds are not swapped on maturity, this does not matter since the theoretical payment and receipt of principal values cancel each other out.

[6] Note that the FI wants to enter swaps to protect itself against rising rates. Thus, it will pay fixed and receive floating. In the context of swap transactions, when an FI pays fixed, it is said to be "buying swaps." Thus, we are solving for the optimal number of swaps contracts the FI should buy in this example.

**TABLE 24–4**
**On- and Off-Balance Sheet Effects of a Swap Hedge**

| | On-Balance Sheet | Off-Balance Sheet |
|---|---|---|
| Begin hedge, $t = 0$ | Equity exposed to impact of rise in interest rates | Sell interest rate swap |
| End hedge, $t = 1$ | Interest rates rise on assets and liabilities by 1% | Buy interest rate swap |

Opportunity loss on balance sheet:

$$\Delta E = -\left[5 - 0.9(3)\right] \times \$100 \, m \times \left[0.01/(1.1)\right]$$
$$= -\$2.09 \text{ million}$$

Gain on interest rate swap:

$$\Delta S = (7 - 1) \times \$38{,}333{,}333 \times \left[0.01/(1.1)\right]$$
$$= \$2.09 \text{ million}$$

Solving for $N_S$:

$$N_S = \frac{(D_A - kD_L) \times A}{D_{fixed} - D_{float}}$$

**EXAMPLE 24–3**
*Calculating the Notional Value of Swaps in a Macrohedge*

Suppose $D_A = 5$, $D_L = 3$, $k = 0.9$, and $A = \$100$ million. Also, assume the duration of a current 10-year, fixed-rate T-bond with the same coupon as the fixed rate on the swap is seven years, while the duration of a floating-rate bond that reprices annually is one year:[7]

$$D_{fixed} = 7 \qquad D_{float} = 1$$

Then:

$$N_S = \frac{(D_A - kD_L) \times A}{D_{fixed} - D_{float}} = \frac{\$230{,}000{,}000}{(7 - 1)} = \$38{,}333{,}333$$

If each swap contract is \$100,000 in size,[8] the number of swap contracts into which the FI should enter will be \$38,333,333/\$100,000 = 383.33, or 383 contracts, rounding down. Table 24–4 summarizes the key features of the hedge assuming that the initial rate on the T-bond is 10 percent and is expected to rise by 1 percent. As shown in Table 24–4, the loss of \$2.09 million in net worth on the balance sheet is exactly offset by a gain off the balance sheet on the swap hedge.

If the FI engaged in a longer-term swap—for example, 15 years—such that $D_{fixed} = 9$ and $D_{float} = 1$, then the notional value of swap contracts would fall to \$230,000,000/(9 − 1) = \$28,750,000. If each swap contract is \$100,000 in size, the FI should enter into 287 swap contracts.

While it may seem logical that fewer contracts are preferable in the sense of saving on fees and other related costs of hedging, this advantage is offset by the fact that longer-term swaps have greater counterparty default or credit risk (discussed later in this chapter).

---

[7] See Chapter 8 for a discussion of the duration on floating-rate bonds.
[8] The notional value of swap contracts can take virtually any size since they are individually tailored OTC contracts.

---

| **Concept Questions** | 1. In Example 24–1, which of the two FIs has its liability costs fully hedged and which is only partially hedged? Explain your answer. |
| --- | --- |
| | 2. What are some nonstandard terms that might be encountered in an off-market swap? |
| | 3. In Example 24–3, what is the notional size of swap contracts if $D_{fixed} = 5$ and swap contracts require payment every six months? ($N_s = \$51{,}111{,}111$) |

---

# CURRENCY SWAPS

**currency swap**
A swap used to hedge against exchange rate risk from mismatched currencies on assets and liabilities.

Just as swaps are long-term contracts that can hedge interest rate risk exposure, they can also be used to hedge currency risk exposures of FIs. The following section considers a simple plain vanilla example of how **currency swaps** can immunize FIs against exchange rate risk when they mismatch the currencies of their assets and liabilities.

## Fixed-Fixed Currency Swaps

Consider the U.S. FI in Panel A of Table 24–5 with all of its fixed-rate assets denominated in dollars. Assume that the dollar-pound exchange rate is fixed at $1.6/£1. It is financing its asset portfolio with a £50 million issue of four-year, medium-term British pound notes that have a fixed annual coupon of 10 percent. By comparison, the U.K. FI in Panel B of Table 24–5 has all its assets denominated in pounds. It is funding those assets with a $80 million issue of four-year, medium-term dollar notes with a fixed annual coupon of 10 percent.

These two FIs are exposed to opposing currency risks. The U.S. FI is exposed to the risk that the dollar will depreciate against the pound over the next four years, making it more costly to cover the annual coupon interest payments and the principal repayment on its pound-denominated CDs. On the other hand, the U.K. FI is exposed to the dollar appreciating against the pound, making it more difficult to cover the dollar coupon and principal payments on its four-year $80 million note issue out of the pound cash flows on its assets.

The FIs can hedge the exposures either on or off the balance sheet. On the balance sheet, the U.S. FI can issue $80 million in four-year, medium-term dollar notes (at, say, 10.5 percent). The proceeds of the sale can be used to pay off the £50 million of four-year, medium-term pound notes. Similarly, the U.K. FI can issue £50 million in four-year, medium-term pound notes (at, say, 10.5 percent), using the proceeds to pay off the $80 million of four-year, medium-term dollar notes. Both FIs have taken actions on the balance sheet so that they are no longer exposed to movements in the exchange rate between the two currencies.

**TABLE 24–5**
**Balance Sheets of Currency Swap Participants**

| Assets | Liabilities |
| --- | --- |
| **Panel A: U.S. FI** | |
| $80 million U.S. loans (4 year) in dollars, 11% | £50 million U.K. CDs (4 year) in pounds, 10% |
| **Panel B: U.K. FI** | |
| £50 million U.K. loans (4 year) in pounds, 11% | $80 million U.S. notes (4 year) in dollars, 10% |

**FIGURE 24–3**
Fixed-Fixed
Pound-Dollar
Currency Swap

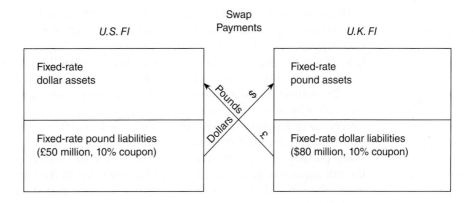

**TABLE 24–6**
**Financing Costs Resulting from the Fixed-Fixed Currency Swap Agreement (in millions of dollars)**

|  | U.S. FI | U.K. FI |
|---|---|---|
| Cash outflows from balance sheet financing | −10% × £50 | −10% × $80 |
| Cash inflows from swap | 10% × £50 | 10% × $80 |
| Cash outflows from swap | −10% × $80 | −10% × £50 |
| Net cash flows | −10% × $80 | −10% × £50 |
| Rate available on: |  |  |
| Dollar-denominated notes | 10.5% |  |
| Pound-denominated notes |  | 10.5% |

**EXAMPLE 24–4**
*Expected Cash Flows on Fixed-Fixed Currency Swap.*

Rather than make changes on the balance sheet, a feasible currency swap into which the U.K. and U.S. FIs can enter is one under which the U.K. FI sends annual payments in pounds to cover the coupon and principal repayments of the U.S. FI's pound note issue, and the U.S. FI sends annual dollar payments to the U.K. FI to cover the interest and principal payments on its dollar note issue.[9] We summarize the currency swap in Figure 24–3 and Table 24–6. As a result of the swap, the U.K. FI transforms fixed-rate dollar payments into fixed-rate pound payments that better match the pound fixed-rate cash flows from its asset portfolio. Similarly, the U.S. FI transforms fixed-rate pound payments into fixed-rate dollar payments that better match the fixed-rate dollar cash flows from its asset portfolio. Further, both FIs transform the pattern of their payments at a lower rate than if they had made changes on the balance sheet. Both FIs effectively obtain financing at 10 percent while hedging against exchange rate risk. Had they gone to the market, we assumed above that they would have paid 10.5 percent to do this. In undertaking this exchange of cash flows, the two parties normally agree on a fixed exchange rate for the cash flows at the beginning of the period.[10] In this example, the fixed exchange rate would be $1.6/£1.

---

[9] In a currency swap, it is usual to include both principal and interest payments as part of the swap agreement. For interest rate swaps, it is usual to include just interest rate payments. The reason for this is that both principal and interest are exposed to FX risk.
[10] As with interest rate swaps, this exchange rate reflects the contracting parties' expectations in regard to future exchange rate movements.

In this example, both liabilities bear a fixed 10 percent interest rate. This is not a necessary requirement for the fixed-fixed currency swap agreement. For example, suppose that the U.S. FI's note coupons were 5 percent per year, while the U.K. FI's note coupons were 10 percent. The swap dollar payments of the U.S. FI would remain unchanged, but the U.K. FI's pound payments would be reduced by £2.5 million (or $4 million) in each of the four years. This difference could be met either by some up-front payment by the U.K. FI to the U.S. FI, reflecting the difference in the present value of the two fixed cash flows, or by annual payments that result in zero net present value differences among the fixed-fixed currency swap participants' payments. Also note that if the exchange rate changed from the rate agreed to in the swap ($1.6/£1), either one or the other side would be losing in the sense that a new swap might be entered into at an exchange rate more favorable to one party. Specifically, if the dollar were to appreciate (rise in value) against the pound over the life of the swap, the agreement would become more costly for the U.S. FI. If, however, the dollar were to depreciate (fall in value), the U.K. FI would find the agreement increasingly costly over the swap's life.

## Fixed-Floating Currency Swaps

By combining an interest rate swap of the fixed-floating type described earlier with a currency swap, we can also produce a fixed-floating currency swap that is a hybrid of the two plain vanilla swaps we have considered so far.

---

**EXAMPLE 24–5**

*Financing Costs Associated with a Fixed-Floating Currency Swap*

Consider a U.S. FI that holds floating-rate, short-term U.S. dollar–denominated assets. It has financed this asset portfolio with a £50 million, four-year note issue with fixed 10 percent annual coupons denominated in pounds. By comparison, a U.K. FI that holds long-term, fixed-rate assets denominated in pounds has financed this portfolio with $80 million short-term dollar-denominated Euro CDs whose rates reflect changes in one-year LIBOR plus a 2 percent premium. As a result, the U.S. FI is faced with both an interest rate risk and a foreign exchange risk. Specifically, if dollar short-term rates fall and the dollar depreciates against the pound, the FI may face a problem in covering its promised fixed-coupon and principal payments on the pound-denominated note. Consequently, it may wish to transform its fixed-rate, pound-denominated liabilities into variable-rate, dollar-denominated liabilities. The U.K. FI also faces interest rate and foreign exchange rate risk exposures. If U.S. interest rates rise and the dollar appreciates against the pound, the U.K. FI will find it more difficult to cover its promised coupon and principal payments on its dollar-denominated CDs out of the cash flows from its fixed-rate pound asset portfolio. Consequently, it may wish to transform its floating-rate, short-term, dollar-denominated liabilities into fixed-rate pound liabilities.

Both FIs can make changes on the balance sheet to hedge the interest rate and foreign exchange rate risk exposure. The U.S. FI can issue $80 million U.S. dollar-dominated, floating-rate, short-term debt (at, say, LIBOR plus 2.5 percent), the proceeds of which can be used to pay off the existing £50 million four-year note. The U.K. FI can issue £50 million in four-year notes (at, say, 11 percent) and use the proceeds to pay off the $80 million in short-term Euro CDs. Both FIs, by changing the financing used on the balance sheet, hedge both the interest rate and foreign exchange rate risk. We again assume that the dollar-pound exchange rate is $1.6/£1.

Alternatively, each FI can achieve its objective of liability transformation by engaging in a fixed-floating currency swap. A feasible swap would be one in which each year, the two FIs swap payments at some prearranged dollar-pound exchange rate, assumed to be $1.6/£1. The U.K. FI sends fixed payments in pounds to cover the cost of the U.S. FI's pound-denominated note issue, while the U.S. FI sends floating payments in dollars to cover the U.K. FI's floating-rate dollar CD costs. The resulting expected financing costs are calculated in Table 24–7. As a result of the fixed-floating currency swap, both FIs have hedged interest rate and foreign exchange rate risk and have done so at a rate below what they could have achieved by making on-balance-sheet changes. The U.S. FI's net financing cost is LIBOR plus 2 percent with the swap, compared to LIBOR plus 2.5 percent in the debt market. The U.K. FI's financing cost is 10 percent with the swap, compared to 11 percent had it refinanced on the balance sheet.

Given the realized LIBOR rates in column (2), we show the relevant payments among the contracting parties in Table 24–8. The realized cash flows from the swap result in a net nominal payment of $1.6 million by the U.S. FI to the U.K. FI over the life of the swap.

**TABLE 24–7**  Financing Costs Resulting from the Fixed-Floating Currency Swap (in millions of dollars)

|  | U.S. FI | U.K. FI |
|---|---|---|
| Cash outflows from balance sheet financing | $-10\% \times £50$ | $-(\text{LIBOR} + 2\%) \times \$80$ |
| Cash inflows from swap | $10\% \times £50$ | $(\text{LIBOR} + 2\%) \times \$80$ |
| Cash outflows from swap | $-(\text{LIBOR} + 2\%) \times \$80$ | $-10\% \times £50$ |
| Net cash outflows | $-(\text{LIBOR} + 2\%) \times \$80$ | $-10\% \times £50$ |
| Rate available on: |  |  |
| Dollar-denominated variable-rate debt | $\text{LIBOR} + 2\frac{1}{2}\%$ |  |
| Pound-denominated fixed-rate debt |  | 11% |

**TABLE 24–8**
Realized Cash Flows on a Fixed-Floating Currency Swap (in millions of dollars)

| | | | Floating Rate Payment by U.S. Bank ($) | Fixed Rate Payment by U.K. FI | | Net Payment by U.S. FI ($) |
| Year | LIBOR | LIBOR + 2% | | Pounds | Dollars at $1.6/£1 | |
|---|---|---|---|---|---|---|
| 1 | 9% | 11% | $ 8.8 | £ 5 | $ 8 | $+0.8 |
| 2 | 7 | 9 | 7.2 | 5 | 8 | −0.8 |
| 3 | 8 | 10 | 8 | 5 | 8 | 0 |
| 4 | 10 | 12 | 89.6 | 55 | 88 | +1.6 |
| Total net payment | | | | | | $+1.6 |

---

**Concept Questions**

1. Referrring to the fixed-fixed currency swap in Table 24–6, if the net cash flows on the swap are zero, why does either FI enter into the swap agreement?

2. Referring to Table 24–8, suppose that the U.S. FI had agreed to make floating payments of LIBOR + 1 percent instead of LIBOR + 2 percent. What would its net payment have been to the U.K. FI over the four-year swap agreement? (−$1.6 m.)

# CREDIT SWAPS

In recent years the fastest-growing types of swaps have been those developed to better allow FIs to hedge their credit risk, so-called credit swaps or credit default swaps (CDSs). In 2000, commercial banks' total notional principal for outstanding credit derivative contracts was $426 billion. By March 2008, this amount had risen to $16.44 trillion, before falling to $13.44 trillion in 2009 during the financial crisis. By June 2012, the notional principal of credit derivative contracts increased only slightly, to $13.64 trillion. Of this amount, $13.36 trillion was CDSs. Credit swaps are important for two reasons. First, credit risk is still more likely to cause an FI to fail than is either interest rate risk or FX risk. Second, CDSs allow FIs to maintain long-term customer lending relationships without bearing the full credit risk exposure from those relationships. Indeed, then Federal Reserve Board Chairman Alan Greenspan credited this market with helping the banking system maintain its strength through an economic recession in the early 2000s. He argued that credit swaps were effectively used to shift a significant part of banks' risk from their corporate loan portfolios.[11] However, the Fed chairman also commented that these derivative securities are prone to induce speculative excesses that need to be contained through regulation, supervision, and private sector action. While commercial banks have been the main buyers of credit risk protection through credit swaps, insurance companies (such as AIG) have been the net sellers of credit risk protection. Thus, they have been more willing than banks to bear credit risk. The result is that the FI bearing the credit risk of a loan is often different from the FI that issued the loan. Indeed, in some recessionary periods, insurance companies have suffered large losses as buyers of credit risk and banks have been well protected. And as discussed above and below, during the financial crisis of 2008–09 insurance or re-insurance company losses from CDSs were so large that some could not pay the promised obligations and, as a result, banks (and other buyers of credit swaps) were exposed to significantly higher credit risk.

The buyer of a CDS makes periodic payments to the seller until the end of the life of the swap or until the credit event specified in the contract occurs. These payments are typically made every quarter, six months, or year. The settlement of the swap in the event of a default involves either physical delivery of the bonds (or loans) or a cash payment. Generally, a CDS specifies that a number of different bonds (loans) can be delivered in the event of a default. The bonds (loans) typically have the same seniority, but they may not sell for the same percentage of face value immediately after a default. This gives the holder of a CDS a cheapest-to-deliver option. When a default happens, the buyer of protection will review alternative deliverable bonds (or loans) and choose the one that can be purchased most cheaply for delivery.

In contrast to actual insurance policies, there is no requirement that the CDS buyer actually own the underlying reference securities, and therefore the notional value of CDS contracts in recent years has exceeded the total value of the outstanding debt instruments. As of 2012, the Bank for International Settlements estimated total global corporate debt instruments (bonds plus loans) outstanding at $10.7 trillion. In contrast, the BIS reported that single name CDSs outstanding in 2012 had a total notional value exceeding $16.9 trillion.[12] This has implications both for settlement of the CDSs contract and systemic risk exposure.

---

[11] Much of this risk exposure was absorbed by domestic and foreign insurance and reinsurance companies.

[12] Single-name CDSs specify a single reference security. In contrast, multi-name CDSs reference more than one name, as in a portfolio or basket CDS or CDS index, such as the Dow Jones CDX. Baskets are credit derivatives based on a small portfolio of loans or bonds, such that all assets included in the underlying pool are individually listed. In contrast, the contents of larger portfolios are described by their characteristics. A basket credit default swap, also known as a first-to-default swap, is structured like a regular CDS, but the reference security consists of several securities. The first reference entity to default triggers a default payment of the par value minus the recovery value, and then all payments end. As of 2012, there was an additional $11.8 trillion notional value in multi-name CDSs.

Similar to options, but different from non-credit-related swaps, the risks on a credit swap are not symmetrical. That is, the protection buyer receives a payment upon the occurrence of a credit event trigger, but the swap "expires worthless" if no trigger occurs.[13] In that event, the protection seller keeps the periodic premiums paid for the swap, similar to the cash flows that characterize options. Thus, the protection buyer transfers the credit risk to the protection seller in exchange for a premium. Although the credit protection buyer hedges exposure to default risk, there is still counterparty credit risk in the event that the seller fails to perform their obligations under the terms of the contract (as was the concern in September 2008 with regard to AIG, an active CDS seller).

Below we look at two types of credit swaps: (1) the total return swap and (2) the pure credit swap. We then look at credit risk concerns with the swaps themselves.

## Total Return Swaps

**total return swap**
A swap involving an obligation to pay interest at a specified fixed or floating rate for payments representing the total return on a specified amount.

Although FIs spend significant resources attempting to evaluate and price expected changes in a borrower's credit risk over the life of a loan, a borrower's credit situation (credit quality) sometimes deteriorates unexpectedly after the loan terms are determined and the loan is issued. A lender can use a total return swap to hedge this possible change in credit risk exposure. A **total return swap** involves swapping an obligation to pay interest at a specified fixed or floating rate for payments representing the total return on a loan or a bond (interest and principal value changes) of a specified amount.

| **EXAMPLE 24–6** *Calculation of Cash Flows on a Total Return Swap* | Suppose that an FI lends $100 million to a Brazilian manufacturing firm at a fixed rate of 10 percent. If the firm's credit risk increases unexpectedly over the life of the loan, the market value of the loan and consequently the FI's net worth will fall. The FI can hedge an unexpected increase in the borrower's credit risk by entering into a total return swap in which it agrees to pay a total return based on an annual fixed rate ($f$) plus changes in the market value of Brazilian (U.S. dollar–denominated) government debt (changes in the value of these bonds reflect the political and economic events in the firm's home country and thus will be correlated with the credit risk of the Brazilian borrowing firm). Also, the bonds are in the same currency (U.S. dollars) as the loans. In return, the FI receives a variable market rate payment of interest annually (e.g., one-year LIBOR rate). Figure 24–4 and Table 24–9 illustrate the cash flows associated with the typical total return swap for the FI. |
| --- | --- |

Using the total return swap, the FI agrees to pay a fixed rate of interest annually and the capital gain or loss on the market value of the Brazilian (U.S. dollar) bond over the period of the hedge. In Figure 24–4, $P_0$ denotes the market value of the bond at the beginning of the swap period and $P_T$ represents the market value of the bond at the end of the swap period. If the Brazilian bond decreases in value over the period of the hedge ($P_0 > P_T$), the FI pays a relatively small (possibly negative) amount to the counterparty equal to the fixed payment on the swap minus the capital loss[14] on the bond. For example, suppose the Brazilian (U.S. dollar) bond was priced at par ($P_0 = 100$) at the beginning of the swap period. At the end of the swap period or the payment date, the Brazilian bond had a secondary market value of 90 ($P_T = 90$) due to an increase in Brazilian country risk. Suppose that the fixed-rate

---

[13] In contrast, an interest rate swap (fixed- for floating-rate swap) will entail symmetric payments such that the swap buyer (the fixed-rate payment on the swap) earns positive cash flows when interest rates increase and the swap seller (the floating-rate payment) earns positive cash flows when interest rates decrease.

[14] Total return swaps are typically structured so that the capital gain or loss is paid at the end of the swap. However, an alternative structure does exist in which the capital gain or loss is paid at the end of each interest period during the swap.

payment (*f*) as part of the total return swap was 12 percent. Then the FI would send to the swap counterparty the fixed rate of 12 percent minus 10 percent (the capital loss on the Brazilian bond), or a total of 2 percent, and would receive in return a floating payment (e.g., LIBOR = 11 percent) from the counterparty to the swap. Thus, the net profit on the swap to the FI lender is 9 percent (11 percent minus 2 percent) times the notional amount of the swap contract. This gain can be used to offset the loss of market value on the loan to the Brazilian firm. This example is illustrated in Table 24–9.

Thus, the FI benefits from the total return swap if the Brazilian bond value deteriorates as a result of a political or economic shock. Assuming that the Brazilian firm's credit risk deteriorates along with the local economy, the FI will offset some of this loss of the Brazilian loan on its balance sheet with a gain from the total return swap.

**FIGURE 24–4**
**Cash Flows on a Total Return Swap**

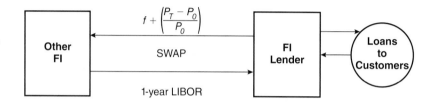

**TABLE 24–9**   Cash Flows on a Total Return Swap

|  | Annual Cash Flow for Year 1 through Final Year | Additional Payment by FI | Total Return |
|---|---|---|---|
| Cash inflow on swap to FI lender | 1-year LIBOR (11%) | — | 1-year LIBOR (11%) |
| Cash outflow on swap to other FI | Fixed rate (*f*) (12%) | $P_T - P_0$ (90 − 100) | $\left[ f + \dfrac{P_T - P_0}{P_0} \right]$ |
|  |  |  | $\left(12\% + \dfrac{90 - 100}{100} = 12\% - 10\% = 2\%\right)$ |
|  | Net profit |  | 9% |

Note that hedging credit risk in this fashion allows the FI to maintain its customer relationship with the Brazilian firm (and perhaps earn fees from selling other financial services to that firm) without bearing a large amount of credit risk exposure. Moreover, since the Brazilian loan remains on the FI's balance sheet, the Brazilian firm may not even know its loan is being hedged. This would not be the case if the FI sought to reduce its risk by selling all or part of the loan (see Chapter 25). Finally, the swap does not completely hedge credit risk in this case. Specifically, basis risk is present to the extent that the credit risk of the Brazilian firm's U.S. dollar loan is imperfectly correlated with Brazilian country risk reflected in the price of the Brazilian (U.S. dollar) bonds.[15]

[15] In many swaps, the total return on a loan (rather than a bond as in this example) is swapped for a floating payment such as LIBOR. In this case, *f* would equal any fees paid for loan origination and $[(P_T - P_0)/P_0]$ would reflect the estimated change in market value of the loan as perceived by brokers/traders in the secondary market for loan sales. The secondary market for loans is described in Chapter 25.

**FIGURE 24–5**
A Pure Credit Swap

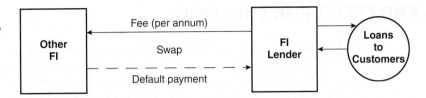

## Pure Credit Swaps

While total return swaps can be used to hedge credit risk exposure, they contain an element of interest rate risk as well as credit risk. For example, in Table 24–9, if the LIBOR rate changes, the *net* cash flows on the total return swap also will change—even though the credit risks of the underlying loans (and bonds) have not changed.

**pure credit swap**
A swap by which an FI receives the par value of the loan on default in return for paying a periodic swap fee.

To strip out the "interest rate" sensitive element of total return swaps, an alternative swap has been developed called a **pure credit swap.** In this case, as shown in Figure 24–5, the FI lender will send (each swap period) a fixed fee or payment (like an insurance premium) to the FI counterparty. If the FI lender's loan or loans do not default, it will receive nothing back from the FI counterparty. However, if the loan or loans default, the FI counterparty will cover the default loss by making a default payment that is often equal to the par value of the original loan (e.g., $P_0 = \$100$) minus the secondary market value of the defaulted loan (e.g., $P_T = \$40$); that is, the FI counterparty will pay $P_0 - P_T$ (or \$60, in this example).[16] Thus, a pure credit swap is like buying credit insurance and/or a multiperiod credit option.

## CDS Indexes

In September 2003, the Dow Jones CDX (DJ CDX) North American Investment Grade Index was introduced. In November 2004, Markit initiated a credit index data service, which included the DJ CDX (which also includes indexes covering emerging market credit derivatives) and the International Index Company's (IIC) iTraxx (which covers the EU, Japan, and non-Japan Asia). Both sets of indexes are made up of 125 of the most liquid, investment-grade credits in the form of CDSs. For example, the DJ CDX consists of a basket of 125 CDS contracts on U.S. firms with liquid, investment-grade corporate debt. The identity of the components in the index changes every six months—every March and September for the DJ CDX. Companies may be dropped from the index if they are downgraded or become illiquid. For example, Ford and General Motors were dropped from the DJ CDX in September 2005 when their debt fell below investment grade. The index is equally weighted, so each CDS component makes up 0.8 percent of the index value. Using indexed CDS to hedge credit risk may be less expensive because of the liquidity of these instruments, although it does expose the hedger to basis risk.[17]

---

[16] While a pure credit swap is like a default option (e.g., the digital default option in Chapter 23), a key difference is that the fee (or premium) payments on the swap are paid over the life of the swap, whereas for a default option the whole fee (premium) is paid up front.

[17] Basis risk results when the fluctuations in the value of the reference securities underlying the derivative do not move in lock step with the hedge position. For example, there is basis risk if an indexed CDS is used to hedge a portfolio of loans to firms that are not identical to the 125 firms in the index.

# SWAPS AND CREDIT RISK CONCERNS

In contrast to futures and options markets, swap markets have historically been governed by very little regulation—there is no central governing body overseeing swap market operations. The International Swaps and Derivatives Association (ISDA) is a global trade association with over 840 members (including most of the world's major financial institutions) from some 59 countries that sets codes and standards for swap markets. Established in 1985, the ISDA establishes, reviews, and updates the code of standards (the language and provisions) for swap documentation. The ISDA also acts as the spokesgroup for the industry on regulatory changes and issues, promotes the development of risk management practices for swap dealers (for example, the ISDA was instrumental in helping to develop the guidelines set by the Bank for International Settlements on capital adequacy in financial institutions—see Chapter 20), provides a forum for informing and educating swap market participants about relevant issues, and sets standards of commercial conduct for its members. Further, because commercial banks are the major swap dealers, the swap markets are subject, indirectly, to regulations imposed by the Board of Governors of the Federal Reserve, the FDIC, and other bank regulatory agencies charged with monitoring bank risk. For example, commercial banks must include swap risk exposure when calculating risk-based capital requirements (see Chapter 20). To the extent that swap activity is part of a bank's overall business, swap markets are monitored for abuses. Investment banks and insurance companies have recently become bigger players in the swap markets, however, and these dealers have generally been subject to few regulations on their swap dealings.

The financial crisis showed just how much risk the swap market can present to FIs and the global financial system. Specifically, as the subprime mortgage market began to fail in the summer of 2008, subprime mortgage pools that FIs bought ended up falling precipitously in value as defaults and foreclosures rose on the underlying mortgage pools. Many credit default swaps were written on these subprime mortgage securities. Thus, as mortgage security losses started to rise, buyers of the CDS contracts wanted to be paid for these losses. AIG was a major writer of these CDS securities. As of June 30, 2008, AIG had written $441 billion worth of swaps on corporate bonds and mortgage-backed securities. And, when mortgage-backed securities started to fall in value, AIG had to make good on billions of dollars of credit default swaps. The problem was exacerbated by the fact that so many FIs were linked to each other through these deals. Lehman Brothers alone had more than $700 billion worth of swaps outstanding, and many of them were backed by AIG. As the value of these subprime CDS fell, AIG had to post more collateral against these swaps. Soon it became clear that AIG was not going to be able to cover its credit default swap market losses. The result was a significant increase in the risk exposure of banks, investment banks, and insurance companies that had purchased AIG CDS contracts. Indeed, the reason the federal government stepped in and bailed out AIG was that the insurer was a dominant player in the CDS market. While banks and hedge funds were playing both sides of the CDS business—buying and trading them and thus offsetting whatever losses they took—AIG was simply selling the CDS. Had AIG defaulted, every FI that had bought a CDS contract from the company would have suffered substantial losses.

Global funding and risk pressures were also evident in the FX swap market during the financial crisis. This risk was driven by demand for dollar funding from global financial institutions, particularly European financial institutions. As

www.isda.org

www.bis.org

www.federalreserve.gov
www.fdic.gov

many of these institutions increasingly struggled to obtain funding in the unsecured cash markets, they turned to the FX swap market as a primary channel for raising dollars. This extreme demand for dollar funding led a sizable shift in FX forward prices, with the implied dollar funding rate observed in FX swaps on many major currencies rising sharply above that suggested by the other relative interest measures such as the dollar OIS (overnight index swap) rate and the dollar LIBOR. Dealers reported that bid–ask spreads on FX swaps increased to as much as 10 times the levels that had prevailed before August 2007. During the last quarter of 2008, the spread of the three month FX swap-implied dollar rate from euro and pound—U.S. dollar FX forward rate—over the dollar LIBOR fixed rate widened to around 330 and 260 basis points, respectively.

Given the role that swaps played in the financial crisis, the federal government has started regulating them more heavily. Specifically, in October 2009, the Over-the-Counter Derivatives Market Act was passed. This was followed by the Wall Street Reform and Consumer Protection Act of 2010. The acts established a framework for the comprehensive regulation of over-the-counter (OTC) derivatives. The regulations require central clearing and exchange trading for specified swaps and established rules for disclosure, reporting, and record keeping of all swaps. The acts require swap dealers and major swap participants to register with either the Commodity Futures Trading Commission (CFTC) or the Securities and Exchange Commission (SEC). The CFTC has jurisdiction over swaps. Swaps are defined as (1) options or other contracts involving the exchange of payments that are linked to, among other things, interest rates, currencies, securities, commodities, instruments of indebtedness, and quantitative measures; (2) event-based contracts, that is, contracts providing for purchase, sale, payment or delivery dependent on event or contingency associated with a potential financial, economic, or commercial consequence; (3) contracts commonly known to the trade as swaps; or (4) any combination or permutation of the above. These includes interest rate swaps, foreign exchange or currency swaps, total return swaps, and credit default swaps that are not security based (i.e., multi-name CDSs). The SEC has jurisdiction over security-based swaps. A security-based swap is defined as any agreement, contract, or transaction that would be a swap and that (1) is based on a narrow-based security index, (2) is based on a single security or, loan, or (3) is a CDS linked to a single issuer of a security or the issuers of securities in a narrow-based security index. Further, the acts grant authority to federal financial regulators (including the SEC, CFTC, the Federal Deposit Insurance Corporation, the Board of Governors of the Federal Reserve System, the National Credit Union Administration, the Office of the Comptroller of the Currency, and all other federal agencies that have authority under law to regulate financial institutions or financial instruments) to oversee any agreements.

Given the events surrounding the financial crisis, and the role that swaps played in the crisis, it is critical that both regulators and market participants have a heightened awareness of credit risks on swap agreements. If a transaction is not structured carefully, it may pass along unintended risks to participants, exposing them to higher frequency and severity of losses than if they had held an equivalent cash position. This raises a question: Is credit or default risk on swaps the same as or different from the credit or default risk on loans? In fact, there are three major differences between the credit risk on swaps and the credit risk on loans. As a result, the credit risk on a swap is generally much less than that on a loan. We discuss these differences next.

### Netting and Swaps

One factor that mitigates the credit risk on swaps is the netting of swap payments. On each swap payment date, a fixed payment is made by one party and a floating payment is made by the other. However, in general, each party calculates the net difference between the two payments and a single payment for the net difference is made by one party to the other. This netting of payments implies that the default exposure of the in-the-money party is limited to the net payment rather than either the total fixed or floating payment. Further, when two parties have large numbers of contracts outstanding against each other, they tend to net across contracts. This process, called *netting by novation*—often formalized through a master netting agreement in the United States—further reduces the potential risk of loss if some contracts are in the money and other are out of the money to the same counterparty.[18]

### Payment Flows Are Interest and Not Principal

While currency swaps involve swaps of interest and principal, interest rate swaps involve swaps of interest payments only measured against some notional principal value. This suggests that the default risk on such swaps is less than that on a regular loan, where both interest and principal are exposed to credit risk.

### Standby Letters of Credit

In cases where swaps are made between parties of different credit standing, such that one party perceives a significant risk of default by the other party, the poor-quality credit risk party may be required to buy a standby letter of credit (or another form of performance guaranty) from a third-party high-quality (AA rated) FI such that if default occurs, the standby letter of credit will provide the swap payments in lieu of the defaulting party. Further, low-quality counterparties are increasingly required to post collateral in lieu of default. This collateral is an incentive mechanism working to deter swap defaults.

| Concept Questions | |
|---|---|
| | 1. What is the link between preserving "customer relationships" and credit derivatives such as total return swaps? |
| | 2. Is there any difference between a digital default option (see Chapter 23) and a pure credit swap? |
| | 3. Are swaps as risky as equivalent-sized loans? |

**Summary**

This chapter evaluated the role of swaps as risk-management vehicles for FIs. We analyzed the major types of swaps: interest rate, currency swaps and credit swaps. Swaps have special features of long maturity, flexibility, and liquidity that make them attractive alternatives relative to shorter-term hedging vehicles such as the futures, forwards, options, and caps discussed in Chapters 22 and 23. However, even though the credit risk of swaps is less than that of loans, because of their OTC nature and long maturities, their credit risk is still generally greater than that for other OTC derivative instruments such as floors and caps. Also, the credit risk on swaps compares unfavorably with that on exchange-traded futures and options, whose credit risk is approximately zero.

[18] In January 1995, FASB Interpretation No. 39 (FIN 39) established the right of setoff under a master netting agreement. Also, since 1995, the BIS has allowed banks to use bilateral netting of swap contracts in calculating their risk-based capital requirements (see Chapter 20). It is estimated that this reduces banks' capital requirements against swaps by up to 40 percent.

**Questions and Problems**

1. Explain the similarity between a swap and a forward contract.

2. Forwards, futures, and options contracts had been used by FIs to hedge risk for many years before swaps were invented. If FIs already had these hedging instruments, why did they need swaps?

3. Distinguish between a swap buyer and a swap seller. In which markets does each have the comparative advantage?

4. An insurance company owns $50 million of floating-rate bonds yielding LIBOR plus 1 percent. These loans are financed with $50 million of fixed-rate guaranteed investment contracts (GICs) costing 10 percent. A bank has $50 million of auto loans with a fixed rate of 14 percent. The loans are financed with $50 million in CDs at a variable rate of LIBOR plus 4 percent.
   a. What is the risk exposure of the insurance company?
   b. What is the risk exposure of the bank?
   c. What would be the cash flow goals of each company if they were to enter into a swap arrangement?
   d. Which FI would be the buyer and which FI would be the seller in the swap?
   e. Diagram the direction of the relevant cash flows for the swap arrangement.
   f. What are reasonable cash flow amounts, or relative interest rates, for each of the payment streams?

5. In a swap arrangement, the variable-rate swap cash flow streams often do not fully hedge the variable-rate cash flow streams from the balance sheet due to basis risk.
   a. What are the possible sources of basis risk in an interest rate swap?
   b. How could the failure to achieve a perfect hedge be realized by the swap buyer?
   c. How could the failure to achieve a perfect hedge be realized by the swap seller?

6. A commercial bank has $200 million of four-year maturity floating-rate loans yielding the T-bill rate plus 2 percent. These loans are financed with $200 million of four-year maturity fixed-rate deposits costing 9 percent. The commercial bank can issue four-year variable-rate deposits at the T-bill rate plus 1.5 percent. A savings bank has $200 million of four-year maturity mortgages with a fixed rate of 13 percent. They are financed with $200 million in four-year maturity CDs with a variable rate of the T-bill rate plus 3 percent. The savings bank can issue four-year long-term debt at 12.5 percent.
   a. Discuss the type of interest rate risk each FI faces.
   b. Propose a swap that would result in each FI having the same type of asset and liability cash flows.
   c. Show that this swap would be acceptable to both parties.
   d. The realized T-bill rates over the four-year contract period are as follows:

| End of Year | T-Bill Rate |
|---|---|
| 1 | 1.75% |
| 2 | 2.00 |
| 3 | 2.25 |
| 4 | 2.50 |

   Calculate the realized cash flows on the swap and the net interest yield for the savings bank and the commercial bank over the contract period.
   e. What are some of the practical difficulties in arranging this swap?

7. Bank 1 can issue five-year CDs at an annual rate of 11 percent fixed or at a variable rate of LIBOR plus 2 percent. Bank 2 can issue five-year CDs at an annual rate of 13 percent fixed or at a variable rate of LIBOR plus 3 percent.
   a. Is a mutually beneficial swap possible between the two banks?
   b. Where is the comparative advantage of the two banks?
   c. What is an example of a feasible swap?

8. First Bank can issue one-year, floating-rate CDs at prime plus 1 percent or fixed-rate CDs at 12.5 percent. Second Bank can issue one-year floating-rate CDs at prime plus 0.5 percent or fixed-rate CDs at 11.0 percent.
   a. What is a feasible swap with all the benefits going to First Bank?
   b. What is a feasible swap with all the benefits going to Second Bank?
   c. Diagram each situation.
   d. What factors will determine the final swap arrangement?

9. Two multinational FIs enter their respective debt markets to issue $100 million of two-year notes. FI A can borrow at a fixed annual rate of 11 percent or a floating rate of LIBOR plus 50 basis points, repriced at the end of the year. FI B can borrow at a fixed annual rate of 10 percent or a floating rate of LIBOR, repriced at the end of the year.
   a. If FI A is a positive duration gap insurance company and FI B is a money market mutual fund, in what market(s) should each firm borrow to reduce its interest rate risk exposure?
   b. In which debt market does FI A have a comparative advantage over FI B?
   c. Although FI A is riskier than FI B and therefore must pay a higher rate in both the fixed-rate and floating-rate markets, there are possible gains to trade. Set up a swap to exploit FI A's comparative advantage over FI B. What are the total gains from the swap? Assume a swap intermediary fee of 10 basis points.
   d. The gains from the swap can be apportioned between FI A and FI B through negotiation. What terms of swap would give all the gains to FI A? What terms of swap would give all the gains to FI B?
   e. Assume swap pricing that allocates all gains from the swap to FI A. If FI A buys the swap from FI B and pays the swap intermediary's fee, what are the realized net cash flows if LIBOR is 8.25 percent?
   f. If FI A buys the swap in part (e) from FI B and pays the swap intermediary's fee, what are the realized net cash flows if LIBOR is 11 percent? Be sure to net swap payments against cash market payments for both FIs.
   g. If all barriers to entry and pricing inefficiencies between FI A's debt markets and FI B's debt markets were eliminated, how would that affect the swap transaction?

10. What are off-market swap arrangements? How are these arrangements negotiated?

11. Describe how an inverse floater works to the advantage of an investor who receives coupon payments of 10 percent minus LIBOR if LIBOR is currently at 4 percent. When is it a disadvantage to the investor? Does the issuing party bear any risk?

12. An FI has $500 million of assets with a duration of nine years and $450 million of liabilities with a duration of three years. The FI wants to hedge its duration gap with a swap that has fixed-rate payments with a duration of six years

and floating-rate payments with a duration of two years. What is the optimal amount of the swap to effectively macrohedge against the adverse effect of a change in interest rates on the value of the FI's equity?

13. A U.S. thrift has most of its assets in the form of Swiss franc–denominated floating-rate loans. Its liabilities consist mostly of fixed-rate dollar-denominated CDs. What type of currency risk and interest rate risk does this FI face? How might it use a swap to eliminate some of those risks?

14. A Swiss bank issues a $100 million, three-year Eurodollar CD at a fixed annual rate of 7 percent. The proceeds of the CD are lent to a Swiss company for three years at a fixed rate of 9 percent. The spot exchange rate is SF1.50/$.
    a. Is this expected to be a profitable transaction?
    b. What are the cash flows if exchange rates are unchanged over the next three years?
    c. What is the risk exposure of the bank's underlying cash position?
    d. How can the Swiss bank reduce that risk exposure?
    e. If the U.S. dollar is expected to appreciate against the SF to SF1.65/$, SF1.815/$, and SF2.00/$ over the next three years, respectively, what will be the cash flows on this transaction?
    f. If the Swiss bank swaps US$ payments for SF payments at the current spot exchange rate, what are the cash flows on the swap? What are the cash flows on the entire hedged position? Assume that the U.S. dollar appreciates at the rates in part (e).
    g. What are the cash flows on the swap and the hedged position if actual spot exchange rates are as follows:

    End of year 1: SF1.55/US$
    End of year 2: SF1.47/US$
    End of year 3: SF1.48/US$

    h. What would be the bank's risk exposure if the fixed-rate Swiss loan was financed with a floating-rate U.S. $100 million, three-year Eurodollar CD?
    i. What type(s) of hedge is appropriate if the Swiss bank in part (h) wants to reduce its risk exposure?
    j. If the annual Eurodollar CD rate is set at LIBOR and LIBOR at the end of years 1, 2, and 3 is expected to be 7 percent, 8 percent, and 9 percent, respectively, what will be the cash flows on the bank's unhedged cash position? Assume no change in exchange rates.
    k. What are the cash flows on the bank's unhedged cash position if exchange rates are as follows:

    End of year 1: SF1.55/US$
    End of year 2: SF1.47/US$
    End of year 3: SF1.48/US$

    l. What are both the swap and the total hedged position cash flows if the bank swaps out its floating rate US$ CD payments in exchange for 7.75 percent fixed-rate SF payments at the current spot exchange rate of SF1.50/$?
    m. If forecasted annual interest rates are 7 percent, 10.14 percent and 10.83 percent over the next three years, respectively, and exchange rates over the next years are those in part (k), calculate the cash flows on an 8.75 percent fixed–floating-rate swap of U.S. dollars to Swiss francs at SF1.50/$.

15. Bank A has the following balance sheet information (in millions):

| Assets | | Liabilities and Equity | |
|---|---|---|---|
| Rate-sensitive assets | $ 50 | Rate-sensitive liabilities | $ 75 |
| Fixed-rate assets | 150 | Fixed-rate liabilities | 100 |
| | | Net worth | 25 |
| Total assets | $200 | Total liabilities and equity | $200 |

Rate-sensitive assets are repriced quarterly at the 91-day Treasury bill rate plus 150 basis points. Fixed-rate assets have five years until maturity and are paying 9 percent annually. Rate-sensitive liabilities are repriced quarterly at the 91-day Treasury bill rate plus 100 basis points. Fixed-rate liabilities have two years until maturity and are paying 7 percent annually. Currently, the 91-day Treasury bill rate is 6.25 percent.

a. What is the bank's current net interest income? If Treasury bill rates increase 150 basis points, what will be the change in the bank's net interest income?

b. What is the bank's repricing or funding gap? Use the repricing model to calculate the change in the bank's net interest income if interest rates increase 150 basis points.

c. How can swaps be used as an interest rate hedge in this example?

16. Use the following information to construct a swap of asset cash flows for the bank in problem 15. The bank is a price taker in both the fixed-rate market at 9 percent and the rate-sensitive market at the T-bill rate plus 1.5 percent. A securities dealer has a large portfolio of rate sensitive assets funded with fixed-rate liabilities. The dealer is a price taker in a fixed-rate asset market paying 8.5 percent and a floating-rate asset market paying the 91-day T-bill rate plus 1.25 percent. All interest is paid annually.

a. What is the interest rate risk exposure to the securities dealer?

b. How can the bank and the securities dealer use a swap to hedge their respective interest rate risk exposures?

c. What are the total potential gains to the swap?

d. Consider the following two-year swap of asset cash flows: An annual fixed-rate asset cash flow of 8.6 percent in exchange for a floating-rate asset cash flow of T-bill plus 125 basis points. The swap intermediary fee is 5 basis points. How are the swap gains apportioned between the bank and the securities dealer if they each hedge their interest rate risk exposures using this swap?

e. What are the realized cash flows if T-bill rates at the end of the first year are 7.75 percent and at the end of the second year 5.5 percent? Assume that the notional value is $107.14 million.

f. What are the sources of the swap gains to trade?

g. What are the implications for the efficiency of cash markets?

17. Consider the following currency swap of coupon interest on the following assets:

5 percent (annual coupon) fixed-rate U.S. $1 million bond

5 percent (annual coupon) fixed-rate bond denominated in Swiss francs (SF)

Spot exchange rate: SF1.5/$.

a. What is the face value of the SF bond if the investments are equivalent at spot rates?

b. What are the realized cash flows, assuming no change in spot exchange rates? What are the net cash flows on the swap?

    c. What are the cash flows if the spot exchange rate falls to SF0.50/$? What are the net cash flows on the swap?

    d. What are the cash flows if the spot exchange rate rises to SF2.25/$? What are the net cash flows on the swap?

    e. Describe the underlying cash position that would prompt the FI to hedge by swapping dollars for Swiss francs.

18. Consider the following fixed-floating-rate currency swap of assets: 5 percent (annual coupon) fixed-rate U.S. $1 million bond and floating-rate SF1.5 million bond set at LIBOR annually. Currently LIBOR is 4 percent. The face value of the swap is SF1.5 million. The spot exchange rate is SF1.5/$.

    a. What are the realized cash flows on the swap at the spot exchange rate?

    b. If the 1-year forward rate is SF1.538 per US$, what are the realized net cash flows on the swap? Assume LIBOR is unchanged.

    c. If LIBOR increases to 6 percent, what are the realized net cash flows on the swap? Evaluate at the forward rate.

19. Give two reasons why credit swaps have been the fastest-growing form of swaps in recent years.

20. What is a total return swap?

21. How does a pure credit swap differ from a total return swap? How does it differ from a digital default option?

22. Why is the credit risk on a swap lower than the credit risk on a loan?

23. What is netting by novation?

24. What role did the swap market play in the financial crisis of 2008–09?

The following problem refers to material in Appendix 24A.

25. The following information is available on a three-year swap contract. One-year maturity zero-coupon discount yields are currently priced at par and pay a coupon rate of 5 percent. Two-year maturity zero-coupon discount yields are currently 5.51 percent. Three-year maturity zero-coupon discount yields are currently 5.775 percent. The terms of a three-year swap of $100 million notional value are 5.45 percent annual fixed-rate payments in exchange for floating-rate payments tied to the annual discount yield.

    a. If an insurance company buys this swap, what can you conclude about the interest rate risk exposure of the company's underlying cash position?

    b. What are the realized cash flows expected over the three-year life of the swap?

    c. What are the realized cash flows that occur over the three-year life of the swap if $d_2 = 4.95$ percent and $d_3 = 6.1$ percent?

# INTEGRATED MINI CASE

# HEDGING INTEREST RATE RISK WITH FUTURES VERSUS OPTIONS VERSUS SWAPS

On January 4, 2015, an FI has the following balance sheet (rates = 8 percent):

| Assets | | | Liabilities/Equity | | |
|---|---|---|---|---|---|
| A | $450 m | $D_A$ = 8 years | L | $396 m | $D_L$ = 4 years |
| | | | E | $ 54 m | |

$DGAP = [8 - (396/450)4] = 4.48$ years $> 0$

The FI manager thinks rates will increase by 0.55 percent in the next three months. If this happens, the equity value will change by:

$$\Delta E = -[8 - \tfrac{396}{450}(4)]450m\,\tfrac{0.0055}{1.08} = -\$10,266,667$$

The FI manager will hedge this interest rate risk with either futures contracts, option contracts, or swap contracts.

If the FI uses futures, it will select June T-bonds to hedge. The duration on the T-bonds underlying the contract is 14.5 years, and the T-bond futures are selling at a price of $110.53125 per $100, or $110,531.25. T-bond futures rates, currently 5 percent, are expected to increase by 0.75 percent over the next three months.

If the FI uses options, it will buy puts on 15-year T-bonds futures with a June maturity, an exercise price of 109, and an option premium of $\tfrac{36}{64}$ percent. The spot price on the T-bond underlying the option is $115.78125 per $100 of face value. The duration on the T-bonds underlying the options is

14.5 years, and the delta of the put options is −0.85. Managers expect these T-bond rates to increase by 0.7 percent from 5.25 percent in the next three months.

If the FI uses swaps, a swap agent offers a swap involving $D_{Fixed} = 8$ years (based on the 15-year Treasury bond rate) and $D_{Floating} = 1$ year (based on Treasury bills).

If by April 4, 2015, balance sheet rates increase by 0.5 percent, futures rates by 0.7 percent, and T-bond rates underlying the option contracts by 0.66 percent, calculate the on- and off-balance-sheet cash flows to the FI when using futures contracts, option contracts, and swap contracts as its hedge instrument.

If by April 4, 2015, balance sheet rates actually fall by 0.25 percent, futures rates fall by 0.35 percent, and T-bond rates underlying the option contract fall by 0.34 percent, calculate the on- and off-balance-sheet cash flows to the FI when using futures contracts, option contracts, and swap contracts as its hedge instrument.

# Appendix 24A

## Setting Rates on an Interest Rate Swap

In this appendix, we discuss how rates are set on a swap at the time the parties enter into the swap agreement. As with much of financial theory, there are important no-arbitrage conditions that should hold in setting rates in a fixed-floating rate swap agreement. The most important no-arbitrage condition is that the expected present value of the cash flow payments made by the fixed-rate payer, the buyer, should equal the expected present value of the cash flow payments made by the floating-rate payer, the seller:

Expected fixed-payment *PV*

= Expected floating-payment *PV*

If this no-arbitrage condition does not hold, one party usually has to compensate the other with an up-front payment equal to the difference

between the two expected present values of the cash flows.

The fixed-rate payment of the swap is usually based on the newly issued or *on-the-run* yield curve of U.S. Treasury notes and bonds. Thus, if four-year Treasuries are currently yielding 10 percent, a quote of 10.25 percent (bid) and 10.35 percent (offer) would mean that the commercial or investment bank acting as a swap dealer is willing to buy or become the fixed-rate payer in a swap agreement at a contractual swap rate of 10.25 percent. It is also willing to take the other side of the swap (become the fixed-rate receiver) if the swap fixed rate is set higher at 10.35 percent. The 10-basis-point spread is the dealer's spread or the return for intermediating the swap. As discussed earlier, in intermediating, the FI has to cover the credit risk assumed in the

**FIGURE 24A–1**
Discount Yield
Curve

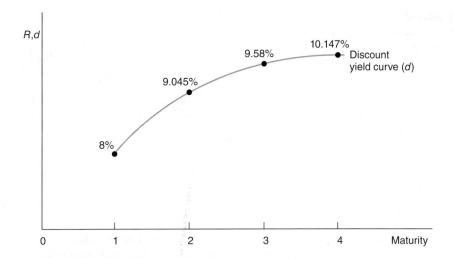

swap transaction and cover its costs of search and intermediation as well. In the next subsection of this appendix, we develop a detailed example of how swap rates might be determined.

## SETTING RATES ON A SWAP: AN EXAMPLE

We develop an example of how rates are set on a swap under simplified assumptions by applying the no-arbitrage condition and pricing swaps off the Treasury yield curve. This provides an understanding of why expected cash flows from the swap agreement can differ from actual or realized cash flows. It also explains why, when yield curves slope upward, the fixed-rate payer (swap buyer) faces an inherent credit risk in any swap contract.

Assume that in a four-year swap agreement, the fixed-rate payer makes fixed-rate payments at the end of each year. Also assume that while these payments are made at the end of each year, interest rates are determined at the beginning of each year.[1] That is,

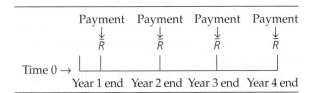

Time $0 \rightarrow$

Year 1 end  Year 2 end  Year 3 end  Year 4 end

---

[1] This is not always the case. Further, in practice many swaps are now priced off the LIBOR yield curve (reflecting some credit risk premuim over Treasuries).

Since this is a four-year swap agreement, the fixed-rate payer knows in advance the annual interest rate to pay each year:

$$\bar{R}_1 = \bar{R}_2 = \bar{R}_3 = \bar{R}_4 = \text{Fixed}$$

Let $R$ be priced off the current zero-coupon *Treasury discount bond yield curve* for four-year, on-the-run Treasury note issues. The assumed current zero-coupon Treasury discount bond yield curve is represented in Figure 24A–1. The four discount yields are represented by the variables $d_1$, $d_2$, $d_3$, and $d_4$. We can use this yield curve to solve for the expected one-year floating rates implied by the zero-coupon yield curve.

We assume that floating interest rate payments are made at the end of each year and are based on the one-year interest rates that are set at the beginning of each year. We can use the zero-coupon bond yield curve to derive the expected one-year forward rates that reflect the expected floating swap payments at the end of each year.

### Solving for the Implied Forward Rates/Floating Payments on a Swap Agreement

*End of Year 1 Payment*
The expected end of year 1 payment $E(\tilde{r}_1)$ must be equal to the current one-year rate set for one-year discount bonds at time 0 since floating rates paid at the end of a period are assumed to depend on rates set or expected at the beginning of that period. That is, the expected first-year floating payment equals the current one-year discount rate:

$$E(\tilde{r}_1) = d_1 = 8\%$$

**FIGURE 24A–2**
Fixed and Expected
Floating Swap
Payments

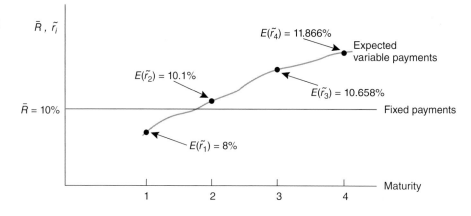

### End of Year 2 Payment

To determine the end of year 2 payment, we need to solve for the expected one-year interest rate or forward rate in year 2. This is the rate that reflects expected payments at the end of year 2. We know that no arbitrage requires:[2]

$$(1 + d_2)^2 = (1 + d_1)[1 + E(\tilde{r}_1)]$$

That is, the yield from holding a two-year zero-coupon bond to maturity must equal the expected yield from holding the current one-year, zero-coupon bond to maturity times the expected yield from investing in a new one-year, zero-coupon bond in year 2. Rearranging this equation, we have:

$$1 + E(\tilde{r}_2) = \frac{(1 + d_2)^2}{(1 + d_1)}$$

Since we already know that $d_2 = 9.045$ percent and $d_1 = 8$ percent, we can solve for $E(\tilde{r}_2)$:

$$1 + E(\tilde{r}_2) = \frac{(1.09045)^2}{(1.08)}$$

$$E(\tilde{r}_2) = 10.1\%$$

### End of Year 3 Payment

In a similar fashion:

$$1 + E(\tilde{r}_3) = \frac{(1 + d_3)^3}{(1 + d_2)^2}$$

Substituting in the $d_2$ and $d_3$ values from the zero-coupon bond yield curve:

$$1 + E(\tilde{r}_3) = \frac{(1.0958)^3}{(1.09045)^2}$$

$$E(\tilde{r}_3) = 10.658\%$$

[2] Under the pure expectations theory of interest rates.

### End of Year 4 Payment

Using the same procedure:

$$1 + E(\tilde{r}_4) = \frac{(1 + d_4)^4}{(1 + d_3)^3} = \frac{(1.10147)^4}{(1.0958)^3}$$

$$E(\tilde{r}_4) = 11.866\%$$

These four expected one-year payments by the floating-rate payer are plotted against the fixed-rate payments by the buyer of the swap in Figure 24A–2. Although expecting to pay a net payment $[\bar{R} - E(\tilde{r}_1)]$ of 2 percent to the floating-rate payer in the first year, the fixed-rate payer expects to receive net payments of 0.1 percent, 0.658 percent, and 1.866 percent from the floating-rate seller in years 2, 3, and 4. This has important credit risk implications. It implies that when the yield curve is upward sloping, the fixed-rate payer can expect not only to pay more than the floating-rate payer in the early years of a swap agreement, but also to receive higher cash flows from the seller or floating-rate payer in the later years of the swap agreement. Thus, the fixed-rate payer faces the risk that if expected rates are actually realized, the floating-rate payer may have an incentive to default toward the end of the swap agreement as a net payer. In this case, the swap buyer might have to replace the swap at less favorable market conditions in the future.

Finally, note that in this appendix we have been comparing expected cash flows in the swap agreement under no-arbitrage conditions. If the term structure shifts after the swap has been entered into, realized one-year rates (and payments) will not equal expected rates for the floating-rate payer. In our example, if the term structure shifts,

$$r_2 \neq E(\tilde{r}_2)$$

$$r_3 \neq E(\tilde{r}_3)$$

$$r_4 \neq E(\tilde{r}_4)$$

where $r_2$, $r_3$, and $r_4$ are realized or actual one-year rates on new one-year discount bonds issued in years 2, 3, and 4, respectively. Of course, the floating-rate payer has to make payments on actual or realized rates rather than expected rates, as we discussed in the first section of this chapter.

# Chapter Twenty-Five

# Loan Sales

## INTRODUCTION

Traditionally, banks and other FIs have relied on a number of contractual mechanisms to control the credit risks of lending. These have included (1) requiring higher interest rate spreads and fees on loans to more risky borrowers, (2) restricting or rationing loans to more risky borrowers, (3) requiring enhanced seniority (collateral) for the bank over the assets of risky borrowers, (4) diversifying across different types of risky borrowers, and (5) placing more restrictive covenants on risky borrowers' actions, such as restrictions on the use of proceeds from asset sales, new debt issues, and dividend payments. These traditional mechanisms for controlling or managing credit risk were described in Chapters 10 and 11.

Additionally, in Chapters 22, 23, and 24 we discussed the increasing use of credit derivatives in the forward, options, and swaps markets to manage credit risk—for example, the use of digital put options to control the credit risk of an individual loan or portfolio of loans. In addition, FIs are increasingly requiring borrowers to hedge their own risks, especially when the FI makes floating-rate loans to borrowers. When interest rates rise, the borrower of a floating-rate loan may have greater difficulty meeting interest rate payments. However, if the borrower has hedged the risk of rising rates in the derivatives market (e.g., by selling interest rate futures or receiving floating payments–paying fixed payments in an interest rate swap), the borrower is in a far better position to meet its contractual payments to the FI. As a result, the credit risk exposure of the FI is reduced.

This and the following chapter on securitization describe the growing role of loan sales and other newer types of techniques (such as the good bank–bad bank structure) increasingly used by FI managers to control credit risk. While loan sales have been in existence for many years, the use of loan sales (by removing existing loans from the balance sheet) is increasingly being recognized as a valuable additional tool in an FI manager's portfolio of credit risk management techniques. Indeed, it has been found that new loan announcements are associated with a positive stock price announcement effect even when a borrower's loans trade on the secondary market. Moreover, when a borrower's existing loans trade for the first time in the secondary loan market, it elicits a positive stock price response. The chapter begins with an overview of the loan sales market. We define and look at the types of loan sales and summarize who are the buyers and sellers of loans. We then discuss why banks and other FIs would sell loans, as well as the factors that deter and encourage loan sales.

# THE BANK LOAN SALES MARKET

## Definition of a Loan Sale

**bank loan sale**
Sale of a loan originated by an FI with or without recourse to an outside buyer.

**recourse**
The ability of a loan buyer to put the loan back to the originator if it goes bad.

Credit derivatives (such as credit swaps) discussed in Chapters 22, 23, and 24 allow FIs to reduce credit risk without physically removing assets from their balance sheet. Loan sales allow FIs to reduce credit risk completely by removing the loan from the balance sheet. Specifically, a **bank loan sale** occurs when an FI originates a loan and sells it either with or without recourse to an outside buyer.

If a loan is sold without recourse, not only is it removed from the FI's balance sheet, but the FI has no explicit liability if the loan eventually goes bad. Panel A of Table 25–1 shows an FI's balance sheet before and after a $20 million loan sale without recourse. The buyer (and not the FI that originated the loan) bears all the credit risk. If, however, the loan is sold with **recourse,** under certain conditions the buyer can put the loan back to the selling FI. Therefore, the FI retains a contingent credit risk liability. Panel B of Table 25–1 shows the FI's balance sheet, including the contingent liability from the loan sale with recourse held off the balance sheet. In practice, most loans are sold without recourse because a loan sale is technically removed from the balance sheet only when the buyer has no future credit risk claim on the FI. Importantly, loan sales involve no creation of new types of securities such as the pass-throughs, CMOs, and MBBs described in Chapter 26. As such, loan sales are a primitive form of securitization in that loan selling creates a secondary market for loans in which ownership of the loan is simply transferred to the loan buyer.

## Types of Loan Sales

The U.S. loan sales market has three segments: two involve the sale and trading of domestic loans, while the third involves emerging-market loan sales and trading. Since we fully described emerging-market loan sales in Chapter 14 on sovereign risk, we concentrate on the domestic loan sales market here.

**TABLE 25–1**   FI Balance Sheet before and after a $20 Million Loan Sale (in millions)

| Before Loan Sale | | | | After Loan Sale | | | |
|---|---|---|---|---|---|---|---|
| **Assets** | | **Liabilities/Equity** | | **Assets** | | **Liabilities/Equity** | |
| **Panel A: Loan Sale without Recourse** | | | | | | | |
| Cash assets | $ 10 | Deposit | $ 90 | Cash assets | $ 10 | Deposits | $ 90 |
| | | | | Loans | 70 | | |
| Loans | 90 | Equity | 10 | New investments | 20 | Equity | 10 |
| | $100 | | $100 | | $100 | | $100 |
| **Panel B Loan Sale with Recourse** | | | | | | | |
| Cash assets | $ 10 | Deposit | $ 90 | Cash assets | $ 10 | Deposits | $ 90 |
| | | | | Loans | 70 | | |
| Loans | 90 | Equity | 10 | New investments | 20 | Equity | 10 |
| | $100 | | $100 | | $100 | | $100 |
| | | | | Off-balance-sheet: Loan sale (contingent liability) | | | $ 20 |

### Traditional Short-Term Loan Sales

In the traditional short-term segment of the market, FIs sell loans with short maturities, often one to three months. This market has characteristics similar to those of the market for commercial paper issued by corporations in that loan sales have similar maturities and issue size. Loan sales, however, usually have yields that are 1 to 10 basis points above those of commercial paper of a similar rating. In particular, the loan sales market in which an FI originates and sells a short-term loan of a corporation is a close substitute for the issuance of commercial paper—either directly or through dealers—for the 1,000 or so largest U.S. corporations. The key characteristics of the short-term loan sales market are:

They are secured by assets of the borrowing firm.

They are made to investment grade borrowers or better.

They are issued for a short term (90 days or less).

They have yields closely tied to the commercial paper rate.

They are sold in units of $1 million and up.

Until 1984 and the emergence of the HLT and emerging market loan markets, traditional short-term loan sales dominated the loan sales market. The growth of the commercial paper market (and its accessibility by over 20,000 corporations), as well as the increased ability of banks (through their Section 20 securities affiliates) to underwrite commercial paper (see Chapter 21), also has reduced the importance of this market segment.

### HLT Loan Sales

**highly leveraged transaction (HLT)**
A loan made to finance a merger and acquisition: a leveraged buyout results in a high leverage ratio for the borrower.

With the growth in M&As and LBOs via **highly leveraged transactions (HLTs),** especially during the period 1985–89, a new segment in the loan sales market appeared. What constitutes an HLT loan has often caused dispute. However, in October 1989 the three U.S. federal bank regulators adopted a definition of an HLT loan as one that (1) involves a buyout, acquisition, or recapitalization and (2) doubles the company's liabilities and results in a leverage ratio higher than 50 percent, results in a leverage ratio higher than 75 percent, or is designated as an HLT by a syndication agent. HLT loans mainly differ according to whether they are nondistressed (bid price exceeds 90 cents per $1 of loans) or distressed (bid price is less than 90 cents per $1 of loans or the borrower is in default).

Virtually all HLT loans have the following characteristics:

They are term loans (TLs).

They are secured by assets of the borrowing firm (usually given senior secured status).

They have a long maturity (often three- to six-year maturities).

They have floating rates tied to LIBOR, the prime rate, or a CD rate (normally 200 to 275 basis points above these rates).

They have strong covenant protection.

**financial distress**
A period when a borrower is unable to meet a payment obligation to lenders and other creditors.

Nevertheless, HLTs tend to be quite heterogeneous with respect to the size of the issue, the interest payment date, interest indexing, and prepayment features. After origination, some HLT borrowers, such as Macy's and El Paso Electric, suffered periods of **financial distress.** As a result, a distinction is usually made between the markets for distressed and nondistressed HLTs. Spreads on HLT loans behave more like investment-grade bonds than like high-yield bonds. A possible reason for this is that HLT loans tend to be more senior in bankruptcy and to have greater collateral backing than do high-yield bonds.

Approximately 100 banks and securities firms make a market in this debt either as brokers or (less commonly) as broker–dealers, including Bank of America Merrill Lynch, J.P. Morgan, Citigroup, and Wells Fargo. Most of these FIs view trading in this debt as similar to trading in junk bonds.

## Types of Loan Sales Contracts

There are two basic types of loan sale contracts or mechanisms by which loans can be transferred between seller and buyer: participations and assignments. Currently, assignments comprise the bulk of loan sales trading.

### Participations

**participation in a loan**
Buying a share in a loan syndication with limited, contractual control and rights over the borrower.

The unique features of **participations in loans** are:

- The holder (buyer) is not a party to the underlying credit agreement so that the initial contract between loan seller and borrower remains in place after the sale.
- The loan buyer can exercise only partial control over changes in the loan contract's terms. The holder can vote only on material changes to the loan contract, such as the interest rate or collateral backing.

The economic implication of these features is that the buyer of the loan participation has a double risk exposure: a risk exposure to the borrower and a risk exposure to the loan selling FI. Specifically, if the selling FI fails, the loan participation bought by an outside party may be characterized as an unsecured obligation of the FI rather than as a true sale if there are grounds for believing that some explicit or implicit recourse existed between the loan seller and the loan buyer. Alternatively, the borrower's claims against a failed selling FI may be set off against its loans from that FI, reducing the amount of loans outstanding and adversely impacting the buyer of a participation in those loans. As a result of these exposures, the buyer bears a double monitoring cost as well.

### Assignments

**assignment**
Buying a share in a loan syndication with some contractual control and rights over the borrower.

Because of the monitoring costs and risks involved in participations, loans are sold on an assignment basis in more than 90 percent of the cases on the U.S. domestic market. The key features of an **assignment** are:

- All rights are transferred on sale, meaning the loan buyer now holds a direct claim on the borrower.
- Transfer of U.S. domestic loans is normally associated with a Uniform Commercial Code filing (as proof that a change of ownership has been perfected).

While ownership rights are generally much clearer in a loan sale by assignment, frequently contractual terms limit the seller's scope regarding to whom the loan can be sold. In particular, the loan contract may require either the FI agent or the borrower to agree to the sale. The loan contract may also restrict the sale to a certain class of institutions, such as those that meet certain net worth/net asset size conditions. (An *FI agent* is an FI that distributes interest and principal payments to lenders in loan syndications with multiple lenders.) Assignments are common in loan syndications, discussed in Chapter 11. In a syndicated loan, two or more banks agree to jointly make a loan to a borrower. The syndicate is formed around the arrangers, which generally include the borrower's relationship banks, who retain a portion of the loan and look for junior participants (e.g., smaller banks).

Currently, the trend appears to be toward loan contracts being originated with very limited assignment restrictions. This is true in both the U.S. domestic and the foreign loan sales markets. The most tradable loans are those that can be assigned without buyer restrictions. Even so, one has to distinguish between floating-rate and fixed-rate assignment loans. For floating-rate loans, most loan sales by assignment occur on the loan's repricing date (which may be two or four times a year), due to complexities for the agent FI in calculating and transferring accrued interest—especially given the heterogeneous nature of floating-rate loan indexes such as fed funds plus, T-bond plus, and LIBOR plus. In addition, the nonstandardization of **accrued interest** payments in fixed-rate loan assignments (trade date, assignment date, coupon payment date) adds complexity and friction to this market. Moreover, while the FI agent may have a full record of the initial owners of the loans, it does not always have an up-to-date record of loan ownership changes and related transfers following trades. This means that great difficulties often occur for the borrower, FI agent, and loan buyer in ensuring that the current holder of the loan receives the interest and principal payments due. Finally, the buyer of the loan often needs to verify the original loan contract and establish the full implications of the purchase regarding the buyer's rights to collateral if the borrower defaults.

**accrued interest**
The loan seller's claim to part of the next interest payment on the loan.

Because of these contractual problems, trading frictions, and costs, some loan sales take as long as three months to complete; reportedly, up to 50 percent eventually fail to be completed at all. In many cases, the incentive to renege on a contract arises because market prices move away from those originally agreed to so that the counterparty finds reasons to delay the completion of a loan sale and/or eventually refuses to complete the transaction.[1]

## Trends in Loan Sales

**correspondent banking**
A relationship entered into between a small bank and a big bank in which the big bank provides a number of deposit, lending, and other services.

Banks and other FIs have sold loans among themselves for over 100 years. In fact, a large part of **correspondent banking** involves small banks making loans that are too big for them to hold on their balance sheets—for lending concentration, risk, or capital adequacy reasons—and selling parts of these loans to large banks with whom they have a long-term deposit-lending correspondent relationship. In turn, the large banks often sell parts of their loans called *participations* to smaller banks. Even though this market has existed for many years, it grew slowly until the early 1980s, when it entered a period of spectacular growth, largely due to expansion in highly leveraged transaction (HLT) loans to finance leveraged buyouts (LBOs) and mergers and acquisitions (M&As). Specifically, the volume of loans sold by U.S. banks grew from less than $20 billion in 1980 to $285 billion in 1989. Between 1990 and 1994 the volume of loan sales fell almost equally dramatically, along with the decline in LBOs and M&As as a result of the credit crunch associated with the 1990–91 recession. In 1994, the volume of loan sales had fallen to approximately $20 billion.

In the late 1990s, the volume of loan sales expanded again, partly due to an expanding economy and a resurgence in M&As. For example, the loan market research firm, Loan Pricing Corporation, reported secondary trading volume in 1999 was more than $77 billion. Loan sales continued to grow to over $175 billion

www.loanpricing.com

---

[1] However, in recent years, completion of a trade within 10 days (or $T + 10$) has become an increasing convention.

in 2005 and $238 billion in 2006 as FIs sold distressed loans (loans trading below 90 cents on the dollar). Triggered by an economic slowdown, distressed loan sales jumped from 11 percent of total loan sales in 1999 to 36 percent in 2001 and 42 percent in 2002. As the U.S. economy improved in the early and mid-2000s, the percent of distressed loan sales fell to 17 percent in 2006. Even as the economy slowed in 2007 and 2008, while loans sales surged to more than $500 billion, distressed loan sales remained low. In 2007 distressed loans were just 9 percent of total loan sales and in 2008 they were under 8 percent of all loan sales. Loan sales fell only slightly (to $474 billion) in 2009, during the worst of the financial crisis. However, as might be expected during a recession, the percent of distressed loans increased significantly, to almost 30 percent. Loan sales decreased slightly in 2010, as the U.S. economy began to improve. However, distressed loans remained high, more than 20 percent. In 2011, the U.S. economy continued to struggle and loan sales increased slightly. However, the percent of distressed loans decreased significantly, to 8.7 percent, as many financial institutions had already sold off their marketable distressed loans in 2009 and 2010. Figure 25–1 shows the growth in loan sales over the 1991–2011 (second quarter) period.

Many of these loans are syndicated, involving many sponsoring banks. For example, through the first three quarters of 2011 the Loan Pricing Corporation reported that J.P. Morgan was the leading loan syndicator in the worldwide secondary loan market sponsoring deals worth 1.096 trillion. Yet J.P. Morgan retained risk for only $257 billion of these loans. Along with J.P. Morgan, Bank of America Merrill Lynch ($1.096 trillion), Citigroup ($877 billion), BNP Paribas ($670 billion), and RBS ($633 billion) were the top five secondary-market loan syndicators in the first three quarters of 2011.

## The Buyers and the Sellers

### The Buyers

Of the wide array of potential buyers, some are concerned with only a certain segment of the market for regulatory and strategic reasons. In particular, an

**FIGURE 25–1**   **Recent Trends in the Loan Sales Market, Secondary Loan Volume (1991–3Q2011)**

Source: Thompson Reuters LPC website, 2012. *www.loanpricing.com*

**vulture fund**
A specialized fund that invests in distressed loans.

increasingly specialized group of buyers of distressed loans includes investment banks and **vulture funds.**

*Investment Banks* Investment banks are predominantly buyers of loans because (1) analysis of these loans utilizes investment skills similar to those used in junk bond trading and (2) investment banks were often closely associated with the distressed borrower in underwriting the original junk bond/HLT deals. As such, large investment banks—for example, Bank of America Merrill Lynch and Goldman Sachs—are relatively more informed agents in this market, either by acting as market makers or in taking short-term positions on movements in the discount from par.

*Vulture Funds* Vulture funds are specialized hedge funds established to invest in distressed loans, often with an agenda that may not include helping the distressed firm to survive (see Chapter 5 for a discussion of hedge funds). These investments can be active, especially for those seeking to use the loans purchased for bargaining in a restructuring deal; this generates restructuring returns that strongly favor the loan purchaser. Alternatively, such loans may be held as passive investments, such as high-yield securities in a well-diversified portfolio of distressed securities. Many vulture funds are in fact managed by investment banks.

For the nondistressed HLT market and the traditional U.S. domestic loan sales market, the five major buyers are other domestic banks, foreign banks, insurance companies and pension funds, closed- and open-end bank loan mutual funds, and nonfinancial corporations.

*Other Domestic Banks* Interbank loan sales are at the core of the traditional market and have historically revolved around correspondent banking relationships and regional banking/branching restrictions. Small banks often sell loan participations to their large correspondents to improve regional/borrower diversification and to avoid regulatory-imposed single-borrower loan concentration ceilings. (Credit exposure to a single borrower should not exceed 10 percent of a bank's capital.) This arrangement also can work in the other direction, with the larger banks selling participations to smaller banks.

The traditional interbank market, however, has been shrinking. This is due to at least three factors. First, the traditional correspondent banking relationship is breaking down in a more competitive and increasingly consolidated banking market. Second, concerns about counterparty risk and moral hazard have increased. In particular, moral hazard is the risk that the selling bank will seek to offload its "bad" loans (via loan sales), keeping the "good" loans in its portfolio. Third, the barriers to nationwide banking were largely eroded with the passage of the Riegle-Neal Interstate Branching and Efficiency Act of 1994. Nevertheless, some small banks find the loan sales market enormously useful as a way to regionally diversify their loan portfolios.

*Foreign Banks* Foreign banks remain an important buyer of domestic U.S. loans. Because of the high cost of branching, the loan sales market allows foreign banks to achieve a well diversified domestic U.S. loan portfolio without developing a costly nationwide banking network.

*Insurance Companies and Pension Funds* Subject to meeting liquidity and quality or investment grade regulatory restrictions, insurance companies and pension funds are important buyers of long-term maturity loans.

*Closed- and Open-End Bank Loan Mutual Funds* First established in 1988, these leveraged mutual funds, such as Highland Capital Management of Dallas, Texas, invest in domestic U.S. bank loans. While they purchase loans on the secondary market, such as loan resales, the largest funds also have moved into primary loan syndications because of the attractive fee income available. That is, these mutual funds participate in funding loans originated by commercial banks. The mutual fund, in turn, receives a fee or part of the interest payment. Indeed, some major center banks, such as J.P. Morgan Chase, have actively encouraged mutual fund participation in primary loan syndications.

*Nonfinancial Corporations*   There are some corporations that buy loans, but this activity is limited mostly to the financial services arms of the very largest U.S. and European companies (e.g., GE Capital and ITT Financial) and amounts to no more than 5 percent of total U.S. domestic loan sales.

### The Sellers

The sellers of domestic loans and HLT loans are major money center banks, foreign banks, investment banks, and the U.S. government and its agencies.

*Major Money Center Banks*   Loan selling has been dominated by the largest money center banks. Initially, market concentration on the loan-selling side was accentuated by the growth of HLTs (and the important role major money center banks have played in originating loans in HLT deals) as well as the growth in real estate loan sales. In recent years, large money center banks have engaged in large (real estate) loan sales directly or have formalized such sales through the mechanism of a "good bank–bad bank" structure.

*Good Bank–Bad Bank*   Bad banks are special-purpose banks that hold portfolios of distressed assets and that are organized to liquidate portfolios of nonperforming loans. As such, their sources of financing can be debt or equity. As the assets are liquidated, the bad bank shrinks and eventually disappears as it pays off debtholders and equity holders from the cash flows on the liquidated "bad" assets. The principal objective in their creation is to maximize asset values by separating good loans (in the "good bank") from bad loans (in the "bad bank"). Past examples of bad banks include Grant Street National Bank (established by Mellon bank), National Loan Bank (established by Chemical), and National Asset Bank (established by First Interstate). For example, Mellon Bank wrote down the face value of $941 million in real estate loans and sold them to a specially created bad bank subsidiary—Grant Street National Bank—for $577 million. This special-purpose bad bank was funded by bond issues and common and preferred stock. Managers of the bad bank were given equity (junior preferred stock) as an incentive mechanism to generate maximum values in liquidating the loans purchased from Mellon (i.e., achieving a market resale value greater than $577 million).

More recently, the good bank–bad bank model was proposed as a way of removing toxic assets from the balance sheets of financial institutions during the financial crisis. The good bank–bad bank proposal called for the use of tax money to buy the toxic assets and put them in a new nationalized financial institution (the bad bank) that would operate under federal control. The toxic assets would be sold off over time. The good bank would be left with the good assets and could then operate free from concerns about troubled assets. Similarly, Spain used this same concept during its banking crisis in 2012. A bad bank, known as SAREB, was set up as a condition of a European aid package received by the country in June 2012. Spanish government debt was used to finance less than 50 percent of the bank. Private investors (such as Deutsche Bank of Germany, British bank Barclays, and French insurer Axa) provided the remaining financing. The bad bank bought billions of euros worth of distressed loans and foreclosed property from Spanish banks for approximately half their book value. The program was expected to remove €60 ($77) billion of toxic assets from banks' balance sheets. All Spanish banks that received European aid were obligated to transfer assets to the bad bank.

Table 25–2 illustrates the sale of nonperforming loans from a good bank to a subsidiary bad bank. In Panel A of Table 25–2, the good bank has $950 million of nonperforming loans along with $2,500 million in performing loans and $500 million in cash assets on its balance sheet before the loan sale. The assets are financed with $2,500 million in deposits, $750 million in purchased funds, and $700 million in equity. If the bad bank, in Panel B, buys the nonperforming loans (with the proceeds of a bond, preferred stock, and common stock financing) for $580 million, the good bank gets these loans off of its balance sheet, incurring a $370 million loss in equity (i.e., $950 million face value of loans minus $580 million received in their purchase). The proceeds of the loan sale are then used to pay off purchased funds, bringing their balance down to $170 million, or $750 million minus $580 million. The bad bank now has the $950 million face value loans (for which it paid $580 million) on its balance sheet. These loans can be restructured or disposed of. If the loans realize more than $580 million, additional returns can be passed through to the bad bank common stockholders in dividends or used to repurchase bonds or preferred stock.

There are at least five reasons for believing that loan sales through a bad bank vehicle will be value enhancing compared to the originating bank itself retaining (and eventually selling) these loans:

1. The bad bank enables bad assets to be managed by loan workout specialists.
2. The good bank's reputation and access to deposit and funding markets tend to be improved once bad loans are removed from the balance sheet.
3. Because the bad bank does not have any short-term deposits (i.e., is a self-liquidating entity), it can follow an optimal disposition strategy for bad assets, as it is not overly concerned with liquidity needs.

**TABLE 25–2** Good Bank–Bad Bank Balance Sheets before and after a Loan Sale (in millions)

| Before Loan Sale | | | | After Loan Sale | | | |
|---|---|---|---|---|---|---|---|
| **Assets** | | **Liabilities/Equity** | | **Assets** | | **Liabilities/Equity** | |
| **Panel A: Good Bank** | | | | | | | |
| Cash assets | $ 500 | Deposits | $2,500 | Cash assets | $ 500 | Deposits | $2,500 |
| Loans | | Purchased | | Loans | | Purchased | |
| Performing | 2,500 | funds | 750 | Performing | 2,500 | funds | 170 |
| Nonperforming | 950 | Equity | 700 | Nonperforming | 0 | Equity | 330 |
| | $3,950 | | $3,950 | | $3,000 | | $3,000 |
| **Panel B: Bad Bank** | | | | | | | |
| Cash assets | $ 600 | Bonds | $ 300 | Cash assets | $ 20 | Bonds | $ 300 |
| Loans | 0 | Preferred | | Loans | 580 | Preferred | |
| | | stock | 100 | | | stock | 100 |
| | | Common | | | | Common | |
| | | stock | 200 | | | stock | 200 |
| | $ 600 | | $ 600 | | $ 600 | | $ 600 |

4. As in the case of Mellon's bad bank, contracts for managers can be created to maximize their incentives to generate enhanced values from loan sales.
5. The good bank–bad bank structure reduces information asymmetries about the value of the good bank's assets (the so-called lemons problem), thus potentially increasing its attractiveness to risk-averse investors.

*Foreign Banks*   To the extent that foreign banks are sellers rather than buyers of loans, these loans come out of branch networks such as Japanese-owned banks in California or through their market-making activities selling loans originated in their home country in U.S. loan sales markets.

*Investment Banks*   Investment banks, such as Merrill Lynch (a subsidiary of Bank of America), act as loan sellers either as part of their market-making function (selling loans they have originated) or as active traders. Again, these loan sales are generally confined to large HLT transactions.

*The U.S. Government and Its Agencies*   In recent years the U.S. government and its agencies have shown an increased willingness to engage in loan sales. This has been aided by the passage of the 1996 Federal Debt Collection Improvements Act, which authorizes federal agencies to sell delinquent and defaulted loan assets. Table 25–3 lists summary information on FDIC asset sales from 1990 to 2011. Loan sales in 1996 produced the lowest loan sales price to book value, 35.2 percent, while 2008 resulted in the highest level of sales price to book value, 57.3 percent, for the FDIC. The Department of Housing and Urban Development also has been an increasingly large seller of mortgage loans on multifamily

www.fdic.gov

www.hud.gov

**TABLE 25–3**   **FDIC Loan Sales Summary, 1990–2011**

Source: Federal Deposit Insurance Corporation, Asset Sales, FDIC website, December 2012. *www.fdic.gov*

| Loan Type | Book Value* | Appraised Value* | Sales Price* | Number Sold | Percent of SP/BV | Percent of SP/AV |
|---|---|---|---|---|---|---|
| **1996 Performing vs. Nonperforming Loan Sales** | | | | | | |
| Performing | $   950 | $   926 | $   910 | 7,013 | 95.8% | 98.3% |
| Nonperforming | 3,196 | 563 | 548 | 10,099 | 17.1 | 97.3 |
| Total 1996 | $   4,146 | $   1,489 | $   1,458 | 17,112 | 35.2% | 97.9% |
| **2008 Performing vs. Nonperforming Loan Sales** | | | | | | |
| Performing | $   571.4 | $   383.0 | $   530.6 | 14,338 | 92.9% | 138.5% |
| Nonperforming | 1,025.9 | 398.1 | 384.9 | 10,188 | 37.5 | 96.7 |
| Total 2008 | $ 1,597.3 | $   781.1 | $   915.5 | 24,526 | 57.3% | 117.2% |
| **Total Performing vs. Nonperforming Loan Sales** | | | | | | |
| Performing | $16,609.2 | $14,126.9 | $14,080.9 | 384,174 | 84.77% | 99.67% |
| Performing/ Nonperforming† | 2,035 | 1,183.9 | 1,362.5 | 120,337 | 66.95 | 115.08 |
| Nonperforming | $18,721.5 | 5,380.3 | 5,538.0 | 395,165 | 29.58 | 102.92 |
| Total 1990–2011 | $37,365.7 | $20,691.1 | $20,981.4 | 899,676 | 56.15% | 101.40% |

\* In millions of dollars.
† Performing/nonperforming loan is a loan on which all payments are made on time but the collateral has decreased in value so that it is no longer sufficient to support the loan. FDIC regulations require the lender to classify the loan as nonperforming. In such a situation, the lender will require additional collateral or will demand payment in full.

apartment properties. However, the largest loan sales by a government agency to date were made by the Resolution Trust Corporation (RTC).

Established in 1989, and disbanded at the end of 1995, the RTC had to resolve more than 700 problem savings institutions through merger, closure, or conservatorship. With respect to the U.S. commercial and industrial loan sale market, RTC dispositions had a relatively moderate supply-side effect largely because the bulk of RTC's asset sales were real estate assets (such as multifamily mortgages). The tendency of the RTC was to combine good and bad loans into loan packages and sell them at auction to bidders. For example, in an April 21, 1995, auction, it offered the highest bidder a package of 29 different commercial assets for sale— located in New Jersey, New York, and Pennsylvania—with aggregate estimated market values of $7.5 million. Bidders had only four days to enter bids on this asset package.

---

| **Concept Questions** | 1. Which loans should have the highest yields: (a) loans sold with recourse or (b) loans sold without recourse? |
|---|---|
| | 2. Which have higher yields, junk bonds or HLT loans? Explain your answer. |
| | 3. Describe the two basic types of loan sale contracts by which loans can be transferred between seller and buyer. |
| | 4. Explain the main reason behind the growth in loan sales in the 1980s and the late 2000s. |
| | 5. What institutions are the major buyers in the traditional U.S. domestic loan sales market? What institutions are the major sellers in this market? |

---

## WHY BANKS AND OTHER FIs SELL LOANS

The introduction to this chapter stated that one reason that FIs sell loans is to manage their credit risk better. Loan sales remove assets (and credit risk) from the balance sheet and allow an FI to achieve better asset diversification. However, other than credit risk management, there are a number of economic and regulatory reasons that encourage FIs to sell loans. These are discussed below.

### Reserve Requirements

Regulatory requirements, such as reserve requirements that a bank has to hold at the central bank, are a form of tax that adds to the cost of funding the loan portfolio. Regulatory taxes such as reserve requirements create an incentive for banks to remove loans from the balance sheet by selling them without recourse to outside parties.[2] Such removal allows banks to shrink both their assets and deposits and, thus, the amount of reserves they have to hold against their deposits.

---

[2] Under current reserve requirement regulations (Regulation D, amended May 1986), bank loan sales with recourse are regarded as a liability and hence are subject to reserve requirements. The reservability of loan sales extends to when a bank issues a credit guaranty as well as a recourse provision. Loans sold without recourse (or credit guarantees by the selling bank) are free of reserve requirements. With the elimination of reserve requirements on nontransaction accounts, the lowering of reserve requirements on transaction accounts in 1991, and the innovation of deposit sweep accounts (see Chapter 18), the reserve tax effect has become a less important feature driving bank loan sales (as well as the recourse/nonrecourse mix) in the future.

### Fee Income

An FI can often report any fee income earned from originating (and then selling) loans as current income, whereas interest earned on direct lending can be accrued (as income) only over time. As a result, originating and quickly selling loans can boost an FI's reported income under current accounting rules.

### Capital Costs

Like reserve requirements, the capital adequacy requirements imposed on FIs are a burden as long as required capital exceeds the amount the FI believes to be privately beneficial. For tax reasons, debt is a cheaper source of funds than equity capital. Thus, FIs struggling to meet a required capital ($K$) to assets ($A$) ratio can boost this ratio by reducing assets ($A$) rather than boosting capital ($K$) (see Chapter 20). One way to downsize or reduce $A$ and boost the $K/A$ ratio is through loan sales.

### Liquidity Risk

In addition to credit risk and interest rate risk, holding loans on the balance sheet can increase the overall illiquidity of an FI's assets. This illiquidity is a problem because FI liabilities tend to be highly liquid. Asset illiquidity can expose an FI to harmful liquidity squeezes whenever liability holders unexpectedly liquidate their claims. To mitigate a liquidity problem, an FI's management can sell some of its loans to outside investors. Thus, the loan sales market has created a secondary market in loans that has significantly reduced the illiquidity of FI loans held as assets on the balance sheet.

| | |
|---|---|
| **Concept Questions** | 1. What are some of the economic and regulatory reasons why FIs choose to sell loans?<br>2. How can an FI use its loans to mitigate a liquidity problem? |

# FACTORS AFFECTING LOAN SALES GROWTH

The loan sales market has gone through a number of up and down phases in recent years (as discussed above). However, notwithstanding the value of loan sales as a credit risk management tool, there remain a number of factors that will both spur and deter the market's growth and development in future years. We first discuss factors that may deter the market's growth.

### Access to the Commercial Paper Market

Beginning with the advent of Section 20 subsidiaries in 1987, large banks have enjoyed much greater powers to underwrite commercial paper (and other securities) directly without legal challenges by the securities industry that underwriting by banks is contrary to the Glass-Steagall Act. With the passage of the Financial Services Modernization Act of 1999 and the abolition of the Glass-Steagall Act, the need to underwrite or sell short-term bank loans as an imperfect substitute for commercial paper underwriting is even less important. In addition, more and more smaller middle market firms are gaining direct access to the commercial paper market. As a result, they have less need to rely on bank loans to finance their short-term expenditures.

## Customer Relationship Effects

As the financial institutions industry consolidates and expands the range of financial services sold, customer relationships are likely to become even more important than they are today. To the extent that a loan customer (borrower) views the sale of its loan by its FI as an adverse statement about the customer's value to the FI, loan sales can harm revenues generated by the FI as current and potential future customers take their business elsewhere.

## Legal Concerns

**fraudulent conveyance**
A transaction such as a sale of securities or transference of assets to a particular party that is ruled illegal.

A number of legal concerns hamper the loan sale market's growth, especially for distressed HLT loans. In particular, while banks are normally secured creditors, this status may be attacked by other creditors if the firm enters bankruptcy. For example, **fraudulent conveyance** proceedings have been brought against the secured lenders to Revco, Circle K, Allied Stores, and RJR Nabisco. More recently, in October 2012 the U.S. Justice Department filed a complaint against Bank of America claiming that the bank and its Countrywide Financial unit generated thousands of defective loans and sold them to Fannie Mae and Freddie Mac. The lawsuit was the sixth brought against a major U.S. bank by the Justice Department in less than 18 months. If such legal moves are upheld, then the sale of loans to a particular party may be found to be illegal. Such legal suits represent one of the factors that have slowed the growth of the distressed loan market. Indeed, in many recent sales, loan buyers have demanded a put option feature that allows them to put the loan back to the seller at the purchase price if a transaction is proved to be fraudulent under the Uniform Fraudulent Conveyance Act.

Further, a second type of distressed-firm risk may result if, in the process of a loan workout, the FI lender acts more like an equity owner than an outside debtor. For example, the FI may get involved in the day-to-day running of the firm and make strategic investment and asset sales decisions. This could open up claims that the FI's loans should be treated like equity rather than secured debt. That is, the FI's loans may be subordinated in the claims priority ranking.

There are at least six factors that point to an increasing volume of loan sales in the future. These are in addition to the credit risk "hedging" value of loan sales.

## BIS Capital Requirements

www.bis.org

The Bank for International Settlements (BIS) risk-based capital rules (see Chapter 20) mean that bankers will continue to have strong incentives to sell commercial loans to other FIs and investors to downsize their balance sheets and boost bank capital ratios.

## Market Value Accounting

www.sec.gov
www.fasb.org

The Securities and Exchange Commission and the Financial Accounting Standards Board (FASB) have advocated the replacement of book value accounting with market value accounting for financial services firms (see Chapter 20). In addition, capital requirements for interest rate risk and market risk have moved banks toward a market value accounting framework (see Chapter 15). The trend toward the marking to market of assets will make bank loans look more like securities and thus make them easier to sell and/or trade.

## Asset Brokerage and Loan Trading

The increased emphasis of large money center banks as well as investment banks on trading and trading income suggests that significant attention will still be paid to those segments of the loan sales market where price volatility is high and thus potential trading profits can be made. Most HLT loans have floating rates so that their underlying values are in large part insulated from swings in the level of interest rates (unlike fixed-income securities such as Treasury bonds). Nevertheless, the low credit quality of many of these loans and their long maturities create an enhanced potential for credit risk volatility. As a result, a short-term, three-month secured loan to a AAA rated company is unlikely to show significant future credit risk volatility compared to an eight-year HLT loan to a distressed company. This suggests that trading in loans to below-investment-grade companies will always be attractive for FIs that use their specialized credit monitoring skills as asset traders rather than as asset transformers in participating in the market.

## Government Loan Sales

With the increased involvement of the federal government in the loan sales market (through its direct purchases of distressed loans held by financial institutions and its takeover of mortgage giants Fannie Mae and Freddie Mac) during the financial crisis, there is a strong likelihood that the sale of loans by the government and its agencies will increase in the future.

## Credit Ratings

There is a growing trend toward the "credit rating" of loans offered for sale. Unlike bonds, a loan credit rating reflects more than the financial soundness of the underlying borrowing corporation. In particular, the value of the underlying collateral can change a loan's credit rating up to one full category above a standard bond rating. As more loans are rated, their attractiveness to secondary market buyers is likely to increase.

## Purchase and Sale of Foreign Bank Loans

With more than $1,200 billion in doubtful and troubled loans on their books in the early 2000s, Japanese banks presented a huge potential market for the sale of distressed loans. Indeed, a number of commercial banks and investment banks established funds to buy up some of these bad loans. For example, in 2003 Goldman Sachs announced a $9.3 billion fund to buy troubled loans from Japan's second largest bank, SMFG. This fund represented the first transfer of a bad loan package of this size to a non-government-affiliated entity in Japan. This deal was watched closely as it provided banks with a way of removing bad loans from their balance sheets while still retaining control over the corporate restructuring process.

More recently, during the early 2010s, inadequate capital levels were such that European banks would need to have decreased in size by more than $2.4 trillion to be adequately capitalized. As such, loan sales increased significantly. For example, in 2012 European banks sold a record $61 billion in loans, after $44 billion sold in 2011. Most of these loans have stopped generating their expected interest streams, and working out how to restructure or dispose of them costs banks significant time and money. The buyers are often large asset managers like "vulture" hedge funds or private equity firms that specialize in generating profits from distressed debts or buying performing debts at a discount from banks that just want to trim their balance sheets.

| **Concept Questions** | 1. What are some of the factors that are likely to deter the growth of the loan sales market in the future? |
| --- | --- |
| | 2. What are some specific legal concerns that have hampered the growth of the loan sales market? |
| | 3. What are some of the factors that are likely to encourage loan sales growth in the future? |
| | 4. Why have the FASB and the SEC advocated that financial services firms replace book value accounting with market value accounting? |

**Summary**

Loan sales provide a primitive alternative to the full securitization of loans through bond packages. In particular, they provide a valuable off-balance-sheet tool to an FI that wishes to manage its credit risk exposure better. The new loan sales market grew rapidly in the 1980s and allowed FIs to sell off short-term and long-term loans of both high and low credit quality. There are a number of important factors that suggest that the loan sales market will continue to grow.

**Questions and Problems**

1. What is the difference between loans sold with recourse and loans sold without recourse from the perspective of both sellers and buyers?
2. A bank has made a three-year $10 million loan that pays annual interest of 8 percent. The principal is due at the end of the third year.
   a. The bank is willing to sell this loan with recourse at an interest rate of 8.5 percent. What price should it receive for this loan?
   b. The bank has the option to sell this loan without recourse at a discount rate of 8.75 percent. What price should it receive for this loan?
   c. If the bank expects a 0.5 percent probability of default on this loan, is it better to sell this loan with or without recourse? It expects to receive no interest payments or principal if the loan is defaulted.
3. What are some of the key features of short-term loan sales?
4. Why are yields higher on loan sales than on commercial paper issues with similar maturity and issue size?
5. What are highly leveraged transactions? What constitutes the federal regulatory definition of an HLT?
6. How do the characteristics of an HLT loan differ from those of a short-term loan that is sold?
7. What is a possible reason why the spreads on HLT loans perform differently than do the spreads on junk bonds?

8. City Bank has made a 10-year, $2 million loan that pays annual interest of 10 percent. The principal is expected to be paid at maturity.
   a. What should City Bank expect to receive from the sale of this loan if the current market interest rate on loans of this risk is 12 percent?
   b. The price of loans of this risk is currently being quoted in the secondary market at bid–offer prices of 88–89 cents (on each dollar). Translate these quotes into actual prices for the above loan.
   c. Do these prices reflect a distressed or nondistressed loan? Explain.
9. What is the difference between loan participations and loan assignments?
10. What are the difficulties in completing a loan assignment?
11. Who are the buyers of U.S. loans and why do they participate in this activity?
    a. What are vulture funds?
    b. What are three reasons the interbank market has been shrinking?
    c. What are reasons a small bank would be interested in participating in a loan syndication?
12. Who are the sellers of U.S. loans and why do they participate in this activity?
    a. What is the purpose of a bad bank?
    b. What are the reasons why loan sales through a bad bank will be value enhancing?
    c. What impact has the 1996 Federal Debt Collection Improvements Act had on the loan sale market?
13. In addition to managing credit risk, what are some other reasons for the sale of loans by FIs?
14. What are factors that may deter the growth of the loan sales market in the future? Discuss.
15. An FI is planning the purchase of a $5 million loan to raise the existing average duration of its assets from 3.5 years to 5 years. It currently has total assets worth $20 million, $5 million in cash (0 duration) and $15 million in loans. All the loans are fairly priced.
    a. Assuming it uses the cash to purchase the loan, should the FI purchase the loan if its duration is seven years?
    b. What asset duration loans should it purchase to raise its average duration to five years?
16. In addition to hedging credit risk, what are five factors that are expected to encourage loan sales in the future? Discuss the impact of each factor.

## Web Question

17. Go to the FDIC website at **www.fdic.gov**. From there, click on "Investors," then click on "Closed Loan Sales," and then click on "Find" to get information on recent loan sales by banks. What percentage of the current year's loan sales consisted of performing versus nonperforming loans? Calculate the average percentage loss on these sales.

www.mhhe.com/saunders8e

See Appendices Online at www.mhhe.com/saunders8e
• Appendix 26A: Fannie Mae and Freddie Mac Balance Sheets

# Securitization

## INTRODUCTION

**asset securitization**
The packaging and selling of loans and other assets backed by securities.

Along with futures, forwards, options, swaps, and loan sales, **asset securitization**—the packaging and selling of loans and other assets backed by securities—is a mechanism that FIs use to hedge their interest rate exposure gaps. Securitization involves a change of strategy from a traditional FI's policy of holding the loans it originates on its balance sheet until maturity. Instead, securitization consists of packaging loans or other assets into newly created securities and selling these asset-backed securities (ABS) to investors. By packaging and selling loans to outside parties, the FI removes considerable liquidity, interest rate, and credit risk from its asset portfolio. Rather than holding loans on the balance sheet until maturity, shortly after origination, the originate-to-distribute model entails the FI's sale of the loan and other asset backed securities for cash, which can then be used to originate new loans/assets, thereby starting the securitization cycle over again. Thus, the process of securitization allows FI asset portfolios to become more liquid, provides an important source of fee income (with FIs acting as servicing agents for the assets sold), and helps reduce the effects of regulatory taxes such as capital requirements, reserve requirements, and deposit insurance premiums. As of 2012, over 66 percent of all residential mortgages were securitized, compared with less than 15 percent in 1980.

Credit derivatives, such as asset securitization, allow investors to separate the credit risk exposure from the lending process itself. That is, FIs can assess the creditworthiness of loan applicants, originate loans, fund loans, and even monitor and service loans without retaining exposure to loss from credit events, such as default or missed payments. This decoupling of the risk from the lending activity allows the market to efficiently transfer risk across counterparties. However, it also loosens the incentives to carefully perform each of the steps of the lending process and can lead to poor loan underwriting, inferior documentation and due diligence, failure to monitor borrower activity, and fraudulent activity on the part of both lenders and borrowers. This loosening of incentives was an important factor leading to the global financial crisis of 2008–09. Although bank regulators attempt to examine the off-balance-sheet activities of banks so as to ascertain their safety and soundness, there is far less scrutiny off the balance sheet than there is for on-balance-sheet activities (i.e., traditional lending and deposit taking). To the extent that counterparty credit risk is not fully disclosed to, or monitored by, regulators, the increased use of these innovations transfers risk in ways that are not necessarily scrutinized or understood. It is in this context of increased risk and inadequate regulation that the credit crisis developed.

This chapter investigates the role of securitization in affecting the return-risk trade-off for FIs. We first describe the mechanisms used by FIs to convert an on-balance-sheet asset to a securitized asset. We then describe the three major forms of asset securitization and analyze their unique characteristics. The major forms of asset securitization are the pass-through security, the collateralized mortgage obligation (CMO), and the mortgage-backed bond. Chapter 25 dealt with a more primitive form of asset securitization—loan sales—whereby loans are sold or traded to other investors and no new securities are created. Although all three forms of securitization originated in the real estate lending market, these techniques are currently being applied to loans other than mortgages—for example, credit card loans, auto loans, student loans, and commercial and industrial (C&I) loans.

# MECHANISMS USED TO CONVERT ON-BALANCE-SHEET ASSETS TO A SECURITIZED ASSET

The basic mechanism of securitization is accomplished via removal of assets (e.g., loans) from the balance sheets of the FIs. This is often done by creating off-balance sheet subsidiaries, such as a special-purpose vehicle (SPV, also known as SPE, special-purpose entity) or a structured investment vehicle (SIV). As discussed in Chapter 21, these shadow banks provide credit, maturity, and liquidity intermediation without access to central bank liquidity provisions or deposit insurance. Further, their activities occur beyond the reach of existing state and federal monitoring and regulation.

Typically, the SPV is used in the more traditional form of securitization. In this form, an FI selects a pool of loans and sells them to an off-balance sheet SPV—a company that is created by an arranger for the purpose of issuing the new securities (see Figure 26–1).[1] The SPV packages the loans together and creates new securities backed by the cash flows from the underlying loan pool (i.e., asset-backed securities, ABS). The SPV sells the newly created asset-backed securities to investors such as insurance companies and pension funds and uses the proceeds to pay the loan-originating FI for the loans. The SPV earns fees from the creation and servicing of the newly created asset-backed securities. However, the underlying loans in the asset pool belong to the ultimate investors in the asset-backed securities. All cash flows from the loans are passed through the SPV and allocated according to the terms of the ABS contract to the ultimate investors. Thus, the SPV acts as a conduit, selling the asset-backed securities to investors and passing the cash back to the originating bank. It is then the ABS security investor who has direct rights to the cash flows on the underlying assets. The life of the SPV is

---

[1] The arranger purchases the assets to be placed in the pool, obtains the credit rating, structures the deals, files with the SEC, and underwrites the asset-backed securities to be issued by the SPV. Thus, the arranger must fund the loans over the period (typically three months or less) after origination and before the asset-backed securities are issued. Bank arrangers use their own funds to finance the loans over this period, but nonbank arrangers typically use third-party warehouse lenders. Indeed, an early step in the credit crisis occurred in January 2007 when warehouse lenders pulled back and demanded more collateral to finance the loans of nonbank arrangers.

**FIGURE 26–1**
The Traditional
Securitization
Process Using a
Special-Purpose
Vehicle

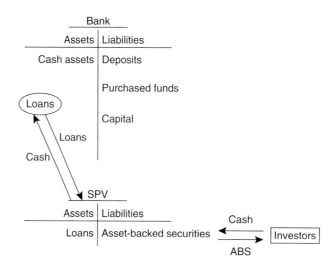

limited to the maturity of the ABS. That is, when the last cash flows of the ABS are paid off, the SPV ceases to exist.

While this method of securitization was lucrative, financial intermediaries soon discovered another method that was even more lucrative. For this form of securitization, an SIV is created. In contrast to the SPV, the SIV's lifespan is not tied to any particular security. Instead, the SIV is a structured operating company that invests in assets that are designed to generate higher returns than the SIV's cost of funds. Rather than selling the asset-backed securities directly to investors in order to raise cash (as do SPVs), the SIV sells commercial paper (or bonds) to investors in order to raise the cash to purchase the bank's loans. The SIV then holds the loans purchased from the banks on its own balance sheet until maturity. These loan assets held by the SIV back the debt instruments issued by the SIV to investors. Thus, in essence the SIV itself becomes an asset-backed security, and the SIV's commercial paper liabilities are considered asset-backed commercial paper (ABCP). The SIV acts similarly to a traditional bank, holding loans or other assets until maturity and issuing short term debt instruments (such as ABCP) to fund its asset portfolio. The major difference between a SIV and a traditional bank is that the SIV cannot issue deposits to fund its asset base (i.e., it is not technically a "bank"; rather, it is a "shadow bank").

Figure 26–2 shows the structure of the SIV method of asset securitization. Unlike an SPV, the SIV does not simply pass through the payments on the loans in its portfolio to the ABCP investors. Indeed, SIV investors have no direct rights to the cash flows on the underlying loans in the portfolio; rather, they are entitled to the payments specified on the SIV's debt instruments. That is, the SIV's ABCP obligations carry interest obligations that are independent of the cash flows from the underlying loan/asset portfolio. Thus, in the traditional form of securitization, the SPV only pays out what it receives from the underlying loans in the pool of assets backing the ABS. In the newer form of securitization, the SIV is responsible for payments on its ABCP obligations whether or not the underlying pool of assets generates sufficient cash flow to cover those costs. Of course, if the cash flows from the asset pool exceed the cost of ABCP liabilities, then the SIV

**FIGURE 26–2**
Securitization
Process Using
a Structured
Investment Vehicle

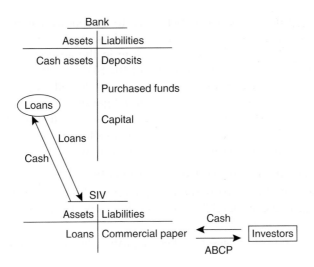

keeps the spread and makes an additional profit. However, if the assets in the underlying pool do not generate sufficient cash flows, the SIV is still obligated to make interest and principal payments on its debt instruments. In such a situation the SIV usually has lines of credit or loan commitments from the sponsoring bank. Thus, ultimately, the loan risk would end up back on the sponsoring bank's balance sheet.

Because of the greater expected return on this newer form of securitization, the SIV became very popular in the years leading up to the financial crisis. Whereas an SPV only earns the fees for the creation of the asset-backed securities, the SIV also earns an expected spread between high yielding assets (such as commercial loans) and low cost commercial paper, as long as the yield curve is upward slopping and credit defaults on the asset portfolio are low. Indeed, because of these high potential spreads, hedge funds owned by Citigroup, Bear Stearns, and others adopted this investment strategy. Until the financial crisis, these instruments appeared to offer investors a favorable return-risk trade-off, i.e., a positive return and an apparently small risk given the asset-backing of the security.

The balance sheet for an SIV in Figure 26–2 looks remarkably similar to the balance sheet of a traditional bank—holding loans or other assets until maturity and issuing short-term debt instruments to fund its asset portfolio. However, to the extent that many SIVs use commercial paper and interbank loans (such as repurchase agreements) to finance their asset portfolios, they are subject to even more liquidity risk than are traditional banks. The reasons for the added liquidity risk are twofold. First, in the financial markets, sophisticated lenders (so-called suppliers of "purchased funds") are prone to "run" at the first sign of trouble, whereas small depositors are slower to react. That is, interbank lenders and commercial paper buyers will withdraw funds (or refuse to renew financing) quicker than traditional "core" depositors, who may rely on their bank deposits for day-to-day business purposes or may be protected by deposit insurance. Second, bank deposits are explicitly insured up to $250,000 and for those in banks viewed as "too big to fail" a full implicit 100 percent. Thus, liquidity risk problems are exacerbated by the liquidity requirements of the SIVs that rely on short-term sources of funding, such as commercial paper, which have to be renewed within a short period of time, i.e., every nine months, and repurchase agreements, which must be fully backed by collateral at all points in time in the absence of a deposit insurance umbrella. Consequently, if the value of the SIV's portfolio declines due to deterioration in credit conditions, the SIV is forced to sell long-term, illiquid assets in order to meet its short-term liquid debt obligations.

Regardless of the form of the off-balance-sheet subsidiary used (SPV or SIV), after the subsidiary is formed, the securitization of loans and the sale of asset-backed securities to investors involves the following steps:

1. The loans are transferred from the originating FI to the SPV or SIV.
2. The SPV or SIV securitizes the loans (either directly or through the issuance of asset-backed commercial paper) and then sells the resulting asset-backed securities to investors.
3. The proceeds of the asset-backed security sale are paid to the FI that originates the loans.

The profitability of securitized assets is largely determined by the SPV or SIV having a high credit rating, since most investors consist of institutional investors who, because they are financial fiduciaries of others, demand or are legally compelled to buy only investment grade securities. Credit rating agencies review all documents of the SPV or SIV before assigning a rating. While the credit rating agency is not a legal party to any of the agreements for setting up the subsidiary, it is listed in all documents as the credit rating agency. Further, once the SPV or SIV is formed, information must be provided to the credit rating agency continually to ensure that the proper procedures are being followed to maintain credit quality, and that credit quality is actually being maintained.

Asset securitization through the use of these off-balance-sheet subsidiaries played a prominent role in the U.S. subprime mortgage crisis, where critics say these securities hid the underlying risk in mortgage investments because the ratings on various securities were based on misleading or incorrect information about the creditworthiness of the borrowers. For a variety of reasons, market participants did not accurately measure the risk inherent with the asset-backed securities or understand the impact of this risk on the overall stability of the financial system. As financial assets became more and more complex, and harder and harder to value, investors were reassured by the fact that both the international bond rating agencies and bank regulators, who came to rely on the rating agencies, accepted as valid some complex mathematical models that theoretically showed the risks of the ABS were much smaller than they actually proved to be in practice. The new products became so complicated that the authorities could no longer calculate the risks and started relying on the risk management methods of the banks themselves. Similarly, the rating agencies relied on the information provided by the originators of synthetic products: a massive abdication of responsibility.

# THE PASS-THROUGH SECURITY

FIs frequently pool mortgages and other assets they originate and offer investors an interest in the pool in the form of *pass-through securities*. Pass-through mortgage securities "pass through" promised payments by households of principal and interest on pools of mortgages created by financial institutions to secondary market investors (mortgage-backed security bondholders) holding an interest in these pools. After a financial institution accepts mortgages, it pools them and sells interests in these pools to pass-through security holders. Each pass-through mortgage security represents a fractional ownership share in a mortgage pool. Thus, a 1 percent owner of a pass-through mortgage security issue is entitled to a 1 percent share of the principal and interest payments made over the life of the mortgages underlying the pool of securities. The originating financial institutions (e.g., bank or mortgage company) or third-party servicer receives principal and interest payments from the mortgage holder and passes these payments (minus a servicing fee) through to the pass-through security holders.

While many different types of loans and assets on FIs' balance sheets are currently being securitized, the original use of securitization is a result of government-sponsored programs intended to enhance the liquidity of the residential mortgage market. These programs indirectly subsidize the growth of home ownership in the United States. Given this, we begin by analyzing the government-sponsored securitization of residential mortgage loans. Three government agencies or government-sponsored enterprises (GSEs) are directly involved in the creation of mortgage-backed, pass-through securities. Informally, they are known as Ginnie Mae (GNMA), Fannie Mae (FNMA), and Freddie Mac (FHLMC).

## GNMA

www.ginniemae.gov

The Government National Mortgage Association (GNMA), or "Ginnie Mae," began in 1968 when it split off from the FNMA (see below). GNMA is a government-owned agency with two major functions. The first is sponsoring mortgage-backed securities programs by FIs such as banks, thrifts, and mortgage bankers. The second is acting as a guarantor to investors in mortgage-backed securities regarding the timely pass-through of principal and interest payments on their sponsored bonds. In other words, GNMA provides **timing insurance.** We describe this more fully later in the chapter. In acting as a sponsor and payment-timing guarantor, GNMA supports only those pools of mortgage loans whose default or credit risk is insured by one of four government agencies: the Federal Housing Administration (FHA), the Veterans Administration (VA), the Department of Housing and Urban Development's Office of Indian and Public Housing, and the USDA Rural Development. Mortgage loans insured by these agencies target groups that might otherwise be disadvantaged in the housing market, such as low-income families, young families, and veterans. As such, the maximum mortgage under the GNMA securitization program is capped.

**timing insurance**
A service provided by a sponsor of pass-through securities (such as GNMA) guaranteeing the bondholder interest and principal payments at the calendar date promised.

## FNMA

www.fanniemae.com

Originally created in 1938, the Federal National Mortgage Association (FNMA), or "Fannie Mae," is the oldest of the three mortgage-backed security sponsoring agencies. While it is now a private corporation owned by shareholders, in the minds of many investors it still has implicit government backing that makes it equivalent to a government-sponsored enterprise (GSE). Indeed, supporting this view is the fact that FNMA has historically had a secured line of credit available from the U.S. Treasury should it need funds in an emergency. Further, and as discussed in more detail below, on September 7, 2008, the Federal Housing Finance Agency (FHFA) placed Fannie Mae (and Freddie Mac, see below) in conservatorship. As conservator, the FHFA was given full powers to control the assets and operations of the firms. Dividends to common and preferred shareholders were suspended, but the U.S. Treasury put in place a set of financing agreements to ensure that the GSEs continue to meet their obligations to bondholders. This means that U.S. taxpayers basically were the guarantors behind about $5 trillion of GSE debt. This step was taken because a default by either Fannie Mae or Freddie Mac, which had been battered by the downturn in housing and credit markets, could have caused severe disruptions in global financial markets, made home mortgages more difficult and expensive to obtain, and had negative repercussions throughout the economy.

FNMA is a more active agency than GNMA in creating pass-through securities. GNMA merely sponsors such programs. FNMA actually helps create pass-throughs by buying and holding mortgages on its balance sheet. It also issues bonds directly to finance those purchases. Specifically, FNMA creates mortgage-backed securities (MBSs) by purchasing packages of mortgage loans from banks and thrifts. It finances such purchases by selling MBSs to outside investors such as life insurers and pension funds. In addition, FNMA engages in swap transactions whereby it swaps MBSs with an FI for original mortgages. Since FNMA guarantees securities as to the full and timely payment of interest and principal, the FI receiving the MBSs can then resell them on the capital market or hold them in its portfolio. Unlike GNMA, FNMA securitizes conventional mortgage loans as well as FHA/VA insured loans, as long as the conventional loans have acceptable loan-to-value or collateral ratios normally not exceeding 80 percent. Conventional loans with high loan-to-value ratios usually require additional private sector credit insurance before they are accepted into FNMA securitization pools.

## FHLMC

www.freddiemac.com

The Federal Home Loan Mortgage Corporation (FHLMC), or "Freddie Mac," performs a function similar to that of FNMA except that its major securitization role has historically involved savings institutions. Like FNMA, FHLMC is a stockholder-owned corporation, yet is currently in conservatorship with the FHFA. Further, like FNMA, it buys mortgage loan pools from FIs and swaps MBSs for loans. FHLMC also sponsors conventional loan pools as well as FHA/VA mortgage pools and guarantees timely payment of interest and ultimate payment of principal on the securities it issues.

## The Incentives and Mechanics of Pass-Through Security Creation

In order to analyze the securitization process, in this section we trace through the mechanics of a mortgage pool securitization to provide insights into the return-risk benefits of this process to the mortgage-originating FI, as well as the attractiveness of these securities to investors. We summarize the steps followed in the creation of a pass-through in Figure 26–3. Given that almost $3 trillion of mortgage-backed securities are outstanding—a large proportion sponsored by GNMA—we analyze an example of the creation of a GNMA pass-through security next.[2]

---

[2] In 2012, outstanding mortgage pools were $7.9 trillion, with GNMA pools amounting to $1.3 trillion; FNMA, $3.0 trillion; and FHLMC, $1.8 trillion.

**FIGURE 26–3**
Summary
of a GNMA
Pass-Through

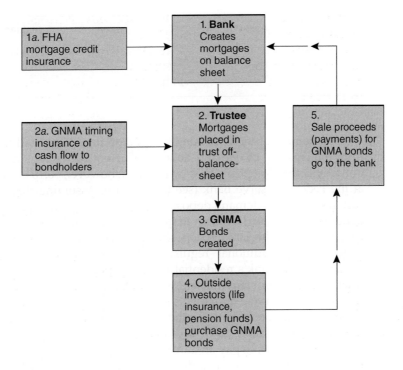

Suppose a bank has just originated 1,000 new residential mortgages in its local area (box 1 in Figure 26–3). The average size of each mortgage is $100,000. Thus, the total size of the new mortgage pool is:

$$1,000 \times \$100,000 = \$100 \text{ million}$$

Each mortgage, because of its small size, will receive credit risk insurance protection from the FHA (box 1a in Figure 26–3). This insurance costs a small fee to the originating bank. In addition, each of these new mortgages has an initial stated maturity of 30 years and a mortgage rate—often called the *mortgage coupon*—of 12 percent per year. Suppose the bank originating these loans relies mostly on liabilities such as demand deposits as well as its own capital or equity to finance its assets. Under current capital adequacy requirements, each $1 of new residential mortgage loans has to be backed by some capital. As discussed in Chapter 20, regular 1–4 family residential mortgages are separated into two risk categories. Category 1 residential mortgages include traditional, first-lien, prudently under-written mortgage loans. Category 2 residential mortgages include junior liens and nontraditional mortgage products. The risk weight assigned to the residential mortgage then depends on the mortgage's category assignment and its loan-to-value ratio. For example, if the loans in the $100 million mortgage pool are classified as category 1 mortgages and have a loan-to-value ratio between 60 and 80 percent, they are assigned a risk weight of 50 percent and the risk-based capital requirement is 8 percent. The bank capital needed to back the $100 million mortgage portfolio would be:

$$\text{Capital requirement} = \$100,000,000 \times 0.5 \times 0.08 = \$4 \text{ million}$$

**TABLE 26–1**
**Bank Balance Sheet (in millions of dollars)**

| Assets | | Liabilities | |
|---|---|---|---|
| Cash reserves | $ 10.67 | Demand deposits | $106.67 |
| Long-term mortgages | 100.00 | Capital | 4.00 |
| | $110.67 | | $110.67 |

We assume that the remaining $96 million needed to fund the mortgages come from the issuance of demand deposits. Current regulations require that for every dollar of demand deposits held by the bank, however, $0.10 in cash reserves be held at the Federal Reserve Bank (see Chapter 19). Assuming that the bank funds the cash reserves with demand deposits, the bank must issue $106.67m [$96m/(1 − 0.1)] in demand deposits (i.e., $96m to fund mortgages and $10.67m to fund the required cash reserves on the demand deposits). The reserve requirement on demand deposits is essentially an additional "regulatory" tax, over and above the capital requirement, on funding the bank's residential mortgage portfolio.[3] Note that since a 0 percent reserve requirement currently exists on CDs and time deposits, the FI needs no extra funds to pay reserve requirements if it uses CDs to fund the mortgage portfolio.

Given these considerations, the bank's initial postmortgage balance sheet may look like that in Table 26–1. In addition to the capital and reserve requirement taxes, the bank has to pay an annual insurance premium to the FDIC based on the risk of the bank. Assuming a deposit insurance premium of 45 basis points (for a low-quality bank), the fee would be:[4]

$$\$106,670,000 \times 0.0045 = \$480,015$$

Although the bank is earning a 12 percent mortgage coupon on its mortgage portfolio, it is facing three levels of regulatory taxes:

1. Capital requirements.
2. Reserve requirements.
3. FDIC insurance premiums.

Thus, one incentive to securitize is to reduce the regulatory tax burden on the FI to increase its after-tax return.[5] In addition to facing regulatory taxes on its residential mortgage portfolio earnings, the bank in Table 26–1 has two risk exposure problems.

### Gap Exposure or $D_A > kD_L$

The FI funds the 30-year mortgage portfolio with short-term demand deposits; thus, it has a duration mismatch.[6] This is true even if the mortgage assets have been funded with short-term CDs, time deposits, or other purchased funds.

---

[3] Implicitly viewing the capital requirement as a tax assumes that regulators set the minimum level above the level that would be privately optimal.

[4] As of 2012 the deposit insurance premium was 12 basis points for the highest-quality banks (see Chapter 19).

[5] Other reasons for securitization include greater geographic diversification of the loan portfolio. Specifically, many FIs originate mortgages from the local community; the ability to securitize facilitates replacing them with MBSs based on mortgages from other cities and regions.

[6] As we discussed in Chapters 8 and 9, core demand deposits usually have a duration of less than three years. Depending on prepayment assumptions, mortgages normally have durations of at least 4.5 years.

### Illiquidity Exposure

The bank is holding a very illiquid asset portfolio of long-term mortgages and no excess reserves. As a result, it is exposed to the potential liquidity shortages discussed in Chapter 12, including the risk of having to conduct mortgage asset fire sales to meet large unexpected demand deposit withdrawals.

One possible solution to these duration mismatch and illiquidity risk problems is to lengthen the bank's on-balance-sheet liabilities by issuing longer-term deposits or other liability claims, such as medium-term notes. Another solution is to engage in interest rate swaps to transform the bank's liabilities into those of a long-term, fixed-rate nature (see Chapter 24). These techniques, however, do not resolve the problem of regulatory taxes and the burden they impose on the FI's returns.

By contrast, creating GNMA pass-through securities can largely resolve the duration and illiquidity risk problems on the one hand and reduce the burden of regulatory taxes on the other. This requires the bank to securitize the $100 million in residential mortgages by issuing GNMA pass-through securities. In our example, the bank can do this since the 1,000 underlying mortgages each have FHA mortgage insurance, the same stated mortgage maturity of 30 years and coupons of 12 percent. Therefore, they are eligible for securitization under the GNMA program if the bank is an approved lender (which we assume it is).

The bank begins the securitization process by packaging the $100 million in mortgage loans and removing them from the balance sheet by placing them with a third-party trustee, in a special-purpose vehicle (SPV) off the balance sheet (box 2 in Figure 26–3). This third-party trustee may be another bank of high creditworthiness, an SPV or SIV, or a legal trustee. Next, the bank determines that (1) GNMA will guarantee, for a fee, the timing of interest and principal payments on the bonds issued to back the mortgage pool and (2) the bank itself will continue to service the pool of mortgages for a fee, even after they are placed in trust (box 2a in Figure 26–3). Then GNMA issues pass-through securities backed by the underlying $100 million pool of mortgages (box 3 in Figure 26–3). These GNMA securities or pass-through bonds are sold to outside investors in the capital market (box 4 in Figure 26–3) and the proceeds (net of any underwriting fees) go to the originating bank (box 5 in Figure 26–3). Large purchasers of these securities include insurance companies and pension funds.

Before we examine the mechanics of the repayment on a pass-through security, we consider the attractiveness of these bonds to investors. In particular, investors in these bonds are protected against two levels or types of default risk.

### Default Risk by the Mortgagees

Suppose that because of rapidly falling house prices, a homeowner walks away from a mortgage, leaving behind a low-valued house to be foreclosed at a price below the outstanding mortgage. This might expose the mortgage bondholders to losses unless there are external guarantors. Through FHA/VA housing insurance, government agencies bear the risk of default, thereby protecting bondholders against such losses.

### Default Risk by Bank/Trustee

Suppose the bank that originated the mortgages goes bankrupt or the trustee absconds with the mortgage interest and principal due to bondholders. Because it guarantees the prompt timing of interest and principal payments on GNMA securities, GNMA bears the cost of making the promised payments in full and on time to GNMA bondholders.

Given this default protection, GNMA bondholders' (or investors') returns from holding these bonds is the monthly repayments of interest and principal on the 1,000 mortgages in the pool, after the deduction of a mortgage-servicing fee by the mortgage-originating bank and a monthly timing insurance fee to be paid to GNMA. The total sum of these fees is around 50 basis points, or ½ percent, with approximately 6 basis points going as a fee to GNMA for timing insurance and the remaining 44 basis points going to the mortgage originator as a servicing fee. As a result, the stated coupons on the GNMA bonds would be set at approximately ½ percent below the coupon rate on the underlying mortgages. In our example:

| | | |
|---|---|---|
| Mortgage coupon rate | = | 12.00% |
| *minus* | | |
| Servicing fee | = | 0.44 |
| *minus* | | |
| GNMA insurance fee | = | 0.06 |
| GNMA pass-through bond coupon | = | 11.50% |

Suppose that GNMA issues $100 million face value bonds at par to back the pool of mortgage loans. The minimum size of a single bond is $25,000; each bondholder gets a pro rata monthly share of all the interest and principal received by the bank minus servicing costs and insurance fees. Thus, if a life insurance company buys 25 percent of the GNMA bond issue (or 1,000 bonds × $25,000 each = $25 million), it gets a 25 percent share of the 360 promised monthly payments from the mortgages comprising the mortgage pool.

**fully amortized**
An equal periodic repayment on a loan that reflects part interest and part principal over the life of the loan.

Every month, each mortgagee makes a payment to the bank. The bank aggregates these payments and passes the funds through to GNMA bond investors via the trustee net of servicing fee and insurance fee deductions. To make things easy, most fixed-rate mortgages are **fully amortized** over the mortgage's life. This means that as long as the mortgagee does not seek to prepay the mortgage early within the 30-year period, either to buy a new house or to refinance the mortgage should interest rates fall, bondholders can expect to receive a constant stream of payments each month analogous to the stream of income on other fixed-coupon, fixed-income bonds. In reality, however, mortgagees do not act in such a predictable fashion. For a variety of reasons, they relocate (sell their house) or refinance their mortgages (especially when current mortgage rates are below mortgage coupon rates). This propensity to **prepay** early, before a mortgage matures, and then refinance with a new mortgage means that *realized* coupons/cash flows on pass-through securities can often deviate substantially from the stated or expected coupon flows in a no-prepayment world. This unique prepayment risk provides the attraction of pass-throughs to some investors but leads other, more risk-averse, investors to avoid these instruments. Before we analyze in greater detail the unique nature of prepayment risk, we summarize the steps followed in the creation of a pass-through in Figure 26–3. Then we analyze how this securitization has helped solve the duration, illiquidity, and regulatory tax problems of the FI manager.

**prepay**
A borrower pays back a loan before maturity to the FI that originated the loan.

In the previous discussion we traced the GNMA securitization process, the origination of mortgages on the balance sheet (Figure 26–3, box 1) through to the sale of GNMA bonds to outside investors (box 4). To close the securitization process, the cash proceeds of the sale of GNMA bonds (box 5) net of any underwriting fees go to the originating bank. As a result, the bank has substituted long-term mortgages for cash by using the GNMA securitization mechanism. Abstracting from the various fees and underwriting costs in the securitization process, the balance sheet of the bank might look like the one in Table 26–2 immediately after the securitization takes place.

There is a dramatic change in the balance sheet exposure of the bank. First, $100 million illiquid mortgage loans is replaced by $100 million cash. Second, the duration mismatch is reduced since both $D_A$ and $D_L$ are now low. Third, the bank has an enhanced ability to deal with and reduce its regulatory taxes. Specifically, it can reduce its capital since capital standards require none be held against cash on the balance sheet compared to the residential mortgages in the pool that require a 4 percent capital ratio. Reserve requirements and deposit insurance premiums are also reduced if the bank uses part of the cash proceeds from the GNMA sale to pay off or retire demand deposits and downsize its balance sheet.

Of course, keeping an all or highly liquid asset portfolio and/or downsizing is a way to reduce regulatory taxes, but these strategies are hardly likely to enhance an FI's profits. The real logic of securitization is that the cash proceeds from the mortgage/GNMA sale can be reused to create or originate new mortgages, which in turn can be securitized. In so doing, the FI is acting more like an asset (mortgage) broker than a traditional asset transformer, as we discussed in Chapter 1. The advantage of being an asset broker is that the FI profits from mortgage pool servicing fees plus up-front points and fees from mortgage origination. At the same time, the FI no longer has to bear the illiquidity and duration mismatch risks and regulatory taxes that arise when it acts as an asset transformer and holds mortgages to maturity on its balance sheet. Put more simply, the FI's profitability becomes more fee dependent than interest rate spread dependent.

The limits of this securitization process clearly depend on the supply of mortgages (and other assets) that can be securitized and the demand by investors for pass-through securities. As was noted earlier, the unique feature of pass-through securities from the demand-side perspective of investors is prepayment risk. To understand the unique nature of this risk and why it might deter or limit investments by other FIs and investors, we next analyze the characteristics of pass-through securities more formally.

**TABLE 26–2**
The Bank's Balance Sheet after Securitization (in millions of dollars)

| Assets | | Liabilities | |
|---|---|---|---|
| Cash reserves | $ 10.67 | Demand deposits | $106.67 |
| Cash proceeds from mortgage securitization | 100.00 | Capital | 4.00 |
| | $110.67 | | $110.67 |

| **Concept** | 1. What is a pass-through security? |
| **Questions** | 2. Should an FI with $D_A > kD_L$ seek to securitize its assets? Why or why not? |

## Prepayment Risk on Pass-Through Securities

To understand the effects of prepayments on pass-through security returns, it is necessary to understand the nature of the cash flows received by investors from the underlying portfolio of mortgages. In the United States, most conventional mortgages are fully amortized. This means that the mortgagee pays back to the mortgage lender (mortgagor) a constant amount each month that contains some principal and some interest. While the total monthly promised payment remains unchanged, the interest component declines throughout the life of the mortgage contract and the principal component increases.

The problem for the FI is to figure a constant monthly payment that exactly pays off the mortgage loan at maturity. This constant payment is formally equivalent to a monthly "annuity" paid by the mortgagee. Consider our example of 1,000 mortgages comprising a $100 million mortgage pool that is to be paid off monthly over 360 months at an annual mortgage coupon rate of 12 percent.

| | |
|---|---|
| Size of pool | = \$100,000,000 |
| Maturity | = 30 years ($n = 30$) |
| Number of monthly payments | = 12 ($m = 12$) |
| $r$ | = Annual mortgage coupon rate = 12 percent |
| $PMT$ | = Constant monthly payment to pay off the mortgage over its life |

Thus, we solve for $PMT$ from the following equation:

$$
\begin{aligned}
\$100,000,000 &= \left[ PMT \left(1 + \frac{r}{m}\right)^{-1} + PMT \left(1 + \frac{r}{m}\right)^{-2} \right.\\
&\quad \left. + \ldots + PMT \left(1 + \frac{r}{m}\right)^{-360} \right]\\
&= PMT \left[ \left(1 + \frac{r}{m}\right)^{-1} + \left(1 + \frac{r}{m}\right)^{-2} + \ldots + \left(1 + \frac{r}{m}\right)^{-360} \right]
\end{aligned}
$$

The term in square brackets is a geometric expansion that in the limit equals:

$$
100,000,000 = \left[ \frac{1 - \dfrac{1}{\left(1 + \dfrac{r}{m}\right)^{mn}}}{\dfrac{r}{m}} \right] \times PMT
$$

**TABLE 26–3**
Fully Amortized
Mortgages

| Month | Outstanding Balance Payment | Fixed Monthly (*PMT*) | Interest Component | Principal Component | Principal Remaining |
|---|---|---|---|---|---|
| 1 | $100,000,000 | $1,028,610 | $1,000,000 | $28,610 | $99,971,390 |
| 2 | 99,971,390 | 1,028,610 | 999,714 | 28,896 | 99,942,494 |
| . | . | . | . | . | . |
| . | . | . | . | . | . |
| . | . | . | . | . | . |
| . | . | . | . | . | . |
| 360 | . | . | . | . | . |

The new term in brackets is the present value of the annuity factor, *PVA*, or $100,000,000 = PMT[PVA]$. Rearranging to solve for *PMT*, the required equal monthly payment on the mortgages, we have:

$$PMT = \frac{100,000,000}{PVA}$$

$$= \frac{100,000,000}{\left[\dfrac{1 - \dfrac{1}{\left(1 + \dfrac{r}{m}\right)^{mn}}}{\dfrac{r}{m}}\right]}$$

$$= \frac{100,000,000}{\left[\dfrac{1 - \dfrac{1}{\left(1 + \dfrac{0.12}{12}\right)^{360}}}{\dfrac{0.12}{12}}\right]} = \$1,028,610$$

As a result, $PMT = \$1,028,610$, or, given 1,000 individual mortgages, $1,028.61 per mortgage rounding to the nearest cent. Thus, payments by the 1,000 mortgagees, with an average monthly mortgage payment of $1,028.61, will pay off the mortgages outstanding over 30 years, assuming no prepayments.

The aggregate monthly payments of $1,028,610 comprise different amounts of principal and interest each month.[7] Table 26–3 breaks down the aggregate monthly amortized mortgage payments of $PMT = \$1,028,610$ into their interest and principal components. In month 1, the interest component is 12 percent divided by 12 (or 1 percent) times the outstanding balance on the mortgage pool ($100 million). This comes to $1,000,000, meaning that the remainder of the aggregate monthly payment, or $28,610, can be used to pay off outstanding principal on the pool. At the

---

[7] Because of the rounding of each monthly payment to the nearest cent, we assume that aggregate monthly cash flows are $1,000 \times \$1,028.61 = \$1,028,610$.

end of month 1, the outstanding principal balance on the mortgages is reduced by $28,610 to $99,971,390. In month 2 and thereafter, the interest component declines and the principal component increases, but the two still sum to $1,028,610. Thus, in month 2, the interest component declines to $999,714 (or 1 percent of the outstanding principal at the beginning of month 2) and the principal component of the payment increases to $28,896.

While 12 percent is the coupon or interest rate the house buyers pay on the mortgages, the rate passed through to GNMA investors is 11½ percent, reflecting an average 6-basis-point insurance fee paid to GNMA and a 44-basis-point servicing fee paid to the originating bank. The servicing fees are normally paid monthly rather than as lump-sum single payments up front to create the appropriate collection/servicing incentives over the life of the mortgage for the originating bank. For example, the bank's incentive to act as an efficient collection/servicing agent over 360 months would probably decline if it received a single large up-front fee in month 1 and nothing thereafter.

The effect of the ½ percent fee is to reduce the cash flows passed through to the bondholders. As can be checked, using a *PVA* that reflects an 11.5 percent annual rate rather than a 12 percent annual rate, GNMA bondholders would collectively receive $990,291 per month over the 30 years instead of $1,028,610 under conditions of no fees.

As we have shown so far, the cash flows on the pass-through directly reflect the interest and principal cash flows on the underlying mortgages minus service and insurance fees. However, over time, mortgage rates change. Let $Y$ be the current annual mortgage coupon rate, which could be higher or lower than 12 percent, and let $y$ be the yield on newly issued par value GNMA pass-through bonds. With no prepayments, the market value of the 12 percent mortgage coupon pool (11½ percent actual coupons) could be calculated as:

$$V = \frac{\$990,291}{\left(1 + \dfrac{y}{12}\right)^{1}} + \frac{\$990,291}{\left(1 + \dfrac{y}{12}\right)^{2}} + \ldots + \frac{\$990,291}{\left(1 + \dfrac{y}{12}\right)^{360}}$$

If $y$ is less than 11½ percent, the market value of the pool will be greater than its original value; if $y$ is greater than 11½ percent, the pool will decrease in value. However, valuation is more complex than this since we have ignored the prepayment behavior of the 1,000 mortgages. In effect, prepayment risk has two principal sources: refinancing and housing turnover.

## Refinancing

As coupon rates on new mortgages fall, there is an increased incentive for individuals in the pool to pay off old, high-cost mortgages and refinance at lower rates. However, refinancing involves transaction costs and recontracting costs. Many banks and thrifts have sought to charge prepayment penalty fees on the outstanding mortgage balance prepaid.[8] In addition, there are often origination costs or points for new mortgages to consider along with the cost of appraisals and credit checks. As a result, mortgage rates may have to fall by some amount below the current coupon rate before there is a significant increase in prepayments in the pool.

---

[8] However, federal regulations typically forbid prepayment penalties on residential first mortgages.

### *Housing Turnover*

The other factor that affects prepayments is the propensity of the mortgagees in the pool to move before their mortgages reach maturity. The decision to move or turn over a house may be due to a complex set of factors, such as the level of house prices, the size of the underlying mortgage, the general health of the economy, and even the season (e.g., spring is a good time to move). In addition, if the existing mortgage is an **assumable mortgage,** the buyer of the house takes over the outstanding mortgage's payments. Thus, the sale of a house in a pool does not necessarily imply that the mortgage has to be prepaid. By contrast, nonassumability means a one-to-one correspondence between sale of a house and mortgage prepayment. Most GNMA pools allow mortgages to be assumable; the reverse holds true for pass-throughs sponsored by FNMA and FHLMC.

Figure 26–4 plots the prepayment frequency of a pool of mortgages in relation to the spread between the current mortgage coupon rate ($Y$) and the mortgage coupon rate ($r$) in the existing pool (12 percent in our example). Notice when the current mortgage rate ($Y$) is above the rate in the pool ($Y > r$), mortgage prepayments are small, reflecting monthly forced turnover as people have to relocate because of jobs, divorces, marriages, and other considerations. Even when the current mortgage rate falls below $r$, those remaining in the mortgage pool do not rush to prepay because up-front refinancing, contracting, and penalty costs are likely to outweigh any present value savings from lower mortgage rates. However, as current mortgage rates continue to fall, the propensity for mortgage holders to prepay increases significantly. Conceptually, mortgage holders have a very valuable call option on the mortgage when this option is in the money.[9] That is, when current mortgage rates fall sufficiently low so that the present value savings of refinancing outweigh the exercise price (the cost of prepayment penalties and other fees and costs), the mortgage will be called.

Since the FI has sold the mortgage cash flows to GNMA investors and must by law pass through all payments received (minus servicing and guaranty fees), investors' cash flows directly reflect the rate of prepayment. As a result, instead of receiving an equal monthly cash flow, *PMT*, as is done under a no-prepayment scenario, the actual cash flows (*CF*) received on these securities by investors fluctuate monthly with the rate of prepayments (see Figure 26–5).

**assumable mortgage**
The mortgage contract is transferred from the seller to the buyer of a house.

**FIGURE 26–4**
**The Prepayment Relationship**

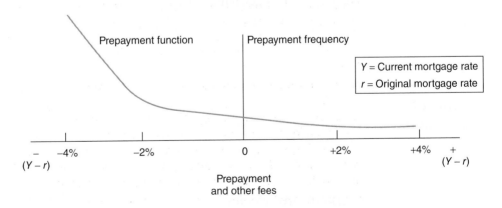

[9] The option is a call option on the value of the mortgage since falling rates increase the value of calling the old mortgage and refinancing a new mortgage at lower rates for the owner of the call option, who is the mortgagee. This option also can be viewed as a put option on interest rates.

**FIGURE 26–5**
The Effects of
Prepayments on
Pass-Through
Bondholders' Cash
Flows

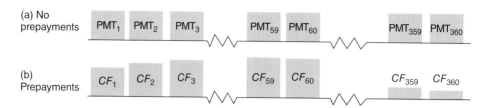

In a no-prepayment world, each month's cash flows are the same: $PMT_1 = PMT_2 = \ldots = PMT_{360}$. However, in a world with prepayments, each month's realized cash flows from the mortgage pool can differ. In Figure 26–5 we show a rising level of cash flows from month 2 onward peaking in month 60, reflecting the effects of early prepayments by some of the 1,000 mortgagees in the pool. This leaves less outstanding principal and interest to be paid in later years. For example, if 300 mortgagees fully prepay by month 60, only 700 mortgagees will remain in the pool at that date. The effect of prepayments is to lower dramatically the principal and interest cash flows received in the later months of the pool's life. For instance, in Figure 26–5, the cash flow received by GNMA bondholders in month 360 is very small relative to month 60 and even months 1 and 2. This reflects the decline in the pool's outstanding principal.

The lowering of current mortgage interest rates and faster prepayments have some good news and bad news effects on the current market valuation of the 12 percent mortgage pool, that is, the 11½ percent GNMA bond.

*Good News Effects*   First, lower market yields reduce the discount rate on any mortgage cash flow and increase the present value of any given stream of cash flows. This would also happen for any fixed-income security. Second, lower yields lead to faster prepayment of the mortgage pool's principal. As a result, instead of principal payments being skewed toward the end of the pool's life, the principal is received (paid back) much faster.

*Bad News Effects*   First, with early prepayment comes fewer interest payments in absolute terms. Thus, instead of receiving scheduled interest payments over 360 months, some of these payments are irrevocably lost as principal outstanding is paid early. That is, mortgage holders are not going to pay interest on mortgage loans they no longer have outstanding. Second, faster cash flow due to prepayments induced by interest rate falls can only be reinvested at lower interest rates when they are received. That is, instead of reinvesting monthly cash flows at 12 percent, investors may reinvest only at lower rates such as 8 percent.

---

**Concept
Questions**

1. What are the two sources of cash flows on a pass-through security?
2. What two factors can cause prepayments on the mortgages underlying pass-through securities?

---

## Prepayment Models

Clearly, managers running FI investment portfolios need to factor in assumptions about the prepayment behavior of mortgages before they can assess the fair value and risk of their GNMA and FNMA/FHLMC bond portfolios. Next, we consider

**FIGURE 26–6**
Pass-Through
Securities,
October 29, 2012

Source: *The Wall Street Journal Online*, October 29, 2012. Reprinted by permission of The Wall Street Journal, © 2012 Dow Jones & Company, Inc. All Rights Reserved Worldwide.

Monday, October 29, 2012

**MORTGAGE-BACKED SECURITIES**

Indicative, not guaranteed; from Bear Stearns Cos./Street Software Technology Inc.

| (1) | | (2) | (3) | (4) | (5) | (6) | (7) | (8) |
|---|---|---|---|---|---|---|---|---|
| | | PRICE | PRICE CHANGE | AVG LIFE | SPREAD TO AVG LIFE | SPREAD CHANGE | PSA (Prepay | YIELD TO |
| | | (Pts-32ds) | (32ds) | (years) | (Bps) | | Spread) | MATURITY* |
| **30-YEAR** | | | | | | | | |
| FMAC GOLD | 4.0% | 106-21 | + 02 | 2.7 | 102 | − 1 | 515 | 1.40 |
| FMAC GOLD | 4.5% | 107-04 | — | 2.3 | 93 | — | 579 | 1.26 |
| FMAC GOLD | 5.0% | 108-04 | — | 2.2 | 73 | 2 | 609 | 1.04 |
| FNMA | 4.0% | 107-02 | + 02 | 2.8 | 87 | − 1 | 513 | 1.25 |
| FNMA | 4.5% | 107-27 | + 01 | 2.4 | 63 | — | 579 | 0.97 |
| FNMA | 5.0% | 109-01 | — | 2.2 | 31 | 1 | 612 | 0.62 |
| GNMA** | 4.0% | 109-11 | + 01 | 3.5 | 67 | — | 455 | 1.17 |
| GNMA** | 4.5% | 108-22 | + 01 | 3.1 | 107 | — | 434 | 1.50 |
| GNMA** | 5.0% | 109-17 | — | 3.2 | 132 | 1 | 426 | 1.77 |
| **15-YEAR** | | | | | | | | |
| FMAC GOLD | 4.0% | 106-03 | — | 2.3 | 84 | 1 | 511 | 1.16 |
| FNMA | 4.0% | 106-24 | — | 2.3 | 56 | 1 | 508 | 0.89 |
| GNMA** | 4.0% | 108-02 | — | 2.8 | 57 | 1 | 380 | 0.95 |

*Extrapolated from benchmarks based on projections from Bear Stearns prepayment model, assuming interest rates remain unchanged.
**Government guaranteed.

**COLLATERIZED MORTGAGE OBLIGATIONS**

Spread of CMO yields above U.S. Treasury securities of comparable maturity, in basis points (100 basis points = 1 percentage point of interest)

| MATURITY | SPREAD | CHG FROM PREV DAY |
|---|---|---|
| SEQUENTIALS | | |
| 2-year | 185 | ... |
| 7-year | 165 | ... |
| 10-year | 150 | ... |
| 20-year | 170 | ... |
| PACS | | |
| 2-year | 150 | ... |
| 5-year | 175 | ... |
| 7-year | 175 | ... |
| 10-year | 135 | ... |
| 20-year | 150 | ... |

www.sifma.com

three alternative ways to model prepayment effects using the Securities Industry and Financial Markets Association (SIFMA) prepayment model, other empirical models, and option valuation models.

To begin, we look carefully at the results of one prepayment model. Look at the reported prices and yields on pass-through securities in Figure 26–6. The first columns in the figure show the sponsor of the issue (GNMA/FNMA/FMAC), the stated maturity of the issue (30 years or 15 years), the mortgage coupons on the mortgages in each pool (e.g., 5 percent), and information about the maximum delay between the receipt of interest by the servicer/sponsor and the actual payment of interest to bondholders. The GOLD next to FMAC indicates a maximum stated delay of 55 days; this is the same as FNMA and FHLMC and 10 days more than GNMA.[10] The current market price is shown in column (2), with the daily price change in column (3) (in 32nds).

Column (4) shows the weighted-average life of the bond reflecting an assumed prepayment schedule. This weighted-average life is not the same as duration, which measures the weighted-average time to maturity based on the relative present values of cash flows as weights. Instead, it is a significant simplification of the duration measure seeking to concentrate on the expected timing of payments of principal. Technically, **weighted-average life (WAL)** is measured by:

**weighted-average life (WAL)**
The sum of the products of the time when principal payments are received and the amount of principal received all divided by total principal outstanding.

$$WAL = \frac{\Sigma\ (\text{Time} \times \text{Expected principal received})}{\text{Total principal outstanding}}$$

For example, consider a loan with two years to maturity and $100 million in principal. Investors expect $40 million of the principal to be repaid at the end of year 1 and the remaining $60 million to be repaid at maturity.

[10] FMAC (or Farmer MAC) stands for the Federal Agricultural Mortgage Corporation. FMAC is smaller than the three main mortgage sponsoring agencies (GNMA, FNMA, and FHLMC) and specializes in agricultural mortgages.

| Time | Expected Principal Payments | Time $\times$ Principal |
|:---:|:---:|:---:|
| 1 | $ 40 | $ 40 |
| 2 | 60 | 120 |
| | $100 | $160 |

$$WAL = \frac{160}{100} = 1.6 \text{ years}$$

Notice in column (4) of Figure 26–6, the WALs of these pools are all 3.5 years or less.

The fifth and sixth columns of Figure 26–6 show the yield spread of mortgage-backed securities over Treasuries and its daily change. The yield spread shown here is the spread to average life, while the more complicated (and most used) is the option-adjusted spread (OAS), which is explained in detail later. Briefly, the OAS can be calculated by using the yield to maturity in the final column [column (8)] and deducting from this the yield on a matched maturity Treasury bond. The yield to maturity in the final column is calculated according to prepayment behavior estimated and valued by the Bear Stearns division of J.P. Morgan Chase, the investment bank. As will be discussed later, allowing for prepayment behavior, the bond is valued and its yield calculated using an explicit prepayment "option" model. This is only one way to calculate the prepayment behavior of mortgagees and the effects of their behavior on yields. Two alternative ways of modeling prepayment behavior are (1) the Public Securities Association (PSA) model approach and (2) the empirical model approach. These two approaches are discussed in the next section, along with the option-based approach. Note that the PSA prepayment speed (see below) of the various securities is shown in column (7) of Figure 26–6. These speeds vary from 380 to 612 "percent" of the SIFMA benchmark prepayment speed.

www.bearstearns.com

### PSA Model

The prepayment model developed by the Public Securities Association (renamed the Bond Market Association in 1997 and merged with the Securities Industry Association in 2006 to form the Securities Industry and Financial Markets Association) is an empirically based model that reflects an average rate of prepayment based on the past experience of pools of FHA-insured mortgages. Essentially, the PSA model assumes that the prepayment rate starts at 0.2 percent (per annum) in the first month, increasing by 0.2 percent per month for the first 30 months, until the annualized prepayment rate reaches 6 percent. This model assumes that the prepayment rate then levels off at a 6 percent annualized rate for the remaining life of the pool[11] (see Figure 26–7). Issuers or investors who assume that their mortgage pool prepayments exactly match this pattern are said to assume 100 percent PSA behavior. Realistically, the actual prepayment rate on any specific mortgage pool backing a specific pass-through security may differ from PSA's assumed pattern for general and economic reasons, including:

www.sifma.com

1. Level of the pool's coupon relative to the current mortgage coupon rate (the weighted-average coupon).
2. Age of the mortgage pool.

---

[11] Or, after month 30, prepayments are made at approximately ½ percent per *month*.

**FIGURE 26–7**
PSA Prepayment Model

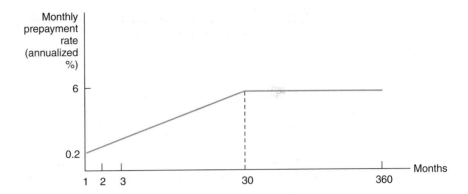

3. Whether the payments are fully amortized.
4. Assumability of mortgages in the pool.
5. Size of the pool.
6. Conventional or nonconventional mortgages (FHA/VA).
7. Geographic location.
8. Age and job status of mortgagees in the pool.

To adjust for these factors, one approach would be to approximately control for them by assuming some fixed deviation of any specific pool from PSA's assumed average or benchmark pattern. For example, one pool may be assumed to be 75 percent PSA and another 125 percent PSA. The former has a slower prepayment rate than historically experienced; the latter, a faster rate. Note these values in Figure 26–8 relative to 100 percent PSA. In column (7) of Figure 26–6 it can be seen that FMAC gold, 4.5 percent 30-year bonds have a PSA of 579. That is, they are expected to prepay at a rate much *faster* than that normally experienced for 30-year mortgage-backed securities. This is because interest rates on new mortgages in October 2012 were well below historic levels.

### *Other Empirical Models*

FIs that are trading, dealing, and issuing pass-throughs have also developed their own proprietary empirical models of prepayment behavior to get a pricing edge on other issuers/investors. Clearly, the FI that can develop the best, most accurate, prepayment model stands to make large profits either in originating and issuing

**FIGURE 26–8**
Deviations from 100 Percent PSA

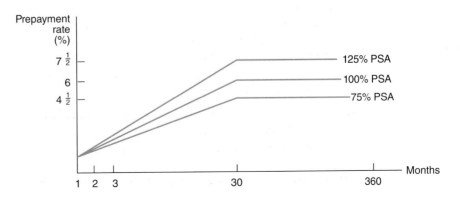

such bonds or in trading such instruments in the secondary market. As a wide variety of empirical models have been developed, we briefly look at the types of methodology followed.

Specifically, most empirical models are proprietary versions of the PSA model in which FIs make their own estimates of the pattern of monthly prepayments. From this modeling exercise, an FI can estimate either the fair price or the fair yield on the pass-through. Of course, those FIs that make the most profits from buying and selling pass-throughs over time are the ones that have most accurately predicted actual prepayment behavior.

In constructing an empirical valuation model, FIs begin by estimating a prepayment function from observing the experience of mortgage holders prepaying during any particular period on mortgage pools similar to the one to be valued. This is conditional, of course, on the mortgages not having been prepaid prior to that period. These conditional prepayment rates in month $i$ ($p_i$) for similar pools would be modeled as functions of the important economic variables driving prepayment—for example, $p_i = f$ (mortgage rate spread, age, collateral, geographic factors, **burn-out factor**).[12] This modeling should take into account the idiosyncratic factors affecting this specific pool, such as its age and burn-out factor, as well as market factors affecting prepayments in general, such as the mortgage rate spread. Once the frequency distribution of the $p_i$'s is estimated, as shown in Figure 26–9, the FI can calculate the expected cash flows on the mortgage pool under consideration and estimate its fair yield given the current market price of the pool.

**burn-out factor**
The aggregate percent of the mortgage pool that has been prepaid prior to the month under consideration.

### *Option Models*

The third class of models uses option pricing theory to figure the fair yield on pass-throughs [see column (8) in Figure 26–6] and, in particular, the fair yield spread of pass-throughs over Treasuries. These so-called option-adjusted spread (OAS) models focus on the prepayment risk of pass-throughs as the essential determinant of the required yield spread of pass-through bonds over Treasuries. As such, they are open to the criticism that they fail to properly include nonrefinancing incentives to prepay and the variety of transaction costs and recontracting costs involved in refinancing.

**FIGURE 26–9**
**Estimated Prepayment Function for a Given Pool**

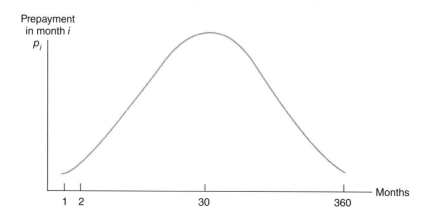

<sup></sup>

[12] A burn-out factor is a summary measure of a pool's prepayments in total prior to month $i$. As such, it is meant to capture heterogeneity of prepayment behavior within any given pool rather than between pools.

Stripped to its basics, the option model views the fair price on a pass-through such as a GNMA as being decomposable into two parts:

$$P_{GNMA} = P_{T\text{-}bond} - P_{prepayment\ option}$$

That is, the value of a GNMA bond to an investor ($P_{GNMA}$) is equal to the value of a standard noncallable Treasury bond of the same duration ($P_{T\text{-}bond}$) minus the value of the mortgage holder's prepayment call option ($P_{prepayment\ option}$). Specifically, the ability of the mortgage holder to prepay is equivalent to the bond investor writing a call option on the bond and the mortgagee owning or buying the option. If interest rates fall, the option becomes more valuable as it moves into the money and more mortgages are prepaid early by having the bond called or the prepayment option exercised. This relationship can also be thought of in the yield dimension:

$$Y_{GNMA} = Y_{T\text{-}bond} + Y_{option}$$

The investors' required yield on a GNMA should equal the yield on a similar duration T-bond plus an additional yield for writing the valuable call option. That is, the fair yield spread or **option-adjusted spread (OAS)** between GNMAs and T-bonds should reflect the value of this option.

**option-adjusted spread (OAS)**

The required interest spread of a pass-through security over a Treasury when prepayment risk is taken into account.

To gain further insights into the option model approach and the OAS, we can develop an example showing how to calculate the value of the option-adjusted spread on GNMAs. To do this, we make a number of simplifying assumptions indicative of the restrictive nature of many of these models:

1. The only reasons for prepayment are due to refinancing mortgages at lower rates; there is no prepayment for turnover reasons.
2. The current discount (zero-coupon) yield curve for T-bonds is flat (this could be relaxed).
3. The mortgage coupon rate is 10 percent on an outstanding pool of mortgages with an outstanding principal balance of $1 million.
4. The mortgages have a three-year maturity and pay principal and interest only once at the end of each year. Of course, real-world models would have 15- or 30-year maturities and pay interest and principal monthly. These assumptions are made for simplification purposes only.
5. Mortgage loans are fully amortized, and there is no servicing fee (again, this could be relaxed). Thus, the annual fully amortized payment under no prepayment conditions is:

$$PMT = \cfrac{1,000,000}{\left[\cfrac{1 - \cfrac{1}{1 + 0.10^3}}{0.1}\right]} = \frac{1,000,000}{2.48685} = \$402,114$$

In a world without prepayments, no default risk, and current mortgage rates ($y$) of 9 percent, we would have the GNMA bond selling at a premium over par:

$$\begin{aligned}
P_{GNMA} &= \frac{PMT}{(1 + y)} + \frac{PMT}{(1 + y)^2} + \frac{PMT}{(1 + y)^3} \\
&= \frac{\$402,114}{(1.09)} + \frac{\$402,114}{(1.09)^2} + \frac{\$402,114}{(1.09)^3} \\
&= \$1,017,869
\end{aligned}$$

**FIGURE 26–10**

Mortgage Rate Changes: Assumed Time Path

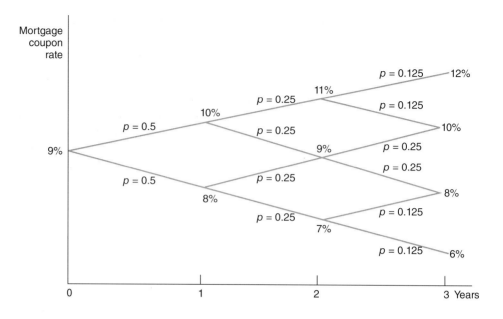

6. Because of prepayment penalties and other refinancing costs, mortgagees do not begin to prepay until mortgage rates, in any year, fall 3 percent or more below the mortgage coupon rate for the pool (the mortgage coupon rate is 10 percent in this example).

7. Interest rate movements over time change a maximum of 1 percent up or down each year. The time path of interest rates follows a binomial process.

8. With prepayments present, cash flows in any year can be the promised payment $PMT = \$402{,}114$, the promised payment (PMT) plus repayment of any outstanding principal, or zero if all mortgages have been prepaid or paid off in the previous year.

In Figure 26–10 we show the assumed time path of interest rates over the three years with associated probabilities ($p$).

***End of Year 1*** Since rates can change up or down by only 1 percent per year, the farthest they can be expected to fall in the first year is to 8 percent. At this level, no mortgage holder would prepay since any mortgage rate savings would be offset by the penalty costs of prepayment, that is, by the assumption it is worth prepaying only when the mortgage rate falls at least 3 percent below its 10 percent coupon rate. As a result, the GNMA pass-through investor could expect to receive $PMT = \$402{,}114$ with certainty. Thus, $CF_1 = \$402{,}114$.

***End of Year 2*** In year 2, there are three possible mortgage interest rate scenarios. However, the only one that triggers prepayment is when mortgage rates fall to 7 percent (3 percent below the 10 percent mortgage coupon rate of the pool). According to Figure 26–10, this occurs with only a 25 percent probability. If prepayment does not occur with 75 percent probability, the investor receives $PMT = \$402{,}114$. If prepayment occurs with 25 percent probability, the investor receives:

$$PMT + \text{Principal balance remaining at end of year 2}$$

We can calculate the principal balance remaining at the end of year 2 as follows. At the end of the first year, we divide the amortized payment, $PMT = \$402,114$, into a payment of interest and a payment of principal. With a 10 percent mortgage coupon rate, the payment of interest component would be $0.10 \times \$1,000,000 = \$100,000$, and the repayment of principal component $= \$402,114 - \$100,000 = \$302,114$. Thus, at the beginning of the second year, there would be $\$1,000,000 - \$302,114 = \$697,886$ principal outstanding. At the end of the second year, the promised amortized payment of $PMT = \$402,114$ can be broken down to an interest component of 10 percent $\times \$697,886 = \$69,788.6$ and a principal component amount of $\$402,114 - \$69,788.6 = \$332,325.4$, leaving a principal balance at the end of year 2 of $\$1,000,000 - \$302,114 - \$332,325.4 = \$365,560.6$.

Consequently, if yields fall to 7 percent, the cash flow received by the investor in year 2 would be:

$$PMT + \text{Principal balance outstanding at end of year 2}$$
$$= \$402,114 + \$365,560.6 = \$767,674.6$$

Thus, expected cash flows at the end of year 2 would be:

$$CF_2 = 0.25(\$767,674.6) + 0.75(\$402,114)$$
$$= \$191,918.64 + \$301,585.5$$
$$= \$493,504.15$$

***End of Year 3*** Since there is a 25 percent probability that mortgages will be prepaid in year 2, there must be a 25 percent probability that the investor will receive no cash flows at the end of year 3 since mortgage holders owe nothing in this year if all mortgages have already been paid off early in year 2. However, there is also a 75 percent probability that mortgages will not be prepaid at the end of year 2. Thus, at the end of year 3 (maturity), the investor has a 75 percent probability of receiving the promised amortized payment $PMT = \$402,114$. The expected cash flow in year 3 is:

$$CF_3 = 0.25(0) + 0.75(\$402,114) = \$301,585.5$$

***Derivation of the Option-Adjusted Spread*** As just discussed, we conceptually divide the required yield on a GNMA, or other pass-throughs, with prepayment risk, into the required yield on T-bonds plus a required spread for the prepayment call option given to the mortgage holders:

$$P = \frac{E(CF_1)}{(1 + d_1 + O_S)} + \frac{E(CF_2)}{(1 + d_2 + O_S)^2} + \frac{E(CF_3)}{(1 + d_3 + O_S)^3}$$

where

$P$ = Price of GNMA
$d_1$ = Discount rate on one-year, zero-coupon Treasury bonds
$d_2$ = Discount rate on two-year, zero-coupon Treasury bonds
$d_3$ = Discount rate on three-year, zero-coupon Treasury bonds
$O_S$ = Option-adjusted spread on GNMA

Assume that the T-bond yield curve is flat, so that:

$$d_1 = d_2 = d_3 = 8\%$$

We can now solve for $O_S$:

$$\$1,017,869 = \frac{\$402,114}{(1 + 0.08 + O_S)} + \frac{\$493,504.15}{(1 + 0.08 + O_S)^2} + \frac{\$301,185.5}{(1 + 0.08 + O_S)^3}$$

Solving for $O_S$, we find that:

$$O_S = 0.96\% \text{ (to two decimal places)}$$
$$Y_{GNMA} = Y_{Tbond} + O_S$$
$$= 8\% + 0.96\%$$
$$= 8.96\%$$

Notice that when prepayment risk is present, the expected cash flow yield at 8.96 percent is four basis points less than the required 9 percent yield on the GNMA when no prepayment occurs. The slightly lower yield results because the positive effects of early prepayment (such as earlier payment of principal) dominate the negative effects (such as loss of interest payments). Note, however, that this result might well be reversed if we altered our assumptions by allowing a wider dispersion of possible interest rate changes and having heavier penalties for prepayment.

Nevertheless, the option-adjusted spread approach is useful for FI managers in that they can place lower bounds on the yields they are willing to accept on GNMA and other pass-through securities before they place them in their portfolios. Realistically, some account has to be taken of nonrefinancing prepayment behavior and patterns; otherwise significant mispricing may occur.

---

**Concept Questions**

1. Should an FI with $D_A < kD_L$ seek to securitize its assets? Why or why not?
2. In general terms, discuss the three approaches developed by analysts to model prepayment behavior.
3. In the context of the option model approach, list three ways in which transaction and other contracting costs are likely to interfere with the accuracy of its predictions regarding the fair price or interest spread on a pass-through security.

---

## Government Sponsorship and Oversight of FNMA and Freddie Mac

Together FNMA and FHLMC represent a huge presence in the financial system as they have more than 60 percent of the single-family mortgage pools in the United States. Some regulators and politicians have argued that these two government-sponsored enterprises have gained too much of a market share. In the early 2000s, their credit losses increased as did their debt-to-equity ratios. Debt to equity for these two agencies ranged from 30 to 97 percent depending on the assumptions made about off-balance-sheet exposures. Recent balance sheets for the two agencies are reported in Appendix 26A, located at the book's website (**www.mhhe.com/saunders8e**).

Also, in the early 2000s, these two agencies came under fire for several reasons. First, in September 2002 Fannie Mae was criticized for allowing a sharp increase in interest rate risk to exist on its balance sheet. The Office of Federal Housing

Enterprise Oversight (OFHEO), a main regulator of Fannie Mae, required Fannie Mae to submit weekly reports to the OFHEO on the company's exposure to interest rate risk. The OFHEO also instructed Fannie Mae to keep regulators apprised of any challenges associated with returning its interest rate risk measure to more acceptable levels, and warned that the office may take additional action if there were adverse developments with Fannie Mae's management's effectiveness in lowering interest rate risk. In October 2003, Fannie Mae and Freddie Mac came under new criticism for allegedly overcharging lenders for services they provide. The overcharges came in the fees that the companies collect from banks, thrifts, and other lenders for guaranteeing repayment of their mortgages. If true, the overcharges hurt mortgage lenders, squeezing their profit margins and perhaps home buyers, too, as lenders increased mortgage interest rates to recover the increased fees. Later that same month, Fannie Mae announced that it miscalculated the value of its mortgages, forcing it to make a $1.1 billion restatement of its stockholders' equity. Earlier in the year, Freddie Mac announced a $4.5 billion misstatement of its earnings. While both were claimed to be computational errors, the episodes reinforced fears that Fannie Mae and Freddie Mac lack the necessary skills to operate their massive and complex businesses, which some investors and political critics worried could pose risk to the nation's financial system if not properly managed. Finally, in February 2004, then Federal Reserve Chairman Alan Greenspan stated that Fannie Mae and Freddie Mac pose very serious risks to the U.S. financial system and urged Congress to curb their growth sooner rather than later.

Underlying the concerns about the actions of these two GSEs was the widespread perception among investors that neither would be allowed to fail if they got into trouble. This perception created a subsidy for the agencies and allowed them to borrow more cheaply than other firms with similar balance sheets. The fear was that the two agencies used their implicit federal backing to assume more risk and finance expansion through increased debt. Such actions created a source of systemic risk for the U.S. financial system. These fears and concerns became reality during the financial crisis. The turmoil in the housing and credit markets that began in 2007 put extreme financial pressure on Fannie Mae and Freddie Mac. The value of their mortgage assets fell, but the debt they issued to purchase those assets remained on their balance sheets. To maintain a positive net worth in the face of falling asset values, financial firms have several options to raise capital, none of which were readily available to Fannie or Freddie. If they sold assets, they would depress the prices of mortgage loans and MBSs even further, worsening both their own balance sheet positions and those of many other financial firms. They could not use retained earnings to increase capital because their operations had not earned a profit since 2006. Finally, rapidly falling share prices made it difficult to raise capital by selling new common stock.

GSE status, however, enabled them to continue to fund their operations by selling debt securities, because the market believed that Fannie and Freddie debt was implicitly guaranteed by the government. In July 2008, however, Fannie and Freddie's share prices fell sharply, resulting in the possibility that market participants might refuse to extend credit to Fannie and Freddie under any terms. Even though Fannie and Freddie maintained access to the debt markets (albeit at higher than usual interest rates), their inability to raise new capital cast doubts on their long-term viability. As a result, the federal government concluded that "the companies cannot continue to operate safely and soundly and fulfill their critical public mission, without significant action" to address their financial weaknesses.

The Housing and Economic Recovery Act of 2008, enacted July 30, 2008, gave the authority for the government's takeover of the GSEs. The act created a new GSE regulator, the Federal Housing Finance Agency (FHFA), with the authority to take control of either GSE to restore it to a sound financial condition. The act also gave the Treasury emergency authority to purchase an unlimited amount of GSE debt or equity securities if necessary to provide stability to the financial markets, prevent disruptions in the availability of mortgage finance, and protect the taxpayer. On September 7, 2008, the FHFA established a conservatorship for both Fannie and Freddie. As conservator, the FHFA took over the assets and assumed all the powers of the shareholders, directors, and officers. Stockholders' voting rights were suspended during the conservatorship, and both firms' replaced their CEOs. Dividends on common and preferred stock were suspended, although the shares continued to trade. (However, in June 2010 the NYSE, through the FHFA, notified Fannie and Freddie that they no longer met NYSE listing standards. The FHFA ordered the two GSEs to delist their common and preferred shares from the NYSE to the over-the-counter market.) The conservatorship will end when the FHFA finds that a safe and solvent condition has been restored.

The takeover of Fannie and Freddie, and specifically the commitment to meet all of the firms' obligations to debtholders, exposes the U.S. government to a potentially large financial risk. At the time the FHFA took over, debt issued or guaranteed by the GSEs totaled more than $5 trillion. The risks of not acting, however, clearly appeared intolerable to the government. A failure or default by either Fannie or Freddie would have severely disrupted financial markets around the world. If the GSE portfolios of mortgage loans and MBSs had to be liquidated, prices would have plunged even further, the secondary market for mortgages would have been decimated, and the supply of new mortgage credit would have been severely restricted.

| **Concept Questions** | 1. Why did Fannie Mae and Freddie Mac come under fire from regulators in the early 2000s? |
| | 2. What problems did Fannie Mae and Freddie Mac experience during the financial crisis? |

## THE COLLATERALIZED MORTGAGE OBLIGATION (CMO)

**CMO**
Collateralized mortgage obligation is a mortgage-backed bond issued in multiple classes or tranches.

While pass-throughs are still the primary mechanism for securitization, the CMO is a second and growing vehicle for securitizing FI assets. Innovated in 1983 by the FHLMC and First Boston, the CMO is a device for making mortgage-backed securities more attractive to investors. The CMO does this by repackaging the cash flows from mortgages and pass-through securities in a different fashion to attract different types of investors. While a pass-through security gives each investor a pro rata share of any promised and prepaid cash flows on a mortgage pool, the **CMO** is a multiclass pass-through with a number of different bondholder classes or tranches. Unlike a pass-through, each bondholder class has a different guaranteed coupon just like a regular T-bond. But more importantly, the allocation of early cash flows due to mortgage prepayments is such that at any one time, all prepayments go to retiring the principal outstanding of only one class of bondholders at a time, leaving the other classes' prepayment protected for a period of time. Thus, a CMO serves as a way to mitigate or reduce prepayment risk.

**FIGURE 26–11**
**The Creation of a CMO**

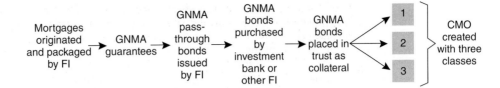

## Creation of CMOs

CMOs can be created either by packaging and securitizing whole mortgage loans or, more usually, by placing existing pass-throughs in a trust off the balance sheet. The trust or third-party FI holds the GNMA pass-through as collateral against issues of new CMO securities. The trust issues these CMOs in three or more different classes. For example, the first CMO that Freddie Mac issued in 1983, secured by 20,000 conventional home mortgages worth $1 billion, had three classes: A, $215 million; B, $350 million; and C, $435 million. We show a three-class or tranche CMO in Figure 26–11.

Issuing CMOs is often equivalent to double securitization. Mortgages are packaged, and a GNMA pass-through is issued. An investment bank such as Goldman Sachs or another CMO issuer such as FHLMC, a commercial bank, a savings institution, or a SPV or SIV, may buy this whole issue or a large part of the issue. Goldman Sachs would then place these GNMA securities as collateral with a trust and issue three new classes of bonds backed by the GNMA securities as collateral.[13] As a result, the investors in each CMO class have a sole claim to the GNMA collateral if the issuer fails. The investment bank or other issuer creates the CMO to make a profit by repackaging the cash flows from the single-class GNMA pass-through into cash flows more attractive to different groups of investors. The sum of the prices at which the three CMO bond classes can be sold normally exceeds that of the original pass-through:

$$\sum_{i=1}^{3} P_{i,\,CMO} > P_{GNMA}$$

To understand the gains from repackaging, it is necessary to understand how CMOs restructure prepayment risk to make it more attractive to different classes of investors. We explain this in the following simple example.

**EXAMPLE 26–1**
*The Value Additivity of CMOs*

Suppose an investment bank buys a $150 million issue of GNMAs and places them in trust as collateral. It then issues a CMO with these three classes:

Class A: Annual fixed coupon 7 percent, class size $50 million
Class B: Annual fixed coupon 8 percent, class size $50 million
Class C: Annual fixed coupon 9 percent, class size $50 million

Under the CMO, each class has a guaranteed or fixed coupon. By restructuring the GNMA as a CMO, the investment bank can offer investors who buy bond class C a higher degree of mortgage prepayment protection compared to a pass-through. Those who buy bond class B receive an average degree of prepayment protection, and those who take class A receive virtually no prepayment protection.

---

[13] These trusts are sometimes called *REMICs*, or real estate mortgage investment conduits.

Each month, mortgagees in the GNMA pool pay principal and interest on their mortgages. Each payment includes the promised amortized amount (PMT) plus any additional payments as some of the mortgage holders prepay principal to refinance their mortgages or because they have sold their houses and are relocating. These cash flows are passed through to the owner of the GNMA bonds, in our example Goldman Sachs. The CMO issuer uses the cash flows to pay promised coupon interest to the three classes of CMO bondholders. Suppose that in month 1 the promised amortized cash flows (PMT) on the mortgages underlying the GNMA pass-through collateral are $1 million, but an additional $1.5 million cash flow results from early mortgage prepayments. Thus, the cash flows in the first month available to pay promised coupons to the three classes of bondholders would be

$$PMT + \text{Prepayments} = \$1\,\text{million} + \$1.5\,\text{million} = \$2.5\,\text{million}$$

This cash flow is available to the trustee, who uses it in the following fashion.

1. *Coupon payments.* Each month (or more commonly, each quarter or half year), the trustee pays out the guaranteed coupons to the three classes of bondholders at annualized coupon rates of 7 percent, 8 percent, and 9 percent, respectively. Given the stated principal of $50 million for each class, the class A (7 percent coupon) bondholders receive approximately $291,667 in coupon payments in month 1, the class B (8 percent coupon) receive approximately $333,333 in month 1, and the class C (9 percent coupon) receive approximately $375,000 in month 1. Thus, the total promised coupon payments to the three classes amount to $1,000,000 (equal to PMT, the no-prepayment cash flows in the GNMA pool).

2. *Principal payments.* The trustee has $2.5 million available to pay out as a result of promised mortgage payments plus early prepayments, but the total payment of coupon interest amounts to $1 million. For legal and tax reasons, the remaining $1.5 million has to be paid out to the CMO bondholders. The unique feature of the CMO is that the trustee would pay this remaining $1.5 million only to class A bondholders to retire these bondholders' principal. This retires early some of these bondholders' principal outstanding. At the end of month 1, only $48.5 million ($50 million − $1.5 million) of class A bonds remains outstanding, compared to $50 million class B and $50 million class C. These payment flows are shown graphically in Figure 26–12.

Let's suppose that in month 2 the same thing happens. The cash flows from the mortgage/GNMA pool exceed the promised coupon payments to the three classes of bondholders. Again, the trustee uses any excess cash flows to pay off or retire the principal of class A bondholders. If the excess cash flows again amount to $1.5 million, at the end of month 2 there will be only $47 million ($48.5 million − $1.5 million) of class A bonds outstanding. Given any positive flow of prepayments, it is clear that within a few years the class A bonds will be fully retired. In practice, this often occurs between 1.5 and 3 years after issue. After the trustee retires class A, only classes B and C remain.

As before, out of any cash flows received from the mortgage/GNMA pool, the trustee pays the bondholders their guaranteed coupons, $C_B = \$333,333$ and $C_C = \$375,000$ for a total of $708,333. Suppose that total cash flows received by the trustee are $1,208,333 in the first month after the total retirement of class A bonds, reflecting amortized mortgage payments by the remaining mortgagees in the pool plus any new prepayments. The excess cash flows of $500,000 ($1,208,333 − $708,333) then go to retire the principal outstanding of CMO bond class B. At the end of that month, there are only $49.5 million class B bonds outstanding. This is shown graphically in Figure 26–13.

As the months pass, the trustee will use any excess cash flows over and above the promised coupons to class B and C bondholders to retire bond class B's principal. Eventually, all of the $50 million principal on class B bonds will be retired—in practice, five to seven years after the CMO issue. After class B bonds are retired, all remaining cash flows will be dedicated to paying the promised coupon of class C bondholders and retiring the $50 million principal on class C bonds. In practice, class C bonds can have an average life as long as 20 years.

**FIGURE 26–12**
**Allocation of Cash Flows to Owners of CMO Tranches**

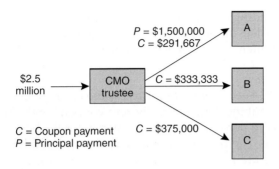

**FIGURE 26–13**
**Allocation of Cash Flows to Remaining Tranches of CMO Bonds**

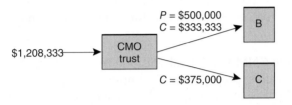

## Class A, B, and C Bond Buyers

### Class A

These bonds have the shortest average life with a minimum of prepayment protection. They are, therefore, of great interest to investors seeking short-duration mortgage-backed assets to reduce the duration of their mortgage-related asset portfolios. In recent years depository institutions have been large buyers of CMO class A securities.

### Class B

These bonds have some prepayment protection and expected durations of five to seven years depending on the level of interest rates. Pension funds and life insurance companies primarily purchase these bonds, although some depository institutions buy this bond class as well.

### Class C

Because of their long expected duration, class C bonds are highly attractive to insurance companies and pension funds seeking long duration assets to match their long duration liabilities. Indeed, because of their failures to offer prepayment protection, regular GNMA pass-throughs may not be very attractive to these institutions. Class C CMOs, with their high but imperfect degree of prepayment protection, may be of greater interest to the FI managers of these institutions.

In summary, by splitting bondholders into different classes and by restructuring cash flows into forms more valued by different investor clienteles, the CMO issuer stands to make a profit.

## Other CMO Classes

CMOs can always have more than the three classes described in the previous example. Indeed, issues of up to 17 different classes have been made. Clearly, the 17th-class bondholders would have an enormous degree of prepayment protection since the first 16 classes would have had their bonds retired before the principal outstanding on this bond class would be affected by early prepayments. In addition, trustees have created other special types of classes as products to attract investor interest; we discuss these classes next.

### Class Z

**Z class**
An accrual class of a CMO that makes a payment to bond-holders only when preceding CMO classes have been retired.

Frequently, CMO issues contain a **Z class** as the last regular class. The Z implicitly stands for zero, but these are not really zero-coupon bonds. This class has a stated coupon such as 10 percent and accrues interest for the bondholder on a monthly basis at this rate. The trustee does not pay this interest, however, until all other classes of bonds are fully retired. When the other classes have been retired, the Z-class bondholder receives the promised coupon and principal payments plus accrued interest payments. Thus, the Z class has characteristics of both a zero-coupon bond (no coupon payments for a long period) and a regular bond.

### Class R

**R class**
The residual class of a CMO giving the owner the right to any remaining collateral in the trust after all other bond classes have been retired plus any reinvestment income earned by the trust.

In placing the GNMA collateral with the trustee, the CMO issuer normally uses very conservative prepayment assumptions. If prepayments are slower than expected, there is often excess collateral left over in the pool when all regular classes have been retired. Further, trustees often reinvest funds or cash flows received from the underlying instrument (GNMA) in the period prior to paying interest on the CMOs. In general, the size of any excess collateral and interest on interest gets bigger when rates are high and the timing of coupon intervals is semiannual rather than monthly. This residual **R class** or "garbage class" is a high-risk investment class that gives the investor the rights to the overcollateralization and reinvestment income on the cash flows in the CMO trust. Because the value of the returns in this bond class increases when interest rates increase, while normal bond values fall with interest rate increases, class R often has a negative duration. Thus, it is potentially attractive to depository institutions seeking to hedge their regular bond and fixed-income portfolios.[14]

---

**Concept Questions**

1. In our example, the coupon on the class C bonds was assumed to be higher than that on the class B bonds and the coupon on class B bonds was assumed to be higher than that on class A bonds. Under what term structure conditions might this not be the case?
2. Would thrifts or insurance companies prefer Z-class CMOs? Explain your answer.
3. Are Z-class CMOs exactly the same as T-bond strips? If not, why not?

---

## THE MORTGAGE-BACKED BOND (MBB) OR COVERED BOND

**mortgage (asset)-backed bonds**
Bonds collateralized by a pool of assets.

**Mortgage (asset)-backed bonds** (MBBs), or covered bonds, are the third asset-securitization vehicle. These bonds differ from pass-throughs and CMOs in two key dimensions. First, while pass-throughs and CMOs help depository institutions remove mortgages from their balance sheets as forms of off-balance-sheet securitization, MBBs normally remain on the balance sheet. Second, pass-throughs and CMOs have a direct link between the cash flows on the underlying mortgages and the cash flows on the bond vehicles. By contrast, the relationship for MBBs is one

---

[14] Negative duration implies that bond prices increase with interest rates. That is, the price–yield curve is positively sloped.

of collateralization—there is no direct link between the cash flow on the mortgages backing the bond and the interest and principal payments on the MBB.

An FI issues an MBB to reduce risk to the MBB bondholders, who have a first claim to a segment of the FI's mortgage assets. Practically speaking, the FI segregates a group of mortgage assets on its balance sheet and pledges, or covers, this group as collateral against the MBB issue. A trustee normally monitors the segregation of assets and makes sure that the market value of the collateral exceeds the principal owed to MBB holders. That is, FIs back most MBB issues by excess collateral. This excess collateral backing of the bond, in addition to the priority rights of the bondholders, generally ensures that these bonds can be sold with a high credit rating such as AAA. In contrast, the FI, when evaluated as a whole, could be rated BBB or even lower. A high credit rating results in lower coupon payments than would be required if significant default risk had lowered the credit rating (see Chapter 10). To explain the potential benefits and the sources of any gains to an FI from issuing MBBs, we examine the following simple example.

| | |
|---|---|
| **EXAMPLE 26–2**<br><br>*Gains to an FI from Issuing MBBs* | Consider an FI with $20 million in long-term mortgages as assets. It is financing these mortgages with $10 million in short-term uninsured deposits (e.g., wholesale deposits over $250,000) and $10 million in insured deposits (e.g., retail deposits of $250,000 or less). In this example, we ignore the issues of capital and reserve requirements. Look at the balance sheet structure in Table 26–4.<br><br>This balance sheet poses problems for the FI manager. First, the FI has a positive duration gap ($D_A > kD_L$). Second, because of this interest rate risk and the potential default and prepayment risk on the FI's mortgage assets, uninsured depositors are likely to require a positive and potentially significant risk premium to be paid on their deposits. By contrast, the insured depositors may require approximately the risk-free rate on their deposits as they are fully insured by the FDIC (see Chapter 19).<br><br>To reduce its duration gap exposure and lower its funding costs, the FI can segregate $12 million of the mortgages on the asset side of its balance sheet and pledge them as collateral backing a $10 million long-term MBB issue. Because of this overcollateralization, the mortgage-backed bond issued by the FI may cost less to issue, in terms of required yield, than uninsured deposits; that is, it may well be rated AAA while uninsured deposits might be rated BBB. The FI can therefore use the proceeds of the $10 million bond issue to retire the $10 million of uninsured deposits.<br><br>Consider the FI's balance sheet after the issue of the MBBs in Table 26–5. It might seem that the FI has miraculously engineered a restructuring of its balance sheet that has resulted in a better matching of $D_A$ to $D_L$ and a lowering of funding costs. The bond issue has lengthened the average duration of liabilities by replacing short-term deposits with long-term MBBs and lowered funding costs because AAA rated bond coupon rates are below BBB rated uninsured deposit rates. However, this outcome occurs only because the insured depositors do not worry about risk exposure since they are 100 percent insured by the FDIC. The result of the MBB issue and the segregation of $12 million of assets as collateral backing the $10 million bond issue is that the $10 million insured deposits are now backed only by $8 million in free or unpledged assets. If smaller depositors were not insured by the FDIC, they would surely demand very high risk premiums to hold these risky deposits. The implication of this is that the FI gains only because the FDIC is willing to bear enhanced credit risk through its insurance guarantees to depositors.[15] As a result, the FI is actually gaining at the expense of the FDIC. Consequently, it is not surprising that the FDIC is concerned about the growing use of this form of securitization by risky depository institutions. |

---

[15] And does not make the risk-based deposit insurance premium to banks and thrifts sufficiently large to reflect this risk.

**TABLE 26–4**
Balance Sheet of
Potential MBB
Issuer (in millions
of dollars)

| Assets | | Liabilities | |
|---|---|---|---|
| Long-term mortgages | $20 | Insured deposits | $10 |
| | | Uninsured deposits | 10 |
| | $20 | | $20 |

**TABLE 26–5**
FI's Balance Sheet
after MBB Issue (in
millions of dollars)

| Assets | | Liabilities | |
|---|---|---|---|
| Collateral = (market value of segregated mortgages) | $12 | MBB issue | $10 |
| Other mortgages | 8 | Insured deposits | 10 |
| | $20 | | $20 |

There are other return reasons why an FI might prefer the pass-through/CMO forms of securitization to issuing MBBs. First MBBs tie up mortgages on the FI's balance sheet for a long time. This increases the illiquidity of the asset portfolio. Second, the amount of mortgages tied up is enhanced by the need to overcollateralize to ensure a high-quality credit risk rating for the bond issue; in our example, the overcollateralization was $2 million. Third, by keeping mortgages on the balance sheet, the FI continues to be liable for capital adequacy and reserve requirement taxes. Because of these problems, MBBs are the least used of the three basic vehicles of securitization in the United States. However, German banks use these instruments extensively, where they are called Pfandbrief or covered bonds. Similarly, Danish banks are extensive users of these covered bonds. Recently, after the mortgage-backed security crisis, some U.S. regulators have reconsidered their opposition to these types of bonds because of their greater security offered to investors.

---

**Concept Question**

1. Would an AAA rated FI ever issue mortgage-backed bonds? Explain your answer.

---

# INNOVATIONS IN SECURITIZATION

We now turn our attention to the growing innovations in FIs' asset securitization. We discuss two major innovations and their use in return-risk management by FIs: mortgage pass-through strips and the extension of the securitization concept to other assets.

## Mortgage Pass-Through Strips

The mortgage pass-through strip is a special type of a CMO with only two classes. The fully amortized nature of mortgages means that any given monthly payment, *PMT*, contains an interest component and a principal component. Beginning in 1987, investment banks and other FI issuers stripped out the interest component from the principal component and sold each payment stream separately to different bond class investors. They sold an interest only (IO) class and a principal only (PO) class. These two bond classes have very special cash flow characteristics, especially regarding the interest rate sensitivity of these bonds. We show this stripping of the cash flows in Figure 26–14 and consider the effects of interest rate changes on the value of each of these stripped instruments below.

### IO Strips

**IO strip**
A bond sold to investors whose cash flows reflect the monthly interest payments received from a pool of mortgages.

The owner of an **IO strip** has a claim to the present value of interest payments made by the mortgage holders in the GNMA pool—that is, to the IO segments of each month's cash flow received from the underlying mortgage pool:

$$P_{IO} = \frac{IO_1}{\left(1 + \frac{y}{12}\right)} + \frac{IO_2}{\left(1 + \frac{y}{12}\right)^2} + \frac{IO_3}{\left(1 + \frac{y}{12}\right)^3} + \dots + \frac{IO_{360}}{\left(1 + \frac{y}{12}\right)^{360}}$$

When interest rates change, they affect the cash flows received on mortgages. We concentrate on two effects: the discount effect and the prepayment effect on the price or value of IOs, denoted by $P_{IO}$.

*Discount Effect*    As interest rates ($y$) fall, the present value of any cash flows received on the strip—the IO payments—rises, increasing the value ($P_{IO}$) of the bond.

*Prepayment Effect*    As interest rates fall, mortgagees prepay their mortgages. In absolute terms, the number of IO payments the investor receives is likely to shrink. For example, the investor might receive only 100 monthly IO payments instead of the expected 360 in a no-prepayment world. The shrinkage in the size and value of IO payments reduces the value ($P_{IO}$) of the bond.

Specifically, one can expect that as interest rates continue to fall below the mortgage coupon rate of the bonds in the pool, the prepayment effect gradually dominates the discount effect, so that over some range the price or value of the IO bond falls as interest rates fall. Note the price–yield curve in Figure 26–15 for an IO strip

**FIGURE 26–14**
**IO/PO Strips**

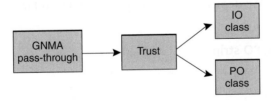

**FIGURE 26–15**
**Price–Yield Curve of an IO Percent Strip**

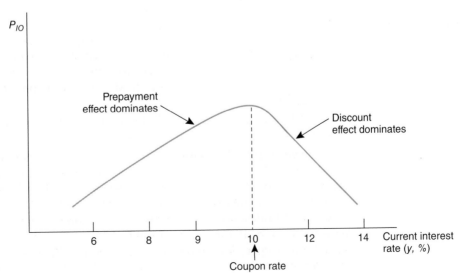

**FIGURE 26–16**   **Hedging with IOs**

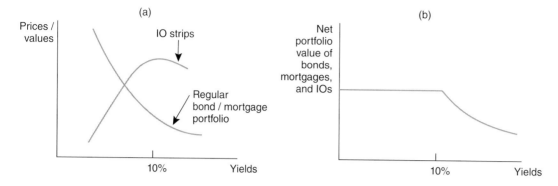

on a pass-through bond with 10 percent mortgage coupon rates. The price–yield curve slopes upward in the interest rate range below 10 percent. This means that as current interest rates rise or fall, IO values or prices rise or fall. As a result, the IO is a rare example of a **negative duration** asset that is very valuable as a portfolio-hedging device for an FI manager when included with regular bonds whose price–yield curves show the normal inverse relationship. That is, while as interest rates rise the value of the regular bond portfolio falls, the value of an IO portfolio may rise. Note in Figure 26–15 that at rates above the pool's mortgage coupon of 10 percent, the price–yield curve changes shape and tends to perform like any regular bond. In recent years, thrifts have been major purchasers of IOs to hedge the interest rate risk on the mortgages and other bonds held as assets in their portfolios. We depict the hedging power of IOs in Figure 26–16.

**negative duration**
Relationship in which the price of a bond increases (decreases) as yields increase (decrease).

### PO Strips

**PO strip**
A bond sold to investors whose cash flows reflect the monthly principal payments received from a pool of mortgages.

The value of the **PO strip** ($P_{PO}$) is defined by:

$$P_{PO} = \frac{PO_1}{\left(1 + \dfrac{y}{12}\right)} + \frac{PO_2}{\left(1 + \dfrac{y}{12}\right)^2} + \frac{PO_3}{\left(1 + \dfrac{y}{12}\right)^3} + \ldots + \frac{PO_{360}}{\left(1 + \dfrac{y}{12}\right)^{360}}$$

where the $PO_i$ represents the mortgage principal components of each monthly payment by the mortgage holders. This includes both the monthly amortized payment component of $PMT$ that is principal and any early prepayments of principal by the mortgagees. Again, we consider the effects on a PO's value ($P_{PO}$) of a change in interest rates.

***Discount Effect***   As yields ($y$) fall, the present value of any principal payments must increase and the value of the PO strip rises.

***Prepayment Effect***   As yields fall, the mortgage holders pay off principal early. Consequently, the PO bondholder receives the fixed principal balance outstanding on the pool of mortgages earlier than stated. Thus, this prepayment effect must also work to increase the value of the PO strip.

As interest rates fall, both the discount and prepayment effects point to a rise in the value of the PO strip. The price–yield curve reflects an inverse relationship, but with a steeper slope than for normal bonds. That is, PO strip bond values are very interest rate sensitive, especially for yields below the stated mortgage

**FIGURE 26–17**
Price–Yield Curve
of a PO Strip

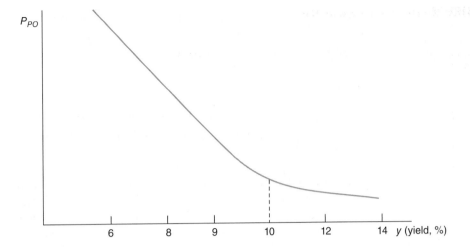

coupon rate. We show this in Figure 26–17 for a 10 percent PO strip. (Note that a regular coupon bond is affected only by the discount effect.) As you can see, when yields fall below 10 percent, the market value or price of the PO strip can increase very fast. At rates above 10 percent, it tends to behave like a regular bond (as the incentive to prepay disappears).

The IO–PO strip is a classic example of financial engineering. From a given GNMA pass-through bond, two new bonds have been created: the first with an upward-sloping price–yield curve over some range and the second with a steeply downward-sloping price–yield curve over some range. Each class is attractive to different investors and investor segments. The IO is attractive to depository institutions as an on-balance-sheet hedging vehicle. The PO is attractive to FIs that wish to increase the interest rate sensitivity of their portfolios and to investors or traders who wish to take a naked or speculative position regarding the future course of interest rates. This high and complex interest sensitivity has resulted in major traders such as J.P. Morgan Chase and Bank of America Merrill Lynch, as well as many investors such as hedge funds, suffering considerable losses on their investments in these instruments when interest rates have moved unexpectedly against them.

## Securitization of Other Assets

While the major use of the three securitization vehicles—pass-throughs, CMOs, and mortgage-backed bonds—has been in packaging fixed-rate mortgage assets, these techniques can and have been used for other assets, including:

Automobile loans.
Credit card receivables (certificates of amortizing revolving debts).
Small business loans guaranteed by the Small Business Administration.
Junk bonds.
Adjustable rate mortgages.
Commercial and industrial loans [collateralized loan obligations (CLOs)].

To examine the securitization of other assets, we use the example of certificates of amortizing revolving debts.

**FIGURE 26–18**
The Structure
of a Credit Card
Securitization

### Certificates of Amortizing Revolving Debts (CARDs)

**CARDs**
Asset-backed securities backed by credit card receivables.

Rather than holding all credit card receivables until they pay off, an FI can segregate a set of receivables and sell them to an off-balance-sheet trust, e.g., an SIV. A good example is J.P. Morgan Chase, which is a major sponsor of credit cards. (J.P. Morgan Chase retains the role of servicing the credit card pool, including collection, administration, and bookkeeping of the underlying credit card accounts.) J.P. Morgan Chase recently sold $280 million of receivables to a trust. The trust in turn issued asset-backed securities **(CARDs)** in which investors had a pro rata claim on the cash flows from the credit card receivables. As the trust received payments on the credit card receivables each month, they were passed through to the bondholders. In practice, bonds of a lesser principal amount than the $280 million credit card pool are issued. In this example, $250 million in bonds were issued, with the difference—$30 million—being a claim retained by J.P. Morgan Chase. The reason for this is that credit card holders can either increase or repay their credit card balances at any time. The risk of variations in principal outstanding and thus collateral for the bonds is borne solely by the FI (i.e., the $30 million component), while the investors' collateral claim remains at $250 million until maturity unless a truly exceptional rate of debt repayment occurs. Indeed, J.P. Morgan Chase's segment is structured to bear even the most extreme cases of early repayment of credit card debt. We show this credit card example in Figure 26–18. Notice from the figure that this securitization of credit card assets is very similar in technology to the pass-through mortgage bond.

---

**Concept Questions**

1. Would an FI with $D_A < kD_L$ be interested in buying an IO strip for hedging purposes?
2. To which investors or investor segments is the IO attractive? To which investors or investor segments is the PO attractive? Explain your answer.

---

## CAN ALL ASSETS BE SECURITIZED?

The extension of securitization technology to other assets raises questions about the limits of securitization and whether all assets and loans can be securitized. Conceptually the answer is that they can, so long as it is profitable to do so or the benefits to the FI from securitization outweigh the costs of securitization. In Table 26–6, we summarize the benefits versus the costs of securitization.

From Table 26–6, given any set of benefits, the more costly and difficult it is to find asset packages of sufficient size and homogeneity, the more difficult and expensive it is to securitize. For example, commercial and industrial (C&I) loans have maturities running from a few months up to eight years. Further, they have

**TABLE 26–6**
Benefits versus Costs of Securitization

| Benefits | Costs |
|---|---|
| 1. New funding source (bonds versus deposits) | 1. Cost of public/private credit risk insurance and guarantees |
| 2. Increased liquidity of FI loans | 2. Cost of overcollateralization |
| 3. Enhanced ability to manage the duration gap of $(D_A - kD_L)$ | 3. Valuation and packaging costs (the cost of asset heterogeneity) |
| 4. If off-balance-sheet, the issuer saves on reserve requirements, deposit insurance premiums, and capital adequacy requirements | |

varying interest rate terms (fixed, LIBOR floating, federal funds–rate floating) and fees. In addition, they contain differing covenants and are made to firms in a wide variety of industries. Despite this, FIs have still been able to issue securitization packages called CLOs (collateralized loan obligations) containing high-quality low–default risk C&I loans and CDOs (collateralized debt obligations) containing a diversified collection of junk bonds or risky bank loans. The interest and principal payments on a CLO or CDO are linked to the timing of default losses and repayments on a pool of underlying loans or bonds. The riskiest of the CDOs, sometimes called "toxic waste," pay out only if everything goes right. The best CDOs will pay out unless the entire portfolio defaults. A synthetic CDO is a type of CDO in which the underlying credit exposures are credit default swaps (CDS) rather than a pool of loans or bonds. Thus, the periodic payments are linked to the cash flows from the credit default swaps. If the credit event occurs in the underlying portfolio, the synthetic CDO (and any investors) become responsible for the losses. Synthetic CDOs are securitized securities that can offer extremely high returns to investors. However, investors can lose more than their initial investments if several credit events occur in the underlying portfolio.

The volume of CDO issues grew from $10 billion in 1995 to more than $500 billion in 2006, before the financial crisis. As discussed below, CDOs were at the very heart of the financial crisis, and this market decreased in size significantly as a result, to $31.1 billion in 2011 and $39.5 billion in the first three quarters of 2012. The major sellers of CDOs are commercial and investment banks, through their SIVs or SPVs (discussed earlier). The major buyers are hedge funds, commercial banks, investment banks, and pension funds. While the banks that create and sell the CDOs distribute the cash flows from the underlying assets to the CDO buyers, the valuation of these credit derivatives is not based solely on the estimated cash flows from underlying assets. Rather, the valuation of CDOs involves the use of metrics and algorithms developed by traders and mathematicians. Generally, it has been much harder to securitize low-quality loans into CDOs. Specifically, the harder it is to value a loan or asset pool, the greater the costs of securitization due to the need for overcollateralization or credit risk insurance.

Of all of the instruments that caused damage to SIVs and SPVs, the FIs that owned them, and the world's financial markets in general during the financial crisis, the most damaging was the cash flow CDOs backed by subprime and Alt-A CMO tranches. Alt-A mortgages are rated lower than prime quality, but are generally higher quality than subprime mortgages. Many SIVs had invested heavily in these CDOs. Cash flow CDOs have as their underlying collateral real securities, such as bonds, CMO tranches, and asset-backed securities tranches. The most naive investors simply looked at the ratings on these CDO tranches and then bought the tranche if they liked the rating. They did not attempt or did not have the models to confirm if the price they were asked to pay was a fair value.[16] Other investors accepted what CDO arrangers and rating agencies recommended for valuation technology. However, these models consistently underestimated the worst-case scenario and overvalued CDO tranches.[17] The best practice in valuing cash flow CDOs is to simulate the performance of the mortgage loans underlying the CMO tranches, loan by loan, then simulate the losses and cash flows of the CMO tranches in the CDO structure. Most investors until recently have done no analysis—because they did not have such software capabilities at their disposal. As a result, they consistently overpaid for cash flow CDO tranches, and they took on risk that they did not understand.

The potential boundary to securitization may well be defined by the relative degree of heterogeneity and credit quality of an asset type or group. It is not surprising that 30-year fixed-rate residential mortgages were the first assets to be securitized since they are the most homogeneous of all assets in FI balance sheets. For example, the existence of secondary markets for houses provides price information that allows reasonably accurate market valuations of the underlying asset to be made, and extensive data are available on mortgage default rates by locality.

| **Concept Question** | 1. Can all assets and loans be securitized? Explain your answer. |
|---|---|

| **Summary** | In Chapter 1 we distinguished between FIs that are asset transformers and those that are asset brokers. By becoming increasingly reliant on securitization, banks and thrifts are moving away from being asset transformers that originate and hold assets to maturity. They are becoming asset brokers more reliant on servicing and other fees. This makes banks and thrifts look more similar to securities firms. Thus, over time, we can expect the traditional financial technology differences between commercial (and savings) banking and investment banking to diminish as more loans and assets are securitized. Three major forms of securitization— pass-through securities, collateralized mortgage obligations (CMOs), and mortgage backed bonds—were discussed. Also, the impact of prepayment behavior on MBS valuation was discussed. Finally, recent innovations in securitization were described. |
|---|---|

[16] These investors ignored the fact that the rating agencies are paid by the CDO arranger and that they have a bias in favor of a rating that is better than the real risk level. Unless CDO tranches were rated favorably, arrangers could not make money by packaging securities freely available in the market and then reselling them at a higher price in the form of tranches.

[17] Note that this technique also maximizes CDO arrangers' profits by getting investors to buy CDO tranches that they would not purchase if they had accurately measured value.

**Questions and Problems**

1. What has been the effect of securitization on the asset portfolios of financial institutions?
2. What are the primary functions of GNMA? What is timing insurance?
3. How does FNMA differ from GNMA?
4. How does FHLMC differ from FNMA? How are they the same?
5. What three levels of regulatory taxes do FIs face when making loans? How does securitization reduce the levels of taxation?
6. An FI is planning to issue $100 million in BB rated commercial loans. The FI BB rated will finance the loans by issuing demand deposits.
   a. What is the minimum amount of capital required under Basel III?
   b. What is the minimum amount of demand deposits needed to fund this loan assuming there is a 10 percent average reserve requirement on demand deposits?
   c. Show a simple balance sheet with total assets, total liabilities, and equity if this is the only project funded by the bank.
   d. How does this balance sheet differ from Table 26–1? Why?
7. Consider the FI in problem 6.
   a. What additional risk exposure problems does the FI face?
   b. What are some possible solutions to the duration mismatch and the illiquidity problems?
   c. What advantages does securitization have in dealing with the FI's risk exposure problems?
8. How are investors in pass-through securities protected against default risk emanating from the mortgagees and the FI/trustee?
9. What specific changes occur on the balance sheet at the completion of the securitization process? What adjustments occur to the risk profile of the FI?
10. Consider the mortgage pass-through example presented in Table 26–3. The total monthly payment by the borrowers reflecting a 12 percent mortgage rate is $1,028,610. The payment passed through to the ultimate investors reflecting an 11.5 percent return is $990,291. Who receives the difference between these two payments? How are the shares determined?
11. Consider a GNMA mortgage pool with principal of $20 million. The maturity is 30 years with a monthly mortgage payment of 10 percent per year. Assume no prepayments.
    a. What is the monthly mortgage payment (100 percent amortizing) on the pool of mortgages?
    b. If the GNMA insurance fee is 6 basis points and the servicing fee is 44 basis points, what is the yield on the GNMA pass-through?
    c. What is the monthly payment on the GNMA in part (b)?
    d. Calculate the first monthly servicing fee paid to the originating FI.
    e. Calculate the first monthly insurance fee paid to GNMA.
12. Calculate the value of (a) the mortgage pool and (b) the GNMA pass-through in question 11 if market interest rates increase 50 basis points. Assume no prepayments.
13. What would be the impact on GNMA pricing if the pass-through was not fully amortized? What is the present value of a $10 million pool of 15-year mortgages with an 8.5 percent per year monthly mortgage coupon if market rates are 5 percent? The GNMA guarantee fee is 6 basis points and the FI servicing fee is 44 basis points.

    a. Assume that the GNMA is fully amortized.

    b. Assume that the GNMA is only half amortized. There is a lump sum payment at the maturity of the GNMA that equals 50 percent of the mortgage pool's face value.

14. What is prepayment risk? How does prepayment risk affect the cash flow stream on a fully amortized mortgage loan? What are the two primary factors that cause early payment?

15. Under what conditions do mortgage holders have a call option on their mortgages? When is the call option in the money?

16. What are the benefits of market yields that are less than the average rate in the GNMA mortgage pool? What are the disadvantages of this rate inversion? To whom do the good news and the bad news accrue?

17. What is the weighted-average life (WAL) of a mortgage pool supporting pass-through securities? How does WAL differ from duration?

18. If 150 $200,000 mortgages in a $60 million 15-year mortgage pool are expected to be prepaid in three years and the remaining 150 $200,000 mortgages are to be prepaid in four years, what is the weighted-average life of the mortgage pool? Mortgages are fully amortized, with mortgage coupon rates set at 10 percent to be paid annually.

19. A FI originates a pool of 500 30-year mortgages, each averaging $150,000 with an annual mortgage coupon rate of 8 percent. Assume that the GNMA credit risk insurance fee is 6 basis points and that the FI's servicing fee is 19 basis points.

    a. What is the present value of the mortgage pool?

    b. What is the monthly mortgage payment?

    c. For the first two payments, what portion is interest and what portion is principal repayment?

    d. What are the expected monthly cash flows to GNMA bondholders?

    e. What is the present value of the GNMA pass-through bonds? Assume that the risk-adjusted market annual rate of return is 8 percent compounded monthly.

    f. Would actual cash flows to GNMA bondholders deviate from expected cash flows as in part (d)? Why or why not?

    g. What are the expected monthly cash flows for the FI and GNMA?

    h. If all the mortgages in the pool are completely prepaid at the end of the second month, what is the pool's weighted-average life? Hint: Use your answer to part (c).

    i. What is the price of the GNMA pass-through security if its weighted-average life is equal to your solution for part (h)? Assume no change in market interest rates.

    j. What is the price of the GNMA pass-through with a weighted-average life equal to your solution for part (h) if market yields decline 50 basis points?

20. What is the difference between the yield spread to average life and the option adjusted spread on mortgage-backed securities?

21. Explain precisely the prepayment assumptions of the Public Securities Association prepayment model.

22. What does an FI mean when it states that its mortgage pool prepayments are assumed to be 100 percent PSA equivalent?

23. What factors may cause the actual prepayment pattern to differ from the assumed PSA pattern? How would an FI adjust for the presumed occurrence of some of these factors?

24. What is the burnout factor? How is it used in modeling prepayment behavior? What other factors may be helpful in modeling the prepayment behavior of a given mortgage pool?

25. What is the goal of prepayment models that use option pricing theory? How do these models differ from the PSA or empirical models? What criticisms often are directed toward these models?

26. How does the price on a GNMA bond relate to the yield on a GNMA option from the perspective of the investor? What is the option-adjusted spread (OAS)?

27. Use the options prepayment model to calculate the yield on a $30 million, three-year, fully amortized mortgage pass-through where the mortgage coupon rate is 6 percent paid annually. Market yields are 6.4 percent paid annually. Assume that there is no servicing or GNMA guarantee fee.
    a. What is the annual payment on the GNMA pass-through?
    b. What is the present value of the GNMA pass-through?
    c. Interest rate movements over time are assumed to change a maximum of 0.5 percent per year. Both an increase of 0.5 percent and a decrease of 0.5 percent in interest rates are equally probable. If interest rates fall 1.0 percent below the current mortgage coupon rates, all of the mortgages in the pool will be completely prepaid. Diagram the interest rate tree and indicate the probabilities of each node in the tree.
    d. What are the expected annual cash flows for each possible situation over the three-year period?
    e. The Treasury bond yield curve is flat at a discount yield of 6 percent. What is the option-adjusted spread on the GNMA pass-through?

28. Use the options prepayment model to calculate the yield on a $12 million, five-year, fully amortized mortgage pass-through where the mortgage coupon rate is 7 percent paid annually. Market yields are 8 percent paid annually. Assume that there is no servicing or GNMA guarantee fee.
    a. What is the annual payment on the GNMA pass-through?
    b. What is the present value of the GNMA pass-through?
    c. Interest rate movements over time are assumed to change a maximum of 1 percent per year. Both an increase of 1 percent and a decrease of 1 percent in interest rates are equally probable. If interest rates fall 3 percent below the current mortgage coupon rates, all mortgages in the pool will be completely prepaid. Diagram the interest rate tree and indicate the probabilities of each node in the tree.
    d. What are the expected annual cash flows for each possible situation over the five-year period?
    e. The Treasury bond yield curve is flat at a discount yield of 6 percent. What is the option-adjusted spread on the GNMA pass-through?

29. What conditions would cause the yield on pass-through securities with prepayment risk to be less than the yield on pass-through securities without prepayment risk?

39. What is a collateralized mortgage obligation (CMO)? How is it similar to a pass-through security? How does it differ? In what way does the creation of a CMO use market segmentation to redistribute prepayment risk?

31. Consider $200 million of 30-year mortgages with a coupon of 10 percent per year paid quarterly.
    a. What is the quarterly mortgage payment?
    b. What are the interest and principal repayments over the first year of life of the mortgages?

c. Construct a 30-year CMO using this mortgage pool as collateral. The pool has three tranches, where tranche A offers the least protection against prepayment and tranche C offers the most protection against prepayment. Tranche A of $50 million receives quarterly payments at 9 percent per year, tranche B of $100 million receives quarterly payments at 10 percent per year, and tranche C of $50 million receives quarterly payments at 11 percent per year.

d. Assume nonamortization of principal and no prepayments. What are the total promised coupon payments to the three classes? What are the principal payments to each of the three classes for the first year?

e. If, over the first year, the trustee receives quarterly prepayments of $10 million on the mortgage pool, how are these funds distributed?

f. How are the cash flows distributed if prepayments in the first half of the second year are $20 million quarterly?

g. How can the CMO issuer earn a positive spread on the CMO?

32. Consider $100 million of 30-year mortgages with a coupon of 5 percent per year paid quarterly.

a. What is the quarterly mortgage payment?

b. What are the interest and principal repayments over the first year of life of the mortgages?

c. Construct a 30-year CMO using this mortgage pool as collateral. The pool has three tranches, where tranche A offers the least protection against prepayment and tranche C offers the most protection against prepayment. Tranche A of $25 million receives quarterly payments at 4 percent per year, tranche B of $50 million receives quarterly payments at 5 percent per year, and tranche C of $25 million receives quarterly payments at 6 percent per year.

d. Assume nonamortization of principal and no prepayments. What are the total promised coupon payments to the three classes? What are the principal payments to each of the three classes for the first year?

e. If, over the first year, the trustee receives quarterly prepayments of $5 million on the mortgage pool, how are these funds distributed?

f. How are the cash flows distributed if prepayments in the first half of the second year are $10 million quarterly?

33. How does a class Z tranche of a CMO differ from a class R tranche? What causes a Z class to have characteristics of both a zero-coupon bond and a regular bond? What factors can cause an R class to have a negative duration?

34. Why would buyers of class C tranches of collateralized mortgage obligations (CMOs) be willing to accept a lower return than purchasers of class A tranches?

35. What are mortgage-backed bonds (MBBs)? How do MBBs differ from pass-through securities and CMOs?

36. From the perspective of risk management, how does the use of MBBs by an FI assist the FI in managing credit and interest rate risk?

37. Consider a bank with $50 million in long-term mortgages as assets. It is financing these mortgages with $30 million in short-term uninsured deposits and $20 million in insured deposits. To reduce its interest rate risk exposure and to lower its funding costs, the bank can segregate $35 million of the mortgages on the asset side of its balance sheet and pledge them as collateral backing a $30 million long-term MBB issue. Because the $30 million in MBBs is backed

by mortgages worth $35 million, the mortgage-backed bond issued by the bank costs less to issue, in terms of required yield, than uninsured deposits. Thus, the FI can then use the proceeds of the $30 million bond issue to replace the $30 million of uninsured deposits. Show the bank's balance sheet before and after the issue of the MBB.

38. What are four reasons why an FI may prefer the use of either pass-through securities or CMOs to the use of MBBs?

39. What is an interest only (IO) strip? How do the discount effect and the prepayment effect of an IO create a negative duration asset? What macroeconomic effect is required for this negative duration effect to be possible?

40. What is a principal only (PO) strip? What causes the price–yield profile of a PO strip to have a steeper slope than a normal bond?

41. An FI originates a pool of real estate loans worth $20 million with maturities of 10 years and paying interest rates of 9 percent per year.
    a. What is the average payment received by the FI, including both principal and interest, if no prepayment is expected over the life of the loan?
    b. If the loans are converted into pass-through certificates and the FI charges a servicing fee of 50 basis points, including insurance, what is the payment amount expected by the holders of the pass-through securities if no prepayment is expected?
    c. Assume that the payments are separated into interest only (IO) and principal only (PO) payments, that prepayments of 5 percent occur at the end of years 3 and 4, and that the payment of the remaining principal occurs at the end of year 5. What are the expected annual payments for each instrument? Assume discount rates of 9 percent.
    d. What is the market value of IOs and POs if the market interest rates for instruments of similar risk decline to 8 percent?

42. What are the factors that, in general, allow assets to be securitized? What are the costs involved in the securitization process?

43. How does an FI use securitization to manage interest rate, credit, and liquidity risks? Summarize how each of the possible methods of securitization products affects the balance sheet and profitability of an FI in the management of these risks.

## Web Question

44. Go to the Federal Reserve Board's website at **www.federalreserve.gov**. From there, click on "Economic Research and Data." Click on "Flow of Funds Accounts of the United States Releases," then click on the most recent date. Click on "Level tables." Go to the table titled "Total Mortgages" to get the most recent data on total mortgages held by government-sponsored and federally related mortgage pools. How have these values changed since 2012?

## Appendix 26A: Fannie Mae and Freddie Mac Balance Sheets

View Appendix 26A at the website for this textbook (**www.mhhe.com/saunders8e**).

# Index

Note: Page numbers followed by *n.* indicate material in notes.